**Professional P**

# Professional Palm OS® Programming

Lonnon R. Foster and Glenn Bachmann

WILEY

Wiley Publishing, Inc.

# Professional Palm OS® Programming

Published by
Wiley Publishing, Inc.
10475 Crosspoint Boulevard
Indianapolis, IN 46256
www.wiley.com

Published simultaneously in Canada

ISBN-13: 978-0-7645-7373-6
ISBN-10: 0-7645-7373-X

Manufactured in the United States of America

10 9 8 7 6 5 4 3 2 1

1B/QU/QU/QV/IN

For general information on our other products and services or to obtain technical support, please contact our Customer Care Department within the U.S. at (800) 762-2974, outside the U.S. at (317) 572-3993 or fax (317) 572-4002.

Wiley also publishes its books in a variety of electronic formats. Some content that appears in print may not be available in electronic books.

Library of Congress Cataloging-in-Publication Data

Foster, Lonnon R., 1972-
 Professional Palm OS programming / Lonnon R. Foster & Glenn Bachmann.
   p. cm.
 Includes index.
 ISBN 0-7645-7373-X (pbk.)
 1. Palm OS. 2. Pocket computers. I. Bachmann, Glenn. II. Title.
 QA76.76.O63F597185 2005
 004.16—dc22

                              2005000594

# About the Authors

**Lonnon R. Foster** is a programmer and writer who has spent the past nine years creating desktop applications, database front ends, Web sites, communications software, technical documentation, and handheld applications. He has been developing Palm OS applications almost as long as the platform has existed, starting with his first Pilot 5000 and progressing to more complicated wireless software for Symbol's 1700 series. Lonnon fills his sparse free time with tactical tabletop gaming, recreational Perl coding, and reading everything he can get his hands on.

**Glenn Bachmann** is a noted author of several books and articles on Palm OS programming and mobile computing. Glenn is also president and founder of Bachmann Software, a leading provider of wireless file management, networking, backup, and printing software products for Palm OS, Pocket PC, and Symbian handheld computing platforms. Founded in 1994, Bachmann Software (www.bachmannsoftware.com) has established itself as a leading contributor to the mobile and wireless economy through its utility software products and partnerships with many of the key companies in the mobile computing arena. Bachmann's PrintBoy, FilePoint, Mobile Backup, and Mobile Utilities are among the best-selling software utilities for handhelds and smartphones.

*First and foremost I thank my acquisitions editor, Chris Webb, for remembering me from our previous collaborations and providing me with the opportunity to participate in writing this book. I also thank my development editor, Eileen Bien Calabro, who bore the difficult task of keeping the book on track with just the right amount of poking and prodding to the author.*

*I also thank Lonnon Foster for creating the phenomenally successful* Palm OS Programming Bible, *the second edition of which is the predecessor and foundation of this book. Through Lonnon's clear and concise writing style and attention to detail, he has helped programmers around the world become Palm OS programmers.*

*There are so many people in the Palm OS developer community—at PalmSource, palmOne, and other software companies—who continue to be the heroes of our little mobile computing industry. These fine folks are responsible for the fantastic handhelds, smartphones, operating systems, and software applications that make it such a delight to participate in and contribute to the success of the Palm Economy. My hat goes off to you all.*

*Thanks are also due to the team at Bachmann Software, truly the finest and most dedicated people I have ever worked with.*

*Finally, I thank my wife for supporting me in my never-ending adventures in growing a software company. I also thank my three wonderful children, who seem to have grown up under the impression that it is entirely normal for their father to possess 58 different handhelds.*

# Credits

**Executive Editor**
Chris Webb

**Development Editor**
Eileen Bien Calabro

**Technical Reviewer**
JB Parrett

**Copy Editors**
Stefan Gruenwedel
Nancy Rapoport

**Vice President & Executive Group Publisher**
Richard Swadley

**Vice President and Publisher**
Joseph B. Wikert

**Project Coordinator**
Erin Smith

**Graphics and Production Specialists**
April Farling
Carrie A. Foster
Lauren Goddard
Denny Hager
Joyce Haughey
Jennifer Heleine
Lynsey Osborn
Julie Trippetti

**Quality Control Technicians**
Laura Albert
Amanda Briggs
John Greenough
Leeann Harney
Carl William Pierce
Brian H. Walls

**Proofreading and Indexing**
TECHBOOKS Production Services

In loving memory of Robert B. Hyslop (1909–2002)

# Contents

# Contents

Contents

# Contents

# Contents

# Contents

# Contents

# Contents

# Contents

# Introduction

The convenience, power, and ease of use of Palm OS handheld devices make them attractive to a wide variety of users. More than 35 million Palm Powered handheld devices have found their way into the shirt pockets of doctors, lawyers, sales personnel, business professionals, and other segments of society not normally given to using small electronic gadgetry. With more than 320,000 registered developers and 20,000 third-party applications, Palm OS also has proven to be popular with software authors, which is where this book comes in.

*Professional Palm OS® Programming* is written for the present and future developers of Palm OS applications. It is designed to help both aspiring and experienced handheld developers master the ins and outs of creating a full-fledged Palm OS handheld application.

Whether you are a developer for a large organization that is integrating Palm Powered handhelds into its sales force or a hobbyist who wants to get the most from your organizer, you will find this book to be a useful guide to creating software for the Palm OS platform.

## What This Book Covers

*Professional Palm OS Programming* shows you how to create applications that run on handhelds and smartphones from palmOne, Sony, Kyocera, Samsung, and other licensees of Palm OS.

This book specifically covers both Palm OS Garnet and the new Palm OS Cobalt, representing the next-generation operating system for Palm OS developers. As of this writing, Palm OS Cobalt 6.1 is complete; however, Palm OS Cobalt–based handhelds have yet to ship. Furthermore, PalmSource Palm OS Cobalt development tools are being updated. Accordingly, the book focuses on Palm OS Garnet as the standard handheld operating system and supplements those chapters with Palm OS Cobalt–specific information where the introduction of Palm OS Cobalt tools, APIs, and concepts is appropriate.

The primary focus of this book is Palm OS development in the C language, using CodeWarrior for Palm OS Platform, or PalmSource's PODS as a development environment. Other tools exist for developing Palm OS applications, but these environments are popular with the largest developer audience and offer the most complete access to the many features of Palm OS and the handhelds that run it.

# Whom This Book Is For

This book was written with the experienced C programmer in mind. If you know nothing at all about Palm OS programming, this book will get you started with the fundamentals, teaching you how Palm OS works, showing you the tools available for Palm OS development, and providing you with tips to make your own applications work seamlessly within PalmSource's programming guidelines.

Even if you already have delved into the world of creating Palm OS applications, you will find this book a useful resource because it covers almost every aspect of Palm OS development in depth. Palm OS is multifaceted, and this book can serve as a guide to exploring those parts of the operating system that you have not yet dealt with.

If you wish to create applications that make use of TCP/IP communications options on appropriately equipped wireless Palm Powered handhelds, you will need to know the basics of socket programming and TCP/IP protocols. Similarly, although this book covers how to perform serial communications on Palm OS, it will not teach you the basics of serial communications.

Conduit programming is a very complex topic and uses a completely different set of tools from those used for handheld programming. This book provides a basic overview of conduits, as well as a description of the tools used to create them. An in-depth discussion of conduit programming would require a book in itself, so that subject is beyond the scope of this volume. For those who are interested in conduits, conduit programming requires solid knowledge of C++, as well as a working knowledge of creating desktop applications for either Windows or Mac OS. Palm's Conduit Development Kit (CDK) provides tools for writing conduits in Java and Visual Basic (or any other COM-compliant language), but this book focuses on C++ conduit development.

# How This Book Is Structured

Each chapter in this book focuses on a specific area of Palm OS programming. The first eight chapters, essential reading for programmers new to the Palm OS, introduce readers to the operating system itself, the development tools, and the basics of creating a simple application. It is critical that new Palm OS programmers master the information and concepts presented in these chapters before moving on to more advanced material.

Once the earlier chapter concepts are mastered, for the most part each of the remaining chapters is self-contained and can be read as a topic unto itself. The following is an overview of what is covered in each chapter:

- ❑ Chapter 1, "The Palm OS Success Story, " introduces the Palm OS platform and discusses design issues that are generally important for any Palm OS programmer to understand.

- ❑ Chapter 2, "Understanding the Palm OS" covers the operating system in more depth, including a historical overview of Palm OS versions up to and including Palm OS Garnet and Palm OS Cobalt.

- ❑ Chapter 3, "Introducing the Development Tools," provides an introduction to using Metrowerks CodeWarrior and PalmSource's PODS to create and work with Palm OS programming projects.

❑  Chapter 4, "Writing Your First Palm OS Application," walks you through the basics of a simple Palm OS application.

❑  Chapter 5, "Debugging Your Program," discusses Palm OS Emulator and Palm Simulator, as well as the debugging tools available in both CodeWarrior and PODS.

❑  Chapter 6, "Creating and Understanding Resources," covers the creation of project resources with Metrowerks' Constructor and PalmSource's Palm OS Resource Editor.

❑  Chapter 7, "Building Forms and Menus," describes how to design forms and menus that make up the primary user interface for most Palm OS applications.

❑  Chapter 8, "Programming User Interface Elements," teaches you how to incorporate resources such as forms, menus, and alerts into your source code.

❑  Chapter 9, "Managing Memory," discusses how memory is managed on Palm OS Garnet and Palm OS Cobalt and provides information on how to allocate and use memory in your application.

❑  Chapter 10, "Programming System Elements," covers system topics such as operating system version checking, fonts, events, and the Clipboard.

❑  Chapter 11, "Programming Graphics," describes how to draw on the device display using the Palm OS Garnet and Palm OS Cobalt windowing and graphics models.

❑  Chapter 12, "Programming Multimedia," covers how to use beeps and sounds within your application, as well as how to make use of media playback and recording functionality.

❑  Chapter 13, "Programming Alarms and Time," discusses the Palm OS time and date facilities, using alarms, and the attention manager

❑  Chapter 14, "Programming Tables," describes how to incorporate tables to display rows and columns of data within your applications user interface.

❑  Chapter 15, "Storing and Retrieving Data," introduces the Palm OS Database Manager and also covers Palm OS Cobalt Schema databases.

❑  Chapter 16, "Manipulating Records," builds on Chapter 15 by examining the programming APIs used to work with database records.

❑  Chapter 17, "Using Secondary Storage," describes how to enhance your application to read and write data stored on memory expansion cards.

❑  Chapter 18, "Sharing Data Through the Exchange Manager," covers the Palm OS Exchange Manager.

❑  Chapter 19, "Using the Serial Port," introduces the Serial Manager as a method for programming serial communications on Palm OS handhelds.

❑  Chapter 20, "Communicating Over a Network," covers the TCP/IP implementation on Palm OS Garnet and Palm OS Cobalt.

❑  Chapter 21, "Learning Conduit Basics," introduces the concept of conduits as a method of exchanging and synchronizing data between the handheld and desktop through HotSync.

❑ Chapter 22, "Building Conduits," builds on Chapter 21 by examining the tools used to build conduits.

❑ Chapter 23, "Programming Navigation Hardware," discusses how to program your application to work correctly with five-way navigation buttons and scroll wheels.

❑ Chapter 24, "Odds and Ends," covers a variety of miscellaneous Palm OS programming topics, including large projects, segmentation, custom fonts, localization, and file streaming.

# How to Approach This Book

Readers who are completely new to Palm OS development will benefit most by first reading Chapters 1–8 in their entirety. These chapters provide an excellent introduction to Palm OS, the development tools, setting up your first projects, and creating a basic application. Following these chapters, you should at least review Chapters 9, 15, and 16 to get an idea of how storage and memory work. After that, the other chapters can generally be read in any order, based on specific topics of interest to the reader.

For readers who have already done some Palm OS development, the first eight chapters form a good review. However, they are also an essential read if you plan to work with PODS and Palm OS Cobalt. The new and updated chapters on graphics, memory management, networking, database storage, and multimedia will also serve as useful references as well as introductions to how these topics are handled differently under Palm OS Cobalt than in Palm OS Garnet.

Anyone interested in creating conduits can obtain a high-level overview of this complex topic from Chapters 21 and 22. Developers who wish to delve right into conduit programming are advised to obtain the most current version of the Conduit Development Kit, available from PalmSource's Web site. The CDK remains the best reference available on this topic.

# What's New in This Edition?

Since the publication of the second edition of *Palm OS Programming Bible*, PalmSource, formerly the Palm OS subsidiary of Palm, Inc., has released updates to Palm OS 5, now known as Palm OS Garnet. PalmSource has also introduced a brand new version of the operating system, known as Palm OS Cobalt. In conjunction with these advances in the operating system, PalmSource for the first time released its very own suite of tools for developing Palm OS applications, known as PODS.

In terms of devices, besides the inexorable march forward in improvements to the screen display and memory capacity, the past year has seen the growth of the smartphone as a tremendously important handheld device that represents the convergence of voice, wireless data, and traditional handheld applications.

*Professional Palm OS Programming* is a brand new Wrox Pro book that builds on *Palm OS Programming Bible, Second Edition* to cover new capabilities and changes for developers of Palm OS Garnet and Palm OS Cobalt applications. In addition to the considerable material provided from *Palm OS Programming Bible* on programming for Palm OS, the following new topics in Palm OS programming are specifically covered in this book:

- ❑ Changes to the Palm OS platform and operating system, including Palm OS Garnet and Palm OS Cobalt

- ❑ New and updated coverage of Palm OS development tools, including Metrowerks' CodeWarrior 9.3 and the new PODS from PalmSource

- ❑ Creating and working with resources using the latest resource editors from PalmSource

- ❑ Debugging Palm OS Garnet and Palm OS Cobalt programs from within the PODS integrated debugger

- ❑ The new Palm OS Cobalt graphics model

- ❑ Working with the new Palm OS Cobalt Schema databases

- ❑ Programming the five-way navigator buttons found on most new handhelds

- ❑ New multimedia functionality for audio and video recording and playback

# What You Need to Use This Book

To make the best use of this book, you should obtain at least one Palm OS handheld. Just about any reasonable modern device from palmOne, Sony, or other handheld vendor should do, although the Palm OS Garnet discussions will make more sense to you if you are working with a Palm OS 5.x–based color device. palmOne's Tungsten series is a good choice if you are looking to purchase a handheld at this time.

It is possible to learn Palm OS programming without a handheld, but there is nothing like working with an actual device to gain the best understanding of what it is like to create software for handhelds.

You will also need access to a computer that is capable of running either Metrowerks' CodeWarrior or PalmSource's PODS development tools. For information on minimum computer requirements, please visit www.metrowerks.com or www.palmsource.com.

# Conventions

To help you get the most from the text and keep track of what's happening, we've used a number of typographic conventions throughout the book.

> **Boxes like this one hold important, not-to-be-forgotten information that is directly relevant to the accompanying text.**

*Tips, hints, tricks, and asides to the current discussion are offset and placed in italics like this.*

As for styles in the text:

- ❑ We *highlight* new terms and important words when we introduce them.

- ❑ We show keyboard strokes like this: Ctrl-A.

- ❑ We show most filenames, URLs, functions, classes, objects, and code within the text like so: `persistence.properties`.

- ❑ We present code in two different ways:

```
In code examples we highlight new and important code with a gray background.
The gray highlighting is not used for code that's less important in the present
context, or has been shown before.
```

Note that depending on the topic, in some cases code listings are presented for both Palm OS Garnet and Palm OS Cobalt.

# Errata

We make every effort to ensure that there are no errors in the text or in the code. However, no one is perfect and mistakes do occur. If you find an error in one of our books, like a spelling mistake or faulty piece of code, we would be very grateful for your feedback. By sending in errata you may save another reader hours of frustration, and at the same time you will be helping us provide even higher quality information.

To find the errata page for this book, go to `www.wrox.com` and locate the title using the Search box or one of the title lists. Then, on the book details page, click the Book Errata link. On this page you can view all errata that has been submitted for this book and posted by Wrox editors. A complete book list, including links to each book's errata, is also available at `www.wrox.com/misc-pages/booklist.shtml`.

If you don't spot "your" error on the Book Errata page, go to `www.wrox.com/contact/techsupport.shtml` and complete the form there to send us the error you have found. We'll check the information and, if appropriate, post a message to the book's errata page and fix the problem in subsequent editions of the book.

# p2p.wrox.com

For author and peer discussion, join the P2P forums at `p2p.wrox.com`. The forums are a Web-based system for you to post messages relating to Wrox books and related technologies and to interact with other readers and technology users. The forums offer a subscription feature to e-mail you topics of interest of your choosing when new posts are made to the forums. Wrox authors, editors, other industry experts, and your fellow readers are present on these forums.

At `http://p2p.wrox.com` you will find a number of different forums that will help you not only as you read this book, but also as you develop your own applications. To join the forums, just follow these steps:

1. Go to `p2p.wrox.com` and click the Register link.
2. Read the terms of use and click Agree.

3. Complete the required information to join as well as any optional information you wish to provide and click Submit.

4. You will receive an e-mail with information describing how to verify your account and complete the joining process.

*You can read messages in the forums without joining P2P, but you must join in order to post your own messages.*

Once you join, you can post new messages and respond to messages other users post. You can read messages at any time on the Web. If you would like to have new messages from a particular forum e-mailed to you, click the Subscribe to This Forum icon by the forum name in the forum listing.

Be sure to read the P2P FAQs for answers to questions about how the forum software works as well as many common questions specific to P2P and Wrox books. To read the FAQs, click the FAQ link on any P2P page.

# 1

# The Palm OS Success Story

Since the release of the Pilot 1000 in 1996, devices running Palm OS have become synonymous with the term "handheld computer." Through the years, the designers of Palm OS have consistently been able to combine just the right mix of features to make a personal digital assistant (PDA) that is easy to integrate into almost any user's lifestyle. Designing an application that takes advantage of the strengths of the Palm OS platform requires an understanding of not only how the platform works but also why it was designed the way it was.

This chapter explains some of the thinking that has made the Palm OS platform so successful. It also points out important design considerations for developers of handheld applications. Finally, it provides an overview of the increasingly diverse world of Palm OS devices and the array of hardware capabilities they encompass.

## The Palm OS Success Story

How has Palm OS maintained its position as the leader in handheld platforms, even in the face of capable challengers such as Microsoft Windows Mobile and Symbian OS?

One could debate the pros and cons of these and other worthy contenders for the title of "best handheld operating system" but the truth is that Palm OS continues to achieve a magic combination of simplicity and extensibility that attracts device manufacturers, developers, and users to the platform.

This success is all the more impressive when you consider that Palm OS has remained the leader throughout a period of time when the definition of a "PDA" has expanded from a simple personal organizer to a robust application platform — all the way through to the present time when it is becoming increasingly difficult to find a handheld that does not play music, take pictures, play games, or double as your cell phone.

What makes Palm OS a great platform for so many developers and handheld users? There are many reasons, but these are among the most important:

❑ **Palm OS is small, fast, and efficient.** Rather than suffer inevitable bloat as new features are added to the latest handhelds, Palm OS remains true to its core values and instead offers extensibility to its licensees, enabling them to build devices that add advanced features to the core operating system.

❑ **Palm OS is easy to use.** Devices that use Palm OS allow users to perform common tasks with a minimum of dialog boxes, menus, and screen navigation. Many common tasks are accomplished with a single button press or stylus tap.

❑ **Palm OS allows simple and fast desktop synchronization.** The Palm OS HotSync design enables one-button synchronization of data between the desktop and handheld. Despite having years to learn from Palm OS, other platforms have yet to approach the simplicity and ease of use that Palm OS HotSync offers.

❑ **Palm OS embraces diversity.** The number and diversity of licensees is a testament to how well the designers of Palm OS enable handheld manufacturers to adapt it to a wide variety of tasks, from multimedia to wireless communications. This is in direct contrast to other platforms, where devices tend to be fairly similar in form and function.

Palm hit upon a perfect combination of these factors with its first device, and it has resisted the temptation to cram marginally useful features into new Palm devices. Intelligent selection of such features has fashioned these devices into handy tools instead of merely expensive toys.

# Comparing Desktop and Handheld Application Design

There are significant differences between a desktop computer and a handheld device—enough differences that designing a handheld application must be approached differently from designing a desktop application. Many elements must be kept in mind when designing a Palm OS application:

❑ Diversity of handheld form factors

❑ Expectation of performance

❑ Limited input methods

❑ Small screen size

❑ Processing power

❑ Battery life

❑ Limited memory

❑ RAM as permanent data storage

## Diversity of Handheld Form Factors

Although certainly some desktop computers are more capable than others and often come with varying sets of peripherals, in general the vast majority of desktop computers are reasonably suited to run just about any desktop software application. By contrast, Palm OS handhelds are an extremely diverse target for the application developer to consider. The form factor and capabilities built into a given target handheld device may in fact determine whether or not your application makes sense for the target user, or indeed whether it will run at all.

Consider an application that depends on Internet connectivity. Whether or not a given target device supports a way to connect to the Internet is clearly going to dictate whether the device and its user will be a reasonable target for the application. What about smartphones? Are you willing to limit your application's audience by including functionality that depends on the presence of telephony features? How about if your application requires a high-resolution color screen? Is it worth it to create a low-resolution, grayscale version of your application for older devices?

Although this can be considered a challenge for the application developer, it is also a benefit. The designers of Palm OS have produced a unique platform that is adaptable to a wide range of handheld form factors. Handheld manufacturers have responded by producing Palm OS handhelds that, in many cases, are specifically oriented toward a certain type of user (for example GPS, telephony, or entertainment). As the developer, you can elect to take advantage of the knowledge that the owner of a given device is guaranteed to have a specific capability available to them.

## Expectation of Performance

Desktop application users usually don't mind waiting a few seconds for a program to load because they plan to use the application for an extended period of time — and they probably aren't going anywhere anytime soon.

Compare this with a handheld user on the go. A person using a Palm OS handheld will need to look up a piece of data (such as a phone number) quickly or spend a few seconds jotting down a note, while in the middle of performing some other task. Someone who is talking to clients on the phone or trying to catch a bus doesn't have time to watch a "wait" cursor spin while an application loads.

Speed and efficiency are key to a successful Palm OS application. Writing fast code is only a small part of the equation; the user interface must be simple, intuitive, and quick to use. The application should allow for rapid selection and execution of commands. Functions that people use the most should require less interaction than those that are used less frequently.

## Limited Input Methods

A desktop system is ideal for entering large quantities of data. A keyboard and a fast processor allow desktop users to input lots of text easily into the computer in a short period of time.

Modern Palm OS handhelds come with a variety of supported data input methods. Virtually all support the standard Graffiti method of entering special shorthand strokes using a stylus on the handheld screen. Graffiti works remarkably well for many users. Palm OS also supports a popup, onscreen keyboard. However, there are now several handhelds with tiny built-in QWERTY keyboards (such as the palmOne

Treo smartphone) and there are handhelds with a larger, laptop-sized keyboard (the Alphasmart Dana). There are also third-party add-on keyboards that communicate with the handheld by serial connector, IrDA, or Bluetooth.

With the possible exception of the Alphasmart Dana, and despite the numerous attempts made by hand-held and smartphone manufacturers to make it easier to enter data on their devices, developers must realize that expecting a user to enter anything longer than a short note is asking a lot of the user.

As an alternative to direct input on the device, HotSync technology provides an easy way to get large amounts of data from the desktop to the handheld. One of the major advantages of Palm OS over other competing mobile platforms is the attention paid to making synchronization powerful yet easy to use. Many software applications leverage this capability by assuming that mass data entry will be performed on desktop machines, which then synch that data to their handheld. This kind of symbiosis between the desktop computer and the handheld plays to the strengths of both devices.

However, don't let this discourage you from writing applications that use a Palm OS handheld as a data collection tool. With intelligent interface design, you can perform data entry quickly and efficiently on such a device.

## Small Screen Size

Current desktop machines have large monitors that generally run at a minimum resolution of $640 \times 480$ pixels, although with prices of display monitors continuing to decline, most computer users choose to run their systems at even higher resolutions. With this kind of screen real estate to play with, displaying large amounts of information and a complex user interface in the same space is easy.

By contrast, most Palm OS handhelds have a screen about six centimeters on a side, with a resolution of $160 \times 160$ pixels. Current high-resolution models support up to only $320 \times 320$ pixels of screen space, a far cry from the acreage available on a desktop computer. Even the new Cobalt version of Palm OS is designed to support a maximum of $320 \times 480$ pixels. Unlike desktop displays, keeping devices small enough for users to carry in their shirt pocket is a unique requirement for handhelds.

Designing applications to use such a small screen is a challenge. Displaying the right information is more important than fitting as much information on the screen as possible. You must strike a balance between showing enough information and keeping the interface uncluttered and simple to use.

Requiring users to scroll through several data screens to find the information they want will make your application frustrating to use. Find logical groupings of data and offer the user a way to filter different views of that data. The To Do List application is a good example of data filtering; its preferences allow users to choose quickly what subset of the list to display. Implementing the standard Palm OS user-defined categories also can help users zero in on exactly the data they want to view.

Unlike desktop machines, which are plugged into wall outlets and sport powerful and fast processors, Palm OS handhelds must rely on batteries for power, which limits them to slower processors. The small processor on such a device is not well suited to intense computations.

If your application has both handheld and desktop components, consider doing all the intensive number crunching on the desktop portion. A great example of relegating processor-intensive tasks to the desktop machine is Doc, the *de facto* standard for large text documents on Palm OS. Several converter applications exist for the desktop machine, which perform the computationally intensive conversion and compression of a large text document to Doc format. The newly formatted document then can be transferred to the handheld during the next HotSync session. All that the Doc viewer application on the handheld needs to concern itself with is displaying the document; the faster desktop computer has handled all the hard stuff.

## Processing Power

Most handheld models sold today sport ARM (Advanced RISC Machine) processors, which are much more powerful than the slower processors of the earlier Palm OS devices. Although developers must consider the fact that there are millions of older handhelds out there, some of the processing power limitations imposed on developers in the early days have been lifted, at least to a certain degree.

Graphics-intensive games and processor-intensive image converters and viewers are two examples of applications that only a few years ago would have been unthinkable. If you are faced with a similar computationally intensive task that is part of the application you are developing, you are still advised strongly to consider how important it is for that task to be performed on the handheld instead of being offloaded to the desktop. However, at least now you have an option.

## Battery Life

Another factor related to processing power is the issue of battery life and your application's impact on it. Although a proliferation of devices can play music, video, and games and surf the Internet, these tasks take their toll on battery life. At a minimum, your application should not be such a drain on battery life that the handheld cannot survive a typical full day of usage without needing to be recharged.

## Limited Memory

As memory prices continue to drop, desktop applications can afford to be less choosy about how they deal with memory. When your application has 64 MB or more to play with, it can load huge data structures into RAM and leave them there the entire time the program is running.

Compared to desktop computers, Palm OS handhelds have very limited memory space for running applications. Though Palm OS handhelds continue to grow in their total amount of RAM, with some topping out at 16 MB, only a small fraction of that (one-sixteenth or less) is available for dynamic memory allocation, application global variables, and static variables. Application stack space is even tighter, often only 4K or less. Versions of Palm OS prior to 3.0 have considerably less room, so designing applications that are compatible with older Palm OS handhelds can be somewhat challenging.

When designing your application, consider that such things as deeply recursive routines, large global variables, and huge dynamically allocated data structures are not Palm OS–friendly.

## RAM as Permanent Data Storage

Hard drives provide desktop computers with abundant permanent storage for vast amounts of data. Palm OS handhelds have considerably more limited storage space because they must store both applications and data in RAM. Although many Palm OS handhelds support secondary storage on memory expansion cards, this storage is usually limited to data. Applications cannot run directly from an expansion card, so they must either reside in RAM or be copied to RAM from the card before running.

5

As of this writing, available memory on a reasonably modern Palm OS handheld ranges between 8 MB and 128 MB. This type of limited storage dictates that handheld applications remain as small as possible. Avoid adding features to your application that will be used infrequently; if a feature will be used by fewer than 20 percent of users, leave it out.

For example, features that globally modify an application's data, but will see only infrequent use, are prime candidates for inclusion in a companion program on the desktop. A command that removes duplicate entries in a database would be perfect for the desktop; it's not likely to be used very often on the handheld, and omitting it from the handheld application makes the program smaller and more efficient.

Your application should pack its data tightly before writing the data to memory. Not only will this reduce the amount of RAM required to store your application's data but it will decrease the amount of time that HotSync needs to synchronize the data with the desktop computer.

# Designing Applications for Smartphones and Other Wireless Devices

From a communications perspective, the way in which a handheld or smartphone connects to other computers and peripherals definitely impacts how developers must think about features that they take for granted on desktop computers: accessing the Internet, local area networks, and peripherals such as printers. Considering the following:

- ❑ Many connection types
- ❑ Connection speed
- ❑ Mobile-user expectations
- ❑ Connection reliability

## *Many Connection Types*

The primary method for a desktop computer to connect to the outside world is through a standard Ethernet jack. Although not as commonly as before, many computer users still connect to the Internet using a dialup modem. By contrast, smartphones and handhelds come equipped with many different connectivity options. Smartphones provide Internet access via wireless radios that support wide-area carrier data networks. Many handheld devices come with a built-in Bluetooth radio that enables short-range connectivity to other computers or even the Internet via a cell phone or access point connection. Some handhelds possess an 802.11b Wi-Fi radio that can connect over a somewhat larger distance to local area networks and the Internet from access points. Last but not least, every modern Palm OS handheld comes with infrared connectivity.

Consider an application that seeks connectivity to the Internet or other networked computers. Although the TCP/IP support in the Palm OS can insulate the application developer from needing to worry about the exact type of connection made, for short range connectivity TCP/IP may not be the most appropriate mechanism for the function in question. Furthermore, you must consider the ease with which the average user can make the connection required by your application.

## Connection Speed

Desktop connectivity on today's networks generally occurs at 10 Mbps or greater. Fast Internet connection options afford the typical user connectivity to e-mail and the Web at bandwidths far in excess of 100Kbps.

Connection speed on smartphones and wireless handhelds varies greatly. Browsing the Web on a smartphone connection, often at speeds lower than that of a 56 Kbps dialup modem, can still be an exercise in frustration. Yet at the other end of the spectrum, multi-megabit connections can be achieved by Wi-Fi–enabled handhelds. Also to be considered are the upper limits of infrared (115 Kbps maximum) and Bluetooth (less than 1 Mbps).

Depending on what services and data transfer your application requires, the type of connection achievable by the user's handheld will significantly impact the end-user experience with your application.

## Mobile-User Expectations

As we mentioned earlier in this chapter, a desktop user is comfortably seated in a chair and has the time and patience to wait for an application to deliver information. The structure of the Web, with its endlessly intricate links among pages of related information, is well-suited to the desktop user, allowing the user to browse the Web at a leisurely pace, for minutes or even hours at a time.

Mobile handheld users, on the other hand, are always in motion: standing, not sitting; on the go and in a hurry. Rather than leisurely browsing the Internet, handheld users who go online are doing so to find a quick answer to a question or to view a specific piece of information. If it takes more than a minute or two to find that information, odds are that the opportunity is lost and the user will simply become frustrated, give up, and move on to another task. Needless to say, the failure to deliver the information to the user in a timely fashion reflects poorly on the application as well as the device.

Accordingly, wireless applications need to be aware of a target average user who has an extremely short attention span. Needless to say, data access methods and screen navigation must be constructed so as to be as fast and direct as possible.

## Connection Reliability

Glenn will never forget when he was a naïve young developer working on a piece of software that transferred data across a network between two personal computers. He had worked hard on his piece of the project and, when he was done, he proudly walked up to his boss and boasted that the work was complete and he could demo it for him. His boss walked over to the computer where his code was running and transferring data at a furious rate. He casually reached behind the computer and yanked the Ethernet cable away from the computer. With horror Glenn watched as his code died an ignominious death with its precious connection pulled out from beneath it. "Come back and let me know when you are really done," his boss said with a smile. Sheepishly, he walked back to his desk and began working on making his code much more bulletproof and robust in the face of a lost connection.

Today's desktop network connections seem fast and ubiquitous. The Ethernet cables snaking through our offices serve as a pleasant reminder that a connection is always there. Things are far different on smartphones and handhelds, where wireless, not wired, connections are the norm and the network can (and often does) disappear at a moment's notice. Wireless applications need to be designed with the idea of an inherently unreliable connection in mind. Extended operations and protocols which rely on a lengthy, unbroken network session are generally not a good design. This is not to say that an application cannot be designed to download a 100K file. Rather, the application that does the downloading should consider the very likely possibility that the transfer will be interrupted by a break in the connection. How can your application plan for this possibility and reward, not frustrate, the end user?

# Connecting to the Desktop

Sharing data with the desktop is a key ingredient in the popularity of Palm OS handhelds. It is one of the key competitive strengths of Palm OS versus other handheld platforms. The connection between the desktop and handheld allows each device to borrow the strengths of the other. A desktop computer is great for large-scale data entry and crunching numbers but not so great for carrying in your pocket when visiting clients. A handheld device is perfect for taking quick notes and reminding you of appointments but not so perfect for analyzing financial reports or writing a book. Together, both devices become greater than the sum of their parts.

The software component that forms the vital link between the Palm OS device and the desktop computer is the *conduit*. During synchronization with your handheld application, HotSync calls code in a conduit, which resides on the desktop computer. This code controls exactly what data HotSync transfers between the two devices. There are several different scenarios in which a conduit plays a vital role; the following are just a few examples:

❑ Two applications, one on the handheld and one on the desktop, use the conduit to keep records in their databases in synch with each other. This is how the conduit for the Date Book and the three other main Palm OS applications works. In this scenario, the conduit is responsible for looking at the records in both databases and determining which records are different between them, as well as in which direction the data must be transferred.

❑ The conduit keeps data in a handheld application synchronized with data in a centralized corporate database, either stored on the machine running HotSync or another machine on a corporate network. In this case, the conduit also might sift the data and transfer only a customized subset to the handheld based on user preferences. For example, a contact application for a sales force might download only information about businesses that a specific salesperson has been working with. Customization like this keeps the size of the data manageable and reduces the time required for HotSync to run.

❑ When syncing, the conduit compares content on the handheld with the contents of a Web page, mail server, or Usenet newsgroup. If the information on the server is newer than what the handheld application has stored, the conduit downloads the new data, processes it into a form that the handheld application can read, and then transfers it to the handheld. The conduit also may instruct the handheld application to discard out-of-date pages, messages, or articles. Because Internet connections are prone to delays, this sort of conduit should probably look only at information previously cached by a desktop application. A HotSync operation should be as short as possible because having the serial port open rapidly drains a Palm OS handheld's batteries.

If your application does not require the level of detailed synchronization logic that a conduit can provide, you may be able to use the default *backup conduit*. Instead of comparing the handheld application's database record by record with the data on the desktop, the backup conduit simply makes a copy of the entire database and transfers it to the desktop computer. Although this works perfectly well for small application databases, it can slow down the HotSync process if your application stores a lot of data. For example, an address book database containing thousands of contacts may synchronize through a properly designed conduit in less time than it takes to copy the entire database to the desktop.

*Chapter 21 provides an introduction to developing Palm OS conduits. Further details on writing conduits follow in Chapter 22.*

# Comparing Palm OS Handheld Devices

For earlier Palm OS developers, the main challenge in managing compatibility with the various handheld models out in the market was in maintaining support for devices running several earlier versions of Palm OS. Physically, the main variations to be found among these devices were the amount of memory and the availability of an expansion card slot. Except for applications that sought specifically to work with expansion cards, well-written application code could be expected, generally speaking, to function across the range of devices available on the market.

Since 2003, the proliferation of form factors and hardware features in devices has been remarkable. The variations among devices today are far greater than just a few years ago. You can categorize these variations as follows:

- ❏ Multimedia (audio/video)
- ❏ Screen size and orientation
- ❏ Voice/telephony
- ❏ Imaging/photo capture
- ❏ Data input/keyboard
- ❏ Navigation/scrolling
- ❏ Wireless data connectivity

As a result of these variations, developers are less focused on the basic device specs (amount of memory, processor speed) and much more concerned instead on the type of user who will buy a given device, and the types of applications and functionality that user will be interested in.

Complicating matters is the fact that most devices on the market today combine several of these variations into one device. For example, the palmOne Tungsten C has wireless data, navigation, and a built-in keyboard. The Alphasmart Dana has an extended screen size, keyboard, and wireless data. The popular palmOne Treo 600 smartphone has managed to cram in just about all of these categories: It's a phone, it can play music, it can take pictures, and it has advanced navigation and data entry features.

There are those who have long sought after the elusive one perfect device that replaces their phone, PDA, personal audio player, and so on. The reality is that although there will be attempts to produce such a device, they will inevitably involve compromises in one or more areas of functionality. Most devices, instead, will continue to focus on being excellent at the kinds of things that the devices' target users want to do with them. This doesn't make one device better than another; it just makes it different.

Even in a time when most people are predicting that the majority of handhelds in the future will be smartphones, and voice capability will be commonplace in PDAs, the mix of other capabilities included on these smartphones will continue to be fine-tuned to the needs of the target user. As a case in point, the ubiquity of the expansion card slot — a feature that was brand new just a few years ago — did not result in Palm OS devices' becoming boring and homogeneous. Rather, it simply graduated from being a bonus feature in high-end handhelds to becoming a standard part of every handheld.

# Looking to the Future

The official Palm OS documentation stresses the importance of developers not making assumptions about the hardware that underlies their applications. This is important because the hardware may change. If your code ignores the Palm OS APIs and directly accesses the hardware, your application is very likely to break on future devices. Furthermore, as we've detailed in this chapter, the diversity of Palm OS devices virtually guarantees that your application will encounter different hardware options and configurations from one handheld to the next.

PalmSource, the company that publishes Palm OS, continues to meet the challenge of extending the platform to embrace new and wonderful handheld capabilities, while at the same time minimizing the impact of these changes on developers and their applications. The divergence of Palm OS into the Garnet and Cobalt versions is a perfect example of this kind of tradeoff: offering developers the assurance that their investment in Palm OS code will be preserved, while offering new APIs and functionality to new devices and applications.

*Use the Palm OS APIs instead of making direct calls to hardware. The Palm OS APIs are very complete. If you stick with using the provided functions, your application should continue to run smoothly on new devices.*

# Summary

This chapter explained the philosophy behind the Palm OS platform and introduced you to the unique mindset required to design effective handheld applications. You should now know the following:

❑ The Palm OS platform's success is based upon a compact and efficient operating system, ease of use, excellent desktop integration, and support for diverse handheld form factors.

❑ Handheld application development is very different from desktop application development because it requires you to work within a number of constraints.

❑ Applications that run on smartphones and wireless devices can expect to have different connectivity options, user expectations, and connection reliability from applications running on desktop systems.

❑ The diversity of Palm OS handhelds is on the increase. A variety of different hardware features is becoming available in various combinations oriented toward specific user types.

# Understanding the Palm OS

The previous chapter introduced you to the philosophy behind Palm OS handhelds and the mind-set required to write applications for them. Even with the limitations imposed upon a Palm OS application by the hardware and mobile nature of handheld usage, Palm OS provides a wealth of features for the developer because it handles everything from user interaction to database management and serial communications. This chapter provides an overview of the structure of Palm OS and how it affects application design.

In addition to the overview of operating system features, this chapter describes some of the PalmSource recommendations for creating a Palm OS user interface. Following these guidelines ensures that your application is consistent with other applications on the Palm OS platform, resulting in an application that is easier for people to use.

## Understanding a Palm OS Handheld's Power Usage

Because of its small size, a Palm OS handheld must deal with power in a different way than a desktop computer does. Palm OS is designed to minimize power usage, making even ecologically conscious, modern, power-saving desktop systems look like energy hogs by comparison. Desktop machines use power-saving features to save money on the electric bill but Palm OS devices have to be energy efficient for a different reason: battery life.

Older Palm OS devices run on a pair of AAA alkaline batteries, while newer devices with rechargeable lithium ion batteries have little power to spare. Palm OS manages to stretch the small amount of power available to it for weeks of normal operation, which is really amazing when you consider that the device is never actually turned off.

A handheld running Palm OS constantly supplies power to important subsystems. The On/Off button simply toggles the device between a low-power mode and a more active mode. Power must not be ever completely turned off because the memory, real-time clock, and interrupt-generation circuitry require a constant supply of some small amount of power to operate properly. This is particularly important in the case of memory because the device stores applications and permanent data in RAM, which loses data if the handheld loses power.

Palm OS supports the following three modes of operation:

❑ **Sleep mode.** This is the mode that a user identifies with the device being turned "off." Everything on the device that does not require power is shut down, including the display, digitizer, and main system clock. Only essential systems such as interrupt-generation circuitry and the real-time clock remain active, along with a trickle of power to keep the RAM from losing its data. When the device is in sleep mode, only certain interrupts, such as input from the serial port or a hardware button press, "wake it up." After a user-customizable period of time (from one to three minutes), the device drops automatically into sleep mode.

❑ **Doze mode.** Most of the time that the device appears to be "on," it is in doze mode. The main clock, digitizer, and LCD screen are turned on, and the processor clock is running but not executing instructions. When there is no user input to process, the system enters doze mode. Any hardware interrupt (such as text input) that the processor receives brings the processor out of doze mode, which is much faster than its coming out of sleep mode because the device does not need to power up any of its peripheral hardware.

❑ **Running mode.** In running mode, the processor is actively executing instructions. User input in doze mode puts the device into running mode, as will an interrupt while in doze mode or sleep mode, such as the system alarm's going off or the user's pressing a hardware button. The device remains in running mode long enough to process the user input, which is usually less than a second, and then it immediately reverts to doze mode. Most applications cause the system to enter running mode only five percent of the time.

# Running Under Different Processors

Palm OS 5, upon which Palm OS Garnet is based, represented a significant step forward for Palm OS. Version 5 was the first version to support a processor architecture other than the Motorola 68K series. Palm OS Garnet and Palm OS Cobalt run on ARM (Advanced RISC Machine) processors, which are far faster than the 68K series. Because a variety of different chip manufacturers produce ARM processors, Palm OS is open to a wide variety of hardware for different purposes, from simple organizers to smartphones.

Porting an operating system from one processor architecture to another normally requires developers to recompile applications for the new processor. For example, the machine instructions for an ARM chip are different from those used by 68K processors. However, both Palm OS Garnet and Palm OS Cobalt contain the Palm Application Compatibility Environment (PACE), which emulates a 68K environment. The PACE allows applications compiled for the 68K architecture to run without modification on ARM hardware. This means that you can use the same tools to create applications that will run on Palm OS Garnet and Palm OS Cobalt as you would to create applications for earlier versions of Palm OS.

Emulation often results in poor performance, however. Extra overhead is usually required to translate data and machine instructions from the format required by one architecture into the format required by another. Because all the operating system routines in Palm OS Garnet and Palm OS Cobalt are native

ARM code, they take full advantage of the speed increase inherent in the new processor architecture. When a 68K application makes a call to a Palm OS function, the PACE executes the ARM equivalent of that function, allowing operating system routines to run at the full speed of the ARM processor. Most Palm OS applications spend the majority of their processing time calling system APIs. Because Palm OS Garnet and Palm OS Cobalt are native to ARM, and because ARM processors tend to be much faster than the 68K series, most 68K applications actually run faster on ARM versions of Palm OS than they would on their native 68K architecture.

For those Palm OS Garnet applications that perform a lot of intensive number crunching, such as games or encryption products, it is possible to create a native ARM code module, called a Palm Native Object (PNO), to handle processor-intensive computation. The PNO may then be linked into a regular 68K application. At runtime, the application uses the Palm OS Garnet PceNativeCall routine to invoke the ARM routine, resulting in much faster performance for those tasks that require it. However, most applications do not require any native ARM code to run at acceptable speeds. The PceNativeCall function is detailed in Chapter 24.

In addition to handing 68K operating system calls off to their native ARM counterparts, the PACE converts 68K data structures into their ARM equivalents. Unlike the big-endian 68K architecture, ARM stores multibyte integers in little-endian format. ARM hardware also requires that 4-byte integers be aligned on 4-byte boundaries; such integers need to be aligned only on an even boundary in the 68K architecture. These differences in data storage mean that Palm OS structures, such as those used to contain information about a form, differ significantly between 68K and ARM.

Because data storage is so different on ARM hardware than on 68K hardware, it is important to use only Palm OS routines to view and modify the internal members of system structures instead of modifying those structures directly. The PACE maintains "shadow structures," which allow data stored in ARM format to look like 68K data. Directly modifying data in a system structure modifies only the shadow copy — without changing what is actually stored by the ARM processor, which could result in crashes or unpredictable behavior. The safe way to manipulate the internal members of a data structure is to call Palm OS routines; such routines work with the PACE to perform the necessary translation between ARM and 68K data structures.

On Palm OS Garnet, your application can access many members of Palm OS data structures by calling regular Palm OS functions, but some members require that you use functions from the PalmOSGlue static library. For more information about linking your application with the PalmOSGlue library, see Chapter 8.

Palm OS Cobalt does away with the PalmOSGlue library entirely. In many cases, it completely hides the innards of operating system data structures. However, Palm OS Cobalt provides a more complete set of APIs for modifying such structures, which makes the PalmOSGlue library unnecessary.

# Using Programming Protein

Although you may still create 68K applications for Palm OS Cobalt, the latest version of Palm OS offers an alternate application development path: native ARM programming. *Palm OS Protein* is the name that PalmSource has given to native ARM development for Palm OS Cobalt. Palm OS Protein applications are entirely ARM-native and they do not require the PACE to run on a Palm OS Cobalt device.

The newest features of Palm OS, such as schema databases and advanced multimedia, are available only to Palm OS Protein applications. However, fully ARM-native applications are not compatible with earlier versions of Palm OS, including Palm OS Garnet. You need to decide which platform to develop for when you write a Palm OS application:

❑ If your application needs to run on Palm OS Cobalt and on earlier versions of the operating system, write it as a standard 68K application and allow the PACE to run your application on Palm OS Cobalt devices. The latest features in Palm OS Cobalt won't be available to your application but chances are good that those features would be difficult or impossible to implement in a 68K application anyway. It can be extraordinarily difficult to maintain a single code base that supports both 68K and ARM versions of the same application, so this development path is a good choice if you need to support legacy Palm OS devices.

❑ If your application needs to take advantage of the latest Palm OS Cobalt APIs and capabilities, write it as an ARM-native Palm OS Protein application. The new features in Palm OS Cobalt are not available to earlier versions of the Palm OS, so backward compatibility isn't really an issue. Only Palm OS Cobalt will be able to run the application.

Porting an application from 68K to Palm OS Protein is not only possible but also relatively painless if your application already runs well on Palm OS Garnet. Details about porting from 68K to Palm OS Protein are available in Chapter 4.

# Running a Palm OS Application

The low-level architecture of the operating system differs significantly between Palm OS Garnet and Palm OS Cobalt. Despite these differences in basic architecture, most applications run in a similar fashion on both versions of the operating system.

## Understanding the Palm OS Garnet Kernel

Palm OS Garnet and earlier versions of Palm OS have a preemptive multitasking kernel. However, the User Interface Application Shell (UIAS), the part of the operating system responsible for managing applications that display a user interface, runs only one application at a time. Normally, the only task running is the UIAS, which calls application code as a subroutine. The UIAS doesn't gain control again until the currently running application quits, at which point the UIAS immediately calls the next application as another subroutine.

*Applications may not be multithreaded on Palm OS Garnet because they must run within the single thread of the UIAS.*

Applications may also *sublaunch* other applications. A sublaunch calls another application as a subroutine of the calling application. Applications use sublaunching to request other programs to perform services on their behalf. An example of sublaunching is the Palm OS global find function, which sublaunches other applications to search their data for a particular string. The code that performs the actual search belongs to the applications that own the data but the search code runs as a subroutine of the application that started the global find operation. All of this takes place within the UIAS task.

Certain calls in an application cause the operating system to launch a new task. For instance, the HotSync application starts another task in addition to the UIAS, which handles serial communication with the desktop computer. Because the serial communication task has a lower priority than the main user interface task, a user can interrupt communications by tapping the screen or pressing a hardware button.

This creation of a new task allows for more optimized communication, both with the desktop and the user. If the user taps the screen to cancel the synch, the higher-priority user interface task processes the tap immediately, allowing for quick response to a user's input, even when the serial task is using most of the processor's time to talk to the desktop. However, because there usually isn't any user interaction during a HotSync session, the serial task gets all the processor time it needs for rapid communication.

> Only the system software can launch a new task in Palm OS Garnet. Application code does not have direct access to the Palm OS multitasking APIs.

## Understanding the Palm OS Cobalt Kernel

Palm OS Cobalt allows for multithreaded applications. Each *thread* is an independent unit of program execution, including a stack, register variables, program counter, and other data required to keep track of the thread's state. Multiple threads may be executed simultaneously; the kernel determines which thread gets access to the CPU at a given time, based on each thread's priority. A multithreaded application can perform potentially lengthy tasks, such as network communications, without becoming unresponsive to the user. For example, an e-mail application can use one thread to download mail in the background, while the application's main user interface thread continues to handle user input, which allows the user to compose a new message instead of being forced to wait for the mail to finish downloading.

One or more threads run inside a *process*, which is a protected environment that contains all the memory, executable code, and state data necessary for the threads to operate. A thread may not inhabit more than one process. By default, Palm OS Cobalt prevents threads in one process from accessing resources contained by a different process. Such restricted access allows for better stability and security than in prior versions of the operating system. It is possible for code in one process to grant access to a thread in a different process. Palm OS also supports a variety of methods for threads to communicate with one another, both within a single process and across process lines.

When the system first starts, it creates its own set of processes to handle system tasks, manage stored data, control basic I/O, and perform tasks defined by the Palm OS licensee that created the device, such as managing special navigation hardware. Palm OS Cobalt does not allow an application to arbitrarily create its own processes. Instead, when an application starts, the system creates a process called the *UI Process*, in which the application's threads may run. In similar fashion to older versions of Palm OS, only one application may run in the UI Process at a time. When an application switch occurs, the currently running application quits, the system destroys the UI Process, and the system creates a brand new UI Process for the new application.

Palm OS Cobalt applications have a number of options when it comes to sublaunching. An application may perform a traditional sublaunch, in which the system loads the sublaunched code into the UI Process and executes it as a subroutine of the calling application. This is identical to the way in which Palm OS Garnet performs a sublaunch but it is inherently insecure because the sublaunched code has full access to the calling application's data in the UI Process.

To allow for secure execution of another application's code, Palm OS Cobalt provides *remote sublaunching*. A remote sublaunch starts a temporary process and then runs the sublaunched code within the new process. While the sublaunched code is executed, the temporary process is treated as the UI Process so the calling application is blocked while the sublaunch is running. Once the sublaunched code completes its task, the operating system destroys the temporary process containing the sublaunched code and returns control to the calling application in the UI Process.

Because the UI Process is destroyed when an application exits, application threads cannot normally continue executing when the user switches to another application. However, Palm OS Cobalt provides the *Background Process* as an area where applications may create threads that remain after an application exits. For example, a Background Process thread could allow an e-mail application to download mail in the background while the user checks appointments in the Date Book; upon returning to the e-mail application, the mail is ready for the user to read.

Any application may have one or more threads running in the Background Process. This means that the address space in the Background Process is inherently insecure; memory in the Background Process is accessible to all threads running there. Any secure operations should be performed in the UI Process, where an application has total control over what code is allowed to run.

Poorly written code can crash the entire Background Process, thereby killing all the threads running there. However, applications may request to be notified when a thread crashes the Background Process, allowing the applications to restart their background threads.

## Responding to Launch Codes

When the system launches an application, it calls a function named `PilotMain` (similar to the `main` function in a C program) and passes it a launch code. The launch code may tell the application to start and display its user interface, in which case it starts up its event loop and processes the event queue. This kind of startup is called a *normal launch*.

Alternatively, the launch code may tell the application to perform some small task, without displaying its user interface, and then exit. The Palm OS global find function works this way, sending a launch code to each application on the device, requesting that it search its own databases for a particular string. Applications that support the global find function then perform the requested search; other applications ignore the launch code. Launch codes also exist for many other purposes, such as opening an application to a specific record or notifying an application that a HotSync operation has just been completed.

When an application receives any launch code other than a normal launch, control passes not to the event loop but rather to another function in the application that does its job outside the event loop. Launch codes are covered in more detail in Chapter 4.

## Handling Events

A Palm OS application is event-driven. It receives events from the operating system and either handles them or passes them back to be handled by the operating system itself. An event structure describes the type of event that has taken place (for example, a stylus tap on an onscreen button) as well as information related to that event, such as the screen coordinates of a stylus tap. During a normal launch, execution passes to the application's *event loop*, which retrieves events from the event queue and dispatches them according to the type of event.

The event loop passes most of the events back to the OS because the system already has facilities for dealing with common tasks, such as displaying menus or determining which onscreen button was tapped. Events that are not handled by the operating system go to the application's own event handler, which either handles the events if they are interesting to the application or passes them back to the event loop.

A typical Palm OS application remains in the event loop until it receives an event telling it to close the application, at which point the event loop passes control to another function that performs cleanup operations and prepares the program to be shut down.

The standard event loop is an important ingredient in power management in a Palm OS application. A standard event loop calls operating system functions to process the event queue, and these functions know enough about managing power to put the device into doze mode if no events currently need processing. Using a standard event loop also ensures that if the user leaves the handheld on for a few minutes, the operating system's auto-off feature will put the device into sleep mode. The event loop is covered in more detail in Chapter 4.

# Using Resources

A Palm OS application is composed of *resources*, which are blocks that represent data, executable code, user interface elements, and other pieces of the application. Resources may be relocated in memory; therefore, each is identified with a four-byte resource type (such as tBTN for a command button) and a two-byte ID number.

A Palm OS application is really a resource database. It contains all the code, user interfaces, and other resources necessary to make the application run properly. On the desktop, resource database files end in the extension .prc, so resource databases are often referred to as *PRC files*.

Resources also allow for easier localization of an application. Because all the user interface elements and strings of an application may be kept in separate resources from the application code, translating an application's text resources to another human language is a simple matter of rebuilding the resources in the new language. Using this modularity ensures that the code running the application need not be changed or recompiled to localize the application. Chapter 6 covers the creation of resources in detail.

# Designing an Application's User Interface

Palm OS provides a variety of resources that represent user interface elements. The visible portion of an application is where user interaction happens, so it is important to know what tools are available and how they work. More than any other part of an application, the user interface separates a good Palm OS application from one that is frustrating to use.

Every user interface element in Palm OS is a resource that you build and then compile into your application. Different development environments provide different ways of generating interface resources; your code deals with them the same way no matter where they were originally located.

This section introduces the user interface elements available in Palm OS, describes their function, and gives examples of each. Find complete details on programming user interface elements in Chapter 8.

# *Forms*

A form provides a container, both visual and programmatic, for different types of user interface elements. Forms contain other user interface elements. A given form usually represents a single screen in an application or a modal dialog box. Figure 2-1 shows different forms from the built-in applications. Notice that different sizes of forms are possible.

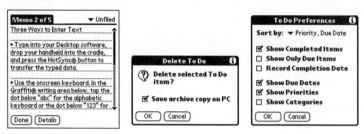

**Figure 2-1**

Every application that presents a user interface must consist of at least one form; most contain more than one to display different views and dialog boxes. Most forms occupy the entire screen area, except for dialog boxes, which may occupy less height than a full-screen form but still occupy the entire width of the screen, and are justified with the bottom of the screen.

Optionally, forms may have the following features:

❑   Title bar

❑   Associated menu bar

❑   Tips icon (only in modal forms)

The tips icon appears as a small, circled "i" in the upper right corner of a form with a title bar (refer to the second and third forms in Figure 2-1). If the user taps the tips icon, another dialog box opens, displaying helpful information about the dialog box that contained the icon. Adding tips to a dialog box is covered in Chapter 7.

# *Alerts*

Alerts provide a facility for displaying simple modal dialog boxes to the user. An alert dialog box is a special kind of form with a title bar, a text message, one or more buttons, and an icon. In addition, alerts also may have a tips icon, just as forms do.

An alert can be one of the following four types:

❑   **Information.** An information dialog box displays an "i" icon, which is similar to the tips icon but larger. It is used to give the user simple information, or to inform the user that the requested action cannot or should not be performed. Such an action does not generate an error or cause data loss. Information alerts also can serve as simple application "about" boxes.

❑ **Confirmation.** A dialog box of the confirmation type displays a "?" icon. It asks the user for input or confirmation and provides a number of buttons from which the user can choose.

❑ **Warning.** A warning dialog box displays an "!" icon. This type of dialog box should be used to ask for confirmation when the user requests a potentially dangerous action. The difference between a warning and a confirmation dialog box is whether the action is reversible or not. Use a confirmation dialog box if the action can be reversed or if data deleted as a result of the action can be backed up to the desktop. Use a warning dialog box if permanent data loss may result from the action.

❑ **Error.** An error dialog box displays a circular stop sign that contains a white "X." Use this type of alert to inform the user that the most recent action caused an error or could not be completed.

If sounds are enabled on the device, different types of alerts will produce different audio cues when displayed. Figure 2-2 shows examples of all four types of alerts from the built-in applications (clockwise from upper left: information, confirmation, error, and warning).

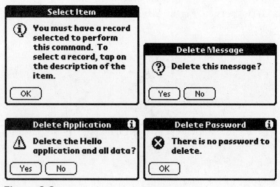

Figure 2-2

# Menus

Menus provide access to commands without occupying precious screen real estate. Each menu contains one or more *menu items*, each of which may have a *command shortcut* assigned to it. A command shortcut is a single character that allows Graffiti to access a menu item's command. If the user enters the Graffiti command stroke (see Figure 2-3) followed by a menu shortcut character, the corresponding menu item is activated. (The dot in Figure 2-3 represents where the stroke begins.)

Figure 2-3

In Palm OS 3.5 and later, making the Graffiti command stroke displays the *command toolbar* (see Figure 2-4).

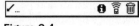

Figure 2-4

The command toolbar contains a number of iconic buttons, each of which is assigned to a particular menu item. Tapping one of these buttons activates a menu item, just as if the user had tapped the menu item itself. Certain common menu commands, such as the editing commands for cutting and copying text, automatically appear on the command toolbar without requiring any application code. Applications may override these default icons and provide their own.

Context determines what icons appear on the command toolbar. For example, the Copy and Cut icons appear only when text is highlighted in a text field. Chapter 7 covers the creation of command toolbar icon resources, while Chapter 8 discusses how to add buttons programmatically to and remove them from the command toolbar.

To group menu items visually, use a *separator bar*. In the menu resource, a separator bar is simply another menu item that has special properties. Figure 2-5 shows a separator bar between the "Select All" and "Keyboard" menu items.

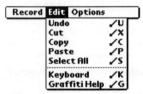

Figure 2-5

Menus themselves are contained in a *menu bar*. There can be only one menu bar assigned to any given form. Figure 2-5 also shows a single menu bar, one of its menus, and the menu items of that particular menu. Creating menu resources is covered in Chapter 7 and programming them is detailed in Chapter 8.

## Tables

Tables are a way to display data in such a way that the user can edit it directly on the screen. A table can organize a number of other user interface elements within its rows and columns. Objects within a table row or column often contain the same kind of objects. For example, in a two-column table, the first column might contain labels and the second column text fields.

You can scroll a table vertically to display more rows of data than fit on the screen at one time. Tables cannot be scrolled horizontally, though. Figure 2-6 shows tables from the built-in To Do List (left) and Date Book (right) applications. Notice the variety of different things that a table's cells may contain. This kind of flexibility makes tables one of the more difficult user interface elements to implement correctly. It also makes them one of the most useful.

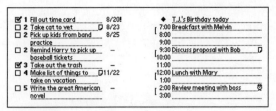

Figure 2-6

## Lists

A list is ideal for displaying multiple rows of data for selecting instead of editing. As with a table, you can scroll it vertically to display more items than fit on the screen at one time. Palm OS draws scroll indicators (small arrows) in the corners of a list to indicate that the list may be scrolled up or down to display hidden items. Unlike a table, a list is not well-suited for displaying dynamic data. Use a list to offer static choices to the user; use a table to allow the user to edit displayed rows directly.

You can display list resources in two different ways. If you include a list directly in a form and set it to be visible, the system will draw the list with square corners and display it as a static user interface element. Alternatively, you can associate a nonvisible list with a pop-up trigger to create a pop-up list. Drawn on the screen with rounded corners, a pop-up list saves screen real estate by staying hidden until the user actually needs to select an item from it. Instead of occupying screen space with numerous list items, only a single item, displayed in the associated pop-up trigger, needs to appear onscreen. Both types of lists are shown in Figure 2-7 (static list on the left, pop-up list on the right).

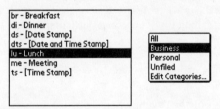

Figure 2-7

## Pop-up Triggers

A pop-up trigger consists of a downward-pointing arrow to the left of a text label, which can change its width to accommodate changes in the text. Pop-up triggers allow the user to choose an item from an associated list without using screen real estate to display the entire list. Only the currently selected list item is displayed in the pop-up trigger's label.

When the user taps the arrow or text label in a pop-up trigger, the trigger's associated list is displayed. If the user taps a new item from the list, the list disappears and the pop-up trigger's caption changes to the newly selected item. If the user decides not to make a change and taps outside the list while it is displayed, the list disappears and the pop-up trigger's text remains the same.

The most common place where pop-up triggers appear in the built-in applications is the upper right corner of a form for the selection of a category. Pop-up triggers make efficient use of screen space. Figure 2-8 shows a pop-up trigger (left) and the list that appears (right) when the pop-up trigger is tapped.

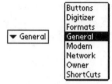

**Figure 2-8**

# Buttons

Buttons are used to launch commands or switch to other screens in an application with a single tap of the stylus. A button usually has a rounded frame and contains a text caption, but rectangular and frameless buttons also are possible, as are buttons containing a bitmap image. Buttons highlight (change color) when tapped until the user lifts the stylus or drags the stylus outside the button's boundaries. Figure 2-9 shows some sample buttons from the built-in applications.

( New ) ( Details... ) ( Show... )

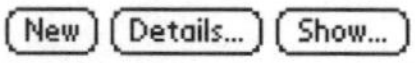

**Figure 2-9**

Use buttons for the most frequently used functions in an application. Requiring only a single tap to activate a command, buttons are the quickest user interface element with which to interact. Buttons are perfect for creating new records, calling up details on a particular record, and switching between major forms in an application.

# Repeating Buttons

Unlike a button, which sends only one event when tapped, a repeating button continues to put events in the event queue while the user holds the stylus on it. Repeating buttons are commonly used for scrolling other user interface elements, such as tables.

Although repeat buttons may look exactly like normal buttons, they are usually defined without borders. Palm OS has a few symbol fonts that contain arrow characters suitable for use as captions in repeating buttons. Most built-in applications use a pair of repeating buttons with arrows in them as scroll controls. Figure 2-10 shows the pair of repeating buttons used for scrolling the To Do List.

**Figure 2-10**

Chapter 7 contains more details about setting up repeating-button resources to mimic the arrow buttons in the built-in applications.

## Selector Triggers

A selector trigger displays a value inside a rectangular box that has a dotted-line border. When the user taps the box, a dialog box appears allowing the user to change the data displayed within the box. Selector triggers grow or shrink to match the width of the values they display.

The most common use of a selector trigger is to allow time or date selection. Palm OS has functions for displaying standard time and date picker dialog boxes, and these work perfectly with selector triggers. If the data you display in a selector trigger is not a time or date, or you wish to show a different dialog box from those supplied by the operating system, you must supply the dialog box that appears when the user taps a selector trigger.

Figure 2-11 shows selector triggers from the Event Details dialog box in the built-in Date Book application. Notice that the caption of a selector trigger may be any string of text you choose.

**Figure 2-11**

## Push Buttons

Push buttons perform the same function as radio buttons in other graphical interfaces. Push buttons always appear in groups of two or more. Only one button in the group may be selected at a time, and that button is highlighted. Use a group of push buttons when you need to present the user with only a small number of options for a particular value. If you need the user to choose from a large number of values, or if those values may change from time to time, use a list instead.

Figure 2-12 shows examples of push buttons from the various built-in applications.

**Figure 2-12**

## Check Boxes

Use a check box to indicate a setting that you can switch on or off. A check box consists of a square and text caption. If the setting indicated by the check box is off, the square is empty; if the setting is on, the square contains a check. Tapping either the box or the text caption toggles the value of a check box. By default, the text caption of a check box always appears to the right of the square. If you want a check box to be labeled on the left, leave the check box's text caption empty and place a label resource to the left of the check box (see the "Labels" section later in this chapter).

As with push buttons, you can arrange check boxes into groups so that only one check box in the group can be checked at a time. Push buttons are best for indicating exclusive choices because they provide a better visual cue that they are part of a group. Check boxes are better for situations where more than one setting may be turned on at a time.

Two check boxes, one checked and the other empty, are shown in Figure 2-13.

**Figure 2-13**

# Sliders

Slider controls are available in Palm OS 3.5 and later. A slider allows the user to select a value graphically that falls within a certain range. For example, a slider could be used as a volume control, ranging from 0 (mute) at the left end of the slider to 11 (maximum volume) at the right end. Figure 2-14 shows a slider control.

**Figure 2-14**

A slider can be adjusted in two ways:

❑ The user can tap and hold the *thumb,* which is the part of the slider that moves back and forth and indicates its current value relative to the endpoint values. While holding the stylus on the thumb, the user can move the thumb left and right.

❑ The user can tap and release on either side of the thumb. As with a scroll bar in other GUIs, doing so causes the thumb to jump toward the direction of the tap by a certain number of units defined by the application that owns the slider.

Sliders come in two flavors: regular and feedback. These two types of sliders are identical in appearance; they differ only in behavior. A *regular slider* queues an event only when the user lifts the stylus from the control. Use a regular slider if your application is interested in retrieving only the final value that the user sets in the slider control. A *feedback slider* sends events while the user holds the stylus to the screen, registering an event each time the thumb moves at least a pixel. Use a feedback slider if your application needs to update the display continuously while the user drags the thumb side to side.

# Labels

A label is simply a bit of noneditable text that appears on a form or in a table. Use labels to provide descriptions of other user interface elements. For example, placing a label containing the text "Date:" to the left of a selector trigger tells the user that tapping the selector trigger will change the date listed in the selector. Labels work also to provide instructions or information in dialog boxes.

Figure 2-15 shows labels from a few different built-in applications.

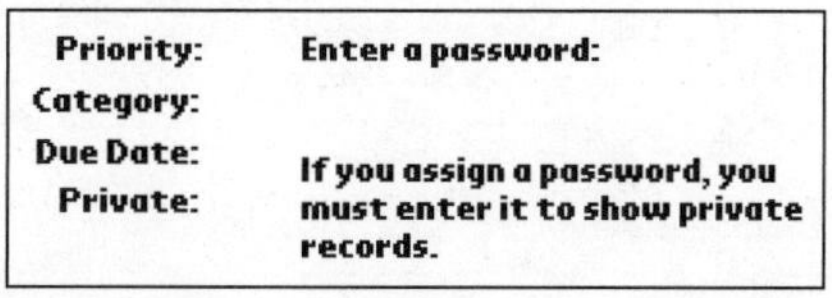

| Priority: | Enter a password: |
|---|---|
| Category: | |
| Due Date: | If you assign a password, you |
| Private: | must enter it to show private records. |

Figure 2-15

## Form Bitmaps

Every form may have one or more form bitmaps associated with it. Form bitmaps are typically used to display icons, such as those used by alert dialog boxes. A form bitmap also works well as a logo for an "about" box.

Form bitmaps simply attach a predefined bitmap resource to a form and specify where on the form the bitmap should appear. Figure 2-16 shows an example of a form bitmap.

Figure 2-16

> If a bitmap must be able to change locations within a form — a technique commonly used for animation in games — you must use the `WinDrawBitmap` function. Chapter 8 explains how to do so.

## Fields

Fields allow for in-place editing of text using any method of text input. A text field also is useful for displaying noneditable text that may change as the program runs. For example, an application could display data from its records in a noneditable text field. Labels could be used for this purpose but they are somewhat more limited than text fields in what they can do.

Fields may consist of a single line or multiple lines. Single-line fields may be either left- or right-justified, and they do not accept Tab or Return characters. Multiline fields may be set to change height dynamically, so that when text is added to or removed from the field, its height expands or contracts to accommodate the text accordingly. Scroll bars are often used in conjunction with multiline fields to allow them to contain many pages of text.

Palm OS keeps track of the current *insertion point* — a blinking cursor that indicates which field in a form is currently active — as well as where the newly entered text will appear. Usually you won't need to worry about the location of the insertion point because the operating system handles all the nitty-gritty implementation details.

Figure 2-17 shows both single-line and multiline text fields.

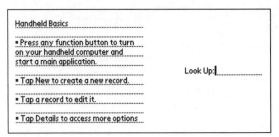

**Figure 2-17**

# *Graffiti Shift Indicator*

Every form with editable text fields should contain a Graffiti shift indicator, preferably in the lower right corner of the form. The state indicator shows the current shift state of the Graffiti text entry system: punctuation, symbol, uppercase shift, or uppercase lock. This provides the user with an important visual cue that aids accurate data entry. Failing to add one to a form with fields will make your application somewhat less than user-friendly.

> *If your application is designed to run on Palm OS version 1.0, be sure to leave extra horizontal space for the Graffiti shift indicator. Instead of the underlined arrow used by current versions of the operating system to indicate uppercase lock, version 1.0 actually displays the letters "Caps" as the shift indicator.*

Fortunately, a Graffiti shift indicator is an easy user interface element to implement. Simply include one as a resource on a form and the Palm OS Graffiti manager automatically updates it as necessary. Figure 2-18 shows a Graffiti shift indicator in its four states: punctuation, symbol, uppercase shift, and uppercase lock (from left to right). The bottom row represents the different symbols used in Palm OS 1.0.

**Figure 2-18**

# *Scroll Bars*

The scroll bar element allows the user to scroll vertically through tables, lists, and multiline fields. The arrow buttons at the top and bottom of a scroll bar help to scroll a single line at a time. A solid bar in the middle of the scroll bar, called the *scroll car*, provides a visual indicator of what percentage of the total data contained in the attached field, list, or table is currently being displayed on the screen. Users may tap the shaded area above or below the scroll car to move through the data a page at a time, or they may drag the scroll car to navigate directly to a specific location in the data.

> *Scroll bars are available only in Palm OS version 2.0 and later. If your application must run on version 1.0, use repeating buttons and the hardware scroll buttons instead of a scroll bar.*

Implementing a scroll bar requires a certain amount of effort on your part. You must provide two-way communication between the scroll bar and the attached list, table, or field in the following manner:

❑   When the data in the element attached to the scroll bar changes, your code must alert the scroll bar to the change so it can properly position and size the scroll car.

❑   When the user taps the scroll bar or its arrows, or drags the scroll car, your code needs to update the list, field, or table to display the appropriate portion of its data. Your application may update the data display in two ways:

 ❑   **Dynamic updating.** As users hold the stylus down on the scroll bar, the data display changes. This method of updating the data provides users with instant feedback about their current location in the data but it can be slow if the data display is a complex table with many different types of data to draw.

 ❑   **Static updating.** The data display changes only after users release the stylus from the scroll bar. This method requires less processing and may be more appropriate for complex tables. It can be frustrating to users, however, because there is no indication of where they are in the data until they release the stylus, at which point they must use the scroll bar again if the field, list, or table is not displaying the data they wanted to see.

Figure 2-19 shows a scroll bar.

Figure 2-19

# Gadgets

If none of the other user interface elements in Palm OS suit your purpose, you can make a custom user interface element using a *gadget*. For example, you could use a gadget to create a monthly calendar view that allows selection of a particular day by tapping on that day in the calendar. A gadget contains information about its screen location, whether it is currently usable or not, and a pointer to a piece of data. You must implement everything else, from drawing the gadget to responding to the stylus taps.

Because you have to do the bulk of the work to implement a gadget anyway, you may be thinking that you might as well code your own custom interface object from scratch. The gadget does offer some advantages over rolling your own object, though:

❑   Gadgets keep track of their rectangular bounds on the screen, making it easy for an application to detect whether a particular tap on the screen was on the gadget or not. This also makes any drawing code for your gadget more portable because it can draw relative to the gadget's bounds instead of requiring hard-coded screen coordinates. You can then use your gadget code in a different application, or even in a different location on the same form, without having to rewrite a lot of code.

❑    A gadget maintains a pointer to whatever data you wish to associate with the gadget. For example, a calendar gadget could store the currently selected date.

❑    The Palm OS Emulator (POSE) and Palm OS Simulator have a testing feature called Gremlins that can randomly poke at your application and uncover obscure bugs that you might otherwise miss. Gremlins occasionally tap on random areas of the screen that don't contain any controls, but they are particularly attracted to standard user interface elements. Coding a custom element as a gadget ensures that Gremlins will give your custom interface a good workout.

More information about POSE and Gremlins is available in Chapter 5.

Figure 2-20 shows a gadget from the built-in Date Book's month view. This complex gadget draws a calendar view and indicates appointments with symbols. The user can pick a particular day by tapping it; doing so displays that particular day in a different screen.

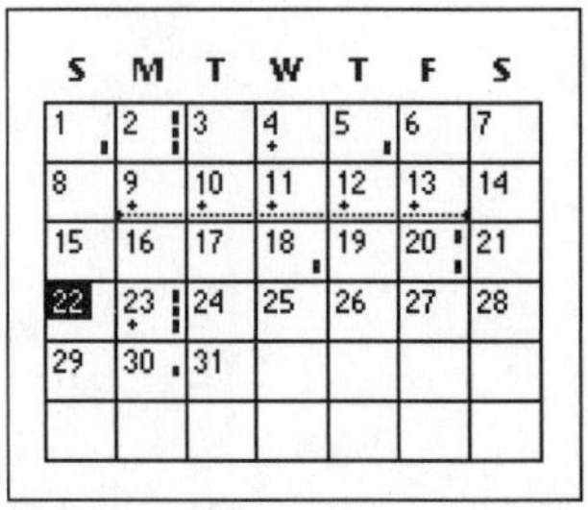

Figure 2-20

# Following Palm OS User Interface Guidelines

Although the philosophy behind the Palm OS platform is responsible for many of PalmSource's user interface guidelines, many of these guidelines apply equally well to any program running on any platform. User interface is the art of striking a balance between screen space and ease of use that makes an application useful to the largest number of people.

The Palm OS user interface guidelines dictate three basic rules:

❑    Programs must be fast.

❑    Frequently used functions should be more accessible than infrequently used functions.

❑    Programs should be easy to use.

You can read the official PalmSource guidelines, "Palm OS User Interface Guidelines," in the Palm OS SDK.

## Making Fast Applications

Creating a fast application is more than just writing good algorithms and optimizing your code. Good handheld applications have an efficient interface that makes it possible to use them quickly. Navigating through different screens, activating commands, and retrieving data should require little time. For example, when the user enters Graffiti strokes in the list view of the built-in Memo Pad application, the application automatically creates a brand-new memo containing the newly entered text; there is no need for the user to tap the New button explicitly to create a new memo. Looking up information in all the standard Palm applications is just as simple, often requiring only one hand, because the hardware buttons can scroll through the most useful information without you having to use the stylus.

Always try to reduce the number of taps required to perform a particular action. The best way to accomplish this is through intelligent selection of controls; some user interface elements are faster at some tasks than others. Keep the following in mind when designing your application's interface:

❑ Buttons provide the quickest access to a program's functions. They occupy a fair amount of screen real estate, though, and having too many buttons on a form is inefficient because users must spend more time visually searching the screen for the button they want.

❑ Because push buttons are faster than pop-up lists (push buttons require only one tap instead of two to make a selection), use push buttons when you have enough screen space for them.

❑ A check box is a fast way to change a setting that can be turned on or off because only a single tap is required to toggle the box. Unless you need to fit a lot of controls into a single screen, avoid using pop-up lists that contain only two items; a single check box will perform the same action in half the number of taps.

❑ A pop-up list is faster than Graffiti or onscreen keyboard input. If your application can offer choices from a list instead of requiring the user to enter text manually, the user will spend much less time entering data. For example, if an application requires the user to enter the name of a state, selecting a state from a pop-up list is much more convenient for the user than having to enter the name of the state as text.

❑ Pop-up lists that contain a lot of elements are slower to use than short lists. Just like having too many buttons on one form, too many list items are hard to take in at a glance. Also, with a large number of list items, the user may have to scroll the list to find the right item, requiring yet another tap.

❑ Menus require an extra tap to display the menu in the first place, so they should be reserved for functions that are used less frequently. A good example of a feature that is appropriate for a menu is a command that displays a dialog box for altering application preferences. Once users have set their preferences, there probably won't be much need for them to get to the preferences quickly.

❑ One exception to the rule for including only infrequently used items on menus is menu items that include a Graffiti command shortcut. Power users appreciate the ability to fire off commands quickly by making a couple of gestures with the stylus.

❑   There is no need for an "exit" or "close" command in a Palm OS application. Palm OS users exit an application by starting another application. This departure from desktop application design has important ramifications for how your application saves its data. Instead of explicitly requiring the user to save before leaving, your application should automatically save its data as it closes.

## *Highlighting Frequently Used Features*

Commands in an application that the user uses frequently should be easier to access than those that the user needs only occasionally. Not only should a frequently used command be easy to spot on a form but the physical actions required to activate the command should be few as well.

Something the user is likely to do several times in an hour, such as checking today's events in the Date Book, should be accessible with a single tap. If a particular action may be performed a number of times in a single day, such as adding an item to the To Do List, a couple taps or a little bit of text entry is appropriate. Adding a repeating event to the Date Book or other things that the user might need only a few times every week can require more taps or an entire dialog box devoted to the task.

The following tips can help you match accessibility to frequency of use:

❑   Important data that you expect a user to look at most of the time should be the first thing displayed when the application starts. The built-in Date Book is a good example of this because it shows today's events when it opens. Just by launching the application, a user can check what is going on without even having to use the stylus.

❑   Keep to a minimum the need to flip through different screens. The more navigation required to move between particular views of the application's data, the more time it takes the user to retrieve that data. Not only is it important to keep this in mind when designing user interface but it also is vital when determining how your application stores its data. Structure the data so that retrieving records does not require much navigation. Chapter 16 deals with data structure concerns more fully.

❑   Use command buttons for the most common tasks that the user must perform. All four major built-in applications have a New button for creating records because quickly adding a new record is a vital part of these programs. Command buttons also are perfect for launching frequently used dialog boxes, such as the Details dialog box in the Date Book and To Do List applications.

❑   Avoid using a dialog box if you don't really need one. Notice that the built-in applications do not prompt the user for a new record's category when the user taps the New button. Instead, the applications assign a reasonable default category to the new item, usually based on the category currently displayed in the list view, and immediately allow the user to start entering data. If the user wants to change the category, another tap on the Details button, or the category pop-up list, allows the user to perform this task. Try to anticipate how someone will use an application and design it accordingly.

❑   Except for infrequently used features, try to avoid displaying a dialog box from another dialog box. Digging back out of nested dialog boxes slows down the application's usage.

# Designing for Ease of Use

Ideally a Palm OS application should be usable with little or no instruction. Within five minutes of picking up a Palm OS device for the first time, a user ought to be able to perform basic tasks and freely navigate among applications. More advanced commands should still be easy to find and use but they should not obscure the most basic functions of a program.

Consistency is key to making a user interface that new users can learn easily. Memorizing a completely new way of interacting with the device for each different application is difficult, time-consuming, and annoying. When every Palm OS application operates in a similar fashion, the skills learned from interacting with one application easily applies to any other program.

One of the best ways to ensure that your Palm OS applications are familiar to users — both new and experienced — is to emulate the interface design of the built-in applications. Study how the standard applications display data and offer choices, and design your own user interface to parallel the placement of controls in the built-in applications. Not only is imitation the sincerest form of flattery, but it will make your applications easier to use.

These suggestions will help you write applications that are easy to use:

❑   In the title bars of forms, let the user know what application is running and what view is currently displayed. This kind of context is necessary to prevent the user from becoming lost while navigating among screens and different applications.

❑   Use clearly labeled buttons for the most important commands. Not only are buttons quick to use but they catch the eye like no other user interface element, making them ideal for stressing key actions to perform. Ensure that the label on the button adequately describes its function. You must strike a balance between saving screen space and providing enough text to avoid confusing the user about the button's function. One possibility for saving some screen real estate with buttons is to label them with icons instead of words. For example, a small picture of a trash can might replace a "Delete" caption. Be careful when using icons, though. What may be intuitive to you may leave your application's users hopelessly confused if they don't make the same logical connection you made between an icon and its function. In particular, be careful with icons in applications intended for a global audience. Different cultures often use completely different images and idioms; to a user in another country, a small icon may mean something far different than what you intended.

❑   Keep the design of forms and dialog boxes clean and simple. You may be tempted to put everything right up front on the screen to allow quick access to as many commands as possible. However, doing so makes the application more difficult to learn and can actually slow users down, forcing them to scan the screen in search of the proper control. A few well-placed buttons that open simple dialog boxes are preferable to trying to cram your entire interface into a single screen.

❑   Make sure that actions are consistent throughout the application. For example, if pressing the hardware scroll buttons browses records a screenful at a time in one view but switches between entry fields in another view, the application becomes harder to learn and use. If each application has its own idiosyncrasies, the user is being asked to remember a lot of information just to use a handheld that is supposed to simplify one's life. Reduce the burden on the user's memory by making similar actions perform similar functions throughout an application.

❏ Navigation between different views in the application should be obvious to the user. The best way to do this is by using command buttons. The address view in Address Book is a good example. The three buttons — Done, Edit, and New — do what most users expect they will do when tapped: return to the main list view, edit the currently displayed record, or make a new record, respectively.

❏ Minimize the number of steps required to perform a particular task. This not only speeds use of the application but also reduces its complexity, making it easier for the user to remember how to perform that task.

❏ Menus are hidden from view by default; the user must tap either the Menu silkscreen button or (in Palm OS version 3.5 or later) the title bar to display the menu bar. Less sophisticated users may not even realize that menus exist. If possible, use menu commands only for functions that are not absolutely necessary for basic, day-to-day operation of the program.

❏ Always provide the standard Edit menu whenever editable text fields are present in a form or dialog box. This ensures that the Clipboard and text editing commands are always available. More importantly, make sure the onscreen keyboard is accessible to those users who prefer it to Graffiti text entry. On Palm OS version 2.0 and later, be sure to provide access to the system Graffiti reference dialog box from this menu. The standard Edit menu is described in Chapter 7.

❏ In addition to the Edit menu, any form that has editable text fields also needs to have a Graffiti shift indicator. This user interface element makes it obvious to the user what character a particular gesture will create. In addition, in Japanese versions of Palm OS, the Graffiti shift indicator indicates whether the front-end processor (FEP) is on or off, as well as whether the FEP is converting text to Hiragana or Katakana characters.

❏ When a form containing text fields opens, the first editable field should have the focus. This does not happen automatically; your application must call the `FrmSetFocus` function to set the focus manually. Putting the focus in a field prevents the user from having to tap the field before entering text, allowing the user to get a running start entering data. The `FrmSetFocus` function is covered in detail in Chapter 8.

# Maintaining Palm OS Style

There are a number of other considerations to keep in mind when designing an application to fit the expectations of users of Palm OS devices. Anyone used to the standard applications installed on such a handheld will count on certain things working in a particular way. Also, some elements of Palm OS style are necessary to ensure that your application is a good citizen and performs the way the operating system expects.

## Navigating Within and Between Applications

Typically users switch applications by pressing the physical application buttons or using the application launcher. If your application intercepts the hardware buttons for its own purposes (a common occurrence for navigation in game programs), be sure to leave the silkscreen application launcher button alone. Otherwise, there will be no way to switch out of your application without resetting the device.

Depending on what information your application must display, it may be appropriate to have two different views of its data: a list view and an edit view. The Memo Pad application operates in this fashion (see Figure 2-21). The list view (left) shows some or all of the application's records one screenful at a time, providing some useful information at a glance. Selecting a record from the list view starts an edit view (right), where a user may change the data in an individual record. Tapping the Done button in the edit view returns the user to the list view. The Details button in the edit view provides a way to change settings that affect the entire record, such as its category or whether it should be marked private.

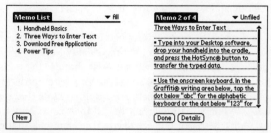

**Figure 2-21**

Even applications such as Date Book and To Do List, both of which display and allow editing of a record in the same screen, have a Details button that operates in similar fashion. Instead of going to an edit view when tapping on a record in these applications, the program enters an editing mode. When the application is in edit mode, the Details button offers the same record-level settings changes that can be made in the Memo Pad and Address Book applications.

If it's appropriate for your application, consider implementing user-defined categories to allow users to organize the program's data. A pop-up list in the upper right corner of the screen provides category switching in the standard applications. Palm OS provides facilities to manage categories easily, including a dialog box to allow adding, renaming, and removing categories. See Chapter 16 for more information about implementing categories.

Repeatedly pressing the hardware application button assigned to one of the built-in applications causes the application to switch between displaying different categories of data. If your application is one that a user might consider assigning to one of the hardware application buttons (using the Preferences application), copying this particular behavior is a good idea.

When providing a number of text entry fields on one screen, be sure your application supports the next-field and previous-field Graffiti strokes, shown in Figure 2-22 (next-field stroke on the left, previous-field stroke on the right). These strokes do not exist in Graffiti 2, and many users do not take the time to learn them, but power users appreciate their inclusion in an application.

**Figure 2-22**

You identify these two characters in code with the constants `nextFieldChr` and `prevFieldChr`. These strokes save time during data entry because the user can just enter the appropriate navigation stroke instead of lifting the stylus from the Graffiti area and tapping in another field. Also, many add-on keyboards map these strokes to Tab and Shift-Tab, respectively, allowing a keyboard user to quickly tab between fields without having to use the stylus at all. The built-in Address Book's edit view is a good example of using Graffiti strokes to switch fields. In the edit view, you can jump from field to field without ever moving the stylus out of the Graffiti entry area.

Because of the small size of the screen, users often need to scroll the display, both to see many records from a database and to view the information in long records. For onscreen scrolling, provide either a pair of arrow-shaped repeating buttons or a scroll bar. Also, handle the `pageUpChr` and `pageDownChr` key events to allow scrolling with the hardware scroll buttons. The hardware buttons should scroll data one page at a time. Although Palm OS user interface guidelines state that repeating buttons used for scrolling should scroll data one line at a time, both the Address Book and To Do List applications scroll one page at a time when the onscreen buttons are used. This is more a matter of what works well with your application's data rather than a hard-and-fast rule. Scrolling is a complex topic, covered in detail in Chapter 14.

## Designing Screen and Dialog Box Layout

The screens and dialog boxes in a standard Palm OS program should follow certain layout rules to achieve a consistent look between applications. The screen from the built-in Memo Pad application shown in Figure 2-23 is a fine example of how to design a screen for a Palm OS application.

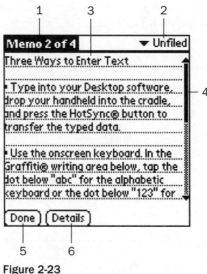

Figure 2-23

The numbers in the following guidelines refer to those in Figure 2-23:

1. **Each screen should have a title bar.** If there is enough room, include the name of the application and current view. The title bar's text should not only let users know what application they are looking at but also should provide context within the program. Carefully worded title bars prevent users from becoming lost in applications that contain many different possible views.

2. **If the application uses categories to organize records, put a category pop-up list in the upper right corner.** In a screen that displays multiple records, this pop-up should change the view to display records from different categories; in a screen that displays a single record, the category pop-up should change the category of the currently displayed record.

3. **Use the whole screen, all the way out to the edge.** As it is, there is precious little screen real estate on a Palm OS handheld. Wasting even a couple pixels to draw a border makes it difficult to fit user interface elements on the screen without crowding them. The hardware case surrounding the screen makes a perfectly suitable frame for your application.

4. **Whenever possible, use the standard Palm OS user interface resources.** Unless your application has unique interface requirements (for example, games tend to have special interface elements), sticking with the default buttons, fields, and other parts of the default operating system provides users with a familiar environment. Familiarity makes the program easier to use.

5. **Line up and left-justify command buttons along the bottom of the screen.** In particular, any buttons used to navigate between screens in an application will be quicker to use if they are all in a consistent location because users will be able to tap in the same region of the screen without moving the stylus very far.

6. **In buttons and other places where text is contained in a border, be sure to leave at least one pixel above and one pixel below the height of the text.** Many characters in the default Palm OS fonts are difficult to read when a line touches them. PalmSource provides recommended settings for individual user interface elements. These guidelines are detailed with their appropriate resources in Chapter 8.

Dialog boxes serve a different function from screens in a Palm OS program. A dialog box provides a place for the application to query the user for input, or for the user to change record and application settings. The dialog box from the To Do List application shown in Figure 2-24 demonstrates good dialog box design principles.

Figure 2-24

Numbered guidelines below refer to Figure 2-24:

1. **Palm OS provides facilities for online help in dialog boxes.** Tips, accessed from the "i" icon in the upper right corner of a dialog box, are an easy way to provide users with details about what all the interface elements in a dialog box actually do. Adding tips to a dialog box is easy and requires no code at all; simply create a string resource and associate it with the dialog box form. Chapter 7 tells you how.

2. **Labels in a dialog box should be right-justified, followed by left-justified elements that may be edited.** Use bold text for the labels and nonbold text for editable items to differentiate among them visually.

3. **Dialog boxes need four pixels of space between buttons and the edge of the dialog box.** Screens do not require this because they have no border.

4. **Be sure to put positive response buttons on the left and negative responses on the right, particularly in alerts that prompt the user to make a decision.** Maintaining this kind of consistency speeds use of the program and helps prevent the user from making errors.

5. **Dialog boxes should always be aligned with the bottom of the screen.** Placing dialog boxes shorter than the full height of the screen at the bottom ensures that the title bar of the screen behind the dialog box will still be visible, thereby reminding users of what application is currently running and where they are within that program.

## Keeping Other PalmSource Guidelines in Mind

There are a number of other considerations to keep in mind to ensure that your application looks and behaves like other Palm OS applications:

❑ Every application should have an icon to identify it in the launcher, as well as a short name to identify the icon. For programs running on Palm OS version 3.0 or later, you also should provide a small icon for the launcher's list view. If you intend for your application to run on hardware that supports high-density screen resolutions, you should include high-density icons to ensure that your application looks its best in the launcher. Although an application can run without any icons at all, your application's icon is the first thing the user sees when launching your program. An application that includes both large and small icons at various color depths and resolutions makes a good first impression on a user. Adding icons and icon names is covered in Chapter 6.

❑ Palm OS applications contain a version resource, which the launcher in Palm OS version 3.0 and later can display from the Options ➪ Info menu command. Version resources are useful if you wish to write multiple applications that cooperate with one another or share data. Should the data format of one of the applications change between versions, the other programs can query that application to determine its version and act accordingly. Adding version resources is detailed also in Chapter 6.

❑ All functions of an application that require tapping the screen should be accessible with a single tap. Double-clicking in a desktop environment can be difficult for some users to manage because a mouse tends to move around a bit when its buttons are clicked; double-tapping on a handheld can be even more difficult because the device is usually held in the other hand instead of resting on a stable surface. Double taps are also counterintuitive. Without explicit instruction, it is impossible to tell from looking at an application that certain commands are activated by double taps.

❑ Where possible, make buttons large enough to allow finger navigation. Navigating between different views in the application should be possible without using the stylus. The buttons in the Palm OS built-in applications are a good size for this purpose.

❑ If a menu item or user interface element is currently disabled or not available, remove it from the screen entirely. Palm OS does not provide any facilities for "graying out" controls and menus. Because of the limited screen space available, removing the item entirely is preferable.

❑ Many desktop applications duplicate commands by making them accessible from a button and from the application's menus. Avoid this kind of duplication in Palm OS applications. Not only does it increase the size of the program but it also goes against the paradigm of highlighting frequently used functions. Important commands that the user accesses regularly should be on the screen itself; commands used less often should be relegated to menus.

❑ Provide Graffiti command shortcuts only for menu items that really need them. For example, cutting, copying, and pasting text are actions that need to be performed quickly and often, so these commands are good candidates for command shortcuts. On the other hand, an "about" box for an application is something that the user will look at only occasionally, if at all, so displaying it does not require a shortcut.

### Evaluating Palm Guidelines for Your Application

A final word on user interface design and the Palm OS User Interface Guidelines: These guidelines are not unbreakable laws of nature; they are just as they are presented — guidelines for the development of user-friendly handheld applications. Without looking too hard, one can fairly easily find many examples, even among the leading Palm OS software applications, that break one or more of the guidelines.

This does not diminish the collective wisdom of the User Interface Guidelines, but rather points out that there are other factors that can influence user interface design — not the least of which is your own creativity. The guidelines simply remind developers to temper that creativity with an acknowledgement of the real-world constraints facing the average handheld user. If after reading and understanding the guidelines you feel you have good reasons to choose an alternative design, by all means do so.

# Communicating with Other Devices

A key part of the Palm OS platform's success is its ability to communicate with other devices. Current versions of Palm OS offer several different communications protocols.

## Serial

Palm OS devices use the serial protocol to synchronize through a cradle with a desktop computer. With the right cable or third-party hardware, Palm OS can talk to just about anything, from modems to temperature probes to GPS (Global Positioning System) receivers. The Palm OS serial communications architecture supports several layers of varying utility and complexity, including byte-level serial I/O and high-level, error-correcting protocols. Palm OS serial communications are covered in detail in Chapter 19.

## TCP/IP

The standard protocol of the Internet, TCP/IP, allows a Palm OS device with the proper attached hardware, such as a modem, to connect to any machine on the Internet and exchange data with it. In Palm

OS Garnet and earlier versions of Palm OS, most of the functions in the Palm OS net library are the spitting image of functions in the Berkeley UNIX sockets API, which is the *de facto* standard for Internet applications. Palm OS Cobalt does away with the net library entirely and simply uses the familiar Berkeley sockets API. Applications written to use Berkeley sockets can be easily recompiled for Palm OS with only a few changes. See Chapter 20 for information about adding network support to Palm OS applications.

# Bluetooth

Bluetooth is a short-range, low-cost wireless networking technology that uses the 2.4 GHz radio band. First envisioned by mobile phone manufacturers and then adopted by other companies, Bluetooth allows small devices to be connected to one another within a range of 10 meters without the need for a tangle of cables to hook everything together.

Aside from making small electronic gizmos easier to connect to one another, Bluetooth presents some exciting possibilities. For example, a Bluetooth-enabled handheld could use a Bluetooth-enabled mobile phone's connection to the Internet for browsing the Web. Two Palm OS handhelds that support Bluetooth could automatically exchange business cards as they come within range of each other without requiring that the users of either handheld manually initiate the exchange. Boring meetings could be enlivened considerably with multiplayer games played around the conference table. On a more businesslike note, attendees of the same meeting could quickly share data and participate in collaborative applications by means of a "whiteboard."

Palm OS has extensive Bluetooth support, both for low-level network communications and for high-level object exchange. Bluetooth communication is covered in Chapter 18.

# Telephony

Palm OS 4.0 introduced support for connecting Palm OS to mobile phones. Later versions of Palm OS have added to this support with a growing library of telephony APIs. The telephony support in Palm OS works both with embedded phones (such as the Handspring Treo, Kyocera QCP 6035, and Samsung I300) and with phones connected to the handheld by a cable or infrared. Among other features, the Palm OS telephony manager handles dialing, phone configuration, and Short Messaging Service (SMS) communication.

PalmSource also provides a Virtual Phone tool, which makes debugging a telephony application possible on a development PC, without the need to use actual phone hardware. Telephony and the Virtual Phone tool are covered in detail in Chapter 20, "Communicating Over a Network."

# IrDA

Starting with the Palm III and Palm OS version 3.0, Palm devices can communicate using the industry-standard Infrared Data Association (IrDA) protocol. This low-level communications protocol can be used to communicate by infrared (IR) with a growing variety of similarly equipped devices, including cell phones, pagers, and even desktop or laptop computers. Like the serial manager, the Palm OS infrared library offers low-level control of IR data transfer. IrDA communication is covered in Chapter 18.

## *Data Exchange*

The Palm OS exchange manager provides facilities for sending individual records and applications between two devices via infrared, SMS, and Bluetooth. Although this procedure is primarily used to beam information between two Palm OS handhelds, the exchange manager is a generic communications method that allows the exchange of typed data objects between different devices. The exchange manager runs on top of other Palm OS communications systems, such as the Palm OS infrared library, the telephony manager's SMS routines, or the Bluetooth library. This modular architecture lets an application use the same code to send data using a variety of transfer mechanisms without having to know anything about the inner workings of each kind of networking technology. More information on beaming via the exchange manager is available in Chapter 18.

# Comparing Palm OS Versions

Many of the changes between different models of Palm OS devices that you need to keep in mind are changes to Palm OS itself. Fortunately, just as PalmSource and its licensees have changed the hardware incrementally, Palm OS also has evolved at an easy pace, making backward compatibility much easier to implement. This section provides a brief overview of what has changed since Palm OS version 1.0.

Because a number of new functions have been added to the operating system with each new version, the system provides facilities to determine easily what features are supported in the currently running environment. If your application uses functions from newer versions of the operating system, it will run more smoothly if you check for the existence of those features before calling them. Checking for the version number of the operating system alone is not enough because future versions of Palm OS will not necessarily implement all the features of earlier versions. Instead, the system can query whether specific *feature sets* are present in the version of Palm OS on which your application is running. For more details about checking for the presence of feature sets, see Chapter 10.

While maintaining backward compatibility all the way back to Palm OS 1.0 is a laudable goal, it does require significant effort. This effort may be wasted if you are developing an application intended for use by the majority of Palm OS handheld owners. According to marketing data gathered by NPD Intelect, more than 86 percent of Palm OS handhelds sold during 2001 run Palm OS 3.5 or later. Even if you include the sales figures for 2000, the number of devices running 3.5 or later drops to only 70 percent of all Palm OS devices sold.

If your application is intended for general use, you owe it to yourself not to worry about supporting the lowest common denominator. Palm OS 3.5 not only introduces features that are more convenient for the user, it provides new features that make it more friendly for developers as well. However, if you know for a fact that your user base includes people with older versions of Palm OS, you should make the effort to support those older versions. For example, owners of the HandEra 330 (which runs Palm OS 3.3) tend to be vocal supporters of their chosen handheld. In an enterprise setting, you also may be limited by the supply of handhelds that a corporation already has on hand.

Finding a happy medium between backward compatibility and support for the latest features of Palm OS is a balancing act that should be performed during the design phase of an application. Retrofitting compatibility onto an application is extraordinarily difficult at best and is often impossible.

# Changes in Version 2.0

Features added to version 2.0 include the following:

- ❏ Scroll bars and associated functions for manipulating them
- ❏ New launch codes to support phone lookup and access to the system preferences panel
- ❏ TCP/IP support (only on devices with 1 MB RAM or more)
- ❏ IEEE floating-point math, including 32-bit floats and 64-bit doubles
- ❏ System-wide Graffiti reference dialog box
- ❏ New string manipulation functions

Features changed from those in earlier versions include the following:

- ❏ Application preferences
- ❏ System keyboard dialog box
- ❏ Edit categories dialog box

# Changes in Version 3.0

Features added to version 3.0 include the following:

- ❏ IR beaming
- ❏ A large bold font
- ❏ Dynamic user interface functions
- ❏ Custom fonts
- ❏ Progress dialog manager
- ❏ Unique device ID on hardware with Flash ROM
- ❏ File streaming to support records larger than 64K
- ❏ Support for Standard MIDI Files (SMF) and asynchronous sound playback

Features changed from those in earlier versions include the following:

- ❏ Further changes to the edit categories dialog box
- ❏ Dynamic heap increased to 96K
- ❏ Storage RAM configured as a single heap instead of multiple 64K heaps
- ❏ Application launcher as an actual application rather than a system pop-up

# Changes in Version 3.1

Features added to version 3.1 include the following:

❑   Contrast adjustment dialog box (Palm V family devices only)

❑   Support for the DragonBall EZ processor

Features changed from those in earlier versions include the following:

❑   Character encoding changed to match Microsoft Windows code page 1252

❑   Text fields allowed to have either dotted or solid underlines

❑   Character variables changed to two bytes long

## Changes in Version 3.2

Features added to version 3.2 include the following:

❑   Function to append data to the Clipboard without erasing its current contents

❑   Alert dialog box for runtime errors, to be used when a runtime error is not the application's fault (for instance, in networking applications)

## Changes in Version 3.3

Features added to version 3.3 include the following:

❑   Support for the Euro currency symbol

❑   New serial manager that introduced more flexible serial connection capabilities, such as serial connections via infrared and support for the IrCOMM standard

❑   Login script enhancements for connecting to remote systems that use token-based authentication

❑   Faster HotSync operations, as well as HotSync operations via infrared

## Changes in Version 3.5

Features added to version 3.5 include the following:

❑   Color screen and drawing support

❑   New data type definitions (for example, `UInt16` instead of `Word`)

❑   Command bar containing buttons for commonly used menu items

❑   Slider and repeating slider controls

❑   Graphical controls

❑   Overlay manager to allow easier localization of applications without requiring complete recompilation

❑   New security routines to allow changing hidden record status from within an application, instead of having to rely on the Security applet

❑   New table routines to implement masked records

Features changed from earlier versions include the following:

❏ Extended gadget support, including the ability to assign a callback function to a gadget to handle gadget events

❏ Text fields that allow double taps to select words, or triple taps to select lines of text

❏ Menus displayed by tapping an application's title bar, a feature previously available only with third-party software

## Changes in Version 4.0

Features added to version 4.0 include the following:

❏ Telephony support

❏ Attention manager, which provides a common interface for getting the user's attention, whether as a result of alarms or wireless contact from outside the handheld

❏ Direct color support for devices with 16-bit or better color displays

Features changed from earlier versions include the following:

❏ Extended exchange manager and exchange library support to add new transport methods, such as SMS and Bluetooth

## Changes in Version 5.0

Features added to version 5.0 include the following:

❏ ARM processor support

❏ Support for high-density displays that break the traditional 160 × 160 pixel barrier

❏ Sampled sound routines for handling high-quality digital sound

❏ Improved security, including encryption routines

## Changes in Palm OS Garnet

Features added to version 5.4 (Garnet) include the following:

❏ QVGA (Quarter VGA) support for 1.5× density displays (240 × 320 pixels)

❏ PinMgr APIs to provide cross-platform support for Dynamic Input Areas (DIA)

❏ Extended text manager routines

## Changes in Palm OS Cobalt

Features added to version 6.0 (Cobalt) include the following:

- ❏ Fully ARM-native application development (Palm OS Protein)
- ❏ Multithreaded application support
- ❏ Graphics Context drawing system
- ❏ Schema databases
- ❏ Multimedia support for high-quality video and audio
- ❏ Dynamic Input Area (DIA), status bar, and slip applications
- ❏ Authentication and authorization managers added to improve security
- ❏ Improved HotSync infrastructure

Features changed from earlier versions include the following:

- ❏ Net library replaced with Berkeley sockets APIs

# Summary

This chapter provided a whirlwind tour of the features of Palm OS and explained a little about how many of them work. You should now know the following:

- ❏ Palm OS user interface guidelines are a combination of making fast programs, matching frequency-of-use to accessibility, and making programs that are easy to use.
- ❏ The Palm OS power management scheme works in such a way that the device is never really "off," only resting.
- ❏ Palm OS applications developed for 68K processors still run on more recent ARM-based Palm OS hardware, thanks to PACE.
- ❏ You can develop fully ARM-native applications for Palm OS Cobalt by using the Palm OS Protein development model.
- ❏ Palm OS applications respond to launch codes when they start. If the code calls for a normal launch, they enter an event loop to process the system event queue.
- ❏ A Palm OS application is composed of resources, some of which are built by the development environment and some of which must be supplied by the developer.
- ❏ User interface elements abound in Palm OS. If none of the provided elements does the job in your application, you can always create your own using the gadget resource.
- ❏ Following PalmSource's user interface guidelines helps produce an application that is easy to use and conforms to what a user expects to see in a Palm OS application.
- ❏ Palm OS provides numerous protocols for communicating with other devices.
- ❏ If your application uses features that were introduced in a recent version of Palm OS, it can easily check its environment to see what features are available before calling a potentially unsupported function.

# 3

# Introducing the Development Tools

You can create Palm OS applications in a great number of development environments. Of the many tools available, C and C++ are the most common languages used to develop applications for the Palm OS platform.

This chapter introduces the two primary suites of tools available for C/C++ Palm development. Metrowerks CodeWarrior for Palm OS Platform is a full-featured integrated development environment (IDE) and has long been the most popular commercial C/C++ development suite for Palm OS developers. Many of the most well-known Palm OS software programs are written using CodeWarrior. In 2004, PalmSource for the first time introduced its very own development tools, called the Palm OS Developer Suite, or PODS for short. PODS is available as a free download from www.palmsource.com. PODS incorporates several aspects of the original GNU PRC-Tools development system used by many developers as a free alternative to CodeWarrior. Given that PalmSource has positioned PODS as the standard development toolset for Palm OS applications, and considering its comprehensive support for both targeted Palm OS Garnet and Palm OS Cobalt development, PODS effectively replaces the GNU PRC-Tools.

In addition to the development tools themselves, you will need an up-to-date copy of the Palm OS SDK (Software Development Kit), which is available for free download from the PalmSource Web site (www.palmsource.com). CodeWarrior and PODS provide the resource creation, code editing, compilation, and debugging tools you need to create Palm OS applications, but these are of little use without the Palm OS header files that are included in the Palm OS SDK.

PODS comes with a copy of the Palm OS SDK and, in general, PODS and the Palm OS SDK are kept updated as a combined toolset. CodeWarrior also comes with a copy of the Palm OS SDK, but because the SDK is updated more frequently than the CodeWarrior tools, it is important to check the PalmSource Web site periodically to make sure you have the latest copy of the SDK.

The SDK also includes complete reference documentation for Palm OS, as well as various other useful guides for programming various aspects of the platform.

Finally, it is common for newer handheld devices to contain features that are specific to that device and that are not yet effectively supported as common features within the Palm OS SDK. Good examples of this are the various navigation methods available on different handhelds, such as Sony's jog-dial and palmOne's five-way navigation buttons. Special SDKs that augment the Palm OS SDK by providing access to these device-specific features are available directly from the handheld manufacturers.

Because programmers will be using either CodeWarrior or PODS as their development environment, the chapter is organized to provide users of either system with a self-contained introduction to creating and working with projects. The first half of the chapter is devoted to CodeWarrior, while the second half focuses on PODS.

# Using CodeWarrior for Palm OS

Metrowerks CodeWarrior for Palm OS Platform is an integrated development environment, containing all the tools you need to develop Palm OS applications in a single interface. CodeWarrior was the first development environment that Palm officially supported, and it continues to be the most popular C/C++ development tool, especially for commercial software applications.

It is important to note that CodeWarrior only supports the development of 68K applications, along with PNO applications and libraries. Developers seeking to create native Palm OS Cobalt applications and work with the Palm OS Protein API must use the Palm OS Developer Suite. This book describes CodeWarrior for Palm OS Platform version 9.0.

The CodeWarrior package contains a number of tools:

❑ **CodeWarrior IDE.** The CodeWarrior IDE is the interface for all the CodeWarrior tools except for Constructor. From within the IDE, you can edit source code, compile and link applications, debug your program, and organize your project's source code and resource files. Many of the tools in CodeWarrior for Palm OS Platform are plug-ins that attach to the IDE. The IDE also contains CodeWarrior's source-level debugger, which can debug applications running on either the Palm OS Emulator or on a real Palm OS handheld connected to the computer via a serial cable.

❑ **CodeWarrior compiler.** CodeWarrior's compiler turns ANSI C/C++ code into object code for Motorola 68K series processors.

❑ **CodeWarrior linker.** The linker used by CodeWarrior to link compiled object code is actually the same linker used in other versions of CodeWarrior to create 68K Mac OS programs.

❑ **CodeWarrior assembler.** The assembler creates executable code from Motorola 68K assembly instructions. CodeWarrior's C/C++ compiler also supports inline assembly statements.

❑ **PalmRez.** The PalmRez plug-in changes the linked object code generated by other parts of CodeWarrior into a `.prc` file suitable for installation and execution on a Palm OS device or on the Palm OS Emulator. PalmRez also merges user interface resources with the linked object code.

❏ **Constructor for Palm OS.** Constructor is a resource editor with a graphical interface. You use it to build the user interface elements of your application, which the other CodeWarrior tools then combine with your source code to create a finished program. Complete details of using Constructor to create and edit Palm OS resources are available in Chapters 6 and 7.

❏ **Palm OS Emulator and Palm Simulator.** Also known as POSE, the Palm OS Emulator imitates most of the hardware and software functions of a 68K-based Palm OS handheld hosted on a Windows PC. You can load real Palm OS applications and databases into POSE and run your applications without modification, making it an invaluable tool for testing and debugging your code. The Palm Simulator, also known as PalmSim, performs a similar set of functions for ARM-based Palm OS handhelds, providing a Windows-hosted simulation of the Palm OS Garnet and Palm OS Cobalt environments. There are many versions of PalmSim, for Palm OS Garnet and Palm OS Cobalt, as well as versions provided by handheld manufacturers such as palmOne to target specific handheld models. Both POSE and PalmSim receive a lot of development attention from both PalmSource and other developers, owing largely to the tremendous productivity benefit of being able to run and test applications under development without constantly having to load them on physical devices. As mentioned earlier, these tools, which are also part of the Palm OS SDK, are updated more frequently than the CodeWarrior tools, so you should periodically check PalmSource's Web site (www.palmsource.com) for newer versions than the one that ships with CodeWarrior.

❏ **Palm Debugger.** The Palm Debugger directly communicates with POSE, PalmSim, or an actual Palm Powered handheld, providing source- and assembly-level debugging facilities. In addition, the Palm Debugger can modify databases in an attached POSE session or on a handheld.

❏ **PilRC Plugin.** Although not officially supported by Metrowerks (it is written and maintained by Neil Rhodes), the PilRC plug-in is a valuable addition to the CodeWarrior programmer's toolbox. The PilRC plug-in allows a CodeWarrior project to compile resources described in a text file, using the same format as the PilRC command-line compiler normally used with the original PRC-Tools toolset.

PilRC and the PRC-Tools toolset have been replaced by the new Palm OS Developer Suite from PalmSource, which includes an entirely new resource editor. For more information on creating resources in PODS, see Chapter 6. PODS itself is covered later in this chapter.

## *Familiarizing Yourself with the IDE*

The CodeWarrior IDE (see Figure 3-1) is a multiple document interface (MDI) application that provides a container for the IDE's various menus, buttons, and windows. The multiple-window support in the IDE makes it possible to work on more than one source file at a time, or even more than one application project at a time. Among other benefits, this makes it easy to compare source files and copy and paste source code and resources from one program to use in another.

CodeWarrior organizes application developments into *projects*. A project contains references to all the different source code and resource files that make up a particular application. You also use projects to save settings for building your application in different ways, each one of which is called a *target*. Having multiple targets within a single project is a useful way to generate both debug and release versions of an application, or to create many versions easily that are localized for various human languages. Different targets may compile entirely different files or use completely different compiler and linker settings.

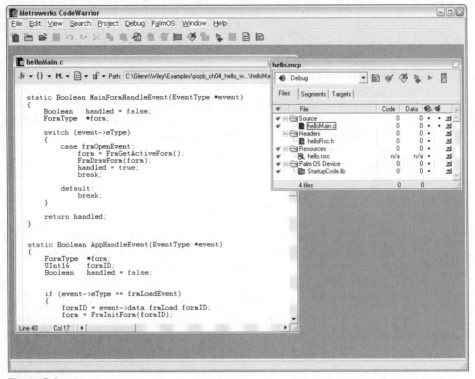

Figure 3-1

## Opening an Existing Project

All the information about a particular CodeWarrior project resides in a *project file*, which has an .mcp extension in Windows. To open an existing project file, select File ➪ Open or press Ctrl-O. You also may use CodeWarrior's recently opened file list to open a project or source code file that you worked on in a previous session. Select File ➪ Open Recent to access the list of the most recently used files. Finally, double-clicking an .mcp file in Windows Explorer automatically launches the project in CodeWarrior.

## Creating a New Project

When creating a new project, you have the following three options to choose from:

❑ Create an empty project

❑ Create a project based on project stationery

❑ Use the Palm OS Application Wizard

Regardless of which method you choose, start the project creation process by selecting File ➪ New Project or pressing Ctrl-Shift-N. CodeWarrior presents you with the New dialog box (see Figure 3-2).

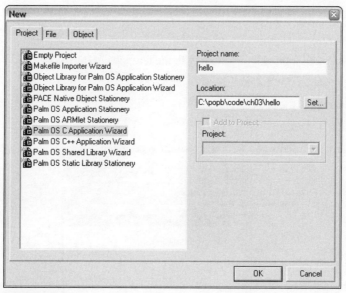

**Figure 3-2**

## Creating an Empty Project

An empty project is just that: empty. It contains no source code or resource files, and its build settings are not calibrated for producing a Palm OS application. Unless you need to create a nonstandard Palm OS application or you really like to work from a completely blank slate, you should create a project from stationery or use the wizard.

To create an empty project, follow these steps:

1.  Select the Project tab at the top of the New dialog box.

2.  Select Empty Project in the left pane of the dialog box.

3.  Choose a location for the project. Either enter the path into the Location text box or click the Set button and choose a folder.

4.  Enter a name for the project in the Project Name text box. As you enter the name, CodeWarrior appends the project name to the folder displayed in the Location text box, creating a new subfolder for your project.

5.  Click OK.

## Creating a Project from Stationery

CodeWarrior's *project stationery* is often a more convenient starting point than creating an empty project. Project stationery is a template for creating a particular kind of application. It contains boilerplate code for common parts of the application and build settings for generating appropriate output. After creating a project from stationery, add your own code to the appropriate parts of the source files that CodeWarrior generates.

To create a project from stationery, follow these steps:

1. Select the Project tab at the top of the New dialog box.

2. Select Palm OS Application Stationery in the left pane of the dialog box.

3. Choose a location for the project.

4. Enter a name for the project.

5. Click OK.

6. CodeWarrior presents you with the New Project dialog box (see Figure 3-3).

**Figure 3-3**

7. Select the appropriate template for your project. For a standard Palm OS C++ application, choose Palm OS C++ App.

8. Click OK.

At first glance, it appears that a stationery project should save you a lot of time. Projects created from stationery already contain a lot of the code necessary for a basic Palm OS application, which saves you from having to type a lot of code that you will use repeatedly for different Palm OS applications. Stationery projects provide a rudimentary resource framework already in place, such as main and about box forms and the beginnings of a menu system. Using stationery also configures project settings to compile a Palm OS application properly; the default settings in an empty project do not work. The stationery code also has the distinct advantage of working. Before you add your own code to it, a stationery project compiles without error, giving you a bug-free baseline on which to base your project.

Unfortunately, CodeWarrior's default Palm OS stationery invariably creates a project called "Starter," whose filenames also are based on the word "Starter" instead of the name you assigned to the new project. The automatically generated source code and resource files compile and run perfectly but they probably include more features than you need in your own application. As if that weren't enough, you still need to edit the target settings to properly set things like output filenames and PalmRez options. By the time you finish renaming the files, changing the resources, ripping out unwanted code, and modifying target settings, you may not save any time over creating the whole project from scratch.

Stationery is not entirely useless, however. CodeWarrior allows you to create your own stationery projects, which may contain all the settings and boilerplate code that you want to use in your own application development. Any project located in a subdirectory of CodeWarrior's Stationery folder may be used as the basis for a new project. To create a stationery project, all you need to do is make a new project using any of the methods described in this chapter. Modify the settings for the project and add to the project whatever generic code or resources you wish to have available when building a new project. Then save the project and copy its .mcp file, Src folder, and Rsc folder to a subdirectory of the Stationery folder. The next time you use the File ➪ New command to create a new project, your stationery project appears in the New dialog box.

Creating your own custom stationery project is a great way to have all your personal project settings, code fragments, and resources on hand to start a new project quickly. It takes time to develop a good stationery project but it is a time investment well worth making.

Alternatively, many developers maintain their own skeleton projects of different types outside the stationery system, which serve as convenient templates when starting a new project.

## Using the Palm OS Application Wizard

The Palm OS Application Wizard is by far the easiest method of creating a new application. The wizard produces a complete project in much the same way that project stationery does but it gives you more options for customizing your project.

To create a project with the Palm OS Application Wizard, follow these steps:

1. Select the Project tab at the top of the New dialog box.

2. Select Palm OS Application Wizard in the left pane of the dialog box.

3. Choose a location for the project.

4. Enter a name for the project.

5. Click OK.

6. CodeWarrior displays the first page of the Palm OS Application Wizard dialog box (see Figure 3-4).

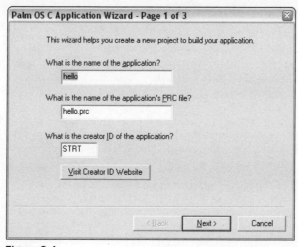

Figure 3-4

Fill in these text boxes to customize your project:

❑ **Application Name.** This field controls the name of your application as it appears in the application launcher on a Palm OS handheld. The name entered in the Application Name text box also becomes the database name for your application.

❑ **Release PRC Filename.** This is the name of the executable .prc file that the project builds when creating a release version of the application.

❑ **Palm OS Creator ID.** This field is where you can set your application's *Creator ID*, a four-byte code that uniquely identifies your application. The wizard provides a handy Visit Creator Code Website button; clicking this button opens your browser to the official PalmSource Creator ID Web site, where you can register your own unique Creator ID for your application. Registration is a free service maintained by PalmSource on www.palmsource.com.

*Creator IDs must be unique across all applications on a Palm OS handheld, so you should never ship an application with the default STRT value that the wizard supplies to you. You application is sure to conflict with applications released by other developers who unwisely released their applications with the same default Creator ID.*

When you have the settings modified to your liking, click the Next button.

**7.** The second page of the wizard (see Figure 3-5) appears.

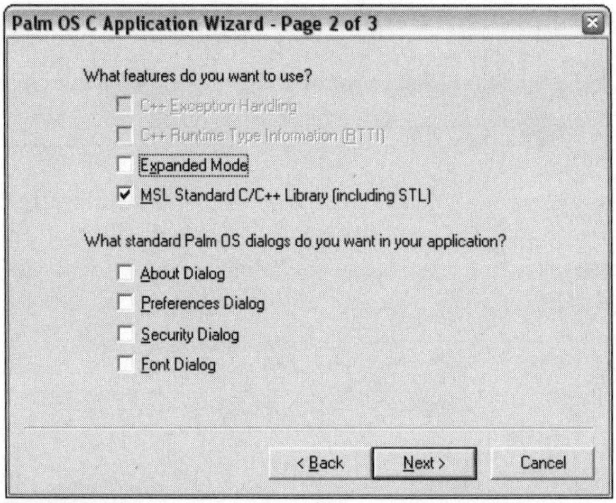

**Figure 3-5**

This page of the wizard allows you to specify language features as well as a selection of standard Palm OS dialog boxes that can be included in your application. When you have finished selecting the options, click Next.

**8.** The third and final page of the wizard (see Figure 3-6) appears.

## What Is a Creator ID?

All Palm OS applications and databases have a four-byte Creator ID to identify them uniquely to the operating system. To prevent your application from conflicting with others, you need to register a Creator ID with PalmSource, which maintains a database of registered IDs. Creator ID registration is simple; just point your browser at `www.palmos.com/dev` and follow the Quick Index to Creator ID. From there, you may browse the list of registered Creator IDs and choose one that is not already in use.

Creator IDs are case-sensitive and they are composed of four ASCII characters in the range 33–127, decimal. PalmSource has reserved Creator IDs composed entirely of lowercase letters for their own use, so your own Creator IDs must have at least one capital letter, number, or symbol character.

Any application you release to the public, or even within a corporation, should have its own unique Creator ID. When the built-in application launcher deletes an application, it also deletes all databases that share the same Creator ID with the deleted application.

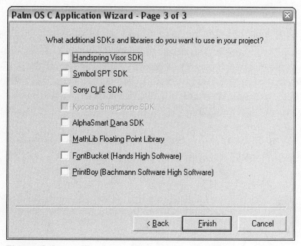

Figure 3-6

This page of the wizard allows you to specify additional SDKs and libraries that your application needs to use, whether supplied by Palm or one of its licensees or approved third-party libraries. Selecting different options changes which header files the wizard-generated code includes, and it also sets up access paths in the project's build settings. When you have finished selecting SDKs and libraries, click Finish.

## Exploring the Project Window

Once you have created or opened a project, CodeWarrior displays the project window (see Figure 3-7). From the project window, you can control which source files a particular project contains, how CodeWarrior compiles and links those files, and what build targets are available.

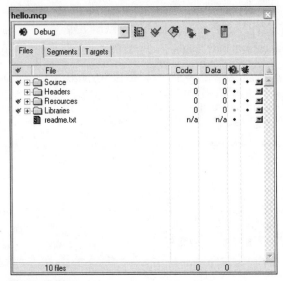

**Figure 3-7**

Use the pop-up menu in the upper left corner of the project window to select the current build target. Changing the target displayed in the pop-up menu changes the rest of the window's display to reflect the settings for that particular target. Also, when the project window has the focus, the currently displayed target in this pop-up menu is what CodeWarrior builds when running a Make, Debug, or Bring Up To Date command from the Project menu.

The project window has three views: Files, Segments, and Targets. To display a particular view, select the appropriate tab at the top of the project window.

## Managing Files in the Files View

The Files view gives you control over what source code and resource files are part of a project (see Figure 3-8).

The columns in the Files view, from left to right, are described as follows:

❑ **Touch column.** The column with a check mark at the top indicates which files have been changed, or *touched*, since the last build, and therefore need to be compiled when building the project. Touched files have a check mark next to them. You can toggle whether a file is touched or not by clicking next to that file in the touch column. In Windows, holding down Alt while clicking in this column toggles the touch status of all the files in the project.

❑ **File column.** This column lists all the files contained in the project. You can use *groups* to organize files. Selecting Project ➪ Create Group creates a new group, and selecting Project ➪ Add Files presents you with a dialog from which to select new files to add to the project. You may change the order in which files are displayed, as well as which groups the files occupy, by dragging them around the project window. Double-clicking a file, or pressing Enter if the file is currently selected, opens the file for editing. Groups also may contain subgroups if your project is complex enough to require that kind of organization. Adding, removing, or reorganizing files in the project window has no effect on the real files, which may be located anywhere you wish to put them on your computer.

❑ **Code column.** Code shows the size of the compiled object code associated with a particular source file or group of source files. A zero in this column indicates code that CodeWarrior has not compiled yet. The total of the values does not necessarily add up to the total size of the compiled program. When linking object code into an application, CodeWarrior may not use all the object code from a particular source because it's leaving out dead code that the rest of the project does not reference.

❑ **Data column.** The Data column shows the size of any nonexecutable data residing in the object code for a particular source file. If the source file is uncompiled, or if it contains no data section, this column displays a zero.

❑ **Target column.** The Target column has a bull's-eye with an arrow pointing to it at the head of the column. CodeWarrior displays this column only if a project contains multiple targets, so many simple Palm OS applications will never need this column. A black dot in this column indicates that a particular file is part of the currently selected target.

❑ **Debug column.** Indicated by a small green insect, the debug column displays a dot next to any file that should contain debugging information when built. Clicking in this column toggles whether or not CodeWarrior includes debugging information in a file when building it.

❑ **Interface pop-up column.** The column full of small buttons with downward-pointing arrows is the interface pop-up column. Clicking one of these buttons displays a pop-up menu that performs different functions, depending upon the type of item displayed in that row:

   ❑ For file groups, the pop-up list contains a list of all files in that group. Choosing a file from this list opens that file for editing.

   ❑ For files, the pop-up list shows a list of header files included by that source file. Picking one of the files from the list opens it for editing. The interface pop-up menu also offers an option to touch or untouch that file.

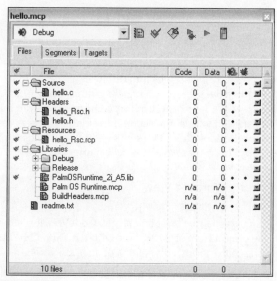

Figure 3-8

Removing files from the project may be accomplished by selecting them and then either choosing Edit ⇨ Delete or pressing the Delete key.

In addition, you also may remove a file in Windows by right-clicking it and then selecting Delete from the pop-up menu that appears. In Mac OS, holding down the Ctrl key while clicking a file opens the same pop-up menu.

## Controlling Link Order with the Segments View

The Segments view of the project window (see Figure 3-9) controls the order in which CodeWarrior links your project's source files together. The linker follows the same order, from top to bottom, that is displayed in the Segments view. To change the link order, simply drag the files in the list until they are in the appropriate positions.

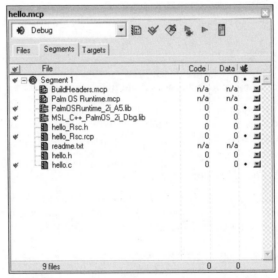

**Figure 3-9**

Within the Segments view, you may group files into different *segments*. In a small application, segments are mostly just a way to organize the project into logical groups. They function similarly to file groups in the project window's Files view. For large applications composed of more than 64K of compiled code, segments must be used to partition your source code into smaller chunks, resulting in a *multi-segment application*. Most Palm OS applications should be small enough not to require segmentation. Full details on building multisegment applications are available in Chapter 24.

## Creating Different Builds in the Targets View

The Targets view of the project window (see Figure 3-10) is where you define different build targets for the application. A project must contain at least one target. CodeWarrior generates release and debug targets when you create a new project from stationery or with the Palm OS Application Wizard. Targets also are useful for generating many localized versions of an application from a single set of source files.

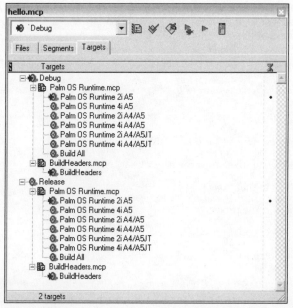

**Figure 3-10**

To create a new target, select Project ⇨ Create Target. The New Target dialog box (see Figure 3-11) appears.

**Figure 3-11**

The New Target dialog box prompts you for a name to call the target you are creating. This name may be anything mnemonic to you that describes what purpose the target has. You also can choose to create an empty target by selecting the Empty Target option, or to copy the settings from an existing target by choosing the Clone Existing Target option. Once you have named and determined the contents of the new target, click OK.

*Because the default settings of an empty target do not work for compiling a Palm OS application, you can save yourself a lot of time by cloning an existing target whose settings already work. Before adding new targets to a project, change all the settings in your project's first target to the appropriate values. Then clone the first target when you add more targets to the project.*

Once you have all the targets you need for your application, you may assign files to those targets from the Files view of the project window. You also may assign targets for a particular file from the Project Inspector window, described later in this chapter.

## Saving a Project

CodeWarrior automatically saves changes to the project when you perform any of the following actions:

- ❑ Close the project
- ❑ Change the Preferences or Target Settings of the project
- ❑ Add files to or delete files from the project
- ❑ Compile any file in the project
- ❑ Edit any groups in the project
- ❑ Remove any object code from the project
- ❑ Quit the CodeWarrior IDE

When saving changes to your project, CodeWarrior saves the names of your project's files and their locations, all the configuration options for the project, dependency information and touch state for all files, and object code compiled from the project's source files. Because CodeWarrior saves all this information automatically, even when closing the IDE, you never have to save your project manually. Should you wish to make a second copy of your project, however, select the File ➪ Save a Copy As command to do so.

# Changing Target Settings

The Target Settings dialog box (see Figure 3-12) is where you can change a wide variety of options that affect how the compiler and linkers assemble your project's code for a specific target. To access the dialog box, select Edit ➪ *target* settings, where *target* represents the name of the current target selected in the project window. Double-clicking the target's name in the project window's Targets view also opens the Target Settings dialog box; and in Windows, you can just press Alt-F7.

The left pane of the Target Settings dialog box, labeled Target Settings Panels, shows a list of all the different settings panels, which appear in the right pane of the dialog box. Select an item from the list to display its panel. There are a bewildering number of options in this dialog box, not all of which are directly applicable to Palm OS development. The CodeWarrior documentation does a good job of describing all the bells and whistles, so only selected panels and those settings that are critical for the compiling of a conventional Palm OS application appear in the following discussion. Less common Palm OS projects, such as shared libraries, require different settings.

The Factory Settings button returns all the panels in the dialog box to their default state. After you make any changes to settings, the Revert button becomes active. Clicking Revert restores the current settings panel to the state it was in the last time you saved the settings. Click OK or Apply to save changes you have made to the target settings.

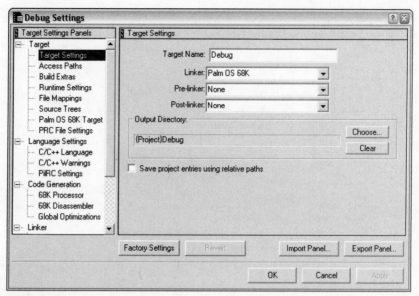

**Figure 3-12**

*The name in the title bar of the Target Settings dialog box varies. The title bar always displays "Target Settings," where Target is the actual name of the selected target. For example, in Figure 3-12, the selected target is called "Debug."*

*The default state of the panels in the Target Settings dialog box does not properly compile working Palm OS applications. The Factory Settings button is a useful feature for other versions of CodeWarrior that target different platforms, but you should never need to use it when developing for Palm OS. If you did not use project stationery or the Palm OS Application Wizard to create your project, or if you created an empty target, be sure to copy the settings from a stationery project to avoid compilation errors.*

The first panel listed is Target Settings, underneath the Target category. This panel controls very general settings for the current target. You can rename the target in the Target Name text box. The pop-up menus allow you to choose the linkers that CodeWarrior should use to link the application. For Palm OS development, Linker should be set to **MacOS 68K Linker**, Pre-linker should be **None**, and Post-linker should be **PalmRez Post Linker**. Checking the Save Project Entries Using Relative Paths check box allows you to move a project to another location without disturbing the paths saved in the project file.

Farther down the Target category, and visible only if Linker in the Target Settings panel is set to MacOS 68K Linker, is the Palm OS 68K Target panel (see Figure 3-13). For Palm OS applications, the Project Type pop-up menu should read **68K Application (Standard)** and the File Name text box should contain the name of the .prc file that represents the executable filename that this target should create, such as **hello.prc**.

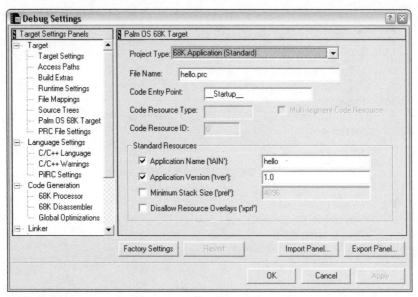

**Figure 3-13**

The last panel with important Palm OS development settings is PRC File Settings (see Figure 3-14). This controls the settings for PalmRez, which is responsible for converting the Motorola 68K code compiled by CodeWarrior, as well as the application's resources created by Constructor, into the .prc format understood by Palm OS. The Type field should be set to **appl** for a standard Palm OS application. The Creator field should contain your application's Creator ID.

**Figure 3-14**

Every database on a Palm OS device, including each application, has a database name, which you can set in the Database Name field. Applications and databases must have unique names. Setting the application's database name using the Database Name field is optional, though; if you leave this field blank, CodeWarrior strips the .prc from the end of the filename in the **Output File** field and uses that as the database name for the application. Just be sure to pick a filename that will be unique once it is on the handheld. One way to help ensure a unique database name is to append your application's unique Creator ID to the end of the database name.

Checking the Reset on Install check box signals Palm OS to reset the device after your application has been installed through a HotSync operation. This feature is needed only by applications that modify basic operating system behavior, such as add-on hardware or communications drivers; most applications do not need the system to reset the device when they are installed. The Backup check box controls whether or not the HotSync Manager should copy this .prc file to the user's backup folder when synchronizing with the desktop. The Hidden check box signals the application launcher to hide this application's icon from view; most applications should not have this option selected. Disallow Copying, when checked, prevents Palm OS version 3.0 or later from beaming the application to another device via the infrared port. It also inhibits the copying of an application or database to an external storage card. It has no effect on versions of Palm OS that do not include IR beaming.

## Compiling and Linking in CodeWarrior

CodeWarrior gives you the option to compile source files one at a time, a few at a time, or all source files at once. Compiling produces only the object code for the appropriate source files without linking them into a complete application. To compile one or more source files, select the desired files in the project window and then do one of the following:

❑    Select Project ⇨ Compile.

❑    In Windows, press Ctrl-F7. In Mac OS, press Command-K.

❑    In Windows, right-click the selected file (or files) and choose Compile from the pop-up menu. In Mac OS, hold down Ctrl while clicking to access the same menu.

If you have changed or added many files, you may wish to update the entire project at once. To do this, select Project ⇨ Bring Up to Date. This command compiles all source code that has either not been compiled or has not been touched.

> *CodeWarrior sometimes does not recognize that you have made changes to a file. To force recompiling, touch the file first and then compile it.*

To link all object code in your project into a completed binary file, select Project ⇨ Make or press F7 in Windows (Command-M in Mac OS). Running the Make command first checks for newly added, modified, or touched files and then compiles them. Then Make runs the compiled object code through the linkers to produce a finished executable program.

Because the CodeWarrior IDE allows you to work on multiple projects containing multiple targets, determining which files CodeWarrior compiles and links can be confusing. When running a global command like Bring Up to Date or Make, CodeWarrior determines which target to build from which project based on the following rules:

❑    If a project window has the focus, CodeWarrior builds the currently selected target in that project window's target pop-up menu.

❑    If a different window has the focus, such as a source code editing window, CodeWarrior relies on its *default project* and *default target* settings.

To set the default project, select Project ➪ Set Default Project and then select the appropriate project file. Likewise, to set the default target, select Project ➪ Set Default Target and then select the appropriate target.

# Using the Palm OS Development Suite (PODS)

The PalmSource Palm OS Development Suite, known as PODS, is a full-featured IDE similar in scope to CodeWarrior. Like CodeWarrior, PODS contains an integrated set of all the tools you need to develop complete Palm OS applications. PODS is available as a free download from PalmSource at www.palmsource.com. Although new at the time of this writing, PalmSource has invested heavily in the creation of PODS and has positioned it as the standard development environment for Palm OS applications moving forward.

PODS is based on the Eclipse version 3.x IDE. It contains a series of plug-ins that, together, provide an adaptation within the Eclipse workbench for developing Palm OS applications. Although this chapter focuses exclusively on Palm OS support within PODS, you may be interested to know that the Eclipse environment can support many such adaptations, which are specific to enabling features of various development targets and platforms. This book describes Palm OS Development Suite (PODS) version 1.1.

PODS contains the following integrated set of development tools:

❑    **Eclipse Workbench.** The Eclipse Workbench is the visual IDE for creating and managing projects, editing source code and resources, and compiling, linking, and debugging your Palm OS applications. The Workbench ties together a large number of underlying compiler, linker, and editor tools that collectively allow Palm OS developers easily to target older 68K applications, Palm OS Garnet applications, Palm OS Cobalt applications, and nonapplication targets such as shared libraries and PACE Native Objects (PNO). All of the PODS and Palm OS SDK documentation is integrated and readily accessible from within the Workbench. The Eclipse Workbench also supports the Palm OS Debugger in PODS, enabling source-level debugging of both Palm OS Protein as well as 68K application and shared library code. As a Palm OS developer, you will spend most of your time working within the Eclipse Workbench portion of PODS.

❑    **Palm OS compiler and linker tools.** PODS includes a variety of compilers, assemblers, and linkers which create Palm OS Protein and legacy 68K applications by translating your source code into the necessary object code that runs on the actual target processor.

❑    **Palm OS Resource Tools.** PODS comes with a suite of tools which can create and edit Palm OS application resources. For most developers, the most visible component of these tools is the Palm OS Resource Editor, an advanced graphical tool for visually creating and managing the forms, menus, icons, and other resource portions of your application. The Palm OS Resource Editor uses a form of XML called XML Resource Description files, or XRD, for storing a program's resources. Other included Palm OS Resource Tools components handle more specific tasks, such as managing overlays, migrating resources into the XRD format, and comparing and merging resources in multiple applications. Complete details of using the Palm OS Resource Editor to create and edit Palm OS resources are available in Chapters 6 and 7.

❑ **Palm OS Emulator and Palm Simulator.** The Palm OS Emulator imitates most of the hardware and software functions of a 68K-based Palm OS handheld hosted on a Windows PC. You can load real Palm OS applications and databases into POSE and run your applications without modification, making it an invaluable tool for testing and debugging your code. The Palm Simulator, also known as PalmSim, performs a similar set of functions for ARM-based Palm OS handhelds, providing a Windows-hosted simulation of the Palm OS Garnet and Palm OS Cobalt environments. Both the Emulator and PalmSim receive a lot of development attention from both PalmSource and other developers, owing largely to the tremendous productivity benefit of being able to run and test applications under development without having to load them constantly on physical devices. PODS comes with a version of the Emulator for 68K applications, a Palm OS Garnet-compatible Simulator, and a Palm OS Cobalt Simulator. As mentioned earlier, these tools, which are also part of the Palm OS SDK, are updated more frequently than the CodeWarrior tools, so you should periodically check PalmSource's Web site (www.palmsource.com) for newer versions than the one that ships with CodeWarrior.

❑ **Integrated Workbench Debugger.** The integrated debugger in PODS provides source-level debugging against POSE, Palm OS Garnet, and Palm OS Cobalt Simulators and physical devices, all within the Eclipse Workbench.

*As of this writing, the currently available versions of CodeWarrior and PODS are unable to recognize each other's project file formats. Developers seeking either to migrate from one tool to the other or support both tools in a hybrid environment need to maintain different project files for each tool.*

## Familiarizing Yourself with the Eclipse Workbench

The Eclipse Workbench (see Figure 3-15) is a visual IDE for working with your Palm OS application projects. The Workbench integrates hierarchical project views and source editors for C/C++ code, as well as resources and other file types, and other various windows to create a full-featured development environment for creating and working with Palm OS projects.

Inside the Eclipse Workbench, you work with projects, which are stored in containers called *workspaces*. A workspace can contain one or more projects. By default your workspace and your projects are stored in the same location where you installed PODS (typically \Program Files\PalmSource) under the workspace folder, with each project stored in subfolders under the workspace folder. Alternatively, for any given project you can specify a location of your own choosing for your project, outside the workspace folder. Note that projects created with a storage location outside the workspace folder still belong to your workspace; they are simply not stored in the workspace folder.

*If you choose a location outside the workspace to create a new project, Eclipse will not automatically create a folder for your project. However, there is a New Folder button in the Browse window of the Workbench, which you can use to create a unique subfolder to contain your project.*

Eclipse projects organize all of the application components and source files that come together to build your program. Typically projects consist of one or more C/C++ source files and associated headers, along with a resource file containing the user interface definitions for your program. Finally, projects contain settings that dictate how your project is built, and which define attributes such as the output name of your program, Creator ID, and dependencies on other projects. Even though your projects are grouped in a single workspace, each Eclipse project has its own unique settings.

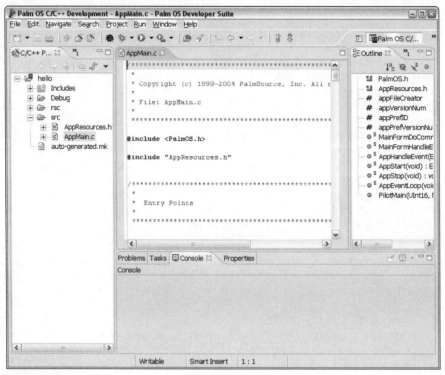

Figure 3-15

## Opening an Existing Project

After you install PODS, you will want to create a shortcut to the Eclipse Workbench on your Windows Start menu or Windows Desktop (the program name is `eclipse.exe` and is found under `/Program Files/PalmSource/Palm OS Developer Suite`). To run Eclipse, double-click your shortcut. Eclipse will automatically open your workspace and show all your projects. To work with any individual project in your workspace, select it with your mouse if the project is already open. If the project is not open, simply select it from the Navigator window and choose Project ➪ Open Project from the Eclipse menu. Projects cannot be automatically opened in Eclipse from Windows Explorer.

PODS stores your project settings in a series of project files in the root directory of your project folder. Three of these files — `.ctdbuild`, `.ctdproject`, and `.project` — are XML files that define your project and its settings. The fourth file is a "makefile," which defines how to build your project and any interdependencies among the components of your project. A makefile can be either autogenerated by Eclipse for you, or you can supply your own homegrown makefiles.

## Creating a New Project

Eclipse Workbench comes with a wizard that helps you create different types of Palm OS projects: 68K, 68K PNO, or Protein. Whichever type of project you choose is dictated by whether you are targeting Palm OS Garnet or Palm OS Cobalt, and which features of Palm OS you wish to make use of in your application. For more details on Palm OS Garnet, Palm OS Cobalt, and Palm OS Protein, please see Chapter 2.

Within these project types, if you are starting from scratch, the wizard can also help you automatically generate a skeleton project complete with source code, resources, and default project settings. Alternatively, if you are porting a project from another development environment, you can create an empty project and import these components yourself.

> *Eclipse does not recognize CodeWarrior MCP project files. If you are porting a project from CodeWarrior to PODS you need to create an empty project and manually import your source files into the new project.*

To create a new project, select File ➪ New Project. Choose the Palm OS Development Wizard by clicking Palm OS Development from the list of wizards in the left panel (see Figure 3-16).

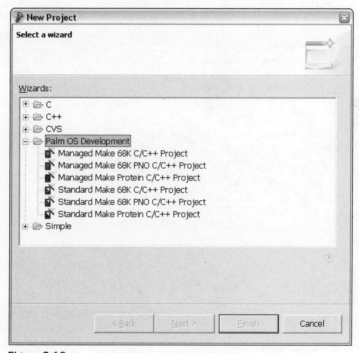

**Figure 3-16**

After you click Palm OS Development, you will see a list of project types appear in the right-hand window. As mentioned before, you can choose a 68K, PNO, or Protein project. Within each project type, you can choose to create a Standard Make project or a Managed Make project. If you intend to work exclusively within the Eclipse IDE in maintaining your project settings and components, choose the Managed Make option. This option ensures that Eclipse automatically updates your project's makefile based on your IDE project settings.

Some developers prefer to exercise fine control over how their projects are built, or they need to incorporate external procedures into their project build scripts. For these developers, PODS offers the Standard Make option. This option lets you manually edit and maintain the makefile that controls how your project is built, as long as you follow some basic Eclipse requirements. If you choose Standard Make, you are responsible for keeping your makefile updated to reflect any changes you make in the IDE project view, such as adding a source file.

## Using the New Project Wizard

After choosing the type of project and make options, the New Project Wizard presents a series of screens to help you create and configure your project. Figure 3-17 presents the first screen for a new Managed Make 68K C/C++ Project.

In the Name field, enter the name you would like to use for the new project in your workspace. This can be any descriptive name you like; it does not need to be tied to the name of the physical Palm OS .prc file that is the output of your project builds.

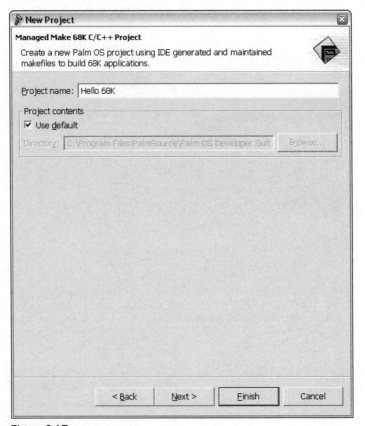

Figure 3-17

In new Eclipse projects, the Use Default option is checked by default. This causes Eclipse to store your project under the \workspace folder within your PODS installation. If you are running through the New Project wizard for the first time and want to learn the Eclipse Workbench, you can leave this option checked. However, because most developers want to store their projects in a location of their own choosing outside the \Program Files\Windows folder, when you go to create your actual development projects you will probably wish to uncheck this box and use the Browse button to navigate to an existing or new folder to store your project.

Click the Next button to proceed to the next Wizard screen.

## Palm OS Settings

This Wizard screen presents you with various options that control the type of Palm component your project will output, and other attributes associated with your output file (see Figure 3-18).

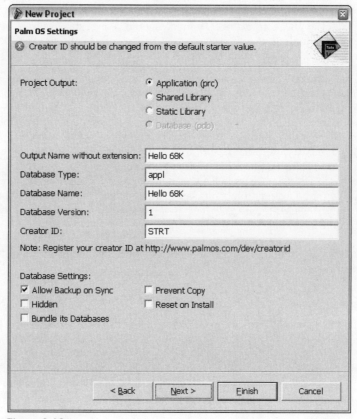

**Figure 3-18**

Fill in these fields to customize your project settings:

- ❑ **Project Output.** This field controls the type of component your project emits after a build. The three choices are Application (prc), Shared Library, or Static Library. Unless you are specifically looking to create a shared library or static library, you should accept the default choice of Application (prc), which results in a standard Palm application.

- ❑ **Output Name.** This is the name of the executable .prc file that the project builds when creating a release version of the application.

❑ **Database Type.** Standard Palm OS applications have a database type of "appl," which identifies them to the Palm OS launcher as an application and specifies that it should be shown in the launcher list of applications. Nonapplication-built targets such as shared libraries, or applications that purposefully need to be hidden from the Palm OS launcher, may use a different four-character code for this field.

❑ **Database Name.** This is the unique name for the database to be used on the target handheld.

❑ **Creator ID.** This field is where you can set your application's four-byte Creator ID code that uniquely identifies your application. The wizard reminds you to visit the Palm Source Creator ID Web site, where you can register your own unique Creator ID for your application. Registration is a free service maintained by PalmSource at www.palmsource.com. By default, the Wizard puts "STRT" as the application creator ID but you should change this to a four-character code that is unique to your application to make sure it does not conflict with other applications on a given handheld device.

❑ **Database Settings.** This is a set of check box settings that control how Palm OS deals with an application when it is resident on a handheld device. Allow Backup on Sync specifies whether or not you want HotSync to back up your program file automatically during synchronization. Unless you have reason to not want this behavior, you should leave this option checked. Hidden causes your application to be hidden from view by the Palm OS launcher (as noted earlier, using a database type that is not "appl" can accomplish much the same thing). Bundle Its Databases tells Palm OS that when your application is run from an expansion card, it should copy any associated databases to RAM in addition to your application .prc file. Prevent Copy prevents your application from being beamable to other handhelds. Reset on Install causes Palm OS to instruct the user to soft-reset the handheld after your application is installed through HotSync onto a handheld device.

For most applications, you will need to change only the Output Name and Creator ID. Leave the rest of the settings at their default values.

## Project Code Generation

The next screen in the Project Wizard after completing project settings is the Project Code Generation screen (see Figure 3-19).

This screen presents you with optional code generation options for your new project. Depending on what you need, you can use this screen to designate anything from a barebones Palm OS project up to a fully coded sample application to use as a starting point for your new application.

The following code generation choices are available:

❑ **Source File Import Project.** This option generates only the basic project settings and makes the necessary files in order to build a Palm OS application correctly with the settings you specified in prior screens. No C/C++ source code or resources are generated for you, however; it is up to you to add these source files yourself.

❑ **PilotMain Starter.** This option generates the basic project settings and makefiles, and it provides you with a single C/C++ source file with the requisite PilotMain() function coded.

❏ **Simple Application.** This option generates the basic project settings and makefiles, and it provides you with a more complete skeleton application than the Basic option, with an event-loop handler and main form processing.

❏ **Sample Application.** This option generates the basic project settings and makefiles, and it provides you with source code for a basic puzzle game.

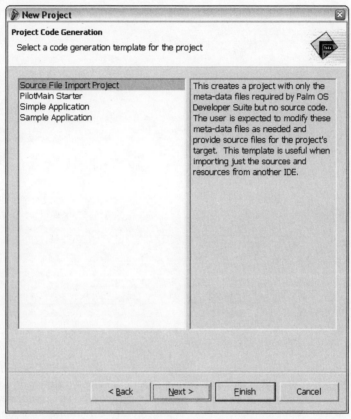

**Figure 3-19**

Whichever code generation option you select depends on what your project is about. If you are learning Palm OS programming, it can be useful to generate a fully working application quickly like Puzzle and learn from its source code. On the other hand, if you were to use Puzzle as the starting point for a new application, there is code that you will most likely need to tear out and rework. Given that virtually every application requires the basic boilerplate startup and event-loop handling code, as well as a main form, the Simple Application option presents an excellent starting point for both newbies and more experienced programmers who are looking to get a quick, basic working project going in PODS.

## Additional Project Settings

The final screen in the Project Wizard is the Additional Project Settings screen (see Figure 3-20).

**Figure 3-20**

If you have other projects in your workspace, this screen presents you with the ability to designate inter-dependencies between your new project and existing projects. Why would you want to do this? As your projects grow, you may wind up with multiple projects that build different components as part of your overall application. For example, you may have a static library, containing common helper functions, and two applications, each of which links in the static library in order to get at the common functions. In this case, each of the two applications would use this Project Settings screen to designate the static library project as a dependency.

If you have no other projects, or if your project is not dependent on other projects within your workspace, you can simply click the Finish button without selecting a dependency.

## Exploring the Project Window

Once you create or open a project, the Eclipse Workbench displays your project in a series of windows in your current view (see Figure 3-21).

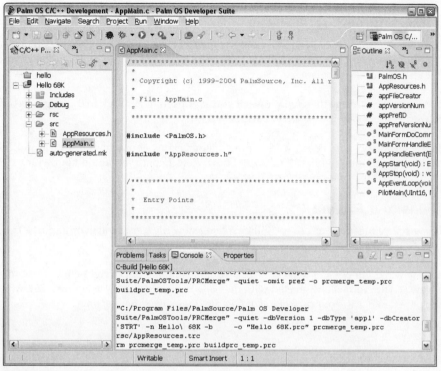

Figure 3-21

The Eclipse Workbench consists of a series of tiled windows, each of which can contain information on a different aspect of your project and workspace. By default in the Palm OS Perspective, these windows are preset to the following:

❑ **C/C++ Projects.** This view shows a hierarchical list of your projects. Each project in your workspace is listed, along with expandable folders containing your source, resources, and make/build files. Double-clicking a file within one of your projects results in Eclipse's launching the associated editor for the specified file. If the file type is one for which an editor is available within the Workbench, such as a C/C++ file, Eclipse opens the file within the Editor view. If you select a file for which there is no built-in editor, such as a Word document, Eclipse launches the associated viewer (if any) in a separate window outside Eclipse.

❑ **Editor.** This view presents the contents of the selected view in an editable window. Eclipse comes with a fully functional source editor that you can use to create and edit your source code. The Editor can have multiple files open simultaneously. Each open file is listed as a tab at the top of the Editor view.

❑ **Outline.** This view presents a high-level overview of the functions and shows a hierarchical list of the "main structural elements" of the currently open file in the editor. Exactly what elements are shown depends on the type of file you are editing. For C/C++ source files, the Outline view presents a list of referenced header files, static data members, functions, and class members. In this sense the Outline view is similar to class browsers found in other development environments. Using this view, you can quickly jump to different functions within your source, which can be helpful especially with larger source files. Note that in the C/C++ Projects view the same elements can be viewed by expanding the node representing a C or C++ file.

❏ **Tasks.** This view is designed to show any errors or warnings found when attempting to compile or build your project. Each problem is listed as a "task," which you can double-click to jump to the source of the problem.

Although you can rearrange these windows, if you ever need to get back to the original configuration you can always select Window ⇨ Reset Perspective.

These views are the primary ones used in normal Palm OS development, but several additional views are available as well, found under Window ⇨ Show View. Experiment to find out which views and window arrangements suit your preferences best.

## Adding Files to a Project

To add new source files to your project, either create a new file from scratch or import a file from another location.

To create a new file, choose File ⇨ New ⇨ File from the main menu or right-click your project and choose New ⇨ File. You will be greeted with the New File dialog box (see Figure 3-22), which lets you select the parent folder in your project to contain the file, as well the filename.

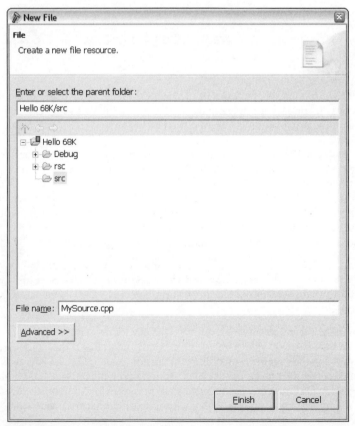

Figure 3-22

The new file is automatically created, added to your project in the folder specified, and stored in the proper physical location relative to your project.

To import an existing file from a location on your hard drive or network, choose File ➪ Import, which brings up the Import dialog box (see Figure 3-23).

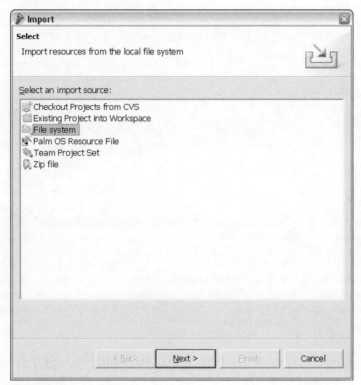

**Figure 3-23**

Because you can import different types of files and resources, the first screen prompts you for the type of file you wish to import. Choose File System to import a stored C/C++ file. The next screen prompts you to navigate to and select the source file(s). Clicking the Browse button lets you explore your local hard drives and network drives for files to import. Recently selected locations are available conveniently for quick recall by clicking the pop-up menu below the From Directory field.

## Changing Project Settings

If, after you create your project, you need to change your project settings, such as the Creator ID, you can do so by choosing Project ➪ Properties. The Properties dialog box appears (see Figure 3-24).

Two of these panels should look familiar to you. The Palm OS Options panel is the same as the Palm OS Settings screen you saw in the New Project Wizard, as is the Project References screen. Here you can adjust most of the settings described on those pages.

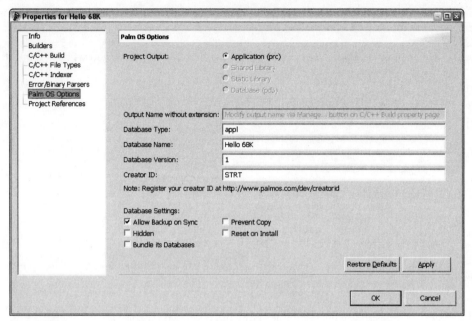

**Figure 3-24**

You can adjust additional project settings in the C/C++ Build panel. In this panel you can specify standard compiler and linker options, such as include paths and external libraries. Do not change any of the default settings until you have had a chance to read the *Introduction to Palm OS Developer Suite* and *Palm OS Protein C/C++ Compiler Tools Guide* documents.

## Compiling and Linking in the Eclipse Workbench

Eclipse lets you build at the project level. You can also build all projects within your workspace. To build your project, select any component within the project and choose Project ➪ Rebuild Project or Project ➪ Rebuild All.

> *Close all projects other than the one on which you are working. Having one project open at a time speeds up the creation of new projects and provides for better performance during builds and searches.*

During the build process, output from the build is shown in the C-Build view, which appears at the bottom of the IDE. Any errors or warnings found during the build will cause the Tasks window to appear with each problem listed as an open task.

> *In PODS 1.0, the Tasks view can sometimes omit some information necessary to fix bugs and warnings. To get better information, double-click the C-Build view title bar to expand it and examine its contents. Double-click the title bar again to restore it back to its original location and size when you are done.*

# Summary

In this chapter, you took a look at the two most popular C/C++ development environments for Palm OS programming. After reading this chapter, you should know the following:

❑ Metrowerks CodeWarrior is a commercial IDE for Palm OS development used by many C/C++ developers.

❑ CodeWarrior stores information about an application and how it should be built in a *project*, which may contain multiple *targets* to direct the CodeWarrior tools to build the project in different ways.

❑ You control how CodeWarrior compiles and links an application by changing the settings in the *project window* and *target settings* dialog box.

❑ The Palm OS Development System, known as PODS, is a freely downloadable tool created and maintained by PalmSource as the officially supported development environment for creating Palm OS applications.

❑ PODS contains project windows and settings to control how your Palm OS application components are built.

❑ The Eclipse Workbench is the primary visual development tool used with PODS to create and manage projects as well as compile, edit, and debug your code.

# 4

# Writing Your First
# Palm OS Application

Chapter 3 showed you the tools you need to build applications for Palm OS. Now it's time to look under the hood of a simple application and see what makes it work. In the longstanding tradition of computer programming examples, this chapter will walk you through the code of a "Hello, World" program, introducing you to the general layout of a Palm OS application. Along the way, you also will learn about how Palm OS starts your application and how the application responds to events.

This chapter takes a two-part approach to presenting the Hello World application. The first part introduces you to Hello World 1, which is a bare-minimum Palm OS application. Hello World 1 does nothing more than display an empty form; it's not much to look at but there are a number of important things going on behind the scenes that form the foundation of every Palm OS application.

Because user interaction is such an integral part of Palm OS, the second part of the chapter turns the Hello World 1 application into Hello World 2, which features a text field, menus, buttons, and a second form. Hello World 2 shows off the basic concepts of handling user input and memory in Palm OS.

This chapter concludes with a discussion of syntactic differences between different versions of Palm OS. Twice during the life of Palm OS, PalmSource changed data type definitions in the Palm OS header files — changes that can be confusing if you need to port code from one version of Palm OS to another. This chapter's final section clarifies these differences in the syntax.

# Creating Hello World 1

There isn't a whole lot of user interface in Hello World 1. When launched, the program displays a blank form (see Figure 4-1). This form does not respond to user input in any way; the only option the user has is to admire the Zen-like emptiness of the form for a while, before launching a different application.

**Figure 4-1**

Now that you have some idea what Hello World 1 looks like, it is time to take a close look at how it works. Despite its minimalist appearance, Hello World 1 must perform a number of tasks before it can display its form. Although the user doesn't get much say in how Hello World 1 operates, the program must still respond properly to directives that it receives from the operating system.

The file `helloMain.c` contains the bulk of the code for the Hello World 1 application. This section deals with a small piece of the application code at a time. A complete listing of `helloMain.c` appears near the end of this chapter in the section "Putting It All Together."

## *Including Header Files*

At the top of `helloMain.c` are the following `#include` directives:

```
#include <PalmOS.h>
#include "helloResources.h"
```

The `PalmOS.h` file contains further includes for most of the header files in Palm OS. In the CodeWarrior environment, `PalmOS.h` includes a prebuilt header to assist in faster compilation. Because Hello World 1 is a simple application, the headers included by `PalmOS.h` are more than sufficient for everything that the application must accomplish.

*Prior to Palm OS SDK 3.5, the main include file for the Palm OS SDK was called Pilot.h. If you are compiling an application using headers that are older than SDK 3.5, use `Pilot.h` instead of `PalmOS.h`. See the section titled "Understanding Changes in Palm OS Header Files" later in this chapter for more details on the differences between different versions of the Palm OS headers.*

Hello World 1 also includes the file `helloResources.h`, which defines resource constants used throughout the application. In a more complicated program, `helloResources.h` might contain constants to identify menus, controls, alerts, and other resources. However, Hello World 1 needs to work with only one resource, which is the form called `MainForm`.

*This chapter deals only with the constants that refer to resources in the two Hello World applications. Chapters 6 and 7 contain details for building the resources themselves.*

In the CodeWarrior and PRC-Tools environments, the PilRC tool generates `helloResources.h` automatically. The following code is an example of a resource constant file generated by PilRC:

```
/* pilrc generated file.  Do not edit!*/
#define MainForm 1001
```

In Palm OS Developer Studio, you create the resource constant file yourself. The following code shows how this handmade file looks:

```
// Main form
#define MainForm                1000
```

## Entering the Application

The first code that Palm OS executes in your application is the `PilotMain` routine, which looks like this in Hello World 1:

**Palm OS Garnet**

```
UInt32 PilotMain(UInt16 cmd, MemPtr cmdPBP,
                UInt16 launchFlags)
{
    Err  error = errNone;


    switch (cmd)
    {
        case sysAppLaunchCmdNormalLaunch:
            error = AppStart();
            if (error == 0)
            {
                AppEventLoop();
                AppStop();
            }
            break;

        default:
            break;
    }

    return error;
}
```

**Palm OS Cobalt**

```
uint32_t PilotMain(uint16_t cmd, MemPtr cmdPBP,
                   uint16_t launchFlags)
{
    status_t error = errNone;


    if ((error = SysGetModuleDatabase(SysGetRefNum(), NULL,
        &gAppDB)) < errNone)
        return error;

    switch (cmd)
    {
        case sysAppLaunchCmdNormalLaunch:
            error = AppStart();
            if (error == errNone)
            {
                AppEventLoop();
                AppStop();
            }
            break;

        default:
            break;

    }

    return error;
}
```

The first parameter to `PilotMain` is a launch code telling your application how to start itself. In a normal application launch, which occurs when the user taps your application's icon in the launcher, Palm OS passes the constant `sysAppLaunchCmdNormalLaunch` to the `PilotMain` routine.

During a normal launch, the `cmdPBP` and `launchFlags` parameters are not used. They contain extra parameters and flags that are used when the operating system calls the application with a different launch code. For example, the `sysAppLaunchCmdFind` launch code, sent by the operating system during a global find, uses the `cmdPBP` parameter to pass a pointer to the text to search for in your application. The following table lists some common launch codes and what they indicate.

| Launch Code | Description |
|---|---|
| sysAppLaunchCmdAddRecord | Signals that another application wants to add a record to your application's database |
| sysAppLaunchCmdDisplayAlarm | Tells the application to display a specified alarm dialog box or perform other lengthy alarm-related actions |
| sysAppLaunchCmdFind | Finds a text string somewhere in the application's stored data |
| sysAppLaunchCmdGoto | Goes to a specific record in the application's database |
| sysAppLaunchCmdNormalLaunch | Launches the application normally |
| sysAppLaunchCmdSystemReset | Allows the application to respond to a system reset |

Palm OS supports many other launch codes. Fortunately, your application does not need to respond to all of them. If a particular launch code is inappropriate for your application, simply leave that code out of your application's PilotMain routine.

PilotMain in the Hello World 1 application deals only with the sysAppLaunchCmdFind launch code. When it receives this code, it passes execution to AppStart to take care of initialization chores.

## Starting the Application

The AppStart routine in Hello World 1 is listed here:

**Palm OS Garnet**

```
static Err AppStart(void)
{
    FrmGotoForm(MainForm);
    return errNone;
}
```

**Palm OS Cobalt**

```
static status_t AppStart(void)
{
    FrmGotoForm(gAppDB, MainForm);
    return errNone;
}
```

AppStart is where more complex programs would carry out database initialization and retrieval of user preferences prior to running the rest of the application. Hello World 1 does not have any data to save between the times the user runs it, but its AppStart routine does perform one important task. AppStart calls the Palm OS function FrmGotoForm to start up the main form that contains the application's interface. The FrmGotoForm function puts frmLoadEvent and frmOpenEvent events into the event queue, signaling the specified form to load itself and open. PilotMain passes the constant MainForm to FrmGotoForm, a constant that represents the form resource for the Hello World 1 program's main form.

Notice that the Palm OS Cobalt version of FrmGotoForm takes an extra argument. Resources are handled differently in Palm OS Cobalt than in prior versions of Palm OS. As a result, the first argument to FrmGotoForm is a reference to the application's database. FrmGotoForm uses the database reference as a starting point to locate the form resource itself. Hello World 1 retrieves its own database reference in its PilotMain function by calling the Palm OS SysGetModuleDatabase function:

```
if ((error = SysGetModuleDatabase(SysGetRefNum(), NULL,
    &gAppDB)) < errNone)
    return error;
```

SysGetModuleDatabase returns a pointer to the Hello World 1 database reference in the global gAppDB variable. Many functions other than FrmGotoForm also require the application's database reference, so most applications should contain a similar call to SysGetModuleDatabase in their PilotMain functions. Storing the database reference in a global variable ensures that the reference need only be retrieved once; the reference never changes between the time an application starts and stops. More details about SysGetModuleDatabase, and the SysGetRefNum function that it calls, are presented in Chapter 15.

## Closing the Application

Skipping ahead a bit, you can see that the AppStop routine runs when the AppEventLoop routine has exited and the application is shutting down. Here is AppStop from Hello World 1:

```
static void AppStop(void)
{
    FrmCloseAllForms();
}
```

AppStop is where a Palm OS program should perform tasks prior to the program's ending execution. Because Hello World 1 does not need to perform any cleanup before closing down, its AppStop routine is devoid of code to close the application's database and save user preferences. The AppStop routine in any Palm OS application should call the system routine FrmCloseAllForms, which sends a frmCloseEvent to every open form. This allows each form to clean up after itself, removing its own structures and data from memory before the application exits.

*Failure to call FrmCloseAllForms before exiting your application could cause a memory leak.*

## Handling Events

After PilotMain calls AppStart to initialize the program, execution passes to the AppEventLoop routine:

**Palm OS Garnet**

```
static void AppEventLoop(void)
{
    EventType   event;
    Err         error;


    do
    {
        EvtGetEvent(&event, evtWaitForever);

        if (SysHandleEvent(&event))
            continue;

        if (MenuHandleEvent(0, &event, &error))
            continue;

        if (AppHandleEvent(&event))
            continue;

        FrmDispatchEvent(&event);
    }
    while (event.eType != appStopEvent);
}
```

**Palm OS Cobalt**

```
static void AppEventLoop(void)
{
    EventType  event;
    status_t   error;


    do
    {
        EvtGetEvent(&event, evtWaitForever);

        if (SysHandleEvent(&event))
            continue;

        if (MenuHandleEvent(0, &event, &error))
            continue;

        if (AppHandleEvent(&event))
            continue;

        FrmDispatchEvent(&event);
    }
    while (event.eType != appStopEvent);
}
```

The event loop is responsible for processing events that are received by the application. Incoming events enter the *event queue*, where AppEventLoop processes one event at a time. AppEventLoop grabs events from the queue with the EvtGetEvent function and then dispatches those events to the event handling routines. Each of the four event handlers gets an opportunity to process the event in turn, in this order:

**1.** SysHandleEvent handles system events, such as the user's pressing the power button to turn off the handheld.

**2.** MenuHandleEvent takes care of menu events, such as the user's tapping the Menu silkscreened button or selecting a displayed menu item.

**3.** AppHandleEvent loads form resources and sets up form-specific event handlers.

**4.** FrmDispatchEvent passes the event to the application's own event handler or lets the operating system perform default actions for that event.

Once the event has been handled, the event loop starts again, retrieving the next event from the event queue and repeating the process. The AppEventLoop routine continues until it pulls an appStopEvent from the queue, at which point it stops and passes execution back to PilotMain.

The EvtGetEvent function warrants further discussion. Its first parameter merely provides an address to which the function should copy the next event it retrieves. The second parameter to EvtGetEvent is a timeout value in *ticks*, which is a unit used by the CPU to keep time. The length of a system tick varies between different models of Palm OS handhelds; you can call the SysTicksPerSecond routine in Palm OS Garnet or the SysTimeToSecs routine in Palm OS Cobalt to find the actual value. If no event enters the queue before the timeout value elapses, EvtGetEvent returns the value nilEvent in the first parameter.

Most applications should pass the constant evtWaitForever (equal to -1) as the second parameter of EvtGetEvent. The evtWaitForever constant tells EvtGetEvent to put the system into doze mode to conserve power until another event enters the queue. Timeout values greater than or equal to zero are primarily useful in applications that must animate screen images, such as games, or those that must handle network traffic, such as telnet or chat programs.

## Processing System Events in SysHandleEvent

The first event handler that receives an event from the event loop is SysHandleEvent, which gives the operating system an opportunity to handle important system events. The system handles such things as Graffiti input, hardware button presses, and taps on the silkscreened buttons. SysHandleEvent also takes care of low battery notifications, the global find function, and other systemwide events that may interrupt whatever the application is currently doing.

Depending on the event, SysHandleEvent often puts more events back into the queue. For example, when the user enters strokes in the Graffiti area, the system interprets the resulting Graffiti events and places corresponding key events into the queue. The event loop eventually pulls these key events out of the queue and processes them.

If it handles the event completely, SysHandleEvent returns true. The event loop then calls EvtGetEvent to process the next event in the queue.

## Handling Menu Events in MenuHandleEvent

If the system was not interested in handling an event, MenuHandleEvent gets the next crack at it. MenuHandleEvent cares about only three kinds of events:

❑ Any taps from the user that invoke a menu, in which case MenuHandleEvent displays the appropriate menu

❑ Taps inside a menu that activate a menu item, which cause MenuHandleEvent to remove the menu from the screen and put events corresponding to the selected command into the event queue

❑ Taps outside a displayed menu, which cause MenuHandleEvent to close the menu and remove it from the screen

Like SysHandleEvent, MenuHandleEvent also returns true if it completely processes an event.

## Preparing Forms in AppHandleEvent

Events that make it this far into the event loop are of potential interest to the application itself. AppHandleEvent is a function you must write yourself; its only purpose is to handle the frmLoadEvent. In the AppHandleEvent function, your program loads and activates form resources. This function also is where the application sets up a callback function to serve as an event handler for the current active form.

AppHandleEvent is covered in more detail later in this chapter.

## Dealing with Form Events in FrmDispatchEvent

The FrmDispatchEvent function is like a miniature event loop within the more complicated AppEventLoop. FrmDispatchEvent first passes the event to the active form's event handler, which was set up previously in AppHandleEvent. Because Hello World 1 has only one form, FrmDispatchEvent passes events to the MainFormHandleEvent callback function. If the form event handler fully processes the event, it returns true, causing FrmDispatchEvent to return execution to the event loop.

FrmDispatchEvent passes events not handled by the application to FrmHandleEvent, a function that lets the system perform default processing of the event. This processing usually involves standard user interface actions, such as highlighting a button tapped by the user. In any case, all events not previously handled in the event loop meet their final resting place in the FrmHandleEvent function, which does not return any value.

# Setting Up Forms

Events not handled by SysHandleEvent or MenuHandleEvent make their way to AppHandleEvent. Unlike the first two event handlers, AppHandleEvent is not part of Palm OS. You must provide this function yourself because its contents vary from program to program, depending on how many forms each program contains. The AppHandleEvent function from Hello World 1 is listed as follows:

**Palm OS Garnet**

```
static Boolean AppHandleEvent(EventType *event)
{
    FormType   *form;
    UInt16     formID;
    Boolean    handled = false;


    if (event->eType == frmLoadEvent)
    {
        formID = event->data.frmLoad.formID;
        form = FrmInitForm(formID);
        FrmSetActiveForm(form);

        switch (formID)
        {
            case MainForm:
                FrmSetEventHandler(form,
                                    MainFormHandleEvent);
                break;

            default:
                break;
        }
        handled = true;
    }

    return handled;
}
```

**Palm OS Cobalt**

```
static Boolean AppHandleEvent(EventType *event)
{
    FormType  *form;
    uint16_t  formID;
    Boolean   handled = false;


    if (event->eType == frmLoadEvent)
    {
        formID = event->data.frmLoad.formID;
        form = FrmInitForm(gAppDB, formID);
        FrmSetActiveForm(form);

        switch (formID)
        {
            case MainForm:
                FrmSetEventHandler(form,
                                        MainFormHandleEvent);
                break;

            default:
                break;
        }
        handled = true;
    }

    return handled;
}
```

AppHandleEvent is responsible for two things:

❏    Initializing form resources

❏    Setting callback event handlers for forms

The AppHandleEvent function accomplishes the first of these two goals by calling two system functions, FrmInitForm and FrmSetActiveForm. FrmInitForm loads the form resource into memory and initializes its data structure, returning a pointer to that form. Then FrmSetActiveForm takes the pointer to the newly initialized form and makes that form into the *active form*. Only one form may be active at a time in Palm OS.

In Palm OS Garnet and earlier versions, there is only one event queue, which belonging to the current application. The current application's event queue has complete control of event processing, and the currently active form receives all input from the user, both pen and key events. All drawing occurs within the active form.

In Palm OS Cobalt, every thread that displays user interface has its own event queue. However, only one thread ever has *input focus*. Only the thread that currently holds input focus receives key events. Forms displayed by other threads may still receive pen events, and any thread may draw to its forms at any time.

Once the form has been initialized and activated, it needs an event handler so it knows what to do with all the input it will soon be receiving. AppHandleEvent sets the form's event handler with the

`FrmSetEventHandler` function. Each form's event handler is a separate callback function that you provide. Once this event handler is set, the operating system passes all events that are not handled by the system or the menu manager to this form event handler.

Only one form exists in Hello World 1, and its event handler is `MainFormHandleEvent`. In more complex applications, `AppHandleEvent` sets a different event handler for each form in the application.

## Responding to Form Events

The `MainFormHandleEvent` routine in Hello World 1 is a callback function to which `FrmDispatchEvent` sends form-related events for processing. Because the main form in Hello World 1 does not actually interact with the user, `MainFormHandleEvent` is a simple function:

**Palm OS Garnet**

```
static Boolean MainFormHandleEvent(EventType *event)
{
    Boolean    handled = false;
    FormType   *form;


    switch (event->eType)
    {
        case frmOpenEvent:
            form = FrmGetActiveForm();
            FrmDrawForm(form);
            handled = true;
            break;

        default:
            break;
    }

    return handled;
}
```

**Palm OS Cobalt**

```
static Boolean MainFormHandleEvent(EventType *event)
{
    Boolean    handled = false;


    switch (event->eType)
    {
        case frmOpenEvent:
            PrvInvalidateFormWindow(MainForm);
            handled = true;
            break;

        default:
            break;
    }

    return handled;
}
```

In Hello World 1, `MainFormHandleEvent` must respond to only one type of event: `frmOpenEvent`. Palm OS queues a `frmOpenEvent` as a request for your application to open and display a form.

In a more complicated application, `MainFormHandleEvent` would also handle events generated by user input. Tapping buttons, entering Graffiti characters, pressing scroll buttons, and other types of user interaction with the currently displayed form generate events that `MainFormHandleEvent` should take care of. Hello World 1 just doesn't present anything for the user to do, so it handles only `frmOpenEvent`.

In the Palm OS Garnet version of Hello World 1, `MainFormHandleEvent` handles a `frmOpenEvent` by first retrieving a pointer to the active form with `FrmGetActiveForm`. Then `MainFormHandleEvent` passes that pointer to `FrmDrawForm`, a system routine that actually draws the form on the screen.

Palm OS Cobalt handles the drawing of forms differently. Instead of explicitly drawing the form, a Palm OS Cobalt application invalidates the window that contains the form. A *window* in Palm OS is simply a rectangular region that can accept user input. Invalidating the window simply tells the operating system that the window's contents are no longer up to date; when the system next gets around to drawing, it knows that the window needs to be redrawn.

Because Palm OS Cobalt is multithreaded, its windows may need to be redrawn at any time. For example, a pop-up application might briefly obscure part of an application, and when the pop-up is dismissed, the portion of the application that was covered by the pop-up must be redrawn.

As a signal that it needs to redraw its interface, Palm OS queues a `frmUpdateEvent`. Normally, an application ignores a `frmUpdateEvent` and allows the system to respond to it at the end of the event loop. The system responds to `frmUpdateEvent` by redrawing the invalid portions of the screen.

To force the system to draw the form, the Palm OS Cobalt version of Hello World 1 invalidates its window by calling its `PrvInvalidateFormWindow` function:

```
static void PrvInvalidateFormWindow(uint16_t formID)
{
    WinHandle   window;
    FormType    *form;

    if ((form = FrmGetFormPtr(formID)) == NULL)
        return;

    if ((window = FrmGetWindowHandle(form)) == NULL)
        return;

    WinInvalidateWindow(window);
}
```

`PrvInvalidateFormWindow` calls the `FrmGetFormPtr` function to get a pointer to a form, based on the form's resource ID. Then `PrvInvalidateFormWindow` passes the form pointer to `FrmGetWindowHandle` to retrieve the window handle of the form. Finally, `PrvInvalidateFormWindow` passes the window handle to the `WinInalidateWindow` function to mark the window area as invalid.

# Creating Hello World 2

Before delving into the code in the Hello World 2 application, a quick description of what the program looks like and what it does is in order. Hello World 2 picks up where Hello World 1 left off by adding user interaction to the application. This sample program does a little more than simply print an impersonal "Hello World" on the screen. Hello World 2 has a text field for the user's name. Figure 4-2 shows the application's main form after some text has been entered into the field.

Figure 4-2

Buttons at the bottom of the form display alerts when tapped. They are customized with a string entered by the user in the name field. The program also has an "about" box (accessible through the application's menus) to display a little information about the program. Figure 4-3 shows the alerts that appear when the user taps the Say Hello or Say Goodbye buttons.

Figure 4-3

Hello World also implements the standard Palm Edit menu to provide text-editing commands for the form's name field. An Options menu offers an About Hello World 2 item to display the application's "about" box. Figure 4-4 shows the menus in the Hello World 2 application.

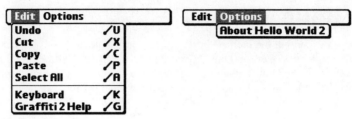

Figure 4-4

The "about" box is a separate form from the main one that constitutes most of the Hello World 2 interface. Although the "about" box form is mostly just a collection of text labels to provide a little information about the program, it does have a single OK button at the bottom to return the user to the main form (see Figure 4-5).

Figure 4-5

The resources for the Hello World 2 application's form, alerts, and menus are defined in separate files from the source code shown in this chapter. These files, and the processes used to generate them, are different among the Palm OS Developer Studio, CodeWarrior, and PRC-Tools environments. Creating resources is covered in detail in Chapters 6 and 7.

## Defining Resource Constants

Because Hello World 2 uses more resources to define its user interface than the single form used by Hello World 1, the Hello World 2 version of `helloResources.h` contains many more resource constant definitions. The following code shows the automatically generated `helloResources.h` file made by PilRC in the CodeWarrior and PRC-Tools environments:

```
/* pilrc generated file.  Do not edit!*/
#define GoodbyeAlert 1020
#define HelloAlert 1019
#define AboutOKButton 1018
```

```
#define AboutForm 1009
#define OptionsAboutHelloWorld2 1008
#define MainGoodbyeButton 1006
#define MainHelloButton 1005
#define MainNameField 1004
#define MainMenuBar 1002
#define MainForm 1001
```

The following code shows the handmade `helloResources.h` file used by Palm OS Developer Studio:

```
// Main form
#define MainForm                 1000
#define MainNameField            1000
#define MainHelloButton          1001
#define MainGoodbyeButton        1002

// Main form menus
#define MainMenuBar              1000
#define OptionsAboutHelloWorld2  1000

// About form
#define AboutForm                1001
#define AboutOKButton            1000

// Alerts
#define HelloAlert               1000
#define GoodbyeAlert             1001

// Bitmaps
#define BmpFamilyAppIcon         1000
```

# Responding to Form Events

The `MainFormHandleEvent` function in Hello World 2 processes input to the application's main form, so it has a bit more to do than the `MainFormHandleEvent` function from Hello World 1. The Hello World 2 version of `MainFormHandleEvent` is shown as follows:

**Palm OS Garnet**
```
static Boolean MainFormHandleEvent(EventType *event)
{
    Boolean   handled = false;
    FormType  *form;
    UInt16    fieldIndex;

    switch (event->eType)
    {
        case frmOpenEvent:
            form = FrmGetActiveForm();
            FrmDrawForm(form);

            fieldIndex = FrmGetObjectIndex(form,
                                           MainNameField);
            FrmSetFocus(form, fieldIndex);
```

```
                handled = true;
                break;
        case ctlSelectEvent:
            switch(event->data.ctlSelect.controlID)
            {
                case MainHelloButton:
                    SaySomething(HelloAlert);
                    handled = true;
                    break;

                case MainGoodbyeButton:
                    SaySomething(GoodbyeAlert);
                    handled = true;
                    break;

                default:
                    break;
            }
            break;

        case menuEvent:
            handled =
                MainMenuHandleEvent(event->data.menu.itemID);
            break;


        default:
            break;
    }

    return handled;
}
```

**Palm OS Cobalt**

```
static Boolean MainFormHandleEvent(EventType *event)
{
    Boolean   handled = false;
    FormType  *form;
    uint16_t  fieldIndex;

    switch (event->eType)
    {
        case frmOpenEvent:
            form = FrmGetFormPtr(MainForm);
            PrvInvalidateFormWindow(MainForm);
            fieldIndex = FrmGetObjectIndex(form,
                                            MainNameField);
            FrmSetFocus(form, fieldIndex);
            handled = true;
            break;
        case ctlSelectEvent:
            switch(event->data.ctlSelect.controlID)
            {
                case MainHelloButton:
                    SaySomething(HelloAlert);
```

```
                    handled = true;
                    break;

                case MainGoodbyeButton:
                    SaySomething(GoodbyeAlert);
                    handled = true;
                    break;

                default:
                    break;
            }
            break;

        case menuEvent:
            handled =
                MainMenuHandleEvent(event->data.menu.itemID);
            break;

        default:
            break;
    }

    return handled;
}
```

Just as it does in Hello World 1, `MainFormHandleEvent` in Hello World 2 handles the `frmOpenEvent` by drawing the form on the screen with the `FrmDrawForm` function or invalidating the form's window with the `PrvInvalidateFormWindow` function. In addition, because there is a text field on the screen, it also is a good idea to put the focus in that field so that the user may immediately begin entering text without first tapping the field. The `FrmSetFocus` function performs this task.

> *Setting field focus with `FrmSetFocus` is a technique you should use in any application that displays text fields. Doing so makes your application quicker and friendlier to use.*

If the user taps and releases either button on the main form, a `ctlSelectEvent` enters the queue and eventually makes its way to `MainFormHandleEvent`. Depending on which button was tapped, `MainFormHandleEvent` displays one of two alerts using the `SaySomething` function, which is explained later in this chapter.

The `MainFormHandleEvent` function also can handle menu events. To keep the function small and easy to read, though, `MainFormHandleEvent` defers menu handling to `MainMenuHandleEvent`, another function provided by the application instead of the operating system.

## Handling Menu Events

In Hello World 2, `MainFormHandleEvent` passes menu events to another function, `MainMenuHandleEvent`, which is shown in the following example:

**Palm OS Garnet**
```
static Boolean MainMenuHandleEvent(UInt16 menuID)
{
    Boolean    handled = false;
    FormType   *form;
```

```
        FieldType   *field;


        form = FrmGetActiveForm();
        field = FrmGetObjectPtr(form,
            FrmGetObjectIndex(form, MainNameField));

        switch (menuID)
        {
            case OptionsAboutHelloWorld2:
                MenuEraseStatus(0);

                form = FrmInitForm(AboutForm);
                FrmDoDialog(form);
                FrmDeleteForm(form);

                handled = true;
                break;

            default:
                break;
        }

        return handled;
}
```

**Palm OS Cobalt**

```
static Boolean MainMenuHandleEvent(uint16_t menuID)
{
    Boolean    handled = false;
    FormType   *form;


    form = FrmGetActiveForm();

    switch (menuID)
    {
        case OptionsAboutHelloWorld2:
            form = FrmInitForm(gAppDB, AboutForm);
            FrmDoDialog(form);
            FrmDeleteForm(form);

            handled = true;
            break;

        default:
            break;
    }

    return handled;
}
```

Hello World 2 has a standard Edit menu that contains commands for editing text, such as copying to and pasting from the Clipboard. MainMenuHandleEvent does not need to handle Edit menu commands explicitly because they are defined in the Hello World 2 resources with special resource ID numbers. Palm OS recognizes a certain series of resource ID numbers as Edit menu commands, and the system automatically handles those commands when it processes events in the `MenuHandleEvent` portion of the event loop. For more details about setting up standard Edit menu resources, see Chapter 7.

The only menu option handled by `MainMenuHandleEvent` displays the application's "about" box, which is another form resource. The "about" box is a modal form; Hello World 2 cannot perform any other tasks until the user taps the OK button. To display the "about" box modally, `MainMenuHandleEvent` must first initialize the `AboutForm` resource by calling `FrmInitForm`. Then `MainMenuHandleEvent` calls `FrmDoDialog` to display the "about" box form. When `FrmDoDialog` is finished, `MainMenuHandleEvent` calls `FrmDeleteForm` to free up memory no longer needed by the "about" box.

Even though the "about" box is a form in its own right, it does not require its own event handler because its only control is the OK button. `FrmDoDialog` displays a form until the user taps a button on that form or switches to another application. If there were other user interface elements in the "about" box (such as a menu), Hello World 2 would need to define a function to handle other events in the box and add a couple lines of code to `AppHandleEvent` to register the event handler. For example, assuming that the event handler for the "about" box were called `AboutFormHandleEvent`, the following code would need to be added to `AppHandleEvent`:

```
switch (formID)
{
    case MainForm:
        FrmSetEventHandler(form,
                        MainFormHandleEvent);
        break;

    case AboutForm:
        FrmSetEventHandler(form,
                        AboutFormHandleEvent);

    default:
        break;
}
```

## Displaying Alerts and Using the Text Field

`MainFormHandleEvent` calls the `SaySomething` function when the user taps one of the main form's two buttons. `SaySomething` is listed in the following example:

**Palm OS Garnet**
```
static void SaySomething(UInt16 alertID)
{
    FormType    *form = FrmGetActiveForm();
    FieldType   *field;


    field = FrmGetObjectPtr(form, FrmGetObjectIndex(form,
                        MainNameField));
    if (FldGetTextLength(field) > 0)
    {
```

```
        FrmCustomAlert(alertID, FldGetTextPtr(field), NULL,
                    NULL);
    }
    else
    {
        // No text in field, so display a "whoever you are"
        // dialog.
        FrmCustomAlert(alertID, "whoever you are", NULL,
                    NULL);
    }
}
```

**Palm OS Cobalt**

```
static void SaySomething(uint16_t alertID)
{
    FormType    *form = FrmGetActiveForm();
    FieldType   *field;


    field = FrmGetObjectPtr(form, FrmGetObjectIndex(form,
                        MainNameField));
    if (FldGetTextLength(field) > 0)
    {
        FrmCustomAlert(gAppDB, alertID, FldGetTextPtr(field),
                    NULL, NULL);
    }
    else
    {
        // No text in field, so display a "whoever you are"
        // dialog.
        FrmCustomAlert(gAppDB, alertID, "whoever you are",
                    NULL, NULL);
    }
}
```

SaySomething takes a single argument—the resource ID of an alert that it should display. Instead of popping up a static alert box with FrmAlert, SaySomething customizes the alerts it displays by using the FrmCustomAlert function, which replaces up to three special characters in the alert resource that it displays with strings supplied in three of its arguments. Hello World 2 needs to fill in only one piece of custom text in each alert, so SaySomething passes NULL for the third and fourth arguments to FrmCustomAlert. More information on displaying custom alerts is in Chapter 7.

In order for SaySomething to grab the string entered in the form's text field, the function needs a pointer to that field. SaySomething provides this pointer with the FrmGetObjectIndex and FrmGetObjectPtr functions. FrmGetObjectIndex takes the resource ID of the text field and returns its *object index*. Every object on a form has a unique object index, starting at zero. FrmGetObjectPtr takes the object index obtained by FrmGetObjectIndex and returns a pointer to the field.

The construct FrmGetObjectPtr(form, FrmGetObjectIndex(form, objectID)) is common in Palm OS programming, and you will find yourself using it throughout your applications. If you wish to save some typing while writing your code, a function similar to the following may come in handy:

**Palm OS Garnet**

```
static void * GetObjectPtr (UInt16 objectID)
{
    FormType   *form;

    form = FrmGetActiveForm();
    return (FrmGetObjectPtr(form,
        FrmGetObjectIndex(form, objectID)));
}
```

**Palm OS Cobalt**

```
static void * GetObjectPtr (uint16_t objectID)
{
    FormType   *form;

    form = FrmGetActiveForm();
    return (FrmGetObjectPtr(form,
        FrmGetObjectIndex(form, objectID)));
}
```

Now that SaySomething has a pointer to the field, the function checks to see if the field contains any text by calling the system function FldGetTextLength. The FldGetTextLength function returns the number of bytes of text contained in a field. If there is no text in the field, SaySomething fills in an appropriate generic name, "whoever you are", so the alert will have something to display to the user.

To extract the text from the field, SaySomething calls the FldGetTextPtr function. FldGetTextPtr returns a pointer to the memory that contains a field's text. SaySomething passes this pointer to FrmCustomAlert to display a short message to the user, a message that includes the contents of the field.

FldGetTextPtr should be used only to read data from a text field. Because the text in a field may change size dynamically as the user edits it, Palm OS uses a moveable chunk of memory to store the field's text. The system uses handles to keep track of a moveable chunk's location instead of pointers, which indicate specific, immobile chunks of memory. Allowing chunks of memory to be mobile ensures that the operating system can relocate memory as it sees fit to make room for more memory allocations, which is a useful feature indeed on a platform with so little dynamic memory available. As the user changes the text in a field, the system might move the memory chunk that contains the field's text, thereby invalidating the pointer returned by FldGetTextPtr. You must use other Palm OS functions to alter the contents of a text field. See Chapter 8 for information about changing the text in a field.

# Putting It All Together

This section contains the complete code listing for both Hello World 1 and Hello World 2.

## Hello World 1: helloMain.c

**Palm OS Garnet**

```
#include <PalmOS.h>
#include "helloResources.h"
```

*(continued)*

```c
static Boolean MainFormHandleEvent(EventType *event)
{
    Boolean    handled = false;
    FormType   *form;


    switch (event->eType)
    {
        case frmOpenEvent:
            form = FrmGetActiveForm();
            FrmDrawForm(form);
            handled = true;
            break;

        default:
            break;
    }

    return handled;
}


static Boolean AppHandleEvent(EventType *event)
{
    FormType   *form;
    UInt16     formID;
    Boolean    handled = false;


    if (event->eType == frmLoadEvent)
    {
        formID = event->data.frmLoad.formID;
        form = FrmInitForm(formID);
        FrmSetActiveForm(form);

        switch (formID)
        {
            case MainForm:
                FrmSetEventHandler(form,
                                MainFormHandleEvent);
                break;

            default:
                break;
        }
        handled = true;
    }

    return handled;
}
```

```c
static void AppEventLoop(void)
{
    EventType   event;
    Err         error;


    do
    {
        EvtGetEvent(&event, evtWaitForever);

        if (SysHandleEvent(&event))
            continue;

        if (MenuHandleEvent(0, &event, &error))
            continue;

        if (AppHandleEvent(&event))
            continue;

        FrmDispatchEvent(&event);
    }
    while (event.eType != appStopEvent);
}


static Err AppStart(void)
{
    FrmGotoForm(MainForm);
    return errNone;
}


static void AppStop(void)
{
    FrmCloseAllForms();
}


UInt32 PilotMain(UInt16 cmd, MemPtr cmdPBP,
                UInt16 launchFlags)
{
    Err  error = errNone;


    switch (cmd)
    {
        case sysAppLaunchCmdNormalLaunch:
            error = AppStart();
            if (error == 0)
            {
                AppEventLoop();
                AppStop();
            }
            break;
```

*(continued)*

**Hello World 1: helloMain.c** *(continued)*

```c
        default:
            break;
    }

    return error;
}
```

**Palm OS Cobalt**

```c
#include <PalmOS.h>
#include "helloResources.h"


/************************************************************
 * Global variables
 ************************************************************/
DmOpenRef   gAppDB;


/************************************************************
 * Internal functions
 ************************************************************/
static void PrvInvalidateFormWindow(uint16_t formID)
{
    WinHandle   window;
    FormType    *form;

    if ((form = FrmGetFormPtr(formID)) == NULL)
        return;

    if ((window = FrmGetWindowHandle(form)) == NULL)
        return;

    WinInvalidateWindow(window);
}


static Boolean MainFormHandleEvent(EventType *event)
{
    Boolean   handled = false;

    switch (event->eType)
    {
        case frmOpenEvent:
            PrvInvalidateFormWindow(MainForm);
            handled = true;
            break;

        default:
            break;
    }
```

```
        return handled;
}


static Boolean AppHandleEvent(EventType *event)
{
    FormType   *form;
    uint16_t   formID;
    Boolean    handled = false;


    if (event->eType == frmLoadEvent)
    {
        formID = event->data.frmLoad.formID;
        form = FrmInitForm(gAppDB, formID);
        FrmSetActiveForm(form);

        switch (formID)
        {
            case MainForm:
                FrmSetEventHandler(form,
                                   MainFormHandleEvent);
                break;

            default:
                break;
        }
        handled = true;
    }

    return handled;
}


static void AppEventLoop(void)
{
    EventType   event;
    status_t    error;


    do
    {
        EvtGetEvent(&event, evtWaitForever);

        if (SysHandleEvent(&event))
            continue;

        if (MenuHandleEvent(0, &event, &error))
            continue;

        if (AppHandleEvent(&event))
            continue;

        FrmDispatchEvent(&event);
```

*(continued)*

**Hello World 1: helloMain.c** *(continued)*

```c
    }
    while (event.eType != appStopEvent);
}


static status_t AppStart(void)
{
    FrmGotoForm(gAppDB, MainForm);
    return errNone;
}


static void AppStop(void)
{
    FrmCloseAllForms();
}


uint32_t PilotMain(uint16_t cmd, MemPtr cmdPBP,
                   uint16_t launchFlags)
{
    status_t error = errNone;


    if ((error = SysGetModuleDatabase(SysGetRefNum(), NULL,
        &gAppDB)) < errNone)
        return error;

    switch (cmd)
    {
        case sysAppLaunchCmdNormalLaunch:
            error = AppStart();
            if (error == errNone)
            {
                AppEventLoop();
                AppStop();
            }
            break;

        default:
            break;

    }

    return error;
}
```

**Hello World 2: helloMain.c**

**Palm OS Garnet**
```c
#include <PalmOS.h>
#include "helloResources.h"
```

```
static void SaySomething(UInt16 alertID)
{
    FormType   *form = FrmGetActiveForm();
    FieldType  *field;


    field = FrmGetObjectPtr(form, FrmGetObjectIndex(form,
                     MainNameField));
    if (FldGetTextLength(field) > 0)
    {
        FrmCustomAlert(alertID, FldGetTextPtr(field), NULL,
                    NULL);
    }
    else
    {
        // No text in field, so display a "whoever you are"
        // dialog.
        FrmCustomAlert(alertID, "whoever you are", NULL,
                    NULL);
    }
}


static Boolean MainMenuHandleEvent(UInt16 menuID)
{
    Boolean    handled = false;
    FormType   *form;


    form = FrmGetActiveForm();

    switch (menuID)
    {
        case OptionsAboutHelloWorld2:
            MenuEraseStatus(0);

            form = FrmInitForm(AboutForm);
            FrmDoDialog(form);
            FrmDeleteForm(form);

            handled = true;
            break;

        default:
            break;
    }

    return handled;
}


static Boolean MainFormHandleEvent(EventType *event)
{
```

*(continued)*

**Hello World 2: helloMain.c** *(continued)*

```c
    Boolean   handled = false;
    FormType  *form;
    UInt16    fieldIndex;

    switch (event->eType)
    {
        case frmOpenEvent:
            form = FrmGetActiveForm();
            FrmDrawForm(form);
            fieldIndex = FrmGetObjectIndex(form,
                                      MainNameField);
            FrmSetFocus(form, fieldIndex);
            handled = true;
            break;

        case ctlSelectEvent:
            switch(event->data.ctlSelect.controlID)
            {
                case MainHelloButton:
                    SaySomething(HelloAlert);
                    handled = true;
                    break;

                case MainGoodbyeButton:
                    SaySomething(GoodbyeAlert);
                    handled = true;
                    break;

                default:
                    break;
            }
            break;

        case menuEvent:
            handled =
                MainMenuHandleEvent(event->data.menu.itemID);
            break;

        default:
            break;
    }

    return handled;
}


static Boolean AppHandleEvent(EventType *event)
{
    FormType  *form;
    UInt16    formID;
    Boolean   handled = false;
```

```
    if (event->eType == frmLoadEvent)
    {
        formID = event->data.frmLoad.formID;
        form = FrmInitForm(formID);
        FrmSetActiveForm(form);

        switch (formID)
        {
            case MainForm:
                FrmSetEventHandler(form,
                            MainFormHandleEvent);
                break;

            default:
                break;
        }
        handled = true;
    }

    return handled;
}


static void AppEventLoop(void)
{
    EventType   event;
    Err         error;


    do
    {
        EvtGetEvent(&event, evtWaitForever);

        if (SysHandleEvent(&event))
            continue;

        if (MenuHandleEvent(0, &event, &error))
            continue;

        if (AppHandleEvent(&event))
            continue;

        FrmDispatchEvent(&event);
    }
    while (event.eType != appStopEvent);
}


static Err AppStart(void)
{
    FrmGotoForm(MainForm);
    return errNone;
}
```

*(continued)*

**Hello World 2: helloMain.c** *(continued)*

```
static void AppStop(void)
{
    FrmCloseAllForms();
}


UInt32 PilotMain(UInt16 cmd, MemPtr cmdPBP,
                 UInt16 launchFlags)
{
    Err  error = errNone;


    switch (cmd)
    {
        case sysAppLaunchCmdNormalLaunch:
            error = AppStart();
            if (error == 0)
            {
                AppEventLoop();
                AppStop();
            }
            break;

        default:
            break;
    }

    return error;
}
```

**Palm OS Cobalt**

```
#include <PalmOS.h>
#include "helloResources.h"


/**********************************************************
 * Global variables
 **********************************************************/
DmOpenRef  gAppDB;

FormLayoutType gMainFormLayout[] = {
    { sizeof(FormLayoutType), MainHelloButton, 0,
      frmFollowBottom },
    { sizeof(FormLayoutType), MainGoodbyeButton, 0,
      frmFollowBottom },
    { 0,0,0,0 }
};


/**********************************************************
 * Internal functions
 **********************************************************/
static void PrvInvalidateFormWindow(uint16_t formID)
```

```
{
    WinHandle  window;
    FormType   *form;

    if ((form = FrmGetFormPtr(formID)) == NULL)
        return;

    if ((window = FrmGetWindowHandle(form)) == NULL)
        return;

    WinInvalidateWindow(window);
}


static void SaySomething(uint16_t alertID)
{
    FormType   *form = FrmGetActiveForm();
    FieldType  *field;


    field = FrmGetObjectPtr(form, FrmGetObjectIndex(form,
                        MainNameField));
    if (FldGetTextLength(field) > 0)
    {
        FrmCustomAlert(gAppDB, alertID, FldGetTextPtr(field),
                    NULL, NULL);
    }
    else
    {
        // No text in field, so display a "whoever you are"
        // dialog.
        FrmCustomAlert(gAppDB, alertID, "whoever you are",
                    NULL, NULL);
    }
}


static Boolean MainMenuHandleEvent(uint16_t menuID)
{
    Boolean    handled = false;
    FormType   *form;


    form = FrmGetActiveForm();

    switch (menuID)
    {
        case OptionsAboutHelloWorld2:
            form = FrmInitForm(gAppDB, AboutForm);
            FrmDoDialog(form);
            FrmDeleteForm(form);

            handled = true;
            break;
```

*(continued)*

**Hello World 2: helloMain.c** *(continued)*

```
            default:
                break;
        }

    return handled;
}


static Boolean MainFormHandleEvent(EventType *event)
{
    Boolean   handled = false;
    FormType  *form;
    uint16_t  fieldIndex;

    switch (event->eType)
    {
        case frmOpenEvent:
            form = FrmGetFormPtr(MainForm);
            PrvInvalidateFormWindow(MainForm);
            fieldIndex = FrmGetObjectIndex(form, MainNameField);
            FrmSetFocus(form, fieldIndex);
            handled = true;
            break;

        case ctlSelectEvent:
            switch(event->data.ctlSelect.controlID)
            {
                case MainHelloButton:
                    SaySomething(HelloAlert);
                    handled = true;
                    break;

                case MainGoodbyeButton:
                    SaySomething(GoodbyeAlert);
                    handled = true;
                    break;

                default:
                    break;
            }
            break;

        case menuEvent:
            handled =
                MainMenuHandleEvent(event->data.menu.itemID);
            break;

        default:
            break;
    }

    return handled;
```

```
}


static Boolean AppHandleEvent(EventType *event)
{
    FormType   *form;
    uint16_t   formID;
    Boolean    handled = false;


    if (event->eType == frmLoadEvent)
    {
        formID = event->data.frmLoad.formID;
        form = FrmInitForm(gAppDB, formID);
        FrmSetActiveForm(form);

        switch (formID)
        {
            case MainForm:
                FrmSetEventHandler(form,
                                   MainFormHandleEvent);
                FrmInitLayout(form, gMainFormLayout);
                break;

            default:
                break;
        }
        handled = true;
    }

    return handled;
}


static void AppEventLoop(void)
{
    EventType   event;
    status_t    error;


    do
    {
        EvtGetEvent(&event, evtWaitForever);

        if (SysHandleEvent(&event))
            continue;

        if (MenuHandleEvent(0, &event, &error))
            continue;

        if (AppHandleEvent(&event))
            continue;

        FrmDispatchEvent(&event);
```

*(continued)*

**Hello World 2: helloMain.c** *(continued)*

```c
    }
    while (event.eType != appStopEvent);
}


static status_t AppStart(void)
{
    FrmGotoForm(gAppDB, MainForm);
    return errNone;
}


static void AppStop(void)
{
    FrmCloseAllForms();
}


uint32_t PilotMain(uint16_t cmd, MemPtr cmdPBP,
                   uint16_t launchFlags)
{
    status_t error = errNone;


    if ((error = SysGetModuleDatabase(SysGetRefNum(), NULL,
        &gAppDB)) < errNone)
        return error;

    switch (cmd)
    {
        case sysAppLaunchCmdNormalLaunch:
            error = AppStart();
            if (error == errNone)
            {
                AppEventLoop();
                AppStop();
            }
            break;

        default:
            break;

    }

    return error;
}
```

# Understanding Changes in Palm OS Header Files

With the release of Palm OS version 3.5, and again with the release of Palm OS Cobalt, PalmSource made significant changes to the header files in the Palm OS SDK. For starters, prior to the version 3.5 headers, the basic file to include in a Palm OS application was `Pilot.h`; in SDK 3.5 and later versions, this file is called `PalmOS.h`.

Within the header files themselves, there are different data type definitions, intended by PalmSource to improve clarity and consistency. For example, the version 3.5 headers use `UInt32` instead of `DWord`, and `Int16` instead of `Int`, to indicate the size of particular data types better, and whether or not those types are signed. Palm OS Cobalt redefines basic data types to be compliant with the 1999 update to the ISO C standard, or "C99." For example, `UInt32` and `Int16` from Palm OS 3.5 become `uint32_t` and `int16_t`, respectively, in Palm OS Cobalt. If you're familiar with the contents of the `stdint.h` header file in UNIX and other operating systems, you should feel right at home with Palm OS Cobalt data types.

*Palm OS Garnet uses the same data types first introduced in Palm OS 3.5.*

Also, early versions of the headers made `typedef` declarations of the form `FooPtr`, where `FooPtr` is simply a pointer to a `FooType` structure. PalmSource has retired this convention in favor of using the standard C convention of `FooType *` to refer to a pointer to a `FooType` structure.

If you are working with code originally written using headers earlier than those included with Palm OS SDK 3.5, you will need to search for the older-style data types and replace them with their new equivalents. There is a file called `PalmCompatibility.h` in SDK 3.5 that maps the older-style data types to their new names. You can include `PalmCompatibility.h` in an older project to help it deal with compilation under the version 3.5 headers, but you are probably better off in the long run to bite the bullet and search and replace the data types yourself. Your code will be easier to read and less likely to break in the future if you fix it properly instead of patching it with `PalmCompatibility.h`.

Palm OS Cobalt has a similar header file called `PalmTypesCompatibility.h` that maps Palm OS 3.5 data types to their Palm OS Cobalt equivalents. Again, you may include `PalmTypesCompatibility.h` to get your project to compile but replacing the data types is a better, long-term solution.

Still, the `PalmCompatibility.h` and `PalmTypesCompatibility.h` files do make good references for what needs to be changed in your source files. The following section of `PalmCompatibility.h` points out the key differences in data types between the Palm OS 3.5 headers and earlier versions of the SDK:

```
typedef Int8    SByte;
typedef UInt8   Byte;

typedef Int16   SWord;
typedef UInt16  Word;

typedef Int32   SDWord;
typedef UInt32  DWord;


// Logical data types
```

```
typedef Int8     SChar;
typedef UInt8    UChar;

typedef Int16    Short;
typedef UInt16   UShort;

typedef Int16    Int;
typedef UInt16   UInt;

typedef Int32    Long;
typedef UInt32   ULong;


// Pointer Types
typedef MemPtr       VoidPtr;
typedef MemHandle    VoidHand;

typedef MemPtr       Ptr;
typedef MemHandle    Handle;


// Because "const BytePtr" means "const pointer to Byte"
// rather than "pointer to const Byte", all these XXXXPtr
// types are deprecated: you're better off just using
//   "Byte *" and so on. (Even better, use "UInt8 *"!)

typedef SByte*     SBytePtr;
typedef Byte*      BytePtr;

typedef SWord*     SWordPtr;
typedef Word*      WordPtr;
typedef UInt16*    UInt16Ptr;

typedef SDWord*    SDWordPtr;
typedef DWord*     DWordPtr;

// Logical data types
typedef Boolean*   BooleanPtr;

typedef Char*      CharPtr;
typedef SChar*     SCharPtr;
typedef UChar*     UCharPtr;

typedef WChar*     WCharPtr;

typedef Short*     ShortPtr;
typedef UShort*    UShortPtr;

typedef Int*       IntPtr;
typedef UInt*      UIntPtr;

typedef Long*      LongPtr;
typedef ULong*     ULongPtr;
```

The following section of `PalmTypesCompatibility.h` shows some of the differences between data types in Palm OS 3.5 and Palm OS Cobalt:

```
typedef char                    Char;

typedef int8_t                  Int8;
typedef int16_t                 Int16;
typedef int32_t                 Int32;
typedef int64_t                 Int64;

typedef uint8_t                 UInt8;
typedef uint16_t                UInt16;
typedef uint32_t                UInt32;
typedef uint64_t                UInt64;
```

Another important difference introduced in Palm OS Cobalt is the use of `status_t` instead of `Err` as the data type for error codes. Not only does the name change but `status_t` is a 32-bit signed integer instead of the 16-bit unsigned integer used for `Err`. Also, Palm OS Cobalt errors are always negative numbers; some functions might return a positive value as a status code, even when the function executes successfully. If you are porting older code to Palm OS Cobalt, you may need to change how you check for error conditions, as shown in the following example:

**Palm OS Garnet**
```
Err  error;

error = VFSFileClose(fileRef);
if (error)
{
    // handle error here
}
```

**Palm OS Cobalt**
```
status_t  error;

error = VFSFileClose(fileRef);
if (error < errNone)
{
    // handle error here
}
```

Keep in mind that no matter how recent the version of the Palm OS SDK you are using, it can still be used to make applications for any prior version of the operating system. For example, the headers in version 5.3 of the Palm OS SDK can still be used to make an application that runs on Palm OS 1.0. You do not need to dig up an ancient copy of Palm OS SDK 1.0 to build applications for the oldest version of Palm OS.

# Summary

In this chapter, you were introduced to the inner workings of a simple Palm OS application. After reading this chapter, you should understand the following:

❑ All Palm OS applications begin execution in the function `PilotMain`, which handles launch codes and starts the application's event loop.

❑ The event loop of a Palm OS application (`AppEventLoop`) is responsible for dispatching events from the event queue to the appropriate event handlers.

❑ Most events can be handled by the system using the functions `SysHandleEvent`, `MenuHandleEvent`, and `FrmHandleEvent`.

❑ The `AppHandleEvent` function, which is not provided by the operating system, initializes forms and sets event handlers for them. These event handlers are callback functions that you write.

❑ The callback event handler for each form responds to user input. For example, an event handler might respond to taps on buttons, hardware button presses, or taps on commands in the application's menus.

# Debugging Your Program

Between contributions from PalmSource and those of the Palm OS development community, a rich set of tools is available for debugging Palm OS applications. Emulators, source-level debuggers, an assembly-level debugger, and some developers' aids built into Palm OS itself all help to make the operating system a programmer-friendly environment for writing bug-free applications. This chapter takes a look at some tools and Palm OS features that are designed to make your life easier when it comes time to hunt down and squash bugs in your applications.

## Using Palm OS Emulator (POSE)

Debugging your Palm OS applications would be a frustrating and laborious process if you were required to install the applications on an actual handheld device for testing. The debugging process usually involves a repeated cycle of compiling, testing, and fixing code before all bugs have been worked out of a program. Installing an application on an actual Palm OS device is rather slow, which bogs down the testing portion of the debugging cycle.

Fortunately, Palm OS Emulator (POSE) provides a much faster alternative. Originally based on Copilot, an emulator written by Greg Hewgill, POSE emulates a Palm OS handheld at the hardware level, right down to the Motorola DragonBall processor. The emulator can do almost anything that an actual handheld is capable of doing, with only a few omissions due to differences in the hardware between a desktop system and a handheld device. Because the emulator runs on the same system you use to do your development work, installing and testing applications is fast and simple. The emulator even looks just like a Palm OS handheld (see Figure 5-1).

Figure 5-1

In addition to simple emulation, POSE provides a wealth of useful debugging features:

❑ Ability to enter text using the desktop computer's keyboard instead of having to use Graffiti or the onscreen keyboard

❑ Support for source-level debugging in external debuggers

❑ Configurable memory size, up to 16 MB

❑ Automated random testing facility (Gremlins)

❑ Profiling code to determine what routines the code spends the most time in (which is very useful for optimization)

❑ Extensive monitoring of memory actions to ensure that your application does not try to access memory that it should leave alone, such as low memory or hardware registers

❑ Complete logging of all application activities, including handled events, called functions, and executed CPU operation codes

❑ Easy screenshot-capturing facility, great for showing off an application on Web sites (or in programming books)

❑ Redirection of network library calls to the host system's TCP/IP stack

❑ Redirection of serial I/O to the host system's own serial ports

❑ Emulation of expansion card storage for testing applications that use the Virtual File System (VFS)

*If you have read any of the PalmSource documentation, there is a good chance you read about the Palm OS Simulator or Palm OS Simulator libraries for Mac OS. Do not confuse the two Simulators with the Palm OS Emulator; they are not the same tool.*

*The Palm OS Simulator, described later in this chapter, is a Windows program for emulating Palm OS 5 applications, which are executed on ARM processors.*

*The Palm OS Simulator libraries are available as part of the Mac OS version of CodeWarrior only. They allow you to build a standalone Macintosh application that simulates your application. If you have POSE for Mac OS, you can probably ignore the Simulator libraries entirely; POSE is a newer and much more versatile debugging tool.*

PalmSource supports versions of POSE for Windows, Mac OS, and UNIX. The Windows and Mac OS versions, as well as their source code, are available as free downloads from the PalmSource Web site at www.palmos.com; the UNIX version is available as a source distribution only. With the source code at your disposal, you can alter the emulator to suit your own tastes. If you come up with a modification (or a bug fix) that might be useful to other developers, be sure to send the changes back to PalmSource so that they can roll them into the emulator's code base. Much of the emulator has actually been developed in this way, from contributions by programmers outside PalmSource. This spirit of cooperation, combined with outstanding efforts on the part of PalmSource, has made the emulator an indispensable tool for Palm OS development.

In addition to the wonderful features mentioned previously, POSE is an economical way for you to test software on a variety of different Palm OS systems without having to drop a large amount of cash for several pieces of hardware. The emulator can mimic the hardware side of most Palm OS devices on the market, and Palm provides ROM images for every release of Palm OS since version 1.0.

Even though POSE is able to perform most of the testing required to make a reasonably bug-free Palm OS application, there are subtle differences between the emulator and an actual Palm OS device. As a final step in testing an application, install it on an actual Palm OS handheld to ensure that it works in a real environment, rather than just in the virtual environment provided by the emulator. In particular, the emulator has the following limitations:

❑ Graffiti input is difficult using a mouse, trackball, or touch pad. Although the emulator allows easy text input using the desktop computer's keyboard, if your application needs to deal with Graffiti input at a lower level (such as processing individual stylus strokes), it can be difficult to test such input using the emulator.

❑ The current version of the emulator has no way to simulate an infrared port. You can perform some infrared testing by setting the emulator in infrared loopback mode using the t shortcut, or by switching the emulator into serial IR mode with the s shortcut (see the "Using Developer Graffiti Shortcuts" section later in this chapter for details). However, in the final equation, the only real way to fully test IR beaming is with a pair of suitably equipped Palm OS handhelds.

❑ Execution speed in the emulator is directly affected by the speed of the desktop system, and by whatever other processes you might be running on that system. This means that the emulator may run slower or faster than an actual handheld, thus making code optimization tricky.

*This book describes POSE version 3.5, which is under constant development. The folks at PalmSource release new versions rapidly. Keep an eye on the Palm OS Developer Home site at* **www.palmos.com/ dev** *for information on the latest release of POSE. Better yet, subscribe to the Emulator Forum mailing list for an up-to-the-minute report on POSE development.*

# Controlling POSE

Interacting with applications running in POSE is simple. Just use the mouse as if it were a stylus; the emulator will respond the same way a real Palm OS handheld does. The emulator also recognizes Graffiti characters drawn in its silkscreen Graffiti area. Because it is rather difficult (and time-consuming) to use a mouse for Graffiti input, you also may type on the desktop computer's keyboard to enter text into the emulator.

Clicking the hardware buttons on the emulator display is identical to pressing hardware buttons on a real device. You can even press and hold the buttons to perform actions such as continuous scrolling. Try clicking and holding down the power button for a few seconds to activate the emulator's "backlight." In addition to using the mouse with the onscreen buttons, you can use keyboard shortcuts for these buttons, as outlined in the following table. These keyboard shortcuts produce the same results as clicking the onscreen buttons in the emulator's display.

| Button | Keyboard Shortcut |
|---|---|
| Power | Esc |
| Date Book | F1 |
| Address Book | F2 |
| To Do List | F3 |
| Memo Pad | F4 |
| Scroll Up | Page Up |
| Scroll Down | Page Down |

In addition to these shortcuts, POSE understands a number of Ctrl-key combinations that send special virtual character codes, which the Palm OS interprets to perform special actions, such as displaying a menu bar. The following table describes some of these shortcuts.

| Shortcut | Description |
|---|---|
| Ctrl-A | Sends a `menuChr` character, opening the menu bar on the current form. |
| Ctrl-B | Sends a `lowBatterChr` character, which the system normally sends when battery power is low as a notification to the current application that it should respond accordingly to the low-power condition. |

| Shortcut | Description |
|---|---|
| Ctrl-C | Sends a `commandChr` character, which is the special Graffiti command stroke that allows for rapid activation of menu commands. |
| Ctrl-D | Sends a `confirmChr` character, which activates the default button in an alert. |
| Ctrl-E | Sends a `launchChr` character, which starts the system application launcher program. |
| Ctrl-F | Sends a `keyboardChr` character, which displays the onscreen keyboard. |
| Ctrl-M | Sends a `linefeedChr` character (a simple linefeed). |
| Ctrl-N | Sends a `nextFieldChr` character, which moves entry to the next text field in applications that handle `nextFieldChr`. |
| Ctrl-P | Sends a `prevFieldChr` character, which moves entry to the previous text field in applications that handle `prevFieldChr`. |
| Ctrl-S | Sends an `autoOffChr` character, which the system sends when the auto-off timeout is reached. |
| Ctrl-T | Sends a `hardContrastChr` character, which launches the contrast adjustment screen on the Palm V and other devices that support software contrast adjustment. |
| Ctrl-U | Sends a `backlightChr` character, which toggles the backlight on and off on devices that have a backlight. |

To control emulator-specific functions, POSE has its own menu. The menu is a pop-up, which you can open in Windows and UNIX by right-clicking anywhere in the emulator's display or by pressing Shift-F10. On Mac OS, you can select menu options from the menu bar above the main POSE display, or you can hold down the Ctrl key and click anywhere in the emulator to display the pop-up menu. Figure 5-2 shows the pop-up menu in the Windows version of the emulator.

The emulator also can copy and paste text between Palm OS text fields and the desktop computer's Clipboard. Any application with text fields that is running in the emulator can share text in this way with the host computer. To copy text from the emulator to a desktop application, follow these steps:

1. Use the mouse to highlight the text to copy in the application running in the emulator.

2. Press Ctrl-C and then press C. Ctrl-C activates the Graffiti command shortcut and C is the accelerator key for the Copy command. The text is now on the desktop computer's Clipboard.

3. Switch to the desktop application to which you wish to copy the text.

4. Use the appropriate command to paste the text into the desktop application. For example, in Windows, press Ctrl-V.

To copy text from a desktop application to the emulator, follow these steps:

1. Copy the text from the desktop application to the Clipboard, using whatever command is appropriate for your operating system. For example, in Windows, press Ctrl-C.

2. Switch to the emulator.

3. Open an application that has a text field and then click the field that should receive the Clipboard text.

4. Press Ctrl-C and then press P. Ctrl-C activates the Graffiti command shortcut and P is the accelerator key for the Paste command. The text is now in the text field in the emulator.

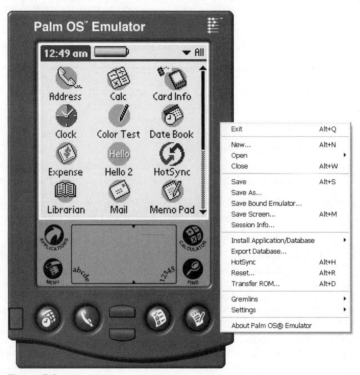

Figure 5-2

## *Running POSE for the First Time*

When you start the emulator for the first time, or if the Caps Lock key is active, the emulator presents you with the dialog box shown in Figure 5-3, but only if you are running POSE in Windows. In Mac OS or UNIX, you see the New Session dialog box instead (see Figure 5-4 for the Windows version of the New Session dialog box, which is very similar to the Mac OS and UNIX versions).

Figure 5-3

The New button fires up the New Session dialog box (Figure 5-4), which prompts you for all the parameters required to start a brand new POSE session. The next section, "Installing a ROM Image," explains more about the New Session dialog box. The Open button opens a File dialog box, which prompts you to select a saved emulator session to load; see the "Saving and Restoring Configurations" section later in this chapter for more details. Clicking the Download button begins the process of downloading a ROM image from a handheld connected to the desktop machine by the cradle; see the "Loading a ROM Image" section for more details. If you click Exit, the emulator quits.

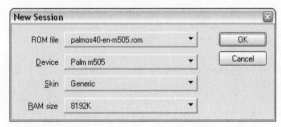

Figure 5-4

## Installing a ROM Image

POSE emulates only the hardware of a Palm OS handheld. In order for the emulator to be truly useful, it needs a ROM image containing the Palm OS system software. Palm has ROM images for all major releases of Palm OS available for download from its Web site. ROM image files have a .rom extension.

For most versions of Palm OS, Palm provides both release and debug versions of each ROM image. Release ROM images are usually identical to the ROM contents of an actual Palm OS handheld, although some release images (labeled "full") contain combinations of features that have never appeared on a real device. Debug ROM images contain extra debugging code to help you track down hard-to-find errors in your code, such as illegal attempts to access protected memory areas.

> Be sure to test your application on debug ROM images if they are available for the platforms you intend to support. The release images do run a bit faster on the emulator (particularly for Palm OS 3.5 and later) but release code is designed to fail gracefully and quietly if anything goes wrong, which prevents you from seeing some kinds of errors, particularly memory leaks. It is well worth the effort to test an application on the debug ROM images because they produce very useful debugging information.

> In particular, if your application runs without difficulty on a Palm OS 4.0 or later debug ROM image, chances are very good that your application will also run well in Palm OS 5. Debug ROM images report many errors that can help prevent serious problems when an application is running under PACE in Palm OS 5, such as direct access to structures or reserved memory locations.

If you click the New button in the emulator's startup dialog box, or if you choose the New item from the Emulator menu, the New Session dialog box appears (see Figure 5-4).

From this dialog box, you can choose a ROM image file, type of hardware you wish to emulate, appearance of the emulator on the desktop, and how much memory the emulated handheld has available.

Click the button next to ROM File to display a pop-up menu of recently used ROM files; this menu is empty the first time you run the emulator. Select Other from the menu to open a file dialog box and browse for an appropriate .rom file to install.

*You also can install a ROM image by dragging the .rom file onto POSE with the mouse. Doing so opens the New Session dialog box (see Figure 5-4) with the appropriate ROM image preselected.*

Clicking the Device button presents a pop-up menu, from which you should select the hardware device you want to emulate. Your choices in this menu are limited by your selection of ROM image; the emulator presents only those devices that actually run the version of Palm OS in the selected ROM image.

The Skin button allows you to customize the appearance of Palm OS Emulator by applying a *skin*, or bitmap image, to the emulator. Skins serve no technical function, but they are a good visual reminder of what device you are currently emulating and they can make for compelling marketing demonstrations of an application during development.

Depending on what hardware you select, different skins are available. The "Default" skin is always an option and results in a generic PalmPilot-shaped case graphic with "Palm OS Emulator" written across it (shown previously in Figure 5-1). The "Standard-English" skin gives you a graphic that looks exactly like the type of hardware you have selected, and the "Standard-Japanese" skin draws the emulator as an equivalent handheld with the Japanese language silkscreen area.

Set the size of the memory available to the emulator with the RAM Size button's menu. You can set the size at various values between 128K and 16 MB. By setting the memory size, you can duplicate the memory available on actual Palm OS handhelds or see what happens when your application is running on a device with very little memory to spare.

## Installing Applications

Because performing an actual HotSync operation to install files to the emulator would be an inefficient use of your time, Palm OS Emulator allows you to install Palm OS applications and databases in a much more direct fashion. Select the Install Application/Database menu item. The emulator presents you with a standard file dialog box, from which you may select any .prc or .pdb files that you want to install.

The emulator cannot install a new copy of a database that already exists in the emulator if the old database is in use. If you are running an application in the emulator and you want to overwrite it (or its database) with a new version, switch to another application in the emulator before installing. The Calculator or the other four built-in applications are good choices because you need to click only once to launch them.

Once you install the applications you want to test, open them just as you would on a real handheld by clicking the application launcher button and then selecting the appropriate icon.

The system application launcher does not update its icons in response to the installation of a new application in the emulator, so a new application's icon will not immediately appear if the launcher is open when you install the new application. Switch to another application and then reopen the launcher; the new icon will appear.

*You also can install applications and databases using the drag-and-drop method (drag them onto the POSE window). To save even more time, select as many files as you want and drag all of them at once for a single, mass installation.*

Palm OS Emulator supports automatic loading of program and data files. Create a folder called `Autoload` in the same folder as `Emulator.exe`, the emulator's executable file. Any time you create a new session or load an old session, POSE automatically installs all the `.prc` and `.pdb` files in the `Autoload` folder. This can be a great timesaver if the application you are debugging is dependent on a number of other applications, databases, or shared libraries.

In addition to automatic loading, POSE can automatically load and run an application. If a folder called `Autorun` exists, the emulator installs all Palm OS files in it and then launches the last `.prc` file in the folder.

POSE can run an application automatically and quit once the application exits, which can be useful for automated testing a script or outside program. To use this feature of the emulator, place all the files that should be loaded in a folder called `AutorunAndQuit`. The emulator executes the last `.prc` file in this folder and then, once that application exits, quits.

## Saving and Restoring Configurations

If you have POSE set up just the way you want it, you can take a snapshot of its current state and save it for later retrieval. Saving an emulator session keeps track of all aspects of the emulator, including the selected hardware type and skin, all the currently installed applications and databases, and even the exact state of the emulated RAM.

To save a session, select the Save or Save As menu options from the pop-up menu. If the current session is loaded from a saved position, the Save command overwrites the currently open session file. Otherwise, Save does the same thing as Save As, which is to present you with a standard file dialog box to prompt you for a filename and location to use for saving the current session. Palm OS Emulator saves session files with the extension `.psf`.

To open a saved session, select Open from the pop-up menu. The emulator presents you with a file dialog box, from which you can select the `.psf` file that contains the configuration of the desired emulator session.

> To save time when testing an application on multiple platforms, create a "clean" session for each ROM image you want to test. Right after creating a new configuration in the New Session dialog box (as shown in Figure 5-4) and before installing any applications or data, save the session with a descriptive name, such as "Palm IIIx 3.5 debug.psf." Then you can quickly retrieve saved sessions by using the Open menu command. You also can drag a .psf file onto the emulator to open a particular saved session.

## Adjusting Emulator Settings

The Palm OS Emulator is incredibly configurable. Most of the configuration options for POSE are located under the Settings option in the pop-up menu. Among other options, you can change the way the emulator looks, how it communicates with the desktop, and how strictly it monitors different kinds of memory access.

### Setting Properties

The Settings ⇨ Properties menu command opens the Properties dialog box (see Figure 5-5).

**Figure 5-5**

From the Properties dialog box, you can control several different kinds of emulator behavior:

❑ **Serial Port.** Use this pop-up list to select a serial port on the desktop computer. POSE redirects serial port calls from applications on the emulator through the selected serial port on the desktop machine. This allows you to test serial communications by connecting a serial cable between the appropriate port and whatever device the emulator should talk to, such as a GPS receiver. You can even connect a pair of serial ports on the desktop machine with a null modem cable to allow the emulator to communicate with a terminal program on the same computer.

❑ **IR Port.** In POSE version 3.3, Palm attempted to add the ability to debug infrared communication by simulating a connection over serial or TCP. Unfortunately, it worked only intermittently so Palm disabled it. The button next to the IR port option is grayed out. With any luck, Palm will get it working again in a future version of the emulator.

❑ **Redirect NetLib Calls to Host TCP/IP.** When checked, this option redirects network library calls in the emulator to the TCP/IP stack on the host computer. This option is a fantastic way to test Internet-enabled Palm OS applications without having to wait for a connection through a handheld modem.

❑ **Enable Sounds.** If this is checked, the emulator attempts to provide audio feedback from Palm OS through the desktop computer. This sound reproduction is not exactly the same as what you would hear on an actual Palm OS handheld; in fact, depending on your desktop system, the emulator might be capable of only primitive beeps and clicks through the system's speaker. For applications where sound is integral to the program, such as music or game programs, test the sound on a real handheld device.

❑ **Closing/Quitting.** The radio buttons in this section of the dialog box control how the emulator saves the current session when it closes. If Always Save Session is selected, the emulator automatically overwrites the current session file with the emulator's current state when the emulator exits. If Ask to Save Session is selected, the emulator prompts you to save the session. If Never Save Session is selected, it simply exits without saving.

❏ **HotSync User Name.** This text box gives you a place to specify the HotSync name to use when emulating a HotSync operation in the emulator. Normally, every Palm OS handheld has a name saved in it to identify its user, which comes in handy when multiple organizers are synchronized with the same desktop machine. See the "Emulating a HotSync Operation" section later in this chapter for more details.

## Setting Debug Options

Selecting Settings ➪ Debugging presents you with the Debug Options dialog box (see Figure 5-6).

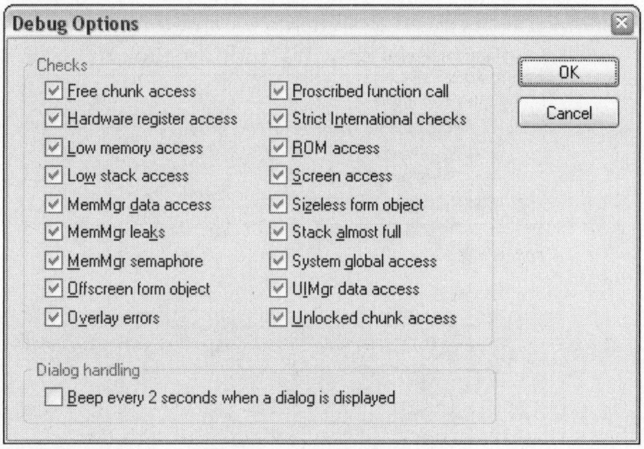

**Debug Options**

Checks

☑ Free chunk access    ☑ Proscribed function call
☑ Hardware register access    ☑ Strict International checks
☑ Low memory access    ☑ ROM access
☑ Low stack access    ☑ Screen access
☑ MemMgr data access    ☑ Sizeless form object
☑ MemMgr leaks    ☑ Stack almost full
☑ MemMgr semaphore    ☑ System global access
☑ Offscreen form object    ☑ UIMgr data access
☑ Overlay errors    ☑ Unlocked chunk access

Dialog handling
☐ Beep every 2 seconds when a dialog is displayed

OK    Cancel

Figure 5-6

In this dialog box, you can set how sensitive the emulator is to certain actions that a program might perform that are either illegal or run counter to recommended Palm OS programming practice. By default, the emulator leaves all these options enabled, and so should you for most applications. If you happen to be writing an application that cannot strictly conform to Palm programming guidelines, such as low-level system hacks that are intended to run only on a single, very specific hardware model, you can disable warnings that you do not want to see.

*The emulator is most useful with all of the debug options enabled. If you leave the Debug Options dialog box alone, POSE can help you ensure that your application runs properly not only on current Palm OS handheld devices but also on future devices by following Palm's recommendations.*

## Changing the Emulator's Appearance

The Settings ➪ Skins menu command opens the Skins dialog box (see Figure 5-7).

From the Skins dialog box, you can set the skin that the emulator uses to display the emulated handheld. Other appearance-related options appear at the bottom of the dialog box as follows:

❏ **Double Scale.** This option doubles the size of Palm OS Emulator on the desktop screen. The double-scale mode is particularly useful for making fine adjustments to screen layout during the design stages of an application because you can count individual pixels without having to squint at an emulator window the size of a real handheld. If you run your desktop machine at 1600 × 1200 pixels or greater resolution, double scale might simply be a necessity if you want the emulator display to be legible at all.

❑ **White Background.** This option replaces the usual LCD green display background with basic white. This option makes for much cleaner screen shots, and you might simply prefer it over the green background because it improves contrast significantly.

❑ **Dim Skin When Inactive.** The emulator dims its skin when it is not the active application. This option is particularly useful when combined with the following Stay on Top option because you can then tell at a glance whether what you type is going to be received by the emulator or by a different application.

❑ **Stay on Top.** This option causes POSE to remain the topmost window, regardless of whether or not it is the active application. This option is useful when running a debugger in another application because it obviates the need to switch back and forth between the debugger and the emulator. The Stay on Top option works only in Windows, though.

Figure 5-7

# Handling Gremlins

Structured functional testing is a good way to make sure that all the parts of an application are working the way they are supposed to be working. However, sometimes the best way to find obscure bugs in an application is by randomly banging on it until something breaks. Gremlins are a testing feature built into Palm OS Emulator that allows you to perform random tests on your application to shake out those bugs that functional testing might not find. More important, each Gremlin test is completely reproducible so you can run the same Gremlin again and get the same error, making it much easier to see what went wrong.

Gremlins use several techniques to torture-test an application. While they are running, Gremlins simulate taps on random areas of the screen, but areas that contain actual user interface elements, such as buttons and pop-up triggers, particularly attract them. Gremlins also enter Graffiti text, such as random strings of garbage and occasional quotes from Shakespeare, into the application.

An individual Gremlin has a seed value from 0 to 999, and each produces its own unique series of random stylus and key input events. You can restrict a Gremlin to stay within a particular application or group of applications. This is particularly useful when you want to concentrate on hammering your own code without wasting time in other programs.

Gremlins also may be run in *Gremlin hordes*. A Gremlin horde runs multiple Gremlins, giving your application a real workout. Setting up a Gremlin horde to run overnight is a good way to ensure that a program has been thoroughly tested.

## Running a Gremlin Horde

To set up Gremlins, select Gremlins ➪ New. The emulator displays the New Gremlin Horde dialog box (see Figure 5-8).

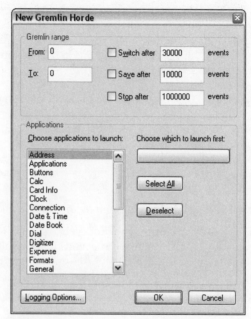

Figure 5-8

The parts of the New Gremlin Horde dialog box are described as follows:

❑ **Gremlin Range.** Set the Gremlins that make up the beginning and end of a Gremlin horde in the From and To text boxes. Enter a number from 0 to 999 in each box to make the emulator run each Gremlin in this range. To run just a single Gremlin, enter the same value in both boxes.

❑ **Switch After.** The emulator will switch to a new Gremlin in the horde when the currently running Gremlin generates the specified number of events; this number of events is called the *switching depth*. If this box is not checked, the emulator will not switch to a new Gremlin in the horde until each Gremlin hits the number of events specified in the Stop After text box. Because a particular Gremlin always repeats the same series of events each time it runs, making Gremlins take turns at attacking your application can add a random element to your testing.

❑ **Save After.** The emulator saves a snapshot of the emulator as a .psf file after the specified number of events. You can open this file in the emulator later to examine the state at that particular moment in time or to begin debugging again from a specific point. Ensure that you have sufficient disk space if you set Save After to a low value because this option can fill your hard drive very quickly with .psf files.

❑ **Stop After.** The emulator stops each Gremlin when it generates the specified number of events. Without this box checked, a Gremlin will run indefinitely, or until it encounters an error.

❑ **Choose Applications to Launch.** Select an application or group of applications to restrict the Gremlin horde while it is running. You can select multiple applications by holding down the Ctrl key (Control on a Mac) while clicking items in the list.

❑ **Choose Which to Launch First.** Select which application should be the first application attacked by the Gremlins session.

❑ **Logging Options.** Click this button to change exactly what events, actions, and errors Gremlins will write to a log file. The default options are sufficient for most debugging purposes, but you also may wish to check other options if your application performs special actions. For example, enabling the Serial Activity and Serial Data options may help you discover the cause of bugs in an application that uses the serial port.

When running a Gremlin horde, POSE steps through the following sequence of events:

1. POSE saves the current state of the emulator to a file called `Gremlin_Root_State.psf`, which is located in a subfolder of the folder containing `Emulator.exe`. The folder is named in the form *Gremlins.date.time*, where `date` and `time` correspond to when the Gremlin horde was started. The emulator stores other information related to the Gremlin horde in the same folder, such as log files and event files.

2. The emulator starts the first Gremlin, indicated by the value of the From text box.

3. The first Gremlin runs until it posts a number of events equal to the Switch After value, at which point the emulator saves its state and suspends that Gremlin. If the Gremlin encounters an error before it hits the switching depth value, the emulator terminates the current Gremlin instead of suspending it.

4. The emulator loads the original saved state.

5. The second Gremlin begins execution and runs until it hits the switching depth or encounters an error.

6. The emulator runs each Gremlin in the horde until each one has been suspended or terminated.

7. The emulator returns to the first suspended Gremlin in the horde and reloads its saved emulator state. The Gremlin then runs from where it left off the last time. The emulator skips over Gremlins that have been terminated because of errors, restarting only those that were suspended after reaching the switching depth.

8. The entire process repeats itself, with the emulator suspending Gremlins as they reach the switching depth again or terminating those that produce errors. Each Gremlin runs until it has finished. A Gremlin is finished when POSE has terminated it because of an error, or when the Gremlin reaches a total number of events equal to the Stop After value specified in the New Gremlin Horde dialog box.

While the emulator is running Gremlins, the Gremlin Control dialog box appears (see Figure 5-9). The Gremlin Control dialog box allows you to control the execution of Gremlins more directly. It displays the current event that is executing, the number of the current Gremlin, and the total elapsed time that the Gremlin horde has been running. Clicking the Stop button pauses execution of the Gremlin horde; clicking Resume continues the horde where it left off. When a horde is stopped, you also can click the Step button to step through a few Gremlins at a time.

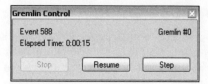

Figure 5-9

*Try running Gremlins when you have a source-level debugger hooked up to POSE. If your application generates an error while a Gremlin is playing with it, the debugger will drop straight to the line of code that triggered the error.*

## Replaying and Minimizing Gremlins

When a Gremlin runs, the emulator saves all events generated by that Gremlin in a Palm event file, which has an extension of .pev. Each Gremlin in a particular horde gets its own event file, in the form *Gremlin_nnn_Events.pev*, where nnn is the seed number for that particular Gremlin. You can later replay the event file by choosing Gremlins ➪ Replay from the pop-up menu. POSE displays a standard file dialog box, from which you can select a .pev file to run.

An application may crash only after a very long series of Gremlins have been run, which makes reproducing the problem tedious if you need to wait for a long replay. Palm OS Emulator can alleviate this problem by *minimizing* the Gremlin events required to cause a crash. To minimize an event file, select Gremlins ➪ Minimize from the pop-up menu and choose a .pev file in the standard file dialog box that appears.

Gremlin minimization is an iterative process, where POSE replays the events in a .pev file, removing ranges of events to see if a crash still occurs. If a crash still occurs after the removal of a range of events, those events are discarded as being unnecessary to the investigation of the crash. If a crash does not occur, POSE puts that range of events back into the events it is replaying and picks a new range to remove.

*Because Gremlin minimization is an iterative process, and because no two applications (or Gremlins) are exactly alike, the amount of time it takes for minimization to run can vary widely. In general, though, the more events contained in a .pev file, the longer that minimization takes. If you have thousands of events to minimize, expect the emulator to run for a few hours.*

After a number of iterations through this process, the emulator produces a minimal set of events required to cause a crash and saves it to a new event file, in the form *Gremlin_nnn_Events_Min.pev*, where nnn is the seed number of the Gremlin that produced the crash in the first place. POSE also creates a text file, named *Gremlin_nnn_Events_Min.txt*, which provides English instructions on how to reproduce the crash. These instructions allow you to reproduce the crash manually without assistance from the Gremlins facility. It is sometimes very useful to be able to walk manually through the steps required to produce a crash when you are trying to determine why it is occurring.

*Gremlin minimization may not produce the same crash that was caused by the events in the original .pev file. Because of the way the minimization process works, the minimized events produced could cause a totally different error. This is still useful information, however, because the new crash probably results from a legitimate bug that should be fixed. Once you have repaired the bug caused by the minimized set of events, you can rerun the full set. If the original error still occurs, you can reminimize the events in another attempt to track down the original error.*

# Emulating a HotSync Operation

Any application that has a close relation with desktop data eventually needs to be tested to see how it behaves during a HotSync operation. Setting up Palm OS Emulator to communicate properly with the desktop during a HotSync operation is somewhat tricky but it can be done. There are two ways to set up the emulator for a HotSync operation:

❑   **Set the emulator to use one of the desktop system's serial ports and the HotSync Manager to use a different serial port. Then connect the two ports with a null modem cable.** This setup is cumbersome and requires a machine with two free serial ports, which can be a problem if, as is common on many PCs, one of the serial ports is in use by a mouse or other peripheral.

❑   **Set up the emulator and HotSync Manager for a Network HotSync operation.** This is a much simpler way to test HotSync connections because it does not require an extra cable connection at the back of the computer. However, it works only with the Windows version of the HotSync Manager.

To set up POSE to use the serial port for HotSync operations, follow these steps:

1.   In the emulator, open the Properties dialog box (shown previously in Figure 5-5). Set the emulator to use one of the host machine's serial ports.

2.   Make sure the HotSync Manager running on the desktop is set to use a different serial port from the one set up in the emulator.

3.   Connect the two serial ports with a null modem cable.

To set up the emulator to use the Network HotSync configuration, follow these steps:

1.   Click the HotSync icon in the system tray and select Network from the pop-up menu that appears if Network does not already have a check mark next to it.

2.   Open the Properties dialog box in the emulator by selecting the Settings ⇨ Properties menu command from the pop-up menu. Check the Redirect NetLib Calls to Host TCP/IP check box and click OK.

3.   Open the HotSync application in the emulator.

4.   Select Options ⇨ Modem Sync Prefs. In the Modem Sync Preferences dialog box that appears (see Figure 5-10), select the Network button. Tap OK.

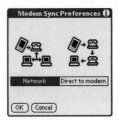

**Figure 5-10**

**5.** Select Options ➪ LANSync Prefs. In the LANSync Preferences dialog box (as shown in Figure 5-11), select the LANSync button. Tap OK.

**Figure 5-11**

**6.** Select Options ➪ Primary PC Setup. In the Primary PC Setup dialog box (see Figure 5-12), enter the network address 127.0.0.1 into the Primary PC Address text field. Tap OK.

**Figure 5-12**

**7.** Depending on which version of Palm OS is running in the emulator, you will need to do one of the following:

❑ On Palm OS 3.1, tap the Select Service selector trigger under the Modem Sync icon to open the Preferences dialog box. Tap the Phone selector trigger, enter two zeroes (00) into the Phone # field, and then tap the OK button. Tap the Done button when you're done.

❑ On Palm OS 3.3 and later, tap the Modem push button and then tap the Select Service selector trigger under the HotSync icon to open the Preferences dialog box. Tap Done when done.

Note that you do not actually have to set up any information for a service profile in Step 7; you need only to select a service. The emulator should now be ready for a Network HotSync operation.

Telling the emulator to start a HotSync operation is easy. Either select the HotSync menu command or open the HotSync application in the emulator and tap the HotSync button in the center of the screen (or the Modem HotSync button, if you are using a Network HotSync setup in Windows).

*The HotSync Manager is processor-intensive, which can cause very slow HotSync operations when both the HotSync Manager and the emulator are fighting for resources on the same machine. To speed up HotSync operations in the emulator, click the emulator window to bring it to the foreground after starting a HotSync operation.*

The emulator uses the value you set for HotSync User Name in the Properties or Preferences dialog box (shown earlier in Figure 5-5) as the user name to identify the emulated handheld. When you first synchronize the emulator with the desktop, the HotSync Manager prompts you for a user profile with which to synchronize.

*Synchronizing the emulator with your own personal data is a sure way to cause all sorts of trouble, including lost data or duplicate records. Your best bet is to create a brand new user profile on the desktop, exclusively for use with the emulator.*

## Emulating Expansion Cards

Palm OS Emulator can emulate expansion card storage, allowing you to test applications that use the Virtual File System (VFS) to access data in secondary storage. However, it does not have a file system built in; for that you must install HostFS, which allows the emulator to treat a folder on the desktop machine as if it were a mounted expansion volume.

*HostFS requires that the emulator be running a ROM image containing Palm OS 4.0 or later with the expansion manager.*

HostFS is available as a separate download, from the same Web site where the emulator is available. The HostFS utility takes the form of a `.prc` file called `HostFS.prc`. To install HostFS and configure the emulator to use it, follow these steps:

**1.** Start a new session in the emulator with an appropriate ROM image.

**2.** Install the `HostFS.prc` file in the emulator.

**3.** Soft reset the emulator by selecting Reset from the pop-up menu, selecting Soft reset, and clicking the Reset button. This step is vital to the proper functioning of HostFS; if you don't reset the emulator, HostFS won't work.

**4.** Create on the desktop computer a folder that you would like to mount as a secondary storage volume. All the files on the emulated expansion card will be stored in this folder.

**5.** Select Settings ⇨ HostFS from the pop-up menu. The HostFS Options dialog box appears (see Figure 5-13).

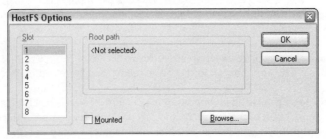

**Figure 5-13**

**6.** Choose a slot from the list. The emulator supports up to eight different expansion slots.

**7.** Click Browse. A standard file dialog box appears. Navigate to the folder you created in Step 4, select the folder, and click OK.

**8.** Click OK to exit the HostFS Options dialog box and save the HostFS settings.

You now have an emulated expansion card mounted in POSE, which applications can access using the expansion manager and VFS functions. To simulate removal of a card, open the HostFS Options dialog box again, deselect the Mounted check box, and click OK. The emulator sends all the proper notifications you would expect upon removal of a real expansion card. To remount the emulated card, select the Mounted check box again. For complete details about expansion cards and VFS, see Chapter 17, "Using Secondary Storage."

## Capturing Screenshots

Capturing screenshots of Palm OS applications in the emulator is simplicity itself. Once you have the screen visible in the emulator's window, select the Save Screen menu option. The emulator presents you with a file dialog box where you can specify the filename and location to save the image file. The emulator saves screenshots as .bmp files in Windows, or as SimpleText images in Mac OS.

*To make screenshots more legible, open the Skins dialog box (shown previously in Figure 5-7) and check the White Background option before capturing the screen.*

## Handling Errors in the Emulator

When the emulator encounters an error during execution of an application, it displays an error dialog box. The text of the error message depends on what the actual error is.

Depending upon the type of error it encounters, the Continue or Debug buttons may be grayed out. These buttons have the following effects when clicked:

❑ **Continue.** The emulator tries to continue executing application code if possible.

❑ **Debug.** The emulator hands over execution to an external debugger if one is running.

❑ **Reset.** The emulator performs a soft reset of the emulated device, which may allow you to continue running the emulator without having to start an entirely new session. You can force a soft reset, or even a hard reset, at other times by selecting the Reset menu command. Forcing a reset can be useful in testing an application that is designed to react to a soft reset through the sysAppLaunchCmdSystemReset launch code. Forcing a hard reset gives you a "clean" emulated handheld, erasing all the applications and data from the emulated handheld's storage memory.

The emulator distinguishes between an *error* and a *warning*:

❑ An error is usually fatal, requiring that the emulator be reset. The Continue button is disabled in the event of an error. Errors include things like address errors and division by zero.

❑ A warning is not fatal; the Continue button is still available if you wish to ignore the warning and continue execution. With a warning, POSE is usually just informing you of a condition that it objects to, such as directly reading from or writing to reserved memory areas like screen memory, procedures that might not work properly on future versions of Palm OS.

The difference between errors and warnings would be mostly academic, were it not for the fact that you can change the behavior of the emulator in response to both. Select Settings ➪ Error Handling to display the Error Handling dialog box (see Figure 5-14).

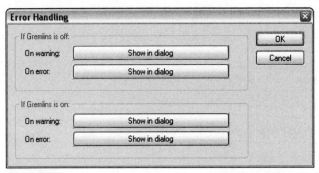

**Figure 5-14**

In the Error Handling dialog box, you can tell the emulator to continue on warnings automatically, and to terminate the emulator automatically in the event of an error. In addition, if Gremlins are running, you have the additional option of telling the emulator to switch to the next Gremlin in its current horde on either an error or warning. These automatic settings are useful if you want to leave the emulator running to perform testing, particularly if you invoke the emulator from a script in an unattended test environment, because they allow it to recover from warnings without any user intervention.

# Using Palm OS Simulator

Palm OS Simulator is essentially Palm OS 5 recompiled to run on a Windows desktop computer. Palm OS 5 is designed with a Device Abstraction Layer (DAL), which isolates the operating system code from the actual hardware. The DAL can be changed to allow Palm OS to run on different types of hardware. By providing a DAL that operates on a Windows computer, Palm OS Simulator can perfectly mimic Palm OS 5 while running on a desktop machine.

The simulator also contains the Palm Application Compatibility Environment (PACE), which is what Palm OS 5 uses to emulate the Motorola 68K environment expected by Palm OS applications that were written for earlier versions of Palm OS. You can use Palm OS Simulator to test whether your existing Palm OS 68K applications work properly on a Palm OS 5 handheld.

You can perform most of the same debugging functions of POSE in Palm OS Simulator, including using Gremlins for automated random torture-testing. In addition, the simulator provides functions unavailable in POSE, including the ability to browse the contents of databases and memory heaps in a simulator session. You can even view events queued by Palm OS in real time as you interact with the simulator.

## Starting the Simulator

When you start Palm OS Simulator for the first time, it prompts you for the location of a ROM image file, which like ROM images for POSE, has a `.rom` extension. For example, the English release ROM image is named NTFull_enUS.rom and the English debug ROM image is named NTFullDbg_enUS.rom. Select an appropriate ROM image and click Open.

*Despite the similarity in file extensions, Palm OS Simulator does not use the same ROM image files as POSE. The simulator cannot open a POSE ROM file and POSE cannot open a Palm OS Simulator ROM file.*

Once you have successfully started Palm OS Simulator, it assumes that you will want to use the same ROM image the next time you run it. The next time you launch the simulator, it will automatically start up the ROM image that you selected when you first ran it. You may also load a different ROM image by holding down the Shift key when you start the simulator. See "Loading a ROM Image" next for more details about loading a different ROM image.

Whenever Palm OS Simulator starts, it displays the digitizer calibration screen, just as if you were configuring a new or hard-reset Palm Powered handheld.

*Clicking through the digitizer screen each time the simulator starts becomes tiresome fairly quickly. Fortunately, there is a faster way to do it. The first two clicks don't actually have to land on the targets displayed in simulator's screen; only the third click, on the target in the center of the screen, needs to be on target. Therefore to start using the simulator quickly, just click twice anywhere on its screen and then click the final target. Now you're off and running.*

## Loading a ROM Image

If you want to choose a different ROM image for Palm OS Simulator to run, you have a number of options:

❏ Palm OS Simulator saves its configuration information in a text file called palmsim.ini, which is located in the same folder as the executable, PalmSim.exe. Open this file in a text editor and change the ROM= line to point to a different ROM image. For example, the following line tells the simulator to load the debug English ROM image located in the C:\palmsim\Debug\enUS folder:

ROM=C:\palmsim\Debug\enUS\NTFullDbg_enUS.rom

❏ If you start Palm OS Simulator from a command line, you can specify a ROM image to load with the -rom option. For example, the following command line launches Palm OS Simulator with the same ROM image specified in the previous example:

palmsim.exe -rom C:\palmsim\Debug\enUS\NTFullDbg_enUS.rom

❏ Hold down the Shift key when you start Palm OS Simulator. It will prompt you for a ROM image file exactly as if this were the first time you ran it.

❏ Drag and drop a ROM image file onto the PalmSim.exe icon in Windows Explorer. You may also drag a ROM image onto a shortcut that points to PalmSim.exe, or you can create a shortcut to PalmSim.exe in the Windows SendTo folder, and then right-click a ROM image file and select the Simulator shortcut from the pop-up Send To menu.

Chapter 5

# Installing Applications and Data

The procedure for installing applications and databases in Palm OS Simulator is almost identical to the installation procedure in POSE. The simulator has a pop-up menu, which appears when you right-click anywhere in the simulator's window. Select Install ⇨ Database from the pop-up menu and choose a .prc, .pdb, or .pqa file to install. Alternatively, you can drag one or more of these files onto Palm OS Simulator to install them.

# Running Gremlins

You can run Gremlins in Palm OS Simulator just as you do in POSE. Select the Gremlins option from the pop-up menu. The Gremlins dialog box appears (see Figure 5-15).

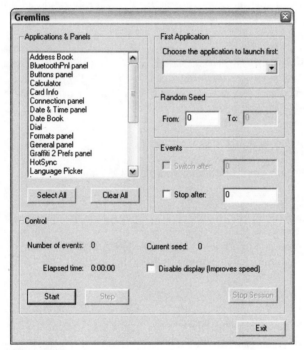

Figure 5-15

Most of the options in the Gremlins dialog box should look familiar from the description of Gremlins in POSE. As of this writing, some features, such as defining a Gremlins horde, are not yet implemented. Instead of displaying a separate Gremlin Control dialog box, you can control a running Gremlin by using the Control section of the Gremlins dialog box. The Control section offers the following options:

❑   **Start.** Click this button to start the Gremlin indicated in the Random Seed section of the dialog box. While a Gremlin is running, the Start button's caption changes to Stop; clicking the Stop button pauses the Gremlin execution and enables the Step button. Click Resume to continue execution of Gremlin events.

❑ **Step.** Initially grayed out, the Step button becomes active as soon as you have paused a running Gremlin. Click Step to walk through the Gremlin's events a handful at a time.

❑ **Stop Session.** Click this button to stop the Gremlin session entirely.

❑ **Disable Display.** Selecting this check box makes Gremlins execute without updating the Palm OS Simulator display; the actions taken by Gremlins do not appear on the screen, allowing Gremlins to run much faster. This option is great for running lengthy Gremlin sessions in a short period of time. Deselect the check box to make Gremlins update the display again.

## Viewing Databases, Memory, and Events

Palm OS Simulator gives you a window into the databases and memory contents contained in the current simulator session, as well as a peek at the events generated by the system and by user interaction with the simulator.

To view a snapshot of the databases stored in the current simulator session, select View ➪ Databases from the pop-up menu. The Databases window appears (see Figure 5-16).

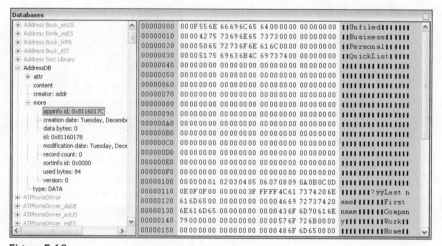

**Figure 5-16**

The Databases window contains a tree view in its left pane, showing all the databases installed in the simulator session. Read-only databases that are contained in simulated ROM are displayed in gray text, and databases in simulated storage RAM are displayed in black text.

Click the plus (+) icons to expand a database node and view the properties and contents of a database. If you click a node that contains actual content, such as a database record, the right pane shows a hex dump of the content.

*The Databases window cannot view the contents of a database that is currently in use by the simulator. For example, if you are currently running the To Do application in the simulator, its database (ToDoDB) cannot be viewed. Exit the application that has a database open before attempting to view that database in the Databases window.*

You also can look at a snapshot of the simulator's memory heaps. Select View ⇨ Heaps to display the Heaps window (see Figure 5-17).

| Heaps | | | | | | | | | | | | |
|---|---|---|---|---|---|---|---|---|

| Heap # | Type | Size | Handles | Free chunks | Movable chunks | Locked chunks | Largest free chunk |
|---|---|---|---|---|---|---|---|
| 0 | RAM (v5) | 512 KB | 200 | 7 chunks (481480 bytes) | 8 chunks (7744 bytes) | 139 chunks (34232 bytes) | 475664 bytes |
| 1 | RAM (v5) | 3583 KB | 200 | 4 chunks (3553904 bytes) | 171 chunks (105688 bytes) | 6 chunks (9320 bytes) | 3553528 bytes |
| 2 | ROM (v4) | 4351 KB | 0 | 1 chunks (25024 bytes) | 0 chunks (0 bytes) | 6499 chunks (4430868 by... | 25016 bytes |

| Chunk # | Ptr | MemHandle | Lock count | Size | Data Size | Owner |
|---|---|---|---|---|---|---|
| 1 | 0x00f00338 | 0x00f00018 | 1 | 32 | 20 | 0 |
| 2 | 0x00f00358 | 0x00f0001c | 1 | 40 | 32 | 0 |
| 3 | 0x00f00380 | 0x00f00020 | 1 | 560 | 552 | 0 |
| 4 | 0x00f005b0 | 0x00f00024 | 1 | 32 | 20 | 0 |
| 5 | 0x00f005d0 | 0x00f00028 | 1 | 40 | 32 | 0 |
| 6 | 0x00f005f8 | 0x00f0002c | 1 | 744 | 732 | 0 |
| 7 | 0x00f008e0 | 0x00f00030 | 1 | 32 | 20 | 0 |
| 8 | 0x00f00900 | 0x00f00034 | 1 | 40 | 32 | 0 |
| 9 | 0x00f00928 | 0x00f00038 | 1 | 64 | 52 | 0 |
| 10 | 0x00f00968 | 0x00f0003c | 1 | 32 | 20 | 0 |
| 11 | 0x00f00988 | 0x00f00040 | 1 | 40 | 32 | 0 |
| 12 | 0x00f009b0 | 0x00f00044 | 1 | 184 | 176 | 0 |
| 13 | 0x00f00a68 | 0x00f00048 | Moveable (0) | 56 | 44 | 0 |
| 14 | 0x00f00aa0 | 0x00f0004c | 1 | 32 | 20 | 0 |
| 15 | 0x00f00ac0 | 0x00f0005c | 1 | 40 | 32 | 0 |
| 16 | 0x00f00ae8 | 0x00f00060 | 1 | 128 | 120 | 0 |
| 17 | 0x00f00b68 | 0x00f00058 | 1 | 32 | 20 | 0 |
| 18 | 0x00f00b88 | 0x00f00068 | 1 | 40 | 32 | 0 |
| 19 | 0x00f00bb0 | 0x00f0006c | 1 | 32 | 20 | 0 |
| 20 | 0x00f00bd0 | 0x00f00050 | Moveable (0) | 56 | 44 | 0 |
| 21 | 0x00f00c08 | 0x00f00078 | Moveable (0) | 16 | 6 | 0 |
| 22 | 0x00f00c18 | 0x00f00064 | Moveable (0) | 24 | 16 | 0 |
| 23 | 0x00f00c30 | 0x00f00054 | Moveable (0) | 6488 | 6480 | 0 |
| 24 | 0x00f02588 | 0x00f00088 | 1 | 32 | 20 | 0 |
| 25 | 0x00f025a8 | 0x00f00084 | 1 | 40 | 32 | 0 |
| 26 | 0x00f025d0 | 0x00f0009c | 1 | 32 | 20 | 0 |
| 27 | 0x00f025f0 | 0x00f00090 | 1 | 40 | 32 | 0 |

**Figure 5-17**

The upper pane of the Heaps window displays general information about the available memory heaps. Click a heap in this section to display the memory chunks contained in that heap in the middle pane of the Heaps window. Select a memory chunk in the middle pane to display its contents, as both hexadecimal and ASCII characters, in the lower pane of the Heaps window.

The Heaps window has its own View menu, which provides the following options:

❑ **Refresh.** This option refreshes the display in the Heaps window.

❑ **Lock.** Selecting this option locks the display, preventing the simulator from updating the heap display. You must select this option if you want to view the contents of a particular memory chunk.

❑ **Unlock.** Selecting this option allows the Heaps window to be updated again.

If you lock the display by selecting View ⇨ Lock, you can view the contents of individual memory chunks. Select the chunk you are interested in; its contents will appear in the bottom pane of the Heaps window.

You also can view events in real time as the simulator queues them. Select View ⇨ Events from the simulator's pop-up menu to open the Events window (see Figure 5-18).

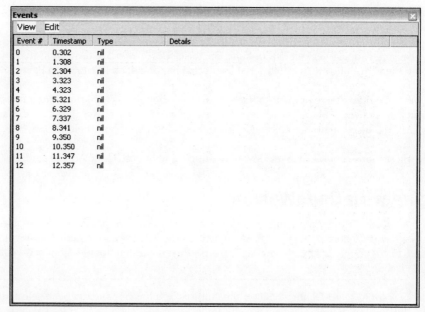

**Figure 5-18**

As Palm OS Simulator queues events, it displays each event in the Events window. The Events window has its own View menu, from which you may choose the following options:

❑ **Clear.** Select this option to clear the contents of the Events window.

❑ **Lock.** Choosing this option prevents the simulator from updating the Events window display. This option allows you to pause the output to the Events window for closer examination.

❑ **Unlock.** This option resumes the updating of the Events window.

## Saving and Loading a Storage Snapshot

You can save the contents of the simulator's emulated memory and load it again. To save a snapshot of the memory, select Storage ⇨ Save from the pop-up menu. The simulator presents you with a standard file dialog box, in which you can choose a location and name for the .ssf (storage snapshot) file you want to save.

To load a storage snapshot, select Storage ⇨ Load from the pop-up menu, and then select the desired .ssf file from the file dialog box that appears. The simulator restores its memory to the exact state in the storage snapshot file.

# Debugging at the Source Level

Source-level debugging is one of the most effective ways to track down and fix bugs in an application. Instead of trying to guess which part of your code is causing an error, you can step through the code line by line and find out exactly what part of it is buggy.

For Palm OS Garnet and earlier versions of Palm OS, the CodeWarrior IDE has a built-in debugger that can debug applications running on an actual serial-connected handheld, on POSE, or on Palm OS Simulator.

In the PalmSource PODS development toolset, Palm OS Debugger (PODS) provides a full source-level debugger that works with 68K applications, as well as newer Protein applications for Cobalt. Like CodeWarrior's debugger, Palm OS Debugger integrates a connected handheld, POSE, or Palm Simulator.

The following sections provide an overview of debugging with both CodeWarrior and PODS.

## Debugging with CodeWarrior

To perform source-level debugging in the CodeWarrior environment, you must first enable the debugger. Select Project ➪ Enable Debugger to enable debugging; if Project ➪ Disable Debugger is displayed in the menu, the debugger is already enabled because this menu item toggles between Enable Debugger and Disable Debugger.

You also may want to select Debug ➪ Show Breakpoints, if it has not already been selected, to display the breakpoint column in the project's code windows. Figure 5-19 shows a CodeWarrior code window with the breakpoint column displayed. Click in the breakpoint column to enable or disable a breakpoint on a particular line of code. Breakpoints are designated with a red dot in the left-hand margin of the code window.

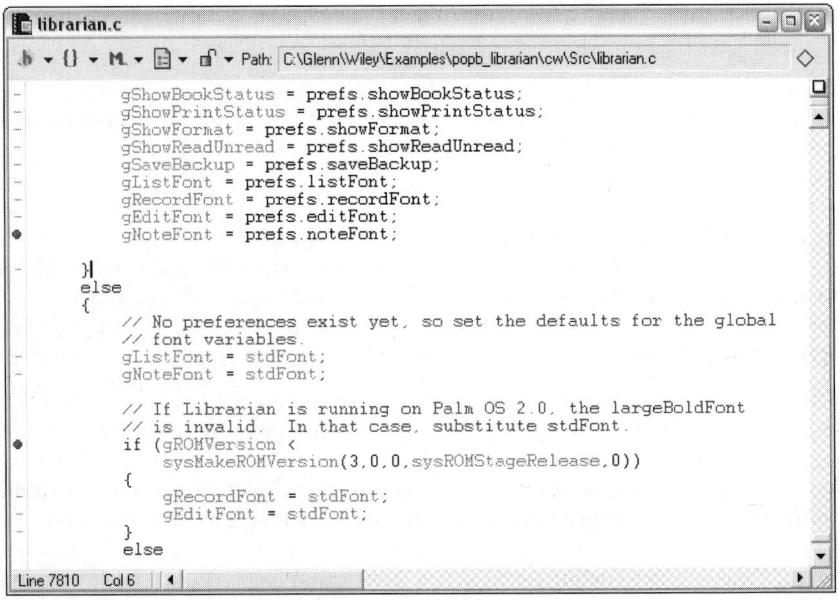

**Figure 5-19**

You also may define a breakpoint by pressing F9; CodeWarrior creates a breakpoint for the line of code where the text cursor is currently located.

## Setting up a Debugging Target

CodeWarrior can debug applications in POSE, Palm OS Simulator, and on an actual handheld. For each project you work with, you will need to set up a target for the debugger to connect to. To set the target, open the project settings dialog, and then under the Debugger category choose the Palm OS Debugging panel (see Figure 5-20).

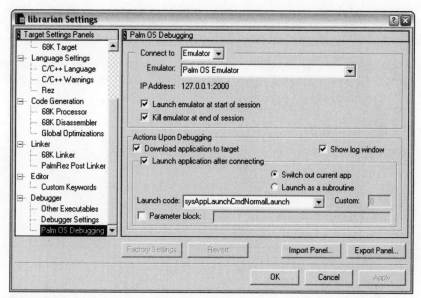

**Figure 5-20**

To connect to either the emulator or the simulator for debugging purposes, choose Emulator from the pop-up menu next to the Connect To label. Underneath Connect To, choose what specific form of Emulator or Simulator target you wish to debug against.

To connect to an actual Palm OS handheld, set the Target pop-up menu to Palm OS Device. You also must also set the Connection pop-up menu to the serial port where the handheld is connected and select an appropriate baud rate for the connection.

## Running the Debugger

To start debugging, select Project ➪ Debug or press F5. If you are debugging in Palm OS Emulator or Palm OS Simulator, ensure that the appropriate emulation program is already running before you start the debugging session or else CodeWarrior will complain and display an error dialog box. Also, the application you wish to debug must not already be running in Palm OS Simulator. Exit the application in the simulator before beginning a new debugging session with the same application.

One more step is necessary to debug on an actual handheld. When you run the Debug command, CodeWarrior shows you the dialog box shown in Figure 5-21, which prompts you to put the handheld into console mode with a special Graffiti shortcut sequence.

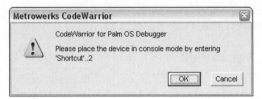

**Figure 5-21**

Enter the console mode debugging shortcut (the Graffiti shortcut symbol followed by a period and the number 2) on the handheld, and then click OK to start debugging. See the "Using Developer Graffiti Shortcuts" section later in this chapter for more details about the console mode debugging shortcut.

*If you are debugging over a serial connection on a Handspring Visor or Sony CLIÉ, you must hold down the Scroll Up button before finishing the debugging shortcut, and then continue holding the Scroll Up button until CodeWarrior finishes downloading the application to the handheld.*

## Controlling the Debugger

When the debugger finishes downloading the application to POSE or to an actual handheld, CodeWarrior stops at the first line of code in the application and displays a debugging window (see Figure 5-22).

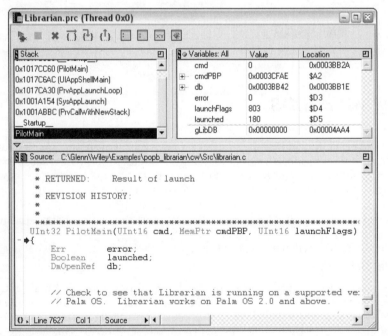

**Figure 5-22**

The buttons across the top of the debugging window, from left to right, have the following functions, also accessible via shortcut keys and menu commands:

❑ **Debug/Resume.** Runs application code until it hits a breakpoint or an error. This button is disabled when the application is running. The Debug command also is available from the menus as Project ⇨ Debug or by pressing F5. Once a debugging session has started, the Debug command changes to Resume in the Project menu. Selecting Project ⇨ Resume continues execution until the application hits another breakpoint or error.

❑ **Run.** Runs your application in POSE or on the attached handheld without enabling the debugger. Select Project ⇨ Run, or press Ctrl-F5, to use the Run command.

❑ **Kill.** Kills the debugger and soft-resets POSE or the attached handheld. Use this command to end a debugging session. The Kill command also is available by selecting Debug ⇨ Kill or by pressing Shift-F5.

❑ **Step Over.** Executes the next line of code, stepping over subroutine calls and remaining in the current routine. Step Over also is available as Debug ⇨ Step Over or by pressing F10.

❑ **Step Into.** Executes the next line of code, stepping into subroutines. Step Into also is in the menu command Debug ⇨ Step Into, in addition to pressing F11.

❑ **Step Out.** Executes the rest of the code in the current routine and then stops again in the current routine's caller. You also can get to the Step Out command by selecting Debug ⇨ Step Out or by pressing Shift-F11.

The debugging window also has a Stack section, which shows the call stack for the application. Selecting a routine from the Stack list displays the code surrounding that particular subroutine call, allowing you to trace which routines called one another to get to the current breakpoint. A Variables list shows you the values for all the variables that are currently in scope in the application.

## Debugging with PODS

The PODS integrated debugger works with Palm OS Garnet and Palm OS Cobalt devices, Palm Simulator, and Palm OS Emulator targets. For most users, a debug session for a program will usually be initiated from within the PODS IDE by choosing Run ⇨ Debug. Doing this automatically launches a debug session for the currently selected project target. PODS prompts you for information on how you wish to configure the current Palm OS Debugger session to debug your code (see Figure 5-23).

To create a debug configuration, click the New button under the Configurations panel.

Within the Debug Configuration dialog box, you can use the five tabs on the right panel to customize your debug configuration:

❑ **Project.** Choose the project in the workspace you wish to debug.

❑ **Launch.** Specify an alternate Palm OS launch code with which to start your program in the debug session. By default, this is the standard sysAppLaunchCmdNormalLaunch code issued in conjunction with a SysUIAppSwitch, but under some circumstances you may wish to simulate being launched via an alternate launch code.

❏ **Target.** Choose from among Palm OS Garnet Simulator, Palm OS Cobalt Simulator, Palm OS Emulator, or an actual physical device (over USB or COM port).

❏ **Source.** Specify additional source code locations with the debugger to display source code when stepping through your debug session. These locations may be in addition to the locations normally associated with your target project.

❏ **Common.** Modify other settings that govern how your debug session is represented within the PODS IDE.

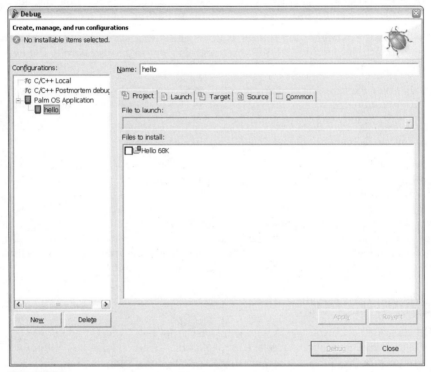

Figure 5-23

After completing customization of your debug settings, launch your debug session by clicking the Debug button. This initiates your debugging session in the target environment (Emulator, Palm Simulator, or device) and launches you into the debugger with your source code, breakpoints, and other windows available to you (see Figure 5-24).

When the debugger finishes downloading the application to POSE, Palm Simulator, or an actual handheld, PODS pauses at the first line of code in the application (normally the first line of PilotMain). At this point you may set breakpoints, run sections of code, and look at variables, just as you would with most source-level debuggers on other programming platforms.

If the Debug view is not already open, you should now open it by selecting Window ⇨ Show View. The Debug view presents you with the standard Step Into, Step Over, and other program control buttons that you will need to use in your debug session.

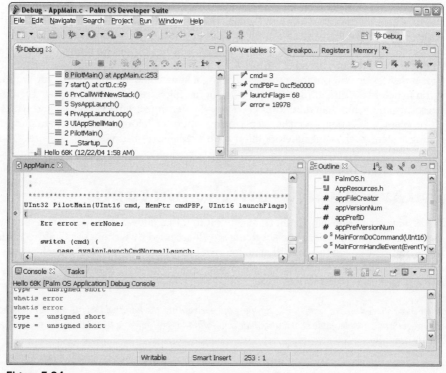

**Figure 5-24**

The buttons across the top of the debugging window, from left to right, support standard debugger options, including Debug/Resume, Suspend, Terminate, Restart, Step Into, Step Over, and Step Out. These options are also available via keyboard shortcut commands.

# Resetting a Palm OS Handheld

When debugging applications on an actual Palm OS handheld, you will need to reset the handheld from time to time. There are a number of different ways to reset a handheld, depending on the situation:

❑ **Soft reset.** A soft reset clears the dynamic memory on the device, leaving the storage memory alone so that applications and data on the device remain intact. You can perform a soft reset by inserting a narrow blunt object, like the end of an unfolded paper clip, into the hole on the back of the handheld to press the reset button.

❑ **Hard reset.** A hard reset wipes out everything in RAM, both dynamic and storage. To perform a hard reset, press the reset button while holding down the power button. The system will ask you to confirm that you want to erase all data on the device before proceeding.

*When using an actual device for debugging, make sure that any important data on that device has been backed up before you perform a hard reset. Once the handheld has been hard-reset, its data is gone forever.*

❏ **No-notification reset.** This kind of reset prevents the system from sending the `sysAppLaunchCmdSystemReset` launch code to all the applications on the device. If you have a bug in the `PilotMain` routine of your application, it is possible for the application to crash the system before it even finishes a reset, sending the device into a vicious cycle of continuous resets. Pressing the reset button while holding the scroll up hardware button allows you to reset the device without the system's sending a launch code to the broken application, enabling you to delete the offending program without having to resort to a hard reset. The no-notification reset also prevents shared libraries and system extensions from loading, so once you have deleted a problem application, you need to perform a soft reset before some important parts of the operating system, such as the network library, are available for use again.

# Using Developer Graffiti Shortcuts

Palm OS has a number of developer shortcuts built into it that allow you to perform a number of useful tasks from within any application. The shortcuts are all accessed by writing the Graffiti shortcut character (a cursive lowercase *L*) in the Graffiti area, followed by two taps (a period character — the first tap puts you in punctuation mode and the second enters the period) and the shortcut code. The following table describes each available shortcut code.

*Some of these shortcuts can leave the serial port open, draining the handheld's batteries. Others, such as the debugger and console mode shortcuts, may cause data loss or damage to existing data. Use these shortcuts carefully.*

| Graffiti | Shortcut | Description |
|---|---|---|
| ℓ .. 1 | .1 | Enters debugger mode. The handheld opens the serial port and waits for a connection from a low-level debugger, such as the Palm Debugger that ships with the Palm OS SDK. You must perform a soft reset to exit this mode and close the serial port. |
| ℓ .. 2 | .2 | Enters console mode. The handheld opens the serial port and waits for a connection from a high-level debugger, such as CodeWarrior. You must perform a soft reset to exit this mode and close the serial port. |
| ℓ .. 3 | .3 | Shuts off the auto-off feature. When this shortcut is made, the device will no longer shut itself off automatically, regardless of the current auto-off time set in the system Prefs application. You must perform a soft reset to enable auto-off again. |
| ℓ .. ℓ | .4 | Briefly displays the username assigned to the device, along with a number that HotSync uses internally to identify the user. |
| ℓ .. 5 | .5 | Erases the username and number assigned to the device. At the start of the next HotSync operation, the HotSync manager treats the device as a brand new handheld that has never been synchronized. This will cause duplicate records to be copied to the handheld from the desktop during the synchronization; to prevent this, perform a hard reset. |

| Graffiti | Shortcut | Description |
|---|---|---|
| ♀ .. 6 | .6 | Displays the date and time at which the ROM was built in the text field that has the focus. |
| ♀ .. ⌐ | .7 | Toggles between alkaline and NiCd modes for keeping track of remaining battery voltage, which is supposed to change when low battery alerts are displayed to the user. Historically, the NiCd mode has never been particularly accurate; you should probably leave this shortcut alone. |
| ♀ .. ⌐ | .i | Temporarily enables the device to receive incoming IR transmissions, even if Beam Receive in the system Preferences application is currently set to "Off." |
| ♀ .. S | .s | Toggles serial IR mode. When active, serial IR mode causes all IR calls to go to the handheld's serial port instead, which can be very useful for debugging low-level infrared code. |
| ♀ .. ⌐ | .t | Toggles loopback mode for the Exchange Manager. When active, loopback mode causes all IR beaming operations to loop back to the device, allowing you to test some beaming functions without using a second handheld. |

*Though you do not need to write these shortcuts in an actual text field, the visual feedback you get from doing so is very useful. Because the Find dialog box contains a text field, and it is available from any application, tapping the Find silkscreen button before entering a shortcut is a quick and easy way to see what you are writing when using these shortcuts.*

# Using the Palm OS Error Manager

The Palm OS error manager is an API that provides mechanisms for displaying errors that might come up during application development. Error manager macros are conditionally compiled, so they become part of your compiled application only if you set certain special constants in your code. During development, the macros are there to help you debug the application. Once you have finished development, you can easily build a version of the application that does not include the error-checking code, resulting in a smaller, faster executable.

The error manager provides three macros for displaying runtime errors: ErrDisplay, ErrFatalDisplayIf, and ErrNonFatalDisplayIf. The ErrDisplay macro always displays an error dialog box, and the other two macros display a dialog box only if their first argument resolves to the value true. Error dialog boxes displayed by these macros also include the line number and filename of the source code that called the error macro, making it easier to find where the error occurred.

The ERROR_CHECK_LEVEL compiler constant controls which error macros the compiler includes in the compiled application. The following table shows the constants defined in Palm OS for each error level, and what each error level means.

| Constant | Value | Description |
|---|---|---|
| ERROR_CHECK_NONE | 0 | Compiler does not compile in any error macros. |
| ERROR_CHECK_PARTIAL | 1 | Compiler compiles only fatal error macros (ErrDisplay and ErrFatalDisplayIf) into the application. |
| ERROR_CHECK_FULL | 2 | Compiler compiles in all error macros. |

To use an error constant, add it in a #define statement at the start of your application, before the application includes the PalmOS.h header file:

```
#define ERROR_CHECK_FULL
#include <PalmOS.h>
```

When you are developing the application, an error-checking value of ERROR_CHECK_FULL is appropriate to catch all the bugs you possibly can. Set ERROR_CHECK_LEVEL to ERROR_CHECK_PARTIAL for alpha and beta tests; the nonfatal errors produced by ErrNonFatalDisplayIf should probably have been handled at this point in the development cycle, anyway, or at the very least they should already be known to you. The ERROR_CHECK_NONE level is appropriate for a final released product.

You can use the ErrDisplay macro always to display an error dialog box. Use the following syntax to call ErrDisplay:

```
ErrDisplay("Insert error message here");
```

The ErrFatalDisplayIf and ErrNonFatalDisplayIf macros take two arguments, the first of which should resolve to a Boolean value. Only if the first argument is true will these two macros display the error message indicated by their second argument. In general, the first argument will be an inline statement of some kind, which makes for neat and tidy error-checking code that is still removed from compilation when you produce a final release build. For example, the following snippet calls a hypothetical function called MyFunc and, if its return value is greater than 4, generates a fatal error dialog box:

```
UInt16 result = MyFunc();
ErrFatalDisplayIf(result > 4,
                  "Illegal result from MyFunc");
```

When ErrDisplay or ErrFatalDisplayIf displays an error dialog box, the user can clear the error only by tapping the supplied Reset button, causing a soft reset of the handheld. The ErrNonFatalDisplayIf macro allows the user to continue execution of the program, so use ErrNonFatalDisplayIf only in situations where you want to check if a certain condition exists but that the condition will not prevent the application from continuing (more or less) normally.

# Summary

In this chapter, you were given an overview of the most important debugging tools available for Palm OS development. After reading this chapter, you should understand the following:

❑ Palm OS Emulator (POSE) is a fantastic tool for debugging Palm OS applications without going through the slow and painful process of repeatedly installing a program to an actual handheld.

❑ POSE does have its limitations, particularly in the areas of IR support and accurate representation of execution speed on a real device, so you should still make a final test pass for your application on an actual Palm OS handheld.

❑ POSE Gremlins let you give your application a really good workout, randomly pounding parts of the program that might not be sufficiently tested using more structured testing techniques.

❑ Palm OS Simulator emulates Palm OS 5 on a Windows computer, allowing you to test applications without needing to run them on actual ARM hardware.

❑ Source-level debugging with CodeWarrior or PODS allows you easily to find which line (or lines) of code in your application is causing a particular bug.

❑ There are multiple ways to reset a Palm OS handheld, including soft resets, hard resets, and no-notification resets.

❑ Special developer Graffiti shortcuts give you access to some more obscure settings of the operating system and hardware.

❑ Adding error manager macros to your application can be a useful debugging tool during the program's development. The macros will not weigh down the application when you release a final version of it to the public.

# Creating and Understanding Resources

As you may recall from Chapter 2, resources fall into three categories: system, form, and project. Because the compiler takes care of creating system resources for you, like the application's executable code, you need to create only the form and project resources to define things such as buttons and application icons.

This chapter explains how to create project resources using the Constructor tool from CodeWarrior, as well as the new Palm OS Resource Editor which is part of PalmSource's PODS toolset. Form resources, which include things like buttons, check boxes, and menus, are covered in Chapter 7.

Before delving into the mechanics of creating resources, though, a discussion about how those resources should be used is in order. PalmSource provides an extensive list of user interface guidelines, which provide a framework for making applications that are best suited to a Palm OS device. If a developer follows them, these Palm OS guidelines ensure that applications look and operate the same way as the built-in Palm OS applications. Emulating the way that the standard applications work helps users interact with your application immediately with little or no instruction because they are already familiar with the interface. The official PalmSource user interface guidelines are available for both Palm OS Protein and Palm OS 68K development at www.palmsource.com.

## Following Palm OS User Interface Guidelines

For many years, PalmSource has provided Palm OS developers with an evolving set of user interface guidelines that address the unique problem of designing an effective user interface for a handheld application. Ultimately, the user interface you design for your applications depends on many factors, but a thorough reading of the PalmSource guidelines is virtually required reading, especially for those new to handheld development.

❑ If a menu item or user interface element is currently disabled or not available, remove it from the screen entirely. The Palm OS does not provide any facilities for "graying out" controls and menus, and there is little enough screen space available that removing the item entirely is preferable.

❑ Many desktop applications duplicate commands by making them accessible from a button and from the application's menus. Avoid this kind of duplication in Palm OS applications. Not only does it increase the size of the program, but it also goes against the paradigm of highlighting frequently used functions. Important commands that the user will access regularly should be on the screen itself; less-often-used commands should be relegated to menus.

❑ Likewise, provide Graffiti command shortcuts only for those menu items that really need them. For example, cutting, copying, and pasting text are actions that need to be performed quickly, so these commands are good candidates for command shortcuts. On the other hand, an "about" box for an application is something that the user will look at only occasionally, if at all, so displaying it does not require a shortcut.

# Creating Resources with Constructor

Constructor is a graphical tool for resource creation with 68K-based applications using Palm OS version 5 or earlier (including Garnet). Its "what you see is what you get" (WYSIWYG) approach to resource editing lets you see exactly what your resources will look like during every step of their creation.

When it opens, Constructor consists of only a title bar and a menu bar underneath it (see Figure 6-1). Only the Windows version of Constructor is pictured in this book; however, the Mac OS version of Constructor is very similar.

**Figure 6-1**

*This book covers Constructor version 1.9.1, which was included with the Palm OS 5.x SDK. With the introduction of the Palm OS Development System ("PODS"), PalmSource has moved away from Constructor and now provides a new Resource Editor as part of its development environment. As of this writing, it does not appear that PalmSource will be continuing to enhance Constructor. The new Resource Editor is covered in depth later in this chapter. For more information on PODS, please refer to Chapter 3.*

Constructor organizes all resources for a particular application in a *project*. To create a new project, select File ➪ New Project File or press Ctrl-N.

> **Understanding Resource Forks**
>
> After saving a project on a Windows machine, you may be wondering why Constructor creates a folder called `Resource.frk` in the same folder where you save the project file. Constructor does this to allow the transfer of resource files between Windows and Mac OS. On Mac OS, Constructor stores resource information in the *resource fork* of the project file. Because Windows files do not contain a resource fork, Constructor saves an empty `.rsrc` file to mimic the Mac OS data fork and then creates the `Resource.frk` folder and saves the resources themselves in that directory, using the same filename as the data file.
>
> Keep in mind that if you wish to move your resource files around in Windows, you need to copy both `.rsrc` files, and the resource fork file must be in a `Resource.frk` folder in the same location as the data fork `.rsrc` file. Failure to copy both files correctly prevents Constructor from working with them.
>
> When opening a project file for editing, you may select either of the `.rsrc` files. Constructor is smart enough to figure out which file contains the data fork and which contains the resource fork.
>
> Note that you may need to adjust your Windows Explorer folder view options if you do not see a Resource.frk folder for your project.

Alternatively, you may open an existing project file by selecting File ➪ Open Project File or by pressing Ctrl-O. Constructor will prompt you for the location of the project file you wish to edit.

*Constructor can also open a `.prc` file. Although Constructor cannot make changes to the `.prc` file, it does allow you to examine resources in the file. You also can use Constructor to copy resources from an open `.prc` file and paste them into your own projects.*

When you have finished making changes to the project, save your work to disk with the File ➪ Save menu command, or press Ctrl-S. Constructor prompts you for a location to which you would like to save the project.

## Exploring the Project Window

The first window Constructor displays when you open an existing project, or when you create a new project, is the *project window*. Figure 6-2 shows the project window for the Hello World 2 application from Chapter 4. Notice that the project window is divided into two sections: the Resource Type and Name list and the Project Settings box.

Besides listing project resources and settings, the project window informs you which resources or settings you have changed since the last time you saved the project. Constructor indicates changed resources or settings with a small black dot to the left of the appropriate item. When you save the project, all the dots disappear.

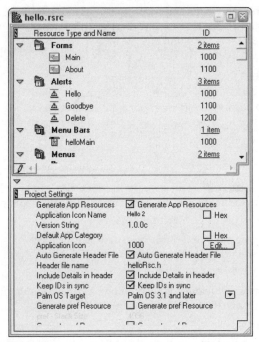

Figure 6-2

Located at the bottom of the project window, the Project Settings box allows you to change settings for the entire project. From top to bottom, the Project Settings box contains the following items:

❑ **Generate App Resources.** When checked, this option tells Constructor to generate application icon name and version resources for the project. Unchecking Generate App Resources disables the Application Icon Name and Version String fields, in case you want to generate other resource types without creating an icon name and version string resources. Leaving the Generate App Resources option unchecked can be useful if you use multiple resource files to create different sections of a large application, because generating application resources in multiple resource files causes the compiler to complain when it encounters duplicate resources for the icon name and version number resources.

❑ **Application Icon Name.** This text field contains the name that appears in the launcher below or next to the program's icon. The Application Icon Name field may contain up to 31 characters, but you should use only half that to prevent the icon name from being truncated by other icon names in the default launcher. It has very little space available for icon names in both its list and icon views. Use the Hex check box to toggle the display of the icon name between hexadecimal and normal text.

❑ **Version String.** The version string is handy for branding the application with its current version. This field accepts up to 15 characters, and it is not limited to just digits and decimal points. Allowing non-numerical characters permits the use of interim version numbers, such as "1.2e," or of beta version numbers, such as "0.9b."

❑ **Default App Category.** In this field, you can specify the name of a default category that the application should be added to when the application is installed on a handheld. If this category does not already exist on the handheld, the system will create it. If this field is left blank, the application becomes part of the Unfiled category on the handheld by default. (The Unfiled category cannot be deleted, so it exists on every handheld.) You should not define a default category for your application unless it clearly falls into one of the following standard categories:

  ❑ **Games:** used for any game application

  ❑ **Main:** used for applications that are likely to be used on a daily basis, such as Date Book or Address applications

  ❑ **System:** used for applications that control how the system behaves, such as the Prefs or HotSync applications

  ❑ **Utilities:** used for applications that assist in system management

  ❑ **Unfiled:** which is the default category

❑ **Application Icon.** This field contains the resource ID number of the application's icon, which is displayed in the launcher. If an icon family with resource ID 1000 already exists in the project, the button is labeled Edit; clicking it opens the existing icon family for editing. Note that changing the ID number to something other than 1000 is a bad idea. Palm OS assumes that an application's icon has an ID of 1000, and if no icon with that ID exists, the operating system displays a blank spot in the launcher instead of an icon.

❑ **Auto Generate Header File.** Checking this option tells Constructor to create a header file automatically containing #define statements that map constant definitions to resource ID numbers. Using resource constants is much easier than trying to remember the four-digit number assigned to each resource in an application, so keeping this option checked will save you a lot of headaches later on. The following two lines in the Project Settings box do not do anything if Auto Generate Header File is not checked.

❑ **Header File Name.** This text field contains the name of the header file to generate if the Auto Generate Header File box is checked. If you do not specify a header filename here, Constructor provides one for you. In Windows, this name is composed of the name of the project file with _res.h appended to it; in Mac OS, the name consists of just the name of the project file with .h appended to it. Likewise, if the filename you enter here does not have an .h extension, Constructor tacks .h onto the end of the name you entered when you save the project.

❑ **Include Details in Header.** Checking this box adds comments to the automatically generated header file, describing individual properties of each of the resources listed in the header. This option is strictly optional because it has no bearing at all on how CodeWarrior compiles the resources.

❑ **Keep IDs in Sync.** When this box is checked, Constructor maintains consistent resource IDs. In particular, Constructor keeps form resource IDs the same as its own internal form IDs. When you change the resource ID of a form, Constructor changes all object IDs of objects in that form to match the beginning of the form's ID. In general, keep this box checked unless you really want mismatched object and form IDs.

❑ **Palm OS Target.** Use this option to define the Palm OS version that Constructor should target when building resources. The following choices are available:

❑ **Palm OS 3.0.x and earlier:** Select this option for all versions of Palm OS 3.0.*x* and earlier.

❑ **Palm OS 3.1 and later:** Select this option for Latin-encoded versions of Palm OS 3.1 and later.

❑ **Palm OS for Japan:** Select this option for Japanese versions of Palm OS. Constructor can handle Japanese text input if it is running on a Japanese system, or if it is running on a Mac OS system with the Japanese Language Kit installed.

❑ **Generate Pref Resource.** Selecting this check box causes Constructor to generate a `pref` resource, which contains information about the environment in which your application should run.

❑ **Pref - Stack Size.** This option is available only if the Generate Pref Resource option is selected. Use this option to set the amount of stack space your application requires, in bytes. When your application runs in Palm OS 3.0 or later, the system attempts to allocate at least this much stack space for your application. Programs without a `pref` resource receive a default amount of stack space that varies depending on the version of the operating system. Most well-designed applications should run without difficulty in the default amount of stack space, so only rarely will you need to set this option.

❑ **Generate xprf Resource.** If you select this check box, Constructor creates a `xprf` resource, which contains instructions for how your application should handle overlays.

❑ **Xprf - Flag No Overlay.** This option is available only if the Generate Xprf Resource option is selected. Selecting this check box signals that your application should not automatically load overlay databases when it starts. An overlay database contains resources for a specific language. Normally, when an application starts, Palm OS looks for an overlay database for that application. If it finds it, it substitutes the overlay database's resource definitions for those contained in the application's `.prc` file. If for some reason you do not want to allow others to localize your application, select the Xprf - Flag No Overlay option.

The Resource Type and Name list shows all the project resources in an application, including forms, alerts, strings, menus, bitmaps, and other resources. Each gray bar represents a different type of resource. Constructor lists underneath that category's gray bar all of the resources in the project that belong to a particular category.

You create new project resources by selecting one of the gray bars and then selecting the Edit ➪ New *Type* Resource menu command, where *Type* represents the kind of resource you have selected. A quicker way is to select the appropriate bar and press Ctrl-K.

Alternatively, you also may select Edit ➪ New *Type* Resource, or press Ctrl-R, to open the Create New Resource dialog box (see Figure 6-3). Clicking the Create button launches a new resource with the properties you set in the dialog box.

You can change the name or resource ID of any resource in the project window by clicking once on its name or ID and then typing the new name or ID number. To edit a particular resource, either double-click it or select it and press Enter. An editor window appropriate to the type of resource appears. You also may use the Edit ➪ Edit Resource command to open the editor for a selected resource.

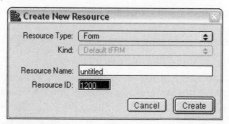

Figure 6-3

*The two commands in the Edit menu for creating new resources look almost identical. Use the first, Edit ⇨ New Type Resource, or the shortcut key Ctrl-K, to create a new resource quickly that is based on the currently selected resource type in the project window. The second command, Edit ⇨ New Type Resource, with the shortcut key Ctrl-R, simply opens the Create New Resource dialog box.*

*To confuse matters further, when no resource type is selected in the project window, both commands open the Create New Resource dialog box. Either command is perfectly valid, but the Ctrl-K method is much quicker.*

Delete resources by selecting them and choosing Edit ⇨ Clear Resource or pressing either the Delete or Backspace key.

Most of the resources you can create from the project window are detailed in the following sections. Forms and menus are complex enough that they merit their own chapter. For detailed information about making form and menu resources, see Chapter 7.

## Alerts

The alert editor window, pictured in Figure 6-4, provides everything you need to make alert dialog boxes. It also shows a preview of what the alert will look like in the finished application.

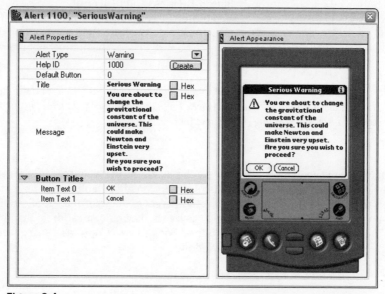

Figure 6-4

From top to bottom, the alert editor window contains the following items:

❏ **Alert Type.** This pop-up menu allows you to select one of the four alert types: information, confirmation, warning, or error.

❏ **Help ID.** This field contains the resource ID of a string resource that serves as the online help for this alert. If you have not assigned a string resource to this alert yet, the resource ID displayed is 0 and the Create button to the right of the ID is disabled. If you set Help ID to a value that does not correspond to any existing string resource, the Create button becomes enabled; clicking it opens a string editor window so you can create a new string resource. If you set the Help ID to the resource ID of an existing string resource, the button's caption changes to Edit; clicking the button opens that string resource in a string editor window.

❏ **Default Button.** You can set the default button for the alert dialog box in this field. If an alert is displayed and the user switches to another application, Palm OS simulates a tap on the default button to dismiss the alert, allowing you to execute appropriate default code on the way out of the dialog box. The Default Button field is disabled if the alert contains only one button.

❏ **Title.** Enter in this field the text to display in the alert's title bar.

❏ **Message.** Whatever message the alert should display goes into this field.

*In addition to the static text that you assign to an alert's message when designing the alert, your application can insert custom text into an alert at runtime by displaying the alert with the FrmCustomAlert function. In order for FrmCustomAlert to work, you must include up to three placeholders (^1, ^2, and ^3) in the Message field. FrmCustomAlert replaces these placeholders with whatever text you like. For more details about using FrmCustomAlert, see Chapter 8.*

❏ **Button Titles.** Clicking the arrow in the left of this item hides or displays the list of buttons for the alert resource. Each button on the form is listed as Item Text *n*, where *n* is the index number of the button; an index of 0 represents the leftmost button. To add more buttons to the alert, select an existing button title and then choose Edit ⇨ New Button Title or press Ctrl-K. A new button title appears below the selected button title. You also can insert a new button before the first button by selecting the gray Button Titles bar and then creating a new button as described previously. You may delete a selected button by selecting the Edit ⇨ Clear Button Title command, or by pressing Backspace. Constructor allows you to add more buttons than Palm OS can actually display in an alert at runtime, so be sure to keep the number of buttons reasonable— only three or four, say, each with short captions.

*Unlike other places in the Windows version of Constructor, where pressing Delete deletes an item, Delete does nothing at all when editing buttons in an alert. Press the Backspace key instead if you want to use a keyboard shortcut instead of selecting the menu option.*

## Strings

A string resource simply contains a string of text characters. String resources are the usual way to provide online help in your applications. They also serve to contain default values for text fields or other miscellaneous text that remains constant between different executions of an application. For example, the Address Book application inserts the string "Copy" at the end of an address that the user duplicates by using the Duplicate Address command. Address Book stores "Copy" as a string resource for easy retrieval. Figure 6-5 shows the string editor window.

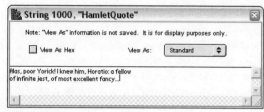

**Figure 6-5**

*Although you could just as easily include such a string as part of your application's code, storing the string as a resource makes your application easier to localize into different languages. You can provide a different set of resources for each language and attach those resources to your application at build time, which is much simpler than having to maintain separate source code modules for each language.*

You may edit the string's text in the lower half of the editor window. The View As Hex check box converts the contents of the window to hexadecimal, and the View As pop-up list allows you to select the font in which to display the text. Note that these two "View As" controls have no effect on the actual resource that Constructor generates; they are for display purposes only.

## String Lists

A string list is an indexed list of text strings with a specific prefix string. Figure 6-6 shows the string list editor window, which has the same "View As" capabilities as the string editor.

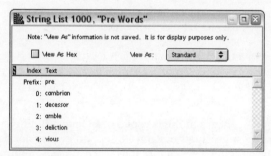

**Figure 6-6**

You can use the `SysStringByIndex` API function to access string list resources from your application. `SysStringByIndex` returns the string list's prefix string, concatenated to a specific string from the list.

To enter the prefix string, click to the right of "Prefix:" in the window and type the prefix string. Note that a prefix string is not required and, in some cases, not desired because the `SysStringByIndex` function tacks the prefix string to the front of every string it returns.

To add individual strings to the list, select Edit ➪ New String, or press Ctrl-K. You also can change the order of items in the list by clicking the index number of a string you wish to move and dragging it to its new location in the list. To delete a particular string, select it and then choose Edit ➪ Clear String or press either the Delete or Backspace key.

## App Info String Lists

An app info string list holds the initial categories for an application. The `CategoryInitialize` function uses this information to set default values for an application's categories. The Palm OS category manager expects to find static category names at the top of an app info string list. If your application will have categories that the user cannot edit, such as the "Unfiled" category common to most built-in applications, be sure to put these category names at the beginning of the list.

Figure 6-7 shows the app info string editor window, which is quite similar to the string list editor window.

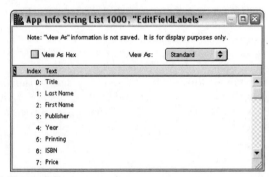

**Figure 6-7**

Except for the lack of a prefix item, you can add, edit, and delete items in an app info string list using the same techniques listed previously for regular string lists.

> *Constructor lets you enter as much text as you like for each category, but Palm OS allows only 15 characters for a category name. Be sure not to exceed this limit when entering category names.*

## App Icon Families

An app icon family resource contains multiple copies of an image at different color depths for use as an application icon. Because not all versions of Palm OS support every color depth, an application that needs to appear properly in multiple versions of the launcher needs multiple icons. The Palm OS default launcher automatically displays the best-quality icon supported in its version of Palm OS; older versions of the launcher ignore icons that are beyond their ability to display.

Applications need two app icon families: one for the program's large icon and one for its small icon. The large app icon family must have a resource ID of 1000; the small app icon family must have a resource ID of 1001.

To create an app icon family, you first need to create a number of bitmaps, one for each color depth that appears in the app icon family (see the "Bitmaps" section next). Usually you should create one bitmap for each color depth you plan to support. For example, an application targeted at a Palm OS 3.5 color device that can handle a maximum of 8-bit color might have one bitmap each at 1-, 2-, 4-, and 8-bit color depths.

*To save space, you can safely skip including a 4-bit grayscale icon. Even on Palm Powered handhelds capable of displaying 4-bit grayscale, the launcher application itself cannot display better than 2-bit grayscale.*

*Also, given the tiny size of an icon, 16-bit color is probably overkill. With such a small space available, the 234 colors of the 8-bit palette are more than sufficient to handle the task. Most users don't spend enough time in the launcher to admire your tiny pixelated masterpiece, anyhow, so leaving 16-bit color out of your icon is a smart way to reduce application size.*

Low-density icon bitmaps should be 22 × 22 pixels for a large application icon, or 15 × 9 for a small icon. A low-density icon also may be 32 pixels wide, but in order to provide some visual separation between icons in the launcher, you should limit yourself to the 22 pixels in the center of the bitmap. High-density icons are 44 × 44 pixels for a large icon, 30 × 18 for a small icon.

The next step is to add the bitmaps to an app icon family resource. In the App Icon Family Editor window (see Figure 6-8), you can add a new image by selecting Edit ➪ New Family Element, or by pressing Ctrl-K. Also, be sure to set the appropriate Width and Height values for the app icon family. Large icon families have Width and Height values of 22, regardless of whether or not they contain high-density icons. Likewise, small icon families should have Width and Height values of 15 and 9, respectively.

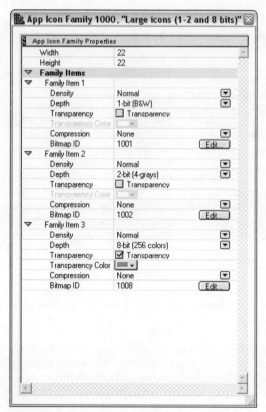

Figure 6-8

*The quickest way to add all the images needed in an app icon family is to select the Family Items line in the editor window and then press Ctrl-K once for each image you need in the family. Using this process also automatically increments the Depth field for each image, so you do not need to set the color depth manually for images one at a time.*

For each image, you can set a number of options as follows:

❑ **Density.** Use this pop-up menu to choose Normal or Double density.

❑ **Depth.** This option specifies the color depth of the bitmap image. There should be only one bitmap of a particular color depth within a particular app icon family.

❑ **Transparency.** If this option is checked, one of the colors in the icon is treated as transparent. Checking the Transparency check box enables the Transparency pop-up menu, from which you may choose one of the colors in the image to be the transparent color. Pixels in the image colored with the selected color are treated as transparent, allowing the background color of the launcher to show through.

❑ **Compression.** This pop-up menu allows you to select the style of compression used for the image. In general, icons should be left uncompressed; compression is intended for other kinds of bitmap images.

❑ **Bitmap ID.** Enter the resource ID of the appropriate bitmap image in this text field. Once an ID has been entered, clicking the Edit button opens the selected bitmap in the bitmap editor window.

*Images in an app icon family must be entered from lowest bit depth to highest, which usually means 1-bit (B&W) at the top of the list and 8-bit (256 colors) at the bottom. In addition, all the low-density icons must precede the high-density icons. Constructor does not enforce this policy; if you enter the images in the wrong order, you will get unpredictable results when the launcher tries to display your application's icon.*

## Bitmap Families

Bitmap families function in exactly the same manner as app icon families, except they are used for general bitmap images rather than for an application's launcher icon. The interface for creating and editing a bitmap family is identical to that for manipulating an app icon family. Also, the same caveat regarding color depth and density order applies to bitmap families; be careful to list the individual low-density images from lowest bit depth to highest, followed by the high-density images from lowest bit depth to highest.

## Bitmaps

The bitmap editor window, pictured in Figure 6-9, provides a space for editing miscellaneous bitmaps to include in your application.

You can create black and white, grayscale, or color bitmaps in the bitmap editor window. To change the color depth of the bitmap, choose an appropriate depth from the Colors menu. The options available are Black & White (1-bit depth), 4 Grays (2-bit depth), 16 Grays (4-bit depth), 256 colors (8-bit depth), and Thousands of Colors (16-bit depth). A single bitmap resource may have only one color depth, so if you need to have multiple depths for a single image, you will need to create a bitmap family to contain a number of bitmaps of varying depths.

**Figure 6-9**

To set the size of the bitmap, select Options ➪ Set Image Size. The Set Image Size dialog box appears, presenting you with text boxes for the Width and Height of the bitmap. Adjust these to the desired values and click Resize.

### Wave Sounds

The sampled sound functions in Palm OS 5 allow an application to play complex recorded sounds. These sounds are stored as a wave sound resource in the application. Constructor converts standard Windows .wav files into wave sound resources.

To add a wave sound to your project's resources, click the Browse button in the Wave Sound editor window. Constructor presents you with a standard file dialog box, from which you can select an appropriate .wav file.

# Creating Resources with the Palm OS Resource Editor

The Palm OS Resource Editor is part of PalmSource's official Palm OS Developer Suite. It is capable of creating and maintaining both 68K and Protein-based resources. Although Resource Editor and Constructor both offer developers a tool for the visual design and creation of Palm OS application resources, they are totally different tools and are in general incompatible with each other. This book describes version 1.1 of PODS and Resource Editor.

Resource Editor is a departure from the .rsrc file standard maintained by Constructor. Instead of .rsrc files, Resource Editor works with XRD files, also known as Resource Description Files, as the storage unit for a set of application resources. Internally, an XRD file is based on the XML standard and contains tags that describe your application's resources. Just like Constructor, Resource Editor allows you to create and edit a variety of resources for your application. When you save your work, your resource definitions are saved in an XRD file as part of your project.

Although most developers make use of the convenient visual design features of Resource Editor, an XRD file is in a human-readable XML format, so you can edit an XRD file directly with your favorite text editor if you wish. Alternatively, you can edit the XRD source directly within the PODS development environment by right-clicking the XRD file and choosing the Edit With ⇨ Text Editor menu option.

For those of you who prefer the convenience of a visual design tool, Resource Editor (see Figure 6-10) is the tool provided with the PODS environment for editing the resources associated with your program. To edit your programs resources in Resource Editor, either double-click the XRD file from within the Navigator window of the PODS IDE, or right-click the XRD file and choose Edit With ⇨ Resource Editor.

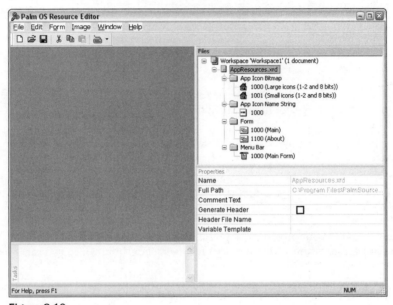

**Figure 6-10**

*Developers who migrate their application from CodeWarrior and Constructor to PODS can use the Import feature in PODS to import existing resources in .rsrc format to the new XRD format. Developers can also take advantage of the GenerateXRD Wizard, or the GenerateXRD command-line tool, both of which are utilities outside PODS.*

Resource Editor's main screen has the following panes:

❑ **Files Pane.** The Files Pane contains a hierarchical view of the resources contained within your XRD. Resources are organized by type, such as Form, Alert, Icon, etc. Under each type is listed an entry for each resource of that type that is defined in the XRD file. To view or edit a resource, double-click its entry in the Files Pane.

❑ **Windows Pane.** As you double-click each resources in the Files Pane, a new window is opened in the Windows Pane representing that resource. Each window is customized with view and toolbar buttons for the purpose of editing the type of resource it contains.

❏ **Tasks Pane.** This is an area below the Windows Pane that displays a scrollable list of messages in response to actions you perform within Resource Editor.

❏ **Properties Pane.** This automatically displays the properties of the currently selected resource within the Files Pane or Windows Pane. Each property has a name and value, and you can edit the value for each property by clicking within the value field.

When you are done editing your resources, you can save your work by using the File ⇨ Save menu option from the main Resource Editor menu.

One notable difference for Palm OS developers who are moving from Constructor to Resource Editor 1.0 is that Resource Editor does not create or update a C header file containing the preprocessor #define's for each resource for use within your application. You are responsible for adding these definitions yourself so that your program code can refer to resources by symbolic name rather than resource ID.

## Creating and Editing Application Resources

You can create new resources within your XRD file by choosing File ⇨ New Resource from either the main menu or by right-clicking in the Files Pane. As with Constructor, Resource Editor supports the creation of forms, alerts, bitmaps, application icons, menus, and strings, as well as other resource types such as category, app info and WAV sounds. These resource types are covered in depth in Chapter 7 and other chapters in this book.

Choosing New ⇨ Resource presents a list of the resource types allowed. Choosing a resource type opens a new window in the Window Pane representing a new instance of the resource type you specified. To complete the definition of the new resource, use the Properties Pane to adjust attributes such as the ID or symbolic name for your resource. For more complex resources, such as forms, you can use a toolbar palette to customize the appearance and behavior of your resource.

To delete a resource, select it in the Files Pane, right-click it, and choose the Clear menu option from the pop-up menu.

### Alerts

When you create a new resource and select an Alert type, a new resource window opens in the Window Pane, containing a new Alert preset with default values. Figure 6-11 shows a sample alert in the Resource Editor.

To alter the appearance and behavior of the alert, change its properties in the properties editor. The following properties are available:

❏ **Type.** This pop-up menu allows you to select a type for the alert: Information, Confirmation, Warning, and Error.

❏ **Help ID.** If you want to attach help information to an alert, specify the ID of a string resource containing the help text. If you include a HelpID in an alert, a small "i" icon appears in the upper-right corner of the alert at runtime. Tapping the icon displays the help text in another dialog box.

❑ **Default Button.** If your alert has more than one button, you should specify a default button. The system simulates a tap on the default button if the user exits the application while the alert is still open, giving your application a chance to save its data accordingly before it quits. Enter a numeric value for Default Button: 0 represents the leftmost button, 1 is the next button to the right, and so on.

❑ **Title.** This property controls the text that appears in the title bar of the alert.

❑ **Message.** Enter in this property the message that should appear in the body of the alert.

❑ **Button 1 Text.** This property defines the text that will appear inside the first button on the alert screen. Additional buttons can be added to the alert resource by pressing the Ins key with the window or Properties Pane in focus.

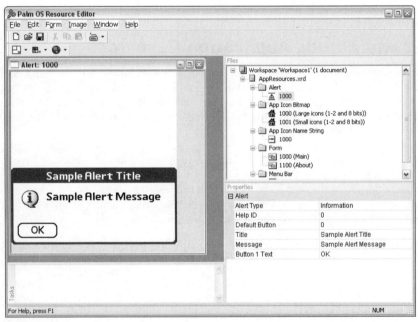

Figure 6-11

## Strings

When you create a new resource and select a String type, a new resource window opens in the Window Pane, containing a new String resource preset with a default value. Figure 6-12 shows a sample string in the Resource Editor.

Edit the text for the string in the String window and save your resource file when you are done.

## Application Icons and Bitmaps

Palm applications can contain both application icons (known as "App Icons") and bitmaps. App Icons are special bitmap resources that are automatically used by the Palm OS launcher when displaying your application in its list or icon views. Bitmaps are bitmap images that you define for use within your application's user interface, such as a logo in an "about" box.

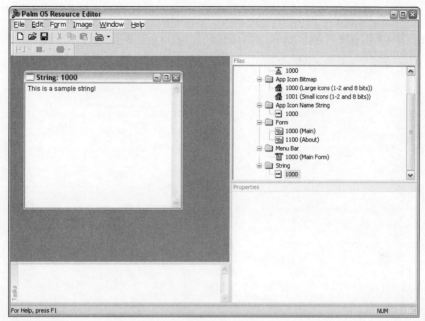

**Figure 6-12**

Each application should have two resource types for App Icons, a large icon and a small icon. If either the large or small App Icon is missing from an application, Palm OS substitutes a default icon. Bitmaps themselves are optional, there are no requirements for the inclusion of bitmaps with your application.

Other than the special designation as an App Icon, creating and editing bitmaps for use as an App Icon or as a Bitmap resource is the same. When either resource type is selected in the resource explorer, Resource Editor displays the bitmaps that make up the bitmap "family" (see Figure 6-13).

As we covered in the section on Constructor, a "bitmap family" is a collection of bitmap images, all of the same width and height but of varying density, resolution, and color depth. When creating bitmaps for use as either App Icon or Bitmap resources, you should add a bitmap corresponding to the most likely devices your application is going to be run on. When your application is run on a device, Palm OS determines the best bitmap in a given family to use for your application based on the available versions in your resources. If there is no bitmap which matches the device resolution, Palm OS chooses the next lowest compatible resolution, with pure 1-bit black and white being the last resort. It is thus in your best interest to provide bitmap families containing bitmaps that match the highest resolutions your application will be run on.

Within the App Icon Editor window, you can add and edit the various bitmaps you wish to use to represent your application when it runs on devices at different resolutions and color depth. As a rule, large icons should be 22 × 22 pixels, and small icons should be 15 × 9 pixels. Bitmap resources may be any size you wish, except that all bitmaps within a bitmap family must be the same dimensions.

When you choose the Add button to add a new version of your bitmap to the family, you are presented with a dialog box that lists all the available combinations of density, resolution, and color depth.

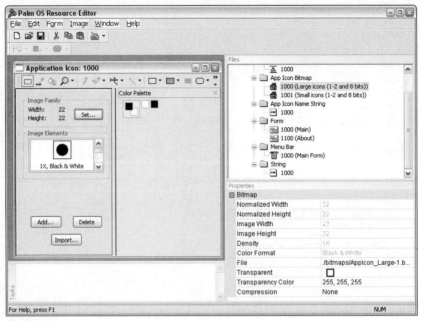

**Figure 6-13**

Both the App Icon and Bitmap Editor Window come equipped with their own toolbar palette full of drawing tools that you can use to hand-draw or touch up the appearance of your bitmap. Alternatively you can import your bitmap from a .bmp file stored on your computer.

# Summary

In this chapter, you learned about Palm's user interface guidelines, as well as resource creation. After reading this chapter, you should understand the following:

❑ Following the Palm OS user interface guidelines helps you write applications that better fit the expectations of Palm OS handheld users, decreasing your application's learning curve and lowering users' level of frustration.

❑ CodeWarrior Constructor is a graphical tool that provides a WYSIWYG interface for creating Palm OS resources.

❑ Resource Editor is the new standard resource editor for use within PalmSource's Palm OS Development System (PODS).

# Building Forms and Menus

The primary interface that a Palm OS application presents to users is contained within forms. Forms are the user's windows to working with an application; they provide displays for the user to view data and controls to allow the user to manipulate that data.

Menus provide a way for users to access application commands that see less frequent use. Because they remain tucked away out of sight until the user needs them, menus also allow your application to perform more functions without you having to make use of valuable screen real estate.

This chapter shows you how to construct the forms, menus, and resources that make up the user interface elements within forms, using CodeWarrior's Constructor and Palm OS Resource Editor from PalmSource's Palm OS Developer Suite (PODS).

The chapter begins by comparing how to create resources using each tool. A review of form object types that are accessible within both editors follows. Once you have a grasp of how to build resources, the chapter concludes by introducing you to Librarian, a sample application used in later chapters to illustrate various aspects of Palm OS programming.

## Building Forms with Constructor

To create a new form in Constructor, select the gray Forms bar in the project window and then select Edit ⇨ New Form Resource or just press Ctrl-K. Double-clicking the name of the newly created form, or selecting it and pressing Enter, opens the *form layout window* (see Figure 7-1). The form layout window is where you add, position, and modify the user interface elements in a particular form.

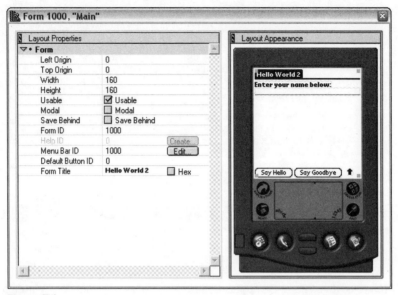

Figure 7-1

The right side of the form layout window, labeled Layout Appearance, displays the form and provides a workspace for selecting, positioning, and resizing the form's contents. Layout Properties, on the left side, shows a list of properties for whatever object is currently selected in the right side of the window.

*When you create a form, the object ID numbers in the Layout Appearance part of the form layout window tend to obscure the user interface objects, making it difficult to see what the completed form will look like. To hide the object IDs, click anywhere in the form display and then select Layout ⇨ Hide Object IDs.*

Simply click an object to select it. You may position a selected object by dragging it around the Layout Appearance view. Use your keyboard's arrow keys to make fine adjustments, one pixel at a time, to an object's position. Dragging the black boxes in the corners of an object resizes it.

Constructor also provides another way to view and select a form's contents. The *Hierarchy window* (see Figure 7-2) lists a form and its contents. To open the Hierarchy window, select Layout ⇨ Show Object Hierarchy or press Ctrl-H.

| Object Type | | Object ID | Title |
|---|---|---|---|
| Form | | 1000 | Main |
| Field | | 1001 | Name |
| Button | | 1002 | Hello |
| Button | | 1003 | Goodbye |
| Graffiti Shift Indicator | | 1004 | Unnamed1004 |
| Label | | 1099 | Unnamed1099 |

Figure 7-2

Selecting an object in the Hierarchy window also selects that object in the form layout window. Likewise, picking different objects from the form layout window changes which object is selected in the Hierarchy window.

> *If your form contains objects that overlap or completely cover one another, it can be difficult to select them in the Layout Appearance side of the form layout window. Use the Hierarchy window to select objects that are buried under other objects.*

The *Catalog window* (see Figure 7-3) is the source for all new form objects. To open the Catalog window, select Window ➪ Catalog or press Ctrl-Y.

**Figure 7-3**

Creating new objects on a form is a simple matter of dragging the appropriate object from the Catalog window to the form layout window, where you can resize and set the new object's properties. You also may copy objects from other forms, even forms in other projects, and paste them into a new form. To copy an object, select it in either the form layout window or the Hierarchy window, and then select Edit ➪ Copy Object or press Ctrl-C. Paste an object into a form by selecting Edit ➪ Paste Object or pressing Ctrl-V. Objects copied in this way retain most of their original properties; Constructor changes only the object ID to a number appropriate to the object's new form.

> *You can save time designing an interface by copying and pasting from the sample applications provided by PalmSource or from other applications you have written yourself. Copying resources from the built-in applications also ensures that your own program has a similar look and feel to the applications with which most Palm OS users are familiar. If you want to use many of the elements in an existing project, you can also open the project and use the File ➪ Save A Copy As command to create a fresh copy of the project, which you can then modify.*

If you want to center an object on a form, either horizontally or vertically, Constructor can do it for you, even though the process is convoluted. Constructor has a center command, but it cannot be used with a single object; it can be used only with groups of two or more selected objects. Follow these steps to center an object horizontally:

1. Select multiple objects in the form that you wish to center. If you want to center only one object, create a temporary dummy object (a button is a good choice) that you can delete later.

2. Select Arrange ⇨ Spread Horizontally in Container. Constructor arranges the objects so that they span the entire width of the form. One object should be touching the left edge and another should be touching the right edge, with any other objects in the selected group distributed evenly across the form.

3. Select Arrange ⇨ Align Centers Horizontally. Constructor centers all the selected objects horizontally in the form.

4. If you created a dummy object in Step 1, delete it. The other object remains centered after you delete the dummy.

To center an object vertically in a form, follow the previous instructions but substitute the Arrange ⇨ Spread Vertically in Container and Arrange ⇨ Align Centers Vertically commands for the menu commands in Steps 2 and 3.

You also can quickly duplicate a selected object by choosing Edit ⇨ Duplicate Object or by pressing Ctrl-D.

To delete an object, select it in the form layout window or the Hierarchy window and then select Edit ⇨ Clear Object or just press Delete.

# Building Menus with Constructor

The system of menus for a particular form consists of two kinds of resources: a *menu bar* and one or more *menu* resources. A menu bar serves as a container for menus, holding the title of each individual menu. Tapping the title of a menu in the menu bar displays that menu's contents, just as in most of the graphical interfaces used on desktop computers.

To create a new menu bar, select the gray Menu Bar line in the project window and then choose Edit ⇨ New Menu Bar Resource or press Ctrl-K. Double-clicking the name of a menu bar resource in the project window, or selecting one and pressing Enter, opens the *menu bar editor window*. When first opened, the menu bar editor window is blank. Figure 7-4 shows the menu bar editor window, both before and after adding menus to a menu bar.

You may add a new menu to a menu bar by selecting Edit ⇨ New Menu or pressing Ctrl-M. Constructor creates a menu called "untitled" and highlights the menu title for editing. To change the menu title, type its new name. If you want to change the menu title at a later time, click the title once to highlight the title text and then type the desired name. If you find that you have created a menu in error, you may remove it by selecting the menu title and then choosing Edit ➪ Remove Menu. You also can change the sequence in which menus appear in the menu bar by dragging them to the appropriate location with the mouse.

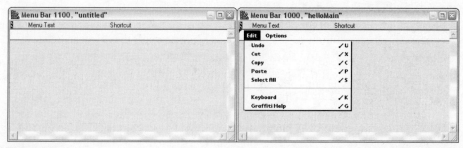

Figure 7-4

In general, clicking any item in the menu bar editor window, whether it is a menu title or menu item, puts that text into *edit mode*. While in edit mode, typing changes the text of the item and Constructor's Edit menu displays different commands that are associated with text editing. Edit mode pops up by default when you click an item, which can be a nuisance if you want only to select the item instead of edit its contents. To depart from edit mode and leave the item selected, simply press Enter.

Once you have a new menu, you need to add items to it. Ensure that the appropriate menu is selected and then choose Edit ➪ New Menu Item or press Ctrl-K to create a new item. When the new menu item appears, type the text that should appear in that item.

You also may enter a Graffiti command shortcut for the menu item. While the item's text is in edit mode, press the Tab key; a highlighted area appears to the right of the menu item. Type the character you wish to use for this menu item's command shortcut. Constructor automatically assigns the key you type to the menu item as its command shortcut.

> *If a menu item is selected but is not currently in edit mode, pressing Tab causes the item to enter edit mode. From there, you can simply press Tab a second time to add a command shortcut.*

Besides normal menu items, you also may add *separator lines* to visually group menu items. To add a separator line, select Edit ➪ New Separator Item or press Ctrl--. You also may turn any normal menu item into a separator by changing its text caption to a single hyphen (-).

To reorder a menu, you may drag menu items with the mouse to new locations within the current menu; by dragging an item over the menu titles, you may move an item from one menu to another. You also may delete a selected menu item by choosing Edit ➪ Clear Menu Item or pressing the Backspace or Delete keys.

> *If an item is in edit mode, the Backspace and Delete keys edit the item's text instead of removing the item from the menu, and the Clear Menu Item command does not appear in the Edit menu. Press Enter to leave edit mode, and then try removing the menu item.*

## Adding Command Shortcuts to Menus

Command shortcuts are a great way to make menu commands quickly accessible to users who are adept at Graffiti. A short command stroke, followed by a single Graffiti character, activates the appropriate menu command without the user having to open and navigate the menu itself.

You should include command shortcuts for any menu item that might be frequently used. The standard text-editing commands of the Edit menu are a good example; they allow the user quickly to cut, copy, and paste text without removing the stylus from the Graffiti entry area of the screen. Commands that create new records or delete existing records also are good candidates for command shortcuts. However, anything that the user is less likely to use on a regular basis should not have a command shortcut. The best example of a command that does not require a shortcut is a menu item to display an application's "about" box.

The Palm OS built-in applications make use of several common shortcuts. Consider adding these shortcuts to your own application to make its interface consistent with the default Palm OS applications.

| Menu | Command | Shortcut |
|---|---|---|
| Record | New <item> | N |
| | Delete <item> | D |
| | Beam <item> | B |
| Edit | Undo | U |
| | Cut | X |
| | Copy | C |
| | Paste | P |
| | Select All | S |
| | Keyboard | K |
| | Graffiti Help | G |
| Options | Preferences | R |

When you add a menu in the menu bar editor window, Constructor automatically creates a separate menu resource, gives it its own resource ID, and associates it with its menu bar. When you close the menu bar editor window, the project window updates to display any newly created menus in its Menus category. You may edit each menu individually by double-clicking its name in the project window, or by selecting it and pressing Enter, which opens the *menu editor window*. The menu editor window operates just like the menu bar editor, except that it can display only a single menu at a time. Because you can perform all the necessary menu-editing functions from the menu bar editor window, editing menus individually is never necessary.

> Manually changing the resource ID of a menu resource can corrupt the menu bar resources that Constructor generates. Leave the assignment of menu resource IDs to Constructor.

If you use the Auto Generate Header File option in the project window to create constant definitions for your resource IDs, be careful to name menu resources differently. Constructor uses the names displayed in the project window to create the constants; if two menus share the same name in the project window, the automatically generated header will define the same constant twice. The best way to avoid this is to change the name of each menu so that it starts with the name of the form it appears in. For example, if an application has two menus titled "Record" appearing in both the List and Edit views of an application, name the menus "List Record" and "Edit Record." When Constructor makes the header file, it then creates two constants called `ListRecordMenu` and `EditRecordMenu`.

## Sharing Menus Between Menu Bars

Although the process for doing so is not intuitive, you can share a menu between two or more menu bars. Menus that are common to more than one form in an application, such as the Edit menu for editing text in fields, are good candidates for sharing. Sharing a menu prevents you from having to create it twice in Constructor. Your application code can deal with the common menu code in one place instead of you having to repeat similar code in multiple locations throughout your program's source.

To share a menu between multiple menu bars, follow these steps:

1. Create the menu bar resources without adding any menus to them.

2. Open one of the menu bars and create the shared menu.

3. Close the menu bar containing the shared menu. Take note of the new menu resource that appears in the project window; this is the resource you will share with other menu bars.

4. Open another menu bar that should contain the shared menu. Position the menu bar editor window so that both it and the project window are visible.

5. Drag the menu resource from the project window into the menu bar editor window.

6. Close the menu bar editor window.

7. To share the menu with more menu bars, repeat Steps 4–6 for each menu bar that should contain the shared menu.

Now any changes to the shared menu will be reflected in all the menu bars containing that menu. If you have the Auto Generate Header File option checked in the project window, Constructor defines a single constant to represent the shared menu, which you can use throughout your code to refer to that menu, no matter which menu bar is currently displayed in the application.

If you find that you have shared a menu with a menu bar by mistake, you may remove the shared menu by selecting it in the menu bar editor window and choosing Edit ➪ Remove Menu. Removing a menu in this fashion, whether it is shared or not, removes only a reference to that menu resource from the menu bar; the actual menu resource remains in the Menus category of the project window. To permanently delete a menu, select it in the project window and choose Edit ➪ Clear Resource or press the Delete or Backspace keys.

# Building Forms with Palm OS Resource Editor

To create a new form in Palm OS Resource Editor, select the `AppResources.xrd` entry in the Files panel of the Resource Editor window and either right-click and select New Resource from the pop-up menu or select Edit ➪ New Resource from the main menu. If there are other forms already existing in your applications resources, you can also simply select the Forms entry in the Files panel of the Resource Editor and press the Insert key on your keyboard. Finally, if you are in a Windows Explorer folder view of your project, you can double-click the `.XRD` file to open it.

Your new form is automatically opened in a window in design mode within the main panel of the Resource Editor (see Figure 7-5). This window contains a WYSIWYG view of your form as it will appear in your application, and it also contains a toolbar that allows you to select new form user interface elements and add them to your form.

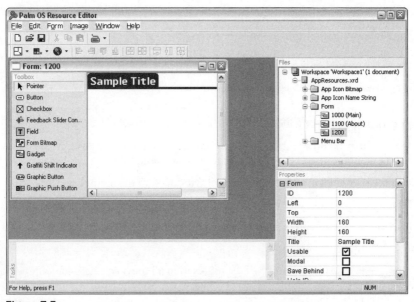

Figure 7-5

Underneath the Files panel of the Resource Editor is the Properties panel. You will notice that when you created your new form, a new entry was created for you in the Files panel under the Forms folder. (If this was the first form in your application, it would have an ID of 1000.) In the Properties panel, various attributes for your new form are displayed and may be modified if you wish.

In general, you add new user interface elements, or objects, to your form by dragging them with your mouse from the Toolbar onto your form. When you release your mouse button, the element is placed on your form. At this point the new element has the main input focus and its attributes are now displayed in the Properties panel. You can also resize an element on your form by selecting it and positioning the mouse cursor above one of the draggable sizer controls located around the border of the element and dragging the border until the size is what you want.

You can move your object when it's selected by using the arrow keys on your keyboard, which moves the object one pixel at a time in the appropriate direction. Finally, you can directly change the size and position coordinates for the currently selected object by clicking the attributes in the Properties panel. Note that some object types such as buttons and fields have a left, top, width, and height attribute. Other types, such as labels, have a left and top but the width and height are automatically determined by the contents of the label.

If you have other forms in your application, you can copy and paste form elements from other forms onto your new form. To copy a form element, select it in the window and choose Edit ➪ Copy or press Ctrl-C. To paste the copied element onto the same form or a different form, select Edit ➪ Paste or press Ctrl-V. Your new element will be automatically assigned a unique ID but will retain all other attributes from the original copied element.

To copy multiple items at the same time, you can select multiple objects by using Shift-left mouse click to add additional objects to your selection. Then use Copy and Paste to create duplicates of the original objects all at once.

> When you paste a copied object onto the same form as the original, Resource Editor will place the new object directly on top of the original object. Because this obscures the original, it can give the impression that a new copy was not created at all. To reveal the new and the original objects after pasting, use the arrow keys to move the new object, which will reveal the original that was hidden underneath the copy.

Aside from copying form elements singly or in groups, you can also copy entire forms. This provides a nice way to reuse a particular layout from one form to another. To do this, right-click your mouse on the form ID listed in the Files panel. Choose Edit ➪ Copy or press Ctrl-C. Now choose Edit ➪ Paste or press Ctrl-V. Resource Editor will ask you if you wish to replace an existing form or create a new one with a unique ID. If your goal is to create a new form using the original as a design template, choose "Unique ID"; your form will be created with a new unique form ID.

Resource Editor supports several convenient menu options that can help you automatically size and align multiple objects so that they look good on your form. For example, it is a common task to align all of your push buttons along the bottom of your form horizontally, or align labels along the left side of your form vertically. To do this, simply select all of the objects that you wish to align and choose the Form menu. In the Form menu you will see menu options that allow you to align left, center or right, vertically or horizontally, and also options for making all of the selected objects the same width, height, or size.

If you need to remove an object from a form, simply select it in your form window and press the Delete key, or choose the Edit ➪ Clear menu option.

# Building Menus with Palm OS Resource Editor

To create a new menu in Palm OS Resource Editor, select the AppResources.xrd entry in the Files panel of the Resource Editor window and either right-click and select New Resource from the pop-up menu or select Edit ▷ New Resource ▷ Menu Bar. If there are other menu bars already existing in your applications resources, you can also simply select the Menu Bar entry in the Files panel of the Resource Editor and press the Insert key on your keyboard.

Your new menu bar is automatically opened in a window in design mode within the main panel of the Resource Editor (see Figure 7-6). This window contains a hierarchical view of your menu bar and menu items. You will notice also that a new Menu resource appears in the Files panel, with an automatically generated unique ID. This ID value is what is set in a form's Menu ID property if you wish to associate a menu with a form.

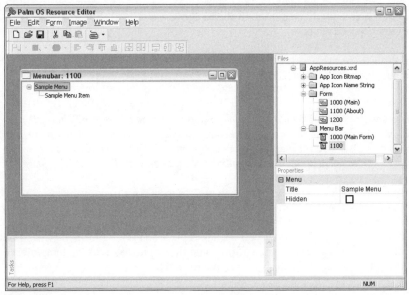

Figure 7-6

The system of menus for a particular form consists of two kinds of resources: a *menu bar* and one or more *menu resources*. A menu bar serves as a container for menus, holding the title of each individual menu. Tapping the title of a menu in the menu bar displays that menu's contents, just as in most of the graphical interfaces used on desktop computers.

In Resource Editor, the top-level item in the visual hierarchy is the menu bar, and the items underneath the menu bar are menu items. In the Properties panel, when a menu bar resource is selected for editing, you can set properties for your menu that control how it appears in your application. Although Resource Editor gives your menu bar a default title, you can change this to the value you wish to appear in your application.

A single menu item is created by default for new menu bars. Selecting a menu item displays a slightly different set of properties in the Properties panel. Once again you can change the default text value for your menu, but for menu items you also assign menu IDs and commands.

You can add more menu items by selecting a menu item and pressing the Insert key. A new menu item with a default title of "Untitled" is created for you directly above the currently selected menu item. To delete a menu item, select the item and press the Delete key. To reorder your menu items, select an item and press the right mouse button, which causes a pop-up context menu to appear. Selecting Move Up or Move Down reorders the menu item within your menu bar's list of items.

The Command property allows you to associate a Graffiti command shortcut for the menu item. Type the character you wish to use for this menu item's command shortcut. Resource Editor automatically assigns the key you type to the menu item as its command shortcut.

# Understanding Form Object Properties

As we've seen, both Constructor and Resource Editor allow you to edit properties associated with form elements, or the form itself. As you use your mouse to select the objects contained in a form, the editing tool reflects the properties that are relevant to the selected form or object.

Form objects have common properties that are found in nearly every object type. There are also a number of individual form object properties that are unique to one or more object types. This section covers both common and individual form object properties which are editable in either Constructor or Resource Editor. (In those few instances where there are variations in property availability or naming in Constructor and Resource Editor, the difference is noted.)

## Common Form Object Properties

Many form objects share common properties, which are described as follows:

❑ **Comment (Resource Editor Only).** The comment property gives you the opportunity to enter notes about an object that will provide helpful information to you and other developers in understanding the object. This is similar to adding comments in your C/C++ source code.

❑ **Object Identifier (Referred to as "ID" in Resource Editor).** Not to be confused with an object's resource ID, the Object Identifier allows you to give a name to an object that is more readable than the numeric resource ID. In Constructor, the Object Identifier also appears next to objects in the Hierarchy window.

❑ **Left Origin and Top Origin (Referred to as "Left" and "Top" in Resource Editor).** These two properties control the location of the upper-left corner of the object in relation to the screen. The upper-left corner of the screen has the coordinates (0, 0). Coordinates increase from left to right and from top to bottom, with the lower-right corner having the coordinates (159, 159).

*If you are writing an application for a high-density handheld with a 320 × 320 pixel display, you are still limited to a 160 × 160 grid when placing user interface objects. Palm OS draws the high-density user interface with more detail, but the objects on a form still occupy the same percentage of screen space as they would on a low-density screen. For example, consider a button that is 35 pixels wide by 12 pixels high. If you place the button at coordinates (1, 147) in the 160 × 160 grid (the bottom-left corner of the screen), the operating system draws the button at coordinates (2, 294) and doubles the size of the button to 70 × 24. The operating system uses the extra resolution it has at its disposal to draw rounder corners on the button and to render the button's text in a high-resolution font.*

*If you want to draw on the screen using the 320 × 320 grid, you must perform such drawing manually; user interface objects always align to a 160 × 160 grid. For more details about high-density drawing, see Chapter 11.*

❑ **Width and Height.** These properties control the width and height of the object in pixels. Most form objects support a width and height property.

❑ **Font.** Many user interface objects display text as part of the object. The Font property controls which font Palm OS uses to draw the object's text. The following table shows examples of the available fonts, both low-density and double-density. Palm OS identifies fonts by means of an enumerated type called `FontID`. Table 7-1 also lists the constants in the `FontID` enumeration.

| Font Name | # | FontID Constant | Example |
| --- | --- | --- | --- |
| Standard | 0 | stdFont | The quick brown fox jumps over<br>The quick brown fox jumps over |
| Bold | 1 | boldFont | **The quick brown fox jumps**<br>**The quick brown fox jumps** |
| Large | 2 | largeFont | The quick brown fox<br>The quick brown fox |
| Symbol | 3 | symbolFont | ◀▮▶▲▼▾↓ ↑ ↟🗋1↥•↘<br>◀▮▶▲▼▾↓ ↑ 🗋1↥•↘ |
| Symbol 11 | 4 | symbol11Font | ☑◀▶🛈<br>☑◀▶🛈 |
| Symbol 7 | 5 | symbol7Font | ▲▼▲▼<br>▲▼▲▼ |
| LED | 6 | ledFont | „e0123456789<br>„e0123456789 |
| Bold 12 | 7 | largeBoldFont | **The quick brown fox**<br>**The quick brown fox** |

❑ **Usable.** If an object's Usable property is unchecked, Palm OS neither draws the object nor allows user interaction with the object. Application code can set the Usable property of an object at runtime. This allows for user interface elements that are hidden when the application first displays a form and then appear in response to user input. For example, if a button is dependent on a check box being selected, your application can start with the button hidden, and then reveal the button when the user taps the check box. Chapter 8 contains further information on changing the Usable property.

# *Individual Form and Form Object Properties*

The following section explains various properties that are specific to individual forms and form object types. Where appropriate, the object descriptions also contain guidelines for properly using each object.

## *Forms*

The property that affects how a form behaves the most is its Modal property. If Modal is checked, Palm OS draws the form with a border and ignores stylus taps outside the form's edges. Check the Modal property when creating a dialog box and leave it unchecked for full-screen views.

Another property that forms have is Save Behind. When Palm OS draws a form with the Save Behind property checked, the system saves the region of the screen occupied by the form and then redraws that region after erasing the form. This can save some time when the application returns from a dialog form because the form underneath does not have to redraw all its contents, just the portion that was covered by the dialog form.

> *There is one case where the system may not restore the pixels behind a modal form. If there is not enough memory available to save the screen area behind the modal form, Palm OS instead posts a `frmUpdate` event to the underlying form, requesting that the underlying form redraw its contents. In fact, the debug versions of Palm OS 3.5 and later, as well as the release version of Palm OS 5, always post an update event in lieu of saving the screen area behind a modal form. Relying on the Save Behind property to redraw a form for you may not always work, so be sure that any form that has modal dialog boxes displayed over it handles frmUpdate in its event handler.*

So when should you use the Save Behind property? To illustrate, imagine an application with two forms, called A and B. If you open form B over the top of form A, and form A is not likely to change its contents while covered, form B should have the Save Behind attribute set. Likewise, if form A might change its contents while form B is open, not setting Save Behind on form B is a better idea, because form A will need to redraw its contents anyhow, and saving the area behind form B is simply a waste of system resources. The Save Behind flag should not be set for modal dialog boxes in Palm OS Cobalt.

You can set the title of the form by changing the Form Title property. In full-screen forms, the system draws the title left-justified at the top of the form; in modal dialog boxes, the title is centered. Regardless of whether the form is modal or not, the title can contain only a single line of text.

In modal dialog boxes, you may set the Help ID to the resource ID of a string resource. If Help ID is set, the operating system draws a small "i" icon in the upper-right corner of the form's title bar. Tapping the icon displays the string resource in a dialog box labeled "Tips." You can provide the user with online help for dialog boxes using the Help ID mechanism.

Setting a form's Menu ID attaches a specific menu bar resource to that form. When the user taps the Menu silkscreen button, the system displays the menu attached to the currently displayed form. Creating menu resources is covered later in this chapter.

Default Button ID specifies which button the operating system should pick in a modal dialog box if the user switches to another application instead of exiting a dialog box after having made a button choice. Default Button ID should contain the resource ID of the appropriate button.

A modal dialog box should occupy the entire width of the screen and rest at the bottom, obscuring any command buttons in the application beneath it and leaving the application's title bar, if any, visible. At least three pixels of space should separate the top of the dialog box's title bar from the bottom of the application's title bar; if the dialog box is too large to allow this, the dialog box should occupy the whole screen.

*The border around a modal dialog box is not included in the width and height that you set for a form, so you should allow for an extra two pixels on the sides, top, and bottom of the form. For example, a full-screen modal dialog box should have both its Left Origin and Top Origin set to 2, and its Width and Height set to 156.*

## Buttons

The Anchor Left property of a button does not actually do anything. Anchor Left is useful in some other controls, such as pop-up triggers and selector triggers, but it serves no useful purpose for buttons, so you can safely ignore it.

Check the Frame property to give the button a frame, which Palm OS draws as a rectangle with rounded corners. Most buttons should have a frame.

Non-Bold Frame controls the thickness of the frame to draw around the button. When checked, the system draws the button with a single-pixel frame. Left unchecked, Non-Bold Frame causes the button to have a bold, two-pixel frame. By default, buttons in Palm OS applications should have non-bold frames.

The Label field controls the text displayed in the button. The system draws button labels centered in the middle of the button, clipping the left and right edges if the text is longer than the width of the button.

In Palm OS 3.5 and later, you can create a graphic button, which displays a graphic image instead of text. A graphic button has two bitmaps associated with it — one that normally appears on the button and another that shows up only when the user taps the button. Set the normal image by entering the resource ID of an existing bitmap resource into the Bitmap Resource field, and set the image to display while selected in the Selected Bitmap field.

*Although prior to Palm OS 3.5 you could not use a bitmap as a button's label, it is still possible to make a button that appears to have a picture on it. Simply create a form bitmap resource at the same size as the button and place both the button and the bitmap in the same location on the form.*

## Check Boxes

The Selected property of a check box controls whether or not the box should appear checked by default when Palm OS draws it on a form. If Selected is checked, so is the check box.

You can group multiple check boxes together to make them mutually exclusive using the Group ID property. Only one check box in a group sharing the same Group ID may be checked at a time. Be sure to set the Selected property of only one check box in a group; setting more than one causes strange behavior at runtime.

*Mutually exclusive check boxes can be confusing to the user; normally, you should use check boxes to allow the user to select several options at a time. If only one option may be selected at a time, use push buttons, a pop-up menu, or a selector trigger.*

In label controls the text is displayed to the right of the check box. Tapping the text in the label toggles the check box just as if the box itself had been tapped. In fact, if you size a check box larger than just the area occupied by its box and label, all the space surrounding the check box, out to the edges of its height and width, will toggle the box when it's tapped.

*Although the check box resource does not offer an option to create a label to the left of the check box, it is possible to create one yourself. Leave the Label property of the check box blank and then create a separate label resource and place it to the left of the check box. Even though the user cannot toggle the check box by tapping this label, tapping the box itself still performs the expected toggling.*

## *Fields*

A text field's Editable property controls whether the user may change the contents of the field. When Editable is checked, the field is user-editable; when it's unchecked, the field does not accept user input. Your application may still change the contents of the field programmatically, even when Editable is not set. A noneditable text field can be used to display variable-length text without resorting to the basic Palm OS drawing APIs to manually write characters to the screen.

*Underline controls whether a field should have a gray (dotted) underline under each row of text. If this property is checked, the field is underlined. Otherwise, the field's text appears without an underline. Editable text fields should always have an underline; without an underline, there is no indication to the user—other than a blinking cursor—that the field even exists.*

Check the Single Line property to create a *single-line field*. This displays only one line of text; it does not accept Tab or Return characters. Depending on the version of Palm OS you are using, attempting to enter text past the end of the line causes the system either to scroll the text to the left or enter characters invisibly at the end of the field. When the Single Line property is not checked, the field becomes a *multi-line field*. This scrolls when the user enters more text than the field can display at once or when the user drags the stylus to select text outside what the field is currently displaying.

The Dynamic Size property, when checked, tells the field to put a `fldChangedEvent` in the event queue when the user enters enough text to cause the field to scroll either up or down. You can intercept this event in your code to allow your application to resize the field as the user enters text. See Chapter 8 for details about handling `fldHeightChangedEvent`.

If a field's Editable property is not set, the Left Justified check box becomes available. Leaving Left Justified checked means that text in the field is justified to the field's left margin; unchecking Left Justified changes the field to right justification. Note that user-editable fields cannot be right-aligned, which is why this property cannot be changed when Editable is checked.

Max Characters sets the maximum number of characters that the field can contain. Palm OS has an absolute maximum of 32,767 characters in a single field. All fields require a Max Characters value if they are to work properly.

If Auto Shift is checked, Palm OS version 2.0 and later will perform automatic capitalization at the beginning of sentences in this field. Setting this property is a good idea in order to maintain consistency with other Palm applications.

The Has Scroll Bar property, when checked, causes the field to put more `fldChangedEvent` events onto the queue. Setting this property is important for text fields with associated scroll bar resources that must be updated regularly as the contents of the field change. For example, the text field that makes up most of the edit view in Memo Pad has this property set to ensure that the scroll bar is properly updated as the user edits text in the field. See Chapter 8 for more information about implementing scrolling text fields.

When checked, the Numeric property restricts character entry to numbers. The field will ignore any input that does not consist of numeric characters (0–9) or the decimal character, as currently defined in the Palm OS number format settings.

> **In versions of Palm OS prior to Palm OS Garnet, it is still possible to paste non-numeric data into a numeric field from the Clipboard, so you cannot rely entirely on the Numeric property to validate the text field's contents.**

## Form Bitmaps

A form bitmap resource serves as an anchor to attach a bitmap resource to a form. The form bitmap's Bitmap Resource ID property contains the resource ID of an existing bitmap. You also may click the Create button in the Bitmap Resource ID field to open the standard bitmap editor; in this case, Constructor creates the bitmap resource for you and assigns its resource ID to the form bitmap's Bitmap Resource ID property.

## Gadgets

Other than setting its position and size, you really can't do a whole lot with a gadget resource at design time. Everything interesting about a gadget occurs at runtime. Chapter 8 contains further information about programming gadget resources.

## Graffiti Shift Indicator

Any form that contains an editable text field should have a Graffiti shift indicator. Only one indicator should be placed on a form; extra shift indicators are not only redundant, they also confuse the Palm OS field-handling routines, resulting in unpredictable field behavior. Place a Graffiti shift indicator in the lower-right corner of a form. Once it has been placed on a form, you can effectively ignore a Graffiti shift indicator when developing your application; Palm OS handles updating the indicator automatically.

## Labels

A label lets you add text to a form that the user cannot edit. Changing a label at runtime through code also is rather limited. Any new text you assign to a label using the `FrmCopyLabel` function may be no longer than the original text, as defined in the Constructor label resource. If your application needs to display only a small amount of changeable text, `FrmCopyLabel` works well, but labels are not well suited to displaying large amounts of dynamic text. Labels are intended for static text display only, such as identifiers next to pop-up triggers or the text in an "about" box.

*If you want to display a large amount of text on the screen that the application can update, but the user cannot change, you have a couple of options. If the text your application displays does not require complex formatting, use a non-editable text field. If your application needs finer control over how the text appears onscreen, such as columnar or other complex formatting, use the* `WinDrawChars` *function to write the text to the screen manually. See Chapter 10 for details on using* `WinDrawChars`.

The Text property of a label contains the text it should display. Keep in mind when editing the Text property that a label's text may contain multiple lines. Pressing Enter while editing a label's caption inserts a line break into the text displayed by the label.

## Lists

List resources serve double-duty. By themselves, lists are stationary interface elements that occupy space on a form. When combined with a pop-up trigger resource, lists consist of hidden elements that appear for selection only when the user needs them. List properties must be set a little differently, depending upon whether or not you plan to use them as-is or in conjunction with pop-up triggers.

A list resource does not have a Height property. Instead, you control how tall the list is by specifying in the Visible Items property the number of rows the list should display. If the list contains more items than the value of the Visible Items property, the list contains arrow buttons to allow scrolling.

If you specify a value of zero for Visible Items, Palm OS will draw all items in the list. Constructor does not show any rows for a list with zero Visible Items, but the operating system draws them anyway, which can result in a bit of a mess if you have another interface element in the "empty" space below the list. You should usually use a Visible Items setting of zero only when the list is intended as a pop-up. Specifying a positive value for Visible Items in a non-pop-up list ensures that the list looks exactly the way you want it to at runtime.

---

**Setting Visible Items to a value greater than the number of items actually in the list can result in an error. If you plan to fill the list dynamically at runtime, you must either include enough placeholder list items to equal or exceed the Visible Items setting or you must call `LstSetListChoices` to set the number of items in the list.**

---

For lists that appear as part of a form's regular interface, be sure to check the Usable property. A pop-up list should have the Usable property turned off to keep the system from drawing it on the form until the user taps its associated pop-up trigger.

To add items to a list, select the List Items row in the Layout Properties side of the form layout window. Then, select Edit ➪ New Item Text or press Ctrl-K. You can remove list items by selecting them and then choosing Edit ➪ Clear Item Text or by pressing Backspace.

When Palm OS displays a list attached to a pop-up trigger, the list appears in the position specified by its Top Origin and Left Origin properties, not relative to the location of the pop-up trigger. Be sure to place the list so that it covers the entire pop-up trigger to prevent ugly bits of the trigger from peeking around the edges of the displayed list. If your pop-up list needs to change location, you must handle this yourself in code. For example, the pop-up triggers for selecting a type of phone number in the Address Book application's Edit view are part of a table, so the program cannot assume that they will always be in the same position. Address Book handles this by changing the location of the phone number type list before displaying it. Chapter 8 explains how to change the location dynamically of a pop-up list.

## *Pop-up Triggers*

A pop-up trigger is useful only when combined with a list resource, but it does not necessarily need to display an item from its attached list. The Label property controls the text initially displayed in a pop-up trigger's label when the system first draws the pop-up trigger control. By default, the system changes a pop-up trigger's label to the most recently selected list item in the pop-up's attached list but you can modify the label in code if you want to display something other than a list value. For example, the Details dialog box in the built-in To Do application has a Due Date pop-up, which displays an actual date instead of "Today," "Tomorrow," or the other values in the pop-up trigger's associated list. Dynamically changing a pop-up trigger's label in response to user input is covered in Chapter 8.

Set the List ID property to the resource ID of the list that the pop-up trigger should display when tapped.

When the pop-up trigger's label text changes, the width of the entire pop-up control also changes to accommodate the new label. Text longer than the current label causes the trigger to grow, whereas shorter text shrinks the control's width. The Anchor Left property, when checked, nails down the left side of the control, causing the right end of the trigger to do all the growing and shrinking. Unchecking Anchor Left reverses this behavior, fixing the position of the right side of the pop-up trigger and causing the system to resize the left end of the control.

> *Keep in mind when designing a form that the size of a trigger is dynamic; user interface elements on the sizable end of a pop-up trigger could collide with the trigger's label if it grows long enough.*

A common use for a pop-up trigger with the Anchor Left property unchecked is for a right-justified category selector in the upper-right corner of the application. Category pop-up triggers in the built-in applications have the following properties:

❑   Left Origin: 160

❑   Top Origin: 0

❑   Width: 0

❑   Height: 13

❑   Anchor Left: Unchecked

## *Push Buttons*

Push buttons are the Palm OS equivalent of radio buttons in other graphical user interfaces, like Windows or Mac OS. Like check boxes, push buttons have a Group ID property to assign a number of push buttons to an exclusive group. Only one push button in a particular group may be selected at a time. Unlike check boxes, it does not make sense to leave push buttons with a Group ID of zero. Push buttons should always occur in groups, never individually; however, Palm OS does not enforce this.

Set the text inside a push button by editing its Label property. Like that on regular buttons, push button text is centered and clipped at the edges of the button.

In Palm OS 3.5 and later, you may create a graphic push button, which can display an image instead of text. Like a graphic button, there are two images associated with a graphic push button, one for normal display and one that appears when the user taps the push button. Set the normal image in the Bitmap ID field and the selected image in the Selected Bitmap ID field.

There is no way to set at design time whether a push button is selected or not. You must set the currently selected push button in a group through code when you initialize the form containing the push buttons. See Chapter 8 for more information about initializing push buttons.

A group of push buttons should be arranged either in a single row or a single column. Buttons in a row should all have the same height; likewise, buttons in a column should all be the same width. Adjacent push buttons share a border with each other, resulting in a single-pixel line between buttons.

Unfortunately, there is no simple way to create a series of push buttons all at once. You must create each button in a group individually, manually sizing it to match the other buttons' height or width. The quickest way to create consistently sized push buttons is to make one button with the proper size and then select Edit ⇨ Duplicate Object or press Ctrl-D to make an exact copy of it.

To align a series of push buttons so that their tops are aligned and they all share edges with one another, do the following:

1.  Select all the push buttons you wish to align.

2.  Choose Arrange ⇨ Arrange Objects to display the Arrange Objects dialog box. In Windows, you may also press Ctrl-L; in Mac OS, press Command-L.

3.  Click the second button from the left in the Vertical panel. This button aligns the tops of the push buttons.

4.  Click the rightmost button in the Horizontal panel and then enter **-1** in the pixels text box. This step arranges the push buttons so that their sides touch one another, with a one-pixel overlap so they will share edges.

5.  Click Apply.

To align a series of push buttons so their left sides are aligned and they all share top or bottom edges with one another, do the following:

1.  Select all the push buttons you wish to align.

2.  Choose Arrange ⇨ Arrange Objects to display the Arrange Objects dialog box. In Windows, you may also press Ctrl+-; in Mac OS, press Command-L.

3.  Click the second button from the left in the Horizontal panel. This button aligns the left sides of the push buttons.

4.  Click the rightmost button in the Vertical panel and then enter **-1** in the pixels text box. This step arranges the push buttons so that their tops and bottoms touch one another, with a one-pixel overlap so they will share edges.

5.  Click Apply.

If you wish to position push buttons manually, you can use the arrow keys to perform fine adjustments to the buttons' positions or just fill in the Top Origin and Left Origin properties. Either of these can be less frustrating than using the mouse to move the buttons into their final positions.

## Repeating Buttons

The properties of a repeating button are exactly the same as those of a regular button; only the button's behavior is different. The built-in applications commonly use repeating buttons to provide scrolling. When used as a scroll button, a repeating button should not have a frame, and its Label property should contain a single arrow character from one of the Palm OS symbol fonts.

In Palm OS 3.5 and later, you may create a graphic repeating button, which can display an image instead of text. You can set the normal image for a graphic repeating button in the Bitmap Resource field and the selected image in the Selected Bitmap field.

## Scroll Bars

A scroll bar resource can scroll only vertically, so you should not alter the default width of 7 pixels that Constructor provides. Height is another story; a scroll bar is usually as tall as the table or multiline text field it controls.

The Value, Min Value, Max Value, and Page Size properties affect the initial appearance and behavior of the *scroll car* — the black bar in the middle of the scroll bar. Min Value, usually zero, represents the numeric value of the scroll bar when the scroll car is at the top of the bar. Similarly, Max Value is the value when the scroll car is all the way at the bottom of the control. Value indicates the starting position of the scroll car when Palm OS initializes the scroll bar control. The Page Size property controls the number of units the scroll car moves when the user taps the gray area above or below the car. Units used by a scroll bar for these four properties are entirely arbitrary; it is up to the application to define what the units represent.

That said, most applications should probably leave the values of all four of these properties set to zero. The data associated with a scroll bar and displayed in an accompanying table or multiline text field is often dynamic in nature, requiring application code to initialize the scroll bar's properties at runtime. If the data controlled by a scroll bar in your application is static, you can get away with setting the scroll bar's properties at design time and leaving them alone, but more likely than not you will need to write code to handle initializing and updating the scroll bar. Setting a scroll bar's properties through code is covered in Chapter 8.

## Selector Triggers

A selector trigger performs a function similar to that provided by a pop-up trigger. Instead of displaying a list when tapped, though, a selector displays an entire dialog box for user input. After the user selects a value from the dialog box and returns to the form containing the selector trigger, the trigger displays a new value based on user input to its attached dialog box. The built-in applications often use selector triggers to invoke the date and time pickers, which are part of Palm OS itself. For other types of selection, you will need to supply your own dialog box as a modal form resource and display it in response to the user's tapping of the selector trigger. Chapter 8 discusses integrating the standard Palm OS date and time pickers into your application, as well as how to display modal forms.

Like the pop-up trigger, a selector trigger's Anchor Left property controls how the trigger resizes as its label text changes. When it is checked, the left side of the selector trigger is fixed in place; when it is unchecked, the right end of the trigger remains stationary.

The Label property provides a place to enter the text the selector trigger initially contains. Not only does the Label property control what displays in the control the first time the application displays the trigger, it also reserves memory space to contain the selector trigger's label. If you try to set a selector trigger's label to a string that is longer than the Label you set at design time, your program will probably crash because it will not have enough memory for the longer string. Be sure to set a Label that is large enough to contain the largest string the application might assign to the trigger label.

## Sliders

A slider's Minimum Value and Maximum Value properties control what value the left and right ends of the slider control represent. You also can set the Initial Value property to define where the thumb (the part of the slider that actually slides) appears on the slider — somewhere between the minimum and maximum values. You can control how far the thumb jumps when the user taps to either side of it by setting the Page Jump Amount property.

You can customize the look of a slider control by assigning bitmap images for its thumb and background. Change the thumb image by entering the resource ID of an existing bitmap into the Thumb Bitmap field and the background image by changing the Background property to an appropriate resource ID.

You can use one background bitmap for multiple sliders of varying width and height because the background bitmap does not have to be large enough to fill the boundaries of the slider control. If the bitmap's height is shorter than the height of the slider, the system centers the bitmap vertically within the slider's boundaries. If the bitmap is not as wide as the slider control, the system draws the bitmap twice. The first time the system draws the bitmap, it draws it against the left side of the slider's boundaries and then clips the right side at the slider's halfway point. The second drawing operation places the bitmap against the right side of the slider and clips its left end at the halfway point. The drawing mechanism described here means that the background image must be at least half as wide as any slider control it is assigned to, or there will be a gap in the middle of the slider.

The properties for a feedback slider are identical to those for a regular slider control.

## Tables

A table's Rows property controls the number of table rows visible at one time. Constructor divides the height of a table by its number of rows to determine how tall each row should be, so if you resize a table by changing its Height property, you also may need to change the Rows property to prevent stretching or shrinking the height of the individual rows.

> Be sure that your rows are all the same height. If a table is even a single pixel too short, the table's last row will not appear at runtime. Tables that are too tall or too short also may result in strange selection behavior or other bugs that are difficult to diagnose. The Height property for a table should be equal to the number of rows times the height of each row. For most tables that use the Standard font, each row should be 11 pixels high.

When you create a table, it already has one column defined. To add more columns, select Column Widths in the form layout window, and then choose Edit ⇨ New Column Width or press Ctrl-K. The value for each of the Column Width properties represents that column's width in pixels.

The types of data that may be displayed in each of a table's cells cannot be set at design time. Instead, you must initialize a table in code before your application can successfully interact with it. See Chapter 14 for more on initializing and using tables.

# Introducing Librarian, a Sample Application

After reading this chapter and Chapter 6, you should have a good grasp of how to create all the resources for a Palm OS application. At this point, I introduce Librarian, a sample application I wrote that appears in this and later chapters to illustrate various points of developing for Palm OS.

Librarian is a database for book collectors. Not only does it store the vital information about books in a collection, such as titles and authors, but because it runs on a handheld device it also allows a user to enter new books into the handheld while looking at them on the shelves, instead of having to drag a pile of them to a desktop computer. The application also can serve as a wish list of books not yet purchased, and it keeps track of books lent to or borrowed from other people.

Trying to fit every nuance of every part of Palm OS into a single application would produce a bloated monster application that would be difficult to use and require hideous amounts of storage space on a Palm OS device. Instead, Librarian focuses more on providing the right interfaces for given tasks, following Palm OS user interface and programming guidelines as closely as possible. In fact, you will notice that Librarian operates in similar fashion to the built-in Address Book application, from which Librarian draws much of its user interface.

That said, the Librarian program uses functions from throughout Palm OS, so it gives a good general picture of how the different parts of the operating system work together in an application. Elements of Palm OS not included in Librarian, such as serial communications, have their own, smaller examples in this book.

## Displaying Multiple Records in List View

The primary display in Librarian is the List view (see Figure 7-7). The List view displays multiple books in Librarian's database at once, providing a lot of information at a glance. When Librarian starts, this is the form it first displays.

Figure 7-7

A large table resource occupies most of the screen space in the List view. Scroll arrows in the lower-right corner of the screen allow the user to scroll the table to display more records; alternatively, pressing the scroll up and scroll down hardware buttons on the device serves the same function. Tapping a book's row in the table shows an expanded view of that particular book.

The pop-up list in the upper-right corner controls which category the List view displays. Users may assign books to different categories to organize them; selecting a category from the pop-up list restricts the display in the List view to books belonging to the selected category.

Two buttons across the bottom of the screen provide access to commonly used functions. The New button opens Librarian's Edit view, described later in the "Editing a Record in Edit View" section, with a blank book record ready for entry.

The Show button opens the Librarian Preferences dialog box (see Figure 7-8). This dialog box controls what information appears in the List view. The Show In List push buttons control both the information displayed for each book and the order in which Librarian sorts the books in the List view table. By default, Librarian displays the last name of the author, followed by the author's first name and the title of the book, sorted alphabetically by the author's last name. Four check boxes toggle the display of other properties associated with each book.

Figure 7-8

## Displaying an Individual Book in Record View

The Record view in Librarian, which is displayed when the user taps a book in the List view's table, shows all the information for a single book record (see Figure 7-9).

Figure 7-9

Because the information displayed in this form varies considerably from record to record, a structured user interface element, such as a table or field, does not work. Instead, Librarian uses custom drawing routines to draw the information straight onto the screen. However, it would be nice to allow the user quick access to the contents of the displayed record by tapping anywhere within the display, so the central portion of the Record view contains a large gadget control. The gadget serves to capture a tap from the user, as well as providing a defined rectangular screen area for the custom drawing routines to work with.

Scroll arrows appear in the lower right of the Record view if the currently displayed book contains more information than the Record view can display at once. The Done button returns to the List view, the Edit button opens the displayed record in Edit view, and the New button opens the Edit view with a blank record, ready for the user to enter data.

## Editing a Record in Edit View

Like the List view, the primary component of the Edit view is a table. The table has two columns, the left column displaying labels describing the contents of the items in the right column (see Figure 7-10).

**Figure 7-10**

Tapping the selector trigger in the upper-right corner displays a pop-up list of categories. Picking an item from the list changes the category of the currently displayed record. The Edit view uses a selector trigger for category selection instead of the pop-up trigger used in the List view, because the function of the category selector is different in Edit view than it is in List view: Choosing a category in Edit view changes the category of the currently displayed record, whereas choosing a category in List view changes which category of records is displayed.

Text fields in the Edit view are expandable, increasing or decreasing in height as necessary to accommodate whatever text the user enters. The user can enter previous and next field Graffiti strokes to move quickly between fields while entering data.

The Done button returns to the application's List view. Tapping Details opens the Book Details dialog box (see Figure 7-11). From this dialog box, the user may set the category of the current book record with the Category pop-up list. Checking the Private check box marks this record as private. If the user has assigned a password in the system's Security application and has chosen to hide private records, any book marked private in Librarian does not show up in the List view — or anywhere else in the application.

Figure 7-11

The Book Details dialog box's Delete button allows the user to delete the current book from Librarian's database. When it is tapped, the Delete Book dialog box appears (see Figure 7-12). The Delete Book dialog box not only confirms that the user really wishes to delete the book, but it offers the user the option to save an archive copy of the book's record on the desktop using Librarian's companion conduit application.

Figure 7-12

Tapping the Note button in the Book Details dialog box, or the Note button in the Edit form, opens Librarian's Note view (see Figure 7-13). This view allows the user to enter any information about the book that does not correspond to any of the regular record fields.

Figure 7-13

From a programming perspective, the Note view is particularly interesting because its resources are not part of the Librarian project itself. Instead, Librarian borrows the shared Note form used by the built-in applications. This form's resources are embedded in ROM along with the standard Palm OS applications, and the Palm OS header files define various constants for use with the Note form. Using the Note form in an application is covered in Chapter 16.

## Examining Librarian's Menus

The List view has a menu bar, providing access to other less frequently accessed functions. Menus in the List view menu bar are shown in Figure 7-14.

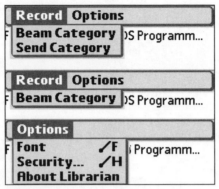

Figure 7-14

The two Record menus in Figure 7-14 appear only when Librarian is running on a Palm OS device that supports infrared beaming or sending records via other communication methods, such as Bluetooth or SMS. To accomplish the feat of displaying different menus on different devices, Librarian actually contains three menu bar resources for the List view: one with the Record menu and a Beam Category command (middle of Figure 7-14), one with a Record menu containing Beam Category and Send Category commands (top of Figure 7-14), and one without any Record menu at all (bottom of Figure 7-14). Code within the application determines whether the device on which Librarian is running is capable of beaming or sending records, and displays the appropriate menu bar resource. Chapter 8 details dynamically displaying menus, and Chapter 10 shows how to determine the features supported by the device on which an application is running.

The user may choose Font from the Options menu to open the Select Font dialog box (see Figure 7-15). Like the Note view, the Select Font dialog box is another form resource stored in ROM, so Librarian does not need to define this form in its own source code. Changing the font in this dialog box causes Librarian to change the font it uses to display information in the current view, allowing a user to customize the program for easier viewing.

The Security command in the Options menu displays the system Change Security dialog box (see Figure 7-16). The Change Security dialog box allows the user to choose how private records are displayed. They may be shown, hidden, or masked. Chapter 16 shows you how to integrate the system Change Security dialog box with your application.

Also available from the Options menu is an About Librarian menu command, which displays the About Librarian dialog box (see Figure 7-17). This dialog box is a simple "about" box, showing information about the Librarian application, such as its version number.

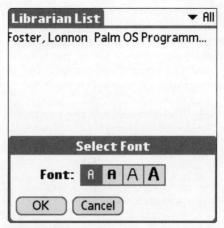

Figure 7-15

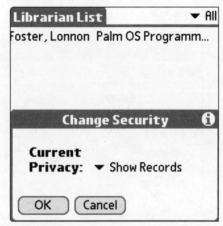

Figure 7-16

Figure 7-17

Librarian's Record view has a menu bar of its own. Like the Record menu in the List view, the Record view's Record menu contains an option related to beaming records, and another for sending records by other means. Unlike the List view menu, the Edit view's Record menu also contains items that are not related to beaming, so Librarian has three Record menus: one with the Beam Book option, one that includes the Beam Book and Send Book options, and one without either. The application displays the appropriate menu for the device on which Librarian is running.

Users can use the Record menu to delete the currently displayed book, duplicate it, attach a text note to it, or remove an existing note. If the device supports it, the user also may beam or send the current book record to another Palm OS device that has the Librarian application installed, adding the record to the Librarian database on the other device.

The Record view's menu bar also has an Options menu, which is the same as that used in the List view's menu bar, save for the absence of a Security option.

In the Edit view, Librarian has similar menus to those in the Record view, with the addition of an Edit menu to provide text-editing functions (see Figure 7-18). Again, there are three different Record menus in this menu bar: one for devices with IR beaming (top), one for devices with IR and other data-sending features (middle), and one for devices without IR capability (bottom).

Figure 7-18

Librarian makes economical use of menu resources by sharing a number of common menus among different forms. The Options menu is shared between the Record and Edit views. Librarian also shares the same Record menus between the Record and Edit views.

Sharing menu resources in this way removes duplicate code from the project because the application handles common menus with common routines. Such sharing reduces the complexity of the application, making it easier to debug and removing precious bytes from the size of the compiled executable. Chapter 8 contains more information about handling common menu items.

# Summary

In this chapter, you learned how to create forms and the user interface elements that they contain, as well as menu bars, menus, and menu items. After reading this chapter, you should understand the following:

❑ You use the *form layout window*, the *Hierarchy window*, and the *Catalog window* to create and edit form and menu resources in Metrowerks Constructor.

❑ Developers working with PODS can use Resource Editor to create and edit form and menu resources.

❑ Using either tool, you integrate forms and menus into your application by designing your form in the visual resource editor, setting common and object-specific properties and then interacting with those resources at runtime in your application source code.

8

# Programming
# User Interface Elements

Palm OS involves a lot of user interaction. Most Palm OS applications serve to collect and display data, and both functions require thoughtful user interface design and implementation if they are to be carried out effectively on such a small device. Earlier chapters showed you how to design and build the resources that make up a Palm OS application's user interface. This chapter shows you how to connect that interface with your application code, forming the vital link between the user and your program.

As you read through this chapter, you may notice a couple of what seem to be major omissions in our coverage of form objects: tables and scroll bars. Tables are the most complex user interface elements in Palm OS; as such, they warrant an entire chapter to themselves. Scrolling, while also linked to fields and lists, is most often associated with tables. Scroll bars and their cousins, repeating arrow buttons, are therefore covered more fully in the chapter on tables. For the complete story on programming tables and scrolling behavior, see Chapter 14.

## Programming Alerts

Alerts are the simplest way to present a dialog box, either to prompt the user for input or simply to display important information. Displaying an alert in your application is very straightforward; simply call the FrmAlert function, passing it the resource ID of the alert you wish to display:

**Palm OS Garnet**
```
UInt16 FrmAlert (UInt16 alertID)
```

**Palm OS Cobalt**
```
uint16_t FrmAlert (DmOpenRef database, uint16_t alertID)
```

The FrmAlert function returns the number of the alert button pressed by the user. The left-most button in the alert is numbered 0, with each button's number increasing sequentially from left to right.

In Garnet and previous versions of Palm OS, the operating system assumes that the alert resource referenced by alertID will be found in the currently open resource database. For most applications this is the application's .prc file. To force Palm OS to load an alert (or another type of resource) from a different resource database than the currently running application, your application code would need to open the resource database, thereby making it current, while displaying the alert.

In Cobalt, Palm OS has done away with this assumption for alerts and other resource types. Developers who use the new Palm OS Cobalt APIs must provide an explicit DmOpenRef reference to the resource database where the alert is found. In the case where the alert is found in your applications .prc file, you can easily obtain this database reference by calling the SysGetModuleDatabase and SysGetRefNum functions, as follows:

```
DmOpenRef database;

SysGetModuleDatabase(SysGetRefNum(), NULL, &database);
```

If all of your resources are found inside your main application .prc file, you can safely call this function in AppStart at the beginning of your program and save the reference in a global variable. This is more efficient, especially in an application which makes heavy use of forms.

The following code displays an alert dialog box, capturing the button tapped by the user in the variable tappedButton:

**Palm OS Garnet**
```
Uint16_t tappedButton;

tappedButton = FrmAlert (MyAlertID);
DmOpenRef database;
```

**Palm OS Cobalt**
```
Uint16_t tappedButton;

SysGetModuleDatabase(SysGetRefNum(), NULL, &database);
tappedButton = FrmAlert (database, MyAlertID);
```

Depending on which button the user taps in the alert, your code can perform different actions. If the alert contains only one button, as is often the case in a purely informational alert, you may safely ignore the return value from FrmAlert.

Otherwise, you will want to respond to the alert differently, depending on which button the user selected. The following code snippet shows how to react to user input from an alert. Figure 8-1 shows the alert dialog box in use.

Figure 8-1

This code determines which button the user tapped and responds accordingly:

**Palm OS Garnet**
```
switch (FrmAlert(RPSAlert)) {
    case 0:
        // user tapped button 1
        break;
    case 1:
        // user tapped button 2
        break;
    case 2:
        // user tapped button 3
        break;
    default:
        // error
        break;
}
```

**Palm OS Cobalt**
```
switch (FrmAlert(database, RPSAlert)) {
    case 0:
        // user tapped button 1
        break;
    case 1:
        // user tapped button 2
        break;
    case 2:
        // user tapped button 3
        break;
    default:
        // error
        break;
}
```

You can customize an alert's message text at runtime. When creating the alert resource, you may insert three placeholders, ^1, ^2, and ^3, which the FrmCustomAlert function replaces with whatever text you like. FrmCustomAlert takes four arguments. The first is the resource ID of the alert to apppear, while the second, third, and fourth arguments are character pointers to the strings that should replace ^1, ^2, and ^3, respectively. If one of the placeholders is missing from the alert, you may pass NULL as its corresponding string argument.

Note that in Palm OS Cobalt, as with FrmAlert, there is an additional first parameter, which is the database reference to the resource database where the alert resource is found.

> Pass NULL as one of the string arguments only if that argument has no corresponding placeholder in the alert. For example, if the alert's message text contains ^1 and you pass NULL as the second placeholder argument to FrmCustomAlert, your application will crash. If you want to ignore an existing placeholder, pass the empty string ("") instead.

Keep in mind that `FrmCustomAlert` does not substitute for placeholder strings in the title or in the button labels of an alert resource; it substitutes placeholder strings only in the alert's message text. For example, a title string containing ^1 will still display "^1" at runtime.

To illustrate `FrmCustomAlert` in action, consider an alert resource with two placeholder strings used in the message portion of the string, as follows:

```
"You are about to delete ^1 records from the "\
          "^2 category. Do you wish to proceed?"
```

When the following call to `FrmCustomAlert` displays the `DeleteAlert` resource, substituting the strings 40 and `Business` for the alert's placeholders, the alert dialog box pictured in Figure 8-2 is the result.

**Palm OS Garnet**
```
tappedButton = FrmCustomAlert (DeleteAlert, "40", "Business", NULL);
```

**Palm OS Cobalt**
```
tappedButton = FrmCustomAlert (database, DeleteAlert, "40", "Business", NULL);
```

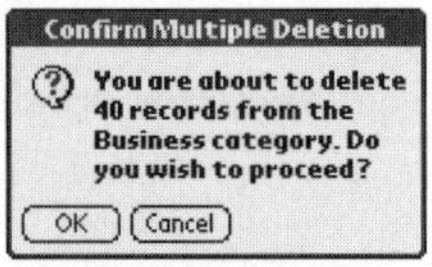

Figure 8-2

# Programming Forms

Depending on the purpose for which you wish to employ different forms in an application, Palm OS offers you a number of options when it comes to displaying forms. The following scenarios outline the most common ways your application might need to display a form:

❑ **Switching to a new form.** In this scenario, the application erases the current form and displays a new one in its place. This most commonly occurs when switching between major, full-screen views in an application. An example of this is changing between the List and Edit modes of the Address Book application when the user taps the New button on the List view's form. This situation calls for the `FrmGotoForm` function.

❑ **Displaying a modal dialog box.** Sometimes you need to display a quick prompt for user input but you need a dialog box with a little more interactivity than an alert resource can provide. A good example of this is the delete confirmation dialog box displayed by the built-in applications when you delete a record. Instead of simply asking you if it is OK to delete the record, the dialog box also provides a check box, giving you the option to save an archive copy of the record on the desktop. If a dialog box contains more than a check box or two, it may also require its own event handler, just like a full-screen form. The `FrmDoDialog` function is the best choice for handling this situation, though you may also use `FrmPopupForm`.

# Switching to a New Form

To allow users to switch between two full-screen views in an application, use the `FrmGotoForm` function. In Palm OS Garnet, `FrmGotoForm` takes a single argument—the resource ID of a form to display. In Palm OS Cobalt, as with `FrmAlert`, `FrmGotoForm` requires passing a database reference as the first parameter. The following example calls `FrmGotoForm` to open and display a form called `EditForm`:

**Palm OS Garnet**
```
FrmGotoForm(EditForm);
```

**Palm OS Cobalt**
```
FrmGotoForm(database, EditForm);
```

`FrmGotoForm` sends a `frmCloseEvent` to the current form and then sends a `frmLoadEvent` and a `frmOpenEvent` to the form you want to display. Located at the end of the application's `EventLoop` function, the system's default form-handling function, `FrmHandleEvent`, automatically takes care of the `frmCloseEvent` by erasing and disposing of the current form. You do not need to do anything special to get rid of the current form. Your application's `ApplicationHandleEvent` function should take care of the `frmLoadEvent` by initializing the form with the `FrmInitForm` function, setting that form as the active form with `FrmSetActiveForm` and associating an event handling function with that form by calling `FrmSetEventHandler`. Now that the form has been initialized in `ApplicationHandleEvent`, the form's event handler needs only to respond to the `frmOpenEvent` by drawing the form with `FrmDrawForm`.

# Displaying a Modal Dialog Box with FrmDoDialog

If a part of your application requires only a small amount of prompting from the user, such as confirmation to delete a record, an alert usually suffices. However, the program may require a little more input than the simple buttons in an alert can provide. In this case, the `FrmDoDialog` function can quickly display a dialog box.

Depending on how complex a dialog box's user interface is, it may or may not require an event handler. If a form that makes up a dialog box contains only user interface elements that the system can handle without intervention from your own code, the form does not require its own event handler. Check boxes and push buttons are ideal for such a dialog box because both user interface elements can store meaningful information and handle user input without any extra code. Your application needs only to display the dialog box with `FrmDoDialog` and then retrieve the user's input when the user dismisses the dialog box.

Tables and selector triggers are good examples of controls that require an event handler because they will not work at all without a fair amount of help from your application's code. Your application must supply an event handler for a dialog box that contains such complex user interface elements. Displaying a complex modal dialog box that has its own event handler is not any different from displaying a simpler dialog box; your application must still call `FrmDoDialog` and then retrieve values from the dialog box's interface.

In much the same way that `FrmAlert` or `FrmCustomAlert` returns the button tapped to dismiss the alert, `FrmDoDialog` returns the resource ID of the button tapped to dismiss its form. Your application's code can then react accordingly, depending upon which button the user tapped.

To use `FrmDoDialog` in your application, follow these steps:

1.  Initialize the form with `FrmInitForm`.

2.  If necessary, set the values of the form's controls with `FrmSetControlValue`.

3.  Display the form with `FrmDoDialog`.

4.  Retrieve the values of the dialog box's controls using `FrmGetControlValue`.

5.  Remove the form from memory with `FrmDeleteForm`.

For example, consider the form resource from the Librarian sample application (introduced in Chapter 7), which defines the delete confirmation dialog box (see Figure 8-3). The only thing that differentiates this dialog box from an alert is the inclusion of a check box control.

**Figure 8-3**

The `DetailsDeleteRecord` function from Librarian, listed in the following example, displays the Date Book dialog box to ask the user to confirm whether the application should really delete a record from its database. Librarian calls this function when the user taps the Delete button while viewing a book's details, or when the user selects the Delete Book menu item:

**Palm OS Garnet**

```
static Boolean DetailsDeleteRecord (void)
{
    UInt16    ctlIndex;
    UInt16    buttonHit;
    FormType *form;
    Boolean   archive;

    // Initialize the dialog form.
    form = FrmInitForm(DeleteBookDialog);

    // Set the "Save archive copy on PC" check box to its
    // previous setting.
    ctlIndex = FrmGetObjectIndex(form,
                                  DeleteBookSaveBackup);
    FrmSetControlValue(form, ctlIndex, gSaveBackup);

    // Display the form and determine which button the user
    // tapped.
    buttonHit = FrmDoDialog(form);

    // Retrieve data from the dialog before deleting the
```

```
    // form.
    archive = FrmGetControlValue(form, ctlIndex);

    // Release the form from memory.
    FrmDeleteForm(form);

    if (buttonHit == DeleteBookCancel)
        return (false);

    // Remember the value of the check box for later.
    gSaveBackup = archive;

    // Code to actually delete the record omitted

    return (true);
}
```

**Palm OS Cobalt**

```
static Boolean DetailsDeleteRecord (void)
{
    uint16_t   ctlIndex;
    uint16_t   buttonHit;
    FormType *form;
    Boolean   archive;
    DmOpenRef database;

    SysGetModuleDatabase(SysGetRefNum(), NULL, &database);

    // Initialize the dialog form.
    form = FrmInitForm(database, DeleteBookDialog);

    // Set the "Save archive copy on PC" check box to its
    // previous setting.
    ctlIndex = FrmGetObjectIndex(form,
                                 DeleteBookSaveBackup);
    FrmSetControlValue(form, ctlIndex, gSaveBackup);

    // Display the form and determine which button the user
    // tapped.
    buttonHit = FrmDoDialog(form);

    // Retrieve data from the dialog before deleting the
    // form.
    archive = FrmGetControlValue(form, ctlIndex);

    // Release the form from memory.
    FrmDeleteForm(form);

    if (buttonHit == DeleteBookCancel)
        return (false);

    // Remember the value of the check box for later.
```

```
        gSaveBackup = archive;

        // Code to actually delete the record omitted

        return (true);
    }
```

The first thing `DetailsDeleteRecord` does is initialize the dialog box form in memory with the `FrmInitForm` function. `FrmInitForm` takes the resource ID of a form as an argument and returns a pointer to the initialized form resource in memory.

Before displaying the dialog box, `DetailsDeleteRecord` needs to set the status of the dialog box's check box. In Librarian, the global variable `gSaveBackup` keeps track of whether or not deleted records should be archived on the PC. `DetailsDeleteRecord` first requires the index of the check box, which it retrieves with the `FrmGetObjectIndex` function. Then `DetailsDeleteRecord` sets the value of the check box via `FrmSetControlValue`.

Now `DetailsDeleteRecord` is ready to display the dialog box. The `FrmDoDialog` function displays a form, given a pointer to a form resource. To close that form, it returns the resource ID of the button the user tapped.

`DetailsDeleteRecord` grabs the value of the check box with `FrmGetControlValue` and then removes the form from memory with `FrmDeleteForm`. This order of events is important; you must retrieve information from a form's controls before deleting it because releasing the form's memory also releases the memory that holds its controls' values.

The `DetailsDeleteRecord` function returns `true` if the user taps the dialog box's OK button or `false` if the user taps its Cancel button. If the user taps OK, `DetailsDeleteRecord` also saves the dialog box's check box value to the global variable `gSaveBackup`. Because the `DeleteBookForm` defines its Cancel button as the form's default button, the operating system simulates a tap on the Cancel button if the user switches applications while the dialog box is open. Therefore, switching applications also causes `DetailsDeleteRecord` to return `false`, ignoring whatever setting is in the dialog box's check box and leaving the contents of `gSaveBackup` alone.

## Displaying a Modal Dialog Box with FrmPopupForm

You also may display a modal dialog box using `FrmPopupForm`. Unlike displaying a dialog box with `FrmDoDialog`, displaying a dialog box with `FrmPopupForm` requires that the dialog box have its own event handler to deal properly with user input, regardless of how simple the user interface elements in the dialog box are.

*Using `FrmDoDialog` results in code that is easier to read and maintain than using `FrmPopupForm`.*

Like `FrmGotoForm`, the `FrmPopupForm` function takes the resource ID of a form as an argument; in the case of Cobalt, the obligatory database reference as the first argument. The `FormType *` argument to `FrmPopupForm` specifies the form to which `FrmPopupForm` sends both a `frmLoadEvent` and a `frmOpenEvent`. By contrast, `FrmGotoForm` sends a `frmCloseEvent` to the current form. The following line of code pops up a form with a resource ID constant of `DetailsForm`:

**Palm OS Garnet**
```
FrmPopupForm(DetailsForm);
```

**Palm OS Cobalt**
```
FrmPopupForm(database, DetailsForm);
```

To exit the dialog box, use the FrmReturnToForm function. As an argument, FrmReturnToForm takes the resource ID of the form to return to. FrmReturnToForm erases the current form from the screen, deletes the form from memory, and sets the active form to the form specified in its argument. The function assumes that the form you pass to it is already loaded into memory.

You also may pass in zero as the argument to FrmReturnToForm, in which case the function returns to the last form that was loaded — in this case, the form displayed by your application before it called FrmPopupForm. The following line of code, then, is all that is required for an application to return from a modal dialog box to its parent form:

```
FrmReturnToForm (0);
```

Typically, the call to FrmReturnToForm should occur in those parts of the modal dialog box's event handler devoted to handling buttons on the dialog form. The following code from a dialog form's event handler closes the form when the user taps that form's OK or Cancel buttons:

```
if (event->eType == ctlSelectEvent)
{
    switch (event->data.ctlSelect.controlID)
    {
        case OkButton:
            FrmReturnToForm (0);
            handled = true;
            break;

        case CancelButton:
            FrmReturnToForm (0);
            handled = true;
            break;

        default:
            break;
    }
}
```

Because **FrmReturnToForm** does not send a **frmCloseEvent** to the current form, be sure to clean up any variables associated with that form before calling **FrmReturnToForm**. Failure to clean up such variables manually could result in a memory leak.

## *Updating a Form*

When Palm OS returns from displaying a modal dialog box, it normally restores the area behind the dialog box automatically, redrawing the underlying form as it appeared before the dialog box was displayed. However, if there isn't enough memory available for the system to save the area behind the dialog box, the system instead queues a frmUpdateEvent, which is an instruction to the application to redraw the entire form.

If your application leaves frmUpdateEvent unhandled, the Palm OS routine FrmHandleEvent automatically redraws the form. If the form contains nothing but standard Palm OS user interface elements, FrmHandleEvent has no trouble restoring the appearance of the form. However, FrmHandleEvent does not know how to redraw any gadgets or other custom user interface elements that your application draws manually. If your application performs any custom drawing, it needs to handle frmUpdateEvent so that the custom parts of the form may be restored along with the rest of the form.

The frmUpdateEvent.data field contains a frmUpdate structure, which looks like this:

**Palm OS Garnet**

```
struct frmUpdate {
    UInt16 formID;
    UInt16 updateCode;
} frmUpdate;
```

**Palm OS Cobalt**

```
struct frmUpdate {
uint16_t formID;
uint16_t updateCode;
RectangleType dirtyRect;
} frmUpdate;
```

The formID member specifies the resource ID of the form to be updated, and updateCode contains a value that tells an application how to redraw the form. If the system queues a frmUpdateEvent when it dismisses a modal dialog box, the system sets updateCode to the constant value frmRedrawUpdateCode, which is a signal to your application that it should redraw the entire form. In Cobalt, the additional member dirtyRect indicates the portion of the form that needs to be drawn, defined as a rectangular area.

You may queue your own frmUpdateEvent by calling FrmUpdateForm; when doing so, you can use any value you wish for updateCode. This technique allows you to request a form in your application to redraw only the portions of the form that have actually changed since the form was last displayed. For example, if the user performs an action in a modal dialog box that changes only a single row of data in a table, the application should redraw only that row of the table instead of having to perform a lengthy refresh of the entire table's data.

In addition, if your application contains table or list data that may have changed in response to a user's actions, handling a custom updateCode gives your form an opportunity to refresh its display in response to new data. For example, if the user selects a new category of records, your application can send an updateCode to tell a form to fill its table or list with records from the new category.

As an example, Librarian's `ListFormHandleEvent` handles `frmUpdateEvent` by passing the event's `updateCode` to another function, `ListFormUpdateDisplay`. The relevant portion of `ListFormHandleEvent` looks like this:

```
static Boolean ListFormHandleEvent(EventType *event)
{
    Boolean  handled = false;
    FormPtr  form;


    switch (event->eType) {
        case frmUpdateEvent:
            ListFormUpdateDisplay(
                event->data.frmUpdate.updateCode);
            handled = true;
            break;

        // Other events omitted.
    }

    return handled;
}
```

The `ListFormUpdateDisplay` routine is responsible for updating the List view form, according to the instructions contained in `updateCode`:

```
static void ListFormUpdateDisplay(UInt16 updateCode)
{
    TablePtr table;
    FormPtr  form;


    table = GetObjectPtr(ListTable);

    if (updateCode == frmRedrawUpdateCode)
    {
        FrmDrawForm(FrmGetActiveForm());
    }

    if ( (updateCode & updateRedrawAll) ||
         (updateCode & updatePopupListChanged) )
    {
        ListFormLoadTable();
        TblRedrawTable(table);
    }

    if ( (updateCode & updateFontChanged) ||
         (updateCode & updateListStatusChanged) )
    {
        form = FrmGetActiveForm();
        ListFormInit(form);
        TblRedrawTable(table);
        if (gCurrentRecord != noRecord)
```

```
                ListFormSelectRecord(gCurrentRecord);
    }

    if (updateCode & updateSelectCurrentRecord &&
        (gCurrentRecord != noRecord) )
    {
        ListFormSelectRecord(gCurrentRecord);
    }
}
```

When `ListFormUpdateDisplay` receives the `frmRedrawUpdateCode` from the operating system, `ListFormUpdateDisplay` redraws the entire List view form by calling `FrmDrawForm`. The other `updateCode` values that `ListFormUpdateDisplay` looks for are defined by the following constants:

```
#define updateRedrawAll            0x01
#define updateCategoryChanged      0x08
#define updateFontChanged          0x10
#define updateListStatusChanged    0x20
#define updatePopupListChanged     0x40
#define updateSelectCurrentRecord  0x80
```

Elsewhere in Librarian's code, various routines pass these constants to `FrmUpdateForm` (or just pass them directly to `ListFormUpdateDisplay`) to request that Librarian redraw the List view in certain ways. For example, if the user changes the font in the List view, Librarian's `SelectFont` function makes the following `FrmUpdateForm` call, passing the resource ID of the List view form for the `formID` parameter:

```
FrmUpdateForm(formID, updateFontChanged);
```

When `ListFormUpdateDisplay` receives an `updateFontChanged` code, it initializes the List view's form with Librarian's `ListFormInit` function, redraws the table with the system call `TblRedrawTable`, and highlights the selected record with the `ListFormSelectRecord` function.

# Programming Objects on Forms

Although the objects that a form may contain vary in form and function, all objects share some common ground when an application handles them in code. The default form handling provided by the `FrmHandleEvent` function not only takes care of visibly reacting to user input, such as inverting a button when it is tapped, but `FrmHandleEvent` also ensures that the system posts to the queue events to which your application can respond.

Internally, Palm OS treats a number of user interface elements as *controls*. The system deals with all controls using similar data structures, events, and functions. Controls consist of the following objects:

- Buttons and graphic buttons
- Push buttons and graphic push buttons
- Check boxes
- Pop-up triggers

❏ Selector triggers

❏ Repeating buttons and graphic repeating buttons

❏ Sliders and feedback sliders

For default processing of user input from controls, FrmHandleEvent actually hands control over to the CtlHandleEvent function, which takes care of all the specifics of user interaction with the control. FrmHandleEvent defers to different functions for other user interface objects: FldHandleEvent for fields, LstHandleEvent for lists, MenuHandleEvent for menus, SclHandleEvent for scroll bars, and TblHandleEvent for tables.

## Handling Form Object Events

Most form objects respond to taps from the user in a similar fashion. When the user first taps within the borders of an object, the control queues an *enter* event. If the user then lifts the stylus while still within the object's screen boundaries, the control posts a *select* event. However, if the user drags the stylus outside the boundaries of the object before lifting, the control instead posts an *exit* event. The repeating button and scroll bar controls generate another type of event, a *repeat* event, when the user holds the stylus down within the boundaries of those objects.

Select events are usually the most interesting to your application because they indicate successful selection of the object. The following select events are possible:

❏ ctlSelectEvent

❏ frmTitleSelectEvent

❏ lstSelectEvent

❏ popSelectEvent

❏ tblSelectEvent

Handling an enter event allows your application to respond to a tap on an object before the user lifts the stylus from the screen. A good use for this style of event handling is to populate the contents of a pop-up list with dynamic data, as the user taps the pop-up trigger to display that list. (See the section "Programming Dynamic Lists" later in this chapter for an example of how to populate a list dynamically.)

Palm OS provides the following enter events:

❏ ctlEnterEvent

❏ fldEnterEvent

❏ frmTitleEnterEvent

❏ lstEnterEvent

❏ sclEnterEvent

❏ tblEnterEvent

Exit events allow for special processing when the user starts to select an object but decides against it and moves the stylus off the object before lifting it from the screen. The exit event is most useful in conjunction

**211**

with an enter event, particularly if the enter event allocates memory for a variable or two. The exit event can then release that memory, preventing a leak. The exit events are as follows:

❑   ctlExitEvent

❑   lstExitEvent

❑   sclExitEvent

❑   tblExitEvent

The scroll bar and repeating button objects continually post repeat events to the queue while the user holds down the stylus within their boundaries, allowing your application to scroll data dynamically until the user lifts the stylus. The two repeat events are as follows:

❑   ctlRepeatEvent

❑   sclRepeatEvent

To respond to any of these events, your application should check for them in the appropriate form event handler. The following event handler captures select events from two buttons (OKButton and CancelButton) and a list:

```
static Boolean MyFormHandleEvent (EventType *event)
{
    Boolean  handled = false;

    if (event->eType == ctlSelectEvent)
    {
        switch (event->data.ctlSelect.controlID)
        {
            case OKButton:
                // Do something in response to the OK
                // button being tapped.
                handled = true;
                break;

            case CancelButton:
                // Do something in response to the Cancel
                // button being tapped.
                handled = true;
                break;

            default:
                break;
        }
    }
    else if (event->eType == lstSelectEvent)
    {
        // Do something in response to the list selection;
        // this code assumes only one list on the form.
        handled = true;
    }

    return (handled);
}
```

Because the form contains two buttons, each of which is capable of generating a `ctlSelectEvent`, the event handler in the previous example must determine which button generated the event. `MyFormHandleEvent` does this by looking at the `data` member of the event structure passed to the event-handling function.

The event structure's `data` member is actually a union of many other structures, each of which holds different data depending upon the type of event represented by the event structure. Each of the different structures stores the resource ID of the object that generated the event in a slightly different place. The following table shows you where to look for the resource ID of an object in an event structure, depending upon the type of event involved.

Notice that `MyFormHandleEvent` assumes that there is only one list in the form. If a form contains only one control capable of generating a particular event, you may forgo checking the event data for the resource ID of the object involved. Simply check for the occurrence of the event and respond to the event accordingly.

| Event Type | Where to Find the Resource ID |
| --- | --- |
| `ctlEnterEvent` | `event->data.ctlEnter.controlID` |
| `CtlExitEvent` | `event->data.ctlExit.controlID` |
| `ctlRepeatEvent` | `event->data.ctlRepeat.controlID` |
| `ctlSelectEvent` | `event->data.ctlSelect.controlID` |
| `fldEnterEvent` | `event->data.fldEnter.fielded` |
| `lstEnterEvent` | `event->data.lstEnter.listID` |
| `lstExitEvent` | `event->data.lstExit.listID` |
| `lstSelectEvent` | `event->data.lstSelect.listID` |
| `popSelectEvent` | `event->data.popSelect.controlID` (ID of the pop-up trigger) <br> `event->data.popSelect.listID` (ID of the attached list resource) |
| `sclEnterEvent` | `event->data.sclEnter.scrollBarID` |
| `sclExitEvent` | `event->data.sclExit.scrollBarID` |
| `sclRepeatEvent` | `event->data.sclRepeat.scrollBarID` |
| `tblEnterEvent` | `event->data.tblEnter.tableID` |
| `tblExitEvent` | `event->data.tblExit.tableID` |
| `tblSelectEvent` | `event->data.tblSelect.tableID` |

## Retrieving an Object Pointer

Before you can do something with an object on a form, you must retrieve a pointer to that object. The `FrmGetObjectPtr` function performs this function, given a pointer to a form and the index of the desired object. Note that the index of an object on a form is different from the object's resource ID. The resource ID is a number that you assign to an object when you build an application's resources in

Constructor or PODS' Palm OS Resource Editor. The index is a number that Palm OS assigns to an object at runtime to differentiate it from other objects on a form.

> *Pay careful attention to whether a particular Palm OS function requires a resource ID, object index, or object pointer. A common source of programming error is passing the wrong number to a function that expects a different kind of information.*

You will usually need to get the index number of an object with `FrmGetObjectIndex` before you can get a pointer to the object with `FrmGetObjectPtr`. Both `FrmGetObjectIndex` and `FrmGetObjectPtr` also require a pointer to the form containing the object you want. Usually, you can simply use the `FrmGetActiveForm` function, which returns a pointer to the currently active form.

> *For modal forms, calling `FrmGetActiveForm` before calling `FrmDoDialog` does not retrieve the correct form pointer because a modal form is not the active form until processing has progressed inside `FrmDoDialog`. You can safely call `FrmDoDialog` from within a form handler in such instances, however.*

The following code retrieves a pointer to the active form and then a pointer to the button whose resource ID is `MainOKButton`:

```
FormType      *form;
ControlType   *ctl;

form = FrmGetActiveForm();
ctl = FrmGetObjectPtr(form, FrmGetObjectIndex(form,
                   MainOKButton));
```

The `ctl` variable now contains a pointer to the `MainOKButton` control, which may be manipulated using other functions.

Calling both `FrmGetObjectPtr` and `FrmGetObjectIndex` is the only way to get an object pointer from a resource ID; Palm OS does not offer a function to turn a resource ID directly into an object pointer. Because retrieving object pointers is a very common action in programming for Palm OS, you may wish to avoid repeating the cumbersome `FrmGetObjectPtr` and `FrmGetObjectIndex` combination throughout your code. The following function is a wrapper for the process of converting a resource ID into a usable object pointer:

**Palm OS Garnet**
```
MemPtr GetObjectPtr (UInt16 objectID)
{
    FormType   *form;

    form = FrmGetActiveForm();
    return (FrmGetObjectPtr(form, FrmGetObjectIndex(form,
            objectID)));
}
```

**Palm OS Cobalt**

```
MemPtr GetObjectPtr (uint16_t objectID)
{
    FormType   *form;

    form = FrmGetActiveForm();
    return (FrmGetObjectPtr(form, FrmGetObjectIndex(form,
            objectID)));
}
```

GetObjectPtr takes the resource ID of an object as its only argument and returns a pointer to that object, assuming that the desired object is on the current active form. Using the GetObjectPtr function, you can shorten the first example in this section to the following single line of code:

```
ControlType *ctl = GetObjectPtr(MainOKButton);
```

Because it is such a useful function, you will see GetObjectPtr used elsewhere in this book, as well as in source code for the built-in applications provided by PalmSource. In fact, this function already exists in any project created with stationery or the Palm OS Application Wizard in Metrowerks CodeWarrior.

*The examples in this section assume you are coding in C, which does not require an explicit cast from a void pointer. In C++, you need to cast the return value of FrmGetObjectPtr and GetObjectPtr to the proper type, as in the following example:*

```
ControlPtr ctl = (ControlPtr)GetObjectPtr(MainOKButton);
```

The FrmGetObjectIndex function allows you to get an index from a resource ID, but what if you need to get an index from an object pointer? Normally, an application is aware of the resource ID of all its user interface objects, and FrmGetObjectIndex suffices. Version 4.0 of Palm OS provides the FrmGetObjectIndexFromPtr function for this purpose.

## Hiding and Showing Form Objects

Sometimes you may wish to hide user interface elements from view, or cause them to appear again, in response to user input. When hidden, an object does not appear onscreen or accept any taps from the user. Palm OS provides two functions for this purpose: FrmHideObject and FrmShowObject. As arguments, both functions take a pointer to the object's form and the object index. Note that the second argument is the object index, not its resource ID or an object pointer; you may retrieve the object index with the FrmGetObjectIndex function.

The following form event handler hides the MyButton control from view when the user selects the form's HideCheckbox control:

**Palm OS Garnet**

```
static Boolean MyFormHandleEvent (EventType *event)
{
    Boolean     handled = false;
    FormType    *form;
    UInt16      buttonIndex;
    ControlType *ctl;
```

```
       if (event->eType == ctlSelectEvent)
       {
           switch (event->data.ctlSelect.controlID)
           {
               case HideCheckbox:
                   form = FrmGetActiveForm();
                   buttonIndex = FrmGetObjectIndex(form,
                                  MyButton);
                   ctl = GetObjectPtr(HideCheckbox);
                   if (CtlGetValue(ctl))
                   {
                       FrmHideObject(form, buttonIndex);
                   }
                   else
                   {
                       FrmShowObject(form, buttonIndex);
                   }
                   handled = true;
                   break;

               case MyButton:
                   // Do something when the user taps MyButton
                   handled = true;
                   break;

               default:
                   break;
           }
       }

       return (handled);
}
```

**Palm OS Cobalt**

```
static Boolean MyFormHandleEvent (EventType *event)
{
    Boolean     handled = false;
    FormType    *form;
    uint16_t      buttonIndex;
    ControlType *ctl;

    if (event->eType == ctlSelectEvent)
    {
        switch (event->data.ctlSelect.controlID)
        {
            case HideCheckbox:
                form = FrmGetActiveForm();
                buttonIndex = FrmGetObjectIndex(form,
                               MyButton);
                ctl = GetObjectPtr(HideCheckbox);
                if (CtlGetValue(ctl))
                {
                    FrmHideObject(form, buttonIndex);
                }
```

```
                    else
                    {
                        FrmShowObject(form, buttonIndex);
                    }
                    handled = true;
                    break;

            case MyButton:
                    // Do something when the user taps MyButton
                    handled = true;
                    break;

            default:
                    break;
        }
    }

    return (handled);
}
```

Notice the use of the `CtlGetValue` function to determine whether the check box is checked or not. `CtlGetValue` returns the value associated with a check box or push button control, either 1 for on or 0 for off. In the preceding code, if the value of the check box is 1 (checked), the event handler hides the `MyButton` control with `FrmHideObject`; if the check box is unchecked, `FrmShowObject` reveals the button again.

## Using PalmOSGlue

For developers who have been programming since Palm OS versions 3 and 4, once you have a pointer to a user interface object, it's tempting to read straight from the structure that defines that object or, worse, bypass the Palm OS APIs and modify the structure's members directly. Unfortunately, any code that accesses internal user interface structures runs the risk of not working properly on future versions of Palm OS. In particular, Palm OS 5 runs on little-endian ARM processors, so byte order and structure alignment differ significantly from the structures described in Palm OS reference documentation — structures that were designed to run on big-endian Motorola 68K chips. The Palm Application Compatibility Environment (PACE) maintains "shadow" structures, which are Motorola 68K versions of the ARM structures used natively by Palm OS 5. However, PACE prevents direct access to these structures. Direct access to user interface structures works reasonably well on older versions of Palm OS but it fails miserably in Palm OS 5.

Fortunately, PalmSource solves this problem with the PalmOSGlue library, a static library that you link into your application. The library contains a variety of functions for retrieving and setting values inside user interface structures. The glue functions know how these structures are arranged on any version of Palm OS, so using glue functions is safe in Palm OS 5 as well as future releases of Garnet.

In Cobalt, PalmSource has done away with direct access to these structures and thus no longer offers the use of glue functions. Rather, Cobalt developers should make use of the underlying operating system functions instead.

The PalmOSGlue library first appeared in Palm OS 3.5 to provide international text-handling functions that were compatible with older versions of Palm OS. PalmOSGlue works in Palm OS 2.0 and later versions.

As an example of using PalmOSGlue to access the innards of a user interface structure, consider the problem of determining what font a button uses to draw its text. Before PalmOSGlue existed, you would get a pointer to the button's ControlType structure and look at the font member of that structure:

```
ControlType   *button;
FormType      *form = FrmGetActiveForm();
FontID        font;
button = FrmGetObjectPtr(form,
    FrmGetObjectIndex(form, myButton));
font = button->font;
```

With PalmOSGlue, you can use the CtlGlueGetFont function:

```
font = CtlGlueGetFont(controlPtr);
```

Then, if you want to change the button's font, you can do so with the CtlGlueSetFont function:

```
CtlGlueSetFont(controlPtr, fontID);
```

In addition to providing safe access to internal user interface structures, PalmOSGlue allows you to use some new functions on older versions of Palm OS that would otherwise not support such functions. As an example, the very useful FrmGetActiveField function, which returns a pointer to the field that currently has the focus, first becomes available in Palm OS 4.0. If you want to use FrmGetActiveField on older versions of Palm OS, you can link PalmOSGlue into your application and call the FrmGlueGetActiveField function, which is otherwise unavailable in older versions of Palm OS.

Glue versions of regular functions first check to see if the native function is present in ROM. If it is, the glue function calls the native version of the function. If the native function does not exist, the glue version executes its own code that duplicates the effects of the native ROM function. So if you were to call FrmGlueGetActiveField on a Palm OS 4.0 handheld, the glue function would call the native FrmGetActiveField function. In versions of Palm OS older than version 4.0, FrmGlueGetActiveField retrieves a pointer to the active field using its own code.

The *Palm OS Programmer's API Reference*, a part of the Palm OS SDK, describes all of the PalmOSGlue functions. In addition, the Palm OS header files have definitions for all the glue functions. Add the following line to the top of your application to include all the PalmOSGlue definitions:

```
#include <PalmOSGlue.h>
```

For Cobalt programmers, the *Porting Applications to Palm OS Cobalt* reference describes the operating system function equivalents to each glue function.

Because PalmOSGlue is a static library, not a shared library, you must explicitly link it into your application. This does add to the size of your application; the more glue functions you use, the larger your application become. Fortunately, the linker strips out any PalmOSGlue functions that you don't use in your application.

To link with PalmOSGlue in a CodeWarrior project, simply add the `PalmOSGlue.lib` file to your project. It is located in the `Palm OS Support\CodeWarrior Libraries\ Palm OS Glue` folder, underneath the folder where you have installed CodeWarrior.

# Programming Check Boxes and Push Buttons

As shown in the previous section, the `CtlGetValue` function returns the value of a check box or push button control, given a pointer to the control. A return value of 1 from `CtlGetValue` indicates a checked check box or a selected push button, whereas 0 represents an unchecked box or an unselected push button.

Besides looking at the value of a check box or push button, you also may set the value using the `CtlSetValue` function. The following lines of code select the `MyPushButton` push button control:

```
ControlType *ctl = GetObjectPtr(MyPushButton);
CtlSetValue(ctl, 1);
```

*Although both `CtlGetValue` and `CtlSetValue` take a pointer to any control type, they work only with check boxes and push buttons. `CtlGetValue` returns an undefined value with other control types, and the system simply ignores calls to `CtlSetValue` for other controls.*

## Handling Control Groups

Check boxes and push buttons may be assigned to mutually exclusive *control groups*. Within a control group, only one check box or push button may be selected at a time. Palm OS provides functions for setting or determining which check box or push button in a group is currently selected.

`FrmSetControlGroupSelection` takes three arguments: a pointer to the form containing the group of controls, the number assigned to the control group, and the resource ID of the control in that group to select. The `FrmSetControlGroupSelection` function selects the specified control and deselects all the other controls that share the same control group, saving you from having to make multiple calls to `CtlSetValue` to turn off manually all the other controls in the group.

`FrmGetControlGroupSelection` returns the index number of the selected control in a control group, given a pointer to the form containing the group and the group's number.

> **FrmGetControlGroupSelection** returns the index of the selected control but
> **FrmSetControlGroupSelection** sets the selection based on the control's resource
> ID. Keep this in mind as you use these functions because passing the wrong number
> is a common error when handling control groups.

As an example, we can take a form that contains a group of push buttons labeled "Rock," "Paper," and "Scissors." The following code selects the MainRockPushButton if it is not already selected:

**Palm OS Garnet**

```
FormType  *form = FrmGetActiveForm();
UInt8      rockIndex = FrmGetObjectIndex(form,
                                           MainRockPushButton)

if (! (FrmGetControlGroupSelection(form, 1) == rockIndex) )
    FrmSetControlGroupSelection(form, 1,
                                 MainRockPushButton);
```

**Palm OS Cobalt**

```
FormType  *form = FrmGetActiveForm();
uint16_t   rockIndex = FrmGetObjectIndex(form,
                                           MainRockPushButton)

if (! (FrmGetControlGroupSelection(form, 1) == rockIndex) )
    FrmSetControlGroupSelection(form, 1,
                                 MainRockPushButton);
```

# Programming Selector Triggers

Without any extra programming, a selector trigger is merely a button surrounded by a gray (dotted) box; Palm OS does not provide most of the behavior users expect from a selector trigger, such as displaying a date or time picker dialog box. Your application is responsible for calling up a dialog box from which the user can pick a value and then displaying that value in the selector trigger.

Fortunately, implementing a selector trigger is not a difficult process. Tapping the selector trigger queues a standard ctlSelectEvent that your application can respond to in a form event handler. Use the FrmPopupForm or FrmDoDialog functions to display a dialog box form, from which the user may pick a value. After the user dismisses the dialog box, your application should change the selector trigger's label with the CtlSetLabel function. CtlSetLabel takes a pointer to a control and a character pointer containing the string to display in the control's label. The following line of code changes the label on a selector trigger to a date string:

```
ControlType *ctl = GetObjectPtr(MySelectorTrigger);
CtlSetLabel(ctl, "Thu 10/31/02");
```

The CtlSetLabel function also works with other controls, not just selector triggers. A companion function, CtlGetLabel, works in reverse, retrieving the current value of a control's label and returning that value as pointer to a null-terminated string.

> Writing a string with **CtlSetLabel** that is longer than the string originally contained by the control's resource can cause a crash. Be sure when you create a control to give it a label at least as long as the longest string you plan to assign using **CtlSetLabel**. Also, the pointer you pass to **CtlSetLabel** must be valid if the form containing that control receives a **frmUpdate** event. This means that if you change a control's label at runtime, the text must come from a global variable, constant, or memory chunk that remains locked for the entire life of the control.

## Selecting Dates and Times

Palm OS contains two built-in dialog boxes from which users can select dates and times. These are perfect candidates for use with selector triggers. The date and time pickers (see Figure 8-4) are accessible through the SelectDay and SelectTime functions.

Figure 8-4

The prototype for the SelectDay function looks like this:

**Palm OS Garnet**
```
Boolean SelectDay (const SelectDayType selectDayBy,
    Int16 *month, Int16 *day, Int16 *year,
    const Char *title)
```

**Palm OS Cobalt**
```
Boolean SelectDay (const SelectDayType selectDayBy,
    int16_t *month, int16_t *day, int16_t *year,
    const char *title)
```

The first argument to SelectDay allows you to specify the granularity of selection allowed by the date picker. SelectDayType is defined in the Palm OS header files, which also define these constant values appropriate for the first argument to SelectDay:

❑ selectDayByDay. This option tells the date picker to allow selection of a single day.

❑ selectDayByWeek. This option restricts selection in the date picker to pick a week at a time when passed this value.

❑ selectDayByMonth. This option restricts selection to a particular month.

Not only do the month, day, and year arguments specify the initial date displayed by the date picker, but these arguments specify variables in which the date picker returns the date selected by the user. The title argument allows you to customize the title bar of the date picker.

SelectDay returns true if the user selects a date from the picker or false if the user taps the picker's Cancel button.

The following form event handler displays a date picker in response to the user's tapping a selector trigger and then changes the label in the selector to the date picked by the user. This event handler assumes that the selector trigger is the only control object on the form.

**Palm OS Garnet**

```
static Boolean MyFormHandleEvent (EventType *event)
{
    Boolean        handled = false;
    ControlType    *ctl;
    Char           *label;
    Int16          month, day, year;
    DateTimeType   now;

    if (event->eType == ctlSelectEvent)
    {
        TimSecondsToDateTime(TimGetSeconds(), &now);
        year = now.year;
        month = now.month;
        day = now.day;

        if (SelectDay(selectDayByDay, &month, &day, &year,
                      "Select a Day"))
        {
            ctl = GetObjectPtr(MySelectorTrigger);
            label = (Char *) CtlGetLabel(ctl);
            DateToDOWDMFormat(month, day, year,
                              dfDMYLongWithComma, label);
            CtlSetLabel(ctl, label);
        }
        handled = true;
    }

    return (handled);
}
```

**Palm OS Cobalt**

```
static Boolean MyFormHandleEvent (EventType *event)
{
    Boolean        handled = false;
    ControlType    *ctl;
    Char           *label;
    int16_t         month, day, year;
    DateTimeType   now;

    if (event->eType == ctlSelectEvent)
    {
```

```
            TimSecondsToDateTime(TimGetSeconds(), &now);
            year = now.year;
            month = now.month;
            day = now.day;

            if (SelectDay(selectDayByDay, &month, &day, &year,
                        "Select a Day"))
            {
                ctl = GetObjectPtr(MySelectorTrigger);
                label = (char *) CtlGetLabel(ctl);
                DateToDOWDMFormat(month, day, year,
                                dfDMYLongWithComma, label);
                CtlSetLabel(ctl, label);
            }
            handled = true;
        }

        return (handled);
}
```

Before displaying the date picker with SelectDay, the preceding example initializes the date first displayed in the dialog box to today's date with the TimSecondsToDateTime and TimGetSeconds functions. Another handy Palm OS date and time function, DateToDOWDMFormat, converts the raw month, day, and year values from SelectDay into a nicely formatted date string. Chapter 13 covers these and other date and time functions, along with the DateTimeType structure they use, in more detail.

The previous example also initializes the label variable, a character pointer to the string displayed in the selector trigger's label, with CtlGetLabel to ensure that label has enough space to hold the date string produced by DateToDOWDMFormat.

*The SelectDay function is available only in Palm OS version 2.0 and later. If your application must run in Palm OS 1.0, use the function SelectDayV10, which allows selection of dates by day only, not by week or month.*

Using SelectTime to present the user with a time picker dialog box is similar to using SelectDay. The prototype for SelectTime looks like this:

**Palm OS Garnet**

```
Boolean SelectTime (TimeType *startTimeP,
    TimeType *EndTimeP, Boolean untimed,
    const Char *titleP, Int16 startOfDay,
    Int16 endOfDay, Int16 startOfDisplay)
```

**Palm OS Cobalt**

```
Boolean SelectTime (TimeType *startTimeP,
    TimeType *EndTimeP, Boolean untimed,
    const char *titleP, int16_t startOfDay,
    int16_t endOfDay, int16_t startOfDisplay)
```

The first two arguments to SelectTime, startTimeP and EndTimeP, are pointers to TimeType structures. TimeType is defined in the standard Palm OS include file DateTime.h as follows:

```
typedef struct {
    UInt8   hours;
    UInt8   minutes;
} TimeType;
```

SelectTime initializes the time picker to display the start and end times given in startTimeP and EndTimeP. The SelectTime function also returns the times the user selects in these two variables. You also may initialize the dialog box to display no selected time by passing true for the value of the untimed parameter. If the user chooses no time in the picker dialog box, SelectTime sets startTimeP and EndTimeP to the constant noTime, which has a value of −1.

The titleP argument to SelectTime contains the text displayed in the time picker's title bar, and startOfDay specifies what hour of the day the picker displays at the top of its hour list. The startOfDay argument must be a value from 0 to 12, inclusive.

The endOfDay argument specifies what hour of the day will be returned if the user taps the All Day button in the time selector dialog box, and startOfDisplay defines what hour will be displayed at the top of the dialog box when it first opens.

> *Prior to version 3.5 of Palm OS, the SelectTime function lacks the endOfDay and startOfDisplay arguments. If you must maintain compatibility with older code, use the SelectTimeV33 function instead of SelectTime.*

SelectTime returns false if the user taps the dialog box's Cancel button; otherwise, SelectTime returns true to indicate that the user changes the time in the picker.

If you wish to prompt the user for a single time, instead of the start and end times, use the SelectOneTime function instead of SelectTime. SelectOneTime displays a different picker dialog box (see Figure 8-5).

Figure 8-5

The SelectOneTime function takes only three arguments, as shown in the following example:

**Palm OS Garnet**
```
Boolean SelectOneTime (Int16 *hour, Int16 *minute,
                       const Char *title)
```

**Palm OS Cobalt**
```
Boolean SelectOneTime (int16_t *hour, int16_t *minute,
                       const char *title)
```

The first two arguments to SelectOneTime determine the time initially displayed in the picker dialog box and provide variables for SelectOneTime to return the time selected by the user. The title argument supplies the text displayed in the picker's title bar. SelectOneTime returns true if the user changes the time in the dialog box, or false if the user taps the Cancel button.

## Selecting Colors

Starting with version 3.5, Palm OS provides a dialog box for choosing colors. You can call this dialog box with the UIPickColor function, which has the following prototype:

**Palm OS Garnet**
```
Boolean UIPickColor (IndexedColorType *indexP,
    RGBColorType *rgbP, UIPickColorStartType start,
    const Char *titleP, const Char *tipP)
```

**Palm OS Cobalt**
```
Boolean UIPickColor (IndexedColorType *indexP,
    RGBColorType *rgbP, UIPickColorStartType start,
    const char *titleP, const char *tipP)
```

The first two arguments to UIPickColor, indexP and rgbP, allow you to specify an initial color that will be selected in the picker dialog box. UIPickColor also returns the selected color in one of these two arguments. The two arguments specify colors in different ways. The indexP argument specifies a color by its index in the system color table, and the rgbP argument specifies a color by its RGB (red, green, blue) value. If you don't want to use one of the two styles of color specification, set the unused argument to NULL to tell UIPickColor to ignore it.

> **Be sure to specify at least one of the two first arguments. If both of them are NULL, the color picker display becomes garbled on some versions of Palm OS.**

If you specify both indexP and rgbP values, UIPickColor always chooses the indexP value over rgbP when determining what color to display in the picker. UIPickColor returns true if the user selects a new color value from the picker, and false if the user taps the Cancel button or chooses the same color that the picker displayed when it opened. If the user selects a new color, UIPickColor sets indexP and rgbP (if they aren't NULL) to the selected color's index and RGB values, respectively.

There are two versions of the color picker that you can display to the user, one that allows selection from a palette of colors (see Figure 8-6) and one that allows selection of an RGB value with sliders (see Figure 8-7). The user can switch between the two pickers by selecting Palette or RGB from the pop-up list in the lower-right corner of the picker.

Figure 8-6

Figure 8-7

The start argument controls which picker appears first. Specify UIPickColorStartPalette to display the palette first, or specify UIPickColorStartRGB to display the RGB slider first. UIPickColor ignores the start argument if you passed NULL for either indexP or rgbP; the function displays only the palette if rgbP is NULL, and it displays only the RGB sliders if indexP is NULL. If either of the first two arguments is NULL, the user cannot switch between the two pickers.

In the titleP argument, you can pass a pointer to a null-terminated string that appears in the title bar of the color picker. The tipP argument is reserved for future use; it has no function in Palm OS 5 or earlier.

As an example, the following code brings up the color picker in RGB mode, titled "Font Color," with indexed color 125 (bright red in the system color table) displayed:

```
IndexedColorType  index = 125;
RGBColorType      rgb;
Boolean           newColor;

newColor = UIPickColor(&index, &rgb,
                  UIPickColorStartPalette,
                  "Font Color", NULL);
```

For more details about using color in an application, including descriptions of indexed and RGB color, see Chapter 11.

# Programming Fields

To the user, text fields seem like very simple user interface objects. However, making a text field simple for the user requires a fair amount of effort on your part. Specifically, fields are rather particular about memory management because the addition or removal of text by the user causes a field object to dynamically change the amount of memory required to store the field's contents.

Palm OS deals with the difficulty of resizable field text by keeping track of the field's storage with a handle instead of a pointer. Each field has its own handle to the memory that stores the field's text contents. The system automatically allocates a new handle for a field if the user enters any text into the field.

## Setting a Handle for a Text Field

To set the text in a field programmatically, you simply point the field at a different handle that contains the new text for the field. The FldSetTextHandle function allows you to change the handle that stores the text for a particular field. In the following example, the FldSetTextHandle function sets the handle for a text field, given a pointer to the field and the handle containing the field's new contents:

```
static void SetFieldHandle (FieldType *field,
                            MemHandle textH)
{
    MemHandle  oldTextH;

    // Retrieve the field's old text handle.
    oldTextH = FldGetTextHandle(field);

    // Set the new text handle for the field.
    FldSetTextHandle(field, textH);
    FldDrawField(field);

    // Free the old text handle to prevent a memory leak.
    if (oldTextH)
        MemHandleFree(oldTextH);
}
```

Notice that the preceding code retrieves the field's original handle with the FldGetTextHandle function and then later explicitly frees the handle with MemHandleFree. Palm OS does not free the handle containing the field's original contents, so the application code must take care of this housekeeping task to prevent a substantial memory leak.

The previous example also calls FldDrawField after setting the field's new handle to ensure that the system draws the new contents of the field to the screen. FldSetTextHandle updates only the handle; your application must manually redraw the field to display the field's new contents.

When a form closes, the system automatically frees the handle associated with each of its fields. To keep the handle, you must remove the association between the field and the handle. To do this, call FldSetTextHandle with NULL as its second argument, as in the following example:

```
FldSetTextHandle(field, NULL);
```

Specifying NULL for a text field's handle disconnects the field from its handle, allowing the handle to persist after the system has disposed of the field.

## Modifying a Text Field

Palm OS keeps track of a good deal of data about each field, such as the position of the insertion point and where line breaks occur in the text. Directly modifying the text in a handle associated with a field can confuse the system, resulting in garbled text on the screen. To avoid this kind of mess, you must disconnect the handle from the field, modify the text in the handle, and then reattach the handle. The `ReverseField` function in the following example reverses a string contained in a field:

```
static void ReverseField (FieldType *field)
{
    MemHandle  textH;

    if (FldGetTextLength(field) > 0)
    {
        textH = FldGetTextHandle(field);
        if (textH)
        {
            char  *str, *p, *q;
            char  temp;
            int   n;

            FldSetTextHandle(field, NULL);
            str = MemHandleLock(textH);
            n = StrLen(str);
            q = (n > 0) ? str + n - 1 : str;
            for (p = str; p < q; ++p, --q)
            {
                temp = *p;
                *p = *q;
                *q = temp;
            }

            MemHandleUnlock(textH);
            FldSetTextHandle(field, textH);
            FldDrawField(field);
        }
    }
}
```

The `ReverseField` function copies the field's text handle into the variable `textH` and then disconnects the handle from the field with `FldSetTextHandle`. Then `ReverseField` calls `MemHandleLock` on the handle to lock it and obtains a character pointer to its contents, which is suitable for a little pointer arithmetic to reverse the order of the string. `MemHandleUnlock` unlocks the handle after the text has been reversed, `FldSetTextHandle` reattaches the modified handle to the field, and then `FldDrawField` redraws the field so that the results of the string reversal are visible to the user.

If you need to modify only a bit of a field's text at a time, instead of the extensive changes performed by the preceding example, note that Palm OS provides a few functions that safely change the field's contents without your having to mess with `FldSetTextHandle`. The functions, and their uses, are described as follows:

❑ FldSetSelection. Sets the start and end of the highlighted selection in a field. FldSetSelection takes three arguments: a pointer to a field, the offset in bytes of the start of the text selection, and the offset of the end of the selection. If the start and end offsets are equal, FldSetSelection does not highlight any text; instead it moves the insertion point to the indicated offset.

❑ FldInsert. Replaces the current selection in a field, if any, with a new string. This function takes three arguments: a pointer to a field, a character pointer containing the string to insert, and the length in bytes of the string to be inserted, not including a trailing null character.

❑ FldDelete. Deletes a specified range of text from a field. FldDelete takes three arguments: a field pointer, the byte offset at the beginning of the text that should be deleted, and the byte offset of the end of the text to delete. This function does not delete the character at the ending offset, just everything up to that point in the field.

> Use these functions to make only small, relatively infrequent changes to a field. Both **FldInsert** and **FldDelete** redraw the entire field. If you call them too often, distracting flickering may occur on the screen as the system rapidly and repeatedly redraws the field. Worse yet, both functions post a **fldChangedEvent** to the queue each time you call them. It is possible to overflow the queue with these events if you call **FldInsert** and **FldDelete** too often.

## Retrieving Text from a Field

You can retrieve the text from a field by using FldGetTextHandle to get the field's text handle and then locking that handle with MemHandleLock to obtain a pointer to the string held in that handle; the last ReverseField example in the previous section does this. However, using FldGetTextHandle in this fashion can be a bit cumbersome if you want your application only to read the text from a field without modifying it. Palm OS also provides the FldGetTextPtr function for this purpose. FldGetTextPtr returns a locked pointer to a field's text string, or NULL if the field is empty.

> The pointer returned by **FldGetTextPtr** becomes invalid as soon as the user edits the text field. Also, any changes you make to the contents of the pointer can muddle the field's internal data for keeping track of text length and word wrapping information, taking the field out of sync with its actual contents. Use **FldGetTextPtr** to take a snapshot of a field's value at only one point in time.

FldGetTextHandle and FldGetTextPtr return NULL if the field has never contained any text, but if the user enters text into the field and deletes all of it, these two functions return a non-NULL pointer that points to a NULL character (\0). You can use the FldGetTextLength function to determine how long the text in a field is:

**Palm OS Garnet**
```
UInt16 length = FldGetTextLength(field);
```

**Palm OS Cobalt**

```
uint16_t length = FldGetTextLength(field);
```

# Setting Field Focus

In a form containing multiple text fields, only one field displays an insertion point and allows text entry at a time. This field has the *focus*. When the user taps in a field, the system automatically shifts the focus to that field. To set the focus within application code, use the FrmSetFocus function. FrmSetFocus has two arguments: a pointer to a form and the index number of the field that should receive the focus. FrmSetFocus uses the index number of a field, not an object pointer or a resource ID. Recall that you can use FrmGetObjectIndex to retrieve an object's index number, given its resource ID.

Set which field in a form initially has the focus when you handle the frmOpenEvent, right after drawing the form with FrmDrawForm. Setting a default field in this way ensures that the user may begin data entry immediately, without having to tap on a field to "wake" it up. Prior to Palm OS 3.5, an application must call FrmSetFocus after drawing the form. In Palm OS 3.5 and later, an application may call FrmSetFocus before calling FrmDrawForm to draw the form.

The FrmGetFocus function is a useful companion to FrmSetFocus. FrmGetFocus returns the index number of the field that currently has the focus, or the constant noFocus if no field has the focus.

Any form with multiple text fields also should support the prevFieldChr and nextFieldChr Graffiti characters, which the user may enter to switch quickly between fields instead of having to move the stylus from the Graffiti entry area to tap another field. You can deal with these two characters in a form event handler by handling the keyDownEvent. The following event handler moves the focus between two fields in a form in response to the prevFieldChr and nextFieldChr characters:

**Palm OS Garnet**

```
static Boolean MyFormHandleEvent (EventType *event)
{
    Boolean  handled = false;

    if (event->eType == keyDownEvent)
    {
        FormType *form = FrmGetActiveForm();
        UInt16 fieldIndex1 = FrmGetObjectIndex(form,
                                           Field1ID);
        UInt16 fieldIndex2 = FrmGetObjectIndex(form,
                                           Field2ID);

        switch (event->data.keyDown.chr)
        {
            case nextFieldChr:
                if (FrmGetFocus(form) == fieldIndex1)
                    FrmSetFocus(form, fieldIndex2);
                handled = true;
                break;

            case prevFieldChr:
                if (FrmGetFocus(form) == fieldIndex2)
                    FrmSetFocus(form, fieldIndex1);
```

```
                        handled = true;
                        break;
                }
        }

        return (handled);
}
```

**Palm OS Cobalt**

```
static Boolean MyFormHandleEvent (EventType *event)
{
    Boolean   handled = false;

    if (event->eType == keyDownEvent)
    {
        FormType *form = FrmGetActiveForm();
        uint16_t fieldIndex1 = FrmGetObjectIndex(form,
                                            Field1ID);
        uint16_t fieldIndex2 = FrmGetObjectIndex(form,
                                            Field2ID);

        switch (event->data.keyDown.chr)
        {
            case nextFieldChr:
                if (FrmGetFocus(form) == fieldIndex1)
                    FrmSetFocus(form, fieldIndex2);
                handled = true;
                break;

            case prevFieldChr:
                if (FrmGetFocus(form) == fieldIndex2)
                    FrmSetFocus(form, fieldIndex1);
                handled = true;
                break;
        }
    }

    return (handled);
}
```

## Setting Field Attributes

Internally, a field stores its attributes in a `FieldAttrType` structure, which the Palm OS header file `Field.h` defines as follows:

**Palm OS Garnet**

```
typedef struct {
    UInt16 usable       :1;
    UInt16 visible      :1;
    UInt16 editable     :1;
    UInt16 singleLine   :1;
    UInt16 hasFocus     :1;
    UInt16 dynamicSize  :1;
```

```
      UInt16 insPtVisible    :1;
      UInt16 dirty           :1;
      UInt16 underlined      :2;
      UInt16 justification   :2;
      UInt16 autoShift       :1;
      UInt16 hasScrollBar    :1;
      UInt16 numeric         :1;
} FieldAttrType;
```

**Palm OS Cobalt**

```
typedef struct {
      uint16_t usable        :1;
      uint16_t visible       :1;
      uint16_t editable      :1;
      uint16_t singleLine    :1;
      uint16_t hasFocus      :1;
      uint16_t dynamicSize   :1;
      uint16_t insPtVisible  :1;
      uint16_t dirty         :1;
      uint16_t underlined    :2;
      uint16_t justification :2;
      uint16_t autoShift     :1;
      uint16_t hasScrollBar  :1;
      uint16_t numeric       :1;
      uint16_t unused        :1;
} FieldAttrType;
```

Most of the time, you will never need to change these attributes at runtime. For those rare occasions where you want to hand-tweak a field's attribute, Palm OS offers the FldGetAttributes and FldSetAttributes functions. The values of many of these attributes also may be affected if an application uses other field functions. For example, FldSetFocus changes the status of the hasFocus field in a field's FieldAttrType structure.

FldGetAttributes has two arguments: a pointer to the field and a pointer to a FieldAttrType structure to receive a copy of the field's attributes. FldSetAttributes takes the same two arguments, only it copies the FieldAttrType structure that it receives into the actual attributes of the specified field. Note that setting the field attributes has no immediate physical effect on the screen; in order to see the changes, you must redraw the field with FldDrawField.

# Programming Gadgets

A gadget object allows you to define your own user interface element. The standard objects included in Palm OS should be sufficient; you should stick with them if at all possible to maintain a consistent look and feel with other Palm OS applications. However, if you need an object that simply cannot be implemented using the normal Palm OS interface elements, you can make your own object using a gadget.

Your application code must handle all taps on the gadget, as well as drawing the gadget to the screen. How you accomplish these tasks depends entirely on what the gadget's function is and what it looks like. The simple gadget pictured in Figure 8-8 illustrates the mechanics of interacting with a gadget. This particular gadget represents a single square from a tic-tac-toe board. Tapping the gadget toggles it from a blank square to an *X*, from an *X* to an *O*, and from an *O* back to a blank square again.

Figure 8-8

The gadget stores its state in a `UInt8` variable. The value 0 represents a blank square, 1 indicates an *X*, and 2 is an *O*. To provide storage space for this variable, the application must allocate a variable for it when it initializes the form containing the gadget:

**Palm OS Garnet**

```
static void MainFormInit(FormType *form)
{
    UInt8    *data;

    data = MemPtrNew(sizeof(UInt8));
    if (data)
    {
        *data = 0;
        FrmSetGadgetData(form, FrmGetObjectIndex(form,
                    MainTicTacToeGadget), data);
    }
}
```

**Palm OS Cobalt**

```
static void MainFormInit(FormType *form)
{
    uint8_t    *data;

    data = MemPtrNew(sizeof(uint8_t));
    if (data)
    {
        *data = 0;
        FrmSetGadgetData(form, FrmGetObjectIndex(form,
                    MainTicTacToeGadget), data);
    }
}
```

`MainFormInit` uses the `MemPtrNew` function to obtain memory space in which to store the gadget's data. Once it has a pointer to this new memory, `MainFormInit` initializes the gadget data to 0 (representing a blank square). To associate the newly allocated handle with the gadget, the `MainFormInit` function calls `FrmSetGadgetData`, passing a pointer to the form containing the gadget, the index number of the gadget object, and the pointer to the gadget's data.

An event handler for the `Main` form calls `MainFormInit` while handling the `frmOpenEvent`. The form event handler takes care of other details related to the gadget when it handles `frmCloseEvent` and `penDownEvent`. You will find details about the latter two events later in this section; for now, take a look at the `frmOpenEvent` part of the event handler:

```
static Boolean MainFormHandleEvent(EventType *event)
{
    Boolean    handled = false;
    FormType   *form = FrmGetActiveForm();

    if (event->eType == frmOpenEvent)
    {
        MainFormInit(form);
        FrmDrawForm(form);
        TicTacToeDraw(form, MainTicTacToeGadget);
        handled = true;
    }
    else if (event->eType == frmCloseEvent)
    {
        // Handle the frmCloseEvent.
    }
    else if (event->eType == penDownEvent)
    {
        // Handle the penDownEvent.
    }

    return (handled);
}
```

After calling `MainFormInit`, the event handler draws the form with `FrmDrawForm` and then draws the gadget with `TicTacToeDraw`:

### Palm OS Garnet

```
static void TicTacToeDraw (FormType *form, UInt16 gadgetID)
{
    RectangleType  bounds;
    UInt16  gadgetIndex = FrmGetObjectIndex(form,
                                      gadgetID);
    MemHandle  dataH = FrmGetGadgetData(form, gadgetIndex);

    if (dataH)
    {
        FontID   originalFont = FntSetFont(boldFont);

        UInt8  *data = MemHandleLock(dataH);

        FrmGetObjectBounds(form, gadgetIndex, &bounds);
        // Draw a border around the gadget.
        WinEraseRectangle(&bounds, 0);
        WinDrawRectangleFrame(rectangleFrame, &bounds);

        // Draw the contents of the tic tac toe square.
        switch(*data)
        {
            case 1:
                WinDrawChars("X", 1, bounds.topLeft.x + 6,
                            bounds.topLeft.y + 4);
                break;
            case 2:
```

```
                    WinDrawChars("O", 1, bounds.topLeft.x + 6,
                                    bounds.topLeft.y + 4);
                break;
            default:
                break;
        }

        MemHandleUnlock(dataH);
        FntSetFont(originalFont);
    }
}
```

**Palm OS Cobalt**

```
static void TicTacToeDraw (FormType *form, uint16_t gadgetID)
{
    RectangleType  bounds;
    Uint16_t  gadgetIndex = FrmGetObjectIndex(form,
                                        gadgetID);
    MemHandle  dataH = FrmGetGadgetData(form, gadgetIndex);

    if (dataH)
    {
        FontID    originalFont = FntSetFont(boldFont);

        uint8_t  *data = MemHandleLock(dataH);

        FrmGetObjectBounds(form, gadgetIndex, &bounds);
        // Draw a border around the gadget.
        WinEraseRectangle(&bounds, 0);
        WinDrawRectangleFrame(rectangleFrame, &bounds);

        // Draw the contents of the tic tac toe square.
        switch(*data)
        {
            case 1:
                WinDrawChars("X", 1, bounds.topLeft.x + 6,
                                    bounds.topLeft.y + 4);
                break;
            case 2:
                WinDrawChars("O", 1, bounds.topLeft.x + 6,
                                    bounds.topLeft.y + 4);
                break;
            default:
                break;
        }

        MemHandleUnlock(dataH);
        FntSetFont(originalFont);
    }
}
```

The `TicTacToeDraw` function first determines the current value of the gadget using `FrmGetGadgetData`, which requires a pointer to the form containing the gadget and the index number of the gadget object. `TicTacToeDraw` locks the handle returned by `FrmGetGadgetData` to obtain a pointer, from which the application may read the gadget's stored value.

Once it has the gadget's value, `TicTacToeDraw` can get down to the business of actually drawing the gadget on the screen. `TicTacToeDraw` retrieves the boundaries of the gadget object, which are stored in a `RectangleType` structure. The Palm OS header file `Rect.h` defines `RectangleType` and the `PointType` structures contained by `RectangleType`, as follows:

```
typedef struct {
    Coord   x;
    Coord   y;
} PointType;

typedef struct {
    PointType   topLeft;
    PointType   extent;
} RectangleType;
```

The `Coord` data type used in `PointType` is simply a `typedef` for `Int16`, defined in the Palm OS header `PalmTypes.h`.

Armed with the gadget's boundaries, `TicTacToeDraw` begins by erasing the gadget's interior with the `WinEraseRectangle` function and then draws a box around the gadget with `WinDrawRectangleFrame`. Then, depending on the value of the gadget, `TicTacToeDraw` draws an *X* or an *O* in the square with `WinDrawChars` or leaves the newly erased square alone if the gadget's value indicates a blank square. `WinEraseRectangle`, `WinDrawRectangleFrame`, `WinDrawChars`, and other drawing functions are detailed in Chapter 11.

Returning to the Main form event handler, the application must free the handle holding the gadget's data when the form no longer has use of it. The `frmCloseEvent` is a perfect place to do just that:

```
else if (event->eType == frmCloseEvent)
{
    MemHandle  dataH = FrmGetGadgetData(form,
        FrmGetObjectIndex(form, MainTicTacToeGadget));

    if (dataH)
        MemHandleFree(dataH);
    handled = true;
}
```

The event handler also must capture the `penDownEvent`, which occurs when the user begins to tap the screen:

**Palm OS Garnet**
```
else if (event->eType == penDownEvent)
{
    UInt16  gadgetIndex = FrmGetObjectIndex(form,
                            MainTicTacToeGadget);
    RectangleType  bounds;
```

```
    FrmGetObjectBounds(form, gadgetIndex, &bounds);
    if (RctPtInRectangle(eventP->screenX, eventP->screenY,
                        &bounds))
    {
        TicTacToeTap(form, MainTicTacToeGadget, eventP);
        handled = true;
    }
}
```

**Palm OS Cobalt**

```
else if (event->eType == penDownEvent)
{
    uint16_t  gadgetIndex = FrmGetObjectIndex(form,
                            MainTicTacToeGadget);
    RectangleType  bounds;

    FrmGetObjectBounds(form, gadgetIndex, &bounds);
    if (RctPtInRectangle(eventP->screenX, eventP->screenY,
                        &bounds))
    {
        TicTacToeTap(form, MainTicTacToeGadget, eventP);
        handled = true;
    }
}
```

MainFormHandleEvent compares the screen coordinates of the tap with the boundaries of the tic-tac-toe gadget. If the tap is within the gadget, the event handler calls the TicTacToeTap function to handle updating the gadget:

**Palm OS Garnet**

```
static void TicTacToeTap (FormType *form, UInt16 gadgetID,
                        EventType *event)
{
    UInt16     gadgetIndex = FrmGetObjectIndex(form,
                                            gadgetID);
    MemHandle dataH = FrmGetGadgetData(form, gadgetIndex);
    Int16     x, y;
    Boolean   penDown;
    RectangleType  bounds;
    Boolean   wasInBounds = true;

    if (dataH)
    {
        FrmGetObjectBounds(form, gadgetIndex, &bounds);
        WinInvertRectangle(&bounds, 0);

        do
        {
            Boolean  nowInBounds;

            PenGetPoint(&x, &y, &penDown);
            nowInBounds = RctPtInRectangle(x, y, &bounds);
```

```
                    if (nowInBounds != wasInBounds) {
                        WinInvertRectangle(&bounds, 0);
                        wasInBounds = nowInBounds;
                    }
            }
        }
        while (penDown);

        if (wasInBounds)
        {
            BytePtr  data = MemHandleLock(dataH);
            if (++(*data) > 2)
                *data = 0;
            MemHandleUnlock(dataH);
            TicTacToeDraw(form, gadgetID);
        }
    }
}
```

**Palm OS Cobalt**

```
static void TicTacToeTap (FormType *form, uint16_t gadgetID,
                          EventType *event)
{
    uint16_t    gadgetIndex = FrmGetObjectIndex(form,
                                                gadgetID);
    MemHandle dataH = FrmGetGadgetData(form, gadgetIndex);
    int16_t    x, y;
    Boolean    penDown;
    RectangleType  bounds;
    Boolean    wasInBounds = true;

    if (dataH)
    {
        FrmGetObjectBounds(form, gadgetIndex, &bounds);
        WinInvertRectangle(&bounds, 0);

        do
        {
            Boolean  nowInBounds;

            //EvtGetPen replaces PenGetPoint in Cobalt
            EvtGetPen(&x, &y, &penDown);
            nowInBounds = RctPtInRectangle(x, y, &bounds);
            if (nowInBounds != wasInBounds) {
                WinInvertRectangle(&bounds, 0);
                wasInBounds = nowInBounds;
            }
        }
        while (penDown);

        if (wasInBounds)
        {
            BytePtr  data = MemHandleLock(dataH);
```

```
            if (++(*data) > 2)
                *data = 0;
            MemHandleUnlock(dataH);
            TicTacToeDraw(form, gadgetID);
        }
    }
}
```

The tic-tac-toe gadget reacts to taps in much the same way as a standard button. The gadget highlights when the user taps it (using the `WinInvertRectangle` function) and remains highlighted for as long as the user holds the stylus on the gadget. Moving the stylus outside the bounds of the gadget returns the gadget's appearance to normal, and releasing the stylus outside the gadget's borders has no lasting effect on the gadget.

If the user taps and releases within the gadget, `TicTacToeTap` rotates the gadget's attached data to the next value and then redraws the gadget by calling `TicTacToeDraw`.

## Programming Extended Gadgets

Palm OS 3.5 introduced *extended gadgets*. An extended gadget's resources are no different from those of a regular gadget. What makes an extended gadget special is that you can assign a callback function to the gadget that handles all of the gadget's user interaction and drawing. The operating system automatically calls your application's custom callback function at appropriate times.

Defining a gadget's behavior and drawing routines in a callback function makes for better encapsulation; extended gadgets are not dependent upon their containing form's event handler. Furthermore, an extended gadget can redraw itself automatically when its containing form needs to be redrawn.

To assign a callback function to an extended gadget, call the `FrmSetGadgetHandler` function, which has the following prototype:

**Palm OS Garnet**
```
void FrmSetGadgetHandler (FormType *formP,
                    UInt16 objIndex,
                    FormGadgetHandlerType *attrP)
```

**Palm OS Cobalt**
```
void FrmSetGadgetHandler (FormType *formP,
                    uint16_t objIndex,
                    FormGadgetHandlerType *attrP)
```

The `formP` parameter is a pointer to the form that contains the gadget, and `objIndex` is the index of the gadget to which you wish to assign a callback function. The final parameter, `attrP`, is a pointer to the callback function itself. A gadget callback must have the following prototype:

**Palm OS Garnet**
```
Boolean (FormGadgetHandlerType)
    (struct FormGadgetTypeInCallback *gadgetP,
     UInt16 cmd, void *paramP)
```

**Palm OS Cobalt**

```
Boolean (FormGadgetHandlerType)
     (struct FormGadgetTypeInCallback *gadgetP,
      uint16_t cmd, void *paramP)
```

The return value from a gadget callback is a signal to the operating system whether the callback handled an action or not. The callback should return `true` if it handled whatever action the system requested of it. If the callback does not handle the action, it should return `false`.

A gadget callback's first parameter is a pointer to the gadget structure itself. Unlike most user interface structures, it is safe to access the fields of this structure directly. On an ARM-based handheld, Palm OS 5 translates its ARM-compatible version of the gadget structure into its Motorola 68K equivalent. The `FormGadgetTypeInCallback` structure looks like this:

**Palm OS Garnet**

```
typedef struct {
     UInt16 id;
     FormGadgetAttrType attr;
     RectangleType rect;
     const void *data;
     FormGadgetHandlerType *handler;
} FormGadgetTypeInCallback;
```

**Palm OS Cobalt**

```
typedef struct {
     uint16_t id;
     FormGadgetAttrType attr;
     RectangleType rect;
     const void *data;
     FormGadgetHandlerType *handler;
} FormGadgetTypeInCallback;
```

The `cmd` parameter is a constant that specifies what action the gadget callback should take. There are four possible values for `cmd`:

❑   `formGadgetDeleteCmd`. The `FrmDeleteForm` system function sends this constant to a gadget as a signal that the system is deleting the gadget object. If the gadget allocates any memory for its own use, it should free that memory in response to this command. If the gadget has any other cleanup tasks to perform, it also should take care of them in response to `formGadgetDeleteCmd`.

❑   `formGadgetDrawCmd`. `FrmDrawForm` and `FrmDrawObject` send this command to tell a gadget to draw or redraw itself. If your gadget performs any drawing, it also should set its `visible` flag:

```
gadgetP->attr.visible = true;
```

If the gadget callback does not set the `visible` flag, `FrmHideObject` won't be able to erase the gadget because `FrmHideObject` returns immediately if an object's `visible` flag is `false`.

❑   `formGadgetEraseCmd`. `FrmHideObject` uses this command to tell a gadget to erase itself from view. The `FrmHideObject` function automatically clears the gadget's `visible` and `usable` flags for you. If you return `false` from the gadget callback function to indicate that the callback did not handle `formGadgetEraseCmd`, `FrmHideObject` also calls `WinEraseRectangle` to erase your gadget. If your gadget draws only within its own borders, it can usually get away with returning `false` to let `FrmHideObject` take care of the erasing.

❑ `formGadgetHandleEventCmd`. `FrmHandleEvent` sends this command to a gadget to give the gadget an opportunity to handle events that occur within the gadget's boundaries. When `cmd` equals `formGadgetHandleEventCmd`, the gadget callback's third parameter, `paramP`, points to an `EventType` structure containing the event to be handled.

There are two possible events that a gadget callback might need to handle: `frmGadgetEnterEvent` and `frmGadgetMiscEvent`. `FrmHandleEvent` sends a `frmGadgetEnterEvent` to a gadget's callback function when a `penDownEvent` occurs within the gadget's boundaries. The gadget should track pen movement and perform highlighting, in much the same way as the `MainFormHandleEvent` function (shown earlier in this section) handles a `penDownEvent`.

# Programming Lists and Pop-up Lists

List objects, depending upon how you use them, can be very simple to implement, or very difficult. The main determining factor in the complexity of a list is whether its elements need to change at runtime or not. Defining all of a list's items at design time, as part of the list resource, results in an easy-to-program static list. If you need to generate the list's items while the program is running, though, programming the list requires more effort.

## Retrieving List Data

If the user taps the screen and releases within a list, the system queues a `lstSelectEvent`, which you can choose to handle in a form event handler. To determine which list item the user selects, you need to use the `LstGetSelection` function. `LstGetSelection` takes a list pointer as its only argument, returning the number of the list item currently selected. List items are numbered sequentially, starting from 0. If no item is selected in the list, `LstGetSelection` returns the constant `noListSelection`, which is defined in the Palm OS headers.

Retrieving the text of a particular item in the list requires the `LstGetSelectionText` function. `LstGetSelectionText` is somewhat misnamed; instead of returning the text of the selected list item, the function actually returns *any* list item's text, given a pointer to the list and the item's number. For example, the following code retrieves the text of the first item in a list:

```
Char *text = LstGetSelectionText(list, 0);
```

You can retrieve the currently selected list item's text by calling `LstGetSelection` within the call to `LstGetSelectionText`. The following example retrieves the text of the currently selected list item:

```
Char *text = LstGetSelectionText(list,
                        LstGetSelection(list));
```

> The character pointer returned by `LstGetSelectionText` is actually a pointer into the list object's internal data, not a copy of that data. Modifying the pointer returned from `LstGetSelectionText` will actually change text in the list itself, causing unexpected results. For example, the following code directly sets the label of a control from the text of the second item in a list, and then changes the control's label again:
>
> ```
> CtlSetLabel(ctl, LstGetSelectionText(list, 1));
> CtlSetLabel(ctl, "This is a bad idea");
> ```
>
> This code does have the desired effect of changing the control's label to the text of the appropriate list item. However, the second call to `CtlSetLabel` overwrites some of the list's contents with the text "This is a bad idea." This spillover happens because the control's label and the list share a pointer. A safer way to set the label from a list item is to copy the list item's text to a new variable and then set the label from the variable:
>
> ```
> Char *label = CtlGetLabel(ctl);
> StrCopy(label, LstGetSelectionText(list, 1));
> CtlSetLabel(ctl, label);
> ```

You also can retrieve the total number of items in a list or the number of visible items, using the `LstGetNumberOfItems` and `LstGetVisibleItems` functions, respectively. `LstGetVisibleItems` is available only in Palm OS version 2.0 and later.

Palm OS 4.0 introduces another useful list function: `LstGetTopItem`. This function returns the index of the topmost item displayed in a list. This function is conspicuously absent from earlier versions of Palm OS but you can still use it on older handhelds by using its PalmOSGlue equivalent, `LstGlueGetTopItem`.

## Manipulating Lists

You can directly set which list item is selected with the `LstSetSelection` function. `LstSetSelection` takes two arguments: a pointer to the list object and the number of the item to select. Like other list functions, 0 represents the first item in the list. You also may pass -1 as the second argument to `LstSetSelection`, which clears the selection entirely.

To make a particular list item visible, use the `LstMakeItemVisible` function. `LstMakeItemVisible` takes a pointer to a list and the number of the list item to make visible. The `LstMakeItemVisible` function changes the top item of the list to make the requested item visible. If the item is already visible, `LstMakeItemVisible` leaves the list alone.

Note that `LstMakeItemVisible` does not update the list display, only the list's internal data. You need to call `LstDrawList` to refresh the list display after a call to `LstMakeItemVisible`. However, even this is not enough to properly redraw the list, because `LstDrawList` does not always erase the highlight from the selected list item before redrawing the list in the new position mandated by `LstMakeItemVisible`. Calling `LstEraseList` before `LstDrawList` removes the highlight, resulting in a clean redraw of the list. Here is an example that scrolls a list to make its fifth item visible and then refreshes the list display:

```
LstMakeItemVisible(list, 4);
LstEraseList(list);
LstDrawList(list);
```

If you are initializing a list before the form containing the list has been drawn, you can safely avoid calling `LstEraseList` and `LstDrawList` because `FrmDrawForm` handles drawing the list for you.

# Programming Dynamic Lists

Palm OS does not provide any functions to insert items into a list or remove them from it. Instead, you have the following two choices for dynamically altering the contents of a list:

❏ Set the entire contents of the list at once by passing an array of strings to `LstSetListChoices`.

❏ Attach a callback function to the list with `LstSetDrawFunction` that the system calls to draw each row of the list.

Both methods of modifying a list are perfectly valid, but using `LstSetDrawFunction` is more flexible and requires less memory overhead. These two methods are described in the next section.

## Populating a List with LstSetListChoices

The `LstSetListChoices` function requires a pointer to a list object, a pointer to an array of strings, and the total number of items in the list. Each member of the array of strings becomes a single item in the list. The prototype for `LstSetListChoices` looks like this:

**Palm OS Garnet**
```
void LstSetListChoices (ListType *listP, Char **itemsText,
                        UInt16 numItems);
```

**Palm OS Cobalt**
```
void LstSetListChoices (ListType *listP, char **itemsText,
                        int16_t numItems);
```

The arguments to `LstSetListChoices` are `list`, a pointer to a list object; `itemsText`, a pointer to an array of strings; and `numItems`, the total number of items in the list. If you have ever dealt with pointers to arrays of strings in C/C++, you should immediately realize that trying to pass all of a list's text at once with `LstSetListChoices` is cumbersome at best. Your application must handle the allocation, initialization, and maintenance of the array of strings without any help from the operating system — a process that can quickly become a nightmare to code and debug if your application needs to change the list's contents often during execution. Also, if the list is long enough, this technique can become a drain on the limited amount of dynamic memory available because you must keep the entire array of strings in memory while the form containing the list is open.

## Filling a List with LstSetDrawFunction

Fortunately, Palm OS offers a simple solution to the problem of changing a list's contents at runtime. Instead of explicitly setting the text of all the list's items at once, you can set a callback function to take care of drawing each individual row in the list using `LstSetDrawFunction`. Once the callback function is in place, whenever the system needs to draw a row in the list, it calls your custom routine to perform

the drawing operation. The one drawback to this approach is that you cannot use the
`LstGetSelectionText` function with the list because none of the list's items are populated with text.

For the sake of simplicity, the example that follows uses this globally defined array of strings:

```
char ListElements[6][10] =
{
    { "Gold" },
    { "Silver" },
    { "Hydrogen" },
    { "Oxygen" },
    { "Argon" },
    { "Plutonium" }
};
```

The event handler for the form containing the list sets a custom drawing function for the list with
`LstSetDrawFunction` while handling the `frmOpenEvent`. Using a callback list drawing function
still requires a call to `LstSetListChoices` to tell the list how many items it should contain.
`MainFormHandleEvent` passes NULL as the second argument to `LstSetListChoices` instead of a
pointer to an array of strings, along with the total number of items in the list as the third argument to
`LstSetListChoices`.

```
static Boolean MainFormHandleEvent (EventType *event)
{
    Boolean    handled = false;

    if (event->eType == frmOpenEvent)
    {
        FormType    *form = FrmGetActiveForm();
        ListType    *list = GetObjectPtr(MainList);
        int         numChoices = 0;

        // Set custom list drawing callback function.
        LstSetDrawFunction(list, MainListDraw);

        // Determine the number of items in the string
        // array, then fill the list with that many items.
        numChoices = sizeof(ListElements) /
                    sizeof(ListElements[0]);
        LstSetListChoices(list, NULL, numChoices);

        // Draw the form, which also draws the list.
        FrmDrawForm(form);
        handled = true;
    }

    return (handled);
}
```

`MainListDraw` is the callback function that handles drawing each item in the list:

**Palm OS Garnet**

```
static void MainListDraw (UInt16 itemNum,
                          RectangleType *bounds,
                          Char **itemsText)
{
    WinDrawChars(ListElements[itemNum],
                 StrLen(ListElements[itemNum]),
                 bounds->topLeft.x,
                 bounds->topLeft.y);
}
```

**Palm OS Cobalt**

```
static void MainListDraw (uint16_t itemNum,
                          RectangleType *bounds,
                          char **itemsText,
                          struct ListType *listP)
{
    WinDrawChars(ListElements[itemNum],
                 StrLen(ListElements[itemNum]),
                 bounds->topLeft.x,
                 bounds->topLeft.y);
}
```

The system passes the number of the item in the list to draw, along with a rectangle defining the screen area occupied by that item. With these two pieces of information, a simple call to `WinDrawChars` can take care of drawing the appropriate list item, retrieving the correct string by using `itemNum` as an index into the `ListElements` array. For example, when drawing the third list item, the system passes the value 2 in the `itemNum` argument, which causes `MainListDraw` to draw the string stored in `ListElements[2]`, or "Hydrogen." In a full-fledged application, you can use `itemNum` as an index into a stored array of string resources, the application's database, or any other appropriate data structure.

This example draws only the text of each list item, but it is simple to add code in the callback for drawing bitmaps if you wish to further customize the list display. The ability to add extra drawing code to the callback function makes this method of filling a list much more flexible than calling `LstSetListChoices` by itself.

## Handling Pop-up Lists

When the user selects an item from a pop-up list, a pop-up trigger sends two events to the queue: a `ctlSelectEvent` and a `popSelectEvent`. The `popSelectEvent` is more useful because it contains data about both the trigger and its attached list, whereas the `ctlSelectEvent` sparked by the user's tapping of a pop-up trigger contains only information about the trigger itself. A `popSelectEvent` also contains other useful bits of information, as outlined in the following table.

| Data | Description |
| --- | --- |
| data.popSelect.controlID | Resource ID of the pop-up trigger |
| data.popSelect.controlP | ControlPtr to the pop-up trigger resource control structure |
| data.popSelect.listID | Resource ID of the list attached to a pop-up trigger |
| data.popSelect.listP | ListPtr to the attached list structure |
| data.popSelect.selection | Item number of the newly selected list item |
| data.popSelect.priorSelection | Item number of the list item selected before the new selection |

When the user selects an item from the pop-up list, the text of that item becomes the new label for the pop-up trigger. However, this behavior works only if you leave popSelectEvent in the queue so FrmHandleEvent has a chance to process it. You can leave the event on the queue by not setting handled = true in the code that reacts to popSelectEvent. For example, the following form event handler reacts to popSelectEvent but leaves it on the queue so that FrmHandleEvent will be able to automatically set the pop-up trigger's label to the text of the item selected in the pop-up list:

```
static Boolean MainFormHandleEvent (EventType *event)
{
    Boolean  handled = false;

    if (event->eType == popSelectEvent)
    {
        // Do something in response to pop-up list
        // selection. Leave handled = false so the event
        // stays in the queue.
    }
}
```

If a pop-up trigger is attached to a list that the application fills dynamically at runtime, you need to initialize the trigger's label to an appropriate value before displaying the form that contains that pop-up trigger. The following code uses the CtlSetLabel function to set a pop-up trigger's label to the text of the selected item in its attached list:

```
ListType    *list = GetObjectPtr(PopupList);
ControlType *popTrig = GetObjectPtr(PopupTrigger);
Char        *label = CtlGetLabel(popTrig);

StrCopy(label, LstGetSelectionText(list,
                        LstGetSelection(list)));
CtlSetLabel(popTrig, label);
```

Note that the code listed previously would work only with either a static list populated at design time or in a list populated using LstSetListChoices, because LstGetSelectionText can retrieve only text that actually exists within the list itself. If you were to use the LstSetDrawFunction method described earlier, you would need to look up the text values yourself, as shown in the following example:

```
StrCopy(label, ListElements[LstGetSelection(list)]);
CtlSetLabel(popTrig, label);
```

# Programming Menus

Dealing with menus in code is mostly straightforward; the "Hello World" application in Chapter 4 covers the basics of handling menu events. Briefly, here are some things to remember when implementing menus in an application:

❑ In the event handler for the form containing a menu, check for an event of type menuEvent.

❑ Look in the event data structure, under event->data.menu.itemID, for the resource ID of the menu item the user selected.

❑ If a form contains more than two or three menu items, it is a good idea to write a separate menu-handling function that actually executes the menu commands and call that function from your event handler. The menu-handling function should take the resource ID of the selected menu as an argument. This technique prevents clutter in the form event handler, making it easier to read.

This information should get you through most menu programming. The rest of this section deals with one potential pitfall of using menu Graffiti shortcuts, along with some methods for doing fancier things with menus in your application.

## *Hiding Menu Items*

Palm OS does not offer any way to "gray out" unusable menu items, as is often the case with desktop GUIs. For the most part, if a menu command is invalid in a certain context in your application, you can simply display an alert dialog box letting the user know why that command cannot be used. The built-in applications use this strategy for a number of commands. Figure 8-9 shows the dialog box that appears when the user tries to invoke Record ➪ Delete Item in the To Do application without first selecting a To Do item from the list.

Figure 8-9

This strategy of displaying a dialog box to inform the user why the command does not work is fine for most context-dependent menu items. However, you may wish to hide a menu item altogether. For example, if an application supports beaming but also can run on devices that do not have an infrared port, removing the beaming-related menu item entirely on non-IR devices removes clutter from the interface. Hiding completely unavailable commands also is more polite because it doesn't tempt the user with menu options that display only a disappointing dialog box when invoked.

Because adding and removing menu items are not standard functions in Palm OS, you must use a brute-force approach to hide menu items. Simply create two menu bars: one that contains the menu item you wish to hide and one without that menu item. You may then programmatically switch with the FrmSetMenu function which menu is displayed. FrmSetMenu takes two arguments: a pointer to a form and the resource ID of a menu bar to associate with that form.

To implement this dual menu bar strategy, assign one of the two menu bars to the form resource at design time, just as you would do for a single menu bar. Then, just before displaying the form containing the switchable menu bar, you can call FrmSetMenu, if necessary, to switch to the second menu. The Librarian sample application uses this strategy to hide the Record ➪ Beam Book command in its Edit view. The following code checks to see if the device running Librarian supports beaming and, if not, sets the menu bar associated with the Edit view to a version that does not contain a Beam Book command:

```
UInt32   romVersion;

FtrGet(sysFtrCreator, sysFtrNumROMVersion, &romVersion);
if (romVersion < gRequiredVersion)
    FrmSetMenu(FrmGetActiveForm(), RecordNoIRMenuBar);
```

Using the FtrGet function to retrieve information about supported features is covered in Chapter 10.

## Programming the Command Toolbar

When the user makes the Graffiti command stroke (a swipe from the lower left to the upper right) in Palm OS 3.5 and later, the system displays a command toolbar (see Figure 8-10).

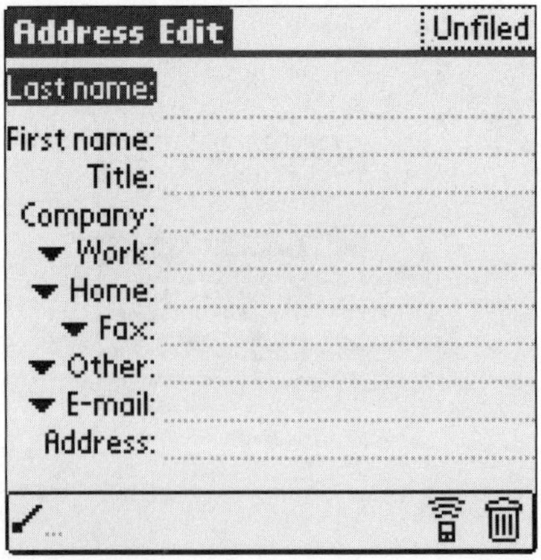

Figure 8-10

The system automatically adds appropriate buttons for text editing commands to the toolbar when there is an active field on the current form. You also can add to the toolbar your own buttons that correspond to menu commands in your application. For example, if your application has a Delete Record menu command, you can add to the toolbar a trash can icon that the user can tap in order to delete a record.

There is limited space available on the command toolbar; it holds a maximum of eight buttons. However, you should limit your application to displaying only four or five to leave space in the left of the command bar, where the system briefly displays the name of the activated menu item when a user taps one of the buttons.

To add a button to the command toolbar, your application should respond to menuCmdBarOpenEvent by calling the MenuCmdBarAddButton function. MenuCmdBarAddButton has the following prototype:

**Palm OS Garnet**
```
Err MenuCmdBarAddButton (UInt8 where,
    UInt16 bitmapId, MenuCmdBarResultType resultType,
    UInt32 result, Char *nameP)
```

**Palm OS Cobalt**
```
Err MenuCmdBarAddButton (uint8_t where,
    uint16_t bitmapId, MenuCmdBarResultType resultType,
    uint32_t result, Char *nameP)
```

The where argument specifies where the new button should appear on the command bar. If you pass the constant menuCmdBarOnLeft, the button appears to the left of any existing buttons; menuCmdBarOnRight places the button to the right of any existing buttons. You also may specify an exact position, numbered from right to left, with the rightmost button occupying position 1. If you specify an exact location and there are no buttons to the right of that position, the command bar contains blank space to the right of the newly added button. For example, if you pass a value of 3 for the where argument and there are no buttons in positions 1 or 2, the command bar is completely blank to the right of the new button at position 3, which may look a little strange to the user.

Use the bitmapId argument to specify the resource ID of a bitmap or bitmap family that contains the image for the button. Buttons must be exactly 16 pixels wide × 13 pixels high; the operating system does not accept buttons with different dimensions.

Palm OS contains a number of built-in bitmap resources for common menu commands. The following table outlines the available icons and the constants used to access them. For the sake of consistency, these commands should always appear in the same order on the command toolbar, from right to left in the same order as they appear in the table.

| Icon | Constant | Menu Command Description |
|------|----------|-------------------------|
| 🗑 | BarDeleteBitmap | Delete a record from the application |
| 📋 | BarPasteBitmap | Paste the contents of the Clipboard into a field at the current cursor position |
| 📑 | BarCopyBitmap | Copy the highlighted text from a field to the Clipboard |
| ✂ | BarCutBitmap | Cut the highlighted text from a field to the Clipboard |
| ↩ | BarUndoBitmap | Undo the last text editing operation |
| 🔒 | BarSecureBitmap | Display the system Change Security dialog box |
| 📶 | BarBeamBitmap | Beam a record to another handheld |
| ℹ | BarInfoBitmap | Display information (this icon is used by the system launcher to display the Info dialog box) |

The resultType argument to MenuCmdBarAddButton defines what kind of data the function returns to the system when the user selects the new button, and the result argument contains the actual data. A command toolbar button typically sends two kinds of information, as defined by the value of resultType:

❑ menuCmdBarResultChar. The system queues a keyDownEvent containing a character that corresponds to the menu item's Graffiti shortcut. In this case, the result argument contains the desired character. This method is inefficient because your application must make another pass through its event loop to pick up the menuEvent queued by the keyDownEvent.

❑ menuCmdBarResultMenuItem. The system queues a menuEvent with the menu item ID of the menu command to activate contained in the result argument. This method is much more efficient than returning a Graffiti command shortcut via menuCmdBarResultChar.

The final argument to MenuCmdBarAddButton, nameP, is a pointer to a null-terminated string that should appear to the left of the buttons on the toolbar when the user selects the button. If you leave this argument set to NULL, the system displays the text of the selected menu item. If the menu item's text is particularly long, you may want to provide a shorter version with the nameP argument. For example, if your application provides an "Import from Memo Pad" command, you could shorten it to "Import" in the command toolbar.

As an example, the Librarian application's EditFormHandleEvent function handles menuCmdBarOpenEvent by adding buttons for common text-editing menu commands, such as copying and pasting. Here are the relevant portions of EditFormHandleEvent:

**Palm OS Garnet**

```
static Boolean EditFormHandleEvent(EventType * event)
{
    Boolean    handled = false;
    FieldPtr   field;
    UInt16     startPos, endPos;
```

```
        switch (event->eType)
        {
            case menuCmdBarOpenEvent:
                field = GetFocusFieldPtr();
                FldGetSelection(field, &startPos, &endPos);

                if (startPos != endPos)
                {
                    MenuCmdBarAddButton(menuCmdBarOnLeft,
                     BarPasteBitmap, menuCmdBarResultMenuItem,
                     EditPaste, NULL);
                    MenuCmdBarAddButton(menuCmdBarOnLeft,
                     BarCopyBitmap, menuCmdBarResultMenuItem,
                     EditCopy, NULL);
                    MenuCmdBarAddButton(menuCmdBarOnLeft,
                     BarCutBitmap, menuCmdBarResultMenuItem,
                     EditCut, NULL);
                }
                else
                {
                    MenuCmdBarAddButton(menuCmdBarOnLeft,
                     BarDeleteBitmap, menuCmdBarResultMenuItem,
                     RecordDeleteBook, NULL);
                    MenuCmdBarAddButton(menuCmdBarOnLeft,
                     BarPasteBitmap, menuCmdBarResultMenuItem,
                     EditPaste, NULL);
                    MenuCmdBarAddButton(menuCmdBarOnLeft,
                     BarUndoBitmap, menuCmdBarResultMenuItem,
                     EditUndo, NULL);
                    MenuCmdBarAddButton(menuCmdBarOnLeft,
                     BarBeamBitmap, menuCmdBarResultMenuItem,
                     RecordBeamBook, NULL);
                }

                // Prevent the field manager from adding its
                // own buttons; this command bar already
                // contains all the buttons it needs.
                event->data.menuCmdBarOpen.preventFieldButtons =
                    true;

                // Leave event unhandled so the system can
                // catch it.
                break;

            // Other events omitted.
        }

    return handled;
}
```

**Palm OS Cobalt**
```
static Boolean EditFormHandleEvent(EventType * event)
{
    Boolean   handled = false;
    FieldPtr  field;
```

```
        Uint16_t    startPos, endPos;


        switch (event->eType)
        {
            case menuCmdBarOpenEvent:
                field = GetFocusFieldPtr();
                FldGetSelection(field, &startPos, &endPos);

                if (startPos != endPos)
                {
                    MenuCmdBarAddButton(menuCmdBarOnLeft,
                     BarPasteBitmap, menuCmdBarResultMenuItem,
                     EditPaste, NULL);
                    MenuCmdBarAddButton(menuCmdBarOnLeft,
                     BarCopyBitmap, menuCmdBarResultMenuItem,
                     EditCopy, NULL);
                    MenuCmdBarAddButton(menuCmdBarOnLeft,
                     BarCutBitmap, menuCmdBarResultMenuItem,
                     EditCut, NULL);
                }
                else
                {
                    MenuCmdBarAddButton(menuCmdBarOnLeft,
                     BarDeleteBitmap, menuCmdBarResultMenuItem,
                     RecordDeleteBook, NULL);
                    MenuCmdBarAddButton(menuCmdBarOnLeft,
                     BarPasteBitmap, menuCmdBarResultMenuItem,
                     EditPaste, NULL);
                    MenuCmdBarAddButton(menuCmdBarOnLeft,
                     BarUndoBitmap, menuCmdBarResultMenuItem,
                     EditUndo, NULL);
                    MenuCmdBarAddButton(menuCmdBarOnLeft,
                     BarBeamBitmap, menuCmdBarResultMenuItem,
                     RecordBeamBook, NULL);
                }

                // Prevent the field manager from adding its
                // own buttons; this command bar already
                // contains all the buttons it needs.
                event->data.menuCmdBarOpen.preventFieldButtons =
                    true;

                // Leave event unhandled so the system can
                // catch it.
                break;

            // Other events omitted.
        }

        return handled;
}
```

*Notice that EditFormHandleEvent does not set handled equal to true but rather leaves it set to false. Your application must leave menuCmdBarOpenEvent unhandled so the system can continue to display the command toolbar properly.*

After you have added your own buttons to the command toolbar, Palm OS checks to see if there is an active text field. If there is, the system automatically adds buttons to the toolbar for common text operations, such as copying and pasting. The operating system adds only those buttons that make sense; for example, Copy and Cut buttons appear only if text is currently selected in a field. If you are running out of room on the toolbar, you can prevent the operating system from adding text-editing buttons by setting menuCmdBarOpen.preventFieldButtons to true, as shown in the previous EditFormHandleEvent example.

# Summary

In this chapter, you learned how to program most of the user interface elements in Palm OS, as well as how to directly draw graphics and text to the screen. After reading this chapter, you should understand the following:

❑   Alerts are an excellent way to quickly display information, or to prompt the user for simple input.

❑   You can display forms as stand-alone screens with FrmGotoForm, complex dialog boxes with FrmPopupForm, or simple dialog boxes with FrmDoDialog.

❑   Many user interface objects post an *enter event* when first tapped, an *exit event* if the user drags the stylus outside the object before lifting it, and a *select event* if the user lifts the stylus within the object's borders.

❑   Most actions you may perform with a form object require a pointer to that object or the object's index number, which you may retrieve with FrmGetObjectPtr and FrmGetObjectIndex, respectively.

❑   You can temporarily remove form objects from the user interface with the FrmHideObject function, and you can make them appear again using FrmShowObject.

❑   To set which check box or push button in a control group is selected, or to determine which object is selected, use the FrmSetControlGroupSelection and FrmGetControlGroupSelection functions.

❑   Selector triggers should be used to display a dialog box for changing the trigger's value; this dialog box may be a form that you program yourself, or the dialog box may be one of the Palm OS standard date and time pickers, which you may display with SelectDay, SelectTime, or SelectOneTime.

❑   Fields require attention to detail to program properly, mostly because Palm OS does not handle much of the memory allocation details of fields, requiring you to do so with your own code.

❑   To implement a gadget, you must provide code to handle taps on the gadget and to handle drawing the gadget on the screen.

❑ In Palm OS 3.5 and later, you can create an extended gadget that handles drawing and user interaction with its own callback function.

❑ You may populate a list at runtime either all at once, using `LstSetListChoices`, or a line at a time, by assigning a list callback function with `LstSetDrawFunction`.

❑ The system takes care of most menu behavior but you do have to do a little extra work if a menu command changes the screen contents, or if you want to show different menus in different situations.

❑ You can add your own buttons to the command toolbar by handling `menuCmdBarOpenEvent` and calling `MenuCmdBarAddButton`.

# 9

# Managing Memory

Memory management is one of the areas of Palm OS programming that highlights the difference between developing a desktop application and developing a handheld application. Even though modern Palm OS handhelds come with dramatically more available memory than those available just a few short years ago, programmers used to writing code that requires the allocation of large amounts of heap memory during program execution are often forced to rethink their memory allocation strategy when designing their handheld applications to run on a platform in which even the most generous scenarios offer less than 1 MB available dynamic RAM.

## Managing Memory

Because Palm OS was designed to run on inexpensive, low-power handheld devices, it is good at dealing with tight memory conditions. Palm OS does not handle all the burden of dealing with such a limited memory space, however. Memory constraints on a Palm OS device require that you pay careful attention to how your application uses memory. Therefore, understanding the memory architecture of Palm OS is important to writing successful applications.

The Palm OS memory architecture has evolved with each new version of the operating system, but the biggest architectural differences are between Palm OS Garnet and Palm OS Cobalt.

### Palm OS Garnet Memory Architecture

On Palm OS Garnet and earlier versions of Palm OS, both the ROM and RAM reside on a memory module called a *card*. In the first Palm devices, this was a physical card that a user could easily replace to upgrade the amount of memory available, exchange the operating system and applications in the ROM for newer versions, or both. However, a card is only a logical abstraction used by Palm OS to describe a memory area used to contain ROM and RAM; a device may have any number of logical cards or no cards at all.

Only one Palm OS handheld has ever used more than one logical card: the Handspring Visor with an installed Springboard memory module. On the Handspring, the device's main memory is card

0 and the Springboard module is card 1. As of the time of this writing, all other Palm OS handhelds have only one card available (card 0). Palm OS Cobalt does away with logical cards entirely.

Many Palm OS functions require a cardNo parameter that specifies the logical memory card upon which to perform a task. Except for the Springboard module case previously mentioned, you should specify 0 for the cardNo argument. Logical memory cards should not be confused with expansion cards, such as SD (Secure Digital) cards or Sony Memory Sticks. Manipulating data on expansion cards requires different functions from those used to manipulate data in RAM (see Chapter 17).

Palm OS Garnet and earlier are built on a 32-bit memory architecture, with data types that are 8, 16, and 32 bits long. Memory addresses are 32 bits long, giving the operating system a 4 GB address space in which to store data and code. The operating system reserves 256 MB of address space for each logical card.

RAM in Palm OS is divided into two separate areas: *dynamic RAM* and *storage RAM*. Figure 9-1 depicts these areas of memory and what they contain.

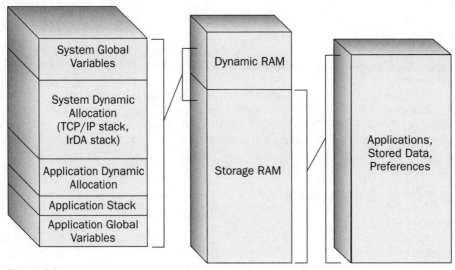

Figure 9-1

Dynamic RAM is used for many of the same purposes as RAM on a desktop computer: It provides a space for temporary storage of global variables and other data that do not require persistence between executions of an application. Storage RAM is used in much the same way that the file system on a desktop machine's hard drive is used: It provides permanent storage for applications and data. Both dynamic and storage RAM are detailed further in the following sections.

## Dynamic RAM on Palm OS Garnet

The entire dynamic area of the device's RAM is used to implement the *dynamic heap*. A *heap* is an area of contiguous memory that manages and contains smaller units of memory, called *chunks*. A chunk is an area of contiguous memory between 1 byte and slightly less than 64K (65,528 bytes to be precise). All data in the Palm OS environment are stored in chunks.

The dynamic heap provides memory for several purposes:

- ❑ Application and system global variables
- ❑ Dynamic allocations by the system, such as the TCP/IP and IrDA (infrared) stacks
- ❑ Stack space for the running application
- ❑ Temporary memory allocations
- ❑ Dynamic allocations by applications

The following table shows how much space is allocated to the dynamic heap in different versions of Palm OS, and it provides a breakdown of what that memory is used for. Notice that even in later versions, the dynamic heap is still a small amount of memory, most of which is used by the operating system itself. Little memory is left for application use.

| Memory Usage | OS 3.5 or later (more than 4 MB total RAM, TCP/IP, and IrDA) | OS 3.5 or later (between 2 and 4 MB total RAM, TCP/IP, and IrDA) | OS 3.0–3.3 (more than 1 MB total RAM; TCP/IP and IrDA) | OS 2.0 (1 MB total RAM; TCP/IP only) | OS 2.0/1.0 (512K total RAM; no TCP/IP or IrDA) |
|---|---|---|---|---|---|
| Total dynamic memory | 256K | 128K | 96K | 64K | 32K |
| System globals (UI globals, screen buffer, database references, etc.) | 40K | 40K | about 2.5K | about 2.5K | about 2.5K |
| TCP/IP stack | 32K | 32K | 32K | 32K | 0 |
| System dynamic allocation (IrDA, "Find" window, temporary allocations) | variable amount | variable amount | variable amount | about 15K | about 15K |
| Application stack (call stack and local variable space) | variable amount | variable amount | 4K (default) | 2.5K | 2.5K |
| Remaining space (dynamic allocations, application global variables, static variables) | 184K | 56K | 36K | 12K | 12K |

*The dynamic heap size in handhelds running Palm OS 3.5 through Palm OS Garnet is actually set by the hardware manufacturer. The table represents values used by palmOne at the time of this writing. Different Palm OS licensees may configure a handheld to have different amounts of memory in the dynamic heap. For example, the Sony CLIÉ PEG-NR70 has 512K of dynamic heap space.*

All of the RAM in the dynamic heap is dedicated to dynamic use. Even if some areas of the dynamic heap are currently not in use (for instance, no TCP/IP communication is currently taking place), that memory is still available only for the dynamic allocations outlined in the preceding table.

Applications use the Palm OS memory manager to allocate, manipulate, and free allocated memory in the dynamic heap. The memory manager functions allow safe use of the dynamic memory on the device, regardless of how the running version of the operating system structures that memory internally.

## Storage RAM on Palm OS Garnet

Any memory on the device that is not dedicated to the dynamic heap is divided into a number of *storage heaps*. The size and number of these storage heaps depend on the version of the operating system and the total amount of RAM available on the device. In Palm OS 1.0 and 2.0, storage RAM is divided into several 64K storage heaps. Versions 3.0 and later treat all the storage RAM available as one big storage heap.

Memory chunks in a storage heap are called *records*. Each record is part of a *database* that is implemented by the Palm OS data manager. A database is simply a list of memory chunks and some database header information. Most of the time, records in a particular database share some kind of association, such as each record representing an appointment in the Date Book.

The Palm OS data manager provides functions for creating, opening, closing, and deleting databases, as well as functions for manipulating records within those databases. A database in Palm OS serves much the same function as a file on a desktop computer. Depending on the contents of a database's records, a given database may represent an application, a shared library, or simply stored application data.

Because memory is such a limited commodity on a Palm OS handheld, applications do not copy data from a storage heap to a dynamic heap to modify it the way desktop computers copy data from the hard drive to memory. The data and memory managers in Palm OS lock individual chunks of memory and edit them in place. RAM is used for permanent storage. Because even the best programmers can introduce errors into their code that write to the wrong memory address, Palm OS does not allow an application to change the contents of any chunk of storage memory without using the memory and data manager APIs. It is still possible to change the contents of dynamic memory without using the APIs, though, so be sure to exercise caution when writing to the dynamic heap.

Records in a database may be scattered across multiple storage heaps on handhelds running Palm OS 2.0 and earlier. On any version of Palm OS, records may be interspersed with records from other databases. They also may be located in ROM as part of the applications that ship with the operating system. The only restriction on the location of individual records is that all the records in a given database must reside on the same logical memory card. Chapters 15 and 16 provide details about using the Palm OS data manager to manipulate databases and records.

## Storage Heaps and Memory Fragmentation

The use of a single large heap in Palm OS 3.0 and later is a big improvement over memory management in earlier versions because it prevents fragmentation of the storage memory. Because most Palm OS devices on the market run version 3.5 or later, memory fragmentation is not something you need to be concerned with when developing applications for the majority of Palm OS handhelds. However, if you do need to support earlier versions, this section explains the problems with memory fragmentation found in those early versions.

Fragmentation occurs as storage heaps fill with data. Even if there is enough total free memory for a new record, there may not be enough contiguous space in any given heap to contain that record.

For example, assume there are four storage heaps, each 64K, with 40K of memory filled in each heap. That's a total of 96K of free memory. If an application tries to allocate 50K, however, it won't be able to because there is, at most, only 24K available in any given heap. Figure 9-2 illustrates this situation and shows how different versions of Palm OS try to deal with this problem. Notice that later versions deal much better with fragmentation than earlier versions.

As shown, Version 1.0 uses an ineffective storage allocation strategy that attempts to keep all heaps equally full. This, in fact, causes every new allocation to be more difficult than the last. Version 2.0 improves upon this somewhat by allocating memory from the heap with the greatest amount of free space. System Update 2.0.4 further improves this scheme, moving chunks of memory from the least-filled heap to other heaps until there is enough space for the new allocation. Palm OS 3.0 finally did away with the fragmentation problems by putting all storage memory in one big heap.

Fragmentation on earlier Palm OS devices is another good reason to make your application as small as possible. Not only is there less total RAM available on earlier devices, but memory fragmentation can make what seems like a reasonably sized application impossible to install.

# Palm OS Cobalt Memory Architecture

Palm OS Cobalt does away with the concept of a logical memory card; memory is a single 32-bit virtual address space. As a result, many Palm OS functions that required a cardNo parameter under Palm OS Garnet and earlier no longer have a cardNo parameter.

RAM is separated into dynamic and storage areas, just as it is in Palm OS Garnet.

## Dynamic RAM on Palm OS Cobalt

Palm OS Cobalt divides memory into *segments*, upon which the operating system bases its memory protection model. Within each segment, the operating system may allocate multiple heaps, each up to 256 MB. Assuming the hardware has enough RAM available, an individual chunk within a heap may be up to 16 MB.

## Storage RAM on Palm OS Cobalt

The system maintains two memory segments for storage heaps. The first segment allows applications to read its data directly, just like a storage heap on Palm OS Garnet. The second segment contains protected and secure databases, which may be accessed only by applications that have permission to read from or write to those databases.

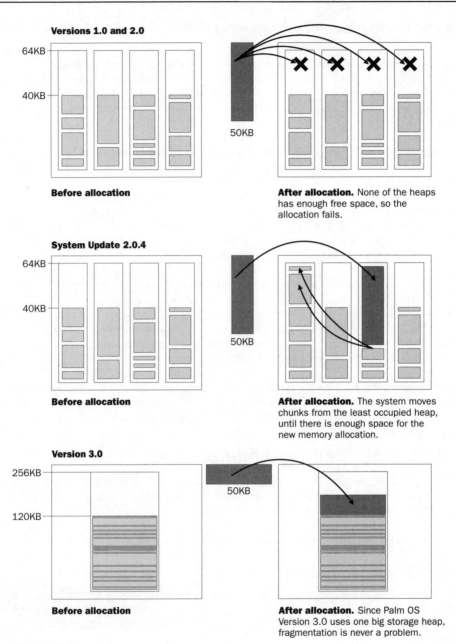

**Versions 1.0 and 2.0**

64KB

40KB

50KB

**Before allocation**

**After allocation.** None of the heaps has enough free space, so the allocation fails.

**System Update 2.0.4**

64KB

40KB

50KB

**Before allocation**

**After allocation.** The system moves chunks from the least occupied heap, until there is enough space for the new memory allocation.

**Version 3.0**

256KB

120KB

50KB

**Before allocation**

**After allocation.** Since Palm OS Version 3.0 uses one big storage heap, fragmentation is never a problem.

Figure 9-2

In addition to separating storage RAM into public and private access, Palm OS Cobalt introduces three new types of databases:

- ❑ **Classic.** This type of database is identical to a Palm OS Garnet database. Each database record is a single chunk of memory, and all the restrictions of earlier databases still apply. Classic databases are an excellent choice if your application must maintain backward compatibility with prior versions of Palm OS.

- ❑ **Extended.** This type of database is similar to a Classic database but with fewer limitations. In particular, records are not limited to 64K. Extended databases allow you to use most of the same techniques you would use for programming Classic database access but without some of the restrictions of the older database model.

- ❑ **Schema.** This type of database is like a relational database. A Schema database may contain one or more tables, each of which contains rows and columns full of data. Among other features, Schema databases provide automatic sorting, iteration, and queries using syntax similar to SQL (Structured Query Language), and the ability to extend a database with new types of data.

Chapters 15 and 16 provide details about using Classic, Extended, and Schema databases in Palm OS Cobalt.

# Using Dynamic Memory in Palm OS Garnet

In Palm OS Garnet most memory manipulation functions fall into two categories: *pointer* functions and *handle* functions. Palm OS Garnet uses the functions `MemPtrNew` and `MemPtrFree` instead of the C standard library calls `malloc` and `free` to allocate and deallocate memory (this deviation from standard C is rectified in Palm OS Cobalt). Other than this syntactic difference, most memory use should be about what you expect from a standard C application. However, `MemPtrNew` returns a pointer to an unmovable chunk of memory; such chunks don't take advantage of the operating system's ability to efficiently manage the small amount of dynamic RAM available.

The `MemHandleNew` function also allocates a chunk of memory. However, instead of returning a pointer to a fixed chunk of memory, `MemHandleNew` returns a handle to a moveable chunk. A handle is simply a pointer to memory that may be moved by the operating system. Whenever the operating system needs to allocate more memory, it relocates moveable chunks until there is enough free contiguous memory for the new allocation. This scheme allows for much more effective use of the limited memory on a Palm OS device.

Because the operating system may freely move the memory connected to a handle, you must first lock a handle with `MemHandleLock` before you can read data from or write data to it. Once you have finished using the handle, unlock it with `MemHandleUnlock` so that the operating system can once again move that handle's chunk around.

How do you know when to use `MemPtrNew` and when to use `MemHandleNew`? It might seem that using `MemHandleNew` would always be the correct choice because it allocates memory chunks that the system can move, if necessary, thus preventing memory fragmentation. However, if you allocate memory with `MemHandleNew` and leave it locked throughout the life of your application, the system still cannot move that chunk of memory. Worse yet, leaving a chunk locked in the middle of the dynamic heap makes it harder for the memory manager to allocate more handles to moveable memory chunks. Leaving a chunk locked for long periods of time actually promotes memory fragmentation instead of alleviating it.

Although the memory allocated by `MemPtrNew` cannot be relocated, `MemPtrNew` always allocates memory from the low part of the heap. If you need to allocate memory and leave it locked for a long period of time, use `MemPtrNew`. On the other hand, if your application can leave a chunk of memory alone most of the time, needing to lock it only occasionally to read or modify the data in that chunk, you should allocate the memory with `MemHandleNew`. You should also use `MemHandleNew` to allocate memory that may need to be resized because the memory manager may need to move the memory chunk to find enough space to hold the contents of an expanded chunk of memory. You can allocate a new memory handle with the `MemHandleNew` function. This function takes an argument specifying the size of the memory chunk to allocate, in bytes. The following code allocates a new, 128-byte handle:

```
MemHandle newHandle = MemHandleNew(128);
```

Palm OS keeps track of how many times you have locked a particular chunk of memory with a *lock count*. Every time you call `MemHandleLock` on a particular handle, the operating system increments the lock count on that handle's memory chunk. Likewise, each call to `MemHandleUnlock` decrements the lock count by one. Only when the lock count reaches zero is the chunk actually unlocked and available to be moved by the operating system again.

> **Because the operating system cannot move a locked chunk of memory, you must be sure to unlock a chunk as soon as possible after it has been locked. Otherwise, memory fragmentation may occur, possibly preventing further memory allocation because Palm OS is unable to locate a large enough area of contiguous memory.**

The other half of the `lock:owner` byte stores the owner ID of the application that owns this particular chunk of memory. When an application exits, the operating system automatically deallocates all chunks of memory with that application's owner ID. This garbage collection prevents a careless programmer from creating a memory leak, which would be a serious problem on a platform with very little dynamic RAM.

*Relying on Palm OS to clean up your memory is sloppy programming. Be sure to explicitly free any memory that you allocate.*

It may be more convenient to unlock a chunk of memory using the `MemPtrUnlock` function. Instead of having to pass the chunk's handle around among different routines in your application, `MemPtrUnlock` will unlock a chunk given a pointer to that chunk, rather than a handle.

When you are through using a chunk of memory, call `MemHandleFree` to dispose of a moveable chunk, or call `MemPtrFree` to deallocate an unmovable chunk:

```
MemHandleFree(someHandle);
MemPtrFree(somePointer);
```

You can retrieve the size of a particular chunk with the `MemHandleSize` and `MemPtrSize` functions:

```
UInt32 sizeOfHandle = MemHandleSize(someHandle);
UInt32 sizeOfPointer = MemPtrSize(somePointer);
```

Resizing a moveable chunk also is possible, using the `MemHandleResize` function:

```
switch (MemHandleResize(someHandle, newSize))
{
    case memErrInvalidParam:
        // Invalid parameter passed
    case memErrNotEnoughSpace:
        // Not enough free space in the current heap
        // to grow the chunk
    case memErrChunkLocked:
        // The chunk passed to MemHandleResize is locked
    case 0:
        // Resizing was successful
}
```

`MemHandleResize` first looks for more memory immediately following the current chunk, so the chunk does not have to be moved. If there is not enough free space directly following the chunk, and if the chunk is not locked, the operating system moves the chunk to a new location that does contain enough contiguous space. There also is a `MemPtrResize` function that works on a locked or immovable chunk of memory, but only if there is enough free space available right after that chunk. Both `MemHandleResize` and `MemPtrResize` always succeed when shrinking the size of the chunk.

Palm OS has a few utility functions for manipulating the contents of memory. `MemMove` copies a certain number of bytes from one location in memory to another, handling overlapping ranges as appropriate:

```
MemMove(void *destination, void *source,
    UInt32 numberOfBytes);
```

`MemSet` sets a certain number of bytes at a particular memory location to a specific value:

```
MemSet(void *changeThis, UInt32 numberOfBytes, Byte value);
```

> **For some strange reason, the engineers at Palm chose not to mimic the parameter order of the standard C memset function. In memset, the last two parameters are the value, followed by the number of bytes, which is the reverse of how MemSet works in Palm OS. Be very careful to use the correct order when calling MemSet. In general, always check the parameters of Palm OS functions against the *Palm OS Programmer's API Reference*, which is part of the Palm OS SDK.**

Finally, MemCmp can be used to compare the values of two different memory locations:

```
Int difference;
difference = MemCmp(void *a, void *b,
                    UInt32 numberOfBytes);
if (difference > 0)
{
    // a is greater than b
}
else if (difference < 0)
{
    // b is greater than a
}
else
{
    // The two blocks are the same
}
```

# Using Dynamic Memory in Palm OS Cobalt

Although the older memory management APIs such as MemPtrNew are still present for compatibility, Palm OS Cobalt offers developers access to standard C library memory APIs such as malloc, free and memcmp. The older APIs — MemPtrNew, MemPtrFree, and MemCmp — still work fine in Palm OS Cobalt, but making use of the standard C routines provides developers with several advantages:

❑   Dynamic memory allocation and usage are simpler for developers, with no more need to work with handles and locking/unlocking pointer code.

❑   Code written to use the standard C library functions is more portable and compatible for programmers who have written code on other computer platforms that make use of the standard C library functions.

❑   The standard C library routines are actually somewhat faster performing than the older memory management APIs.

❑   Allocations made using malloc are tracked in the Cobalt Simulator's Memory Debug feature, which can help track down and resolve memory leaks in your code.

For those developers who are working with code written against earlier versions of Palm OS, the older memory management APIs exist for portability, and programmers can make use of the compatibility header memorymgrcompatibility.h as they transition their code to Palm OS Cobalt.

A significant change for existing Palm OS developers is that memory heaps are now created on a per-process basis. This means that when an application process is torn down, any memory chunks allocated by the application are released by the operating system. One implication of this is that using MemSetOwner no longer works as a way to preserve a memory chunk from destruction after an application is closed.

Any older memory manager functions that referenced a card number, such as MemLocalIDToPtr, have been changed to reflect the removal of the card number concept. Finally, a number of older, less well known APIs found in MemoryMgr.h, such as MemKernelInit and MemInitHeapTable, have been deleted in Palm OS Cobalt.

# Summary

This chapter provided details on memory management and usage in both Palm OS Garnet and Palm OS Cobalt. You should now know the following:

❑   Palm OS memory in both Palm OS Garnet and Palm OS Cobalt is divided into dynamic memory and storage memory.

❑   Available heap memory for use by Palm OS applications has grown since Palm OS version 3.x, but still remains limited compared with desktop operating systems.

❑   Palm OS Garnet applications make use of Palm-specific memory management functions such as `MemPtrNew`.

❑   Palm OS Cobalt applications can use the standard C library memory functions such as `malloc`, `free`, and `realloc`.

# 10

# Programming System Elements

Chapter 8 covered the ins and outs of programming the interface of a Palm OS application, the part that the user interacts with directly. This chapter focuses on what runs under the hood of your application and the functions that Palm OS provides to help you with many common programming tasks. Palm OS supplies a well-stocked toolbox of functions and features to help you with everything from generating random numbers to manipulating text to launching other applications.

## Checking for Supported Features

Not all Palm OS features exist on all versions of the operating system. Infrared beaming, for example, was introduced in Palm OS version 3.0; 1.0 and 2.0 devices do not support beaming. Likewise, different devices running the same version of Palm OS may not share the same hardware capabilities. For example, the palmOne Zire 21 and Tungsten C have the same operating system, but the wireless hardware on the Tungsten C does not exist on a Zire 21. If your application must be compatible with a variety of Palm OS devices, and you plan to support features that are available on only some of those devices, you need to query the system about what features are available.

The Palm OS feature manager allows you to determine what features exist in the operating system and on the handheld. A *feature* is a 32-bit piece of data published by the operating system, or another program, to indicate the presence of a particular software or hardware element. The value of a feature has a specific meaning in the context of the application that publishes the feature. You can identify a particular feature by its *feature creator* and *feature number*. The feature creator is a unique creator ID that is usually the same as the creator ID of the application that publishes the feature. The feature number is simply a 16-bit value used to distinguish between different features that share a creator ID.

The system stores lists of registered features in *feature tables*. System-published features reside in a feature table in the device's ROM, while a separate feature table in RAM holds application-published features. In Palm OS 3.1 and later, the system copies the contents of the ROM feature table into the RAM feature table at startup, making both the system and application features available from the same location.

Your applications can publish features for their own use or for use by other programs, which can be handy if you need quick access to a small amount of data that should persist between closing and reopening an application. This mechanism also comes in handy when an application must operate without access to global variables, allowing you to store small values without resorting to global values. Chapter 15 explains how to publish your own features and use feature memory.

To retrieve the value of a feature, use the FtrGet function. It has three arguments: the creator ID of the application that owns the feature, the application-specific number assigned to the desired feature, and a pointer to a variable that receives the feature value. FtrGet also returns an error value of errNone if the feature was retrieved without incident, or the constant value ftrErrNoSuchFtr if the requested feature does not exist.

## Determining the Operating System Version

One handy feature published by the operating system is the version number of the operating system. The Palm OS header file SystemMgr.h defines the constants sysFtrCreator and sysFtrNumROMVersion to assist in retrieving the version number. Calling FtrGet with the following code places the system version number value in the variable romVersion:

**Palm OS Garnet**

```
UInt32   romVersion;

FtrGet(sysFtrCreator, sysFtrNumROMVersion, &romVersion);
```

**Palm OS Cobalt**

```
uint32_t   romVersion;

FtrGet(sysFtrCreator, sysFtrNumROMVersion, &romVersion);
```

The operating system version number published by the operating system has a specific, if nonintuitive, format. Here is what the format looks like, expressed in the form of a hexadecimal number:

```
0xMMmfsbbb
```

The individual parts of the format have the following meanings:

- ❑   MM: Major version number
- ❑   m: Minor version number
- ❑   f: Bug fix version number
- ❑   s: Release stage, wherein the value for s may be one of the following:
  - ❑   0: Development
  - ❑   1: Alpha

- ❑    2: Beta
- ❑    3: Release
- ❑   bbb: Build number for nonreleases

`SystemMgr.h` defines some useful macros for parsing the system version number. Given the feature value returned from a call to `FtrGet`, these macros mask the appropriate bits of the version number and return a more focused subset of the information contained in the feature. The following macros are available:

- ❑   `sysGetROMVerMajor`
- ❑   `sysGetROMVerMinor`
- ❑   `sysGetROMVerFix`
- ❑   `sysGetROMVerStage`
- ❑   `sysGetROMVerBuild`

For example, the following code retrieves the system version number, parses out the major version, and, based on the version number, changes which code is executed:

**Palm OS Garnet**

```
UInt32  romVersion;

FtrGet(sysFtrCreator, sysFtrNumROMVersion, &romVersion);
switch (sysGetROMVerMajor(romVersion))
{
    case 1:
        // Version 1.x
        break;
    case 2:
        // Version 2.x
        break;
    case 3:
        // Version 3.x
        break;
    default:
        // Not version 1, 2, or 3
        break;
}
```

**Palm OS Cobalt**

```
uint32_t  romVersion;

FtrGet(sysFtrCreator, sysFtrNumROMVersion, &romVersion);
switch (sysGetROMVerMajor(romVersion))
{
    case 1:
        // Version 1.x
        break;
    case 2:
```

```
        // Version 2.x
        break;
    case 3:
        // Version 3.x
        break;
    default:
        // Not version 1, 2, or 3
        break;
    }
```

The following table shows the system version numbers of all Palm OS versions available when this book was written.

| Number | Palm OS Version (and Device) |
| --- | --- |
| 0x01003001 | 1.0 (Pilot 1000, Pilot 5000) |
| 0x02003000 | 2.0 (PalmPilot Personal, PalmPilot Professional) |
| 0x03003000 | 3.0 (Palm III) |
| 0x03103000 | 3.1 (Palm IIIx, Palm IIIe, Palm V; IBM Workpad, Workpad c3) |
| 0x03203000 | 3.2 (Palm VII) |
| 0x03303000 | 3.3 (Original Palm Vx; Palm III, Palm IIIx, or Palm V with software upgrade; Visor, Visor Deluxe; original TRGPro) |
| 0x03503001 | 3.5 (Palm IIIxe, Palm IIIc, newer Palm Vx, Palm VIIx; newer TRGPro; Sony CLIÉ PEG-S300, PEG-S500, PEG-N710) |
| 0x03513000 | 3.5.1 (Palm m100, Palm m105) |
| 0x03523000 | 3.5.2 (Visor Edge, Visor Neo, Visor Platinum, Visor Prism, Visor Pro, Treo 180; Sony CLIÉ PEG-S320, PEG-N610C, PEG-N710C; Kyocera QCP 6035) |
| 0x03533000 | 3.5.3 (HandEra 330) |
| 0x04003000 | 4.0 (Palm m125, Palm m500, Palm m505) |
| 0x04103000 | 4.1 (Palm m130, Palm m515, Palm i705; palmOne Zire; Sony CLIÉ PEG-N760C, PEG-T415, PEG-T615C, PEG-NR70, PEG-NR70V; Sony CLIÉ PEG-N710 with software upgrade; GSPDA Xplore G18; Lenovo Pam 168; Acer s10, s50, s60; Kyocera 7135; Alphasmart Dana, Dana Wireless) |
| 0x04113000 | 4.1.1 (palmOne Tungsten W; Sony CLIÉ PEG-SJ22) |
| 0x04123000 | 4.1.2 (Aceeca Meazura) |
| 0x05003000 | 5.0 (Palm Tungsten T; Sony CLIÉ PEG-NX70V, PEG-NX73V, PEG-NX80V, PEG-NZ90, PEG-TG50; Garmin iQue 3600) |
| 0x05203000 | 5.2 (Sony CLIÉ PEG-TJ22, PEG-TJ33) |

| Number | Palm OS Version (and Device) |
|---|---|
| 0x05213000 | 5.2.1 (palmOne Zire 21, Zire 71, Tungsten E, Tungsten T2, Tungsten T3, Tungsten C) |
| 0x05223000 | 5.2.2 (Sony CLIÉ PEG-UX40, PEG-UX50, PEG-TH55, PEG-TJ27, PEG-TJ37) |
| 0x05233000 | 5.2.3 or Garnet (No devices when this book was written) |
| 0x05263000 | 5.2.6 (Original Tapwave Zodiac) |
| 0x05273000 | 5.2.7 (Tapwave Zodiac with Zodiac 1.1 update) |
| 0x06003000 | 6 or Cobalt (No devices when this book was written) |

## Checking Individual Features

Because future versions of Palm OS may not necessarily include all the features of earlier versions, it is safest to check for specific features before using them, instead of assuming that those features are present on a particular version of the operating system. To help discover what features are available, the Palm OS SystemMgr.h header defines a number of useful constants for checking the presence of individual elements, such as the processor the device uses or whether or not the device has a backlight.

Unfortunately, the system does not publish features for some fairly obvious things that you might wish to check for, such as the presence or absence of an infrared port. For system and device elements that do not have constants defined in SystemMgr.h, checking the system version number is still an available option.

> Normally, an application needs to check for specific features, or for a particular version of Palm OS, but on a rare occasion you may need to determine the exact make and model of the hardware. Unfortunately, the methods that PalmSource and its licensees have used to identify hardware have evolved over time, and they vary from manufacturer to manufacturer.

> Hal Mueller has a Web page that describes the complex and changing landscape of querying Palm OS for hardware details. Visit www.mobilegeographics.com/dev/devices.html for more details.

To find the processor used in a Palm OS device, use FtrGet to query the system for the sysFtrNumProcessorID feature. The following table shows the processor ID values for Palm OS devices that exist at the time of this writing.

| Constant | Value | Description |
|---|---|---|
| sysFtrNumProcessor328 | 0x00010000 | Motorola 68328 (DragonBall) |
| sysFtrNumProcessorEZ | 0x00020000 | Motorola 68EZ328 (DragonBall EZ) |
| sysFtrNumProcessorVZ | 0x00030000 | Motorola 68VZ328 (DragonBall VZ) |
| sysFtrNumProcessorSuperVZ | 0x00040000 | Motorola 68SZ328 (DragonBall Super VZ) |
| sysFtrNumProcessorARM720T | 0x00100000 | ARM 720T |
| sysFtrNumProcessorARM7TDMI | 0x00110000 | ARM7TDMI |
| sysFtrNumProcessorARM920T | 0x00120000 | ARM920T |
| sysFtrNumProcessorARM922T | 0x00130000 | ARM922T |
| sysFtrNumProcessorARM925 | 0x00140000 | ARM925 |
| sysFtrNumProcessorStrongARM | 0x00150000 | StrongARM |
| sysFtrNumProcessorXscale | 0x00160000 | Xscale |
| sysFtrNumProcessorARM710A | 0x00170000 | ARM710A |
| sysFtrNumProcessorx86 | 0x01000000 | Intel CPU (Palm Simulator) |

To determine whether the device has a backlight, query the system for the sysFtrNumBacklight feature. The backlight feature has a value of 0x00000001 if the device has a backlight and 0x00000000 if the backlight is not present.

You also may retrieve a list of features available on the device by repeatedly calling the FtrGetByIndex function. FtrGetByIndex has the following prototype:

**Palm OS Garnet**
```
Err FtrGetByIndex (UInt16 index, Boolean romTable,
                   UInt32 *creatorP, UInt16 *numP,
                   UInt32 *valueP)
```

**Palm OS Cobalt**
```
status_t FtrGetByIndex (uint16_t index, Boolean romTable,
                        uint32_t *creatorP, uint16_t *numP,
                        uint32_t *valueP)
```

The FtrGetByIndex function's return value simply indicates whether an error has occurred while you were attempting to retrieve the requested feature. FtrGetByIndex returns errNone if there was no error, or ftrErrNoSuchFeature if the index argument provided is out of range.

The index argument to FtrGetByIndex is simply a numerical index into the feature table, starting at 0 and incrementing by one for each feature in the table. Passing true for the romTable argument tells FtrGetByIndex to return a feature from the ROM feature table; a false value for romTable retrieves features from the table in RAM.

All three remaining arguments to `FtrGetByIndex` are where the function returns useful information. The `creatorP` argument holds the creator ID of the application that owns the feature, `numP` holds the application-specific feature number, and `valueP` holds the actual value of the feature in question.

The following example loops through the RAM feature table, retrieving each feature registered there:

**Palm OS Garnet**
```
UInt16  index = 0;
UInt32  creator;
UInt16  feature;
UInt32  value;

while (FtrGetByIndex(index, false, &creator, &feature,
                     &value) != ftrErrNoSuchFeature)
{
    // Do something with the values of creator, feature,
    // and value.
    index++;
}
```

**Palm OS Cobalt**
```
uint16_t  index = 0;
uint32_t  creator;
uint16_t  feature;
uint32_t  value;

while (FtrGetByIndex(index, false, &creator, &feature,
                     &value) != ftrErrNoSuchFeature)
{
    // Do something with the values of creator, feature,
    // and value.
    index++;
}
```

# Manipulating Text

Palm OS provides several useful functions and macros for manipulating text. This section covers three groups of functions and macros: font functions, string functions, and character macros. Font functions deal with the actual onscreen representation of characters, string functions allow you to control strings within your program's code, and character macros are handy tools for determining information about individual characters.

## Using Font Functions

Palm OS supports two types of fonts:

❑ **Bitmapped.** These contain a single bitmap for each glyph in the font. A bitmapped font must also contain a separate bitmap for each different size, screen density, and style in which a character appears. For example, there is a separate bitmap for the lowercase "a" character on 160 ×

160 screens than on double-density 320 × 320 screens. Standard Palm OS controls are rendered using bitmapped fonts.

❑ **Scalable.** These are based on TrueType fonts, which are inherently scalable. This means they contain only the definition of a character's shape; there is no need to store a separate glyph for different font sizes. Only Palm OS Cobalt supports scalable fonts, but the scalable font engine is not guaranteed to be present on all Palm OS Cobalt devices. If scalable fonts are not available, the scalable font functions return bitmapped fonts instead of scalable fonts.

The other major difference between bitmapped and scalable fonts is how they are drawn on the screen. Applications draw bitmapped fonts using window manager functions, but they draw scalable fonts using graphics context functions. Most applications that use standard forms and controls have no need for scalable fonts. However, if your application draws custom text to the screen, scalable fonts give you more flexibility in how the text appears.

*More information about drawing with the window manager and graphics context functions is available in Chapter 11.*

## Using Bitmapped Font Functions

Bitmapped font functions in Palm OS depend upon the current font setting in an application. The system keeps track of one font at a time. All font functions, as well as all drawing functions that deal with text (such as `WinDrawChars`), use the current font. To set the current font, use the `FntSetFont` function:

```
FontID  oldFont;

oldFont = FntSetFont(largeFont);
```

The `FntSetFont` function takes a single argument of type `FontID`, specifying an ID for the new font. The function returns whatever font was previously the current font before calling `FntSetFont`, allowing you to store that value for later restoration. It is good coding practice always to save the value of the current font setting before changing it. Once you are done using the new font setting, restore the original font with another call to `FntSetFont`, like this:

```
FntSetFont(oldFont);
```

Palm OS also provides the `FntGetFont` function, which takes no arguments and returns the `FontID` value of the current font. Chapter 7 contains a complete list of constants that you can use to specify a `FontID` value.

Many Palm OS font functions are purely informational in function, providing data about the current font. These information functions take no arguments. The following table briefly describes the return value from each of the informational font functions.

| Function | Return Value |
|---|---|
| FntAverageCharWidth | Width in pixels of the average character in the current font |
| FntBaseLine | Distance in pixels from the top of the character cell to the baseline for the current font |

| Function | Return Value |
|---|---|
| FntCharHeight | Height in pixels of a character in the current font, including accents and descenders |
| FntDescenderHeight | Distance in pixels from the baseline to the bottom of the character cell for the current font |
| FntLineHeight | Height in pixels of a line of text in the current font (the height of a line is equal to the height of a character plus the distance between lines of text) |

A few other simple functions—FntCharWidth, FntCharsWidth, and FntLineWidth—provide the width of individual characters or strings of characters. The FntCharWidth function takes a single character as an argument and returns its width in pixels for the current font. The FntCharsWidth function takes a string and the length of the string in bytes as arguments, and it returns the width of the entire string in pixels, substituting the font's missing character symbol for any character that does not exist in the current font. The FntLineWidth function takes the same arguments as FntCharsWidth, returning the width in pixels of the string for the current font and taking tab characters and missing characters into account.

> *The* WinDrawChars *function does not account for the width of tab characters, and neither does* FntCharsWidth. *If you want to know the exact width of a string to be drawn by* WinDrawChars, *use the* FntLineWidth *function. The* FntLineWidth *function works better for determining the width of a string that will appear at the start of a line in a text field because it properly handles the width of tab characters.*

## Fitting Text to a Specific Screen Width

Some applications require a method for drawing text within a certain amount of space on the screen. The Address List view in the built-in Address Book application is a good example. Each name must fit within a specific area on the screen. If the application called WinDrawChars to draw each name in the list without checking first to see how much of the name would fit, the program would draw over the top of the phone numbers, resulting in an unreadable mess.

Fortunately, there is an easy way around the problem of keeping text within a specific area of the screen. Palm OS 3.1 and later provide the WinDrawTruncChars function, which draws a number of characters on the screen, truncating them if they exceed a certain width in pixels. The prototype for WinDrawTruncChars looks like this:

**Palm OS Garnet**
```
void WinDrawTruncChars (const Char *chars,
    Int16 len, Coord x, Coord y, Coord maxWidth)
```

**Palm OS Cobalt**
```
void WinDrawTruncChars (const char *chars,
    int16_t len, Coord x, Coord y, Coord maxWidth)
```

The first parameter, chars, is a pointer to the beginning of the text to draw, and the len parameter specifies the length of the text in bytes. Use the x and y parameters to specify the horizontal and vertical coordinates, respectively, where the text should appear. The last parameter, maxWidth, specifies the maximum screen width for the text, in pixels.

If WinDrawTruncChars truncates a string to make it fit within the maxWidth value, the function drops one or more characters from the end of the text to make room for an ellipsis (...), which WinDrawTruncChars draws at the end of the text.

> *If the text you pass to WinDrawTruncChars is wider than maxWidth, but shorter than the width of an ellipsis character, WinDrawTruncChars draws nothing.*

On versions of Palm OS prior to 3.1, you can either link your project with the PalmOSGlue library and call the function WinGlueDrawTruncChars or you can produce the same effect with your own code. Palm OS provides the FntCharsInWidth function, which allows you to determine the number of bytes of a particular string that fits within a given width using the current font. The FntCharsInWidth function can be tricky to use, however, because half of its arguments serve as both input parameters and return values. The prototype for FntCharsInWidth looks like this:

**Palm OS Garnet**

```
void FntCharsInWidth (const char *string,
                      Int16 *stringWidthP,
                      Int16 *stringLengthP,
                      Boolean *fitWithinWidth)
```

**Palm OS Cobalt**

```
void FntCharsInWidth(const char* string,
                     Coord *stringWidthP,
                     size_t *stringLengthP,
                     Boolean *fitWithinWidth);
```

The string argument is simply the string to test. As input parameters, stringWidthP tells FntCharsInWidth the maximum width in pixels that the string should occupy, and stringLengthP represents the maximum length of text to allow in bytes. Upon return, FntCharsInWidth sets stringWidthP to the actual width in pixels of the text that fits, and the function sets stringLengthP to the actual length in bytes of the text. The function sets the fitWithinWidth argument to true if the entire string fits within the specified width and length; FntCharsInWidth sets fitWithinWidth to false if the string must be truncated to fit the specified width and length.

The FntCharsInWidth function treats spaces and newlines at the end of a string in a special manner. The function removes any spaces at the end of the string and ignores them, returning true in the fitWithinWidth argument. If there is a newline in the string, FntCharsInWidth ignores any characters after the newline and treats the string as truncated, returning false in the fitWithinWidth argument.

As an example, the list view in the Librarian sample application (introduced in Chapter 7) must deal with similar space restrictions as the Address Book application. The following utility function from Librarian, DrawCharsInWidth, draws as much of a string as will fit a given width, appending an ellipsis (...) as a visual cue to the user that the text continues.

**Palm OS Garnet**

```
static void DrawCharsInWidth (Char *str, Int16 *width,
    Int16 *length, Int16 x, Int16 y, Boolean rightJustify)
{
```

```
    Int16    ellipsisWidth;
    Boolean  fitInWidth;
    Int16    newX;
    char     ellipsisChar;


    // Determine whether the string will fit within the
    // maximum width.
    FntCharsInWidth(str, width, length, &fitInWidth);

    // If the string fits within the maximum width, draw
    // it.
    if (fitInWidth)
    {
        if (rightJustify)
            WinDrawChars(str, *length, x - *width, y);
        else
            WinDrawChars(str, *length, x, y);
    }

    // The string was truncated; append an ellipsis to the
    // end of the string, and recalculate the portion of
    // the string that can be drawn, because the ellipsis
    // shortens the width available.
    else
    {
        // Retrieve an ellipsis character and set its
        // width.
        ChrHorizEllipsis(&ellipsisChar);
        ellipsisWidth = (FntCharWidth(ellipsisChar));

        *width -= ellipsisWidth;
        FntCharsInWidth(str, width, length, &fitInWidth);

        if (rightJustify)
            newX = x - *width - ellipsisWidth;
        else
            newX = x;

        WinDrawChars(str, *length, newX, y);
        newX += *width;
        WinDrawChars(&ellipsisChar, 1, newX, y);

        // Add the width of the ellipsis to return the
        // actual width used to draw the string.
        *width += ellipsisWidth;
    }
}
```

**Palm OS Cobalt**

```
static void DrawCharsInWidth (char *str, int16_t *width,
    int16_t *length, int16_t x, int16_t y,
    Boolean rightJustify)
{
```

```
int16_t  ellipsisWidth;
Boolean  fitInWidth;
int16_t  newX;
char     ellipsisChar;


// Determine whether the string will fit within the
// maximum width.
FntCharsInWidth(str, width, length, &fitInWidth);

// If the string fits within the maximum width, draw
// it.
if (fitInWidth)
{
    if (rightJustify)
        WinDrawChars(str, *length, x - *width, y);
    else
        WinDrawChars(str, *length, x, y);
}

// The string was truncated; append an ellipsis to the
// end of the string, and recalculate the portion of
// the string that can be drawn, because the ellipsis
// shortens the width available.
else
{
    // Retrieve an ellipsis character and set its
    // width.
    ChrHorizEllipsis(&ellipsisChar);
    ellipsisWidth = (FntCharWidth(ellipsisChar));

    *width -= ellipsisWidth;
    FntCharsInWidth(str, width, length, &fitInWidth);

    if (rightJustify)
        newX = x - *width - ellipsisWidth;
    else
        newX = x;

    WinDrawChars(str, *length, newX, y);
    newX += *width;
    WinDrawChars(&ellipsisChar, 1, newX, y);

    // Add the width of the ellipsis to return the
    // actual width used to draw the string.
    *width += ellipsisWidth;
}
}
```

The first three arguments to DrawCharsInWidth mirror the first three arguments of the FntCharsInWidth function: str is the string to draw, width is a pointer to the width in pixels that the string must fit into, and length is a pointer to the maximum length in bytes for the string. The DrawCharsInWidth function has x and y arguments to specify the window-relative coordinates of the upper-left corner of the space the string should occupy; the `rightJustify` argument, if `true`, tells the function to draw the text right-aligned within the given space. If `rightJustify` is `false`, `DrawCharsInWidth` simply starts at the x position when drawing the string.

After declaring variables, `DrawCharsInWidth` calls `FntCharsInWidth` to determine if `str` fits within the constraints of `width` and `length`. If the return value from `FntCharsInWidth`, stored in `fitInWidth`, is `true`, the entire string fits within the given width and length, so `DrawCharsInWidth` calls `WinDrawChars` to draw the string to the screen, modifying the starting horizontal coordinate if the string should be drawn right-aligned.

If the return value from `FntCharsInWidth` is `false`, the string must be truncated to fit within the allotted space. In this situation, `DrawCharsInWidth` attaches an ellipsis character to the end of the string before drawing. Because the ellipsis itself takes up some space, it might be necessary to truncate `str` further to allow for the width of the ellipsis character. The `DrawCharsInWidth` function retrieves the ellipsis character with the `ChrHorizEllipsis` macro, determines the character's width with `FntCharWidth`, and subtracts the character's width from the total width available. Then `DrawCharsInWidth` calls `FntCharsInWidth` again with the new value of `width`, which is modified to accommodate the ellipsis character.

> *Librarian uses the `ChrHorizEllipsis` macro instead of hard-coding the value of the ellipsis character because, starting with Palm OS 3.1, the ellipsis has a different character code than in previous versions of the operating system. The `ChrHorizEllipsis` macro is not available in pre-3.1 header files (such as those that ship with CodeWarrior R5), so if you are building with headers earlier than version 3.1 and your application is not intended for use on Palm OS 3.1 or later devices, use the `horizEllipsisChr` constant instead of `ChrHorizEllipsis`.*
>
> *Alternatively, you can link in the PalmOSGlue library and call the `TxtGlueGetHorizEllipsisChar` function. See the sidebar "Using PalmOSGlue" in Chapter 8 for full details of including the PalmOSGlue library in your application.*

After the second call to `FntCharsInWidth`, `length` points to the number of bytes of `str` that will fit, followed by an ellipsis character, within the constraints originally set by `width` and `length`. Passing the value of `length` as the second argument to `WinDrawChars` draws only those characters in `str` that fit before the ellipsis. After drawing `str`, `DrawCharsInWidth` moves the drawing position, represented by `newX`, to the right of the text and draws an ellipsis character with another call to `WinDrawChars`.

The `DrawCharsInWidth` function treats its `width` and `length` arguments in much the same way as `FntCharsInWidth` treats its `stringWidthP` and `stringLengthP` arguments. Before returning, `DrawCharsInWidth` makes sure that `width` and `length` represent the actual width in pixels and length in bytes of the string that it drew, instead of the values originally passed to the function. For this reason, `DrawCharsInWidth` adds the width of the ellipsis character to `width` if the string was truncated, because the second call to `FntCharsInWidth` sets `width` to the length of the string without the ellipsis.

## Using Scalable Font Functions

Using a scalable font is more complicated than merely specifying a font ID. Before you can use a scalable font, you need to create a handle to the font. The `GcCreateFont` function serves this purpose; it has the following prototype:

```
GcFontHandle GcCreateFont (const char *fontSpec)
```

GcCreateFont may look simple but its fontSpec parameter is a pointer to a string that contains a CSS (Cascading Style Sheets) font specification. CSS is a standard language for formatting Web pages and its font specifications contain a wealth of options, including — but not limited to — font face, style, and size.

> *Palm OS implements only a subset of the CSS font specification. More information about CSS can be found on the Web at www.w3.org/Style/CSS/.*

The string passed as the fontSpec argument has the following format. Items in square braces ([ ]) are optional.

```
[face] [size] [family] [, [size] alternateFamily]
```

The face part of the string specifies the style of the font, such as "normal" or "bold." The strings shown in the following table may be specified for face.

| String | Meaning |
|---|---|
| normal | Uses the normal face of the specified font family |
| bold | Uses the bold face of the specified font family |
| italic | Uses the italic face of the specified font family |
| oblique | Uses the oblique face of the specified font family |

The size part of the string may contain a number that specifies an exact font size, or it may contain a text description of a size that is relative to the current font size. The following table describes the size options.

| String | Meaning |
|---|---|
| numberpx | Font size is number pixels high in native coordinates; for example, 12px specifies a font height of 12 native pixels |
| numberdb | Font size is number standard coordinates high; for example, 10db specifies a font height of 10 standard coordinates |
| number% | Font size is a percentage of the current font size; for example, 50% specifies a font height that is half as tall as the current font |
| xx-small | Font size is three steps smaller than the current font size |
| x-small | Font size is two steps smaller than the current font size |
| small | Font size is one step smaller than the current font size |
| medium | Font size is equal to the current font size |
| larg | Font size is one step larger than the current font size |
| x-large | Font size is two steps larger than the current font size |

| String | Meaning |
|---|---|
| xx-large | Font size is three steps larger than the current font size |
| smaller | Font size is one step smaller than the current font size |
| larger | Font size is one step larger than the current font size |

The family part of the string specifies the name of a TrueType font family. If the name of the font family contains spaces, the name must be surrounded by single quotes ('). For example, 'Times New Roman' would specify the Times New Roman font family.

The alternateFamily part of the string may be used multiple times to provide alternative font families in case the family specified by family is not available.

Instead of naming a TrueType font family, you may specify for the family or alternateFamily one of the following standard system fonts:

- palmos-plain
- palmos-bold
- palmos-large-plain
- palmos-large-bold

The system uses a TrueType font for the standard system fonts if one is available; otherwise, the system substitutes one of the standard Palm OS bitmapped fonts.

The following fontSpec string tells GcCreateFont to create a handle to the Palatino font family, in italic style, at a height of 12 standard coordinates. If Palatino is not available, the specification falls back to Times New Roman. If that is also unavailable, the system uses the normal Palm OS system font:

```
italic 12db Palatino, 'Times New Roman', palmos-plain
```

Instead of calling GcCreateFont, you may also retrieve a font handle by calling GcCreateFontFromFamily:

```
font = GcCreateFontFromFamily("Palatino");
```

GcCreateFontFromFamily returns a handle to the appropriate font in its default style, with a size of zero. If the function cannot find a font that matches the specified name, GcCreateFontFromFamily returns NULL instead of a font handle.

Because GcCreateFontFromFamily returns a font with a size of zero, you must call GcSetFontSize to set the font size to a useful value:

```
GcSetFontSize(font, 12);
```

GcSetFontSize sets the font to a size specified in native pixel coordinates.

You may also create a font handle to a bitmapped font by passing the appropriate font ID to the
`GcCreateFontFromID` function:

```
font = GcCreateFontFromID(id);
```

`GcCreateFontFromID` always creates a font with the same size and style that the specified bitmap font
normally uses. However, the font may be resized or transformed as if it were a scalable font.

> *Though `GcCreateFontFromID` allows you to resize a bitmapped font, such resizing may not produce
> attractive results, particularly if the new size differs radically from the original size. Scalable fonts are a
> better choice if you need text that looks good at a variety of sizes.*

Once you have created a handle to the font you want to use, you can set the current font by passing the
handle to the `GcSetFont` function:

```
GcSetFont(context, font);
```

Like many graphics context functions, the first argument to `GcSetFont` is a handle to the current graphics context. The second argument to `GcSetFont` is a handle to a scalable font.

Instead of using `WinDrawChars`, you must call `GcDrawTextAt` to draw text in a scalable font. For more
information about drawing text using a scalable font, see Chapter 11.

After your application has finished drawing text with a particular font, it should release the memory
allocated for the font handle by calling `GcReleaseFont`:

```
GcReleaseFont(font);
```

> *Creating a font handle can be a relatively slow operation. If your application needs to draw text many
> times, particularly within a tight loop, it should avoid releasing the font handle until it is done using it.*

Like it does for bitmapped fonts, Palm OS provides a variety of informational functions for scalable
fonts. The following table outlines a few of the available functions.

| Function | Description |
| --- | --- |
| GcGetFontBoundingBox | Returns a rectangle, whose dimensions are equal to the average width of a character in the font and height of the tallest possible character in the font, including ascenders and descenders |
| GcGetFontFamilyAndStyle | Returns strings containing the family and style of the font specified by a particular font handle |
| GcGetFontSize | Returns the height, expressed in native coordinates, of the font specified by a particular font handle |
| GcGetFontHeight | Returns a structure that describes the heights of ascenders and descenders, as well as the vertical space between lines of text, of the font specified by a particular font handle |

## Fitting Text to a Specific Screen Width

The graphics context functions in Palm OS Cobalt do not contain an equivalent to the WinDrawTruncChars function for automatically truncating drawn characters to a certain screen width. However, the GcFontStringCharsInWidth function does exist, and it is much easier to use than FntCharsInWidth. GcFontStringCharsInWidth has the following prototype:

```
size_t GcFontStringCharsInWidth (GcFontHandle font,
    const char *string, size_t maxWidth);
```

The font argument to GcFontStringCharsInWidth is a font handle for the font in which a string is to be drawn, string is the string to be printed, and maxWidth is the maximum width available for drawing, expressed in native coordinates. GcFontStringCharsInWidth returns the number of characters in string that fit within maxWidth when drawn with the font specified by font.

> *GcFontStringCharsInWidth returns the number of individual glyphs that fit, not the number of bytes. Depending on the language used, characters may consist of multiple bytes. If you need to determine the number of bytes in a string that may be displayed in a given width, call the GcFontStrongBytesInWidth function instead.*

## Determining Available Fonts

If your application is capable of drawing text in many different fonts, it may be useful to allow the application's user to select a display font from all the fonts installed on the handheld. The GcCountFontFamilies and GcGetFontFamily functions may be used together to iterate over the list of available fonts, as in the following example:

```
int32_t      index;
FontFamily   fontFamily;


for (index = 0; index < GcCountFontFamilies(); index++)
{
    GcGetFontFamily(index, fontFamily);
    // fontFamily now contains the name of an available
    // font family.
}
```

GcCountFontFamilies simply returns the number of fonts installed on the handheld. GcGetFontFamily fills the string specified in its second argument with the name of an installed font, given that font's index in the system's list of fonts. The FontFamily type is simply a character array that is large enough to store the largest possible font family name. In the preceding example, fontFamily could be passed directly to GcCreateFontFromFamily to create a handle to a font with default style, or it could be used to assemble a more complicated CSS font specification for the GcCreateFont function.

Within a given font, there may be one or more available styles. The GcCountFontStyles and GcGetFontStyle functions may be used to iterate over the list of styles available in a given font, as in the following example:

```
int32_t     index;
FontStyle  fontStyle;


for (index = 0; index < GcCountFontStyles("Times New Roman");
     index++)
{
    GcGetFontStyle("Times New Roman", index, fontStyle);
    // fontStyle now contains the name of an available
    // font style.
}
```

GcCountFontStyles returns the number of styles available in a given font family. GcGetFontStyle fills the string specified in its third argument with the name of an available style, given that style's index within the list of styles for a particular font. FontStyle is a character array, so the fontStyle variable in the preceding example could be passed to GcSetFontStyle or used to assemble a CSS font specification string for GcCreateFont.

## Using String Functions

Many of the string functions in Palm OS are familiar to anyone with a reasonable amount of C/C++ programming experience because the system provides its own versions of string functions from the C standard library. The following table lists the Palm OS string functions that mirror standard library calls, as well as each function's equivalent in the standard library.

| Palm OS Function | Standard Library Equivalent |
| --- | --- |
| StrAToI | Atoi |
| StrCat | Strcat |
| StrChr | Strchr |
| StrCompare | Strcmp |
| StrCopy | Strcpy |
| StrLen | Strlen |
| StrNCat | Strncat |
| StrNCompare | Strncmp |
| StrNCopy | Strncpy |
| StrPrintF | Sprintf |
| StrStr | Strstr |
| StrVPrintF | Vsprintf |

The biggest difference between the Palm OS string functions and their C standard library equivalents is that the Palm OS versions properly handle multibyte characters; the standard library functions only handle single-byte characters. A character in Palm OS may be from one to four bytes in length, and a single string could contain both single- and multibyte characters, depending upon the character encoding used.

Furthermore, the standard library functions are not part of the operating system in Palm OS Garnet and earlier. They increase the size of the compiled application because their code is not native to Palm OS. In Palm OS Cobalt, this restriction does not exist.

How do you decide which set of string functions to use? A good rule of thumb is that if the string contains text with which the user interacts, such as the contents of a text field or a label, use the Palm OS versions. Doing so makes your application easier to localize and less likely to produce text-handling errors when installed on Palm OS devices that use a different language. If the strings are entirely internal to the application, they are guaranteed always to contain single-byte characters, and you can safely use the standard library functions.

Palm OS includes the StrIToA and StrIToH functions for converting integer values to strings containing the integer's ASCII or hexadecimal equivalent. The following code shows these two functions in action:

```
int    i = 42;
char   *asciiString, *hexString;

// If necessary, allocate memory for the two strings using
// MemHandleNew and MemHandleLock. This step has been
// omitted.

StrIToA(asciiString, i);
StrIToH(hexString, i);

// asciiString now contains "42".
// hexString now contains "0000002A".
```

In addition to the StrCompare and StrNCompare functions for comparing the values of two strings, Palm OS also offers StrCaselessCompare and StrNCaselessCompare. These caseless versions ignore the case and accent of each character in the two strings to be compared. For example, StrCaselessCompare treats e, E, and é as the same character for purposes of comparison.

*Use StrCompare and StrNCompare to compare strings for the purpose of sorting them alphabetically because these two functions pay attention to case and accent. When comparing strings for the purpose of finding a particular string, use StrCaselessCompare and StrNCaselessCompare. The caseless comparison is particularly useful when trying to find a string based on user input in a text field because it allows the user to enter a search string more quickly by not bothering with capitalization or accented characters, both of which take time to enter using Graffiti. For example, the user could enter "clie" to find the string "CLIÉ."*

## Using Character Macros

Like many of the string functions that mirror functions from the C standard library, Palm OS also contains several character attribute macros that mimic the macros defined in the standard library. These macros take a character argument and return a Boolean response, indicating whether the character belongs to a specific class of characters. For example, the `IsDigit` macro returns `true` if a character is one of the numeric digit characters (0 through 9).

*In Palm OS Garnet and earlier, use the Palm OS versions of the character attribute macros instead of the C standard library versions to avoid compiling extra static library code into your application.*

There are three versions of each character macro in Palm OS. The oldest macro of each triplet has been in Palm OS since version 1.0; newer versions of each macro were added more recently with the *International Feature Set* and with the PalmOSGlue library. The International Feature Set was introduced with Palm OS 3.1 to provide features to support localization of an application to different languages, particularly Asian languages that require double-byte character encoding. To check for the existence of the International Feature Set on a given device, use the following line of code:

```
error = FtrGet(sysFtrCreator, sysFtrNumIntlMgr, &value);
```

If the International Feature Set is present, `value` will be nonzero and the value for `error` will be zero (to indicate no error). The older macros are not available if you are compiling an application using headers from a Palm OS version that includes the International Feature Set.

*The International Feature Set contains much more than the small number of macros included in this chapter. See the "Localizing Applications" section in Chapter 24 for more details.*

To maintain more consistent backward compatibility, Palm added PalmOSGlue equivalents of the International Feature Set macros to Palm OS. When you link the PalmOSGlue library into an application, the same function call works on all versions of Palm OS from 2.0 to Garnet, whether or not they support the International Feature Set. The PalmOSGlue library is not available in Palm OS Cobalt, but Cobalt directly supports the International Feature Set.

*To find out how to link the PalmOSGlue library into your application, see the sidebar "Using PalmOSGlue" in Chapter 8.*

The following table correlates the three Palm OS versions of each character macro with the equivalent macro from the C standard library. The oldest character macros are defined in the Palm OS header file `CharAttr.h`, the newer macros from the international manager are defined in `TextMgr.h`, and the latest macros from the PalmOSGlue library are defined in `TxtGlue.h`.

| Old Palm OS Macro | Macro from Palm OS with International Feature Set | PalmOSGlue Macro | Standard Library Equivalent |
|---|---|---|---|
| IsAlNum | TxtCharIsAlNum | TxtGlueCharIsAlNum | Isalnum |
| IsAlpha | TxtCharIsAlpha | TxtGlueCharIsAlpha | Isalpha |
| IsAscii | TxtCharIsAscii | TxtGlueCharIsAscii | Isascii |
| IsCntrl | TxtCharIsCntrl | TxtGlueCharIsCntrl | Iscntrl |
| IsDigit | TxtCharIsDigit | TxtGlueCharIsDigit | Isdigit |
| IsGraph | TxtCharIsGraph | TxtGlueCharIsGraph | Isgraph |

| Old Palm OS Macro | Macro from Palm OS with International Feature Set | PalmOSGlue Macro | Standard Library Equivalent |
|---|---|---|---|
| IsHex | TxtCharIsHex | TxtGlueCharIsHex | Isxdigit |
| IsLower | TxtCharIsLower | TxtGlueCharIsLower | Islower |
| IsPrint | TxtCharIsPrint | TxtGlueCharIsPrint | Isprint |
| IsPunct | TxtCharIsPunct | TxtGlueCharIsPunct | Ispunct |
| IsSpace | TxtCharIsSpace | TxtGlueCharIsSpace | Isspace |
| IsUpper | TxtCharIsUpper | TxtGlueCharIsUpper | Isupper |

Calling the old character macros is somewhat different from calling the macros from the International Feature Set, PalmOSGlue, or the macros in the C standard library. Except for IsAscii, which takes a single character argument, the old character macros require two arguments. The first argument is the character attribute block, followed by the character itself. Palm OS provides the GetCharAttr function to retrieve the character attribute block, so testing a character for a particular attribute involves code similar to the following:

```
Boolean  itsADigit;
char     c = '2';

itsADigit = IsDigit(GetCharAttr(), c);
```

The new macros in the International Feature Set and PalmOSGlue have longer, more cumbersome names, but they take only one argument — the character to be tested–so they are easier to use in practice:

```
itsADigit = TxtCharIsDigit(c);
// Alternatively:
itsADigit = TxtGlueCharIsDigit(c);
```

Both of the previous examples set itsADigit to true.

Palm OS also has the macro IsDelim (defined as TxtCharIsDelim in the International Feature Set and TxtGlueCharIsDelim in PalmOSGlue) to test whether a character is a text delimiter. A text delimiter in this case is any space or punctuation character.

Another macro not found in the C standard library, ChrIsHardKey (TxtCharIsHardKey in the International Feature Set), tests whether a character code represents one of the four hardware application buttons on the device. Testing an incoming character from a keyDownEvent with ChrIsHardKey allows you to copy the behavior of the built-in applications, which cycle through the categories as the user repeatedly presses, or holds, the button that activates the application. Your own application can take advantage of this behavior if the user redefines one of the buttons to launch your application instead of one of the default programs.

*Oddly enough, there is no PalmOSGlue equivalent of* ChrIsHardKey *or* TxtCharIsHardKey.

**287**

The Librarian sample application implements this category-cycling behavior if the user has defined a hardware button to launch Librarian. Note that, unlike most of the other character attribute macros, the older ChrIsHardKey takes only one argument (the character to test), but TxtCharIsHardKey requires two arguments (the modifiers to the keyDownEvent and the character itself). The following example is the section of Librarian's ListFormHandleEvent event handler that handles a keyDownEvent if it happens to be the result of the user pressing an application button. This example assumes that a version of Palm OS that does not include the International Feature Set (such as Palm OS 3.0 or earlier) is being used:

```
case keyDownEvent:
    if (ChrIsHardKey(event->data.keyDown.chr))
    {
        if (! (event->data.keyDown.modifiers &
            poweredOnKeyMask))
        {
            ListFormNextCategory();
            handled = true;
        }
    }
    else
    {
        // Other keyDownEvent handling omitted.
    }
    break;
```

Here is the same section of event handler, written for version of Palm OS that includes the International Feature Set, such as Palm OS 3.1:

```
case keyDownEvent:
    if (TxtCharIsHardKey(event->data.keyDown.modifiers,
                        event->data.keyDown.chr))
    {
        if (! (event->data.keyDown.modifiers &
            poweredOnKeyMask))
        {
            ListFormNextCategory();
            handled = true;
        }
    }
    else
    {
        // Other keyDownEvent handling omitted.
    }
    break;
```

The event handler checks that the keyDownEvent modifiers do not contain the poweredOnKeyMask value, which would indicate that the application button press was responsible for activating the application; the first press of the hardware button that activates the program should not cycle the categories. Satisfied that the incoming keyDownEvent represents the second or later hardware button press, ListFormHandleEvent calls ListFormNextCategory, another function internal to Librarian, to actually change the category.

*More details about implementing categories are available in Chapter 16.*

# Handling Pen Events

Most of the time, handling user input is best left in the capable hands of user interface elements. However, if you want your application to respond directly to the stylus as the user drags it across the screen (as in, for example, a drawing program), Palm OS provides three events for the direct handling of the stylus input. The system generates three events in response to the user tapping, dragging, and releasing the stylus: penDownEvent, penMoveEvent, and penUpEvent.

The penDownEvent occurs when the user first taps the screen, and the event contains the window-relative coordinates of that tap in the event's screenX and screenY members. See Chapter 11 for more information about window-relative coordinates.

As the user drags the stylus across the screen, the system queues penMoveEvent events. Like the penDownEvent, each penMoveEvent contains the current window coordinates of the stylus.

When the user finally lifts the stylus from the screen, the system queues a penUpEvent, which contains the window-relative coordinates of the place where the stylus left the screen. The penUpEvent also contains two PointType structures in the event's data member: start and end. These two point structures contain the display-relative coordinates of the start and end points of the stylus stroke.

> If you handle penDownEvent completely, returning true in the form event handler, controls and other user interface elements on the form never get a chance to process a stylus tap. If you wish to capture stylus input and allow the user to manipulate user interface objects on the same form (for example, in an application that tracks stylus movement on the screen for drawing or signature capture), you should check the screen coordinates of penDownEvent and return false if the stylus tap occurs on an object.

The following form event handler implements a simple doodling program. This example handles penDownEvent, penMoveEvent, and penUpEvent to draw on the screen wherever the user drags the stylus — except for small regions at the top and bottom of the screen, which prevents the scribbling from overwriting the application's title bar or any command buttons located at the bottom of the form. The drawing area itself is defined by a global RectangleType variable called gDrawRect. The MainFormHandleEvent function also looks in the global variables gX and gY for the current coordinates of the stylus, and in gPenDown for the current state of the stylus, which are either true for down or false for up:

**Palm OS Garnet**

```
static Boolean MainFormHandleEvent(EventType *event)
{
    Boolean  handled = false;


    switch(event->eType)
    {
        case penDownEvent:
            if (RctPtInRectangle(event->screenX,
                event->screenY, &gDrawRect))
            {
                gX = event->screenX;
                gY = event->screenY;
                gPenDown = true;
                handled = true;
```

```
            }
            break;

        case penMoveEvent:
            if (RctPtInRectangle(event->screenX,
                event->screenY, &gDrawRect) && gPenDown)
            {
                Int16 newX = event->screenX;
                Int16 newY = event->screenY;

                WinDrawLine(gX, gY, newX, newY);
                gX = newX;
                gY = newY;
                handled = true;
            }
            break;

        case penUpEvent:
            if (RctPtInRectangle(event->screenX,
                event->screenY, &gDrawRect) && gPenDown)
            {
                Int16 newX = event->screenX;
                Int16 newY = event->screenY;

                WinDrawLine(gX, gY, newX, newY);
                gX = gDrawRect.topLeft.x;
                gY = gDrawRect.topLeft.y;
                gPenDown = false;
                handled = true;
            }
            break;

        default:
            break;

    }

    return handled;
}
```

**Palm OS Cobalt**

```
static Boolean MainFormHandleEvent(EventType *event)
{
    Boolean  handled = false;


    switch(event->eType)
    {
        case penDownEvent:
            if (RctPtInRectangle(event->screenX,
                event->screenY, &gDrawRect))
            {
                gX = event->screenX;
```

```
                    gY = event->screenY;
                    gPenDown = true;
                    handled = true;
                }
                break;

            case penMoveEvent:
                if (RctPtInRectangle(event->screenX,
                    event->screenY, &gDrawRect) && gPenDown)
                {
                    int16_t newX = event->screenX;
                    int16_t newY = event->screenY;

                    WinDrawLine(gX, gY, newX, newY);
                    gX = newX;
                    gY = newY;
                    handled = true;
                }
                break;

            case penUpEvent:
                if (RctPtInRectangle(event->screenX,
                    event->screenY, &gDrawRect) && gPenDown)
                {
                    int16_t newX = event->screenX;
                    int16_t newY = event->screenY;

                    WinDrawLine(gX, gY, newX, newY);
                    gX = gDrawRect.topLeft.x;
                    gY = gDrawRect.topLeft.y;
                    gPenDown = false;
                    handled = true;
                }
                break;

            default:
                break;

    }

    return handled;
}
```

When the form receives any of the pen-related events, the event handler first checks to see if the point passed by the event is within the drawing area. The RctPtInRectangle function is useful for this operation because it returns true if a given point lies within a given rectangle. By comparing the screenX and screenY coordinates passed by the various pen events with the borders of the rectangle, the event handler can tell whether it should take care of the event or hand it off to the system for default processing.

A penDownEvent within the drawing area merely sets the global gX and gY variables to the coordinates of the screen tap. It also sets the gPenDown variable to true, providing a point from which the penMoveEvent and penUpEvent handlers may draw a line and indicating to the rest of the application that the stylus is currently touching the screen. The MainFormHandleEvent function handles the penMoveEvent and

**291**

penUpEvent only if the pen state is currently down (which is to say, gPenDown is true); otherwise, the program would draw some unexpected things on the screen if the user tapped outside the drawing rectangle and then released the stylus within the drawing area.

# Handling Key Events

Whenever the user enters a text character by using Graffiti, the system queues a keyDownEvent. The system also puts a keyDownEvent on the queue when the user presses a hardware button or taps one of the silkscreened buttons, such as the Menu button. Along with these tangible key events, the system generates various virtual key events when certain actions take place, such as when the low battery display appears.

The keyDownEvent stores the value of the character, hardware button, or virtual key in the event's chr member. You can find a large number of useful constants for various key event values in the header file Chars.h. Some of the more common character code constants are listed in the following table.

| Constant | Value | Description |
|---|---|---|
| chrLeftArrow | 0x1C | Character-left Graffiti stroke (not generated by Graffiti 2) |
| chrRightArrow | 0x1D | Character-right Graffiti stroke (not generated by Graffiti 2) |
| vchrNextField | 0x0103 | Graffiti next-field character (not generated by Graffiti 2) |
| vchrPrevField | 0x010C | Graffiti previous-field character (not generated by Graffiti 2) |
| vchrPageUp | 0x0B | Hardware scroll up button |
| vchrPageDown | 0x0C | Hardware scroll down button |
| vchrHard1 | 0x0204 | Date Book hardware button |
| vchrHard2 | 0x0205 | Address hardware button |
| vchrHard3 | 0x0206 | To Do List hardware button |
| vchrHard4 | 0x0207 | Memo Pad hardware button |
| vchrHardPower | 0x0208 | Hardware power button |
| vchrHardCradle | 0x0209 | HotSync button on the cradle |
| vchrLaunch | 0x0108 | Application launcher silkscreened button |
| vchrMenu | 0x0105 | Menu silkscreened button |
| vchrCalc | 0x010B | Calculator silkscreened button |
| vchrFind | 0x010A | Find silkscreened button |
| vchrLowBattery | 0x0101 | Queued when the low battery dialog box appears |
| vchrAlarm | 0x010D | Queued before displaying an alarm |
| vchrRonamatic | 0x010E | Queued upon a stroke from the Graffiti area to the upper half of the screen |

| Constant | Value | Description |
|----------|-------|-------------|
| vchrBacklight | 0x0113 | Toggles the state of the backlight |
| vchrAutoOff | 0x0114 | Queued when the power is about to shut off for inactivity |

The keyDownEvent also has a modifiers member, which is a bit field that stores a number of flags pertaining to the contents of the key event. The Event.h header file contains constant values that you can use as bit masks to test for the presence or absence of certain flags in the modifiers field. The following table shows some of these constants and their values.

| Constant | Value | Description |
|----------|-------|-------------|
| shiftKeyMask | 0x0001 | Graffiti is in case-shift mode |
| capsLockMask | 0x0002 | Graffiti is in caps-lock mode |
| commandKeyMask | 0x0008 | This keyDownEvent is a menu event or a special virtual key code |
| autoRepeatKeyMask | 0x0040 | This keyDownEvent is the result of an autorepeat event (autorepeating usually occurs as a result of holding down one of the hardware buttons, such as the scrolling buttons) |
| poweredOnKeyMask | 0x0100 | This keyDownEvent powered the system on |

Virtual key events always have the commandKeyMask flag set. Checking for the presence of this flag is a good way to separate normal text entry from special system events.

As an example, the following form event handler displays an alert if the user presses the scroll down hardware button (represented by vchrPageDown), but only if the user holds down the button long enough to generate an autorepeat, which requires about half a second of pressing:

```
static Boolean MainFormHandleEvent(EventType *event)
{
    Boolean  handled = false;


    switch (event->eType)
    {
        case keyDownEvent:
            if ((event->data.keyDown.chr == vchrPageDown) &&
                (event->data.keyDown.modifiers &
                 autoRepeatKeyMask))
            {
                FrmAlert(MyAlert);
                handled = true;
            }

        default:
```

```
            break;

    }

    return handled;
}
```

Another quick way to check for a virtual `keyDownEvent` is to use the `EvtKeydownIsVirtual` macro, which returns `true` if an event is a virtual key down event and `false` if it is any other type of event, as follows:

```
if (EvtKeydownIsVirtual(event))
    // event is a virtual keyDownEvent
else
    // event is a different type of event
```

## Understanding Application Button Presses

Normally, `SysHandleEvent` handles application button presses by launching an application that has been assigned to that button. Because `SysHandleEvent` comes before an application's form event handlers in the event loop, `SysHandleEvent` grabs the `keyDownEvent` queued by an application button press before an application's own form event handler even sees the event. The exception to this is if the application assigned to a button is already running, in which case `SysHandleEvent` leaves the event unhandled and the application's event loop passes the `keyDownEvent` along to the active form's event handler.

As an example of how this works, assume the user has chosen the Date Book button to launch Librarian. While Librarian is running, pressing the Date Book button queues a `keyDownEvent`, which `SysHandleEvent` ignores. The event then continues through the event loop to Librarian's current form event handler. Pressing any of the other three hardware application buttons queues an appropriate `keyDownEvent`, which `SysHandleEvent` responds to by closing Librarian and launching a new application. Librarian's form handler never gets a chance to respond to any hardware application button other than the Date Book button.

It is possible to override this behavior and handle an application button before `SysHandleEvent` does.

## Overriding Hardware Application Buttons

The hardware application buttons each send their own `keyDownEvent`. However, the `SysHandleEvent` call at the beginning of an application's event loop gets first crack at handling an application button press. It does so by closing the running application and launching whatever program is assigned to that button. If your application needs to override this behavior, it must have a slightly modified event loop that can grab an application button `keyDownEvent` before `SysHandleEvent` gets ahold of it. Games are the most common type of program that needs to override the `SysHandleEvent` function's default handling of hardware application buttons because games often use those buttons as primary control mechanisms.

Fortunately, overriding the `SysHandleEvent` function's processing of hardware application button presses is simple. The following `AppEventLoop` function passes the handling of an event to another function, `SpecialKeyDown`, before it calls `SysHandleEvent`:

**Palm OS Garnet**

```
static void AppEventLoop(void)
{
    EventType   event;
    UInt16      error;


    do
    {
        EvtGetEvent(&event, evtWaitForever);

        // Intercept hardware application buttons.
        if (SpecialKeyDown(&event))
            continue;

        if (SysHandleEvent(&event))
            continue;

        if (MenuHandleEvent(0, &event, &error))
            continue;

        if (AppHandleEvent(&event))
            continue;

        FrmDispatchEvent(&event);
    }
    while (event.eType != appStopEvent);
}
```

**Palm OS Cobalt**

```
static void AppEventLoop(void)
{
    EventType   event;
    status_t    error;


    do
    {
        EvtGetEvent(&event, evtWaitForever);

        // Intercept hardware application buttons.
        if (SpecialKeyDown(&event))
            continue;

        if (SysHandleEvent(&event))
            continue;

        if (MenuHandleEvent(0, &event, &error))
            continue;

        if (AppHandleEvent(&event))
            continue;

        FrmDispatchEvent(&event);
    }
    while (event.eType != appStopEvent);
}
```

The `SpecialKeyDown` function looks like the following:

```
Boolean SpecialKeyDown (EventType *event)
{
    Boolean  handled = false;


    if (event->eType != keyDownEvent)
        return handled;

    if (event->data.keyDown.modifiers & poweredOnKeyMask)
        return handled;

    switch(event->data.keyDown.chr)
    {
        case vchrHard1:
            // Handle Datebook button.
            handled = true;
            break;

        case vchrHard2:
            // Handle Address button.
            handled = true;
            break;

        case vchrHard3:
            // Handle To Do button.
            handled = true;
            break;

        case vchrHard4:
            // Handle Memo button.
            handled = true;
            break;

        default:
            break;
    }

    return handled;
}
```

`SpecialKeyDown` first checks to see if the event is a `keyDownEvent`:

```
if (event->eType != keyDownEvent)
    return handled;
```

If the event is not a `keyDownEvent`, `SpecialKeyDown` leaves the event unhandled and it passes back to the event loop for regular processing.

Next, `SpecialKeyDown` checks to see if the button press occurred while the handheld was turned off:

```
if (event->data.keyDown.modifiers & poweredOnKeyMask)
    return handled;
```

If the user presses one of the hardware application buttons to turn the handheld on, SpecialKeyDown ignores the keyDownEvent and passes it back to the event loop unhandled. This step is important if the user assigns your application to start when one of the hardware buttons is pressed. Generally, a user expects that turning the power off and on again will not affect the display in whatever application is currently running. Turning the handheld on should be a consistent activity, regardless of whether the user does so by pressing the power button or by pressing the button assigned to launch the currently running application. Having the handheld perform some kind of action just as it powers up can be confusing to the user, particularly if that action modifies what is being displayed on the screen.

The rest of SpecialKeyDown is a switch statement that handles the virtual characters assigned to hardware application buttons. This part of SpecialKeyDown works just like any other event handler; it can respond to a hardware button press directly within SpecialKeyDown or it can hand off the actual event handling to another function.

# Looking Up Phone Numbers

In Palm OS versions 2.0 and later, the operating system provides an easy way for the user to look up a phone number in the built-in Address Book application from any text field. It is almost as simple to add this feature in your own application. All that is required to implement a phone number lookup is a text field and the PhoneNumberLookup function.

The PhoneNumberLookup function takes a single argument—a pointer to a field object. When called, PhoneNumberLookup first searches the Address Book application for whatever text is currently selected in the specified field. If no text is selected in the field, PhoneNumberLookup tries to find whatever word is closest to the insertion point.

If PhoneNumberLookup finds a match, it replaces the current selection, if any, with the full name and phone number of the record that the function found in the Address Book database. If PhoneNumberLookup cannot immediately find an unambiguous match, the function displays the Address Book's Phone Number Lookup form to allow the user to select a record manually.

To maintain consistency with the built-in applications, any program that implements phone number lookup should have an Options ➪ Phone Lookup menu item, with an "L" character for its Graffiti command shortcut. The Librarian sample application, like the built-in applications, implements a phone number lookup in its Note view. The following section of Librarian's NoteViewHandleEvent function launches a phone number lookup when the user selects the Options ➪ Phone Lookup menu item or enters an "L" after a command stroke:

**Palm OS Garnet**

```
static Boolean NoteViewDoCommand(UInt16 command)
{
    FieldType  *field;
    Boolean    handled = true;

    switch (command)
    {
        case notePhoneLookupCmd:
            field = GetObjectPtr(NoteField);
            PhoneNumberLookup(field);
            break;
```

```
        // Other menu items omitted

    default:
        handled = false;
    }

    return (handled);
}
```

**Palm OS Cobalt**

```
static Boolean NoteViewDoCommand(uint16_t command)
{
    FieldType  *field;
    Boolean    handled = true;

    switch (command)
    {
        case notePhoneLookupCmd:
            field = GetObjectPtr(NoteField);
            PhoneNumberLookup(field);
            break;

        // Other menu items omitted

        default:
            handled = false;
    }

    return (handled);
}
```

# Launching Applications

Normally launching an application is a simple matter of tapping the silkscreened Applications button and selecting a program from the Palm OS application launcher. Well-designed Palm OS applications make this a painless operation by saving whatever data the user is working on before switching to the launcher. The constant readiness of a Palm OS application to drop whatever it's doing and allow the user to switch to another application is part of what makes a Palm OS device so convenient.

However, some applications, particularly replacements for the system launcher application, may need to call up the launcher without waiting for the user to tap the Applications button. In other cases, an application may need to launch another program directly, without using the system launcher at all; this technique is a good way for a suite of related applications to provide easy links between those applications. Also, it can be useful for an application to send a specific launch code to another application to request that it perform some sort of action or modify its data in some way. Again, a suite of applications could send launch codes to one another as a means of inter-application communication.

## Calling the System Application Launcher

Starting with Palm OS version 3.0, the application launcher is an independent application stored in the handheld's ROM. Prior to 3.0, the launcher is a pop-up dialog box. The end user of a Palm OS handheld can tell no difference between these two styles of application launcher, but the difference does have some important implications for an application developer. Regardless of this difference, there is a method of displaying the launcher that works on any version of Palm OS. Simply queue a keyDownEvent that contains the special vchrLaunch character; the system takes care of showing the launcher. The following code assembles the keyDownEvent and adds it to the event queue with EvtAddEventToQueue:

```
EventType  newEvent;

newEvent.eType = keyDownEvent;
newEvent.data.keyDown.chr = vchrLaunch;
newEvent.data.keyDown.modifiers = commandKeyMask;
EvtAddEventToQueue(&newEvent);
```

*To display the launcher pop-up in Palm OS 2.0 and earlier, you also may use the SysAppLauncherDialog function, which requires no arguments and has no return value. This function still exists in post-2.0 versions of Palm OS for backward compatibility. However, you should always queue a keyDownEvent containing a vchrLaunch to bring up the system application launcher to ensure that your code continues to work without modification on future versions of the operating system.*

## Launching Applications Directly

Two functions in Palm OS are responsible for launching other applications: SysAppLaunch and SysUIAppSwitch. Both functions allow you to customize how you wish to launch an application, giving you control over the launch code, launch flags, and parameter block to send to the other application. The SysAppLaunch function is for making use of another program and then returning to the original application, while SysUIAppSwitch quits the current application and starts another in its place.

> Do not use **SysAppLaunch** or **SysUIAppSwitch** to call the system application launcher. If another application has replaced the default launcher, that application will not open in place of the default system launcher. Instead, queue a **keyDownEvent** containing a **vchrLaunch** to open the system launcher, as described earlier in this chapter.

The most common use for SysAppLaunch is to send launch codes to other applications, thus enabling an application to make use of another program's features to perform a task. In effect, SysAppLaunch allows a program to call a specific subroutine in another application. As an example, the Palm OS PhoneNumberLookup function, discussed earlier in this chapter, uses SysAppLaunch to send a sysAppLaunchCmdLookup launch code to the Address Book application, telling the Address Book to search its database for a particular name and return the phone number associated with that name.

The prototype for SysAppLaunch looks like this:

**Palm OS Garnet**
```
Err SysAppLaunch (UInt16 cardNo, LocalID dbID,
    UInt16 launchFlags, UInt16 cmd, MemPtr cmdPBP,
    UInt32 *resultP)
```

**Palm OS Cobalt**

```
status_t SysAppLaunch (DatabaseID dbID, uint16_t cmd,
    void *cmdPBP, uint32_t* resultP);
```

The `cardNo` and `dbID` arguments in the Palm OS Garnet version of `SysAppLaunch` identify the application that `SysAppLaunch` should call by specifying the memory card where that application is located and its unique database ID. You can retrieve the values for `cardNo` and `dbID` with the `DmGetNextDatabaseByTypeCreator` function, which returns the card and database ID given to the creator ID of the application. Chapter 15 contains more information about `DmGetNextDatabaseByTypeCreator`.

In Palm OS Cobalt, the `cardNo` parameter does not exist. Use the `DmFindDatabaseByTypeCreator` function to retrieve the database ID of the application to be launched. Chapter 15 contains more information about `DmFindDatabaseByTypeCreator`.

To send a launch code to another application in Palm OS Garnet, pass the value 0 for the `launchFlags` argument. Other launch flags exist but they are usually needed only by the system. Palm OS Cobalt has done away with the `launchFlags` parameter entirely.

The `cmd` argument specifies the launch code to send to the other application, and `cmdPBP` points to a parameter block structure containing information the called application needs in order to process the launch code. When the other application is finished, `SysAppLaunch` uses `resultP` to return a pointer to the result of the called application's `PilotMain` routine.

The `SysUIAppSwitch` function takes the same parameters as `SysAppLaunch` but does not have a `resultP` parameter because `SysUIAppSwitch` tells the current application to quit before launching the new program. However, an extra step may be necessary in Palm OS Garnet or earlier when sending anything other than a `sysAppLaunchCmdNormalLaunch` launch code. If you pass a parameter block to the new application using the `cmdPBP` argument, you should grant ownership of the parameter block to the system with the `MemPtrSetOwner` function. Otherwise, the system will free the memory allocated for the parameter block when the calling application quits. The `MemPtrSetOwner` function takes two parameters — the pointer itself and the ID of the new owning application. Passing 0 for the second parameter assigns ownership of the pointer to the system. For example, the following line of code changes ownership of `cmdPBP` to the system:

```
Err error = MemPtrSetOwner(cmdPBP, 0);
```

The `error` return value from `MemPtrSetOwner` contains 0 if there is no error while changing ownership, or `error` contains the constant `memErrInvalidParam` if an error occurs. Another function, `MemHandleSetOwner`, exists for changing the ownership of handles, which also must be done for any handles within the parameter block. The `MemHandleSetOwner` function works the same way as `MemPtrSetOwner`, by substituting a handle for the pointer in the function's first argument.

In Palm OS Cobalt, it is not necessary to change ownership of the parameter block when changing applications with `SysUIAppSwitch`. Palm OS Cobalt completely tears down the process in which an application runs when the application closes, which would also destroy the parameter block. Instead of passing a pointer to the parameter block to the newly launched application, Palm OS Cobalt copies the block before destroying it and then passes a pointer to the copied parameter block to the newly launched application.

To simplify calls to SysAppLaunch and SysUIAppSwitch, Palm OS provides two macros, AppCallWithCommand and AppLaunchWithCommand, which incorporate a call to DmGetNextDatabaseByTypeCreator. These macros allow an application to send launch codes and launch another application without having to find the application's card number and database ID manually. These macros are available only in Palm OS Garnet and earlier; equivalent macros do not exist in Palm OS Cobalt.

The following code shows the definitions of both of these macros, which are supplied in the Palm OS header file AppLaunchCmd.h:

```
#define AppCallWithCommand(appCreator, appCmd, \
                        appCmdParams) \
{ \
    UInt16    cardNo; \
    LocalID   dbID; \
    DmSearchStateType   searchState; \
    UInt32    result; \
    Err       err; \
    DmGetNextDatabaseByTypeCreator(true, &searchState, \
        sysFileTApplication, appCreator, true, &cardNo, \
        &dbID); \
    ErrNonFatalDisplayIf(!dbID, "Could not find app"); \
    if (dbID) { \
        err = SysAppLaunch(cardNo, dbID, 0, appCmd, (Ptr) \
                        appCmdParams, &result); \
        ErrNonFatalDisplayIf(err, "Could not launch app");\
    } \
}


#define AppLaunchWithCommand(appCreator, appCmd, \
                        appCmdParams)\
{ \
    UInt16    cardNo; \
    LocalID   dbID; \
    DmSearchStateType   searchState; \
    Err       err; \
    DmGetNextDatabaseByTypeCreator(true, &searchState, \
        sysFileTApplication, appCreator, true, &cardNo, \
        &dbID); \
    ErrNonFatalDisplayIf(!dbID, "Could not find app"); \
    if (dbID) { \
        err = SysUIAppSwitch(cardNo, dbID, appCmd, \
                        appCmdParams); \
        ErrNonFatalDisplayIf(err, "Could not launch app");\
    } \
}
```

Both macros have three arguments. The first, appCreator, is the creator ID of the application that should be launched. The second, appCmd, is the launch code to send to the application. The third, appCmdParams, is a pointer to the parameter block that should be passed along with the launch code.

As an example of how to use these macros, CodeWarrior's project stationery for Palm OS includes a function called RomVersionCompatible, which checks the current version of the operating system when the application starts to see if it meets a minimum version requirement. If the system version is older than the required version, RomVersionCompatible alerts the user about the version requirement and then calls AppLaunchWithCommand to launch a "safe" default application that is guaranteed to exist in that version of the operating system. The relevant lines of code from RomVersionCompatible are shown in the following example:

```
if (romVersion <
    sysMakeROMVersion(2,0,0,sysROMStageRelease,0))
    AppLaunchWithCommand(sysFileCDefaultApp,
                         sysAppLaunchCmdNormalLaunch,
                         NULL);
```

The constant sysFileCDefaultApp is defined in every version of the Palm OS headers to refer to a default application that exists in that version of the operating system. In Palm OS 1.0 and 2.0, this default is the Memory application; in Palm OS 3.0 and later, the system Preferences application is the default because memory display in the more recent versions of the operating system is part of the system launcher application and the Memory application no longer exists by default.

## Sending Launch Codes Globally

If you need to send a particular launch code to every application on the device, use the SysBroadcastActionCode function. This function takes two arguments: the launch code to send and a pointer to the parameter block containing information needed by any applications that respond to the launch code.

## Creating Your Own Launch Codes

Palm OS allows you to define your own launch codes. This feature permits two applications to talk to each other and control each other's data behind the scenes without the user ever being aware of what the programs are doing. Using your own launch codes, you can create suites of applications that communicate with one another, shared libraries that may be called from many different applications, and large applications composed of multiple smaller applications that communicate with one another using launch codes.

Launch codes in Palm OS are 16-bit values. Codes from 0 through 32767 are reserved for use by PalmSource for their own launch codes and future enhancements to the operating system, leaving the numbers from 32768 to 65535 for your own applications, which should be more space than any application could realistically need for launch codes. Using your own launch codes is a simple matter of deciding what a particular number represents and then making sure that your applications respond to that number in their PilotMain routines.

# Generating Random Numbers

The SysRandom function is the only pseudo-random number generator built into Palm OS. For most purposes, SysRandom should be sufficient for the task of creating random numbers. Some applications that require very random numbers, such as strong cryptography programs, may not work well with SysRandom. Those applications may require you to provide your own algorithms.

The SysRandom function returns an integer value from 0 to sysRandomMax, which the Palm OS headers define as 32,767. To generate a random number with SysRandom, pass the function an unsigned long integer value to use as a seed value, or 0 to use the last seed value. The best way to ensure that your application produces reasonably random results is to seed the random number generator from the system clock when the user first starts the application. The following line of code in the application's StartApplication function will seed the random number generator from the Palm OS device's onboard clock:

**Palm OS Garnet**
```
SysRandom(TimGetTicks());
```

**Palm OS Cobalt**
```
SysRandom((int32_t)TimGetTicks());
```

*Casting the result of TimGetTicks to an int32_t type is necessary in Palm OS Cobalt because the Cobalt version of TimGetTicks returns a uint64_t data type instead of the int32_t type returned by earlier versions of TimGetTicks.*

After the random number generator has been seeded, call SysRandom with a value of 0 each time you need a new random number. With a little (simple) math, you can use SysRandom to come up with almost any random number. The following simple function returns a number from 0 to n - 1, where n is the total number of possible choices:

**Palm OS Garnet**
```
UInt16 RandomNum(UInt n) {
    return SysRandom(0) / (1 + sysRandomMax / n);
}
```

**Palm OS Cobalt**
```
uint16_t RandomNum(uint8_t n) {
    return SysRandom(0) / (1 + sysRandomMax / n);
}
```

For example, passing the value 52 for n causes RandomNum to return a value between 0 and 51, which would be appropriate for randomly drawing a card from a standard poker deck.

Random numbers, although necessary for some applications, can make debugging a nightmare because the application may not produce the same results each time it is run. When debugging an application that calls SysRandom, seed the random number generator with a constant number instead of with TimGetTicks, like this:

```
SysRandom(1);
```

When seeded in this way, the random number generator produces the same series of "random" numbers each time you run the application, greatly reducing your frustration level when debugging. When you are ready to distribute the application, replace the constant with a call to TimGetTicks so the application genuinely produces a different random number each time the end user runs it.

# Managing Power

Palm OS provides the SysBatteryInfo function for determining information about the handheld's battery settings. The prototype for SysBatteryInfo looks like this:

**Palm OS Garnet**

```
UInt16 SysBatteryInfo (Boolean set, UInt16 *warnThresholdP,
    UInt16 *criticalThresholdP, UInt16 *maxTicksP,
    SysBatteryKind *kindP, Boolean *pluggedIn,
    UInt8 *percentP)
```

**Palm OS Cobalt**

```
uint16_t SysBatteryInfo (Boolean set,
    uint16_t* warnThresholdPercentP,
    uint16_t* criticalThresholdPercentP,
    uint16_t *shutdownThresholdPercentP,
    uint32_t* maxMilliSecsP, SysBatteryKind* kindP,
    Boolean* pluggedInP, uint8_t * percentP);
```

The SysBatteryInfo function returns a value equal to the current battery voltage in hundredths of a volt, which allows the system to store the value as an integer instead of as a floating-point number. Divide the return value from SysBatteryInfo by 100 to obtain the actual voltage level of the batteries.

The first argument, set, should be false to retrieve battery settings. Presumably, a true value for set would change the settings, but the PalmSource documentation states that applications should never change battery settings. This restriction is understandable because changing the voltage threshold levels at which the device warns the user about a low battery condition could potentially result in data loss because of a drained battery. Be careful when using SysBatteryInfo.

Pass NULL for any of the remaining arguments to SysBatteryInfo that you wish to ignore. For any value you wish to retrieve, allocate a variable of the appropriate type and pass a pointer to that variable to the SysBatteryInfo function.

In Palm OS Garnet and earlier, the warnThresholdP argument is a pointer to a variable to receive the system battery warning threshold. The battery warning threshold is the voltage at which the system first displays a warning to the user, stating that the batteries are low and should be changed or recharged. Like the return value of SysBatteryInfo, the value that warnThresholdP points to is the threshold's level in hundredths of a volt. The criticalThresholdP argument points to a variable to receive the critical battery threshold. When the battery voltage reaches the critical threshold level, the device drops to sleep mode without warning and does not return to normal operation until the battery voltage is above the critical threshold again. Note the value that criticalThresholdP points to is the threshold voltage level in hundredths of a volt.

In Palm OS Cobalt, instead of raw voltage values, SysBatteryInfo returns percentages of total voltage for the various threshold levels. The warnThresholdPercentP argument receives the system battery warning threshold, criticalThresholdPercentP receives the critical battery threshold, and shutdownThresholdPercentP receives the percentage of remaining battery power at which the device automatically puts itself into sleep mode to prevent further power loss and potential loss of data.

The maxTicksP argument in Palm OS Garnet points to a variable to receive the value of the system battery timeout value, in system ticks, which the system uses internally to determine when to display the low battery warning dialog box to the user. The Palm OS Cobalt equivalent is maxMilliSecsP, which receives the same value expressed in milliseconds instead of system ticks.

The kindP argument points to a variable that receives the type of battery installed in the device. The battery type alters the values that the system uses to calculate remaining voltage in the battery. Different battery types are defined in the header file SystemMgr.h in Palm OS Garnet, and in CmnBatteryTypes.h in Palm OS Cobalt:

**Palm OS Garnet**
```
typedef enum {
    sysBatteryKindAlkaline = 0,
    sysBatteryKindNiCad,
    sysBatteryKindLiIon,
    sysBatteryKindRechAlk,
    sysBatteryKindNiMH,
    sysBatteryKindLiIon1400,
    sysBatteryKindLast = 0xFF
} SysBatteryKind;
```

**Palm OS Cobalt**
```
enum SysBatteryKindTag {
    sysBatteryKindAlkaline = 0,
    sysBatteryKindNiCad,
    sysBatteryKindLiIon,
    sysBatteryKindRechAlk,
    sysBatteryKindNiMH,
    sysBatteryKindLiIon1400,
    sysBatteryKindFuelCell,
    sysBatteryKindPlutonium237,
    sysBatteryKindAntiMatter,
    sysBatteryKindLast = 0xFF
};
typedef Enum8 SysBatteryKind;
```

The pluggedIn argument indicates whether the device is plugged into external power, which might be the case for most handhelds with rechargeable internal batteries when they are resting in their cradles or plugged into an AC adapter to recharge. A true value for pluggedIn indicates that the device is plugged in; false indicates that the device is not attached to external power.

Finally, the percentP contains the approximate percentage of power left in the device's batteries. Because the power regulation hardware on a Palm OS device is not sophisticated, it is difficult for the system to determine the exact voltage in the device's batteries. Because this inaccuracy can result in a brand new set of batteries appearing to have less than 100 percent power, SysBatteryInfo actually fudges the percentP value, returning 100 when the calculated percentage is 90 or higher.

The Palm OS also provides the function SysBatteryInfoV20 for backward compatibility reasons. The SysBatteryInfoV20 function is exactly like the Palm OS Garnet version of SysBatteryInfo, except that it has no percentP argument.

## *Reacting to Low Battery Conditions*

When the batteries in a Palm OS device reach the battery warning threshold level, the system queues a keyDownEvent containing a special vchrLowBattery character code. Normally, letting this event fall through to the system's SysHandleEvent routine in your application's event loop should be sufficient, because SysHandleEvent reacts to this event by displaying the system low battery dialog box. If, for some reason, your application needs to know when the low battery warning threshold has been reached, your own application's event handlers can react to it by handling the vchrLowBattery event.

> If you do react to a **vchrLowBattery** event, be sure not to mark the event as handled so that **SysHandleEvent** still gets a chance to display the system low battery warning dialog box.

# Identifying the Device

Starting with the Palm III, some Palm OS devices with flash ROM have a unique 12-digit serial number in their ROM storage to identify the device. This serial number is stored in a text buffer with no null terminator. The user can view a device's serial number in the application launcher's Info view. Serial numbers may be used to implement copy protection for an application that is keyed to a specific handheld. In Palm OS devices that support wireless connections, the serial number may be used for authentication purposes to verify the security of a connection between the handheld and a remote server.

To retrieve the serial number from ROM, use the SysGetROMToken function. The prototype for SysGetROMToken looks like this:

**Palm OS Garnet**
```
Err SysGetROMToken (UInt16 cardNo, UInt32 token,
                    UInt8 **dataP, UInt16 *sizeP)
```

**Palm OS Cobalt**
```
status_t SysGetROMToken (uint32_t token, uint8_t **dataP,
                         uint16_t *sizeP);
```

If SysGetROMToken successfully retrieves a valid serial number, the function's return value should be 0. Because of the inner workings of SysGetROMToken, you also should verify that dataP is not NULL. Also, if dataP does contain data, the first character should not be 0xFF. Once you have verified that all these things are true, you can be sure that SysGetROMToken has retrieved a valid serial number.

The cardNo argument in the Palm OS Garnet version is the memory card holding the ROM to be queried; because no Palm OS device currently has more than one card, pass 0 for this value. The Palm OS Cobalt version omits the cardNo parameter.

Pass the constant sysROMTokenSnum, defined in the Palm OS SystemMgr.h header file, for the token argument. The SysGetROMToken function is capable of retrieving information other than the device's serial number from ROM, but the serial number is the only bit of information Palm has made publicly available to developers, so sysROMTokenSnum is the only thing you can pass in the token argument and expect to get a useful result from SysGetROMToken.

The `dataP` argument is a pointer to a text buffer to hold the serial number `SysGetROMToken` retrieves, and `sizeP` is a pointer to a variable to receive the size of the retrieved text, in bytes.

As an example, the following function draws a device's serial number on the screen at a given location, or a short message indicating the device's lack of a serial number:

**Palm OS Garnet**

```
static void DrawSerialNumber(Coord x, Coord y)
{
    char    *buffer;
    UInt16  length;
    Err     error;


    error = SysGetROMToken(0, sysROMTokenSnum, (UInt8 *)
                          &buffer, &length);
    if ( (! error) && (buffer) &&
        ( (UInt8) *buffer != 0xFF) )
        // There is a valid serial number, so draw it.
        WinDrawChars(buffer, length, x, y);
    else
        // There isn't a valid serial number, so draw a
        // message indicating this to the user.
        WinDrawChars("No serial number", 16, x, y);
}
```

**Palm OS Cobalt**

```
static void DrawSerialNumber(Coord x, Coord y)
{
    char     *buffer;
    uint16_t length;
    status_t error;


    error = SysGetROMToken(sysROMTokenSnum, (uint8_t *)
                          &buffer, &length);
    if ( (error == errNone) && (buffer) &&
        ( (uint8_t) *buffer != 0xFF) )
        // There is a valid serial number, so draw it.
        WinDrawChars(buffer, length, x, y);
    else
        // There isn't a valid serial number, so draw a
        // message indicating this to the user.
        WinDrawChars("No serial number", 16, x, y);
}
```

# Using the Clipboard

The built-in applications allow for the cutting, copying, and pasting of data between text fields. The area of memory the system maintains for this kind of temporary data storage is called the *Clipboard*.

There are actually three different clipboards, each of which is used to store a different kind of data. The header file Clipboard.h defines the following enumerated type to identify these different types of Clipboard data:

**Palm OS Garnet**

```
enum clipboardFormats {
    clipboardText,
    clipboardInk,
    clipboardBitmap
};
typedef enum clipboardFormats ClipboardFormatType;
```

**Palm OS Cobalt**

```
enum clipboardFormats {
    clipboardText,
    clipboardInk,
    clipboardBitmap
};
typedef Enum8 ClipboardFormatType;
```

The clipboardText format stores textual data, and the clipboardBitmap format stores bitmap image data. As of this writing, the clipboardInk format is reserved for future use but, as its name implies, it is probably intended for storing "digital ink"—a hybrid between text and bitmap data. Digital ink data represents something that the user has drawn directly on the screen, composed of a doodle or text that has not been converted by the Graffiti engine, or even a mixture of pictures and text.

Adding cut, copy, and paste behavior to a field is the easiest way to give users access to the Clipboard. The functions FldCut, FldCopy, and FldPaste all take a pointer to a field object as an argument:

```
void FldCut (FieldType* fldP)
void FldCopy (const FieldType* fldP)
void FldPaste (FieldType* fldP)
```

Both FldCut and FldCopy copy the currently selected text from the indicated field and place it on the text Clipboard. The FldCut function also deletes the selected text from the field. The FldPaste function replaces the currently selected text in the field with the contents of the text Clipboard, or if there is no selection in the text, it inserts the contents of the Clipboard at the field's insertion point.

If you need to place text data on the Clipboard directly, without using a field, or if you want to put bitmap data on the Clipboard, use the ClipboardAddItem function. ClipboardAddItem is the only way to put data on the Clipboard without using a field. The prototype for ClipboardAddItem looks like this:

**Palm OS Garnet**

```
void ClipboardAddItem (const ClipboardFormatType format,
    const void *ptr, UInt16 length)
```

**Palm OS Cobalt**
```
void ClipboardAddItem (const ClipboardFormatType format,
    const void *ptr, size_t length);
```

The first argument to ClipboardAddItem is format, which specifies which clipboard, text or bitmap, should accept the incoming data. The other two arguments, ptr and length, are a pointer to the beginning of the data and the length of that data in bytes, respectively. Whatever data you place on a Clipboard with ClipboardAddItem overwrites the current contents of that Clipboard. The maximum size of text data on the Clipboard is 1000 bytes.

Starting with Palm OS version 3.2, the ClipboardAppendItem function allows an application to write more data onto the end of the Clipboard without deleting what is already there, thus allowing you to build up larger Clipboard contents from many smaller pieces of text. The ClipboardAppendItem function takes the same parameters as ClipboardAddItem. Because ClipboardAppendItem is intended for use with text data only, be sure to pass the clipboardText constant for the first argument to ClipboardAppendItem.

> **You cannot add null-terminated string data to the Clipboard. Be sure there are no null characters in the text data you add or append to the Clipboard.**

You can retrieve data from the Clipboard with the ClipboardGetItem function, which has the following prototype:

**Palm OS Garnet**
```
MemHandle ClipboardGetItem (
    const ClipboardFormatType format, UInt16 *length)
```

**Palm OS Cobalt**
```
MemHandle ClipboardGetItem (
    const ClipboardFormatType format, size_t *length)
```

The ClipboardGetItem function returns a handle to the actual memory chunk that contains the requested Clipboard data. Because this is a handle to the Clipboard's actual memory, attempting to modify the contents of this handle directly will result in an error. Copy the data out of the handle with the MemMove function before attempting to modify the data. Likewise, do not free the handle returned from ClipboardGetItem; the system frees this handle automatically the next time data is copied to the Clipboard.

> **Text data in the clipboard is not null-terminated, so be sure to use the value returned in the ClipboardGetItem function's length parameter to determine how much text is in the Clipboard.**

# Summary

In this chapter, you got to take a look at functions that help you program the guts of your application, the parts that do all the work but that the user never sees. After reading this chapter, you should understand the following:

❑ Not all features of Palm OS are present in all devices or in all versions of the operating system, but the system does provide a way to query what features exist by using the FtrGet function.

❑ Palm OS provides many functions for manipulating text, including font functions for handling the onscreen display of text and string functions that mirror many basic functions in the C standard library.

❑ You can directly handle pen and key events before the operating system gets them to allow your application to do special things with the stylus and hardware button input.

❑ Palm OS allows you to activate the system's application launcher programmatically, or you can launch applications manually within your program's code using the SysAppLaunch and SysUIAppSwitch functions.

❑ Many other utility functions exist in Palm OS for doing things such as looking up phone numbers in the built-in Address Book, generating random numbers, managing battery power, and retrieving the device's onboard serial number.

# 11

# Programming Graphics

When the Palm OS platform was introduced, graphics color and sound were not features that Palm considered terribly important in a handheld organizer. The original Pilot 1000 and 5000 sported monochrome LCD screens and slow 16 MHz processors, hardly the sort of hardware necessary for a compelling graphical experience.

Despite these limitations, software developers saw the entertainment potential of a portable computing platform, and games began to appear for Palm OS. Often requiring clever hacking in Motorola 68K assembly language to work around the restrictions of early Palm OS handhelds, these pioneering efforts proved that there was interest in using the Palm OS platform for more than just keeping schedules and contacts.

Over the years, with new advances in hardware, Palm OS licensees have added new features to their handhelds. Palm OS licensees, such as HandEra, Handspring, and Sony, added advanced graphics and sound capabilities to their Palm Powered devices, resulting in an explosion of handhelds with high-resolution, high-density color screens and advanced sound capabilities, running on more powerful processors like the 66 MHz DragonBall SuperVZ.

Given the high speed at which ARM processors run, Palm OS 5 handhelds can rely on processing power unheard of in earlier Palm Powered handhelds, allowing Palm and its licensees to create an entirely new class of handhelds. Palm OS 5 Garnet takes advantage of this extra processing power by adding native support for higher screen resolutions and color densities, as well as support for 16-bit multi-channel sound. Palm OS Cobalt takes things a step further by adding a completely new native ARM high-performance engine for drawing graphics on the screen.

It might seem that with all these new features arriving on the Palm OS scene, it would be difficult to maintain compatibility between older applications and a new generation of high-resolution, rich-sounding programs. Fortunately, this entire progression of graphics and sound technology, from simple monochrome line drawing to glorious 16-bit color, is available through a set of APIs that PalmSource has carefully planned and implemented over the life of Palm OS. Given the changes in hardware since the beginning of Palm OS, its graphics routines are remarkably simple to use and maintain a high degree of backward compatibility. Aside from the new Palm OS Cobalt drawing APIs, the majority of the drawing APIs in Palm OS have remained backward compatible.

This chapter covers how drawing and graphics work in Palm OS and shows the techniques required to make use of the screen on both Palm and licensee handhelds. Throughout this chapter, you will find references to Color Test, a sample application that shows off some of the color features of Palm OS (see Figure 11-1). Color Test is based entirely on drawing routines that are present only in Palm OS 3.5 and later. Note that the application actually appears in vibrant color in POSE, Palm Simulator, or on an actual color handheld, not black and white as in this book.

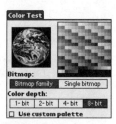

Figure 11-1

The first part of this chapter covers the traditional Palm OS window drawing functions, which work across all modern versions of Palm OS through Garnet. In Palm OS 5, these functions are supported through the PACE layer. Although many window functions still exist and are unchanged in Palm OS Cobalt, a number of window drawing functions (such as `WinSaveBits` and `WinRestoreBits`) described in this section have been deleted in Palm OS Cobalt, so this portion of the chapter omits any discussion of Palm OS Cobalt.

The second part of this chapter introduces the new advanced rendering model and graphics context functions, which are specific to Palm OS Cobalt. The Graphics Context system is completely separate from the legacy window APIs. We recommend that if you are building a Palm OS Cobalt application, you use the new graphics context functions for drawing rather than the legacy window functions.

# Managing the Drawing Surface

Before you can jump in and start drawing on the screen in Palm OS, you should understand a few things about the surface on which you are drawing. Palm OS provides a large number of functions for manipulating color depth, palettes, and the drawing area itself. This first chapter section focuses on the nature of the Palm OS drawing surface, known as the *window*.

## Understanding Windows

Palm OS drawing functions center on the concept of the *window*. A window is a rectangular drawing area, either onscreen or in memory. You are already familiar with one type of window: forms. A form is simply a window with added features for handling various user interface elements. Every form is a window but not every window is a form.

The system keeps track of two special windows. At any given time, there can be only one *draw window* and one *active window*. Usually the operating system treats the same window as both the draw window and active window.

The draw window is where the system renders all output from graphics functions. All coordinates used in the drawing functions are relative to the current draw window. The coordinate (0, 0) refers to the upper-leftmost pixel of the draw window. The system clips output from graphics functions to the edges of the draw window. Normally the system takes care of setting the draw window automatically; the current active form also is usually the draw window. You can manually set the current draw window with the WinSetDrawWindow function. WinSetDrawWindow takes a single argument, the handle of the window to set as the new draw window, and returns the handle of the old draw window.

The active window is the only region of the screen that accepts user input. If the user taps outside the active window, the system discards that input. The system automatically sets the active form as the active window. If you need to set explicitly a different window to be active, you can do so with the WinSetActiveWindow function, which also sets the draw window to be the same as the active window.

By default, whichever form is currently active is both the active window and draw window. All of the various graphics functions with a Win prefix automatically write to the active form if you take no action to set the draw window manually.

You can create a new window with the WinCreateWindow function, whose prototype looks like this:

```
WinHandle WinCreateWindow (RectangleType *bounds,
    FrameType frame, Boolean modal, Boolean focusable,
    UInt16 *error)
```

The bounds argument is a pointer to a RectangleType structure defining the boundaries of the new window. You can define the type of frame that surrounds the window by setting the frame argument, which accepts a FrameType value describing the type of frame to draw. The Palm OS header file Window.h defines a number of constants for window frames; these constants are described in the following table.

| Constant | Value | Description |
| --- | --- | --- |
| noFrame | 0 | No frame. |
| simpleFrame | 1 | One-pixel-wide rectangular frame. |
| rectangleFrame | 1 | Same as simpleFrame. |
| roundFrame | 0x0401 | One-pixel-wide frame with rounded corners. The corners have a diameter of 7 pixels. |
| boldRoundFrame | 0x0702 | Two-pixel-wide frame with rounded corners. The corners have a diameter of 7 pixels. |
| popupFrame | 0x0205 | One-pixel-wide frame with rounded corners and a shadow effect. The corners have a diameter of 2 pixels. Palm OS draws menus using this style of frame. |
| dialogFrame | 0x0302 | Two-pixel-wide frame with rounded corners. The corners have a diameter of 3 pixels. The system draws modal dialog forms and alerts using this style of frame. |
| menuFrame | 0x0205 | Same as popupFrame. |

The system draws a window's frame outside the actual borders of the window, so take this into account if you later need to remove the window from the screen. The `WinGetWindowFrameRect` function can help with this because it retrieves a `RectangleType` defining the rectangular area occupied by a window and its frame.

*Calling `WinCreateWindow` does not draw a window's frame; it merely defines what the frame should look like. You must first set the new window as the draw window with `WinSetDrawWindow` and then call the `WinDrawWindowFrame` function to actually draw the window's frame.*

Two Boolean arguments follow `frame` in a `WinCreateWindow` call. The `modal` argument, if `true`, indicates that the window should be modal, which is to say it won't accept user input outside its bounds. Passing `true` as the `focusable` argument allows the window to become the active window.

Unlike most functions in Palm OS, which indicate an error of some kind in their return value, `WinCreateWindow` returns possible error values via the `error` argument, which is a pointer to a `UInt16` value (`status_t` in Palm OS Cobalt) representing the error encountered. A value of 0 in the `error` argument indicates that `WinCreateWindow` completed successfully.

`WinCreateWindow` does not clear the area occupied by a new window. If you create a new window over an existing window, you must manually clear with the `WinEraseWindow` function the area occupied by the new window. It also may be important to restore the screen area under the window, particularly for a pop-up window. You can use the `WinSaveBits` function to save a screen area to an offscreen window and then restore that area with `WinRestoreBits` after removing the pop-up window.

Once you are finished with a window, you may remove it from memory, and from the screen using the `WinDeleteWindow` function. `WinDeleteWindow` takes two arguments. The first is the handle of the window you wish to delete. The second argument is a Boolean value to indicate whether the window should be erased before being deleted. Passing `true` as this second argument erases the area occupied by the window, and its frame, before removing the window from memory.

> **WinDeleteWindow** releases the memory occupied by the window, but it does not reset the address of the window handle. After a call to **WinDeleteWindow**, the window handle of the deleted window becomes invalid. If you plan to use the same window handle later in your code, setting the window handle to **NULL** is a good idea to prevent the system from crashing by reading from an unallocated chunk of memory.

The following example creates and displays a pop-up window in the middle of the screen, surrounded by a rounded bold border:

```
WinHandle       newWindow, originalWindow, savedWindow;
RectangleType   newBounds, savedBounds;
UInt16          err;

// Set the bounds of the new window.
newBounds.topLeft.x = 20;
newBounds.topLeft.y = 20;
newBounds.extent.x = 120;
newBounds.extent.y = 120;

// Create the window.
```

```
newWindow = WinCreateWindow(&newBounds, boldRoundFrame,
                            false, false, &err);

// Save the bits from the form beneath the new window.
WinGetWindowFrameRect(newWindow, &savedBounds);
savedWindow = WinSaveBits(&savedBounds, &err);

// Draw the new window.
originalWindow = WinSetDrawWindow(newWindow);
WinEraseWindow();
WinDrawWindowFrame();
WinSetDrawWindow(originalWindow);
```

This example starts by setting up the newBounds rectangle that defines the screen area for the new window. Once the rectangle structure is filled, a call to WinCreateWindow creates the window in memory and assigns it to the newWindow handle. Because this window is not intended for user input, the modal and focusable arguments to WinCreateWindow are both false.

At this point in the code, a window exists in memory, but no visible change has happened on the screen. The code continues by saving the screen bits in the area occupied by the form, so they may be restored later. The WinGetWindowFrameRect function ensures that the saved bits include the frame around newWindow; recall that the system draws a window's frame around the outside edge of the rectangle that makes up the frame, so the newBounds rectangle does not actually include the frame. Armed with a savedBounds rectangle containing the window and its frame, a call to WinSaveBits stores the original screen contents under newWindow in the handle savedWindow.

Next the code sets newWindow as the draw window with WinSetDrawWindow, saving the current draw window in originalWindow so it may be restored later. WinEraseWindow clears the screen area occupied by the window and WinDrawWindowFrame draws a border around the frame.

> Be careful about calling erase functions in the corners of a window or form with a rounded frame. Rounded frame corners pass within the actual drawing area of a window, so functions such as **WinEraseWindow**, **WinEraseLine**, and **WinEraseRectangle** can overwrite the corners of a window with white space. The sample code here calls **WinDrawWindowFrame** after it calls **WinEraseWindow** for exactly this reason. If **WinEraseWindow** were called last, it would clip the corners of the window's frame.

The window is now drawn on the screen. Another call to WinSetDrawWindow passes draw window status back to the form underneath the new window.

The following code erases the pop-up window drawn by the previous example:

```
WinDeleteWindow(newWindow, true);
WinRestoreBits(savedWindow, savedBounds.topLeft.x,
               savedBounds.topLeft.y);
newWindow = NULL;
```

WinDeleteWindow releases the window structure from memory, and the true value in its second argument tells the system to erase the window from the screen, frame and all. WinRestoreBits restores the contents of the screen to what they were before displaying the pop-up window, given the savedWindow handle, which was filled earlier by a call to WinSaveBits. As a precaution, the example also sets the newWindow handle to NULL because it is now invalid, and accessing that handle could crash the system.

# Creating Offscreen Windows

If your application has a lot of custom drawing to perform, which is common in games and other programs that perform animation, the screen may show some flickering as successive drawing routines update the screen. Even if an application draws only static graphics on the screen, multiple calls to drawing routines may result in noticeably slow screen updating.

It is possible to speed up screen updates by *double buffering*. This is a technique whereby a program performs all the actual drawing in a memory buffer instead of on the screen itself, and then the program copies the contents of the buffer all at once to the display. In a Palm OS program, the memory buffer requirement of double buffering may be fulfilled by creating an *offscreen window*. An offscreen window is just like a regular window, except that it exists only in memory. Drawing to an offscreen window is much faster than drawing directly to the screen because the system does not need to update the display after each call to a drawing routine.

Use the WinCreateOffscreenWindow function to create an offscreen window. It has the following prototype:

```
WinHandle WinCreateOffscreenWindow (Coord width,
    Coord height, WindowFormatType format,
    UInt16 *error)
```

The width and height parameters of WinCreateOffscreenWindow control the size of the offscreen window created by the function. For double buffering purposes, these values should match the actual width and height of the display.

The format parameter gives you the option to create the offscreen window in one of two formats: screenFormat or genericFormat. A screenFormat window is stored in the native format used by the handheld's video system, which means that it is quicker for the system to copy such a window back to the display. A window in genericFormat is device-independent; genericFormat is a better choice if you wish to store an offscreen window's image in a database, particularly if that database might later be shared with another Palm Powered handheld that uses different video hardware.

Like WinCreateWindow, WinCreateOffscreenWindow returns error values by way of its error parameter. If the call to WinCreateOffscreenWindow succeeds, the return value from the function is the new offscreen window's handle.

The following example shows how to create an offscreen window, draw to it, and copy the contents of the window back to the display:

```
WinHandle  originalWindow, offscreenWindow;
UInt16     err;
RectangleType  r;

offscreenWindow = WinHandle(160, 160, genericFormat, &err);
originalWindow = WinSetDrawWindow(offscreenWindow);

// Call drawing functions here to draw to the offscreen
```

```
// window.

WinGetBounds(offscreenWindow, &r);
WinCopyRectangle(offscreenWindow, originalWindow, &r,
                0, 0, winPaint);
WinSetDrawWindow(originalWindow);
```

The example uses the WinGetBounds routine to fill a RectangleType structure that defines the boundaries of the offscreen window.

> *The WinGetBounds function exists only in Palm OS 4.0 and later. If your application needs to support earlier versions of Palm OS, use the WinGetDrawWindowBounds routine. WinGetDrawWindowBounds retrieves only the bounds of the current draw window, so you must call WinSetDrawWindow to ensure that the window whose bounds you wish to retrieve is the current draw window.*

The previous example transfers the offscreen window to the display by calling WinCopyRectangle. It looks like this:

```
void WinCopyRectangle (WinHandle srcWin, WinHandle dstWin,
    const RectangleType *srcRect, Coord destX, Coord destY,
    WinDrawOperation mode)
```

The first two arguments, srcWin and dstWin, specify the source and destination windows, respectively. Next comes the srcRect argument, which is a pointer to a RectangleType structure that defines the rectangular area in the source window that should be copied. The destX and destY arguments are the horizontal and vertical coordinates where the rectangle should appear in the destination window. Finally, mode specifies the transfer mode that WinCopyRectangle should use when drawing the rectangle in the destination window. Values for mode are part of an enumerated type called WinDrawOperation, which defines various drawing operations that may be performed by the WinCopyRectangle and WinSetDrawMode functions. The following table shows the possible values for mode.

| Constant | Description |
|----------|-------------|
| winPaint | Copy mode; destination pixels are completely replaced by pixels from the source |
| winErase | AND mode; destination pixels are cleared to the background color, where source pixels have color index or RGB value of zero |
| winMask | AND NOT mode; destination pixels are cleared to the background color, where source pixels have a nonzero color index or RGB value |
| winInvert | XOR mode; destination pixels are inverted where source pixels have a nonzero color index or RGB value |
| winOverlay | OR mode; destination pixels are set only where source pixels have a nonzero color index or RGB value |
| winPaintInverse | Copy NOT mode; destination pixels are replaced with inverted source pixels |
| winSwap | Color invert mode; destination foreground and background colors are swapped, leaving any other colors unchanged |

Unless you need to create some kind of special effect, `winPaint` is usually sufficient for copying an entire offscreen window to the display. `WinSetDrawMode` is described later in this chapter in the "Drawing Graphics and Text" section.

## Saving and Restoring the Draw State

Palm OS keeps track of several properties that define how the various drawing functions do their work within a given draw window. For example, a window has a particular font assigned to it, which all calls to text drawing functions use when drawing text in that window. Collectively, the drawing properties for a window are called its *draw state*.

The process of drawing on the screen in Palm OS involves changing a window's draw state to the desired properties, and then calling drawing routines to perform the actual drawing. For example, to draw a red line, an application changes the drawing state's foreground color to red, and then draws the line, as shown in the following example:

```
RGBColorType       redRGB;
IndexedColorType   redIndexed;

redRGB.r = 255; redRGB.g = 0; redRGB.b = 0;
redIndexed = WinRGBToIndex(&redRGB);
WinSetForeColor(redIndexed);
WinDrawLine(0, 0, 159, 159);
```

A number of Palm OS functions begin with `WinSet`, all of which change the current draw window's draw state. Because most drawing functions depend upon the drawing state to define the color they draw, the font they use, or other drawing-related properties, changing the drawing state of a window affects all other calls to drawing routines. For this reason, it is often a good idea to write your application so that it saves the current draw state, performs whatever drawing it needs to do, and then restores the draw state to its original values.

Prior to Palm OS 3.5, the only way to save the draw state is to keep track of individual draw state variables manually. Each of the various `WinSet` functions returns the previous value of the variable it sets, which allows you to save the old value, change the draw state variable, and then restore the old value. The following example saves the current foreground color, changes the foreground color to red, draws a line, and then restores the foreground color:

```
RGBColorType       redRGB;
IndexedColorType   redIndexed, oldIndexed;

redRGB.r = 255; redRGB.g = 0; redRGB.b = 0;
redIndexed = WinRGBToIndex(&redRGB);
oldIndexed = WinSetForeColor(redIndexed);
WinDrawLine(0, 0, 159, 159);
WinSetForeColor(oldIndexed);
```

This system of manually saving draw state variables works, but it can be cumbersome to save and restore the current draw window's font, foreground and background colors, text color, and other properties. It also is easy to forget to save and restore these values, which can result in hard-to-diagnose drawing bugs in your application.

In version 3.5 and later, Palm OS provides a much more elegant method of saving and restoring the draw state. Not only do newer versions of Palm OS keep track of the draw state as a single unit instead of as individual variables, but the operating system provides a stack where you can save old drawing states. The `WinPushDrawState` routine saves a snapshot of the current drawing state and pushes it onto this stack, and the `WinPopDrawState` routine pops a drawing state off the stack and restores its values to the current draw window. As in any stack structure, draw states enter and leave the stack in a first-in, last-out order.

To illustrate the use of the draw state stack, the following code duplicates the effects of the previous example, without the need to explicitly save and restore the old foreground color:

```
RGBColorType       redRGB;
IndexedColorType   redIndexed;

redRGB.r = 255; redRGB.g = 0; redRGB.b = 0;
redIndexed = WinRGBToIndex(&redRGB);
WinPushDrawState();
WinSetForeColor (redIndexed);
WinDrawLine(0, 0, 159, 159);
WinPopDrawState();
```

Using `WinPushDrawState` and `WinPopDrawState` also assists in debugging when testing your application on a debug ROM image in POSE. Debug ROM images warn you when an application exits without popping all the draw states from the stack, and they also tell you when an application attempts to pop a draw state from a stack that has already been emptied.

## Determining and Setting Color Depth

This section provides an overview of the concept of *color depth*. Color depth refers to the capability of the operating system to render to the physical device display at varying levels of grayscale and color quality.

The Palm OS supports five color depths:

❑ **1-bit monochrome.** This is the only mode officially supported in versions of Palm OS earlier than version 3.5. Every Palm OS device can manage 1-bit color depth.

❑ **2-bit grayscale.** This has four colors: white, light gray, dark gray, and black. Noncolor Palm OS devices that have a non-EZ processor can use this mode, but nothing fancier.

❑ **4-bit grayscale.** This includes 16 levels of gray from white to black. Noncolor Palm OS devices with a DragonBall EZ processor can handle this mode.

❑ **8-bit color.** This has a somewhat more complex palette to choose from than lesser color depths. The first part of the Palm OS 8-bit color palette is composed of 216 "Web-safe" colors. These colors have red, green, and blue components at the following levels: 0x00, 0x33, 0x66, 0x99, 0xCC, and 0xFF. Sixteen gray shades, some already part of the first 216 colors, also are part of the palette, including 0x111111, 0x222222, and so on—adding another 10 colors to the palette. Six named HTML colors round out the regular part of the Palm OS palette for a total of 232 colors: 0x0C0C0C (silver), 0x808080 (gray), 0x800000 (maroon), 0x800080 (purple), 0x008000 (green), and 0x008080 (teal). The last 24 color entries are undefined and filled with black in the release version of the operating system; on debug ROM images, these 24 slots are filled with some particularly ugly random colors that are useful for highlighting invalid color choices while testing an application.

❑ **Direct color.** At the time of this book's writing, this means 16-bit color, providing a range of 65,536 colors. Direct color mode is supported only in Palm OS 4.0 and later, and then only on hardware that is capable of displaying so many colors, such as the Palm m515 and the Sony CLIÉ PEG-NR70. Unlike 8-bit mode, which maps available colors to index values, direct color mode sets colors directly, using RGB values. The user interface layer of Palm OS does not support direct color mode, so buttons, text fields, and other user interface elements are displayed at a maximum color depth of 8 bits.

*Future Palm Powered handhelds may include support for direct color depths greater than 16 bits. The current 16-bit implementations use five bits for red, six for green, and another five for blue. The direct color routines in Palm OS can support more than 16 million colors, which corresponds to a bit depth of 24 bits.*

Before attempting to use any color drawing routines, your application should first query the system to find out what its color capabilities are. To determine what color depths are available, use the WinScreenMode function, which has the following prototype:

```
Err WinScreenMode (WinScreenModeOperation operation,
    UInt32 *widthP, UInt32 *heightP, UInt32 *depthP,
    Boolean *enableColorP)
```

The WinScreenMode function is the Swiss Army knife of Palm OS color programming. Not only does it allow you to query supported color depths, but it also may modify screen dimensions and color depth, as well as enable color drawing mode. The key to this function's versatility is its first parameter, operation, which may be one of the constant values described in the following table.

| Constant | Description |
|---|---|
| winScreenModeGet | Retrieves the current display settings |
| winScreenModeGetDefaults | Retrieves the default display settings |
| winScreenModeGetSupportedDepths | Returns a value in the depthP parameter that describes the color depths supported by the hardware |
| winScreenModeGetSupportsColor | Returns true in the enableColorP parameter if it is possible to enable color drawing mode |
| winScreenModeSet | Changes display settings |
| winScreenModeSetDefaults | Changes display settings to their default values |

Depending on the value of operation, the other parameters of WinScreenMode serve double duty as both input and return parameters. The next table outlines how each parameter is used given the operation to be performed; "in" means the parameter passes a value into the function, "out" means that WinScreenMode returns a value in the parameter, and "ignored" means that WinScreenMode ignores the parameter entirely. If you do not wish to change a particular value, or you are not interested in retrieving that value, you may pass NULL for any of the widthP, heightP, depthP, or enableColorP parameters.

| Operation | widthP | heightP | depthP | enableColorP |
|---|---|---|---|---|
| winScreenModeGet | out | out | out | out |
| winScreenModeGetDefaults | out | out | out | out |
| winScreenModeGetSupportedDepths | in | in | out | in |
| winScreenModeGetSupportsColor | in | in | in | out |
| winScreenModeSet | in | in | in | in |
| winScreenModeSetDefaults | ignored | ignored | ignored | ignored |

To find out what color depths the system can handle, pass winScreenModeGetSupportedDepths for the operation parameter of WinScreenMode and supply a pointer for the depthP parameter. For example, the following line from the Color Test application's StartApplication routine sets up a global variable, gSupportedDepths, with the supported color depth information:

```
WinScreenMode(winScreenModeGetSupportedDepths, NULL, NULL,
              &gSupportedDepths, NULL);
```

The value returned in depthP is actually a binary representation of the supported color depths. Each bit in the return value represents support for a given depth if the bit is 1, or no support if the bit is 0. The position of a 1 in the bit field, not the decimal numeric value represented by that bit, determines whether a particular color depth is supported. For example, a return value of 0x0B, whose binary representation is 1011, indicates support for 4-bit, 2-bit, and 1-bit color depths because its fourth, second, and first bits are set to 1. Another example is 0x8B (binary 10001011), which indicates support for 8-bit, 4-bit, 2-bit, and 1-bit drawing.

To check whether a specific color depth is supported, use a logical AND (&) to compare depthP to a particular bit value. The following sample code tests to see if 8-bit color is supported, using the gSupportedDepths value obtained by the last example (0x80 is 10000000 in binary):

```
if (0x80 & gSupportedDepths)
{
    // 8-bit color depth is supported.
}
```

## Retrieving Color Depth

If your application changes the color depth, it is good programming practice to ensure that it returns the color depth to its original state before exiting. To accomplish this, you need to retrieve the color depth when your application starts so that it knows what state to restore when finished. Use the winScreenModeGet operation with WinScreenMode to retrieve the current depth, as in the following example from the Color Test application's StartApplication routine:

```
WinScreenMode(winScreenModeGet, NULL, NULL, &gOldDepth,
              NULL);
```

Because Color Test is not interested in the screen dimensions or availability of color drawing, NULL values are used for the widthP, heightP, and enableColorP parameters.

*The system automatically sets the color depth back to its default when launching a new application. However, PalmSource recommends that you restore the color depth yourself before your application exits because future versions of Palm OS may not reset the color depth for you.*

## Setting Color Depth

Setting color depth involves passing the `winScreenModeSet` operation to `WinScreenMode`, along with the desired depth in the `depthP` parameter. As an example, the Color Test application sets the screen depth when the user selects one of the color depth push buttons. The following `MainFormSelectColorDepth` function is responsible for handling the change in color depth:

```
static void MainFormSelectColorDepth (UInt16 controlID)
{
    FormType  *form = FrmGetActiveForm();
    UInt32    depth;
    UInt32    depthHex;
    UInt16    ctlIndex;


    // If the push button is already selected, there is
    // nothing to do, so return.
    if (controlID == gCurrentPushButtonID)
        return;

    switch (controlID)
    {
        case MainColorDepth1BitPushButton:
            depth = 1;
            depthHex = 0x01;
            break;

        case MainColorDepth2BitPushButton:
            depth = 2;
            depthHex = 0x02;
            break;

        case MainColorDepth4BitPushButton:
            depth = 4;
            depthHex = 0x08;
            break;

        case MainColorDepth8BitPushButton:
            depth = 8;
            depthHex = 0x80;
            break;

        default:
            ErrFatalDisplay("Invalid ID");
    }

    if (depthHex & gSupportedDepths)
    {
        // Change color depth and refresh the screen.
        WinScreenMode(winScreenModeSet, NULL, NULL, &depth,
                    NULL);
```

```
            FrmUpdateForm(MainForm, frmRedrawUpdateCode);
            gCurrentPushButtonID = controlID;

            // Display the custom palette check box if 8-bit
            // mode is selected, or hide it when another color
            // depth is selected.
            ctlIndex = FrmGetObjectIndex(form,
                MainCustomPaletteCheckbox);
            if (depth == 8)
                FrmShowObject(form, ctlIndex);
            else
                FrmHideObject(form, ctlIndex);

    }
    else
    {
        // Alert the user that the selected depth is not
        // supported.
        FrmAlert(UnsupportedDepthAlert);

        // Set push button back to where it was.
        FrmSetControlGroupSelection(form, 1,
                                    gCurrentPushButtonID);
    }
}
```

The only line in `MainFormSelectColorDepth` that actually performs the change in color depth is the call to `WinScreenMode`; everything else is either code to determine which push button was selected or code to let the user know that the push button selected corresponds to a color depth that the system cannot display.

*Palm OS 3.0 first introduced the function `ScrDisplayMode`, which is the direct predecessor to `WinScreenMode`. The `ScrDisplayMode` function operates in much the same fashion as `WinScreenMode` and allows access to grayscale modes on devices that are running Palm OS prior to version 3.5.*

## Using Color Tables

To provide the best performance when drawing, the operating system uses an indexed *color table* to store the available colors in 8-bit or lower color depths. A color table consists of a count of the number of colors in the table, followed by an array of `RGBColorType` structures, one for each color in the table. `RGBColorType` looks like this:

```
typedef struct RGBColorType {
    UInt8 index;
    UInt8 r;
    UInt8 g;
    UInt8 b;
} RGBColorType;
```

The r, g, and b fields in `RGBColorType` represent the level of red, green, and blue in a particular color, respectively. The index value is used differently by various parts of the system. Most of the drawing routines in Palm OS use the index instead of a raw RGB value because it is faster.

If you wish to change the current palette used for drawing in your application, use the `WinPalette` function. The most common use for `WinPalette` is to display bitmaps that use a different color table from the system default. See the section titled "Using Color Bitmaps" later in this chapter for more details about color bitmaps.

Like the `WinScreenMode` function, `WinPalette` is a multipurpose function. Its first parameter specifies what operation it should perform:

```
Err WinPalette (UInt8 operation, Int16 startIndex,
    UInt16 paletteEntries, RGBColorType *tableP)
```

Depending on what `operation` you specify, the `tableP` pointer to an array of `RGBColorType` structures may be used to supply values to `WinPalette` or to retrieve values from the function. The following table describes the operation constants available for `WinPalette`.

| Constant | Description |
|---|---|
| winPaletteGet | Retrieves the current palette; `WinPalette` reads entries from the palette beginning at `startIndex` and places them in `tableP`, starting at index 0 |
| winPaletteSet | Sets entries in the current palette; `WinPalette` reads entries from `tableP`, beginning at index 0, and sets those entries into the current palette, starting at `startIndex` |
| winPaletteSetToDefault | Sets the current palette to the default system palette; during this operation, `WinPalette` does not use the `startIndex` or `tableP` parameters |

> Be sure not to confuse a color table, which begins with a count of its entries, with a simple array of **RGBColorType** structures. Some functions, such as **BmpGetColorTable**, use a full color table, whereas others, such as **WinPalette**, use just an array of RGB color values.

The `paletteEntries` parameter controls how many palette entries should be retrieved or set. Aside from its regular use of indicating the starting index in the palette, you also may pass the constant value `WinUseTableIndexes` for the `startIndex` parameter. Doing so tells `WinPalette` to use the individual index values of each `RGBColorType` structure in `tableP` to determine which color slot to get or set. Specifying anything other than `WinUseTableIndexes` for the `startIndex` parameter causes `WinPalette` to ignore the `index` values stored in `tableP`.

To show `WinPalette` in action, the Color Test application displays a Use custom palette check box when it is in 8-bit color depth mode. Checking this box shifts Color Test into a custom palette, which the application assembles with this code in its `StartApplication` routine:

```
if (0x80 & gSupportedDepths)
{
```

```
        int  i;

        for (i = 0; i < 256; i++)
        {
            gCustomPalette[i].index = i;
            gCustomPalette[i].r = 0;
            gCustomPalette[i].g = 255 - i;
            gCustomPalette[i].b = 0;
        }
    }
```

This custom palette is composed entirely of different shades of green. When the user taps the Use custom palette check box, Color Test calls its `MainFormSwitchPalette` routine to change the palette; `MainFormSwitchPalette` looks like this:

```
    static void MainFormSwitchPalette (void)
    {
        FormType   *form = FrmGetActiveForm();
        ControlType  *ctl =
            GetObjectPtr(MainCustomPaletteCheckbox);

        if (CtlGetValue(ctl) == 1)
        {
            // Switch to the custom palette.
            WinPalette(winPaletteSet, 0, 256, gCustomPalette);
        }
        else
        {
            // Switch to the default palette.
            WinPalette(winPaletteSetToDefault, NULL, NULL,
                    NULL);
        }
    }
```

If the check box is checked, `MainFormSwitchPalette` uses `WinPalette` with the `winPaletteSet` operation to change every entry in the display palette to an entry in the custom green palette. When the check box is empty, `MainFormSwitchPalette` calls `WinPalette` with the `winPaletteSetToDefault` operation to set the palette back to the default system palette.

## Translating RGB to Index Values

Your application may need to convert RGB values to index values in the display palette, or vice versa. Two functions exist for making these conversions: `WinRGBToIndex` and `WinIndexToRGB`. The prototypes for these functions look like this:

```
    IndexedColorType WinRGBToIndex (const RGBColorType *rgbP);
    void WinIndexToRGB (IndexedColorType i,
                    RGBColorType *rgbP);
```

The `IndexedColorType` type is simply a `typedef` for an unsigned 8-bit integer:

```
    typedef UInt8 IndexedColorType;
```

If the color requested in `WinRGBToIndex` is not one of the colors present in the system palette, `WinRGBToIndex` finds the nearest matching color and returns its index. If the current display palette is entirely grayscale (1-bit, 2-bit, or 4-bit), `WinRGBToIndex` tries to match the luminosity of the color to an entry in the palette. For a color palette (8-bit or direct color), `WinRGBToIndex` matches a color by looking for the nearest available RGB value. This kind of shortest-distance algorithm may not always produce a color that is the closest perceptual match to the requested color, but it is much faster than a more complex algorithm and works reasonably well in the default 8-bit system palette, which contains only 232 usable colors.

Unlike `WinRGBToIndex`, `WinIndexToRGB` can always return an exact RGB match for the requested color index.

# Drawing Graphics and Text

Most of the time, you can rely on the standard user interface elements to handle the display of whatever data your application needs to communicate to the user, but sometimes you might need to draw something different on the screen. Palm OS offers a number of functions for directly drawing graphics and text, as well as a wealth of routines for altering the colors and fonts used in such drawing.

Most of the Palm OS drawing functions come in several flavors:

❑ **Draw** functions draw in the current foreground color, overwriting any pixels that fall within their drawing area. The exception to this is `WinDrawBitmap`, which uses the colors already present in a bitmap instead of drawing with the foreground color. All draw functions use the `winPaint` transfer mode.

❑ **Erase** functions draw in the current background color. Calling a draw function, and then calling its companion erase function with the same parameters, erases whatever the draw function rendered onscreen. All erase functions use the `winErase` transfer mode.

❑ **Fill** functions draw the internal area of an object, using the current foreground color and the current pattern to render the object.

❑ **Invert** functions swap the foreground and background colors within the region defined by the function. All invert functions use the `winInvert` transfer mode.

❑ **Paint** functions draw using all the properties of the current draw state, including transfer mode, foreground color, background color, text color, pattern, font, and underline mode. The paint routines are available only in Palm OS 3.5 and later.

For simple drawing tasks, such as rendering your own user interface elements, you will need to use only the draw, erase, and fill functions. The invert functions, particularly `WinInvertRectangle`, are useful for indicating to the user that part of the screen has been selected. The paint functions are primarily useful for rendering special effects, such as transparency.

## Setting the Transfer Mode

To make effective use of the paint functions, change the current transfer mode by calling `WinSetDrawMode`, which has the following prototype:

```
WinDrawOperation WinSetDrawMode (WinDrawOperation newMode)
```

`WinSetDrawMode` takes the new transfer mode as its sole argument, and the function returns the previous transfer mode so you can later restore it. The transfer modes were described earlier in this chapter. The `WinSetDrawMode` function changes the current draw state, so you may wish to save the current draw state with `WinPushDrawState` before calling `WinSetDrawMode`. As an example, the following code uses `WinSetDrawMode` and `WinPaintBitmap` to draw a bitmap, using transparency to allow the screen's original contents to show through parts of the bitmap:

```
WinPushDrawState();
WinSetDrawMode(winOverlay);
WinPaintBitmap(bitmap, 50, 50);
WinPopDrawState();
```

The `winOverlay` transfer mode causes `WinPaintBitmap` to draw only those pixels in the bitmap that have a nonzero color index or RGB value. As a result, empty pixels in the bitmap are not drawn, which leaves those regions of the screen as they were before `WinPaintBitmap` was called.

## Setting Foreground, Background, and Text Colors

Prior to Palm OS 3.5, the implementation of draw and erase functions is very simple: Draw functions always render in black and erase functions always render in white. With the introduction of color to the operating system, drawing and erasing become a little more complicated because they use the current draw state's foreground and background colors, respectively. The default foreground color is black and the default background color is white, so older applications continue to run in Palm OS 3.5 and later without modification. If your application needs to draw in other colors, though, it must set the foreground and background colors to appropriate values before calling any drawing routines.

To change the current foreground color, use either `WinSetForeColor` or `WinSetForeColorRGB`. The `WinSetForeColor` routine sets the foreground color using an indexed color value and the `WinSetForeColorRGB` routine sets the foreground color using an actual RGB value. The prototypes for these functions look like this:

```
IndexedColorType WinSetForeColor (
    IndexedColorType foreColor)
void WinSetForeColorRGB (const RGBColorType *newRgbP,
                    RGBColorType *prevRgbP)
```

`WinSetForeColor` has a single argument, the indexed color that should become the current foreground color. The function returns the previous foreground color so that it may be restored later.

`WinSetForeColorRGB` operates in direct color mode. The function's first argument is a pointer to an `RGBColorType` structure that defines the new foreground color, and the second argument receives a pointer to the previous foreground color.

You can change the background color with `WinSetBackColor` or `WinSetBackColorRGB`, which have the same arguments as their foreground analogs. Likewise, to set the color that text drawing functions will use, call `WinSetTextColor` or `WinSetTextColorRGB`.

> *WinSetForeColorRGB, WinSetBackColorRGB, and WinSetTextColorRGB are available only on Palm OS 4.0 handhelds that support direct color. Be sure to verify that direct color is supported with a call to WinScreenMode before using these functions.*

All of the color-changing functions alter the draw state. It is a good idea to call `WinPushDrawState` before changing colors with these functions and then, once your application is finished drawing with the new colors, call `WinPopDrawState` to restore the original draw state.

# Drawing Pixels

The most basic drawing function in Palm OS is `WinDrawPixel`, which draws a single pixel in the foreground color. `WinDrawPixel` is a simple function:

```
void WinDrawPixel (Coord x, Coord y)
```

`WinDrawPixel` draws its single pixel at the coordinates specified by its two arguments.

There are a number of variations on the pixel drawing theme, all of which take the same arguments as `WinDrawPixel`:

❑   **WinErasePixel** draws a single pixel using the current background color

❑   **WinInvertPixel** inverts the color of a single pixel

❑   **WinPaintPixel** draws a single pixel using all the properties in the current draw state

If drawing one pixel at a time seems a bit slow, note that Palm OS also offers `WinPaintPixels`, which takes as an argument an entire array of pixel coordinates:

```
void WinPaintPixels (UInt16 numPoints, PointType pts[])
```

The first argument, `numPoints`, specifies the number of points in the array of pixels; the second argument, `pts`, specifies the array itself. `WinPaintPixels`, like the other paint functions, draws using the properties of the current draw state.

# Drawing Lines

To draw a line, use the `WinDrawLine` function, which simply draws a line in the current foreground color, one pixel wide, between two points on the screen. `WinDrawLine` takes four arguments. The first two arguments specify the x- and y-coordinates of the line's start point, and the last two arguments are the x- and y-coordinates of the line's end point. For example, the following code draws a line connecting the upper-left and lower-right corners of the screen, assuming that the draw window occupies the entire display area of a low-resolution Palm OS device:

```
WinDrawLine(0, 0, 159, 159);
```

Two companion functions, `WinDrawGrayLine` and `WinEraseLine`, operate in the same fashion. `WinDrawGrayLine` draws every other pixel of the specified line, alternating between the current foreground and background colors, resulting in a dotted line.

> On a color Palm Powered handheld (or one capable of grayscale drawing), `WinDrawGrayLine` does not actually draw in any shade of gray. The name of the function is a holdover from earlier versions of Palm OS that supported only one-bit monochrome displays. The only way to make "gray" on such devices is to draw alternating black and white pixels.

*The other "gray" function in Palm OS,* `WinDrawGrayRectangleFrame`, *operates in a similar fashion on color devices, drawing alternating foreground and background pixels instead of a true gray color. To draw using an actual gray color, call* `WinSetForeColor` *or* `WinSetForeColorRGB` *to change the drawing color to the desired gray, and then draw using the normal* `WinDraw` *functions instead of the* `WinDrawGray` *routines.*

`WinEraseLine` draws background pixels between two points; calling `WinEraseLine` with the same arguments as an earlier `WinDrawLine` call removes a line from the screen entirely.

The `WinFillLine` function draws a line using the current fill pattern set by the `WinSetPattern` function. See the section on drawing rectangles for more information about using `WinSetPattern`.

The `WinInvertLine` function inverts the colors along a line, and the `WinPaintLine` function draws a line using all the properties of the current draw state.

## Drawing Rectangles

Trying to fill a large area of the screen with the line functions requires many calls to `WinDrawLine` or its ilk because that group of functions draws only a single pixel width at a time. It is much more convenient to call `WinDrawRectangle` to fill a rectangular region of the screen. `WinDrawRectangle` takes a pointer to a `RectangleType` structure and a `cornerDiam` value indicating the roundness of the rectangle's corners.

*The* `cornerDiam` *argument is misnamed and, in older Palm OS documentation, described incorrectly. Unlike what its name seems to suggest, the* `cornerDiam` *argument does not specify the diameter of the corners but rather their radius. The system draws the corners as if an imaginary circle with radius equal to* `cornerDiam` *had been placed in each corner of the rectangle, tangent to two sides of the rectangle.*

A larger `cornerDiam` argument results in a rounder corner. In fact, if `cornerDiam` is equal to half the width or height of a perfectly square rectangle structure, `WinDrawRectangle` draws a solid circle with a diameter equal to twice the `cornerDiam` argument. A `cornerDiam` value of 0 results in a rectangle with square corners. The following code draws a circle 80 pixels across in the middle of the screen:

```
RectangleType  rect;
UInt16  cornerDiam = 40;

rect.topLeft.x = 40;
rect.topLeft.y = 40;
rect.extent.x = 80;
rect.extent.y = 80;

WinDrawRectangle(&rect, cornerDiam);
```

`WinEraseRectangle` is the opposite of the `WinDrawRectangle` function, requiring the same arguments that `WinDrawRectangle` requires but drawing pixels in the background color instead of the foreground color.

The `WinInvertRectangle` function inverts the colors within its rectangular drawing region. An identical effect also may be achieved by calling `WinPaintRectangle` with the draw state's transfer mode set to `winInvert`. `WinPaintRectangle` draws according to the properties of the current draw state.

Inverting the colors in a rectangle is one way that you can indicate selection in the user interface, but color inversion gives bitmap images a photonegative look, which isn't always aesthetically pleasing. A better way to show selection, used by some Palm OS system routines, is to use `WinPaintRectangle` and the `winSwap` transfer mode. Instead of inverting all the colors in the rectangle, `winSwap` swaps only the foreground and background colors. Assuming that the foreground and background colors are set to their default values, a bitmap image within the rectangle will have only its black and white values reversed, which looks much nicer than having all its colors inverted.

## Filling with Patterns

Along with creating solid rectangles, Palm OS provides the `WinFillRectangle` function to create rectangles filled with a custom pattern of pixels. `WinFillRectangle` takes the same arguments as the other rectangle creation functions but draws a rectangle using a pattern defined by the `WinSetPattern` function. `WinSetPattern` also sets the pattern used by the `WinFillLine` function.

`WinSetPattern` takes an argument of type `CustomPatternType`, which the Palm OS header file `Window.h` defines as follows:

```
typedef UInt8 CustomPatternType [8];
```

This array of eight `UInt8` variables may not look like much, but it stores a bitmap pattern eight pixels high by eight pixels wide, at a color depth of one bit per pixel. Each byte in the array defines a row in an $8 \times 8$ grid of pixels. For example, the following `CustomPatternType` array represents a 50 percent gray pattern, consisting of alternating foreground color and background color pixels:

```
CustomPatternType  gray50 = { 0xAA, 0x55, 0xAA, 0x55,
                              0xAA, 0x55, 0xAA, 0x55 };
```

In the preceding example, rows alternate between AA, which has a binary representation of 10101010, and 55 (01010101 in binary). Each binary 1 represents a pixel that is set to the foreground color, and each 0 represents a pixel that is set to the background color.

This pattern storage technique is extremely flexible, if a bit difficult to use. Unfortunately, using `CustomPatternType` requires that you perform a fair amount of binary arithmetic each time you want to create a new pattern, and the Palm OS headers do not have any predefined constants for commonly used patterns. Here are a few patterns to get you started:

```
// Light gray dots (12.5%)
CustomPatternType  patternGray12 = { 0x11, 0x00, 0x44, 0x00,
                                     0x11, 0x00, 0x44, 0x00 };
// Medium gray dots (50%)
CustomPatternType  patternGray50 = { 0xAA, 0x55, 0xAA, 0x55,
                                     0xAA, 0x55, 0xAA, 0x55 };
// Dark gray dots (87.5%)
CustomPatternType  patternGray87 = { ~0x11,~0x00,~0x44,~0x00,
                                     ~0x11,~0x00,~0x44,~0x00 };
// Light horizontal stripes (25%)
CustomPatternType  patternStripesHor25 = { 0xFF, 0x00, 0x00, 0x00,
                                           0xFF, 0x00, 0x00, 0x00 };
// Horizontal halftone (50%)
CustomPatternType  patternStripesHor50 = { 0xFF, 0x00, 0xFF, 0x00,
                                           0xFF, 0x00, 0xFF, 0x00 };
// Dark horizontal stripes (75%)
```

```
      CustomPatternType  patternStripesHor75 = { ~0xFF, ~0x00, ~0x00, ~0x00,
                                                 ~0xFF, ~0x00, ~0x00, ~0x00 };
      // Light vertical stripes (25%)
      CustomPatternType  patternStripesVer25 = { 0x88, 0x88, 0x88, 0x88,
                                                 0x88, 0x88, 0x88, 0x88 };
      // Vertical halftone (50%)
      CustomPatternType  patternStripesVer50 = { 0xAA, 0xAA, 0xAA, 0xAA,
                                                 0xAA, 0xAA, 0xAA, 0xAA };
      // Dark vertical stripes (75%)
      CustomPatternType  patternStripesVer75 = { ~0x88, ~0x88, ~0x88, ~0x88,
                                                 ~0x88, ~0x88, ~0x88, ~0x88 };
      // Bold horizontal stripes
      CustomPatternType  patternStripesHorBold = { 0xFF, 0xFF, 0x00, 0x00,
                                                   0xFF, 0xFF, 0x00, 0x00 };
      // Bold vertical stripes
      CustomPatternType  patternStripesVerBold = { 0xCC, 0xCC, 0xCC, 0xCC,
                                                   0xCC, 0xCC, 0xCC, 0xCC };
      // Diagonal stripes, upper left to lower right
      CustomPatternType  patternStripesDiag1 = { 0x88, 0x44, 0x22, 0x11,
                                                 0x88, 0x44, 0x22, 0x11 };
      // Diagonal stripes, upper right to lower left
      CustomPatternType  patternStripesDiag2 = { 0x11, 0x22, 0x44, 0x88,
                                                 0x11, 0x22, 0x44, 0x88 };
      // Polka dots
      CustomPatternType  patternPolkaDots = { 0x60, 0xF0, 0xF0, 0x60,
                                              0x06, 0x0F, 0x0F, 0x06 };
      // Inverse polka dots (white on black)
      CustomPatternType  patternWhitePolkaDots = { ~0x60, ~0xF0, ~0xF0, ~0x60,
                                                   ~0x06, ~0x0F, ~0x0F, ~0x06 };
      // Checkerboard
      CustomPatternType  patternCheckerboard = { 0xF0, 0xF0, 0xF0, 0xF0,
                                                 0x0F, 0x0F, 0x0F, 0x0F };
      // Large grid
      CustomPatternType  patternGridLarge = { 0xFF, 0x80, 0x80, 0x80,
                                              0x80, 0x80, 0x80, 0x80 };
      // Small grid
      CustomPatternType  patternGridSmall = { 0xFF, 0x88, 0x88, 0x88,
                                              0xFF, 0x88, 0x88, 0x88 };
      // Crosshatch
      CustomPatternType  patternCrossHatch = { 0xFF, 0xAA, 0xFF, 0xAA,
                                               0xFF, 0xAA, 0xFF, 0xAA };
```

Before calling `WinSetPattern` to change the fill pattern, call `WinGetPattern` to retrieve the current pattern so that you can restore it when you are done drawing with the new pattern. The following example draws a rectangle in a checkerboard pattern and then restores the original fill pattern:

```
RectangleType      rect;
CustomPatternType  newPattern = { 0xF0, 0xF0, 0xF0, 0xF0,
                                  0x0F, 0x0F, 0x0F, 0x0F };
CustomPatternType  oldPattern;

rect.topLeft.x = 40;
rect.topLeft.y = 40;
rect.extent.x = 80;
```

```
rect.extent.y = 80;

WinGetPattern(oldPattern);
WinSetPattern(newPattern);
WinFillRectangle(&rect, 0);
WinSetPattern(oldPattern);
```

Alternatively, you can use `WinPushDrawState` and `WinPopDrawState` to save and restore the entire draw state.

## Drawing Rectangular Borders

The `WinDrawRectangleFrame` and `WinDrawGrayRectangleFrame` functions draw a hollow rectangular border around a given `RectangleType` structure. `WinDrawRectangleFrame` draws a solid frame and `WinDrawGrayRectangleFrame` draws a dotted border, starting with the upper-left pixel in the foreground color and alternating foreground and background pixels.

*Both rectangle frame functions draw the frame outside the edge of the rectangle you pass to the functions. Keep this in mind when you try to determine the screen area occupied by a rectangle frame; you can use the `WinGetFramesRectangle` function to obtain a `RectangleType` structure that comprises the area occupied by a rectangle and its surrounding frame.*

`WinDrawRectangleFrame` and `WinDrawGrayRectangleFrame` each take two arguments: a `FrameType` value describing the type of border to draw and a pointer to a `RectangleType` structure defining the rectangle around which the function draws a frame. The rectangle frame functions use the same `FrameType` constants described in the first table in this chapter.

You can remove a frame from the screen by calling `WinEraseRectangleFrame`, which takes the same parameters as the other two rectangle frame functions but draws pixels in the background color instead of in the foreground color. `WinInvertRectangleFrame` inverts the colors in a frame and `WinPaintRectangleFrame` draws a frame according to the properties of the current draw state.

# Drawing Text

The `WinDrawChars` function draws a string of characters, using the foreground color, on the screen at a specific location. `WinDrawChars` takes four arguments: a pointer to the characters to draw, the length of the characters in bytes, and the x- and y-coordinates where the characters should appear.

To control the font that `WinDrawChars` uses to draw the characters, call the `FntSetFont` function. Only one font can be the active font at a time, and `FntSetFont` changes the active font given the `FontID` of the new font. `FntSetFont` also returns the current active font before changing it, allowing you to store the old font value so you can restore it when you are done with the new font. Chapter 7 contains a complete list of constants you can use to specify a `FontID` value.

Another function that alters the behavior of `WinDrawChars` is `WinSetUnderlineMode`. The underline mode may be one of three values:

❑  `noUnderline` draws text without any underlining

❑  `grayUnderline` draws a dotted underline beneath the text, much like the dotted underline used by a standard text field

❑  `solidUnderline` draws a solid line under the text

Like `FntSetFont`, `WinSetUnderlineMode` returns the value of the previous underline setting so that you can restore it later.

The following example draws the string "To be, or not to be" near the top of the screen in the Palm OS "large" font, with a gray (dotted) underline:

```
FontID              oldFont;
UnderlineModeType   oldUnderline;

oldFont = FntSetFont(largeFont);
oldUnderline = WinSetUnderlineMode(grayUnderline);
WinDrawChars("To be, or not to be",
             StrLen("To be, or not to be"), 0, 20);

// Restore font and underline values
FntSetFont(oldFont);
WinSetUnderlineMode(oldUnderline);
```

Use the `WinEraseChars` function to erase the pixels occupied by characters in a particular string by drawing the string in the current background color. The `WinEraseChars` function takes the same arguments as `WinDrawChars`. You also may draw color-inverted text with `WinInvertChars` or draw text according to draw state settings with `WinPaintChars`.

Palm OS also provides single-character versions of the text-drawing functions. `WinDrawChar`, `WinEraseChar`, `WinInvertChar`, and `WinPaintChar` all take a single character as an argument instead of a string; otherwise, they work just like their `Chars` counterparts. Palm OS contains a plethora of string and font functions for manipulating text. See Chapter 10 for details.

## Drawing Bitmaps

The `WinDrawBitmap` function takes a pointer to a bitmap resource, along with x- and y-coordinates, and draws the bitmap on the screen at the specified location. Coordinates passed to `WinDrawBitmap` represent the window-relative location of the upper-left corner of the bitmap.

Because bitmaps are defined as resources, you must perform a little resource magic to get a bitmap pointer suitable for passing to `WinDrawBitmap`. The `DmGetResource` function allows you to retrieve a handle to a bitmap resource, which you can then turn into a pointer using `MemHandleLock`. More information about using resources, including a more complete description of `DmGetResource`, is available in Chapter 15.

If your application must draw a lot of bitmaps, consider using a function such as `DrawBitmap` in the following example, which displays a bitmap resource given its resource ID and the screen coordinates where it should appear:

```
void DrawBitmap (UInt16 bitmapID, Int16 x, Int16 y)
{
    MemHandle  bitmapH;

    // Retrieve a handle to the bitmap resource.
    bitmapH = DmGetResource(bitmapRsc, bitmapID);

    if (bitmapH)
```

```
{
    BitmapType  *bitmap;

    // Lock the bitmap handle to retrieve a pointer,
    // then draw the bitmap.
    bitmap = (BitmapPtr)MemHandleLock(bitmapH);
    WinDrawBitmap(bitmap, x, y);
    MemHandleUnlock(bitmapH);

    // Release the bitmap resource.
    DmReleaseResource(bitmapH);
    }
}
```

If `DmGetResource` does not find a matching resource in your application's resource database, the function takes a look in the Palm OS system resources to find a match. This behavior can be handy for using system bitmaps and other resources. If you want to limit the search for a matching resource to your application's resource database, use `DmGet1Resource`.

## Using Color Bitmaps

With color support added to the operating system, you should consider a few extra things when creating and displaying bitmaps in a Palm OS application. One thing to keep in mind is the color depth at which you intend to display a bitmap. If your application is to run on a variety of Palm OS handhelds, define your bitmap resources as *bitmap families* to provide support for more than one color depth in a single image.

A bitmap family is simply a collection of different versions of the same image, each version intended for a specific color depth. Both Constructor and PilRC allow for creation of bitmap families. See Chapter 6 for the specifics of using Constructor and PilRC to create individual bitmaps and bitmap families.

The Color Test sample application has a bitmap family that contains five bitmaps of the earth, one for each possible color depth. Color Test also has a bitmap family containing only one 8-bit color image for comparison. Even if only one image is included in a form bitmap, it must be contained in a bitmap family.

The Bitmap Family and Single Bitmap push buttons toggle the display between showing the complete bitmap family with images in all color depths and the single color bitmap. At 8-bit color depth, both images appear identical, but if you move through the other color depths, you will notice that the bitmap images differ slightly. This is because the system's drawing routines must convert the single bitmap image into the lower color depths to display it, and the grayscale approximations produced by the operating system do not quite match what is contained in the full bitmap family.

It is more efficient for the system to display simply an image of the appropriate color depth than to convert an image into another depth, so always provide bitmaps at whatever color depths an application may need to use.

It is possible to include a color table as part of a bitmap resource. There is no way to attach a color table to a bitmap in Constructor, but PilRC can do so by including the `COLORTABLE` option as part of the `BITMAPCOLOR` or `BITMAPFAMILY` directives, as in the following example:

```
BITMAPCOLOR ID 1000 "color.bmp" COLORTABLE
```

In Palm OS 4.0 and later, direct color bitmaps can always be rendered, whether or not the hardware can handle direct color. The bitmap drawing routines in Palm OS 4.0 and later automatically convert direct color bitmaps into whatever color depth the display is currently using. However, earlier versions of Palm OS do not have this conversion capability, so a direct color bitmap by itself will not work. To maintain compatibility with pre-4.0 versions of Palm OS, always include another bitmap at a lower bit depth in the same bitmap family as the direct color bitmap.

Unfortunately, including a color table with a bitmap degrades application performance because the system converts the bitmap's colors to the current display palette before drawing the bitmap. To keep your application running quickly, use bitmap resources that do not have attached color tables and use the `WinPalette` function to adjust the display palette to display the bitmaps properly that have different palette requirements. Better yet, if you can get away with it, make sure the bitmaps you use are already in the system palette, which will obviate the need for you to fiddle with the display palette at all.

## Coloring the User Interface

Along with the main system color table, the system also keeps lists of colors to use for various user interface elements, one list for each supported color depth. These color lists are stored in the system preferences, so that an application can alter the colors the system uses to draw user interface objects. Palm OS 5 allows the user to customize user interface colors by changing settings in the Preferences application.

The system uses a number of constants to refer to each user interface color in the list. The following table lists the user interface color constants and describes where each color is used.

| Constant | Description |
| --- | --- |
| UIObjectFrame | Border for user interface elements, such as buttons, selector triggers, menus, and check boxes. |
| UIObjectFill | Background color for a solid user interface object. |
| UIObjectForeground | Foreground color for a user interface object; usually applied to the label on the object. |
| UIObjectSelectedFill | Background color for a selected user interface object, whether or not the object itself is solid. |
| UIObjectSelectedForeground | Foreground color for a selected user interface object. |
| UIMenuFrame | Color of the border around a menu. |
| UIMenuFill | Background color of a menu item. |
| UIMenuForeground | Text color in a menu. |
| UIMenuSelectedFill | Background color in a selected menu item. |
| UIMenuSelectedForeground | Text color in a selected menu item. |

*Table continued on following page*

| Constant | Description |
|---|---|
| UIFieldBackground | Background color of an editable text field. |
| UIFieldText | Text color in an editable text field. |
| UIFieldTextLines | Underline color in an editable text field. |
| UIFieldCaret | Insertion point cursor color in an editable text field. |
| UIFieldTextHighlightBackground | Background color of highlighted text in an editable text field. |
| UIFieldTextHighlightForeground | Text color of highlighted text in an editable text field. |
| UIFieldFepRawText | Text color of unconverted text in the inline conversion area of a Front End Processor (FEP), such as that used for the Japanese version of Palm OS. If the FEP colors are identical to normal text field colors (which is usually the case on a monochrome display), unconverted text is indicated with a solid underline. |
| UIFieldFepRawBackground | Background color of unconverted text in the inline conversion area of an FEP. |
| UIFieldFepConvertedText | Text color of converted text in the inline conversion area of an FEP. If the FEP colors are identical to normal text field colors, unconverted text is indicated with a double-thick solid underline. |
| UIFieldFepConvertedBackground | Background color of converted text in the inline conversion area of an FEP. |
| UIFieldFepUnderline | Underline color used in the inline conversion area of an FEP. |
| UIFormFrame | Border and title bar color of a form. |
| UIFormFill | Background color of a form. White is usually the best color to use for UIFormFill because it provides the best contrast with user interface elements on the form. |
| UIDialogFrame | Border and title bar color of a modal form. |
| UIDialogFill | Background color of a modal form. |
| UIAlertFrame | Border and title bar color of an alert dialog box. |
| UIAlertFill | Background color of an alert dialog box. |
| UIOK | Color of an information icon. |
| UICaution | Color of a caution icon. |
| UIWarning | Color of a warning icon. |

*Keep in mind that within a table, objects use the UIField colors instead of the regular UIObject colors. Also, as of this writing, Palm OS does not use the UIOK, UICaution, or UIWarning color constants.*

In the color debug ROM images for Palm OS 3.5 and later, most of the user interface color constants have a unique color assigned to them from the last 24 entries in the system palette. These color choices make the screen in POSE look like a fashion designer's worst nightmare; the colors are fairly hideous and seem to be designed to clash with one another. However, this crime against good taste can actually be a debugging bonus if your application changes user interface colors because you can easily distinguish default system colors from those colors that you assign yourself. In addition, the strange colors make it easier to see if your code fails to erase to the current background color and if your application's icons and bitmaps properly use transparency. If you design a color application, try it on the debug ROM to make sure it does the right thing with the user interface colors, and then test it again on the release version of the ROM to make sure it looks okay with the actual default system colors.

## Retrieving User Interface Colors

If your application needs to know what colors are in use for various user interface elements, it can query these values with the `UIColorGetTableEntryIndex` or `UIColorGetTableEntryRGB` functions. These two functions are very similar to each other:

```
IndexedColorType UIColorGetTableEntryIndex (
    UIColorTableEntries which)
void UIColorGetTableEntryRGB (UIColorTableEntries which,
                            RGBColorType *rgbP)
```

The `which` parameter for both of these functions controls what user interface color they return; use one of the constants from the following table. `UIColorGetTableEntryIndex` returns the indexed color as its return value, and `UIColorGetTableEntryRGB` returns a pointer to the actual RGB value of the color in its `rgbP` parameter.

| Constant | Description |
| --- | --- |
| UIObjectFrame | Border for user interface elements, such as buttons, selector triggers, menus, and check boxes. |
| UIObjectFill | Background color for a solid user interface object. |
| UIObjectForeground | Foreground color for a user interface object; usually applied to the label on the object. |
| UIObjectSelectedFill | Background color for a selected user interface object, whether or not the object itself is solid. |
| UIObjectSelectedForeground | Foreground color for a selected user interface object. |
| UIMenuFrame | Color of the border around a menu. |
| UIMenuFill | Background color of a menu item. |
| UIMenuForeground | Text color in a menu. |
| UIMenuSelectedFill | Background color in a selected menu item. |
| UIMenuSelectedForeground | Text color in a selected menu item. |
| UIFieldBackground | Background color of an editable text field. |

*Table continued on following page*

| Constant | Description |
| --- | --- |
| UIFieldText | Text color in an editable text field. |
| UIFieldTextLines | Underline color in an editable text field. |
| UIFieldCaret | Insertion point cursor color in an editable text field. |
| UIFieldTextHighlightBackground | Background color of highlighted text in an editable text field. |
| UIFieldTextHighlightForeground | Text color of highlighted text in an editable text field. |
| UIFieldFepRawText | Text color of unconverted text in the inline conversion area of a Front End Processor (FEP), such as that used for the Japanese version of Palm OS. If the FEP colors are identical to normal text field colors (which is usually the case on a monochrome display), unconverted text is indicated with a solid underline. |
| UIFieldFepRawBackground | Background color of unconverted text in the inline conversion area of an FEP. |
| UIFieldFepConvertedText | Text color of converted text in the inline conversion area of an FEP. If the FEP colors are identical to normal text field colors, unconverted text is indicated with a double-thick solid underline. |
| UIFieldFepConvertedBackground | Background color of converted text in the inline conversion area of an FEP. |
| UIFieldFepUnderline | Underline color used in the inline conversion area of an FEP. |
| UIFormFrame | Border and title bar color of a form. |
| UIFormFill | Background color of a form. White is usually the best color to use for UIFormFill because it provides the best contrast with user interface elements on the form. |
| UIDialogFrame | Border and title bar color of a modal form. |
| UIDialogFill | Background color of a modal form. |
| UIAlertFrame | Border and title bar color of an alert dialog box. |
| UIAlertFill | Background color of an alert dialog box. |
| UIOK | Color of an information icon. |
| UICaution | Color of a caution icon. |
| UIWarning | Color of a warning icon. |

These routines are particularly useful if you need to draw a gadget and you want it to match the same color scheme used by the default Palm OS user interface elements. As an example, the following code retrieves the color used for the label of a selected user interface element and sets the text color to match:

```
IndexedColorType  textColor;

textColor =
    UIColorGetTableEntryIndex(UIObjectSelectedFill);
WinSetTextColor(textColor);
```

### Setting User Interface Colors

Within an application, you can change the user interface colors using the `UIColorSetTableEntry` function, which has the following prototype:

```
Err UIColorSetTableEntry (UIColorTableEntries which,
    const RGBColorType *rgbP)
```

The `which` parameter is the symbolic color constant from the preceding table that you want to change, and `rgbP` is a standard `RGBColorType` structure containing the RGB color that you wish to assign to the specified user interface element. The `UIColorSetTableEntry` function finds the best fit in the current display palette for the requested color and then sets the user interface color to the best-fit color.

> *Be sure that the drawing window is currently onscreen when using `UIColorSetTableEntry`. If the drawing window is offscreen, the best-fit algorithm used by `UIColorSetTableEntry` might pick a color that is not actually available in the current display palette.*

To find out what color is currently assigned to a particular user interface element, use the `UIColorGetTableEntryIndex` function to retrieve the color's index in the display palette or the `UIColorGetTableEntryRGB` function to retrieve the color's actual RGB value in an `RGBColorType` structure. The prototypes for these two functions look like this:

```
IndexedColorType UIColorGetTableEntryIndex
    (UIColorTableEntries which);
void UIColorGetTableEntryRGB
    (UIColorTableEntries which, RGBColorType *rgbP);
```

> *When the system switches to a new application, it applies the default system user interface colors, losing any changes your application has made. If you want changes to user interface colors to stick between invocations of your application, you will need to save them as application preferences and reset the user interface colors when your application starts up again.*

# Programming High-Resolution Displays

Traditionally, the screen resolution on a Palm OS handheld has always been $160 \times 160$ pixels. However, as LCD display technology has improved, it has become feasible to make handhelds with higher-resolution displays. Palm OS licensees HandEra and Sony were the first handheld manufacturers to lead the charge, releasing their own high-resolution devices even before the operating system contained support for high-resolution programming. Palm OS 5 introduced native high-resolution support to the operating system in its High-Density Display feature set. Since that time, high-resolution displays have become the norm rather than the exception.

# Using the High-Density Display Feature Set

The High-Density Display feature set in Palm OS 5 supports double-density screens, which have a resolution of 320 × 320 pixels. Doubling the pixel density allows older applications, written for a 160 × 160 screen, to run without modification on a high-resolution screen. The Palm OS *blitter*, which is the part of the operating system responsible for actually displaying pixels on the screen, automatically doubles the size of low-density bitmaps, user interface elements, and text when drawing such items onto a high-density screen. As an example, consider a low-density bitmap image 10 pixels wide × 20 pixels high. When displaying this bitmap on a double-density screen, the blitter doubles the dimensions of the bitmap so that it becomes 20 pixels wide × 40 pixels high.

Palm OS makes a distinction between the *standard coordinate system* and a *native coordinate system*. The standard coordinate system, used by Palm Powered handhelds that don't support the High-Density Display feature set, maps exactly one pixel to each standard coordinate. A native coordinate system is what the blitter uses, and it is based on the actual physical pixels of the display hardware. In a native coordinate system, there can be more than one pixel per standard coordinate.

By default, applications running in Palm OS 5 use the standard coordinate system. The blitter converts screen coordinates between the standard low-density system to the native double-density system automatically. For example, an instruction to draw a bitmap at standard coordinates (40, 60) causes the blitter to draw the bitmap at native coordinates (80, 120).

Doubling the display density results in elegant handling of user interface elements and text. User interface elements and text occupy the same percentage of screen space in double-density displays as they do in low-density displays, so the relative positions of objects on a form remain the same between low- and double-resolution displays. For example, relative to the edges of the screen itself, (80, 120) on a double-density display corresponds to the same visual location as (40, 60) on a low-density display.

Applications designed for low-density displays can still make use of better-looking high-resolution text without changing the layout of the application's interface; the double-density fonts occupy the same relative amount of screen space as their low-density equivalents, but they use the extra pixel density to render the text more legibly. Likewise, user interface elements like buttons can have more rounded corners in double-density mode than when drawn on a low-resolution screen.

To illustrate how a low-density application looks in double-density mode, see how the Librarian sample application looks on both low-density and double-density displays (see Figure 11-2). The 160 × 160 low-density screen on the left has been enlarged to double its normal size for easier comparison with the 320 × 320 double-density screen on the right. Notice that the relative positions of user interface elements do not change between resolutions; buttons and table rows occupy the same amount of screen space in double-density that they do in low-density. However, the double-density display has smoother fonts than the low-density display.

> The High-Density Display feature set is actually designed to handle resolutions other than 160 × 160 and 320 × 320, including displays with rectangular rather than square aspect ratios, but the blitter in Palm OS 5 supports only low-density and high-density displays. Future handhelds and versions of Palm OS may have blitters capable of supporting different display densities and aspect ratios.

Before using any of the special functions of the High-Density Display feature set, check to see if it is present. As for any other special set of APIs in Palm OS, detecting the High-Density Display feature set involves a call to the `FtrGet` function:

```
err = FtrGet(sysFtrCreator, sysFtrNumWinVersion, &version);
if (version >= 4)
    // High-Density Display feature set is present.
```

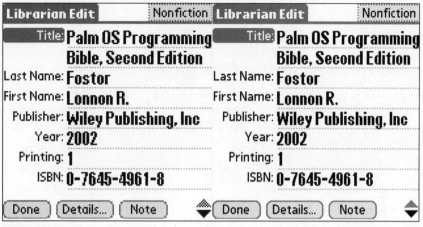

Figure 11-2

## Detecting Available Screen Densities

Knowing that high-density support is present isn't always enough; on devices that can support multiple resolutions, it also is sometimes necessary to know which specific densities are supported on a particular handheld. To determine what densities are available, use the WinGetSupportedDensity routine:

```
Err     error;
UInt16  density = 0;

do
{
    error = WinGetSupportedDensity(&density);
    if (error)
        break;
    else
    {
        // Do something with the density value, like storing
        // it in an array for later use.
    }
}
while (density != 0);
```

WinGetSupportedDensity should be called in a loop. Make sure to set the initial density value to zero before starting. Then, each time WinGetSupportedDensity returns, it sets density to the next highest density value. When WinGetSupportedDensity has gone through all the densities available on the handheld, it sets density back to zero again. Possible density values are defined in the DensityType enumerated type:

```
typedef enum {
    kDensityLow = 72,
    kDensityOneAndAHalf = 108,
    kDensityDouble = 144,
    kDensityTriple = 216,
    kDensityQuadruple = 288
} DensityType;
```

## Setting and Retrieving the Coordinate System

Drawing high-density graphics is much like drawing in color. You must first set the coordinate system to the desired resolution with the `WinSetCoordinateSystem` function, after which subsequent calls to drawing routines will use the new coordinate system. The `WinSetCoordinateSystem` function looks like this:

```
UInt16 WinSetCoordinateSystem (WinHandle winH,
                               UInt16 coordSys)
```

The `coordSys` parameter is one of the values from the `WinCoordinatesType` enumerated type, shown as follows:

```
typedef enum {
    kCoordinatesNative = 0,
    kCoordinatesStandard = 72,
    kCoordinatesOneAndAHalf = 108,
    kCoordinatesDouble = 144,
    kCoordinatesTriple = 216,
    kCoordinatesQuadruple = 288
} WinCoordinatesType;
```

The numbers supplied by `WinCoordinatesType` represent the bitmap density used for the various screen densities. The `kCoordinatesStandard` constant represents normal $160 \times 160$ display density, and `kCoordinatesDouble` represents the $320 \times 320$ double-density mode.

Like other `WinSet` functions, `WinSetCoordinateSystem` modifies the draw state, so consider using `WinPushDrawState` and `WinPopDrawState` to save and restore the draw state before and after using `WinSetCoordinateSystem`.

As an example, the following code pushes the draw state, changes the screen to double-density mode, draws a line from the upper-left corner to the lower-right corner, and then pops the draw state back to its original values:

```
WinHandle  drawWindow;

WinPushDrawState();
drawWindow = WinGetDrawWindow();
WinSetCoordinateSystem(drawWindow, kCoordinatesDouble);
WinDrawLine(0, 0, 319, 319);
WinPopDrawState();
```

You also may need to determine the current density of a window's draw state. To do so, use the `WinGetCoordinateSystem` function:

```
UInt16 WinGetCoordinateSystem (WinHandle winH)
```

`WinGetCoordinateSystem` returns a `WinCoordinatesType` constant that describes the current coordinate system in use in that window.

## Translating Between Coordinate Systems

Palm OS provides a number of functions for translating coordinates between standard and native coordinate systems. Normally, you can rely on the operating system to translate standard coordinates automatically into native coordinates, but one instance where you might need to perform conversion manually is if your application performs high-resolution drawing for a gadget.

When converting from the standard coordinate system to a window's native coordinate system, you can use the `WinScalePoint` and `WinScaleRectangle` functions. These functions have the following prototypes:

```
void WinScalePoint (WinHandle winH, PointType *pointP)
void WinScaleRectangle (WinHandle winH,
                        RectangleType *rectP)
```

Both functions take a `winH` argument, which is the handle of the window containing the native coordinate system to which the functions should convert. In `WinScalePoint`, the next argument is a pointer to a `PointType` structure; in `WinScaleRectangle`, the next argument is a pointer to a `RectangleType` structure. The second argument should initially refer to a point or rectangle in standard coordinates; upon return, these functions convert the point or rectangle in the second argument into its native coordinate equivalent. If the window referenced by `winH` already uses the standard coordinate system, the point or rectangle is left unmodified.

To convert in the other direction — from native coordinates to standard coordinates — use the `WinUnscalePoint` and `WinUnscaleRectangle` functions, which have the same arguments as `WinScalePoint` and `WinUnscaleRectangle`, respectively.

# Using the Palm OS Cobalt Graphics Model

Palm OS Cobalt introduces a brand new model for performing drawing and graphics operations on the display. In contrast with the simpler Window APIs developers have used to date, the new drawing model provides much more powerful and advanced capabilities, such as paths, gradients, anti-aliasing and transformations. In the new model, these functions are all performed against something called a *Graphics Context*.

> *Most of the legacy window APIs are still present and supported in Palm OS Cobalt. In many cases, developers may find that they can build their existing Window-based code with very few changes under Palm OS Cobalt. However there are some Window functions that no longer exist, and given the power and capabilities of the new drawing model it may be worthwhile to investigate updating your drawing code. For details on which functions have been removed from Palm OS Cobalt, please refer to the Porting Guide in the developer documentation.*

# *What Is a Graphics Context?*

In the new drawing model in Palm OS Cobalt, drawing is performed on a Graphics Context (GC). A graphics context can be thought of as an intelligent buffer that sits between your code and the actual target drawing window. The graphics context is responsible for keeping track of the rendering state set by your code and making sure that it correctly updates the target window to match the series of drawing commands you issue.

In Palm OS Cobalt, your code no longer draws directly to a window. Instead it relies on the graphics context to draw to the window on your behalf. In fact, you may be interested to know that drawing performed by the renderer to the graphics context is done in a different operating system process than your application.

Your application forms will know when it is time to draw when they receive a `frmUpdateEvent`. This is a signal from Palm OS Cobalt that your window is ready to be drawn on and you are able to receive a valid graphics context that can process your drawing commands. You should be sure to restrict your form drawing code so that it is only performed in response to a `frmUpdateEvent`.

# *Understanding Paths*

When you draw in a graphics context, you do so by constructing *paths*. Paths are made up of lines, arcs, and curves. Paths are also used when you draw text. A path has one or more of these drawing elements in it. To create a path, you use the `GcMoveTo` function to set the current drawing point on the graphics context. You then call `GcLineTo`, `GcRect`, or other drawing commands to complete your path. When you are done creating your path, you call `GcPaint` which fills, or paints, the shapes in the path based on the current graphics context settings. When you call `GcPaint`, the path you created is cleared from the graphics context and you can either release the graphics context or continue drawing with a new path.

`GcPaint` can also render an outline version of the path instead of a filled version by calling `GcStroke` before calling `GcPaint`.

# *Alpha Blending and Anti-Aliasing*

Alpha blending and anti-aliasing are closely related techniques that can improve the visual appearance of lines, shapes, and text when rendered on a grid against various types of backgrounds

*Alpha blending* allows you to specify a transparency level between 0 and 255, which is then associated with the color in the graphics context. The most basic transparency levels are fully transparent (zero) and fully opaque (255). Thus a level of 0 means the color should be rendered as a fully transparent color, while an alpha level of 255 means the color should be rendered as a fully opaque color. Any values in between 0 and 255 indicate varying degrees of transparency. Palm OS Cobalt then performs a blend between the current color and the color beneath it. Because it is a lot of work for the operating system to determine the final color for every pixel if you use an intermediate transparency value, you should use an opaque alpha level of 255 unless you absolutely need transparency effects.

In addition to alpha blending, Palm OS Cobalt supports a concept called *anti-aliasing*. When anti-aliasing is off, a pixel is either painted with the current color or it is not painted, depending on whether the pixel falls within the line or shape being drawn. With anti-aliasing enabled, a pixel is painted with a color value that reflects the percentage of the pixel that contains the line or shape being drawn. The result of anti-aliasing is that lines and shapes are drawn more smoothly. As with alpha blending, anti-aliasing can adversely affect performance, so you should only enable it if you will actually need it.

# How Drawing Works in a Graphics Context

Drawing to a graphics context always follows the same basic sequence. First you need to obtain a handle to the current graphics context by calling GcGetCurrentContext. This handle is then used when calling other graphics context functions. When you are done with the graphics context, you must remember to release it back to the operating system by calling GcReleaseContext. In between calling GcGetCurrentContext and GcReleaseContext, you can change the state of the graphics context, and you can create and paint one or more paths.

## Setting the Rendering State

A graphics context supports the following attributes, which together define its state:

❑ **Color** is set by the GcColor function and is used to set the fill color for the background of the current path. The default color is black.

❑ **Coordinate System** controls the coordinate system, which is used in drawing your shapes and other elements to the window. Just as with the legacy Window system, Palm OS Cobalt supports native, standard, one and a half, double, triple and quadruple coordinate system constants. The coordinate system is set by GcSetCoordinateSystem.

❑ **Pen Size** controls the width of the pen when drawing lines in stroke mode. The pen size is set by using the GcSetPenSize function, and it is set to a default of one pixel.

❑ **Join** controls how two lines are connected together and can be set by GcSetJoin. By default the join style is set as bevel.

❑ **Font** controls font used when drawing text and is set by calling GcSetFont.

❑ **Transformations** allow you to transform the current coordinate system in a variety of ways using GcTransform and GcSetFontTransform.

❑ **Anti-Aliasing** is controlled by calling GcSetAntialiasing for lines and shapes, and GcSetFontAntialiasing for text.

❑ **Text Hinting** controls whether the system draws characters to exact pixel boundaries. You can turn this setting off by calling GcSetFontHinting.

❑ **Gradients** used in background fills are set using GcInitGradient and GcSetGradient.

If you wish to change any of these graphics context states, it is always a good idea to restore the context back to its original state after you are done with the context. To do this, call GcPushState before you begin changing the state. After you complete your state changes and all of your path creation and drawing, call GcPopState to clear your state and restore the context to its original state, as in the following example:

```
GcHandle gc;

gc = GcGetCurrentContext ();

if (gc)
```

```
{
  // save the original state
  GcPushState (gc);
  // change the color to red (255,0,0) and fully opaque (255)
  GcSetColor (gc, 255, 0, 0, 255);
  // create a path
  // ...
  // draw the path
  GcPaint (gc);
  // restore the original context state
  GcPopState (gc);
  GcReleaseContext (gc);
}
```

## Defining a Path

As previously mentioned, a path is made up of lines, shapes, and text. Using the current coordinate position set by GcMoveTo as the origin for the element to be drawn, you can then call GcLineTo and GcMoveTo to create a series of lines.

If you wish to just draw lines and not closed shapes, you can call GcStroke at any time before GcPaint to cause GcPaint to render your lines as an outline. Otherwise GcPaint attempts to fill a shape defined by your drawing commands. For this reason you should ensure that your drawing commands form a closed area. GcClosePath can be used to close a path by automatically drawing a straight line from the current point to the point specified by the most recent GcMoveTo call.

The following code snippet draws a simple filled blue square:

```
GcHandle gc;

gc = GcGetCurrentContext ();

if (gc)
{
  // save the original state
  GcPushState (gc);
  // change the color to blue (0,0,255) and fully opaque (255)
  GcSetColor (gc, 0, 0, 255, 255);
  // create a path
  GcMoveTo (gc, 0, 0);
  GcLineTo (gc, 100, 0);
  GcLineTo (gc, 100, 100);
  GcLineTo (gc, 0, 100);
  GcClosePath (gc);
  // draw the path
  GcPaint (gc);
  // restore the original context state
  GcPopState (gc);
  GcReleaseContext (gc);
}
```

Although we took the trouble to draw a rectangle in this example manually, Palm OS Cobalt provides as a convenience a couple of functions that can draw common shapes such as rectangles, rounded rectangles, and curved shapes such as circles and ovals with arcs. Shapes other than rectangles and arcs, such as triangles, are left up to developers to define using GcMoveTo and GcLineTo.

## Painting Your Path

It is important to remember that when you create your path with lines and other shapes, your graphics are not rendered until you call GcPaint. It takes the current path and performs a fill with the current color. After you call GcPaint, your path is cleared from the context.

## Drawing Text

You can draw text on a graphics context by calling GcDrawTextAt, which draws text using the currently selected font. GcDrawTextAt is different from the shape-oriented functions described earlier in that it is totally self-contained. It clears any previous path, creates a new path containing the specified text, and immediately calls GcPaint to render it. Thus in order to not lose any path you had been working on prior to calling GcDrawTextAt, you either need to render the path using GcPaint or use GcPushState to save the path and restore it with GcPopState after you call GcDrawTextAt.

## Clipping Regions

Clipping regions are useful in order to have Palm OS Cobalt restrict the effects of your drawing code within a defined region. With a clipping region defined, you can create paths that span the drawing window but the graphics context will only render that portion of your path that lies within the clipping region's coordinates.

To define a clipping region, call GcBeginClip and then use GcMoveTo, GcLineTo, or other shape drawing functions to define the perimeter of the closed clipping region, calling GcPaint to fill the region with white. Finally, complete the definition of the clipping region by calling GcEndClip.

At this point, any paths you create will only be painted within the clipping region, even if you specify coordinates that fall outside the clipping region. You can even have multiple clipping regions defined simultaneously within the same context. If multiple regions overlap, the graphics context will use the intersection of the two regions as the clipping region.

The current clipping region or regions are in effect until you clear the drawing state by calling GcPopState.

# Summary

In this chapter, you learned how to draw graphics and text to the screen, as well as how to play sound. After reading this chapter, you should understand the following:

❑   All Palm OS drawing occurs within the current *draw window,* which you may set with WinSetDrawWindow, and all user input goes to the current *active window,* which you may set with WinSetActiveWindow.

❑   To directly draw on the screen, you may take your pick from a number of drawing functions for creating lines, rectangles, patterns, and text.

❑   Palm OS 3.5 supports five color depths: 1-bit (monochrome), 2-bit (4-color grayscale), 4-bit (16-color grayscale), 8-bit (256 colors), and direct color (16-bit and higher).

❑ Querying supported color depths, retrieving the current color depth, and setting color depth can all be accomplished with the WinScreenMode function.

❑ The WinPalette function allows you to change the current display palette, substituting your own colors for the default colors of the system palette.

❑ For maximum compatibility on various Palm OS handhelds, color bitmap resources should be created as bitmap families, containing different bitmaps for different color depths.

❑ The system keeps a list of user interface colors, which you may customize using the UIColorSetTableEntry function.

❑ Palm OS 5 includes support for double-density displays at a resolution of 320 × 320 pixels.

❑ Palm OS Cobalt introduces a whole new drawing model based on Graphics Contexts.

❑ Drawing on a Graphics Context is accomplished by creating one or more paths consisting of lines, shapes, and text.

# 12

# Programming Multimedia

Not too long ago the concept of supporting multimedia capabilities on a handheld was an unlikely one. True, most early handhelds were capable of emitting basic sounds — beeps and alarms. But those handhelds lacked the hardware, processing power, display screen, and storage necessary to play modern digital audio and video.

In stark contrast, today's Palm Powered handhelds routinely come equipped with high-powered processors, expansion slots capable of supporting gigabyte-sized expansion media, and audio and video hardware that is up to the task of recording and playing digital media. Indeed, handhelds and smartphone devices capable of playing music and video, whether stored locally or accessed wirelessly, are among today's hottest products (witness the unprecedented success of the Apple iPod) and are being sought out in increasing numbers by consumers who want to capture, record, and play their music and video "on the go."

This chapter describes the programming interfaces and subsystems available in Palm OS Garnet and Palm OS Cobalt for developers who seek to work with various forms of audio and video in their handheld applications. The first section of this chapter deals with Sound Manager, which enables playing of simple and somewhat more sophisticated audio sounds on both older and modern versions of Palm OS. The second part of this chapter covers the newer, richer capabilities offered in Palm OS Cobalt Multimedia Services.

## Understanding Sound Manager

Prior to Palm OS 5, Palm Powered devices were very limited in their ability to create sound. With the exception of certain handhelds manufactured by HandEra and Sony, which sported more advanced sound capabilities than other Palm OS hardware, only a single tone could be generated at any particular time through the device's simple speaker. This limitation rendered the handheld unsuitable for music or accurate voice playback without the addition of extra hardware — such as the built-in MP3 player on some Sony models — and it also ruled out other applications, such as using the device to generate phone-dialing tones for use as an autodialer. Even with a better speaker, the slow speed of processors on handhelds prior to Palm OS 5 was not enough to keep up with the demands of real-time digital audio decoding. To be sure, the speaker in older Palm OS devices does work well for simple alarm beeps and user input feedback.

With the introduction of Palm OS 5, coupled with the extra power of available ARM processors, handhelds were able to offer more sophisticated sound capabilities than earlier versions of Palm OS. To encompass both the basic capabilities of earlier handhelds and the more modern ARM-based handhelds, PalmSource offers the Sound Manager, available in both Palm OS Garnet and Palm OS Cobalt. Sound Manager consists of APIs that support the playing of anything from simple beeps to WAV (or "WAVE") sound data.

To distinguish between the older sound capabilities of Palm OS and the new features included in version 5, Palm OS divides its sound APIs into two groups:

❑ Simple sound, which includes all single-tone sound routines prior to Palm OS 5

❑ Sampled sound, which allows Palm OS to play WAV sound data

Both simple and sampled sound capabilities are supported on both Palm OS Garnet and Palm OS Cobalt, making it the best bet for developers who need modest sound support and require greater compatibility across older and newer Palm OS handhelds. Furthermore, Sound Manager is generally easier to program than the Multimedia Services associated with Palm OS Cobalt, albeit certainly less capable.

## Playing Simple Sound

The simplest way to make sounds in any version of Palm OS is the `SndPlaySystemSound` function, which allows you to generate one of the predefined system sounds. The `SndPlaySystemSound` function takes a single argument of type `SndSysBeepType`, which is an enum defined as follows in `SoundMgr.h`:

```
typedef enum SndSysBeepType {
    sndInfo = 1,
    sndWarning,
    sndError,
    sndStartUp,
    sndAlarm,
    sndConfirmation,
    sndClick
} SndSysBeepType;
```

Aside from the predefined system sounds, you also can generate your own tones manually using `SndDoCmd`. The `SndDoCmd` function has the following prototype:

```
Err SndDoCmd (MemPtr chanP, SndCommandType *cmdP,
              Boolean noWait)
```

The `chanP` argument to `SndDoCmd` specifies which audio channel should receive the sound output. Because current implementations of `SndDoCmd` support only a single, default channel, you must pass `NULL` for this argument. Likewise, `noWait` also is not fully implemented. In the future, passing zero for `noWait` tells the system to play the sound synchronously, which is to say `SndDoCmd` plays the entire sound before returning. A nonzero value specifies asynchronous playback, which means that `SndDoCmd` returns immediately, allowing interruption of the sound playback by other processes. For now, you must pass zero for this argument.

All the real work of SndDoCmd is contained in its second argument, cmdP, which is a pointer to a SndCommandType structure. The SndCommandType structure may contain a number of completely different pieces of information, based on the value of its first member, an enum called SndCmdIDType. The Palm OS header file SoundMgr.h defines SndCmdIDType and SndCommandType as follows:

```
typedef enum SndCmdIDType {
    sndCmdFreqDurationAmp = 1,
    sndCmdNoteOn,
    sndCmdFrqOn,
    sndCmdQuiet
} SndCmdIDType;

typedef struct SndCommandType {
    SndCmdIDType  cmd;
    UInt8         reserved;
    Int32         param1;
    UInt16        param2;
    UInt16        param3;
} SndCommandType;
```

The only option available in versions of Palm OS prior to 3.0 is sndCmdFreqDurationAmp. When this value is passed for the cmd member, param1 specifies the frequency of the sound to play (in Hertz), param2 specifies the duration of the sound (in milliseconds), and param3 specifies the amplitude of the sound. When using sndCmdFreqDurationAmp, the SndDoCmd function always plays the sound synchronously, unless param3 is sndMaxAmp (a constant defined in SoundMgr.h that is equal to zero), in which case SndDoCmd plays the sound asynchronously, returning immediately.

> All values for **cmd**, other than **sndCmdFreqDurationAmp**, cause the **SndDoCmd** function to crash on versions of Palm OS prior to 3.0. Be sure to check the version before making **SndDoCmd** calls using the other values in the **SndCmdIDType** enum if you intend your application to run on earlier versions of the operating system.

The sndCmdNoteOn command allows you to specify a tone to play using the MIDI (Musical Instrument Digital Interface) format. When using sndCmdNoteOn, param1 specifies the MIDI key index (a value from 0 to 127), param2 specifies the duration in milliseconds, and param3 specifies the sound's velocity (another value from 0 to 127, which SndDoCmd interpolates into an amplitude for playback).

Using sndCmdFreqOn is similar to using sndCmdFreqDurationAmp but it always plays asynchronously, allowing you to interrupt the sound playback with another call to SndDoCmd. When cmd is sndCmdFreqOn, param1 specifies frequency in Hertz, param2 specifies duration in milliseconds, and param3 specifies amplitude. (Use the sndMaxAmp constant to set the sound at the maximum amplitude.)

The final value in the SndCmdIDType enum is sndCmdQuiet, which stops the play of the current sound. All three param variables should be set to zero when using sndCmdQuiet.

# Playing Sampled Sound

The `SndPlayResource` function can play WAV audio data that has the following properties:

❑ Either no compression (Pulse Code Modulation, or PCM) or Interactive Multimedia Association four-bit adaptive Differential Pulse Code Modulation (IMA-ADPCM) compression

❑ Either one channel (monophonic) or two channels (stereophonic)

❑ Sampling rate of 8, 11, 22.05, 44.1, 48, or 96 kilobits per second

Before playing audio data, an application needs to retrieve a handle to the resource that contains the data. Use the `DmGetResource` function for this purpose, specifying the resource type as `wave`, as in the following example:

```
MemHandle  audioH;

audioH = DmGetResource('wave', myAudioResourceID);
```

Once you have a handle to the audio data, lock the handle with `MemHandleLock` to get a pointer to the data and then pass that pointer to `SndPlayResource`, as follows:

```
if (audioH)
{
    SndPlayResource(MemHandleLock(audioH), sndGameVolume,
                    sndFlagSync);
    MemHandleUnlock(audioH);
}
```

The preceding example plays a sampled sound at the user's current game volume preference, which the user may set in the Preferences application. The sound is also played synchronously, which is to say the entire sound finishes playing before `SndPlayResource` returns control to the application that called it.

The `SndPlayResource` function has the following prototype:

```
Err SndPlayResource (SndPtr sound, Int32 volume,
    UInt32 flags);
```

The first parameter, `sound`, is a pointer to the audio data to be played. The `volume` parameter specifies at what volume the sound should be played. Values for `volume` range from 0, which is silent, to `sndMaxAmp`, which is defined in `SoundMgr.h` as 64. Three convenient constants allow you to set the volume to the user's various volume preferences:

❑ `sndAlarmVolume` is the user's current Alarm Sound setting.

❑ `sndGameVolume` is the user's current Game Sound setting.

❑ `sndSystemVolume` is the user's current System Sound setting.

The `SndPlayResource` function's final parameter, `flags`, defines various flags that alter how `SndPlayResource` plays back the sound. You may pass three constants for the `flags` parameter:

❑ sndFlagSync causes SndPlayResource to play the sound synchronously. With this flag specified, SndPlayResource does not return until sound playback has finished. Because synchronous playback blocks user input until the sound has finished playing, use sndFlagSync for short sounds only.

❑ sndFlagAsync causes SndPlayResource to play the sound asynchronously. With this flag specified, SndPlayResource returns immediately while the sound continues playing. Asynchronous playback is a good choice if you want to play long sounds in the background while the user performs other tasks. For example, a game could play music asynchronously while the user plays the game.

> If you choose to play back sound asynchronously, do not unlock the handle to the sound resource until the sound has finished playing. The earlier example plays back synchronously for this reason because the example unlocks the handle to the sound resource immediately after calling **SndPlayResource**. Unlocking the handle to a sound resource in the middle of playback could result in a crash if the system needs to shuffle the sound resource around in storage RAM to make space for other memory allocations.

❑ sndFlagNormal is equivalent to the sndFlagSync flag.

# Understanding Multimedia Services

Multimedia Services is an entirely new subsystem in Palm OS Cobalt, designed to support an application-level API for controlling media tasks from an application. Applications written to use multimedia library APIs can create and work with the Palm OS Cobalt Movie Server, enabling recording and playback of a variety of media file formats.

## Session Objects

The Movie Server coordinates Palm OS audio, video, storage, and other subsystems and abstracts them as a series of objects:

❑ A *stream* refers to multmedia data in a specific media file format (such as MP3).

❑ A *source* is a specific device that originates one or more streams, each of which can be directed to a different destination. A good example of a source is a video camera.

❑ A *destination* is the target for a given stream. In the case of a recording, the destination may be an audio or video file. In the case of video playback, the destination may be the handheld screen.

❑ A *track* is a pathway for media between a source and destination. Tracks perform the actual encoding and decoding of media content.

Each of these objects is part of a *session*. A session is an object that ties together sources, destinations, streams, and tracks as a single high-level media task.

# Working with Sources and Destinations

In Multimedia Services, sources and destinations contain one or more streams, such as an audio or video stream. When working with the multimedia APIs, a URL scheme is used when referring to a source or destination. For file-based sources and destinations, the URL syntax is as follows:

```
"file://" ["localhost"] "/" [VolumeLabel] "/" Path
```

For example, an MP3 song called "TheSong.mp3" which is stored on an expansion card would be referred to by the following URL:

```
file://localhost/Card1/MyMusic/TheSong.mp3
```

Note that the volume name is optional. However, if the volume name is omitted, all volumes will be searched for the path/file specified.

URLs are also used to access specific devices (such as a camera or a microphone) as a virtual source or destination. In this case, rather than the `file://` scheme, you would use the `palmdev://` scheme. The following table lists a series of default `palmdev://` URLs and the types of devices they refer to.

| Constant | Description |
| --- | --- |
| palmdev:///Media/Null | Refers to a null device |
| palmdev:///Media/Default/AudioIn | Refers to an audio recording device |
| palmdev:///Media/Default/AudioOut | Refers to an audio playback device |
| palmdev:///Media/Default/StillIn | Refers to a capture input for still images |
| palmdev:///Media/Default/VideoIn | Refers to a video recording device |
| palmdev:///Media/Default/VideoOut | Refers to a video playback device |

# Components of a Playback Session

The basic sequence followed in any multimedia playback session is to create the session, define the source data, set up the session object, and start playing.

To create a multimedia session, you need to call `MMSessionCreate`, which has the following prototype:

```
status_t MMSessionCreate (MMSessionClassID sessionClass, int32_t flags,
  MMSessionID *outSession)
```

The `sessionClass` argument refers to the type of multimedia session you wish to create. Palm OS Cobalt defines two class IDs in the `MMSessionClass.h` header file:

❑   `P_MM_SESSION_CLASS_DEFAULT_CAPTURE` is used to create a recording (capture) session class.

❑   `P_MM_SESSION_CLASS_DEFAULT_PLAYBACK` is used to create a playback session class.

The flags argument specifies whether to create the session in any available process (typically a background process) or as a local process. Palm OS Cobalt defines two constants P_MM_SESSION_CREATE_ANY_PROCESS and P_MM_SESSION_CREATE_LOCAL_PROCESS for this purpose.

The outSession argument must be passed in to receive a valid multimedia session ID, if MMSessionCreate was successful.

After successful creation of a session with MMSessionCreate, the next step is to specify a source for the data to be used in the session. To accomplish this, you would call MMSessionAddSource, which has the following prototype:

```
status_t MMSessionAddSource (MMSessionID session,
const char *sourceURL, MMSourceID *outSource)
```

The session argument is a valid session ID returned from MMSessionCreate. The sourceURL argument is the URL of the data source to add to the session. As described in the previous section, this URL can be a file-based URL or a palmdev:// URL. The outSource argument is passed in order to receive a valid multimedia source ID if the function call is successful.

After adding the source, you need to prepare the source as one or more media streams (one for each track in the source content) for use in your session. This is done by calling MMSourceFinalize, which simply takes the source ID returned by MMSessionAddSource. If MMSourceFinalize is successful, Palm OS Cobalt proceeds to open the media source and create the necessary streams for your content.

The next step in preparing for playback is to set up the tracks that are necessary for your content. This is performed by calling MMSessionAddDefaultTracks, which has the following prototype:

```
status_t MMSessionAddDefaultTracks (MMSessionID session,
MMSourceID source, MMDestID dest)
```

In a simple playback session, the destination ID may be specified as P_MM_DEFAULT_DEST, in which case the operating system automatically adds the necessary default destinations appropriate to the content and finalizes them.

The final step in preparation of your media playback session is to call MMSessionFinalize. Calling this function is your signal to Palm OS that your are done adding any sources, destinations, or tracks for the session and you are ready to begin playback (or capture).

At this point, your session is ready for playback. Your code may choose to proceed with playback immediately, or you may wish to return control to the user — for example, by providing a "play" button. MMSessionControl is a master function that provides a mechanism for sending opcodes to the session object to control playback, capture, and preview. The following table describes the opcodes that are supported.

| Constant | Description |
|---|---|
| PP_MM_SESSION_CTL_RUN | Start or continue recording or playback |
| PP_MM_SESSION_CTL_PAUSE | Pause recording or playback |
| PP_MM_SESSION_CTL_STOP | Stop recording or playback |
| PP_MM_SESSION_CTL_PREFETCH | Begin buffering data from the source |
| PP_MM_SESSION_CTL_GRAB | Grab a still image from a video playback or recording session |
| PP_MM_SESSION_CTL_REFRESH | Refresh the display |
| PP_MM_SESSION_CTL_CUSTOM_BASE | Allow licensees to add custom control opcodes |

Playback may begin by calling MMSessionControl (sessionID, PP_MM_SESSION_CTL_RUN). Once playback begins, further opcodes may be issued to pause or stop playback.

Given an open media session, you may wish to allow your users to move forward or backward within the session, return to the beginning, or advance to the end. To move forward or backward within a session, you can call MMSessionSeek, which has the following prototype:

```
status_t MMSessionSeek (MMSessionID session,
MMSeekOrigin origin, int64_t position)
```

MMSessionSeek allows you to reposition to a different location within the current session. The origin argument specifies the point which you wish to seek from. This can be either P_MM_SEEK_ORIGIN_BEGIN to begin the seek at the beginning of the file, PP_MM_SEEK_ORIGIN_CURRENT to begin the seek at the current file location, or PP_MM_SEEK_ORIGIN_END to begin seeking at the end of the file.

The position argument specifies the distance to seek forward or backward. This value is expressed in nanoseconds; a negative value specifies a backward seek (a rewind), while a positive value signifies a forward seek (a fast forward).

## Sample Source Code for Playback

The following short example illustrates that although Palm OS Cobalt's multimedia library exposes a large number of functions, objects, properties, and constants, basic audio playback can be written as a fairly straightforward set of function calls:

```
MMSessionID sessionID;
status_t err;

// create the session as a default playback session
err = MMSessionCreate(P_MM_SESSION_CLASS_DEFAULT_PLAYBACK, 0,
      &sessionID);
if (err == 0)
{
    // specify the url name for the source media file
```

```
      err = MMSessionAddSource (sessionID,
          "file://localhost/Card1/MyMusic/TheSong.mp3", &sourceID);
   if (err == 0)
   {
      // ask Palm OS to prepare the source
      err = MMSourceFinalize (sourceID);
      if (err == 0)
      {
          // set up the default tracks
          err = MMSessionAddDefaultTracks (sessionID, sourceID,
              P_MM_DEFAULT_DEST);
          if (err ==0)
          {
             // Done! Now prepare for playback
            err = MMSessionFinalize (sessionID);
            if (err == 0)
            {
                // play some music!
                MMSessionControl (sessionID, P_MM_SESSION_CTL_RUN);
            }
          }
      }

   }
   }
}
```

# Summary

This chapter provided an overview of the sound and multimedia interfaces available in Palm OS Garnet and Palm OS Cobalt. You should now know the following:

❑   For Palm OS Garnet and Palm OS Cobalt, Sound Manager presents a simplified way to create simple sounds such as beeps and alerts, as well as WAV sounds, on a wide range of Palm OS handhelds.

❑   SndPlaySystemSound and SndDoCmd are the chief methods of making simple noises in all versions of Palm OS.

❑   In Palm OS 5 and later, use the SndPlayResource function to play sampled WAV sounds.

❑   Multimedia services in Palm OS Cobalt provides an advanced interface for interacting with rich media content in playback and recording

❑   Media sessions are used to control recording and playback. They are composed of sources, destinations, tracks, and streams.

# 13

# Programming
# Alarms and Time

One of the primary purposes of most Palm OS handhelds is to serve as organizers. Managing times and dates, therefore, is an important part of the operating system. Besides providing a wealth of time and date conversion and manipulation routines, Palm OS offers alarm facilities for performing actions at specific times or for alerting the user that a certain time has been reached. Alarms may be used not only to tell the handheld's user about upcoming appointments but also for scheduling background tasks. For example, an application could be set up to archive old records at a certain time each day, without any user intervention required.

As Palm OS handhelds become more connected, particularly wirelessly, it becomes possible for more and more events to compete for the user's attention. It's bad enough that a busy person, upon starting a handheld, may need to tap through several expired alarm dialog boxes before being able to use the handheld. This situation becomes more annoying if the handheld also can alert the user when it receives Short Message Service (SMS) messages or incoming e-mail. To alleviate the problems inherent in getting the user's attention, Palm OS 4.0 introduces the attention manager, a common user interface for alerting the user, in a polite and unobtrusive manner, that certain events have taken place.

This chapter shows you how to set and respond to alarms, use the Palm OS time and date facilities, and use the attention manager to make the user politely aware of events.

## Setting Alarms

Palm OS provides facilities for setting alarms based on the device's real-time clock, which may be used to display reminders or perform periodic tasks. Alarms actually wake up the handheld, bringing it out of sleep mode so it can perform some sort of processing, which may or may not include alerting the user with sound, vibration, or a dialog box. Setting and responding to alarms requires some cooperation between the system and your application.

Here are the steps required for setting and responding to an alarm, followed by sections that explain the process in greater detail:

1.  The application sets the alarm with `AlmSetAlarm`. The `AlmSetAlarm` function places a new alarm into the Palm OS alarm manager's queue. If multiple applications request the same alarm time, the alarm manager processes alarms on a first-requested, first-serviced basis. The alarm manager keeps track of only a single alarm for each application.

2.  When an alarm comes due, the system sends a `sysAppLaunchCmdAlarmTriggered` launch code to each application that has an alarm in the queue for the current time.

3.  The application responds to the `sysAppLaunchCmdAlarmTriggered` launch code. This launch code gives applications the chance to perform some sort of quick action, such as setting another alarm, playing a short sound, causing the handheld to vibrate, or performing some quick main-tenance activity. Anything the application does at this point should be very brief; otherwise, the application delays other applications with alarms set at the same time from responding in a timely fashion.

4.  Once all the applications with alarms set for the current time have dealt with the `sysAppLaunchCmdAlarmTriggered` launch code, the alarm manager sends a `sysAppLaunchCmdDisplayAlarm` code to each application with an alarm set for the current time.

5.  The application responds to the `sysAppLaunchCmdDisplayAlarm` launch code. Now that all applications with pending alarms for the current time have had a chance to do something quick with the `sysAppLaunchCmdAlarmTriggered` launch code, the application may perform some lengthy operation in response to the alarm, such as displaying a dialog box.

6.  If the applications are still displaying dialog boxes in response to the `sysAppLaunchCmdDisplayAlarm` launch code when another alarm comes due, the alarm man-ager sends a new `sysAppLaunchCmdAlarmTriggered` launch code to each application with a pending alarm for the new time. However, the system waits until the user dismisses the last alarm dialog box before sending out another batch of `sysAppLaunchCmdDisplayAlarm` codes.

## Setting an Alarm

Use the `AlmSetAlarm` function to set an alarm. The prototype for `AlmSetAlarm` looks like this:

**Palm OS Garnet**
```
Err AlmSetAlarm (UInt16 cardNo, LocalID dbID, UInt32 ref,
                 UInt32 alarmSeconds, Boolean quiet)
```

**Palm OS Cobalt**
```
status_t AlmSetAlarm (DatabaseID dbID, uint32_t ref,
                      uint32_t alarmSeconds, Boolean quiet)
```

The `cardNo` argument (Palm OS Garnet only) specifies the number of the storage card on which the application resides, and `dbID` is the database ID of the application. These two items may be obtained in Palm OS Garnet using the `DmGetNextDatabaseByTypeCreator` function, or in Palm OS Cobalt using the `DmFindDatabaseByTypeCreator` function. See the next example for more details.

Because an application does not have access to its global variables when responding to the two alarm launch codes, the ref argument provides a space for you to store information that the application might require when displaying the alarm. If you find that you need to pass more information than you can comfortably fit in the 32-bit integer provided by the ref argument, you might wish to consider using feature memory to store the extra data. See Chapter 15 for more information about using feature memory.

The alarmSeconds parameter is where you specify the actual time for the alarm, in seconds since January 1, 1904. Palm OS provides a number of useful functions for converting different time values to and from this seconds-since-1/1/1904 format. See the "Manipulating Time Values" section, later in this chapter, for descriptions of some of these functions.

The quiet argument is reserved for future use. For now, just pass the value true for this argument.

A sample code snippet follows, which sets an alarm three hours ahead of the current time. The creator ID for this example is stored in the global variable gAppCreatorID:

**Palm OS Garnet**

```
UInt16   cardNo;
LocalID  dbID;
DmSearchStateType  searchInfo;
UInt32   alarmTime, nowTime;


alarmTime = nowTime = TimGetSeconds();
alarmTime += 10800;  // 10800 seconds is three hours

DmGetNextDatabaseByTypeCreator(true, &searchInfo,
    sysFileTApplication, gAppCreatorID, true, &cardNo,
    &dbID);
AlmSetAlarm(cardNo, dbID, nowTime, alarmTime, true);
```

**Palm OS Cobalt**

```
DatabaseID  dbID;
uint32_t    alarmTime, nowTime;

alarmTime = nowTime = TimGetSeconds();
alarmTime += 10800;  // 10800 seconds is three hours

dbID = DmFindDatabaseByTypeCreator(sysFileTApplication,
    gAppCreatorID, dmFindAllDB, NULL);
if (dbID > 0)
    AlmSetAlarm(dbID, nowTime, alarmTime, true);
```

The preceding example not only sets an alarm three hours in the future, but stores the current time in the alarm's ref parameter via the nowTime variable. As a result, the application knows what time the alarm was set when the alarm goes off and the system sends the two alarm-related launch codes.

Because the alarm manager keeps track of only a single alarm for each application, calling AlmSetAlarm a second time before the first alarm has gone off replaces the first alarm with a new one. You can use the AlmGetAlarm function to retrieve the alarm settings for a particular application before overwriting the application's current alarm. If your application must keep track of more than one alarm time, you need to store that information with the application's data in storage RAM.

*Alarms may trigger a bit late when the handheld is "off," or in sleep mode. This happens because the main system clock (which keeps track of time down to the nearest hundredth of a second) is shut down in sleep mode and the real-time clock on the device (which keeps track of time only to the nearest whole second) — and is still active during sleep mode — does not have the fine granularity of the main system clock. As a result, alarms that trigger while the device is "on" occur at exactly the time you expect them to go off, but alarms that trigger in sleep mode may be up to a minute late.*

# Responding to Alarms

The first launch code your application needs to respond to when an alarm goes off is `sysAppLaunchCmdAlarmTriggered`. At this point, your application should perform only quick actions in response to the alarm to keep from delaying any alarms set by other applications for the same time. Such actions may include setting the application's next alarm or playing a short sound.

When your application handles `sysAppLaunchCmdDisplayAlarm`, it has a chance to perform lengthier actions in response to the alarm, such as displaying a pop-up dialog box to show the user whatever information the application needs to convey as a result of the alarm's going off.

Unless you need only a couple lines of code to respond to `sysAppLaunchCmdAlarmTriggered` and `sysAppLaunchCmdDisplayAlarm`, you should hand off processing of the launch codes from your `PilotMain` routine to other functions. This technique makes the code in your application's `PilotMain` routine more readable and easier to maintain. It also is easier to process the launch codes' parameter blocks if you need to retrieve any information that the system passes with those launch codes. The following `PilotMain` routine passes the handling of the two alarm launch codes to the functions `AlarmTriggered` and `DisplayAlarm`:

**Palm OS Garnet**

```
UInt32 PilotMain(UInt16 cmd, MemPtr cmdPBP, UInt16 launchFlags)
{
    switch (cmd) {
        case sysAppLaunchCmdNormalLaunch:
            // Normal launch code handling omitted.

        case sysAppLaunchCmdAlarmTriggered:
            AlarmTriggered((SysAlarmTriggeredParamType *)
                        cmdPBP);
            break;

        case sysAppLaunchCmdDisplayAlarm:
            DisplayAlarm(
                (SysDisplayAlarmParamType *) cmdPBP);
            break;

        default:
            break;
    }

    return 0;
}
```

**Palm OS Cobalt**

```
uint32_t PilotMain(uint16_t cmd, MemPtr cmdPBP, uint16_t launchFlags)
{
    status_t error = errNone;

    if ((error = SysGetModuleDatabase(SysGetRefNum(), NULL,
        &gAppDB)) < errNone)
        return error;

    switch (cmd)
    {
        case sysAppLaunchCmdNormalLaunch:
            // Normal launch code handling omitted.

        case sysAppLaunchCmdAlarmTriggered:
            AlarmTriggered((SysAlarmTriggeredParamType *)
                        cmdPBP);
            break;

        case sysAppLaunchCmdDisplayAlarm:
            DisplayAlarm(
                (SysDisplayAlarmParamType *) cmdPBP);
            break;

        default:
            break;
    }

    return errNone;
}
```

Because the `cmdPBP` variable that contains the parameter block for a launch code is actually just a pointer to type `void`, `PilotMain` must cast `cmdPBP` to the appropriate structure before passing the parameter block to another function. The Palm OS header file `AlarmMgr.h` defines the following structures for alarm-related launch codes:

**Palm OS Garnet**

```
typedef struct SysAlarmTriggeredParamType {
    UInt32   ref;
    UInt32   alarmSeconds;
    Boolean  purgeAlarm;
    UInt8    padding;
} SysAlarmTriggeredParamType;

typedef struct SysDisplayAlarmParamType {
    UInt32   ref;
    UInt32   alarmSeconds;
    Boolean  soundAlarm;
} SysDisplayAlarmParamType;
```

**Palm OS Cobalt**

```
typedef struct SysAlarmTriggeredParamType {
    uint32_t  ref;
    uint32_t  alarmSeconds;
```

```
        Boolean    purgeAlarm;
        uint8_t    padding;
        uint16_t   padding1;
} SysAlarmTriggeredParamType;

typedef struct SysDisplayAlarmParamType {
        uint32_t   ref;
        uint32_t   alarmSeconds;
        Boolean    soundAlarm;
        uint8_t    padding;
        uint16_t   padding;
} SysDisplayAlarmParamType;
```

In both `SysAlarmTriggeredParamType` and `SysDisplayAlarmParamType`, the `ref` member stores extra application-defined data related to the alarm, and `alarmSeconds` holds the actual time of the alarm, in seconds since January 1, 1904.

If your application sets the `purgeAlarm` member of `SysAlarmTriggeredParamType` to `true`, the alarm manager does not send a `sysAppLaunchCmdDisplayAlarm` code to the application for that alarm. Set `purgeAlarm` to `true` if your application completely handles incoming alarms when it takes care of the `sysAppLaunchCmdAlarmTriggered` launch code. By default, `purgeAlarm` is `false`, so if you do not fiddle with the value of `purgeAlarm`, the system will send a `sysAppLaunchCmdDisplayAlarm` code to your application.

According to PalmSource documentation, the `soundAlarm` member of `SysDisplayAlarmParamType` should be `true` if the alarm is to be sounded; `false` otherwise. However, the system does not currently use `soundAlarm`, so you can safely ignore this value. You can also ignore `padding` and `padding1` in both `SysAlarmTriggeredParamType` and `SysDisplayAlarmParamType`.

Typically, the `AlarmTriggered` function called from the `PilotMain` function in the previous example would contain a call to `SndPlaySystemSound` to trigger the system default alarm sound. If the application stores more than one alarm at a time in its permanent database, `AlarmTriggered` should then look through that database for the next alarm time and set that alarm with a call to `AlmSetAlarm`. Playing sounds in Palm OS is covered in Chapter 12. Retrieving values stored in an application's database is covered in Chapter 15.

Displaying a dialog box in response to `sysAppLaunchCmdAlarmTriggered` can be somewhat tricky because your application might not be running at the time and must display a dialog box over the top of another application. The following example defines a `DisplayAlarm` function to take care of displaying a simple alarm dialog box to the user:

**Palm OS Garnet**

```
static void DisplayAlarm (SysDisplayAlarmParamType *cmdPBP)
{
    FormType    *form, *curForm;


    form = FrmInitForm(AlarmForm);
    curForm = FrmGetActiveForm();
    if (curForm)
        FrmSetActiveForm(form);
```

```
        FrmSetEventHandler(form, AlarmFormHandleEvent);
        FrmDrawForm(form);

        // Do something here with cmdPBP->alarmSeconds or
        // cmdPBP->ref, such as drawing those values to the
        // alarm display using WinDrawChars.

        FrmDoDialog(form);
        FrmDeleteForm(form);
        FrmSetActiveForm(curForm);
}
```

**Palm OS Cobalt**
```
static void DisplayAlarm (SysDisplayAlarmParamType *cmdPBP)
{
    FormType  *form, *curForm;


    form = FrmInitForm(gAppDB, AlarmForm);
    curForm = FrmGetActiveForm();
    if (curForm)
         FrmSetActiveForm(form);
    FrmSetEventHandler(form, AlarmFormHandleEvent);
    FrmDrawForm(form);

    // Do something here with cmdPBP->alarmSeconds or
    // cmdPBP->ref, such as drawing those values to the
    // alarm display using WinDrawChars.

    FrmDoDialog(form);
    FrmDeleteForm(form);
    FrmSetActiveForm(curForm);
}
```

In the previous example, DisplayAlarm first initializes a new form object with FrmInitForm. The DisplayAlarm function then saves the currently displayed form in the variable curForm so that the application can return to whatever form is currently onscreen when the alarm goes off. Storing the active form in this way is important because the application handling the alarm might not be active when the alarm goes off. Suddenly changing to another application in the middle of what the user is doing can be disorienting at best, or downright rude at worst.

After storing the current form for later use, DisplayAlarm sets an event handler for the alarm form. Depending on the needs of the application, the AlarmFormHandleEvent function can be as simple or as complex as the alarm dialog box requires. One thing that should be included in the alarm dialog box's event handler, though, is a response to the appStopEvent that prevents the user from switching to another application until the dialog box has been dismissed. Switching to another application while the alarm dialog box is displayed can cause a system crash because the alarm dialog box is probably displayed over the top of another application. Also, trapping appStopEvent serves a very practical purpose: If the user doesn't hear the alarm go off, or has the system alarm sound turned off, the dialog box will be the first thing the user sees when turning on the device again. Here is a short AlarmFormHandleEvent function that traps appStopEvent:

```
static Boolean AlarmFormHandleEvent(EventType *event)
{
    if (event->eType == appStopEvent)
        return true;
    else
        return false;
}
```

Moving back to the `DisplayAlarm` example, once an event handler has been set for the dialog box, `DisplayAlarm` draws the alarm dialog box with `FrmDrawForm`. At this point, the application can perform any custom drawing required on the alarm dialog box, possibly using the values passed from the parameter block in the `sysAppLaunchCmdDisplayAlarm` launch code. The `DisplayAlarm` function then displays the dialog box using `FrmDoDialog`. Although the preceding example ignores the return value from `FrmDoDialog`, it also could respond differently depending upon which dialog box button the user tapped.

After the user dismisses the alarm dialog box, `DisplayAlarm` removes the dialog box from memory with `FrmDeleteForm` and then restores with `FrmSetActiveForm` the active status of the form that was on the screen before the alarm dialog box appeared.

> **Be sure to set the Save Behind attribute of the alarm dialog box when designing its form resource. Without this attribute, the screen quickly becomes a mess because the system tries to draw the alarm dialog box over the top of the current form without first clearing it from the screen.**

## *Responding to Other Launch Codes*

There are two other launch codes that you should consider responding to in an alarm-enabled application: `sysAppLaunchCmdSystemReset` and `sysAppLaunchCmdTimeChange`.

The Palm OS alarm manager does not keep track of the alarm queue across system resets. This means that after any system reset, all alarms disappear from the system. Fortunately, the system sends a `sysAppLaunchCmdSystemReset` launch code to every application after a system reset. To make your application's alarms persist across system resets, respond to the `sysAppLaunchCmdSystemReset` launch code by retrieving the next appropriate alarm time from your application's stored data and then setting that time in the system alarm queue with `AlmSetAlarm`.

When the user or an application changes the system time, the operating system sends a `sysAppLaunchCmdTimeChange` launch code to every application. Applications that handle alarms might be interested in this event. By default, if an application has an alarm in the queue and the user changes the system clock to a time beyond the set alarm, the alarm immediately goes off when the clock is changed. For most applications, this is desirable behavior because it ensures that the user does not miss any alarms set between the old system time and the new system time. However, some applications may need to reset alarms in response to a change in system time; the `sysAppLaunchCmdTimeChange` launch code allows your application to do just that.

# Manipulating Time Values

Because keeping track of dates and times is a common use for handheld computers, Palm OS provides many functions for retrieving, converting, and altering time values.

Internally, the system's real-time clock keeps track of time as a 32-bit unsigned integer, representing the number of seconds since midnight, January 1, 1904. The real-time clock keeps track of the date and time in one-second increments, even while the device is in sleep mode. A Palm OS device also has a faster timer, which keeps track of time in *system ticks*. System ticks occur 100 times per second on an actual Palm OS device, or 60 times per second in a Palm OS Simulator application running in Mac OS. The system resets the ticks counter to zero whenever the device is reset, and the ticks counter does not update while the device is in sleep mode.

Palm OS uses three basic structures in many of its time functions to keep track of the date, time, or date and time as a single unit. These structures are defined in the Palm OS header file `DateTime.h`, shown in the following example:

**Palm OS Garnet**

```
typedef struct {
    Int16   second;
    Int16   minute;
    Int16   hour;
    Int16   day;
    Int16   month;
    Int16   year;
    Int16   weekDay;  // Days since Sunday (0 to 6)
} DateTimeType;

typedef struct {
    UInt8   hours;
    UInt8   minutes;
} TimeType;

typedef struct {
    UInt16  year  :7;  // Years since 1904 (Mac format)
    UInt16  month :4;
    UInt16  day   :5;
} DateType;
```

**Palm OS Cobalt**

```
typedef struct {
    int16_t  second;
    int16_t  minute;
    int16_t  hour;
    int16_t  day;
    int16_t  month;
    int16_t  year;
    int16_t  weekDay;  // Days since Sunday (0 to 6)
} DateTimeType;

typedef struct {
#if CPU_ENDIAN == CPU_ENDIAN_BIG
    uint16_t hours   :8;
    uint16_t minutes :8;
```

```
#elif CPU_ENDIAN == CPU_ENDIAN_LITTLE
    uint16_t  minutes :8;
    uint16_t  hours   :8;
} TimeType;


#if (BITFIELD_LAYOUT == MSB_TO_LSB)
    typedef struct {
        uint16_t  year  :7;   // Years since 1904 (Mac format)
        uint16_t  month :4;
        uint16_t  day   :5;
    }

#elif (BITFIELD_LAYOUT == LSB_TO_MSB)
    typedef struct {
        uint16_t  day   :5;
        uint16_t  month :4;
        uint16_t  year  :7;   // Years since 1904 (Mac format)
    }
#endif
```

Notice that the TimeType and DateType structures for Palm OS Cobalt contain conditional compilation that defines different structures based on the endianness of the handheld. If your application uses only the Palm OS time and date functions to manipulate TimeType and DateType data, you don't need to worry about endianness. However, if your application must read or write the internal members of TimeType or DateType directly, be sure to pay attention to whether your application's target device is big-endian or little-endian. As of this writing, Palm OS Cobalt devices run on only the ARM platform, which is little-endian, but future Palm OS hardware may use a different, big-endian processor architecture.

## *Retrieving and Setting Time Values*

The TimGetSeconds function retrieves the current time from the system's real-time clock, in seconds since midnight, January 1, 1904. You also can set the system clock by passing the appropriate seconds-past-1/1/1904 value to the TimSetSeconds function.

You can implement finer timing by using the TimGetTicks function, which retrieves the number of ticks that have passed since the last time the device was soft-reset. Because ticks can vary in length between devices, the Palm OS headers define macros that convert system ticks into more conventional units of time. In Palm OS Garnet, use the SysTicksPerSecond macro to retrieve the number of ticks per second on the device and then divide the value from TimGetTicks by the value returned by SysTicksPerSecond to get the actual time in seconds since the device was last reset, as in the following example:

**Palm OS Garnet**
```
UInt16 secondsSinceReset = TimGetTicks() /
    SysTicksPerSecond();
```

Palm OS Cobalt also defines macros for converting time values from system ticks into more conventional units, such as milliseconds. In addition, Palm OS Cobalt defines macros for converting regular time units back into system ticks. The following table describes the time conversion macros available in Palm OS Cobalt.

| Palm OS Cobalt Macro | Description |
|---|---|
| SysTimeInMicroSecs | Converts microseconds to system ticks |
| SysTimeInMilliSecs | Converts milliseconds to system ticks |
| SysTimeInCentiSecs | Converts centiseconds to system ticks |
| SysTimeInSecs | Converts seconds to system ticks |
| SysTimeInMins | Converts minutes to system ticks |
| SysTimeToSecs | Converts system ticks to seconds |
| SysTimeToMilliSecs | Converts system ticks to milliseconds |
| SysTimeToMicroSecs | Converts system ticks to microseconds |

The SysTicksPerSecond macro is defined in Palm OS Cobalt, but it is deprecated and may not be available in future versions of the operating system. Instead of calling TimGetTicks and dividing its result by SysTicksPerSecond, pass the result of the TimGetTicks call directly to the SysTimeToSecs macro to get the time, in seconds, since the device was last reset, as in the following example:

**Palm OS Cobalt**
```
uint64_t secondsSinceReset = SysTimeToSecs(TimGetTicks());
```

> The **TimGetTicks** function was changed in Palm OS Cobalt to return **uint64_t** (a 64-bit unsigned integer) instead of the smaller **UInt16** (16-bit unsigned integer) that is returned by earlier versions of the **TimGetTicks** function. Be sure variables that contain tick counts in Palm OS Cobalt are declared as **uint64_t**.

## Converting Time Values

The TimSecondsToDateTime function converts between the internal seconds-past-1/1/1904 value to a DateTimeType structure. You can convert from a DateTimeType structure back to seconds using TimDateTimeToSeconds. Much as the TimSecondsToDateTime function does, DateSecondsToDate converts seconds since 1/1/1904 into a DateType structure but there is no corresponding function to convert a DateType structure back into seconds.

More functions that use the DateType structure include DateDaysToDate, which converts the number of days since 1/1/1904 into a DateType structure, and DateToDays, which converts a DateType structure into the number of days past 1/1/1904.

The function DateToAscii allows the conversion of a particular date to an ASCII string, suitable for display to the user. The prototype for DateToAscii looks like this:

**Palm OS Garnet**
```
void DateToAscii (UInt8 months, UInt8 days, UInt16 years,
    DateFormatType dateFormat, Char *pString)
```

369

**Palm OS Cobalt**

```
void DateToAscii (uint8_t months, uint8_t days,
    uint16_t years, DateFormatType dateFormat,
    char *pString)
```

The first three arguments to `DateToAscii` allow you to specify the month (from 1 to 12), day (from 1 to 31), and year (in a four-digit format) to convert to text. The `dateFormat` argument specifies the format that the date should take, as defined by the `DateFormatType` enum in the Palm OS header file `DateTime.h`:

```
typedef enum {
    dfMDYWithSlashes,        // 12/31/04
    dfDMYWithSlashes,        // 31/12/04
    dfDMYWithDots,           // 31.12.04
    dfDMYWithDashes,         // 31-12-04
    dfYMDWithSlashes,        // 04/12/31
    dfYMDWithDots,           // 04.12.31
    dfYMDWithDashes,         // 04-12-31

    dfMDYLongWithComma,      // Dec 31, 2004
    dfDMYLong,               // 31 Dec 2004
    dfDMYLongWithDot,        // 31. Dec 2004
    dfDMYLongNoDay,          // Dec 2004
    dfDMYLongWithComma,      // 31 Dec, 2004
    dfYMDLongWithDot,        // 2004.12.31
    dfYMDLongWithSpace,      // 2004 Dec 31

    dfMYMed,                 // Dec '04
    dfMYMedNoPost            // Dec 04
    dfMDYWithDashes          // 12-31-04
} DateFormatType;
```

The `pString` argument is a pointer to a string to receive the converted date text. The string pointed to by `pString` must be of length `dateStringLength` for short date strings, or length `longDateStringLength` for long date formats.

The `DateToDOWDMFormat` takes the same arguments as `DateToAscii` but adds a three-letter day-of-week abbreviation to the front of whatever string format is specified by the `dateFormat` argument. For example, the following call to `DateToDOWDMFormat` fills the variable `dateStr` with the string `Sun Dec 31, 1995`:

```
DateToDOWDMFormat(12, 31, 1995, dfMDYLongWithComma, dateStr);
```

If you need to determine which ordinal day of the month a particular date falls on, use the `DayOfMonth` function. The value returned by this function is not the cardinal date (for example, 31 for the 31st of December) but rather the day's relative position within the month (for example, the last Sunday of December). The `DayOfMonth` function returns a value from the enum `DayOfMonthType`, defined in `DateTime.h` as follows:

```
#define DayOfWeekType DayOfMonthType
typedef enum {
    dom1stSun, dom1stMon, dom1stTue, dom1stWen, dom1stThu,
```

```
        dom1stFri, dom1stSat,
    dom2ndSun, dom2ndMon, dom2ndTue, dom2ndWen, dom2ndThu,
        dom2ndFri, dom2ndSat,
    dom3rdSun, dom3rdMon, dom3rdTue, dom3rdWen, dom3rdThu,
        dom3rdFri, dom3rdSat,
    dom4thSun, dom4thMon, dom4thTue, dom4thWen, dom4thThu,
        dom4thFri, dom4thSat,
    domLastSun, domLastMon, domLastTue, domLastWen,
        domLastThu, domLastFri, domLastSat
} DayOfWeekType;
```

*DayOfMonthType is actually defined as DayOfWeekType to maintain compatibility with existing code. PalmSource recommends that you use DayOfMonthType instead of using the DayOfWeekType enumeration directly for future compatibility.*

The DaysInMonth function returns the number of days in a month, given a month and a year. Palm OS also provides the DayOfWeek function, which — when given a month, day, and year — returns the day of the week as a value from 0 to 6, where 0 represents Sunday.

*The return value from DayOfWeek is not affected by the user preference that determines whether the beginning of the week is on Sunday or Monday. DayOfWeek always returns 0 for Sunday.*

## Altering Time Values

Two functions, DateAdjust and TimAdjust, allow for quick changes in dates, thus freeing you of the burden of manually changing the month or year when simple math on dates (additions or subtractions of a certain amount of time to or from an initial date) would cause the date to wrap to a new month or year.

The DateAdjust function takes a pointer to a DateType structure and a number of days as arguments, altering the passed DateType structure by the specified number of days. If the number of days is positive, DateAdjust adds the days to the date; for a negative number of days, DateAdjust subtracts the number of days.

The TimAdjust function works like DateAdjust, except that it modifies a DateTimeType structure by a specified number of seconds.

# Following User Date and Time Preferences

Palm OS stores a variety of user preferences for how dates and times should be displayed — for example, in 12- or 24-hour format. Users set these preferences in the system Prefs application. It is your application's responsibility to display dates and times in the format chosen by the user.

You can find out what the user's date and time preferences are by passing an appropriate constant to the PrefGetPreference function. The following example retrieves the user's preferred time display format:

```
TimeFormatType  timeFormat;

timeFormat = PrefGetPreference(prefTimeFormat);
```

The following table describes the time and date constants that you can pass to PrefGetPreference, as well as the data type that PrefGetPreference returns for each preference.

| Constant | PrefGetPreference Return Type | Description |
| --- | --- | --- |
| prefDateFormat | DateFormatType | Short date format. For example, "9/24/73" for the 24th of September, 1973. |
| prefLongDateFormat | DateFormatType | Long date format. For example, "Sep 24, 1973" for the 24th of September, 1973. |
| prefTimeFormat | TimeFormatType | Time format. |
| prefWeekStartDay | UInt32 or uint32_t | Starting day of the week. A return value of 0 represents Sunday and a value of 1 represents Monday. |
| prefMinutesWestOfGMT | UInt32 or uint32_t | Local time zone, expressed as the number of minutes *east* of Greenwich Mean Time (GMT). Note that it's east, not west, as the name of the constant erroneously claims. In Palm OS 4.0 or later, use prefTimeZone instead of prefMinutesWestOfGMT. Possible values range from 0 to 1440. |
| prefTimeZone | Int32 or int32_t | Local time zone, expressed as the number of minutes east or west of GMT. The prefTimeZone preference is available only on Palm OS 4.0 or later. Possible values range from -720 to 720. |
| prefDaylightSavings | DaylightSavingsTypes | Local rules for Daylight Saving Time (DST). The DaylightSavingsTypes enumerated type describes different forms of DST according to country or region. For example, dsUSA represents the United States and dsEasternEuropean represents eastern Europe. In Palm OS 4.0 and later, use the more flexible prefDaylightSavingsAdjustment instead of prefDaylightSavings. |

| Constant | PrefGetPreference Return Type | Description |
|---|---|---|
| prefDaylightSavingAdjustment | UInt32 or uint32_t | Number of minutes by which the time should be adjusted for DST. This value is normally 0 for no adjustment or 60 to adjust the time one hour, but prefDaylightSavingAdjustment allows for smaller DST adjustments in those areas of the world that use them. The prefDaylightSavingAdjustment preference is available only in Palm OS 4.0 and later. |

An application also can set date and time preferences programmatically, overriding the preferences the user has set in the Prefs panel, by using the PrefSetPreference function. The following example sets the handheld's time format preference to 24-hour time, using a colon (:) as a separator between hours and minutes:

**Palm OS Garnet**
```
PrefSetPreference(prefTimeFormat, (UInt32) tfColon24h);
```

**Palm OS Cobalt**
```
PrefSetPreference(prefTimeFormat, (uint32_t) tfColon24h);
```

The TimeFormatType enumerated type is defined in DateTime.h as follows:

```
typedef enum
{
    tfColon,
    tfColonAMPM, // 1:00 pm
    tfColon24h,  // 13:00
    tfDot,
    tfDotAMPM,   // 1.00 pm
    tfDot24h,    // 13.00
    tfHoursAMPM, // 1 pm
    tfHours24h,  // 13
    tfComma24h   // 13,00
} TimeFormatType;
```

Changing the time zone or DST preferences does not automatically update the system clock to match the new settings. If your application changes these preferences, it also should adjust the current time by calling TimSetSeconds. If your application adjusts the clock as well as the preferences, ensure that your program alters the preferences before changing the time. When you change the time with TimSetSeconds, Palm OS sends a notification to other applications that the time has just changed, which gives those applications a chance to modify their own settings in accordance with the new information. However, when the user or an application changes the time zone or DST preferences, the operating system does not send any kind of notification to other programs. Setting the time zone or DST preference before changing the time ensures that other applications will know about the new time zone or DST settings when they react to the time change notification. For more details on using `PrefGetPreference` and `PrefSetPreference`, see Chapter 15.

# Getting the User's Attention

On Palm Powered handhelds that can receive communications without any input from the user, such as devices with embedded mobile phones or Bluetooth wireless hardware, it can be difficult for a user to make sense of the many different alarms and messages that a handheld displays. Palm OS 4.0 introduces the attention manager, a common interface for applications to politely bring items to the user's attention.

The attention manager itself does not handle alarms, but an application can use the attention manager in conjunction with the Palm OS alarm facility. Typically, an application sets an alarm and, in response to that alarm's triggering, the application uses the attention manager to display a dialog box, play a sound, vibrate the handheld, flash an LED, or perform a combination of attention-getting actions, depending on the capabilities of the particular hardware. Your application controls how insistent it wants to be about getting the user's attention, ranging from a subtle flashing icon in the title bar of the current application to a dialog box that must be manually dismissed.

> *The attention manager is not intended to prompt the user for immediate action. For example, if your application needs to prompt the user to connect to another handheld, use a regular alert dialog box because most communications time out after a relatively short period of time, often less than a minute. Because the attention manager is intended for use in situations where the handheld may be turned off when the appointed time arrives, use the attention manager to bring items to the user's attention that may be postponed, such as appointments or incoming e-mail messages.*

The most insistent method the attention manager has for getting a user's attention is to display a modal dialog box, which the user then must dismiss before doing anything else with the handheld. This dialog box has space for details about the event that triggered the dialog box, so it is called the detail dialog box. Figure 13-1 shows a typical detail dialog box, which displays an alarm generated by the built-in Date Book application.

Figure 13-1

The attention manager draws the title bar and buttons in the details dialog box, but the application that is requesting attention fills in the rest of the space in the dialog box with information that identifies the reason for the dialog box's existence. Tapping OK dismisses the dialog box, returning the user to the application that is already running. Tapping Snooze dismisses the dialog box for five minutes, at which point the attention manager makes another attempt to get the user's attention. Tapping the Go To button launches the application that called the attention manager. The application displays details about the event that triggered the dialog box.

If a second application makes an attempt to get the user's attention while the detail dialog box is still displayed, or if the original application asks for the user's attention a second time before the user has dismissed the detail dialog box, the attention manager displays the list dialog box (see Figure 13-2).

Figure 13-2

The list dialog box displays a list of all the attempts that the attention manager has made to get the user's attention. The attention manager draws the title bar, buttons, and check boxes in this dialog box, but each application that uses the attention manager is responsible for drawing an icon and a couple of lines of text for each attention item. Tapping the Done button temporarily dismisses the list dialog box, without actually removing any attention items from its display. Tapping Snooze also doesn't remove anything from the list; like the Snooze button in the details dialog box, it dismisses the list dialog box for five minutes, at which point the dialog box reappears. Tapping the Clear All button in the list dialog box removes all pending events from the attention manager's list.

> *There is only one snooze timer, which is used by the attention manager for all events, and the timer always resets to five minutes when the user taps the Snooze button in either a detail or list dialog box.*

If an application chooses to be subtle in its attempt to get the user's attention, the attention manager draws a flashing "star" icon in the title bar of whatever application happens to be running at the time (see Figure 13-3).

Figure 13-3

If the list dialog box contains only items that the user has already seen, either from viewing the list dialog box or from seeing them in a detail dialog box, the attention icon simply flashes on and off. If there are items in the list dialog box that the user has not yet seen, the attention icon performs an "exploding star" animation. In either case, tapping the attention icon opens the list dialog box.

# Requesting Attention

Telling the attention manager to request the user's attention is a simple matter of calling the `AttnGetAttention` function, which has the following prototype:

**Palm OS Garnet**

```
Err AttnGetAttention (UInt16 cardNo, LocalID dbID,
    UInt32 userData, AttnCallbackProc *callbackFnP,
    AttnLevelType level, AttnFlagsType flags,
    UInt16 nagRateInSeconds, UInt16 nagRepeatLimit)
```

**Palm OS Cobalt**

```
status_t AttnGetAttention (DatabaseID dbID,
    uint32_t userData, AttnLevelType level,
    AttnFlagsType flags, uint16_t nagRateInSeconds,
    uint16_t nagRepeatLimit)
```

The `cardNo` and `dbID` parameters define the card number and database ID of the application that is making the attention request. In Palm OS Garnet retrieve these values by calling the `DmGetNextDatabaseByTypeCreator` function. In Palm OS Cobalt, the `cardNo` parameter does not exist; use the `DmFindDatabaseByTypeCreator` function to retrieve the database ID. For details about using `DmGetNextDatabaseByTypeCreator` and `DmFindDatabaseByTypeCreator`, see Chapter 15.

You can pass any data you wish in the `userData` parameter. The attention manager passes this data back to your application through either a callback function or a special `sysAppLaunchCmdAttention` launch code. The data in `userData` can be any 32-bit value, even a pointer to memory containing a larger amount of data. Most applications pass the unique ID of a record that contains data unique to the attention attempt.

The `callbackFnP` parameter is a pointer to a callback function that the attention manager calls when it needs to display or remove an attention item. You also may specify NULL instead of a function pointer, in which case the attention manager communicates with your application through the `sysAppLaunchCmdAttention` launch code instead of directly calling a function in your application. The next section of this chapter, "Responding to the Attention Manager," shows the steps your application must take to properly respond to attention requests.

> Callback functions are not supported under Palm OS Cobalt, so the `callbackFnP` parameter does not exist in the Palm OS Cobalt version of the `AttnGetAttention` function. Palm OS Cobalt applications must use the `sysAppLaunchCmdAttention` launch code to respond to attention manager requests.

The level parameter defines how annoying the attention manager should be when trying to get the user's attention. You can specify two different values for this parameter:

❑ **kAttnLevelInsistent.** The attention manager displays a dialog box that interrupts whatever the user is currently doing on the handheld. Optionally, the attention attempt also may use other effects to get the user's attention, such as playing a sound, vibrating the handheld, or flashing an LED.

❑ **kAttnLevelSubtle.** The attention manager adds an item to its list without displaying a dialog box. A subtle attention attempt may still include special effects like playing sounds but it won't interrupt the user with a modal dialog box that must be dismissed.

You can customize the behavior of the attention request by setting values in the flags parameter. The flags parameter is a bit field, which may have a combination of the constant values described in the following table.

| Constant | Value | Description |
|---|---|---|
| kAttnFlagsSoundBit | 0x0001 | Plays a sound |
| kAttnFlagsLEDBit | 0x0002 | Flashes an LED if the handheld is properly equipped |
| kAttnFlagsVibrateBit | 0x0004 | Vibrates the handheld if it is properly equipped |
| kAttnFlagsCustomEffectBit | 0x0008 | Triggers an application-specific custom effect to get the user's attention |
| kAttnFlagsAllBits | 0xFFFF | Uses all available means to get the user's attention |
| kAttnFlagsUseUserSettings | 0x0000 | Obeys the user's system preferences to determine what methods to use for getting attention |

The Palm OS header file AttentionMgr.h also defines a number of useful constants that allow you to override the user's system preferences. These constants are outlined in the following table.

| Constant | Value | Description |
|---|---|---|
| kAttnFlagsAlwaysSound | kAttnFlagsSoundBit | Plays a sound, regardless of user preferences |
| kAttnFlagsAlwaysLED | kAttnFlagsLEDBit | Flashes an LED, regardless of user preferences |
| kAttnFlagsAlwaysVibrate | kAttnFlagsVibrateBit | Vibrates the handheld, regardless of user preferences |
| kAttnFlagsAlwaysCustomEffect | kAttnFlagsCustomEffectBit | Activates an application-specific custom effect |

*Table continued on following page*

| Constant | Value | Description |
|---|---|---|
| kAttnFlagsEverything | kAttnFlagsAllBits | Uses all available means to get the user's attention, regardless of user preferences |
| kAttnFlagsNoSound | kAttnFlagsSound Bit << 16 | Prevents sound from playing, regardless of user preferences |
| kAttnFlagsNoLED | kAttnFlagsLEDBit << 16 | Prevents an LED from flashing, regardless of user preferences |
| kAttnFlagsNoVibrate | kAttnFlagsVibrate Bit << 16 | Prevents the handheld from vibrating, regardless of user preferences |
| kAttnFlagsNoCustomEffect | kAttnFlagsCustom EffectBit << 16 | Prevents an application-specific custom effect |
| kAttnFlagsNothing | kAttnFlagsAll Bits << 16 | Prevents all attention-getting methods from being triggered, regardless of user preferences |

The various kAttnFlags constants may be combined to selectively turn different attention-getting mechanisms on and off. For example, the following line of code tells the attention manager only to vibrate the handheld (assuming the handheld has that capability), regardless of user preferences:

```
flags = kAttnFlagsNothing ^ kAttnFlagsNoVibrate |
        kAttnFlagsAlwaysVibrate;
```

The nagRateInSeconds parameter controls how often the attention manager attempts to get the user's attention, using the special effects defined by the flags parameter. Every nagRateInSeconds seconds, the attention manger triggers whatever special effects are assigned to the attention attempt. The attention manager continues trying to get the user's attention until either the user dismisses the attention item or a number of attempts equal to the value in the nagRepeatLimit parameter is reached.

As an example of how AttnGetAttention works, the following call displays a dialog box, obeying the user's preferences for what types of special effects should be used. If the user does not immediately dismiss the dialog box, the attention manager repeats the special effects three more times, at one-minute intervals from the time the dialog box first appeared. The application calling AttnGetAttention handles requests for the drawing and removal of an attention item by responding to the sysAppLaunchCmdAttention launch code.

**Palm OS Garnet**
```
AttnGetAttention(cardNo, dbID, NULL, NULL,
                kAttnLevelInsistent,
                kAttnFlagsUseUserSettings, 60, 3);
```

**Palm OS Cobalt**
```
AttnGetAttention(dbID, NULL, kAttnLevelInsistent,
                kAttnFlagsUseUserSettings, 60, 3);
```

# Responding to the Attention Manager

In Palm OS Garnet, you need to define a callback function to respond to requests from the attention manager to draw or remove an attention item only if your application is a shared library or a system extension. Regular applications should use the simpler mechanism of handling the sysAppLaunchCmdAttention launch code.

Palm OS Cobalt does not support callbacks, but shared libraries and system extensions in Palm OS Cobalt do have access to launch codes, so they can handle the sysAppLaunchCmdAttention launch code just like any normal application.

The sysAppLaunchCmdAttention launch code is accompanied by an AttnLaunchCodeArgsType structure, which contains further details about what the attention manager would like your application to do. The AttnLaunchCodeArgsType structure looks like this:

**Palm OS Garnet**

```
typedef struct {
    AttnCommandType command;
    UInt32 userData;
    AttnCommandArgsType *commandArgsP;
} AttnLaunchCodeArgsType;
```

**Palm OS Cobalt**

```
typedef struct {
    AttnCommandType command;
    uint16_t padding;
    uint32_t userData;
    AttnCommandArgsType *commandArgsP;
} AttnLaunchCodeArgsType;
```

The command field specifies the type of action your application should take. The following table describes the possible values for the command field.

| Constant | Value | Requested action |
| --- | --- | --- |
| kAttnCommandDrawDetail | 1 | Draws appropriate information in the detail dialog box. |
| kAttnCommandDrawList | 2 | Draws appropriate information in the list dialog box. |
| kAttnCommandPlaySound | 3 | Plays a sound. |
| kAttnCommandCustomEffect | 4 | Performs some kind of custom attention-getting effect. |
| kAttnCommandGoThere | 5 | Goes to a particular record and displays it. |
| kAttnCommandGotIt | 6 | Takes appropriate action based on the fact that the user dismisses an item. For example, your application may need to free memory allocated for an item. |

*Table continued on following page*

| Constant | Value | Requested action |
| --- | --- | --- |
| kAttnCommandSnooze | 7 | Takes appropriate action based on the fact that the user taps a Snooze button. Applications normally leave this action unhandled. |
| kAttnCommandIterate | 8 | Takes appropriate action while the attention manager iterates through the entire list of queued attention items. This action gives your application an opportunity to update or remove stale and invalid items — for example, after a HotSync operation. |

The padding field only occurs in the Palm OS Cobalt version of AttnLaunchCodeArgsType; it is for system use only, so you can ignore it.

The userData field in AttnLaunchCodeArgsType contains any application-defined data that your program passed to the attention manager via the AttnGetAttention function's userData parameter. This is a good place to put the unique ID of a record from your application's database, or some other value that allows your application to identify an attention item.

The final field in AttnLaunchCodeArgsType is commandArgsP, a pointer to an AttnCommandArgsType structure that holds data pertinent to a particular action. For example, in a Draw Detail or Draw List action, AttnCommandArgsType holds information about the screen area in which your application should perform the drawing. The AttnCommandArgsType structure is a union of different structures, so its contents vary depending upon the type of action requested by the attention manager.

The easiest way to respond to the sysAppLaunchCmdAttention launch code is to pass the launch code's cmdPBP pointer along to another function whose only purpose is to handle attention requests. For example, the following partial PilotMain function captures an incoming sysAppLaunchCmdAttention launch code and hands control to a function called ProcessAttention:

**Palm OS Garnet**
```
UInt32 PilotMain (UInt16 cmd, MemPtr cmdPBP,
                  UInt16 launchFlags)
{
    switch (cmd)
    {
        case sysAppLaunchCmdAttention:
            ProcessAttention((AttnLaunchCodeArgsType*)cmdPBP);

        // Other launch codes omitted.
    }

    return 0;
}
```

**Palm OS Cobalt**
```
uint32_t PilotMain (uint16_t cmd, MemPtr cmdPBP,
                    uint16_t launchFlags)
{
```

```
        switch (cmd)
        {
            case sysAppLaunchCmdAttention:
                ProcessAttention((AttnLaunchCodeArgsType*)cmdPBP);

            // Other launch codes omitted.
        }

        return errNone;
    }
```

> In Palm OS Garnet, if your application is not running when it receives a `sysApp`
> `LaunchCmdAttention` launch code, your program will not have access to its global
> variables. Be sure to use only local variables when responding to `sysAppLaunch`
> `CmdAttention`. Palm OS Cobalt applications do not have this restriction.

The `ProcessAttention` function's purpose is to find out what action the attention manager has
requested and to respond accordingly. A skeleton for `ProcessAttention` looks like this:

```
void ProcessAttention (AttnLaunchCodeArgsType * paramP)
{
    AttnCommandArgsType   *argsP = paramP->commandArgsP;


    switch (paramP->command)
    {
        case kAttnCommandDrawDetail:
            // Draw information in the detail dialog box.
            break;

        case kAttnCommandDrawList:
            // Draw information in the list dialog box.
            break;

        case kAttnCommandPlaySound:
            // Play an alarm sound.
            break;

        case kAttnCommandCustomEffect:
            // Perform a custom attention-getting effect.
            break;

        case kAttnCommandGoThere:
            // Display the item.
            break;

        case kAttnCommandGotIt:
            if (argsP->gotIt.dismissedByUser)
                // The user explicitly dismissed the item.
            break;

        case kAttnCommandIterate:
```

```
                // Update or delete stale or invalid items.
                break;
        }
    }
```

## Handling a Draw Detail Request

The kAttnCommandDrawDetail action is a request for your application to draw information about an attention item in the detail dialog box. During a Draw Detail request, the AttnCommandArgsType union contains the following structure:

**Palm OS Garnet**
```
struct AttnCommandArgsDrawDetailTag {
    RectangleType bounds;
    Boolean firstTime;
    AttnFlagsType flags;
} drawDetail;
```

**Palm OS Cobalt**
```
struct AttnCommandArgsDrawDetailTag {
    RectangleType bounds;
    Boolean firstTime;
    uint8_t padding1;
    uint16_t padding2;
    AttnFlagsType flags;
} drawDetail;
```

The bounds field defines the screen area in which your application may draw. Your application cannot add any user interface elements to this area, such as buttons or check boxes, but it can draw any graphics or text necessary to tell the user why the attention dialog box has appeared. The attention manager sets the clipping region to the same area as the drawing rectangle, so your application will not be able to accidentally draw "outside the lines" and make a mess of the detail dialog box.

If the firstTime field is true, your application can assume that the detail dialog box is empty and immediately commence drawing. However, if firstTime is false, the drawing area may already contain text or graphics, so your application should clear it by calling WinEraseRectangle.

The padding1 and padding2 fields in the Palm OS Cobalt version of the union are for system use and may safely be ignored.

The flags field contains the same attention flags that your application originally specified when it called AttnGetAttention.

For example, the following code, when placed in the ProcessAttention function described earlier, draws the text "Pay attention to me!" in the upper-left corner of the detail dialog box, leaving a two-pixel gap between the top and side of the drawing area:

```
case kAttnCommandDrawDetail:
    WinDrawChars("Pay attention to me!",
                StrLen("Pay attention to me!"),
                argsP->drawDetail.bounds.topLeft.x + 2,
                argsP->drawDetail.bounds.topLeft.y + 2);
    break;
```

## Handling a Draw List Request

A Draw List request is nearly identical to a Draw Detail request. When responding to Draw List, your application also must consider one extra field in the `AttnCommandArgsType` union:

**Palm OS Garnet**

```
struct AttnCommandArgsDrawListTag {
    RectangleType bounds;
    Boolean firstTime;
    AttnFlagsType flags;
    Boolean selected;
} drawList;
```

**Palm OS Cobalt**

```
struct AttnCommandArgsDrawListTag {
    RectangleType bounds;
    Boolean firstTime;
    uint8_t padding1;
    uint16_t padding2;
    AttnFlagsType flags;
    Boolean selected;
    uint8_t padding3;
    uint8_t padding4;
} drawList;
```

The `selected` field is `true` if the item the attention manager wants your application to draw is selected. In that case, your application is responsible for drawing some indication that the item is selected. The simplest way to do this is by inverting the colors in the drawing area. Also, the attention manager always erases the drawing area for you, so you don't have to worry about checking the value of `firstTime`.

There are much tighter constraints on how your application should draw a Draw List request than a Draw Detail request. To keep items in the list dialog box lined up nicely, whatever icon you draw in the list should be no wider than `kAttnListMaxIconWidth`, and your text should begin a number of pixels from the left edge of the drawing area equal to `kAttnListTextOffset`. The following `WinDrawChars` call draws the text "Feed the cats" at the appropriate location:

```
WinDrawChars("Feed the cats", StrLen("Feed the cats"),
            argsP->drawList.bounds.topLeft.x +
            kAttnListTextOffset,
            argsP->drawList.bounds.topLeft.y);
```

For more details about drawing text and graphics, see Chapter 11.

## Handling a Go There Request

Handling the `kAttnCommandGoThere` action is similar to handling the `sysAppLaunchCmdGoTo` launch code, which the system's global find facility sends to an application to have it display a particular record. The `AttnCommandArgsType` structure is empty during a Go There request, but you can use the `AttnLaunchCodeArgsType` structure's `userData` field to look for a specific record that your application can display. Programming the global find facility is covered in Chapter 16.

### Handling a Got It Request

A Got It request is a signal that the operating system automatically sends to your application when the user explicitly dismisses an item. Your application should respond by freeing memory or deleting alarms that may be associated with a particular attention item.

## Managing Attention Attempts

If your application needs to modify a pending attention item, it can call the `AttnUpdate` function. `AttnUpdate` takes the same parameters as the `AttnGetAttention` function and replaces an existing attention item's properties with those specified in the `AttnUpdate` function's parameters. Calling `AttnUpdate` forces the attention manager to tell all its client applications to redraw their items in the list dialog box. If your application needs to modify the text of one of its attention items, change the value that your application draws in the list dialog box, and then call `AttnUpdate`.

Your application may need to remove an item from the attention manager's list. To remove an item, call the `AttnForgetIt` function:

**Palm OS Garnet**
```
Boolean success = AttnForgetIt(cardNo, dbID, userData);
```

**Palm OS Cobalt**
```
Boolean success = AttnForgetIt(dbID, userData);
```

If the attention manager finds an item in its list that matches the card number, database ID, and user data value supplied by the `AttnForgetIt` function, the attention manager removes the item and `AttnForgetIt` returns `true`. Typically, your application should call `AttnForgetIt` as its last action when handling a Go There request; when the user is directly viewing the item that called for attention, there is no need for that item to remain in the attention manager's list.

## Preventing the Attention Indicator from Appearing

If your application does not have a title bar, or if it does something special when the user taps the title bar (such as displaying its own custom pop-up menu), you may wish to prevent the attention indicator from appearing in that application. To disable the attention indicator, call the `AttnIndicatorEnable` function with an argument of `false`:

```
AttnIndicatorEnable(false);
```

You can query the enabled state of the attention indicator with the `AttnIndicatorEnabled` function:

```
if (AttnIndicatorEnabled())
    // Attention indicator is enabled.
else
    // Attention indicator is disabled.
```

If you would like your application to still be able to open the attention manager's list dialog box, you can manually open it with the `AttnListOpen` function:

```
AttnListOpen();
```

AttnListOpen is useful for applications that lack a title bar but still need to offer the user some way to interact with the attention manager.

# Summary

In this chapter, you looked at how alarms, time, and getting the user's attention work in Palm OS. After reading this chapter, you should know the following:

❑ Setting alarms in Palm OS requires calling the AlmSetAlarm function, as well as handling the sysAppLaunchCmdAlarmTriggered, sysAppLaunchCmdDisplayAlarm, sysAppLaunchCmdTimeChange, and sysAppLaunchCmdSystemReset launch codes.

❑ Because managing time is an important function of a handheld organizer, Palm OS provides a complete set of functions for manipulating, converting, and setting time and date values.

❑ You can call PrefGetPreference to retrieve a handheld user's system-wide time, date, time zone, and Daylight Saving Time (DST) preferences.

❑ The attention manager provides a common interface for gaining the user's attention, which comprises a system of dialog boxes, sounds, and other attention-getting mechanisms.

❑ An application adds items to the attention manager's list with the AttnGetAttention function, and the application responds to attention manager requests by handling the sysAppLaunchCmdAttention launch code.

# 14

# Programming Tables

Tables are some of the most complex user interface elements in Palm OS and, therefore, some of the most difficult to implement. Although many internal functions of tables are handled by the Palm OS table manager, the system does not provide much of what users of ROM applications expect as default behavior from a table. In this regard, tables are somewhat like gadgets; Palm OS provides you with a user interface object to attach to your program but much of the hard work that makes the object tick comes from the application itself. Fortunately, the built-in applications provide good examples of how to implement tables that operate in ways users expect to see, and much of the code required to operate a table is simply a boilerplate that you can modify slightly and reuse in your own applications.

> *PalmSource makes the source code for the table manager available on their Web site (*www.palmsource. com*). Looking through the source code is an excellent way to gain insight into the nuances of tables. As of this writing, table manager source code is available for Palm OS 3.0, 3.5, and 4.0.*

Both tables and lists tend to look and act in similar ways. How do you decide which to use, a table or a list? Tables are more suited to editing data in place, and lists are optimized for selecting items. If you want to allow a user to edit data in a tabular format, such as the way the interface for the Date Book and To Do List applications does, use a table. If you just want to present the user with a list of choices, a list is much easier to use.

This chapter is divided into two sections, "Creating a Simple Table" and "Creating More Complex Tables." The first section explains the basic mechanics of creating, initializing, and drawing a simple table by way of a small sample program. The second section examines adding more complex behavior to a table, such as database interaction, scrolling, and expanding text fields, and uses the Librarian sample application to demonstrate these techniques.

> *Most tables are intimately linked to an application's database, so some Palm OS database terminology appears throughout this chapter. Refer to Chapters 15 and 16 for more information about Palm OS database routines.*

# Creating a Simple Table

The sample application in this section demonstrates all the available table item types. Figure 14-1 shows Table Example as it looks after you start the program.

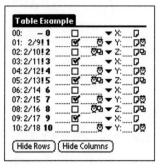

**Figure 14-1**

Table Example contains a single main form, which is host to only four objects: the table, a list (hidden from view until invoked by the table's pop-up triggers), and two buttons for demonstrating how to hide rows and columns in the table. The following PilRC resource definition, from the file `table.rcp`, defines the form and its elements:

```
FORM ID MainForm 0 0 160 160
MENUID MainFormMenuBar
USABLE
BEGIN
    TITLE "Table Example"
    TABLE ID MainTable AT (0 16 160 121) ROWS 11 COLUMNS 9
        COLUMNWIDTHS 12 25 12 18 12 33 17 20 9
    BUTTON "Hide Rows"    ID MainHideRowsButton
        AT (1 147 50 12)
    BUTTON "Hide Columns" ID MainHideColumnsButton
        AT (56 147 64 12)
    GRAFFITISTATEINDICATOR AT (140 PrevTop)
    LIST "X" "Y" "Z" ID MainList AT (120 141 19 33)
        NONUSABLE VISIBLEITEMS 3
END
```

The table in the example program is designed for display on a square screen, with the pen input area currently displayed. The table is 11 rows high. In the standard Palm OS font, it fills most of the screen, leaving just enough room across the bottom of the form for command buttons. There are nine columns in the table, one for each kind of table item supported by the table manager. Table items are described in the next section.

## Understanding How Tables Work

Palm OS tables are essentially containers for a variety of other form elements, such as pop-up lists, text fields, and check boxes. As such, each table maintains a complex array of subordinate controls. Every cell in the table is a *table item*. The Palm OS table manager keeps track of a handful of properties for each table item, and there are table manager functions for retrieving and setting those property values. The use of these functions is covered in more detail later in this chapter. The following table outlines the available properties and their associated functions.

| Property | Get Function | Set Function | Description |
|---|---|---|---|
| Item Style | none | TblSetItemStyle | Defines the user interface element contained by the table item |
| Font | TblGetItemFont | TblSetItemFont | Defines the font used to draw the table item's text |
| Int Value | TblGetItemInt | TblSetItemInt | Specifies an integer value that is associated with the table item |
| Pointer | TblGetItemPtr | TblSetItemPtr | Specifies a pointer to data that is associated with the table item |

The Item Style property determines how the system draws each table item; it also controls which of the other three properties are used with a particular table item. Different table items store different data in the Font, Int Value, and Pointer properties. Some table item types allow the user to edit the value displayed in their table cells, whereas others are for display purposes only. The following table provides an overview of the available values for Item Style and shows which are user-editable and which of the other three properties each item style uses.

| Item Style | Editable By User? | Table Item Properties Used By This Style |
|---|---|---|
| checkboxTableItem | Yes | Int Value |
| customTableItem | Yes | None, although you may store data in the Int Value and Pointer properties if required by your application |
| dateTableItem | No | Int Value |
| labelTableItem | No | Pointer |
| numericTableItem | No | Int Value |
| popupTriggerTableItem | Yes | Int Value, Pointer |
| textTableItem | Yes | Font, Pointer |
| textWithNoteTableItem | Yes | Font, Pointer |
| timeTableItem | N/A | Palm OS does not implement this item style |
| narrowTextTableItem | Yes | Font, Int Value, Pointer |

*Table continued on following page*

| | | |
|---|---|---|
| `tallCustomTableItem` | Yes | None, although you may store data in the Int Value and Pointer properties if required by your application |
| `labelNoColonTableItem` | No | Pointer |
| `popupTriggerNoColonTableItem` | Yes | Int Value, Pointer |

The following sections describe each data type in more detail.

## checkboxTableItem

A `checkboxTableItem` is a simple check box without a label. The user may toggle the check box on or off by tapping the table cell containing the check box. This table item stores the value of the check box in the Int Value property, with 0 representing an unchecked box and 1 representing a checked box.

## customTableItem

The `customTableItem` type is the table equivalent of a gadget object, allowing you to create your own type of table item if none of the others fits the bill. Your application code should install a callback routine to draw the contents of a `customTableItem` cell. The callback function may use the cell's Int Value and Pointer properties to store whatever data might be required by the custom cell.

In Palm OS Garnet, the `customTableItem` style is limited to a height of 11 pixels in the standard coordinate system (the height of the Palm OS standard font). You can make the row containing a `customTableItem` taller than 11 pixels, but when selected, only the top 11 pixels are highlighted. If you need a custom table item taller than this, use `tallCustomTableItem`.

Palm OS Cobalt does not have this restriction. You never need to use `tallCustomTableItem` in Palm OS Cobalt.

## dateTableItem

This table item is display-only, showing the date in the form "month/day." The date itself is stored in the table item's Int Value property, and it should be a value that can be cast as a `DateType`. The Palm OS header file `DateTime.h` defines `DateType` as follows:

**Palm OS Garnet**

```
typedef struct {
    UInt16 year  :7;   // years since 1904 (MAC format)
    UInt16 month :4;
    UInt16 day   :5;
} DateType;
```

**Palm OS Cobalt**

```
typedef struct {
#if CPU_ENDIAN == CPU_ENDIAN_BIG
    uint16_t  year  :7;   // Years since 1904 (Mac format)
    uint16_t  month :4;
    uint16_t  day   :5;
```

```
#elif CPU_ENDIAN == CPU_ENDIAN_LITTLE
    uint16_t  day   :5;
    uint16_t  month :4;
    uint16_t  year  :7;  // Years since 1904 (Mac format)
} DateType;
```

If the value of the Int Value property is -1, the date table item displays a hyphen (-) instead of a date. If the date in Int Value occurs on or before today's date according to the handheld's system clock, the table manager displays an exclamation point (!) after the date. The table manager always draws a dateTableItem in the current font. This display behavior should be familiar to anyone who has used the built-in To Do List application because its due date column is composed of dateTableItem cells.

## labelTableItem

A labelTableItem is simply a text label that the user cannot edit, except that instead of displaying only the string pointed to by its Pointer property, the label table item appends a colon (:) to the text. The table manager draws the label in the system's default font. Selecting the label, or a text field in the same row as the label, highlights the label. Most of the field labels in the Address Book application belong to this type of table item.

## numericTableItem

Numeric table items display the value stored in their Int Value properties. The number cannot be directly edited by the user. The table manager draws the number in the system's small bold font.

## popupTriggerTableItem

A popupTriggerTableItem allows the user to call up a pop-up list and make a selection from the list by tapping the table cell containing the pop-up trigger table item. The popupTriggerTableItem displays the currently selected list item and stores the index of the list selection in its Int Value property. This table item keeps a pointer to the pop-up trigger's associated list in the table item's Pointer property. Keep in mind that, as with an ordinary pop-up trigger object, you must provide a separate list object resource to attach to the pop-up trigger table item. The table manager draws the list and the currently selected item in the system's default font.

## textTableItem

A textTableItem is an editable text field contained within a single table cell. The table item's Font property stores the font used to display the text, and Pointer contains a pointer to the string that contains the field's text. You must provide callback functions to load and save the text in each textTableItem cell.

## textWithNoteTableItem

The textWithNoteTableItem type is identical to the textTableItem type, except that textWithNote TableItem also has a note icon on the right side of the cell.

## timeTableItem

Although the timeTableItem style has existed through several versions of Palm OS, it has never been implemented. If you want a table item that displays a time, use a labelTableItem, customTableItem, or textTableItem.

## narrowTextTableItem

A narrowTextTableItem is similar to a textTableItem but it has a certain amount of space reserved at the right side of the cell. The Int Value property of the table item stores the number of pixels to set aside at the right of the cell. This space is useful for displaying small icons, such as the repeat and alarm indicators used in the built-in Date Book application. Along with the callbacks for loading and saving the text contents of the cell, a narrowTextTableItem also should have a callback function to draw the icons. This drawing callback is similar to the callback function used for a customTableItem.

## labelNoColonTableItem

Available only in Palm OS Cobalt, the labelNoColonTableItem is identical to labelTableItem but it does not append a colon (:) to the text it displays.

## popupTriggerNoColonTableItem

Available only in Palm OS Cobalt, the popupTriggerNoColonTableItem is identical to popupTrigger TableItem but it does not append a colon (:) to the pop-up trigger it displays.

# Initializing a Table

Before you can implement user interaction with a table, or even use the table to display data, you must prepare the table for use. Initializing a table primarily involves telling the table manager what item style each cell of the table should be, along with setting up callback functions for certain columns to perform custom drawing routines or to save and retrieve text from fields in the table.

You need to initialize a table before the system draws it to the screen. The best time to perform this initialization is when handling a form's frmOpenEvent. In Table Example, the main form's event handler, MainFormHandleEvent, delegates initialization of the table to MainFormInit:

```
static Boolean MainFormHandleEvent(EventType *event)
{
    Boolean     handled = false;
    FormType    *form;

    switch (event->eType)
    {
        case frmOpenEvent:
            form = FrmGetActiveForm();
            MainFormInit(form);
            FrmDrawForm(form);
            handled = true;

        // Other event handling omitted.

        default:
            break;

    }

    return handled;
}
```

Before we delve into `MainFormInit`, it would be useful to take a look at some of the constants and global variables used in Table Example because these items furnish the values for some of the labels and text fields in the table. The following global variables are from the top of `table.c`:

```
// Table constants
#define numTableColumns  9
#define numTableRows     11
#define numTextColumns   3

// Global variables
static char *  gLabels[] = {"00", "01", "02", "03", "04",
                            "05", "06", "07", "08", "09",
                            "10"};
MemHandle   gTextHandles[numTextColumns][numTableRows];
Boolean     gRowsHidden = false;
Boolean     gColumnsHidden = false;
```

The constants `numTableColumns` and `numTableRows` are fairly self-explanatory. They simply declare how many columns and rows the table has; `numTextColumns` states the number of columns that contain a text field item. Labels for each row in the table are stored in the `gLabels` array, which Table Example initializes in the `gLabels` variable declaration. The `gTextHandles` two-dimensional array of memory handles stores the handles to each of the text fields in the table. Table Example uses `gRowsHidden` and `gColumnsHidden` to keep track of whether the application is currently hiding any rows or columns in the table.

Before `MainFormInit` can use the `gTextHandles` array, the application must initialize the array. Table Example accomplishes this in its `StartApplication` routine:

**Palm OS Garnet**
```
static Err StartApplication(void)
{
    Int16  i, j;


    for (i = 0; i < numTextColumns; i++)
    {
        for (j = 0; j < numTableRows; j++)
        {
            Char  *str;

            gTextHandles[i][j] = MemHandleNew(1);
            str = MemHandleLock(gTextHandles[i][j]);
            *str = '\0';
            MemHandleUnlock(gTextHandles[i][j]);
        }
    }

    return false;
}
```

**Palm OS Cobalt**
```
static Err StartApplication(void)
{
```

```
    int16_t  i, j;


    for (i = 0; i < numTextColumns; i++)
    {
        for (j = 0; j < numTableRows; j++)
        {
            char  *str;

            gTextHandles[i][j] = MemHandleNew(1);
            str = MemHandleLock(gTextHandles[i][j]);
            *str = '\0';
            MemHandleUnlock(gTextHandles[i][j]);
        }
    }

    return false;
}
```

The `StartApplication` function iterates over the `gTextHandles` array, allocating a new memory handle for each array element and filling the handle's contents with a single trailing null.

Now that all the global variables that Table Example requires have been readied, the program can get to the work of initializing the table with the `MainFormInit` function:

**Palm OS Garnet**

```
static void MainFormInit(FormType *form)
{
    TableType  *table;
    Int16      numRows;
    Int16      i;
    DateType   dates[11], today;
    UInt32     now;
    UInt32     curDate;
    ListType   *list;


    // Initialize the dates. The first date in the table is
    // set to the constant noTime so it will display as a
    // hyphen. The rest of the dates will range from four
    // days ago to five days ahead of the current date on
    // the handheld.
    * ((Int16 *) &dates[0]) = noTime;
    DateSecondsToDate(TimGetSeconds(), &today);
    now = DateToDays(today);
    for (i = 1; i < sizeof(dates) / sizeof(*dates); i++)
    {
        curDate = now - 5 + i;
        DateDaysToDate(curDate, &(dates[i]));
    }

    table = FrmGetObjectPtr(form, FrmGetObjectIndex(form,
                        MainTable));
```

```
list = FrmGetObjectPtr(form, FrmGetObjectIndex(form,
                       MainList));

// Set item types and values.
numRows = TblGetNumberOfRows(table);
for (i = 0; i < numRows; i++)
{
    TblSetItemStyle(table, i, 0, labelTableItem);
    TblSetItemPtr(table, i, 0, gLabels[i]);

    TblSetItemStyle(table, i, 1, dateTableItem);
    TblSetItemInt(table, i, 1, DateToInt(dates[i]));

    TblSetItemStyle(table, i, 2, numericTableItem);
    TblSetItemInt(table, i, 2, i);

    TblSetItemStyle(table, i, 3, textTableItem);

    TblSetItemStyle(table, i, 4, checkboxTableItem);
    TblSetItemInt(table, i, 4, i % 2);

    TblSetItemStyle(table, i, 5, narrowTextTableItem);
    TblSetItemInt(table, i, 5, ((i % 3) * 7) + 6);

    TblSetItemStyle(table, i, 6, popupTriggerTableItem);
    TblSetItemInt(table, i, 6, i % 3);
    TblSetItemPtr(table, i, 6, list);

    TblSetItemStyle(table, i, 7, textWithNoteTableItem);

    TblSetItemStyle(table, i, 8, customTableItem);
    TblSetItemInt(table, i, 8, i % 3);

    TblSetRowStaticHeight(table, i, true);
}

// Set columns usable and adjust column spacing.
for (i = 0; i < numTableColumns; i++)
{
    TblSetColumnUsable(table, i, true);
    switch (i)
    {
        case 2:
            TblSetColumnSpacing(table, i, 2);
            break;

        default:
            TblSetColumnSpacing(table, i, 0);
            break;
    }
}

// Set callback functions for loading, saving, and
```

```
      // drawing.
    TblSetLoadDataProcedure(table, 3, LoadTextTableItem);
    TblSetLoadDataProcedure(table, 5, LoadTextTableItem);
    TblSetLoadDataProcedure(table, 7, LoadTextTableItem);

    TblSetSaveDataProcedure(table, 3, SaveTextTableItem);

    TblSetCustomDrawProcedure(table, 5,
                              DrawNarrowTextTableItem);
    TblSetCustomDrawProcedure(table, 8, DrawCustomTableItem);

    // Draw the form.
    FrmDrawForm(form);
}
```

**Palm OS Cobalt**

```
static void MainFormInit(FormType *form)
{
    TableType   *table;
    int16_t     numRows;
    int16_t     i;
    DateType    dates[11], today;
    uint32_t    now;
    uint32_t    curDate;
    ListType    *list;


    // Initialize the dates. The first date in the table is
    // set to the constant noTime so it will display as a
    // hyphen. The rest of the dates will range from four
    // days ago to five days ahead of the current date on
    // the handheld.
    * ((int16_t *) &dates[0]) = noTime;
    DateSecondsToDate(TimGetSeconds(), &today);
    now = DateToDays(today);
    for (i = 1; i < sizeof(dates) / sizeof(*dates); i++)
    {
        curDate = now - 5 + i;
        DateDaysToDate(curDate, &(dates[i]));
    }

    table = FrmGetObjectPtr(form, FrmGetObjectIndex(form,
                            MainTable));
    list = FrmGetObjectPtr(form, FrmGetObjectIndex(form,
                           MainList));

    // Set item types and values.
    numRows = TblGetNumberOfRows(table);
    for (i = 0; i < numRows; i++)
    {
        TblSetItemStyle(table, i, 0, labelTableItem);
        TblSetItemPtr(table, i, 0, gLabels[i]);

        TblSetItemStyle(table, i, 1, dateTableItem);
```

```
            TblSetItemInt(table, i, 1, DateToInt(dates[i]));

            TblSetItemStyle(table, i, 2, numericTableItem);
            TblSetItemInt(table, i, 2, i);

            TblSetItemStyle(table, i, 3, textTableItem);

            TblSetItemStyle(table, i, 4, checkboxTableItem);
            TblSetItemInt(table, i, 4, i % 2);

            TblSetItemStyle(table, i, 5, narrowTextTableItem);
            TblSetItemInt(table, i, 5, ((i % 3) * 7) + 6);

            TblSetItemStyle(table, i, 6, popupTriggerTableItem);
            TblSetItemInt(table, i, 6, i % 3);
            TblSetItemPtr(table, i, 6, list);

            TblSetItemStyle(table, i, 7, textWithNoteTableItem);

            TblSetItemStyle(table, i, 8, customTableItem);
            TblSetItemInt(table, i, 8, i % 3);

            TblSetRowStaticHeight(table, i, true);
        }

        // Set columns usable and adjust column spacing.
        for (i = 0; i < numTableColumns; i++)
        {
            TblSetColumnUsable(table, i, true);
            switch (i)
            {
                case 2:
                    TblSetColumnSpacing(table, i, 2);
                    break;

                default:
                    TblSetColumnSpacing(table, i, 0);
                    break;
            }
        }

        // Set callback functions for loading, saving, and
        // drawing.
        TblSetLoadDataProcedure(table, 3, LoadTextTableItem);
        TblSetLoadDataProcedure(table, 5, LoadTextTableItem);
        TblSetLoadDataProcedure(table, 7, LoadTextTableItem);

        TblSetSaveDataProcedure(table, 3, SaveTextTableItem);

        TblSetCustomDrawProcedure(table, 5,
                                DrawNarrowTextTableItem);
        TblSetCustomDrawProcedure(table, 8, DrawCustomTableItem);

        // Draw the form.
        FrmDrawForm(form);
}
```

The first part of `MainFormInit` simply fills `dates`, an array of `DateType` structures, with a few dates so the table's second column will have data to display:

```
// Initialize the dates. The first date in the table is
// set to the constant noTime so it will display as a
// hyphen. The rest of the dates will range from four days
// ago to five days ahead of the current date on the
// handheld.
* ((int16_t *) &dates[0]) = noTime;
DateSecondsToDate(TimGetSeconds(), &today);
now = DateToDays(today);
for (i = 1; i < sizeof(dates) / sizeof(*dates); i++)
{
    curDate = now - 5 + i;
    DateDaysToDate(curDate, &(dates[i]));
}
```

After `MainFormInit` fills in the `dates` array, the real work of initializing the table begins. The first task is to iterate over the rows of the table and set the table item type for each cell.

## Setting item types

Use the `TblSetItemStyle` function to set the item type for a particular cell column. The `TblSetItemStyle` function takes four arguments: a pointer to a table, the row of the cell to set, the column of the cell to set, and a `TableItemStyleType` value. It is possible to set cells within a column to different item types, although it is more common to make all of a column's cells share the same type.

> In particular, the **textTableItem, textWithNoteTableItem,** and **narrowTextTableItem** styles do not play well with other styles of table item because the functions for setting load and save callback functions for text type table items, **TblSetLoadDataProcedure** and **TblSetSaveDataProcedure,** allow you to specify only an entire column. Setting a text-loading or text-saving callback function for a cell that does not have a text field in it will cause your application to crash.

Because `MainFormInit` is iterating over the table's rows with a `for` loop, this is a handy time to set the Int Value and Pointer properties for each cell that requires these values. The `TblSetItemInt` and `TblSetItemPtr` functions accomplish this task in `MainFormInit`.

The first three columns of the table contain data types that the user cannot directly alter. Column one is a simple label. `MainFormInit` fills in the text for the labels from the global `gLabels` array:

```
TblSetItemStyle(table, i, 0, labelTableItem);
TblSetItemPtr(table, i, 0, gLabels[i]);
```

Values for the second column were set earlier in `MainFormInit` in the `dates` array. After `MainFormInit` sets the second column's type to `dateTableItem`, it fills in the date for each date cell with `TblSetItemInt`:

```
TblSetItemStyle(table, i, 1, dateTableItem);
TblSetItemInt(table, i, 1, DateToInt(dates[i]));
```

> *The DateToInt "function" used here is not documented anywhere in the Palm OS Programmer's API Reference. Instead, DateToInt is a macro defined in the Palm OS header file DateTime.h. Because the DateType structure is exactly 16 bits long, the DateToInt macro is useful for shoehorning a DateType into a normal 16-bit integer value, such as the Int Value property of a table item.*

The third column, the last of the columns that are not user-editable, is a numericTableItem. MainFormInit simply tosses the index of the current row into the Int Value for each item in this column:

```
TblSetItemStyle(table, i, 2, numericTableItem);
TblSetItemInt(table, i, 2, i);
```

The table's fourth column is a textTableItem. Because a text table item's Int Value property is unused and its Pointer property is set using a callback function later in MainFormInit, the only thing initially set in this for loop is the cell's style:

```
TblSetItemStyle(table, i, 3, textTableItem);
```

The fifth column is a check box. After MainFormInit sets the cell's item type to checkboxTableItem, it sets alternating check boxes in the column to be checked:

```
TblSetItemStyle(table, i, 4, checkboxTableItem);
TblSetItemInt(table, i, 4, i % 2);
```

After the check box comes the sixth column, which contains another type of text field: a narrowText TableItem. A narrow text item's Int Value indicates the amount of space to reserve at the right side of the text field for custom drawing. In Table Example, the space is reserved for drawing the alarm and repeat icons from the built-in Address Book application. Each of these icons is seven pixels wide, and the for loop initializes space for neither, one, or both icons, depending upon the row's index number:

```
TblSetItemStyle(table, i, 5, narrowTextTableItem);
TblSetItemInt(table, i, 5, ((i % 3) * 7) + 6);
```

The extra six pixels added to the space provide leeway to ensure that the icons at the right of the field are not cut off by the next column's pop-up triggers. Pop-up triggers are ill-behaved when it comes to staying within their allotted space in a table. Because they are right-justified, they will gladly overlap anything to their left if the text displayed in the trigger is too long to fit, as is the case in Table Example.

The seventh column contains pop-up triggers. Besides setting the item type for this column, MainFormInit also sets the Int Value property to 0, 1, or 2, depending on the table row, and sets the Pointer property to point to MainList, a pop-up list containing three items. The Int Value determines which list element from MainList is currently selected and therefore drawn as the trigger's label. Note that a popupTriggerTableItem appends a colon (:) to the end of the pop-up trigger label, but this colon does not display in the pop-up list itself.

```
TblSetItemStyle(table, i, 6, popupTriggerTableItem);
TblSetItemInt(table, i, 6, i % 3);
TblSetItemPtr(table, i, 6, list);
```

Occupying the eighth column is the last type of table text field, a textWithNoteTableItem. Like the textTableItem in column four, the item type is the only thing that needs to be set in this for loop:

```
TblSetItemStyle(table, i, 7, textWithNoteTableItem);
```

The ninth and last column contains a `customTableItem`. In the Table Example program, the custom widget displayed in this column's cells displays nothing, the alarm icon, or the repeat icon, depending upon whether the value of the cell's Int Value property is 0, 1, or 2, respectively. Tapping in the last column causes the cell to cycle to the next icon. The `for` loop sets up the initial value for each of this column's cells, but the code that actually handles drawing and responding to taps is elsewhere in the application:

```
TblSetItemStyle(table, i, 8, customTableItem);
TblSetItemInt(table, i, 8, i % 3);
```

## Setting Static Row Height

In ROM applications, tables that contain text fields automatically expand and contract the height of the row containing a text field when the user enters more text than will fit in the field. As a matter of fact, expansion and contraction of table fields is their default behavior, and the table manager handles adjustments to the height of the row automatically. Unfortunately, the table manager does only half the work required. The system will resize a row without help from your application, but if expanding the field shoves other table rows off the bottom of the table, and then the user deletes enough text to allow other rows to have space again, the table manager does not redraw the rows, resulting in a large blank space in the bottom part of the table.

Properly implementing expanding text fields in a table requires a fair amount of complex scrolling code in your application. Because Table Example is supposed to be a simple example without any scrolling, preventing rows from automatically resizing as text is added to their fields is necessary. Fortunately, Palm OS provides the `TblSetRowStaticHeight` function, which takes a pointer to a table, the row in the table to set, and a Boolean value indicating whether the row's height should be unchangeable (`true`) or resizable (`false`). The `MainFormInit` function in Table Example calls `TblSetRowStaticHeight` as its last action while iterating over each row in the table:

```
TblSetRowStaticHeight(table, i, true);
```

## Setting Column Usability and Spacing

After iterating over the rows of the table, `MainFormInit` needs to iterate over the columns to further set up the table:

```
for (i = 0; i < numTableColumns; i++)
{
    TblSetColumnUsable(table, i, true);
    switch (i) {
        case 2:
            TblSetColumnSpacing(table, i, 2);
            break;

        default:
            TblSetColumnSpacing(table, i, 0);
            break;
    }
}
```

By default, table columns are not usable and, hence, not drawn by the table manager. To make each column visible, `MainFormInit` calls the `TblSetColumnUsable` function. A companion function,

`TblSetRowUsable`, also exists to set the usability (and visibility) of table rows, but because rows default to usable, it is not necessary to call `TblSetRowUsable` in the table initialization.

After setting column usability, `MainFormInit` sets the spacing between columns. Without any intervention from your application code, each column in a cell automatically has a single space following it to separate it from the next column. Because the Table Example program is pressed for available screen space, `MainFormInit` uses `TblSetColumnSpacing` to set most of the columns to have no trailing space at all.

> *In a real application, text fields are easier to use with a bit of leading space before them;* `MainFormInit` *sets the spacing in the third column (column index 2) to two pixels to make the* `textTableItem` *in column four easier to read. Compare column four of Table Example with columns six and eight, which have no leading space, to see the difference that leaving space in front of a text field can make.*

## Setting Custom Load Routines

The `MainFormInit` function, having finished with formatting and loading data into the table's cells, must now turn its attention to setting up callback functions for retrieving and saving the text in each of the table's text fields. First, `MainFormInit` sets the callbacks for loading data:

```
TblSetLoadDataProcedure(table, 3, LoadTextTableItem);
TblSetLoadDataProcedure(table, 5, LoadTextTableItem);
TblSetLoadDataProcedure(table, 7, LoadTextTableItem);
```

Setting a table item's data loading callback function requires the use of `TblSetLoadDataProcedure`. As parameters, `TblSetLoadProcedure` takes a pointer to the table, the index of the column that will use the callback function to load its data, and a pointer to a function of type `TableLoadDataFuncType`. The prototype for `TableLoadDataFuncType` looks like this:

**Palm OS Garnet**
```
Err TableLoadDataFuncType (void *tableP, Int16 row,
    Int16 column, Boolean editable, MemHandle *dataH,
    Int16 *dataOffset, Int16 *dataSize, FieldType *fld)
```

**Palm OS Cobalt**
```
status_t TableLoadDataFuncType (void *tableP, int16_t row,
    int16_t column, Boolean editable, MemHandle *dataH,
    int16_t *dataOffset, int16_t *dataSize, FieldType *fld)
```

In `TableLoadDataFuncType`, `tableP` is a pointer to a table, and `row` and `column` indicate the row and column of the cell in `tableP` that should be loaded. If the system passes a value of `true` for the `editable` parameter, a text cell somewhere in the table is currently being edited; if `editable` is `false`, the table is merely being drawn, not edited. The `dataH` parameter is a pointer to a handle, which your application should fill with the unlocked handle of a block of memory containing a null-terminated string. You need to set `dataOffset` to the offset within `dataH`, in bytes, where the string data begins.

The `dataOffset` parameter allows you to store string data for table use in a memory structure other than a simple string. For example, consider the following structure:

```
typedef struct {
    int16_t   someValue;
    char[10]  string;
} MyDataType;
```

The `MyDataType` structure contains an integer value before its string data, but you can still pass a handle to memory containing this structure in the `dataH` parameter of `TableLoadDataFuncType` if you also pass the value `sizeof(int16_t)` in the `dataOffset` parameter to indicate that the string data begins after the `int16_t` value in the structure.

Your application should set `dataSize` to the allocated size of the text string in bytes; be sure not to set `dataSize` to the length of the string because this may be different from its memory size. Finally, the `fld` parameter contains a pointer to the field in the cell that should be loaded.

Table Example's implementation of `TableLoadDataFuncType` is `LoadTextTableItem`, which looks like this:

**Palm OS Garnet**
```
static Err LoadTextTableItem (void *table, Int16 row,
    Int16 column, Boolean editable, MemHandle *dataH,
    Int16 *dataOffset, Int16 *dataSize, FieldType *field)
{
    *dataH = gTextHandles[GetTextColumn(column)][row];
    *dataOffset = 0;
    *dataSize = MemHandleSize(*dataH);

    return 0;
}
```

**Palm OS Cobalt**
```
static status_t LoadTextTableItem (void *table, int16_T row,
    int16_t column, Boolean editable, MemHandle *dataH,
    int16_t *dataOffset, int16_t *dataSize, FieldType *field)
{
    *dataH = gTextHandles[GetTextColumn(column)][row];
    *dataOffset = 0;
    *dataSize = MemHandleSize(*dataH);

    return errNone;
}
```

The `LoadTextTableItem` function is simple, merely retrieving the cell's text from the previously initialized `gTextHandles` array and passing it to the table manager. The `GetTextColumn` function called in `LoadTextTableItem` is a Table Example helper function that maps table column indices to the indices of the first dimension in the `gTextHandles` array. Here is what `GetTextColumn` looks like:

**Palm OS Garnet**
```
static Int16 GetTextColumn(Int16 column)
{
    Int16   result;


    switch (column)
    {
        case 3:
            result = 0;
            break;

        case 5:
```

```
                result = 1;
                break;

        case 7:
            result = 2;
            break;

        default:
            ErrFatalDisplay("Invalid text column");
            break;
    }

    return result;
}
```

**Palm OS Cobalt**
```
static int16_t GetTextColumn(int16_t column)
{
    int16_t  result;


    switch (column)
    {
        case 3:
            result = 0;
            break;

        case 5:
            result = 1;
            break;

        case 7:
            result = 2;
            break;

        default:
            ErrFatalError("Invalid text column");
            break;
    }

    return result;
}
```

Because the data stored in the handles in gTextHandles are composed of the desired strings only, LoadTextTableItem sets dataOffset to 0 to indicate the start of the data in the handle. Then LoadTextTableItem calls the Palm OS function MemHandleSize to retrieve the amount of memory occupied by the string and passes this value back using the dataSize parameter.

## Setting Custom Save Routines

Strictly speaking, a custom save routine is not necessary if your application needs to save only the text entered in each table field verbatim. If you want to perform some processing on the text before saving it, such as changing capitalization, you also should set up a callback function to customize the data saving behavior with TblSetSaveDataProcedure:

```
TblSetSaveDataProcedure(table, 3, SaveTextTableItem);
```

The `TblSetSaveDataProcedure` function takes three parameters: a pointer to a table, the index of a column in that table whose save behavior should be modified, and a callback function of type `TableSaveDataFuncType` to perform the saving. The `TableSaveDataFuncType` callback type is simpler than `TableLoadDataFuncType`, and its prototype looks like this:

**Palm OS Garnet**
```
Boolean TableSaveDataFuncType (void *tableP, Int16 row,
                               Int16 column);
```

**Palm OS Cobalt**
```
Boolean TableSaveDataFuncType (void *tableP, int16_t row,
                               int16_t column);
```

In `TableSaveDataFuncType`, the `tableP` parameter is a pointer to a table object, and `row` and `column` contain the row and column of the cell in that table whose data should be processed before saving. A function implementing `TableSaveDataFuncType` should return `true` if the callback function changed the text in the field, or it should return `false` if the function left the text alone.

The Table Example program uses a custom save routine for the first column of text fields (column number 3). The implementation of `TableSaveDataFuncType` in Table Example is `SaveTextTableItem`. The `SaveTextTableItem` routine capitalizes the text in the first text field of the current row when the user selects another row in the table. `SaveTextTableItem` looks like this:

**Palm OS Garnet**
```
static Boolean SaveTextTableItem (void *table, Int16 row,
                                  Int16 column)
{
    Boolean     result = false;
    FieldType   *field;
    MemHandle   textH;
    Char        *str;
    Int16       i;


    field = TblGetCurrentField(table);

    // If the field has been changed, uppercase its text.
    if (field && FldDirty(field))
    {
        textH = gTextHandles[GetTextColumn(column)][row];
        str = MemHandleLock(textH);
        for (i = 0; str[i] != '\0'; i++)
        {
            if (str[i] >= 'a' && str[i] <= 'z')
                str[i] -= 'a' - 'A';
        }

        MemHandleUnlock(textH);
        TblMarkRowInvalid(table, row);
        result = true;
```

```
    }

    return result;
}
```

**Palm OS Cobalt**

```
static Boolean SaveTextTableItem (void *table, int16_t row,
                                  int16_t column)
{
    Boolean    result = false;
    FieldType  *field;
    MemHandle  textH;
    char       *str;
    int16_t    i;


    field = TblGetCurrentField(table);

    // If the field has been changed, uppercase its text.
    if (field && FldDirty(field))
    {
        textH = gTextHandles[GetTextColumn(column)][row];
        str = MemHandleLock(textH);
        for (i = 0; str[i] != '\0'; i++)
        {
            if (str[i] >= 'a' && str[i] <= 'z')
                str[i] -= 'a' - 'A';
        }

        MemHandleUnlock(textH);
        TblMarkRowInvalid(table, row);
        result = true;
    }

    return result;
}
```

The SaveTextTableItem function first uses the TblGetCurrentField function to retrieve a pointer to the field the user is currently editing. If no field currently has the focus in the table, TblGetCurrentField returns NULL, which is why the next if statement first checks to see if field has a value. The if also uses FldDirty to see if the field has been changed at all; if the field hasn't been changed, there is no need to run the rest of the code in SaveTextTableItem.

If the user changes the contents of the field, SaveTextTableItem retrieves and locks a handle to the field's text and then converts the characters in the field to uppercase letters. Then SaveTextTableItem unlocks the handle and marks the row invalid with TblMarkRowInvalid. The call to TblMarkRowInvalid is important, as it forces the table manager to redraw the row and display the changes that SaveText TableItem made to the field's text. Finally, SaveTextTableItem sets the return value of the function to true to indicate to the table manager that the text has been changed by the callback function.

*Because Table Example does not have an actual database, Table Example does not actually use SaveTextTableItem to save any data, only to capitalize text before moving on to another row in the table.*

## Setting Custom Drawing Routines

Table Example uses two custom drawing routines, one for adding icons to the ends of the narrowText TableItem cells in the table's sixth column and one for drawing the customTableItem in the ninth column. The MainFormInit function sets the custom drawing callback functions using TblSetCustomDrawProcedure:

```
TblSetCustomDrawProcedure(table, 5, DrawNarrowTextTableItem);
TblSetCustomDrawProcedure(table, 8, DrawCustomTableItem);
```

The TblSetCustomDrawProcedure function takes three parameters: a pointer to a table, the column in that table that should have custom drawing behavior, and a pointer to a TableDrawItemFuncType function. The TableDrawItemFuncType prototype looks like this:

**Palm OS Garnet**
```
void TableDrawItemFuncType (TablePtr tableP, Int16 row,
    Int16 column, RectangleType *bounds)
```

**Palm OS Cobalt**
```
void TableDrawItemFuncType (void *tableP, int16_t row,
    int16_t column, RectangleType *bounds)
```

In TableDrawItemFuncType, tableP is a pointer to a table, row and column are the row and column of the table cell to draw, and bounds is a pointer to a rectangle that defines the boundaries of the table cell.

Table Example implements two versions of TableDrawItemFuncType. The first, DrawNarrowTextTableItem, draws the icons on the end of the narrowTextTableItem in column six:

**Palm OS Garnet**
```
static void DrawNarrowTextTableItem(void *table, Int16 row,
    Int16 column, RectangleType *bounds)
{
    Char    symbol[3];
    Int16   i;
    Int16   length = 0;


    for (i = 0; i < 3; i++)
        symbol[i] = '\0';

    switch(TblGetItemInt(table, row, column))
    {
        case 13:
            symbol[0] = symbolAlarm;
            length = 1;
            break;

        case 20:
            symbol[0] = symbolAlarm;
            symbol[1] = symbolRepeat;
            length = 2;
            break;

        default:
```

```
            break;
    }

    if (symbol[0] != '\0')
    {
        FontID  curFont = FntSetFont(symbolFont);
        Coord   x;

        x = (bounds->topLeft.x + bounds->extent.x) -
            ((length * 7) + 6);
        WinDrawChars(&symbol[0], length, x,
                    bounds->topLeft.y);
        FntSetFont(curFont);
    }
}
```

**Palm OS Cobalt**

```
static void DrawNarrowTextTableItem(void *table, int16_t row,
    int16_t column, RectangleType *bounds)
{
    char     symbol[3];
    int16_t  i;
    int16_t  length = 0;


    for (i = 0; i < 3; i++)
        symbol[i] = '\0';

    switch(TblGetItemInt(table, row, column))
    {
        case 13:
            symbol[0] = symbolAlarm;
            length = 1;
            break;

        case 20:
            symbol[0] = symbolAlarm;
            symbol[1] = symbolRepeat;
            length = 2;
            break;

        default:
            break;
    }

    if (symbol[0] != '\0')
    {
        FontID  curFont = FntSetFont(symbolFont);
        Coord   x;

        x = (bounds->topLeft.x + bounds->extent.x) -
            ((length * 7) + 6);
        WinDrawChars(&symbol[0], length, x,
                    bounds->topLeft.y);
```

```
                FntSetFont(curFont);
        }
}
```

The `DrawNarrowTextTableItem` function starts by setting up a three-character-long string (`symbol`) and initializing its characters to trailing nulls. Then the callback function uses the `TblGetItemInt` function to retrieve the Int Value stored in this table cell. As we mentioned earlier in this chapter, the Int Value in a `narrowTextTableItem` represents the number of pixels to reserve at the right of the cell. The `MainFormInit` function sets up space for 0, 1, or 2 icons, each of which is seven pixels wide, with six pixels of padding to allow space for the pop-up trigger in the next column. As a result, the value stored in Int Value will be 0, 13 (7 x 1 + 6), or 20 (7 x 2 + 6), which form the comparison values for the `switch` statement in `DrawNarrowTextTableItem`.

Depending upon the number of icons that should be drawn, `DrawNarrowTextTableItem` fills the first part of the `symbol` string with `symbolAlarm` and `symbolRepeat` characters from the Palm OS symbol font, as appropriate, and then draws `symbol` at the correct screen location, using the rectangle pointed to by `bounds` as a guide.

The `DrawCustomTableItem` function in Table Example requires much less math to accomplish its simple goals. Depending upon the value stored in the custom table cell's Int Value property, `DrawCustomTableItem` draws nothing, an alarm icon, or a repeat icon:

**Palm OS Garnet**

```
static void DrawCustomTableItem(void *table, Int16 row,
        Int16 column, RectangleType *bounds)
{
        FontID   curFont;
        Char     symbol[2];
        Int16    i;


        for (i = 0; i < 2; i++)
            symbol[i] = '\0';

        switch(TblGetItemInt(table, row, column))
        {
            case 1:
                symbol[0] = symbolAlarm;
                break;

            case 2:
                symbol[0] = symbolRepeat;
                break;

            default:
                break;
        }

        if (symbol[0] != '\0')
        {
            curFont = FntSetFont(symbolFont);
            WinDrawChars(&symbol[0], 1, bounds->topLeft.x + 1,
                        bounds->topLeft.y);
```

```
                FntSetFont(curFont);
        }
}
```

**Palm OS Cobalt**

```
static void DrawCustomTableItem(void *table, int16_t row,
    int16_t column, RectangleType *bounds)
{
    FontID   curFont;
    char     symbol[2];
    int16_t  i;


    for (i = 0; i < 2; i++)
        symbol[i] = '\0';

    switch(TblGetItemInt(table, row, column))
    {
        case 1:
            symbol[0] = symbolAlarm;
            break;

        case 2:
            symbol[0] = symbolRepeat;
            break;

        default:
            break;
    }

    if (symbol[0] != '\0')
    {
        curFont = FntSetFont(symbolFont);
        WinDrawChars(&symbol[0], 1, bounds->topLeft.x + 1,
                    bounds->topLeft.y);
        FntSetFont(curFont);
    }
}
```

# Handling Table Events

The tblSelectEvent provides a mechanism for reacting to taps within the bounds of a table. In a fully fledged application (which Table Example is not), a form's event handler would look for a tblSelectEvent and perform some action in response to the user's tapping a particular column and row, such as launching another form or dialog box.

Because it is only a sample program, Table Example does not require this level of interactivity. However, it does handle the tblEnterEvent to toggle the icon displayed by the customTableItem in the last column of the table. The following code from MainFormHandleEvent takes care of taps on cells in the last column; this technique is suitable for responding to pen events for any customTableItem.

**Palm OS Garnet**

```
case tblEnterEvent:
{
    Int16   row = event->data.tblEnter.row;
    Int16   column = event->data.tblEnter.column;

    if (column == 8)
    {
        TableType *table = event->data.tblEnter.pTable;
        Int16     oldValue = TblGetItemInt(table, row,
                                            column);

        TblSetItemInt(table, row, column,
                      (oldValue + 1) % 3);
        TblMarkRowInvalid(table, row);
        TblRedrawTable(table);
        handled = true;
    }
}
break;
```

**Palm OS Cobalt**

```
case tblEnterEvent:
{
    int16_t   row = event->data.tblEnter.row;
    int16_t   column = event->data.tblEnter.column;

    if (column == 8)
    {
        TableType *table = event->data.tblEnter.pTable;
        int16_t    oldValue = TblGetItemInt(table, row,
                                            column);

        TblSetItemInt(table, row, column,
                      (oldValue + 1) % 3);
        TblMarkRowInvalid(table, row);
        TblRedrawTable(table);
        handled = true;
    }
}
break;
```

When the main form receives a `tblEnterEvent`, `MainFormEventHandler` checks to see if the stylus came down within the last column. If so, `MainFormEventHandler` uses `TblSetItemInt` to cycle the tapped cell's Int Value to the next number and then marks the row invalid with `TblMarkRowInvalid` to ensure that the table manager will redraw the row. A call to `TblRedrawTable` forces the system to redraw invalid rows, causing the `customTableItem` cell's custom drawing routine to draw the appropriate new icon for the cell's new Int Value.

# Hiding Rows and Columns

Often an application with a table needs to be able to hide rows and columns from view. For example, hiding parts of the table allows for customizing the display by adding or removing columns. The built-in

To Do application uses column hiding to great effect, letting the user choose how much information should be shown for each To Do item.

Hiding a column requires the `TblSetColumnUsable` function, which was introduced earlier in this chapter as part of Table Example's `MainFormInit` function. Columns are set unusable by default, so it is necessary to activate them in the initialization of your table. After the table is up and running, you can use `TblSetColumnUsable` to toggle columns on and off. Likewise, the `TblSetRowUsable` function allows you to turn rows in the column on and off.

To demonstrate hiding and showing parts of a table, Table Example has two buttons at the bottom of its main form, `MainHideRowsButton` and `MainHideColumnsButton`. The `MainFormHandleEvent` routine handles `ctlSelectEvents` from these buttons by calling the `ToggleRow` or `ToggleColumn` function, as appropriate:

```
case ctlSelectEvent:
    switch (event->data.ctlSelect.controlID)
    {
        case MainHideRowsButton:
            ToggleRows();
            handled = true;
            break;

        case MainHideColumnsButton:
            ToggleColumns();
            handled = true;
            break;

        default:
            break;
    }
    break;
```

Figure 14-2 shows what the Table Example program looks like when the user taps the two buttons in all their permutations (clockwise from upper left: nothing hidden, rows hidden, both rows and columns hidden, columns hidden). Notice that when the columns are hidden, the slightly oversized pop-up triggers overlap part of the check box column to their left. When all the columns are visible, this overlap is not apparent because the code in `MainFormInit` and `DrawNarrowTextTableItem` compensates for the six pixels of overlap by drawing the narrow text table item's icons six pixels farther to the left.

The `ToggleRows` function appears as shown in the following example:

**Palm OS Garnet**
```
static void ToggleRows(void)
{
    FormType     *form;
    TableType    *table;
    ControlType  *ctl;
    Int16        i;


    form = FrmGetActiveForm();
    table = FrmGetObjectPtr(form,
            FrmGetObjectIndex(form, MainTable));
```

```
    ctl = FrmGetObjectPtr(form,
        FrmGetObjectIndex(form, MainHideRowsButton));

    for (i = 0; i < numTableRows; i++)
    {
        if (i % 2)
            TblSetRowUsable(table, i , gRowsHidden);
        TblMarkRowInvalid(table, i);
    }

    if (gRowsHidden)
        CtlSetLabel(ctl, "Hide Rows");
    else
        CtlSetLabel(ctl, "Show Rows");

    TblRedrawTable(table);
    gRowsHidden = !gRowsHidden;
}
```

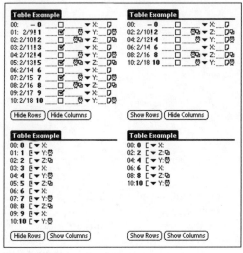

**Figure 14-2**

**Palm OS Cobalt**

```
static void ToggleRows(void)
{
    FormType     *form;
    TableType    *table;
    ControlType  *ctl;
    int16_t      i;


    form = FrmGetActiveForm();
    table = FrmGetObjectPtr(form,
            FrmGetObjectIndex(form, MainTable));
    ctl = FrmGetObjectPtr(form,
```

```
                     FrmGetObjectIndex(form, MainHideRowsButton));

    for (i = 0; i < numTableRows; i++)
    {
        if (i % 2)
            TblSetRowUsable(table, i , gRowsHidden);
        TblMarkRowInvalid(table, i);
    }

    if (gRowsHidden)
        CtlSetLabel(ctl, "Hide Rows");
    else
        CtlSetLabel(ctl, "Show Rows");

    TblRedrawTable(table);
    gRowsHidden = !gRowsHidden;
}
```

The ToggleRows function iterates over the rows of the table, hiding or showing every other row with TblSetRowUsable, depending upon the value of gRowsHidden. Also, TblSetRowUsable marks every row in the table invalid with TblMarkRowInvalid; in order to hide or show rows, the entire table needs to be redrawn. After invalidating rows, ToggleRows changes the text of the MainHideRowsButton to an appropriate caption, redraws the table with TblRedrawTable, and toggles the value of gRowsHidden.

Table Example's ToggleColumns function is almost identical to ToggleRows:

**Palm OS Garnet**

```
static void ToggleColumns(void)
{
    FormType     *form;
    TableType    *table;
    ControlType  *ctl;
    Int16        i;


    form = FrmGetActiveForm();
    table = FrmGetObjectPtr(form,
            FrmGetObjectIndex(form, MainTable));
    ctl = FrmGetObjectPtr(form,
            FrmGetObjectIndex(form, MainHideColumnsButton));

    for (i = 0; i < numTableColumns; i++)
    {
        if (i % 2)
            TblSetColumnUsable(table, i , gColumnsHidden);
    }

    for (i = 0; i < numTableRows; i++)
        TblMarkRowInvalid(table, i);

    if (gColumnsHidden)
        CtlSetLabel(ctl, "Hide Columns");
    else
```

```
                CtlSetLabel(ctl, "Show Columns");


        TblRedrawTable(table);
        gColumnsHidden = !gColumnsHidden;
}
```

**Palm OS Cobalt**

```
static void ToggleColumns(void)
{
    FormType      *form;
    TableType     *table;
    ControlType   *ctl;
    int16_t       i;


    form = FrmGetActiveForm();
    table = FrmGetObjectPtr(form,
            FrmGetObjectIndex(form, MainTable));
    ctl = FrmGetObjectPtr(form,
            FrmGetObjectIndex(form, MainHideColumnsButton));

    for (i = 0; i < numTableColumns; i++)
    {
        if (i % 2)
            TblSetColumnUsable(table, i , gColumnsHidden);
    }

    for (i = 0; i < numTableRows; i++)
        TblMarkRowInvalid(table, i);

    if (gColumnsHidden)
        CtlSetLabel(ctl, "Hide Columns");
    else
        CtlSetLabel(ctl, "Show Columns");

    TblRedrawTable(table);
    gColumnsHidden = !gColumnsHidden;
}
```

Notice that `ToggleColumns` contains an extra `for` loop to invalidate table rows. This step is necessary because columns cannot be invalidated, only rows; the first `for` loop iterates over the table's columns, not its rows.

# Creating More Complex Tables

Now that you have been introduced to the basics of initializing and interacting with tables, it is time to look at a more complicated example. The Librarian sample application has two forms that contain tables: the List view and Edit view (see Figure 14-3—List view on the left, Edit view on the right). The List view's table is mostly for display purposes; it contains a variable number of columns depending upon what kind of status information the user wishes to display in the view. Status information may be altered by tapping a status cell, which pops up a list for the selection of a new status value. The Edit view's table has only two columns: a set of row labels and a series of variable-height text fields.

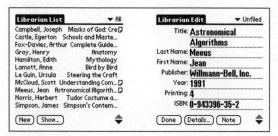

**Figure 14-3**

The biggest difference between these tables and the table in Table Example is that Librarian's tables are scrollable, allowing them to provide access to more information than will fit on a single screen. Before getting too far into the intricacies of scrolling tables, though, this chapter will look at how Librarian initializes its tables.

# Connecting a Table to Data

This section uses Librarian's List view table to demonstrate one of the most common uses for tables, which is to display information from an application's database. Each row in the table represents a single record from Librarian's database. The List view table has the following PilRC resource definition:

```
TABLE ID ListTable AT (0 16 160 121) ROWS 11 COLUMNS 6
    COLUMNWIDTHS 113 10 10 10 10 6
```

The six columns in the List view table, from left to right, are used to display a record's title, book status, print status, format, read or unread status, and a note indicator to let the user know that a particular record has an attached note. Librarian uses a number of constants to identify these columns, defined in librarian.h as follows:

```
// List view constants
#define titleColumn         0
#define bookStatusColumn    1
#define printStatusColumn   2
#define formatColumn        3
#define readColumn          4
#define noteColumn          5
```

## Initializing the List View Table

To initialize this table, the form handler for the List view, ListFormHandleEvent, calls ListFormInit in response to a frmOpenEvent. ListFormInit looks like this:

**Palm OS Garnet**
```
static void ListFormInit(FormType *form)
{
    UInt16       row;
    UInt16       rowsInTable;
    TableType    *table;
    ControlType  *ctl;
    Int16        statusWidth;
```

```
FontID       curFont;
char         noteChar;
Boolean      statusExists;
RectangleType  tableBounds;


curFont = FntSetFont(gListFont);

// Initialize the book list table.
table = FrmGetObjectPtr(form,
        FrmGetObjectIndex(form, ListTable));
rowsInTable = TblGetNumberOfRows(table);
for (row = 0; row < rowsInTable; row++)
{
    TblSetItemStyle(table, row, titleColumn,
                    customTableItem);
    TblSetItemStyle(table, row, bookStatusColumn,
                    customTableItem);
    TblSetItemStyle(table, row, printStatusColumn,
                    customTableItem);
    TblSetItemStyle(table, row, formatColumn,
                    customTableItem);
    TblSetItemStyle(table, row, readColumn,
                    customTableItem);
    TblSetItemStyle(table, row, noteColumn,
                    customTableItem);

    if (gROMVersion >=
        sysMakeROMVersion(3,0,0,sysROMStageRelease,0))
    {
        TblSetItemFont(table, row, titleColumn,
                       gListFont);
        TblSetItemFont(table, row, bookStatusColumn,
                       gListFont);
        TblSetItemFont(table, row, printStatusColumn,
                       gListFont);
        TblSetItemFont(table, row, formatColumn,
                       gListFont);
        TblSetItemFont(table, row, readColumn,
                       gListFont);
    }

    TblSetRowUsable(table, row, false);
}

TblSetColumnUsable(table, titleColumn, true);
TblSetColumnUsable(table, bookStatusColumn,
                   gShowBookStatus);
TblSetColumnUsable(table, printStatusColumn,
                   gShowPrintStatus);
TblSetColumnUsable(table, formatColumn, gShowFormat);
TblSetColumnUsable(table, readColumn, gShowReadUnread);
TblSetColumnUsable(table, noteColumn, true);

// Set the width of the book status column.
if (gShowBookStatus)
```

```
    {
        TblSetColumnWidth(table, bookStatusColumn,
            FntCharWidth(libWidestBookStatusChr));
        if (gShowPrintStatus || gShowFormat ||
            gShowReadUnread)
            TblSetColumnSpacing(table, bookStatusColumn, 0);
        else
            TblSetColumnSpacing(table, bookStatusColumn, 1);
    }

    // Set the width of the print status column.
    if (gShowPrintStatus)
    {
        TblSetColumnWidth(table, printStatusColumn,
            FntCharWidth(libWidestPrintStatusChr));
        if (gShowFormat || gShowReadUnread)
            TblSetColumnSpacing(table, printStatusColumn, 0);
        else
            TblSetColumnSpacing(table, printStatusColumn, 1);
    }

    // Set the width of the format column.
    if (gShowFormat)
    {
        TblSetColumnWidth(table, formatColumn,
            FntCharWidth(libWidestFormatStatusChr));
        if (gShowReadUnread)
            TblSetColumnSpacing(table, formatColumn, 0);
        else
            TblSetColumnSpacing(table, formatColumn, 1);
    }

    // Set the width of the read column.
    if (gShowReadUnread)
    {
        TblSetColumnWidth(table, readColumn,
            FntCharWidth(libWidestReadUnreadChr));
        TblSetColumnSpacing(table, readColumn, 1);
    }

    // Set the width of the note column.
    FntSetFont(symbolFont);
    noteChar = symbolNote;
    TblSetColumnWidth(table, noteColumn,
                    FntCharWidth(noteChar));
    FntSetFont(gListFont);

    statusExists = (gShowBookStatus || gShowPrintStatus ||
                    gShowFormat || gShowReadUnread);

    // Set the width and column spacing of the title
    // column.
    statusWidth = ((statusExists ? spaceBeforeStatus + 1 :
                    1) +
                    (gShowBookStatus ?
```

```
                    TblGetColumnWidth(table,
                        bookStatusColumn) : 0) +
                (gShowPrintStatus ?
                    TblGetColumnWidth(table,
                        printStatusColumn) : 0) +
                (gShowFormat ? TblGetColumnWidth(table,
                    formatColumn) : 0) +
                (gShowReadUnread ?
                    TblGetColumnWidth(table,
                        readColumn) : 0) +
                    TblGetColumnWidth(table, noteColumn) +
                    1);

    TblGetBounds(table, &tableBounds);
    TblSetColumnWidth(table, titleColumn,
                    tableBounds.extent.x -
                    statusWidth);
    if (statusExists)
        TblSetColumnSpacing(table, titleColumn,
                            spaceBeforeStatus);
    else
        TblSetColumnSpacing(table, titleColumn, 1);

    // Set the callback routine that will draw the records.
    TblSetCustomDrawProcedure(table, titleColumn,
                            ListFormDrawRecord);
    TblSetCustomDrawProcedure(table, bookStatusColumn,
                            ListFormDrawRecord);
    TblSetCustomDrawProcedure(table, printStatusColumn,
                            ListFormDrawRecord);
    TblSetCustomDrawProcedure(table, formatColumn,
                            ListFormDrawRecord);
    TblSetCustomDrawProcedure(table, readColumn,
                            ListFormDrawRecord);
    TblSetCustomDrawProcedure(table, noteColumn,
                            ListFormDrawRecord);

    // Load records into the address list.
    ListFormLoadTable();

    FntSetFont(curFont);

    // Other form initializing code omitted.
}
```

**Palm OS Cobalt**

```
static void ListFormInit(FormType *form)
{
    uint16_t    row;
    uint16_t    rowsInTable;
    TableType   *table;
    ControlType *ctl;
    int16_t     statusWidth;
    FontID      curFont;
    char        noteChar;
```

```
Boolean      statusExists;
RectangleType  tableBounds;


curFont = FntSetFont(gListFont);

// Initialize the book list table.
table = FrmGetObjectPtr(form,
        FrmGetObjectIndex(form, ListTable));
rowsInTable = TblGetNumberOfRows(table);
for (row = 0; row < rowsInTable; row++)
{
    TblSetItemStyle(table, row, titleColumn,
                 customTableItem);
    TblSetItemStyle(table, row, bookStatusColumn,
                 customTableItem);
    TblSetItemStyle(table, row, printStatusColumn,
                 customTableItem);
    TblSetItemStyle(table, row, formatColumn,
                 customTableItem);
    TblSetItemStyle(table, row, readColumn,
                 customTableItem);
    TblSetItemStyle(table, row, noteColumn,
                 customTableItem);

    TblSetItemFont(table, row, titleColumn,
                 gListFont);
    TblSetItemFont(table, row, bookStatusColumn,
                 gListFont);
    TblSetItemFont(table, row, printStatusColumn,
                 gListFont);
    TblSetItemFont(table, row, formatColumn,
                 gListFont);
    TblSetItemFont(table, row, readColumn,
                 gListFont);

    TblSetRowUsable(table, row, false);
}

TblSetColumnUsable(table, titleColumn, true);
TblSetColumnUsable(table, bookStatusColumn,
                 gShowBookStatus);
TblSetColumnUsable(table, printStatusColumn,
                 gShowPrintStatus);
TblSetColumnUsable(table, formatColumn, gShowFormat);
TblSetColumnUsable(table, readColumn, gShowReadUnread);
TblSetColumnUsable(table, noteColumn, true);

// Set the width of the book status column.
if (gShowBookStatus)
{
    TblSetColumnWidth(table, bookStatusColumn,
        FntCharWidth(libWidestBookStatusChr));
    if (gShowPrintStatus || gShowFormat ||
        gShowReadUnread)
```

```
                    TblSetColumnSpacing(table, bookStatusColumn, 0);
        else
                TblSetColumnSpacing(table, bookStatusColumn, 1);
}


// Set the width of the print status column.
if (gShowPrintStatus)
{
    TblSetColumnWidth(table, printStatusColumn,
        FntCharWidth(libWidestPrintStatusChr));
    if (gShowFormat || gShowReadUnread)
        TblSetColumnSpacing(table, printStatusColumn, 0);
    else
        TblSetColumnSpacing(table, printStatusColumn, 1);
}


// Set the width of the format column.
if (gShowFormat)
{
    TblSetColumnWidth(table, formatColumn,
        FntCharWidth(libWidestFormatStatusChr));
    if (gShowReadUnread)
        TblSetColumnSpacing(table, formatColumn, 0);
    else
        TblSetColumnSpacing(table, formatColumn, 1);
}


// Set the width of the read column.
if (gShowReadUnread)
{
    TblSetColumnWidth(table, readColumn,
        FntCharWidth(libWidestReadUnreadChr));
    TblSetColumnSpacing(table, readColumn, 1);
}


// Set the width of the note column.
FntSetFont(symbolFont);
noteChar = symbolNote;
TblSetColumnWidth(table, noteColumn,
                FntCharWidth(noteChar));
FntSetFont(gListFont);

statusExists = (gShowBookStatus || gShowPrintStatus ||
                gShowFormat || gShowReadUnread);

// Set the width and column spacing of the title
// column.
statusWidth = ((statusExists ? spaceBeforeStatus + 1 :
                1) +
                (gShowBookStatus ?
                TblGetColumnWidth(table,
                    bookStatusColumn) : 0) +
                (gShowPrintStatus ?
                TblGetColumnWidth(table,
                    printStatusColumn) : 0) +
```

```
                    (gShowFormat ? TblGetColumnWidth(table,
                        formatColumn) : 0) +
                    (gShowReadUnread ?
                     TblGetColumnWidth(table,
                        readColumn) : 0) +
                    TblGetColumnWidth(table, noteColumn) +
                    1);

    TblGetBounds(table, &tableBounds);
    TblSetColumnWidth(table, titleColumn,
                    tableBounds.extent.x -
                    statusWidth);
    if (statusExists)
        TblSetColumnSpacing(table, titleColumn,
                        spaceBeforeStatus);
    else
        TblSetColumnSpacing(table, titleColumn, 1);

    // Set the callback routine that will draw the records.
    TblSetCustomDrawProcedure(table, titleColumn,
                        ListFormDrawRecord);
    TblSetCustomDrawProcedure(table, bookStatusColumn,
                        ListFormDrawRecord);
    TblSetCustomDrawProcedure(table, printStatusColumn,
                        ListFormDrawRecord);
    TblSetCustomDrawProcedure(table, formatColumn,
                        ListFormDrawRecord);
    TblSetCustomDrawProcedure(table, readColumn,
                        ListFormDrawRecord);
    TblSetCustomDrawProcedure(table, noteColumn,
                        ListFormDrawRecord);

    // Load records into the address list.
    ListFormLoadTable();

    FntSetFont(curFont);

    // Other form initializing code omitted.
}
```

The first thing `ListFormInit` takes care of is defining what kind of data each table cell contains. Just as in the Table Example program, Librarian iterates over each row in the table with a `for` loop; unlike Table Example, however, Librarian sets every single cell to the `customTableItem` style. Although the `labelTableItem` style allows for static display of text, which is primarily what the `ListTable` is for, `labelTableItem` cells tack a colon (`:`) onto the end of their text strings, an unwelcome side effect for the List view's table.

> *In Palm OS Cobalt, Librarian could use the `labelNoColonTableItem` style to avoid using having a colon appended, but for the sake of keeping the code similar between the Palm OS Garnet and Palm OS Cobalt versions, Librarian uses `customTableItem` cells in both.*

Within the first `for` loop, `ListFormInit` also sets the font of the title and four status cells:

```
if (gROMVersion >=
    sysMakeROMVersion(3,0,0,sysROMStageRelease,0))
```

```
    {
        TblSetItemFont(table, row, titleColumn, gListFont);
        TblSetItemFont(table, row, bookStatusColumn, gListFont);
        TblSetItemFont(table, row, printStatusColumn, gListFont);
        TblSetItemFont(table, row, formatColumn, gListFont);
        TblSetItemFont(table, row, readColumn, gListFont);
    }
    TblSetItemFont(table, row, titleColumn, gListFont);
    TblSetItemFont(table, row, bookStatusColumn, gListFont);
    TblSetItemFont(table, row, printStatusColumn, gListFont);
    TblSetItemFont(table, row, formatColumn, gListFont);
    TblSetItemFont(table, row, readColumn, gListFont);
```

The code differs slightly between Palm OS Garnet and Palm OS Cobalt. The Palm OS Garnet version is backward-compatible to versions of Palm OS prior to 3.0, in which PalmSource introduced the `TblSetItemFont` function. Prior to Palm OS 3.0, attempting to call this function results in an error. The Palm OS Cobalt version does not need to check the version because it cannot run on prior versions of Palm OS at all.

Palm OS versions 3.0 and later have the big, legible `largeBoldFont` available, and Librarian allows the user to customize the display font used in the List view. The user can select the standard Palm OS font to fit as much information on the screen as possible, or the larger font when readability from a distance is an issue. Calling `TblSetItemFont` for each of the table's cells to set that cell's font to `gListFont` (a Librarian global variable that keeps track of the current font for the List view) ensures that the cells are the proper height to hold their contents, whether those contents are in `stdFont`, `boldFont`, or `largeBoldFont`. Note that it is unnecessary to set the last column's font because the note icon it contains will never be taller than the default `stdFont` height.

After setting fonts for each row's cells, `ListFormInit` makes all the rows of the table unusable:

```
    TblSetRowUsable(table, row, false);
```

Librarian makes all the rows unusable by default because there may not be enough records displayed to fill the entire screen, which would result in empty rows that still responded to user interaction. The rows become usable only if they contain data, which the `ListFormLoadTable` function (described in the next section) handles as it fills the table from Librarian's database.

Next, `ListFormInit` sets the usability of the table's columns:

```
    TblSetColumnUsable(table, titleColumn, true);
    TblSetColumnUsable(table, bookStatusColumn,
                       gShowBookStatus);
    TblSetColumnUsable(table, printStatusColumn,
                       gShowPrintStatus);
    TblSetColumnUsable(table, formatColumn, gShowFormat);
    TblSetColumnUsable(table, readColumn, gShowReadUnread);
    TblSetColumnUsable(table, noteColumn, true);
```

The `titleColumn` and `noteColumn` are always visible in the List view, but Librarian allows the user to turn the four status columns on or off. Librarian uses four global variables—`gShowBookStatus`, `gShowPrintStatus`, `gShowFormat`, and `gShowReadUnread`—to keep track of which fields should be displayed. A `true` value in any of these variables indicates that the appropriate column should show up in the List view. Figure 14-4 shows three views of the List form with varying numbers of the status columns turned on or off (all columns displayed on the left, only two status columns displayed in the middle, and none of the status columns displayed on the right).

**Figure 14-4**

To make the most efficient use of the handheld's limited screen real estate, Librarian resizes the columns in the List view to allow the largest amount of space possible for the first column. To determine the size of the first column, `ListFormInit` first calculates and sets the widths of the four status columns and the note indicator column:

```
// Set the width of the book status column.
if (gShowBookStatus)
{
    TblSetColumnWidth(table, bookStatusColumn,
        FntCharWidth(libWidestBookStatusChr));
    if (gShowPrintStatus || gShowFormat ||
        gShowReadUnread)
        TblSetColumnSpacing(table, bookStatusColumn, 0);
    else
        TblSetColumnSpacing(table, bookStatusColumn, 1);
}

// Set the width of the print status column.
if (gShowPrintStatus)
{
    TblSetColumnWidth(table, printStatusColumn,
        FntCharWidth(libWidestPrintStatusChr));
    if (gShowFormat || gShowReadUnread)
        TblSetColumnSpacing(table, printStatusColumn, 0);
    else
        TblSetColumnSpacing(table, printStatusColumn, 1);
}

// Set the width of the format column.
if (gShowFormat)
{
    TblSetColumnWidth(table, formatColumn,
        FntCharWidth(libWidestFormatStatusChr));
    if (gShowReadUnread)
        TblSetColumnSpacing(table, formatColumn, 0);
    else
        TblSetColumnSpacing(table, formatColumn, 1);
```

```
    }

    // Set the width of the read column.
    if (gShowReadUnread)
    {
        TblSetColumnWidth(table, readColumn,
            FntCharWidth(libWidestReadUnreadChr));
        TblSetColumnSpacing(table, readColumn, 1);
    }

    // Set the width of the note column.
    FntSetFont(symbolFont);
    noteChar = symbolNote;
    TblSetColumnWidth(table, noteColumn,
                        FntCharWidth(noteChar));
    FntSetFont(gListFont);
```

The widest character that can appear in each status column is stored in a constant value, one of `libWidestBookStatusChr`, `libWidestPrintStatusChr`, `libWidestFormatStatusChr`, or `libWidestReadUnreadChr`. Feeding the character constant to the `FntCharWidth` function determines the width in pixels of the character, which is suitable to pass to `TblSetColumnWidth` to actually set the width of each column.

To conserve screen space, the four status columns are jammed next to one another with no intervening space; but to provide a little visual separation between the status columns and the note indicator, the last visible status column should have a single pixel of separation between it and the note column. The `ListFormInit` function uses `TblSetColumnSpacing` to set the after-column spacing of each status column.

After the widths of the last five columns have been calculated, it is possible to set the width of the `titleColumn`:

```
statusExists = (gShowBookStatus || gShowPrintStatus ||
                gShowFormat || gShowReadUnread);

// Set the width and column spacing of the title column.
statusWidth = ( (statusExists ? spaceBeforeStatus + 1 : 1)+
                (gShowBookStatus ? TblGetColumnWidth(table,
                    bookStatusColumn) : 0) +
                (gShowPrintStatus ? TblGetColumnWidth(table,
                    printStatusColumn) : 0) +
                (gShowFormat ? TblGetColumnWidth(table,
                    formatColumn) : 0) +
                (gShowReadUnread ? TblGetColumnWidth(table,
                    readColumn) : 0) +
                TblGetColumnWidth(table, noteColumn) + 1);

TblSetColumnWidth(table, titleColumn,
                    table->bounds.extent.x - statusWidth);
if (statusExists)
    TblSetColumnSpacing(table, titleColumn, spaceBeforeStatus);
else
    TblSetColumnSpacing(table, titleColumn, 1);
```

The Boolean value statusExists, if true, indicates that at least one status column is visible in the table. Armed with this information, ListFormInit can fill in statusWidth with the width in pixels of any visible status column plus the width of the note column, using the Palm OS function TblGetColumnWidth to determine the widths of the appropriate columns. Then ListFormInit can calculate the width of titleColumn as the total width of the table, less statusWidth.

Finally, if any status columns are displayed, ListFormInit sets the spacing after titleColumn to the constant value spaceBeforeStatus (three pixels), which provides some visual separation between titleColumn and the first status column. This separation is important because titleColumn and the status columns are composed of text in the same font; and without a little extra space, it is hard to tell where the title ends and the status indicators begin.

The ListFormInit function uses TblSetCustomDrawProcedure to set the same callback function for all the table's columns:

```
TblSetCustomDrawProcedure(table, titleColumn,
                          ListFormDrawRecord);
TblSetCustomDrawProcedure(table, bookStatusColumn,
                          ListFormDrawRecord);
TblSetCustomDrawProcedure(table, printStatusColumn,
                          ListFormDrawRecord);
TblSetCustomDrawProcedure(table, formatColumn,
                          ListFormDrawRecord);
TblSetCustomDrawProcedure(table, readColumn,
                          ListFormDrawRecord);
TblSetCustomDrawProcedure(table, noteColumn,
                          ListFormDrawRecord);
```

Now that the table has been initialized, all that remains is to fill it with data from Librarian's database. The ListFormInit function calls another of Librarian's functions, ListFormLoadTable, to accomplish this task.

## Loading Data Into the Table

The ListFormLoadTable function, which is responsible for filling the List form's table with data, looks like this:

**Palm OS Garnet**

```
static void ListFormLoadTable(void)
{
    UInt16    row, numRows, visibleRows;
    UInt16    lineHeight;
    UInt16    recordNum;
    FontID    curFont;
    TableType *table;


    table = GetObjectPtr(ListTable);

    TblUnhighlightSelection(table);

    // Try going forward to the last record that should be
```

```
    // visible.
    visibleRows = ListFormNumberOfRows(table);
    recordNum = gTopVisibleRecord;
    if (! SeekRecord(&recordNum, visibleRows - 1,
        dmSeekForward))
    {
        // At least one line has no record. Fix it.
        // Try going backwards one page from the last
        // record.
        gTopVisibleRecord = dmMaxRecordIndex;
        if (! SeekRecord(&gTopVisibleRecord, visibleRows -
                        1, dmSeekBackward))
        {
            // Not enough records to fill one page. Start
            // with the first record.
            gTopVisibleRecord = 0;
            SeekRecord(&gTopVisibleRecord, 0,
                    dmSeekForward);
        }
    }

    curFont = FntSetFont(gListFont);
    lineHeight = FntLineHeight();
    FntSetFont(curFont);

    recordNum = gTopVisibleRecord;

    for (row = 0; row < visibleRows; row++)
    {
        if (! SeekRecord(&recordNum, 0, dmSeekForward))
            break;

        // Make the row usable.
        TblSetRowUsable(table, row, true);

        // Mark the row invalid so that it will draw when we
        // call the draw routine.
        TblMarkRowInvalid(table, row);

        // Store the record number as the row ID.
        TblSetRowID(table, row, recordNum);

        TblSetRowHeight(table, row, lineHeight);

        recordNum++;
    }

    // Hide the items that don't have any data.
    numRows = TblGetNumberOfRows (table);
    while (row < numRows)
    {
        TblSetRowUsable(table, row, false);
        row++;
```

```
    }

    // Update the List view's scroll buttons.
    ListFormUpdateScrollButtons();
}
```

**Palm OS Cobalt**

```
static void ListFormLoadTable(void)
{
    uint16_t  row, numRows, visibleRows;
    uint16_t  lineHeight;
    uint32_t  recordNum;
    FontID    curFont;
    TableType *table;


    table = GetObjectPtr(ListTable);

    TblUnhighlightSelection(table);

    // Try going forward to the last record that should be
    // visible.
    visibleRows = ListFormNumberOfRows(table);
    recordNum = gTopVisibleRecord;
    if (! SeekRecord(&recordNum, visibleRows - 1,
        dmSeekForward))
    {
        // At least one line has no record. Fix it.
        // Try going backwards one page from the last
        // record.
        gTopVisibleRecord = dmMaxRecordIndex;
        if (! SeekRecord(&gTopVisibleRecord, visibleRows -
                        1, dmSeekBackward))
        {
            // Not enough records to fill one page. Start
            // with the first record.
            gTopVisibleRecord = 0;
            SeekRecord(&gTopVisibleRecord, 0,
                    dmSeekForward);
        }
    }

    curFont = FntSetFont(gListFont);
    lineHeight = FntLineHeight();
    FntSetFont(curFont);

    recordNum = gTopVisibleRecord;

    for (row = 0; row < visibleRows; row++)
    {
        if (! SeekRecord(&recordNum, 0, dmSeekForward))
            break;

        // Make the row usable.
```

```
        TblSetRowUsable(table, row, true);

        // Mark the row invalid so that it will draw when we
        // call the draw routine.
        TblMarkRowInvalid(table, row);

        // Store the record number as the row ID.
        TblSetRowData(table, row, recordNum);

        TblSetRowHeight(table, row, lineHeight);

        recordNum++;
    }

    // Hide the items that don't have any data.
    numRows = TblGetNumberOfRows (table);
    while (row < numRows)
    {
        TblSetRowUsable(table, row, false);
        row++;
    }

    // Update the List view's scroll buttons.
    ListFormUpdateScrollButtons();
}
```

Because `ListFormLoadTable` completely redraws the items displayed in the table, the highlighted selection becomes invalid. The first thing `ListFormLoadTable` does is to retrieve a handle to the List form's table and unhighlight the table's current selection with the `TblUnhighlightSelection` function.

The `ListFormLoadTable` function then retrieves the number of rows the table can display at one time by using the helper function `ListFormNumberOfRows`:

**Palm OS Garnet**

```
static UInt16 ListFormNumberOfRows(TableType *table)
{
    UInt16  rows, rowsInTable;
    UInt16  tableHeight;
    FontID  curFont;
    RectangleType  r;


    rowsInTable = TblGetNumberOfRows(table);

    TblGetBounds(table, &r);
    tableHeight = r.extent.y;

    curFont = FntSetFont(gListFont);
    rows = tableHeight / FntLineHeight();
    FntSetFont(curFont);

    if (rows <= rowsInTable)
```

```
            return (rows);
        else
            return (rowsInTable);
}
```

**Palm OS Cobalt**

```
static uint16_t ListFormNumberOfRows(TableType *table)
{
    uint16_t  rows, rowsInTable;
    uint16_t  tableHeight;
    FontID  curFont;
    RectangleType  r;


    rowsInTable = TblGetNumberOfRows(table);

    TblGetBounds(table, &r);
    tableHeight = r.extent.y;

    curFont = FntSetFont(gListFont);
    rows = tableHeight / FntLineHeight();
    FntSetFont(curFont);

    if (rows <= rowsInTable)
        return (rows);
    else
        return (rowsInTable);
}
```

The `ListFormNumberOfRows` function simply compares the height of a line in the current font, determined using the `FntLineHeight` function, with the height of the table itself. If the user changes the display font Librarian uses for drawing the List form's data, the number of displayable rows changes because some fonts are taller than others. For example, the `stdFont` allows for 11 table rows, whereas the `largeBoldFont` allows space for only eight.

Once the number of visible rows is stored in the variable `visibleRows`, `ListFormLoadTable` looks for an appropriate record in the database to use as a starting point for filling in the table. The global variable `gTopVisibleRecord` stores the index of the record at the top of the table. If the program is just starting up, `gTopVisibleRecord` is equal to 0, representing the first record in Librarian's database. In order for a record to be a good candidate for `gTopVisibleRecord`, the following things must be true:

❑ There must be enough displayable records after `gTopVisibleRecord` in Librarian's database to fill the entire table, leaving no blank rows at the end

❑ Failing that, `gTopVisibleRecord` should be the first displayable record in the database

The `ListFormLoadTable` function determines the viability of `gTopVisibleRecord` with the following code:

```
// Try going forward to the last record that should be visible.
visibleRows = ListFormNumberOfRows(table);
recordNum = gTopVisibleRecord;
```

```
if (! SeekRecord(&recordNum, visibleRows - 1,
    dmSeekForward))
{
    // At least one line has no record. Fix it.
    // Try going backwards one page from the last record.
    gTopVisibleRecord = dmMaxRecordIndex;
    if (! SeekRecord(&gTopVisibleRecord, visibleRows - 1,
                    dmSeekBackward))
    {
        // Not enough records to fill one page. Start with
        // the first record.
        gTopVisibleRecord = 0;
        SeekRecord(&gTopVisibleRecord, 0, dmSeekForward);
    }
}
```

In the Palm OS Garnet version, Librarian's SeekRecord function is a wrapper for the Palm OS function DmSeekRecordInCategory, which looks for the next available record in the database that is a certain offset from the current record. The Palm OS Cobalt version of Librarian uses the equivalent DmFindRecordByOffsetInCategory function. The details of using DmSeekRecordInCategory or DmFindRecordByOffsetInCategory are best left for Chapter 16, but for the purpose of understanding how ListFormLoadTable works, all that is necessary is to know what SeekRecord does. Here is the prototype for SeekRecord:

**Palm OS Garnet**
```
static Boolean SeekRecord(UInt16 *index, Int16 offset,
                            Int16 direction)
```

**Palm OS Cobalt**
```
static Boolean SeekRecord(uint32_t *index, int16_t offset,
                            int16_t direction)
```

The index parameter is the index of a record in the database, offset is an integer value indicating how many records from index the search should start at, and direction tells SeekRecord whether to search forward or backward through the database. See Chapter 16 for details on how to use DmSeekRecordInCategory, DmFindRecordByOffsetInCategory, and other database-related functions.

The first thing ListFormLoadTable attempts to do is search forward through the database for a record that is visibleRows - 1 records away from the current record at the top of the list. If such a record does not exist, there will be one or more empty rows at the bottom of the table. To prevent empty rows, ListFormLoadTable then searches backward through the database, starting with the last record, again looking visibleRows - 1 records away. If no record exists to satisfy that condition either, then there are not enough records in the entire database to fill the table. In that case, ListFormLoadTable resigns itself to using the first record in the database as the top of the table, assigning 0 to gTopVisibleRecord.

One more call to SeekRecord is necessary, though, because the first record might not be in the category Librarian is currently displaying; therefore, this last call to SeekRecord advances to the first displayable record in the database.

Now that ListFormLoadTable has determined a starting point in the database, it can get to the business of actually filling in the table:

**Palm OS Garnet**

```
curFont = FntSetFont(gListFont);
lineHeight = FntLineHeight();
FntSetFont(curFont);

recordNum = gTopVisibleRecord;

for (row = 0; row < visibleRows; row++)
{
    if (! SeekRecord(&recordNum, 0, dmSeekForward))
        break;

    // Make the row usable.
    TblSetRowUsable(table, row, true);

    // Mark the row invalid so that it will draw when we
    // call the draw routine.
    TblMarkRowInvalid(table, row);

    // Store the record number as the row ID.
    TblSetRowID(table, row, recordNum);

    TblSetRowHeight(table, row, lineHeight);

    recordNum++;
}
```

**Palm OS Cobalt**

```
curFont = FntSetFont(gListFont);
lineHeight = FntLineHeight();
FntSetFont(curFont);

recordNum = gTopVisibleRecord;

for (row = 0; row < visibleRows; row++)
{
    if (! SeekRecord(&recordNum, 0, dmSeekForward))
        break;

    // Make the row usable.
    TblSetRowUsable(table, row, true);

    // Mark the row invalid so that it will draw when we
    // call the draw routine.
    TblMarkRowInvalid(table, row);

    // Store the record number as the row ID.
    TblSetRowData(table, row, recordNum);

    TblSetRowHeight(table, row, lineHeight);

    recordNum++;
}
```

For each visible row, `ListFormLoadTable` searches for the next displayable record using `SeekRecord`; if it doesn't find one, `ListFormLoadTable` is finished filling in records and breaks out of the `for` loop. The `ListFormLoadTable` function sets each row that does have a record usable with `TblSetRowUsable` and then marks that row invalid with `TblMarkRowInvalid` so that the table manager redraws the row when it next draws the table.

Most important, in the Palm OS Garnet version, the `for` loop stores the index of the record as the row's ID number with the `TblSetRowID` function. Every row in a table has an ID value, which you may use to store whatever unsigned 16-bit integer value you wish. In an application that uses classic databases, this ID number is an ideal place to stash the database index of the record displayed in a particular row. Palm OS also provides the companion functions `TblGetRowID` and `TblFindRowID`. The `TblGetRowID` function simply returns the ID value assigned to a row, given the row number. If you need to retrieve the row number and all you have is the row's ID number, use the `TblFindRowID` function instead.

Palm OS Cobalt's schema databases use an unsigned 32-bit integer to store the index of a particular row in a database. This large a value will not fit into the 16-bit row ID, so the Palm OS Cobalt version of Librarian uses the row data field instead. Every row in a table has a 32-bit data value associated with it, which may be filled with any application-defined data you wish to put there by calling the `TblSetRowData` function. Palm OS Cobalt also provides `TblGetRowData` for retrieving the data value assigned to a row, given the row number, as well as `TblFindRowData` for retrieving the row number given a row data value.

The `for` loop finishes by setting the height of each row with the `TblSetRowHeight` function.

After filling in the table, `ListFormLoadTable` hides, with a `while` loop, the rows that do not contain any data:

```
// Hide the items that don't have any data.
numRows = TblGetNumberOfRows (table);
while (row < numRows) {
    TblSetRowUsable(table, row, false);
    row++;
}
```

Finally, `ListFormLoadTable` calls Librarian's `ListFormUpdateScrollButtons` function, which ensures that any changes to the table made by `ListFormLoadTable` are reflected in the appearance of the arrow buttons in the lower-right corner of the List form:

```
// Update the List view's scroll buttons.
ListFormUpdateScrollButtons();
```

The details of `ListFormUpdateScrollButtons` are omitted here; see the next section's description of the Edit form's table for more information about implementing scrolling tables.

## Drawing Individual Rows

The part of Librarian that does all the drawing work in the List form's table is the `ListFormDrawRecord` callback function, which `ListFormInit` sets up for all six columns in the table. `ListFormDrawRecord` looks like this:

**Palm OS Garnet**

```
static void ListFormDrawRecord (void *table, Int16 row,
    Int16 column, RectangleType *bounds)
{
    UInt16  recordNum;
    Err     error;
    MemHandle  recordH;
    char    noteChar;
    FontID  curFont;
    LibDBRecordType  record;
    char    statusChr;
    Int16   x;
    UInt8   showInList;


    curFont = FntSetFont(gListFont);

    // Get the record number that corresponds to the table
    // item to draw.
    recordNum = TblGetRowID(table, row);

    // Retrieve a locked handle to the record. Remember to
    // unlock recordH later when finished with the record.
    error = LibGetRecord(gLibDB, recordNum, &record,
                         &recordH);
    ErrNonFatalDisplayIf((error), "Record not found");
    if (error)
    {
        MemHandleUnlock(recordH);
        return;
    }

    switch (column)
    {
        case titleColumn:
            showInList = LibGetSortOrder(gLibDB);
            DrawRecordName(&record, bounds, showInList,
                        &gNoAuthorRecordString,
                        &gNoTitleRecordString);
            break;

        case bookStatusColumn:
            switch (record.status.bookStatus)
            {
                case bookStatusHave:
                    statusChr = libHaveStatusChr;
                    break;

                case bookStatusWant:
                    statusChr = libWantStatusChr;
                    break;

                case bookStatusOnOrder:
                    statusChr = libOnOrderStatusChr;
```

```
                    break;

            case bookStatusLoaned:
                statusChr = libLoanedStatusChr;
                break;

            default:
                break;
        }
        x = bounds->topLeft.x + (bounds->extent.x / 2)-
            (FntCharWidth(statusChr) / 2);
        WinDrawChars(&statusChr, 1, x,
                    bounds->topLeft.y);
        break;

    case printStatusColumn:
        switch (record.status.printStatus)
        {
            case printStatusInPrint:
                statusChr = libInPrintStatusChr;
                break;

            case printStatusOutOfPrint:
                statusChr = libOutOfPrintStatusChr;
                break;

            case printStatusNotPublished:
                statusChr = libNotPublishedStatusChr;
                break;

            default:
                break;
        }
        x = bounds->topLeft.x + (bounds->extent.x / 2)-
            (FntCharWidth(statusChr) / 2);
        WinDrawChars(&statusChr, 1, x,
                    bounds->topLeft.y);
        break;

    case formatColumn:
        switch (record.status.format)
        {
            case formatHardcover:
                statusChr = libHardcoverStatusChr;
                break;

            case formatPaperback:
                statusChr = libPaperbackStatusChr;
                break;

            case formatTradePaperback:
                statusChr = libTradePaperStatusChr;
                break;

            case formatOther:
```

```
                        statusChr = libOtherStatusChr;
                        break;

                    default:
                        break;
                }
                x = bounds->topLeft.x + (bounds->extent.x / 2)-
                    (FntCharWidth(statusChr) / 2);
                WinDrawChars(&statusChr, 1, x,
                            bounds->topLeft.y);
                break;

            case readColumn:
                if (record.status.read)
                    statusChr = libReadStatusChr;
                else
                    statusChr = libUnreadStatusChr;
                x = bounds->topLeft.x + (bounds->extent.x / 2)-
                    (FntCharWidth(statusChr) / 2);
                WinDrawChars(&statusChr, 1, x,
                            bounds->topLeft.y);
                break;

            case noteColumn:
                // Draw a note symbol if the field has a note.
                if (record.fields[libFieldNote])
                {
                    FntSetFont(symbolFont);
                    noteChar = symbolNote;
                    WinDrawChars (&noteChar, 1,
                                bounds->topLeft.x,
                                bounds->topLeft.y);
                    FntSetFont(gListFont);
                }
                break;

            default:
                break;
        }

    // Since the handle returned from LibGetRecord
    // (recordH) is no longer needed, unlock it.
    MemHandleUnlock(recordH);

    FntSetFont(curFont);
}
```

**Palm OS Cobalt**

```
static void ListFormDrawRecord (void *table,
    int16_t row, int16_t column, RectangleType *bounds)
{
    uint32_t  recordNum;
    status_t  error;
    MemHandle recordH;
    char      noteChar;
```

```
FontID    curFont;
LibDBRecordType  record;
char      statusChr;
int16_t   x;
uint8_t   showInList;


curFont = FntSetFont(gListFont);

// Get the record number that corresponds to the table
// item to draw.
recordNum = TblGetRowData(table, row);

// Retrieve a locked handle to the record. Remember to
// unlock recordH later when finished with the record.
error = LibGetRecord(gLibDB, recordNum, &record,
                     &recordH);
DbgOnlyFatalErrorIf((error), "Record not found");
if (error)
{
    MemHandleUnlock(recordH);
    return;
}

switch (column)
{
    case titleColumn:
        showInList = LibGetSortOrder(gLibDB);
        DrawRecordName(&record, bounds, showInList,
                     &gNoAuthorRecordString,
                     &gNoTitleRecordString);
        break;

    case bookStatusColumn:
        switch (record.status.bookStatus)
        {
            case bookStatusHave:
                statusChr = libHaveStatusChr;
                break;

            case bookStatusWant:
                statusChr = libWantStatusChr;
                break;

            case bookStatusOnOrder:
                statusChr = libOnOrderStatusChr;
                break;

            case bookStatusLoaned:
                statusChr = libLoanedStatusChr;
                break;

            default:
                break;
        }
```

```
        x = bounds->topLeft.x + (bounds->extent.x / 2)-
            (FntCharWidth(statusChr) / 2);
        WinDrawChars(&statusChr, 1, x,
                    bounds->topLeft.y);
        break;

case printStatusColumn:
    switch (record.status.printStatus)
    {
        case printStatusInPrint:
            statusChr = libInPrintStatusChr;
            break;

        case printStatusOutOfPrint:
            statusChr = libOutOfPrintStatusChr;
            break;

        case printStatusNotPublished:
            statusChr = libNotPublishedStatusChr;
            break;

        default:
            break;
    }
    x = bounds->topLeft.x + (bounds->extent.x / 2)-
        (FntCharWidth(statusChr) / 2);
    WinDrawChars(&statusChr, 1, x,
                bounds->topLeft.y);
    break;

case formatColumn:
    switch (record.status.format)
    {
        case formatHardcover:
            statusChr = libHardcoverStatusChr;
            break;

        case formatPaperback:
            statusChr = libPaperbackStatusChr;
            break;

        case formatTradePaperback:
            statusChr = libTradePaperStatusChr;
            break;

        case formatOther:
            statusChr = libOtherStatusChr;
            break;

        default:
            break;
    }
    x = bounds->topLeft.x + (bounds->extent.x / 2)-
        (FntCharWidth(statusChr) / 2);
    WinDrawChars(&statusChr, 1, x,
```

```
                              bounds->topLeft.y);
            break;

        case readColumn:
            if (record.status.read)
                statusChr = libReadStatusChr;
            else
                statusChr = libUnreadStatusChr;
            x = bounds->topLeft.x + (bounds->extent.x / 2)-
                (FntCharWidth(statusChr) / 2);
            WinDrawChars(&statusChr, 1, x,
                              bounds->topLeft.y);
            break;

        case noteColumn:
            // Draw a note symbol if the field has a note.
            if (record.fields[libFieldNote])
            {
                FntSetFont(symbolFont);
                noteChar = symbolNote;
                WinDrawChars (&noteChar, 1,
                              bounds->topLeft.x,
                              bounds->topLeft.y);
                FntSetFont(gListFont);
            }
            break;

        default:
            break;
    }

    // Since the handle returned from LibGetRecord
    // (recordH) is no longer needed, unlock it.
    MemHandleUnlock(recordH);

    FntSetFont(curFont);
}
```

When called by the table manager, ListFormDrawRecord first determines from the row's ID number or data field the database index of the record displayed in a particular row, using the TblGetRowID or TblGetRowData function. Then ListFormDrawRecord passes this index to Librarian's LibGetRecord function to retrieve the actual record from the database as follows:

**Palm OS Garnet**
```
// Get the record number that corresponds to the table item
// to draw.
recordNum = TblGetRowID(table, row);

// Retrieve a locked handle to the record. Remember to
// unlock recordH later when finished with the record.
error = LibGetRecord(gLibDB, recordNum, &record, &recordH);
ErrNonFatalDisplayIf((error), "Record not found");
if (error)
```

```
{
    MemHandleUnlock(recordH);
    return;
}
```

**Palm OS Cobalt**
```
// Get the record number that corresponds to the table item
// to draw.
recordNum = TblGetRowData(table, row);

// Retrieve a locked handle to the record. Remember to
// unlock recordH later when finished with the record.
error = LibGetRecord(gLibDB, recordNum, &record, &recordH);
DbgOnlyFatalErrorIf((error), "Record not found");
if (error)
{
    MemHandleUnlock(recordH);
    return;
}
```

*The details of LibGetRecord are not important to this discussion; see Chapter 16 for more information about Librarian's database handling routines.*

After retrieving the record, ListFormDrawRecord enters a large switch statement to perform different drawing tasks based on the column value passed to the callback function by the table manager.

If the column that should be drawn is the titleColumn, ListFormDrawRecord calls the LibGetSortOrder and DrawRecordName helper functions to draw the appropriate record title data into the first column in the table:

```
case titleColumn:
    showInList = LibGetSortOrder(gLibDB);
    DrawRecordName(&record, bounds, showInList,
                &gNoAuthorRecordString,
                &gNoTitleRecordString);
    break;
```

The LibGetSortOrder function retrieves the current display style for the List form, which is one of three things:

- ❑ Author of the book followed by title
- ❑ Title of the book followed by author
- ❑ Title of the book only

Passing the showInList value retrieved by LibGetSortOrder to DrawRecordName allows the latter function to know which database fields it should pull from Librarian's database and the order in which they should be displayed. The DrawRecordName function performs the actual drawing to the screen, within the limits of the bounds parameter provided to ListFormDrawRecord by the table manager.

*The LibGetSortOrder and DrawRecordName functions both involve a fair amount of database access, which is a topic better left to another chapter of this book. Chapter 16 covers these Librarian functions in detail.*

If the column to be drawn is one of the status columns, `ListFormDrawRecord` looks at the database record to determine the correct character to display in the cell and then draws that character in the appropriate place on the screen. The four status column sections of the `switch` statement and the note column section perform nearly identical operations, so only the part that handles the `bookStatusColumn` is shown in the following example for reference:

```
case bookStatusColumn:
    switch (record.status.bookStatus)
    {
        case bookStatusHave:
            statusChr = libHaveStatusChr;
            break;

        case bookStatusWant:
            statusChr = libWantStatusChr;
            break;

        case bookStatusOnOrder:
            statusChr = libOnOrderStatusChr;
            break;

        case bookStatusLoaned:
            statusChr = libLoanedStatusChr;
            break;

        default:
            break;
    }
    x = bounds->topLeft.x + (bounds->extent.x / 2) -
        (FntCharWidth(statusChr) / 2);
    WinDrawChars(&statusChr, 1, x, bounds->topLeft.y);
    break;
```

Based on the value of `bounds`, which is a rectangle defining the edges of the cell to draw in, `ListFormDrawRecord` centers the status character horizontally in the cell and draws it with the `WinDrawChars` function.

After drawing the status and note columns, `ListFormDrawRecord` performs some cleanup, unlocking the handle to the row's database record and setting the font back to its former state before `ListFormDrawRecord` started playing around with it:

```
// Since the handle returned from LibGetRecord (recordH) is
// no longer needed, unlock it.
MemHandleUnlock(recordH);

FntSetFont(curFont);
```

## Scrolling Tables

Librarian's Edit form contains a table that is ideal for demonstrating table scrolling. One of the form's two columns is full of text fields that expand and contract in height as the user adds text to or removes it from the fields, which is a fairly complex scenario to implement. Figure 14-5 illustrates what happens to the table as a user enters more text than fits in a field at once. On the left, the user has entered text almost to the end of a line in a text field ("Astronomical Algorit"). On the right, the field has expanded by one line to accommodate more text ("Astronomical Algorithms"), pushing the table rows underneath down a line, which causes the last line in the table to disappear entirely.

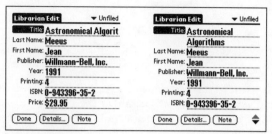

**Figure 14-5**

## Initializing a Table with Resizable Text Fields

The PilRC resource definition of the Edit form's table looks like this:

```
TABLE ID EditTable AT (0 18 160 121) ROWS 11 COLUMNS 2
    COLUMNWIDTHS 45 115
```

Librarian initializes the table in the function EditFormInit. The most important things that happen in EditFormInit are setting the table item styles and setting the callback functions for loading and saving data in the text field column. The EditFormInit function also is responsible for setting the widths of the table's two columns as follows:

```
// Initialize the edit table.
table = FrmGetObjectPtr(form, FrmGetObjectIndex(form,
                    EditTable));
rowsInTable = TblGetNumberOfRows(table);
for (row = 0; row < rowsInTable; row++)
{
    TblSetItemStyle(table, row, labelColumn,
                labelTableItem);
    TblSetItemStyle(table, row, dataColumn, textTableItem);
    TblSetRowUsable(table, row, false);
}

TblSetColumnUsable(table, labelColumn, true);
TblSetColumnUsable(table, dataColumn, true);

TblSetColumnSpacing(table, labelColumn, spaceBeforeData);

// Set the callback routines that will load and save the data
// column.
TblSetLoadDataProcedure(table, dataColumn,
                    EditFormGetRecordField);
TblSetSaveDataProcedure(table, dataColumn,
                    EditFormSaveRecordField);

// Compute the width of the data column; account for the
// space between the two columns.
```

```
TblGetBounds(table, &bounds);
dataColumnWidth = bounds.extent.x - spaceBeforeData -
    gEditLabelColumnWidth;

TblSetColumnWidth(table, labelColumn,
                  gEditLabelColumnWidth);
TblSetColumnWidth(table, dataColumn, dataColumnWidth);

EditFormLoadTable();
```

After setting up the table itself, `EditFormInit` calls `EditFormLoadTable`, which performs a similar function to that of the List view's `ListFormLoadTable`. The `EditFormLoadTable` function is somewhat more complex than `ListFormLoadTable`'s because, unlike those in List view, rows in the Edit view's table can have different heights:

**Palm OS Garnet**

```
static void EditFormLoadTable(void)
{
    UInt16     row, numRows;
    UInt16     lineHeight;
    UInt16     fieldIndex, lastFieldIndex;
    UInt16     dataHeight;
    UInt16     tableHeight;
    UInt16     columnWidth;
    UInt16     pos, oldPos;
    UInt16     height, oldHeight;
    FontID     fontID;
    FontID     curFont;
    FormType   *form;
    TableType  *table;
    Boolean    rowUsable;
    Boolean    rowsInserted = false;
    Boolean    lastItemClipped;
    RectangleType  r;
    LibDBRecordType  record;
    MemHandle  recordH;
    LibAppInfoType  *appInfo;
    Boolean    fontChanged;


    appInfo = MemHandleLock(LibGetAppInfo(gLibDB));

    form = FrmGetActiveForm();

    // Get the current record
    LibGetRecord(gLibDB, gCurrentRecord, &record,
                 &recordH);

    // Get the height of the table and the width of the
    // data column.
    table = GetObjectPtr(EditTable);
    TblGetBounds(table, &r);
    tableHeight = r.extent.y;
```

```
columnWidth = TblGetColumnWidth(table, dataColumn);

// If a field is currently selected, make sure that it
// is not above the first visible field.
if (gCurrentFieldIndex != noFieldIndex) {
    if (gCurrentFieldIndex < gTopVisibleFieldIndex)
        gTopVisibleFieldIndex = gCurrentFieldIndex;
}

row = 0;
dataHeight = 0;
oldPos = pos = 0;
fieldIndex = gTopVisibleFieldIndex;
lastFieldIndex = fieldIndex;

// Load fields into the table.
while (fieldIndex <= editLastFieldIndex) {
    // Compute the height of the field's text string.
    height = EditFormGetFieldHeight(table, fieldIndex,
                columnWidth, tableHeight, &record, &fontID);

    // Is there enough room for at least one line of the
    // data?
    curFont = FntSetFont(fontID);
    lineHeight = FntLineHeight();
    FntSetFont (curFont);
    if (tableHeight >= dataHeight + lineHeight) {
        rowUsable = TblRowUsable(table, row);

        // Get the height of the current row.
        if (rowUsable)
            oldHeight = TblGetRowHeight(table, row);
        else
            oldHeight = 0;

        // If the field is not already displayed in the
        // current row, load the field into the table.
        if (gROMVersion >=
            sysMakeROMVersion(3, 0, 0,
                              sysROMStageRelease, 0))
            fontChanged = (TblGetItemFont(table, row,
                            dataColumn) != fontID);
        else
            fontChanged = false;

        if ((! rowUsable) ||
            (TblGetRowID(table, row) != fieldIndex) ||
            fontChanged)
        {
            EditInitTableRow(table, row, fieldIndex,
                            height, fontID,
                            &record, appInfo);
        }

        // If the height or the position of the item
```

```
                    // has changed, draw the item.
            else if (height != oldHeight)
            {
                TblSetRowHeight(table, row, height);
                TblMarkRowInvalid(table, row);
            }
            else if (pos != oldPos)
            {
                TblMarkRowInvalid(table, row);
            }

            pos += height;
            oldPos += oldHeight;
            lastFieldIndex = fieldIndex;
            fieldIndex++;
            row++;
        }

    dataHeight += height;

    // Is the table full?
    if (dataHeight >= tableHeight)
    {
        // If a field is currently selected, make sure
        // that it is not below the last visible field.
        // If the currently selected field is the last
        // visible record, make sure the whole field is
        // visible.
        if (gCurrentFieldIndex == noFieldIndex)
            break;

        // Above last visible?
        else if (gCurrentFieldIndex < fieldIndex)
            break;

        // Last visible?
        else if (fieldIndex == lastFieldIndex)
        {
            if ((fieldIndex == gTopVisibleFieldIndex)
                || (dataHeight == tableHeight))
                break;
        }

        // Remove the top item from the table and
        // reload the table again.
        gTopVisibleFieldIndex++;
        fieldIndex = gTopVisibleFieldIndex;

        row = 0;
        dataHeight = 0;
        oldPos = pos = 0;
    }
}

// Hide the items that don't have any data.
```

```
    numRows = TblGetNumberOfRows(table);
    while (row < numRows)
    {
        TblSetRowUsable(table, row, false);
        row++;
    }

    // If the table is not full and the first visible field
    // is not the first field in the record, display enough
    // fields to fill out the table by adding fields to the
    // top of the table.
    while (dataHeight < tableHeight)
    {
        fieldIndex = gTopVisibleFieldIndex;
        if (fieldIndex == 0) break;
        fieldIndex--;

        // Compute the height of the field.
        height = EditFormGetFieldHeight(table, fieldIndex,
            columnWidth, tableHeight, &record, &fontID);

        // If adding the item to the table will overflow
        // the height of the table, don't add the item.
        if (dataHeight + height > tableHeight)
            break;

        // Insert a row before the first row.
        TblInsertRow(table, 0);

        EditInitTableRow(table, 0, fieldIndex, height,
                        fontID, &record, appInfo);

        gTopVisibleFieldIndex = fieldIndex;
        rowsInserted = true;
        dataHeight += height;
    }

    // If rows were inserted to fill out the page,
    // invalidate the whole table; it all needs to be
    // redrawn.
    if (rowsInserted)
        TblMarkTableInvalid(table);

    // If the height of the data in the table is greater
    // than the height of the table, then the bottom of the
    // last row is clipped and the table is scrollable.
    lastItemClipped = (dataHeight > tableHeight);

    // Update the scroll arrows.
    EditFormUpdateScrollers(form, lastFieldIndex,
                            lastItemClipped);

    MemHandleUnlock(recordH);
    MemPtrUnlock(appInfo);
}
```

**Palm OS Cobalt**

```
static void EditFormLoadTable(void)
{
    uint16_t   row, numRows;
    uint16_t   lineHeight;
    uint16_t   fieldIndex, lastFieldIndex;
    uint16_t   dataHeight;
    uint16_t   tableHeight;
    uint16_t   columnWidth;
    uint16_t   pos, oldPos;
    uint16_t   height, oldHeight;
    FontID     fontID;
    FontID     curFont;
    FormType   *form;
    TableType  *table;
    Boolean    rowUsable;
    Boolean    rowsInserted = false;
    Boolean    lastItemClipped;
    RectangleType  r;
    LibDBRecordType  record;
    MemHandle  recordH;
    LibAppInfoType  appInfo;
    Boolean    fontChanged;


    LibGetAppInfo(gLibDB, &appInfo);

    form = FrmGetActiveForm();

    // Get the current record
    LibGetRecord(gLibDB, gCurrentRecord, &record,
                 &recordH);

    // Get the height of the table and the width of the
    // data column.
    table = GetObjectPtr(EditTable);
    TblGetBounds(table, &r);
    tableHeight = r.extent.y;
    columnWidth = TblGetColumnWidth(table, dataColumn);

    // If a field is currently selected, make sure that it
    // is not above the first visible field.
    if (gCurrentFieldIndex != noFieldIndex) {
        if (gCurrentFieldIndex < gTopVisibleFieldIndex)
            gTopVisibleFieldIndex = gCurrentFieldIndex;
    }

    row = 0;
    dataHeight = 0;
    oldPos = pos = 0;
    fieldIndex = gTopVisibleFieldIndex;
    lastFieldIndex = fieldIndex;

    // Load fields into the table.
    while (fieldIndex <= editLastFieldIndex) {
```

```
// Compute the height of the field's text string.
height = EditFormGetFieldHeight(table, fieldIndex,
        columnWidth, tableHeight, &record, &fontID);

// Is there enough room for at least one line of the
// data?
curFont = FntSetFont(fontID);
lineHeight = FntLineHeight();
FntSetFont (curFont);
if (tableHeight >= dataHeight + lineHeight) {
    rowUsable = TblRowUsable(table, row);

    // Get the height of the current row.
    if (rowUsable)
        oldHeight = TblGetRowHeight(table, row);
    else
        oldHeight = 0;

    // If the field is not already displayed in the
    // current row, load the field into the table.
    if (gROMVersion >=
        sysMakeROMVersion(3, 0, 0,
                           sysROMStageRelease, 0))
        fontChanged = (TblGetItemFont(table, row,
                        dataColumn) != fontID);
    else
        fontChanged = false;

    if ((! rowUsable) ||
        (TblGetRowID(table, row) != fieldIndex) ||
        fontChanged)
    {
        EditInitTableRow(table, row, fieldIndex,
                        height, fontID,
                        &record, &appInfo);
    }

    // If the height or the position of the item
    // has changed, draw the item.
    else if (height != oldHeight)
    {
        TblSetRowHeight(table, row, height);
        TblMarkRowInvalid(table, row);
    }
    else if (pos != oldPos)
    {
        TblMarkRowInvalid(table, row);
    }

    pos += height;
    oldPos += oldHeight;
    lastFieldIndex = fieldIndex;
    fieldIndex++;
    row++;
```

```
        }

        dataHeight += height;

        // Is the table full?
        if (dataHeight >= tableHeight)
        {
            // If a field is currently selected, make sure
            // that it is not below the last visible field.
            // If the currently selected field is the last
            // visible record, make sure the whole field is
            // visible.
            if (gCurrentFieldIndex == noFieldIndex)
                break;

            // Above last visible?
            else if (gCurrentFieldIndex < fieldIndex)
                break;

            // Last visible?
            else if (fieldIndex == lastFieldIndex)
            {
                if ((fieldIndex == gTopVisibleFieldIndex)
                    || (dataHeight == tableHeight))
                    break;
            }

            // Remove the top item from the table and
            // reload the table again.
            gTopVisibleFieldIndex++;
            fieldIndex = gTopVisibleFieldIndex;

            row = 0;
            dataHeight = 0;
            oldPos = pos = 0;
        }
    }

    // Hide the items that don't have any data.
    numRows = TblGetNumberOfRows(table);
    while (row < numRows)
    {
        TblSetRowUsable(table, row, false);
        row++;
    }

    // If the table is not full and the first visible field
    // is not the first field in the record, display enough
    // fields to fill out the table by adding fields to the
    // top of the table.
    while (dataHeight < tableHeight)
    {
        fieldIndex = gTopVisibleFieldIndex;
```

```
            if (fieldIndex == 0) break;
            fieldIndex--;

            // Compute the height of the field.
            height = EditFormGetFieldHeight(table, fieldIndex,
                columnWidth, tableHeight, &record, &fontID);

            // If adding the item to the table will overflow
            // the height of the table, don't add the item.
            if (dataHeight + height > tableHeight)
                break;

            // Insert a row before the first row.
            TblInsertRow(table, 0);

            EditInitTableRow(table, 0, fieldIndex, height,
                            fontID, &record, &appInfo);

            gTopVisibleFieldIndex = fieldIndex;
            rowsInserted = true;
            dataHeight += height;
        }

        // If rows were inserted to fill out the page,
        // invalidate the whole table; it all needs to be
        // redrawn.
        if (rowsInserted)
            TblMarkTableInvalid(table);

        // If the height of the data in the table is greater
        // than the height of the table, then the bottom of the
        // last row is clipped and the table is scrollable.
        lastItemClipped = (dataHeight > tableHeight);

        // Update the scroll arrows.
        EditFormUpdateScrollers(form, lastFieldIndex,
                            lastItemClipped);

        MemHandleUnlock(recordH);
}
```

In the Palm OS Garnet version of Librarian, the EditFormLoadTable function begins by retrieving Librarian's application info block with the helper function LibGetAppInfo and the current record from Librarian's database with LibGetRecord. The Palm OS Cobalt version of Librarian does not have an application info block but it retrieves the equivalent information from its database by calling a different version of LibGetAppInfo.

*See Chapter 15 for more information about application info blocks and Librarian's LibGetAppInfo function. See Chapter 16 for more information about retrieving records from databases and Librarian's LibGetRecord function.*

After setting up a few values that will come in handy later in the function, EditFormLoadTable checks to see whether the field currently selected — represented by the global variable gCurrentFieldIndex — is less than the first displayable field in the table, which is held in the global variable gTopVisibleFieldIndex. If gCurrentFieldIndex is less than gTopVisibleFieldIndex, EditFormLoadTable sets gTopVisibleFieldIndex equal to the currently selected field index:

```
// If a field is currently selected, make sure that it is not
// above the first visible field.
if (gCurrentFieldIndex != noFieldIndex)
{
    if (gCurrentFieldIndex < gTopVisibleFieldIndex)
        gTopVisibleFieldIndex = gCurrentFieldIndex;
}
```

The EditFormLoadTable then starts to load data into the table. This process is tricky because, unlike in the List view's table, there is not a one-to-one relationship between the number of data fields in each record and the number of rows available in the Edit view's table. Each field may occupy more than one row. Figure 14-6 shows the extremes involved in filling the table. The EditFormLoadTable function must be able to handle the table having fewer data fields than table rows (left), fewer table rows than data fields (right), and everything in between.

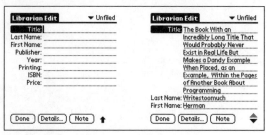

**Figure 14-6**

The logic in the massive while loop at the heart of EditFormLoadTable goes something like this:

1. Starting with the topmost visible data field, stored in gTopVisibleFieldIndex, iterate through the data fields until the last data field, represented by the constant editLastFieldIndex, has been reached.

2. Call the helper function EditFormGetFieldHeight to retrieve the amount of vertical space the current field would occupy onscreen and store that value in the variable height for later use.

3. Check to see if at least one line of the current field's data will fit within the table:

```
if (tableHeight >= dataHeight + lineHeight)
```

The while loop uses the variable dataHeight to keep track of the total height of the data displayed in the field, tableHeight is the total height available in the table itself, and lineHeight is the height of a single line of table text. If the first line of the current field does not fit, skip to Step 9.

4. Determine if the current table row is usable by calling TblRowUsable:

```
rowUsable = TblRowUsable(table, row);
```

5. If the row is usable, find the height of the current table row with TblGetRowHeight and store this value in the variable oldHeight:

```
oldHeight = TblGetRowHeight(table, row);
```

If the row is not usable, set `oldHeight` equal to 0.

**6.** Determine whether the current table row needs to be initialized. The row needs to be initialized if any of the following criteria are met:

- ❑ The row is not usable (`rowUsable != true`). A usable row has already been initialized.

- ❑ The row's ID does not match the index of the current field (`TblGetRowID(table, row) != fieldIndex`). If it does match, the current field is already drawn in the current row.

- ❑ The font has changed (`fontChanged == true`).

If the row requires initialization, call the helper function `EditInitTableRow` to do the job.

**7.** If the row's height or position has changed, mark the row invalid so it will be redrawn:

```
else if (height != oldHeight)
{
    TblSetRowHeight(table, row, height);
    TblMarkRowInvalid(table, row);
}
else if (pos != oldPos)
{
    TblMarkRowInvalid(table, row);
}
```

**8.** Increment and set values for the next pass through the `while` loop:

```
pos += height;
oldPos += oldHeight;
lastFieldIndex = fieldIndex;
fieldIndex++;
row++;
```

**9.** Check to see if the table is full:

```
if (dataHeight >= tableHeight)
```

If the table is not full, the `while` loop repeats with the new values set in Step 8.

**10.** If the table is full, check to see that the currently selected field (`gCurrentFieldIndex`) appears onscreen. The selected field is visible if its index is less than the index of the current `fieldIndex` used by the `while` loop, or if the selected field is the only field displayed in the table. If the selected field is visible, break out of the `while` loop:

```
if (gCurrentFieldIndex == noFieldIndex)
    break;

// Above last visible?
else if (gCurrentFieldIndex < fieldIndex)
    break;

// Last visible?
else if (fieldIndex == lastFieldIndex)
{
```

```
        if ((fieldIndex == gTopVisibleFieldIndex) ||
            (dataHeight == tableHeight))
            break;
    }
```

**11.** The field is full, but the selected field is not visible. Peel the top row off the table to bump all the other rows up one slot and start at the beginning of the `while` loop again:

```
// Remove the top item from the table and reload the table
// again.
gTopVisibleFieldIndex++;
fieldIndex = gTopVisibleFieldIndex;

row = 0;
dataHeight = 0;
oldPos = pos = 0;
```

Once this `while` loop is completed, `EditFormLoadTable` hides any table rows that do not contain data:

```
numRows = TblGetNumberOfRows(table);
while (row < numRows)
{
    TblSetRowUsable(table, row, false);
    row++;
}
```

At this point, you might be thinking that this function (not to mention the developer who wrote it) should take a long and well-deserved vacation, but `EditFormLoadTable` is not quite finished. After `EditFormLoadTable` has run through all the preceding code, it is still possible that the table is not quite filled and that the first field visible in the table is not the first field in the record. In this case, `EditFormLoadTable` tries to pad out the empty space in the table by adding more fields at the *top* of the table, pushing the rest of the table data down the page. Another `while` loop kicks off this whole process, which is set to run while the height of the displayed data is less than the height of the table itself:

```
while (dataHeight < tableHeight)
```

The new `while` loop walks backward through all the fields before the field currently displayed at the top of the table. If the height of the previous field, as returned by `EditFormGetFieldHeight`, is short enough to fit within the table, `EditFormLoadTable` calls the Palm OS function `TblInsertRow` to put a new row at the top of the table as follows:

```
// Insert a row before the first row.
TblInsertRow(table, 0);

EditInitTableRow(table, 0, fieldIndex, height, fontID,
                 &record, appInfo);

gTopVisibleFieldIndex = fieldIndex;
rowsInserted = true;
dataHeight += height;
```

The `TblInsertRow` function does not actually increase the total number of table rows; it merely bumps all the other rows down by one, losing the last row of the table. A companion to `TblInsertRow` is

`TblRemoveRow`, which also does not affect the number of rows in a table but rather moves the indicated row to the bottom of the table and marks it unusable. Neither `TblInsertRow` nor `TblRemoveRow` redraws the display, so the application must call `TblRedrawTable` to make the changes made by these row insertion and deletion functions visible.

After inserting the new row with `TblInsertRow`, `EditFormLoadTable` calls `EditInitTableRow` to set up the new row. Once the `while` loop either runs out of previous fields to try or encounters a field that would make the total data height larger than the height of the table, `EditFormLoadTable` is in the home stretch. All that remains is to mark the entire table invalid, using `TblMarkTableInvalid`, if the second `while` loop inserted any rows; update the Edit form's scroll buttons by calling `EditFormUpdateScrollers`; and unlock the record and application info block handles:

**Palm OS Garnet**

```
// If rows were inserted to fill out the page, invalidate
// the whole table, it all needs to be redrawn.
if (rowsInserted)
    TblMarkTableInvalid(table);

// If the height of the data in the table is greater than
// the height of the table, then the bottom of the last row
// is clipped and the table is scrollable.
lastItemClipped = (dataHeight > tableHeight);

// Update the scroll arrows.
EditFormUpdateScrollers(form, lastFieldIndex,
                        lastItemClipped);

MemHandleUnlock(recordH);
MemPtrUnlock(appInfo);
```

**Palm OS Cobalt**

```
// If rows were inserted to fill out the page, invalidate
// the whole table, it all needs to be redrawn.
if (rowsInserted)
    TblMarkTableInvalid(table);

// If the height of the data in the table is greater than
// the height of the table, then the bottom of the last row
// is clipped and the table is scrollable.
lastItemClipped = (dataHeight > tableHeight);

// Update the scroll arrows.
EditFormUpdateScrollers(form, lastFieldIndex,
                        lastItemClipped);

MemHandleUnlock(recordH);
```

The `EditInitTableRow` function, used in a couple of places in `EditFormLoadTable` to initialize individual table rows, looks like this:

**Palm OS Garnet**

```
static void EditInitTableRow(TableType *table, UInt16 row,
    UInt16 fieldIndex, Coord rowHeight, FontID fontID,
    LibDBRecordType *record, LibAppInfoType *appInfo)
```

```
{
    // Make the row usable.
    TblSetRowUsable(table, row, true);

    // Set the height of the row to the height of the data
    // text field.
    TblSetRowHeight(table, row, rowHeight);

    // Store the record number as the row ID.
    TblSetRowID(table, row, fieldIndex);

    // Mark the row invalid so that it will draw when
    // calling the draw routine.
    TblMarkRowInvalid(table, row);

    // Set the text font if Librarian is running on version
    // 3.0 or later.
    if (gROMVersion >=
        sysMakeROMVersion(3,0,0,sysROMStageRelease,0))
        TblSetItemFont(table, row, dataColumn, fontID);

    // Set the labels in the label column.
    TblSetItemPtr(table, row, labelColumn,
                appInfo->fieldLabels[fieldIndex]);
}
```

**Palm OS Cobalt**

```
static void EditInitTableRow(TableType *table, uint16_t row,
    uint16_t fieldIndex, Coord rowHeight, FontID fontID,
    LibDBRecordType *record, LibAppInfoType *appInfo)
{
    // Make the row usable.
    TblSetRowUsable(table, row, true);

    // Set the height of the row to the height of the data
    // text field.
    TblSetRowHeight(table, row, rowHeight);

    // Store the record number as the row ID.
    TblSetRowID(table, row, fieldIndex);

    // Mark the row invalid so that it will draw when
    // calling the draw routine.
    TblMarkRowInvalid(table, row);

    TblSetItemFont(table, row, dataColumn, fontID);

    // Set the labels in the label column.
    TblSetItemPtr(table, row, labelColumn,
                appInfo->fieldLabels[fieldIndex]);
}
```

## Scrolling a Table

Most of the hard work required to scroll the Edit view's table has already been taken care of by the
EditFormLoadTable function. Scrolling involves changing the top visible field index (stored in the global

gTopVisibleFieldIndex), marking the table invalid, and then calling EditFormLoadTable to redraw the table in its new position. The following sample shows the EditFormScroll function, which determines what the new value of gTopVisibleFieldIndex should be, given a direction in which to scroll.

**Palm OS Garnet**

```
static void EditFormScroll(WinDirectionType direction)
{
    UInt16      row;
    UInt16      height;
    UInt16      fieldIndex;
    UInt16      columnWidth;
    UInt16      tableHeight;
    TableType *table;
    FontID      curFont;
    RectangleType  r;
    LibDBRecordType  record;
    MemHandle   recordH;


    curFont = FntSetFont(stdFont);

    table = GetObjectPtr(EditTable);
    TblReleaseFocus(table);

    // Get the height of the table and the width of the
    // description column.
    TblGetBounds(table, &r);
    tableHeight = r.extent.y;
    height = 0;
    columnWidth = TblGetColumnWidth(table, dataColumn);

    // Scroll the table down.
    if (direction == winDown)
    {
        // Get the index of the last visible field; this
        // will become the index of the top visible field,
        // unless it occupies the whole screen, in which
        // case the next field will be the top field.
        row = TblGetLastUsableRow(table);
        fieldIndex = TblGetRowID(table, row);

        // If the last visible field is also the first
        // visible field, then it occupies the whole
        // screen.
        if (row == 0)
            fieldIndex = min(editLastFieldIndex,
                            fieldIndex + 1);
    }

    // Scroll the table up.
    else
    {
        // Scan the fields before the first visible field
        // to determine how many fields we need to scroll.
        // Since the heights of the fields vary, total the
        // height of the records until we get a screenful.
```

```
            fieldIndex = TblGetRowID(table, 0);
            ErrFatalDisplayIf(fieldIndex > editLastFieldIndex,
                              "Invalid field Index");
            // If we're at the top of the fields already, there
            // is no need to scroll.
            if (fieldIndex == 0) {
                FntSetFont(curFont);
                return;
            }


            // Get the current record.
            LibGetRecord(gLibDB, gCurrentRecord, &record,
                         &recordH);

            height = TblGetRowHeight(table, 0);
            if (height >= tableHeight)
                height = 0;

            while (height < tableHeight && fieldIndex > 0)
            {
              height +=
                FldCalcFieldHeight(record.fields[fieldIndex-1],
                                   columnWidth) *
                                   FntLineHeight();
                if ( (height <= tableHeight) ||
                     (fieldIndex == TblGetRowID(table, 0)) )
                    fieldIndex--;
            }

            MemHandleUnlock(recordH);
        }

    TblMarkTableInvalid(table);
    gCurrentFieldIndex = noFieldIndex;
    gTopVisibleFieldIndex = fieldIndex;
    gEditRowIDWhichHadFocus = editFirstFieldIndex;
    gEditFieldPosition = 0;

    // Remove the highlight before reloading the table to
    // prevent the selection information from being out of
    // bounds, which can happen if the newly loaded data
    // has fewer rows than the old data.
    TblUnhighlightSelection(table);
    EditFormLoadTable();
    TblRedrawTable(table);
    FntSetFont(curFont);
}
```

**Palm OS Cobalt**

```
static void EditFormScroll(WinDirectionType direction)
{
    uint16_t  row;
    uint32_t  height;
    uint16_t  fieldIndex;
    uint16_t  columnWidth;
```

```
uint16_t  tableHeight;
TableType *table;
FontID    curFont;
RectangleType  r;
LibDBRecordType  record;
MemHandle  recordH;


curFont = FntSetFont(stdFont);

table = GetObjectPtr(EditTable);
TblReleaseFocus(table);

// Get the height of the table and the width of the
// description column.
TblGetBounds(table, &r);
tableHeight = r.extent.y;
height = 0;
columnWidth = TblGetColumnWidth(table, dataColumn);

// Scroll the table down.
if (direction == winDown)
{
    // Get the index of the last visible field; this
    // will become the index of the top visible field,
    // unless it occupies the whole screen, in which
    // case the next field will be the top field.
    row = TblGetLastUsableRow(table);
    fieldIndex = TblGetRowID(table, row);

    // If the last visible field is also the first
    // visible field, then it occupies the whole
    // screen.
    if (row == 0)
        fieldIndex = min(editLastFieldIndex,
                         fieldIndex + 1);
}

// Scroll the table up.
else
{
    // Scan the fields before the first visible field
    // to determine how many fields we need to scroll.
    // Since the heights of the fields vary, total the
    // height of the records until we get a screenful.
    fieldIndex = TblGetRowID(table, 0);
    ErrFatalErrorIf(fieldIndex > editLastFieldIndex,
                    "Invalid field Index");
    // If we're at the top of the fields already, there
    // is no need to scroll.
    if (fieldIndex == 0) {
        FntSetFont(curFont);
        return;
    }

    // Get the current record.
```

```
            LibGetRecord(gLibDB, gCurrentRecord, &record,
                        &recordH);

        height = TblGetRowHeight(table, 0);
        if (height >= tableHeight)
            height = 0;

        while (height < tableHeight && fieldIndex > 0)
        {
          height +=
            FldCalcFieldHeight(record.fields[fieldIndex-1],
                              columnWidth) *
                              FntLineHeight();
          if ( (height <= tableHeight) ||
               (fieldIndex == TblGetRowID(table, 0)) )
               fieldIndex--;
        }

        MemHandleUnlock(recordH);
    }

    TblMarkTableInvalid(table);
    gCurrentFieldIndex = noFieldIndex;
    gTopVisibleFieldIndex = fieldIndex;
    gEditRowIDWhichHadFocus = editFirstFieldIndex;
    gEditFieldPosition = 0;

    // Remove the highlight before reloading the table to
    // prevent the selection information from being out of
    // bounds, which can happen if the newly loaded data
    // has fewer rows than the old data.
    TblUnhighlightSelection(table);
    EditFormLoadTable();
    TblRedrawTable(table);
    FntSetFont(curFont);
}
```

When the user scrolls down, the EditFormScroll finds the last visible field in the table and makes it the topmost field — unless the last visible field occupies the entire screen, in which case EditFormScroll scrolls to the next field after the last visible one:

```
row = TblGetLastUsableRow(table);
fieldIndex = TblGetRowID(table, row);

// If the last visible field is also the first visible
// field, then it occupies the whole screen.
if (row == 0)
    fieldIndex = min(editLastFieldIndex,
                    fieldIndex + 1);
```

The TblGetLastUsableRow function returns the index of the last usable row in the table. From this index, EditFormScroll can determine which field occupies the last usable row by calling TblGetRowID, because the row IDs in the Edit view's table store the indices of each row's associated field.

*Unlike Librarian's List view table, which in Palm OS Cobalt must use the table's row data property to store record indices, the Edit view displays fewer than a dozen fields of data in the table, so there is no need to use the larger 32-bit capacity of the table's row data property. The 16-bit row ID suffices.*

Scrolling up is somewhat more complex because `EditFormScroll` must iterate through the fields prior to the current top visible field, calculating their total height until a screenful has been accumulated or until there are no more prior fields to look at. The `EditFormScroll` function calls Librarian's `LibGetRecord` to retrieve the current record so it may look through the record's fields and directly calculate the height of each using the Palm OS function `FldCalcFieldHeight`.

*In Palm OS Garnet, `FldCalcFieldHeight` returns an unsigned 16-bit value, but it returns an unsigned 32-bit value in Palm OS Cobalt. Therefore, the Palm OS Cobalt version of the `EditFormScroll` function declares the height variable as `uint32_t` instead of the smaller `UInt16` used by the Palm OS Garnet version.*

The `FldCalcFieldHeight` function determines the number of lines long a field will be in the current font, given a pointer to the text occupying the field and the width of the field in pixels. From this information, multiplying the number of lines in the field by the height of a single line gives the total vertical space occupied by the text field:

```
height += FldCalcFieldHeight(record.fields[fieldIndex - 1],
                             columnWidth) * FntLineHeight();
```

Once `EditFormScroll` has determined what the new top visible field index is, it sets appropriate variables related to the table's new position, marks the entire table invalid, reloads the table with `EditFormLoadTable`, and redraws it with `TblRedrawTable`:

```
TblMarkTableInvalid(table);
gCurrentFieldIndex = noFieldIndex;
gTopVisibleFieldIndex = fieldIndex;
gEditRowIDWhichHadFocus = editFirstFieldIndex;
gEditFieldPosition = 0;

// Remove the highlight before reloading the table to
// prevent the selection information from being out of
// bounds, which can happen if the newly loaded data has
// fewer rows than the old data.
TblUnhighlightSelection(table);
EditFormLoadTable();
TblRedrawTable(table);
FntSetFont(curFont);
```

The Edit form's event handler, `EditFormHandleEvent`, calls `EditFormScroll` in response to a `ctlRepeatEvent` from either of the form's two repeating arrow buttons, or in response to a `keyDownEvent` containing either a `pageUpChr` or a `pageDownChr`, both of which are generated by the hardware scroll buttons or other navigation hardware.

One more thing is required to keep scrolling running smoothly in the Edit form: The repeating scroll buttons must be visually updated to reflect the current scroll state of the form. The Palm OS function `FrmUpdateScrollers`, given the right information, takes care of redrawing a pair of scroll arrows so they reflect a specific scroll status. Librarian contains an `EditFormUpdateScrollers` function that wraps `FrmUpdateScrollers` and gives it the information it needs:

**Palm OS Garnet**

```
static void EditFormUpdateScrollers(FormType *form,
    UInt16 bottomFieldIndex, Boolean lastItemClipped)
{
    UInt16 upIndex;
    UInt16 downIndex;
    Boolean scrollableUp;
    Boolean scrollableDown;

    // If the first field displayed is not the first field
    // in the record, enable the up scroller.
    scrollableUp = gTopVisibleFieldIndex > 0;

    // If the last field displayed is not the last field in
    // the record, enable the down scroller.
    scrollableDown = (lastItemClipped ||
                    (bottomFieldIndex <
                    editLastFieldIndex));

    // Update the scroll button.
    upIndex = FrmGetObjectIndex(form,
                            EditScrollUpRepeating);
    downIndex = FrmGetObjectIndex(form,
                            EditScrollDownRepeating);
    FrmUpdateScrollers(form, upIndex, downIndex,
                    scrollableUp, scrollableDown);
}
```

**Palm OS Cobalt**

```
static void EditFormUpdateScrollers(FormType *form,
    uint16_t bottomFieldIndex, Boolean lastItemClipped)
{
    uint16_t  upIndex;
    uint16_t  downIndex;
    Boolean   scrollableUp;
    Boolean   scrollableDown;

    // If the first field displayed is not the first field
    // in the record, enable the up scroller.
    scrollableUp = gTopVisibleFieldIndex > 0;

    // If the last field displayed is not the last field in
    // the record, enable the down scroller.
    scrollableDown = (lastItemClipped ||
                    (bottomFieldIndex <
                    editLastFieldIndex));

    // Update the scroll button.
    upIndex = FrmGetObjectIndex(form,
                            EditScrollUpRepeating);
    downIndex = FrmGetObjectIndex(form,
                            EditScrollDownRepeating);
    FrmUpdateScrollers(form, upIndex, downIndex,
                    scrollableUp, scrollableDown);
}
```

The FrmUpdateScrollers function takes five arguments: a pointer to a form, the index of the scroll up button, the index of the scroll down button, a Boolean value indicating whether it is currently possible to scroll up, and another Boolean to indicate the possibility of scrolling down. Depending on the values of scrollableUp and scrollableDown, FrmUpdateScrollers will enable, disable, or redraw the scroll buttons according to the values listed in the following table.

| scrollableUp | scrollableDown | Result |
|---|---|---|
| True | True | Both arrows drawn solid |
| True | False | Up arrow draw solid, down arrow drawn grayed out |
| False | True | Down arrow drawn solid, up arrow drawn grayed out |
| False | False | Both arrows disabled (not visible) |

The EditFormUpdateScrollers function knows that the table may be scrolled up if the top visible field index is not the first field in the record. Likewise, if the last field displayed in the table is not the last field in the record, or if the bottom of the last displayed field is clipped, scrolling down is possible.

# Handling Table Text Fields

When tables (already a complex user interface object) collide with text fields (yet another complex object), all manner of mysterious behavior can result. Text fields contained within a table require some special handling above and beyond what a regular text field requires. This section attempts to unravel some of the mystery and point out a few "gotchas" you might encounter when implementing text field table items.

## Understanding Fields in Tables

The basic underlying principle behind text fields in a table is that *there is only ever one field object associated with a table at any one time.* Only the field that is currently being edited actually exists; the table manager creates, draws, and discards field objects as needed to give the illusion of multiple fields in a table.

What effect does this amazing fact have on your Palm OS table programming? Because the table manager maintains only one active field at a time, it discards the text handle for a field as soon as it finishes drawing that field, unless the field is currently being edited. Whenever an application performs an action that releases the focus from the current field, the system calls the TableSaveDataFuncType callback function you have set up (using the TblSetSaveDataProcedure function) for the column that contains the current field.

Within the save data callback, copy any value contained in the current field's text handle rather than just save a pointer to the handle itself because when the table manager destroys the field, it deallocates the field's text handle. You can retrieve a reference to the current field with the TblGetCurrentField function. As an example, here are the relevant portions of Librarian's EditFormSaveRecordField function, which EditFormInit attaches to the text fields in the Edit view's data column:

**Palm OS Garnet**

```
static Boolean EditFormSaveRecordField (void *table,
    Int16 row, Int16 column)
{
    FieldType   *field;
```

```
    MemHandle   textH;
    Char        *text;
    Boolean     redraw = false;


    field = TblGetCurrentField(table);
    textH = FldGetTextHandle(field);

    if (FldDirty(field))
    {
        if (textH == 0)
            text = NULL;
        else
        {
            text = MemHandleLock(textH);
            if (text[0] == '\0')
                text = NULL;
        }

        // EditFormSaveRecordField saves the text data to
        // Librarian's database here, using the contents of
        // the text character pointer. Most of the code has
        // been omitted for clarity.
        if (text)
            MemPtrUnlock(text);
    }

    // Free the memory used for the field's text.
    FldFreeMemory(field);

    // The code that actually sets
    // EditFormSaveRecordField's return value has been
    // omitted.
    return redraw;
}
```

**Palm OS Cobalt**

```
static Boolean EditFormSaveRecordField (void *table,
    int16_t row, int16_t column)
{
    FieldType   *field;
    MemHandle   textH;
    char        *text;
    Boolean     redraw = false;


    field = TblGetCurrentField(table);
    textH = FldGetTextHandle(field);

    if (FldDirty(field))
    {
        if (textH == 0)
            text = NULL;
        else
        {
```

```
            text = MemHandleLock(textH);
            if (text[0] == '\0')
                text = NULL;
        }


        // EditFormSaveRecordField saves the text data to
        // Librarian's database here, using the contents of
        // the text character pointer. Most of the code has
        // been omitted for clarity.
        if (text)
            MemPtrUnlock(text);
    }

    // Free the memory used for the field's text.
    FldFreeMemory(field);

    // The code that actually sets
    // EditFormSaveRecordField's return value has been
    // omitted.
    return redraw;
}
```

After retrieving the current field's text handle, the `EditFormSaveRecordField` function checks to see if any changes have been made to the field by calling `FldDirty`. If so, `EditFormSaveRecordField` locks the text handle, which allows the rest of the function to gain access to its contents via the `text` character pointer.

Once the callback has saved the data contained in `text`, `EditFormSaveRecordField` unlocks the text handle and frees the memory allocated for the field object by calling `FldFreeMemory`. This last step is important to prevent memory leaks; although the system discards the text handle, it does not deallocate it. Any handle you allocate within the save callback function must be deallocated before the end of the function.

Tables have an *edit mode*, which is activated as soon as a `tblEnterEvent` occurs within an editable text field in the table, or when your application calls the `TblGrabFocus` function to deliberately select a specific text cell for editing. You can check whether a table is in edit mode by calling the `TblEditing` function, which returns `true` if a text field is currently active for editing. It also is possible to retrieve a pointer to the current field, if any, by calling `TblGetCurrentField`.

The table manager calls the save data callback function any time the current field loses the focus. This can occur when the user changes the focus by tapping in a different table cell, when the user taps a note indicator in a `textWithNoteTableItem` cell, or if your code explicitly calls `TblReleaseFocus`. Calling `TblReleaseFocus` manually is necessary any time your code redraws the table in such a way that the current field may no longer appear in the table, thus causing it to lose the focus. For example, Librarian's `EditFormScroll` function calls `TblReleaseFocus` before attempting to scroll the table.

## Handling Resizable Text Table Items

The event handler for a form with a table that contains resizable text fields, such as those in Librarian's Edit view or the built-in Date Book and Address Book applications, needs to handle the `fldHeightChangedEvent` to deal properly with changes to a text field's height. Whenever the height of a field changes in response to user input, the system posts a `fldHeightChangedEvent` to the event queue.

Librarian's `EditFormHandleEvent` takes care of a `fldHeightChangeEvent` by calling the `EditFormResizeData` function, shown here:

**Palm OS Garnet**

```
static void EditFormResizeData(EventType *event)
{
    UInt16      pos;
    Int16       row, column;
    UInt16      lastRow;
    UInt16      fieldIndex, lastFieldIndex, topFieldIndex;
    FieldType   *field;
    TableType   *table;
    Boolean     restoreFocus = false;
    Boolean     lastItemClipped;
    RectangleType  itemR;
    RectangleType  tableR;
    RectangleType  fieldR;


    // Get the current height of the field;
    field = event->data.fldHeightChanged.pField;
    FldGetBounds(field, &fieldR);

    // Have the table object resize the field and move the
    // items below the field up or down.
    table = GetObjectPtr(EditTable);
    TblHandleEvent(table, event);

    // If the field's height has expanded, we're done.
    if (event->data.fldHeightChanged.newHeight >=
        fieldR.extent.y)
    {
        topFieldIndex = TblGetRowID(table, 0);
        if (topFieldIndex != gTopVisibleFieldIndex)
            gTopVisibleFieldIndex = topFieldIndex;
        else
        {
            // Since the table has expanded we may be able
            // to scroll when before we might not have.
            lastRow = TblGetLastUsableRow(table);
            TblGetBounds(table, &tableR);
            TblGetItemBounds(table, lastRow, dataColumn,
                            &itemR);
            lastItemClipped =(itemR.topLeft.y +
                itemR.extent.y > tableR.topLeft.y +
                tableR.extent.y);
            lastFieldIndex = TblGetRowID(table, lastRow);

            EditFormUpdateScrollers(FrmGetActiveForm(),
                lastFieldIndex, lastItemClipped);

            return;
        }
    }

    // If the field's height has contracted and the first
```

```
    // edit field is not visible, then the table may be
    // scrolled. Release the focus, which will force saving
    // the currently edited field.
    else if (TblGetRowID (table, 0) != editFirstFieldIndex)
    {
        TblGetSelection(table, &row, &column);
        fieldIndex = TblGetRowID(table, row);

        field = TblGetCurrentField(table);
        pos = FldGetInsPtPosition(field);
        TblReleaseFocus(table);

        restoreFocus = true;
    }

    // Add items to the table to fill in the space made
    // available by shortening the field.
    EditFormLoadTable();
    TblRedrawTable(table);

    // Restore the insertion point position.
    if (restoreFocus)
    {
        TblFindRowID(table, fieldIndex, &row);
        TblGrabFocus(table, row, column);
        FldSetInsPtPosition(field, pos);
        FldGrabFocus(field);
    }
}
```

**Palm OS Cobalt**

```
static void EditFormResizeData(EventType *event)
{
    uint16_t    pos;
    int16_t     row, column;
    uint16_t    lastRow;
    uint16_t    fieldIndex, lastFieldIndex, topFieldIndex;
    FieldType   *field;
    TableType   *table;
    Boolean     restoreFocus = false;
    Boolean     lastItemClipped;
    RectangleType   itemR;
    RectangleType   tableR;
    RectangleType   fieldR;


    // Get the current height of the field;
    field = event->data.fldHeightChanged.pField;
    FldGetBounds(field, &fieldR);

    // Have the table object resize the field and move the
    // items below the field up or down.
    table = GetObjectPtr(EditTable);
    TblHandleEvent(table, event);

    // If the field's height has expanded, we're done.
```

```
        if (event->data.fldHeightChanged.newHeight >=
            fieldR.extent.y)
    {
        topFieldIndex = TblGetRowID(table, 0);
        if (topFieldIndex != gTopVisibleFieldIndex)
            gTopVisibleFieldIndex = topFieldIndex;
        else
        {
            // Since the table has expanded we may be able
            // to scroll when before we might not have.
            lastRow = TblGetLastUsableRow(table);
            TblGetBounds(table, &tableR);
            TblGetItemBounds(table, lastRow, dataColumn,
                            &itemR);
            lastItemClipped =(itemR.topLeft.y +
                itemR.extent.y > tableR.topLeft.y +
                tableR.extent.y);
            lastFieldIndex = TblGetRowID(table, lastRow);

            EditFormUpdateScrollers(FrmGetActiveForm(),
                lastFieldIndex, lastItemClipped);

            return;
        }
    }

    // If the field's height has contracted and the first
    // edit field is not visible, then the table may be
    // scrolled. Release the focus, which will force saving
    // the currently edited field.
    else if (TblGetRowID (table, 0) != editFirstFieldIndex)
    {
        TblGetSelection(table, &row, &column);
        fieldIndex = TblGetRowID(table, row);

        field = TblGetCurrentField(table);
        pos = FldGetInsPtPosition(field);
        TblReleaseFocus(table);

        restoreFocus = true;
    }

    // Add items to the table to fill in the space made
    // available by shortening the field.
    EditFormLoadTable();
    TblRedrawTable(table);

    // Restore the insertion point position.
    if (restoreFocus)
    {
        TblFindRowID(table, fieldIndex, &row);
        TblGrabFocus(table, row, column);
        FldSetInsPtPosition(field, pos);
        FldGrabFocus(field);
    }
}
```

The EditFormResizeData function determines if expanding or contracting a text field requires redrawing the form, which can occur when a text field shrinks, causing new rows to appear at the bottom of the table. It also checks to see if the change in size of a text field enables previously disabled scrolling, which happens when the expansion of a text field causes the field to expand below the bottom of the table.

## Enabling Autoshifting in Table Text Fields

Autoshifting in a standard text field is easy to set up, and it is standard behavior in the built-in applications, so adding it to your own application presents a more consistent experience to the user. Simply define autoshifting as part of the field's properties when you create the field resource.

Unfortunately, this easy solution is not possible for text fields in a table. Because of the "virtual" nature of a table's fields, there is no way to set the autoshifting property at design time. Instead, you must enable it via application code.

Librarian's Edit table enables autoshifting in the EditFormGetRecordField function, which is the callback that EditFormInit sets up for the Edit table's dataColumn. Within EditFormGetRecordField is a call to a helper function, EditSetGraffitiMode, which is listed in the following example:

```
static void EditSetGraffitiMode(FieldType *field)
{
    FieldAttrType  attr;


    if (field)
    {
        FldGetAttributes(field, &attr);
        attr.autoShift = true;
        FldSetAttributes(field, &attr);
    }
}
```

The EditSetGraffitiMode function manually sets a field's autoshift attribute. Because the table manager calls EditFormGetRecordField every time it needs to draw one of the Edit view's text fields, all the fields in the table gain the autoshift attribute when they are initialized.

## Setting Edit Indicators

When a text field in a table has the focus in edit mode, the table manager automatically indicates that the table row containing the text field is active by highlighting other table items in the row that are not text fields. Such a highlighted table item is called an *edit indicator*. By default, all table item styles except textTableItem, textWithNoteTableItem, and narrowTextTableItem are edit indicators. The edit indicator attribute is set on a per-column basis; an entire column's table items either are, or are not, edit indicators.

Use the TblSetColumnEditIndicator function to change whether or not a particular column is an edit indicator. The following example sets column as an edit indicator:

```
TblSetColumnIndicator(table, column, true);
```

In Palm OS Garnet, only the leftmost set of contiguous edit indicators are highlighted when the table enters edit mode. For example, if columns 1, 2, and 4 are set as edit indicators, but column 3 is not, only columns 1 and 2 are highlighted. The behavior is different in Palm OS Cobalt; all columns set as edit indicators are highlighted when the table enters edit mode.

# Summary

In this chapter, you have learned the ins and outs of programming tables, the most complex user interface element in Palm OS. After reading this chapter, you should know the following:

❑   Palm OS tables can be composed of 12 different item types.

❑   A table must be initialized before it can be used.

❑   Initializing a table involves defining each cell's item type with `TblSetItemStyle`, setting initial values for nontext table items with `TblSetItemInt` and `TblSetItemPtr`, and attaching callback functions for drawing, loading, and saving with `TblSetCustomDrawProcedure`, `TblSetLoadDataProcedure`, and `TblSetSaveDataProcedure`.

❑   You can hide and display rows and columns of a table with the `TblSetRowUsable` and `TblSetColumnUsable` functions.

❑   Tables that must support scrolling require a function to load and redraw the table whenever its data changes.

❑   Only one text field ever exists at any one time in a table.

# 15

# Storing and Retrieving Data

In its role as a portable data storage and display device, a handheld running Palm OS must be able to store data in many forms and allow the user quick access to that data. Because primary data storage in the Palm OS occurs in RAM, creating and maintaining space for permanent data in Palm OS requires an approach different from that which desktop systems use to store files on nonvolatile storage media. In Palm OS, the primary mechanism for long-term data storage is the database. Thus, the first part of this chapter details the mechanics of creating, finding, and accessing Palm OS databases in both Palm OS Garnet and Palm OS Cobalt. For information on handling individual records within a database, see Chapter 16.

Not all data that should be saved between invocations of a particular program is appropriate for storage in a database. For example, keeping track of the last view the user visited in an application, or storing the user's preferred display font, requires saving a trivial amount of data, probably too little to go to the trouble of trying to store it in a database. For this kind of small data storage, Palm OS offers *application preferences*, which this chapter also covers.

Finally, some special applications may require the use of another Palm OS storage technique called *feature memory*. The last part of this chapter discusses what feature memory is and how to use it.

## Understanding Palm OS Databases

Prior to the introduction of Palm OS Cobalt, Palm OS databases were represented as collections of memory chunks in the handheld's storage RAM. These chunks are commonly referred to as "records." There was little structure imposed on these records from the data manager—records did not possess any inherent concept of fields, field types, or field lengths. Records were seen through the data manager as unstructured memory chunks, with any structure or layout determined and managed totally by the application developer. This arrangement provided much flexibility in terms of how database content was stored and accessed. However, the unstructured nature of the record arrangement required developers to invest a lot of work in their application code in interpreting and formatting data in database record storage.

These unstructured databases, now referred to as "classic" databases, are still supported across all versions of Palm OS, including Palm OS Cobalt. However, with the introduction of Palm OS Cobalt, PalmSource has now provided developers who wish to target Palm OS Cobalt with the option of using a new type of database, called "schema" databases. As opposed to classic databases, schema databases resemble relational database systems found in other platforms. Schema databases are organized into two-dimensional tables, and data access is row/column-oriented, not record-oriented. The Palm OS APIs for working with schema databases are specific to Palm OS Cobalt and are different than the APIs used when working with classic databases.

With Palm OS Cobalt there is also the option of using "extended" databases. These are based on the original classic database, with a small number of enhancements to functionality. Most of the original classic database APIs are the same for both classic and extended databases. For developers who, for compatibility reasons, wish to continue using the original classic database mechanism, extended databases offer some benefits when used on Palm OS Cobalt handhelds, yet do not require significant changes in source code written to work with classic databases.

Because of their similarities, classic and extended databases are now referred together as "non-schema" databases. Although schema databases represent a break from the original "classic" Palm OS data manager familiar to developers, the use of schema databases offers significant advantages over classic databases. As with other Palm OS Cobalt-specific APIs and features, Palm OS developers need to assess how important it is for their applications to be compatible with earlier versions of the operating system and balance that against the advantages of using schema databases over classic databases.

Because of the significant differences between schema and non-schema databases, the discussion of databases in this chapter is accordingly separated in two sections. The first section discusses how to use non-schema databases (classic and extended). This is followed by a section devoted to working with the newer schema databases.

# Understanding Non-Schema Databases

As we previously mentioned, classic and extended databases are represented to the developer as a list of memory chunks in the handheld's storage RAM, along with some header information that describes the database itself. These memory chunks are unstructured and have no inherent understanding of fields or a record layout. It is up to the application developer to read, write, and interpret the content of these records manually using the data manager APIs. Unless specifically noted otherwise, the concepts and information in this section apply to both classic and extended databases.

Within the database's record list, each record is identified by its *LocalID*, a memory offset from the beginning address of the card that contains the record. Storing record locations as LocalIDs, instead of using pointers to the records, lets the system relocate an entire memory card without needing to adjust the location of each record stored in a database's record list.

> **The system can relocate data at will within the handheld's storage area, so LocalIDs are valid only between the time an application opens a database and the time it closes the database. Saving the LocalID of a database record or even of the start of a database is futile because once your application has closed a database, the system could move the data anywhere, thereby invalidating the LocalID you saved.**

Even though the database's record list uses LocalIDs to keep track of its records, application code actually requests records by their index within the record list. The Palm OS data manager uses the index to look up the LocalID of the requested record, converts the LocalID to a handle based on the card the database header is located in, and then returns the handle to the requesting application. More details about getting, modifying, and deleting database records are available in Chapter 16.

## Record Databases

The database header consists of a number of fields, outlined in the following table, that describe everything from the name of the database to the number of records the database contains.

> The format of the database header may change in future versions of Palm OS. When working with database structures, never assume that the database has a specific format; always use the Palm OS database functions.

| Field | Size in Bytes | Description |
| --- | --- | --- |
| name | 32 | Null-terminated string containing the name of the database |
| attributes | 2 | Flags specifying properties of the database |
| version | 2 | Version number of the database format, a value that is application-defined and does not necessarily equal the version number of the application itself |
| creationDate | 4 | Date and time when the database was created, expressed in seconds since midnight, January 1, 1904 |
| modificationDate | 4 | Date and time when the database was last modified, expressed in seconds since midnight, January 1, 1904 |
| lastBackupDate | 4 | Date and time when the database was last backed up during a HotSync operation |
| modificationNumber | 4 | Incremented every time an application adds, modifies, or deletes a record in the database |
| appInfoID | 4 | LocalID where the database's application info block, if any, begins |
| sortInfoID | 4 | LocalID where the database's sort info block, if any, begins |
| type | 4 | Application-defined database type |
| creator | 4 | Creator ID of the database |
| uniqueIDSeed | 4 | Used by the system to generate a unique ID number for each record in the database |
| recordList | 4 | LocalID of the first record list, a value that is 0 if there is only one record list for this database |

The `recordList` field of the header holds the LocalID of the database's first record list. A database can contain only one record list structure if it has few enough records to fit the entire list within the database header; otherwise, the record list's `nextRecordList` field will contain the LocalID of the next list of records. The structure of a record list is outlined in the following table.

| Field | Size in Bytes | Description |
|---|---|---|
| nextRecordListID | 4 | LocalID of the next list of records; this value is 0 if there are no other record lists beyond the current list |
| numRecords | 2 | Number of records in this record list |
| firstEntry | 2 | Placeholder for the memory address of the first record entry in this list |

Starting at the memory location of the `firstEntry` field in the record list, each record list contains an array of record entries, whose structure is outlined in the following table. This structure holds the LocalID of the actual record, the record's attribute flags, and a unique ID for the record within its database. The HotSync Manager uses the unique ID of each record when performing synchronization with the desktop version of a database; if the unique ID of a record on the desktop matches the unique ID of a handheld record, the HotSync Manager considers them to be the same record. For details on the inner workings of the HotSync Manager, see Chapter 21.

| Field | Size in Bytes | Description |
|---|---|---|
| localChunkID | 4 | LocalID of the actual record |
| attributes | 1 | Attribute and category information for this record |
| uniqueID | 3 | Unique ID for this record |

A record entry's `attributes` field contains four flags and a 4-bit number indicating which category the record belongs to. The next table shows the byte offsets and meanings of the contents of the `attributes` byte.

| Field | Offset | Description |
|---|---|---|
| category | 0x00 | Category of the record |
| secret | 0x10 | If set, indicates that this record is marked private |
| busy | 0x20 | If set, indicates that this record is currently in use |
| dirty | 0x40 | If set, indicates that this record should be archived at the next HotSync operation |
| delete | 0x80 | If set, indicates that this record should be deleted at the next HotSync operation |

# Resource Databases

The database format described so far in this chapter is what Palm OS uses to store record information. There also is a database format in Palm OS for storing resources. Unlike standard records, a resource contained in a database is tagged with a resource type and an ID number. Palm OS applications are simply resource databases containing the data, code, and user interface resources necessary to run a program.

Resource databases differ from record databases in the structure used in the record list to indicate each resource stored in the database. Applications must also use a different set of functions to manipulate resources from the functions used to manipulate records. The following table outlines the structure of a resource entry.

| Field | Size in Bytes | Description |
|---|---|---|
| type | 4 | Resource type |
| id | 2 | ID number for the resource, which is unique among all resources in a database that share the same type |
| localChunkID | 4 | LocalID of the actual resource |

More details about handling individual resources within a database are available in Chapter 16.

# Working with Non-Schema Databases

Non-schema databases on a Palm OS handheld are roughly analogous to files on a desktop computer, except that Palm OS databases reside in RAM instead of the permanent storage medium (your hard drive) that holds desktop files. Using functions in the Palm OS API, your application can create and delete databases, as well as open and close them, much as a desktop system handles its files. Where a Palm OS database differs most from a desktop file is in the way an application reads data from, and writes data to, the database. Instead of positioning a file pointer as you would in most desktop file systems, when you manipulate records on Palm OS you are directly reading from and writing to memory.

## Creating Databases

To create a new database, call the DmCreateDatabase function. The prototype for DmCreateDatabase looks like this:

**Palm OS Garnet**
```
Err DmCreateDatabase (UInt16 cardNo, const Char * nameP,
                      UInt32 creator, UInt32 type,
                      Boolean resDB)
```

**Palm OS Cobalt**
```
status_t DmCreateDatabase (const char * nameP,
                      uint32_t creator, uint32_t type,
                      Boolean resDB)
```

The cardNo parameter is the memory card on which you wish to create the database.

*The concept of multiple card numbers never became a reality on handhelds, and most applications long ago defaulted the* cardNo *parameter to zero on* Dm *API calls. In fact, if you are programming to the Palm OS Cobalt SDK, the* cardNo *parameter has officially been removed from* Dm *functions. Also, do not confuse a memory card, which refers to the handheld's internal RAM, with an expansion card, which is removable storage available only through a different set of functions. See Chapter 17 for details on expansion cards.*

The nameP parameter of DmCreateDatabase accepts a string to use as the human-readable name for the database. As we showed earlier in this chapter, only 32 bytes are available in the database header to store this name, which includes one byte for the terminating null, so database names can be a maximum of 31 ASCII characters long.

Aside from meeting the size requirement for a database name, you also must take steps to ensure that the name of your database is unique. The best way to do this is to append the application's creator ID to the end of the database name. For example, the Librarian sample application's database is named Librarian-LFlb.

The creator parameter takes a four-byte creator ID code. Every database belonging to a particular application should be marked with that application's creator ID. Among other things, this ensures that the system application launcher can properly delete all of a program's data along with the program itself when the user removes it from the device.

Another four-byte code goes into the type parameter. This code is application-specific; it identifies what type of data the database contains. Unlike the creator ID, the type code does not need to be unique among all Palm OS applications. Palm OS reserves the code appl to represent executable applications; other than this, you can assign just about any four-byte code you wish, preferably a mnemonic to help you identify the kind of data in the database. By convention, most applications use the code Data or DATA to indicate a normal database that contains an application's main records instead of supplementary data.

Many applications require only one database, which is true of most basic ROM applications: The built-in applications all use the type DATA for their databases. A good example of multiple database usage is the Expense application, which uses three databases. Expense stores its main records in a DATA database, a list of cities in a city database, and a list of vendors in a vend database.

The last parameter to DmCreateDatabase, resDB, is a Boolean value that tells the data manager to create a resource database instead of a record database if resDB is set to true. For most normal application databases, leave resDB set to false.

In general, an application should check for the existence of its database in its StartApplication routine, or from a helper routine that StartApplication calls. If the database does not exist, StartApplication (or its helper) can then call DmCreateDatabase to make a new database for the application.

Librarian's StartApplication routine calls a function called LibGetDatabase, which opens Librarian's database if it already exists or creates it if the database does not exist. The following excerpt is from Librarian's LibGetDatabase routine:

**Palm OS Garnet**

```
#define libDBName      "LibrarianDB-LFlb"
#define libDBType      'DATA'
```

```
#define libCreatorID  'LFlb'

Err      error = 0;
UInt16   mode;


// Code to set the database mode omitted

// Find Librarian's database. If it doesn't exist,
// create it.
gLibDB = DmOpenDatabaseByTypeCreator(libDBType,
                                     libCreatorID, mode);
if (! gLibDB)
    {
    error = DmCreateDatabase(0, libDBName, libCreatorID,
                             libDBType, false);
    if (error)
        return error;

    gLibDB = DmOpenDatabaseByTypeCreator(libDBType,
                                         libCreatorID,
                                         mode);
    if (! gLibDB)
        return DmGetLastErr();

    // Code for initializing the application info block
    // omitted
}
```

**Palm OS Cobalt**

```
#define libDBName     "LibrarianDB-LFlb"
#define libDBType     'DATA'
#define libCreatorID  'LFlb'

status_t error = 0;
uint16_t mode;


// Code to set the database mode omitted

// Find Librarian's database. If it doesn't exist,
// create it.
gLibDB = DmOpenDatabaseByTypeCreator(libDBType,
                                     libCreatorID, mode);
if (! gLibDB)
    {
    error = DmCreateDatabase(libDBName, libCreatorID,
                             libDBType, false);
    if (error)
        return error;

    gLibDB = DmOpenDatabaseByTypeCreator(libDBType,
                                         libCreatorID,
                                         mode);
```

```
      if (! gLibDB)
          return DmGetLastErr();

      // Code for initializing the application info block
      // omitted
}
```

*When creating a classic database in a Protein application, the calls to* DmCreateDatabase *and* DmOpenDatabase *need to be replaced with* DmCreateDatabaseV50 *and* DmOpenDatabaseV50, *respectively.*

The LibGetDatabase routine first checks to see if Librarian's database exists by attempting to open it with DmOpenDatabaseByTypeCreator, which returns either a reference to the open database or the value 0. If the database does not exist, LibGetDatabase calls DmCreateDatabase with Librarian's database name, creator ID, and the type DATA to create the new database. Then LibGetDatabase opens the newly created database so that Librarian will have access to it. If this second database opening fails — a situation that should happen only rarely — LibGetDatabase calls the DmGetLastErr function to get the code of the last error encountered by the data manager and passes this error code back to the StartApplication routine, which in turn passes the error back to PilotMain.

## Opening Databases

The DmOpenDatabaseByTypeCreator function, shown in the previous example, opens a database given the type and creator ID of the database and returns a reference to the open database if successful. The Palm OS type used for an open database reference, and for the gLibDB global variable in the previous example, is DmOpenRef.

A third parameter to DmOpenDatabaseByTypeCreator sets the mode in which the database should be opened. Palm OS provides a number of constants, shown in the following table, for defining database access modes. Your code should OR these values together to form the mode parameter to DmOpenDatabaseByTypeCreator.

| Constant | Description |
|---|---|
| dmModeReadWrite | Read/write access |
| dmModeReadOnly | Read-only access |
| dmModeWriteOnly | Write-only access |
| dmModeLeaveOpen | Leave the database open after the application quits |
| dmModeExclusive | Exclude other applications from opening this database |
| dmModeShowSecret | Show records in this database that are marked private |

Most of the time, you should use the dmModeReadWrite mode when your application starts because that mode allows modification and display of the application's data. To support private records in your application, also check the system preferences to see if the user currently has private records hidden or not and then set the dmModeShowSecret mode as appropriate. The following code from Librarian's StartApplication sets the mode to read/write access and sets the mode to show or hide private records:

```
if (gPrivateRecordStatus == hidePrivateRecords)
    mode = dmModeReadWrite;
else
    mode = dmModeReadWrite | dmModeShowSecret;
```

The global `gPrivateRecordStatus` variable is of type `privateRecordViewEnum`, an enumeration defined in the Palm OS 3.5 header `PrivateRecords.h` as follows:

```
typedef enum privateRecordViewEnum {
    showPrivateRecords = 0x00,
    maskPrivateRecords,
    hidePrivateRecords
} privateRecordViewEnum;
```

Librarian uses `gPrivateRecordStatus` in various parts of its code to determine how private records should be displayed.

> *You are entirely responsible for implementing private-record behavior in your application if you want to allow the user to mark records as private; the only thing the operating system does to maintain private records is to keep track of how they should be displayed. Your application code must do all the work of checking the system preferences and making sure that hidden records are displayed, masked, or hidden, as appropriate.*

Besides `DmOpenDatabaseByTypeCreator`, Palm OS also allows opening databases with `DmOpenDatabase`. Instead of the type and creator ID of the desired database, `DmOpenDatabase` requires the database's card number and LocalID. See the "Finding Databases" section coming up in this chapter for information on how to determine a database's LocalID.

## Closing Databases

When your application is finished with a database, it should call `DmCloseDatabase` to close it. The `DmCloseDatabase` function takes a `DmOpenRef` type reference to an open database as a parameter:

```
DmCloseDatabase(gLibDB);
```

An application's `StopApplication` function is a good place to put a call to `DmCloseDatabase`, right after any code that performs any other cleanup required by the application.

> *The system allocates approximately 50 to 100 bytes of memory from the dynamic heap for each open database, so be sure to close databases when they are no longer needed. More important, any future attempt to open a database that is already open will fail, including attempts from a desktop conduit during synchronization. Only a soft reset closes databases that are left open. Records that are either busy or locked remain in that state after the application closes the database.*

## Finding Databases

A number of functions exist for finding databases on the handheld, given different criteria. The most basic is `DmFindDatabase`, which returns the LocalID of a database header given a card number and the name of the database to search for:

**Palm OS Garnet**
```
LocalID  dbID;

dbID = DmFindDatabase(0, "Librarian-LFlb");
```

**Palm OS Cobalt**
```
LocalID  dbID;
DmDatabaseInfoType dbInfo

dbID = DmFindDatabase("Librarian-LFlb", libCreatorID,
dmFindAllDB, &dbInfo );
```

*Within a Palm OS Protein application* DmFindDatabase *needs to be replaced with* DmFindDatabaseV50.

If DmFindDatabase cannot find a database that matches the given name, it returns 0; in this case, call DmGetLastErr to find out the exact reason DmFindDatabase failed. In Palm OS Cobalt, this function has been changed in a number of ways. First, the cardNo parameter has been removed. In addition, the function looks based on both the database name and the creator ID. Third, the function takes a DmFindType parameter that allows the caller to specify whether databases of type schema, classic, extended, or combinations of these three types should be searched. Finally, for convenience it takes a pointer to a DmDatabaseInfoType structure to receive information about the database.

The DmGetDatabase function returns the LocalID of a database given a card number and the index of the database on the card. Use DmGetDatabase to retrieve a list of all the databases on a card. Index numbers for databases range from 0 to the total number of databases on the card, minus one. If you pass the card number to the function DmNumDatabases to determine the number of databases, you can then iterate over all the databases on that card:

**Palm OS Garnet**
```
LocalID  dbID;
Int16    i;

for (i = 0; i < DmNumDatabases(0); i++)
{
    dbID = DmGetDatabase(0, i);
    // Do something with the dbID, the database's LocalID.
}
```

**Palm OS Cobalt**
```
LocalID  dbID;
int16_t  i;

for (i = 0; i < DmNumDatabases(); i++)
{
    dbID = DmGetDatabase(i);
    // Do something with the dbID, the database's LocalID.
}
```

*Within a Palm OS Protein application* DmGetDatabase *needs to be replaced with* DmGetDatabaseV50.

Finally, Palm OS offers `DmGetNextDatabaseByTypeCreator` for more complex searches. The `DmGetNextDatabaseByTypeCreator` function searches for a database given a type, creator ID, or both. It has the following prototype:

```
Err DmGetNextDatabaseByTypeCreator (Boolean newSearch,
    DmSearchStatePtr stateInfoP, UInt32 type,
    UInt32 creator, Boolean onlyLatestVers,
    UInt16* cardNoP, LocalID* dbIDP)
```

The `DmGetNextDatabaseByTypeCreator` function returns 0 if it successfully found a matching database, or the constant `dmErrCantFind` if no database matching the supplied `type` or `creator` can be found.

It is necessary to call `DmGetNextDatabaseByTypeCreator` more than once to get all the databases on the handheld with the specified criteria. The first parameter, `newSearch`, tells `DmGetNextDatabaseByTypeCreator` to start a brand new search if its value is `true`. Passing a pointer to a `DmSearchStateType` structure in the `stateInfoP` parameter allows the function to keep track of its search state, so subsequent calls to the function with a `newSearch` value of `false` can pick up the search where it left off after the last call to `DmGetNextDatabaseByTypeCreator`.

The `type` and `creator` parameters accept the database type and creator ID, respectively, that you wish to search for. You may pass `NULL` for either of these parameters to specify a wildcard search. If `type` is `NULL`, the routine returns databases of any type that match the specified `creator`. Likewise, if `creator` is `NULL`, the search returns databases of the specified `type`, but with any creator ID. Passing `NULL` to both parameters returns every database on the handheld.

Pass `true` for the value of the `onlyLatestVers` parameter to restrict the search to the latest version of each database. A `false` value for `onlyLatestVers` allows for retrieval of all databases matching the specified `type` and `creator`, regardless of their versions.

*Databases in RAM are always considered a more recent version than databases stored in ROM. This allows you to replace any of the built-in applications stored in ROM with your own by creating an application with the same type and creator ID as the built-in application you wish to replace.*

A special case to look out for when `onlyLatestVers` is set to `true` has to do with changes in implementation of `DmGetNextDatabaseByTypeCreator` between Palm OS versions 3.0 and 3.1. If multiple databases exist on the handheld that all share the same type, creator ID, and version, Palm OS 3.0 and earlier return all of those databases. However, Palm OS 3.1 and later return only one of the multiple databases when `onlyLatestVers` is `true`, effectively selected at random. If `onlyLatestVers` is `false`, `DmGetNextDatabaseByTypeCreator` works the same way across all versions of Palm OS.

*To ensure that calls to `DmGetNextDatabaseByTypeCreator` work in the same way across all versions of Palm OS, you have two options. The first option is to set `onlyLatestVers` to false when specifying both the type and creator parameters. The second option is to pass NULL for the value of `type` or `creator`, or for both `type` and `creator`.*

The two remaining parameters to `DmGetNextDatabaseByTypeCreator`, `cardNoP` and `dbIDP`, receive the card number in which a found database resides and the database's LocalID on that card.

The following helper function counts the number of databases on the handheld matching a given type and creator ID:

```
Int16 CountDatabases(UInt32 type, UInt32 creator)
{
    DmSearchStateType  searchState;
    Int16    count = 0;
    UInt16   cardNo;
    LocalID  dbID;


    if (DmGetNextDatabaseByTypeCreator(true, &searchState,
        type, creator, false, &cardNo, &dbID))
    {
        do
        {
            count++;
            // Do something with each database here, if
            // desired, using cardNo and dbID.
        }
        while (DmGetNextDatabaseByTypeCreator(false,
               &searchState, myType, myCreator, false,
               &cardNo, &dbID);
    }

    return count;
}
```

Note that on Palm OS Cobalt, DmGetNextDatabaseByTypeCreator has been changed considerably, and now must be used in conjunction with DmOpenIteratorByTypeCreator. A compatibility function DmGetNextDatabaseByTypeCreatorV50 has been supplied for those who wish to retain compatibility with existing code.

## Deleting Databases

To remove a database and all its records from the handheld, call the DmDeleteDatabase function. The function takes two parameters, the card number where the database is located and the database's LocalID, and it returns 0 if successful or an error code if the deletion failed for some reason. Use one of the functions in the previous section to retrieve the card and LocalID for the database you wish to delete.

> **Other than restoring from a backup on the desktop, there is no way to recover data deleted using DmDeleteDatabase. Be careful when using this function.**

A related function, DmDatabaseProtect, allows you to prevent a database from being deleted, thus allowing you to keep a particular record or resource in a database locked without keeping the database open. The DmDatabaseProtect function operates by increasing or decreasing the *protection count* on a particular database. If the protection count assigned to a database is greater than 0, the database cannot be deleted. The prototype for DmDatabaseProtect looks like this:

```
Err DmDatabaseProtect (UInt16 cardNo, LocalID dbID,
                       Boolean protect)
Err DmSetDatabaseProtection (DatabaseID dbID,
                             Boolean protect)
```

The `cardNo` and `dbID` parameters accept the card number and LocalID of the database to modify, respectively. Passing a value of `true` to the `protect` parameter increments the protection count; a `false` `protect` value decrements the protection counter. Note that the system keeps protection count information in dynamic memory, so all databases become "unprotected" whenever the handheld is reset.

## Retrieving and Modifying Database Information

A database stores a lot of information about itself in its header. The Palm OS function for retrieving this information is `DmDatabaseInfo`, which has the following prototype:

```
Err DmDatabaseInfo (UInt16 cardNo, LocalID dbID,
    Char* nameP, UInt16* attributesP, UInt16* versionP,
    UInt32* crDateP, UInt32* modDateP, UInt32* bckUpDateP,
    UInt32* modNumP, LocalID* appInfoIDP, LocalID*
    sortInfoIDP, UInt32* typeP, UInt32* creatorP)
Err DmDatabaseInfo (DatabaseID dbID, DmDatabaseInfoPtr dbInfo *)
```

In Palm OS Cobalt the lengthy list of parameters has been replaced by a single `DmDatabaseInfoPtr` structure, which contains essentially the same information in one handy package.

The `cardNo` and `dbID` parameters take the card number and LocalID of the database whose information you wish to retrieve. Only the first two parameters provide input to `DmDatabaseInfo`; everything else receives return values from the function. Pass `NULL` for the value of any of the remaining parameters to ignore that particular piece of information.

First in the long list of properties is `nameP`, which retrieves the name of the database. Ensure that the character array whose pointer you pass in `nameP` is 32 bytes long so it has enough room to contain the longest possible database name string.

The `attributesP` parameter receives the attribute flags associated with the database. In the Palm OS header file `DataMgr.h`, a number of constants are defined for handling database attributes. The following table shows the attribute constants and what they mean.

| Constant | Value | Description |
| --- | --- | --- |
| dmHdrAttrResDB | 0x0001 | Set if database is a resource database. |
| dmHdrAttrReadOnly | 0x0002 | Set if database is read-only. |
| dmHdrAttrAppInfoDirty | 0x0004 | Set if application info block is dirty. |
| dmHdrAttrBackup | 0x0008 | Set if this database should be backed up to the desktop during a HotSync operation. This bit should be set if there is no conduit associated with this application to perform backup duties. |
| dmHdrAttrOKToInstallNewer | 0x0010 | Set if it is OK for the HotSync backup conduit to install a newer version of this database with a different name if this database is currently open. |

*Table continued on following page*

| Constant | Value | Description |
|---|---|---|
| dmHdrAttrResetAfterInstall | 0x0020 | Set if the handheld requires a reset after installing this database. |
| dmHdrAttrCopyPrevention | 0x0040 | Set if the database should not be copied via IR beaming or other methods. |
| dmHdrAttrStream | 0x0080 | Set if this database is a file stream. |
| dmHdrAttrHidden | 0x0100 | Set if this database should be hidden from view. For example, the application launcher in Palm OS 3.2 and later hides applications with this bit set. For record databases, setting this bit hides the record count in the application launcher's Info screen. |
| dmHdrAttrLaunchableData | 0x0200 | Set on a non-application database if this database may be "launched" by its name being passed to its owner (an application database with the same creator ID) via the sysAppLaunchCmdOpenNamedDB launch code. For example, Palm Query Applications (PQAs) have this bit set so they will appear in the application launcher, even though they are not actually applications. |
| dmHdrAttrOpen | 0x8000 | Set if the database is open. |

The DataMgr.h header also defines the constants dmAllHdrAttrs and dmSysOnlyHdrAttrs, which are bit masks representing all the header attributes and attributes, respectively, that may be altered only by the system:

```
#define dmAllHdrAttrs (dmHdrAttrResDB | \
                       dmHdrAttrReadOnly | \
                       dmHdrAttrAppInfoDirty | \
                       dmHdrAttrBackup | \
                       dmHdrAttrOKToInstallNewer | \
                       dmHdrAttrResetAfterInstall | \
                       dmHdrAttrCopyPrevention | \
                       dmHdrAttrStream | \
                       dmHdrAttrOpen)

#define dmSysOnlyHdrAttrs (dmHdrAttrResDB | \
                          dmHdrAttrOpen)
```

The versionP parameter receives the version number for this database. By default, databases all have a version number of 0.

If you change the format of the records within a database between different versions of your application, it also is a good idea to increment the database version so your application can tell the difference between old and new database formats and deal with them appropriately. For an example of how to convert a database from one version to another, see the section titled "Changing Database Structures Between Versions" in Chapter 16.

Three parameters, crDateP, modDateP, and bckUpDateP, receive timestamps related to the database; crDateP is the database's creation date, modDateP is the data of the last modification made to the database, and bckUpDateP is the last time the database was backed up via a HotSync operation. All of these values are stored as the number of seconds since midnight on January 1, 1904.

*Different versions of Palm OS have dealt differently with the modification date field. Version 1.0 never updated the modification date, and version 2.0 updated the modification date when a database open in writable mode was closed. Not until version 3.0 did the system actually update the modification date only when something in the database actually changed, such as adding, deleting, archiving, rearranging, or resizing records; setting a record's dirty bit via DmReleaseRecord; rearranging or deleting categories; or updating the database's header fields using DmSetDatabaseInfo. If you need to ensure that the modification date is updated the same way across all versions of Palm OS, set the modification date manually with the DmSetDatabaseInfo function.*

The modNumP parameter receives the database's modification number, a value that the system increments every time a record in the database is added, modified, or deleted.

Retrieving the appInfoIDP and sortInfoIDP values gives you the LocalIDs of the application info block and sort info block for this database, respectively. Because both of these blocks are optional in any database, these values will be NULL if no application info block or sort info block exists for the database.

The typeP and creatorP parameters receive the type and creator ID of the database, respectively.

To set database header information, use DmSetDatabaseInfo. Like its companion DmDatabaseInfo, DmSetDatabaseInfo has many parameters:

```
Err DmSetDatabaseInfo (UInt16 cardNo, LocalID dbID,
    const Char* nameP, UInt16* attributesP,
    UInt16* versionP, UInt32* crDateP, UInt32* modDateP,
    UInt32* bckUpDateP, UInt32* modNumP,
    LocalID* appInfoIDP, LocalID* sortInfoIDP,
    UInt32* typeP, UInt32* creatorP)
Err DmSetDatabaseInfo (DatabaseID dbID, DmDatabaseInfoPtr dbInfo *)
```

Just as in DmDatabaseInfo, the first two parameters to DmSetDatabaseInfo are the card number and LocalID of the database to work with. All the other parameters are pointers to values that should be modified in the database. Passing NULL for any parameter leaves that parameter's associated value unchanged in the database header.

As an example of how to use DmSetDatabaseInfo, the following code snippet from Librarian's LibGetDatabase routine sets the backup bit on a newly created database:

```
UInt16    cardNo;
LocalID   dbID;
UInt16    attributes;


DmOpenDatabaseInfo(gLibDB, &dbID, NULL, NULL, &cardNo,
                   NULL);
DmDatabaseInfo(cardNo, dbID, NULL, &attributes, NULL, NULL,
               NULL, NULL, NULL, NULL, NULL, NULL, NULL);
attributes |= dmHdrAttrBackup;
DmSetDatabaseInfo(cardNo, dbID, NULL, &attributes, NULL,
```

```
                    NULL, NULL, NULL, NULL, NULL, NULL,
                    NULL);
DatabaseID    dbID;
uint16_t      attributes;
DmDatabaseInfo dbInfo;


DmGetOpenInfo(gLibDB, &dbID, NULL, NULL, NULL);
dbInfo.pAttributes = &attributes;
DmDatabaseInfo(dbID, &dbInfo);
attributes |= dmHdrAttrBackup;
DmSetDatabaseInfo(dbID, &dbInf0);
```

Setting a database's `attributes` field is a two-step process. First, you must retrieve the existing attributes using `DmDatabaseInfo`. Then, you can OR the retrieved attributes together with one or more of the database attribute constants, such as `dmHdrAttrBackup`.

*If you do not plan to write a conduit for an application, set the backup bit on its database so the HotSync backup conduit makes a copy of the application's data in the user's backup folder on the desktop machine. If you wish to convert a Palm OS application's saved data to a more desktop-friendly format, you need to write either a conduit or a desktop application that can perform the conversion.*

Aside from the database header functions we just mentioned, Palm OS also provides functions for retrieving other pieces of valuable data about databases on the handheld. The `DmOpenDatabaseInfo` function returns information about an open database. It has the following prototype:

```
Err DmOpenDatabaseInfo (DmOpenRef dbP, LocalID* dbIDP,
    UInt16* openCountP, UInt16* modeP, UInt16* cardNoP,
    Boolean* resDBP)
```

*In Palm OS Cobalt this function is obsolete. Palm OS Cobalt developers should use `DmGetOpenInfo` instead.*

The first parameter, `dpP`, is a pointer to an open database reference. Much as its cousin `DmDatabaseInfo` does, the rest of the parameters retrieve various pieces of data about the database. Pass NULL for the value of any parameter you are not interested in.

Retrieving `dpIDP` gives you the LocalID of the database. The `openCountP` parameter receives the number of applications that have this database open, `modeP` receives the mode used to open the database, `cardNoP` holds the number of the card where this database resides, and `resDBP`, if requested, contains `true` if this is a resource database or `false` if it is a regular record database.

Use the `DmGetDatabaseLockState` function to retrieve information about the number of locked and busy records in a database:

```
void DmGetDatabaseLockState (DmOpenRef dbR, UInt8* highest,
                    UInt32* count, UInt32* busy)
```

Pass an open database reference for the value of the `dbR` parameter, and `DmGetDatabaseLockState` returns the highest lock count of any of the database's records in `highest`. This lock count is specified by `highest` in the `count` parameter and the number of records with their busy bits set in `busy`. As usual, pass NULL for any value that you do not wish to retrieve.

The `DmDatabaseSize` function returns information about the size of the database:

**Palm OS Garnet**

```
Err DmDatabaseSize (UInt16 cardNo, LocalID dbID,
                    UInt32* numRecordsP,
                    UInt32* totalBytesP,
                    UInt32* dataBytesP)
```

**Palm OS Cobalt**

```
Err DmDatabaseSize (DatabaseID dbID,
                    uint32_t* numRecordsP,
                    uint32_t* totalBytesP,
                    uint32_t* dataBytesP)
```

Given the card number and LocalID of a database, `DmDatabaseSize` returns the number of records in the database via the `numRecordsP` parameter, the total size in bytes occupied by the database in `totalBytesP`, and the total memory occupied by just the data, not counting the overhead in the database's header, in the `dataBytesP` parameter.

*If you need to find quickly the card number and database ID of the currently running application, use the `SysCurAppDatabase` function:*

```
UInt16   cardNo;
LocalID  dbID;
SysCurAppDatabase(&cardNo, &dbID);
```

*Palm OS Protein applications should instead use `SysGetModuleDatabase`.*

## Creating an Application Info Block

The *application info block* is an optional block that stores application-defined data related to the database as a whole, as opposed to the data stored in individual records. Among other things, most of the ROM applications use an application info block to keep track of the user-customizable category names in the application. The memory devoted to an application info block, much like the memory used for individual records, may be located anywhere on the same card as a database's header, which keeps track of the LocalID of the application info block.

Databases also may have an optional *sort info block*, which PalmSource originally intended to contain information about how the records in the database should be sorted. However, under current implementations of Palm OS, the HotSync manager does not back up the sort info block, so it is not a good place to store information that needs to persist across synchronizations. You could use the sort info block to temporarily cache information about the database that can be regenerated from other data, but most Palm OS applications do not use it at all.

*Schema databases do not support an application info block.*

When you first create a new database that has an application info block, you should initialize the new database's application info block. The Librarian sample application calls a helper function, `LibAppInfoInit`, from its `LibGetDatabase` routine to take care of creating the new application info block:

```
error = LibAppInfoInit(gLibDB);
if (error) {
    DmCloseDatabase(gLibDB);
```

```
        DmDeleteDatabase(cardNo, dbID);
        return error;
}
```

Notice that if `LibAppInfoInit` fails for some reason to create the application info block, `LibGetDatabase` cannot successfully complete its mission to create Librarian's database, so it calls `DmCloseDatabase` to close the empty database it just created, then `DmDeleteDatabase` to remove it.

Librarian's application info block is a structure called `LibAppInfoType`, defined as follows in `librarianDB.h`:

```
typedef struct {
    UInt16  renamedCategories;  // bit field of categories
                                // with a different name
    char  categoryLabels[dmRecNumCategories]
                    [dmCategoryLength];
    UInt8 categoryUniqIDs[dmRecNumCategories];
    UInt8 lastUniqID;
    UInt8 reserved1;  // from the compiler word aligning
                    // things
    UInt16  reserved2;
    // End of category structure; Librarian-specific
    // application info starts here.
    UInt8       showInList;  // Current sort order for
                            // database
    libLabel   fieldLabels[libNumFieldLabels];  // Labels in
                                            // Edit view
    // The following are status strings for the Record view:
    libLabel   bookStatusStrings[libNumBookStatusStrings];
    libLabel   printStatusStrings[libNumPrintStatusStrings];
    libLabel   formatStatusStrings[libNumFormatStatusStrings];
    libLabel   readStatusStrings[libNumReadStatusStrings];
} LibAppInfoType;
```

The first six fields in `LibAppInfoType` are required in the application info block of any application that supports the standard implementation of Palm OS categories; just tack these fields onto the front of any application info structure you define for your own application, and the various Palm OS category functions will be able to function properly. Chapter 16 covers the category functions in detail.

The `showInList` field stores the current sort order used to display records in Librarian's List view. Librarian's `librarianDB.h` header defines the following constants for keeping track of sort order:

```
#define libShowAuthorTitle   0
#define libShowTitleAuthor   1
#define libShowTitleOnly     2
```

The rest of the fields in `LibAppInfoType` store the various strings used to display status information about a record in Librarian's Record view. These strings are things like "Got this book," "Paperback," and "Unread," and Librarian has application info string resources containing these string values. To save time while the application is running, Librarian avoids retrieving these resource strings from the application's resources every time it needs them. Instead, it copies these resources into the application info block when it creates and initializes its database. In that way, Librarian needs to open the application info block only once each time it runs to retrieve these values, instead of having to retrieve each individual string every time it is needed. More details of the mechanism Librarian uses to keep track of status strings in the Record view are available in Chapter 16.

The relevant portions of Librarian's `LibAppInfoInit` function look like this:

```
Err LibAppInfoInit(DmOpenRef db)
{
    UInt16        cardNo;
    LocalID       dbID, appInfoID;
    MemHandle     h;
    LibAppInfoType *appInfo;


    if (DmOpenDatabaseInfo(db, &dbID, NULL, NULL, &cardNo,
        NULL))
        return dmErrInvalidParam;
    if (DmDatabaseInfo(cardNo, dbID, NULL, NULL, NULL,
        NULL, NULL, NULL, NULL, &appInfoID, NULL, NULL,
        NULL))
        return dmErrInvalidParam;

    // If there isn't an app info block make space for one.
    if (appInfoID == NULL)
    {
        h = DmNewHandle(db, sizeof(LibAppInfoType));
        if (!h)
            return dmErrMemError;

        appInfoID = MemHandleToLocalID(h);
        DmSetDatabaseInfo(cardNo, dbID, NULL, NULL, NULL,
                          NULL, NULL, NULL, NULL,
                          &appInfoID, NULL, NULL, NULL);
    }

    appInfo = MemLocalIDToLockedPtr(appInfoID, cardNo);

    // Clear the app info block.
    DmSet(appInfo, 0, sizeof(LibAppInfoType), 0);

    // Code for initializing categories and fields omitted

    MemPtrUnlock(appInfo);

    return 0;
}
```

The `LibAppInfoInit` function first retrieves the card number and LocalID of the database using the `DmOpenDatabaseInfo` function, and then it passes these values to `DmDatabaseInfo` to retrieve `appInfoID`, the LocalID of the database's application info block.

If `appInfoID` is equal to NULL, then no application info block is defined for the database, in which case `LibAppInfoInit` proceeds to make space for a new application info block by calling `DmNewHandle`. Notice that `LibAppInfoInit` uses the `DmNewHandle` function here instead of `MemHandleNew`.

`DmNewHandle` allocates space in the same storage heap occupied by Librarian's database, as opposed to `MemHandleNew`, which would allocate space in the dynamic heap. Also, because handles cannot be stored in the database, `LibAppInfoInit` converts the handle to a LocalID with the `MemHandleToLocalID` function and then passes this value to `DmSetDatabaseInfo` to set the application info block location in the database's header.

Then `LibAppInfoInit` locks a pointer to the new application info block using the `MemLocalIDToLocketPtr` function. With this pointer, `LibAppInfoInit` can zero the memory of the application info block using `DmSet`, the storage heap equivalent of the `MemSet` function.

After creating the new application info block, `LibAppInfoInit` initializes the categories and other fields in the `appInfo` structure. This initialization delves into managing categories and retrieving individual resources, topics left for a later chapter. Chapter 16 revisits the `LibAppInfoInit` function and fills in the details of initializing individual fields in an application info block.

Once all the values have been initialized, `LibAppInfoInit` is finished with the pointer to the application info block, so it unlocks it with `MemPtrUnlock`.

## Working with Extended Databases

In Palm OS Cobalt, a variation of the classic database, called the extended database, offers several enhancements and changes:

❑    Database records can now exceed 64K in length.

❑    Data can now be stored in either little-endian or big-endian format.

❑    Databases are now identified by using a combination of name and creator ID (classic databases are uniquely identified only by name).

If you are coding to the Palm OS Cobalt SDK, your call to `DmCreateDatabase` will automatically create an extended database. To create an old-style classic database using the Palm OS Cobalt SDK you must call `DmCreateDatabaseV50`. With the exception of the now-obsolete `cardNo` parameter, the parameters for `DmCreateDatabase` and `DmCreateDatabaseV50` are identical.

Note that if you are creating a 68K application, but running on a Palm OS Cobalt device, your call to `DmCreateDatabase` will still result in a classic database. Extended databases are only a consideration if you are both coding specifically to Palm OS Cobalt and running on a Palm OS Cobalt device.

With few exceptions, the remainder of the "Dm" set of database functions for classic databases are supported for extended databases.

## Working with Schema Databases

Schema databases are specific to Palm OS Cobalt and represent a very different way of storing and retrieving data, both in terms of the Palm OS functions involved and the methods used. As opposed to classic or extended databases, schema databases have a defined structure and layout that makes reading and writing data less work and more automatic for the Palm OS developer.

Each schema database can contain one or more tables. Each table is defined by a table schema, which details the column layout for the table, and the properties associated with each column in the table. A given table stores its data as rows, each of which conforms to the table schema in terms of column definitions.

## Creating Databases

To create a new schema database, call the DbCreateDatabase function as follows:

```
status_t DbCreateDatabase (const char *name, uint32_t creator,
uint32_t type,
uint32_t numTables,
const DbTableDefinitionType schemaListP[],
DatabaseID *dbIDP)
```

The name parameter of DbCreateDatabase accepts a string to use as the human-readable name for the database. As with other databases in Palm OS, a maximum of 32 bytes are available for this name, including one byte for the terminating null.

The creator and type parameters are the same as for classic databases, representing a four-byte creator ID code and data type for the database to be created. In schema databases, uniqueness is determined by a combination of database name and creator ID.

The numTables parameter indicates how many tables will be defined within the database after its successful creation. The value of this parameter can be zero, which means the database will be created without any initial tables. Alternatively you may specify a number of tables that shall be created. If nonzero, each table must be defined with a DbTableDefinitionType structure in the schemaListP parameter.

> *It is not required that tables be defined at database creation time. You can add tables to a database anytime after the database is created. Adding tables to an existing database is covered later in this section.*

The schemaList parameter is a pointer to a list of DbTableDefinitionType structures, each of which defines a table schema for one of the tables specified to be precreated in the numTables parameter. If numTables is zero, this parameter may be null.

The dbIDP parameter is a pointer to a DatabaseID value, which is filled by DbCreateDatabase and passed back to the caller upon successful creation of the database. This ID is used in most schema database functions.

A version of the Librarian program that uses a schema database can thus be coded as follows:

```
#define libDBName      "LibrarianDB-LFlb"
#define libDBType      'DATA'
#define libCreatorID   'LFlb'


status_t error = 0;
DatabaseID   dbID;


// Code to set the database mode omitted

// Find Librarian's database. If it doesn't exist,
```

```
// create it.
gLibDB = DmOpenDatabaseByTypeCreator(libDBType,
                                     libCreatorID, mode);
if (! gLibDB)
    {
    error = DbCreateDatabase(libDBName, libCreatorID,
                             libDBType, 0, NULL, &dbID);
    if (error)
        return error;

    // now go on to add a table definition to the database...
    }
```

In this version, `LibGetDatabase` calls `DbCreateDatabase` with Librarian's database name, creator ID, and the type `DATA` to create the new database. It specifies that zero tables should be defined at creation, and it provides a pointer to a database ID to receive the ID of the newly created database.

## Opening Databases

To open a schema database you need to call the `DbOpenDatabase` function. `DbOpenDatabase` opens a schema database and returns a database reference.

The `dbID` parameter of `DbOpenDatabase` is obtained by `DmFindDatabase` or `DbCreateDatabase`.

The second parameter mode specifies the database access mode in which your application will be working with the open database. Possible values are `dmModeExclusive`, `dmModeReadOnly`, `dmModeReadWrite`, `dmModeShowSecret`, and `dmModeWrite`.

The `share` parameter specifies how the database may be used by other applications while your application has it open. Since Palm OS Cobalt and future versions of Palm OS Cobalt enable background tasks, it is possible for multiple applications to be using the same database simultaneously. Possible values for this parameter are `dbShareNone`, `dbShareRead`, and `dbShareReadWrite`.

You may also use `DbOpenDatabaseByName` to directly open a database without needing to first obtain a database ID. This function substitutes creator ID and database name instead of the database ID.

## Closing Databases

The `DbCloseDatabase` function closes a database that was previously opened with `DbOpenDatabase` or `DbOpenDatabaseByName`. `DbCloseDatabase` simply takes a `DmOpenRef` reference to the open database.

## Tables, Columns, and Schemas

As you've seen, you may add a table to a database at database creation time, or you may add tables later. To add a table to an existing database, use the `DbAddTable` function, which is prototyped as follows:

```
status_t DbAddTable (DmOpenRef dbRef,
                     const DbTableDefinitionType *schemaP)
```

The first parameter to `DbAddTable` is an open database reference. The second parameter is a pointer to a `DbTableDefinitionType` structure. A `DbTableDefinitionType` essentially defines the table's schema:

```
typedef struct {
char name[dbDBNameLength];
uint32_t numColumns;
DbSchemaColumnDefnType *columnListP;
} DbTableDefinitionType
```

The name member provides a human-readable name for the table. The numColumns and columnListP members together define the columns that will be represented for each row in the database, with columnListP providing a list of column definitions—one for each column in the table. In turn, the DbSchemaColumnDefnType structure, which defines a single column, is as follows:

```
typedef struct {
uint32_t id;
uint32_t maxSize;
char name[dbDBNameLength];
DbSchemaColumnType type;
uint8_t attrib;
uint16_t reserved;
status_t errCode;
} DbSchemaColumnDefnType
```

The id member is simply a user defined value that can be used to reference the column.

The maxSize member specifies the maximum size of the data in the column for any given row.

The type member specifies the data type associated with the column. These can be any type supported by the DbSchemaColumnType definition. You will find that most Palm OS data types have a parallel supported type as a DbSchemaColumnType.

The attrib member specifies additional attributes that describe how the column is treated by the data manager.

The following piece of code illustrates how to put all this together and successfully add a new table containing a single column to an existing database:

```
#define libDBName       "LibrarianDB-LFlb"
#define libDBType       'DATA'
#define libCreatorID    'LFlb'

DmOpenRef ref;
Status_t err;

ref = DbOpenDatabaseByName(libCreatorID, libDBName,
                           dmModeReadWrite, dbShareNone);
if (ref) {
   DbTableDefinitionType       dbSchema;
   DbSchemaColumnDefnType      column;

   // Initialize the schema structure
   dbSchema.numColumns      = 2;
   dbSchema.columnListP     = &column;
```

```
        strcpy(dbSchema.name, "MyTable");

        // set up the column definition
        MemSet(&column, sizeof(DbSchemaColumnDefnType), 0);
        column.id                = 1;
        column.maxSize           = 20;
        column.type              = dbVarChar;
        strcpy(column.name, "LastName");

        // now add the table
        err = DbAddTable (ref, &dbSchema);
}
```

Given a reference to an open, existing database, the main job is to set up a column definition, which in this simple example is the lone table column.

You can enumerate tables within an existing database by calling DbNumTables, and then calling DbGetTableName and DbGetTableSchema once for each table in the database. Once a database contains one or more tables, you can also get information about the columns in a table by using DbNumColumns, DbGetColumnDefinitions, DbGetAllColumnDefinitions, and DbGetColumnID, depending on what information you need.

Tables also support dynamic column addition and removal. You can add a column to an existing database table by calling DbAddColumn. All existing row values for that column will be initialized to NULL. Removal of a column is performed by calling DbRemoveColumn, after which all data for that column is removed from the table.

If you need to delete a table from a database, you can call DbRemoveTable. Note that you will first need to remove any and all rows from the table. For information on how to add, query, and delete row data from schema databases, see Chapter 16.

# Storing Application Preferences

Devoting an entire database to the storage of small pieces of data, such as which columns are visible in a given application view, is simply overkill. Databases are well suited to storing many pieces of data with a common format, but there is a better way to keep track of smaller odds and ends that a program needs to remember between invocations, such as *application preferences*. These are somewhat analogous to .ini files in Windows or .rc files in UNIX, in that they are a handy place to store configuration data for an application.

Palm OS maintains a database of preference information for all applications on the device that wish to use it. Each record in this database is application-defined, so a program can store whatever data it needs to for its own purposes.

Before using application preferences, you need to define a structure to contain them. As an example, the following code from librarian.c defines LibPreferenceType, the structure used in Librarian to store application preferences:

```
typedef struct {
    UInt16    currentCategory;
    Boolean   showAllCategories;
    Boolean   showBookStatus;
    Boolean   showPrintStatus;
    Boolean   showFormat;
    Boolean   showReadUnread;
    Boolean   saveBackup;
    FontID    listFont;
    FontID    recordFont;
    FontID    editFont;
    FontID    noteFont;
} LibPreferenceType;
```

None of the data stored in LibPreferenceType is particularly lengthy; it is simply a mishmash of values that should be maintained between invocations of Librarian for consistency's sake but that don't really fit anywhere in its database. The currentCategory and showAllCategories fields keep track of the category currently displayed by Librarian. The showBookStatus, showPrintStatus, showFormat, and showReadUnread fields store which columns of the List view are visible, and saveBackup saves whether the check box in the delete confirmation dialog box is checked or not. Finally, the various FontID fields save the user's font preferences for various views in Librarian.

Once you have determined the format required to store application preferences, your application needs to retrieve these settings when it opens, usually in its StartApplication routine. The parts of Librarian's StartApplication function that deal with retrieving Librarian's preferences look like this:

```
LibPreferenceType   prefs;
UInt16  prefsSize;


prefsSize = sizeof(LibPreferenceType);
if (PrefGetAppPreferences(libCreatorID, libPrefID, &prefs,
    &prefsSize, true) != noPreferenceFound)
{
    gCurrentCategory = prefs.currentCategory;
    gShowAllCategories = prefs.showAllCategories;
    gShowBookStatus = prefs.showBookStatus;
    gShowPrintStatus = prefs.showPrintStatus;
    gShowFormat = prefs.showFormat;
    gShowReadUnread = prefs.showReadUnread;
    gSaveBackup = prefs.saveBackup;
    gListFont = prefs.listFont;
    gRecordFont = prefs.recordFont;
    gEditFont = prefs.editFont;
    gNoteFont = prefs.noteFont;
}
else
{
    // No preferences exist yet, so set the defaults for
    // the global font variables.
    gListFont = stdFont;
```

```
        gNoteFont = stdFont;

        // If Librarian is running on Palm OS 2.0, the
        // largeBoldFont is invalid. In that case, substitute
        // stdFont.
        if (gROMVersion <
            sysMakeROMVersion(3,0,0,sysROMStageRelease,0))
        {
            gRecordFont = stdFont;
            gEditFont = stdFont;
        }
        else
        {
            gRecordFont = largeBoldFont;
            gEditFont = largeBoldFont;
        }
    }
```

Librarian's `StartApplication` routine calls `PrefGetAppPreferences` to retrieve Librarian's `LibPreferenceType` structure from the system's list of application preferences. The `PrefGetAppPreferences` function has the following prototype:

```
Int16 PrefGetAppPreferences (UInt32 creator, UInt16 id,
    void* prefs, UInt16* prefsSize, Boolean saved)
```

The first parameter to `PrefGetAppPreferences`, `creator`, is the creator ID of the application whose preferences should be retrieved.

It is possible for an application to have more than one preference type, which is where the `id` parameter comes into play. The `id` lets you assign an application-defined `UInt16` value to identify each of the application's preference types. Librarian has only one preference type, defined by the constant `libPrefID` in `librarian.h`, which has a value of `0`.

The `void` pointer `prefs` receives the actual preferences structure. To let the system know how large this structure is, you also must pass the size of the structure, in bytes, via the `prefsSize` parameter. It also is possible to retrieve variable-length structures from application preferences. To find out how large the structure stored in an application's preferences is, call `PrefGetAppPreferences` once with a `NULL` pointer for the `prefs` parameter and a `prefsSize` of `0`. The `PrefGetAppPreferences` functions sets `prefsSize` to the actual size of the buffer holding the application's preferences. Once you have the actual size of the structure, you can allocate a buffer large enough to hold the preferences and call `PrefGetAppPreferences` a second time to retrieve them.

The `PrefGetAppPreferences` function's last parameter, `saved`, specifies whether to retrieve saved preferences or unsaved preferences. The system maintains two lists of preferences, those that should be saved during a HotSync operation and those that do not need to be backed up. If your application's preferences require backing up, you should set `saved` to `true` so that your application's preferences are saved by the HotSync manager. However, if your application needs only a place to store data temporarily, it can get away with using unsaved preferences. For example, a game program might save its current state, which is relevant only while the application is running, in unsaved preferences. The game's high score list, which contains more valuable data that the user may wish to back up, might be stored in saved preferences.

If `PrefGetAppPreferences` is unable to find the specified application preferences, it returns the constant `noPreferenceFound`. If the preferences were retrieved, Librarian's `StartApplication` function sets a series of global variables based on the contents of the saved preferences. If the preferences do not exist yet, Librarian sets the same global variables to reasonable defaults.

Once your application is ready to exit, it should save its preferences again with the `PrefSetAppPreferences` function, which takes almost the same parameters as `PrefGetAppPreferences`, with the addition of an `Int16` value to indicate what version of the application's preferences should be saved. Librarian's `StopApplication` function saves application preferences with the following code:

```
LibPreferenceType  prefs;


// Save Librarian's preferences.
prefs.currentCategory = gCurrentCategory;
prefs.showAllCategories = gShowAllCategories;
prefs.showBookStatus = gShowBookStatus;
prefs.showPrintStatus = gShowPrintStatus;
prefs.showFormat = gShowFormat;
prefs.showReadUnread = gShowReadUnread;
prefs.saveBackup = gSaveBackup;
prefs.listFont = gListFont;
prefs.recordFont = gRecordFont;
prefs.editFont = gEditFont;
prefs.noteFont = gNoteFont;

PrefSetAppPreferences(libCreatorID, libPrefID,
    libPrefVersionNum, &prefs, sizeof(prefs), true);
```

After filling `prefs` with the data from several of Librarian's global variables, `StopApplication` calls `PrefSetAppPreferences` to store these values in the system's application preferences database.

You may have noticed that it is possible to create preferences with `PrefSetAppPreferences` that do not match your application's creator ID, simply by passing a different creator ID to the function. However, when the user deletes an application, the system removes only those preferences that match the creator ID of the deleted application. Any other preferences created by the application remain on the device, occupying precious storage space and unnecessarily slowing down HotSync operations, because the system preferences database is updated on the desktop system at every synchronization.

Some shareware developers have used this quirk of the Palm OS preferences mechanism to implement programs that disable themselves after they have been installed for a certain period of time. These applications store a timestamp of when the application was first run in a preference whose creator ID does not match that of the application itself. When the shareware trial period is up, deleting the application and reinstalling it will not reset the timestamp, resulting in an application that is still disabled.

The issue of whether or not to write Palm OS applications that leave orphaned preferences behind has been hotly debated in Palm OS programming forums. On one hand, it is a reasonably effective way to enforce shareware trial periods. On the other hand, it is rude to a handheld user to leave garbage data behind, data that slows down every HotSync operation. Weigh the advantages of using orphaned preferences carefully against their disadvantages before using them.

# Reading and Setting System Preferences

Palm OS maintains a database of global settings for the system itself. Some of these settings, such as whether private records are currently hidden or what the current date and time formats are, may be of interest to your application. The PrefGetPreferences function allows you to retrieve the system preferences, which the function returns as a SystemPreferencesType structure:

```
SystemPreferencesType  sysPrefs;

PrefGetPreferences(&sysPrefs);
```

Because the SystemPreferencesType occupies a good-sized chunk of memory, if you need to retrieve only a single value from the system preferences, use the PrefGetPreference function instead of PrefGetPreferences. In fact, the documentation from PalmSource recommends that you use the newer PrefGetPreference instead of PrefGetPreferences. The PrefGetPreference function takes a member of the enum SystemPreferencesChoice, defined in the Palm OS header Preferences.h as an argument, which determines the preference the function retrieves and returns as a UInt32 value. You may have to cast the return value because the data stored in the system preferences are not all UInt32 values. As an example, here is the section of Librarian's StartApplication function that retrieves the private records system preference:

```
if (gROMVersion >=
    sysMakeROMVersion(3,5,0,sysROMStageRelease,0))
    gPrivateRecordStatus = (privateRecordViewEnum)
{
        PrefGetPreference(prefShowPrivateRecords);
}
else
{
    if ((Boolean)
        PrefGetPreference(prefHidePrivateRecordsV33))
        gPrivateRecordStatus = hidePrivateRecords;
    else
        gPrivateRecordStatus = showPrivateRecords;
}
```

Prior to Palm OS 3.5, record masking did not exist, so the system preference controlling whether or not private records should be shown is a simple Boolean value, prefHidePrivateRecordsV33, which the code in the example translates into an appropriate privateRecordViewEnum value for use in Librarian.

*If you are using earlier Palm OS header files than those that ship with the 3.5 SDK, retrieve private record display status by passing the prefHidePrivateRecords constant to PrefGetPreference. The prefHidePrivateRecordsV33 constant was introduced with the advent of Palm OS 3.5 because some restructuring of the SystemPreferencesChoice enumerated type was necessary to squeeze in the new prefShowPrivateRecords constant.*

Palm OS also offers PrefSetPreference for directly setting systemwide preferences, such as sound volume or time zone. The PrefSetPreference function has the following prototype:

```
void PrefSetPreference (SystemPreferencesChoice choice,
                        UInt32 value)
```

You must cast any value you wish to set via `PrefSetPreference` into a `UInt32` value before passing it to the function, even though many values in the `SystemPreferencesType` structure are not of type `UInt32`. For example, the following code sets the handheld's default long date format to display dates in the form of `31 Oct 2002`:

```
PrefSetPreference(prefLongDateFormat, (UInt32) dfDMYLong);
```

You also may use the older `PrefSetPreferences` function to set system preferences but, like `PrefGetPreferences`, doing so requires making space in memory for the entire `SystemPreferencesType` structure. PalmSource recommends that you not use `PrefSetPreferences` in current versions of Palm OS.

# Using Feature Memory

Starting with version 3.1, Palm OS supports the use of *feature memory*. This stores data in a storage heap rather than the dynamic heap, allowing stored values to persist between invocations of an application. However, feature memory will not survive a soft reset, so you should not store exclusively in feature memory any data that requires actual permanence. Also, because feature memory exists in a storage heap, it is no quicker to write to than it is to write to a database, so anything stored in feature memory should not require frequent modification. Feature memory is useful primarily for storage of data chunks larger than 64K, which is larger than what may be stored in a normal database record. In some rare cases, using feature memory might also optimize performance. Memory chunks larger than 64K are supported only in Palm OS 3.5 or later.

To allocate a chunk of feature memory, call the `FtrPtrNew` function, which has the following prototype:

```
Err FtrPtrNew (UInt32 creator, UInt16 featureNum,
               UInt32 size, void **newPtrP)
```

The `creator` parameter is the creator ID of the application requesting a chunk of feature memory, and `featureNum` is the application-defined number identifying the feature itself. Specify the size of the desired memory chunk, in bytes, in the `size` parameter. The `FtrPtrNew` function returns a pointer to the newly allocated chunk via the `newPtrP` parameter.

Once you have allocated feature memory, you write to it using the `DmWrite`, `DmSet`, or `DmStrCopy` functions because memory in the storage area does not support direct writing:

```
DmWrite(myData, 0, &myData, sizeof(myData));
```

You can retrieve values from feature memory using the `FtrGet` function:

```
Err  error;

error = FtrGet(myCreator, myFeatureNum, (UInt32 *)&value);
```

The `FtrGet` function returns 0 if it successfully retrieves a feature or an error code if it could not find the requested feature. Because the values normally stored by the feature manager are simple `UInt32` numeric values, you must cast the return value in the `FtrGet` function's third parameter to a pointer type. Once you have the pointer, you may read from it like any other pointer; if you want to modify the value at the pointer, though, be sure to use `DmWrite`.

An example of the proper use of feature memory is a function that needs to access an application's preferences in response to a launch code other than sysAppLaunchCmdNormalLaunch. If this function is called frequently, opening the preferences database each time could be quite slow. The following example allocates a chunk of feature memory and caches the application's preferences within it so that the function needs to perform the slow-database-opening routine only once after a soft reset instead of every time the function is called:

```
MyAppPreferencesType  prefs,
void  *newPrefs;


if (FtrGet(myCreator, myFeatureNum, (UInt32 *)&prefs) != 0)
{
    // The feature memory does not exist, so allocate it.
    FtrPtrNew(myCreator, myFeatureNum, 32, &newPrefs);

    // Open the preferences database.
    PrefGetAppPreferences(myCreator, myPrefID, &prefs,
                          sizeof(prefs), true);

    // Write the preferences to feature memory.
    DmWrite(newPrefs, 0, &prefs, sizeof(prefs));
}
```

Palm OS also offers other functions for manipulating feature memory, such as FtrPtrResize for resizing a chunk of feature memory and FtrPtrFree for explicitly releasing the memory allocated to a chunk of feature memory. The FtrPtrFree function also unregisters the feature that holds the pointer to the feature memory chunk, which clears the reference to the freed memory from the system feature table, thereby preventing accidental use of memory that no longer exists.

# Summary

In this chapter, you were shown three different persistent storage techniques in Palm OS—databases, preferences, and feature memory—and how to use them. You also saw how Palm OS Cobalt introduces the concept of schema databases for structured data access. After reading this chapter, you should understand the following:

❑   With the advent of Palm OS Cobalt, developers can now store data in classic, extended or schema databases.

❑   Classic databases are backward compatible with earlier versions of Palm OS through Palm OS Cobalt, and provide low-level unstructured access to data storage on RAM.

❑   Extended databases provide several enhancements and changes to Palm OS classic databases when used with Palm OS Cobalt.

❑   Schema databases, new in Palm OS Cobalt, provide developers with a structured way to deal with databases and tables through the use of schemas, or column definitions.

❑   An important part of creating a new database is the creation and initialization of its *application info block*, a section of memory that maintains information about the database as a whole.

❑ *Application preferences* provide a way to store information that is not appropriate for storage in the application's database but that should still be saved between invocations of the application.

❑ Use the `PrefGetPreference` and `PrefSetPreference` functions to retrieve and set the values of system preferences.

❑ *Feature memory* is a way to store large amounts of data that does not need to persist over soft system resets.

# 16

# Manipulating Records

The previous chapter discussed manipulation of databases on a grand scale, covering their creation, deletion, and modification using classic, extended, and schema types of databases. This chapter looks at databases on a smaller scale, concentrating on individual records within a database. Most of the work that a Palm OS application must perform to save, retrieve, and modify its data happens at the record level.

As with Chapter 15, coverage of database programming in this chapter is broken into sections devoted to non-schema (classic and extended) and schema databases. This is because working with records in Cobalt schema databases is markedly different than working with records in non-schema databases.

Once you have an understanding of how to use database records, you can implement one of the most useful features of Palm OS: the global find system. The last section of this chapter shows you what you need to add to your application to make it support the global find facility.

## Working with Non-Schema Database Records

Before we dive into the specifics of manipulating records, an explanation of the Palm OS philosophy behind organizing records is in order. In the interests of efficiency, the ROM applications and Palm OS database routines rely on a presorted database model. It is not a requirement that your database be sorted, and Palm OS can handle unsorted databases, but storing records in a sorted order allows for rapid population of tables and lists from database records. Decreasing the time required to display data in this way causes data to appear more quickly onscreen, thereby not irritating impatient users. In a database containing many records, it is much quicker for an application to iterate over record indices in a sorted database than it is to skip around through the database, searching for individual records.

So if the Palm OS database model prefers a presorted set of records, does this mean you are stuck with sorting your database in only one way? Not at all. Instead of trying to sort records every time you try to display them, you can re-sort the database only when the user wants to change the sort order. The built-in Address Book application and Librarian both use this approach. When the user changes the sort order in either application's preferences dialog box, the application sorts the entire database when the user closes the dialog box. In this way, the lengthy sorting process happens only infrequently, when the user requests a change in the sort order, instead of every single time the records must be drawn in a table or list.

## Looking at Records in the Librarian Sample Application

Librarian's record format is designed to use as little space as possible to store each record. Because a record in Librarian is composed mostly of variable-length strings, devoting a fixed amount of space to each record would be wasteful. Only enough space to store each string is really required.

To achieve this kind of storage efficiency, Librarian uses the same technique employed by the built-in Address Book application. Librarian effectively has two database formats: `LibPackedDBRecord`, a packed format for actual record storage, and `LibDBRecordType`, an expanded format that is easier to access once a record has been retrieved. The `LibPackedDBRecord` structure, along with a couple of structures it relies on, is defined in `librarianDB.h` as follows:

```
typedef struct {
    unsigned reserved      :1;
    unsigned bookStatus    :2;
    unsigned printStatus   :2;
    unsigned format        :2;
    unsigned read          :1;
} LibStatusType;

typedef union {
    struct {
        unsigned reserved     :7;
        unsigned note         :1;
        unsigned price        :1;
        unsigned isbn         :1;
        unsigned printing     :1;
        unsigned year         :1;
        unsigned publisher    :1;
        unsigned firstName    :1;
        unsigned lastName     :1;
        unsigned title        :1;
    } bits;
    UInt16 allBits;
} LibDBRecordFlags;

typedef struct {
    LibStatusType      status;
    LibDBRecordFlags   flags;
    UInt16             lastNameOffset;
    UInt16             firstNameOffset;
    UInt16             yearOffset;
    UInt16             noteOffset;
    char               firstField;
} LibPackedDBRecord;
```

The `LibStatusType` structure contains fixed-length information that every Librarian record must keep track of, such as whether the book is in print or in what format (hardcover or paperback) the book was printed. These pieces of information are stored in bit fields, which Librarian accesses using the following enumerated types, which also are defined in `librarianDB.h`:

```
// BookStatusType
// Enum for the general status of a book. Used with the
// bookStatus member of LibStatusType.

typedef enum {
    bookStatusHave = 0,
    bookStatusWant,
    bookStatusOnOrder,
    bookStatusLoaned,
    bookStatusCount
} BookStatusType;


// PrintStatusType
// Enum for the print status of a book record. Note that
// the status field is actually four bits long, but
// Librarian only makes use of three of those bits. Used
// with the printStatus member of LibStatusType.

typedef enum {
    printStatusInPrint = 0,
    printStatusOutOfPrint,
    printStatusNotPublished,
    printStatusCount
} PrintStatusType;


// FormatType
// Enum for the format of the book. Used with the format
// member of LibStatusType.

typedef enum {
    formatHardcover = 0,
    formatPaperback,
    formatTradePaperback,
    formatOther,
    formatCount
} FormatType;
```

The second field in `LibPackedDBRecord` is of type `LibDBRecordFlags`, which is a union used to keep track of which fields in a record actually contain data. The `lastNameOffset`, `firstNameOffset`, `yearOffset`, and `noteOffset` fields store the offsets of important fields from the start of `firstField` so they may be quickly accessed in place elsewhere in the application.

Starting at `firstField`, which is actually just a placeholder for the first character of the first string stored in the packed record, Librarian crams each field's data into the record, one after another, terminating each one with a trailing null character. This scheme means that the total size of a Librarian record varies widely, depending entirely on its contents. Librarian's `LibUnpackedSize` function provides an easy way to determine how big a record is:

```
static UInt32 LibUnpackedSize (LibDBRecordType *record)
{
    UInt32  size;
```

```
    Int16   i;

    // Initial size is the size of a packed record, minus
    // the character placeholder that provides the position
    // of the first field.
    size = sizeof(LibPackedDBRecord) - sizeof(char);

    // Add the length of each field that contains data,
    // plus one byte for each to accommodate a terminating
    // null character.
    for (i = 0; i < libFieldsCount; i++)
    {
        if (record->fields[i] != NULL)
            size += StrLen(record->fields[i]) + 1;
    }
    return size;
}
```

An unpacked record in Librarian, and the enumerated type used to access its fields, looks like this:

```
typedef enum {
    libFieldTitle = 0,
    libFieldLastName,
    libFieldFirstName,
    libFieldPublisher,
    libFieldYear,
    libFieldPrinting,
    libFieldIsbn,
    libFieldPrice,
    libFieldNote,
    libFieldsCount
} LibFields;

typedef struct {
    LibStatusType   status;
    char            *fields[libFieldsCount];
} LibDBRecordType;
```

The `LibDBRecordType` structure is much easier to work with than the packed record structure because all the text fields are readily available through the `fields` array.

In order for Librarian to make use of this dual record structure scheme, it needs to be able to translate records between the two formats. The `PackRecord` and `UnpackRecord` functions serve this purpose. These two functions look like this:

```
static void PackRecord (LibDBRecordType *record,
                        MemPtr recordDBEntry)
{
    UInt32  offset;
    Int16   index;
    UInt16  length;
    MemPtr  p;
    LibDBRecordFlags  flags;
    LibPackedDBRecord  *packed = 0;
```

```
UInt16  lastNameOffset = 0, firstNameOffset = 0,
        yearOffset = 0, noteOffset = 0;


flags.allBits = 0;

// Write book status structure into packed record.
DmWrite(recordDBEntry, (UInt32)&packed->status,
        &record->status, sizeof(record->status));
offset = (UInt32)&packed->firstField;

for (index = 0; index < libFieldsCount; index++)
{
    if (record->fields[index] != NULL)
    {
        p = record->fields[index];
        length = StrLen(p) + 1;

        // Write text field data to packed record.
        DmWrite(recordDBEntry, offset, p, length);
        offset += length;
        SetBitMacro(flags.allBits, index);
    }
}

// Write field flags to packed record.
DmWrite(recordDBEntry, (UInt32)&packed->flags.allBits,
        &flags.allBits, sizeof(flags.allBits));

// Set or clear field offsets, as necessary.
index = 0;
if (record->fields[libFieldTitle] != NULL)
    index += StrLen(record->fields[libFieldTitle]) + 1;
if (record->fields[libFieldLastName] != NULL)
{
    lastNameOffset = index;
    index += StrLen(record->fields[libFieldLastName]) +
                    1;
}
if (record->fields[libFieldFirstName] != NULL)
{
    firstNameOffset = index;
    index += StrLen(record->fields[libFieldFirstName])
                    + 1;
}
if (record->fields[libFieldPublisher] != NULL)
    index += StrLen(record->fields[libFieldPublisher])
                    + 1;
if (record->fields[libFieldYear] != NULL) {
    yearOffset = index;
    index += StrLen(record->fields[libFieldYear]) + 1;
}
if (record->fields[libFieldPrinting] != NULL)
    index += StrLen(record->fields[libFieldPrinting]) +
                    1;
```

```
        if (record->fields[libFieldIsbn] != NULL)
            index += StrLen(record->fields[libFieldIsbn]) + 1;
        if (record->fields[libFieldPrice] != NULL)
            index += StrLen(record->fields[libFieldPrice]) + 1;
        if (record->fields[libFieldNote] != NULL)
            noteOffset = index;

        DmWrite(recordDBEntry,
                (UInt32)(&packed->lastNameOffset),
                &lastNameOffset, sizeof(lastNameOffset));
        DmWrite(recordDBEntry,
                (UInt32)(&packed->firstNameOffset),
                &firstNameOffset, sizeof(firstNameOffset));
        DmWrite(recordDBEntry, (UInt32)(&packed->yearOffset),
                &yearOffset, sizeof(yearOffset));
        DmWrite(recordDBEntry, (UInt32)(&packed->noteOffset),
                &noteOffset, sizeof(noteOffset));
}
static void UnpackRecord (LibPackedDBRecord *packed,
                          LibDBRecordType *record)
{
    Int16   index;
    UInt16  flags;
    char    *p;


    record->status = packed->status;
    flags = packed->flags.allBits;
    p = &packed->firstField;

    for (index = 0; index < libFieldsCount; index++)
    {
        if (GetBitMacro(flags, index) != 0)
        {
            record->fields[index] = p;
            p += StrLen(p) + 1;
        }
        else
        {
            record->fields[index] = NULL;
        }
    }
}
```

The PackRecord function has a much harder job than UnpackRecord because PackRecord must calculate the offsets of the last name, first name, year, and note fields, and write these values into the packed record structure. Also PackRecord must set and clear the appropriate flags in its flags field to indicate which text fields contain data and which are empty.

The UnpackRecord function needs only to look through the flags field of a packed record to determine which fields have data and then iterate over the pile of strings starting at the firstField member of the packed record, separating the strings into the fields array of an unpacked record.

These two packing functions, as well as other functions in other parts of Librarian, make use of the following macros to easily retrieve, set, and clear flag bits in bit fields:

```
#define BitAtPosition(pos) ((UInt16)1 << (pos))
#define GetBitMacro(bitfield, index) \
    ((bitfield) & BitAtPosition(index))
#define SetBitMacro(bitfield, index) \
    ((bitfield) |= BitAtPosition(index))
#define RemoveBitMacro(bitfield, index) \
    ((bitfield) &= ~BitAtPosition(index))
```

## Comparing Records

Because every application stores different kinds of data, a single Palm OS function for sorting databases is impractical. Instead, each application provides its own callback function for comparing records, which the system uses to sort the records into the proper order. Various Palm OS functions, detailed later in this chapter, use this callback to sort the database and to find the proper location to insert new records.

The application-defined callback for comparing two records in a database should have the following prototype:

```
typedef Int16 DmComparF (void* rec1, void* rec2,
    Int16 other, SortRecordInfoPtr rec1SortInfo,
    SortRecordInfoPtr rec2SortInfo, MemHandle appInfoH)
```

The first two parameters, rec1 and rec2, are pointers to the two records that should be compared. Along with the information contained in each record, the system provides other information that may be useful for sorting the records. The other parameter holds a value that is specific to your application. You may use other for any extra integer information you want to pass along when using the other Palm OS functions that require the callback function. For example, if your application allows for more than one way of sorting records, you can use the other parameter to specify which sort order should be assumed when comparing records. The Address Book uses this kind of scheme to allow sorting by surname or company name.

The next two parameters contain a SortRecordInfoType structure for each of the two records. Within the Palm OS header file DataMgr.h, SortRecordInfoType is defined as follows:

```
typedef struct {
    UInt8  attributes;
    UInt8  uniqueID[3];
} SortRecordInfoType;
```

In SortRecordInfoType, the attributes field contains the attributes for a particular record, which include the category of the record and all its status flags, such as whether or not the record is marked private. The uniqueID parameter contains the record's unique ID within the database.

The information in the rec1SortInfo and rec2SortInfo parameters to DmComparF may be useful for sorting records that might otherwise be identical according to your application's normal sorting criteria. Along with all the other information provided to DmComparF, the system supplies a handle to the database's application info block in the appInfoH parameter.

*For most applications, the rec1SortInfo, rec2SortInfo, and appInfoH parameters are overkill; just having pointers to the two records and the other parameter usually supplies more than enough information to compare two records. Still, the other three parameters might be useful if your application needs to perform more unusual sorting tasks, such as sorting records by their categories.*

To indicate how the two records compare, the DmComparF callback must return a signed integer value *n*, where *n* is one of the following values:

❑ n < 0 if the first record should come before the second record

❑ n > 0 if the first record should come after the second record

❑ 0 if the two records can occupy exactly the same place in the sort order

*Notice that these return values are exactly the same as the return values of the standard C function str-cmp and its Palm OS cousin, StrCompare. This fact should make it easier for you to remember what to return when writing a callback comparison function.*

As an example, the following implementation of DmComparF makes a simple string comparison between two records' name fields. Note that the other, rec1SortInfo, rec2SortInfo, and appInfoH parameters are completely unused in this function:

```
Int16 MyCompareFunc (RecordType* rec1, RecordType* rec2,
    Int16 other, SortRecordInfoPtr rec1SortInfo,
    SortRecordInfoPtr rec2SortInfo, MemHandle appInfoH)
{
    return StrCompare(rec1->name, rec2->name);
}
```

Unlike this basic example, the Librarian sample application's LibComparePackedRecords function is quite complex. There are multiple sort orders possible in the Librarian application. Each one changes which of Librarian's record fields should be compared, and in what order, to determine the relative sort values of two records. Also, empty fields are possible in Librarian records, which further complicates matters. The following listing shows the LibComparePackedRecords function:

```
static Int16 LibComparePackedRecords (
    LibPackedDBRecord *r1, LibPackedDBRecord *r2,
    Int16 showInList, SortRecordInfoPtr info1,
    SortRecordInfoPtr info2, MemHandle appInfoH)
{
    UInt16  whichKey1, whichKey2;
    char    *key1, *key2;
    Int16   result;


    // Records that don't contain data in the primary sort
    // field for the current sort order should be sorted
    // before records that do contain data. For example, in
    // libShowAuthorTitle sort order, any record containing
    // author data should come after a record without an
    // author.
    switch (showInList)
    {
        case libShowAuthorTitle:
            // Does r1 have empty author data?
            if ( (! r1->flags.bits.lastName) &&
                 (! r1->flags.bits.firstName) )
            {
                // Does r2 have empty author data?
```

```
            if ( (! r2->flags.bits.lastName) &&
                 (! r2->flags.bits.firstName) )
                // Neither r1 nor r2 contains author
                // data, so LibComparePackedRecords
                // needs to compare the records field
                // by field to determine sort order.
                break;
            // r1 has no author data, r2 does have
            // author data. Therefore, r1 < r2.
            else
            {
                result = -1;
                return result;
            }
        }
        else
        {
            // r1 has author data, r2 does not have
            // author data. Therefore, r1 > r2.
            if ( (! r2->flags.bits.lastName) &&
                 (! r2->flags.bits.firstName) )
            {
                result = 1;
                return result;
            }
        }
        break;

    case libShowTitleAuthor:
    case libShowTitleOnly:
        // Does r1 have empty title data?
        if (! r1->flags.bits.title)
        {
            // Does r2 have empty title data?
            if (! r2->flags.bits.title)
                // Neither r1 nor r2 contains title
                // data, so LibComparePackedRecords
                // needs to compare the records field
                // by field to determine sort order.
                break;
            // r1 has no title data, r2 does have title
            // data. Therefore, r1 < r2.
            else
            {
                result = -1;
                return result;
            }
        }
        else
        {
            // r1 has title data, r2 does not have
            // title data. Therefore, r1 > r2.
            if (! r2->flags.bits.title)
            {
                result = 1;
```

```
                    return result;
                }
            }
        break;

    default:
        break;
}

// Both records contain primary key data, or both
// records have empty primary key data. Either way,
// LibComparePackedRecords must now compare the two
// records field by field to determine sort order.
whichKey1 = 1;
whichKey2 = 1;

do
{
    LibFindKey(r1, &key1, &whichKey1, showInList);
    LibFindKey(r2, &key2, &whichKey2, showInList);

    // A key with NULL loses the StrCompare.
    if (key1 == NULL)
    {
        // If both are NULL then return them as equal.
        if (key2 == NULL)
        {
            result = 0;
            return result;
        }
        else
            result = -1;
    }
    else if (key2 == NULL)
        result = 1;
    else
    {
        result = StrCaselessCompare(key1, key2);
        if (result == 0)
            result = StrCompare(key1, key2);
    }

}
while (! result);

return result;
}
```

The first thing LibComparePackedRecords tries to determine is whether the primary key field for each record contains any data. The primary key is the field that has first priority when LibComparePackedRecords tries to compare two records. To determine which field is the primary key, LibComparePackedRecords looks at the value of its showInList parameter.

The LibComparePackedRecords function sorts empty fields before those that contain data so that they will appear at the top of the list. If one of the records has an empty primary key field and the other record's primary key contains data, LibComparePackedRecords will have enough data to compare the records without even looking at the contents of their fields and it will return the appropriate value and then exit.

If both records have primary key data, or if both records have empty primary keys, LibComparePackedRecords compares the records field by field to determine which record should come first. To accomplish this task, LibComparePackedRecords calls a helper function, LibFindKey, within a do ... while loop to get the offsets of the appropriate strings within each record. The LibFindKey function is shown in the following listing:

```
static void LibFindKey (LibPackedDBRecord *record,
                        char **key, UInt16 *whichKey,
                        Int16 showInList)
{
    LibDBRecordFlags  fieldFlags;


    fieldFlags.allBits = record->flags.allBits;

    ErrFatalDisplayIf(*whichKey == 0 || *whichKey == 6,
                      "Bad sort key");

    switch (showInList)
    {
        case libShowAuthorTitle:
            if (*whichKey == 1 && fieldFlags.bits.lastName)
            {
                *whichKey = 2;
                goto returnLastNameKey;
            }
            if (*whichKey <= 2 &&
                fieldFlags.bits.firstName)
            {
                *whichKey = 3;
                goto returnFirstNameKey;
            }
            if (*whichKey <= 3 && fieldFlags.bits.title)
            {
                *whichKey = 4;
                goto returnTitleKey;
            }
            if (*whichKey <= 4 && fieldFlags.bits.year)
            {
                *whichKey = 5;
                goto returnYearKey;
            }
            break;

        case libShowTitleAuthor:
        case libShowTitleOnly:
            if (*whichKey == 1 && fieldFlags.bits.title)
            {
                *whichKey = 2;
```

```
                    goto returnTitleKey;
            }
            if (*whichKey <= 2 && fieldFlags.bits.lastName)
            {
                *whichKey = 3;
                goto returnLastNameKey;
            }
            if (*whichKey <= 3 &&
                fieldFlags.bits.firstName)
            {
                *whichKey = 4;
                goto returnFirstNameKey;
            }
            if (*whichKey <= 4 && fieldFlags.bits.year)
            {
                *whichKey = 5;
                goto returnYearKey;
            }
            break;

        default:
            break;
    }

    // All possible fields have been tried.
    *whichKey = 7;
    *key = NULL;
    return;

returnTitleKey:
    *key = &record->firstField;
    return;

returnLastNameKey:
    *key = (char *) &record->firstField +
        record->lastNameOffset;
    return;

returnFirstNameKey:
    *key = (char *) &record->firstField +
        record->firstNameOffset;
    return;

returnYearKey:
    *key = (char *) &record->firstField +
        record->yearOffset;
    return;
}
```

If Librarian's current sort order is libShowAuthorTitle, LibFindKey returns fields from a record in the following order: author's last name, author's first name, title of the book, and year of publication. If the sort order is libShowTitleAuthor or libShowTitleOnly, LibFindKey uses this order instead: title of the book, author's last name, author's first name, and year of publication. The LibFindKey function looks for the first field in this order that contains data and returns a pointer to that field's string via the key parameter. If LibFindKey cannot find any key field that contains data, it returns NULL in the key parameter. The function also advances the whichKey parameter to an appropriate value so that the next time LibComparePackedRecords calls LibFindKey, the search for a valid key field can start after the fields that have already been tried.

As an example of how this works, assume that whichKey has a value of 1 and that showInList is libShowAuthorTitle. With these values, LibFindKey looks for data in the record's lastName field. If it finds data there, the function returns a pointer to the beginning of the lastName string in the key parameter and advances whichKey to 2; if lastName is empty, LibFindKey looks next in the record's firstName field, followed by title, followed by year, returning the first field in which it finds data or NULL if they are all empty.

Once LibComparePackedRecords has isolated a key field in each record that contains data, it calls StrCaselessCompare, passing the strings returned from LibFindKey. If these two strings are unequal, LibComparePackedRecords returns the value returned by StrCaselessCompare. Otherwise, LibComparePackedRecords continues its do ... while loop, comparing the next key field in the first record with the next key field in the second record until either StrCaselessCompare returns a nonzero value, or all of the key fields in both records have been exhausted; in either case, the two records are equal.

## Finding Records

Use the DmFindSortPosition function to find where a record belongs in a sorted database. Given a record that is currently unattached from a database, DmFindSortPosition performs a binary search to locate the record's proper position in the database. The prototype for DmFindSortPosition looks like this:

```
UInt16 DmFindSortPosition (DmOpenRef dbP, void* newRecord,
    SortRecordInfoPtr newRecordInfo, DmComparF *compar,
    Int16 other)
```

The dbP parameter is a reference to an open database, which your application can retrieve with the DmOpenDatabaseByTypeCreator or DmOpenDatabase functions. For more information about opening databases, see Chapter 15.

You should pass a pointer to a database record, with all its appropriate key fields filled in, via the newRecord parameter. The newRecordInfo parameter may be used to pass in extra information about the record. You usually will not need to use newRecordInfo. Simply pass the value NULL for this parameter if you do not wish to specify any extra record information.

The compar parameter is a pointer to your application's record comparison callback, and the other parameter allows you to send extra information to that callback function via its own other parameter.

Because Librarian must call DmFindSortPosition in a similar fashion from several locations throughout its code, Librarian has a LibFindSortPosition function that wraps DmFindSortPosition:

```
static UInt16 LibFindSortPosition (DmOpenRef db,
    LibPackedDBRecord *record)
{
    UInt8   showInList;
    LibAppInfoType  *appInfo;


    // Retrieve the current sort order from Librarian's
```

```
        // application info block.
        appInfo = MemHandleLock(LibGetAppInfo(db));
        showInList = appInfo->showInList;
        MemPtrUnlock(appInfo);

        return DmFindSortPosition(db, (MemPtr) record, NULL,
            (DmComparF *) &LibComparePackedRecords,
            (UInt16) showInList);
    }
```

The `LibFindSortPosition` function reduces to two the number of parameters needed to find the sort position of a record: an open database reference and a pointer to the record itself. Because Librarian never needs to pass extra record information to the `DmFindSortPosition` function, `LibFindSortPosition` just passes NULL for the `newRecordInfo` parameter. Likewise, the record comparison callback never changes, so `LibFindSortPosition` just passes the address of `LibComparePackedRecords` for the `compar` parameter. The current sort order of Librarian's database does change, so the `LibFindSortPosition` function looks up the current sort order in Librarian's application info block and passes it as the special value in the `other` parameter of `DmFindSortPosition`. More details about using `DmFindSortPosition`, and Librarian's `LibFindSortPosition` wrapper function, may be found later in this chapter in the sections on creating and modifying records.

If you already know the unique ID of the record you want to find, you can use the `DmFindRecordByID` function to return the record's index in the database:

```
Err DmFindRecordByID (DmOpenRef dbP, UInt32 uniqueID,
                      UInt16* indexP)
```

The `DmFindRecordByID` function takes three arguments: an open database reference, the unique ID of the desired record, and a pointer to a variable that receives the index of the requested record. If for some reason `DmFindRecordByID` is unable to locate a record with the given unique ID, the function returns an error code. A successful search for the unique ID results in a 0 return value.

One last function for finding records is `DmSearchRecord`. This function looks through all of the open record databases for a record with a given handle and returns an open database reference and the index of the record in that database if it finds the record. The `DmSearchRecord` function has the following prototype:

```
UInt16 DmSearchRecord (MemHandle recH, DmOpenRef* dbPP)
```

The pointer to the database where the record is found is returned in the `dbPP` parameter, and the function's return value contains the index of the found record. If `DmSearchRecord` is unable to find a record, it returns -1, and `dbPP` is NULL.

## Creating Records

There are two ways to create a new record in a Palm OS database. The first method allocates space for a new record with `DmNewRecord` and then writes data to the new record. The second method involves creating the record in its own memory chunk and then attaching that chunk to the database with `DmAttachRecord`. Both methods are perfectly valid; each has its uses.

## Creating Records with DmNewRecord

Using DmNewRecord to create records works well if your application needs to view or edit the new record immediately, because DmNewRecord sets the *busy bit* on the record it creates. The busy bit is a flag that indicates to the data manager that a record is currently open and should be left alone. A busy record may not be opened by another application until its busy bit is cleared with the DmReleaseRecord function.

The DmNewRecord function takes three parameters: an open database reference, a pointer to the desired index for the new record, and the size of the record in bytes. If DmNewRecord successfully creates a new record, it returns a handle to the new record. The prototype for DmNewRecord looks like this:

```
MemHandle DmNewRecord (DmOpenRef dbP, UInt16* atP,
                       UInt32 size)
```

When you call DmNewRecord, the atP parameter should point to a variable containing the index where you would like to insert the record; when DmNewRecord returns, it replaces the contents of what atP points to with the actual index of the newly created record. Record indices range from 0 to the total number of records minus one. If you specify 0 as the index for the new record, DmNewRecord adds the record at the beginning of the database:

```
MemHandle  newRecordH;
UInt16     index = 0;

newRecordH = DmNewRecord(gDB, &index, size);
```

If the index number is greater than the number of records in the database, DmNewRecord adds the record to the end of the database. You can ensure that a record is appended to the end of the database by using the constant dmMaxRecordIndex:

```
UInt16  index = dmMaxRecordIndex;

newRecordH = DmNewRecord(gDB, &index, size);
```

After the previous call, index contains the actual index of the new record.

> Usually, you should not add records to the end of the database because that is where the data manager sorts deleted and archived records during a call to **DmQuickSort** or **DmInsertionSort**. Adding records to the end of the database can confuse record-sorting functions like **DmFindSortPosition**, which assumes that deleted records always have a higher index than undeleted records.

Most of the time, you will want to add a new record at its proper sort position in the database. Use the DmFindSortPosition function to find where the new record belongs and then create the new record using DmNewRecord:

```
UInt16        index;
MyRecordType  newRecord;
MemHandle     newRecordH;
```

```
MyRecordType   *newRecordP;


// Initialize the fields of the newRecord structure.

index = DmFindSortPosition(gDB, &newRecord, NULL,
                                (DmComparF *) MyCompareFunc,
                                NULL);
newRecordH = DmNewRecord(gDB, &index, sizeof(newRecord));
newRecordP = MemHandleLock(newRecordH);
DmWrite(newRecordP, 0, &newRecord, sizeof(newRecord));
MemHandleUnlock(newRecordH);
DmReleaseRecord(gDB, index, true);
```

This example goes one step further than previous examples and actually writes the new record's data into the database with DmWrite. The DmWrite function has four parameters: a pointer to a locked chunk of storage memory, the offset from the beginning of that memory where DmWrite should start writing data, a pointer to the data to write, and the size of the data in bytes. In the preceding example, the DmWrite function writes the entire newRecord structure to memory.

After you are finished reading from and writing to a record created with DmNewRecord, call DmReleaseRecord to clear the busy bit on the new record. The DmReleaseRecord function has three parameters: an open database reference, the index of the record to release, and a Boolean value to indicate whether the record should be marked dirty or not. Passing a true value for the DmReleaseRecord function's last parameter sets the record's *dirty bit*, and a false value leaves the dirty bit alone.

*A record's dirty bit is important during a HotSync operation. The HotSync Manager uses the dirty bit to determine whether a record has changed. Be sure that your application sets the dirty bit if it changes a record. Not setting the dirty bit can cause an application's conduit to improperly synchronize a record because the conduit doesn't know that the record has changed.*

## Creating Records with DmAttachRecord

The second method for creating a new database record first creates the record in its own independent storage memory chunk and then attaches that chunk to a database using the DmAttachRecord function. This method works well if your application does not view or edit the new record immediately because DmAttachRecord does not set the busy bit on the new record. Likewise, it is not necessary to remember to call DmReleaseRecord after creating a new record using the DmAttachRecord function.

To start creating a new record with DmAttachRecord, first allocate a chunk of storage memory and fill it with the new record's data. Use the DmNewHandle function to accomplish this task:

```
MyRecordType   newRecord;
MemHandle      newRecordH;
MyRecordType   *newRecordP;
UInt16         index;
Err            error;

// Initialize the fields of the newRecord structure.

newRecordH = DmNewHandle(gDB, sizeof(newRecord));
newRecordP = MemHandleLock(recordH);
DmWrite(newRecordP, 0, &newRecord, sizeof(newRecord));
```

After this code executes, you have a chunk of memory containing the new record. To attach this chunk to the database, first use `DmFindSortPosition` to find where the record belongs and then use `DmAttachRecord` to attach the record at that position:

```
index = DmFindSortPosition(gDB, &newRecord, NULL,
                             (DmComparF *) MyCompareFunc,
                             NULL);
MemHandleUnlock(recordH);
error = DmAttachRecord(gDB, &index, newRecordH, NULL);

// If all went well, index now contains the actual index
// where the record was inserted into the database.

if (error)
    MemHandleFree(newRecordH);
```

The `DmAttachRecord` function has four parameters: an open database reference, a pointer to a variable containing the desired index for the new record, the handle of the new record, and a pointer to another record handle. The last parameter of `DmAttachRecord` can be used to replace an existing record in the database. If you pass a pointer to a handle for the last parameter, `DmAttachRecord` replaces the record at the requested index with the new record and returns a handle to the old record via this pointer; see the "Modifying Records" section coming up in this chapter for an example. A `NULL` value for the fourth parameter tells `DmAttachRecord` to insert the record instead of replacing an existing one, in much the same way that `DmNewRecord` works. Another similarity between `DmNewRecord` and `DmAttachRecord` is in how the functions deal with their `index` parameters; `DmAttachRecord` returns the actual index of the new record via its `index` parameter, just as `DmNewRecord` does.

The Librarian sample application uses the `DmAttachRecord` method to add new records to its database, and it wraps the whole new record-creation process in the `LibNewRecord` function:

```
Err LibNewRecord (DmOpenRef db, LibDBRecordType *record,
                  UInt16 *index)
{
    MemHandle   recordH;
    Err         error;
    LibPackedDBRecord  *packed;
    UInt16      newIndex;


    // Allocate a chunk large enough to hold the new
    // record.
    recordH = DmNewHandle(db, LibUnpackedSize(record));
    if (recordH == NULL)
        return dmErrMemError;

    // Copy the data from the unpacked record to the packed
    // one.
    packed = MemHandleLock(recordH);
    PackRecord(record, packed);

    // Get the index of the new record.
    newIndex = LibFindSortPosition(db, packed);
```

```
        MemPtrUnlock(packed);

        // Attach new record in place and return the index of
        // the new record in the index parameter.
        error = DmAttachRecord(db, &newIndex, recordH, 0);
        if (error)
            MemHandleFree(recordH);
        else
            *index = newIndex;

        return error;
    }
```

## Deleting Records

Deleting records from a Palm OS database requires a bit of finesse because the data manager expects to find deleted and archived records at the end of the database. In an application with a conduit, deleted records need to stick around on the handheld until the next HotSync operation, at which point the application's conduit can delete the corresponding records from the desktop version of the application's database. Likewise, archived records need to remain on the handheld until a HotSync operation can allow the conduit to properly archive a record on the desktop before completing the process of removing it from the handheld.

Because of these deletion and archival requirements, Palm OS provides three functions for deleting records from a database, appropriate for different circumstances: DmRemoveRecord, DmDeleteRecord, and DmArchiveRecord.

The first record-deletion function, DmRemoveRecord, actually deletes a record outright without giving the application's conduit a chance to look at it. This function is appropriate when the user creates a record on the handheld but then deletes it before the next HotSync operation. In this case, there is no corresponding record on the desktop, so there is no need to keep the record at the end of the database until the next HotSync operation. The DmRemoveRecord function needs only an open database reference and the index of the record to remove:

```
    Err error = DmRemoveRecord(gDB, index);
```

The DmDeleteRecord function frees the memory chunk associated with a record's data but marks the record as deleted in the database header. A similar function, DmArchiveRecord, frees a record's data chunk and sets the record's archive bit in the database header. Just as with DmRemoveRecord, these two functions require an open database reference and the index of the record to delete or archive.

You must be sure that your application moves deleted and archived records to the end of the database itself using the DmMoveRecord function; the system does not perform this important step for you. The following code takes care of deleting or archiving a record and moving it to the end of the database:

```
    if (gArchive)
        DmArchiveRecord(gDB, index);
    else
        DmDeleteRecord(gDB, index);
    DmMoveRecord(gDB, index, DmNumRecords(gDB));
```

The last parameter of the DmMoveRecord indicates the index where a record should be moved to, which causes the indices of all of the records following this insertion point to increase by one. You may pass a value one greater than the index of the last record to move a record to the end of the database. The preceding example uses the function DmNumRecords to determine the number of records in the database and uses that function's return value as the index to which a deleted or archived record should be moved (recall that record indices are zero-based).

An accompanying function, DmDetachRecord, allows you to remove a database record's entry in the database header deliberately while leaving its data chunk intact. DmDetachRecord turns the record into an unattached orphan that is not associated with a parent database. The prototype for DmDetachRecord looks like this:

```
Err DmDetachRecord (DmOpenRef dbP, UInt16 index,
    MemHandle* oldHP)
```

The first two parameters to DmDetachRecord take an open database reference and the index of the record you would like to detach. If you supply a pointer to a memory handle in the third parameter, DmDetachRecord returns the handle of the detached record in this pointer. The DmDetatchRecord function is a good way to start moving a record from one database to another. Use DmDetachRecord to cut the record from the first database and then attach it to the second database using DmAttachRecord.

Librarian encapsulates the code it needs to delete records in its DeleteRecord function, shown as follows:

```
static void DeleteRecord (Boolean archive)
{
    // Show the prior record. This provides context for the
    // user, as it shows where the record was, and it
    // allows a return to the same location in the database
    // if the user is working through the records
    // sequentially. If there isn't a prior record, show
    // the following record. If there isn't a following
    // record, don't show a record at all.
    gListFormSelectThisRecord = gCurrentRecord;
    if (! SeekRecord(&gListFormSelectThisRecord, 1,
        dmSeekBackward))
        if (! SeekRecord(&gListFormSelectThisRecord, 1,
            dmSeekForward))
            gListFormSelectThisRecord = noRecord;

    // Delete or archive the record.
    if (archive)
        DmArchiveRecord(gLibDB, gCurrentRecord);
    else
        DmDeleteRecord(gLibDB, gCurrentRecord);

    // Deleted records are stored at the end of the
    // database.
    DmMoveRecord(gLibDB, gCurrentRecord,
                DmNumRecords(gLibDB));

    // Since we just moved the gCurrentRecord to the end,
    // the gListFormSelectThisRecord may need to be moved
    // up one position.
```

```
        if (gListFormSelectThisRecord >= gCurrentRecord &&
            gListFormSelectThisRecord != noRecord)
            gListFormSelectThisRecord--;

        // Use whatever record we found to select.
        gCurrentRecord = gListFormSelectThisRecord;
}
```

Librarian keeps track of the current record via a global variable, gCurrentRecord. When the user deletes the current record, DeleteRecord ensures that gCurrentRecord is set to an appropriate value because deleting a record makes it invalid for display purposes. Likewise, Librarian also keeps track of which record in its List view should be highlighted using the global gListFormSelectThisRecord; DeleteRecord also ensures that this global variable is updated properly. The SeekRecord function used in DeleteRecord is described later in this chapter in the section "Categorizing Records."

# Reading Records

If your application needs to read values from a record without writing to it, the data manager allows the application to lock a handle to the record without marking it busy by using the DmQueryRecord function. Calling DmQueryRecord looks like this:

```
MemHandle recordH = DmQueryRecord(gDB, index);
MyRecordType *recordP = MemHandleLock(recordH);
// Read values from recordP here.
MemHandleUnlock(recordH);
```

# Modifying Records

Just as there is more than one way to create records, there is more than one way to open a record so that your application may write to it. The first requires DmGetRecord to retrieve a handle to the record, marking the record busy in the process. The second method allocates a completely new memory chunk for the changed record with DmNewHandle, copies the old values from the record to the new chunk with DmQueryRecord, modifies the new chunk's values, and then replaces the original record with the new one using DmAttachRecord. A third method, useful for text data displayed in fields in a table, relies on the field manager's FldSetText function to allow the user to edit the data in place.

## Modifying Records with DmGetRecord

The DmGetRecord function marks a record as busy so that no other applications can modify the record while your application is doing so. Just as when you're creating a new record with DmNewRecord, you must call DmReleaseRecord to clear the record's busy bit after you are done making changes, and to set the record's dirty bit if necessary. Also, because all memory in the storage area is protected, you can write to it using the DmWrite or DmStrCopy functions only, or DmSet to set a memory range to a particular value.

Changing a record with DmGetRecord requires the following steps:

1. Open the record with DmGetRecord.

2. Create a temporary record structure and copy the original record into it.

3. Change the temporary record structure's fields to their new values.

**4.** Copy the changes from the temporary record to the actual record using DmWrite.

**5.** Check to see if changes to the record have altered its sort position within the database. If so, release the record and mark it dirty with DmReleaseRecord and then move the record to its proper index with DmMoveRecord.

**6.** If the record did not change position, release it and mark it dirty with DmReleaseRecord.

Note that you need not always write out the full record structure with DmWrite. If you have a very large data structure you can also use DmWrite to update individual fields within a record, based on offsets.

The following function takes an open database reference and a pointer to the index of a record and changes the record according to the six steps outlined previously:

```
Err ChangeRecord (DmOpenRef db, UInt16 *index)
{
    MemHandle       recordH;
    MyRecordType    tempRecord;
    MyRecordType    *record;
    MyRecordType    *cmp;
    UInt16          attributes;
    Boolean         move = true;
    Int16           i;

    recordH = DmGetRecord(db, *index);
    if (recordH == NULL)
        return DmGetLastErr();
    record = MemHandleLock(recordH);

    // Copy the values from the actual record to a
    // temporary record.
    tempRecord = *record;

    // Modify the temporary record here.
    tempRecord.field = newValue;

    // Copy the modified temporary record into the actual
    // storage space of the real record.
    DmWrite(record, 0, &tempRecord, sizeof(tempRecord));

    // Determine if the record is in the proper sort order.
    if (*index > 0)
    {
        // Compare this record to the record before it.
        cmp = MemHandleLock(DmQueryRecord(db, *index - 1));
        move = (MyCompareFunc(cmp, record, 0, NULL, NULL,
                              NULL) > 0);
        MemPtrUnlock(cmp);
    }
    else
    {
        move = false;
    }

    if (*index + 1 < DmNumRecords(db))
```

```
    {
        // Be sure not to move the record beyond the
        // deleted records at the end of the database.
        DmRecordInfo(db, *index + 1, &attributes,
                     NULL);
        if (! (attributes & dmRecAttrDelete))
        {
            // Compare this record to the record after it.
            cmp = MemHandleLock(DmQueryRecord(db, *index +
                                              1));
            move = (! move) && (MyCompareFunc(record,
                                cmp, 0, NULL, NULL, NULL) >
                                0);
            MemPtrUnlock(cmp);
        }
    }

    if (move)
    {
        // The record isn't in the right position, so move
        // it.
        i = DmFindSortPosition(db, record, NULL,
                               &MyCompareFunc, 0);

        // Unlock and release the record before moving it.
        MemHandleUnlock(recordH);
        DmReleaseRecord(db, index, true);

        DmMoveRecord(db, *index, i);
        if (i > *index)
            i--;
        *index = i;  // Return new record database
                     // position.
    }
    else
    {
        MemHandleUnlock(recordH);
        DmReleaseRecord(db, index, true);
    }

    return 0;
}
```

If you have changed any key fields that your application uses to sort records, use DmMoveRecord to put the changed record into its proper sort order within the database. By calling the application-defined MyCompareFunc callback function directly, the ChangeRecord function determines whether the modified record should be moved. First, the example compares the changed record with the record before it, which is the record located at *index - 1. Then, ChangeRecord compares the modified record with the record following it, at *index + 1. If the record is out of place, ChangeRecord finds the record's proper sort position using DmFindSortPosition and then moves the record to the new location with DmMoveRecord. Afterward, ChangeRecord modifies its index parameter to reflect the altered record's new index.

## Modifying Records with DmAttachRecord

A slightly different approach to modifying records involves the DmAttachRecord function. Instead of modifying an existing record, this method allocates a brand new chunk of storage memory to contain the changed record. An application should follow these steps when modifying a record with DmAttachRecord:

1. Create a temporary record structure and copy the original record into it.

2. Change the temporary record structure's fields to their new values.

3. Allocate a chunk of memory with DmNewHandle to hold the changed record.

4. Copy the temporary record into the new chunk of memory. You now have an orphaned record, floating freely in storage RAM.

5. Check to see if changes to the record have altered its sort position within the database. If so, move the original record to the correct index with DmMoveRecord.

6. Replace the original record with the new memory chunk using DmAttachRecord.

7. Dispose of the original record, which has now become an orphaned chunk of memory.

The following ChangeRecord2 function performs exactly the same function as the ChangeRecord function from the previous section, but it uses the DmAttachRecord method outlined previously instead of DmGetRecord:

```
Err ChangeRecord2 (DmOpenRef db, UInt16 *index)
{
    Err           result;
    MemHandle     recordH, changedRecordH, oldH;
    MyRecordType  tempRecord;
    MyRecordType  *record;
    MyRecordType  *changedRecord;
    MyRecordType  *cmp;
    UInt16        attributes;
    Boolean       move = true;
    Int16         i;

    recordH = DmQueryRecord(db, *index);
    record = MemHandleLock(recordH);

    // Copy the values from the actual record to a
    // temporary record.
    tempRecord = *record;

    // The original record has been copied and is no longer
    // needed.
    MemHandleUnlock(recordH);

    // Modify the temporary record here.
    tempRecord.field = newValue;

    // Allocate a chunk for the changed record.
    changedRecordH = DmNewHandle(db, sizeof(tempRecord));
```

```
if (changedRecordH == NULL)
{
    MemHandleUnlock(recordH);
    return dmErrMemError;
}
changedRecord = MemHandleLock(changedRecordH);

// Copy the modified temporary record into the new
// memory chunk.
DmWrite(changedRecord, 0, &tempRecord,
        sizeof(tempRecord));

// Make sure the record is in the proper sort order.
if (*index > 0)
{
    // Compare this record to the record before it.
    cmp = MemHandleLock(DmQueryRecord(db, *index - 1));
    move = (MyCompareFunc(cmp, changedRecord, 0, NULL,
                          NULL, NULL) > 0);
    MemPtrUnlock(cmp);
}
else
{
    move = false;
}

if (*index + 1 < DmNumRecords(db))
{
    // Be sure not to move the record beyond the
    // deleted records at the end of the database.
    DmRecordInfo(db, *index + 1, &attributes, NULL,
                 NULL);
    if (! (attributes & dmRecAttrDelete))
    {
        // Compare this record to the record after it.
        cmp = MemHandleLock(DmQueryRecord(db, *index +
                                          1));
        move = (! move) &&
            (MyCompareFunc(changedRecord, cmp, 0, NULL,
             NULL, NULL) > 0);
        MemPtrUnlock(cmp);
    }
}

if (move)
{
    // The record isn't in the right position, so move
    // it.
    i = DmFindSortPosition(db, changedRecord);
    DmMoveRecord(db, *index, i);
    if (i > *index)
        i--;
    *index = i;   // Return new record database
                  // position.
```

```
    }

    // Replace the original record, now located in its
    // proper sort order, with the memory chunk containing
    // the changed record.
    result = DmAttachRecord(db, index, changedRecordH,
                            &oldH);
    MemHandleUnlock(changedRecordH);
    if (result) return result;

    // The original record is now a detached orphan, so its
    // memory may be freed.
    MemHandleFree(oldH);
    return 0;
}
```

Because the previous method never marks the record to change as busy with DmGetRecord, and the DmAttachRecord function sets the dirty bit on a newly attached record, there is no need to call DmReleaseRecord when done to clear the busy bit or set the dirty bit. The DmReleaseRecord call in ChangeRecord2 also returns a handle, oldH, to the original record; this example does not need to do anything with the original record once it has been replaced, and so ChangeRecord2 disposes of the handle with MemHandleFree.

*The DmAttachRecord function is very handy for cutting and pasting between two databases.*

The Librarian sample application uses the DmAttachRecord method for committing changes to a record in its database. Librarian's LibChangeRecord function, shown as follows, takes care of all the necessary work:

```
Err LibChangeRecord (DmOpenRef db, UInt16 *index,
                     LibDBRecordType *record,
                     LibDBRecordFlags changedFields)
{
    LibDBRecordType  src;
    MemHandle        srcH;
    Err              result;
    MemHandle        recordH = 0;
    MemHandle        oldH;
    Int16            i;
    UInt32           changes = changedFields.allBits;
    Int16            showInList;
    LibAppInfoType   *appInfo;
    Boolean          move = true;
    UInt16           attributes;
    LibPackedDBRecord* cmp;
    LibPackedDBRecord* packed;


    // LibChangeRecord does not assume that record is
    // completely valid, so it retrieves a valid pointer
    // to the record.
    if ((result =
        LibGetRecord(db, *index, &src, &srcH)) != 0)
```

```
        return result;

    // Apply the changes to the valid record.
    src.status = record->status;
    for (i = 0; i < libFieldsCount; i++)
    {
        // If the flag is set, point to the string,
        // otherwise point to NULL.
        if (GetBitMacro(changes, i) != 0)
        {
            src.fields[i] = record->fields[i];
            RemoveBitMacro(changes, i);
        }
        if (changes == 0)
            break;      // no more changes
    }

    // Make a new chunk with the correct size.
    recordH = DmNewHandle(db, LibUnpackedSize(&src));
    if (recordH == NULL)
    {
        MemHandleUnlock(srcH);
        return dmErrMemError;
    }
    packed = MemHandleLock(recordH);

    // Copy the data from the unpacked record to the packed
    // record.
    PackRecord(&src, packed);

    // The original record is copied and no longer needed.
    MemHandleUnlock(srcH);

    // Check if any of the key fields have changed. If they
    // have not changed, this record is already in its
    // proper place in the database, and LibChangeRecord
    // can skip re-sorting the record.
    if ((changedFields.allBits & sortKeyFieldBits) == 0)
        move = false;

    // Make sure *index - 1 < *index < *index + 1; if so,
    // the record is already in sorted order. Deleted
    // records are stored at the end of the database, so
    // LibChangeRecord must also make sure not to sort this
    // record past the end of any deleted records.
    if (move)
    {
        appInfo = MemHandleLock(LibGetAppInfo(db));
        showInList = appInfo->showInList;
        MemPtrUnlock(appInfo);

        if (*index > 0)
        {
            // Compare this record to the record before it.
            cmp = MemHandleLock(DmQueryRecord(db,
```

```
                                                *index - 1));
            move = (LibComparePackedRecords(cmp, packed,
                    showInList, NULL, NULL, NULL) > 0);
            MemPtrUnlock(cmp);
        }
        else
        {
            move = false;
        }


        if (*index + 1 < DmNumRecords(db))
        {
            // Be sure not to move the record beyond the
            // deleted records at the end of the database.
            DmRecordInfo(db, *index + 1, &attributes, NULL,
                    NULL);
            if (! (attributes & dmRecAttrDelete))
            {
                // Compare this record to the record after
                // it.
                cmp = MemHandleLock(DmQueryRecord(db,
                                *index + 1));
                move = (! move) &&
                    (LibComparePackedRecords(packed, cmp,
                    showInList, NULL, NULL, NULL) > 0);
                MemPtrUnlock(cmp);
            }
        }
    }

    if (move)
    {
        // The record isn't in the right position, so move
        // it.
        i = LibFindSortPosition(db, packed);
        DmMoveRecord(db, *index, i);
        if (i > *index)
            i--;
        *index = i;  // Return new record database
                     // position.
    }

    // Attach the new record to the old index, which
    // preserves the category and record ID.
    result = DmAttachRecord(db, index, recordH, &oldH);
    MemPtrUnlock(packed);
    if (result) return result;

    MemHandleFree(oldH);
    return 0;
}
```

Note that because LibChangeRecord receives a LibDBRecordFlags structure (changedFields) that indicates what fields in the record have changed, LibChangeRecord saves itself a lot of work by looking in changedFields for changed key fields before checking whether the record is in the right position or not. If none of the key fields that Librarian uses to sort its data have been changed, then the record is still in its proper sort order and does not need to be moved. The sortKeyFieldBits macro that LibChangeRecord uses to make this decision is defined as follows in librarianDB.c:

```
#define BitAtPosition(pos)   ((UInt16)1 << (pos))
#define sortKeyFieldBits  ( \
    BitAtPosition(libFieldTitle) | \
    BitAtPosition(libFieldLastName) | \
    BitAtPosition(libFieldFirstName) | \
    BitAtPosition(libFieldYear) )
```

## Editing Records in Place

A field object can be used to edit a string in place within a record. In-place editing is particularly useful in large text fields that may contain a lot of data, such as the Note view in the various ROM applications. Less dynamic memory is required to edit a large field in place than to copy all the data from the field to a database record.

With a little bit of setup, the field manager takes care of resizing the handle containing the string as the user edits the text in the field. This method even works for string values that are stored within a larger structure in an application's records; you simply need to pass an offset from the start of the record where the string data begins.

To illustrate editing in place, consider the following record structure:

```
typedef struct {
    Int16   data1;
    Int32   data2;
    Char    stringData[20];
} MyRecordType;
```

The text string stored in stringData is a null-terminated string and may be of any length, not just 20 characters. The following code sets up a text field for in-place editing of the stringData field:

```
FormType    *form;
FieldType   *field;
MemHandle   recordH;
MemHandle   oldTextH;
MyRecordType   *record;

form = FrmGetActiveForm();
field = FrmGetObjectPtr(form, FrmGetObjectIndex(form,
                                         MyField));
oldTextH = FldGetTextHandle(field);

// Dispose of the old handle to prevent a memory leak.
if (oldTextH)
    MemHandleFree(oldTextH);

recordH = DmGetRecord(gDB, index);
record = MemHandleLock(recordH);
```

```
FldSetText(field, recordH, offsetof(MyRecordType,
                                    stringData),
    StrLen(record.stringData) + 1);

MemHandleUnlock(recordH);
```

Now the `MyField` text field is set up for in-place editing of a record's `stringData` field. You can actually dispense with calling `MemHandleFree` to free up the memory occupied by the field's old text handle if you are setting up in-place editing on a form that has just been opened, because a text field that has just been initialized does not have a text handle allocated for it yet; just in case, though, it's never a bad idea to dispose of the old handle, because doing so will prevent a memory leak if the field did, indeed, have a text handle before your application called `FldGetTextHandle`.

Once editing is finished, you must perform a few cleanup tasks. Normally, you will call something similar to the following code when closing the form that contains the text field you are working with:

```
Boolean  dirty = FldDirty(field);

if (dirty)
    FldCompactText(field);
FldSetTextHandle(field, NULL);
DmReleaseRecord(gDB, index, dirty);
```

The first thing you should do is to compact the handle containing the text if the field has been modified. Because the field manager resizes the text handle several bytes at a time instead of one byte at a time, there might be more space allocated for the string than is actually required. Call `FldCompactText` to trim the handle down to the proper size so that you are not wasting storage space with unnecessary empty bytes.

Once you have compacted the text handle, disconnect the handle from the field by calling `FldSetTextHandle` with `NULL` as its second parameter. The system frees the memory allocated for a field's text handle when disposing of the field. Because the text handle in this case is actually the data stored in the application's database, freeing this memory will cause a crash, because `MemHandleFree`, which the system calls when the form closes, cannot free a handle in the storage heap. Disconnecting the text handle from the field with `FldSetTextHandle` prevents this crash.

Finally, you must release the record so the system can clear its busy bit. The `DmReleaseRecord` function serves this purpose here, also setting the dirty bit for the record if necessary.

> **The in-place editing technique cannot connect more than one text field to multiple strings in a database record. If two or more fields were hooked up to the same record, they might both try to resize the handle, and the field manager is not set up to deal with that situation.**

Librarian uses the in-place editing technique in its Note view to allow in-place editing of a large field. The `NoteViewLoadRecord` function takes care of setting up in-place editing in the Note view:

```
static void NoteViewLoadRecord (void)
{
    FieldType    *field;
    LibPackedDBRecord  *packed;
    MemHandle  packedH;
    Char       *ptr;
    UInt16     offset;


    // Get a pointer to the memo field.
    field = GetObjectPtr(NoteField);

    // Set the font used in the memo field.
    FldSetFont(field, gNoteFont);

    // Retrieve the note field from the current database
    // record. Librarian calls CreateNote before getting to
    // NoteViewLoadRecord, which guarantees that the note
    // field already exists.
    packedH = DmQueryRecord(gLibDB, gCurrentRecord);
    ErrFatalDisplayIf((! packedH), "Bad record");
    packed = MemHandleLock(packedH);

    // Set a pointer to the location of the note field,
    // using the note field offset stored in the packed
    // database record.
    ptr = &packed->firstField;
    ptr += packed->noteOffset;

    // Calculate the offset of the note field from the
    // front of the packed database record, not from the
    // beginning of the first field, since FldSetText wants
    // the offset from the start of the record's memory
    // chunk.
    offset = ptr - (char *)packed;

    // Set the note field text to the contents of the note
    // field.
    FldSetText(field, packedH, offset, StrLen(ptr) + 1);

    MemHandleUnlock(packedH);
}
```

Notice that `NoteViewLoadRecord` does not use the `offsetof` macro to determine the offset of the record's note field. Because Librarian uses variable-length records, and a number of strings of different lengths may or may not exist before the note field in a record, a simple `offsetof` call will not return the correct location of the note field. Instead, `NoteViewLoadRecord` uses the record structure's `noteOffset` field to determine where the note field begins.

The `NoteViewSave` function takes care of in-place editing cleanup in Librarian:

```
static void NoteViewSave (void)
{
    FieldType  *field;
```

```
UInt16      length;


field = GetObjectPtr(NoteField);

// If the field wasn't modified then don't do anything.
if (FldDirty(field))
{
    // Release any free space in the note field.
    FldCompactText(field);
    DirtyRecord(gCurrentRecord);
}

length = FldGetTextLength(field);

// Clear the handle value in the field, otherwise the
// handle will be free when the form is disposed of.
// This call also unlocks the handle that contains the
// note string.
FldSetTextHandle(field, 0);

// Empty fields are not allowed because they cause
// problems.
if (length == 0)
    DeleteNote();
}
```

Because of Librarian's record structure, an empty string does not work well in one of its fields, because such a string would still contain a single terminating null character. Other routines in Librarian expect that an empty field will take up zero space in a record, and leaving the trailing null of an empty string in the record would cause problems later, so NoteViewSave deletes the note entirely with the DeleteNote function if the note's text field is empty.

# Changing Database Structures Between Versions

As an application evolves, it may become necessary for you to change its data format to accommodate new features. Unfortunately, if you alter the way your application stores its records between versions, the new version will no longer be able to read the old version's data. Convincing users of your application to upgrade to the latest version can be a very hard sell if they must re-enter all their data for the new version.

Fortunately, the Palm OS provides an easy way to mark the version of a record database. The DmSetDatabaseInfo function, introduced in Chapter 13, allows you to set many properties of a database, including its version. Using that function's companion, DmDatabaseInfo, your application can retrieve the version of its database. If the database version is older than the database version supported by the application, it can convert the database to the newer format automatically.

*There is a difference between a database version and the version of an application. Database version is a property of a record database, stored in the database's header, and it shouldn't be confused with the version of the application itself, which is usually stored in a version resource as part of the application .prc file. It is necessary to increment the database version only when its record format changes. Thus, unless you change the record format with every new version of your application, chances are that your application's version number will increase more often than its database version.*

The best place to check for the database version is in your application's StartApplication routine, where the program first opens its database. After opening the database with DmOpenDatabase or DmOpenDatabaseByTypeCreator and retrieving the database's card number and database ID with DmOpenDatabaseInfo, you can call DmDatabaseInfo to retrieve the database's version, as shown in the following example:

```
DmOpenRef   db;
UInt16      cardNo;
LocalID     dbID;
UInt16      dbVersion;

db = DmOpenDatabaseByTypeCreator(MyDBType, MyCreatorID,
                        dmModeReadWrite);
DmOpenDatabaseInfo(db, &dbID, NULL, NULL, &cardNo, NULL);
DmDatabaseInfo(cardNo, dbID, NULL, NULL, &dbVersion, NULL,
            NULL, NULL, NULL, NULL, NULL, NULL, NULL);
```

Once it has retrieved the database version, your application can take appropriate action, depending upon the version of the database. Usually, this action will take the form of converting the existing database to the new version, then marking the database with the new version number using DmSetDatabaseInfo. The following example shows how to set the database version to the value 1:

```
dbVersion = 1;
DmSetDatabaseInfo(cardNo, dbID, NULL, NULL, &dbVersion,
            NULL, NULL, NULL, NULL, NULL, NULL,
            NULL, NULL);
```

*Keep in mind that when you create a database with DmCreateDatabase, the database's default version number is 0. In the previous example, the value 1 represents the second version of the database, not the first.*

If your application uses a very complex data format, or if you have made enough changes to the data format between versions that the conversion code would be long and complex, including the code to convert between database versions in your main application may increase its size unnecessarily. In this case, you may want to consider creating a separate application that is devoted entirely to converting data from one version to the next. Your main application would simply display a warning alert if it encountered an old database version, instructing the user to install and run your conversion utility. Then, the converter could be deleted, thereby saving space on the handheld.

For most programs, though, conversion code shouldn't add too much to the size of the main application. It also is a much simpler and more pleasant experience for the user if your application simply takes care of conversion in the background, without any user intervention.

For a complete example of detecting and converting old database versions, consider the Librarian sample application. Since publication of the first edition of this book, I discovered a bug in Librarian that was directly related to the packed record structure in the first version of Librarian. Here is the old version of Librarian's LibPackedDBRecord structure, which has been renamed to LibPackedDBRecordV0 in the new version of Librarian:

```
typedef struct {
    LibStatusType       status;
    LibDBRecordFlags    flags;
```

```
      unsigned char     lastNameOffset;
      unsigned char     firstNameOffset;
      unsigned char     yearOffset;
      unsigned char     noteOffset;
      char              firstField;
} LibPackedDBRecordV0;
```

Notice that `lastNameOffset`, `firstNameOffset`, `yearOffset`, and `noteOffset` are all defined as type `unsigned char`. Librarian uses these four structure members to store the offsets of text field data in a record, for purposes of retrieving those pieces of data quickly without having to completely unpack the record. For example, the `noteOffset` member stores the number of bytes from the beginning of a record until the start of the note data in that record.

The problem is that the largest number that an `unsigned char` can store is 255. There are eight text fields' worth of data stored in a Librarian record, each of which may hold up to 256 bytes of text, including null string terminators. If the first few text fields contain a lot of data, the offsets to later fields may be larger than the maximum limit of 255 that is imposed by an `unsigned char`. For example, if there is enough text in early fields to put the note data at an offset of 1,000 bytes from the beginning of the record, that 1,000 is converted to 235 to fit in the `unsigned char` variable (1,000 modulus 255 equals 235), which is clearly the incorrect location for the note's data. The result is that Librarian displays incorrect data in the Note view, because the offset of 235 bytes into the record points to data somewhere in one of the record's other text fields, not to the note.

To fix this problem, the new version of Librarian uses `UInt16` variables to store the offset values. The largest number that may be stored in a `UInt16` is 65,535, which is larger than the maximum size of a record imposed by the HotSync architecture; a `UInt16` is more than sufficient to store correct offset values. The new `LibPackedDBRecord` structure looks like this:

```
typedef struct {
    LibStatusType      status;
    LibDBRecordFlags   flags;
    UInt16             lastNameOffset;
    UInt16             firstNameOffset;
    UInt16             yearOffset;
    UInt16             noteOffset;
    char               firstField;
} LibPackedDBRecord;
```

Other code in Librarian, primarily in the `PackRecord` function, expects the `LibPackedDBRecord` structure's offsets to be `UInt16` values, so the new version of Librarian would produce errors if it tried to read the older packed record format's `unsigned char` values. Before Librarian can open an older database, it must convert all its records to the new `LibPackedDBRecord` structure.

Librarian first checks the version of the database in its `LibGetDatabase` function, which `StartApplication` calls directly. The relevant portion of `LibGetDatabase` looks like this:

```
DmOpenDatabaseInfo(db, &dbID, NULL, NULL, &cardNo, NULL);
DmDatabaseInfo(cardNo, dbID, NULL, NULL, &dbVersion, NULL,
           NULL, NULL, NULL, NULL, NULL, NULL, NULL);
if (dbVersion == libDatabaseVersion1_0_0)
{
    LibConvertDB(db, libDatabaseVersion1_0_0,
```

```
                            libDatabaseVersion2_0_0);
        dbVersion = libDatabaseVersion2_0_0;
        DmSetDatabaseInfo(cardNo, dbID, NULL, NULL,
                          &dbVersion, NULL, NULL, NULL, NULL,
                          NULL, NULL, NULL, NULL);
    }
```

The constants libDatabaseVersion1_0_0 and libDatabaseVersion2_0_0 correspond to the
database versions used by versions 1.0.0 and 2.0.0 of Librarian, respectively. The constants are defined as
follows in librarianDB.h:

```
#define libDatabaseVersion1_0_0    0
#define libDatabaseVersion2_0_0    1
```

If LibGetDatabase detects that the database version is equal to libDatabaseVersion1_0_0, it calls
LibConvertDB to convert the database's records to the new format. After converting the database's
records, LibGetDatabase sets the database's version to libDatabaseVersion2_0_0. The next time
Librarian starts, it detects that the database is already in the new format, so it skips calling LibConvertDB
unnecessarily. LibConvertDB is shown in the following code:

```
Err LibConvertDB (DmOpenRef db, UInt16 fromVersion,
                  UInt16 toVersion)
{
    UInt16      index;
    UInt32      oldSize, newSize;
    MemHandle   oldRecordH, newRecordH;
    LibPackedDBRecordV0  *oldRecord, *tempRecord;
    LibPackedDBRecord  *newRecord;
    LibPackedDBRecord  *offsetRecord = 0;
    UInt16      lastNameOffset, firstNameOffset,
        yearOffset, noteOffset;
    UInt16 numRecords;


    if (fromVersion == libDatabaseVersion1_0_0 &&
        toVersion == libDatabaseVersion2_0_0)
    {
        // Retrieve number of undeleted records in the
        // database.  Deleted records don't need to be
        // converted.
        numRecords = DmNumRecordsInCategory(db,
            dmAllCategories);
        for (index = 0; index < numRecords; index++)
        {
            oldRecordH = DmGetRecord(db, index);
            oldSize = MemHandleSize(oldRecordH);
            tempRecord = MemPtrNew(oldSize);
            if (!tempRecord)
            {
                DmReleaseRecord(db, index, false);
                return -2;
            }
            MemSet(tempRecord, oldSize, 0);

            oldRecord = MemHandleLock(oldRecordH);
```

```
MemMove(tempRecord, oldRecord, oldSize);
MemHandleUnlock(oldRecordH);

newSize = oldSize + sizeof(LibPackedDBRecord) -
    sizeof(LibPackedDBRecordV0);

newRecordH = DmResizeRecord(db, index, newSize);
if (! newRecordH)
{
    DmReleaseRecord(db, index, false);
    MemPtrFree(tempRecord);
    return -2;
}

newRecord = MemHandleLock(newRecordH);

// Copy status structure and field flags to new
// record.
DmWrite(newRecord, 0, tempRecord,
        sizeof(LibStatusType) +
        sizeof(LibDBRecordFlags));

// Copy offsets to new record.
lastNameOffset =
    (UInt16) tempRecord->lastNameOffset;
firstNameOffset =
    (UInt16) tempRecord->firstNameOffset;
yearOffset = (UInt16) tempRecord->yearOffset;
noteOffset = (UInt16) tempRecord->noteOffset;

DmWrite(newRecord,
        (UInt32) &offsetRecord->lastNameOffset,
        &lastNameOffset,
        sizeof(lastNameOffset));
DmWrite(newRecord,
        (UInt32) &offsetRecord->firstNameOffset,
        &firstNameOffset,
        sizeof(firstNameOffset));
DmWrite(newRecord,
        (UInt32) &offsetRecord->yearOffset,
        &yearOffset, sizeof(yearOffset));
DmWrite(newRecord,
        (UInt32) &offsetRecord->noteOffset,
        &noteOffset, sizeof(noteOffset));

// Copy data to new record.
DmWrite(newRecord,
        (UInt32) &offsetRecord->firstField,
        &tempRecord->firstField, newSize -
        sizeof(LibStatusType) -
        sizeof(LibDBRecordFlags) -
        sizeof(lastNameOffset) -
        sizeof(firstNameOffset) -
        sizeof(yearOffset) -
```

```
                              sizeof(noteOffset));

            MemPtrFree(tempRecord);
            MemHandleUnlock(newRecordH);
            DmReleaseRecord(db, index, false);
        }
    }
    return -1;
}
```

`LibConvertDB` is designed to be expandable. It currently converts only between versions 0 and 1 of the Librarian database, but the first two arguments to `LibConvertDB` allow the function to be told to convert between any two versions of the database. If the database format needs to be further modified in a future version, it is a simple matter to add another `if` statement to `LibConvertDB` that checks for other versions of the database and provides code to convert between them.

> *Notice that `LibConvertDB` uses `DmNumRecordsInCategory` instead of `DmNumRecords` to retrieve the total number of records in the database. This is because `DmNumRecords` incorporates in its count the deleted records stored at the end of the database. Deleted records do not contain any data for `LibConvertDB` to convert, so it ignores these records by iterating over the undeleted records only.*

To actually convert each record, `LibConvertDB` performs the following steps:

1. Retrieves a handle to the record using `DmGetRecord`

2. Creates a temporary space in memory (`tempRecord`) with `MemPtrNew` and copies the contents of the record into that space using `MemMove`

3. Calculates the space required for the new record format (`newSize`), and then resizes the record using `DmResizeRecord`

4. Copies the status structure and field flags from `tempRecord` into the newly resized record with `DmWrite`

5. Converts the old `unsigned char` offset values into `UInt16` values by simply casting them as `UInt16`, then writes the offsets into the record with `DmWrite`

6. Copies the rest of the record data from `tempRecord` into the new record with `DmWrite`

7. Disposes of the temporary record

## Sorting Records

The Palm OS provides two functions for sorting all the records in a database: `DmInsertionSort` and `DmQuickSort`. As its name implies, `DmInsertionSort` performs an insertion sort of a database's records, which works its way through the database one record at a time, comparing each record with the preceding record and inserting it into its proper sorted position if the value of the record is less than the value of the preceding record. The `DmInsertionSort` algorithm is acceptably fast on a database that is already mostly sorted, or on a small database containing about 20 or fewer records. In a situation where your application has moved a single record out of place, `DmInsertionSort` is ideal to place the database back in order. To call `DmInsertionSort`, pass an open database reference, a pointer to a `DmComparF` callback comparison function, and any special value the callback might need to perform its job:

```
Err error = DmInsertionSort(gDB, &MyCompareFunc, other);
```

The DmQuickSort function sorts records using a quicksort algorithm, which sorts the database by partitioning the records repeatedly. Use DmQuickSort when you don't know how sorted the database is. For example, changing the sort order of a database from sorting by name to sorting by date (a different field in the database record) is best done with DmQuickSort. Call DmQuickSort the same way you call DmInsertionSort:

```
Err error = DmQuickSort(gDB, &MyCompareFunc, other);
```

Keep in mind that the sort performed by DmInsertionSort is stable, whereas DmQuickSort performs an unstable sort. In a stable sort, two records that compare as the same value maintain their relative positions in the database; an unstable sort may cause equal records to change positions. Also, DmQuickSort can work with a maximum of 16K records, whereas DmInsertionSort can handle up to 32K records.

## Retrieving and Modifying Record Information

Each record in a database has a number of properties related to it that are stored in the record list in the database's header. You can retrieve this information using the DmRecordInfo function:

```
UInt16    attributes;
UInt16    uniqueID;
LocalID   chunkID;
Err       error;

error = DmRecordInfo(db, index, &attributes, &uniqueID,
                     &chunkID);
```

The DmRecordInfo function returns the record's unique ID, as well as the LocalID of the chunk where the record's data resides. Usually, the best way to modify a record is to retrieve a handle to it using DmGetRecord or DmQueryRecord, but the unique ID and LocalID are available through DmRecordInfo should you need them.

*You can pass NULL for the* attributes, uniqueID, *or* chunkID *parameters of* DmRecordInfo *if you want to ignore any of these values.*

The attributes parameter for a record includes flags for the record's deleted, dirty, busy, and secret bits, along with half a byte containing the record's category. The Palm OS header file DataMgr.h provides the following handy constants for accessing the flags and masking the category in this bit field:

```
#define dmRecAttrCategoryMask   0x0F
#define dmUnfiledCategory       0
#define dmRecAttrDelete         0x80
#define dmRecAttrDirty          0x40
#define dmRecAttrBusy           0x20
#define dmRecAttrSecret         0x10
```

*Even though the* DmRecordInfo *function returns a pointer to an unsigned 16-bit integer containing a record's attributes, current implementations of the Palm OS use only half of this space (one byte) to store the attributes. As with any implementation-specific details of the Palm OS, you should not rely on the size of specific structures used by the system. Code defensively; always use the Palm OS API functions and the appropriate constants in the Palm OS headers when dealing with record attributes.*

For example, the following code retrieves the current deletion status of a record:

```
UInt16  attributes;

DmRecordInfo(db, index, &attributes, NULL, NULL);
Boolean deleted = attributes & dmRecAttrDelete;
```

You can set record information with the `DmSetRecordInfo` function. Everything available through `DmRecordInfo` may be set, except for the LocalID of the record's data chunk:

```
Err error = DmSetRecordInfo(db, index, &attributes,
                            &uniqueID);
```

Passing `NULL` for the `attributes` or `uniqueID` parameters leaves that particular piece of record information alone.

> *As a general rule, leave the unique ID of a record alone. The data manager automatically creates a unique ID when you create a record with `DmNewRecord`, so applications usually do not have to change a record's unique ID.*

The following example sets a record's secret bit, which controls whether or not a record is considered private:

```
UInt16 attributes;

DmRecordInfo(db, index, &attributes, NULL, NULL);
attributes |= dmRecAttrSecret;
DmSetRecordInfo(db, index, &attributes, NULL);
```

See the sections "Setting a Record's Category," "Selecting and Modifying Categories," and "Implementing Private Records" later in this chapter for more examples of how to use `DmRecordInfo` and `DmSetRecordInfo`.

# Categorizing Records

Every record in a Palm OS database has an attributes field, which contains half a byte of category information about the record. This mechanism allows you to provide user-customizable categories for classifying records, in the same way that the built-in Address Book, To Do List, and Memo Pad applications do. The Palm OS provides a category manager to make managing categories easier.

## Initializing Categories

In order to provide some default categories in your application, such as the "Business," "Personal," and "Unfiled" categories that are common in the built-in applications, you will need to initialize those categories in the application info block. The best place to store these default category names is in an app info string resource, which you create with either Constructor or PilRC, depending on your development environment.

Librarian has the default categories "Fiction," "Nonfiction," and "Unfiled." Figure 16-1 shows Librarian's category app info string, as defined in Constructor. Notice that "Unfiled" is listed first. Any categories that you do not want the user to edit or remove must appear first in the app info string.

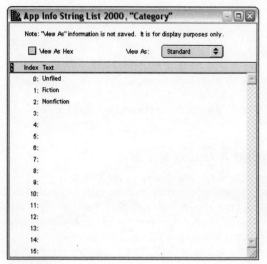

**Figure 16-1**

The PilRC definition for Librarian's categories looks like this:

```
CATEGORIES ID CategoryAppInfoStr
    "Unfiled"
    "Fiction"
    "Nonfiction"
    ""
    ""
    ""
    ""
    ""
    ""
    ""
    ""
    ""
    ""
    ""
    ""
    ""
    ""
```

Once you have default categories defined in your application's resources, you can initialize the application info block with these default names using the `CategoryInitialize` function, which has the following prototype:

```
void CategoryInitialize (AppInfoPtr appInfoP,
    UInt16 localizedAppInfoStrID)
```

The `CategoryInitialize` function needs a pointer to an application info block and the resource ID of an app info string containing the default category names. Librarian calls `CategoryIntialize` from its `LibAppInfoInit` function when it first creates a new application info block for the program, like this:

```
LibAppInfoType    *appInfo;


// Code to retrieve appInfo omitted.

CategoryInitialize((AppInfoPtr) appInfo, CategoryAppInfoStr);
```

For the complete story on initializing a new application info block for a database, see Chapter 13, "Storing and Retrieving Data."

## Finding Records Within a Category

The function `DmSeekRecordInCategory` allows an application to search for records in a database, restricting the records returned to those that match a particular category. In addition, `DmSeekRecordInCategory` skips over deleted records; it also skips private records if the database was opened without the `dmModeShowSecret` mode constant. This function is particularly useful when an application displays records in a table or list, in conjunction with a pop-up list for selecting categories. Figure 16-2 shows the Librarian's category pop-up list in action. Selecting a category from the list changes which category is displayed in Librarian's List view.

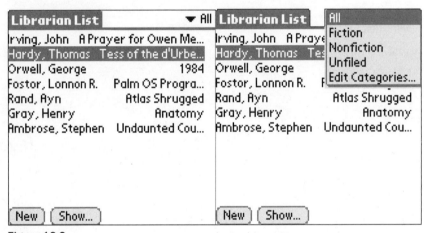

Figure 16-2

To restrict record retrieval to a specific category, call the `DmSeekRecordInCategory` function when filling a table or list, passing the desired category to `DmSeekRecordInCategory`, which has the following prototype:

```
Err DmSeekRecordInCategory (DmOpenRef dbP, UInt16* indexP,
     Int16 offset, Int16 direction, UInt16 category)
```

The first parameter to `DmSeekRecordInCategory` is an open database reference. Specify a category to restrict the search to using the `category` parameter, or pass the constant `dmAllCategories` to specify all records.

The offset parameter allows you to skip a number of records that match the requested category before returning a record. Starting at index, DmSeekRecordInCategory looks through the records in the direction specified by direction (either of the constants dmSeekForward or dmSeekBackward). When DmSeekRecordInCategory finds a record in the appropriate category, it decrements offset and continues searching for the next matching record until offset equals 0 and another match is found, at which point the function returns the index of the found record in the index parameter.

If DmSeekRecordInCategory successfully finds an appropriate record, it returns 0; otherwise, it returns dmErrIndexOutOfRange or dmErrSeekFailed to indicate why it was unable to find a matching record.

Depending upon whether or not the starting record at indexP is in the current category, you need to specify different values for offset to get the next matching record. If the record at indexP is in the specified category, an offset of 0 will return the current record. To find the next record in the category, you must call DmSeekRecordInCategory with an offset of 1 to skip over the current record.

As an example, the following code iterates over all the records in a database belonging to a specific category:

```
UInt16  i;
UInt16  recordNum;

recordNum = 0;

// Find the first record in the category.
if (! DmSeekRecordInCategory(db, &recordNum, 0,
                             dmSeekForward, category))
{

    // Do something with the first record at index
    // recordNum.

    for (i = 1; i < DmNumRecordsInCategory(db, category);
         i++)
    {
        // Use offset == 1 to skip over current record.
        if (! DmSeekRecordInCategory(db, &recordNum, 1,
                                     dmSeekForward,
                                     category))
            break;

        // Do something with the record at index recordNum.

        recordNum++;
    }
}
```

The previous example first calls DmSeekRecordInCategory with an offset of 0 to ensure that if the record at index 0 in the database is in the correct category, the record is returned properly. Then, the code iterates over the rest of the records matching category, using DmNumRecordsInCategory to return the number of records in the category. Subsequent calls to DmSeekRecordInCategory in the body of the for loop use an offset of 1 to skip over the current record, because the current record in this loop will always match the desired category.

> The **DmNumRecordsInCategory** function must examine all the records in the
> database; in a large database, this can take some time. Use
> **DmNumRecordsInCategory** sparingly; calling this function from within a tight loop
> can cause significant performance problems.

Librarian uses the DmSeekRecordInCategory function extensively, as will any application that implements scrolling tables filled with records from a database. To make calling this function easier, Librarian
wraps it in the SeekRecord function:

```
static Boolean SeekRecord (UInt16 *index, Int16 offset,
                           Int16 direction)
{
    DmSeekRecordInCategory(gLibDB, index, offset,
                           direction, gCurrentCategory);
    if (DmGetLastErr()) return (false);

    return (true);
}
```

The SeekRecord function cuts down to three the number of parameters required for a
DmSeekRecordInCategory call, because it always looks in the global gLibDB variable for the database
reference and it relies on the global gCurrentCategory to supply the proper category to search through.
Also, SeekRecord returns a simple Boolean value to indicate whether or not a matching record was
found. See Chapter 12, "Programming Tables," for examples of the SeekRecord function in action.

You also can use DmQueryNextInCategory to find records in a specific category. The
DmQueryNextInCategory function returns a handle to the next record in the database in the specified
category:

```
recordH = DmQueryNextInCategory(db, &index, category);
```

Because DmQueryNextInCategory does not have an offset parameter like DmSeekRecordInCategory's,
you must increment the index parameter to skip over a known record in the correct category to get the next
record in the category. Also, DmQueryNextInCategory does not allow you to specify a direction; it searches
only forward through the database. The handle returned by this function is read-only;
DmQueryNextInCategory does not set the busy bit in the record it finds.

Another useful function is DmPositionInCategory, which returns the position of a record within its
own category, using a zero-based indexing system:

```
UInt16 position = DmPositionInCategory(db, index,
                                       category);
```

For example, if a record is the fourth record in the category passed to DmPositionInCategory, the
function returns the value 3.

## Setting a Record's Category

To set the category for a particular record, use the following code:

```
DmRecordInfo(db, index, &attributes, NULL, NULL);
attributes &= ~dmRecAttrCategoryMask;
attributes |= category;
attributes |= dmRecAttrDirty;
DmSetRecordInfo(gLibDB, gCurrentRecord, &attr, NULL);
```

The previous example sets the category of the record at `index` to the category specified by the `category` variable. Setting the dirty bit ensures that the HotSync Manager will deal properly with the record at synchronization time.

## Selecting and Modifying Categories

When the user taps a category pop-up trigger, your application should display a list of available categories from which the user may select a new category. To match the behavior of category triggers in the built-in applications, the pop-up list should have an "Edit Categories..." item at the bottom of the list that launches the system category editing dialog box, pictured in Figure 16-3. From the editing dialog box the user may add, remove, and rename categories in the current application, with the exception of those categories at the beginning of the list that the application has designated as uneditable.

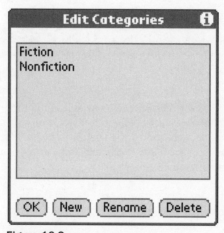

Figure 16-3

The `CategorySelect` function makes displaying a category list with appropriate behavior a fairly painless process. Call `CategorySelect` in response to a `ctlSelectEvent` triggered by the category pop-up trigger; it has the following prototype:

```
Boolean CategorySelect (DmOpenRef db, const FormType *frm,
    UInt16 ctlID, UInt16 lstID, Boolean title,
    UInt16 *categoryP, char *categoryName,
    UInt8 numUneditableCategories, UInt32 editingStrID)
```

You must supply an open database reference in the first parameter to `CategorySelect` so that the function can retrieve category names from the database's application info block. The `frm`, `ctlID`, and `lstID` parameters are pointers to the form, pop-up trigger, and list objects that `CategorySelect` should use when displaying the category list.

Pass true for the value of the title parameter if the category trigger is located on the title line of a form; if title is true, CategorySelect adds an "All" choice to the top of the pop-up list. Pass a title value of false if the trigger is intended to select the category for a single record, instead of for a list of records, where an "All" list item is not appropriate. A good example of this second kind of category trigger is in Librarian's Details dialog box, pictured in Figure 16-4. The category trigger in this dialog box changes the category of the current record instead of changing the current display category.

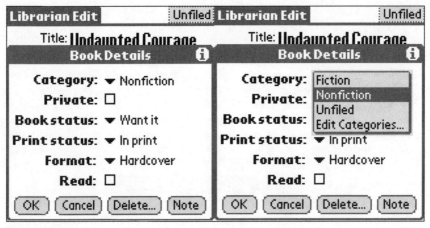

Figure 16-4

In the categoryP parameter, supply a pointer to a variable containing the category that should be selected in the pop-up list. When CategorySelect returns, it modifies the contents of the categoryP pointer to match the new category selected by the user, if any. Likewise, the categoryName parameter should point to a string containing the name of the selected category, and CategorySelect changes this string to the name of the new selected category.

You can retrieve the name of a category with the CategoryGetName function, which requires an open database reference, the category's index, and a pointer to a string to fill with the category name:

```
char   categoryName[dmCategoryLength];

CategoryGetName(db, category, categoryName);
```

The CategorySelect function's numUneditableCategories allows you to specify how many uneditable categories the application's category list contains. Usually, there is only one, the "Unfiled" category, but you can make applications with more uneditable categories if you want certain categories to always appear in the list.

Finally, the editingStrID parameter allows you to specify the resource ID of a string that appears at the bottom of the category list and in the title of the category editing dialog box. By default, this string is "Edit Categories…"; you can specify this default string by passing 0, or the constant categoryDefaultEditCategoryString, defined in the Palm OS header file Category.h. You also may use the constant categoryHideEditCategory to prevent the user from editing categories entirely; this constant removes the editing item from the bottom of the category pop-up list. If you want to customize the string that appears here, pass in the ID of your own string resource, and it will appear in the pop-up list and as the title of the editing dialog box.

> Be sure not to make your custom string resource longer than **dmCategoryLength** (15 characters, plus a terminating null). Anything longer causes a crash when the system tries to display the category list, because the system allocates only 16 bytes to hold the list item text.

When the user selects the "Edit Categories..." list item (or its customized equivalent), CategorySelect calls the CategoryEdit function to launch the system category editing dialog box, shown earlier in Figure 16-3. You can call the CategoryEdit function directly from your application's code to launch the editing dialog box:

```
Boolean result = CategoryEdit(db, category, titleStrID,
    numUneditableCategories);
```

Both CategorySelect and CategoryEdit return a Boolean value to indicate that the user made some major change to the categories while the category list was displayed. The return value is true if any of the following occurred:

- ❑ The user renamed a category.
- ❑ The user deleted a category.
- ❑ The user renamed a category with the name of another category, merging those two categories.

If your application checks the return value from CategorySelect or CategoryEdit, it can react appropriately to the changes in the categories, reloading records into a table or list if the current form displays a list of records, or re-categorizing the current record as appropriate in a details dialog box.

*The category selection and editing process has evolved as new versions of the Palm OS have been released. In Palm OS version 2.0, the numUneditableCategories parameter to CategoryEdit is unavailable, and Palm OS 1.0 does not allow customization of the category editing dialog box because CategoryEdit on version 1.0 does not have a titleStrID parameter. Palm OS 3.0 and later contain CategoryEditV20 and CategoryEditV10 functions to provide compatibility with applications written for earlier versions of the operating system.*

*Likewise, CategorySelect is different between versions 1.0 and 2.0 of the Palm OS, with both the numUneditableCategories and titleStrID parameters in version 2.0. Even though numUneditableCategories is not available in the 2.0 version of CategoryEdit, the 2.0 CategorySelect does support this option. Starting with Palm OS 2.0, a backward-compatible CategorySelectV10 function is available to support applications that must maintain compatibility with Palm OS 1.0.*

You also can programmatically set a category's name with the CategorySetName function, which may be called as follows:

```
CategorySetName(db, category, newNameString);
```

Pass a null-terminated string in the newNameString parameter to change the specified category's name. Your application also may use the CategorySetName function to delete a category; pass NULL for the new name instead of a string, and CategorySetName deletes the category instead of renaming it.

One more function, `DmMoveCategory`, allows your application to move all the records from one of its categories to another category:

```
Boolean  dirty = true;

Err error = DmMoveCategory(db, toCategory, fromCategory,
                           dirty);
```

The last parameter to `DmMoveCategory` controls whether or not records re-categorized by this function should be marked dirty; a `true` value marks them dirty, and a `false` value leaves the records' dirty bits alone.

## Cycling Through Categories

The built-in applications that support categories, as well as the Librarian sample application, allow the user to cycle through the categories in the application by repeatedly pressing the hardware key assigned to launch the application. For example, pressing the Memo Pad hardware button while the Memo Pad application is already open and displaying its List view causes Memo Pad to change its display to the next available category. When it gets to the end of the list of categories, Memo Pad displays all the categories, then goes on to the first category in the list again.

To implement this behavior in your application, you need to handle the `keyDownEvent` and look for hard key presses and, in response, call the `CategoryGetNext` function to retrieve the next available category. The following bit of code from Librarian's `ListFormHandleEvent` function handles a hard key press while the application is already running:

```
case keyDownEvent:
    if (TxtCharIsHardKey(event->data.keyDown.modifiers,
                    event->data.keyDown.chr))
    {
        if (! (event->data.keyDown.modifiers &
            poweredOnKeyMask))
        {
            ListFormNextCategory();
            handled = true;
        }
    }
}
```

The `ListFormNextCategory` function called previously looks like this:

```
static void ListFormNextCategory (void)
{
    UInt16      category;
    TableType   *table;
    ControlType *ctl;


    category = CategoryGetNext(gLibDB, gCurrentCategory);

    if (category != gCurrentCategory)
    {
```

```
        if (category == dmAllCategories)
            gShowAllCategories = true;
        else
            gShowAllCategories = false;

        ChangeCategory(category);

        // Set the label of the category trigger.
        ctl = GetObjectPtr(ListCategoryPopTrigger);
        CategoryGetName(gLibDB, gCurrentCategory,
                        gCategoryName);
        CategorySetTriggerLabel(ctl, gCategoryName);

        // Display the new category.
        ListFormLoadTable();
        table = GetObjectPtr(ListTable);
        TblEraseTable(table);
        TblDrawTable(table);

        // By changing the category the current record is
        // lost.
        gCurrentRecord = noRecord;
    }
}
```

The first thing ListFormNextCategory does is call CategoryGetNext, passing the Librarian open database reference and the current category, which Librarian keeps track of through the global gCurrentCategory variable.

> *The CategoryGetNext function's behavior is dependent upon what version of the Palm OS is running. In Palm OS 1.0, CategoryGetNext cycles through the "All" category — all of the named categories in alphabetical order — and the "Unfiled" category, then it starts again with the "All" category. Starting with Palm OS 2.0, CategoryGetNext skips over categories that do not contain any records and the "Unfiled" category.*

After retrieving the new category, ListFormNextCategory calls a small utility function, ChangeCategory, to update some Librarian global variables in response to a category change:

```
static void ChangeCategory (UInt16 category)
{
    gCurrentCategory = category;
    gTopVisibleRecord = 0;
}
```

Then ListFormNextCategory sets the label of the List view's category pop-up trigger, using the Palm OS function CategorySetTriggerLabel, which is far more convenient than having to deal with the CtlSetLabel function, because CategorySetTriggerLabel takes care of all of the details normally required for setting a control label.

Finally, ListFormNextCategory reloads the List form's table to reflect the change of category.

### Deleting All Records in a Category

The `DmDeleteCategory` function deletes all the records in a given category. Use the function as follows:

```
Err error = DmDeleteCategory(db, category);
```

If no error occurs while deleting the records, `DmDeleteCategory` returns 0.

*Despite its name, `DmDeleteCategory` does nothing to modify the name of the category given to it; `DmDeleteCategory` merely deletes the records within a category, leaving its name intact. If you want to delete a category's name, call the `CategorySetName` function and pass it a NULL for the string you would like to use to rename the category:*

```
CategorySetName(db, category, NULL);
```

## Implementing Private Records

The Palm OS provides a facility to enable the user to mark records in applications across the handheld as private, so that they may be shown only when the user enters the correct password in the device's Security application. To enable the use of private records in your application, you must pay attention to the system-wide private records preference and program your application to respond appropriately, depending upon what the current private record status is on the handheld.

*Private records are marked with a secret bit only in the record's entry in the database header; the Palm OS does not take any steps to encrypt private records, and private information may easily be read by someone's synchronizing the device and opening a database's backed-up .pdb file on the desktop in a text editor. If you need real security in a Palm OS application, you will have to program your own encryption, a subject that is beyond the scope of this book.*

You can retrieve the current private records status of the device by querying the system preferences with the `PrefGetPreference` function. Most applications should retrieve the system's current private record status in their `StartApplication` functions and assign the privacy status to a global variable for later use throughout the application. For example, Librarian stores the system private records status in the global variable `gPrivateRecordStatus`. Then, the application should open the database in the appropriate mode; if private records are not hidden, use the `dmModeShowSecret` mode, which allows the various database functions to display hidden records. Without the `dmModeShowSecret` mode turned on, the `DmOpenDatabaseByTypeCreator` and `DmOpenDatabase` functions prevent access to records marked private. For more information about retrieving the private record status, see the "Reading and Setting System Preferences" section in Chapter 13, "Storing and Retrieving Data." See the "Opening Databases" section in the same chapter to learn how to set the mode when opening a database.

Once you have the database opened in the appropriate mode, functions like `DmSeekRecordInCategory`, `DmQueryNextInCategory`, and `DmNumRecordsInCategory` skip over private records when the database has not been opened in `dmModeShowSecret` mode.

To change a record's privacy status, use `DmRecordInfo` and `DmSetRecordInfo` to retrieve and set the record's secret bit. The following code toggles the secret bit as appropriate:

```
DmRecordInfo(db, index, &attributes, NULL, NULL);
if (secret)
    attributes |= dmRecAttrSecret;
```

```
    else
        attributes &= ~dmRecAttrSecret;
    DmSetRecordInfo(db, index, &attributes, NULL);
```

## Deleting All Private Records

If for some reason you need your application to delete all the private records in a database, call the DmRemoveSecretRecords function and pass it an open database reference. This function exists primarily for system use; if a user forgets the password assigned to show private records in the Security application and taps that application's Forgotten Password button to reset the password, the Security application deletes all the private records on the device, using this function on every database.

Because the user may delete private records in this manner, it is a bad idea to use the secret bit for any purpose other than to mark a record as private, such as using the secret bit to flag a record as read-only. If the user reset the system password, all the "read-only" records in your application would suddenly disappear.

> Be careful how you use **DmRemoveSecretRecords**, if you use it at all. It can cause a lot of damage very quickly.

## Resizing Records

The DmResizeRecord function allows you to change the size of a record's data chunk. This function comes in handy if your application's records are of variable length. To resize a record, call DmResizeRecord as follows:

```
    MemHandle newHandle = DmResizeRecord(db, index, newSize);
```

The newSize parameter should contain the new size of the record, in bytes. If the heap that currently contains the record is not large enough to resize the record, DmResizeRecord reallocates the record in a different heap on the same card. If this happens, the handle to the record's data chunk changes, so be sure to use the handle returned by the DmResizeRecord function after resizing a record, because the original handle may be invalid. If for some reason DmResizeRecord is unable to allocate enough space for the record, it returns NULL; in this case, call DmGetLastErr to retrieve an error code that indicates what went wrong.

# Working with Schema Database Records

As described in Chapter 15, "Storing and Retrieving Data," Palm OS Cobalt introduces a brand new way of working with Palm OS databases, known as schema databases. Schema databases offer a highly structured method of defining and working with database tables and relieve developers from needing to write low-level code that formats and parses physical database records.

This section covers the new schema database and how to navigate, retrieve, insert, and update records in schema databases.

# Working with Cursors

In order to work with schema database records it is essential to understand how to use cursors. Whereas with non-schema databases you literally navigate each physical record in the database, cursors allow you to create logical views of a given database table at runtime. These views are constructed based on a query statement that uses a subset of the SQL standard to define the set of records to be included in the view. One way to think about cursors is as a reference to a subset of records in a database table that matches a sort order and selection criteria of your own choosing. Once created, a cursor then provides you with a mechanism for moving forward or backward within that record subset.

Creating and using cursors gives developers much more convenient methods for locating and navigating only those records that are relevant to the application in a specific situation. For example, imagine a real estate application that shows lists of houses for sale in each state. Your job is to display a scrollable list of properties that are located in a state that the user selects. Using non-schema data manager functions, you would need to start at the first record and iterate through every record in the database, checking each record to see if it satisfied the state selection criteria. Using a cursor, you would specify the state selection when you created the cursor, and as a result only the matching records would be in the result set.

## Creating a Cursor

To create a cursor, use the `DbCursorOpen` function. DbCursorOpen has the following prototype:

```
status_t DbCursorOpen (DmOpenRef dbRef,
                       const char *sql, uint32_t flags,
                       uint32_t *cursorID);
```

The `dbRef` parameter is required as a handle to an open database. The `sql` parameter is the key to this function, and it is your way of specifying:

❑   Which table in your database will be queried

❑   Which rows of the database table will be returned

❑   What order the rows will be returned in

For those readers familiar with SQL syntax, the `sql` parameter uses a simplified form of the standard SQL SELECT statement. The SQL implementation is functional, but fairly basic (more advanced concepts such as joins and subqueries are not supported at all).

The SELECT statement used in creating a cursor is an ASCII string that takes the form:

```
[SELECT * FROM] tableName [WHERE column op arg]
[ORDER BY (col1, col2, ...) [DESC | ASC | CASED | CASELESS]
[, col...]]
```

Let's look at each part of the SELECT statement:

❑   *SELECT * FROM* is actually optional. Most relational database systems on other platforms offer programmers a way to specify a subset of the target table's columns that will be returned in the result. With Cobalt's implementation of schema databases, all table columns are always returned, so the SELECT * FROM portion of the syntax is actually unnecessary.

❑ *tablename* is the name of the table within your database that you wish to query records from. For more information on creating and naming tables, please refer to Chapter 15.

❑ *WHERE column op arg* allows you to apply a filter on the set of rows in the table. For example, to return only those rows where the house is in New York, you might specify "WHERE state = NY". Aside from equality, operators are available for not equal, less than, greater than, less than or equal, greater than or equal, and other expressions. See the table below for a complete list of operators that are available. The WHERE clause can also be used to combine multiple filters against different table columns, using AND and OR to combine filters. Note that the WHERE clause is actually optional – you can skip it altogether if you want your cursor to reflect all rows in the target table.

❑ *ORDER BY (col1, col2, ...) [DESC | ASC | CASED | CASELESS]* allows you to apply a sort order to the rows that are returned in your cursor. The sort order is defined by the columns specified in the ORDER BY clause, with col1 representing the first sort column, col2 representing the second sort column, and so on. For each column, you can also specify whether that column should be sorted in ascending or descending order, and whether the sorting should take case into account when comparing column values.

❑ The *flags* parameter of the DbCursorOpen function specifies details that can customize how the cursor is to be opened. Supported options appear in the following table.

| Flag | Value | Description |
|------|-------|-------------|
| DbCursorEnableCaching | 0x00010000 | Enables the caching of row data locally in the cursor. |
| DbCursorIncludeDeleted | 0x00000001 | Specifies that the cursor should contain rows that are marked as archived or deleted. |
| dbCursorOnlyDeleted | 0x00000002 | Specifies that the cursor should contain only rows that are marked as archived or deleted. |
| dbCursorOnlySecret | 0x00000004 | Specifies that the cursor should contain only rows that are marked as secret. |
| DbCursorSortByCategory | 0x10000000 | Specifies that the cursor should sort its rows by category. |

❑ The *cursorID* parameter returns the ID of the newly created cursor, if the DbCursorOpen function is successful.

According to the SDK documentation, the sort order used in the ORDER BY clause must match an actual sort index that is present in the database.

## Closing a Cursor

When you are done with a cursor, you need to free up the resources associated with the cursor. This is done by calling DbCursorClose. After calling DbCursorClose, the cursor ID associated with the cursor is no longer valid.

## Navigating with Cursors

Upon successfully opening a new cursor with DbCursorOpen, you use the returned cursor ID to move forward and backward within the result set represented by the cursor. It is important to understand that a cursor represents a snapshot in time of the table rows that match the SQL SELECT statement you submitted in DbCursorOpen. As such, the cursor is not automatically updated as changes are made to the database. If you make changes to the target table while a cursor is open, you can force the cursor to be updated by calling `DbCursorRequery`.

A cursor has the concept of a current position within the result set represented by the cursor. The default cursor position after DbCursorOpen is the first row in the cursor result set. Navigating within the rows represented by a cursor is done using `DbCursorMove`. DbCursorMove allows you to change the current cursor position by specifying the number of rows to move, and the direction to move in. As an added convenience, a number of functions such as `DbCursorMoveFirst`, `DbCursorMoveLast`, `DbCursorMovePrev`, `DbCursorMoveToRowID`, and `DbCursorSetAbsolutePosition` provide finer levels of control as to where to move the current cursor position. These, along with helper functions that allow you to test whether you are at the beginning or end of the cursor's set of rows, allows you to easily iterate forward or backward within the cursor data.

## Accessing Row Data

Given a current cursor position, you can access a single column value for a row explicitly by calling `DbGetColumnValue`. With DbGetColumnValue, you specify the row ID and the column ID, and in return you are given a pointer to the column value for that row. You can obtain the column ID for any given column by calling `DbGetColumnID`.

If you would like to obtain multiple column values for a row with just one function call, you can use `DbGetColumnValues`, in which you pass an array of column IDs and are given in return a pointer to an array of column values. Because you don't need to actually allocate your own storage memory to receive these values, using this technique is referred to as retrieving by reference.

> *Although the Data Manager allocates the storage for the values, you are responsible for freeing the memory associated with the pointer returned by DbGetColumnValue and DbGetColumnValues, by calling `DbReleaseStorage`.*

As an alternative to using DbGetColumnValue or DbGetColumnValues, you can use `DbCopyColumnValue` or `DbCopyColumnValues`. The main difference is that with DbCopyColumnValue, you provide your own pre-allocated memory buffer which receives the requested column value. There is also a noticeable performance hit for using the Copy routines, so if possible developers should make use of the Get APIs.

Probably the most common method for accessing row data in an SQL-based system is through the use of *data binding*. With data binding, you associate program variables with table columns, thereby *binding* each column to a variable. The huge benefit of data binding is that once you have successfully bound columns to variables, as you iterate through rows in a cursor your program variables are automatically updated with the values of the bound columns for each row. This is considerably less work than using DbGetColumnValues or DbCopyColumnValues for each row.

To bind a program variable to a cursor column, you need to call `DbCursorBindData`, which has the following prototype:

```
status_t DbCursorBindData (uint32_t cursorID,
                 uint32_t columnID, void *dataBufferP,
                 uint32_t dataBufferLength,
                 uint32_t *dataSizeP, status_t *errCodeP)
```

With DbCursorBindData, you supply the columnID for the column you wish to bind, as well as a void pointer to a variable that will receive the column data and the actual size of the program variable. You also need to supply a pointer to a variable to receive the actual size of the column value returned for each row, as well as an error code that will be set for each row.

The following example illustrates the use of data binding with the Last Name and First Name cursor columns in our Librarian program:

```
uint32_t cursor;
char firstName[32];
char lastName[32];
uint32_t sizeFirstName;
uint32_t sizeLastName;
status_t errFirstName;
status_t errLastName;

// open the database referenced by dbID
dbRef = DbOpenDatabase(dbID, dmModeReadWrite, dbShareNone,
idSortByName);

// Create a cursor for the table
err = DbCursorOpen(dbRef, "SELECT * FROM mytable", 0, &cursor);

// Bind a local variable for first name and last name
// to the corresponding table columns
DbCursorBindData(cursor, idColFirstName, firstName, 32,
&sizeFirstName, &errFirstName);

DbCursorBindData(cursor, idColLastName, lastName, 32,
&sizeLastName, &errLastName);

// Position ourselves at the first row in the cursor
err = DbCursorMoveFirst(cursor);

// now iterate through each row in the cursor
while (err == errNone)
{
// Do something with the column values for first and last
// name for this row
HandleRow(firstName, lastName);
// Get data for next row
err = DbCursorMoveNext(cursor);
}
// close the cursor
DBCursorClose(cursor);
```

## Creating Records in a Table

To create new rows in a database table, you use the function DbInsertRow, which has the following prototype:

```
status_t DbInsertRow (DmOpenRef dbRef,
            const char *table, uint32_t numColumnValues,
            DbSchemaColumnValueType *columnValuesP,
            uint32_t *rowIDP)
```

Using DbInsertRow, you supply the name of the target table, the number of column values you will be providing, and an array of the column values in the form of DbSchemaColumnValueType structures. Any columns in the table schema for which column values are not supplied will contain NULL as a value. In fact, you may create a "blank" record by supplying zero for the numColumnValues parameter and NULL for the columnValuesP parameter.

The DbInsertRow function works independently of any cursors you may be using in your program. New rows are physically added to the end of the target database table and are not automatically reflected in any open cursors, even if the new row would have qualified for the cursor given the SELECT statement used in creating the cursor. If you are adding new records to a table while a cursor is open and you wish to update the cursor to reflect the new rows, you must explicitly call DbCursorRequery.

## Updating Records in a Table

You can update a column value in a row by calling DbWriteColumnValue, or you can perform an update of multiple columns by using DbWriteColumnValues. As with DbInsertRow, DbWriteColumnValue functions independently of any open cursors. To update an open cursor that encompasses records updated with DbWriteColumnValues, you must call DbCursorRequery.

## Removing, Deleting, and Archiving Records

You can remove rows by calling DbRemoveRow with the row ID, once for each row you wish to physically remove from the database. If you wish to only mark a record for deletion by HotSync, you would instead call DbDeleteRow.

If instead you wish to archive a row, you may call DbRemoveRow. This function simply marks the record as archived and leaves the physical row intact within the database.

## Using Sort Indices

As mentioned earlier in this chapter, you can specify the order that you wish rows to be sorted in as part of the SELECT statement you pass into DbCursorOpen. One very important restriction in the use of sorting criteria in your SELECT statement is that the sort column must match an existing *sort index* that has been created for the target database table. As opposed to other SQL-based systems developers may be familiar with on other platforms, Palm OS Cobalt's implementation of schema databases will not perform a live runtime sort of the records in a table based on an arbitrary column-sort specification supplied in a SELECT statement.

Although this may seem like a serious restriction, in actual practice it almost always makes sense for performance reasons to ensure your sorted queries take advantage of predefined database indices. By enforcing this practice, Palm OS can maintain multiple sorted lists of rows for each sort index, and automatically add to, delete from, and update them when row operations are performed. Using this mechanism, the operating system does not suffer the performance penalty associated with having to re-sort table rows every time a cursor is opened. This is in marked contrast to non-schema databases, which have no indexing support and require you to physically sort your database records if you wish to retrieve them in a specific order.

To create an index, you call DbAddSortIndex, which has the following prototype:

```
status_t DbAddSortIndex (DmOpenRef dbRef,
                         const char *orderBy)
```

The orderBy parameter is simply a SELECT statement in the same format as described previously in the section "Creating a Cursor." By calling DbAddSortIndex, the data manager immediately will construct a new sort order for all of the rows in the target database table.

Existing sort indices can be can be removed by calling DbRemoveSortIndex. In addition, your application can check for the existence of a matching sort index by calling DbHasSortIndex. Finally, all of the sort indices for a given database can be enumerated by calling DbNumSortIndices and then calling DbGetSortDefinition for each index by position within the list of indices.

You are permitted to define as many sort indices as you would like within your schema database. Because each index must be updated by the data manager every time you insert, update, or delete a row, it is best to maintain as few indices as necessary to support your application's sorting needs.

*If you know you are going to be performing bulk changes to your database (such as during a large import of data), you can temporarily disable live index updating by calling DbEnableSorting.*

## Categories and Schema Databases

As we've seen, non-schema databases can make use of the Palm OS category system to assign database records to one of 15 categories, or the "Unfiled" category. Palm OS Cobalt extends the category system for schema databases as follows:

❑   There are now up to 255 categories that a row may be assigned to

❑   A row may belong to more than one category

❑   If a row does not belong to any category, it is not associated with the Unfiled category.

As with non-schema databases, categories are maintained on a per-database basis, enabling your application to make use of categories that are different from those in use by other applications.

To enable this expanded category support, the data manager introduces a set of new category functions. The function DbAddCategory adds one or more categories to the list of categories a given row is a member of. DbSetCategory overwrites the list of categories for a given row with a new set of categories. Conversely, DbRemoveCategory removes membership in one or more categories for a given row.

In terms of enumerating category membership, DbNumCategory returns the number of categories that a given row is a member of, and DbGetCategory retrieves the list of category IDs for a given row.

# Implementing the Global Find Facility

Any application that stores text data can benefit from the Palm OS global find feature. Activated by means of the silk-screen Find button, the Find dialog box, pictured in Figure 16-5, allows the user to search for a particular text string through any applications that support global find.

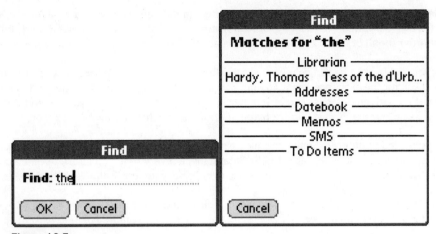

**Figure 16-5**

To implement the global find feature, an application should handle three launch codes: sysAppLaunchCmdSaveData, sysAppLaunchCmdFind, and sysAppLaunchCmdGoto. The following list outlines the sequence of events that occur when the user enters text in the Find dialog box and taps the dialog box's OK button:

1. The system sends a sysAppLaunchCmdSaveData launch code to the currently active application. This launch code allows an application that supports find to save its own unsaved data if the application happens to be open when the find operation begins.

2. The system sends a sysAppLaunchCmdFind launch code to each application. Any program that supports the global find responds to this launch code by querying its database for the search text supplied by the user, returning a list of records that contain the appropriate text. The Find dialog box displays a list of matching records in all applications that support the find feature.

3. If the user selects a matching record from the list, the system sends a sysAppLaunchCmdGoto launch code to the application that owns the selected record. The owning application can then respond to the launch code by displaying the appropriate record from its database.

Keep in mind that in a multi-segment application, any function referenced from PilotMain, including any functions used to implement the global find facility, must be located in the same code segment as PilotMain. For more information about multi-segment applications, turn to Chapter 24, "Odds and Ends."

## Handling sysAppLaunchCmdSaveData

If a Find-aware application is currently open when the user performs a global find, it needs to save any unsaved data, because the find operation can display a different record from the record that is currently displayed, or even open a different application. This sudden switch to a new record can cause data loss if the application has a record open for editing.

Fortunately, the sysAppLaunchCmdSaveData launch code that the system sends before a sysAppLaunchCmdFind code provides an easy way to ensure that everything is saved in the application. The simplest thing to do in response to sysAppLaunchCmdSaveData is call the FrmSaveAllForms function, which sends a `frmSaveEvent` to all of the open forms in an application. Then, in the event handler for any form that might have unsaved data when a global find occurs, respond to the `frmSaveEvent` by saving unsaved data.

As an example, here is the portion of the Librarian application's `PilotMain` routine that takes care of an incoming `sysAppLaunchCmdSaveData` launch code:

```
switch (cmd)
{
    case sysAppLaunchCmdSaveData:
        FrmSaveAllForms();
        break;
    // Other launch codes omitted
}
```

The only form in Librarian that might contain unsaved data when a global find occurs is the Edit form, which might have one unsaved text field within its table. Librarian's `EditFormHandleEvent` function takes care of the `frmSaveEvent` by releasing the focus from whichever field in the Edit form is currently being edited:

```
switch (event->eType)
{
    case frmSaveEvent:
        table = GetObjectPtr(EditTable);
        TblReleaseFocus(table);
        break;
    // Other events omitted
}
```

For more details about how Librarian handles text editing in its Edit form, see Chapter 14, "Programming Tables."

## Handling sysAppLaunchCmdFind

When handling a `sysAppLaunchCmdFind` launch code, an application should perform the following actions:

1. Open the application's database.

2. Draw an appropriate header string, using the `FindDrawHeader` function, in the Find results dialog box to differentiate matching records in the currently running application from those found in other applications.

3. Search through the application's records for matching text using the `FindStrInStr` function.

4. For each successful match, call `FindSaveMatch` to let the system know that a match has been found so that the system can update its own internal data about the progress of the global find operation. Also, retrieve the screen location of the next line in the Find results dialog box with `FindGetLineBounds` and draw an appropriate string in the dialog box to identify the record that was found.

5. Close the application's database.

The Librarian sample application's `PilotMain` function passes handling of the `sysAppLaunchCmdFind` launch code to another function called `Search`. The `PilotMain` function also casts the parameter block received with the launch code to a `FindParamsType` for use by the various find functions in the `Search` routine:

```
UInt32 PilotMain(UInt16 cmd, MemPtr cmdPBP,
                 UInt16 launchFlags)
{
    switch (cmd)
    {
        case sysAppLaunchCmdFind:
            Search( (FindParamsType *) cmdPBP);
            break;

        // Other launch codes omitted
    }

    return 0;
}
```

The following listing shows Librarian's `Search` function. The listing includes the numbered steps listed previously for reference.

```
static void Search (FindParamsPtr params)
{
    LibAppInfoType  *appInfo;
    LibDBRecordType  record;
    MemHandle   recordH;
    Boolean   done, match;
    DmOpenRef   db;
    DmSearchStateType   searchState;
    Err       error;
    Char       *header;
    MemHandle   headerStringH;
    RectangleType  r;
    LocalID   dbID;
    UInt16    cardNo = 0;
    UInt16    recordNum;
    UInt16    i;
    UInt16    pos;
    Char      *noAuthor = NULL;
    Char      *noTitle = NULL;


    // Find the Librarian database.
    error = DmGetNextDatabaseByTypeCreator(true,
                                       &searchState,
        libDBType, libCreatorID, true, &cardNo, &dbID);
    if (error)
    {
        params->more = false;
        return;
    }

    // Open the Librarian database.
```

```
db = DmOpenDatabase(cardNo, dbID, params->dbAccesMode);
if (! db)
{
    params->more = false;
    return;
}

// Display the heading line.
headerStringH = DmGetResource(strRsc,
                                FindHeaderString);
header = MemHandleLock(headerStringH);
done = FindDrawHeader(params, header);
MemHandleUnlock(headerStringH);
DmReleaseResource(headerStringH);
if (done)
    goto Exit;

// Search the description and note fields for the
// "find" string.
recordNum = params->recordNum;
while (true)
{
    // Applications may take a long time to finish a
    // find, so it is a good idea to allow the user to
    // interrupt the find at any time. This allows the
    // user to immediately go to a displayed record by
    // tapping on it, even before the global find
    // finishes filling the screen, or to cancel the
    // find entirely by tapping the Stop button. To
    // accomplish this, check to see if an event is
    // pending, and stop the find if there is an
    // event. This call slows down the search, so it
    // should only be performed every sixteen records
    // instead of at each and every record. If that
    // 16th record is marked secret, and the system is
    // currently set to hide private records, the check
    // does not occur, because DmQueryNextInCategory
    // respects the database access mode used earlier
    // to open the database.
    if ((recordNum & 0x000f) == 0 &&
        EvtSysEventAvail(true))
    {
        // Stop the search process.
        params->more = true;
        break;
    }

    recordH = DmQueryNextInCategory(db, &recordNum,
                                    dmAllCategories);

    // Stop searching if there are no more records.
    if (! recordH)
    {
        params->more = false;
        break;
```

```
    }

        // Search all the fields of the Librarian record.
        LibGetRecord(db, recordNum, &record, &recordH);
        match = false;
        for (i = 0; i < libFieldsCount; i++)
        {
            if (record.fields[i])
            {
                match = FindStrInStr(record.fields[i],
                                     params->strToFind,
                                     &pos);
                if (match)
                    break;
            }
        }

        if (match)
        {
            done = FindSaveMatch(params, recordNum, pos, i,
                                 0, cardNo, dbID);
            if (done)
            {
                MemHandleUnlock(recordH);
                break;
            }

            // Get the bounds of the region where we will
            // draw the results.
            FindGetLineBounds(params, &r);

            appInfo = MemHandleLock(LibGetAppInfo(db));

            // Display the title of the description.
            FntSetFont(stdFont);
            DrawRecordName(&record, &r,
                           appInfo->showInList, &noAuthor,
                           &noTitle);

            MemPtrUnlock(appInfo);

            params->lineNumber++;
        }

        MemHandleUnlock(recordH);
        recordNum++;
    }

// Unlock handles to unnamed items.
if (noAuthor != NULL)
    MemPtrUnlock(noAuthor);
```

```
        if (noTitle != NULL)
            MemPtrUnlock(noTitle);

Exit:
    DmCloseDatabase(db);
}
```

The search performed by the `FindStrInStr` function is case-insensitive. Another thing to keep in mind is that `FindStrInStr` matches only the beginnings of words. For example, a search for *bar* will match the word *bark* but not the word *embarrassed*.

## Handling sysAppLaunchCmdGoto

An application supporting global find that receives a `sysAppLaunchCmdGoto` launch code should display the record requested by the system. This can be a bit tricky, because the application that is handling the `sysAppLaunchCmdGoto` launch code may or may not already be running. The `sysAppLaunchCmdGoto` launch code also is integral to the process of beaming records from one handheld to another. See the "Displaying Beamed Records" section of Chapter 18, "Sharing Data Through the Exchange Manager," for more details.

An application can tell if it was launched by the `sysAppLaunchCmdGoto` launch code, or if it is already running, by checking its `PilotMain` function's `launchFlags` parameter for the `sysAppLaunchFlagNewGlobals` flag, which indicates that the launch code comes with its own brand new set of global variables. A new set of global variables means that the application was not already running.

If the application is already running, you must take care to close any open dialog boxes in the application before switching to whatever view displays the requested record. If the application is not already running, you need to take care of some of the same responsibilities that the `sysAppLaunchCmdNormalLaunch` launch code takes care of, namely running the application's `StartApplication` function before displaying the found record and then calling the application's `EventLoop` and `StopApplication` functions. A `sysAppLaunchCmdGoto` launch is essentially a second entry point into the application.

As an example of how to handle `sysAppLaunchCmdGoto`, here are the appropriate parts of Librarian's `PilotMain` function:

```
UInt32 PilotMain(UInt16 cmd, MemPtr cmdPBP,
            UInt16 launchFlags)
{
    Err      error;
    Boolean  launched;


    switch (cmd)
    {
        case sysAppLaunchCmdGoTo:
            launched = launchFlags &
                sysAppLaunchFlagNewGlobals;

            if (launched)
```

```
            {
                error = StartApplication();
                if (error)
                    return (error);
            }

            GoToItem( (GoToParamsType *) cmdPBP, launched);

            if (launched)
            {
                EventLoop();
                StopApplication();
            }
            break;

        // Other launch codes omitted
    }

    return 0;
}
```

Librarian's `PilotMain` function defers most of the processing of the `sysAppLaunchCmdGoto` launch code to another function, `GoToItem`, by first casting the launch code's parameter block to a `GoToParamsType` and then passing the parameter block to `GoToItem`. The `GoToItem` function looks like this:

```
static void GoToItem (GoToParamsPtr goToParams,
                    Boolean launchingApp)
{
    UInt16    formID;
    UInt16    recordNum;
    UInt16    attr;
    UInt32    uniqueID;
    EventType event;
    UInt32    romVersion;


    recordNum = goToParams->recordNum;
    DmRecordInfo(gLibDB, recordNum, &attr, &uniqueID,
                NULL);

    // Change the current category if necessary.
    if (gCurrentCategory != dmAllCategories)
    {
        gCurrentCategory = attr & dmRecAttrCategoryMask;
    }

    // If the application is already running, close all the
    // open forms. If the record currently displayed is
    // blank, it will be deleted, which knocks all the
    // record indices off by one. Use the found record's
    // unique ID to find the record index again once all
    // the forms are closed.
    if (! launchingApp)
    {
        FrmCloseAllForms();
```

```
            DmFindRecordByID(gLibDB, uniqueID, &recordNum);
    }

    // Set global variable to keep track of the current
    // record.
    gCurrentRecord = recordNum;

    // Set gPriorFormID so the Note view returns to the
    // List view.
    gPriorFormID = ListForm;

    if (goToParams->matchFieldNum == libFieldNote)
    {
        // If running on Palm OS 3.5 or above, use the
        // NewNoteView form; otherwise, stick with the
        // original NoteView.
        FtrGet(sysFtrCreator, sysFtrNumROMVersion,
                &romVersion);
        if (romVersion >=
            sysMakeROMVersion(3,5,0,sysROMStageRelease,0))
            formID = NewNoteView;
        else
            formID = NoteView;
    }
    else
    {
        formID = RecordForm;
    }

    MemSet(&event, sizeof(EventType), 0);

    // Send an event to load the form.
    event.eType = frmLoadEvent;
    event.data.frmLoad.formID = formID;
    EvtAddEventToQueue(&event);

    // Send an event to go to a form and select the
    // matching text.
    event.eType = frmGotoEvent;
    event.data.frmGoto.formID = formID;
    event.data.frmGoto.recordNum = recordNum;
    event.data.frmGoto.matchPos = goToParams->matchPos;
    event.data.frmGoto.matchLen = goToParams->searchStrLen;
    event.data.frmGoto.matchFieldNum =
        goToParams->matchFieldNum;
    EvtAddEventToQueue(&event);
}
```

The GoToItem function first retrieves the record information for the found record by calling DmRecordInfo. Both the record's attributes and unique ID are interesting to GoToItem. The attributes allow GoToItem to change the current category if the category to which the record belongs is not the category currently displayed in Librarian, and the unique ID allows GoToItem to find the record again after calling FrmCloseAllForms. If Librarian is already running, and it is currently displaying an empty record in its Edit view, that record is deleted as soon as FrmCloseAllForms closes the Edit form; deleting the record bumps all the record indices following the deleted record down by one, invalidating the index provided by the GoToItem function's goToParams parameter. Passing the unique ID of the record to DmFindRecordByID allows GoToItem to recover the correct record index.

If the found text is part of the note field, GoToItem launches Librarian's Note view; otherwise, GoToItem launches the Record view. To launch the appropriate form, GoToItem must queue a frmLoadEvent for the form, and then a frmGotoEvent to actually go to that form. The frmGotoEvent also contains data about the position and length of the found text so that the form can highlight the text in its display.

The last part of implementing sysAppLaunchCmdGoto involves handling the frmGotoEvent in the forms that might pop up in response to a sysAppLaunchCmdGoto launch code. In Librarian, both the Record and Note views handle frmGotoEvent. Here is the appropriate section of the NoteViewHandleEvent function, which demonstrates how Librarian highlights the found text in the Note view:

```
case frmGotoEvent:
    form = FrmGetActiveForm();
    gCurrentRecord = event->data.frmGoto.recordNum;
    NoteViewInit(form);
    field = GetObjectPtr(NoteField);
    FldSetScrollPosition(field,
                        event->data.frmGoto.matchPos);
    FldSetSelection(field, event->data.frmGoto.matchPos,
                    event->data.frmGoto.matchPos +
                    event->data.frmGoto.matchLen);
    NoteViewDrawTitle(form);
    NoteViewUpdateScrollBar();
    FrmSetFocus(form, FrmGetObjectIndex(form, NoteField));
    handled = true;
    break;
```

# Summary

This chapter showed you how to read and write records and resources, as well as how to implement the Palm OS global find facility. After reading this chapter, you should understand the following:

❑   Most Palm OS record databases keep their records in sorted order to permit rapid population of lists and tables from record data.

❑   You should implement a callback comparison function for your record database for the system to call when you use the DmFindSortPosition, DmInsertionSort, or DmQuickSort functions.

❑   You can find a record, or the position it should occupy, using the DmFindSortPosition, DmFindRecordByID, and DmSearchRecord functions.

❑   An application may create records with the DmNewRecord function or by allocating a new memory chunk and attaching it to the database with DmAttachRecord.

❑   Deleted and archived records remain at the end of a database's record list, so that an application's conduit can update the desktop version of the application's database.

❑   The DmRecordInfo and DmSetRecordInfo functions allow you to retrieve and set attributes and other properties of database records.

❑ After initializing default category names with `CategoryIntialize`, you can implement the standard Palm OS category selection list by calling `CategorySelect` and `CategoryEdit`.

❑ All implementation of private records is up to your application; the system takes care only of keeping track of the global security setting and a secret bit on each record.

❑ Schema databases in Palm OS Cobalt use an entirely different set of functions to perform record retrieval, insertion, and update.

❑ The cursor is the primary method for navigating rows in a schema database, and is based on a subset of SQL syntax.

❑ Querying rows in sorted order from a schema database requires the existence of a matching sort index.

❑ To implement the system global find facility, you must handle three application launch codes: `sysAppLaunchCmdSaveData`, `sysAppLaunchCmdFind`, and `sysAppLaunchCmdGoto`.

# 17

# Using Secondary Storage

RAM works well for storing most Palm OS applications and data, provided they don't require huge amounts of space. However, some kinds of software and data—such as dictionaries, mapping programs, photo albums, electronic books, and games—require a large amount of memory to store raw data. Even some of the newest Palm OS handhelds, with 32 MB RAM or more, have difficulty storing more than a handful of such large applications and their associated data.

Seeing a need for add-on storage, as well as an opportunity to provide a universal mechanism for attaching additional hardware to a Palm OS handheld, PalmSource added support for expansion cards to Palm OS 4.0. The expansion manager and its companion, the Virtual File System (VFS), give a Palm OS application the ability to interact with data on removable storage media. This chapter explains how to add support for expansion media to a Palm OS application.

## Understanding the Expansion Manager

The architecture of the expansion manager is modular, allowing hardware manufacturers to write their own expansion slot drivers to support other types of media, or even add-on peripheral hardware like digital cameras and Global Positioning System (GPS) receivers. Some expansion media also could be ROM cards, holding dedicated applications and read-only data, or even new types of I/O hardware, such as modems and Bluetooth wireless transceivers.

The expansion manager also provides a bridge between peripherals and the serial port on newer handhelds from palmOne. On such handhelds, the serial port is called the *universal connector*. The universal connector offers applications easy access to peripherals attached to the serial port. A special slot driver makes such a connection appear to applications to be a card inserted into an expansion slot, allowing the expansion manager to handle peripherals that, traditionally, would require use of the serial manager to manage their connection.

*Despite the fact that the expansion manager can deal with virtually anything that a hardware manufacturer can dream of attaching to a Palm OS handheld, for simplicity's sake the rest of this chapter will refer to any peripheral that can be connected through the expansion manager as simply an "expansion card."*

The expansion manager presents a unified interface to an application. Whether or not the expansion card is inserted into a slot or hooked onto the bottom of the handheld, an application can check for the same notifications to determine when a peripheral is connected or disconnected.

Individual hardware manufacturers provide their own expansion slot drivers, which are standard Palm OS shared libraries. When the handheld first boots up after a reset, the expansion manager automatically loads the appropriate slot drivers, allowing applications to communicate with the hardware connected to those slots. Once the slot drivers are loaded and running, the user may insert and remove cards at will, and the slot drivers automatically perform any low-level tasks required to establish and break connection with the expansion cards. A handheld may have any number of slots.

The expansion manager provides the following services:

❏ Notifications of card insertion and removal

❏ Automatic installation of slot drivers

❏ Information about which slots contain cards, and what kinds of cards are inserted

# Understanding Secondary Storage

The Palm OS makes a distinction between *primary storage*, or storage space in RAM on the handheld itself, and *secondary storage*, or add-on memory. Primary storage may be directly addressed by an application, either through memory manager functions that modify data in dynamic RAM or through data and resource manager functions that modify data in storage RAM. Secondary storage, on the other hand, has a lot more in common with a desktop file system, including a serial interface to data that allows access to data only one bit, byte, or block at a time.

The Virtual File System (VFS) manager is the Palm OS interface to the file system on a secondary storage card. Applications use VFS manager functions to create, delete, and modify files located on secondary storage media, as well as to manage directories and format media inserted in an expansion slot.

A file system located on secondary storage media is called a *volume*. When you first insert an expansion card containing a volume into an expansion slot, the expansion manager looks for a volume on the card; if it finds one, it *mounts* that volume. Mounting a volume provides the operating system a way to identify a volume and also gives applications a way to find the volume and access its files and directories. Because a handheld may possess more than one expansion slot, mounting a volume is necessary if the device is to differentiate one expansion card from another. Removing a card from an expansion slot causes the expansion manager to unmount the volume contained on that card.

To support the widest possible number of external storage formats, the VFS manager provides a unified set of functions for manipulating secondary storage. It is possible for the storage card itself to have virtually any file system, but Palm OS applications do not need to know exactly how the data is stored on the expansion media. The VFS manager uses a file system library provided by the manufacturer of the handheld or the storage medium to translate actions requested by an application into the specific instructions needed to manipulate data in a particular file system.

Because the VFS manager abstracts file system details from a Palm OS application, the same application code can access files on Secure Digital (SD) cards, Sony's Memory Stick, MultiMedia Cards (MMC), CompactFlash, or whatever new kind of media comes along. Palm OS 4.0 natively supports VFAT, the industry standard for flash memory cards. The VFAT (Virtual File Allocation Table) library in Palm OS 4.0 recognizes and mounts FAT (File Allocation Table) and VFAT file systems located on secondary storage media.

Aside from offering the ability to cram more data onto a Palm OS handheld, the VFS support for multiple file systems allows expansion media to be used to transfer data between different kinds of devices. For example, it is possible to remove a card from a digital camera, put it in a Palm OS handheld, and view or modify the images on the handheld. As long as the proper file system library is installed on the handheld, the VFS manager can read data from any number of different file systems.

## *Organizing Files and Directories*

Palm OS uses a standard hierarchy of directories that all applications should be aware of, whether the applications are designed to manage files or merely to use an expansion card to store their data. Although there is nothing preventing you from writing your application's files and directories wherever you want to on an expansion card, following the standards set by PalmSource make for a more consistent and user-friendly experience for whomever will be running your application. Furthermore, you can prevent conflicts with other applications by following PalmSource's guidelines when you want to determine where to put your application's data. The recommended directory structure is detailed in the following table.

| Directory | Description |
|---|---|
| / | This is the root directory of the secondary storage volume. The root directory is reserved for operating system use and for use by non–Palm OS applications that might be sharing the expansion media. |
| /PALM | Built-in applications, or those actually written by Palm, Inc., store their data in subdirectories of /PALM. For example, Palm Reader, Palm's eBook reading program, stores eBooks in /PALM/Books. |
| /PALM/Backup | Reserved by Palm OS for backing up data and applications. Writing your own data to this directory is a really bad idea because it could interfere with the proper operation of backup software, resulting in possible data loss or corruption. |
| /PALM/Programs | Third-party applications should store their data in a subdirectory of /PALM/Programs. For example, an application called MyApp might store its data in /PALM/Programs/MyApp. |
| /PALM/Launcher | Applications in /PALM/Launcher appear in their own category in the built-in Launcher application. |

When a user inserts an expansion card containing a writable volume (as opposed to, say, a dictionary/thesaurus card, the information on which is read-only), the system creates the /PALM and /PALM/Launcher directories if they don't already exist. The launcher then looks for an application named start.prc in the /PALM directory and runs it if it exists. This behavior allows a software developer to create a program that runs automatically as soon as a card is inserted, allowing for distribution of the software on expansion media. This method of starting an application is much simpler for the user than having to use the Palm Install Tool to copy the program to storage RAM during a HotSync operation, particularly if the application relies on a number of separate data files. Instead of relying on an application's user to remember to copy all the data files over to the handheld, the data can accompany the application on the same card, making for a tidy distribution package.

If there is no `start.prc` file and `/PALM/Launcher` already exists and contains one or more application files, the Launcher automatically switches to the list of applications available on the card, ready for the user to select an application to run.

*The Sony CLIÉ series also has an application called MS Autorun, which allows the user of the handheld to choose an application, either on the Memory Stick or in main storage memory, that will automatically run when the Memory Stick is inserted. MS Autorun works in much the same way as the `start.prc` launching mechanism provided by the Palm OS 4.0 Launcher, except that it is customizable by the user.*

## Running Applications from Secondary Storage

Palm OS can directly run only applications stored in RAM. Data access in secondary storage is completely different from the method the operating system uses in RAM to run an application, so application code stored on expansion media cannot be executed.

So how does Palm OS run an application from an expansion card? The process is almost identical to what a desktop computer does when it runs an application: Palm OS copies the file from the expansion card into storage RAM and then runs the application there. Applications located in the `/PALM/Launcher` directory on an expansion card are easy for the user to run; the Launcher application takes care of copying the application from the expansion card and launches it once the copy is located in storage RAM. When the user switches to another application, the operating system deletes the application from storage memory, once again freeing the space for other applications and data.

Because it is possible for the user to copy any application onto the card, it is important to know the following things about this procedure:

❑ Only the actual application is located on the expansion card, not its data. Databases created by an application remain in storage memory because most applications are designed to use storage RAM to save data. Unless an application had been written specifically to work with data located on expansion media, its data would be inaccessible if the data also were copied to the card. This also means that if the user deletes an application from an expansion card, the application's data remains in storage memory.

❑ There is some amount of delay when launching and closing an application stored on an expansion card. It takes time for the operating system to copy the program from the card to storage memory when the application starts, and to remove the program from RAM when the application exits. For smaller applications, this isn't a concern, but larger applications can cause a noticeable delay on launch.

❑ An application in secondary storage cannot receive notifications or special launch codes. This means that applications that use alarms cannot respond to them, and programs that support the global find feature are not searched.

❑ Launch codes tell an application if it was launched from a card so, if necessary, it is possible to program an application to behave differently when it is launched from a card than if it is launched from RAM. For example, an application launched from a card could avoid setting alarms to which it would be unable to respond.

Palm OS sends a `sysAppLaunchCmdCardLaunch` launch code to an application that is about to be launched from an expansion card. This launch code gives the application the opportunity to react differently when run from secondary storage than when run from main memory. As with most other launch codes, global variables are not available to the application when it receives `sysAppLaunchCmdCardLaunch`. After the program is finished handling the `sysAppLaunchCmdCardLaunch` code, the operating system sends the application the usual `sysAppLaunchCmdNormalLaunch` code. The program should not present the user with any interface while handling `sysAppLaunchCmdCardLaunch` but rather store in the application's preferences or databases whatever information the application needs to know to handle a card-based launch. When the application receives the `sysAppLaunchCmdNormalLaunch` code, it can check for those stored values and change how the program behaves accordingly.

> *For more information about handling launch codes other than* `sysAppLaunchCmdNormal`, *see the "Setting Alarms" section of Chapter 13 or the "Implementing the Global Find Facility" section of Chapter 16.*

# Using the Virtual File System

To illustrate how to use the VFS manager, this chapter draws from an example application called VFS Test. Figure 17-1 shows a couple of views of the simple user interface in the VFS Test application.

**Figure 17-1**

VFS Test presents a bare minimum user interface for the creation and deletion of files and directories in secondary storage. It also allows for reading data from and writing data to files on an expansion card. The functions of the Name and Data text fields, as well as the Do It button at the bottom of the screen, change depending upon which push buttons are selected. The following table outlines the possibilities.

| Selected Push Buttons | Name, Data, and Do It Function |
| --- | --- |
| Create, File | Tapping Do It creates a new file with the name and location given in the Name field. The Data field is hidden. |
| Create, Directory | Tapping Do It creates a new directory with the name and location given in the Name field. The Data field is hidden. |
| Delete, File | Tapping Do It deletes the file indicated by the path and filename in the Name field. The Data field is hidden. |

*Table continued on following page*

| Selected Push Buttons | Name, Data, and Do It Function |
|---|---|
| Delete, Directory | Tapping Do It deletes the directory indicated by the path and filename in the Name field. The Data field is hidden. |
| Read, File | Tapping Do It reads the data from the file indicated by the Name field and then displays that data in an alert dialog box. The Data field is hidden. |
| Write, File | Tapping Do It writes the text in the Data field to the file indicated by the Name field. |

Note that the Directory push button is not available when either the Read or Write push buttons are selected because applications cannot read data from or write data to directory entries, only to files.

## Verifying Presence of the VFS Manager

Before attempting to use any of the features of the VFS manager, an application should first check to make sure that the VFS manager exists. Use the following call to `FtrGet` to perform this check:

**Palm OS Garnet**
```
UInt32  vfsMgrVersion;

Err error = FtrGet(sysFileCVFSMgr, vfsFtrIDVersion,
                    &vfsMgrVersion);
```

**Palm OS Cobalt**
```
uint32_t  vfsMgrVersion;

status_t error = FtrGet(sysFileCVFSMgr, vfsFtrIDVersion,
                        &vfsMgrVersion);
```

If the VFS manager is installed, the `vfsMgrVersion` parameter will be nonzero and `error` will have the value 0, representing no error.

*It is not necessary to check also for the presence of the expansion manager because it will always be included on any device that has the VFS manager installed.*

## Detecting Card Insertion and Removal

Unlike primary storage, secondary storage media is designed to be and exists for the purpose of being removable. This means that the user can swap out expansion cards at any time, while any application is running. Applications that make use of secondary storage therefore need to be able to determine when a card is present in an expansion slot.

Although a user can remove an expansion card at any time, it is inadvisable to do so while an application is writing data to secondary storage. Because of the nature of flash memory, removing an expansion card while the handheld is writing data to it can corrupt data on the card and, in some cases, even damage the memory in the card itself. If your application spends more than a second or two writing data to an expansion card, it should display a warning that instructs the user not to remove the card until the data has been written.

The Expansion and VFS managers use *notifications* to alert interested applications that a card has been inserted or removed. A notification is similar to a launch code, but Palm OS sends notifications only to applications that have registered to receive them. Applications may receive notifications even while they are not currently running, just as they may receive launch codes while inactive. For more details on using Palm OS notifications, see Chapter 24.

An application can register to receive the following four card-related notifications:

❑ sysNotifyCardInsertedEvent

❑ sysNotifyCardRemovedEvent

❑ sysNotifyVolumeMountedEvent

❑ sysNotifyVolumeUnmountedEvent

The first two notifications are low-level events that occur at the hardware level when the card is inserted or removed. For the most part, an application dealing with secondary storage is not interested in these low-level events. The sysNotifyCardInsertedEvent notification occurs before the expansion manager has mounted any volumes on the inserted card, so there isn't anything available for VFS routines to work with at this point. Likewise, when the sysNotifyCardRemovedEvent notification occurs, the volume has already been unmounted, so the data on the card is unavailable to VFS routines. These two notifications are primarily for the creation of device drivers for special hardware—such as a digital camera or Bluetooth wireless card—that connects to an expansion slot or the universal connector.

Most applications that use secondary storage are much more interested in sysNotifyVolumeMounted Event and sysNotifyVolumeUnmountedEvent. These two notifications occur when the volume is actually mounted or unmounted, respectively. Once a volume has been mounted, its contents are accessible to VFS manager routines. This section deals with these two volume-related notifications.

## Registering to Receive Notifications

Before an application can receive the mount and unmount notifications, it must register to receive them. To register to receive a notification, use the SysNotifyRegister function:

**Palm OS Garnet**
```
Err SysNotifyRegister (UInt16 cardNo, LocalID dbID,
    UInt32 notifyType, SysNotifyProcPtr callback,
    Int8 priority, void *userData)
```

**Palm OS Cobalt**
```
status_t SysNotifyRegister (DatabaseID dbID,
    uint32_t notifyType, SysNotifyProcPtr callback,
    int32_t priority, void *userData, uint32_t userDataSize)
```

The first two parameters specify the card number (cardNo) and database ID (dbID) of the application that should receive the notification—except in Palm OS Cobalt, which omits the cardNo parameter. The notifyType parameter specifies the type of notification the application should receive.

If a shared library were to call SysNotifyRegister, it would use the callback parameter to pass a pointer to a callback function that the operating system should call when the notification event occurs. A regular application, however, can just pass NULL for the callback parameter; applications normally receive notifications through the launch code mechanism.

*This section of the book assumes a regular application, using launch codes to receive notifications.*

The priority parameter specifies what priority this application has when Palm OS is deciding which applications get to handle a notification in what order. It is best to pass the constant sysNotifyNormal Priority for this parameter, which gives the registration whatever default priority Palm OS normally assigns to the notification.

The userData parameter is a pointer to application-specific data that the operating system can send back along with the notification. In Palm OS Cobalt, there is also a userDataSize parameter that states the size, in bytes, of the data pointed to by the userData parameter.

When should an application register to receive mounting notifications? It depends on whether the application needs to respond to these notifications only while it is active, or while it is not the active application as well. If it must respond to insertion and removal of cards while other applications are active, the best time for the application to register for notifications is right after it has been installed. To do this, your application should respond to the sysAppLaunchCmdSyncNotify launch code, which the application receives after being installed via a HotSync operation.

*Because the user can copy an application directly from an expansion card to storage memory, an action that does not generate a sysAppLaunchCmdSyncNotify launch code, you also may want your application to register for notifications when your application first starts, as described in the following paragraphs. The user must then run the application once before it is registered if it is to receive insertion and removal notifications. Unfortunately, there is no way for an application to register itself when it is copied to the handheld's memory from an expansion card, so the user must either install the application via a HotSync operation or run it once before it can receive notifications.*

Unless you are writing a utility program that performs some sort of action whenever a card is inserted or removed, you probably need to deal with these notifications only while your application is currently running. In this case, you can get away with registering for notification when the program first starts up, which makes the application's StartApplication routine ideal for the purpose.

This method is exactly what the VFS Test sample application uses. Here are the relevant parts of the StartApplication function from VFS Test:

**Palm OS Garnet**
```
UInt16    cardNo;
LocalID   dbID;

SysCurAppDatabase(&cardNo, &dbID);
SysNotifyRegister(cardNo, dbID,
                  sysNotifyVolumeMountedEvent, NULL,
                  sysNotifyNormalPriority, NULL);
SysNotifyRegister(cardNo, dbID,
                  sysNotifyVolumeUnmountedEvent, NULL,
                  sysNotifyNormalPriority, NULL);
```

**Palm OS Cobalt**
```
DatabaseID  dbID;

SysCurAppDatabase(&dbID);
SysNotifyRegister(dbID,
                  sysNotifyVolumeMountedEvent, NULL,
                  sysNotifyNormalPriority, NULL, 0);
SysNotifyRegister(dbID,
                  sysNotifyVolumeUnmountedEvent, NULL,
                  sysNotifyNormalPriority, NULL, 0);
```

VFS Test first retrieves the memory card number and database ID of the VFS Test application itself using SysCurAppDatabase. Then it passes these two values to SysNotifyRegister, once with sysNotifyVolumeMountedEvent and once with sysNotifyVolumeUnmountedEvent. VFS Test has no need to send any data through the notification process, so it simply passes NULL to SysNotifyRegister for the userData parameter—and in Palm OS Cobalt, it passes 0 for the userDataSize parameter.

## Responding to Notifications

Applications receive notifications via the launch code mechanism, so the first place to add code for handling these notifications is to the program's PilotMain routine. Palm OS sends notifications through the sysAppLaunchCmdNotify launch code. The following excerpt from the VFS Test program's PilotMain function shows how it deals with the launch code:

```
case sysAppLaunchCmdNotify:
    // Only respond if VFS Test is currently running.
    if (launchFlags & sysAppLaunchFlagSubCall)
    {
        HandleNotification( (SysNotifyParamType *) cmdPBP);
    }
    break;
```

Because VFS Test is interested in card insertion and removal only while it is the active application, it checks the PilotMain routine's launchFlags parameter for the sysAppLaunchFlagSubCall flag. If sysAppLaunchFlagSubCall is present, VFS Test is already running, in which case PilotMain hands off actual processing of the notification to the HandleNotification routine. Because VFS Test handles these notifications only when it is already running, global variables are always available, even while running in Palm OS Garnet.

*Keep in mind that if your application handles the* `sysAppLaunchCmdNotify` *launch code when it is not the active application in Palm OS Garnet, global variables are not available and attempting to use them will cause a crash. The global variable restriction does not exist in Palm OS Cobalt.*

The `HandleNotification` routine looks like this:

```
void HandleNotification (SysNotifyParamType *param)
{
    FormType   *form = FrmGetActiveForm();


    switch (param->notifyType)
    {
        case sysNotifyVolumeMountedEvent:
            if (FrmGetFormId(form) == frmAbout)
                FrmReturnToForm(0);
            InitVFS();
            param->handled = true;
            break;

        case sysNotifyVolumeUnmountedEvent:
            if (FrmGetFormId(form) == frmAbout)
                FrmReturnToForm(0);
            gVolRefNum = 0;
            PrintVolume(NULL);
            param->handled = true;
            break;
    }
}
```

VFS Test needs to know when a volume has been mounted or unmounted so that it can update a text string in the upper-right corner of its title bar. This string is the name of whatever volume is currently mounted, or the text "No volume mounted" if that's the case. When the notification is `sysNotifyVolume MountedEvent`, `HandleNotification` calls `InitVFS`. The `InitVFS` routine is covered in detail in the next section, but one important task it performs is to retrieve the name of the mounted volume and pass it to a routine called `PrintVolume`. The `sysNotifyVolumeUnmountedEvent` case also calls `PrintVolume`, a helper routine that simply updates the volume text in the upper-right corner.

## Retrieving a Volume Reference

Before an application can perform any operations on files or directories in secondary storage, it must obtain a reference to a mounted volume. Many of the VFS manager functions require this volume reference as their first argument. The function used for finding this reference is `VFSVolumeEnumerate`:

**Palm OS Garnet**
```
Err VFSVolumeEnumerate (UInt16 *volRefNumP,
    UInt32 *volIteratorP)
```

**Palm OS Cobalt**
```
status_t VFSVolumeEnumerate (uint16_t *volRefNumP,
    uint32_t *volIteratorP)
```

The VFSVolumeEnumerate function is designed to allow an application to iterate over all the volumes currently mounted on the handheld. The function is designed to be called as part of a loop, returning mounted volumes one at a time each time it is called. The first argument to VFSVolumeEnumerate, volRefNumP, is a pointer that receives a reference to the next mounted volume the function can find. The second argument, volIterator, is a pointer to a value that keeps track of which volume VFSVolumeEnumerate should return next.

To find all mounted volumes, call VFSVolumeEnumerate from a loop, like this:

**Palm OS Garnet**

```
UInt16  volRefNum;
UInt32  volIterator = vfsIteratorStart;
Err error;

while (volIterator != vfsIteratorStop)
{
    error = VFSVolumeEnumerate(&volRefNum, &volIterator);
    if (error == errNone)
    {
        // Do something with the volume referenced in
        // volRefNum.
    }
    else
    {
        // An error occurred.
    }
}
```

**Palm OS Cobalt**

```
uint16_t  volRefNum;
uint32_t  volIterator = vfsIteratorStart;
status_t  error;

while (volIterator != vfsIteratorStop)
{
    error = VFSVolumeEnumerate(&volRefNum, &volIterator);
    if (error == errNone)
    {
        // Do something with the volume referenced in
        // volRefNum.
    }
    else
    {
        // An error occurred.
    }
}
```

This code snippet starts the loop by setting volIterator equal to the constant value vfsIteratorStart, which indicates to VFSVolumeEnumerate that it should return the first mounted volume it finds. If there is a mounted volume, VFSVolumeEnumerate returns a reference to that volume in volRefNum and then increments volIterator so the next call to VFSVolumeEnumerate returns the next mounted volume.

The `InitVFS` function in VFS Test is responsible for finding a volume reference to be used throughout the rest of the application. VFS Test is interested in only the first mounted volume it comes across, so `InitVFS` doesn't bother calling `VFSVolumeEnumerate` from within a loop. Here is what `InitVFS` looks like:

**Palm OS Garnet**

```
void InitVFS (void)
{
    Err     error;
    UInt32  volIterator = vfsIteratorStart;
    Char    *volName;


    error = VFSVolumeEnumerate(&gVolRefNum, &volIterator);
    if (error)
    {
        gVolRefNum = 0;
        PrintVolume(NULL);
    }
    else
    {
        volName = MemPtrNew(256);
        MemSet(volName, 256, 0);
        error = VFSVolumeGetLabel(gVolRefNum, volName, 255);
        ErrFatalDisplayIf(error,
            "Couldn't retrieve volume label");
        PrintVolume(volName);
        MemPtrFree(volName);
    }
}
```

**Palm OS Cobalt**

```
void InitVFS (void)
{
    status_t  error;
    uint32_t  volIterator = vfsIteratorStart;
    char      *volName;


    error = VFSVolumeEnumerate(&gVolRefNum, &volIterator);
    if (error < errNone)
    {
        gVolRefNum = 0;
        PrintVolume(NULL);
    }
    else
    {
        volName = malloc(256);
        memset(volName, 0, 256);
        error = VFSVolumeGetLabel(gVolRefNum, volName, 255);
        ErrFatalErrIf(error < errNone,
            "Couldn't retrieve volume label");
        PrintVolume(volName);
        free(volName);
    }
}
```

VFS Test maintains a global variable, gVolRefNum, that stores the volume reference number for use throughout the application. If VFSVolumeEnumerate does not return a mounted volume, InitVFS sets gVolRefNum to 0, indicating to other routines in the application that no mounted volume is available.

## Getting and Setting Volume Labels

InitVFS also is responsible for retrieving the name of the mounted volume. To accomplish this task, InitVFS calls VFSVolumeGetLabel. The VFSVolumeGetLabel routine has the following prototype:

**Palm OS Garnet**
```
Err VFSVolumeGetLabel (UInt16 volRefNum, Char *labelP,
    UInt16 bufLen)
```

**Palm OS Cobalt**
```
status_t VFSVolumeGetLabel (uint16_t volRefNum,
    char *labelP, uint16_t bufLen)
```

VFSVolumeGetLabel takes as its parameters a volume reference (volRefNum), a pointer to a buffer to receive the volume name (labelP), and the length of the buffer (bufLen). Volume labels in the Virtual File System can be a maximum of 255 characters in length, so InitVFS allocates a buffer of 256 bytes — enough room for the longest possible volume label plus one byte for a terminating null.

The complementary function to VFSVolumeGetLabel is VFSVolumeSetLabel, which has the following prototype:

**Palm OS Garnet**
```
Err VFSVolumeSetLabel (UInt16 volRefNum,
                const Char *labelP)
```

**Palm OS Cobalt**
```
status_t VFSVolumeSetLabel (uint16_t volRefNum,
                const char *labelP)
```

The first argument to VFSVolumeSetLabel, volRefNum, is a volume reference that refers to the volume that should be relabeled. The second argument, labelP, is a pointer to a null-terminated string that contains the new name of the volume.

Volume names in the Virtual File System are at most 255 characters in length, and they are case-insensitive. The following characters are valid in volume names:

❑  Numbers

❑  Alphabetic characters, both uppercase and lowercase, in any character set

❑  Spaces

❑  The following special characters: $ % ' - _ @ ~ ` ! ( ) ^ # & + , ; = [ ]

*Some underlying file systems use volume names that don't adhere to these naming guidelines. Fortunately, it is the responsibility of the file system library to translate whatever name you pass to the VFS manager into a name that the file system can handle. These names are then converted back to their*

**579**

*VFS equivalent when an application retrieves them from such a file system. As an example, many file systems do not natively support long filenames. If this is the case, VFSVolumeSetLabel creates a file called* `volume.nam` *in the root directory of the volume. This file contains information necessary for the file system to preserve the long volume name information.*

# Finding Volume Information

The VFS manager provides a wealth of information about a mounted volume. One of the most common pieces of data an application might need is how much space is available on a volume—both the total size of the volume and the space remaining on the volume. The VFSVolumeSize function provides such information. Its prototype looks like this:

**Palm OS Garnet**
```
Err VFSVolumeSize (UInt16 volRefNum, UInt32 *volumeUsedP,
    UInt32 *volumeTotalP)
```

**Palm OS Cobalt**
```
status_t VFSVolumeSize (uint16_t volRefNum,
    uint32_t *volumeUsedP, uint32_t *volumeTotalP)
```

The first argument is simply the volume reference number. VFSVolumeSize fills in the pointers you provide for the volumeUsedP and volumeTotalP arguments with the number of bytes occupied on the volume and the total size of the volume, respectively.

Another function, VFSVolumeInfo, provides more general information about a mounted volume, such as the type of media the volume is on. Pass VFSVolumeInfo a pointer to a VolumeInfoType structure, and the function fills in the structure with all kinds of information. Here is an example of calling VFSVolumeInfo:

**Palm OS Garnet**
```
Err   error;
VolumeInfoType  info;

error = VFSVolumeInfo(volRefNum, &info);
```

**Palm OS Cobalt**
```
status_t  error;
VolumeInfoType  info;

error = VFSVolumeInfo(volRefNum, &info);
```

The VolumeInfoType structure is defined in the Palm OS header file VFSMgr.h. It has the following definition:

**Palm OS Garnet**
```
typedef struct VolumeInfoTag
{
    UInt32  attributes; // Read-only, hidden, etc.
    UInt32  fsType;     // File system type for this volume
    UInt32  fsCreator;  // Creator code of file system driver
                        //   for this volume.
```

```
    UInt32  mountClass; // Mount class that mounted this
                        //   volume
    UInt16  slotLibRefNum; // Library on which the volume
                           //   is mounted
    UInt16  slotRefNum;    // ExpMgr slot number of card
                           //   containing volume
    UInt32  mediaType;  // Type of card media
                        //   (mediaMemoryStick,
                        //    mediaCompactFlash, etc.)
    UInt32  reserved;   // reserved for future use
} VolumeInfoType, *VolumeInfoPtr;
```

**Palm OS Cobalt**

```
typedef struct VolumeInfoTag
{
    uint32_t  attributes; // Read-only, hidden, etc.
    uint32_t  fsType;     // File system type for this volume
    uint32_t  fsCreator;  // Creator code of file system driver
                          //   for this volume.
    uint32_t  mountClass; // Mount class that mounted this
                          //   volume
    uint16_t  slotLibRefNum;  // Library on which the volume
                              //   is mounted
    uint16_t  slotRefNum;     // ExpMgr slot number of card
                              //   containing volume
    uint32_t  mediaType;  // Type of card media
                          //   (mediaMemoryStick,
                          //    mediaCompactFlash, etc.)
    uint32_t  reserved;   // reserved for future use
} VolumeInfoType, *VolumeInfoPtr;
```

# Creating Directories

You can create a directory in a volume by calling VFSDirCreate:

**Palm OS Garnet**

```
Err VFSDirCreate (UInt16 volRefNum, const Char *dirNameP)
```

**Palm OS Cobalt**

```
status_t VFSDirCreate (uint16_t volRefNum,
    const char *dirNameP)
```

The first parameter, volRefNum, is the volume reference number. The second parameter, dirNameP, is a pointer to a null-terminated string containing the full path and name of the directory you wish to create.

*Keep in mind that there is no such concept as a "current" or "working" directory in the VFS. All path names are absolute, so you must pass in the entire path to a file or directory when working with VFS manager routines.*

VFS Test wraps VFSDirCreate in its CreateDirectory function, shown here:

**Palm OS Garnet**

```
void CreateDirectory (Char *name)
{
    Err     error;
    Char    *badPath;
    Char    *errString;
    Int8    i;


    if (! name)
    {
        FrmAlert(altNoDirectoryNamed);
        return;
    }

    error = VFSDirCreate(gVolRefNum, name);
    switch (error)
    {
        case errNone:
            FrmCustomAlert(altCreateDir, name, "", "");
            break;

        case vfsErrBadName:
            FrmCustomAlert(altCreateDirInvalid, name, "",
                        "");
            break;

        case vfsErrDirectoryNotFound:
            badPath = MemPtrNew(StrLen(name) + 1);
            for (i = StrLen(name); i > 0; --i)
            {
                if ( (name[i] == '/') || (name[i] == '\\') )
                    break;
            }
            if (i == 0)
                i = StrLen(name);
            StrNCopy(badPath, name, i);
            FrmCustomAlert(altCreateDirBadPath, name,
                        badPath, "");
            MemPtrFree(badPath);
            break;

        case vfsErrFileAlreadyExists:
            FrmCustomAlert(altCreateDirExists, name, "",
                        "");
            break;

        default:
            errString = MemPtrNew(maxStrIToALen);
            FrmCustomAlert(altCreateDirError, name,
                        StrIToA(errString, error), "");
            MemPtrFree(errString);
    }
}
```

**Palm OS Cobalt**

```
void CreateDirectory (char *name)
{
    status_t    error;
    char        badPath[maxStrIToALen];
    char        errString[maxStrIToALen];
    int8_t      i;


    if (! name)
    {
        FrmAlert(altNoDirectoryNamed);
        return;
    }

    error = VFSDirCreate(gVolRefNum, name);
    switch (error)
    {
        case errNone:
            FrmCustomAlert(altCreateDir, name, "", "");
            break;

        case vfsErrBadName:
            FrmCustomAlert(altCreateDirInvalid, name, "",
                            "");
            break;

        case vfsErrDirectoryNotFound:
            memset(badPath, 0, maxStrIToALen);
            for (i = strlen(name); i > 0; --i)
            {
                if ( (name[i] == '/') || (name[i] == '\\') )
                    break;
            }
            if (i == 0)
                i = strlen(name);
            strncpy(badPath, name, i);
            FrmCustomAlert(altCreateDirBadPath, name,
                            badPath, "");
            break;

        case vfsErrFileAlreadyExists:
            FrmCustomAlert(altCreateDirExists, name, "",
                            "");
            break;

        default:
            FrmCustomAlert(altCreateDirError, name,
                            StrIToA(errString, error), "");
    }
}
```

`CreateDirectory` receives the path name of the new directory as its sole argument. The path name consists of whatever text is in VFS Test's Name text field. Because the user could enter literally anything into the Name field, the bulk of `CreateDirectory` is error-handling code that deals with most of the common mistakes that the user might make when entering the new directory name. The most common `VFSDirCreate` errors you might have to deal with are outlined in the following table.

| Error Constant | Description |
|---|---|
| `vfsErrBadName` | Directory name contains invalid characters. |
| `vfsErrDirectoryNotFound` | Path leading up to the new directory name does not exist. For example, if you attempt to create a directory called `/PALM/Programs/foo/bar`, and the directory `/PALM/Programs/foo` does not exist, `VFSDirCreate` returns `vfsErrDirectoryNotFound`. |
| `vfsErrFileAlreadyExists` | Directory you are attempting to create, or a file with the same name, already exists. |

Directory names and filenames follow the same naming rules as VFS volume labels. The directory separator used by the VFS manager is the forward slash (/), though functions that require a path as an argument also accept a backslash (\).

As for volume labels, the file system library handles translation of VFS long filenames to names that are usable by the underlying file system. For example, the standard VFAT library present on all expansion-capable Palm OS devices uses the following rules when converting long filenames to the "8.3" naming convention used in the FAT file system:

❑ The first six valid, nonspace characters form the first part of the filename. Valid characters include A–Z, 0–9, $, %, ', –, _, @, ~, `, !, (, ), ^, #, and &.

❑ The first occurrence of a shortened filename has ~1 appended to its first six characters. Subsequent occurrences increment this number, which means the second occurrence of a shortened name has ~2 appended to it, and so on. When the number reaches 10, the first part of the filename is truncated to the first five valid characters in the original long filename, and the VFAT library appends ~10 to the filename. This process of shortening the first part of the name occurs at each order of magnitude the number following the tilde (~) reaches: 10, 100, 1000, and so on.

❑ The extension is composed of the first three valid characters following the rightmost period (.) in the filename. This can result in no extension at all if there are no valid characters, or if there is no period in the filename.

When creating directories, be sure to pay attention to the standard directory hierarchy created by PalmSource and presented earlier in this chapter. Creating directories wherever you please on an expansion card can cause serious conflicts with system utilities like the application launcher. There is plenty of space under the `/PALM/Programs` directory for whatever your application needs to write to the card.

> It's a good idea to add the creator ID of your application to its directory name to ensure there won't be conflict with another application's data. For example, a program called MyApp with a creator ID of myAP might create a directory called `/PALM/Programs/MyApp-myAP` in which to store its files. This is the same convention recommended by PalmSource for databases in regular storage RAM.

*At the time of this book's writing, we have seen few applications that adhere to this convention, including programs written by palmOne and Sony. This is unfortunate because adding this kind of unique identification to directories could prevent applications from competing for the same piece of expansion media real estate.*

## Handling VFS Manager Errors Gracefully

The key to a positive user experience with an application that uses secondary storage is good error handling. There are many little things that can go wrong when accessing files on expansion media, and users will quickly become frustrated if your application spits back the same error message for all of them. The VFS manager routines return many different error codes, which are valuable clues to help diagnose what the problem is so that you can present a helpful and informative error message to the user.

For example, the VFS Test application could just check the return value from the VFS manager routines it calls and, if they're nonzero, return a generic error message, as in the following code snippet:

```
error = VFSDirCreate(gVolRefNum, name);
if (error < errNone)
    FrmAlert(altGenericErrorMessage);
```

While this simplistic error handling fulfills the application's obligation to not crash the handheld, it doesn't provide the user with any idea at all of what might have gone wrong. Did the directory name contain invalid characters? Does the directory already exist? Is the volume out of space? There is no way for the user to find out any of this information.

Instead of presenting the user with a single error message for every occasion, VFS Test pays attention to the most common errors that occur with each VFS manager routine it calls and responds with error messages tailored to the situation. There are 35 different alerts in VFS Test's resources that are devoted to providing specific information about VFS errors. Most functions in VFS Test that interact with the file system contain lengthy `switch` statements to find out what errors have occurred and display the proper alert to the user. VFS Test also makes extensive use of `FrmCustomAlert` to add more information, such as the path name input by the user, to the alert dialog box. Figure 17-2 shows some of the alerts generated by the `CreateDirectory` routine. Clockwise from upper left, they are successful creation, `vfsErrBadName`, `vfsErrDirectoryNotFound`, and `vfsErrFileAlreadyExists`.

The errors that `CreateDirectory` pays special attention to consist of things that the user can correct by entering different, valid data in the Name text field. For more esoteric errors, `CreateDirectory` has a `default` case in its `switch` statement that catches the error and displays an error message (see Figure 17-3) that contains the error number.

Errors that get to the `default` case are caused by situations that the user probably can't do anything about. For example, if the file system on the expansion media cannot create new directories (unlikely, but possible), `VFSDirCreate` returns `vfsErrNoFileSystem`. The user of VFS Test probably won't have any idea what to do about this error condition, but with the information presented in the alert, the user could make a useful bug report to the developer.

This kind of error handling may sound like a lot of effort, but it isn't difficult to implement, merely tedious. A little tedium can make your application much friendlier and less confusing to use and allow users of your application to give you much better feedback if they encounter bugs.

**Figure 17-2**

**Figure 17-3**

# Creating Files

Creating files is much like creating directories, except that you use the VFSFileCreate function:

**Palm OS Garnet**
```
Err VFSFileCreate (UInt16 volRefNum, const Char *pathNameP)
```

**Palm OS Cobalt**
```
status_t VFSFileCreate (uint16_t volRefNum,
                        const char *pathNameP)
```

The volRefNum parameter should look familiar by now; it holds the volume reference number. The pathNameP parameter takes a pointer to a null-terminated string representing the full path and name for the new file.

*Creating a file does not open it for reading and writing; see the "Opening and Closing Files" section later in this chapter for details on opening files.*

VFSTest wraps VFSFileCreate and some error-checking in its CreateFile function:

**Palm OS Garnet**

```
void CreateFile (Char *name)
{
    Err    error;
    Char   *badPath;
    Int8   i;
    Char   *errString;


    if (! name)
    {
        FrmAlert(altNoFileNamed);
        return;
    }

    error = VFSFileCreate(gVolRefNum, name);
    switch (error)
    {
        case errNone:
            FrmCustomAlert(altCreateFile, name, "", "");
            break;

        case vfsErrBadName:
            FrmCustomAlert(altCreateFileInvalid, name, "",
                           "");
            break;

        case vfsErrFileAlreadyExists:
            FrmCustomAlert(altCreateFileExists, name, "",
                           "");
            break;

        case vfsErrDirectoryNotFound:
            badPath = MemPtrNew(StrLen(name) + 1);
            MemSet(badPath, StrLen(name) + 1, 0);
            for (i = StrLen(name); i > 0; --i)
            {
                if ( (name[i] == '/') || (name[i] == '\\') )
                    break;
            }
            if (i == 0)
                i = StrLen(name);
            StrNCopy(badPath, name, i);
            FrmCustomAlert(altCreateFileBadPath, name,
                           badPath, "");
            MemPtrFree(badPath);
            break;

        default:
            errString = MemPtrNew(maxStrIToALen);
            FrmCustomAlert(altCreateFileError, name,
                           StrIToA(errString, error), "");
            MemPtrFree(errString);
    }
}
```

**Palm OS Cobalt**

```
void CreateFile (char *name)
{
    status_t  error;
    char      badPath[maxStrIToALen];
    char      errString[maxStrIToALen];
    int8_t    i;


    if (! name)
    {
        FrmAlert(altNoFileNamed);
        return;
    }

    error = VFSFileCreate(gVolRefNum, name);
    switch (error)
    {
        case errNone:
            FrmCustomAlert(altCreateFile, name, "", "");
            break;

        case vfsErrBadName:
            FrmCustomAlert(altCreateFileInvalid, name, "",
                        "");
            break;

        case vfsErrFileAlreadyExists:
            FrmCustomAlert(altCreateFileExists, name, "",
                        "");
            break;

        case vfsErrDirectoryNotFound:
            memset(badPath, 0, maxStrIToALen);
            for (i = strlen(name); i > 0; --i)
            {
                if ( (name[i] == '/') || (name[i] == '\\') )
                    break;
            }
            if (i == 0)
                i = strlen(name);
            strncpy(badPath, name, i);
            FrmCustomAlert(altCreateFileBadPath, name,
                        badPath, "");
            break;

        default:
            FrmCustomAlert(altCreateFileError, name,
                        StrIToA(errString, error), "");
    }
}
```

Quick examination of the code for CreateFile reveals it to be nearly identical to the code for CreateDirectory. This is not all that surprising, given that VFSDirCreate and VFSFileCreate return most of the same error values. The primary difference is that CreateFile calls slightly different alerts, all of which replace the word *directory* with the word *file* so as not to confuse the user who reads the alerts.

# Deleting Files and Directories

An application can delete both files and directories with the same function: VFSFileDelete. The prototype for VFSFileDelete looks like this:

**Palm OS Garnet**
```
Err VFSFileDelete(UInt16 volRefNum, const Char *pathNameP)
```

**Palm OS Cobalt**
```
status_t VFSFileDelete(uint16_t volRefNum,
                       const char *pathNameP)
```

The parameters for VFSFileDelete are the same as those described earlier in this chapter for VFSDir Create and VFSFileCreate. The VFSFileDelete function can delete only a file or directory that is not open. If you want to delete a file that is open, you need to close it with VFSFileClose before calling VFSFileDelete.

VFS Test calls VFSFileDelete from two functions: DeleteDirectory and DeleteFile. The two functions look like this:

**Palm OS Garnet**
```
void DeleteDirectory (Char *name)
{
    Err    error;
    Char   *errString;


    if (! name)
    {
        FrmAlert(altNoDirectoryNamed);
        return;
    }

    error = VFSFileDelete(gVolRefNum, name);
    switch (error)
    {
        case errNone:
            FrmCustomAlert(altDeleteDir, name, "", "");
            break;

        case vfsErrBadName:
            FrmCustomAlert(altDeleteDirInvalid, name, "",
                           "");
            break;

        case vfsErrFileNotFound:
            FrmCustomAlert(altDeleteDirFileNotFound, name,
                           "", "");
            break;
```

```
            case vfsErrDirNotEmpty:
                FrmCustomAlert(altDeleteDirNotEmpty, name, "",
                            "");
                break;

        default:
            errString = MemPtrNew(maxStrIToALen);
            FrmCustomAlert(altDeleteDirError, name,
                        StrIToA(errString, error), "");
            MemPtrFree(errString);
    }
}


void DeleteFile (Char *name)
{
    Err        error;
    Char       *errString;
    FileRef    fileRef;
    UInt32     attributes;


    if (! name)
    {
        FrmAlert(altNoFileNamed);
        return;
    }

    // Make sure the file isn't actually a directory.
    error = VFSFileOpen(gVolRefNum, name, vfsModeRead,
                    &fileRef);
    if (! error)
    {
        error = VFSFileGetAttributes(fileRef, &attributes);
        if (! error)
        {
            if (attributes & vfsFileAttrDirectory)
            {
                VFSFileClose(fileRef);
                FrmCustomAlert(altDeleteFileIsDirectory,
                            name, "", "");
                return;
            }
            VFSFileClose(fileRef);
        }
    }

    error = VFSFileDelete(gVolRefNum, name);
    switch (error)
    {
        case errNone:
            FrmCustomAlert(altDeleteFile, name, "", "");
            break;
```

```
        case vfsErrBadName:
            FrmCustomAlert(altDeleteFileInvalid, name, "",
                            "");
            break;

        case vfsErrFileNotFound:
            FrmCustomAlert(altDeleteFileFileNotFound, name,
                            "", "");
            break;

        default:
            errString = MemPtrNew(maxStrIToALen);
            FrmCustomAlert(altDeleteFileError, name,
                            StrIToA(errString, error), "");
            MemPtrFree(errString);
    }
}
```

**Palm OS Cobalt**

```
void DeleteDirectory (char *name)
{
    status_t    error;
    char        errString[maxStrIToALen];


    if (! name)
    {
        FrmAlert(altNoDirectoryNamed);
        return;
    }

    error = VFSFileDelete(gVolRefNum, name);
    switch (error)
    {
        case errNone:
            FrmCustomAlert(altDeleteDir, name, "", "");
            break;

        case vfsErrBadName:
            FrmCustomAlert(altDeleteDirInvalid, name, "",
                            "");
            break;

        case vfsErrFileNotFound:
            FrmCustomAlert(altDeleteDirFileNotFound, name,
                            "", "");
            break;

        case vfsErrDirNotEmpty:
            FrmCustomAlert(altDeleteDirNotEmpty, name, "",
                            "");
            break;
```

```
            default:
                FrmCustomAlert(altDeleteDirError, name,
                            StrIToA(errString, error), "");
    }
}


void DeleteFile (Char *name)
{
    status_t  error;
    char      errString[maxStrIToALen];
    FileRef   fileRef;
    uint32_t  attributes;


    if (! name)
    {
        FrmAlert(altNoFileNamed);
        return;
    }

    // Make sure the file isn't actually a directory.
    error = VFSFileOpen(gVolRefNum, name, vfsModeRead,
                        &fileRef);
    if (error == errNone)
    {
        error = VFSFileGetAttributes(fileRef, &attributes);
        if (error == errNone)
        {
            if (attributes & vfsFileAttrDirectory)
            {
                VFSFileClose(fileRef);
                FrmCustomAlert(altDeleteFileIsDirectory,
                            name, "", "");
                return;
            }
            VFSFileClose(fileRef);
        }
    }

    error = VFSFileDelete(gVolRefNum, name);
    switch (error)
    {
        case errNone:
            FrmCustomAlert(altDeleteFile, name, "", "");
            break;

        case vfsErrBadName:
            FrmCustomAlert(altDeleteFileInvalid, name, "",
                        "");
            break;

        case vfsErrFileNotFound:
            FrmCustomAlert(altDeleteFileFileNotFound, name,
                        "", "");
            break;
```

```
        default:
            FrmCustomAlert(altDeleteFileError, name,
                        StrIToA(errString, error), "");
    }
}
```

Even though both `DeleteDirectory` and `DeleteFile` call `VFSFileDelete` to do their work, they do a couple of things differently. First of all, `DeleteFile` checks the file to see if it is a directory and, if it is, refuses to delete it. `DeleteFile` could just as easily delete a directory as it could a file, given that `VFSFileDelete` happily deletes either. However, it could be confusing to the user to have a Delete File command remove a directory, so `DeleteFile` opens the file or directory first using `VFSFileOpen`, which is covered in more detail next in the "Opening and Closing Files" section. Once open, `DeleteFile` can determine whether it is dealing with a file or a directory by calling `VFSFileGetAttributes`, which is detailed later in the "Retrieving and Setting File Information" section.

The other way in which `DeleteDirectory` and `DeleteFile` differ is in their handling of errors. `DeleteFile` rules out the possibility of the file's being a directory early on when it checks the file attributes, so the routine does not need to deal with directory-specific errors, like `vfsErrDirNotEmpty`, which `VFSFileDelete` returns when it tries to delete a directory that contains files or subdirectories. The following table outlines the most common errors returned by `VFSFileDelete`.

| Error Constant | Description |
|---|---|
| `vfsErrBadName` | File or directory name contains invalid characters. |
| `vfsErrFileNotFound` | File or directory path passed to `VFSFileDelete` does not exist. |
| `vfsErrDirNotEmpty` | `VFSFileDelete` attempted to delete a directory that still contains files or subdirectories. |

## Opening and Closing Files

Many VFS manager routines work only on a file that is open. To open a file or directory, call the `VFSFileOpen` routine:

**Palm OS Garnet**
```
Err VFSFileOpen (UInt16 volRefNum, const Char *pathNameP,
    UInt16 openMode, FileRef *fileRefP)
```

**Palm OS Cobalt**
```
status_t VFSFileOpen (uint16_t volRefNum,
    const char *pathNameP, uint16_t openMode,
    FileRef *fileRefP)
```

The `volRefNum` parameter contains the volume reference number, and `pathNameP` is a pointer to a null-terminated string representing the path to the file or directory to open.

The `openMode` parameter is a bit field whose flags determine how the file should be opened. The following table describes the different open mode constants.

| Constant | Value | Description |
|---|---|---|
| vfsModeExclusive | 0x0001U | Locks the file or directory, preventing other callers from using the file or directory until it is closed with VFSFileClose. |
| vfsModeRead | 0x0002U | Opens the file or directory for reading. |
| vfsModeWrite | 0x0004U \| vfsModeExclusive | Opens the file or directory for writing. The vfsModeWrite mode includes vfsModeExclusive, implicitly preventing access to the file until by other callers until the file is closed. |
| vfsModeReadWrite | vfsModeWrite \| vfsModeRead | Opens the file or directory for reading and writing. |
| vfsModeCreate | 0x0008U | Creates the file or directory if it doesn't already exist. This is a shortcut that allows you to create and open a file in one step, without first calling VFSFileCreate or VFSDirCreate to create the file or directory. This mode is implemented in the VFS layer rather than by the file system library. |
| vfsModeTruncate | 0x0010U | Truncates the file to zero bytes in length upon opening. Use this mode with care because it deletes all data that was contained in the file. Like vfsModeCreate, this mode also is implemented as part of the VFS layer. |
| vfsModeLeaveOpen | 0x0020U | Leaves the file open, even after the opening application exits. |

VFSFileOpen returns a unique file reference number in its final argument, fileRefP. Much like the volume reference number required by many VFS functions, this file reference is required by any function that works with open files or directories.

When you are done working with a file, close it using VFSFileClose:

**Palm OS Garnet**
```
Err VFSFileClose (FileRef fileRef)
```

**Palm OS Cobalt**
```
status_t VFSFileClose (FileRef fileRef)
```

VFSFileClose takes a single argument—the file reference number of an open file.

# Retrieving and Setting File Information

Every file in an expansion module has attributes—a series of flags that identify specific properties of the file. To retrieve these values, use the VFSFileGetAttributes routine:

**Palm OS Garnet**
```
Err VFSFileGetAttributes (FileRef fileRef,
    UInt32 *attributesP)
```

**Palm OS Cobalt**
```
status_t VFSFileGetAttributes (FileRef fileRef,
    uint32_t *attributesP)
```

As arguments, VFSFileGetAttributes takes a reference to an open file and a pointer to a UInt32 value that receives the file's attributes. The attributes are in the form of a bit field. The following table details the constants defined for flags in this bit field and what they mean.

| Constant | Value | Description |
|---|---|---|
| vfsFileAttrReadOnly | 0x00000001UL | File or directory is read-only. |
| vfsFileAttrHidden | 0x00000002UL | File or directory is hidden. |
| vfsFileAttrSystem | 0x00000004UL | File or directory is marked for special use by the operating system. |
| vfsFileAttrVolumeLabel | 0x00000008UL | File is a volume label. |
| vfsFileAttrDirectory | 0x00000010UL | File is a directory. |
| vfsFileAttrArchive | 0x00000020UL | File or directory is marked for archival. |
| vfsFileAttrLink | 0x00000040UL | File is actually a link to another file or directory. |

By comparing the attributes returned from VFSFileGetAttributes with the constants in the table, an application can discover a file or directory's properties. For example, VFS Test's DeleteFile routine uses the vfsFileAttrDirectory to determine whether a file is actually a directory, as shown in this excerpt:

**Palm OS Garnet**
```
Err      error;
FileRef  fileRef;
UInt32   attributes;

error = VFSFileGetAttributes(fileRef, &attributes);
if (! error)
{
    if (attributes & vfsFileAttrDirectory)
    {
        // File is a directory.
    }
}
```

**Palm OS Cobalt**

```
status_t  error;
FileRef   fileRef;
uint32_t  attributes;

error = VFSFileGetAttributes(fileRef, &attributes);
if (error == errNone)
{
    if (attributes & vfsFileAttrDirectory)
    {
        // File is a directory.
    }
}
```

You also can change most of the file attributes with the VFSFileSetAttributes routine, which has the following prototype:

**Palm OS Garnet**

```
Err VFSFileSetAttributes (FileRef fileRef,
    UInt32 attributes)
```

**Palm OS Cobalt**

```
status_t VFSFileSetAttributes (FileRef fileRef,
    uint32_t attributes)
```

The arguments to VFSFileSetAttributes are similar to those for VFSFileGetAttributes. Using VFSFileSetAttributes is a simple matter of assembling the attributes and then passing them to the routine. The following example shows how to set a file or directory to be read-only:

**Palm OS Garnet**

```
Err    error;
UInt32 attributes = 0;

attributes |= vfsFileAttrReadOnly;
error = VFSFileSetAttributes(fileRef, attributes);
```

**Palm OS Cobalt**

```
status_t  error;
uint32_t  attributes = 0;

attributes |= vfsFileAttrReadOnly;
error = VFSFileSetAttributes(fileRef, attributes);
```

*You cannot use VFSFileSetAttributes to set the vfsFileAttrDirectory or vfsFileAttrVolumeLabel attributes. VFSDirCreate sets the vfsFileAttrDirectory attribute for you when it creates a directory, and VFSVolumeSetLabel performs a similar function with the vfsFileAttrVolumeLabel attribute when it creates a volume.nam file.*

## Getting and Setting File Dates

If you need to know when a file was created, last modified, or last accessed, you can call VFSFileGetDate:

**Palm OS Garnet**
```
Err VFSFileGetDate (FileRef fileRef, UInt16 whichDate,
    UInt32 *dateP)
```

**Palm OS Cobalt**
```
status_t VFSFileGetDate (FileRef fileRef,
    uint16_t whichDate, uint32_t *dateP)
```

The fileRef parameter is a reference to an open file. The second parameter, whichDate, specifies which date you want to retrieve: creation, modification, or last access. You can choose from the following constant values:

❑ vfsFileDateCreated

❑ vfsFileDateModified

❑ vfsFileDateAccessed

The final parameter, dateP, is a pointer to a UInt32 (uint32_t in Palm OS Cobalt) value that receives the date. File dates are expressed in standard Palm OS date format (seconds past midnight on January 1, 1904).

You also can set file dates using the VFSFileSetDate function, which looks similar to VFSFileGetDate:

**Palm OS Garnet**
```
Err VFSFileSetDate (FileRef fileRef, UInt16 whichDate,
    UInt32 date)
```

**Palm OS Cobalt**
```
status_t VFSFileSetDate (FileRef fileRef,
    uint16_t whichDate, uint32_t date)
```

The following example sets a file's modification date to the current time and date:

**Palm OS Garnet**
```
Err      error;
UInt32   date;

date = TimGetSeconds();
error = VFSFileSetDate(fileRef, vfsFileDateModified, date);
```

**Palm OS Cobalt**
```
status_t   error;
uint32_t   date;

date = TimGetSeconds();
error = VFSFileSetDate(fileRef, vfsFileDateModified, date);
```

## Determining File Size

One other important piece of data you might want to know about a file is its size. You can retrieve a file's size using the VFSFileSize function:

**Palm OS Garnet**
```
Err VFSFileSize (FileRef fileRef, UInt32 *fileSizeP)
```

**Palm OS Cobalt**
```
status_t VFSFileSize (FileRef fileRef, uint32_t *fileSizeP)
```

The `fileRef` parameter is a reference to an open file, and the `fileSizeP` parameter is a pointer that receives the size of the file in bytes.

# Reading Data from Files

An application can read data from a file only if that file has first been opened with `VFSFileOpen`. Once the file is open, there are a couple options for reading the data, depending upon where you want the data to go. The most common destination for data is dynamic memory. Your application could, for example, read text from secondary storage into dynamic memory, and then immediately display that text onscreen. An application may also read data into storage memory, a process which could be used to populate a database from information stored on an expansion card.

If you want to read the data into dynamic memory, usually so you can use it immediately in your application, use `VFSFileRead`:

**Palm OS Garnet**
```
Err VFSFileRead (FileRef fileRef, UInt32 numBytes,
    void *bufP, UInt32 *numBytesReadP)
```

**Palm OS Cobalt**
```
status_t VFSFileRead (FileRef fileRef, uint32_t numBytes,
    void *bufP, uint32_t *numBytesReadP)
```

As with other routines requiring an open file, the first argument to `VFSFileRead` is a file reference. The next argument, `numBytes`, specifies the number of bytes of data to attempt to read from the file. The `bufP` argument is a pointer to a buffer that receives the data read. This pointer must point to an allocated chunk of memory large enough to hold however many bytes you specified in the `numBytes` argument.

The final argument, `numBytesReadP`, is a pointer that receives the number of bytes actually read by `VFSFileRead`. The value you point to does not need to be initialized because `VFSFileRead` automatically sets this value, returning 0 if no bytes were actually read. If you aren't interested in how many bytes were actually read, you can pass `NULL` for the `numBytesReadP` parameter.

Most of the time, you will probably use `VFSFileRead` to read data from a file into dynamic memory, from which it may be used immediately by your application. However, it also is possible to read data directly into storage RAM with the `VFSFileReadData` routine:

**Palm OS Garnet**
```
Err VFSFileReadData (FileRef fileRef, UInt32 numBytes,
    void *bufBaseP, UInt32 offset, UInt32 *numBytesReadP)
```

**Palm OS Cobalt**
```
status_t VFSFileReadData (FileRef fileRef, uint32_t numBytes,
    void *bufBaseP, uint32_t offset, uint32_t *numBytesReadP)
```

The `fileRef`, `numBytes`, and `numBytesReadP` parameters are exactly as for `VFSFileRead`. The `bufBaseP` pointer is similar to the `VFSFileRead` function's `bufP`, but it points to the beginning of a chunk of storage RAM allocated by one of the data manager functions, such as `DmNewRecord`.

The `offset` parameter allows you to write data at a specific byte offset beyond the location pointed to by `bufBaseP`. An offset of 0 means data is written starting at the beginning of the storage memory chunk. Specifying `offset` can be convenient because you can pass in a pointer to the beginning of a record in `bufBaseP` and then write data to a specific part of that record simply by setting `offset` to the location where you want to put the data.

> *If you want to write an application that can store its data both in RAM and on an expansion card, you need to write two different sets of functions in your application: one set that reads and writes data in primary storage and another set that reads and writes data in secondary storage. Because the techniques used to store data in RAM differ significantly from those used to store data on an expansion card, you should also use two different data formats that are designed to work well with each type of storage, and then write conversion routines to change the data from one format to the other. VFSFileReadData is a handy function when performing conversion from the secondary storage format to the primary storage format because it allows your application to copy data directly from an expansion card without first copying it to RAM, thus speeding up the conversion process.*

VFS Test can read data from a file and display it in an alert. The function in VFS Test that accomplishes this task is `ReadFile`:

**Palm OS Garnet**

```
void ReadFile (Char *name)
{
    Err     error;
    Char    *errString;
    Char    *data;
    FileRef fileRef;
    UInt32  fileSize;


    if (! name)
    {
        FrmAlert(altNoFileNamed);
        return;
    }

    error = VFSFileOpen(gVolRefNum, name, vfsModeRead,
                        &fileRef);
    if (error)
    {
        switch (error)
        {
            case vfsErrBadName:
                FrmCustomAlert(altReadFileInvalid, name, "",
                            "");
                break;

            case vfsErrFileNotFound:
                // Note: uses the same alert as DeleteFile.
```

```
                        FrmCustomAlert(altDeleteFileFileNotFound,
                                    name, "", "");
                        break;

                default:
                        errString = MemPtrNew(maxStrIToALen);
                        FrmCustomAlert(altReadFileError, name,
                                    StrIToA(errString, error), "");
                        MemPtrFree(errString);
        }
}
else
{
    error = VFSFileSize(fileRef, &fileSize);
    if (error)
    {
        if (error == vfsErrIsADirectory)
            FrmCustomAlert(altReadFileIsDirectory, name,
                        "", "");
        else
        {
            errString = MemPtrNew(maxStrIToALen);
            FrmCustomAlert(altReadFileError, name,
                        StrIToA(errString, error), "");
            MemPtrFree(errString);
        }
        VFSFileClose(fileRef);
        return;
    }
    else
    {
        // Allocate a buffer large enough to store the
        // file, plus an extra byte to hold a
        // terminating null.
        data = MemPtrNew(fileSize + 1);
        if (! data)
        {
            FrmCustomAlert(altReadFileOutOfMemory, name,
                        "", "");
            VFSFileClose(fileRef);
            return;
        }
        MemSet(data, fileSize + 1, 0);
        error = VFSFileRead(fileRef, fileSize, data,
                        NULL);
        if (error)
        {
            switch (error)
            {
                case vfsErrFileEOF:
                    FrmCustomAlert(altReadFileNoData,
                                name, "", "");
                    break;

                default:
                    errString =
```

```
                             MemPtrNew(maxStrIToALen);
                     FrmCustomAlert(altReadFileError,
                         name, StrIToA(errString, error),
                         "");
                     MemPtrFree(errString);
                }
            }
            else
                FrmCustomAlert(altReadFile, name, data, "");

            VFSFileClose(fileRef);
            MemPtrFree(data);
        }
    }
}
```

**Palm OS Cobalt**

```
void ReadFile (char *name)
{
    status_t  error;
    char      errString[maxStrIToALen];
    char      *data;
    FileRef   fileRef;
    uint32_t  fileSize;


    if (! name)
    {
        FrmAlert(altNoFileNamed);
        return;
    }

    error = VFSFileOpen(gVolRefNum, name, vfsModeRead,
                        &fileRef);
    if (error < errNone)
    {
        switch (error)
        {
            case vfsErrBadName:
                FrmCustomAlert(altReadFileInvalid, name, "",
                            "");
                break;

            case vfsErrFileNotFound:
                // Note: uses the same alert as DeleteFile.
                FrmCustomAlert(altDeleteFileFileNotFound,
                            name, "", "");
                break;

            default:
                FrmCustomAlert(altReadFileError, name,
                            StrIToA(errString, error), "");
        }
    }
    else
```

```
    {
        error = VFSFileSize(fileRef, &fileSize);
        if (error < errNone)
        {
            if (error == vfsErrIsADirectory)
                FrmCustomAlert(altReadFileIsDirectory, name,
                               "", "");
            else
            {
                FrmCustomAlert(altReadFileError, name,
                               StrIToA(errString, error), "");
            }
            VFSFileClose(fileRef);
            return;
        }
        else
        {
            // Allocate a buffer large enough to store the
            // file, plus an extra byte to hold a
            // terminating null.
            data = malloc(fileSize + 1);
            if (! data)
            {
                FrmCustomAlert(altReadFileOutOfMemory, name,
                               "", "");
                VFSFileClose(fileRef);
                return;
            }
            memset(data, 0, fileSize + 1);
            error = VFSFileRead(fileRef, fileSize, data,
                               NULL);
            if (error < errNone)
            {
                switch (error)
                {
                    case vfsErrFileEOF:
                        FrmCustomAlert(altReadFileNoData,
                                       name, "", "");
                        break;

                    default:
                        FrmCustomAlert(altReadFileError,
                            name, StrIToA(errString, error),
                            "");
                }
            }
            else
                FrmCustomAlert(altReadFile, name, data, "");

            VFSFileClose(fileRef);
            free(data);
        }
    }
}
```

`ReadFile` reads files in an unsophisticated way:

1. `ReadFile` opens the file with `VFSFileOpen`.

2. The `ReadFile` function determines how large the file is using `VFSFileSize` and allocates a buffer called `data` using `MemPtrNew` in Palm OS Garnet, or `malloc` in Palm OS Cobalt. This buffer is large enough to store the file, plus an extra byte for a terminating null.

3. `ReadFile` calls `VFSFileRead` to read the entire file into the allocated memory buffer.

4. `ReadFile` calls `FrmCustomAlert`, passing `data` as one of the parameters, to display the file's data in a custom alert.

5. `ReadFile` cleans up by closing the file with `VFSFileClose` and freeing `data` with `MemPtrFree` or `free`.

This procedure works well for small text files, but it has a number of important limitations:

❑ If the file passed to `ReadFile` is particularly large, there may not be enough dynamic memory available on the handheld to read the entire file into the `data` buffer, in which case `ReadFile` displays an alert to tell the user that there isn't enough available memory to complete the operation.

❑ An alert dialog box can display only a limited amount of text. Even if there is enough memory to read in the whole file, only a short section of the top of the file is actually displayed (see Figure 17-4).

Figure 17-4

❑ If the file contains any null characters near the beginning of the file, the display will be further shortened because `FrmCustomAlert` treats such a null as the end of the string that it should display.

## Positioning a File Pointer

VFS Test is only a small sample application; in a real application, you will probably need to use more complicated techniques to read and display data from secondary storage. Not only is it likely that data stored on the expansion card is larger than the dynamic RAM your application has available, but reading in an entire file before displaying it is inefficient and requires that the user sit and wait for data to be displayed.

The strategy most applications should employ is to read in data a little bit at a time. Not only does this prevent the application from running out of dynamic memory in which to keep the data, but it also allows your application to perform other tasks in between reads, such as updating a progress meter or the display itself.

*The optimum length of data to read with each call to VFSFileRead or VFSFileReadData varies depending on the type of data being read and what your application intends to do with the data. Experiment with different values for the numBytes parameter to find what works best.*

For each file that is open, the VFS manager keeps track of a *file pointer*, which is the offset into the file where read and write operations occur. By default, when VFSFileOpen opens a file, the file pointer of that file is set to the start of the file's data. VFSFileRead, VFSFileReadData, and VFSFileWrite all advance the pointer as they read data from or write data to the file. For example, consider the following call to VFSFileRead, made on a newly opened file:

```
error = VFSFileRead(fileRef, 8, buffer, NULL);
```

Assuming that there are at least eight bytes of data to read from the file, the file pointer is now located eight bytes from the beginning of the file. The next call to VFSFileRead will begin reading data from the new position of the file pointer.

You can retrieve the current position of the file pointer by calling VFSFileTell:

**Palm OS Garnet**
```
Err VFSFileTell (FileRef fileRef, UInt32 *filePosP)
```

**Palm OS Cobalt**
```
status_t VFSFileTell (FileRef fileRef, uint32_t *filePosP)
```

VFSFileTell takes the usual file reference as its first argument and returns the file pointer position by way of a pointer in its second argument. The value returned by VFSFileTell in its filePosP argument represents the number of bytes from the start of the file.

Although the various read and write functions in the VFS manager move the file pointer automatically as they work, it is sometimes desirable to move the file pointer manually. Putting the file pointer exactly where you want it allows you to create fixed-width data structures within a file, which can be a reasonably efficient way to access data that is buried deep within the file. The function that allows you to position the file pointer is VFSFileSeek:

**Palm OS Garnet**
```
Err VFSFileSeek (FileRef fileRef, FileOrigin origin,
    Int32 offset)
```

**Palm OS Cobalt**
```
status_t VFSFileSeek (FileRef fileRef, FileOrigin origin,
    int32_t offset)
```

The first argument to VFSFileSeek is the reference number of an open file. Next is the origin parameter, which tells VFSFileSeek what it should count as the origin point when moving the file pointer. The following table details the constant values you can use with the origin parameter.

| Constant | Description |
|---|---|
| vfsOriginBeginning | Moves the file pointer relative to the beginning of the file |
| vfsOriginCurrent | Moves the file pointer relative to the current position of the file pointer |
| vfsOriginEnd | Moves the file pointer relative to the end of the file |

The offset parameter specifies how many bytes to move the file pointer, relative to whatever position you specified in the origin parameter. You may specify positive or negative values for offset; positive values move the file pointer toward the end of the file, and negative values move the file pointer toward the beginning of the file. Only positive values of offset are allowed if origin is vfsOriginBeginning, and only negative values are allowed if origin is vfsOriginEnd. A value of 0 sets the file pointer to the position specified by the origin parameter.

*If you attempt to set the file pointer to a position beyond the end of the file, VFSFileSeek positions the file pointer at the end of the file instead.*

The following code snippet shows how you can use VFSFileSeek to position the file pointer at the beginning of a fixed-width record in a file:

**Palm OS Garnet**
```
UInt32 offset = recordIndex * (sizeof(MyRecordStructure));
error = VFSFileSeek(fileRef, vfsOriginBeginning, offset);
```

**Palm OS Cobalt**
```
uint32_t offset = recordIndex * (sizeof(MyRecordStructure));
error = VFSFileSeek(fileRef, vfsOriginBeginning, offset);
```

This example assumes that records are stored consecutively in the file, and each record consists of a specific data structure called MyRecordStructure. The offset is calculated by multiplying the index of the desired record (recordIndex) by the length of MyRecordStructure.

One more useful file pointer tool is the VFSFileEOF function, which can be used to determine if the file pointer is located at the end of the file. The prototype for VFSFileEOF looks like this:

**Palm OS Garnet**
```
Err VFSFileEOF (FileRef fileRef)
```

**Palm OS Cobalt**
```
status_t VFSFileEOF (FileRef fileRef)
```

The VFSFileEOF function returns vfsErrFileEOF if the file pointer is located at the end of the file, or errNone if the file pointer is located elsewhere in the file. VFSFileEOF is primarily useful when looping through a file toward its end. Checking if VFSFileEOF equals vfsErrFileEOF provides a handy way of terminating the loop.

The following example reads data from a file a byte at a time, until either the end of the file or the end of the receiving buffer has been reached:

**Palm OS Garnet**
```
Err     error;
UInt16  maxSize = 4096;
UInt16  bytesRead = 0;
Char    *buffer = MemPtrNew(maxSize);

while ( ((error = VFSFileEOF(fileRef)) == errNone) &&
        (bytesRead < maxSize) )
{
    error = VFSFileRead(fileRef, 1, buffer, NULL);
    if (error)
    {
        // Handle the error, possibly by breaking from
        // the loop.
    }
    bytesRead++;
}
MemPtrFree(buffer);

if (error != vfsErrFileEOF)
{
    // An actual error terminated the loop instead of
    // reaching the end of the file.
}
```

**Palm OS Cobalt**
```
status_t  error;
uint16_t  maxSize = 4096;
uint16_t  bytesRead = 0;
char      buffer[maxSize];

while ( ((error = VFSFileEOF(fileRef)) == errNone) &&
        (bytesRead < maxSize) )
{
    error = VFSFileRead(fileRef, 1, buffer, NULL);
    if (error < errNone)
    {
        // Handle the error, possibly by breaking from
        // the loop.
    }
    bytesRead++;
}

if (error != vfsErrFileEOF)
{
    // An actual error terminated the loop instead of
    // reaching the end of the file.
}
```

# Writing Data to Files

To write data to an open file, use the VFSFileWrite function:

**Palm OS Garnet**
```
Err VFSFileWrite (FileRef fileRef, UInt32 numBytes,
    const void *dataP, UInt32 *numBytesWrittenP)
```

**Palm OS Cobalt**
```
status_t VFSFileWrite (FileRef fileRef, uint32_t numBytes,
    const void *dataP, uint32_t *numBytesWrittenP)
```

The arguments for VFSFileWrite are nearly identical to those for VFSFileRead. The familiar fileRef heads up the list, followed by numBytes, which represents the number of bytes to write to the file. The dataP argument is a pointer to a buffer containing the data to be written, and numBytesWrittenP is a pointer that accepts the number of bytes actually written when VFSFileWrite returns. If you don't need to know how many bytes were written, pass NULL for the numBytesWrittenP argument.

VFS Test uses VFSFileWrite in its WriteFile routine:

**Palm OS Garnet**
```
void WriteFile (Char *name, Char *data)
{
    Err     error;
    Char    *errString;
    FileRef fileRef;
    UInt32  fileSize;
    UInt32  attributes;


    if (! name)
    {
        FrmAlert(altNoFileNamed);
        return;
    }

    if (! data)
    {
        FrmAlert(altNoData);
        return;
    }

    error = VFSFileOpen(gVolRefNum, name, vfsModeReadWrite,
                    &fileRef);
    if (error)
    {
        switch (error)
        {
            case vfsErrBadName:
                FrmCustomAlert(altWriteFileInvalid, name,
                            "", "");
```

```
                    break;

            case vfsErrFileNotFound:
                // Note: uses the same alert as DeleteFile.
                FrmCustomAlert(altDeleteFileFileNotFound,
                            name, "", "");
                break;

            default:
                errString = MemPtrNew(maxStrIToALen);
                FrmCustomAlert(altWriteFileError, name,
                            StrIToA(errString, error), "");
                MemPtrFree(errString);
        }
    }
    else
    {
        error = VFSFileWrite(fileRef, StrLen(data), data,
                        NULL);
        if (error)
        {
            switch (error)
            {
                case vfsErrIsADirectory:
                    FrmCustomAlert(altWriteFileIsDirectory,
                                name, "", "");
                    break;

                case vfsErrVolumeFull:
                    FrmCustomAlert(altWriteFileVolumeFull,
                                name, "", "");
                    break;

                default:
                    errString = MemPtrNew(maxStrIToALen);
                    FrmCustomAlert(altWriteFileError, name,
                                StrIToA(errString, error),
                                "");
                    MemPtrFree(errString);
            }
            VFSFileClose(fileRef);
            return;
        }
        else
        {
            FrmCustomAlert(altWriteFile, name, "", "");
            VFSFileClose(fileRef);
        }
    }
}
```

**Palm OS Cobalt**

```
void WriteFile (char *name, char *data)
{
    status_t  error;
```

```
char      errString[maxStrIToALen];
FileRef   fileRef;
uint32_t  fileSize;
uint32_t  attributes;


if (! name)
{
    FrmAlert(altNoFileNamed);
    return;
}

if (! data)
{
    FrmAlert(altNoData);
    return;
}

error = VFSFileOpen(gVolRefNum, name, vfsModeReadWrite,
                    &fileRef);
if (error < errNone)
{
    switch (error)
    {
        case vfsErrBadName:
            FrmCustomAlert(altWriteFileInvalid, name,
                           "", "");
            break;

        case vfsErrFileNotFound:
            // Note: uses the same alert as DeleteFile.
            FrmCustomAlert(altDeleteFileFileNotFound,
                           name, "", "");
            break;

        default:
            FrmCustomAlert(altWriteFileError, name,
                           StrIToA(errString, error), "");
    }
}
else
{
    error = VFSFileWrite(fileRef, StrLen(data), data,
                         NULL);
    if (error < errNone)
    {
        switch (error)
        {
            case vfsErrIsADirectory:
                FrmCustomAlert(altWriteFileIsDirectory,
                               name, "", "");
                break;

            case vfsErrVolumeFull:
                FrmCustomAlert(altWriteFileVolumeFull,
```

```
                                name, "", "");
                    break;

            default:
                FrmCustomAlert(altWriteFileError, name,
                            StrIToA(errString, error),
                            "");
            }
            VFSFileClose(fileRef);
            return;
        }
        else
        {
            FrmCustomAlert(altWriteFile, name, "", "");
            VFSFileClose(fileRef);
        }
    }
}
```

WriteFile is a straightforward function. It receives the contents of VFS Test's Data text field and writes that text as a null-terminated string to the file specified in VFS Test's Name text field. Most of the code in WriteFile is a series of error handlers to let the user know what is going on if the write operation was unsuccessful. The following table outlines the most common errors that occur when calling VFSFileWrite.

| Error | Description |
|---|---|
| vfsErrIsADirectory | File reference passed to VFSFileWrite refers to a directory, not a file. VFSFileWrite cannot write to directories, only to files. |
| vfsErrVolumeFull | Volume does not have enough space remaining to write the requested data. |

*If VFSFileWrite returns vfsErrFilePermissionDenied, and you're sure that the file and the volume containing it are not set to read-only, check to make sure you opened the file by passing vfsModeWrite or vfsModeReadWrite to VFSFileOpen. Opening a file with vfsModeRead and then attempting to write to it can make for a frustrating debugging experience.*

## Finding Files

There are times when an application may need to find a file without knowing exactly where it is located, or when an application needs to present the user with a list of files available on the expansion card. The VFSDirEntryEnumerate function allows an application to iterate over the entries in an open directory:

**Palm OS Garnet**
```
Err VFSDirEntryEnumerate (FileRef dirRef,
    UInt32 *dirEntryIteratorP, FileInfoType *infoP)
```

**Palm OS Cobalt**
```
status_t VFSDirEntryEnumerate (FileRef dirRef,
    uint32_t *dirEntryIteratorP, FileInfoType *infoP)
```

The dirRef parameter is simply the file reference returned from the VFSFileOpen routine.

VFSDirEntryEnumerate operates in much the same fashion as VFSVolumeEnumerate, discussed earlier in this chapter. VFSDirEntryEnumerate uses the dirEntryIteratorP parameter to keep track of its place in the directory. By making multiple calls to VFSDirEntryEnumerate, the function traverses all the files and subdirectories within a directory, returning information about each in turn. Before calling VFSDirEntryEnumerate for the first time on a given directory, set the variable that dirEntryIteratorP points to equal to the constant vfsIteratorStart. Each time VFSDirEntryEnumerate returns, it increments the value pointed to by dirEntryIteratorP.

The infoP parameter is a pointer to a FileInfoType structure, which looks like this:

**Palm OS Garnet**

```
typedef struct FileInfoTag {
    UInt32 attributes;
    Char *nameP;
    UInt16 nameBufLen;
} FileInfoType, *FileInfoPtr;
```

**Palm OS Cobalt**

```
typedef struct FileInfoTag {
    uint32_t attributes;
    char *nameP;
    uint16_t nameBufLen;
    uint16_t reserved;
} FileInfoType, *FileInfoPtr;
```

The attributes member of this structure is where VFSDirEntryEnumerate returns the file attributes of the file or directory that it has found. The nameP member points to a chunk of memory that VFSDirEntryEnumerate fills with the name of the file or directory, and nameBufLen contains the length of the nameP buffer in bytes. You must initialize the nameP and nameBufLen members of this structure before calling VFSDirEntryEnumerate.

The following sample code shows VFSDirEntryEnumerate in action, enumerating the contents of the root directory:

**Palm OS Garnet**

```
Err       error;
FileInfoType  info;
FileRef  dirRef;
UInt32   dirIterator;
Char *fileName = MemPtrNew(256);

error = VFSFileOpen(volRefNum, "/", vfsModeRead, &dirRef);
if (error)
{
    // Handle directory opening error.
}
else
{
    info.nameP = fileName;
    info.nameBufLen = MemPtrSize(fileName);
    dirIterator = vfsIteratorStart;
    while (dirIterator != vfsIteratorStop)
    {
```

```
            error = VFSDirEntryEnumerate(dirRef, &dirIterator,
                                        &info);
            if (error)
            {
                // Handle the error, possibly breaking out of
                // the while loop.
            }
            else
            {
                // Do something with the information in the
                // info structure.
            }
        }
        VFSFileClose(dirRef);
}
MemPtrFree(fileName);
```

**Palm OS Cobalt**

```
status_t   error;
FileInfoType  info;
FileRef    dirRef;
uint32_t   dirIterator;
char       fileName[256];


error = VFSFileOpen(volRefNum, "/", vfsModeRead, &dirRef);
if (error)
{
    // Handle directory opening error.
}
else
{
    info.nameP = fileName;
    info.nameBufLen = MemPtrSize(fileName);
    dirIterator = vfsIteratorStart;
    while (dirIterator != vfsIteratorStop)
    {
        error = VFSDirEntryEnumerate(dirRef, &dirIterator,
                                    &info);
        if (error < errNone)
        {
            // Handle the error, possibly breaking out of
            // the while loop.
        }
        else
        {
            // Do something with the information in the
            // info structure.
        }
    }
    VFSFileClose(dirRef);
}
```

# Retrieving Default File Locations

The Virtual File System supports the concept of a *default directory,* which is a place on the expansion card where files with a specific extension or MIME (Multipurpose Internet Mail Extensions) type should go. The default directory for a particular file type is dependent on the manufacturer of the handheld and the expansion slot driver that manufacturer provides. For example, the SD slot driver provided by palmOne registers files with a .jpg extension to the /DCIM directory.

Default file locations exist to provide easy compatibility with other devices that use the same expansion media but don't run Palm OS. For example, many digital cameras that use SD media store their images in the /DCIM directory, which is why the SD slot driver puts .jpg images in that directory.

To find the default directory for a particular type of file, use the VFSGetDefaultDirectory function, which has the following prototype:

**Palm OS Garnet**

```
Err VFSGetDefaultDirectory (UInt16 volRefNum,
    const Char *fileTypeStr, Char *pathStr,
    UInt16 *bufLenP)
```

**Palm OS Cobalt**

```
status_t VFSGetDefaultDirectory (uint16_t volRefNum,
    const char *fileTypeStr, char *pathStr,
    uint16_t *bufLenP)
```

The first argument, volRefNum, is the reference number of the volume. The fileTypeStr argument is a pointer to a null-terminated string you provide that contains either the MIME type or file extension you are interested in. VFSGetDefaultDirectory uses the pointer in the pathStr argument to return the default directory path; you must allocate a buffer for pathStr to point to before calling VFSGetDefaultDirectory. When calling VFSGetDefaultDirectory, set the variable pointed to by the final argument, bufLenP, to the length of the pathStr buffer, in bytes. VFSGetDefaultDirectory returns in the bufLenP argument the actual number of bytes written to pathStr.

The following example determines the path for files with a .jpg extension:

**Palm OS Garnet**

```
Err     error;
UInt16  pathLength = 256;
Char    *pathStr = MemPtrNew(pathLength);

error = VFSGetDefaultDirectory(volRefNum, ".jpg", pathStr,
                               &pathLength);
// Do something with pathStr here.
MemPtrFree(pathStr);
```

**Palm OS Cobalt**

```
status_t error;
uint16_t pathLength = 256;
char     pathStr[pathLength];

error = VFSGetDefaultDirectory(volRefNum, ".jpg", pathStr,
                               &pathLength);
// Do something with pathStr here.
```

If you want to find the default directory for files based on their MIME type, you can do something similar to the next example, which looks for the default directory of files with MIME type image/jpeg:

```
error = VFSGetDefaultDirectory (volRefNum, "image/jpeg",
                                pathStr, &pathLength);
```

# Dealing with Palm OS Databases

The VFS manager provides a few convenient functions for dealing with standard Palm OS databases that reside in secondary storage. These functions allow an application to access information and data from record databases, which have a file extension of .pdb, and from resource databases, which have a file extension of .prc.

> The functions described in this section do not allow access to schema databases stored in secondary storage. They are used only with classic and extended databases.

The VFSFileDBGetRecord function is similar to DmGetRecord, in that it provides access to the attributes and data of a record in a Palm OS database. VFSFileDBGetRecord takes a reference to an open .pdb file and a record number and returns a handle to the record's data, the attributes of the record, and the unique identifier of that record. The prototype for VFSFileDBGetRecord looks like this:

**Palm OS Garnet**
```
Err VFSFileDBGetRecord (FileRef ref, UInt16 recIndex,
    MemHandle *recHP, UInt8 *recAttrP, UInt32 *uniqueIDP)
```

**Palm OS Cobalt**
```
status_t VFSFileDBGetRecord (FileRef ref, uint16_t recIndex,
    MemHandle *recHP, uint8_t *recAttrP, uint32_t *uniqueIDP)
```

You can retrieve a resource from a resource database using VFSFileDBGetResource, which is analogous to DmGetResource. VFSFileDBGetResource looks like this:

**Palm OS Garnet**
```
Err VFSFileDBGetResource (FileRef ref, DmResType type,
    DmResID resID, MemHandle *resHP)
```

**Palm OS Cobalt**
```
status_t VFSFileDBGetResource (FileRef ref, DmResType type,
    DmResID resID, MemHandle *resHP)
```

If you need information about an open .pdb or .prc file only, use the VFSFileDBInfo function:

**Palm OS Garnet**
```
Err VFSFileDBInfo (FileRef ref, Char *nameP,
    UInt16 *attributesP, UInt16 *versionP, UInt32 *crDateP,
    UInt32 *modDateP, UInt32 *bckUpDateP, UInt32 *modNumP,
    MemHandle *appInfoHP, MemHandle *sortInfoHP,
    UInt32 *typeP, UInt32 *creatorP, UInt16 *numRecordsP)
```

**Palm OS Cobalt**

```
status_t VFSFileDBInfo (FileRef ref, char *nameP,
    uint16_t *attributesP, uint16_t *versionP,
    uint32_t *crDateP, uint32_t *modDateP,
    uint32_t *bckUpDateP, uint32_t *modNumP,
    MemHandle *appInfoHP, MemHandle *sortInfoHP,
    uint32_t *typeP, uint32_t *creatorP,
    uint16_t *numRecordsP)
```

> It is tempting to add quick and dirty VFS support to an application by copying its databases to secondary storage using **VFSExportDatabaseToFile**, and then using **VFSFileDBGetRecord** and **VFSFileDBGetResource** to read data directly from the native Palm OS databases. However, parsing the Palm OS database format from a file stored on expansion media is not an efficient process. Frequent calls to **VFSFileDBGetRecord** and **VFSFileDBGetResource** can slow your application to a crawl. If you need to support secondary storage, you are much better off designing your application to store data with **VFSFileWrite** and retrieve information with either **VFSFileRead** or **VFSFileReadData**, even if it means writing your own routines to convert data between a Palm OS native format and a format more suited to VFS storage.

## Moving Palm OS Databases

The VFS manager also provides functions for transferring Palm OS databases between RAM and secondary storage. VFSExportDatabaseToFile copies a database from main memory to an expansion card, and VFSImportDatabaseFromFile copies a database from an expansion card to main memory.

Because moving large databases can be a lengthy process, the VFS manager also provides the VFSExportDatabaseToFileCustom and VFSImportDatabaseFromFileCustom functions, which call a custom callback function you provide to take care of informing the user of the progress of the operation. These two functions make use of the exchange manager, best known for its use in beaming files between handhelds, to perform most of the work involved in transferring the file between main memory and secondary storage.

> Designing the callback functions for **VFSExportDatabaseToFileCustom** and **VFSImportDatabaseFromFileCustom** is similar to designing data transfer for an application that uses the exchange manager. See Chapter 18 for more details.

# Summary

This chapter described how secondary storage works and how to use it in your own applications. After reading this chapter, you should know the following:

❏   The expansion manager is responsible for handling the low-level aspects of expansion slots and drivers, and the VFS manager provides a high-level interface for manipulating volumes, directories, and files.

❏   Palm OS applications can run from an expansion card, but there are limitations to this process.

❏   Detection of card insertion and removal is accomplished through the Palm OS notification mechanism.

❏   Before accessing any files or directories on a volume, you must retrieve a reference to it using `VFSVolumeEnumerate`.

❏   Files may be created using `VFSFileCreate`, directories may be created using `VFSDirCreate`, and both may be deleted using `VFSFileDelete`.

❏   Before any operations can take place on a file or directory, it must be opened with the `VFSFileOpen` function.

❏   Once a file is open, you may read data from it with `VFSFileRead` or `VFSFileReadData`, and you may write to it using `VFSFileWrite`.

❏   You can find the default directory for a particular type of file by calling `VFSGetDefaultDirectory`.

❏   The VFS manager provides facilities for dealing with non-schema Palm OS databases stored on expansion media, including the `VFSFileDBGetRecord`, `VFSFileDBGetResource`, and `VFSFileDBInfo` functions.

# 18

# Sharing Data Through the Exchange Manager

First introduced in Palm OS 3.0, the exchange manager allows the exchange of data objects between two Palm OS handhelds, or between a Palm OS handheld and another suitably equipped device. The exchange manager can handle a variety of transport mechanisms, including infrared (IR), Short Message Service (SMS), and Bluetooth, making it possible to send and receive data on a Palm OS handheld without having to connect devices with cables.

The exchange manager connects to different transport methods through *exchange libraries*, plug-in modules that know how to transfer data over their respective protocols. Regardless of how the data actually travels, your application can use the same simple interface to talk to a wide variety of devices.

When it was first introduced, the primary focus of the exchange manager was transmission of discrete units of data, rather than constant streaming communication. In Palm OS 3.0, the only transport mechanism available to the exchange manager was IR beaming, so it was optimized for beaming records or applications between two handhelds. With the introduction of new types of communication in Palm OS 4.0, Palm expanded the exchange manager to handle more complicated two-way communication.

The exchange manager is still most commonly used to exchange *typed data objects,* which are streams of data that include identifying information about the stream's contents. Palm OS identifies a typed data object in one of three ways:

- ❑  By the creator ID of the application that is responsible for receiving the object

- ❑  By the Multipurpose Internet Mail Extensions (MIME) data type, a system commonly used to identify attachments in e-mail

- ❑  By the filename and extension

Even with its more recent two-way communication ability, the exchange manager is not necessarily the most efficient way to keep a Palm OS handheld in constant communication with another device. In some cases, there might not be an exchange library that implements the type of communication you want to use. In other cases, using the exchange manager might simply add too much overhead to communications. Palm OS provides other interfaces that are much more suited to some kinds of communication, like the serial manager for serial port connections, the IR Library for low-level infrared communication, and the net library for TCP/IP networking. For more details about using the serial port and IR Library, see Chapter 19. TCP/IP networking is covered in Chapter 20.

# Using the Exchange Manager

Central to using the exchange manager is the ExgSocketType structure. Defined in the Palm OS header ExgMgr.h, ExgSocketType holds information about the connection and the type of data being transferred. When sending data, an application needs to fill in the appropriate fields in this structure. Likewise, when receiving data, an application can retrieve information about an incoming data stream and its contents from the socket structure.

*The term "socket," as used by the exchange manager, has nothing to do with socket communications programming.*

The ExgSocketType structure looks like this:

**Palm OS Garnet**

```
typedef struct ExgSocketType {
    UInt16  libraryRef;
    UInt32  socketRef;
    UInt32  target;
    UInt32  count;
    UInt32  length;
    UInt32  time;
    UInt32  appData;
    UInt32  goToCreator;
    ExgGoToType  goToParams;
    UInt16  localMode:1;
    UInt16  packetMode:1;
    UInt16  noGoTo:1;
    UInt16  noStatus:1;
    UInt16  preview:1;
    UInt16  reserved:11;
    Char    *description;
    Char    *type;
    Char    *name;
}
```

**Palm OS Cobalt**

```
typedef struct ExgSocketTag{
    uint16_t    libraryRef;
    uint16_t    socketRefSize;
    uint32_t    socketRef;
    uint32_t    target;
    uint32_t    count;
    uint32_t    length;
    uint32_t    time;
    uint32_t    appData;
    uint32_t    goToCreator;
    ExgGoToType goToParams;
```

```
    uint16_t    localMode:1;
    uint16_t    packetMode:1;
    uint16_t    noGoTo:1;
    uint16_t    noStatus:1;
    uint16_t    preview:1;
    uint16_t    cnvFrom68KApp:1;
    uint16_t    acceptedSocket:1;
    uint16_t    reserved:9;
    uint8_t     componentIndex;
    uint8_t     padding_1;
    char        *description;
    char        *type;
    char        *name;
} ExgSocketType;
```

The following table describes the fields in the ExgSocketType structure.

| Field | Description |
|-------|-------------|
| libraryRef | Internal field used by the exchange manager to identify the exchange library that is in use. Normally, an application does not need to specify the library to use directly; instead it indicates what library to use in the name member of ExgSocketType. The exchange manager fills in libraryRef for you. |
| socketRef | Identifier for the connection itself, used internally by the exchange manager. You should leave this field alone. |
| target | Creator ID of the application that the data is being sent to. This field is optional; you can leave determination of what application receives the data to the receiving device, based on the filename or MIME type of the data. |
| count | Number of data objects in this connection. This value is usually 1, even if the application is sending multiple records. This field is optional. |
| length | Total length in bytes of all the objects being transferred. This field is optional. |
| time | Time when the object was last modified. This field is optional. |
| appData | Application-specific data. This field is optional. |
| goToCreator | Creator ID of the application to launch after the transfer is complete. The exchange manager assigns this value when it determines what application on the receiving end is registered to handle the transmitted data. |
| goToParams | Structure containing information about where to go if goToCreator is specified. |
| localMode | If set to 1, transfer takes place only with the local machine; if set to 0, transfer is enabled with a remote device. The default is 0. |
| packetMode | If set to 1, use connectionless packet mode (Ultra mode) for the transfer. The default is 0 because, as of Palm OS 5, Ultra mode is not supported. |
| noGoTo | If set to 1, the exchange manager does not launch the application specified in goToCreator after completion of the transfer. The default is 0. |

*Table continued on following page*

| Field | Description |
|---|---|
| noStatus | If set to 1, the exchange manager does not display any transfer progress dialog boxes. This option is useful if your application opens a two-way connection between two devices and you don't want progress dialog boxes to pop up repeatedly during a communication session. The default is 0. |
| preview | If set to 1, the exchange manager is currently displaying preview information about the transmitted data. The exchange manager sets this bit for you; there is no need to set it yourself. |
| cnvFrom68KApp | Palm OS Cobalt only. If set to 1, the socket structure was created by a 68K application. The exchange manager sets this bit to indicate to the exchange library that it needs to convert the data from 68K to ARM format in some parts of the socket structure. There is no need to set this bit yourself. |
| acceptedSocket | Palm OS Cobalt only. If set to 1, the socket structure was passed to the ExgAccept function. The exchange manager sets this bit for you; there is no need to set it yourself. |
| reserved | Reserved for future use. |
| componentIndex | Palm OS Cobalt only. Identifies the exchange manager C++ component that holds this socket, if any. The exchange manager sets this bit for you; there is no need to set it yourself. |
| padding_1 | Palm OS Cobalt only. Structure padding; this field is not used. |
| description | Pointer to a string containing a text description of the data object that is being transferred. This description is displayed to the user on both the sending and receiving ends of the transfer. |
| type | Pointer to a string describing the MIME type of the data object. This field is optional. |
| name | Pointer to a string holding the name of the data object, usually a filename. This field also commonly contains a special Uniform Resource Locator (URL) that identifies which exchange library should handle transfer of the data object. This field is optional. |

The exchange manager modifies and reads the fields in the ExgSocketType structure at several points during the process of transferring data objects. The rest of this chapter gives more detail about how to use the ExgSocketType structure.

Every application that is to receive data must register with the exchange manager the type(s) of data that it can handle, using the ExgRegisterDatatype function. When the exchange manager detects incoming data that can be handled by one of the programs on the handheld, it sends three launch codes to the registered application so it can receive the data:

❑ sysAppLaunchCmdAskUser to present a customized dialog box to the user for accepting or rejecting incoming data

❑ sysAppLaunchCmdReceiveData to actually receive the incoming data

❑    `sysAppLaunchCmdGoTo` to display the newly received record

*If the user has turned off the Beam Receive option in the Preferences application, the exchange manager does not send these launch codes to any application, whether or not any applications are registered to handle incoming data.*

# Registering a Data Type

If you wish to write an application that communicates only with another copy of itself on another Palm OS handheld, such as a game or a whiteboard application, simply specify the application's creator ID in the `target` field of the `ExgSocketType` structure. The exchange manager will send the appropriate launch codes to that application on the receiving handheld. However, this scenario is somewhat limited. The exchange manager was built with enough flexibility to allow transfer between Palm OS and completely different applications, operating systems, and devices. In order to allow a Palm OS application to receive data from so many different sources, the application must register with the exchange manager the types of data that it can handle.

At least one of the following three pieces of identifying information about a data object is required if an application is to receive it:

❑    Creator ID of the specific Palm OS application that will receive the data

❑    Filename identifying the data, usually with some kind of file extension (for example, `.txt` for text files)

❑    Multipurpose Internet Mail Extensions (MIME) data type (for example, `text/html` for HTML documents)

*If no application on the receiving handheld is registered to handle the data transmitted by another handheld, the exchange manager on the sending handheld informs the user that there is nothing on the receiving handheld that knows what to do with the transmitted data.*

An application should call `ExgRegisterDatatype` immediately after it has been installed on the handheld to let the exchange manager know what kinds of data the program would like to receive. `ExgRegisterDatatype` is available only in Palm OS 4.0 and later. Its prototype looks like this:

**Palm OS Garnet**
```
Err ExgRegisterDatatype (UInt32 creatorID, UInt16 id,
    const Char *dataTypesP, const Char *descriptionsP,
    UInt16 flags)
```

**Palm OS Cobalt**
```
status_t ExgRegisterDatatype (uint32_t creatorID,
    uint16_t id, const char *dataTypesP,
    const char *descriptionsP, uint16_t flags);
```

The `creatorID` parameter specifies the application to register to handle a data type. Use the `id` parameter to define exactly what kind of data type to register. The `ExgMgr.h` header file defines four registry ID constants that you may pass for the `id` parameter. The following table describes these constants.

| Constant | Value | Description |
|---|---|---|
| exgRegCreatorID | 0xfffb | Registers the application to handle data tagged for a specific creator ID. Normally the application whose creator ID matches the target field in the ExgSocketType structure receives such data, but by registering for a different program's creator ID, an application can take over the receiving of that program's data. |
| exgRegSchemeID | 0xfffc | Registers the application to handle a particular URL scheme. Normally only exchange libraries register to handle a URL scheme. |
| exgRegExtensionID | 0xfffd | Registers a file extension. Everything following the last period in the name field of ExgSocketType is that data object's file extension. An application registered to handle a certain file extension receives all data objects with that file extension. |
| exgRegTypeID | 0xfffe | Registers a MIME data type. The type field in ExgSocketType defines a data object's MIME type. If a data object's type matches the MIME type for which an application has registered, the application receives that data object. |

Pass a pointer to a null-terminated string containing the file extensions or MIME types to register in the dataTypesP parameter. You can specify multiple file extensions or MIME types in the same string by delimiting types with tab characters.

The descriptionsP parameter is a pointer to a null-terminated string that contains descriptions of the data type or types in the dataTypesP parameter. The exchange manager displays these descriptions in dialog boxes, allowing the user to preview data before actually accepting it. When the only transport mechanism supported by the exchange manager was infrared, this was not necessary; you could just ask the person with whom you shared data what you were about to receive. With longer-range protocols, like SMS, it is important that the user have as much information about the incoming data as possible, thus letting the user make an informed decision about whether to accept or reject the incoming data.

Within the descriptionsP string, you may specify one of the following:

❏ A single description for all the types in the dataTypesP parameter.

❏ One description for each data type in the dataTypesP string. Like the types in dataTypesP, descriptions are separated by tab characters. The number of descriptions must match the number of data types.

❏ NULL, which skips defining any descriptions for the registered data types.

Descriptions may have a number of characters up to exgMaxDescriptionLength. In Palm OS 5, exgMaxDescriptionLength is defined as 80.

The final ExgRegisterDatatype parameter, flags, specifies options that affect data type registration. In Palm OS Garnet and earlier, you can set only one flag. If your application passes the constant exgUnwrap for the `flags` parameter, it registers to receive objects that are wrapped up in an object of a different type. For example, if your application registers to receive data with a MIME type of `image/jpeg`, and the exchange manager received an e-mail message with a JPEG image attachment, the exchange manager would unwrap the image and send it along to your application.

In Palm OS Cobalt, the `flags` parameter is deprecated; wrapping an object in an object of a different type is not supported. This flag should always have the value `0` in Palm OS Cobalt.

Here are some examples of using `ExgRegisterDatatype`. The following `ExgRegisterDatatype` call registers an application to handle files with a `.txt` file extension:

```
Err error = ExgRegisterDatatype(myCreatorID,
    exgRegExtensionID, "txt", "Text file", 0);
```

This example registers an application to handle HTML documents, which have a MIME type of `text/html`:

```
Err error = ExgRegisterDatatype(myCreatorID, exgRegTypeID,
    "text/html", "HTML document", 0);
```

> The Internet Assigned Numbers Authority (IANA) maintains the central registry of MIME types. A complete list of MIME types is available on the Web at www.iana.org/assignments/media-types/.

If you want your application to handle multiple data types, call `ExgRegisterDatatype` only once for each registry type. For example, if your application should handle both JPEG and GIF format images, it can register to receive both types of data with the following `ExgRegisterDatatype` call:

```
Err error = ExgRegisterDatatype(myCreatorID, exgRegTypeID,
    "image/jpeg\timage/gif", "JPEG image\tGIF image", 0);
```

The best time to register an application for handling data is right after the application has been installed to the handheld. If an application were to call `ExgRegisterDatatype` only in its `AppStart` routine, the program would be able to respond to incoming data transmissions only after it has been run once. Instead, you can call `ExgRegisterDatatype` in response to the `sysAppLaunchCmdSyncNotify` launch code. The system sends this launch code to an application whose databases have been changed during the most recent HotSync operation. Installing the application itself counts as a change in the application's database, so an application can catch the `sysAppLaunchCmdSyncNotify` launch code and use it to register itself with the exchange manager.

There are situations, however, where registering your application in response to `sysAppLaunchCmdSyncNotify` might not be enough. If a user installs the application by copying it from an expansion card, `sysAppLaunchCmdSyncNotify` won't be triggered for that application until the next time the user performs a HotSync operation. Ironically enough, this scenario also applies to applications received through the exchange manager; if your application was beamed onto a handheld, it might not be able to register itself to handle beamed records.

As a backup plan, your application can call `ExgRegisterDatatype` when it starts for the first time. This still requires that your application run once before it is registered to receive data, but this is the best your application can do.

*This same registration problem applies to applications installed in POSE or Palm OS Simulator. If you plan to test your application's data exchange in either emulator, your application needs to register data types in its AppStart function or in another routine that the application calls when it runs for the first time.*

Keep in mind that ExgRegisterDatatype is available only in Palm OS 4.0 and later. If you want to support data exchange in Palm OS 3.0 through 3.5, you need to use the ExgRegisterData function, which has the following prototype:

```
Err ExgRegisterData (UInt32 creatorID, UInt16 id,
                     const Char *dataTypesP)
```

ExgRegisterData is nearly identical to ExgRegisterDatatype. The only things missing in ExgRegisterData are descriptions for the data types the function registers and the flags parameter. In addition, the only registry ID constants available for the id parameter are exgRegExtensionID and exgRegTypeID. ExgRegisterData cannot register an application to handle another application's creator ID, nor can it handle a URL scheme.

As an example, the following relevant parts of the Librarian application's PilotMain function call another Librarian function, LibRegisterData, to register Librarian to handle incoming Librarian data:

**Palm OS Garnet**
```
UInt32 PilotMain(UInt16 cmd, MemPtr cmdPBP,
                 UInt16 launchFlags)
{
    switch (cmd)
    {
        case sysAppLaunchCmdSyncNotify:
            LibRegisterData();
            break;
    }

    return 0;
}
```

**Palm OS Cobalt**
```
uint32_t PilotMain(uint16_t cmd, MemPtr cmdPBP,
                   uint16_t launchFlags)
{
    switch (cmd)
    {
        case sysAppLaunchCmdSyncNotify:
            LibRegisterData();
            break;
    }

    return 0;
}
```

Librarian registers to receive two file extensions:

❑     .lib, which represents a single book record

❑     .lbc, which represents an entire category of Librarian records

Librarian defines in `librarianTransfer.h` a number of constants that hold the file extensions and descriptions used by the application's data exchange routines:

```
#define libFileExtension        "lib"
#define libCategoryExtension    "lbc"
#define libFileExtensionLength  3
#define libExgFileDesc          "Librarian book record"
#define libExgCategoryDesc \
        "Librarian category (multiple book records)"
```

The `LibRegisterData` function looks like this:

### Palm OS Garnet

```
void LibRegisterData(void)
{
    UInt32   romVersion;


    // ExgRegisterDatatype is available only in Palm OS 4.0
    // and later, and ExgRegisterData is available only on
    // Palm OS 3.0 and later.
    FtrGet(sysFtrCreator, sysFtrNumROMVersion,
           &romVersion);
    if (romVersion >=
        sysMakeROMVersion(4,0,0,sysROMStageRelease,0))
    {
        ExgRegisterDatatype(libCreatorID,
            exgRegExtensionID,
            libFileExtension "\t" libCategoryExtension,
            libExgFileDesc "\t" libExgCategoryDesc,
            0);
    }
    else if (romVersion >=
             sysMakeROMVersion(3,0,0,sysROMStageRelease,0))
    {
        ExgRegisterData(libCreatorID, exgRegExtensionID,
            libFileExtension "\t" libCategoryExtension);
    }
}
```

### Palm OS Cobalt

```
void LibRegisterData(void)
{
    ExgRegisterDatatype(libCreatorID,
        exgRegExtensionID,
        libFileExtension "\t" libCategoryExtension,
        libExgFileDesc "\t" libExgCategoryDesc,
        0);
}
```

The Palm OS Garnet version of Librarian must jump through some hoops to determine on what version of Palm OS it is running. Because beaming and the exchange manager are available only in Palm OS 3.0 and later, Librarian registers itself only if it is installed on an appropriate version of the operating system. Librarian chooses the `ExgRegisterDatatype` if it is running on a Palm OS 4.0 handheld, and the application falls back to ExgRegisterData if 4.0 is not available. Also, Librarian uses three different sets of menus: one with beaming commands, for 3.0 through 3.5; one with send commands for 4.0 and later; and one without any exchange commands, for running Librarian in Palm OS 2.0. Data exchange functions appear in Librarian's interface only if the program is running on a device that supports the exchange manager.

> Take a look at the "Programming Menus" section of Chapter 8 for details about changing the menus displayed by a form.

The Palm OS Cobalt version of Librarian has it easy. Because it can only run in Palm OS Cobalt, it doesn't need to check for operating system version; it simply calls ExgRegisterDatatype.

# Sending Data

Sending data through the exchange manager is a four-step process:

1. Initialize an ExgSocketType structure.
2. Call ExgPut to begin the transfer.
3. Call ExgSend from within a loop to send the data.
4. Call ExgDisconnect to end the transfer.

## Initializing an ExgSocketType Structure

Every data exchange operation requires an ExgSocketType structure to define how the transfer should take place. Before using the socket structure, it is important to set all of its fields to zero with the MemSet function; random bits left over from declaring the ExgSocketType structure can cause unpredictable (and undesirable) results when it comes time to actually send data. The following lines of code declare an exchange socket structure and wipe it clean:

**Palm OS Garnet**
```
ExgSocketType   exgSocket;

MemSet(&exgSocket, sizeof(exgSocket), 0);
```

**Palm OS Cobalt**
```
ExgSocketType   exgSocket;

memset(&exgSocket, 0, sizeof(exgSocket));
```

Once the socket structure is zeroed, set appropriate fields in the structure to control how the send operation should proceed.

### Specifying a Description

The first field to initialize is the description field, which is a pointer to a string that describes the data that is about to be sent. This description string appears in the beaming dialog boxes on both the sending and receiving devices. Figure 18-1 shows beaming dialog boxes as used by the Librarian sample application when beaming the "Nonfiction" category. Pictured here are the sending dialog box (upper left), the receiving dialog box (upper right), and a dialog box to prompt the user to accept the data (lower left).

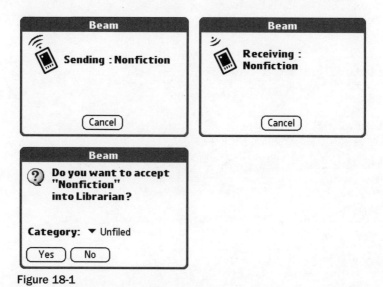

Figure 18-1

When beaming an individual record, it is customary to use part of the record's data for the description field:

```
exgSocket.description = myRecord->name;
```

Librarian's `LibSendRecord` function, shown in the following code sample, goes to considerable lengths to assemble an appropriate string for the description because not all of the fields in a Librarian record may contain data. Librarian uses a book record's title by default; records that lack a title have a description beginning with "a book by" and ending with the author's name; records with neither title nor author simply use "a book." Assembling a good description string may be as simple or complex a process as you want. Ideally, the description should give the user enough information to decide whether to accept or reject the incoming record.

**Palm OS Garnet**

```
void LibSendRecord(DmOpenRef db,
                const Char * const urlPrefix,
                Int16 recordNum, UInt16 noDataAlertID)
{
    LibDBRecordType  record;
    MemHandle   recordH = NULL;
    LibPackedDBRecord *packed;
    MemHandle   packedH;
    MemHandle   descH;
    UInt16      descSize = 0;
    Coord       descWidth;
    Boolean     descFit;
    UInt16      newDescSize;
    MemHandle   prefixH;
    Char        *prefix;
```

```
MemHandle    nameH;
Err          error;
ExgSocketType exgSocket;
UInt8        prefixLength;
Coord        ignoreHeight;


// If the record number is actually "no record", return.
if (recordNum == noRecord)
    return;

// Initialize the exchange socket structure to zero.
MemSet(&exgSocket, sizeof(exgSocket), 0);

// Assemble a description of the record to send. This
// description is displayed by the system send and
// receive dialogs on both the sending and receiving
// devices.
error = LibGetRecord(db, recordNum, &record, &recordH);
ErrNonFatalDisplayIf(error, "Can't get record.");

if (RecordContainsData(&record))
{
    // Use the title of the book, if it exists. If the
    // book record is untitled, use the author's name.
    // Failing that, fall back to a generic string
    // stored in Librarian's resources.
    descH = NULL;
    exgSocket.description = NULL;
    if (record.fields[libFieldTitle])
    {
        // Use title of book for the description.
        descSize =
            StrLen(record.fields[libFieldTitle]) +
            sizeOf7BitChar('\0');
        descH = MemHandleNew(descSize);
        if (descH)
        {
            exgSocket.description =
                MemHandleLock(descH);
            StrCopy(exgSocket.description,
                    record.fields[libFieldTitle]);
        }
    }
    else if (record.fields[libFieldFirstName] ||
             record.fields[libFieldLastName])
    {
        // Use "a book by <author>" for the
        // description.
        prefixH = DmGetResource(strRsc,
                                UntitledSendString);
        prefix = (Char *) MemHandleLock(prefixH);
        descSize = StrLen(prefix);

        if (record.fields[libFieldFirstName] &&
```

```
                record.fields[libFieldLastName])
            descSize += sizeOf7BitChar(' ') +
                sizeOf7BitChar('\0');
        else
            descSize += sizeOf7BitChar('\0');

        if (record.fields[libFieldFirstName])
            descSize +=
              StrLen(record.fields[libFieldFirstName]);

        if (record.fields[libFieldLastName])
            descSize +=
              StrLen(record.fields[libFieldLastName]);

        descH = MemHandleNew(descSize);
        exgSocket.description = MemHandleLock(descH);
        StrCopy(exgSocket.description, prefix);
        MemHandleUnlock(prefixH);
        DmReleaseResource(prefixH);

        if (record.fields[libFieldFirstName])
        {
            StrCat(exgSocket.description,
                    record.fields[libFieldFirstName]);
            if (record.fields[libFieldLastName])
                StrCat(exgSocket.description, " ");
        }

        if (record.fields[libFieldLastName])
            StrCat(exgSocket.description,
                    record.fields[libFieldLastName]);
    }

    // Truncate the description if it's too long.
    if (descSize > 0)
    {
        newDescSize = descSize;
        WinGetDisplayExtent(&descWidth, &ignoreHeight);
        FntCharsInWidth(exgSocket.description,
                        &descWidth,
                        (Int16 *) &newDescSize,
                        &descFit);

        if (newDescSize > 0)
        {
            if (newDescSize != descSize)
            {
                exgSocket.description[newDescSize] =
                    nullChr;
                MemHandleUnlock(descH);
                MemHandleResize(descH, newDescSize +
                            sizeOf7BitChar('\0'));
                exgSocket.description =
                    MemHandleLock(descH);
            }
```

```
        }
        else
        {
            MemHandleFree(descH);
        }
        descSize = newDescSize;
    }

    // If the description has a length of 0, it
    // indicates that:
    //   a. The record's title, last name, and first
    //      name fields are empty, or
    //   b. One of those fields contained data, but it
    //      consisted entirely of space or tab
    //      characters, and the FntCharsInWidth call
    //      during truncation wiped the description
    //      string out.
    // To remedy either situation, use "a book" for the
    // description.
    if (descSize == 0)
    {
        prefixH = DmGetResource(strRsc,
                               NoAuthorSendString);
        prefix = (Char *) MemHandleLock(prefixH);
        descSize = StrLen(prefix) +
            sizeOf7BitChar('\0');

        descH = MemHandleNew(descSize);
        exgSocket.description = MemHandleLock(descH);
        StrCopy(exgSocket.description, prefix);
        MemHandleUnlock(prefixH);
        DmReleaseResource(prefixH);
    }

    // Create a filename from the description. The
    // filename conforms to Internet Mail Consortium
    // spec (maximum 32 characters in length). Prefix
    // the filename with the appropriate URL prefix,
    // and truncate the description so it and the
    // ".lib" file extension fit within the
    // 32-character maximum.
    prefixLength = StrLen(urlPrefix);
    nameH = MemHandleNew(prefixLength +
                        imcFilenameLength);
    exgSocket.name = MemHandleLock(nameH);
    StrCopy(exgSocket.name, urlPrefix);
    StrNCat(exgSocket.name, exgSocket.description,
        prefixLength + imcFilenameLength -
        libFileExtensionLength -
        sizeOf7BitChar('.'));
    StrCat(exgSocket.name, ".");
    StrCat(exgSocket.name, libFileExtension);

    // Clean up the filename.
```

```
            CleanFileName(exgSocket.name);

            // Send the record.
            error = ExgPut(&exgSocket);
            if (! error) {
                packedH = DmQueryRecord(db, recordNum);
                packed = MemHandleLock(packedH);
                error = SendData(&exgSocket, packed,
                             MemHandleSize(packedH));
                MemHandleUnlock(packedH);

                // Calling ExgDisconnect with an empty library
                // reference causes a fatal error. Because
                // Librarian specifies a library by URL and not
                // by explicit library reference, it is
                // possible that the library reference in the
                // exchange socket structure doesn't get filled
                // in by ExgPut; this happens when the
                // particular handheld Librarian is running on
                // doesn't support the library requested in the
                // URL. This is why the call to ExgDisconnect
                // is located within this branch of the if
                // statement; ExgDisconnect should not be
                // called if ExgPut returned an error, because
                // exgSocket.libraryRef might not be filled in
                // properly.
                ExgDisconnect(&exgSocket, error);
            }
            else if (error != exgErrUserCancel)
            {
                FrmAlert(ExchangeErrorAlert);
            }

            if (nameH)
            {
                MemHandleUnlock(nameH);
                MemHandleFree(nameH);
            }

            if (descH)
            {
                MemHandleUnlock(descH);
                MemHandleFree(descH);
            }
        }
        else
        {
            FrmAlert(noDataAlertID);
        }

        MemHandleUnlock(recordH);
    }
```

```
void LibSendRecord(DmOpenRef db,
                   const char * const urlPrefix,
                   int16_t recordNum, uint16_t noDataAlertID)
{
    LibDBRecordType  record;
    MemHandle   recordH = NULL;
    LibPackedDBRecord  *packed;
    MemHandle   packedH;
    MemHandle   descH;
    uint16_t    descSize = 0;
    Coord       descWidth;
    Boolean     descFit;
    uint16_t    newDescSize;
    MemHandle   prefixH;
    char        *prefix;
    MemHandle   nameH;
    status_t    error;
    ExgSocketType exgSocket;
    uint8_t     prefixLength;
    Coord       ignoreHeight;


    // If the record number is actually "no record", return.
    if (recordNum == noRecord)
        return;

    // Initialize the exchange socket structure to zero.
    memset(&exgSocket, 0, sizeof(exgSocket));

    // Assemble a description of the record to send. This
    // description is displayed by the system send and
    // receive dialogs on both the sending and receiving
    // devices.
    error = LibGetRecord(db, recordNum, &record, &recordH);
    DebugOnlyFatalErrorIf((error < errNone),
                          "Can't get record.");

    if (RecordContainsData(&record))
    {
        // Use the title of the book, if it exists. If the
        // book record is untitled, use the author's name.
        // Failing that, fall back to a generic string
        // stored in Librarian's resources.
        descH = NULL;
        exgSocket.description = NULL;
        if (record.fields[libFieldTitle])
        {
            // Use title of book for the description.
            descSize =
                StrLen(record.fields[libFieldTitle]) +
                sizeOf7BitChar('\0');
            descH = MemHandleNew(descSize);
            if (descH)
            {
```

```
                    exgSocket.description =
                        MemHandleLock(descH);
                    StrCopy(exgSocket.description,
                            record.fields[libFieldTitle]);
        }
}
else if (record.fields[libFieldFirstName] ||
            record.fields[libFieldLastName])
{
        // Use "a book by <author>" for the
        // description.
        prefixH = DmGetResource(strRsc,
                                UntitledSendString);
        prefix = (char *) MemHandleLock(prefixH);
        descSize = StrLen(prefix);

        if (record.fields[libFieldFirstName] &&
            record.fields[libFieldLastName])
            descSize += sizeOf7BitChar(' ') +
                sizeOf7BitChar('\0');
        else
            descSize += sizeOf7BitChar('\0');

        if (record.fields[libFieldFirstName])
            descSize +=
                StrLen(record.fields[libFieldFirstName]);

        if (record.fields[libFieldLastName])
            descSize +=
                StrLen(record.fields[libFieldLastName]);

        descH = MemHandleNew(descSize);
        exgSocket.description = MemHandleLock(descH);
        StrCopy(exgSocket.description, prefix);
        MemHandleUnlock(prefixH);
        DmReleaseResource(prefixH);

        if (record.fields[libFieldFirstName])
        {
            StrCat(exgSocket.description,
                    record.fields[libFieldFirstName]);
            if (record.fields[libFieldLastName])
                StrCat(exgSocket.description, " ");
        }

        if (record.fields[libFieldLastName])
            StrCat(exgSocket.description,
                    record.fields[libFieldLastName]);
}

// Truncate the description if it's too long.
if (descSize > 0)
{
    newDescSize = descSize;
```

```
            WinGetDisplayExtent(&descWidth, &ignoreHeight);
            FntCharsInWidth(exgSocket.description,
                            &descWidth,
                            (int16_t *) &newDescSize,
                            &descFit);

        if (newDescSize > 0)
        {
            if (newDescSize != descSize)
            {
                exgSocket.description[newDescSize] =
                    nullChr;
                MemHandleUnlock(descH);
                MemHandleResize(descH, newDescSize +
                                sizeOf7BitChar('\0'));
                exgSocket.description =
                    MemHandleLock(descH);
            }
        }
        else
        {
            MemHandleFree(descH);
        }
        descSize = newDescSize;
    }

    // If the description has a length of 0, it
    // indicates that:
    //   a. The record's title, last name, and first
    //      name fields are empty, or
    //   b. One of those fields contained data, but it
    //      consisted entirely of space or tab
    //      characters, and the FntCharsInWidth call
    //      during truncation wiped the description
    //      string out.
    // To remedy either situation, use "a book" for the
    // description.
    if (descSize == 0)
    {
        prefixH = DmGetResource(strRsc,
                            NoAuthorSendString);
        prefix = (char *) MemHandleLock(prefixH);
        descSize = StrLen(prefix) +
            sizeOf7BitChar('\0');

        descH = MemHandleNew(descSize);
        exgSocket.description = MemHandleLock(descH);
        StrCopy(exgSocket.description, prefix);
        MemHandleUnlock(prefixH);
        DmReleaseResource(prefixH);
    }

    // Create a filename from the description. The
    // filename conforms to Internet Mail Consortium
    // spec (maximum 32 characters in length). Prefix
```

```
// the filename with the appropriate URL prefix,
// and truncate the description so it and the
// ".lib" file extension fit within the
// 32-character maximum.
prefixLength = StrLen(urlPrefix);
nameH = MemHandleNew(prefixLength +
                        imcFilenameLength);
exgSocket.name = MemHandleLock(nameH);
StrCopy(exgSocket.name, urlPrefix);
StrNCat(exgSocket.name, exgSocket.description,
        prefixLength + imcFilenameLength -
        libFileExtensionLength -
        sizeOf7BitChar('.'));
StrCat(exgSocket.name, ".");
StrCat(exgSocket.name, libFileExtension);

// Clean up the filename.
CleanFileName(exgSocket.name);

// Send the record.
error = ExgPut(&exgSocket);
if (error == errNone) {
    packedH = DmQueryRecord(db, recordNum);
    packed = MemHandleLock(packedH);
    error = SendData(&exgSocket, packed,
                    MemHandleSize(packedH));
    MemHandleUnlock(packedH);

    // Calling ExgDisconnect with an empty library
    // reference causes a fatal error. Because
    // Librarian specifies a library by URL and not
    // by explicit library reference, it is
    // possible that the library reference in the
    // exchange socket structure doesn't get filled
    // in by ExgPut; this happens when the
    // particular handheld Librarian is running on
    // doesn't support the library requested in the
    // URL. This is why the call to ExgDisconnect
    // is located within this branch of the if
    // statement; ExgDisconnect should not be
    // called if ExgPut returned an error, because
    // exgSocket.libraryRef might not be filled in
    // properly.
    ExgDisconnect(&exgSocket, error);
}
else if (error != exgErrUserCancel)
{
    FrmAlert(ExchangeErrorAlert);
}

if (nameH)
{
    MemHandleUnlock(nameH);
```

```
                MemHandleFree(nameH);
        }

        if (descH)
        {
                MemHandleUnlock(descH);
                MemHandleFree(descH);
        }
    }
    else
    {
        FrmAlert(noDataAlertID);
    }

    MemHandleUnlock(recordH);
}
```

## Specifying the Target, Type, or Name

After setting the description, the sending application needs to set at least one of the following three fields in the socket structure:

❑     `target`

❑     `type`

❑     `name`

Setting `target` to the creator ID of a specific application (usually the same as the sending application's creator ID) tells the exchange manager to send the appropriate launch codes to that application so it can receive the data. This is perfectly sufficient for an application that needs to send data only to another copy of the same application already installed on another Palm OS handheld. However, setting `target` prevents any other application from receiving the data on the other end of the transfer, so if your application needs to be able to send data to other programs, you are better off setting the `name` or `type` fields instead. For example, a handheld user may wish to replace the built-in Memo Pad application with a third-party program. If you send text data with `target` equal to memo, the text data goes straight to the Memo Pad application, but if you instead specify a `name` parameter that has a `.txt` file extension, the third-party replacement program has an opportunity to process the incoming data.

If you want to describe the outgoing data using a particular MIME type, set the `type` field in the socket structure to point to a string describing an appropriate MIME type. For example, the following code sets a socket's `type` to an HTML document:

```
exgSocket.type = "text/html";
```

Instead of specifying a MIME type, you also can specify a filename by pointing the socket's `name` parameter at a string containing the appropriate filename. The following example sets a socket's `name` field to send a file with a `.txt` extension:

```
exgSocket.name = "myRecord.txt";
```

## Specifying an Exchange Library by URL

Although you can specify a simple filename, the real power of the `name` field is its ability to define what transport mechanism you wish to use for transmitting data. Every exchange library is registered to handle specific URL schemes, and the `name` field can contain a URL. An exchange manager URL is composed of a scheme, followed by a colon (:) and the data object's filename, as shown in the following example:

```
_beam:myRecord.txt
```

The `_beam` URL scheme in the preceding example tells the exchange manager to use the IR library to send a data object. The data object itself has a filename of `myRecord.txt`.

> *If the name field contains a colon, the exchange manager automatically interprets name as a URL, and if the name field does not contain a valid URL, the exchange manager produces an error. Other than the colon that separates the URL scheme from the rest of the URL, strip colons out of any text in the name field.*

You may leave the selection of an appropriate exchange library to the user by including a question mark (?) in front of the URL scheme. This also allows you to include multiple URL schemes in the same URL, separated by semicolons (;). For example, the following URL prompts the user to choose between the IR library and whatever exchange libraries are installed that support the `_send` scheme:

```
?_beam;_send:myRecord.txt
```

If more than one exchange library can handle the specified URL scheme(s), the exchange manager displays a dialog box that prompts the user to select a transport mechanism for the data exchange. If only one installed exchange library supports a specified URL scheme, the exchange manager uses that library without bothering to prompt the user.

The first scheme listed in a URL is highlighted in the dialog box. For example, specifying the following URL causes the exchange manager to highlight the Transfer option; the Transfer option sends data to the local exchange library:

```
?_local;_beam:
```

The exchange libraries installed on many Palm OS handhelds register to handle a variety of URL schemes. The Bluetooth exchange library adds its own URL schemes to the list, making for numerous options when it comes time to specify a URL in the `name` field. The following table describes available URL schemes in Palm OS.

| Scheme | Description |
|---|---|
| _beam | IR library for beaming between devices via infrared |
| _local | Local exchange library for passing data between sending and receiving applications that reside on the same handheld |
| _sms | SMS library for sending data via Short Message Service |
| _btobex | Bluetooth object exchange for transmitting data between Bluetooth-enabled devices |
| _send | Generic scheme, supported by multiple libraries, for implementing a Send command in applications |

The `ExgMgr.h` header file defines two constants that define the _beam and _send schemes:

```
#define exgBeamScheme  "_beam"
#define exgSendScheme  "_send"
```

Using these constants as building blocks, `ExgMgr.h` also defines constants for assembling a URL scheme prefix. In addition, the Bluetooth exchange library comes with its own header file, `BtExgLib.h`, that defines constants for the various Bluetooth URL schemes. Other exchange libraries also supply their own constants describing their own URL schemes. The following table describes the constants for building URL schemes, as well as which header files define the constants.

| Constant | Value | Header File |
|---|---|---|
| exgBeamPrefix | _beam: | ExgMgr.h |
| exgSendPrefix | ?_send: | ExgMgr.h |
| exgSendBeamPrefix | ?_send;_beam: | ExgMgr.h |
| exgLocalPrefix | _local: | ExgMgr.h |
| kSmsScheme | _sms | SmsLib.h |
| btexgPrefix | _btobex:// | BtExgLib.h |
| btexgSimplifiedPrefix | _btobex: | BtExgLib.h |
| btexgSingleSufix | ?_single/ | BtExgLib.h |
| btexgMultiSufix | ?_multi/ | BtExgLib.h |

*The btexgSingleSufix and btexgMultiSufix constants really are misspelled in the header file. Be sure not to replace "Sufix" with "Suffix" when using these constants. The meanings of the two "Sufix" constants are described next in the "Using Bluetooth Object Exchange" section.*

Librarian uses the `description` of a record for its filename, tacking a `.lib` file extension onto the end of the string to form the name. `LibSendRecord` prefixes the name with an appropriate URL scheme, depending upon the value of the function's `urlPrefix` argument. If the user selected one of Librarian's Beam commands, `HandleCommonMenus` calls `LibSendRecord` with the `exgBeamPrefix` constant. `HandleCommonMenus` uses the `exgSendPrefix` constant in response to the selection of a Send menu command.

`LibSendRecord` uses the following code to assemble a URL:

```
prefixLength = StrLen(urlPrefix);
nameH = MemHandleNew(prefixLength + imcFilenameLength);
exgSocket.name = MemHandleLock(nameH);
StrCopy(exgSocket.name, urlPrefix);
StrNCat(exgSocket.name, exgSocket.description,
        prefixLength + imcFilenameLength -
        libFileExtensionLength - sizeOf7BitChar('.'));
StrCat(exgSocket.name, ".");
StrCat(exgSocket.name, libFileExtension);
```

The `sizeOf7BitChar` macro that appears throughout `LibSendRecord` is defined in the Palm OS header file `TextMgr.h` as follows:

```
#define  sizeOf7BitChar(c)  1
```

At first glance, this macro may seem a waste of typing time. However, it helps a great deal when one is trying to write self-documenting code. Many uses of `sizeof` result in a size of 2 bytes (`sizeof('\0')`, for example) because `sizeof` treats many character constants as `int` values instead of `char` values. The `sizeOf7BitChar` macro is safer to use than `sizeof` when assembling string values and provides a clearer picture of what is going on in the code than something like the following:

```
StrNCat(exgSocket.name, exgSocket.description,
        prefixLength + imcFilenameLength -
        libFileExtensionLength - 1);
```

There is no way to tell at a glance what the significance of the 1 is in this example. Replacing 1 with `sizeOf7BitChar('.')` lets you see immediately that the value represents the length of a period character.

## Using Bluetooth Object Exchange

Bluetooth's URL schemes require a bit more discussion. Because Bluetooth can connect to a number of devices within range of a handheld's Bluetooth transceiver, it is necessary to narrow down which device(s) the user wishes to send data to. There are two ways to accomplish this task:

❑   Ask the user which device(s) should receive the data. The Bluetooth exchange library searches for all the other Bluetooth devices within range, and then presents a list of available devices to the user. To ask the user to choose a single destination device, use the following URL style:

```
_btobex://?_single/myRecord.txt
```

To ask the user to choose multiple destination devices, use this URL style:

```
_btobex://?_multi/myRecord.txt
```

❑   Explicitly send data to a specific device(s), given the destination device's Bluetooth address. Bluetooth addresses are in the form xx:xx:xx:xx:xx:xx, where each x is a hexadecimal digit. To send data to a single Bluetooth address, use this URL form:

```
_btobex:// 12:34:56:78:90:ab/myRecord.txt
```

To send data to multiple Bluetooth devices, specify multiple addresses, separated by commas:

```
_btobex://12:34:56:78:90:ab,cd:ef:12:34:56:78/myRecord.txt
```

A Bluetooth URL prefix may be in either of two forms: with or without a double slash (//) following the colon:

```
_btobex://
_btobex:
```

Before attempting to use Bluetooth object exchange, check to see if the Bluetooth exchange library is installed. You can determine the presence of the library by calling `FtrGet`, as shown in the following example:

**Palm OS Garnet**

```
UInt32   btExgLibVersion;

Err error = FtrGet(btexgFtrCreator, btexgFtrNumVersion,
                   &btExgLibVersion);
```

**Palm OS Cobalt**

```
uint32_t   btExgLibVersion;

status_t error = FtrGet(btexgFtrCreator, btexgFtrNumVersion,
                        &btExgLibVersion);
```

FtrGet returns errNone if the Bluetooth exchange library is present and btExgLibVersion contains the version number of the installed Bluetooth exchange library.

## Setting Optional ExgSocketType Fields

Once you have a description for the data to be transferred, and a target, name, or type, you may proceed to initiate the data transfer. However, there are some optional fields in the socket structure that you may wish to consider setting:

❑   length. If you have calculated in advance the length of the data to transfer, setting length to equal the total length of the data in bytes can pre-empt the transfer if the receiving device does not have enough memory to receive the data object. Instead of having to transfer a significant part of a large piece of data before failing because of memory constraints, the receiving device can look at the length before transfer even begins and determine whether there is enough space for the object. By using the length field, you can prevent the user from having to wait a long time for an unsuccessful data transfer.

❑   localMode. Setting localMode to 1 prevents the application from sending the data out via the handheld's infrared port and, instead, loops the data back to the local device. A localMode value of 1 is equivalent to specifying a URL scheme of _local in the ExgSocketType structure's name field. The localMode option is primarily useful when you are debugging the beaming features of an application because it means you can debug most of the beaming process using only one handheld, or just Palm OS Emulator.

❑   noGoTo. Setting noGoTo to 1 prevents the receiving application from displaying the record that was just transferred. This setting works only when localMode also is set to 1. You can use noGoTo to export data to another application on the local handheld, without actually launching the other program.

*The built-in Memo Pad application is registered to handle data with a file extension of .txt. If you want your application to export text data to the Memo Pad, set the socket's name to a filename with a .txt extension and then set localMode to 1. If you want to export the data and remain in the current application, you also should set noGoTo to 1 instead of jumping straight to the Memo Pad.*

## Beginning a Transfer with ExgPut

The ExgPut function initiates a data transfer. Pass a pointer to the exchange socket structure as an argument to ExgPut:

**Palm OS Garnet**
```
Err error = ExgPut(&exgSocket);
```

**Palm OS Cobalt**
```
status_t error = ExgPut(&exgSocket);
```

If `ExgPut` does not return an error, the connection was successful and you must follow up with a call to either `ExgSend` or `ExgDisconnect`. The `ExgPut` function displays a dialog box (see Figure 18-2) to let the user know that the application is busy assembling data to export.

Figure 18-2

## Sending Data with ExgSend

The `ExgSend` function does the actual work necessary to send data across the connection formed by `ExgPut`. Here is the prototype for `ExgSend`:

**Palm OS Garnet**
```
UInt32 ExgSend(ExgSocketPtr socketP,
               const void * const bufP,
               const UInt32 bufLen, Err *err)
```

**Palm OS Cobalt**
```
uint32_t ExgSend(ExgSocketPtr socketP,
                 const void * const bufP,
                 const uint32_t bufLen, status_t *err)
```

The `socketP` parameter is a pointer to the exchange socket structure to use for the transfer. The `bufP` parameter should point to the start of the data to transmit, and `bufLen` should contain the length of the data in that buffer, in bytes. You can check for errors in the transfer process by passing a pointer to an `Err` type variable in the `err` parameter in Palm OS Garnet, or a pointer to a `status_t` type variable in Palm OS Cobalt.

The `ExgSend` function returns the number of bytes of data that it successfully sent. You must call `ExgSend` in a loop, changing the `bufP` and `bufLen` parameters to reflect the remaining data in the buffer at each call. The `ExgSend` function may not send all the data that you instruct it to send because of connection problems between the two devices; instead, it may require multiple attempts to send the data.

Wrapping `ExgSend` in its own routine is the easiest way to use it. As an example of one approach to looping over `ExgSend`, here is the `SendData` function from Librarian:

**Palm OS Garnet**
```
static Err SendData (ExgSocketType *exgSocket,
                     void *buffer, UInt32 bytes)
{
```

```
    Err   error = errNone;


    while ( (! error) && (bytes > 0) )
    {
        UInt32  bytesSent = ExgSend(exgSocket, buffer,
                                     bytes, &error);
        bytes -= bytesSent;
        buffer = ( (Char *) buffer) + bytesSent;
    }

    return error;
}
```

**Palm OS Cobalt**
```
static status_t SendData (ExgSocketType *exgSocket,
                           void *buffer, uint32_t bytes)
{
    status_t  error = errNone;


    while ( (error == errNone) && (bytes > 0) )
    {
        uint32_t  bytesSent = ExgSend(exgSocket, buffer,
                                       bytes, &error);
        bytes -= bytesSent;
        buffer = ( (char *) buffer) + bytesSent;
    }

    return error;
}
```

*To make your data transfers more efficient, try to call ExgSend as few times as possible. If possible, allocate a large buffer and send all of the buffer's data at once.*

## Ending a Transfer with ExgDisconnect

After you have finished sending data with ExgSend, call ExgDisconnect to sever the connection:

```
ExgDisconnect(&exgSocket, error);
```

The first argument to ExgDisconnect is a pointer to the exchange socket used for the transfer. For the second argument, pass whatever error value has been returned by calls to ExgSend, which lets the exchange manager know what kind of cleanup it needs to perform and which dialog boxes it should display to the user to indicate either a completed transfer or one that failed because of some sort of interruption.

*If ExgPut returns an error, you should not call ExgDisconnect. Usually when ExgPut encounters problems opening a connection, it does not fill in the libraryRef field of the ExgSocketType structure. ExgDisconnect relies on the libraryRef field to determine which exchange library should be disconnected; if libraryRef is still 0 when ExgDisconnect tries to use it, ExgDisconnect causes a fatal error.*

## Beaming Multiple Records

It might be useful to allow an application to send many records all at once. For example, the built-in applications that support categories, and Librarian, all present the option to send an entire category of records. There are a number of ways to send multiple records, but the primary thing to remember when designing data transfer for multiple records is that the receiving application must be able to tell multiple records from single records and handle them properly. Librarian uses a simple system to differentiate single-record transfer from category transfer. Single records have a file extension of .lib, and beamed categories have an extension of .lbc.

Librarian's LibSendCategory function is responsible for sending a whole category full of records. Other than the data that LibSendCategory sends, the function differs little from LibSendRecord. The LibSendCategory function sends the following information:

❑    An unsigned 16-bit value containing the total number of records in the transfer

❑    For each record in the category:

   ❑    An unsigned 16-bit value containing the length of the record in bytes

   ❑    The record's actual data

Here is the LibSendCategory function in its entirety:

**Palm OS Garnet**

```
void LibSendCategory(DmOpenRef db,
                     const Char * const urlPrefix,
                     UInt16 category)
{
    Err        error;
    Char       desc[dmCategoryLength];
    UInt16     index;
    Boolean    foundAtLeastOneRecord;
    ExgSocketType exgSocket;
    UInt16     mode;
    LocalID    dbID;
    UInt16     cardNo;
    Boolean    databaseReopened;
    UInt16     numRecords;
    LibPackedDBRecord  *packed;
    MemHandle  packedH;


    // If the database is currently opened to show private
    // records, reopen it with private records hidden to
    // prevent private records from being accidentally sent
    // along with a large batch of normal records. Private
    // records should only be sent one at a time.
    DmOpenDatabaseInfo(db, &dbID, NULL, &mode, &cardNo,
                       NULL);
    if (mode & dmModeShowSecret)
    {
        db = DmOpenDatabase(cardNo, dbID, dmModeReadOnly);
        databaseReopened = true;
```

```
    }
    else
        databaseReopened = false;

    // Verify that there is at least one record in the
    // category. It's possible to just use
    // DmNumRecordsInCategory for this purpose, but that
    // function has to look over the entire database, which
    // can be slow if there are many records. This
    // technique is quicker, since it stops searching at
    // the first successful match.
    index = 0;
    foundAtLeastOneRecord = false;
    while (true)
    {
        if (DmSeekRecordInCategory(db, &index, 0,
                                   dmSeekForward,
                                   category) != 0)
            break;

        foundAtLeastOneRecord =
            (DmQueryRecord(db, index) != 0);
        if (foundAtLeastOneRecord)
            break;

        index++;
    }

    // If at least one record exists in the category, send
    // the category.
    if (foundAtLeastOneRecord)
    {
        // Initialize the exchange socket structure to
        // zero.
        MemSet(&exgSocket, sizeof(exgSocket), 0);

        // Assemble a description of the record to send.
        // This description is displayed by the system send
        // and receive dialogs on both the sending and
        // receiving devices.
        CategoryGetName(db, category, desc);
        exgSocket.description = desc;

        // Create a filename from the description.
        exgSocket.name = MemPtrNew(StrLen(urlPrefix) +
            StrLen(desc) + sizeOf7BitChar(chrFullStop) +
            StrLen(libCategoryExtension) +
            sizeOf7BitChar(chrNull));
        if (exgSocket.name)
        {
            StrCopy(exgSocket.name, urlPrefix);
            StrCat(exgSocket.name, desc);
            StrCat(exgSocket.name, ".");
```

```
            StrCat(exgSocket.name, libCategoryExtension);
}

// Initiate transfer.
error = ExgPut(&exgSocket);
if (! error)
{
    // Now use DmNumRecordsInCategory to get the
    // number of records to send, since it's
    // certain at this point that the category will
    // be sent.
    numRecords = DmNumRecordsInCategory(db,
                                         category);

    // Send the number of records across first.
    error = SendData(&exgSocket, &numRecords,
                    sizeof(numRecords));

    index = dmMaxRecordIndex;
    while ( (! error) && (numRecords-- > 0) )
    {
        UInt16  seekOffset = 1;
        UInt16  recordSize;

        // Be sure to check the last record instead
        // of skipping over it.
        if (index == dmMaxRecordIndex)
            seekOffset = 0;

        error = DmSeekRecordInCategory(db, &index,
                seekOffset, dmSeekBackward,
                category);
        if (! error)
        {
            packedH = DmQueryRecord(db, index);
            ErrNonFatalDisplayIf(! packedH,
                "Couldn't query record.");

            // Send the size of the record.
            recordSize = MemHandleSize(packedH);
            error = SendData(&exgSocket,
                            &recordSize,
                            sizeof(recordSize));

            // Send the record itself.
            if (! error)
            {
                packed = MemHandleLock(packedH);
                error = SendData(&exgSocket,
                                packed,
                                recordSize);
                MemHandleUnlock(packedH);
            }
```

```
                }
            }
            ExgDisconnect(&exgSocket, error);
        }
        else if (error != exgErrUserCancel)
        {
            FrmAlert(ExchangeErrorAlert);
        }

        // Free the filename string to prevent a memory
        // leak.
        MemPtrFree(exgSocket.name);
    }

    if (databaseReopened)
        DmCloseDatabase(db);
}
```

**Palm OS Cobalt**

```
void LibSendCategory(DmOpenRef db,
                     const char * const urlPrefix,
                     uint16_t category)
{
    status_t    error;
    char        desc[dmCategoryLength];
    uint16_t    index;
    Boolean     foundAtLeastOneRecord;
    ExgSocketType exgSocket;
    uint16_t    mode;
    DatabaseID  dbID;
    Boolean     databaseReopened;
    uint16_t    numRecords;
    LibPackedDBRecord *packed;
    MemHandle   packedH;


    // If the database is currently opened to show private
    // records, reopen it with private records hidden to
    // prevent private records from being accidentally sent
    // along with a large batch of normal records. Private
    // records should only be sent one at a time.
    DmOpenDatabaseInfo(db, &dbID, NULL, &mode, NULL);
    if (mode & dmModeShowSecret)
    {
        db = DmOpenDatabase(dbID, dmModeReadOnly);
        databaseReopened = true;
    }
    else
        databaseReopened = false;

    // Verify that there is at least one record in the
    // category. It's possible to just use
    // DmNumRecordsInCategory for this purpose, but that
    // function has to look over the entire database, which
    // can be slow if there are many records. This
```

```
    // technique is quicker, since it stops searching at
    // the first successful match.
    index = 0;
    foundAtLeastOneRecord = false;
    while (true)
    {
        if (DmFindRecordByOffsetInCategory(db, &index, 0,
            dmSeekForward, category) < errNone)
            break;

        foundAtLeastOneRecord =
            (DmQueryRecord(db, index) != NULL);
        if (foundAtLeastOneRecord)
            break;

        index++;
    }


    // If at least one record exists in the category, send
    // the category.
    if (foundAtLeastOneRecord)
    {
        // Initialize the exchange socket structure to
        // zero.
        memset(&exgSocket, 0, sizeof(exgSocket));

        // Assemble a description of the record to send.
        // This description is displayed by the system send
        // and receive dialogs on both the sending and
        // receiving devices.
        CategoryGetName(db, category, desc);
        exgSocket.description = desc;

        // Create a filename from the description.
        exgSocket.name = malloc(StrLen(urlPrefix) +
            StrLen(desc) + sizeOf7BitChar(chrFullStop) +
            StrLen(libCategoryExtension) +
            sizeOf7BitChar(chrNull));
        if (exgSocket.name)
        {
            StrCopy(exgSocket.name, urlPrefix);
            StrCat(exgSocket.name, desc);
            StrCat(exgSocket.name, ".");
            StrCat(exgSocket.name, libCategoryExtension);
        }

        // Initiate transfer.
        error = ExgPut(&exgSocket);
        if (error == errNone)
        {
            // Now use DmNumRecordsInCategory to get the
            // number of records to send, since it's
            // certain at this point that the category will
            // be sent.
            numRecords = DmNumRecordsInCategory(db,
```

```
                                                category);

        // Send the number of records across first.
        error = SendData(&exgSocket, &numRecords,
                         sizeof(numRecords));

        index = dmMaxRecordIndex;
        while ( (error == errNone) && (numRecords-- > 0) )
        {
            uint16_t   seekOffset = 1;
            uint16_t   recordSize;

            // Be sure to check the last record instead
            // of skipping over it.
            if (index == dmMaxRecordIndex)
                seekOffset = 0;

            error = DmSeekRecordInCategory(db, &index,
                        seekOffset, dmSeekBackward,
                        category);
            if (error == errNone)
            {
                packedH = DmQueryRecord(db, index);
                DebugOnlyFatalErrorIf(! packedH,
                    "Couldn't query record.");

                // Send the size of the record.
                recordSize = MemHandleSize(packedH);
                error = SendData(&exgSocket,
                                 &recordSize,
                                 sizeof(recordSize));

                // Send the record itself.
                if (error == errNone)
                {
                    packed = MemHandleLock(packedH);
                    error = SendData(&exgSocket,
                                     packed,
                                     recordSize);
                    MemHandleUnlock(packedH);
                }
            }
        }
        ExgDisconnect(&exgSocket, error);
    }
    else if (error != exgErrUserCancel)
    {
        FrmAlert(ExchangeErrorAlert);
    }

    // Free the filename string to prevent a memory
    // leak.
    free(exgSocket.name);
```

```
    }

    if (databaseReopened)
        DmCloseDatabase(db);
}
```

## Customizing the Data Acceptance Dialog Box

The first launch code that an application registered to receive data receives is
`sysAppLaunchCmdAskUser`. If the application simply ignores this launch code, no harm is done; the
exchange manager presents a default dialog box prompting the user to either accept or reject the incoming data (see Figure 18-3).

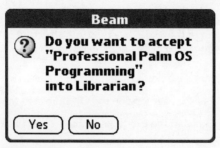

Figure 18-3

Quite often, the default dialog box is perfectly fine; most applications do not require any more than a
simple "yes" or "no" when they ask whether or not data should be accepted. However, if you would like
to do something more interesting with the incoming data, such as assign it to a specific category, the
application needs to handle `sysAppLaunchCmdAskUser` and present a custom dialog box to the user.
Librarian, when running in Palm OS 3.5 or later, displays such a custom dialog box (see Figure 18-4),
which allows the user to place incoming data in a specific category.

Figure 18-4

A `sysAppLaunchCmdAskUser` launch code comes with a parameter block that is a pointer to an
`ExgAskParamType` structure. This structure is defined as follows in `ExgMgr.h`:

**Palm OS Garnet**

```
typedef struct {
    ExgSocketPtr        socketP;
    ExgAskResultType    result;
    UInt8               reserved;
} ExgAskParamType;
```

**Palm OS Cobalt**

```
typedef struct {
    ExgSocketPtr        socketP;
    ExgAskResultType    result;
    uint8_t             reserved;
    uint16_t            padding_1;
} ExgAskParamType;
```

The `ExgAskParamType` structure contains a pointer to the exchange structure used to transfer the data. You should set the `result` field of the `ExgAskParamType` structure to one of the following values, depending upon how you want the exchange manager to proceed:

❑   `exgAskDialog` presents the default dialog box to the user

❑   `exgAskOk` pretends that the user taps on the OK button in the default dialog box

❑   `exgAskCancel` pretends that the user taps on the Cancel button in the default dialog box

*You do not need to provide your own replacement for the default data acceptance dialog box at all. Instead, simply use sysAppLaunchCmdAskUser as an opportunity to accept or reject incoming data based on criteria other than user input. This kind of scenario could work for constant, low-bandwidth infrared traffic between two copies of a game that is played via IR although, for efficiency's sake, you are probably better off using the IR Library to provide this kind of "always on" connection between two handhelds.*

Setting the `result` parameter takes care of the basic function of the default dialog box, but what about adding other return values, such as category selection? For this, you have the `appData` field of the socket structure contained within the launch code's parameter block. The `appData` field is a `UInt32` value (`uint32_t` in Palm OS Cobalt) that may contain any data you wish. When the application handles the `sysAppLaunchCmdReceiveData` launch code (see the "Receiving Data" section later in this chapter), it may then take action based on the value of the `appData` field.

## Setting the Category of Incoming Records

Starting with Palm OS 3.5, the exchange manager provides the `ExgDoDialog` function, which makes it easy to display a default data acceptance dialog box containing a category selector. Palm OS 3.5 and later versions of the built-in applications use this dialog box, and so does Librarian. Here is the relevant section of Librarian's `PilotMain` function as an example of how to prompt the user for a category:

**Palm OS Garnet**

```
UInt32 PilotMain(UInt16 cmd, MemPtr cmdPBP,
                UInt16 launchFlags)
{
    Err         error;
```

```
        DmOpenRef  db;


        switch (cmd)
        {
            case sysAppLaunchCmdExgAskUser:
                // If Librarian is not already running, open
                // its database.
                if (! (launchFlags & sysAppLaunchFlagSubCall))
                {
                    error = LibGetDatabase(&db,
                                    dmModeReadWrite);
                }
                else
                {
                    db = gLibDB;
                }

                if (db != NULL)
                {
                    CustomReceiveDialog(db,
                        (ExgAskParamType *) cmdPBP);
                    if (! (launchFlags &
                            sysAppLaunchFlagSubCall))
                        error = DmCloseDatabase(db);
                }
                break;

                // Other launch codes omitted
        }

        return 0;
}
```

**Palm OS Cobalt**

```
uint32_t PilotMain(uint16_t cmd, MemPtr cmdPBP,
                uint16_t launchFlags)
{
    status_t   error;
    DmOpenRef  db;


    switch (cmd)
    {
        case sysAppLaunchCmdExgAskUser:
            // If Librarian is not already running, open
            // its database.
            if (! (launchFlags & sysAppLaunchFlagSubCall))
            {
                error = LibGetDatabase(&db,
                                    dmModeReadWrite);
            }
            else
            {
```

```
                        db = gLibDB;
                }

                if (db != NULL)
                {
                        CustomReceiveDialog(db,
                            (ExgAskParamType *) cmdPBP);
                        if (! (launchFlags &
                                sysAppLaunchFlagSubCall))
                            error = DmCloseDatabase(db);
                }
                break;

                // Other launch codes omitted
        }

        return errNone;
}
```

If Librarian is not already running, which `PilotMain` determines by looking through the launch code's flags for a `sysAppLaunchFlagSubCall` flag, `PilotMain` opens Librarian's database. Access to the database is required because the database's application info block contains all the strings for Librarian's category names.

Whether the database is open or closed, `PilotMain` then throws the ball to `CustomReceiveDialog`, listed in the following code, to handle most of the details:

**Palm OS Garnet**

```
Err CustomReceiveDialog (DmOpenRef db,
                        ExgAskParamType *askInfo)
{
    ExgDialogInfoType  exgInfo;
    Err       error;
    Boolean   result;
    UInt32    romVersion;


    // The custom category-enabled dialog box is available
    // only in Palm OS 3.5 or later.
    FtrGet(sysFtrCreator, sysFtrNumROMVersion,
        &romVersion);
    if (romVersion <
        sysMakeROMVersion(3,5,0,sysROMStageRelease,0))
        return 1;

    // Set the default category to Unfiled.
    exgInfo.categoryIndex = dmUnfiledCategory;

    // Store the database reference for use by the event
    // handler.
    exgInfo.db = db;

    // Display the custom dialog box.
```

```
    result = ExgDoDialog(askInfo->socketP, &exgInfo,
                    &error);

    if (! error && result)
    {
        // Accept the data; pretend that the user tapped
        // OK.
        askInfo->result = exgAskOk;

        // Stuff the category index into the appData field.
        askInfo->socketP->appData = exgInfo.categoryIndex;
    }
    else
    {
        // Reject the data; pretend that the user tapped
        // Cancel.
        askInfo->result = exgAskCancel;
    }

    return error;
}
```

**Palm OS Cobalt**

```
status_t CustomReceiveDialog (DmOpenRef db,
                        ExgAskParamType *askInfo)
{
    ExgDialogInfoType  exgInfo;
    status_t  error;
    Boolean   result;


    // Set the default category to Unfiled.
    exgInfo.categoryIndex = dmUnfiledCategory;

    // Store the database reference for use by the event
    // handler.
    exgInfo.db = db;

    // Display the custom dialog box.
    result = ExgDoDialog(askInfo->socketP, &exgInfo,
                    &error);

    if ( (error == errNone) && result)
    {
        // Accept the data; pretend that the user tapped
        // OK.
        askInfo->result = exgAskOk;

        // Stuff the category index into the appData field.
        askInfo->socketP->appData = exgInfo.categoryIndex;
    }
    else
    {
```

```
            // Reject the data; pretend that the user tapped
            // Cancel.
            askInfo->result = exgAskCancel;
        }


    return error;
}
```

The Palm OS Garnet version of `CustomReceiveDialog` first checks the version of the operating system. Because `ExgDoDialog` and the custom dialog box resource it uses do not exist before Palm OS 3.5, `CustomReceiveDialog` returns immediately on earlier versions, allowing the exchange manager to display the default dialog box without any category-selection capability. The Palm OS Cobalt version does not need to check the Palm OS version because it can only run in Palm OS Cobalt, which is guaranteed to have the custom dialog box resource.

After checking the Palm OS version, `CustomReceiveDialog` declares and initializes `exgInfo`, an `ExgDialogInfoType` structure, with the default category that should appear in the custom dialog box and an open reference to Librarian's database so that the dialog box can display the names of the categories in its pop-up list. The `ExgDialogInfoType` structure, declared in `ExgMgr.h`, looks like this:

**Palm OS Garnet**
```
typedef struct {
    UInt16   version;
    DmOpenRef  db;
    UInt16   categoryIndex;
} ExgDialogInfoType;
```

**Palm OS Cobalt**
```
typedef struct {
    uint16_t    version;
    uint16_t    padding_1;
    DmOpenRef   db;
    CategoryID  categoryIndex;
} ExgDialogInfoType;
```

The `version` field of `ExgDialogInfoType` represents the version of the structure itself. This value is for possible future changes to the structure; for now, just use a value of 0 for `version`, even in Palm OS Cobalt.

Once `exgInfo` is initialized, `CustomReceiveDialog` calls the `ExgDoDialog` function, passing in a pointer to the exchange socket structure for the transfer, a pointer to `exgInfo`, and a pointer to an `Err` or `status_t` value to receive any errors encountered during the display of the dialog box. The `ExgDoDialog` function returns a Boolean result: `true` if the user taps the dialog box's Yes button, `false` if the user taps No. If the return result was `true`, and no errors occurred, `CustomReceiveDialog` sets the `result` field of the launch code's parameters to mimic a tap on OK in the default beam dialog box. Also, `CustomReceiveDialog` fills the socket structure's `appData` field with the category selected in the custom dialog box, which is stored in the `categoryIndex` field of `exgInfo`. A `false` return value from `ExgDoDialog` causes `CustomReceiveDialog` to act as if the user tapped on Cancel in the default dialog box.

# Receiving Data

When the exchange manager receives data that is targeted to a particular application's creator ID, or that has a file extension or MIME type registered by an application, the manager sends a sysAppLaunchCmdReceiveData launch code to the appropriate application. Handling this launch code allows an application to receive beamed data.

The application handling sysAppLaunchCmdReceiveData must open its database if it is not already the active application. Librarian takes care of this step in its PilotMain routine and then hands off processing of the incoming data to another function:

**Palm OS Garnet**

```
UInt32 PilotMain(UInt16 cmd, MemPtr cmdPBP,
                 UInt16 launchFlags)
{

    case sysAppLaunchCmdExgReceiveData:
        // If Librarian is not already running, open its
        // database.
        if (! (launchFlags & sysAppLaunchFlagSubCall))
        {
            error = LibGetDatabase(&db, dmModeReadWrite);
        }
        else
        {
            db = gLibDB;
            FrmSaveAllForms();
        }

        if (db != NULL)
        {
            error = LibReceiveData(db,
                (ExgSocketType *) cmdPBP);
            if (! (launchFlags & sysAppLaunchFlagSubCall))
                error = DmCloseDatabase(db);
        }
        break;
    }

    return 0;
}
```

**Palm OS Cobalt**

```
uint32_t PilotMain(uint16_t cmd, MemPtr cmdPBP,
                   uint16_t launchFlags)
{

    case sysAppLaunchCmdExgReceiveData:
        // If Librarian is not already running, open its
        // database.
        if (! (launchFlags & sysAppLaunchFlagSubCall))
        {
            error = LibGetDatabase(&db, dmModeReadWrite);
        }
        else
        {
            db = gLibDB;
            FrmSaveAllForms();
        }

        if (db != NULL)
```

```
        {
            error = LibReceiveData(db,
                (ExgSocketType *) cmdPBP);
            if (! (launchFlags & sysAppLaunchFlagSubCall))
                error = DmCloseDatabase(db);
        }
        break;
    }

    return errNone;
}
```

The function that takes care of receiving data in Librarian is `LibReceiveData`:

**Palm OS Garnet**

```
Err LibReceiveData (DmOpenRef db,
                    ExgSocketType *exgSocketP)
{
    Err     error;
    UInt16  index = 0;
    Char    *startOfExtension;
    Boolean singleRecord = false;
    UInt16  numRecords;
    UInt16  recordSize;


    // Determine whether the input stream contains a single
    // record or an entire category by looking at the file
    // extension.
    if (exgSocketP->name)
    {
        startOfExtension = exgSocketP->name +
            StrLen(exgSocketP->name) -
            libFileExtensionLength;
        if (StrCaselessCompare(startOfExtension,
                               libFileExtension) == 0)
            singleRecord = true;
    }

    // Accept connection from remote device.
    error = ExgAccept(exgSocketP);

    // Import records from data stream.
    if (! error)
    {
        if (singleRecord)
        {
            // Import a single record.
            error = LibImportRecord(db, exgSocketP,
                                    libEntireStream,
                                    &index);
        }
        else
        {
            // Import a whole category, starting with the
```

```
            // number of records in the transfer.
            ExgReceive(exgSocketP, &numRecords,
                    sizeof(numRecords), &error);
            while ( (! error) && (numRecords-- > 0) )
            {
                // Retrieve the size of the next record.
                ExgReceive(exgSocketP, &recordSize,
                        sizeof(recordSize), &error);

                // Import the record.
                if (! error)
                    error = LibImportRecord(db, exgSocketP,
                        recordSize, &index);
            }
        }

        // Disconnect the transfer.
        ExgDisconnect(exgSocketP, error);
    }

    // Set the socket structure's goTo information so the
    // system can fire off a sysAppLaunchCmdGoTo launch
    // code to open the newly transmitted record in
    // Librarian.
    if (! error)
    {
        DmOpenDatabaseInfo(db,
            &exgSocketP->goToParams.dbID, NULL, NULL,
            &exgSocketP->goToParams.dbCardNo, NULL);
        exgSocketP->goToParams.recordNum = index;
        exgSocketP->goToCreator = libCreatorID;
    }

    return error;
}
```

**Palm OS Cobalt**

```
status_t LibReceiveData (DmOpenRef db,
                    ExgSocketType *exgSocketP)
{
    status_t   error;
    uint16_t   index = 0;
    char       *startOfExtension;
    Boolean    singleRecord = false;
    uint16_t   numRecords;
    uint16_t   recordSize;


    // Determine whether the input stream contains a single
    // record or an entire category by looking at the file
    // extension.
    if (exgSocketP->name)
    {
        startOfExtension = exgSocketP->name +
            StrLen(exgSocketP->name) -
```

```
                    libFileExtensionLength;
        if (StrCaselessCompare(startOfExtension,
                                libFileExtension) == 0)
            singleRecord = true;
    }

    // Accept connection from remote device.
    error = ExgAccept(exgSocketP);

    // Import records from data stream.
    if (error == errNone)
    {
        if (singleRecord)
        {
            // Import a single record.
            error = LibImportRecord(db, exgSocketP,
                                    libEntireStream,
                                    &index);
        }
        else
        {
            // Import a whole category, starting with the
            // number of records in the transfer.
            ExgReceive(exgSocketP, &numRecords,
                        sizeof(numRecords), &error);
            while ( (error == errNone) &&
                    (numRecords-- > 0) )
            {
                // Retrieve the size of the next record.
                ExgReceive(exgSocketP, &recordSize,
                            sizeof(recordSize), &error);

                // Import the record.
                if (error == errNone)
                    error = LibImportRecord(db, exgSocketP,
                        recordSize, &index);
            }
        }

        // Disconnect the transfer.
        ExgDisconnect(exgSocketP, error);
    }

    // Set the socket structure's goTo information so the
    // system can fire off a sysAppLaunchCmdGoTo launch
    // code to open the newly transmitted record in
    // Librarian.
    if (error == errNone)
    {
        DmGetOpenInfo(db, &exgSocketP->goToParams.dbID,
                    NULL, NULL, NULL);
        exgSocketP->goToParams.recordNum = index;
```

```
        exgSocketP->goToCreator = libCreatorID;
    }

    return error;
}
```

Receiving records is a four-step process:

1. Call ExgAccept to accept the connection.

2. Call ExgReceive within a loop to retrieve the data.

3. Call ExgDisconnect to end the transfer.

4. Set up goTo parameters to display the transferred record.

## Accepting a Connection with ExgAccept

The ExgAccept function is similar to ExgPut: It merely opens a connection, and you must call ExgReceive or ExgDisconnect next to either retrieve data or close the connection. Pass a pointer to the exchange socket structure to ExgAccept:

**Palm OS Garnet**
```
Err error = ExgAccept(&exgSocket);
```

**Palm OS Cobalt**
```
status_t error = ExgAccept(&exgSocket);
```

## Receiving Data with ExgReceive

If ExgAccept did not return an error, your application may now start receiving data using the ExgReceive function. Just as with ExgSend, you must call ExgReceive repeatedly from within a loop to retrieve all the incoming data. The prototype for ExgReceive is nearly identical to that for ExgSend:

**Palm OS Garnet**
```
UInt32 ExgReceive (ExgSocketPtr socketP, void *bufP,
                   UInt32 bufLen, Err *err)
```

**Palm OS Cobalt**
```
uint32_t ExgReceive (ExgSocketPtr socketP, void *bufP,
                     uint32_t bufLen, status_t *err);
```

The ExgReceive function returns the number of bytes actually read from the incoming data stream. The easiest way to use ExgReceive is from within another function that contains the loop necessary to make ExgReceive work. Librarian uses the LibImportRecord function for this purpose:

**Palm OS Garnet**
```
Err LibImportRecord (DmOpenRef db,
                     ExgSocketType *exgSocketP,
                     UInt32 bytes, UInt16 *indexP)
{
    Char     buffer[libImportBufferSize];
```

```
Err      error;
UInt16   index = 0;
UInt16   insertIndex;
UInt32   bytesReceived;
MemHandle  recordH = NULL;
Char     *record;
UInt32   recordSize = 0;
MemHandle  packedH;
LibPackedDBRecord  *packed;
Boolean  allocated = false;
UInt16   category;


do
{
    UInt32  bytesToRead = min(bytes, sizeof(buffer));


    bytesReceived = ExgReceive(exgSocketP, buffer,
                               bytesToRead, &error);
    bytes -= bytesReceived;
    if (! error)
    {
        if (! recordH)
            recordH = DmNewRecord(db, &index,
                                     bytesReceived);
        else
            recordH = DmResizeRecord(db, index,
                recordSize + bytesReceived);

        if (! recordH)
        {
            error = DmGetLastErr();
            break;
        }

        allocated = true;
        record = MemHandleLock(recordH);
        error = DmWrite(record, recordSize, buffer,
                        bytesReceived);
        MemHandleUnlock(recordH);

        recordSize += bytesReceived;
    }
}
while ( (! error) && (bytesReceived > 0) &&
        (bytes > 0) );

if (recordH)
{
    DmReleaseRecord(db, index, true);

    // Grab the category for the new record from the
    // socket's appData field.
```

```
        category = exgSocketP->appData;

        // Put the record in the proper category.
        if (category)
        {
            UInt16  attr;


            // Get the record's attributes.
            error = DmRecordInfo(db, index, &attr, NULL,
                            NULL);

            // Set the category and mark the record dirty.
            if ((attr & dmRecAttrCategoryMask) != category)
            {
                attr &= ~dmRecAttrCategoryMask;
                attr |= category | dmRecAttrDirty;
                error = DmSetRecordInfo(db, index, &attr,
                                NULL);
            }
        }

        // Move the record to its proper sort position.
        packedH = DmQueryRecord(db, index);
        packed = MemHandleLock(packedH);
        insertIndex = LibFindSortPosition(db, packed);
        error = DmMoveRecord(db, index, insertIndex);
        if (! error)
            index = insertIndex - 1;
        MemHandleUnlock(packedH);
    }

    if (error && allocated)
        DmRemoveRecord(db, index);

    *indexP = index;
    return error;
}
```

**Palm OS Cobalt**

```
status_t LibImportRecord (DmOpenRef db,
                    ExgSocketType *exgSocketP,
                    uint32_t bytes, uint16_t *indexP)
{
    char      buffer[libImportBufferSize];
    status_t  error;
    uint16_t  index = 0;
    uint16_t  insertIndex;
    uint32_t  bytesReceived;
    MemHandle recordH = NULL;
    char      *record;
    uint32_t  recordSize = 0;
    MemHandle packedH;
    LibPackedDBRecord  *packed;
    Boolean   allocated = false;
```

```
        uint8_t   category;


do
{
    uint32_t  bytesToRead = min(bytes, sizeof(buffer));


    bytesReceived = ExgReceive(exgSocketP, buffer,
                                bytesToRead, &error);
    bytes -= bytesReceived;
    if (error == errNone)
    {
        if (! recordH)
            recordH = DmNewRecord(db, &index,
                                    bytesReceived);
        else
            recordH = DmResizeRecord(db, index,
                recordSize + bytesReceived);

        if (! recordH)
        {
            error = DmGetLastErr();
            break;
        }

        allocated = true;
        record = MemHandleLock(recordH);
        error = DmWrite(record, recordSize, buffer,
                        bytesReceived);
        MemHandleUnlock(recordH);

        recordSize += bytesReceived;
    }

}
while ( (error == errNone) && (bytesReceived > 0) &&
        (bytes > 0) );

if (recordH)
{
    DmReleaseRecord(db, index, true);

    // Grab the category for the new record from the
    // socket's appData field.
    category = exgSocketP->appData;

    // Put the record in the proper category.
    if (category)
    {
        uint8_t  attr;


        // Get the record's attributes.
```

```
                    error = DmGetRecordAttr(db, index, &attr);

                    // Set the category and mark the record dirty.
                    error = DmSetRecordCategory(db, index,
                                                   &category);
                    attr |= dmRecAttrDirty;
                    error = DmSetRecordAttr(db, index, &attr);
               }

               // Move the record to its proper sort position.
               packedH = DmQueryRecord(db, index);
               packed = MemHandleLock(packedH);
               insertIndex = LibFindSortPosition(db, packed);
               error = DmMoveRecord(db, index, insertIndex);
               if (error == errNone)
                    index = insertIndex - 1;
               MemHandleUnlock(packedH);
          }

          if ( (error < errNone) && allocated)
               DmRemoveRecord(db, index);

          *indexP = index;
          return error;
     }
```

The LibImportRecord function begins by creating a new record with DmNewRecord; then it progressively calls ExgReceive to fill the new record, resizing the record as necessary with DmResizeRecord. Once the record has been successfully retrieved, LibImportRecord checks the appData field of the exchange socket structure to see if the user assigned a new category to the record using the custom beam acceptance dialog box. Because the Unfiled category has a value of 0, LibImportRecord takes no action when the appData field equals 0, resulting in the record's landing in the Unfiled category. Otherwise, LibImportRecord assigns the record to the category specified in appData.

*Making many calls to ExgReceive using small buffers is better than allocating a large buffer to receive incoming data because the application receiving the data is not necessarily the currently running application. The active application is already occupying a great deal of dynamic memory with its own variables, so there might not be a lot of space available for ExgReceive to do its work. If you have verified that your application is indeed the active application, you can get away with allocating a large buffer but, in general, you should stick with smaller buffers when receiving data than you use when sending data.*

One more step remains. As it currently stands, the newly created record is the first record in the database (index equal to 0), which is not necessarily where the record belongs. The LibImportRecord function retrieves a handle to the new record with DmQueryRecord and then finds its proper sort position by calling Librarian's LibFindSortPosition function, which is just a wrapper for the Palm OS Garnet function DmFindSortPosition or the Palm OS Cobalt function DmGetRecordSortPosition. Once the record's real location is determined, LibImportRecord moves the record to the correct location with DmMoveRecord. See Chapter 16 for more information about creating, resizing, sorting, and moving records.

## Ending a Transfer with ExgDisconnect

After receiving all the incoming data, your application should end the transfer by calling `ExgDisconnect`, passing it a pointer to the exchange socket structure and the error value, if any, received from any `ExgAccept` or `ExgReceive` calls:

```
ExgDisconnect(&exgSocket, error);
```

## Setting Up goTo Parameters

After receiving a record, your application should modify the socket structure's `goToParams` and `goToCreator` fields so that the exchange manager knows which record to display, and in what application it should display it. The `goToParams` field is an `ExgGoToType` structure that contains a number of values necessary for an application to jump to a particular record and display it. The Palm OS header file `ExgMgr.h` defines the `ExgGoToType` as follows:

**Palm OS Garnet**
```
typedef struct {
    UInt16    dbCardNo;
    LocalID   dbID;
    UInt16    recordNum;
    UInt32    uniqueID;
    UInt32    matchCustom;
} ExgGoToType;
```

**Palm OS Cobalt**
```
typedef struct {
    DatabaseID  dbID;
    uint32_t    recordNum;
    uint32_t    uniqueID;
    uint32_t    matchCustom;
} ExgGoToType;
```

The following table briefly describes the fields in the `ExgGoToType` structure.

| Field | Description |
|---|---|
| dbCardNo | Card number containing the database that holds the record (Palm OS Garnet only) |
| dbID | Local ID of the database that holds the record |
| recordNum | Index of the record to display |
| uniqueID | Unique ID of the record that was added (this field is not used) |
| matchCustom | Custom information for use by the application |

Librarian's `LibReceiveData` fills in `goToParams` and `goToCreator` with the following lines of code:

**Palm OS Garnet**
```
DmOpenDatabaseInfo(db, &exgSocketP->goToParams.dbID,
    NULL, NULL, &exgSocketP->goToParams.dbCardNo, NULL);
exgSocketP->goToParams.recordNum = index;
exgSocketP->goToCreator = libCreatorID;
```

**Palm OS Cobalt**

```
DmGetOpenInfo(db, &exgSocketP->goToParams.dbID,
            NULL, NULL, NULL);
exgSocketP->goToParams.recordNum = index;
exgSocketP->goToCreator = libCreatorID;
```

## Receiving Multiple Records

Librarian can tell whether it is receiving a single record or category by the file extension of the incoming data object (see the section "Beaming Multiple Records" earlier in this chapter). If a single record is on its way in, the `LibReceiveData` function just calls `LibImportRecord` to loop over the data stream and extract a record from it.

If `LibReceiveData` determines that a whole category is inbound, it calls `ExgReceive` to pull the two-byte number of records included in the transfer into the `numRecords` variable:

```
ExgReceive(exgSocketP, &numRecords, sizeof(numRecords),
        &error);
```

Retrieving the number of incoming records allows `LibReceiveData` to set up a loop for retrieving individual records from the data stream. In each iteration of the loop, `LibReceiveData` calls `ExgReceive` to grab the two-byte record size number that precedes each record's actual data and then passes that size to `LibImportRecord` to retrieve the record itself:

**Palm OS Garnet**

```
ExgReceive(exgSocketP, &numRecords,
        sizeof(numRecords), &error);
while ( (! error) && (numRecords-- > 0) )
{
    // Retrieve the size of the next record.
    ExgReceive(exgSocketP, &recordSize, sizeof(recordSize),
            &error);

    // Import the record.
    if (! error)
        error = LibImportRecord(db, exgSocketP, recordSize,
                            &index);
}
```

**Palm OS Cobalt**

```
ExgReceive(exgSocketP, &numRecords,
        sizeof(numRecords), &error);
while ( (error == errNone) && (numRecords-- > 0) )
{
    // Retrieve the size of the next record.
    ExgReceive(exgSocketP, &recordSize, sizeof(recordSize),
            &error);

    // Import the record.
    if (! error)
        error = LibImportRecord(db, exgSocketP, recordSize,
                            &index);
}
```

665

# Displaying Beamed Records

The final step in receiving a record is displaying that record to the user. In order to accomplish this task, the exchange manager sends a `sysAppLaunchCmdGoTo` launch code to the application, based on the `goToParams` and `goToCreator` fields in the transfer's socket structure, which specifies the record to display. The `sysAppLaunchCmdGoTo` launch code is actually shared between the exchange manager and the global find facility, which both use it to display specific data within an application.

*See the "Implementing the Global Find Facility" section in Chapter 16 for more information about how to handle the `sysAppLaunchCmdGoTo` launch code.*

Unlike the find facility, the exchange manager generally does not need to highlight specific information within a record that it displays. Therefore, the `matchPos` and `matchFieldNum` fields in the `sysAppLaunchCmdGoTo` launch code's parameter block are not set. However, you may pass an application-defined value to the launch code parameter block's `matchCustom` field by setting the `matchCustom` field in the socket's `goToParams` when you are handling the `sysAppLaunchCmdReceiveData` launch code:

**Palm OS Garnet**
```
UInt32  myCustomValue;

// Set myCustomValue here.

exgSocketP->goToParams.matchCustom = myCustomValue;
```

**Palm OS Cobalt**
```
uint32_t  myCustomValue;

// Set myCustomValue here.

exgSocketP->goToParams.matchCustom = myCustomValue;
```

# Debugging Beaming

Other than setting the exchange socket's `localMode` field to 1, a couple of other tricks can make debugging beaming operations much easier. Both of these methods are special developer Graffiti shortcuts that you can make by writing the Graffiti shortcut stroke in the Graffiti area, followed by a period (two dots) and a letter (see Figure 18-5).

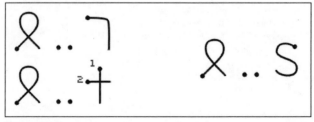

**Figure 18-5**

*The "t"-shortcut differs between Graffiti and Graffiti 2. Pictured in the figure are the original Graffiti "t" (top) and the Graffiti 2 "t" (bottom).*

A Graffiti shortcut character, followed by a period and the letter *t*, toggles `localMode` on and off. The *t*-shortcut is useful for debugging data exchange in POSE. Although you cannot send data from one copy of POSE to another, looping data back to the same copy of POSE that sent the data still executes all the code in an application that sends and receives data. As with any communication code, however, you should perform final testing on real hardware.

*In an application that supports beaming records, you can use the t-shortcut as a quick-and-dirty record copier. Turn on local beaming and beam yourself the record you wish to copy. Just accept the record back into the application. Now you have a duplicate record. Just be sure to make the t-shortcut a second time when you're done to enable beaming to other devices again.*

A Graffiti shortcut character, followed by a period and the letter *s*, sends infrared data to the handheld's serial port. This is primarily useful when you are debugging using POSE, which does not actually have an IR port but can simulate a serial connection using the desktop machine's own serial ports.

You may also run two copies of Palm OS Simulator for Palm OS Cobalt at the same time to test beaming. Simply start a beaming operation from one copy of Simulator, and the other accepts the incoming "beamed" data, just as if it were a second handheld receiving real IR data.

## Sending Applications and Databases

The default system application launcher allows you to send applications between Palm OS handhelds. You also can implement application transfer from within your own application, as well as perform a few tricks that the launcher cannot do, such as sending any arbitrary database on the handheld, whether or not it is an application.

Sending databases is similar to sending any other type of data with the exchange manager. Two extra functions are required to make the whole process work: `ExgDBWrite` and a callback function that `ExgDBWrite` uses to actually send the database's bytes across the connection.

The `ExgDBWrite` function converts a database from its internal format on the handheld to its equivalent `.prc` or `.pdb` file format on the desktop and then uses a callback function to perform some kind of write operation with the converted database information. Most commonly, this write operation will be used to send the database through the exchange manager, but this function also might be used for other purposes, such as to make a backup copy of a database on the handheld. The `ExgDBWrite` function has the following prototype:

**Palm OS Garnet**
```
Err ExgDBWrite (ExgDBWriteProcPtr writeProcP,
                void* userDataP, const char* nameP,
                LocalID dbID, UInt16 cardNo)
```

**Palm OS Cobalt**
```
status_t ExgDBWrite (ExgDBWriteProcPtr writeProcP,
                     void* userDataP, const char* nameP,
                     DatabaseID dbID);
```

The first parameter to `ExgDBWrite` is a pointer to the callback function that will be responsible for sending the actual data. This callback must have the following prototype:

**Palm OS Garnet**

```
Err ExgDBWriteProc (const void *dataP, UInt32 *sizeP,
                         void *userDataP)
```

**Palm OS Cobalt**

```
status_t ExgDBWriteProc (const void *dataP, uint32_t *sizeP,
                            void *userDataP)
```

Next, the `ExgDBWrite` function has a `userDataP` parameter, where you may pass application-defined data to `ExgDBWrite`. This data also is passed along to the callback function's `userDataP` parameter. When using `ExgDBWrite` to beam a database, pass a pointer to the exchange socket structure in the `userDataP` parameter.

If `nameP` is not `NULL`, `ExgDBWrite` looks for a database that has a name matching the string that `nameP` points to. You may alternatively specify a value for `dbID` if you know the LocalID of the database to send. In either case, you need to use the `cardNo` parameter in Palm OS Garnet to specify the number of the card on which the database resides; Palm OS Cobalt omits the `cardNo` parameter.

The following simple function takes the name of a database as an argument and sends the corresponding database to another handheld using the exchange manager:

**Palm OS Garnet**

```
Err SendDatabase (Char *dbName)
{
    ExgSocketType  exgSocket;
    Err    error;
    Char   name[36];  // max length for a database name
                      // (32), plus a period and
                      // three-letter file extension


    // Initialize the socket structure.
    MemSet(&exgSocket, sizeof(exgSocket), 0);
    StrCopy(name, dbName);
    StrCat(name, ".prc");

    exgSocket.description = dbName;
    exgSocket.name = name;

    // Make a connection to send the database.
    error = ExgPut(&exgSocket);
    if (! error) {
        error = ExgDBWrite(WriteDatabase, &exgSocket,
                        dbName, NULL, 0);
        error = ExgDisconnect(&exgSocket, error);
    }
    return error;
}
```

**Palm OS Cobalt**

```
status_t SendDatabase (char *dbName)
{
    ExgSocketType  exgSocket;
    status_t  error;
```

```
        char  name[36];   // max length for a database name
                          // (32), plus a period and
                          // three-letter file extension


        // Initialize the socket structure.
        memset(&exgSocket, 0, sizeof(exgSocket));
        StrCopy(name, dbName);
        StrCat(name, ".prc");

        exgSocket.description = dbName;
        exgSocket.name = name;

        // Make a connection to send the database.
        error = ExgPut(&exgSocket);
        if (error == errNone) {
            error = ExgDBWrite(WriteDatabase, &exgSocket,
                          dbName, NULL);
            error = ExgDisconnect(&exgSocket, error);
        }
        return error;
}
```

The operating system is registered to handle the file extensions `.prc` (application database), `.pdb` (record database), and `.pqa` (Palm Query Application). If you specify any of these file extensions for the socket's filename, the system on a receiving Palm OS handheld will automatically try to receive the database that you have sent.

> *The exchange manager is built on IrDA standards, so as long as you include an appropriate file extension for the database you are sending, the technique demonstrated by the* `SendDatabase` *function may be used to send files to a desktop or laptop PC equipped with IR or Bluetooth instead of another Palm OS handheld.*

The `WriteDatabase` callback passed to `ExgDBWrite` in the `SendDatabase` function is similar to Librarian's `SendData` function but does not need to call `ExgSend` in a loop, because `ExgDBWrite` already calls the callback function multiple times until it sends the entire database or times out. Here is what the `WriteDatabase` function should look like:

### Palm OS Garnet

```
Err WriteDatabase (const void *buffer, UInt32 *bytes,
                void *exgSocket)
{
    Err  error;


    ExgSend( (ExgSocketType *) exgSocket, buffer, bytes,
            &error);

    return error;
}
```

**Palm OS Cobalt**

```
status_t WriteDatabase (const void *buffer, uint32_t *bytes,
                        void *exgSocket)
{
    status_t  error;


    ExgSend( (ExgSocketType *) exgSocket, buffer, bytes,
             &error);

    return error;
}
```

*You also may send the currently running application to another handheld by passing the name of the application to the SendDatabase function described earlier. By providing this ability to the user — perhaps through a "Beam This Application" menu item — you can let your application's users distribute your program from handheld to handheld. This scenario is an excellent way to expose a freeware or shareware program to a larger user base.*

# Receiving Databases

Normally, you do not have to do anything to receive an incoming database if it was sent with the .prc, .pdb, or .pqa file extensions; the system automatically takes care of receiving databases with these extensions. However, if you want an application to receive a database and subject it to special processing — such as converting the data to a different format before saving the database — you can use ExgDBRead to receive a database with a different file extension. The ExgDBRead function has the following prototype:

**Palm OS Garnet**

```
Err ExgDBRead (ExgDBReadProcPtr readProcP,
    ExgDBDeleteProcPtr deleteProcP, void* userDataP,
    LocalID* dbIDP, UInt16 cardNo, Boolean* needResetP,
    Boolean keepDates)
```

**Palm OS Cobalt**

```
status_t ExgDBRead (ExgDBReadProcPtr readProcP,
    ExgDBDeleteProcPtr deleteProcP, void* userDataP,
    DatabaseID* dbIDP, Boolean* needResetP,
    Boolean keepDates);
```

The first two parameters to ExgDBRead are pointers to callback functions. The first callback, specified by readProcP, is the receiving equivalent of the send callback function used by ExgDBWrite. ExgDBRead calls this function repeatedly until the entire database has been received or ExgDBRead times out. The reading callback function must have the following prototype:

**Palm OS Garnet**

```
Err ReadProc (void* dataP, UInt32* sizeP, void* userDataP)
```

**Palm OS Cobalt**

```
status_t ReadProc (void* dataP, uint32_t* sizeP,
                   void* userDataP)
```

After the read callback function is a delete callback. The ExgDBRead function calls the function specified by deleteProcP if a database already exists with the same name as the incoming database. The delete callback function is responsible for deleting, renaming, moving, or otherwise dealing with the name conflict. If the delete callback successfully deals with the situation, it returns `true`; otherwise, it returns `false`. The delete callback function must have the following prototype:

**Palm OS Garnet**
```
Boolean DeleteProc (const char* nameP, UInt16 version,
    UInt16 cardNo, LocalID dbID, void* userDataP)
```

**Palm OS Cobalt**
```
Boolean DeleteProc (const char* nameP, uint16_t version,
    DatabaseID dbID, void* userDataP)
```

> **A bug in the default application launcher on some versions of Palm OS prior to version 3.5 can cause data loss if users beam an application from one handheld to another. If the launcher is currently running on the receiving handheld, the launcher not only replaces the application with the incoming new version, but it also deletes any databases that share the application's creator ID. When the launcher is not running, only the application itself is replaced.**
>
> **Unfortunately, there is no easy workaround for this problem. If you write an application that can beam itself or another program to another Palm OS handheld, it would be a good idea to inform users of your application that they should not run the launcher when receiving beamed applications. Luckily, the vast majority of Palm OS handhelds in use run Palm OS 3.5 or later, which doesn't have this bug.**

# Summary

This chapter showed you how to use the exchange manager to send data and applications between Palm OS handhelds or from a Palm OS handheld to another type of device. After reading this chapter, you should understand the following:

❑ To enable transfer of data between the Palm OS and other platforms, you can register Palm OS applications to handle data with either a specific file extension or a particular MIME data type.

❑ The `ExgSocketType` structure contains all the information about an exchange manager data transfer, and you set and read its fields throughout the process of beaming data.

❑ Beaming data requires four steps: initializing an `ExgSocketType` structure, calling `ExgPut` to begin the transfer, calling `ExgSend` within a loop to send the actual data, and calling `ExgDisconnect` to end the transfer.

❑ An application that is to receive data should handle the `sysAppLaunchCmdAskUser`, `sysAppLaunchCmdReceiveData`, and `sysAppLaunchCmdGoTo` launch codes.

❑ The `ExgDoDialog` function, available starting with Palm OS version 3.5, makes it easy to prompt the user for a category in which to place a transferred record.

❑ Receiving data requires four steps: accepting the connection with `ExgAccept`, calling `ExgReceive` within a loop to receive the actual data, calling `ExgDisconnect` to end the transfer, and setting up the exchange socket structure's `goTo` parameters to allow the exchange manager to display the newly transferred record.

# Using the Serial Port

Part of the success of the Palm OS platform can be attributed to its ability to connect to and share data with other devices using standard methods of communication. The serial port on a Palm OS device is a perfect example of this kind of easy connectivity. Because a Palm OS handheld uses standard RS-232 serial signals, the only obstacle to direct communication between the handheld and another device is finding a cable with the correct wiring for both ends of the connection. You can hook up a wide variety of electronics to a Palm OS handheld, including modems, printers, Global Positioning System (GPS) receivers, and desktop computers, just to name a few. In fact, HotSync technology, the primary method for synchronizing data between Palm OS and the desktop computer, relies on a serial connection through a cradle as one of the methods to take care of shoving bits back and forth between the two systems.

> *The cradle on newer Palm OS handhelds connects to a USB port instead of a serial port, but the communication that takes place between handheld and desktop is still essentially serial.*

This chapter shows you how to use the Palm OS serial manager to send and receive data using the handheld's serial port, including an overview of the hardware and software layers that make up the Palm OS serial communications system.

## Understanding Palm OS Serial Communications

The serial port on current Palm OS devices is a slightly stripped-down version of what you might be used to in a desktop computer's serial port. The UART (Universal Asynchronous Receiver and Transmitter) chip in a Palm OS handheld uses the following five external signals:

- ❑ SG (signal ground)
- ❑ TD (transmit data)

❏   RD (receive data)

❏   CTS (clear to send)

❏   RTS (request to send)

A few Palm Powered handhelds also have a configurable DTR (data terminal ready) signal, which is almost always set high.

Some signals used by desktop serial ports, such as RI (ring indicator), are not present in a Palm Powered handheld's UART. The hardware UART send and receive buffers also hold only eight bytes apiece, compared with the 16-byte UART buffers commonly found on desktop computers.

The Palm OS serial port supports serial communications at speeds between 300 and 115,200 bps. Another thing to keep in mind when designing Palm OS programs that communicate with other devices through the serial port is that all data that enters or leaves the device is arranged in Motorola's big-endian byte order. In other words, multibyte data types like UInt16 and UInt32 are arranged with their most significant bytes at the lowest address. This is an important distinction when connecting to an Intel-based machine, all of which use little-endian byte ordering. If your program needs to send multibyte data to an Intel system, you will need to reverse the byte order, either in the handheld application or, preferably, in whatever program serves as the handheld application's counterpart on the desktop, if any.

*The byte-ordering is changed for Palm OS Protein applications, which send data in little-endian order.*

On the software side, the serial communications system in Palm OS comprises several layers. Each layer adds to and relies upon the capabilities of the layer beneath it. The following layers make up the Palm OS serial communications stack:

❏   **Serial manager.** At the lowest level, the serial manager provides direct control of RS-232 signals and the hardware serial port. This layer allows for byte-level serial input and output, which makes this layer the most flexible for use in custom applications.

❏   **Modem manager.** Built directly on top of the serial manager, the modem manager provides a small API for modem dialing and control, which is capable of handling a modem attached either directly to the handheld's serial port or through a Palm modem cable.

❏   **Serial Link Protocol (SLP).** Also built on the serial manager, this protocol provides an efficient send-and-receive system for data packets, including CRC-16 error checking. Both the HotSync desktop program and the Palm Debugger use this protocol for communicating with a Palm OS handheld resting in its cradle. Palm OS also offers an API for your own applications to use SLP, called the Serial Link Manager (SLM), which offers a socket-like implementation of SLP and provides support for remote debugging and Remote Procedure Calls (RPC).

❏   **Packet Assembly/Disassembly Protocol (PADP).** Built on the Serial Link Protocol, PADP provides buffered data transmission capabilities for the Desktop Link Protocol, described below. PADP is entirely internal, and your applications do not have access to this layer.

❏   **Desktop Link Protocol (DLP).** DLP is built on top of PADP and provides remote access to various Palm OS subsystems, including data storage. HotSync technology uses DLP to perform synchronization and to install and back up databases. Although you cannot directly access DLP's features through a Palm OS application, you indirectly can make use of it if you write a HotSync conduit for a desktop computer.

❑ **Connection Management Protocol (CMP).** CMP is built directly on the serial manager layer. It is another protocol that the system uses for negotiating baud rates and exchanging basic information with outside communication software. Only the operating system has access to CMP. You can, however, alter connection profiles used by Palm OS to connect applications via IR, serial, or network communications using the connection manager.

Figure 19-1 shows how the different layers of the Palm OS serial communications stack relate to one another.

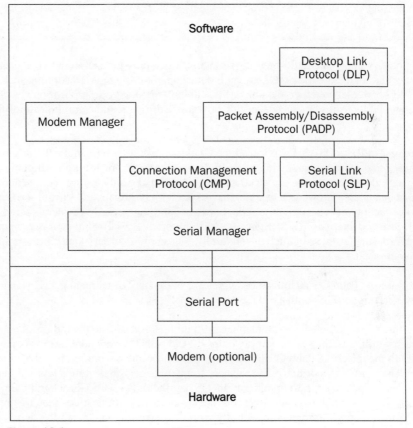

**Figure 19-1**

# Using the Serial Manager

Because the serial manager is the basic underlying layer for all serial communications on a Palm OS handheld, having the most direct control over the device's hardware, the serial manager is the most flexible way to connect a Palm OS application to another device. Of course, this flexibility comes with a price: You are entirely responsible for implementing your own communications protocols. The higher-level serial protocols available on Palm OS, such as SLP, do provide more advanced communications capabilities than the basic serial manager but they are rather limited in scope. For example, SLP works well for communicating with a debugger but it is difficult to adapt to any other purpose. Whatever you connect the handheld to is likely to require its own arbitrary communication format, so handling data transfer at the byte level with the serial manager lets you adapt a Palm OS application to fit the needs of whatever device is attached to the handheld.

> **The single most important thing to remember about serial communications on the Palm OS platform is that the serial port is extremely power-intensive. An open serial connection drains a handheld's batteries faster than almost any other system on the device.**

To prolong battery life, you should keep the serial port open only long enough to perform the necessary data transfer, and then close the port. Leaving the port open for long periods of time sucks the life out of the handheld's batteries (whether alkaline or lithium ion), making your application very unpopular with users. You will find various tips on conserving power use during serial communications throughout this chapter.

With the release of Palm OS 3.3, Palm introduced the *new serial manager*. Unlike the original serial manager, the new serial manager can maintain multiple serial connections through different communications devices on a single handheld; the old serial manager could make only a single connection at a time. The new serial manager also allows you to write drivers for both hardware and virtual serial devices, providing an abstraction layer between the serial hardware and the operating system's serial management routines. This new driver-based system is more efficient on devices that have more than one serial device installed, such as those in the Palm III family, whose physical serial and IR ports are both capable of serial communications.

Even more recently, Palm OS 4.0 introduced version 2 of the new serial manager. This new version has virtual serial drivers for Bluetooth and USB connections.

Handhelds that support the new serial manager still understand calls to the old serial manager functions. In such handhelds, the system simply maps the old calls to equivalent routines in the new serial manager. With the release of Palm OS 5, PalmSource has officially decommissioned the old serial manager, so this chapter focuses primarily on the new serial manager, presenting a few pointers later on if you need to write code to support an older Palm OS handheld. Palm OS Garnet and Palm OS Cobalt both support the new serial manager functions and structures, so applications that are dependent on new serial manager are assured of compatibility with the newest Palm OS handhelds.

*Unless your application must be able to perform serial communications on handhelds running an operating system prior to Palm OS 3.3, be sure to use the new calls rather than the original serial manager routines.*

Just to be safe on older handhelds, before calling new serial manager functions it is a good idea to determine whether the system supports them. Use the following call to `FtrGet` to perform this check:

```
UInt32  value;

Err error = FtrGet(sysFileCSerialMgr,
                   sysFtrNewSerialPresent, &value);
```

If the new serial manager is installed, the `value` parameter will be non-zero, and `error` will have the value 0, representing no error.

To determine if version 2 of the new serial manager is available, use the following code:

```
Err     error;
UInt32  value;
UInt32  romVersion;

error = FtrGet(sysFileCSerialMgr, sysFtrNewSerialVersion,
            &value);
error = FtrGet(SysFtrCreator, sysFtrNumROMVersion,
            &romVersion);
```

The new serial manager version 2 is present if the `value` parameter is 2, `romVersion` equals `0x04003000`, and both calls to `FtrGet` return 0 for no error.

> Checking that the operating system version is greater than version 3.3 is not a reliable way to ensure that the new serial manager is installed. Not all future Palm OS devices necessarily include any serial manager at all, so checking for the manager directly is a good idea if you want your code to continue working on upcoming versions of Palm OS.

## Using the New Serial Manager

To demonstrate the use of the new serial manager, this chapter refers to a sample application called Serial Chat (see Figure 19-2), which allows a Palm OS handheld to chat with a connected terminal program on the desktop via the cradle, or even with another handheld connected to the first one with a null modem cable.

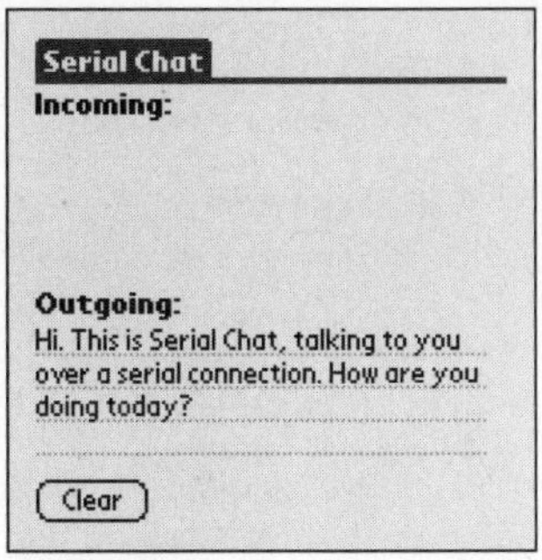

Figure 19-2

Serial Chat automatically opens a serial connection when it starts up and then closes the connection when it exits. Text to send to the desktop may be entered in the Outgoing field at the bottom of the screen; entering a linefeed character sends the contents of the field over the serial connection. Data coming back from the desktop appears in the read-only Incoming field at the top of the screen. The Clear button erases the contents of both fields.

Before you can use the serial manager to send or receive data, you must open an appropriate serial device with either `SrmOpen` or `SrmOpenBackground`, depending upon whether you want a foreground or background port connection. A foreground connection, made with the SrmOpen function, can read from and write to the port. There can be only one foreground connection at a time. A background connection, made with SrmOpenBackground, can receive only incoming data. If an application makes a foreground connection, the background connection relinquishes the port to the foreground task. Like a foreground connection, only one application or task can have background ownership of the port. Background connections are primarily useful for providing hardware support for an external device, such as a keyboard, which requires only one-way communication from outside the handheld.

To open a connection using either function, you must specify either a *logical port number* or a four-character creator ID that identifies a specific piece of serial hardware on the handheld. Logical port numbers are generic identifiers for different kinds of ports. If you specify a logical port number, the system finds an appropriate port on the handheld and opens it. If you use a creator ID instead, the system attempts to open the specific device identified by the creator ID. The Palm OS header file SerialMgr.h defines the following constants for logical port numbers:

```
#define serPortLocalHotSync    0x8000  // Physical HotSync
                                       //   port
#define serPortCradlePort      0x8000  // Cradle port (auto
                                       //   detect cradle
                                       //   type)
#define serPortIrPort          0x8001  // Use available IR
                                       //   port.
#define serPortConsolePort     0x8002  // Console port
#define serPortCradleRS232Port 0x8003  // Cradle RS232 Port
#define serPortCradleUSBPort   0x8004  // Cradle USB Port
```

You can find useful constants for serial device creator IDs in SystemResources.h:

```
#define sysFileCUart328    'u328' // Creator type for '328
                                  //   UART plug-in
#define sysFileCUart328EZ  'u8EZ' // Creator type for
                                  //   '328EZ UART plug-in
#define sysFileCUart650    'u650' // Creator type for '650
                                  //   UART plug-in (IR port
                                  //   on an upgraded Palm
                                  //   III device)
#define sysFileCVirtIrComm 'ircm' // Creator type for
                                  //   IrComm virtual port
                                  //   plug-in
#define sysFileCVirtRfComm 'rfcm' // Creator type for
                                  //   RfComm (Bluetooth)
                                  //   virtual port plug-in
```

For compatibility with different versions of Palm OS, you are better off using a logical port number than the creator ID of a specific hardware port. I ran across this kind of compatibility problem when developing the Serial Chat example program for this chapter because I had originally used the u328 code to specify the serial port directly. Although this works fine on POSE when it emulates a Palm III running Palm OS 3.3, when I installed the application on my Palm IIIx running Palm OS 3.5, the SrmOpen call at the start of the program returned the error serErrBadPort. This is because the IIIx has a DragonBall EZ processor, whose serial UART has a creator ID of u8EZ instead of u328, which is the code for non-EZ devices like the Palm III. Specifying the logical port ID of 0x8000 ensures that Serial Chat works on devices with either the DragonBall or the DragonBall EZ processor.

## Opening the Serial Port

Both SrmOpen and SrmOpenBackground are used to open a serial port in Palm OS. Both functions take the same parameters, the first of which is the logical port number, or the 4-character creator ID. Here is the prototype for SrmOpen:

```
Err SrmOpen (UInt32 port, UInt32 baud, UInt16* newPortIdP)
```

After the port identifier, specify an initial baud rate for the connection. The third parameter to SrmOpen and SrmOpenBackground is a pointer to a variable to receive the *port ID*. The port ID must be passed to other serial manager functions so that they can find the open connection and work with it.

A return value of 0 from SrmOpen and SrmOpenBackground indicates that the port was opened successfully. You also should specifically check for the error value serErrAlreadyOpen. If either open function returns this value, the port was successfully opened, but another task is already installed as the foreground or background port owner. In this case, the system increments an open count for the port to keep track of how many tasks are using the port concurrently. If SrmOpen returns serErrAlreadyOpen, close the port and open it before attempting to use it.

> It is possible for two tasks to use the port at the same time, but I do not recommend sharing reads and writes between two applications unless you like vast amounts of pain. Sharing the port is more likely to result in corrupt data and debugging headaches than in anything useful.

Version 2 of the new serial manager also gives you the option of using the SrmExtOpen and SrmExtOpenBackground functions. These two functions serve identical purposes to their SrmOpen and SrmOpenBackground equivalents but they allow you to specify more detailed configuration information for the port connection. This configuration information is necessary for opening Bluetooth or USB connections. Bluetooth and USB automatically negotiate baud rate, so they are more concerned with the reason a connection is being opened than with the minutiae of serial communications.

SrmExtOpen and SrmExtOpenBackground have the following prototypes:

```
Err SrmExtOpen (UInt32 port, SrmOpenConfigType *configP,
            UInt16 configSize, UInt16 *newPortIdP)
Err SrmExtOpenBackground (UInt32 port,
    SrmOpenConfigType *configP, UInt16 configSize,
    UInt16 *newPortIdP)
```

Both SrmExtOpen and SrmExtOpenBackground take a pointer to an SrmOpenConfigType structure as an argument, along with a configSize argument that specifies the length in bytes of the structure. The Palm OS header file SerialMgr.h defines SrmOpenConfigType as follows:

```
typedef struct SrmOpenConfigType {
    UInt32 baud;         // Baud rate for the connection
    UInt32 function;     // Purpose of the connection
    MemPtr drvrDataP;    // Pointer to driver-specific data
    UInt16 drvrDataSize; // Size of the driver-specific
                         //  data block
```

```
    UInt32 sysReserved1; // System reserved
    UInt32 sysReserved2; // System reserved
} SrmOpenConfigType;
```

For protocols that require a baud rate, such as generic RS-232 serial communication, specify the baud rate of the connection in the structure's baud member. Serial drivers that do not require a baud rate, such as USB, ignore the baud member.

The function member defines the reason the connection has been opened. You should specify either the Creator ID of the application that is opening the serial port or one of the predefined Palm OS constant values, as shown in the following table.

| Constant | Description |
| --- | --- |
| serFncUndefined | Purpose is undefined; this is the default value for function. |
| serFncPPPSession | Connection will be used for a PPP (Point-to-Point Protocol) interface. |
| serFncSLIPSession | Connection will be used for a SLIP (Serial Line IP) interface. |
| serFncDebugger | Connection will be used to hook up to a debugger. |
| serFncHotSync | Connection will be used for a HotSync operation. |
| serFncConsole | Connection will hook up to a debugging console. |
| serFncTelephony | Connection will hook up to the telephony library. |

Protocols such as Bluetooth and USB use the function member to perform different startup tasks depending upon how the connection is to be used. RS-232 serial drivers ignore the function member. Be sure to check for the presence of the new serial manager version 2 before calling SrmExtOpen or SrmExtOpenBackground.

If your application receives a serErrAlreadyOpen error when trying to open a serial connection, the application should call SrmClose to decrement the open count and then display an appropriate error message. Failure to call SrmClose after a serErrAlreadyOpen error will leave the serial port open after your application exits, a surefire way to drain battery power.

Serial Chat calls SrmOpen from its OpenSerial function to make a foreground connection. The OpenSerial function, called from Serial Chat's StartApplication routine, looks like this:

```
static Err OpenSerial (void)
{
    Err     error = 0;


    // Open the serial port with an initial baud rate of
    // 9600.
    error = SrmOpen(serPortCradlePort, 9600, &gPortID);
    ErrNonFatalDisplayIf(error == serErrBadPort,
                         "serErrBadPort");
    switch (error)
    {
        case errNone:
```

```
                    break;

            case serErrAlreadyOpen:
                SrmClose(gPortID);
                FrmAlert(SerialBusyAlert);
                return error;
                break;

            default:
                FrmAlert(SerialOpenAlert);
                return error;
                break;
    }

    gConnected = true;

    // Clear the port in case garbage data is hanging
    // around.
    SrmReceiveFlush(gPortID, 100);

    // Code to set connection parameters omitted.

    return error;
}
```

The OpenSerial function calls SrmOpen with the serPortCradlePort logical port number (0x8000), setting an initial baud rate of 9600. Serial Chat uses the global variable gPortID to store the port ID obtained by SrmOpen for use with other new serial manager functions. After a bit of error checking, including displaying appropriate alerts to the user if there is a problem opening the serial connection, OpenSerial sets the global variable gConnected to true. Serial Chat uses gConnected to determine whether or not the application is connected.

Once the connection has been made, OpenSerial empties the serial receiving queue with the SrmReceiveFlush routine. This step ensures that any stale data remaining in the queue from earlier uses of the serial port is discarded before Serial Chat starts to use the port. The SrmReceiveFlush function has two parameters: the port ID returned from SrmOpen, and a timeout value:

```
Err SrmReceiveFlush (UInt16 portId, Int32 timeout)
```

When flushing the port, SrmReceiveFlush first discards all the waiting data and then waits a number of system ticks equal to timeout. If more data arrives at the port before the timeout period is up, SrmReceiveFlush empties the queue again, resets its timer to the timeout value, and waits again. As soon as SrmReceiveFlush waits the entire timeout period without seeing any more data, the function returns. If you want to just empty the queue once without letting SrmReceiveFlush wait for more data, call SrmReceiveFlush with a timeout value of 0.

Right after opening the serial port also is a good time to set communications parameters for the connection, such as the number of bits per character and the parity. The code that does this in OpenSerial has been omitted in this section; see the "Changing Serial Port Settings" section later in this chapter for more information.

## Closing the Serial Port

When you are ready to close the serial port, you must use SrmClose. This closes the open communications channel and also frees up the port resource and makes it available for use by other applications. SrmClose has the following prototype:

**Palm OS Garnet**
```
Err SrmClose (UInt16 portID)
```

**Palm OS Cobalt**
```
status_t SrmClose (uint16_t portID)
```

The portID parameter of SrmClose is the port ID as returned by the SrmOpen or SrmOpenBackground call that opened the port in the first place. The SrmClose function returns 0 if it successfully closes the port, or serErrBadPort if the specified port ID is invalid. Be sure to pair every successful call to SrmOpen or SrmOpenBackground with a call to SrmClose to ensure that the serial port is not left open when your application exits.

Serial Chat wraps a call to SrmClose in its CloseSerial function, which the application calls in its StopApplication routine just before exiting. The CloseSerial function looks like this:

**Palm OS Garnet**
```
static void CloseSerial (void)
{
    Err   error;


    error = SrmSendWait(gPortID);
    ErrNonFatalDisplayIf(error == serErrBadPort,
                         "SrmClose: bad port");
    if (error == serErrTimeOut)
        FrmAlert(SerialTimeoutAlert);

    SrmClose(gPortID);

    gConnected = false;
}
```

**Palm OS Cobalt**
```
static void CloseSerial (void)
{
    status_t   error;


    error = SrmSendWait(gPortID);
    ErrNonFatalDisplayIf(error == serErrBadPort,
                         "SrmClose: bad port");
    if (error == serErrTimeOut)
    {
        // pass the database reference containing the alert
        FrmAlert(database, SerialTimeoutAlert);
    }

    SrmClose(gPortID);

    gConnected = false;
}
```

Before calling SrmClose, CloseSerial makes a call to SrmSendWait. The SrmSendWait function waits until all the data in the transmit queue has been sent, and then returns. Calling SrmSendWait ensures that all the data sent by your application is transmitted before the application exits; simply closing the port immediately stops transmission and might strand a few bytes in the outgoing queue before they get a chance to leave the port, resulting in lost data.

The SrmSendWait function has only one parameter — the port ID as returned by SrmOpen or SrmOpenBackground. A return value of 0 from SrmSendWait means that the function was able to send successfully all the data remaining in the outgoing queue. If SrmSendWait times out before it finishes its task, the function returns the serErrTimeOut error code, which causes Serial Chat's CloseSerial routine to display an alert to inform the user that some of the data may not have been transmitted. You can control the timeout value used by SrmSendWait by setting the ctsTimeout value with the SrmControl function; see the "Changing Serial Port Settings" section later in this chapter.

## Sending Data

Sending data over a serial connection is a simple matter of calling SrmSend. This routine has the following prototype:

**Palm OS Garnet**
```
UInt32 SrmSend (UInt16 portId, void *bufP, UInt32 count,
            Err* errP)
```

**Palm OS Cobalt**
```
uint32_t SrmSend (uint16_t portId, void *bufP, uint32_t count,
            status_t * errP)
```

The first parameter of SrmSend is simply the familiar port ID reference obtained with SrmOpen or SrmOpenBackground. The bufP parameter should be a pointer to the data to send, and count is the length of that buffer in bytes. If SrmSend encounters an error, it returns it through the errP parameter.

The SrmSend routine returns the number of bytes actually sent. If SrmSend successfully transmits all the data in the buffer, it sets errP to NULL, and SrmSend returns a value equal to the count parameter. If errP is not NULL, check the return value to determine how many bytes SrmSend managed to send before it encountered an error.

Serial Chat uses SrmSend in its WriteSerial function, which is responsible for retrieving the contents of the application's Outgoing field and sending it over the serial connection. After it has sent the field's contents, the WriteSerial routine sends a linefeed character to signal the end of the message. Here is what WriteSerial looks like:

**Palm OS Garnet**
```
static void WriteSerial (void)
{
    Err        error;
    FieldType  *field;
    Char       *text = NULL;
    Char       lineFeed = chrLineFeed;


    // Bail out if not connected.
```

```
    if (gConnected == false) return;

    // Retrieve a pointer to the outgoing field's text.
    field = GetObjectPtr(MainOutgoingField);
    text = FldGetTextPtr(field);
    if (text)
    {
        // Send the contents of the outgoing field.
        SrmSend(gPortID, text, StrLen(text), &error);
        if (error)
            FrmAlert(SerialSendAlert);

        // Send a linefeed character.
        SrmSend(gPortID, &lineFeed, 1, &error);
        if (error)
            FrmAlert(SerialSendAlert);
    }
}
```

**Palm OS Cobalt**

```
static void WriteSerial (void)
{
    status_t    error;
    FieldType  *field;
    char    *text = NULL;
    char    lineFeed = chrLineFeed;


    // Bail out if not connected.
    if (gConnected == false) return;

    // Retrieve a pointer to the outgoing field's text.
    field = GetObjectPtr(MainOutgoingField);
    text = FldGetTextPtr(field);
    if (text)
    {
        // Send the contents of the outgoing field.
        SrmSend(gPortID, text, StrLen(text), &error);
        if (error)
            FrmAlert(database, SerialSendAlert);

        // Send a linefeed character.
        SrmSend(gPortID, &lineFeed, 1, &error);
        if (error)
            FrmAlert(database, SerialSendAlert);
    }
}
```

The new serial manager also has some useful utility functions to assist an application with sending data. SrmSendCheck checks the transmission queue and returns the number of bytes that have not been sent yet. The prototype for SrmSendCheck looks like this:

**Palm OS Garnet**

```
Err SrmSendCheck (UInt16 portId, UInt32* numBytesP)
```

```
status_t SrmSendCheck (uint16_t portId, uint32_t* numBytesP)
```

The SrmSendCheck function's second parameter is a pointer to a variable that receives the number of bytes left in the queue. If SrmSendCheck encounters an error, it returns an appropriate error code. In particular, be on the lookout for a serErrorNotSupported error, which indicates that checking the status of the outgoing queue is not supported by the serial hardware. Not all serial devices are capable of providing this information.

Another useful function is SrmSendFlush, the send queue equivalent of SrmReceiveFlush, which empties the transmission queue instead of the receiving queue. The SrmSendFlush routine takes a single argument, the port ID of the serial connection, and the function returns an error code if it was unable to flush the queue. Unlike SrmReceiveFlush, SrmSendFlush does not have a timeout feature.

## Receiving Data

In order to allow an application to receive and process data as it becomes available from the serial port, you need to modify the event loop in your application. Most applications use the constant evtWaitForever for the timeout argument to EvtGetEvent, which means that the event loop is triggered only when user input places a new event in the queue. If you change the timeout value to an actual number of system ticks, the event loop can be used to service the serial port at regular intervals, while still allowing for user input to be handled. For example, the following call to EvtGetEvent sets the timeout period to 100 ticks:

```
EvtGetEvent(&event, 100);
```

*If your application needs to receive serial data in a tight loop that does not call EvtGetEvent, you can still process user input with periodic calls to EvtEventAvail to see if any user events are in the queue. These EvtEventAvail calls should probably be no more than a second apart to allow the user ample opportunity to interrupt the application. Putting the application in a loop that cannot be canceled, particularly when the loop is draining the battery through a serial port connection, is a sure way to annoy users.*

With EvtGetEvent set up with a timeout value, you can add code to the event loop that checks the serial port for data. As an example, here is the EventLoop routine from Serial Chat:

**Palm OS Garnet**

```
static void EventLoop (void)
{
    Err         error;
    EventType   event;
    static UInt32  lastResetTime;


    lastResetTime = TimGetSeconds();
    do
    {
        // Retrieve an event about once every second.
        EvtGetEvent(&event, 100);

        // Prevent the auto-off timer from putting the
        // handheld into sleep mode by resetting the
        // auto-off timer every 50 seconds.
```

```
        if (TimGetSeconds() - lastResetTime > 50)
        {
            EvtResetAutoOffTimer();
            lastResetTime = TimGetSeconds();
        }

        // Read data from the serial port.
        ReadSerial();

        if (! SysHandleEvent(&event))
            if (! MenuHandleEvent(0, &event, &error))
                if (! ApplicationHandleEvent(&event))
                    FrmDispatchEvent(&event);

    }
    while (event.eType != appStopEvent);

}
```

**Palm OS Cobalt**

```
static void EventLoop (void)
{
    status_t    error;
    EventType   event;
    static uint32_t  lastResetTime;


    lastResetTime = TimGetSeconds();
    do
    {
        // Retrieve an event about once every second.
        EvtGetEvent(&event, 100);

        // Prevent the auto-off timer from putting the
        // handheld into sleep mode by resetting the
        // auto-off timer every 50 seconds.
        if (TimGetSeconds() - lastResetTime > 50)
        {
            EvtResetAutoOffTimer();
            lastResetTime = TimGetSeconds();
        }

        // Read data from the serial port.
        ReadSerial();

        if (! SysHandleEvent(&event))
            if (! MenuHandleEvent(0, &event, &error))
                if (! ApplicationHandleEvent(&event))
                    FrmDispatchEvent(&event);

    }
    while (event.eType != appStopEvent);

}
```

Serial Chat's `EventLoop` routine calls the `ReadSerial` function to do the actual receiving of incoming serial data. Before we get to `ReadSerial`, we should look at another feature of the `EventLoop` function. The `EventLoop` routine calls `EvtResetAutoOffTimer` every 50 seconds to prevent the system auto-off timer from putting the handheld in sleep mode. Preventing the system from going to sleep means that Serial Chat can continue to receive and display data uninterrupted, even if there has been no user input on the handheld side of the connection. If you plan to use this technique to keep the handheld from sleeping during communication, you need to call `EvtResetAutoOffTimer` at least once a minute because one minute is the smallest auto-off timer that the user can normally set.

The `ReadSerial` function is where Serial Chat does its actual processing of incoming serial data:

**Palm OS Garnet**

```
static void ReadSerial (void)
{
    static Char  buffer[maxFieldLength];
    static UInt16  index = 0;
    Err    error;
    UInt32  bytes;


    if (gConnected == false) return;

    // See if there is anything in the queue.
    error = SrmReceiveCheck(gPortID, &bytes);
    if (error)
    {
        FrmAlert(SerialCheckAlert);
        return;
    }

    // Make sure the data in the queue won't overflow the
    // buffer. If there is too much data waiting, only
    // retrieve as much data as will fit in the buffer.
    if (bytes + index > sizeof(buffer))
    {
        bytes = sizeof(buffer) - index -
                sizeOf7BitChar('\0');
    }

    // Retrieve data.
    while (bytes)
    {
        SrmReceive(gPortID, &buffer[index], 1, 0, &error);
        if (error)
        {
            SrmReceiveFlush(gPortID, 1);
            index = 0;
            return;
        }
        switch (buffer[index])
        {
            case chrCarriageReturn:
                // Treat a carriage return as the end of an
```

```
                     // incoming message, since some terminals
                     // may send CR instead of linefeed. Convert
                     // the CR to a LF so the message is
                     // displayed correctly in the incoming text
                     // field.
                     buffer[index] = chrLineFeed;

                     // Fall through...

            case chrLineFeed:
                     // Treat a linefeed as the end of an
                     // incoming message. Leave the linefeed
                     // intact in the incoming data to properly
                     // format the incoming text field, tack a
                     // terminating null onto the string in the
                     // buffer, and then display the message in
                     // the incoming field.
                     buffer[index + 1] = chrNull;
                     MainFormDisplayMessage(buffer);
                     index = 0;
                     break;

            default:
                     index++;
                     break;
        }
        bytes--;
    }
}
```

**Palm OS Cobalt**

```
static void ReadSerial (void)
{
    static char  buffer[maxFieldLength];
    static uint16_t  index = 0;
    status_t      error;
    uint32_t  bytes;


    if (gConnected == false) return;

    // See if there is anything in the queue.
    error = SrmReceiveCheck(gPortID, &bytes);
    if (error)
    {
        FrmAlert(database, SerialCheckAlert);
        return;
    }

    // Make sure the data in the queue won't overflow the
    // buffer. If there is too much data waiting, only
    // retrieve as much data as will fit in the buffer.
    if (bytes + index > sizeof(buffer))
    {
        bytes = sizeof(buffer) - index -
```

```
                    sizeOf7BitChar('\0');
    }

    // Retrieve data.
    while (bytes)
    {
        SrmReceive(gPortID, &buffer[index], 1, 0, &error);
        if (error)
        {
            SrmReceiveFlush(gPortID, 1);
            index = 0;
            return;
        }
        switch (buffer[index])
        {
            case chrCarriageReturn:
                // Treat a carriage return as the end of an
                // incoming message, since some terminals
                // may send CR instead of linefeed. Convert
                // the CR to a LF so the message is
                // displayed correctly in the incoming text
                // field.
                buffer[index] = chrLineFeed;

                // Fall through...

            case chrLineFeed:
                // Treat a linefeed as the end of an
                // incoming message. Leave the linefeed
                // intact in the incoming data to properly
                // format the incoming text field, tack a
                // terminating null onto the string in the
                // buffer, and then display the message in
                // the incoming field.
                buffer[index + 1] = chrNull;
                MainFormDisplayMessage(buffer);
                index = 0;
                break;

            default:
                index++;
                break;
        }
        bytes--;
    }
}
```

The ReadSerial function uses a two-step process to retrieve data from the incoming serial queue. First, it checks to see if there is any data in the queue with SrmReceiveCheck. Second, if there is data in the queue, ReadSerial receives it with SrmReceive.

The SrmReceiveCheck function retrieves the number of bytes sitting in the serial port's receive queue. This is the prototype for SrmReceiveCheck:

**Palm OS Garnet**
```
Err SrmReceiveCheck(UInt16 portId, UInt32* numBytesP)
```

**Palm OS Cobalt**
```
status_t SrmReceiveCheck(uint16_t portId, uint32_t * numBytesP)
```

As usual for new serial manager functions, the SrmReceiveCheck routine's first parameter is the port ID of the serial connection. The second parameter is a pointer to a UInt32 (uint32_t in Palm OS Cobalt) variable that receives the number of bytes waiting in the queue. If SrmReceiveCheck succeeds, it returns a 0 value, indicating no error.

If SrmReceiveCheck reports that there is data to retrieve, ReadSerial then calls SrmReceive from within a while loop to retrieve the data one byte at a time, checking each incoming character to see if it is a linefeed or a carriage return. Serial Chat uses these two characters to indicate the end of a message. If one of these end-of-message characters is encountered, ReadSerial calls MainFormDisplayMessage to display the message in the Incoming field.

The SrmReceive function has the following prototype:

**Palm OS Garnet**
```
UInt32 SrmReceive (UInt16 portId, void *rcvBufP,
                   UInt32 count, Int32 timeout, Err* errP)
```

**Palm OS Cobalt**
```
uint32_t SrmReceive (uint16_t portId, void *rcvBufP,
                     uint32_t count, int32_t timeout, status_t* errP)
```

The SrmReceive routine's second parameter is a pointer to a buffer to receive data from the serial queue, and the third parameter specifies the number of bytes to retrieve. The timeout parameter is the number of system ticks that the new serial manager waits to receive the requested block of data; if the timeout period is reached before the requested number of bytes has been received, SrmReceive returns the error code serErrTimeOut via the errP parameter. Regardless of any errors encountered, SrmReceive reports in its return value the actual number of bytes received.

If a line error occurs while receiving data, SrmReceive returns the error code serErrLineErr in its errP parameter. When your application receives a serErrLineErr result from a SrmReceive call, clear the error using the SrmClearErr function, which takes the port ID of the connection as its only parameter. Alternatively, you can simply flush the receive queue with SrmReceiveFlush to ensure that no garbage data remains in the queue for the next read; the SrmReceiveFlush function also calls SrmClearErr internally to clear any line errors from the port.

If your application needs to receive records of a specific size, and it cannot handle partial records, you may want to consider using SrmReceiveWait. The SrmReceiveWait function waits a specified amount of time for a certain amount of data to enter the receive queue, and then returns. The prototype for SrmReceiveWait looks like this:

**Palm OS Garnet**
```
Err SrmReceiveWait(UInt16 portId, UInt32 bytes,
                   Int32 timeout)
```

**Palm OS Cobalt**
```
status_t SrmReceiveWait(uint16_t portId, uint32_t bytes,
                        int32_t timeout)
```

The `bytes` parameter specifies the number of bytes to wait for before returning. In Palm OS Garnet, the `timeout` value is the length of time in system ticks that `SrmReceiveWait` stalls while waiting to accumulate the required number of bytes. In Palm OS Cobalt, the timeout value is expressed in microseconds. The `SrmReceiveWait` routine returns the error code `srmErrTimeOut` if it cannot retrieve all the bytes requested before the `timeout` period is up.

> *The `SrmReceiveWait` function puts the system into doze mode while it waits for data. Using `SrmReceiveWait` is a battery-friendly way to await large blocks of incoming data.*

## Retrieving Serial Port Information

Should you wish to see what line errors were encountered when `SrmReceive`, `SrmReceiveCheck`, or `SrmReceiveWait` returns a `serErrLineErr` error code, you can use `SrmGetStatus` to retrieve them. The `SrmGetStatus` function has the following prototype:

**Palm OS Garnet**
```
Err SrmGetStatus (UInt16 portId, UInt32* statusFieldP,
                  UInt16* lineErrsP)
```

**Palm OS Cobalt**
```
status_t SrmGetStatus (uint16_t portId, uint32_t* statusFieldP,
                       uint16_t* lineErrsP)
```

The `lineErrsP` parameter should specify a pointer to a variable that will hold the line error status. The line error value is a bit field that may contain a number of constant values, defined in the Palm OS header file `SerialMgr.h`. The following table shows the constants, their values, and what error each represents.

| Constant | Value | Description |
|---|---|---|
| serLineErrorParity | 0x0001 | Parity error |
| serLineErrorHWOverrun | 0x0002 | Hardware overrun |
| serLineErrorFraming | 0x0004 | Framing error |
| serLineErrorBreak | 0x0008 | Break signal detected |
| serLineErrorHShake | 0x0010 | Line handshake error |
| serLineErrorSWOverrun | 0x0020 | Software overrun |
| serLineErrorCarrierLost | 0x0040 | Carrier Detect (CD) signal dropped |

The variable pointed to by the `statusFieldP` parameter receives a bit field containing hardware status information for the port. The `SerialMgr.h` header also defines constants for use with this status field, as described in the following table.

| Constant | Value | Description |
|---|---|---|
| srmStatusCtsOn | 0x00000001 | CTS line is active. |
| srmStatusRtsOn | 0x00000002 | RTS line is active. |
| srmStatusDsrOn | 0x00000004 | DSR line is active. |
| srmStatusBreakSigOn | 0x00000008 | Break signal is active. |

Two more functions, SrmGetDeviceCount and SrmGetDeviceInfo, are useful if you want to take a peek at what serial devices are available on a given handheld and what capabilities those devices have. SrmGetDeviceCount requires a pointer to a UInt16 value that will receive the total number of serial devices, both physical and virtual, present on the handheld:

**Palm OS Garnet**
```
Err SrmGetDeviceCount (UInt16* numOfDevicesP)
```

**Palm OS Cobalt**
```
status_t SrmGetDeviceCount (uint16_t* numOfDevicesP)
```

The SrmGetDeviceInfo function provides a description of a given serial port. It has the following prototype:

**Palm OS Garnet**
```
Err SrmGetDeviceInfo (UInt32 deviceID,
                      DeviceInfoType* deviceInfoP)
```

**Palm OS Cobalt**
```
status_t SrmGetDeviceInfo (uint32_t deviceID,
                      DeviceInfoType* deviceInfoP)
```

You have a number of options for specifying the deviceID parameter, which identifies the particular serial port you are interested in retrieving information from. The deviceID parameter may be a valid port ID returned from SrmOpen or SrmOpenBackground, the creator ID of a specific device, or a zero-based index. The index number is particularly useful when paired with the SrmGetDeviceCount function because it allows you to enumerate the existing serial devices and retrieve information for all of them. The following code walks through the serial ports on a device and retrieves information about each:

**Palm OS Garnet**
```
UInt16  index;
UInt32  i;
DeviceInfoType  deviceInfo;

SrmGetDeviceCount(&index);
for (i = 0; i < index; i++)
{
    SrmGetDeviceInfo(i, &deviceInfo);
    // Do something with the information here.
}
```

**Palm OS Cobalt**
```
uint16_t  index;
uint32_t  i;
```

```
DeviceInfoType  deviceInfo;

SrmGetDeviceCount(&index);
for (i = 0; i < index; i++)
{
    SrmGetDeviceInfo(i, &deviceInfo);
    // Do something with the information here.
}
```

The DeviceInfoType that SrmOpenBackground returns via its deviceInfoP parameter is defined in SerialMgr.h as follows:

```
typedef struct DeviceInfoType {
    UInt32 serDevCreator;        // Four Character creator
                                 //  type for serial driver
                                 //  ('sdrv')
    UInt32 serDevFtrInfo;        // Flags defining features
                                 //  of this serial
                                 //  hardware
    UInt32 serDevMaxBaudRate;    // Maximum baud rate for
                                 //  this device
    UInt32 serDevHandshakeBaud;  // HW Handshaking is
                                 //  recommended for baud
                                 //  rates over this value
    Char *serDevPortInfoStr;     // Description of serial
                                 //  HW device or virtual
                                 //  device
    UInt8 reserved[8];           // Reserved
} DeviceInfoType;
```

*Note that in Palm OS Cobalt, SrmOpenBackground is no longer supported.*

You can retrieve values from the serDevFtrInfo bit field by using the constants described in the following table.

| Constant | Value | Description |
|---|---|---|
| serDevCradlePort | 0x00000001 | Serial hardware controls RS-232 serial from cradle connector of Palm OS device. |
| serDevRS-232Serial | 0x00000002 | Serial hardware has RS-232 line drivers. |
| serDevIRDACapable | 0x00000004 | Serial hardware has IR line drivers and generates IrDA mode serial signals. |
| serDevModemPort | 0x00000008 | Serial hardware drives modem connection. |
| serDevCncMgrVisible | 0x00000010 | Serial device port name string should be displayed in the Connection panel. |

## Changing the Size of the Receive Buffer

The default receive buffer provided by the new serial manager is 512 bytes long. If you need a larger buffer, you can provide your own and install it with SrmSetReceiveBuffer. The SrmSetReceiveBuffer function has the following prototype:

**Palm OS Garnet**

```
Err SrmSetReceiveBuffer (UInt16 portId, void *bufP,
                         UInt16 bufSize)
```

**Palm OS Cobalt**

```
status_t SrmSetReceiveBuffer (uint16_t portId, void *bufP,
                              uint16_t bufSize)
```

Like most other new serial manager functions, the first argument to SrmSetReceiveBuffer must be the port ID of the serial connection. The bufP parameter is a void pointer to the buffer itself, and bufSize is the size of that buffer in bytes.

Call SrmSetReceiveBuffer after a successful call to SrmOpen to install the new buffer:

**Palm OS Garnet**

```
Err      error;
UInt16   portID;
Char     *buffer;

buffer = MemPtrNew(2048);
error = SrmOpen(serPortCradlePort, 9600, &portID);
if (! error)
    SrmSetReceiveBuffer(portID, buffer, bufferSize);
```

**Palm OS Cobalt**

```
status_t error;
uint16_t  portID;
char     *buffer;

buffer = MemPtrNew(2048);
error = SrmOpen(serPortCradlePort, 9600, &portID);
if (! error)
    SrmSetReceiveBuffer(portID, buffer, bufferSize);
```

When your application is done using the serial port, it must reinstall the default buffer before closing the port. To accomplish this task, call SrmSetReceiveBuffer again, specifying NULL for both the bufP and bufSize parameters:

```
SrmSetReceiveBuffer(portID, NULL, NULL);
MemPtrFree(buffer);
```

## Changing Serial Port Settings

Depending upon what sort of device you are connecting a Palm OS handheld to, you may need to alter various communications settings, such as baud rate and parity, to be able to communicate with the other device. By default, the new serial manager opens a port with the following properties:

❑   A 512-byte-long receive queue

- ❑    A CTS timeout of five seconds

- ❑    One stop bit

- ❑    Eight data bits

- ❑    Hardware handshaking

- ❑    Flow control enabled

- ❑    Whatever baud rate you specified when opening the port, if the connection is a standard RS-232 connection

The SrmControl routine is the function to use when retrieving or establishing communications settings for a serial port, and it has the following prototype:

**Palm OS Garnet**
```
Err SrmControl (UInt16 portId, UInt16 op, void *valueP,
                UInt16 *valueLenP)
```

**Palm OS Cobalt**
```
status_t SrmControl (uint16_t portId, uint16_t op, void *valueP,
                     uint16_t *valueLenP)
```

The usual port ID heads the list of parameters for SrmControl. The next parameter, op, is a control code that specifies what action you want SrmControl to perform. This control code turns what looks like a simple four-parameter function into a tool of Swiss Army knife capabilities, both complex and versatile. Values for the op parameter should be from the enumerated type SrmCtlEnum, which is defined in SerialMgr.h. Depending upon the value of the control code, the valueP parameter may specify either the address of a value to pass to the function, or the address of a variable that will receive data from SrmControl. If the requested control code uses the valueP parameter, then the valueLenP parameter specifies the address of a variable that contains the length of the data in valueP. Not all control codes use the valueP and valueLenP parameters; for those that do not require a value, pass NULL for valueP and valueLenP.

The possible control codes in SrmCtlEnum, and how they should be used, are described in the following table.

| Control Code | Description |
| --- | --- |
| srmCtlSetBaudRate | Sets the baud rate for the connection. valueP should point to an Int32 value that specifies the baud rate, and valueLenP should point to sizeof(Int32). |
| srmCtlGetBaudRate | Retrieves the current baud rate of the connection. valueP should point to an Int32 value that will receive the baud rate, and valueLenP should point to sizeof(Int32). |
| srmCtlSetFlags | Sets flags for the serial hardware. These flags control things like parity, number of stop bits, and bits per character. valueP should point to a UInt32 bit field containing the flags to set, and valueLenP should point to sizeof(UInt32). |

*Table continued on following page*

| Control Code | Description |
|---|---|
| srmCtlGetFlags | Retrieves flags for the serial hardware. valueP should point to a UInt32 variable to receive the flags, and valueLenP should point to sizeof(UInt32). |
| srmCtlSetCtsTimeout | Sets the length of the CTS timeout. valueP should point to an Int32 value containing the timeout value, and valueLenP should point to sizeof(Int32). |
| srmCtlGetCtsTimeout | Retrieves the length of the CTS timeout. valueP should point to an Int32 variable to receive the timeout value, and valueLenP should point to sizeof(Int32). |
| srmCtlStartBreak | Turns on the RS-232 break signal. Make sure to leave the break signal on long enough to generate a valid break on whatever device the handheld is connected to. |
| srmCtlStopBreak | Turns off the RS-232 break signal. |
| srmCtlStartLocalLoopback | Starts local loopback test. |
| srmCtlStopLocalLoopback | Stops local loopback test. |
| srmCtlIrDAEnable | Enables IrDA connection on the serial port. |
| srmCtlIrDADisable | Disables IrDA connection on the serial port. |
| srmCtlRxEnable | Enables receiver for IrDA communications. |
| srmCtlRxDisable | Disables receiver for IrDA communications. |
| srmCtlUserDef | Passes the valueP and valueLenP pointers to the SdrvControl function for a serial driver, or the VdrvControl function for a virtual driver. This control code is used by serial driver developers, who may need to send or receive custom control information that the regular serial manager interface cannot handle. |
| srmCtlGetOptimalTransmitSize | Asks the port for the most efficient buffer size for transmitting data packets. If the serial or virtual driver does not support this control code, SrmControl returns the error code serErrNotSupported, in which case no buffering should be done. If the port wants some kind of buffering, but it is not choosy about the buffer size, this control code sets valueP to point to 0. Otherwise, valueP points to a number that specifies the most efficient block size, in bytes, for transmitting data through this port. valueLenP points to sizeof(Int32). |

The flags for the srmCtlSetFlags and srmCtlGetFlags control codes may be accessed by means of a number of constant values, defined in SerialMgr.h. The following table describes what each flag represents.

| Constant | Value | Description |
|---|---|---|
| srmSettingsFlagStopBitsM | 0x00000001 | Mask for stop bits field. |
| srmSettingsFlagStopBits1 | 0x00000000 | One stop bit. |
| srmSettingsFlagStopBits2 | 0x00000001 | Two stop bits. |
| srmSettingsFlagParityOnM | 0x00000002 | Mask for parity on. |
| srmSettingsFlagParityEvenM | 0x00000004 | Mask for parity even. |
| srmSettingsFlagXonXoffM | 0x00000008 | Mask for Xon/Xoff flow control. Not implemented as of Palm OS 3.5. |
| srmSettingsFlagRTSAutoM | 0x00000010 | Mask for RTS receive flow control. |
| srmSettingsFlagCTSAutoM | 0x00000020 | Mask for CTS transmit flow control. |
| srmSettingsFlagBitsPerCharM | 0x000000C0 | Mask for bits per character field. |
| srmSettingsFlagBitsPerChar5 | 0x00000000 | Five bits per character. |
| srmSettingsFlagBitsPerChar6 | 0x00000040 | Six bits per character. |
| srmSettingsFlagBitsPerChar7 | 0x00000080 | Seven bits per character. |
| srmSettingsFlagBitsPerChar8 | 0x000000C0 | Eight bits per character. |
| srmSettingsFlagFlowControl | 0x00000100 | Enables software overrun protection. If this flag and srmSettingsFlagRTSAutoM are both set, the new serial manager asserts the RTS signal when the receive buffer is full to prevent the transmitting device from overrunning the buffer. When the application receives data from the buffer, the system turns off the RTS assertion to allow more incoming data into the buffer. Using this feature prevents software overrun line errors, but it may cause CTS timeouts on the connected device if the RTS line is asserted longer than the current CTS timeout value. |

*The default settings for the serial port are eight bits per character, one stop bit, and no parity, with RTS flow control engaged and a CTS timeout value of five seconds. The constant srmDefaultCTSTimeout, defined in SerialMgr.h, specifies the default CTS timeout length; all the other defaults are part of the srmDefaultSettings constant.*

To demonstrate using SrmControl, here are the relevant parts of Serial Chat's OpenSerial function that were omitted earlier in this chapter:

**Palm OS Garnet**

```
Err      error;
UInt32   flags = 0;
UInt16   flagsSize = sizeof(flags);

flags = srmSettingsFlagBitsPerChar8 |
        srmSettingsFlagStopBits1 |
        srmSettingsFlagRTSAutoM;
error = SrmControl(gPortID, srmCtlSetFlags, &flags,
                    &flagsSize);
```

**Palm OS Cobalt**

```
status_t  error;
uint32_t  flags = 0;
uint16_t  flagsSize = sizeof(flags);

flags = srmSettingsFlagBitsPerChar8 |
        srmSettingsFlagStopBits1 |
        srmSettingsFlagRTSAutoM;
error = SrmControl(gPortID, srmCtlSetFlags, &flags,
                    &flagsSize);
```

Serial Chat sets the port up with eight bits per character, no parity, one stop bit, and RTS hardware flow control. It could just as easily have used seven bits per character, even parity, and one stop bit — in which case, the `flags` variable would have been set like this:

```
flags = srmSettingsFlagBitsPerChar7 |
        srmSettingsFlagParityOnM |
        srmSettingsFlagParityEvenM |
        srmSettingsFlagStopBits1 |
        srmSettingsFlagRTSAutoM;
```

If you are experimenting with the Serial Chat sample application by connecting it to a terminal program on the desktop, be sure to set the terminal program to use eight bits per character, no parity, and one stop bit to ensure that the data passed over the serial connection does not become garbled.

*If you plan to connect at speeds faster than 19,200 bps, use hardware handshaking to make a successful connection:*

```
flags = srmSettingsFlagRTSAutoM |
        srmSettingsFlagCTSAutoM;
```

## Using the Old Serial Manager

If you need to write an application that can use the serial port on pre-Palm OS 3.3 devices that do not support the new serial manager, you will have to use the old serial manager. Fortunately, the two serial managers are very similar. In fact, the names of functions in the old serial manager are almost identical to their counterparts in the new serial manager, beginning with a `Ser` prefix instead of `Srm`. Most of the information already presented about using the new serial manager is applicable to using the old serial manager, so this section concentrates on the differences between the two managers.

*To use any of the old serial manager functions with Palm OS 3.5 or later SDK headers, be sure to include the file `SerialMgrOld.h` in your project. Even better, it is probably easiest to build with* *version 3.1 headers to avoid duplication of the enumerated types and constants that are used by both the old and new serial managers.*

The first major difference between the old and new serial managers is that the old serial manager does not use the port ID value required by most of the new serial manager functions. Instead, old serial manager functions require a reference to the serial manager library, which you must retrieve with the `SysLibFind` function, like this:

```
UInt16 serialRefNum;

Err error = SysLibFind("Serial Library", &serialRefNum);
```

You must retrieve the serial library reference even before you call `SerOpen` to open the connection because `SerOpen` also requires the reference as an argument.

## Opening and Closing the Serial Port

Just as with the New Serial Manager, the basic open and close operations are supported.

The `SerOpen` function has the following prototype:

```
Err SerOpen (UInt16 refNum, UInt16 port, UInt32 baud)
```

The first parameter, `refNum`, is the serial library reference retrieved by `SysLibFind`. The old serial manager supports only the standard physical serial port; to indicate this port, pass 0 for the `port` parameter. Specify the baud rate for the connection using the `baud` parameter.

Just as with the new serial manager, if `SerOpen` returns an error code of `serErrAlreadyOpen`, another task is currently using the port. Unless you want to deal with the nightmare of sharing the serial port with another application, you should close the connection with the `SerClose` function.

After opening the port, you may wish to flush the receive buffer with the `SerReceiveFlush` function, which operates just like its cousin `SrmReceiveFlush`.

When you are finished with the serial port, close it with the `SerClose` function. Optionally, you may wish to first drain the transmit queue with `SerSendWait`, which has an additional `timeout` parameter not present in `SrmSendWait`:

```
Err SerSendWait (UInt16 refNum, Int32 timeout)
```

The `timeout` parameter was never really implemented before the new serial manager made its debut, so you should pass the value –1 for `timeout`.

## Sending Data

The `SerSend` function operates in the same fashion as `SrmSend`. If you require compatibility with Palm OS 1.0 instead, use `SerSend10`, which has the following prototype:

```
Err SerSend10 (UInt16 refNum, void *bufP, UInt32 size)
```

The `SerSend10` function works in much the same fashion as `SerSend` and `SrmSend`; it just returns less useful information than later versions of the function.

**699**

# Chapter 19

## Receiving Data

You can use `SerReceive` in the same way that you would use `SrmReceive`; they have the same parameters. An older version of the function, `SerReceive10`, exists to support Palm OS 1.0:

```
Err SerReceive10 (UInt16 refNum, void *bufP, UInt32 bytes,
                   Int32 timeout)
```

Just like `SerSend10`, `SerReceive10` is somewhat less useful than its newer counterpart because it returns less information about the transfer.

## Getting Serial Port Information

The old serial manager does not have functions equivalent to `SrmGetDeviceCount` and `SrmGetDeviceInfo`. If you want to check on the status of the connection after receiving a `serErrLineErr` error code from `SerReceive`, `SerReceiveCheck`, or `SerReceiveWait`, call `SerGetStatus`. The `SerGetStatus` function looks and operates differently from `SrmGetStatus`:

```
UInt16 SerGetStatus (UInt16 refNum, Boolean *ctsOnP,
                      Boolean *dsrOnP)
```

The values returned to the `ctsOnP` and `dsrOnP` parameters actually have no meaning; they were never implemented before the new serial manager was created. The return value from `SerGetStatus` is equivalent to the bit field returned in the `lineErrsP` parameter of `SrmGetStatus`; see the discussion of `SrmGetStatus` in the "Retrieving Serial Port Information" section earlier in this chapter for some useful constants to use when reading this bit field.

## Changing the Size of the Receive Buffer

Just as the new serial manager's `SrmSetReceiveBuffer` function does, `SerSetReceiveBuffer` allows you to install your own buffer in place of the default 512-byte buffer. The same warnings as for `SrmSetReceiveBuffer` apply; be sure to reinstall the default buffer before closing the port.

## Altering Serial Port Settings

In the new serial manager, `SrmControl` is responsible for a great number of tasks. The old serial manager divides these duties among three functions: `SerControl`, `SerGetSettings`, and `SerSetSettings`. The `SerControl` function handles everything except for basic communications properties like baud rate and parity. The prototype for `SerControl` looks like this:

```
Err SerControl (UInt16 refNum, UInt16 op, void *valueP,
                 UInt16 *valueLenP)
```

There are fewer control codes available for the `op` parameter of `SerControl` than for the `SrmControl` function, all of which are part of the `SerCtlEnum` enumerated type defined in `SerialMgrOld.h`. Most of the control codes are similar to those required by `SrmControl`; notable omissions are codes for setting and retrieving baud rate, retrieving optimal block size, and passing data to a custom serial driver.

Use `SerGetSettings` to retrieve communications parameters for the serial port and `SerSetSettings` to change the same parameters. These functions have the following prototypes:

700

```
Err SerGetSettings (UInt16 refNum,
                    SerSettingsPtr settingsP)
Err SerSetSettings (UInt16 refNum,
                    SerSettingsPtr settingsP)
```

The SerSettingsType structure is required by both of these functions; this structure is defined as follows in SerialMgrOld.h:

```
typedef struct SerSettingsType {
    UInt32  baudRate;    // Baud rate
    UInt32  flags;       // Miscellaneous settings
    Int32   ctsTimeout;  // Max # of ticks to wait for CTS
                         //  to become asserted before
                         //  transmitting; used only when
                         //  configured with
                         //  serSettingsFlagCTSAutoM.
} SerSettingsType;
```

The flags parameter is a bit field that uses constants similar to those used by the flags in the srmCtlGetFlags and srmCtlSetFlags control codes of the SrmControl function; just use the same constants, with a ser prefix instead of srm. Note that there is no equivalent in the old serial manager to the special srmSettingsFlagFlowControl mode for preventing software buffer overrun.

# Summary

In this chapter, you learned how to use the Palm OS serial manager to communicate with other devices via the handheld's serial port. After reading this chapter, you should understand the following:

❑ The serial communications stack in Palm OS is based on the byte-level control of the serial manager. The following protocols are built on top of the serial manager: the modem manager, Serial Link Protocol (SLP), Packet Assembly/Disassembly Protocol (PADP), Desktop Link Protocol (DLP), and Connection Management Protocol (CMP).

❑ The new serial manager is the preferred interface to basic serial input and output, but there is still backwards compatibility with the old serial manager to allow serial communications programming for older devices.

❑ Palm OS Garnet and Palm OS Cobalt only support the new serial manager.

❑ It is very important to close the serial port when your application does not actually need it to be open because an open serial port rapidly drains the batteries.

❑ New serial manager functions require a port ID, which you retrieve by passing a logical port number or a serial device creator ID to SrmOpen, SrmExtOpen, SrmOpenBackground, or SrmExtOpenBackground. Old serial manager functions require a reference to the serial library, which you retrieve with the SysLibFind function.

❑ Unless you want to deal with the nightmare of sharing a connection between two applications, call SrmClose and don't use the serial port if SrmOpen or SrmOpenBackground returns the serErrAlreadyOpen error code.

❑ When receiving incoming data, take care not to shut out user input completely; the simplest way to achieve this is by passing a timeout parameter to the `EvtGetEvent` call in your application's event loop.

❑ You can change the size of the receive buffer with `SrmSetReceiveBuffer` but you must make sure to reinstall the default buffer before closing the port.

# 20

# Communicating Over a Network

When the first Palm OS handheld was introduced, it was called the "Pilot Connected Organizer." At the time, "connected" referred only to the HotSync connection between a desktop computer and the handheld. As Palm OS evolved, Palm added networking capabilities to the platform, allowing the operating system to become truly connected. Since version 2.0, Palm OS has had the ability to connect directly to and communicate with computers and other devices via TCP/IP—the network protocol suite that forms the backbone of the Internet.

There are a number of ways a Palm OS handheld can connect to a network. Modern Palm OS handhelds offer built-in TCP/IP connectivity primarily over 802.11b "Wi-Fi," over Bluetooth, or over a cellular data "smartphone" connection. For those Palm OS handhelds that do not possess these built-in connectivity options, add-on cards and sleds are available that can provide Wi-Fi, Bluetooth, and cellular data connectivity. Finally, TCP/IP connectivity is available via many wired and wireless add-on products, including landline dialup modems, Ethernet cradles, direct serial connections, and IrDA-to-Ethernet bridges and access points.

Regardless of the physical method used to connect a Palm OS handheld to the network, applications access the network in the same way: through the built-in network APIs provided as part of the PalmSource SDK. Using APIs ensures that an application can make use of network services without any changes in code to handle the different types of physical connection.

For Palm OS Garnet as well as earlier versions of the Palm OS SDK, TCP/IP support is provided via the net library. This is a proprietary abstraction of TCP/IP sockets that has been part of the PalmSource SDK since Palm OS 3.x. Although Berkeley sockets is not inherently supported at the system level in Palm OS Garnet and earlier Palm OS versions, as a convenience PalmSource also provides a thin Berkeley sockets API interface that sits on top of the net library.

With the introduction of Palm OS Cobalt, PalmSource has done away with the original net library interface in favor of the widely supported Berkeley sockets API, which is now built in as a system service. Applications built against non-Palm OS Cobalt versions of the SDK, and which use the net library APIs, will continue to work when run in Palm OS Cobalt. However, developers who are targeting the Palm OS Cobalt SDK for their Palm OS application will need to modify them to use the sockets API.

# Understanding TCP/IP Networking

TCP/IP and its sister protocol, UDP, are the glue that connects computers to one another on the Internet and within many intranets worldwide. The IP (Internet Protocol) portion of both protocols provides routing, which ensures that data are marked with their intended destination on the network. IP is a connectionless protocol; it takes care of directing data to the proper network or subnetwork, but it makes no guarantee that the data will actually reach the intended destination.

TCP (Transmission Control Protocol) is a connection-oriented protocol. It sets up a link between both ends of a connection and provides reliable transport of data, ensuring that all the bytes sent from one end of a connection make it safely to the other end. TCP uses IP to transmit data to the correct destination, but TCP also verifies that no errors in transmission occurred. TCP breaks up data into individual packets, each of which must be acknowledged by the other end of the connection. If the sender does not receive an acknowledgment for a packet, TCP requests that the packet be resent until it reaches the other end of the connection intact. TCP also makes sure that packets are reassembled in the correct order, ensuring that whatever data enters the connection always comes out the other end unmodified.

Unlike TCP, UDP (User Datagram Protocol) is connectionless, and it provides no guarantee of delivery. However, TCP requires a lot of network bandwidth to send acknowledgments back and forth. On an unreliable network, TCP can take a long time to retransmit data that didn't make it across the network intact. UDP encapsulates data into *datagrams*, which are indivisible chunks of data. If the datagram makes it to its destination, it already contains the sum total of the transmission without the need for reassembly. UDP is well suited for slow or unreliable networks, or for communications that involve only tiny amounts of data.

TCP and IP form two layers of the *network protocol stack*. The network protocol stack is a series of layers that define protocols for handling different parts of a networked application's communication. Four layers make up the stack as follows:

- ❑ **Transport Layer.** Controls how data is divided into packets. Both TCP and UDP are transport-level protocols.

- ❑ **Network Layer.** Controls the routing of packets to their intended destinations. IP is a network-level protocol.

- ❑ **Data Link Layer.** Consists of network drivers that transmit the data from higher levels in the protocol stack to the actual network adapter. The Palm OS protocol stack provides PPP (Point to Point Protocol) and SLIP (Serial Link Internet Protocol) as data link protocols.

- ❑ **Physical Layer.** Converts data into a physical representation of that data. Depending upon the actual transmission medium, the physical form of the data can be varying electrical voltages, modulations of radio frequencies, pulses of light, or whatever magic hardware engineers dream up next.

The application itself is a fifth layer, the *application layer*, which sits on top of the network protocol stack. In Palm OS Garnet and earlier version of Palm OS, the Palm OS net library forms the interface between the application layer and the top of the network protocol stack. In Palm OS Cobalt, the sockets API provides this interface. Figure 20-1 shows the relationships between the layers of the protocol stack.

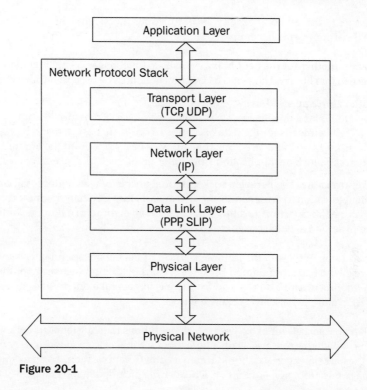

Figure 20-1

# Programming the Palm OS Garnet Net Library

Berkeley sockets is the de facto model used for programming TCP/IP applications. The Berkeley model negotiates a connection, called a *socket*, between two hosts on a network. A socket hides many of the details of making and maintaining a TCP/IP connection and allows applications to treat the connection as a pipe. Applications on either end of the socket are free to toss data into the pipe, or pull data from the pipe, at will without regard to how TCP/IP manages the data. Effectively, applications can read from the network and write to it in a fashion similar to how they might read data from and write data to a file system.

The Palm OS Garnet net library mirrors the Berkeley sockets model, with a few small additions to make it better suited to running on a handheld with limited resources. Networking in Palm OS is implemented as a shared library instead of being a core part of the system software.

Palm OS provides the following two interfaces to the net library:

❑   Net library native interface

❑   Berkeley sockets interface

The native interface to the net library is a series of functions that begin with the *Net* prefix. Many of these functions have three arguments in common:

❑ **Reference number for the net library.** All calls to functions in a Palm OS shared library require a reference to that library. The `SysLibFind` function must be used to retrieve this reference number.

❑ **Timeout value, specified in system ticks.** Because of network conditions, network operations can sometimes take time to complete, which may make a networked application appear to be "frozen" while it waits for the data exchange to finish. To ensure that a handheld application remains responsive to the user, this timeout may be used to limit the amount of time a network operation can block the application from other tasks, such as processing user input events.

❑ **Error return value.** The Berkeley sockets model normally uses a global variable called `errno` to alert an application to error conditions. Because a Palm OS shared library cannot have global variables, net library functions that might return an error return it in one of their arguments instead of setting a global error variable.

Other than the addition of these extra arguments, most of the net library functions should look very familiar to anyone who has programmed Berkeley sockets. Although the names of the primary sockets APIs have been modified with a `NetLib` prefix, there is in general a one-to-one correspondence between the net library APIs and the Berkeley sockets interface.

The Palm OS Berkeley sockets interface uses macro definitions to map standard Berkeley sockets function calls to the native net library routines. With a little bit of setup work, code written for other operating systems that uses the Berkeley interface should run in a Palm OS application. As an example, the following macro definition comes from `sys_socket.h`, a header file included in the Palm OS SDK:

```
#define  socket(domain, type, protocol) \
    NetLibSocketOpen(AppNetRefnum, domain, type, \
                    protocol, AppNetTimeout, &errno)
```

Using the Berkeley sockets interface to the net library provides a number of advantages. There is already a lot of free sockets code available on the Internet, and much of it is usable in a Palm OS program with only a little modification. If you already know how to program sockets, you can use familiar syntax to program networking in a Palm OS application. Also, it is easier to debug the networking part of an application on another platform, like UNIX or Windows, than it is to debug network code using Palm OS tools. Once you have the network code up and running on the other platform, you can drop it into a Palm OS program.

Finally, if you must target multiple versions of Palm OS — including Palm OS Garnet, Palm OS 3.x/4.x, and Palm OS Cobalt — using the sockets interface under Palm OS Garnet can reduce the effort required to maintain both Palm OS Garnet and Palm OS Cobalt versions of your application networking code.

*Because the Palm OS Garnet Berkeley sockets interface to the net library requires the use of global variables, it can be used only in situations where an application has access to its global variables, such as the* `sysAppLaunchCmdNormalLaunch` *launch code.*

To use the Berkeley sockets interface in your application, follow these steps:

**1.** Include the header file `<unix/sys_socket.h>`, which is part of the Palm OS SDK. The `sys_socket.h` file and other header files included by `sys_socket.h` define macros that map Berkeley style network routines to equivalent Palm OS net library function calls.

2. Link the file NetSocket.c, also included in the Palm OS SDK, with your project. The NetSocket.c file contains the implementations of various utility functions, along with global variable declarations for the net library reference number (AppNetRefnum) and timeout value (AppNetTimeout).

3. Retrieve the net library reference number with SysLibFind and assign it to the global variable AppNetRefnum:

```
Err error = SysLibFind("Net.lib", &AppNetRefnum);
```

The Berkeley sockets macros need this global variable so they can pass the library reference to native net library functions.

4. Adjust the value of AppNetTimeout. The following example sets the timeout to 10 seconds:

```
AppNetTimeout = 10 * SysTicksPerSecond();
```

Many net library functions require a timeout value, but Berkeley sockets function calls do not include a timeout. AppNetTimeout is needed so that the Berkeley macros can pass a timeout value to the native net library functions.

5. Declare the global variable errno in your code:

```
Err  errno;
```

Berkeley macros retrieve the error value from native net library function calls and assign it to the global errno variable, which duplicates the standard behavior exhibited by regular Berkeley sockets functions.

## Retrieving a Net Library Reference

Before using any net library calls, your application must obtain a reference to the net library itself by calling the SysLibFind function:

```
UInt16  gNetRefNum;

Err error = SysLibFind("Net.lib", &gNetRefNum);
```

SysLibFind takes two arguments; the first argument is the name of the library to open, and the second is a pointer that receives the reference number of the library. Most of the functions in the net library require the reference number as their first argument. If the return value from SysLibFind is sysErrLibNotFound, the net library does not exist on this particular handheld and your application does not have access to the net library interface.

Unless your application needs to only briefly make a network connection, it is a good idea to save the net library reference in a global variable. That way, the reference is available throughout your application. In fact, if you use the Berkeley sockets interface to the net library, the reference number *must* be in a global variable. The NetSocket.c module declares the global variable AppNetRefnum, which the Berkeley sockets macros use when they call the various net library functions.

## Opening the Net Library

Before you can make any calls to net library functions, you must open the library. To open the net library, use the NetLibOpen routine:

```
UInt16  ifErrs;

Err error = NetLibOpen(gNetRefNum, &ifErrs);
```

The two arguments to `NetLibOpen` are the reference to the net library and a pointer that receives any error encountered while attempting to start up the network interfaces. A nonzero return value from `NetLibOpen` may not indicate failure to open the net library; `NetLibOpen` returns `netErrAlreadyOpen` if the net library is already open. Other return values from `NetLibOpen`, other than 0, indicate that an actual error of some kind occurred while opening the library. The following example shows how `NetLibOpen` should typically be called in order to provide proper error handling:

```
error = NetLibOpen(gNetRefNum, &ifErrs);
if (! error)
{
    // No errors; opening the net library succeeded.
}
else if (error == netErrAlreadyOpen)
{
    // No errors; the library was already open.
}
else
{
    // An error occurred while opening the net
    // library. Check to see if it was an interface error.
    if (ifErrs)
    {
        // An interface error occurred.
    }
}
```

The net library keeps track of how many times it has been opened. If the net library is already open, `NetLibOpen` merely increases the open count of the library by one. The function to close the net library, `NetLibClose`, decreases the open count by one each time it is called. `NetLibClose` doesn't attempt to actually close the network library until the open count reaches zero, which allows multiple applications to keep the library open until they no longer need it. `NetLibClose` is described fully later in this chapter, in the section "Closing the Net Library."

If you need to determine how many times the net library has been opened, you can retrieve the open count with the `NetLibOpenCount` function:

```
UInt16  count;

Err error = NetLibOpenCount(gNetRefNum, &count);
```

## Resolving Hostnames and Addresses

An *IP address* (also called an *Internet address*) is a 32-bit integer value that uniquely identifies a single host on the network. IP addresses are often represented in *dotted decimal notation*, in which the address is separated by periods into its constituent bytes, in the form `1.2.3.4`. For example, say the hexadecimal IP address of this book's Web site is `D8F0933D`, which corresponds to the dotted decimal value `216.240.147.61`.

The hexadecimal form of an IP address is easy to work with if you happen to be a computer, but it's not very readable to human beings. Even the friendlier dotted decimal notation, while more readable, is still difficult for a human to remember. For this reason, each IP address may have a *hostname* assigned to it, which uses words or abbreviations instead of numbers to easily identify a host.

Hostnames use a hierarchical naming system to identify the *domain* to which a host belongs. A domain is a logical group of hosts, other subordinate domains, or both. At the highest level of the hierarchy are top-level domains, such as `.com`, which is reserved for commercial purposes. Below that level are the second-level domains, which belong to individuals, corporations, or organizations. In this example, this book's Web site is hosted on the domain `palmosbible.com`.

The next level in the hierarchy usually identifies a host within the second-level domain. For example, `www.palmosbible.com` represents the host that handles Web access to the `palmosbible.com` domain, and `ftp.palmosbible.com` identifies the host that handles FTP (File Transfer Protocol) services. It is possible for the third hierarchy level to be yet another subdomain, and so on, which allows the owner of a domain to split it into different logical units by tacking more names onto the front of the address.

Within a given domain, each host's name must be unique. As an example, within the `palmosbible.com` domain, there can be only one host named `www`, and within the `.com` top-level domain, there can be only one host named `palmosbible`. It is possible, however, for another `palmosbible` to exist on a different top level domain, such as `.org` or `.net`.

## Resolving Hostnames

In order for any computer to use a hostname, it must first resolve that name into a 32-bit IP address. The net library provides the `NetLibGetHostByName` function for resolving hostnames. `NetLibGetHostByName` has the following prototype:

```
NetHostInfoPtr NetLibGetHostByName (UInt16 libRefNum,
    const Char *nameP, NetHostInfoBufPtr bufP,
    Int32 timeout, Err *errP)
```

Like most net library functions, the first argument to `NetLibGetHostByName` is the reference to the net library. Following that argument is a pointer to a string containing the hostname. The fourth and fifth arguments are the usual timeout and error arguments present in most net library calls.

The third argument, `bufP`, and the `NetLibGetHostByName` function's return value are entwined with each other. The `bufP` argument is a pointer to a `NetHostInfoBufType` structure, which is a buffer you must allocate for storage of address information. On successful name resolution, `NetLibGetHostByName` fills the `NetHostInfoBufType` structure with variable-length address information and then returns a pointer to a structure that your application uses to access the contents of the `NetHostInfoBufType` buffer.

When calling `NetLibGetHostByName`, you first need to initialize a `NetHostInfoBufType` structure to hold the results from the function call. Because stack space is extremely limited on Palm OS, and because `NetHostInfoBufType` is a large structure, you should allocate space for the structure from the heap by calling `MemPtrNew`, as shown in the following example:

```
NetHostInfoBufPtr hostInfoBufP;

hostInfoBufP = (NetHostInfoBufPtr)
    MemPtrNew(sizeof(NetHostInfoBufType));
```

*Because* `MemPtrNew` *returns a variable of type* `MemPtr`, *you must cast its return value to type* `NetHostInfoBufPtr`. *Also, be sure to free the memory allocated for the* `NetHostInfoBufType` *structure when you are finished with it by calling* `MemPtrFree`:

```
MemPtrFree(hostInfoBufP);
```

The `NetHostInfoBufType` structure is defined in the Palm OS header file `NetMgr.h` as follows:

```
typedef struct {
    NetHostInfoType  hostInfo;  // high level results of
                                //  call are here

    // The following fields contain the variable length
    // data that hostInfo points to
    Char   name[netDNSMaxDomainName+1];  // hostInfo->name
    Char   *aliasList[netDNSMaxAliases+1];
    Char   aliases[netDNSMaxAliases][netDNSMaxDomainName+1];
    NetIPAddr  *addressList[netDNSMaxAddresses];
    NetIPAddr  address[netDNSMaxAddresses];
} NetHostInfoBufType, *NetHostInfoBufPtr;
```

`NetHostInfoBufType` is a complicated structure. Fortunately, you don't need to know anything about its internals to use it. `NetHostInfoBufType` is merely a buffer that the net library fills with address information. The `hostInfo` member of `NetHostInfoBufType` presents a simple interface to the complex insides of the `NetHostInfoBufType` structure. The `hostInfo` member is a structure of type `NetHostInfoType`. Also defined in `NetMgr.h`, `NetHostInfoType` looks like this:

```
typedef struct {
    Char    *nameP;          // official name of host
    Char    **nameAliasesP;  // array of aliases for the
                             //  hostname
    UInt16  addrType;        // address type of return
                             //  addresses
    UInt16  addrLen;         // the length, in bytes, of
                             //  the address
    UInt8   **addrListP;     // array of pointers to IP
                             //  addresses
} NetHostInfoType, *NetHostInfoPtr;
```

`NetHostInfoType` is a much simpler structure than `NetHostInfoBufType`, but it may not be obvious which of its members contains the IP address retrieved by `NetLibGetHostByName`. The `NetHostInfoType` structure is the Palm OS equivalent of the Berkeley sockets `hostent` structure, which is designed to handle a variety of addressing schemes. Fortunately, the current implementation of the net library supports only the standard 32-bit IP Version 4 (IPv4) address format, so retrieving the IP address from `NetHostInfoType` is a simple matter of casting the first pointer in the address list (`addressListP`):

```
NetIPAddr *addrP = (NetIPAddr*) hostInfoP->addrListP[0];
```

`NetIPAddr` is simply an alias for a `UInt32` variable, which also is defined in `NetMgr.h`:

```
typedef UInt32  NetIPAddr;
```

It also is possible to retrieve host information if you already have an IP address by calling the `NetLibGetHostByAddr` function. This function comes in handy if your application accepts incoming connections from outside hosts, and your application needs to look up information about the hosts that made the connections. `NetLibGetHostByAddr` looks like this:

```
NetHostInfoPtr NetLibGetHostByAddr (UInt16 libRefNum,
    UInt8 *addrP, UInt16 len, UInt16 type,
    NetHostInfoBufPtr bufP, Int32 timeout, Err *errP)
```

Many of the arguments to `NetLibGetHostByAddr` are identical in name and function to their counterparts in `NetLibGetHostByName`. The three different arguments, `addrP`, `len`, and `type`, define the IP address to look up. The `addrP` argument is a pointer to the address to resolve. `NetLibGetHostByAddr` is designed to be protocol-independent, which is why `addrP` is a pointer to a `UInt8` value instead of a 32-bit `NetIPAddr` value. You also must specify the length of the address value in the `len` parameter, as well as the type of address in the `type` parameter.

*Currently, the net library supports only 32-bit IP addresses, so you should specify 4 for the `len` value and netSocketAddrINET for the type value. Future versions of the net library may support other protocols, such as the 128-bit addresses to be used in the upcoming IP Version 6 (IPv6) standard.*

## Converting IP Addresses

At times, it may be necessary for an application to convert dotted decimal IP addresses into their 32-bit form, and vice versa. The `NetLibAddrAToIN` and `NetLibAddrINToA` functions perform these conversions:

```
NetIPAddr NetLibAddrAToIN (UInt16 libRefnum, const Char *a)
Char *NetLibAddrINToA (UInt16 libRefnum, NetIPAddr inet,
                        Char *spaceP)
```

Call `NetLibAddrAToIN` to convert an IP address in dotted decimal notation to an actual 32-bit IP address:

```
char  dottedAddr[] = "216.240.147.61";

NetIPAddr addr = NetLibAddrAToIN(gNetRefNum, dottedAddr);
```

`NetLibAddrINToA` performs the conversion from the 32-bit IP address back to a string containing a dotted decimal address:

```
NetIPAddr addr = 0xD8F0933D;

Char *dottedAddr = MemPtrNew(netMaxIPAddrStrLen);
MemSet(dottedAddr, netMaxIPAddrStrLen, 0);
NetLibAddrINToA(gNetRefNum, addr, dottedAddr);
// Do something with the address in dottedAddr.
MemPtrFree(dottedAddr);
```

## Changing the Byte Order

A 32-bit IP address value seems straightforward, but be aware of one catch. Computers with different chip architecture store multibyte integers differently. The order in which a computer stores multibyte integers is called its *byte order*. The Motorola processors used on most Mac OS and UNIX systems, and on pre–Palm OS 5 handhelds, store integers in *big-endian* order, with the most significant bytes coming first. For example, the IP address 1.2.3.4 would be stored as 0x01020304 on a big-endian system.

The Intel processors used by Windows systems, and the ARM processors used on many Palm OS 5 handhelds, store integers in *little-endian* order, with the least significant byte stored first. On a little-endian system, the IP address 1.2.3.4 would be stored as 0x04030201. Obviously, passing an IP address between little-endian and big-endian systems without some kind of conversion process will result in address resolution errors.

The TCP networking standard forces all systems to use big-endian IP addresses, which is referred to as *network byte order*. Little-endian hosts must convert from their own byte order, in this case called *host byte order*, to the network byte order before sending information over a network connection.

Palm OS has macros to convert between network and host byte orders. NetHToNL converts a 32-bit (4-byte) integer from host byte order to network byte order, and its companion function, NetNToHL, converts from network byte order back to host byte order. These macros are designed to do the right thing, whether or not the handheld they are on uses big-endian or little-endian byte order, so they are safe to use no matter which processor is present on the handheld. For example, on a Palm Powered handheld with a Motorola processor, these macros do nothing because the big-endian host byte order already matches the network byte order. On an ARM device, such as a Palm OS 5 handheld, the macros actually perform conversion between the little-endian host byte order and the big-endian network byte order.

> *The net library also provides the NetHToNS and NetNToHS macros, which convert word values (two-byte integers) between host and network byte orders.*

## Putting It All Together

Resolving a host with NetLibGetHostByName involves the following steps:

1.  Initialize a NetHostInfoBufType structure to hold the address information returned by NetLibGetHostByName.

2.  Call NetLibGetHostByName, passing it a pointer to the NetHostInfoBufType structure you allocated in Step 1.

3.  Use the pointer returned by NetLibGetHostByName to retrieve the actual IP address from the depths of the NetHostInfoBufType structure.

4.  Convert the IP address to host byte order by calling the NetNToHL function.

5.  Free the memory allocated for the NetHostInfoBufType structure.

As an example of this process, the following code presents a complete function, GetIPAddress, which takes a string containing a hostname as an argument and returns the IP address for that host. GetIPAddress assumes that a valid reference to the net library already exists in the global variable gNetRefNum:

```
NetIPAddr GetIPAddress (Char *hostName)
{
    Err  error = 0;
    NetHostInfoBufPtr  hostInfoBufP = NULL;
    NetHostInfoPtr  hostInfoP = NULL;
    NetIPAddr  address = 0;
```

```
NetIPAddr  *addressP = NULL;

// Allocate a buffer to receive host information.
hostInfoBufP = (NetHostInfoBufPtr)
    MemPtrNew(sizeof(NetHostInfoBufType));

if (! hostInfoBufP)
    return 0;
// Retrieve host information.
hostInfoP = NetLibGetHostByName(gNetRefNum, hostName,
    hostInfoBufP, 10 * SysTicksPerSecond(), &error);

if (hostInfoP)
{
    // Retrieve a pointer to the first IP address in
    // the array.
    addressP = (NetIPAddr*) hostInfoP->addrListP[0];

    // Convert the address to host byte order.
    address = NetNToHL(*addressP);
}
else
{
    // Depending on the value of error, the application
    // could take action at this point to inform the
    // user of the error condition.
}

// Free the memory used by the address buffer.
MemPtrFree(hostInfoBufP);

return address;
```

## Finding a Service Port

Knowing the IP address of the machine that you want to connect to isn't quite enough information to form a connection; you also must determine which service should handle the connection. Network services represent different ways to connect to and communicate with a host, such as e-mail, Web, and telnet. Each service has both a human-readable name (for example, smtp for e-mail) and a 16-bit port number (for example, 25 for e-mail).

The net library provides the NetLibGetServByName function for retrieving a port number based on the human-readable name of a service. The prototype for NetLibGetServByName looks like this:

```
NetServInfoPtr NetLibGetServByName (UInt16 libRefNum,
    const Char *servNameP, const Char *protoNameP,
    NetServInfoBufPtr bufP, Int32 timeout, Err *errP)
```

By now, the libRefNum, timeout, and errP parameters should be familiar to you. The NetLibGetServByName function's servNameP parameter is a pointer to a null-terminated string containing the desired service name; possible values for servNameP are chargen, discard, daytime, echo, finger, ftp, ftp-data, imap2, name, nntp, pop2, pop3, qotd, smtp, ssh, telnet, and time.

The `protoNameP` parameter is a pointer to a null-terminated string containing the protocol that you wish to use for the connection. Your choices for protocol are `tcp` and `udp`.

Much as the `NetLibGetHostByName` function does, `NetLibGetServByName` returns its information in a complicated structure. You must allocate space for this structure and initialize its members ahead of time. The `bufP` parameter is a pointer to a `NetServInfoBufType` structure, which is declared as follows in the `NetMgr.h` header file:

```
typedef struct {
    NetServInfoType  servInfo;  // high level results of
                                //  call are here

    // The following fields contain the variable length
    // data that servInfo points to.
    Char   name[netServMaxName+1];  // servInfo->name
    Char   *aliasList[netServMaxAliases+1];
    Char   aliases[netServMaxAliases][netServMaxName];
    Char   protoName[netProtoMaxName+1];
    UInt8  reserved;
} NetServInfoBufType, *NetServInfoBufPtr;
```

The `NetServInfoType` structure serves as a friendlier interface to the internals of `NetServInfoBufType`. `NetServInfoType` looks like this:

```
typedef struct {
    Char    *nameP;        // official name of service
    Char    **nameAliasesP; // array of aliases for the
                            //  service name
    UInt16  port;          // port number for this
                           //  service
    Char    *protoP;       // name of protocol to use
} NetServInfoType, *NetServInfoPtr;
```

On a successful call, `NetLibGetServByName` returns a pointer to a `NetServInfoType` structure. You can retrieve the port number by accessing the `port` member of that structure. The following example presents a function called `GetServicePort`, which takes a string containing a service name and returns the port number associated with that service. Notice that `GetServicePort` assumes the protocol is TCP:

```
UInt16 GetServicePort (Char *servName)
{
    Err  error = 0;
    NetServInfoBufPtr  servInfoBufP = NULL;
    NetServInfoPtr  servInfoP = NULL;
    UInt16  port = 0;
    UInt16  *portP = NULL;


    // Allocate a buffer to receive service information.
    servInfoBufP = (NetServInfoBufPtr)
        MemPtrNew(sizeof(NetServInfoBufType));

    if (! servInfoBufP)
```

```
        return 0;

    // Retrieve service information.
    servInfoP = NetLibGetServByName(gNetRefNum, servName,
        "tcp", servInfoBufP, 10 * SysTicksPerSecond(),
        &error);

    if (servInfoP)
    {
        // Retrieve the port from the service structure.
        port = servInfoP->port;
    }
    else
    {
        // Depending on the value of error, the application
        // could take action at this point to inform the
        // user of the error condition.
    }

    // Free the memory used by the service buffer.
    MemPtrFree(servInfoBufP);

    return address;
}
```

# Opening a Socket

To connect to a remote host, your application must first open a socket. You open a socket with the NetLibSocketOpen function, which has the following prototype:

```
NetSocketRef NetLibSocketOpen (UInt16 libRefnum,
    NetSocketAddrEnum domain, NetSocketTypeEnum type,
    Int16 protocol, Int32 timeout, Err *errP)
```

The libRefNum, timeout, and errP parameters are the same as in other net library functions. The domain parameter contains the type of address that the socket should expect; usually, you should use the value netSocketAddrINET to specify Internet-style addresses.

> *It also is possible to create raw sockets by specifying netSocketAddrRaw, which gives your application low-level access to the network and data link layers of the network protocol stack. This advanced technique isn't officially supported by PalmSource, although the routines necessary to make raw sockets work do exist in the Palm OS header files if you need that level of control in your application. This book focuses on the netSocketAddrINET variety of socket only.*

Use the type parameter to specify the type of connection to create. Your choices here are netSocketTypeStream (used for TCP connections), netSocketTypeDatagram (used for UDP connections), and netSocketTypeRaw. NetLibSocketOpen ignores the protocol parameter, so you can safely specify 0 here.

If successful, NetLibSocketOpen returns a NetSocketRef value, which is a reference to the open socket. Other functions that make use of an open socket need to know this reference number. To conserve system resources, the net library allows only four sockets to be opened at a time.

# Connecting a Socket

Once you have successfully opened a socket, you need to connect it to the remote host before you can send and receive data. Connecting a socket also causes the handheld to perform whatever routine is necessary to connect the handheld to the network — whether that is dialing a modem, searching for a nearby wireless base station, or whatever else might be required by the network hardware.

*Because connecting a socket may be a lengthy operation that blocks the user from making any input until the connection has been made, make it obvious in your application that it is about to spend some time making a connection. Silently connecting to the network in the background serves only to make your application look sluggish or even unresponsive.*

Use the `NetLibSocketConnect` function to make the connection:

```
Int16 NetLibSocketConnect (UInt16 libRefnum,
    NetSocketRef socket, NetSocketAddrType *sockAddrP,
    Int16 addrLen, Int32 timeout, Err *errP)
```

`NetLibSocketConnect` requires a reference to an open socket, which you supply in the `socket` parameter. You also must specify in a `NetSocketAddrType` structure the address and port that you wish to connect to. `NetSocketAddrType`, declared in `NetMgr.h`, looks like this:

```
typedef struct NetSocketAddrType {
    Int16  family;
    UInt8  data[14];
} NetSocketAddrType;
```

The `NetSocketAddrType` structure is generic; it can hold addresses in a number of different formats, depending upon the value of its `family` member. For standard Internet addresses, Palm OS provides the `NetSocketAddrINType` structure:

```
typedef struct NetSocketAddrINType {
    Int16   family;    // Address family in host byte order
    UInt16  port;      // Port in network byte order
    NetIPAddr  addr;   // IP address in network byte order
} NetSocketAddrINType;
```

`NetSocketAddrINType` just happens to be the same size as `NetSocketAddrType`, so it is possible to cast the `NetSocketAddrType` structure as `NetSocketAddrINType` to fill in the necessary data. The following example shows how to fill in the `NetSocketAddrType` structure, assuming that the port and IP address have already been retrieved in the variables `port` and `ipAddr`, respectively:

```
NetSocketAddrType      addr;
NetSocketAddrINType    *inetAddrP;

addrINP = (NetSocketAddrINType*) &addr;
inetAddrP->family = netSocketAddrINET;
inetAddrP->port = NetHToNS(port);
inetAddrP->addr = NetHToNL(ipAddr);
```

Notice that the example uses the `NetHToNS` and `NetHToNL` macros to convert the port and IP address from host to network byte order.

Once you have the `NetSocketAddrType` structure filled in, you are ready to call `NetLibSocketConnect`, as shown in the following example:

```
Err  error;

Int16  result = NetLibSocketConnect(gNetRefNum, socketRef,
    &addr, sizeof(addr), 10 * SysTicksPerSecond(), &error);
```

If successful, `NetLibSocketConnect` returns 0; otherwise, it returns -1, and you should check the value of the `errP` parameter to see what error occurred while the connection was being made. One common error that `NetLibSocketConnect` returns is `sysErrorTimeout`, which indicates that the connection operation timed out before a link could actually be established.

# Sending and Receiving Data

Once you have successfully navigated through the pitfalls of resolving a hostname, opening a socket, and connecting the socket, you are finally ready to transmit and receive data. All the preparation work of setting up and connecting a socket ensures that actual data exchange is a relatively simple process.

## Sending Data

To send data, use the `NetLibSend` function:

```
Int16 NetLibSend (UInt16 libRefNum, NetSocketRef socket,
                  void *bufP, UInt16 bufLen, UInt16 flags,
                  void *toAddrP, UInt16 toLen,
                  Int32 timeout, Err *errP)
```

The `socket` parameter is a reference to an open socket, and the usual `libRefNum`, `timeout`, and `errP` parameters also are present. The other `NetLibSend` parameters can be divided into three groups:

❑  The `bufP` and `bufLen` parameters specify the actual data to transmit and its length.

❑  The `flags` parameter allows you to specify special values for fine-tuning how the data is processed. For normal network usage, you can safely set this parameter to 0.

❑  The `toAddrP` and `toLen` parameters are used with UDP networking to specify an address to which the data should be sent. This allows a single socket to broadcast to a number of different IP addresses, without the need to disconnect and reconnect the socket. For TCP streaming data exchange, you can set both `toAddrP` and `toLen` to 0.

The `bufP` parameter points to the beginning of the data you wish to send, and `bufLen` contains the length of the data pointed to by `bufP`. If `NetLibSend` succeeds in sending all the data, it returns a value equal to `bufLen`.

Depending upon how much space is currently available in the outgoing buffer, `NetLibSend` may not always send all the data that you thought you sent. The return value from `NetLibSend` is the number of bytes actually sent to the socket's outgoing buffer. `NetLibSend` does not resend data that is too large to fit in the outgoing buffer, so you should normally call `NetLibSend` in a loop to ensure that all the data you want to transmit is actually sent. The following example defines a function called `SendData`, which sends a null-terminated string over an open socket:

```
Err SendData (NetSocketRef socketRef, Char *string)
{
    Err     error = 0;
    UInt16  bytesToSend;
    UInt16  bytesSent;
    Char    *dataP;


    bytesToSend = StrLen(string);
    dataP = string;
    while ((bytesToSend > 0) && (! error))
    {
        bytesSent = NetLibSend(gNetRefNum, socketRef,
                               dataP, bytesToSend, 0,
                               NULL, 0,
                               10 * SysTicksPerSecond(),
                               &error);

        if (bytesSent == 0)
        {
            // Connection was closed by remote host. The
            // application should close the socket.
        }

        if (! error)
        {
            dataP += bytesSent;
            bytesToSend -= bytesSent;
        }
    }

    return error;
}
```

NetLibSend returns –1 if an error occurred while it was sending data; if this happens, your application can check the errP value to find out what went wrong. Occasionally, the remote host might close the connection before NetLibSend can transmit any data, in which case NetLibSend returns 0. If this happens, your application should close the socket because that socket is no longer valid.

## Receiving Data

The counterpart to NetLibSend is NetLibReceive, which has the following prototype:

```
Int16 NetLibReceive (UInt16 libRefNum, NetSocketRef socket,
                     void *bufP, UInt16 bufLen,
                     UInt16 flags, void *fromAddrP,
                     UInt16 *fromLenP, Int32 timeout,
                     Err *errP);
```

The parameters for NetLibReceive are nearly identical in function to the parameters for NetLibSend, the primary difference being that bufP and bufLen define a receiving buffer rather than point to data to be sent. NetLibReceive attempts to read bufLen bytes from the incoming data buffer and the function returns the number of bytes actually read.

Like `NetLibSend`, `NetLibReceive` returns 0 if the remote host closed the connection, and it returns –1 if there was an error while receiving data. Check the `errP` value to determine what went wrong.

`NetLibReceive` should be called from a loop. The following example shows a function called `ReceiveData`, which wraps the `NetLibReceive` function. The parameters to `ReceiveData` are a reference to an open socket, a pointer to a buffer to receive incoming data, and the length of the buffer in bytes. `ReceiveData` attempts to read in as many bytes as fills the receiving buffer:

```
Err ReceiveData (NetSocketRef socketRef, Char *buffer,
            UInt16 bufLen)
{
    Err     error = 0;
    UInt16  bytesToRead;
    UInt16  bytesRead;
    Char    *dataP;


    bytesToRead = bufLen;
    dataP = buffer;
    do
    {
        bytesRead = NetLibReceive(gNetRefNum, socketRef,
                            dataP, bytesToRead, 0,
                            NULL, 0,
                            10 * SysTicksPerSecond(),
                            &error);

        if (bytesRead == 0)
        {
            // Connection was closed by remote host. The
            // application should close the socket.
        }

        if (! error)
        {
            dataP += bytesRead;
            bytesToRead -= bytesRead;
        }
    }
    while ((bytesToRead > 0) && (! error))

    return error;
}
```

`NetLibReceive` works well for reading data into a buffer located in heap memory, but it may be more convenient for your application to read directly into storage RAM. For this purpose, you can use the `NetLibDmReceive` function, which looks like this:

```
Int16 NetLibDmReceive (UInt16 libRefNum,
    NetSocketRef socket, void *recordP,
    UInt32 recordOffset, UInt16 rcvLen, UInt16 flags,
    void *fromAddrP, UInt16 *fromLenP, Int32 timeout,
    Err *errP)
```

The primary difference between `NetLibDmReceive` and `NetLibReceive` is the addition of a `recordOffset` parameter to `NetLibDmReceive`, which specifies where within a database record incoming data should be copied. The `recordOffset` parameter is based on a byte offset from the pointer given in the `recordP` parameter. For example, the following example copies incoming data into a record beginning 200 bytes from the `record` pointer location:

```
recordH = DmGetRecord(db, index);
record = MemHandleLock(recordH);
bytesRead = NetLibDmReceive(gNetRefNum, socketRef,
                           record, 200, bytesToRead, 0,
                           NULL, 0,
                           10 * SysTicksPerSecond(),
                           &error);
```

For complete details on handling database records and data, see Chapter 16.

## Disconnecting a Socket

When you have finished sending data from your application, you need to disconnect the socket. Either the local host or the remote host may shut down a connection; disconnecting is a way for one host to signal to the other that it has finished sending data and it is now safe for the other host to stop listening for more data.

You disconnect a socket with the `NetLibSocketShutdown` function:

```
Int16 NetLibSocketShutdown (UInt16 libRefnum,
    NetSocketRef socket, Int16 direction, Int32 timeout,
    Err *errP)
```

The `libRefNum`, `timeout`, and `errP` parameters work as they do for other net library functions, and `socket` is a reference to an open socket that should be disconnected. The remaining parameter, `direction`, tells `NetLibSocketShutdown` to close the connection in the sending direction, the receiving direction, or both.

Typically, your application should specify `netSocketDirOutput` when it is finished sending data and needs to close the connection. Possible values for `direction` are `netSocketDirInput`, `netSocketDirOutput`, and `netSocketDirBoth`. To avoid losing incoming data from the remote host, you usually shouldn't disconnect data in the incoming direction. Instead, check the return values from `NetLibSend` and `NetLibReceive`; if they ever equal 0, the remote host has disconnected and it is safe to close the connection.

Be careful not to open and close sockets too quickly because the sockets may not recycle quickly enough to be available for use once the net library has disposed of them. Opening and closing sockets too quickly can have a number of undesirable effects:

- If you open and close sockets in a tight loop, you might quickly exhaust the four sockets available in the Palm OS net library, resulting in a `netErrNoMoreSockets` error.

- UNIX sockets take time to recycle before they are available again, sometimes up to a couple of minutes. In an enterprise scenario, if hundreds of handheld network clients attempt to connect to a single server, it is possible to exhaust the number of sockets available to the server if the client application tries to reopen sockets too quickly.

❑ Many firewall servers view rapid connection and disconnection to a particular service as a denial-of-service attack. Connecting and disconnecting many times over a short time will not only cause such servers to disconnect your application but it may also raise the ire of the owner of the firewall system.

You can avoid the problems of quick connection and disconnection by leaving sockets open and reusing them until your application exits, at which point you can safely disconnect the sockets.

## Closing a Socket

If you are finished using a particular socket, it is time to use the NetLibSocketClose function to close it:

```
Int16 NetLibSocketClose (UInt16 libRefnum,
    NetSocketRef socket, Int32 timeout, Err *errP)
```

NetLibSocketClose is a simple function. Aside from the usual net library reference, timeout, and error parameters, it requires only a reference to the open socket that should be closed.

The NetLibSocketClose function can handle the disconnection of a socket without a prior call to NetLibSocketShutdown, but this is not a recommended procedure. If NetLibSocketClose disconnects a socket, it doesn't always do so in a polite fashion; it's possible that the socket will be shut down while one or both ends of the connection are in the middle of sending data, which can result in lost data packets. Most of the time, you should call NetLibSocketShutdown first to ensure that the socket is disconnected cleanly.

## Closing the Net Library

If your application is about to exit, or if it is finished using the network, it should shut down the net library so the operating system no longer needs to devote resources to running the network protocol stack. There are a couple of options to choose from when shutting down the net library:

❑ Shut down the net library immediately.

❑ Defer network shutdown, waiting to see if another application (or the one that requested the network shutdown) wants to open the net library again.

The first option immediately frees up the resources taken by the network protocol stack. This means that a significant amount of system memory is once again made available for applications. However, there is a catch: If another application needs to open the network library, there may be an extended wait while the net library establishes contact with the network and loads the network protocol stack. Ideally, the user shouldn't be subjected to an annoying wait every time an application needs to connect to the network.

Fortunately, the net library doesn't need to be immediately closed when leaving an application. It can remain open for a certain period of time, called the *idle timeout*, which the user may set in the Network panel of the Prefs application. This allows the user, for example, to leave a networked application briefly to look something up in another program and then return without having lost the network connection.

The NetLibClose function gives you the option of either closing the net library immediately or deferring network shutdown. NetLibClose looks like this:

```
Err NetLibClose (UInt16 libRefnum, UInt16 immediate)
```

The `immediate` parameter can be either `true` or `false`. If `immediate` is `true`, `NetLibClose` shuts down the net library immediately. If `immediate` is `false`, `NetLibClose` starts a countdown equal to the idle timeout length, and the net library enters the *close-wait* state.

In the close-wait state, if the countdown reaches zero before `NetLibOpen` is called—either by another application or by the application that initiated the countdown—the system closes the net library and frees the resources taken by the network protocol stack. If an application calls `NetLibOpen` before the countdown runs out, the countdown halts and the net library stays open and resumes normal operation.

If for some reason your application needs to shut the network down immediately while the net library is in the close-wait state, it can call the `NetLibFinishCloseWait` function.

# Using the Palm OS Cobalt Berkeley Sockets APIs

In Palm OS Cobalt, PalmSource has replaced the Network Library with a native version of the Berkeley Sockets API. To be specific, Palm OS Cobalt introduces native 4.3BSD sockets support:

❑ New applications written to target Palm OS Cobalt exclusively need only code to the sockets API, which provides excellent cross-platform compatibility between your Palm OS application and sockets code written for other platforms.

❑ Applications which must be written to target Palm OS Garnet, earlier versions of Palm OS, and Palm OS Cobalt will either need to use `#ifdef` conditional compilation and maintain both net library and sockets interfaces, or will need to take advantage of the Palm OS Garnet sockets layer found in `netsocket.c`.

❑ Applications which are written to the Palm OS Garnet or earlier net library APIs, but which must also run in Palm OS Cobalt, should work unmodified. Only applications coded using the Palm OS Cobalt SDK will find net library support removed from the SDK headers.

*In applications built for Palm OS Cobalt, you cannot link in the NetSockets.c source or use the macros found in* `sys_socket.h`. *Instead, you must include the various headers required by Berkeley sockets.*

Developers who use the Berkeley sockets support in Palm OS Cobalt do need to be aware of a small number of unsupported items, primarily in the area of UNIX compatibility:

❑ `AF_UNIX`/`PF_UNIX` is not supported (these are UNIX address and protocol families)

❑ `socketpair()` is not available (this only applies to UNIX domain sockets)

❑ UNIX-like asynchronous signals/options/flags are not supported

## Learning More About Sockets

This book does not purport to teach the Berkeley sockets API to Palm OS programmers, nor is the sockets API unique to the Palm OS environment. Quite the opposite: Sockets is available on most platforms in existence, and there is an overwhelming amount of information, references, books, articles and sample code available on this topic. Palm OS Cobalt application developers unfamiliar with sockets programming are strongly encouraged to seek out one of these references as a guide to using the sockets API.

The following table serves as a helpful guide in mapping the Palm OS Garnet net library API calls to the appropriate sockets API. Supported sockets APIs are listed in the header file `sys/socket.h`, found in the OS6 folder in the PODS distribution.

| Socket API | Palm OS Garnet API |
|------------|-------------------|
| Accept | NetLibSocketAccept |
| Bind | NetLibSocketBind |
| Connect | NetLibSocketConnect |
| Getpeername | NetLibSocketAddr |
| getsockname | NetLibSocketAddr |
| Getsockopt | NetLibSocketOptionGet |
| Listen | NetLibSokcetListen |
| Recv | NetLibReceive |
| Recvfrom | NetLibReceive |
| Recvmsg | NetLibReceive |
| Send | NetLibSend |
| Sendmsg | NetLibSend |
| Sendto | NetLibSend |
| setsocketopt | NetLibSocketOptionSet |
| Shutdown | NetLibSocketShutdown |
| Socket | NetLibSocketOpen |

## Advantages of Using Sockets with Palm OS Cobalt

Aside from providing compatibility with the standard Berkeley sockets interface, the Palm OS Cobalt sockets subsystem provides the following benefits to programmers:

❏ The system can now support up to 64 open sockets. Earlier versions of Palm OS were severely limited in the number of sockets available for use by applications.

❏ Restrictions in using the sockets interface under Palm OS Garnet, such as the global variable requirement, are now gone.

❏ The sockets interface is now an integral part of the operating system and no longer needs to be explicitly loaded as a shared library, thus dispensing with the cumbersome `refNum` parameter accompanying all net library APIs.

❏ It is now much easier to code, test, and debug your Palm OS networking code on other platforms that are more debugging-friendly.

# Summary

This chapter showed you the ins and outs of using the Palm OS net library to connect an application to remote hosts over a TCP/IP network. After reading this chapter, you should know the following:

❑ TCP and its companion protocol, UDP, form the transport layer of a network protocol stack.

❑ IP, which makes up the network layer of the protocol stack, handles the routing of data to the intended destination.

❑ The Palm OS net library is based on the Berkeley sockets model of network programming.

❑ The Palm OS Cobalt SDK makes the legacy net library API obsolete in favor of the industry-standard sockets interface.

❑ Most net library functions require three common arguments: a reference to the net library, a timeout value, and an error return variable.

❑ Prior to use, the net library must be opened with the `NetLibOpen` function, which also makes whatever connection is necessary for the handheld to communicate with a network.

❑ Hostname resolution is performed by the `NetLibGetHostByName` function, and IP address resolution is accomplished with the `NetLibGetHostByAddr` function.

❑ Sockets must be opened before use with `NetLibSocketOpen`, and then connected with `NetLibSocketConnect`. When communication is finished, the sockets should be disconnected with `NetLibSocketShutdown`, and then closed with `NetLibSocketClose`.

❑ An application sends data by calling `NetLibSend`, and it receives data by calling `NetLibReceive`.

❑ The `NetLibClose` function closes the net library but allows you to defer closing for a user-specified idle period, allowing other network applications an opportunity to reuse the open net library.

❑ The Palm OS Cobalt sockets interface and subsystem provides many advantages to network programmers over the earlier net library interface.

# 21

# Learning Conduit Basics

Conduits are code modules that perform synchronization between Palm OS handheld applications and data on a desktop computer. The HotSync Manager calls conduits during a HotSync operation to keep records in synch between the desktop and the handheld, back up data from the handheld to the desktop, or download data from the desktop to the handheld.

The Conduit Development Kit (CDK), available as a free download from PalmSource, contains all the templates, object classes, and documentation necessary to create conduits for the Mac OS and Windows. To develop conduits for the Mac OS, you also need to have Metrowerks CodeWarrior (the full version of CodeWarrior, not just Metrowerks CodeWarrior for Palm OS platform).

To create conduits for Windows, you need to use one of the following development environments:

❏ **Microsoft Visual C++ 6.0 and the CDK for Windows.** Use the C/C++ Sync Suite, included in the CDK for Windows, for development.

❏ **Any COM-compliant programming environment and the CDK for Windows.** Use the COM Sync Suite, included in the CDK for Windows, for development. PalmSource designed the COM Sync Suite for use with Microsoft Visual Basic, but any language that supports COM (for example, Delphi, Borland C/C++, Visual Basic for Applications, Java, or Visual C/C++) will work with the COM Sync Suite.

❏ **WebGain VisualCafé and the CDK for Windows.** Use the JSync Suite, included in the CDK for Windows, for development. You also may use any other standard Java development tools, such as Sun Microsystems Java SDK or Microsoft Visual J++, but PalmSource supports Java conduit development using VisualCafé only.

Chapters 21 and 22 focus on conduit development for Windows, using Visual C++ and the C/C++ Sync Suite. However, much of the information in this chapter is conceptual and applies just as well to Java, COM, and Mac OS conduit development as it does to Visual C++ conduit development. The next chapter, "Building Conduits," delves into the actual details of conduit programming using Visual C++, so it will not be as useful as this chapter for Mac OS, COM, or Java conduit developers.

*Because conduit development involves creating software to run on a desktop machine instead of a Palm OS handheld, it requires a different set of skills and tools from those needed for handheld application development. You should be familiar with object-oriented programming in C++, Java, or a COM-compliant language, depending upon the part of the CDK you wish to use, and it also helps to have some experience with creating dynamic link libraries (if using the CDK for Windows) or Code Fragment Manager plug-ins (if using the CDK for Mac OS). Knowing your way around Microsoft Foundation Classes (MFC) is a must if you plan to build a conduit based on the Palm MFC Base Classes.*

# Understanding Conduits

A standard Windows conduit is a DLL module with entry points called by the HotSync Manager. (Mac OS conduits are Code Fragment Manager plug-in modules, Java conduits are Java classes that use the `jsync.dll` module to communicate with the HotSync Manager, and COM conduits are programs that communicate with the HotSync Manager through the COM Sync Module.) A conduit is only one piece of software that must cooperate with a number of other programs to transfer data between a handheld and a desktop computer. Some or all of the following components may be involved in a given HotSync operation:

❏ **HotSync Manager.** This program controls the entire HotSync process. The HotSync Manager runs in the background on the desktop computer, watching appropriate communications ports for a HotSync request from a Palm OS handheld. The HotSync Manager handles basic communication between the desktop and a handheld, manages multiple users synchronizing with the same desktop machine, provides an interface with which users can customize the behavior of individual conduits, installs new applications and databases to a handheld, and restores data on the handheld in the event of a hard reset or other catastrophic data loss.

❏ **Conduits.** Conduits are plug-in modules that handle the actual transfer of data between a handheld application and a desktop data source. During a HotSync operation, the HotSync Manager calls each registered conduit in turn to synchronize a handheld application with its desktop data. A conduit does not require any user interaction to perform its duties; instead it relies on internal logic to correctly modify data on the desktop, the handheld, or both. This lack of interaction is important to remember when designing a conduit; if a user synchronizes a handheld remotely, there is no way for the conduit to prompt the user for input.

❏ **Notifier DLLs.** If both a conduit and a desktop application can modify the same data, it may be necessary to tell the desktop application to leave the data alone during the course of a HotSync operation, thereby preventing data loss, duplicate records, or just plain mangled data. The HotSync Manager uses a process called *notification* to prevent this sort of mess. Before the HotSync Manager launches a conduit to perform data transfer, the manager calls a *notifier DLL* for that particular conduit. The notifier DLL in turn passes information to the appropriate desktop application in a format that the application understands. The best example of this process is the Palm Desktop application, which does not allow the user to change any data during a HotSync operation; the Palm Desktop knows that a HotSync operation is in progress because it was notified by its notifier DLL, `pdn20.dll`.

❏ **Handheld applications.** A handheld application may serve as a quick data collection tool for a desktop application or as a portable viewer for information imported from the desktop. Also, an application on the handheld may simply share data with a desktop application, just as the four main ROM applications share data with the Palm Desktop program. If you follow standard Palm OS programming guidelines, there is nothing that you need to add to a handheld application to allow it to work with the HotSync process. See Chapter 16 for more details about handling data in a Palm OS application.

❑ **Desktop applications.** Because of the flexibility inherent in conduit design, virtually any desktop application may share data with a Palm OS handheld. A desktop application can create data to send to the handheld, process data retrieved from the handheld, or share data with the handheld.

❑ **Sync Manager API.** This application programming interface allows conduits to communicate with the handheld, regardless of how the handheld is connected to the desktop computer. The Sync Manager API can directly read and write data on the handheld, and it forms the most basic layer in conduit programming.

Figure 21-1 shows the relationships between the various components that may be present in a Palm OS synchronization scheme. The arrows in the figure show how data flows between different pieces of software. In most cases, components perform two-way communication, sending data in both directions between the components; notification, however, usually flows in one direction only, from the HotSync Manager to a notifier DLL to a desktop application.

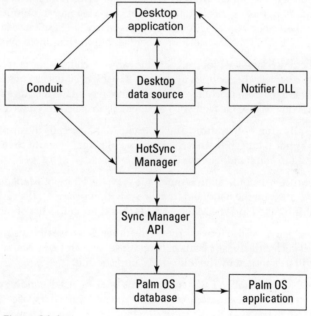

**Figure 21-1**

# *Stepping Through the HotSync Process*

When the user initiates a HotSync operation, either by pressing the HotSync button on the cradle or by tapping the HotSync button in the HotSync application on the handheld, the HotSync Manager springs into action, following a particular series of steps to synchronize the desktop and the handheld.

*A HotSync operation may be initiated only from the handheld. Because of limitations in current cradle hardware, there is no way to start the synchronization process from the desktop computer.*

The following steps outline the actions taken by the HotSync Manager during a HotSync operation:

1. **User validation and location.** Each Palm OS handheld has a unique *user ID* associated with it. When the user synchronizes the handheld for the first time, the HotSync Manager assigns a pseudo-random number to that particular handheld, which allows a single desktop computer to synchronize with multiple handhelds and still keep their data separate. At the beginning of a HotSync operation, the HotSync Manager ensures that the user ID on the handheld is valid and then locates the path to that particular user's data on the desktop computer. For example, my own user path is `c:\Palm\FosterL`. Most conduits save their information in subdirectories of the user path.

2. **Determination of synchronization type.** A conduit may perform two kinds of synchronization: *SlowSync* and *FastSync*. In a SlowSync, the conduit compares each record in the handheld database with its corresponding record in the desktop data source. In a FastSync, the conduit compares only records whose modification flag is set.

   The HotSync Manager determines which type of synchronization to perform by looking at the *PC ID* stored on the handheld from its last HotSync operation. Like a user ID, the PC ID is a pseudo-random number generated by the HotSync Manager to uniquely identify a desktop computer. Whenever a HotSync operation takes place, the HotSync Manager stores on the handheld itself the PC ID of the last desktop machine that the handheld synchronized with.

   If the handheld was last synchronized with the same machine as the current HotSync operation, the HotSync Manager tells the conduits to perform a FastSync. If the last machine the handheld synchronized with was a different machine, conduits cannot rely on the modification flag of each record being valid, so in this case the HotSync Manager tells installed conduits to perform a SlowSync.

3. **Desktop application notification.** The HotSync Manager calls the appropriate notifier DLLs to let desktop applications know that the HotSync Manager is about to modify the data shared between desktop and handheld applications.

4. **Conduit setup.** Once notification is out of the way, the HotSync Manager retrieves the creator ID of each application on the handheld (databases with type `appl`). If a conduit is installed for a particular creator ID, the HotSync Manager adds that conduit to a list of modules that should be run.

   The HotSync Manager also looks through the other databases on the handheld that are not of type DATA. If such a database has its backup bit set, the HotSync Manager adds that database to a list that will be handled by the built-in Backup conduit.

5. **Installation.** Now the HotSync Manager uses its built-in Install conduit to install any databases that are queued up on the desktop computer. Typically, these databases were queued by the Palm Install Tool (`instapp.exe`). In Windows, the HotSync Manager knows there are databases to install when a particular Registry key is present, namely `\HKEY_CURRENT_USER\Software\U.S.` `Robotics\Pilot Desktop\HotSync Manager\Install`*NNNNN*, where *NNNNN* is the pseudo-random user ID assigned to the handheld. The Palm Install Tool creates this Registry key when it queues databases for installation and then copies those databases to the `Install` subdirectory of the appropriate user data folder. For example, files awaiting installation on my machine go into the `c:\Palm\FosterL\Install` directory. The Install conduit looks in this particular directory for databases to install.

---

Careless modification of the Windows Registry is a great way to cause irreparable damage to Windows or applications installed on a Windows computer. Unless you know exactly what you are doing, you should let the HotSync Manager take care of changing Registry settings for you.

---

6. **Conduit execution.** The HotSync Manager cycles through the list of conduits it assembled in Step 4, calling each in turn to synchronize data between the handheld and desktop applications.

7. **Second Installation.** Version 3.0.1 or later of the HotSync Manager calls the Install conduit a second time, which gives the HotSync operation a chance to pick up any databases queued for installation by any of the conduits. This step allows a conduit to generate a database and "push" it out to the handheld, which can be very useful for conduits that retrieve information from the Web or other network sources. For example, the AvantGo conduit uses this mechanism to install newly down-loaded Web pages to the handheld. Note that prior to HotSync Manager version 3.0.1, this second installation phase does not happen.

8. **Database backup.** The HotSync Manager calls the Backup conduit to copy databases queued for backup in Step 4. These databases are stored in a `Backup` subdirectory of the appropriate user data directory. For example, my own backup directory is `c:\Palm\FosterL\Backup`.

9. **Synchronization information update.** Now that the HotSync Manager has completed most of its tasks, it updates the synch time, PC ID, and user ID, if necessary, in the HotSync application on the handheld. At this point, the HotSync Manager also transfers a shortened version of the HotSync log to the handheld, which the user may view to determine the nature of any errors or warnings generated by the HotSync operation.

10. **Second desktop application notification.** The HotSync Manager calls the appropriate notifier DLLs a second time, to alert applications that the HotSync operation is complete and it is now safe for desktop applications to modify shared data sources again.

11. **Handheld application notification.** Palm OS itself gives notification of a finished HotSync operation to newly installed handheld applications and those whose data was modified during the HotSync process by sending a `sysAppLaunchCmdSyncNotify` launch code to each of these applications. Any application that needs to perform some operation immediately after installation or having its data modified by a HotSync operation, such as resetting alarms or registering to receive beamed data, may do so by handling the `sysAppLaunchCmdSyncNotify` launch code.

# Designing Conduits

You can build a conduit to synchronize a custom Palm OS application with a custom data source on the desktop, or to synchronize one of the built-in handheld applications with a custom desktop data source. You also could hijack the Palm Desktop data and synchronize it with your own handheld application or even replace one of the built-in conduits so it synchronizes a built-in handheld application with the default Palm Desktop in a different way, although these two scenarios are less likely.

Given the different databases that you can synchronize with one another, there also are four different types of synchronization you can perform. Listed from most complex to least complex, here are the different styles of synchronization:

❑ **Transaction-based.** In a transaction-based scenario, the desktop computer must perform some sort of processing between each record synchronization. For example, a conduit that updates information on the handheld from a live Internet source would require a transaction-based approach. This style of synchronization takes a lot longer than other types and should be used only when absolutely necessary because it slows down the entire HotSync process.

❑ **Mirror image.** In this scenario, modifications to records may be made on both the handheld and the desktop, and the conduit makes the databases identical on both platforms. The conduit also must resolve conflicts when the user modifies the same record on both the desktop and the handheld. Palm's four basic built-in applications use mirror image synchronization with the Palm Desktop.

❑ **One-directional.** Only one side of the connection — either the desktop or the handheld — may modify data in a one-directional scenario. This type of synchronization is ideal for desktop applications that update some sort of data, such as stock quotes, and then dump that data to the handheld for remote viewing. One-directional synchronization also works well the other way, for applications that use the handheld as a data collection device and then port that raw data to the desktop computer for further processing.

❑ **Backup.** If an application does not have a desktop component, it can rely on the default Backup conduit provided with the HotSync Manager. This also could work as a "poor man's" one-directional synchronization if a desktop application can parse the .pdb file used by Palm OS to store the handheld application's records on the desktop. An actual one-directional conduit is easier to use, however.

Consider speed when picking a style of synchronization. Try not to over-engineer your conduit; use the simplest type of synchronization that will get the job done.

*Rapid synchronization is a vital part of the Palm OS philosophy, and it has been a key factor in the popularity of Palm Powered handhelds. Also, because most HotSync operations take place through the handheld's serial port, which is a major drain on the batteries, it is imperative to keep the total synchronization time as short as possible. Try to design conduits to execute quickly and efficiently.*

## Choosing a Development Path

The C/C++ Sync Suite gives you three basic starting points for building a conduit, each with its own strengths and weaknesses:

❑ Start with the *Palm MFC Base Classes* and customize them for your application.

❑ Start with the *Palm Generic Conduit Base Classes* and customize them for your application.

❑ Start from scratch, calling *Sync Manager API* functions directly from your conduit.

The Palm MFC Base Classes are a set of C++ object classes based on the Microsoft Foundation Classes (MFC), and they provide a high-level interface to the HotSync process. You must customize the base classes to interact properly with the handheld application's data format. On the desktop side, an MFC conduit reads and writes data using the MFC serialization format. To access this data from your own desktop application, that application must be an MFC program that also makes use of the Palm MFC Base Classes. The Palm MFC Base Classes provide all the logic necessary to perform mirror image synchronization; simply fill in the details about the data format from the handheld side of the HotSync operation.

The Palm Generic Conduit Base Classes are a different set of C++ object classes that also provide a high-level interface to the HotSync process. Unlike the Palm MFC Base Classes, a generic conduit may be customized for different data formats on both the handheld and on the desktop, so the Palm Generic Conduit

Base Classes are ideal for connecting a handheld application with a standard desktop database format, such as ODBC or plain old comma-delimited value format. The generic base classes also are designed with portability in mind; the same source code works on both Mac OS and Windows, making generic conduits ideal for cross-platform conduit development. Like the Palm MFC Base Classes, the generic conduit classes also provide their own synchronization logic, allowing you to concentrate on filling in code to convert between handheld and desktop data formats.

*Generic conduits are the wave of the future as far as PalmSource is concerned. The Palm MFC Base Classes were originally the only high-level conduit development classes available, but starting with CDK version 3.0, Palm released the newer Palm Generic Conduit Base Classes as an unsupported feature, and as of CDK version 4.02, they are officially supported. Because generic conduits are more flexible and can be used for cross-platform development, PalmSource is phasing out support for MFC conduits; they probably will not be included in future versions of the CDK. PalmSource suggests that developers who are new to conduit development start with generic conduits instead of MFC conduits.*

The Sync Manager API is a set of low-level functions that directly control interaction between the desktop and the handheld. Both MFC and generic conduits use the Sync Manager API to perform the basic tasks of sending and receiving data during a HotSync operation. The base classes take care of all the synchronization logic required to keep a desktop data source in mirror image synchronization with a handheld application. If your application does not require mirror image synchronization, or if you want to implement your own synch logic, directly controlling the handheld through the Sync Manager API requires less overhead than using the base classes and can result in a much quicker and more efficient conduit.

# Installing Conduits

A conduit cannot run without first being properly registered. Registration tells the HotSync Manager that it should call your conduit when synching databases with a specific creator ID. For a conduit to be a good HotSync citizen and play nicely with other conduits, its installation program must be able to register and unregister the conduit without any user intervention and, more importantly, without damaging the HotSync process by overwriting or removing conduit registration information that belongs to other conduits.

Prior to version 3.0 of the CDK, conduit registration involved adding entries directly to the Windows Registry. This situation was tenuous at best because there was no mechanism in place to prevent one developer's registration or unregistration code from destroying the registration information of other conduits. Worse yet, uninstalling conduits often involved renaming existing Registry entries and, if not done carefully, could prevent the entire HotSync process from working properly.

With the introduction of CDK 3.0, Palm added the Conduit Manager—a set of functions for conduit registration and unregistration. The Conduit Manager functions reside in a DLL called CondMgr.dll, which ships with version 3.0 and later of the HotSync Manager. As of this writing, the HotSync Manager still uses the Windows Registry to store conduit registration information, but the Conduit Manager API hides the details of registration storage from developers, providing a much cleaner and safer interface for registering conduits. Not only is it easier to use the Conduit Manager than it is to try tiptoeing your way through the minefield of HotSync Registry entries, it separates the act of registering and unregistering conduits from the method used to store registration data, so it is possible that future versions of the HotSync Manager may not use the Windows Registry at all.

# Installing Conduits Manually

When developing and testing a conduit, you can manually register and unregister it using the Conduit Configuration tool supplied with the CDK. This tool, pictured in Figure 21-2, provides a graphical interface for registering and unregistering conduits.

**Figure 21-2**

The Conduit Configuration tool itself is an executable called CondCfg.exe, which resides in the bin\HSM\ Release and bin\HSM\Debug directories, underneath the directory where you installed the CDK. Use the copy in the Release directory with the release version of the HotSync Manager, and the copy in the Debug directory when using the debug version of the HotSync Manager.

> **If you use the same desktop machine for both conduit development and for synching your own Palm OS handheld, be very careful when using the Conduit Configuration tool. Improper use of the tool can cause unpredictable HotSync behavior, preventing you from backing up your handheld's data. Use the Conduit Switch tool, described later in this section, to back up your HotSync registration settings before modifying them.**

The View Conduits and View Notifiers buttons in the configuration tool display the currently registered conduits or notifier DLLs, respectively. Clicking the HotSync Settings button brings up a dialog box, pictured in Figure 21-3, from which you may change basic settings of the HotSync Manager itself.

On the main Conduit Configuration tool screen, if the list is currently displaying conduits, clicking the Add button brings up the Conduit Information dialog box, shown in Figure 21-4. From this dialog box, you can enter the settings for a new conduit that you want to register.

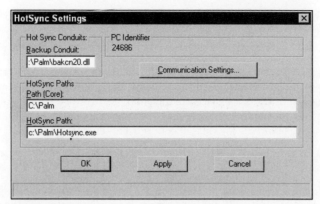

**Figure 21-3**

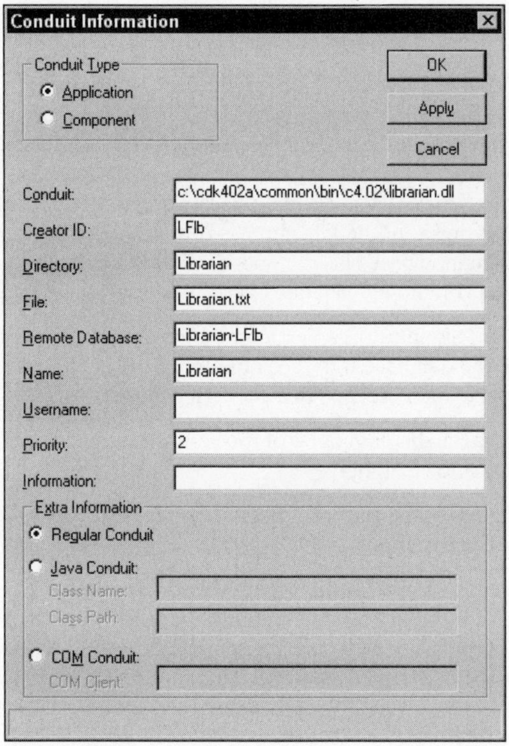

**Figure 21-4**

Figure 21-4 shows the settings required by the Librarian sample conduit, which is covered in detail in the next chapter, "Building Conduits."

The Conduit Type section at the top of the dialog box specifies whether the conduit is independent (Application) or integrated as part of the Palm Desktop application (Component). Generally, most third-party conduits are of the Application variety.

The text boxes in the rest of the dialog box are pieces of registration information for the conduit. The first three are required to properly register a conduit, while the rest are optional. These entries are described as follows:

- ❏ **Conduit.** This is the filename of the conduit DLL. Without a complete path name, the file needs to be located either in the same directory as the HotSync Manager or somewhere on the system path. Most conduit DLLs are placed in the HotSync directory. If your conduit is written in Java, the DLL listed here should be JSync.dll, which is a C++ DLL that communicates between the HotSync Manager and the Java-based conduit. This entry is required.

- ❏ **Creator ID.** Enter into this text box the creator ID of the database(s) on the handheld that this conduit should synch with. This entry is required and is case-sensitive.

  *Although a conduit may be registered for only a single Creator ID, once the conduit is running, it is free to synchronize desktop data with any of the databases installed on the handheld.*

- ❏ **Directory.** This should be the name of a directory where your conduit's data files will be stored. The HotSync Manager creates this directory within each individual user's directory; such a directory structure serves to separate your conduit's files from those used by other conduits. This entry is required. Depending on the conduit's needs, it may or may not actually use this directory, but the Conduit Configuration tool still requires a directory name.

- ❏ **File.** The filename of the desktop data file with which your conduit synchronizes goes here. Without a complete path, this file is assumed to be in the conduit's Directory, which is entered above the filename. This entry is optional because your conduit might synchronize with more than one file on the desktop; the File entry is provided as a convenience for conduits based on the Palm MFC or generic base classes, which use this filename by default for the desktop data file. This field must contain at least one character, however, even if it is unused.

- ❏ **Remote Database.** This should be the name of the database on the handheld, which the conduit may use to create the database if it does not already exist. The name is case-sensitive and, like the File entry, must contain at least one character.

- ❏ **Name.** This entry is the display name of the conduit, which the HotSync Manager shows in its Custom dialog box and elsewhere.

- ❏ **Username.** This entry is not currently used, but it is intended to store the name of the user for whom this conduit is installed.

- ❏ **Priority.** Every conduit has a priority value that determines the order in which the HotSync Manager executes conduits. This value should be from 0 to 4, with 2 being the normal value for most conduits. The HotSync Manager runs conduits with lower values in the Priority field before conduits with higher values in this field. For example, a priority 1 conduit runs before one with priority 3.

- ❏ **Information.** This entry is used to display extra information to the user if there is a conflict between your conduit and another that wishes to access the same database on the handheld. A conduit installer might display this string and ask the user which of two conflicting conduits should be permitted to handle a particular database.

The two entries under Java Information are for Java-based conduits. See the CDK for Windows, Java Edition, for more information.

Back on the main Conduit Configuration tool screen again, clicking the Details button also brings up the Conduit Information dialog box but with certain fields disabled. The conduit currently selected in the main screen's list is displayed. You can edit many of the registration entries for an installed conduit in this way.

To uninstall a conduit, select it from the list in the main screen, and then click Delete. In the confirmation dialog box that appears, click OK to delete the conduit's registration entries. Note that this does not delete the actual DLL file, only its registration with the HotSync Manager.

*Any changes you make using the Conduit Configuration tool will not take effect until you restart the HotSync Manager.*

### Backing Up and Restoring HotSync Configurations

Because changes made using the Conduit Configuration tool can potentially cause strange things to happen during a HotSync operation, it is a good idea to back up a working HotSync configuration before making changes so that you can restore it later if necessary. Saving different configurations also is useful during development if you want to quickly switch back and forth between saved states to try out different scenarios.

The CDK comes with a command-line tool for easily making backups of the HotSync Manager's registration settings and restoring them again later. The Conduit Switch tool, an executable called CondSwitch.exe, is located in the bin\HSM\Release directory under the directory where you installed the CDK. To save the current HotSync configuration to a file, call the Conduit Switch tool with the following parameters:

```
CondSwitch -b backup_file.txt
```

Later, when you want to restore a configuration you saved earlier, use this syntax:

```
CondSwitch -d -i backup_file.txt
```

*As in the Conduit Configuration tool, any changes you make to the HotSync configuration with the Conduit Switch tool will not take effect until you restart the HotSync Manager. To save time, you can tack the -r switch onto the CondSwitch command line to restart the HotSync Manager automatically.*

## Creating Automatic Conduit Installations

Because your conduit's users do not have access to the Conduit Configuration tool (nor should they!), whatever program you use to install your conduit must take care of registering and unregistering your conduit at installation and de-installation time. The CDK for Windows contains a sample install script for version 5.5 or later of the popular InstallShield Professional program, a script you can modify for your own conduit.

*The InstallShield sample included with the CDK does not work with the free version of InstallShield that comes with Microsoft Visual C++. The free edition cannot call functions in a DLL, an action that is required for proper conduit registration.*

If you want to create your own installation program, you will need to use the Conduit Manager API, contained in CondMgr.dll, to register or unregister your conduit. The first hurdle you must clear during installation is finding the CondMgr.dll file.

## Finding CondMgr.dll

One of the benefits of using a DLL to store the Conduit Manager functions is that if PalmSource decides to change the way it stores conduit registration information, it can simply replace CondMgr.dll with a new version, and your installation program will be none the wiser. Unfortunately, PalmSource does not install the DLL in the Windows system folder, where it would be easily accessible. Instead, CondMgr.dll is in the same directory as the HotSync Manager executable.

Finding the location of the HotSync Manager and all the core Palm Desktop programs is actually very simple: Use the CmGetCorePath function from the Conduit Manager. However, this function, as you may have already guessed, is located in CondMgr.dll with the rest of the Conduit Manager API. This makes CmGetCorePath somewhat difficult to use because the point of this whole exercise is to find the location of the CondMgr.dll file itself.

You can solve this problem by including a copy of CondMgr.dll with your installation program. That way, the installer can call CmGetCorePath from its local copy of CondMgr.dll to find out where the "real" CondMgr.dll is located and then use the up-to-date copy to register the conduit. The sequence of events your installer should follow looks like this:

1. Look for CondMgr.dll on the system path and use that version if you find it because it is probably from a more recent version of the Palm Desktop software than the version you are shipping with your conduit.

2. If CondMgr.dll is not on the path, use the CmGetCorePath function from the version bundled with your installer to find where the Palm Desktop is installed, and look in that directory for CondMgr.dll. Use this version if it exists because it might be newer than the version included with your installer.

3. If you still cannot find CondMgr.dll in the Palm Desktop's directory, use the copy included with your installer. You may have to do this if the Palm Desktop software installed on the user's computer is older than version 3.0 because CondMgr.dll did not ship with earlier versions of the Palm Desktop.

> Your installer should not replace **CondMgr.dll** or other HotSync **.dll** files on the user's computer with newer versions. Doing so may render the HotSync Manager inoperable.

## Registering with the Conduit Manager

Once you have located CondMgr.dll, you can call its functions to register your conduit. There are two basic ways to accomplish this task:

❑ Build an installation structure and call a single function to register the conduit.

❑ Call many individual functions to set configuration entries for the conduit.

The first technique uses a CmConduitType structure with the CmInstallConduit function. The CmConduitType structure looks like this:

```
typedef struct {
    int iStructureVersion;
```

```
        int iStructureSize;
        int iType;
        char szCreatorID[CREATOR_ID_SIZE];
        DWORD dwPriority;
        int iConduitNameOffset;
        int iDirectoryOffset;
        int iFileOffset;
        int iRemoteDBOffset;
        int iUsernameOffset;
        int iTitleOffset;
        int iInfoOffset;
    } CmConduitType;
```

All of the various `Offset` fields in this structure specify the offset in bytes from the beginning of the structure to the first character of a string value. This method of storing strings saves some space because it does not need to store empty string values for those entries that you do not wish to include in your call to `CmInstallConduit`. When you allocate space for a `CmConduitType` structure, make sure to include memory for the string values themselves.

The `CmInstallConduit` function takes a handle to a `CmConduitType` structure:

```
        int CmInstallConduit (HANDLE hStruct)
```

The alternative, and much simpler, method of installing a conduit is to call individual functions to set the various registration entries. First, you need to call `CmInstallCreator` to set the creator ID that your conduit is registered to handle:

```
        int CmInstallCreator (const char *pCreator, int iType)
```

For `iType`, specify the constant value `CONDUIT_APPLICATION`; `pCreator` should point to a string containing the creator ID to register.

After calling `CmInstallCreator`, you can call other functions, in any order you like, to set other registration entries:

❑ **CmSetCreatorName.** This function sets the filename of the conduit DLL, and it corresponds to the Conduit field in the Conduit Configuration tool.

❑ **CmSetCreatorDirectory.** This function sets the conduit's data directory.

❑ **CmSetCreatorFile.** This function sets the filename the conduit uses to store desktop data.

❑ **CmSetCreatorRemote.** This function sets the name of the database on the handheld that should be created if it does not already exist; it corresponds to the Remote Database field in the Conduit Configuration tool.

❑ **CmSetCreatorTitle.** This function sets the display name for the conduit; it corresponds to the Name field in the Conduit Configuration tool.

❑ **CmSetCreatorUser.** This function sets the username for which this conduit was installed; it corresponds to the Username field in the Conduit Configuration tool.

❑ **CmSetCreatorPriority.** This function sets the conduit's priority.

❑ **CmSetCreatorInfo.** This function sets the conflict-resolution information string for the conduit; it corresponds to the Info field in the Conduit Configuration tool.

All of these functions take, as their first argument, a pointer to a string containing the creator ID that the conduit is registered to handle. For example, here is the prototype for the `CmSetCreatorName` function:

```
int CmSetCreatorName(const char *pCreatorID,
    const TCHAR *pConduitName)
```

## Unregistering with the Conduit Manager

In the uninstall portion of your conduit's installation program, cleanly uninstall the conduit by calling the `CmRemoveConduitByCreatorID` function:

```
int CmRemoveConduitByCreatorID(const char *pCreatorID)
```

The `CmRemoveConduitByCreatorID` function removes all the conduits registered under the creator ID you supply and returns the number of conduits removed.

> *In the current implementation of `CmRemoveConduitByCreatorID`, the return value is always 1 if there is no error because the HotSync Manager will allow only one conduit per creator ID.*

# Logging Actions in the HotSync Log

The HotSync Manager keeps a log of its actions, along with certain errors it might encounter, in a text file on the desktop computer, as well as a smaller version of the log accessible from the HotSync application on the handheld. Although the HotSync Manager does not actually write out the log file until after it has run all its conduits, the Sync Manager API provides a number of functions to allow conduits to add their own messages to the log. The HotSync Manager appends its own messages, and those added by conduits, to the end of the log file. To keep the HotSync log file from becoming too large, the HotSync Manager also trims the log file so that it contains information about the ten most recent HotSync operations only.

> *By default, the log file generated by the HotSync Manager is called `HotSync.log`, and it resides in the current user's directory on the desktop.*

The simplest function for adding a message to the log is `LogAddEntry`, which has the following prototype:

```
long LogAddEntry (LPCTSTR pszEntry, Activity act,
    BOOL bTimeStamp)
```

The `pszEntry` parameter is a pointer to a null-terminated string containing the text that should be entered into the log. If `bTimeStamp` is `TRUE`, `LogAddEntry` appends a timestamp to the log entry. The `act` parameter specifies the kind of activity that you want to log, which must be a member of the `Activity` enumerated type. The following table contains descriptions of most of the activity constants.

| Constant | Description |
|---|---|
| slArchiveFailed | An archive operation failed. |
| slCategoryDeleted | A category was deleted. |
| slChangeCatFailed | Changing the category of a record failed. |

| Constant | Description |
|---|---|
| slDateChanged | The date was changed. |
| slDoubleModify | A record was modified on both the desktop and the handheld. |
| slDoubleModifyArchive | A record that was modified on both desktop and the handheld was archived. |
| slDoubleModifySubsc | A file link record was modified on the desktop. |
| slFileLinkCompleted | File link processing has finished. |
| slLocalAddFailed | Adding a record to the desktop failed. |
| slLocalSaveFailed | Saving the desktop data file failed. |
| slRecCountMismatch | The number of records on the desktop and the number of records on the handheld do not match. |
| slRemoteAddFailed | Adding a record to the handheld failed. |
| slRemoteChangeFailed | Changing a record on the handheld failed. |
| slRemoteDeleteFailed | Deleting a record from the handheld failed. |
| slRemotePurgeFailed | Purging a record from the handheld failed. |
| slRemoteReadFailed | Reading a record on the handheld failed. |
| slResetFlagsFailed | Resetting synchronization flags failed. |
| slSyncAborted | Synchronization was aborted. |
| slSyncFinished | The synchronization operation completed successfully. |
| slSyncStarted | The synchronization operation started. |
| slText | This indicates a simple text entry. |
| slTooManyCategories | The maximum number of categories has already been reached. |
| slWarning | This logs a warning. |
| slXMapFailed | The position cross-map function failed. |

Most of the time, you will need to use only five of the activity logging constants:

❑    slSyncStarted. Call LogAddEntry with this constant and an empty string when your conduit first starts up:

```
LogAddEntry("", slSyncStarted, FALSE);
```

❑    slSyncAborted. Use this constant if your conduit encounters an error that forces it to quit synchronization:

```
LogAddEntry("MyConduit", slSyncAborted, FALSE);
```

❏ slSyncFinished. This constant signals to the log that your application successfully completed its synchronization:

```
LogAddEntry("MyConduit", slSyncFinished, FALSE);
```

❏ slWarning. When this activity constant is specified, the HotSync Manager displays a dialog box at the end of the HotSync operation to alert the user that there are messages of interest in the log. This constant should be used to warn the user about errors that did not cause the conduit to abort.

❏ slText. Use this constant to add a simple message to the log without alerting the user at the end of the HotSync process. This constant is a good choice to use if you want to quietly add diagnostic information to the HotSync log that you could later use in resolving possible synchronization bugs in your conduit. These messages do not require immediate attention from the user, but if the user reports problems with your conduit, you can look through the user's HotSync log and find out exactly what your conduit was doing when the problem occurred.

In addition to LogAddEntry, there is a LogAddFormattedEntry function; it allows you to use standard C sprintf format specifiers to format a log entry. The LogAddFormattedEntry function has the following prototype:

```
long LogAddFormattedEntry (Activity act, BOOL bTimeStamp,
    const char* dataString, ...);
```

Use the dataString parameter the same way you would use the format specifier for a sprintf call:

```
LogAddFormattedEntry(slWarning, false,
    "%d terrible things happened during synchronization.",
    nTerrible);
```

> The **LogAddFormattedEntry** function uses a 256-byte internal buffer to hold the formatted string. If the data you pass to **LogAddFormattedEntry** exceeds the size of this buffer, **LogAddFormattedEntry** will crash.

You also can find out how many errors were logged using LogTestCounters, which has the following prototype:

```
WORD LogTestCounters()
```

This function simply returns the number of error entries in the log, or 0 if the log contains no errors. The following activity constants do not count as errors for the purposes of the LogTestCounters function:

❏ slSyncAborted

❏ slSyncFinished

❏ slSyncStarted

❏ slText

The LogTestCounters function treats every other type of log entry as an error and adds it to its return value.

*Internally, this function enables the HotSync Manager to determine whether or not to display a dialog box to the user mentioning the presence of messages in the HotSync log. Although explicit use of the* slWarning *constant will trigger the dialog box, any of the other entry types that* LogTestCounters *counts also will cause the dialog box to be displayed.*

# Summary

In this chapter, you learned some of the basics of how conduits work, as well as the mechanical aspects of installing conduits and logging their actions to the HotSync log. After reading this chapter, you should understand the following:

- ❏ A conduit is a code module that the HotSync Manager calls to synchronize data between a handheld application and a data source on the desktop.

- ❏ The four types of synchronization a conduit can perform, from most complex to least, are transaction-based, mirror image, one-directional, and backup.

- ❏ There are three basic paths to developing a conduit: starting with the Palm MFC Base Classes, starting with the Palm Generic Conduit Base Classes, or calling Sync Manager API functions directly.

- ❏ During development, you can manually install conduits using the Conduit Configuration tool, and you can use the Conduit Switch tool to save backups of your configurations and restore them later on.

- ❏ To provide for smooth installation of a conduit, your conduit's install program needs to register the conduit using the Conduit Manager API.

- ❏ You can add entries to the HotSync log with the LogAddEntry and LogAddFormattedEntry functions.

# 22

# Building Conduits

No matter which set of base classes you decide to use for your conduit, or even if you decide to forgo using the base classes at all and use the Sync Manager API directly, the Conduit Development Kit for Windows provides one easy way to start any conduit project: the Conduit Wizard. The Conduit Wizard is installed in Visual C++ when you install the rest of the CDK for Windows.

*You do not have to use the Conduit Wizard to build a conduit in Visual C++, but it certainly saves you a lot of time and frustration to let the wizard generate boilerplate code for you to fill in. If you really need to start from scratch (or if pain is something you enjoy), you can build a conduit DLL without the wizard, but be sure to build it as a regular DLL, not as an extension DLL.*

## Using the Conduit Wizard

To create a new conduit project in Visual C++ using the Conduit Wizard, select File ➪ New. The New dialog box, pictured in Figure 22-1, appears.

Select the Projects tab in the dialog box, and then select "Palm Conduit Wizard (dll)" from the list of available project types. Enter a name for your project in the Project name text box, and then enter an appropriate path for the project in the Location text box. Click OK when you have set everything to your satisfaction.

After you click OK, the Conduit Wizard launches and begins to prompt you for parameters that control what kind of conduit project you want to create. The Conduit Wizard has five steps:

1.  Select the type of conduit.

2.  Choose a handheld application with which to synchronize.

3.  Select a type of data transfer.

4.  Select conduit features.

5.  Confirm the classes to be created by the Conduit Wizard.

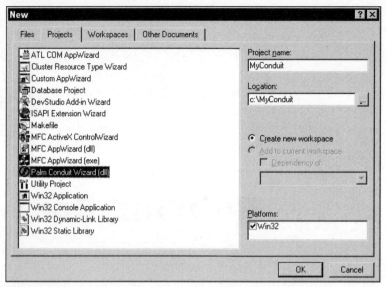

**Figure 22-1**

*If you choose to create only conduit entry points in Step 1 instead of using the base classes, the Conduit Wizard skips Steps 2 and 3 and proceeds straight to feature selection in Step 4.*

## Selecting a Conduit Type

Step 1 in the Conduit Wizard prompts you for the set of base classes you want to use for building the conduit. Figure 22-2 shows the Conduit Wizard at this stage of the process.

The Conduit Wizard presents you with three choices:

❑ **Generic.** Choose Generic if you want to build a conduit using the Palm Generic Conduit Base Classes.

❑ **MFC (Table Based).** Select this option if you want to build a conduit using the Palm MFC Base Classes.

❑ **Conduit entry points only (no synch logic).** Pick this option if you do not want to use either set of base classes but instead merely wish to use the Conduit Manager to generate a framework for a Sync Manager API–based conduit.

Click Next to proceed to the next step or Back to return to the New dialog box.

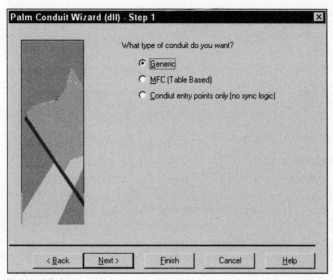

Figure 22-2

# Choosing a Handheld Application

From Step 2, pictured in Figure 22-3, you can choose with which handheld application the conduit interfaces.

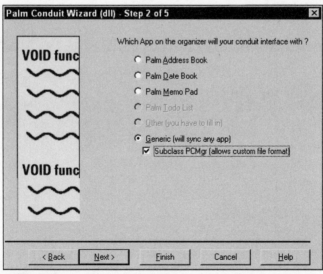

Figure 22-3

The Conduit Wizard can generate code for connecting to any of the four main Palm OS ROM applications, or it can assemble a framework for you to fill in for synchronization with your own custom handheld application. The options presented by the handheld application selection screen are as follows:

❑ **Palm Address Book.** Synchronize with the Address Book application.

❑ **Palm Date Book.** Synchronize with the Date Book application.

❑ **Palm Memo Pad.** Synchronize with the Memo Pad application.

❑ **Palm Todo List.** Synchronize with the To Do List application.

❑ **Other (you have to fill in).** Synchronize with a custom application. This option is for MFC conduits only and is not available if you selected Generic in Step 1.

❑ **Generic (will synch any app).** Synchronize with a custom application. This option is for generic conduits only and is not available if you selected MFC (Table Based) in Step 1. In addition, when you select this option you also may select the Subclass PCMgr (allows custom file format) check box, which allows you to implement your own storage format on the desktop. Without this box checked, the code generated by the Conduit Wizard saves to the same MFC-serialized format as an MFC conduit, so checking the box is important if you want to synchronize with a different data source on the desktop.

Click Next to proceed to the next step or Back to return to Step 1.

## Selecting a Data Transfer Type

Step 3 in the Conduit Wizard, shown in Figure 22-4, allows you to choose what type of data transfer you want in your conduit.

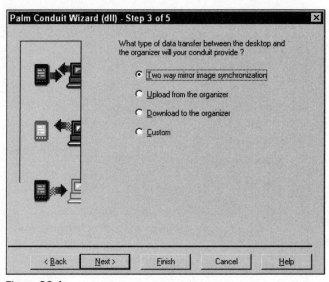

Figure 22-4

The choices available in this step are described as follows:

❑ **Two-way mirror image synchronization.** If you select this option, the Conduit Wizard creates code to implement mirror image synchronization between the desktop and handheld, as described in Chapter 21. This is by far the easiest way to add mirror image synchronization to a conduit because the base classes can take care of all of the ugly details of resolving record conflicts without your having to write a single line of code.

❑ **Upload from the organizer.** With this option selected, the code produced by the Conduit Wizard is geared toward retrieving information from the handheld and storing it on the desktop, probably performing some kind of operation on the data in the process.

*If you are interested only in backing up data from the handheld application, rely on the standard Backup conduit instead of building a conduit with the Upload from the organizer data transfer option. You need to use this option only if you want to convert the data to another format before storing it on the desktop. For example, if you want your handheld application's data to be stored in a Microsoft Access database on the desktop computer, use the Upload from the organizer option.*

❑ **Download to the organizer.** This option creates application code that moves data from the desktop computer to the handheld. If your data may be modified only on the desktop computer and then transferred to the handheld, this is a good option to select.

❑ **Custom.** Select this option if the other options listed previously do not suit your application.

Click Next to proceed to the next step or Back to return to Step 2.

## Selecting Conduit Features

Step 4 in the Conduit Wizard, pictured in Figure 22-5, allows you to add optional features to your conduit.

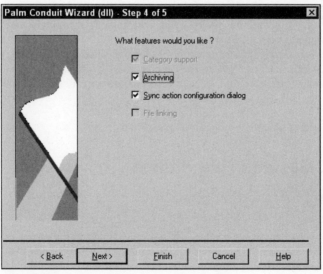

**Figure 22-5**

Depending upon your selections in Steps 1 and 2, some of the features listed in Step 4 may not be available, in which case they will be grayed out in the dialog box. Others may be required by the conduit type and application, and they will be grayed out but checked, to indicate that you cannot tell the Conduit Wizard to skip making code for that feature. The features are as follows:

❏ **Category support.** If this feature is selected, the Conduit Wizard generates code to synchronize the standard system of record categories used by many Palm OS applications.

❏ **Archiving.** Selecting Archiving causes the Conduit Wizard to add support for archiving deleted and modified records to a separate location from the normal desktop data source.

❏ **Sync action configuration dialog box.** Select this option to have the wizard add code implementing a standard conduit configuration dialog box, pictured in Figure 22-6. This dialog box appears when the user chooses the Custom option in the HotSync Manager's menu, and it allows the user to change how the conduit synchronizes its data.

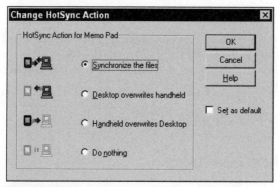

**Figure 22-6**

❏ **File linking.** If this option is selected, the Conduit Wizard adds functions to support *file linking* to your conduit project. File linking is a way to automatically update handheld data from a file on the desktop. For example, you could link a handheld application to an address database kept on the desktop; changes made to the desktop database would then be made automatically to the handheld application's data during every HotSync operation. A file link updates data in only one category of the handheld database.

Click Next to proceed to the next step or Back to return to Step 3.

## Confirming Class and File Names

The final step in the Conduit Wizard, shown in Figure 22-7, allows you to customize the names of classes and files generated by the wizard.

By default, the Conduit Wizard creates class and file names based on the project name that you supplied when you first started the wizard. Sometimes, these names can be somewhat unwieldy to use when actually programming the conduit, so this step gives you an opportunity to change the names to something more aesthetically pleasing or mnemonic.

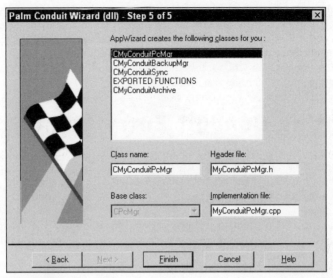

**Figure 22-7**

To change a class, header file, or implementation filename, select a class name from the list at the top of the dialog box. Modify the names in the Class name, Header file, and Implementation file text boxes. When you have altered the names to your taste, click Finish to proceed to the New Project Information dialog box, shown in Figure 22-8. You also may click Back to return to Step 4.

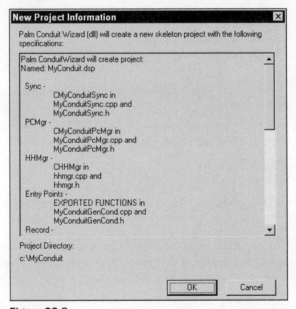

**Figure 22-8**

The New Project Information dialog box summarizes the classes and files that the Conduit Wizard will create, and it also lists the options you select for the project. Verify that everything is set up the way you want it, and then click OK to actually create the new conduit project. If you find that you would like to change something, click Cancel, and Visual Studio returns you to the Conduit Wizard so that you can make changes to the project. You will not lose the changes you have already made if you click Cancel.

# Implementing Conduit Entry Points

Now that you have created an application framework with the Conduit Wizard, you can get to the actual work of coding your conduit. Whether you use the base classes or not, every conduit has certain entry points that you must implement and several that are optional if you want to add other features to your conduit. The following four functions are required entry points to any conduit:

❑ GetConduitInfo. This function returns various bits of information about the conduit, including its name, whether MFC is used to build the conduit, and the conduit's default action.

❑ GetConduitName. This function returns the name of the conduit.

❑ GetConduitVersion. This function returns the version number of the conduit.

❑ OpenConduit. This function is the main entry point into the conduit. When the HotSync Manager needs to call a conduit to perform synchronization, it calls the conduit's OpenConduit function.

In addition to the required entry points, you will need to implement additional functions to provide certain features in your conduit:

❑ ConfigureConduit and CfgConduit. These two functions serve an identical purpose, which is to display a configuration dialog box to allow the user to customize how the conduit synchronizes its data. The CfgConduit function is a newer version of the ConfigureConduit function that provides more data to your conduit; CfgConduit is available in version 3.0 and later of the HotSync Manager.

❑ ConfigureSubscription. This function allows the HotSync Manager to retrieve file-linking details from your conduit.

❑ ImportData. This function loads data from a linked file and displays a dialog box, allowing the user to choose how fields should be mapped between the linked file and the data source.

❑ SubscriptionSupported. The HotSync Manager calls this function to determine if a conduit supports file linking.

❑ UpdateTables. This function updates a desktop data source with information from a file-linking operation, such as changes to category names.

External entry points to a conduit DLL, just like any DLL entry point built with Visual C++, must have a return type of __declspec( dllexport ). One of the header files created by the Conduit Wizard provides a bit of syntactic sugar for this unwieldy expression:

```
#define ExportFunc __declspec( dllexport )
```

All of the entry point functions generated by the Conduit Wizard are declared with an ExportFunc return type.

## *Implementing GetConduitInfo*

The Conduit Wizard generates all of the code you will normally need for the `GetConduitInfo`, `GetConduitName`, and `GetConduitVersion` functions. For the most part, you should not have to customize these functions. Instead, you should customize some of the strings in the string table created by the Conduit Wizard. Click the ResourceView tab in the Visual C++ workspace toolbar, and then find the String Table resource and double-click it to view the strings in the conduit project. Figure 22-9 shows the string table open for editing.

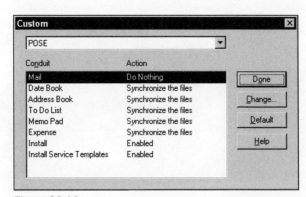

| ID | Value | Caption |
|---|---|---|
| IDS_CONDUIT_NAME | 1 | Generic Conduit |
| IDS_CONNECTION | 3311 | Please check your connections and try again. |
| IDS_DEVICE_FULL | 3312 | Your Palm organizer may be full. Check the Palm organizer's Memory Application |
| IDS_DESKTOP_FULL | 3313 | Your Desktop disk may be full. Check the disk space and HotSync again. |
| IDS_BAD_ADD_REC | 3315 | Could not copy the following record to Palm organizer: %s |
| IDS_BAD_PURGE_REMOTE | 3316 | Could not purge the deleted records on Palm organizer. %s |
| IDS_BAD_DEL_REC | 3317 | Could not delete the following record on Palm organizer: %s |
| IDS_BAD_CHANGE_REC | 3318 | Could not modify the following record on Palm organizer: %s |
| IDS_BAD_LOCALADD_REC | 3319 | Could not copy the following record to the Desktop: %s |
| IDS_REMOTE_BAD_CHANGE | 3320 | Could not move the Palm organizer records in category '%s' to 'Unfiled'. |
| IDS_BAD_READ_RECORD | 3322 | Could not read the next Palm organizer record. |
| IDS_REMOTE_TOOMANY_C | 3323 | Only 15 categories are allowed. All records in remote category %s were change— |
| IDS_REMOTE_CAT_DELETE | 3325 | -- Remote category %s has been deleted. The records in this category have bee |
| IDS_DOUBLE_MODIFIED | 3328 | The following record was modified on both Palm organizer and the Desktop: %s. |
| IDS_ARCH_DOUBLE_MOD1 | 3331 | The following record was modified on both Palm organizer and the Desktop: %s. |
| IDS_REVERSE_DELETE | 3334 | The following record, %s, was modified on one platform and deleted on the othe |
| IDS_RECCOUNT_DESKTOP1 | 3338 | Some Palm organizer records were not copied to the Desktop. Your computer m |
| IDS_RECCOUNT_PILOT1 | 3341 | Some Desktop records were not copied to Palm organizer. Your Palm organizer |
| IDS_CUSTOM_LABEL | 3343 | A custom label was modified on the Desktop and Palm organizer. The Palm org |
| IDS_BAD_XMAP | 3345 | Records may not be sorted correctly on the Desktop. |
| IDS_BAD_ARCHIVE_ERR | 3346 | Some or all of your deleted records were not archived. |
| IDS_BAD_RESET_FLAGS_RE | 3348 | Could not clear Palm organizer's status flags. Error Code %s |
| IDS_DOUBLE_MODIFY_SUB! | 3358 | The following record in a subscription category was modified: %s. This record ma |
| IDS_LOG_SPACING | 3360 | - |

**Figure 22-9**

The two strings you should modify are `IDS_CONDUIT_NAME`, found at the top of the list, and `IDS_SYNC_ACTION_TEXT`, found at the bottom of the list. The `IDS_CONDUIT_NAME` string is simply the name of your conduit as it will appear in the HotSync Manager's Custom dialog box (pictured in Figure 22-10) and in the HotSync log. Typically, this will be the same as the name of the handheld application with which the conduit synchronizes.

**Figure 22-10**

The IDS_SYNC_ACTION_TEXT string appears in the default configuration dialog box (refer to Figure 22-6) that the Conduit Wizard provides if you select the Sync action configuration dialog box feature during Step 4 of the Conduit Wizard. You should set this string to something like HotSync Action for *MyApp*, where *MyApp* is the name of your application.

Once you have the string table set up properly, you need only to alter GetConduitInfo, GetConduitName, and GetConduitVersion if you want to make them return information other than just information from the string table. Here is the wizard-generated GetConduitInfo function:

```
ExportFunc long GetConduitInfo (ConduitInfoEnum infoType,
                                void *pInArgs, void *pOut,
                                DWORD *pdwOutSize)
{
    if (!pOut)
        return CONDERR_INVALID_PTR;
    if (!pdwOutSize)
        return CONDERR_INVALID_OUTSIZE_PTR;

    switch (infoType)
    {
        case eConduitName:
            if (!pInArgs)
                return CONDERR_INVALID_INARGS_PTR;
            ConduitRequestInfoType *pInfo;
            pInfo = (ConduitRequestInfoType *)pInArgs;
            if ((pInfo->dwVersion !=
                    CONDUITREQUESTINFO_VERSION_1) ||
                (pInfo->dwSize != SZ_CONDUITREQUESTINFO))
                return CONDERR_INVALID_INARGS_STRUCT;

            if (!::LoadString((HINSTANCE)hLangInstance,
                            IDS_CONDUIT_NAME,
                            (TCHAR*)pOut, *pdwOutSize))
                return CONDERR_CONDUIT_RESOURCE_FAILURE;
            break;

        case eDefaultAction:
            if (*pdwOutSize != sizeof(eSyncTypes))
                return CONDERR_INVALID_BUFFER_SIZE;
            (*(eSyncTypes*)pOut) = eFast;
            break;

        case eMfcVersion:
            if (*pdwOutSize != sizeof(DWORD))
                return CONDERR_INVALID_BUFFER_SIZE;
            (*(DWORD*)pOut) = MFC_NOT_USED;
            break;

        default:
            return CONDERR_UNSUPPORTED_CONDUITINFO_ENUM;
    }
    return 0;
}
```

The `GetConduitInfo` function must deal with three possible requests for information:

- ❏   `eConduitName`. A request for the name of the conduit
- ❏   `eDefaultAction`. A request for the conduit's default action, expressed as a member of the `eSyncTypes` enumerated type
- ❏   `eMfcVersion`. A request for the version of MFC used to build the conduit

Boilerplate code generated by the Conduit Wizard for `GetConduitInfo` returns the `IDS_CONDUIT_NAME` string when `GetConduitInfo` receives an `eConduitName` request, and it returns `eFast` as the default action for the conduit. The `eSyncTypes` enumerated type, defined in the CDK header file `syncmgr.h`, looks like this:

```
enum eSyncTypes {eFast,
                 eSlow,
                 eHHtoPC,
                 ePCtoHH,
                 eInstall,
                 eBackup,
                 eDoNothing,
                 eProfileInstall,
                 eSyncTypeDoNotUse=0xffffffff
};
```

If your application should perform a default action other than a FastSync, simply replace the `eFast` constant in `GetConduitInfo` with the appropriate `eSyncTypes` constant. For example, if your conduit does nothing more than back up a handheld application's data to a database on the desktop computer, you should choose `eBackup`.

If you used the Conduit Wizard to generate an MFC conduit, the `GetConduitInfo` function will return different values in response to an `eMfcVersion` request than if you used the Conduit Wizard to create a conduit based on the Palm Generic Conduit Classes. These values are defined as follows in the CDK header file `Condapi.h`:

```
#define MFC_VERSION_41   0x00000410
#define MFC_VERSION_50   0x00000500
#define MFC_VERSION_60   0x00000600
#define MFC_NOT_USED     0x10000000
```

*The versions in these constants correspond to the version of Visual C++ that MFC shipped with, not the version number included in the MFC libraries themselves.*

## Implementing GetConduitName

The default `GetConduitName` function provided by the Conduit Wizard merely returns the `IDS_CONDUIT_NAME` string:

```
ExportFunc long GetConduitName (char* pszName, WORD nLen)
{
    long retval = -1;

    if (::LoadString((HINSTANCE)hLangInstance,
```

```
                         IDS_CONDUIT_NAME, pszName, nLen))
        retval = 0;

    return retval;
}
```

## Implementing GetConduitVersion

The GetConduitVersion function is even simpler than GetConduitName, returning a constant from one of the conduit project's header files; the following code from a wizard-generated generic conduit implements GetConduitVersion:

```
ExportFunc DWORD GetConduitVersion()
{
    return GENERIC_CONDUIT_VERSION;
}
```

Within the DWORD value you return from GetConduitVersion, you must pack the major version number in the high byte of the return value's low word, and the minor version number goes into the low byte of the low word. For example, a standard generic conduit created by the Conduit Wizard defines the following constant, equivalent to a version number of 1.2:

```
#define GENERIC_CONDUIT_VERSION 0x00000102
```

> **Never use a conduit version of 0x00000100 (1.0). Although it seems intuitive for a new conduit to have a version of 1.0, a bug in version 2.x of the Palm Desktop software prevents any conduit from running with a version of 1.0. This affects all Macintosh Palm Desktop users. The default version constant provided by the Conduit Wizard is 0x00000101, which you should leave alone until you need to increment your conduit's version number.**

## Implementing OpenConduit

The OpenConduit function is responsible for actually performing synchronization between a specific handheld application and its desktop data source. If you used the Conduit Wizard to create a conduit framework based on the generic or MFC base classes, OpenConduit already contains some code that calls base class methods to perform the synchronization. If you used the Conduit Wizard only to create entry points, the OpenConduit function is rather sparse, providing you with only a placeholder to fill in with your own code:

```
ExportFunc long OpenConduit (PROGRESSFN pFn,
                             CSyncProperties& rProps)
{
    long retval = -1;
    if (pFn)
    {
        // TODO - create your own custom sync class, and
```

```
        // run it
    }
    return(retval);
}
```

The pFn argument to OpenConduit is a pointer to a callback function provided by the HotSync Manager, which allows you to update the HotSync Manager with status messages regarding the progress of your conduit.

*None of the conduits for the four built-in applications actually makes use of the callback, and documentation regarding it is scant at best. The MFC boilerplate generated by the Conduit Wizard assigns the function pointer to the m_pfnProgress member of the conduit's subclass of CBaseConduitMonitor, but it never actually calls the function. The following comment from the basemon.cpp source file, which implements the MFC CBaseConduitMonitor class, might provide a starting place if you want to explore further:*

```
// The Progress Callback is not currently used, but
// here is an example of how you could use it:
//      char probString[64];
//      memset(probString,0,sizeof(probString));
//      strcpy(probString, "Joe");
//      (*m_pfnProgress)(probString);
```

The HotSync Manager fills the rProps argument to OpenConduit with a pointer to a CSyncProperties object, which contains a wealth of information about the environment in which the conduit is running. The CDK header file Syncmgr.h defines CSyncProperties as follows:

```
class CSyncProperties
{
public:
    eSyncTypes  m_SyncType;
    char        m_PathName[BIG_PATH];
    char        m_LocalName[BIG_PATH];
    char        m_UserName[BIG_PATH];
    char*       m_RemoteName[SYNC_DB_NAMELEN];
    CDbListPtr  *m_RemoteDbList;
    int         m_nRemoteCount;
    DWORD       m_Creator;
    WORD        m_CardNo;
    DWORD       m_DbType;
    DWORD       m_AppInfoSize;
    DWORD       m_SortInfoSize;
    eFirstSync  m_FirstDevice;
    eConnType   m_Connection;
    char        m_Registry[BIG_PATH];
    HKEY        m_hKey;
    DWORD       m_dwReserved;
};
```

The following table describes the data members of the CSyncProperties class.

| Member | Description |
|---|---|
| m_SyncType | Current synchronization type. |
| m_PathName | Pathname that precedes files on the desktop computer. |
| m_LocalName | File name of the data source on the desktop. |
| m_UserName | Username used for this HotSync operation. |
| m_RemoteName | An array of names of databases on the handheld to synchronize with. |
| m_RemoteDbList | Pointer to a CDbList class that contains further information about the remote databases, including various status flags and modification dates. |
| m_nRemoteCount | Number of databases on the handheld that should be synchronized. |
| m_Creator | Creator ID of the handheld databases. |
| m_CardNo | Card number containing the handheld databases. |
| m_DbType | Database type for databases on the handheld. |
| m_AppInfoSize | Size of the handheld database's application info block, stored here for convenience. |
| m_SortInfoSize | Size of the handheld database's sort info block, stored here for convenience. |
| m_FirstDevice | Specifies if this is the first time this particular desktop or handheld has been synchronized, using the eFirstSync enumerated type, which has the following possible values: eNeither, ePC, and eHH. |
| m_Connection | Connection medium used for this HotSync operation. This value comes from the eConnType enumerated type, which has the following possible values: eCable and eModemConnType. |
| m_Registry | Full Windows Registry path for the conduit. |
| m_hKey | Primary Windows Registry key for the conduit. |
| m_dwReserved | Reserved for future use. Set this field to NULL before using a CSyncProperties object. |

Within the OpenConduit function, you should create a new instance of whatever class you are using to implement synchronization logic, call an appropriate method of that class to begin the actual synchronization process, and then delete the object. If you are working from a bare bones conduit with only the entry points created by the Conduit Wizard, you have your work cut out for you. If you are using either the generic or MFC base classes, the Conduit Wizard will have already filled in the appropriate code for the OpenConduit function. In a generic conduit, OpenConduit looks like this:

```
ExportFunc long OpenConduit (PROGRESSFN pFn,
                             CSyncProperties& rProps)
{
    long retval = -1;
    if (pFn)
    {
        CLibCondSync* pGeneric;
```

```
        pGeneric = new CLibCondSync(rProps,
            GENERIC_FLAG_CATEGORY_SUPPORTED |
            GENERIC_FLAG_APPINFO_SUPPORTED );
        if (pGeneric)
        {
            retval = pGeneric->Perform();

            delete pGeneric;
        }
    }
    return(retval);
}
```

An MFC-based conduit has the following OpenConduit implementation:

```
ExportFunc long OpenConduit (PROGRESSFN pFn,
                             CSyncProperties& rProps)
{
    AFX_MANAGE_STATE(AfxGetStaticModuleState());
    long retval = -1;
    if (pFn)
    {
        CLibCondMonitor* pMonitor;

        pMonitor = new CLibCondMonitor(pFn, rProps,
                                       myInst);
        if (pMonitor)
        {
            retval = pMonitor->Engage();

            delete pMonitor;
        }
    }
    return(retval);
}
```

*Calling the AFX_MANAGE_STATE macro at the start of each exported function in an MFC DLL is required if the DLL is to function properly. The Conduit Wizard puts the macro in the proper places when it generates a framework for your conduit, and you should not delete any occurrence of AFX_MANAGE_STATE.*

The "Using Palm MFC Base Classes" and "Using Generic Conduit Base Classes" sections later in this chapter provide more details about customizing the base classes so that they will perform appropriate actions for your own conduits.

## *Implementing Configuration Entry Points*

The ConfigureConduit and CfgConduit entry points allow the user to change how the conduit synchronizes its data. You can think of the dialog box displayed by these functions as a control panel from which the user can not only select synchronization types (such as choosing between "Synchronize the files" and "Do nothing") but also change any other settings that might be specific to your own conduit (such as setting paths to other files that your conduit might need on the desktop).

*Although doing so is not strictly required, you should implement* `ConfigureConduit` *or* `CfgConduit` *in every conduit because without one of these functions, nothing happens when the user tries to config-ure the conduit from the HotSync Manager's Custom dialog box (see Figure 22-10). At the very least, you should display a dialog box explaining that there is nothing to configure in your conduit, or per-haps just display an "about" box.*

The `CfgConduit` function is a newer version of `ConfigureConduit`, which PalmSource added with the introduction of version 3.0 of the HotSync Manager. When the user chooses to change a conduit's HotSync action, 3.0 and later versions of the HotSync Manager attempt to call `CfgConduit` first; if that function is not implemented, the HotSync Manager tries to call `ConfigureConduit`. Earlier versions of the HotSync Manager call only `ConfigureConduit`.

If you used the Conduit Wizard to generate a generic conduit, or only conduit entry points, the boiler-plate code already contains a default dialog box resource (`IDD_CONDUIT_ACTION`) and the code to implement it in `CfgConduit` and `ConfigureConduit`. Figure 22-11 shows `IDD_CONDUIT_ACTION` as it appears in the Visual C++ resource editor.

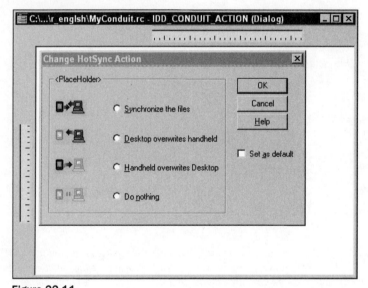

**Figure 22-11**

The `IDD_CONDUIT_ACTION` dialog box is a good starting point if you want to offer the user more, or pos-sibly fewer, configuration options for your conduit. You simply need to modify the resource and then add code to `CfgConduit` and `ConfigureConduit` to implement user interaction with the new dialog box. The base code for the wizard-generated `ConfigureConduit` function in generic and bare bones conduits looks like this:

```
ExportFunc long ConfigureConduit (CSyncPreference& pref)
{

    long nRtn = -1;
    CfgConduitInfoType cfg;
```

```
        cfg.dwVersion = CFGCONDUITINFO_VERSION_1;
        cfg.dwSize  = sizeof(CfgConduitInfoType);
        cfg.dwCreatorId = 0;
        cfg.dwUserId = 0;
        memset(cfg.szUser , 0, sizeof(cfg.szUser));
        memset(cfg.m_PathName, 0, sizeof(cfg.m_PathName));
        cfg.syncPermanent = pref.m_SyncType;
        cfg.syncTemporary = pref.m_SyncType;
        cfg.syncNew = pref.m_SyncType;
        cfg.syncPref = eTemporaryPreference;

        int iResult;
        iResult = DialogBoxParam((HINSTANCE)hLangInstance,
                MAKEINTRESOURCE(IDD_CONDUIT_ACTION),
                GetForegroundWindow(),
                (DLGPROC)ConfigureDlgProc,
                (LPARAM)&cfg);
        if (iResult == 0)
        {
            pref.m_SyncType = cfg.syncNew;
            pref.m_SyncPref = cfg.syncPref;
            nRtn = 0;
        }
        return nRtn;
    }
```

A wizard-generated MFC conduit project also contains fully implemented CfgConduit and ConfigureConduit functions. Instead of a resource that is included as part of the project, an MFC conduit created by the Conduit Wizard uses a CHotSyncActionDlg object, which is a descendant of the MFC CDialog class. The resulting dialog box is identical to that produced by the generic conduit code, but changing the dialog box requires that you subclass CHotSyncActionDlg and make modifications there instead of altering a dialog resource. The ConfigureConduit function in an MFC conduit project looks like this:

```
ExportFunc long ConfigureConduit (CSyncPreference& pref)
{
    AFX_MANAGE_STATE(AfxGetStaticModuleState());
    long nRtn = -1;
    char szName[81];
    CHotSyncActionDlg actDlg(CWnd::GetActiveWindow());

    pref.m_SyncPref = eNoPreference;

    GetConduitName(szName,80);
    actDlg.m_csGroupText = szName;

    switch (pref.m_SyncType)
    {
        case eFast:
        case eSlow:
            actDlg.m_nActionIndex = 0;
            break;
        case ePCtoHH:
            actDlg.m_nActionIndex = 1;
            break;
```

```
                case eHHtoPC:
                    actDlg.m_nActionIndex = 2;
                    break;
                case eDoNothing:
                default:
                    actDlg.m_nActionIndex = 3;
        }

        if (actDlg.DoModal() == IDOK)
        {
            switch (actDlg.m_nActionIndex)
            {
                case 0:
                    pref.m_SyncType = eFast;
                    break;
                case 1:
                    pref.m_SyncType = ePCtoHH;
                    break;
                case 2:
                    pref.m_SyncType = eHHtoPC;
                    break;
                case 3:
                default:
                    pref.m_SyncType = eDoNothing;
                    break;
            }

            pref.m_SyncPref = (actDlg.m_bMakeDefault) ?
                ePermanentPreference : eTemporaryPreference;

            nRtn = 0;
        }
        return nRtn;
}
```

The pref argument that the HotSync Manager passes to ConfigureConduit is a CSyncPreference
object containing information about the current HotSync settings for the conduit. Defined in the CDK
header file Syncmgr.h, this is what the CSyncPreference class looks like:

```
class CSyncPreference
{
public:
    char        m_PathName[BIG_PATH];
    char        m_Registry[BIG_PATH];
    HKEY        m_hKey;
    eSyncPref   m_SyncPref;
    eSyncTypes  m_SyncType;
    DWORD       m_dwReserved;
};
```

The following table describes what the data members of the CSyncPreference class mean.

| Member | Description |
|---|---|
| m_PathName | Indicates the pathname that precedes files on the desktop computer. |
| m_Registry | Specifies the full Windows Registry path for the conduit. |
| m_hKey | Indicates the primary Windows Registry key for the conduit. |
| m_SyncPref | Specifies whether the user's selected synchronization preferences should be applied temporarily (on the next HotSync action only) or permanently. This field uses the eSyncPref enumerated type, which can have the following values: eNoPreference, ePermanentPreference, or eTemporaryPreference. |
| m_SyncType | Specifies the synchronization type using a constant from the eSyncTypes enumerated type. |
| m_dwReserved | Reserved for future use. Set this field to NULL before using a CSyncPreference object. |

Not only does the CSyncPreference object serve to provide the ConfigureConduit function with information it needs, CSyncPreference also returns values to the HotSync Manager in response to changes the user makes to the conduit's settings. In particular, the m_SyncPref and m_SyncType members of CSyncPreference should be set to appropriate values before returning from ConfigureConduit.

The CfgConduit function allows later versions of the HotSync Manager to pass more data to the conduit than can be done through the ConfigureConduit function. Instead of passing data through a CSyncPreference object, CfgConduit accepts a CfgConduitInfoType structure. Here is the prototype for CfgConduit:

```
long CfgConduit (ConduitCfgEnum cfgType, void *pArgs,
                DWORD *pdwArgsSize);
```

The first argument to CfgConduit indicates what version of the CfgConduit function that the HotSync Manager is attempting to call, as defined by the ConduitCfgEnum enumerated type. As of this writing, there is only one version of the CfgConduit function, which you should specify using the eConfig1 constant.

The pArgs argument contains a pointer to the incoming CfgConduitInfoType structure, and pdwArgsSize is a pointer to a variable containing the size of that structure, in bytes. Defined in the CDK header file Condapi.h, the CfgConduitInfoType structure looks like this:

```
typedef struct CfgConduitInfoType {
    DWORD dwVersion;
    DWORD dwSize;
    DWORD dwCreatorId;
    DWORD dwUserId;
    TCHAR szUser[64];
    char  m_PathName[BIG_PATH];
    eSyncTypes syncPermanent;
    eSyncTypes syncTemporary;
    eSyncTypes syncNew;
    eSyncPref  syncPref;
} CFGCONDUITINFO;
```

The following table describes the fields in the `CfgConduitInfoType` structure.

| Field | Description |
|---|---|
| dwVersion | Version number of the `CfgConduitInfoType` structure |
| dwSize | Size of the `CfgConduitInfoType` structure |
| dwCreatorId | Creator ID of the handheld application this conduit is registered to handle |
| dwUserId | User ID number for whom the conduit should be configured |
| szUser | Name of the user for whom the conduit should be configured |
| m_PathName | Pathname that precedes files on the desktop computer |
| syncPermanent | Type of synchronization to perform on a permanent basis |
| syncTemporary | Type of synchronization to perform temporarily (on the next HotSync operation) |
| syncNew | Type of synchronization to perform for a handheld that has never been synchronized before |
| syncPref | Specifies whether the user's selected synchronization preferences should be applied temporarily (on the next HotSync action only) or permanently |

Like the `CSyncPreference` class, the `CfgConduitInfoType` structure carries return values back to the HotSync Manager. In particular, make sure the `syncPermanent`, `syncTemporary`, and `syncPref` values are set appropriately before the end of the `CfgConduit` function.

As an example of how to use values from the `CfgConduitInfoType` structure, here is the default `CfgConduit` function from a generic conduit project:

```
ExportFunc long CfgConduit (ConduitCfgEnum cfgType,
                            void *pArgs, DWORD *pdwArgsSize)
{
    long nRtn = -1;
    TCHAR szName[256];
    DWORD dwNamesize;
    ConduitRequestInfoType infoStruct;
    CfgConduitInfoType *pCfgInfo;


    dwNamesize = sizeof(szName);


    if (!pArgs)
        return CONDERR_INVALID_INARGS_PTR;
    if (!pdwArgsSize)
        return CONDERR_INVALID_ARGSSIZE_PTR;
    if (*pdwArgsSize != SZ_CFGCONDUITINFO)
        return CONDERR_INVALID_ARGSSIZE;

    if (cfgType != eConfig1)
```

```
                    return CONDERR_UNSUPPORTED_CFGCONDUIT_ENUM;

    pCfgInfo = (CfgConduitInfoType *)pArgs;
    if (pCfgInfo->dwVersion != CFGCONDUITINFO_VERSION_1)
        return CONDERR_UNSUPPORTED_STRUCT_VERSION;

    infoStruct.dwVersion = CONDUITREQUESTINFO_VERSION_1;
    infoStruct.dwSize = SZ_CONDUITREQUESTINFO;
    infoStruct.dwCreatorId = pCfgInfo->dwCreatorId;
    infoStruct.dwUserId = pCfgInfo->dwUserId;
    strcpy(infoStruct.szUser, pCfgInfo->szUser);
    nRtn = GetConduitInfo(eConduitName,
                          (void *)&infoStruct,
                          (void *)szName, &dwNamesize);
    if (nRtn)
        return nRtn;

    int iResult;
    iResult = DialogBoxParam((HINSTANCE)hLangInstance,
            MAKEINTRESOURCE(IDD_CONDUIT_CFG_DETAILED),
            GetForegroundWindow(),
            (DLGPROC)ConfigureDlgProc,
            (LPARAM)pCfgInfo);

    return 0;
}
```

## Understanding Native Synchronization Logic

Synchronizing two sets of records that may have been modified on both the desktop computer and the handheld requires a large amount of complex logic to resolve conflicts. If the user alters the same record in both places, or deletes the record on one platform and changes it on another, the conduit must be sure to do the "right thing" with the data, ensuring that the result of the synch makes sense to the user and that no data is ever lost that the user did not explicitly delete. Writing code to handle all the possible combinations of modification on two different devices can be sheer hell, particularly when it comes time to debug it.

Fortunately, the developers at PalmSource have already gone through the agony of implementing native synchronization logic in both sets of base classes. If you use the base classes as a foundation for your conduit, you can concentrate on the details of customizing the conduit for your handheld and desktop application data formats, instead of spending time trying to implement your own two-way mirror synchronization code.

Because it may be helpful for you to know what is going on under the hood, the following table describes what the native synch logic does when it encounters each possible combination of changes that can be made to handheld and desktop records.

| Record Status on Handheld | Record Status on Desktop | Conduit Action |
|---|---|---|
| Added | No record | Add the handheld record to the desktop database. |
| Archived | Deleted | Archive the handheld record, and then delete the record from both the handheld and desktop databases. |
| Archived | No changes | Archive the handheld record, and then delete the record from both the handheld and desktop databases. |
| Archived | No record | Archive the handheld record. |
| Archived and changed | Changed | Archive both the handheld record and the desktop record if the changes are identical. If the changes are not identical, do not archive the handheld record; instead, add the desktop record to the handheld database, and add the handheld record to the desktop database. |
| Archived, no changes | Changed | Do not archive the handheld record; instead, replace it with the desktop record. |
| Changed | Archived and changed | Archive the handheld record if the changes are identical, and then delete the record from both the handheld and desktop databases. If the changes are not identical, do not archive the desktop record; instead, add the desktop record to the handheld database and add the handheld record to the desktop database. |
| Changed | Archived, no changes | Do not archive the desktop record; instead, replace the record in the desktop database with the handheld record. |
| Changed | Changed | Take no action if the changes are identical. If the changes are not identical, add the handheld record to the desktop database and add the desktop record to the handheld database. |

| Record Status on Handheld | Record Status on Desktop | Conduit Action |
|---|---|---|
| Changed | Deleted | Do not delete the desktop record; instead, replace the desktop record with the handheld record. |
| Changed | No changes | Replace the desktop record with the handheld record. |
| Deleted | Changed | Do not delete the handheld record; instead, replace the handheld record with the desktop record. |
| Deleted | No changes | Delete the record from the desktop and handheld databases. |
| No changes | Archived | Archive the desktop record, and then delete the record from both the desktop and handheld databases. |
| No changes | Changed | Replace the handheld record with the desktop record. |
| No changes | Deleted | Delete the record from both the desktop and handheld databases. |

Keeping records in synch is not the only task a conduit implementing mirror-image synchronization needs to worry about. It is equally important to maintain consistency between categories of records on the desktop and the handheld. Like record synchronization logic, this is rather difficult and time-consuming to code, so category synching also is part of the native synchronization logic.

Maintaining harmony between categories on two devices requires that the synch logic keep an eye on each category's name, category ID, and index location in relation to other categories. The following table shows how the native synch logic deals with different category situations between desktop and handheld.

| Name | Category ID | Index | Conduit Action |
|---|---|---|---|
| Desktop name matches handheld name | Not applicable | Desktop index matches handheld index | Take no action. |
| Desktop name matches handheld name | Not applicable | Desktop index does not match handheld index | Change all desktop records in the category to match the handheld's category ID. |
| Desktop name does not exist on handheld and | Desktop ID matches handheld ID | Not applicable | Change the category name on the handheld to match the desktop. |

| Name | Category ID | Index | Conduit Action |
|---|---|---|---|
| Desktop name does not exist on the handheld | Desktop ID does not exist on the handheld | Desktop index is not in use on the handheld | Add desktop category to the handheld. |
| Desktop name does not exist on the handheld | Desktop ID does not exist on the handheld | Desktop index is already in use on the handheld | Add desktop category at the next free index on the handheld, and update desktop records in the category to use the new index. |

# Using the Generic Conduit Base Classes

To create a conduit using the generic conduit base classes, you must make your own subclasses of the various base classes, and then override virtual methods of those classes to customize the conduit's behavior for your own purposes. In order to do all that, you need to know what the base classes are and how they interact with one another. The following list introduces and briefly describes the base classes:

❑ CSynchronizer. The synchronizer object is responsible for performing the actual synchronization of records, categories, and the handheld program's application info block. All of the native synch logic is implemented in CSynchronizer.

❑ CPDbBaseMgr. This class serves as the foundation for CPcMgr and CHHMgr. The various manager classes control storage and retrieval of records, from both the desktop and the handheld.

❑ CPcMgr. The CPcMgr class deals with storing records on and retrieving them from the desktop. Your generic conduit will have at least one subclass of CPcMgr (named something like CMyConduitPcMgr), customized for handling whatever desktop format you choose to implement in the conduit. There might also be subclasses of this subclass, used for archiving (CMyConduitArchiveMgr) and backing up (CMyConduitBackupMgr) records on the desktop.

❑ CHHMgr. The counterpart to CPcMgr, CHHMgr stores and retrieves data on the handheld end of the conduit. In general, there should be no need to subclass CHHMgr; in fact, the Conduit Wizard does not even bother to generate a CMyConduitHHMgr function.

❑ CPCategoryMgr and CPCategory. The synchronizer object uses these classes to synch categories between the handheld and the desktop.

❑ CPalmRecord. This class provides a generic record storage format on the desktop. The CPalmRecord class contains methods for converting itself to and from the raw record format used on the handheld, as well as routines for making common conversions between Intel and Motorola byte ordering.

❑ CMyConduitRecord. This is not really a base class but rather a class you should define yourself. If you want to store data in something other than the default serialization format used by the base classes, you need to provide your own class to define the data format of your records on the desktop.

*Throughout this section, any class name you see that contains* MyConduit *will actually contain the project name you supplied to the Conduit Wizard instead of* MyConduit. *For example, the Librarian sample conduit discussed in this chapter has a class called* CLibPcMgr *instead of* CMyConduitPcMgr.

Figure 22-12 shows how the various generic conduit base classes, and the subclasses you derive from them, relate to one another.

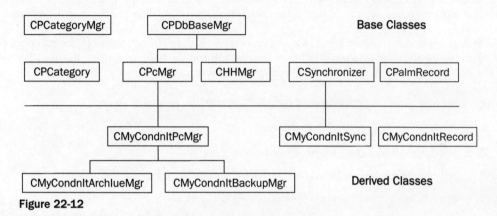

**Figure 22-12**

# Following Generic Conduit Flow of Control

Like any other conduit, a generic conduit starts synching in its OpenConduit function. The OpenConduit function instantiates your subclass of CSynchronizer, and then invokes the synchronizer object's Perform method to start the entire synch process. After the synchronizer has finished its job, OpenConduit destroys the synchronizer and exits. The OpenConduit function generated by the Conduit Wizard looks like this:

```
ExportFunc long OpenConduit (PROGRESSFN pFn,
                            CSyncProperties& rProps)
{
    long retval = -1;
    if (pFn)
    {
        CLibCondSync* pGeneric;
        pGeneric = new CLibCondSync(rProps,
            GENERIC_FLAG_CATEGORY_SUPPORTED |
            GENERIC_FLAG_APPINFO_SUPPORTED);
        if (pGeneric)
        {
            retval = pGeneric->Perform();
            delete pGeneric;
        }
    }
    return(retval);
}
```

The synchronizer object's `Perform` method creates two manager objects, one for the desktop (`CMyConduitPcMgr`) and one for the handheld (`CHHMgr`). Depending upon the type of synchronization that should be performed, the managers retrieve records from the handheld and the desktop (all of them in the case of a SlowSync, only modified records for a FastSync).

Next, the synchronizer creates and uses `CPCategoryMgr` and `CPCategory` objects to synchronize categories between handheld and desktop. Then, the synchronizer synchs the database's application info block if it contains any extra information besides just categories, such as the database's sort order.

Once category and application info block synchronization is out of the way, the synchronizer can concentrate on getting the records in synch between the desktop and the handheld, using the native synch logic built into the `CSynchronizer` class. When finished, the synchronizer destroys the managers it created.

To get your own generic conduit up and running, perform the following steps:

1. Describe the format of records on the desktop.
2. Implement desktop record storage and retrieval.
3. Implement conversion between your own data format and `CPalmRecord`.
4. Implement synchronization of the application info block.

# Describing the Desktop Record Format

You can use a generic conduit created by the Conduit Wizard "out of the box," without adding a single line of code to it. If you make no modifications, a wizard-generated generic conduit will interface with any Palm OS record database and store its contents on the desktop in MFC serialized format. However, this makes the generic conduit no different from a conduit developed from the Palm MFC Base Classes. To truly make use of the flexibility of a generic conduit, you need to make some changes to it so that it can read from and write to any arbitrary data format you want.

Because the `CPalmRecord` class is more than adequate for the task of representing records on the handheld, you need to provide only a class or structure to correspond to records on the desktop. Using a class instead of a structure is entirely for your own convenience; a generic conduit can get along just fine with a structure, but having a desktop record class can make your life easier when you have to implement storage and retrieval of desktop records. Plus, a well-formed class could be included in other desktop applications that access the same data, without your having to rewrite the code that accesses the desktop data.

If your application's records store very simple data, or if you don't need to perform extensive processing of a record during synchronization, you can skip creating a class and instead represent a desktop record with a simple structure. The Librarian conduit example in this chapter uses the structure approach.

## Using a Class for Desktop Data

The Conduit Wizard does not create even a skeleton for a desktop record class so you will need to make your own from scratch. The Visual C++ WizardBar's `New Class` option provides an easy way to start this task because it creates new `.h` and `.cpp` files to contain the class, along with a very basic code framework to fill out. What follows is a sample declaration for a very simple record class, one that contains only a single string for its data:

```
class CMyConduitRecord
{
public:
    CMyConduitRecord(void);
    ~CMyConduitRecord();

public:
    DWORD m_dwRecordID;
    DWORD m_dwStatus;
    DWORD m_dwPosition;
    CPString m_csData;
    DWORD m_dwPrivate;
    DWORD m_dwCategoryID;

public:
    void Reset(void);
};
```

The CPString class used previously to store the record's data is a string class provided by the CDK. A CPString object is essentially a PalmSource implementation of the standard MFC CString class, containing all the useful string-handling methods and operators that you might be used to in the CString class. Be sure to include "CPString.h" at the head of your record's .h file if you want to take advantage of the CPString class.

Here is the actual implementation of the CMyConduitRecord class declared previously:

```
CMyConduitRecord::CMyConduitRecord (void)
{
    Reset();
}


CMyConduitRecord::~CMyConduitRecord()
{
}


void CMyConduitRecord::Reset(void)
{
    m_dwRecordID = 0;
    m_dwStatus = 0;
    m_dwPosition = 0;
    m_dwPrivate = 0;
    m_dwCategoryID = 0;
    m_csData.Empty();
}
```

There is nothing fancy here; the CMyConduitRecord class is pretty much just a structure that initializes its own fields. If you want to, you can declare and implement other methods in your record class to aid in storing and retrieving its contents from whatever storage format you use on the desktop computer. You also can provide better encapsulation of a record's data by declaring its members private instead of public, and then creating access methods to get and set the values of those members.

### Using a Structure for Desktop Data

Sometimes, the effort required to create a class to model desktop records is overkill. The Librarian conduit stores data on the desktop in a tab-delimited text file, which is very straightforward to read from and write to. Instead of a class, the Librarian conduit uses the following structure:

```
typedef struct {
    DWORD   dwBookStatus;
    DWORD   dwPrintStatus;
    DWORD   dwFormat;
    DWORD   dwRead;
    char    szTitle[256];
    char    szLastName[256];
    char    szFirstName[256];
    char    szPublisher[256];
    char    szYear[256];
    char    szPrinting[256];
    char    szIsbn[256];
    char    szPrice[256];
    char    szNote[4096];
    DWORD   dwCategory;
    DWORD   dwPrivate;
    DWORD   dwAttributes;
    DWORD   dwRecordID;
} LibrarianRecord;
```

The `LibrarianRecord` structure stores all the data that Librarian would normally keep in one of its records on the handheld. Because there is a lot more storage space and memory available to work with on the desktop than on a handheld, the Librarian conduit need not be concerned with packing data into as small a space as possible. The Librarian application on the handheld goes to great lengths to pack data into a smaller format for storage, but the Librarian conduit has the luxury of allocating 256 bytes for each of the text fields from Librarian, regardless of whether that text field actually contains any data.

Also note that the `LibrarianRecord` structure uses four `DWORD` variables, a total of 128 bytes, to store small pieces of information about a record, such as its print status (in or out of print) and the format the book was printed in (hardcover, trade paperback, and so on). The handheld-side `LibStatusType` structure accomplishes the same task in only 8 bytes. Not only is there plenty of memory to work with on the desktop, but accessing this kind of simple structure is faster than having to pack and unpack records, and fast conduit code means that HotSync operations take less time to complete. See Chapter 16 for more details about how Librarian stores data on a handheld.

## Implementing Storage and Retrieval

Once you have defined a class that describes your desktop data format, you need to override a couple of functions in your conduit's subclass of `CPcMgr` to implement storage and retrieval of desktop records. The two methods you need to concern yourself with are `RetrieveDB` and `StoreDB`. By default, the code generated by the Conduit Wizard simply defers to the `RetrieveDB` and `StoreDB` methods of the actual `CPcMgr` class, which read and write data in the MFC serialization format.

## Implementing RetrieveDB

The following partial RetrieveDB function takes care of some required bookkeeping tasks, such as reading in the database and application info blocks. The RetrieveDB function that follows also leaves a spot in the middle for your own code to retrieve data from the desktop. Much of this code is drawn straight from the RetrieveDB method of the base CPcMgr class; there is no need to reinvent the wheel here when much of the required code already exists.

```
long CMyConduitPcMgr::RetrieveDB (void)
{
    m_bNeedToSave = FALSE;

    // Check validity of the desktop file name and the
    // handle to that file.
    if (!_tcslen(m_szDataFile))
        return GEN_ERR_INVALID_DB_NAME;
    if (m_hFile == INVALID_HANDLE_VALUE)
        return GEN_ERR_INVALID_DB;

    // Initialize a space for the database info block.
    BOOL bDone = FALSE;
    long retval = 0;
    retval = CreateDBInfo();
    if (retval)
    {
        CloseDB();
        return retval;
    }

    // Read in the database info block from disk.
    retval = ReadInData((LPVOID)m_pDBInfo,
                    CM_STORAGE_HEADER_SIZE);

    if (retval)
    {
        CloseDB();
        if (retval == GEN_ERR_STORAGE_EOF)
            return 0;
        return GEN_ERR_READING_DBINFO;
    }

    // Read the application info block from disk.
    if (m_pDBInfo->dwAppInfo > 0)
    {
        m_pAppInfo = (STORAGE_INFO_PTR)
            malloc(m_pDBInfo->dwAppInfo);
        if (!m_pAppInfo)
            retval = GEN_ERR_LOW_MEMORY;
        if (!retval) {
            retval = ReadInData((LPVOID)m_pAppInfo,
                            m_pDBInfo->dwAppInfo);
        }
        if (retval)
        {
```

```
            CloseDB();
            return GEN_ERR_READING_APPINFO;
        }
    }

    // Code for reading data from the desktop goes here.

    CloseDB();
    m_bNeedToSave = FALSE;
    return retval;
}
```

The m_szDataFile and m_hFile data members of the manager class store the filename for the desktop data source and a handle to that file, respectively. When it calls OpenConduit to start record synchronization, the HotSync Manager passes the name of the desktop data file as part of a CSyncProperties object, which eventually trickles its way down to the desktop manager object and becomes the m_szDataFile and m_hFile members. You can use the file handle provided in m_hFile to read data from the desktop data source.

> *The generic conduit code assumes that your data source on the desktop is a file. If you want to pipe in data from a different source, you also will need to override the Open, OpenDB, Close, and CloseDB methods of CPcMgr to handle opening and closing the unusual data source.*

After checking that m_szDataFile and m_hFile contain valid data, your RetrieveDB method should initialize space in memory for a database information block. The CreateDBInfo method of CPcMgr takes care of this task, setting a pointer to the initialized memory block in the manager object's m_pDBInfo member variable. The pointer stored in m_pDBInfo points to a STORAGE_HEADER structure, which is defined as follows in the CDK header file pcmgr.h:

```
typedef struct StorageHeaderType {
    DWORD   dwStructSize;
    WORD    wVersion;

    char    szName[DB_NAMELEN];
    DWORD   dwDBVersion;
    DWORD   dwDBCreator;
    DWORD   dwDBType;
    WORD    wDBFlags;

    long    lDBModDate;
    DWORD   dwDBModNumber;
    long    lDBCreateDate;
    long    lDBBackupDate;
    long    lDBRecCount;
    long    dwAppInfo;
    long    dwSortInfo;
} STORAGE_HEADER;
```

The STORAGE_HEADER structure contains information about the database itself, including its number of records. It also contains the length of the database's application info block, in bytes, in its dwAppInfo field. The RetrieveDB method should look in dwAppInfo for the length of the database's application info block; armed with this value, RetrieveDB then can copy that many bytes of data into a memory block pointed to by the desktop manager object's m_pAppInfo variable.

In the previous example, as in the CPcMgr base class itself, RetrieveDB uses the ReadInData method of the manager object to retrieve the database and application info blocks from the desktop data source. The ReadInData function provided in CPcMgr is set up to read data from a file, but you can supply your own override of ReadInData to read data from whatever format you wish to use on the desktop. For example, if your conduit needs to read records from a database, you will need to override ReadInData. The arguments that ReadInData takes are a pointer to a buffer to receive data and the number of bytes to read in.

## Implementing RetrieveDB in the Librarian Conduit

The Librarian conduit must perform a bit more processing to read data from a tab-delimited file into the LibrarianRecord structure used elsewhere in the conduit. The RetrieveDB method in the Librarian conduit looks like this:

```
long CLibPcMgr::RetrieveDB(void)
{
    long err = 0;


    m_bNeedToSave = FALSE;
    if (! _tcslen(m_szDataFile))
        return GEN_ERR_INVALID_DB_NAME;

    if (m_hFile == INVALID_HANDLE_VALUE)
        return GEN_ERR_INVALID_DB;

    CPalmRecord newRecord;
    while (ReadRecord(newRecord, err) && err == 0)
        AddRec(newRecord);

    return err;
}
```

RetrieveDB in the Librarian conduit is a much simpler function because it hands most of the actual work to a method called ReadRecord. The ReadRecord method returns a record that has been converted from the tab-delimited desktop format into an instance of the CPalmRecord class. RetrieveDB uses the CPcMgr::AddRec method to add each retrieved and converted record to an in-memory record database, which the CSynchronizer class uses to perform actual synchronization.

Here is the ReadRecord method:

```
bool CLibPcMgr::ReadRecord(CPalmRecord &rec, long &err)
{
    char    buffer[MAX_RECORD_SIZE];
    char    *p;


    if ((err = ReadString(buffer, sizeof(buffer))) != 0)
    {
        if (err = GEN_ERR_STORAGE_EOF)
            // This is the last record, so it's not really
            // an error.
```

```
            err = 0;
        return false;
    }

    // Read values from text file into PC-side record
    // format.
    LibrarianRecord record;
    p = buffer;

    strncpy(record.szTitle, ReadToNextTab(&p), 255);
    strncpy(record.szLastName, ReadToNextTab(&p), 255);
    strncpy(record.szFirstName, ReadToNextTab(&p), 255);
    strncpy(record.szPublisher, ReadToNextTab(&p), 255);
    strncpy(record.szYear, ReadToNextTab(&p), 255);
    strncpy(record.szPrinting, ReadToNextTab(&p), 255);
    strncpy(record.szIsbn, ReadToNextTab(&p), 255);
    strncpy(record.szPrice, ReadToNextTab(&p), 255);
    strncpy(record.szNote, ReadToNextTab(&p), 4095);
    record.dwBookStatus = atol(ReadToNextTab(&p));
    record.dwPrintStatus = atol(ReadToNextTab(&p));
    record.dwFormat = atol(ReadToNextTab(&p));
    record.dwRead = atol(ReadToNextTab(&p));
    record.dwCategory = atol(ReadToNextTab(&p));
    record.dwPrivate = atol(ReadToNextTab(&p));
    record.dwAttributes = atol(ReadToNextTab(&p));
    record.dwRecordID = atol(ReadToNextTab(&p));

    ConvertPcToGeneric(&record, &rec);

    return true;
}
```

The ReadRecord method combines the role of reading records from the desktop with the job of converting those records into the handheld data format. Format conversion actually takes place in the ConvertPcToGeneric routine, described later in this chapter.

ReadRecord makes use of the routine ReadString, which reads a line of data from the tab-delimited file into a buffer. ReadString looks like this:

```
long CLibPcMgr::ReadString(char *buffer, long size)
{
    long  err;
    long  i;

    for (i = 0; i < size - 1; i++)
    {
        err = ReadInData(buffer + i, 1);
        if (err)
            break;
        if ((i > 0) && (buffer[i - 1] == '\r' ) &&
            (buffer[i] == '\n'))
        {
            buffer[i - 1] = '\0';
```

```
            return 0;
        }
    }

    buffer[i] = '\0';

    // It's not really an error if the last line isn't
    // null-terminated.
    if (err == GEN_ERR_STORAGE_EOF && i > 0)
        err = 0;
    return err;
}
```

ReadString uses the CPcMgr::ReadInData method. ReadInData and the CPcMgr class take care of all the actual details of file access, including opening and closing the file. ReadString calls ReadInData in a loop to retrieve a single byte at a time from the tab-delimited file. When ReadString encounters a carriage return followed by a linefeed (\r\n), it knows that it has reached the end of a record, so it returns.

ReadRecord also makes extensive use of another helper function, ReadToNextTab, which separates the data in a record at tab characters. ReadToNextTab looks like this:

```
char *CLibPcMgr::ReadToNextTab(char **p)
{
    char *startOfString = *p;

    while ((**p != '\0') && (**p != '\t'))
    {
        // Replace right guillemot with tabs.
        if (**p == '\273')
            **p = '\t';

        // Replace paragraph characters with newlines.
        if (**p == '\266')
            **p = '\n';

        (*p)++;
    }
    if (**p == '\t')
    {
        // Replace the tab character with a terminating
        // null.
        **p = '\0';
        (*p)++;
    }

    return startOfString;
}
```

ReadToNextTab keeps its place in the string via its p parameter. When ReadToNextTab begins, it treats the value referred to by p as the offset in the string to start reading from. ReadToNextTab increments the p value as it goes and returns its place in the string via p when finished. The ReadToNextTab function also returns the starting position of the string so its caller knows where the string that ReadToNextTab has just parsed begins.

When `ReadToNextTab` finds a tab, it replaces it with a null to serve as a string terminator. `ReadToNextTab` also replaces certain characters, used on the desktop as placeholders for characters that make parsing a tab-delimited file difficult or impossible. Tab characters from the handheld become a right guillemot (», or octal 273) on the desktop, and newlines become a paragraph character (¶, or octal 266), so when `ReadToNextTab` encounters these characters, it changes them back to the proper values used on the handheld.

## Implementing StoreDB

Many parts of `StoreDB` will look similar to your `RetrieveDB` function, only in reverse because it writes information to disk instead of reading.

```
long CMyConduitPcMgr::StoreDB (void)
{
    // Check to see if there were any changes to the data.
    // If not, save time by not saving unnecessarily.
    if (!m_bNeedToSave)
    {
        if ((!m_pCatMgr) || (!m_pCatMgr->IsChanged()))
            return 0;
    }

    // Open the desktop database for writing.
    long retval = OpenDB();
    if (retval)
        return GEN_ERR_UNABLE_TO_SAVE;

    // Store database info block. If there is no info
    // block, then there is nothing to store.
    if (!m_pDBInfo)
    {
        CloseDB();
        return 0; // No error if nothing to store
    }

    if (m_pDBInfo)
    {
        m_pDBInfo->lDBRecCount = (long)m_dwRecordCount;
        if (m_pAppInfo)
            m_pDBInfo->dwAppInfo =
                m_pAppInfo->dwStructSize;
        else
            m_pDBInfo->dwAppInfo = 0;

        retval = WriteOutData(m_pDBInfo,
                              m_pDBInfo->dwStructSize);
        if (retval != 0)
        {
            CloseDB();
            return GEN_ERR_UNABLE_TO_SAVE;
        }
    }

    // Store application info block, if it exists.
    if (m_pAppInfo)
```

```
        {
            retval = WriteOutData(m_pAppInfo,
                                  m_pAppInfo->dwStructSize);
            if (retval != 0)
            {
                CloseDB();
                return GEN_ERR_UNABLE_TO_SAVE;
            }
        }

        // Code for writing data to the desktop goes here.

        CloseDB();
        m_bNeedToSave = FALSE;
        return 0;
    }
```

The first thing StoreDB does is to check the desktop manager object's m_bNeedToSave variable. If m_bNeedToSave is FALSE, then there have been no changes to the data that would require saving. In this case, StoreDB can simply exit because it has nothing to do.

If StoreDB does, indeed, have something to do, it calls the CPcMgr class method OpenDB to open the desktop file for writing. Then, StoreDB writes the database information block to the beginning of the file, followed by the application info block, but only if these pieces of information are available. Once the header information is out of the way, StoreDB can get to the work of writing actual records to the desktop.

Like its sibling ReadInData, the WriteOutData method of CPcMgr writes raw bytes of data to the desktop file. You will need to replace WriteOutData with your own code to write to something other than a file.

Besides overriding RetrieveDB and StoreDB, if your conduit supports archiving of deleted records or keeping a backup copy of the desktop database, the Conduit Wizard will generate subclasses of your CPcMgr subclass to handle archive and backup databases. Unless you need to do something special with the archive and backup databases, such as saving these two databases in a different format from your main desktop database, you can leave the CMyConduitArchive and CMyConduitBackupMgr classes generated by the Conduit Wizard alone; they will automatically handle archiving and backing up your desktop data.

## Implementing StoreDB in the Librarian Conduit

Like the Librarian conduit's RetrieveDB method, its StoreDB method is relatively short, given its use of helper functions to perform most of its work. StoreDB looks like this in the Librarian conduit:

```
long CLibPcMgr::StoreDB(void)
{
    // If there are no changes, there is no need to save
    // anything.
    if (!m_bNeedToSave)
    {
        return 0;
    }

    long err = Open();
    if (err)
```

```
            return GEN_ERR_UNABLE_TO_SAVE;

    for (DWORD dwIndex = 0;
         (dwIndex < m_dwMaxRecordCount) && (!err);
         dwIndex++)
    {
        // Skip to the next record if there is no
        // record at this index.
        if (!m_pRecordList[dwIndex])
            continue;
        err = WriteRecord(m_pRecordList[dwIndex]);
    }

    Close();
    if (err == 0)
    {
        m_bNeedToSave = FALSE;
        return 0;
    }
    else
        return GEN_ERR_UNABLE_TO_SAVE;
}
```

Most of the real work occurs in the WriteRecord routine, which writes records, converted from CPalmRecord format to tab-delimited text, to the desktop file. Here is what WriteRecord looks like:

```
long CLibPcMgr::WriteRecord(CPalmRecord *pPalmRec)
{
    char    buf[MAX_RECORD_SIZE];
    DWORD   recordSize = MAX_RECORD_SIZE;
    long    retval;
    DWORD dwRawSize = pPalmRec->GetRawDataSize();
    if (!dwRawSize) {
        // invalid record
        return 0;
    }
    LibrarianRecord *libRecord = new LibrarianRecord;
    ConvertGenericToPc(pPalmRec, libRecord);
    // Write out the record.  Format is tab-delimited, with
    // the following fields:
    //    <title> <last name> <first name> <publisher> <year>
    //    <printing> <isbn> <price> <note> <bookStatus>
    //    <printStatus> <format> <read> <category> <private>
    //    <attributes> <record ID>
    // Status fields are stored as their numeric values, and
    // the private record indicator is simply 1 if the
    // record's private bit is set, 0 otherwise.  Attributes
    // are not written, but a space is left for them; the
    // attribute values are only used to determine how to
    // sync a record from the desktop to the handheld, so
    // there is never a reason for the conduit to write
    // attribute information to desktop storage.
    sprintf(
        buf,
```

```
        "%s\t%s\t%s\t%s\t%s\t%s\t%s\t%s\t%d\t%d\t%d\t%d\t%d\t%d\t\t%d\r\n",
        libRecord->szTitle,
        libRecord->szLastName,
        libRecord->szFirstName,
        libRecord->szPublisher,
        libRecord->szYear,
        libRecord->szPrinting,
        libRecord->szIsbn,
        libRecord->szPrice,
        libRecord->szNote,
        libRecord->dwBookStatus,
        libRecord->dwPrintStatus,
        libRecord->dwFormat,
        libRecord->dwRead,
        pPalmRec->GetCategory(),
        pPalmRec->IsPrivate() ? 1 : 0,
        pPalmRec->GetID()
        );
    retval = WriteOutData(buf, strlen(buf));
    delete libRecord;
    return retval;
}
```

StoreDB first converts the record from the CPalmRecord class to the LibrarianRecord structure used to define a desktop record. The conversion takes place in the ConvertGenericToPc routine, described later in this chapter.

Once the conversion to the LibrarianRecord structure has taken place, StoreDB prepares the data for the desktop data file by writing all of the data to a string. StoreDB then passes this string to the CPcMgr method WriteOutData, which actually writes the data to the file.

## Converting Data to and from CPalmRecord

The next step in making a generic conduit is implementing conversion between your desktop record format and the generic CPalmRecord class. To do this, you must override the ConvertGenericToPc and ConvertPcToGeneric methods of CPcMgr. The following is an example of a ConvertGenericToPc method, using the CMyConduitRecord class defined earlier in the chapter:

```
long CMyConduitPcMgr::ConvertGenericToPc (
    CPalmRecord &palmRec,
    CMyConduitRecord &rec, BOOL bClearAttributes)
{
    BYTE    *pBuff;
    long    retval    = 0;
    int     nLength;

    rec.Reset();

    if (palmRec.GetRawDataSize() == 0)
    {
        // This is a deleted record because it has no data.
        return GEN_ERR_EMPTY_RECORD;
    }
```

```
      // Fill in the record ID.
      rec.m_dwRecordID = palmRec.GetID();

      // Unless the attributes should be thrown out
      // (bClearAttributes == TRUE), fill in record attributes.
      if (bClearAttributes)
          rec.m_dwStatus = 0;
      else {
          rec.m_dwStatus = palmRec.GetAttribs();
      }

      // Fill in position, category ID, and the private status.
      rec.m_dwPosition   = palmRec.GetIndex();
      rec.m_dwCategoryID = palmRec.GetCategory();
      rec.m_dwPrivate    = palmRec.IsPrivate();

      DWORD dwRawSize = palmRec.GetRawDataSize();
      if (!dwRawSize)
      {
          // This is an invalid record.
          return 0;
      }

      pBuff = palmRec.GetRawData();

      // Convert the actual record data. Add carriage
      // returns.
      nLength = _tcslen((char *)pBuff);

      AddCRs((char *)pBuff,
             rec.m_csData.GetBuffer(nLength * 2), nLength);
      rec.m_csData.ReleaseBuffer();

      pBuff += nLength + 1;

      return retval;
}
```

Most of the previous example `ConvertGenericToPc` function involves copying members of the `CPalm Record` object `palmRec`, such as the record ID and attributes, straight into members of the `CMyConduit Record` object `rec`, using `CPalmRecord` methods to retrieve the appropriate values because `CPalmRecord` stores just about anything of interest in protected member variables. Retrieving the actual data relies on the `CPalmRecord` class `GetRawData` method, which returns a pointer to the raw data of a record.

The only real conversion performed by `CMyConduitPcMgr::ConvertGenericToPc` is to add carriage return characters to the data because Windows ends lines of text with both carriage return and linefeed characters, and Palm OS uses only linefeeds. This conversion is made easy by the use of the `CPcMgr::AddCRs` method. The `CPcMgr` class also has a companion `StripCRs` method for removing carriage returns when converting data back to the handheld database.

Here is the companion `ConvertPcToGeneric` function:

```
long CMyConduitPcMgr::ConvertPCtoGeneric(
    CMyConduitRecord &rec,
    CPalmRecord &palmRec)
{
    long    retval = 0;
    char    *pBuff;
    int     destLen;
    BYTE    szRawData[MAX_RECORD_SIZE];
    DWORD   dwRecSize = 0;


    // Copy over all the record fields and attributes.
    palmRec.SetID(rec.m_dwRecordID);

    palmRec.SetCategory(rec.m_dwCategoryID);

    if (rec.m_dwPrivate)
        palmRec.SetPrivate(TRUE);
    else
        palmRec.SetPrivate(FALSE);

    palmRec.SetArchived((BOOL)(rec.m_dwStatus &
                            fldStatusARCHIVE));
    palmRec.SetDeleted((BOOL)(rec.m_dwStatus &
                            fldStatusDELETE));
    palmRec.SetUpdate((BOOL)(rec.m_dwStatus &
                            fldStatusUPDATE));

    // Convert the actual record data.
    pBuff = (char*)szRawData;

    int nLength;
    nLength = rec.m_csData.length();
    if (nLength > 0)
    {
        // Strip carriage returns. StripCRs places its
        // result directly into pBuff.
        destLen = StripCRs(pBuff, rec.m_csData.c_str(),
                        nLength);

        pBuff += destLen;
        dwRecSize += destLen;
    }

    if (dwRecSize == 0)
    {
        // A record without any data has been deleted.
        palmRec.SetDeleted();
    }

    retval = palmRec.SetRawData(dwRecSize, szRawData);

    return(retval);
}
```

The MAX_RECORD_SIZE constant, used to define the size of the buffer that ConvertPcToGeneric puts the record's actual raw data into, is defined in the CDK header file CPalmRec.h as the value 0xfff0, or 65,520 bytes, which is the largest possible record allowed by the HotSync Manager.

## Converting to CPalmRecord in the Librarian Conduit

The Librarian conduit converts its internal LibrarianRecord structure to a CPalmRecord object using the CLibPcMgr::ConvertPcToGeneric method. ReadRecord fills in a LibrarianRecord structure, and then passes it to ConvertPcToGeneric for conversion. The Librarian conduit version of Convert PcToGeneric is shown in the following code.

```
void CLibPcMgr::ConvertPcToGeneric (LibrarianRecord *pRec,
                                    CPalmRecord *palmRec)
{
    BYTE    szRawData[MAX_RECORD_SIZE];
    char    *pRawData, *pFlags, *pFirstField;
    WORD    *pLastNameOffset, *pFirstNameOffset,
            *pYearOffset, *pNoteOffset;
    DWORD   dwRecSize = 0;


    palmRec->SetID(pRec->dwRecordID);
    palmRec->SetCategory(pRec->dwCategory);
    palmRec->SetPrivate(pRec->dwPrivate);

    palmRec->ResetAttribs();
    LibRecordAttributes attr;

    memmove(&attr, &pRec->dwAttributes, sizeof(DWORD));
    if (attr.newRec)
        palmRec->SetNew();
    if (attr.updated)
        palmRec->SetUpdate();
    if (attr.archived)
        palmRec->SetArchived();
    if (attr.deleted)
        palmRec->SetDeleted();

    // Set a pointer to the start of the buffer.
    pRawData = (char *) szRawData;

    // Fill the status structure.
    LibStatusType  status;

    memset(&status, 0, sizeof(status));
    status.bookStatus = pRec->dwBookStatus;
    status.printStatus = pRec->dwPrintStatus;
    status.format = pRec->dwFormat;
    status.read = pRec->dwRead;

    // Copy status structure to the buffer.
    WORD wStatus = 0;
    memmove(&wStatus, &status, sizeof(BYTE));
    memmove(pRawData, &wStatus, sizeof(WORD));
```

```
    // Advance the pointer and add the status structure to
    // the record's total size.
    pRawData += sizeof(WORD);
    dwRecSize += sizeof(WORD);

    // Zero out the flags structure, and save its location;
    // it will be filled in below later when the text field
    // data is written to the buffer.
    LibDBRecordFlags  flags;

    memset(&flags, 0, sizeof(WORD));
    pFlags = pRawData;

    // Advance the pointer and add the flags structure to
    // the record's total size.
    pRawData += sizeof(WORD);
    dwRecSize += sizeof(WORD);

    // Initialize offsets to zero, and skip past them;
    // they'll be filled in after all the field data is
    // copied to the buffer.
    pLastNameOffset = pRawData;
    memset(pLastNameOffset, 0, sizeof(WORD));
    pRawData += sizeof(WORD);
    dwRecSize += sizeof(WORD);

    pFirstNameOffset = pRawData;
    memset(pFirstNameOffset, 0, sizeof(WORD));
    pRawData += sizeof(WORD);
    dwRecSize += sizeof(WORD);

    pYearOffset = pRawData;
    memset(pYearOffset, 0, sizeof(WORD));
    pRawData += sizeof(WORD);
    dwRecSize += sizeof(WORD);

    pNoteOffset = pRawData;
    memset(pNoteOffset, 0, sizeof(WORD));
    pRawData += sizeof(WORD);
    dwRecSize += sizeof(WORD);

    // Save location of the first text field.
    pFirstField = pRawData;

    int            length;
    unsigned char  loc;

    // Title
    if ((length = strlen(pRec->szTitle)) > 0)
    {
        flags.title = 1;
        strncpy(pRawData, pRec->szTitle, 255);
        pRawData += length + 1;
        dwRecSize += length + 1;
    }
```

```
    // Last name
    if ((length = strlen(pRec->szLastName)) > 0)
    {
        // Store last name field offset.
        loc = pRawData - pFirstField;
        memmove(pLastNameOffset, &loc, sizeof(loc));

        flags.lastName = 1;
        strncpy(pRawData, pRec->szLastName, 255);
        pRawData += length + 1;
        dwRecSize += length + 1;
    }

    // First name
    if ((length = strlen(pRec->szFirstName)) > 0)
    {
        // Store first name field offset.
        loc = pRawData - pFirstField;
        memmove(pFirstNameOffset, &loc, sizeof(loc));

        flags.firstName = 1;
        strncpy(pRawData, pRec->szFirstName, 255);
        pRawData += length + 1;
        dwRecSize += length + 1;
    }
    // Publisher
    if ((length = strlen(pRec->szPublisher)) > 0)
    {
        flags.publisher = 1;
        strncpy(pRawData, pRec->szPublisher, 255);
        pRawData += length + 1;
        dwRecSize += length + 1;
    }

    // Year
    if ((length = strlen(pRec->szYear)) > 0)
    {
        // Store year field offset.
        loc = pRawData - pFirstField;
        memmove(pYearOffset, &loc, sizeof(loc));

        flags.year = 1;
        strncpy(pRawData, pRec->szYear, 255);
        pRawData += length + 1;
        dwRecSize += length + 1;
    }

    // Printing
    if ((length = strlen(pRec->szPrinting)) > 0)
    {
        flags.printing = 1;
        strncpy(pRawData, pRec->szPrinting, 255);
        pRawData += length + 1;
        dwRecSize += length + 1;
    }
```

```
        // ISBN
        if ((length = strlen(pRec->szIsbn)) > 0)
        {
            flags.isbn = 1;
            strncpy(pRawData, pRec->szIsbn, 255);
            pRawData += length + 1;
            dwRecSize += length + 1;
        }

        // Price
        if ((length = strlen(pRec->szPrice)) > 0)
        {
            flags.price = 1;
            strncpy(pRawData, pRec->szPrice, 255);
            pRawData += length + 1;
            dwRecSize += length + 1;
        }

        // Note
        if ((length = strlen(pRec->szNote)) > 0)
        {
            // Store note field offset.
            loc = pRawData - pFirstField;
            memmove(pNoteOffset, &loc, sizeof(loc));

            flags.note = 1;
            strncpy(pRawData, pRec->szNote, 4095);
            pRawData += length + 1;
            dwRecSize += length + 1;
        }

        // Now that the flags information has been filled in,
        // copy it to the buffer.  Be sure to byte-swap the
        // flags so they'll show up on the handheld in
        // big-endian order.
        WORD  wSwappedFlags = 0;
        memmove(&wSwappedFlags, &flags, sizeof(WORD));
        wSwappedFlags = CPalmRecord::FlipWord(wSwappedFlags);
        memmove(pFlags, &wSwappedFlags, sizeof(WORD));

        // Write the raw record data to the record.
        palmRec->SetRawData(dwRecSize, szRawData);
    }
```

ConvertPcToGeneric in the Librarian conduit is analogous to the PackRecord function in Librarian itself. Both routines must compress an expanded record format into the space-efficient storage format Librarian writes to its database. ConvertPcToGeneric and PackRecord differ in that they convert from a different unpacked record format. The unpacked Librarian record format on the handheld (LibDBRecordType) is still more memory efficient than the LibrarianRecord structure used on the desktop. With the considerable resources available on a desktop computer, the Librarian conduit can afford to use more memory to store a record. For a detailed discussion of PackRecord and the LibDbRecordType structure, see Chapter 16.

`ConvertPcToGeneric` also converts from the little-endian byte order of an Intel-based Windows desktop machine to the big-endian byte order used on a Motorola-based Palm OS handheld. The flags that signal whether a particular text field contains data or not are stored as a 2-byte word, which must be swapped before moving it to the handheld. `CPalmRecord` provides the handy `FlipWord` method for just such an occasion, which `ConvertPcToRecord` uses to flip the flags around the right way. If your conduit needs to exchange 4-byte `DWORD` values between the desktop and handheld, use `CPalmRecord::SwapDWordTo Intel` to convert from handheld to desktop and the `CPalmRecord::SwapDWordToMotor` method to convert from desktop to handheld.

## Converting from CPalmRecord in the Librarian Conduit

`WriteRecord` in the Librarian conduit calls `CLibPcMgr::ConvertGenericToPc` to change the data in a `CPalmRecord` object into a `LibrarianRecord` desktop format before writing the data out to a tab-delimited file. The `ConvertGenericToPc` method is shown in the following listing:

```
void CLibPcMgr::ConvertGenericToPc (CPalmRecord *palmRec,
                                    LibrarianRecord *pRec)
{
    LibStatusType   status;
    LibDBRecordFlags  flags;
    char   *p;


    p = (char *) palmRec->GetRawData();

    // Copy status information from the front of the record.
    // Although only a single byte in size on the handheld,
    // the LibStatusType structure at the start of a
    // Librarian record gets word-aligned when transferred
    // via CPalmRecord's GetRawData method.  Only the low
    // byte contains the actual status data, so it's
    // necessary to mask out the high byte.
    WORD wStatus;
    memmove(&wStatus, p, sizeof(WORD));
    BYTE nStatus = wStatus & 0xff;
    memmove(&status, &nStatus, sizeof(BYTE));

    pRec->dwBookStatus = status.bookStatus;
    pRec->dwPrintStatus = status.printStatus;
    pRec->dwFormat = status.format;
    pRec->dwRead = status.read;

    // Advance pointer past the status byte.
    //p += sizeof(BYTE);
    p += sizeof(WORD);

    // Copy text field flags.  Be sure to byte-swap them to
    // little-endian Intel byte order.
    WORD  wSwappedFlags;
    memmove(&wSwappedFlags, p, sizeof(WORD));
    wSwappedFlags = CPalmRecord::FlipWord(wSwappedFlags);
    memmove(&flags, &wSwappedFlags, sizeof(wSwappedFlags));
```

```
    // Advance pointer past flags and text field offset
    // values.
    p += sizeof(WORD) + sizeof(WORD) +
        sizeof(WORD) + sizeof(WORD) +
        sizeof(WORD);

    // Now the pointer is at the start of the first text
    // field's data.  Check each field flag in turn to see
    // if that field's data exists, and if it does, copy the
    // data.  Palm OS uses only LF to end lines, but Windows
    // uses CR/LF pairs, so normally a conduit might add CRs
    // to the text here.  However, Librarian's conduit
    // stores its data as tab-delimited text on the desktop,
    // one record to a line, and a CR/LF pair signifies end
    // of line, so LF characters are converted to paragraph
    // markers (ASCII 182) to prevent records being broken
    // up in the wrong place.
    if (flags.title)
    {
        strncpy(pRec->szTitle, p, 255);
        Untabify(pRec->szTitle);
        p += strlen(p) + 1;
    }
    else
        memset(pRec->szTitle, 0, 256);

    if (flags.lastName)
    {
        strncpy(pRec->szLastName, p, 255);
        Untabify(pRec->szLastName);
        p += strlen(p) + 1;
    }
    else
        memset(pRec->szLastName, 0, 256);

    if (flags.firstName)
    {
        strncpy(pRec->szFirstName, p, 255);
        Untabify(pRec->szFirstName);
        p += strlen(p) + 1;
    }
    else
        memset(pRec->szFirstName, 0, 256);

    if (flags.publisher)
    {
        strncpy(pRec->szPublisher, p, 255);
        Untabify(pRec->szPublisher);
        p += strlen(p) + 1;
    }
    else
        memset(pRec->szPublisher, 0, 256);
```

```
    if (flags.year)
    {
        strncpy(pRec->szYear, p, 255);
        Untabify(pRec->szYear);
        p += strlen(p) + 1;
    }
    else
        memset(pRec->szYear, 0, 256);

    if (flags.printing)
    {
        strncpy(pRec->szPrinting, p, 255);
        Untabify(pRec->szPrinting);
        p += strlen(p) + 1;
    }
    else
        memset(pRec->szPrinting, 0, 256);

    if (flags.isbn)
    {
        strncpy(pRec->szIsbn, p, 255);
        Untabify(pRec->szIsbn);
        p += strlen(p) + 1;
    }
    else
        memset(pRec->szIsbn, 0, 256);

    if (flags.price)
    {
        strncpy(pRec->szPrice, p, 255);
        Untabify(pRec->szPrice);
        p += strlen(p) + 1;
    }
    else
        memset(pRec->szPrice, 0, 256);

    if (flags.note)
    {
        strncpy(pRec->szNote, p, 4095);
        Untabify(pRec->szNote);
        p += strlen(p) + 1;
    }
    else
        memset(pRec->szNote, 0, 4096);
}
```

ConvertGenericToPc is similar to Librarian's UnpackRecord function on the handheld. The Convert GenericToPc method expands a record from its packed handheld storage format into the less efficient, but easier to access, LibrarianRecord structure. As it makes the conversion, ConvertGenericToPc uses the Librarian conduit's Untabify helper function to convert tabs and newlines into characters that will make parsing the tab-delimited text file easier. Untabify looks like this:

```
void CLibPcMgr::Untabify(char *string)
{
    char  *p;


    p = string;
    for (unsigned int i = 0; i < strlen(string); ++i)
    {
        if (p[i] == '\t')
            p[i] = '\273';
        if (p[i] == '\n')
            p[i] = '\266';
    }
}
```

## Synching the Application Info Block

The last thing to implement in a generic conduit is synchronization of the database's application info block. The synchronizer object uses the CCategoryMgr object to automatically convert category information stored at the head of an application info block, so only extra information stored in the application info block needs to be synched. Because not every Palm OS application stores extra information in its application info block, not all conduits need to explicitly synch this data. Overriding CPcMgr::Synchronize AppInfo allows you to perform special processing of the application info block data on its way between the handheld and the desktop.

# Using the Palm MFC Base Classes

Just like creating a conduit using the Palm Generic Conduit Base Classes, making a conduit using the Palm MFC Base Classes is a matter of subclassing the base classes and overriding certain functions to provide your conduit with its own custom behavior. This is where the similarity ends between the two sets of base classes; the MFC classes have a different structure and flow of control from those of the generic conduit classes. The following list briefly describes the function of each of the Palm MFC Base Classes:

❑   CBaseMonitor. The base monitor class controls the entire synchronization operation, creating, using, and destroying instances of the other base classes as necessary to perform its job. In fact, the CBaseMonitor class contains, as data members, a CBaseDTLinkConverter object, four CBaseTable objects, and two CCategoryMgr objects. The monitor class also contains most of the methods responsible for running the synchronization process, including the Engage method, which OpenConduit calls to set the entire synch procedure in motion.

❑   CBaseDTLinkConverter. A link converter object is responsible for converting records from the handheld into their equivalent format on the desktop computer. It can convert data both ways, from handheld to desktop and vice versa.

❑   CCategoryMgr. Category manager objects manage the categories to which records belong. There are two CCategoryMgr objects in the CBaseMonitor class: one to keep track of desktop categories and one for handheld categories. Category managers also are present in the CBaseTable class.

❑ CBaseTable. A table object contains records in a linear format. The CbaseMonitor class uses a number of table objects for storing records from the desktop database, an archive copy of the desktop database, and the handheld.

❑ CBaseIterator. Every table object has an iterator object associated with it that takes care of sorting and searching for records within the table.

❑ CBaseSchema. Each table object also has an associated schema object, which serves as a template for identifying individual records within the linear format the table object uses for storage.

❑ CBaseRecord. All records within a table object are accessed by an object derived from the CBaseRecord class. In order for desktop data to mesh properly with the database format used on the handheld, you must heavily modify whatever subclass of CBaseRecord you create for your conduit.

Figure 22-13 shows how the various Palm MFC Base Classes are all closely related to one another. Some classes are nested within others (for example, there are four CBaseTable objects within CBaseMonitor), whereas others allow one another access to their internals using the C++ friend mechanism (for example, all the functions in CBaseTable are friends of CBaseRecord).

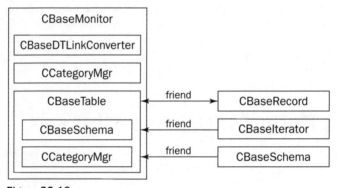

**Figure 22-13**

In order to allow customization of the conduit's actions, the Conduit Wizard generates subclasses of the base classes. You must add the custom behavior by overriding virtual functions in the subclasses. The default subclass names provided by the Conduit Wizard look just like the base class names described previously, substituting your project name for the Base part of the name. For example, if your project is named MyConduit, the wizard-generated monitor subclass is CMyConduitMonitor.

## Following MFC Conduit Flow of Control

The flow of control through an MFC-based conduit starts in the OpenConduit function, which creates an instance of your conduit's CBaseMonitor subclass and then calls the monitor's Engage method to start the synch process. After the monitor object has done its job, OpenConduit destroys the monitor and returns. Here is a sample OpenConduit function, as generated by the Conduit Wizard:

```
ExportFunc long OpenConduit (PROGRESSFN pFn,
                             CSyncProperties& rProps)
{
    AFX_MANAGE_STATE(AfxGetStaticModuleState());
    long retval = -1;
    if (pFn)
    {
        CMyConduitMonitor* pMonitor;

        pMonitor = new CMyConduitMonitor(pFn, rProps,
                                         myInst);
        if (pMonitor)
        {
            retval = pMonitor->Engage();

            delete pMonitor;
        }
    }
    return(retval);
}
```

Once the monitor object is in control, it creates a pair of table objects (CBaseTable subclasses): one to represent the records on the desktop and one to contain records from the handheld database. Using an iterator object (CBaseIterator subclass), the monitor steps through the records in the handheld table object, retrieving only modified records from the handheld if the HotSync operation is a FastSync or retrieving all the handheld records in the case of a SlowSync.

As it retrieves handheld records, the monitor converts each record into its desktop format by calling methods from a link converter object (CBaseDTLinkConverter subclass). Once the handheld and desktop records are in the same format, the monitor can compare them using the conduit's native synch logic and deal with each record appropriately. See the sidebar "Understanding Native Synchronization Logic" in this chapter for more details about how the native synch logic works.

## Implementing a Monitor Class

To make your conduit's subclass of CBaseMonitor work, you need to override five of its virtual methods:

❑   ConstructRecord. This method creates a new record object within a table, derived from the CBaseRecord class.

❑   CreateTable. This method creates a new table, derived from CBaseTable.

❑   LogApplicationName. This method returns the name of your conduit, for purposes of writing the conduit's name to the HotSync log.

❑   LogRecordData. If the monitor object has to report errors with synchronizing a specific record, it needs to write a string describing the problem record to the HotSync log. The LogRecordData function assembles this string, based on the unique record format of the handheld application to which the conduit is attached.

❑   SetArchiveFileExt. This method sets up the file extension your conduit appends to its desktop archive file.

The Conduit Wizard makes light work of most of the function overrides; a wizard-generated conduit already has minimal implementations for all but the LogRecordData function. Because every handheld application's record format is different, the wizard cannot automatically generate LogRecordData. Some handheld applications may store their data as simple text strings, such as the storage method used by the built-in Memo Pad application, but other applications such as Address Book use a more complicated structure containing multiple fields of data for each record. The string you return from LogRecordData should uniquely identify a single record in the handheld database. For example, if the conduit connects to Address Book, LogRecordData should generate a string consisting of the first name, last name, and company fields in an address book record.

As an example, the following LogRecordData function is from the Address Book conduit. Notice that the function casts the CBaseRecord rRec parameter as the address conduit's own CAddressRecord class, and then uses methods from CAddressRecord to retrieve the appropriate field values needed for the log string.

```
void CAddressConduitMonitor::LogRecordData (CBaseRecord&
    rRec, char * errBuff)
{

    CAddressRecord &rLocRec = (CAddressRecord&)rRec;
    CString  csStr;
    int      len = 0;

    rLocRec.GetName(csStr);
    len = csStr.GetLength();
    if (len > 20)
        len = 20;

    strcpy(errBuff, "        ");
    strncat(errBuff, csStr, len);
    strcat(errBuff, ", ");

    rLocRec.GetFirst(csStr);
    len = csStr.GetLength();
    if (len > 20)
        len = 20;

    strncat(errBuff, csStr, len);
    strcat(errBuff, ", ");

    rLocRec.GetCompany(csStr);
    len = csStr.GetLength();
    if (len > 30)
        len = 30;

    strncat(errBuff, csStr, len);
}
```

## Implementing a Table Class

A CBaseTable object stores records in a linear format, relying upon the position and size of each record to identify individual records within the table. All of the size and position data for a table lies within its associated CBaseSchema object, which is described in the next section of this chapter. Most of the really tricky work that goes on in a table is handled by the schema and record objects, but you do need to perform a little bit of customization before the table subclass provided by the Conduit Wizard will work properly.

Conceptually, a conduit table object looks just like a table in a database or spreadsheet. The table is composed of rows and columns; each row represents a single record from the database, and each column is a particular field within that record. Usually, the logical storage structure to use for this sort of construct would be a two-dimensional array, but CBaseTable actually keeps the entire mess in a big single-dimensional array, packing records in one after another. A table object relies on its associated schema object to position a CBaseRecord object at the right place in the array for changing an individual record. Each table object is able to read itself from and write itself out to disk in the standard MFC data serialization format.

To implement a table class, you need to override its AppendDuplicateRecord method, which adds a new row to the table. The Conduit Wizard generates a skeleton for the AppendDuplicateRecord method, which looks something like this:

```
long CMyConduitTable::AppendDuplicateRecord(CBaseRecord&
    rFrom, CBaseRecord& rTo, BOOL bAllFlds)
{
    long  retval = -1;

    CMyConduitRecord& rFromRec = (CMyConduitRecord&)rFrom;
    CMyConduitRecord& rToRec = (CMyConduitRecord&)rTo;

    //
    // Source record must be positioned at valid data.
    //
    if (rFromRec.m_Positioned)
    {
        if (!CBaseTable::AppendBlankRecord(rToRec))
        {
            // TODO - successfully added blank record, now
            // copy the data into it
            if (bAllFlds)
            {
                // copy record ID and status as well
            }
            // copy all remaining field data
        }
    }
    return(retval);
}
```

The monitor object passes AppendDuplicateRecord the addresses of a pair of record objects derived from CBaseRecord. Of these two record objects, rFrom is the address of a record to copy data from, and rTo is the address of a newly created blank record where the data should be copied. Note that the first action AppendDuplicateRecord takes is to cast the incoming classes as your own conduit's subclass of CBaseRecord; in the previous example, this happens to be CMyConduitRecord. This step is necessary because AppendDuplicateRecord relies upon the methods of the derived record class to retrieve and set record fields. Implementing these Get and Set methods is covered in more detail under "Implementing a Record Class" in this chapter.

The bAllFlds argument to AppendDuplicateRecord will be true if the monitor wants to make an exact copy of a record, including its record ID and status bits. If bAllFlds is false, the monitor needs only AppendDuplicateRecord to copy the record's data and not the information describing the record itself.

What follows is an example of what AppendDuplicateRecord might look like for a hypothetical database containing only one field:

```
long CMyConduitTable::AppendDuplicateRecord(CBaseRecord&
    rFrom, CBaseRecord& rTo, BOOL bAllFlds)
{
    long    retval = -1;
    int     nTemp;
    CString csTemp;

    CMyConduitRecord& rFromRec = (CMyConduitRecord&)rFrom;
    CMyConduitRecord& rToRec = (CMyConduitRecord&)rTo;


    //
    // Source record must be positioned at valid data.
    //
    if (rFromRec.m_Positioned)
    {
        if (!CBaseTable::AppendBlankRecord(rToRec))
        {
            if (bAllFlds)
            {
                // If bAllFlds is true, copy all fields,
                // including the record ID.
                retval = rFromRec.GetRecordId(nTemp) ||
                    rToRec.SetRecordId(nTemp);
                if (retval != 0)
                    return retval;

                retval = rFromRec.GetStatus(nTemp) ||
                    rToRec.SetStatus(nTemp);
                if (retval != 0)
                    return retval;

                retval = rToRec.SetArchiveBit(
                    rFromRec.IsArchived() );
                if (retval != 0)
                    return retval;
            }

            // Copy remaining field data.
            retval = rToRec.SetPrivate(
                rFromRec.IsPrivate() );
            if (retval != 0)
                return retval;

            retval = rFromRec.GetData(csTemp) ||
                rToRec.SetData(csTemp);
            if (retval != 0)
```

```
            return retval;

        return 0;
    }
}
    return(retval);
}
```

There is one other method in CBaseTable that you may need to override if your application's data requires special initialization or sorting: AppendBlankRecord. This function has a single parameter, which is the address of a CBaseRecord object. The declaration of AppendBlankRecord looks like this:

```
virtual long CBaseTable::AppendBlankRecord
    (CBaseRecord& rec);
```

# Implementing a Schema Class

Because the schema object is responsible for positioning records within a table object, it must be custom-built to work with the record format used in the table. The subclass of CBaseSchema created by the Conduit Wizard also has a DiscoverSchema method, which you need to override because it sets up data members of the schema object according to the record format.

Before setting up the DiscoverSchema function, you should #define some constants to identify the fields in each record. These constant definitions should go in the header file that contains the declaration of your conduit's CBaseSchema subclass. For example, here are some sample definitions for a very simple record format:

```
#define myFLDRecordID      0
#define myFLDStatus        1

#define myFLDData          2

#define myFLDPrivate       3
#define myFLDCategoryID    4
#define myFLDPosition      5

#define myFLDLast myFLDPosition
```

In this example, the actual data stored by the record format is in the myFLDData field; everything else describes various properties of the record itself.

The DiscoverSchema function tells the schema object what type of data is present in each field. Another task that DiscoverSchema must perform is to let the schema object know where certain key fields are located in the record, such as the record ID and status. Here is an implementation of DiscoverSchema that sets up a schema object for the fields described previously:

```
long CMyConduitSchema::DiscoverSchema (void)
{
    // Define the number of fields per record.
    m_FieldsPerRow = myFLDLast + 1;
    m_FieldTypes.SetSize(m_FieldsPerRow);
```

```
    // Set field positions.
    m_FieldTypes.SetAt(myFLDRecordID,   (WORD)eInteger);
    m_FieldTypes.SetAt(myFLDStatus,     (WORD)eInteger);

    m_FieldTypes.SetAt(myFLDData,       (WORD)eString);

    m_FieldTypes.SetAt(myFLDPrivate,    (WORD)eBool);
    m_FieldTypes.SetAt(myFLDCategoryID, (WORD)eInteger);
    m_FieldTypes.SetAt(myFLDPosition,   (WORD)eInteger);

    // Set the location of the four common fields.
    m_RecordIdPos     = myFLDRecordID;
    m_RecordStatusPos = myFLDStatus;
    m_CategoryIdPos   = myFLDCategoryID;
    m_PlacementPos    = myFLDPosition;

    return 0;
}
```

## Implementing a Record Class

Instances of a record class are not used to actually store record data; that data resides in a table object. Instead, an object derived from `CBaseRecord` provides other parts of the conduit with read and write methods for accessing and modifying the data stored in a table. Your conduit's subclass of `CBaseRecord` will probably require more customization than the other classes in the conduit, simply because you must provide `Set` and `Get` functions for each and every data field in a record. The base class provides methods for reading and writing the record ID, status, category ID, and position of a record, but you must provide your own methods for everything else.

> Make sure that the fields you define in your record subclass match the fields you defined in your schema subclass. Any disagreement between them will be very messy.

To continue with the simple record format shown in the most recent example, here is the declaration of a `CMyConduitRecord` class:

```
class CMyConduitRecord : public CBaseRecord
{
protected:
    friend  CLibCondTable;

public:
    CMyConduitRecord   (CBaseTable &rTable,
                        WORD wModAction = MODFILTER_STUPID) :
                        CBaseRecord (rTable, wModAction){};

    CMyConduitRecord   (CMyConduitTable &rTable,
                        WORD wModAction = MODFILTER_STUPID) :
                        CBaseRecord (rTable, wModAction){};
```

```
long GetData      (CString &csData);
BOOL IsPrivate    (void);

long SetData      (CString csData);
long SetPrivate   (BOOL bPrivate);

// Required function overrides
long Assign(const CBaseRecord&);
BOOL operator==(const CBaseRecord&);

};
```

Constructors for a record subclass do not actually need to do anything special so they simply call the CBaseRecord constructor. The MODFILTER_STUPID constant used for the wModAction parameter's value indicates that the conduit will mark a record dirty if any of its Set methods are called to alter its data. If your conduit changes the contents of records during synchronization instead of just keeping them in synch between the desktop and handheld ("smart" filtering, as opposed to the default "stupid" filtering provided by MODFILTER_STUPID), you should pass a value of 0 for wModAction.

The CMyConduitRecord class described previously defines two methods for each data field in the record, one for retrieving its value and one for setting its value. The GetData and IsPrivate functions look like this:

```
long CMyConduitRecord::GetData (CString &csData)
{
    CStringField* pFld;

    if (m_Positioned &&
        (pFld = (CStringField*) m_Fields.GetAt(myFLDData) )
        && pFld->GetValue(csData) == 0)
        return 0;
    else
        return DERR_RECORD_NOT_POSITIONED;
}

BOOL CMyConduitRecord::IsPrivate (void)
{

    CBoolField* pFld;

    if (m_Positioned &&
        (pFld =
         (CBoolField*) m_Fields.GetAt(myFLDPrivate)))
    {
        if (pFld->IsTrue() )
            return TRUE;
        else
            return FALSE;
    }
    else
        return DERR_RECORD_NOT_POSITIONED;
}
```

Aside from the `CStringField` and `CBoolField` classes used previously for retrieving string and Boolean field values, the Palm MFC Base Classes also provide `CIntegerField` for integer values, `CDateField` for date values, and `CAlphaField` for fixed-length byte fields. All of these classes are defined in the CDK header file `bfields.h` as subclasses of `CBaseField`, which also are defined in `bfields.h`.

Before retrieving data, the `Get` functions check the value of the `m_Positioned` member of the record object. This data member keeps track of whether or not the table is positioned on the record in question. If the table is not positioned on the correct record, the `Get` methods return the error constant `DERR_RECORD_NOT_POSITIONED`.

Following is `SetData`, the partner function to `GetData`. `SetPrivate` is almost identical so it is not listed here. Notice that `SetData` leaves the modification status of the record alone if the new value of the field is equal to the old value; if they are identical, no changes have really been made so no update is required.

```
long CMyConduitRecord::SetData (CString csData)
{
    BOOL        bFlipStatus = FALSE;
    int         nStatus     = 0;
    long        retval      = DERR_RECORD_NOT_POSITIONED;
    CString*    pFld        = NULL;


    if (m_Positioned &&
        (pFld = (CString*) m_Fields.GetAt(myFLDData)))
    {
        if (m_wModAction == MODFILTER_STUPID) {
            GetStatus(nStatus);
            if (nStatus != fldStatusADD) {
                CString csTemp(csData);
                if (pFld->Compare(&csTemp))
                    bFlipStatus = TRUE;
            }
        }
        if (!pFld->SetValue(csData))
        {
            if (bFlipStatus)
                SetStatus(fldStatusUPDATE);
            retval = 0;
        }
    }

    return retval;
}
```

The `fldStatusADD` and `fldStatusUPDATE` constants used previously are part of a family of status constants defined in the CDK header file `tables.h`. These constants describe the status of a desktop record. The following table describes each of the constants and what they signify.

| Constant | Value | Description |
|---|---|---|
| FldStatusNONE | 0 | The record has not changed since the last synch. |
| FldStatusADD | 0x01 | The record has been added since the last synch. |
| FldStatusUPDATE | 0x02 | The record has been modified since the last synch. |
| FldStatusDELETE | 0x04 | The record has been deleted since the last synch. |
| FldStatusPENDING | 0x08 | The record requires some kind of action at the end of the synchronization, depending upon other circumstances. |
| FldStatusARCHIVE | 0x80 | The record has been archived since the last synch. |

Not only do you need to provide the various Get and Set methods, you need to override a pair of virtual functions before your subclass of CBaseRecord will work properly. You first need to override Assign, which copies one record object into another. The conduit passes the address of the record object to copy from, which you should cast to your own subclass of CBaseRecord before iterating over the record's fields and copying them.

```
long CMyConduitRecord::Assign (const CBaseRecord& rSubj)
{
    if (!m_Positioned)
        return -1;
    for (int i = myFLDRecordID; i <= myFLDLast; i++)
    {
        CBaseField* pMyFld =
            (CBaseField*) m_Fields.GetAt(i);
        CBaseField* pSubjFld = (CBaseField*)
            ( (CMyConduitRecord&) rSubj).m_Fields.GetAt(i);
        if (pMyFld && pSubjFld)
            pMyFld->Assign(*pSubjFld);
    }

    return 0;
}
```

You also need to override the comparison operator (operator==) to compare two record objects for equality. This routine should ignore the record ID and status, relying on the record's own fields for the comparison. If you were clever and defined the record ID and status field constants as the first two #define statements earlier on, simply begin at the next available field and start iterating through the fields, comparing each one.

```
BOOL CMyConduitRecord::operator== (
    const CBaseRecord& rSubj)
{
    if (!m_Positioned)
        return FALSE;
    for (int i = myFLDData; i <= myFLDLast; i++)
    {
```

```
        CBaseField* pMyFld =
            (CBaseField*) m_Fields.GetAt(i);
        CBaseField* pSubjFld = (CBaseField*)
            ( (CMyConduitRecord&)rSubj).m_Fields.GetAt(i);
        if (!pMyFld || !pSubjFld)
            return FALSE;
        if (pMyFld->Compare(pSubjFld) != 0)
            return FALSE;
    }

    return TRUE;
}
```

## Implementing a Link Converter Class

The last class you need to implement is the link converter, which translates records between their hand-held format and the format used by your subclass of CBaseRecord. To implement the link converter, you must override two functions: ConvertToRemote and ConvertFromRemote. These functions have the following prototypes:

```
long ConvertToRemote    (CBaseRecord &rRec,
                         CRawRecordInfo &rInfo);

long ConvertFromRemote (CBaseRecord &rRec,
                         CRawRecordInfo &rInfo);
```

The first thing these functions should do is to cast rRec as your own conduit's subclass of CBaseRecord and then use the Get and Set methods of the record subclass to retrieve or set values in rRec as appropriate. When the conduit calls either function, it allocates a buffer in rInfo.m_pBytes, which you should write to in ConvertToRemote or read from in ConvertFromRemote. The CRawRecordInfo class is defined in the CDK header file Syncmgr.h as follows:

```
class CRawRecordInfo
{
public:
    BYTE    m_FileHandle;
    DWORD   m_RecId;
    WORD    m_RecIndex;
    BYTE    m_Attribs;
    short   m_CatId;
    int     m_ConduitId;
    DWORD   m_RecSize;
    WORD    m_TotalBytes;
    BYTE*   m_pBytes;
    DWORD   m_dwReserved;
};
```

The following table describes the data members that make up CRawRecordInfo and, by extension, the rInfo parameter.

| Member | Description |
|---|---|
| m_FileHandle | Handle to the database on the handheld |
| m_RecId | Record ID |
| m_RecIndex | Sequential index of the record within the handheld database |
| m_Attribs | Record attribute flags |
| m_CatId | Category ID |
| m_ConduitId | Unused |
| m_RecSize | Actual amount of data in the record, in bytes |
| m_TotalBytes | Size of the buffer allocated for data |
| m_pBytes | Pointer to a buffer containing the record's data |
| m_dwReserved | Reserved for future use |

Following earlier examples in this section, here is a ConvertToRemote function to convert a CMyConduitRecord object to its handheld data format:

```
long CMyConduitDTLinkConverter::ConvertToRemote (
    CBaseRecord& rRec, CRawRecordInfo& rInfo)
{
    long    retval = 0;
    char    *pBuff;
    CString csTemp;
    DWORD   length;
    int     nTemp, destLen;
    char    *pSrc;

    CMyConduitRecord& rAddrRec = (CMyConduitRecord &)rRec;
    rInfo.m_RecSize = 0;

    // Convert the record ID and category ID.
    retval = rAddrRec.GetRecordId(nTemp);
    rInfo.m_RecId = (long)nTemp;
    retval = rAddrRec.GetCategoryId(nTemp);
    rInfo.m_CatId = nTemp;

    // Convert record attributes.
    rInfo.m_Attribs = 0;
    if (rAddrRec.IsPrivate())
        rInfo.m_Attribs |= PRIVATE_BIT;
    if (rAddrRec.IsArchived())
        rInfo.m_Attribs |= ARCHIVE_BIT;
    if (rAddrRec.IsDeleted())
        rInfo.m_Attribs |= DELETE_BIT;
    if (rAddrRec.IsModified() || rAddrRec.IsAdded())
        rInfo.m_Attribs |= DIRTY_BIT;
```

```
    pBuff = (char*)rInfo.m_pBytes;

    // Convert the body of the record.
    retval = rAddrRec.GetData(csTemp);
    length = csTemp.GetLength();
    if (length != 0)
    {
        // Strip the carriage returns; StripCRs places its
        // result directly into pBuff.
        pSrc    = csTemp.GetBuffer(length);
        destLen = StripCRs(pBuff, pSrc, length);
        csTemp.ReleaseBuffer(-1);

        // If there were more fields in the record, the
        // following lines would advance the buffer pointer
        // and add to the record's total size:
        //      pBuff += destLen;
        //      rInfo.m_RecSize += destLen;
    }

    return retval;
}
```

Here is the counterpart to the last example, ConvertFromRemote:

```
long CAddrCondDTLinkConverter::ConvertFromRemote (
    CBaseRecord& rRec, CRawRecordInfo& rInfo)
{
    long     retval = 0;
    char     *pBuff;
    int      nTemp;
    CString  csTemp;

    CMyConduitRecord& rAddrRec = (CMyConduitRecord &)rRec;

    // Convert record attributes.
    retval = rAddrRec.SetRecordId(rInfo.m_RecId);
    retval = rAddrRec.SetCategoryId(rInfo.m_CatId);
    if (rInfo.m_Attribs & ARCHIVE_BIT)
        retval = rAddrRec.SetArchiveBit(TRUE);
    else
        retval = rAddrRec.SetArchiveBit(FALSE);

    if (rInfo.m_Attribs & PRIVATE_BIT)
        retval = rAddrRec.SetPrivate(TRUE);
    else
        retval = rAddrRec.SetPrivate(FALSE);

    retval = rAddrRec.SetStatus(fldStatusNONE);
    if (rInfo.m_Attribs & DELETE_BIT)
        retval = rAddrRec.SetStatus(fldStatusDELETE);
    else if (rInfo.m_Attribs & DIRTY_BIT)
        retval = rAddrRec.SetStatus(fldStatusUPDATE);
```

```
    // Only convert the body of the record if the remote
    // record is not deleted.
    if (!(rInfo.m_Attribs & DELETE_BIT))
    {
        pBuff = (char*)rInfo.m_pBytes;

        // Add in any necessary carriage returns; AddCRs
        // places its result in m_TransBuff.
        AddCRs(pBuff, strlen(pBuff));
        csTemp = m_TransBuff;
        retval = rAddrRec.SetName(csTemp);

        // If there were more fields in the record, the
        // following line would advance the pointer in the
        // buffer to the next field:
        //     pBuff += strlen(pBuff) + 1;
    }

    return retval;
}
```

Although the previous example does not require them, the CBaseDTLinkConverter class contains methods to easily swap byte orders between the handheld and the desktop, which is quite useful when you consider that many Palm OS handhelds use Motorola big-endian byte order and a Windows desktop machine uses Intel little-endian. The functions available are as follows:

❑   SwapDWordToMotor. This function translates a little-endian Intel DWORD into a big-endian Motorola DWORD.

❑   SwapDWordToIntel. This function performs the reverse conversion from that made by SwapDWordToMotor.

❑   FlipWord. You can use FlipWord to flip a WORD value back and forth between Intel and Motorola formats.

The CBaseDTLinkConverter class also has methods for converting between the date format used in the Palm OS (DateType in the Palm OS headers, TdDateType in the conduit base classes) and the MFC CTime format. The ConvertToTdDate translates CTime to DateType, and ConvertFromTdDate reverses the process.

# Using the Sync Manager API

If your conduit does not keep records in mirror image synch between the desktop and handheld, or if your conduit is very simple and does not require the record-synchronization logic provided by the Palm MFC or Generic Classes, you can use the Sync Manager API directly. The Sync Manager API contains a large number of very low-level functions for communicating directly with a Palm OS handheld during a HotSync operation. This section is only a brief overview of using Sync Manager functions; for exhaustive details, see the *C/C++ Sync Suite Companion*, which ships as part of the CDK.

*If any call to a Sync Manager function results in an error, treat the other return values from the function as unusable. Using any of these undefined values is likely to cause data corruption.*

# Registering and Unregistering a Conduit

Before a conduit can make any other Sync Manager calls, it must be registered with the Sync Manager by calling the `SyncRegisterConduit` function. This registration is not the same as registering the conduit upon installation. See Chapter 20 for information about registering a conduit when it is installed.

The prototype for `SyncRegisterConduit` looks like this:

```
long SyncRegisterConduit (CONDHANDLE &rHandle)
```

The handle returned in the `rHandle` parameter is required by some other calls your conduit makes to Sync Manager functions. The `SyncRegisterConduit` function returns 0 if it successfully registered your conduit, or -1 if another conduit that ran before yours did not unregister itself properly. Only one conduit may be registered at a time, so it is imperative that you unregister your conduit before it exits, using the `SyncUnRegisterConduit` function:

```
long SyncUnRegisterConduit (CONDHANDLE handle)
```

The `SyncUnRegisterConduit` function returns 0 if it successfully unregisters your conduit, or -1 if you provide the function with an invalid `handle` parameter.

# Opening and Closing Handheld Databases

Typically, you will use the `SyncOpenDB` function to open an existing database on the handheld. The prototype for `SyncOpenDB` looks like this:

```
long SyncOpenDB (char *pName, int nCardNum, Byte& rHandle,
    Byte openMode)
```

The `pName` parameter is a null-terminated string containing the name of the database to open, and `nCardNum` receives the number of the card on which the database is located (0 on all current Palm OS handhelds). You can specify the mode in which to open the database using the `openMode` parameter, which should be one or more `eDbOpenModes` constants combined with the OR operator (|). The CDK headers define `eDbOpenMode` like this:

```
enum eDbOpenModes {eDbShowSecret = 0x0010,
                   eDbExclusive  = 0x0020,
                   eDbWrite      = 0x0040,
                   eDbRead       = 0x0080
};
```

In general, you should almost always include the `eDbShowSecret` constant because it enables access to records marked private on the device. The `eDbShowSecret` flag affects how the `SyncReadNextRecIn Category` and `SyncReadNextModifiedRecInCategory` functions (see the "Iterating Over Database Records" section, later in this chapter) operate. These two functions skip over private records if the database was opened without the `eDbShowSecret` flag.

The `eDbExclusive` flag opens the database in exclusive mode, which prevents any other application on the handheld from accessing the database while it is open. This flag is of only limited utility, however, because the Sync Manager does not allow any applications to run during a HotSync operation anyway.

Including the eDbWrite flag opens a database for writing, and the eDbRead flag opens a database for reading. You can use both of these flags together to allow reading and writing to a database in the same open action. For example, to open a database in read/write mode, with access to private records, pass the following value for openMode:

```
(eDbShowSecret | eDbWrite | eDbRead)
```

The SyncOpenDB function returns a handle to the opened database in its rHandle parameter, as well as a value of 0 in its return value for a successful opening, or an error code if the database could not be opened for some reason.

If the database you want to access does not already exist on the handheld, you can create and open a brand new database using the SyncCreateDB function, which has the following prototype:

```
long SyncCreateDB (CDbCreateDB& rDbStats)
```

The rDbStats parameter is an object of class CDbCreateDB, which looks like this:

```
class CDbCreateDB
{
public:
    BYTE m_FileHandle;
    DWORD m_Creator;
    eDbFlags m_Flags;
    BYTE m_CardNo;
    char m_Name[SYNC_DB_NAMELEN];
    DWORD m_Type;
    WORD m_Version;
    DWORD m_dwReserved;
};
```

The following table describes the data members of the CDbCreateDB class as they relate to the SyncCreateDB function.

| Data Member | Description |
| --- | --- |
| m_FileHandle | Receives a handle to the newly created and opened database when SyncCreateDB returns. |
| m_Creator | Creator ID for the new database. |
| m_Flags | Database creation flags, a combination of eDbFlags constants. |
| m_CardNo | Number of the card in which to create the database. Use the value 0 for current Palm OS handhelds. |
| m_Name | Null-terminated string containing the name for the new database. |
| m_Type | Four-character type of the new database. |
| m_Version | Database version. |
| m_dwReserved | Reserved for future use. |

*Although the Sync Manager API contains a number of different classes, none of these classes contains any actual methods, only data members. You can use them in much the same way you would use structures in a C application.*

The eDbFlags enumerated type, used in the m_Flags member of the CDbCreateDB class, is defined like this:

```
enum eDbFlags {
    eRecord             = 0x0000,
    eResource           = 0x0001,
    eReadOnly           = 0x0002,
    eAppInfoDirty       = 0x0004,
    eBackupDB           = 0x0008,
    eOkToInstallNewer   = 0x0010,
    eResetAfterInstall  = 0x0020,
    eCopyPrevention     = 0x0040,
    eOpenDB             = 0x8000
};
```

With the exception of eRecord and eResource, which are mutually exclusive, you can OR these values together. The following table describes the individual flags in eDbFlags.

| Flag | Description |
|------|-------------|
| eRecord | Creates a record database. This option is the default. |
| eResource | Creates a resource database. |
| eReadOnly | Indicates that the database is read-only, which is usually indicative of databases stored in ROM. |
| eAppInfoDirty | Indicates that the database's application info block has been modified. |
| eBackupDB | Sets the backup flag so the HotSync backup conduit will back up this database if no other conduit has been assigned to handle the database's creator ID. |
| eOkToInstallNewer | Indicates that the backup conduit may install a newer version of this database with a different name if this database is currently open. This is primarily used by the system to update the Graffiti shortcuts database because it is still open when the user starts a HotSync operation. |
| eResetAfterInstall | Tells the system to perform a soft reset once the synch operation that installs this database is complete. |
| eCopyPrevention | Prevents the system launcher from beaming this database to other handhelds. |
| eOpenDB | Indicates that the database is already open. This flag is for system use only; never pass this flag when creating a database. |

The SyncCreateDB function opens the newly created database in exclusive mode for reading and writing, with private records shown; this is the equivalent of the conduit's having opened the database with SyncOpenDB by passing the following openMode parameter:

```
(eDbShowSecret | eDbExclusive | eDbWrite | eDbRead)
```

## Closing Databases

When you have finished using a database opened with either SyncOpenDB or SyncCreateDB, you need to close the database with the SyncCloseDB function, whose prototype looks like this:

```
long SyncCloseDB(BYTE fHandle)
```

This function is very simple; it takes as an argument only the handle of the database you want to close. The SyncCloseDB function returns 0 if it successfully closed the database and destroyed its handle or an error code if something went wrong while closing the database.

> The Sync Manager allows you to have only one database open at a time. If you forget to close a database with **SyncCloseDB**, you will prevent other conduits from being able to open their own databases. Be sure to pair every successful **SyncOpenDB** or **SyncCreateDB** call with a call to **SyncCloseDB**.

# Iterating Over Database Records

Most conduits need some way to walk through the records in a database, and the Sync Manager contains a variety of functions to handle this task. Before iterating over database records, however, call SyncResetRecordIndex to ensure that the record index points at the first record in the database. The SyncResetRecordIndex function has the following prototype:

```
long SyncResetRecordIndex (BYTE fHandle)
```

The fHandle parameter is simply the handle to the database, as it was returned by the SyncOpenDB or SyncCreateDB function.

*The Sync Manager automatically resets the record index when it first opens a database so you can skip calling SyncResetRecordIndex if you know for sure that the database was just opened.*

There are three functions for iterating over records using the Sync Manager API:

❑    SyncReadNextModifiedRec retrieves the next modified record from the database.

❑    SyncReadNextRecInCategory retrieves the next record belonging to a specific category.

❑    SyncReadNextModifiedRecInCategory retrieves the next modified record that belongs to a specific category.

The prototypes for these functions look like this:

```
long SyncReadNextModifiedRec (CRawRecordInfo &rInfo);
long SyncReadNextRecInCategory (CRawRecordInfo &rInfo);
long SyncReadNextModifiedRecInCategory (
    CRawRecordInfo &rInfo);
```

All of the functions use the CRawRecordInfo class, which is used by many other functions in the Sync Manager API that read and write record information. The definition of CRawRecordInfo looks like this:

```
class CRawRecordInfo
{
public:
    BYTE m_FileHandle;
    DWORD m_RecId;
    WORD m_RecIndex;
    BYTE m_Attribs;
    short m_CatId;
    int m_ConduitId;
    DWORD m_RecSize;
    WORD m_TotalBytes;
    BYTE* m_pBytes;
    DWORD m_dwReserved;
};
```

The following table describes the members of the CRawRecordInfo class. Notice that some members of the class have subtly different meanings, depending upon whether the function using the CRawRecordInfo class is reading, writing, or iterating over records.

| Data Member | Description |
|---|---|
| m_FileHandle | Handle to the database, as returned by SyncOpenDB or SyncCreateDB. |
| m_RecId | Unique record ID for the record. Supply this value when calling a function that reads or deletes a record based on its record ID. Functions that iterate over records return a retrieved record's ID in this field. |
| m_RecIndex | The index of a record. Supply this value if you are calling a function that reads records by index value. Version 2.1 or later of the Sync Manager API fills in this value with the actual index of a record retrieved from the handheld. |
| m_Attribs | Record attribute flags, a combination of constants in the eSyncRecAttrs enumerated type. Supply this value if you are calling a function that writes a record. Functions that read a record return the record's attributes in this field. |
| m_CatId | Category index for a record. Supply this value if you are calling a function that writes a record. Functions that read a record return the record's category index in this field. |
| m_ConduitId | Currently unused. |

| Data Member | Description |
|---|---|
| m_RecSize | Actual amount of data in the record, in bytes. If you are calling a function to write a record, you must specify this value, and it should be equal to the m_TotalBytes value. Functions that read a record return the record's actual data size in this field. If the data size is larger than the buffer you allocated to contain the incoming record, m_RecSize will be larger than m_TotalBytes, and depending upon the version of the Sync Manager API, one of two things may happen. In 2.1 or later, only m_TotalBytes of data are copied from the record; in versions earlier than 2.1, nothing is copied at all. |
| m_TotalBytes | Size of a buffer you have allocated for sending data to or receiving data from a record. If you are writing a record, this field should equal the size of the record in bytes. If you use a function to read a record, m_TotalBytes should indicate the size of the buffer pointed to by m_pBytes, in bytes. |
| m_pBytes | Pointer to a buffer you have allocated for reading or writing records. You must allocate this buffer before calling any Sync Manager function that reads or writes records using the CRawRecordInfo class. |
| m_dwReserved | Reserved for future use. Set this field to NULL before passing a CRawRecordInfo object to one of the Sync Manager functions. |

The eSyncRecAttrs enumerated type, used in the m_Attribs member of CRawRecordInfo, has the following definition:

```
enum eSyncRecAttrs {eRecAttrDeleted  = 0x80,
                    eRecAttrDirty    = 0x40,
                    eRecAttrBusy     = 0x20,
                    eRecAttrSecret   = 0x10,
                    eRecAttrArchived = 0x08
};
```

> **Modifying a database while iterating over its records is not supported by the Sync Manager. Be sure to structure your conduit so it does not intersperse record modification with iteration. The exception to this rule is that Palm OS version 2.0 and later supports deletion of records during iteration using the SyncDeleteRec function.**

As an example of how to use the Sync Manager iteration functions, the following function walks through all the modified records in a database, given a handle to an open database as a parameter:

```
long WalkThroughModifiedRecs (BYTE myHandle)
{
    long retval = 0, err = 0;
    CRawRecordInfo rawRecord;

    memset(&rawRecord, 0, sizeof(rawRecord));
    rawRecord.m_FileHandle = myHandle;
    rawRecord.m_RecId      = 0;
```

```
        // Allocate memory for rawRecord data.
        rawRecord.m_TotalBytes = 0;
        rawRecord.m_pBytes = (BYTE*) new char [8000];
        if (rawRecord.m_pBytes)
        {
            rawRecord.m_TotalBytes = wRawRecSize;
            memset(rawRecord.m_pBytes, 0, wRawRecSize);
        }
        else
            return CONDERR_RAW_RECORD_ALLOCATE;

        // Read in each modified remote record one at a time.
        while (!err && !retval)
        {
            if (!(err = SyncReadNextModifiedRec(rawRecord)))
            {

                // Do something with each modified record here.

            }

            // Reset data buffer between each record retrieval.
            memset(rawRecord.m_pBytes, 0,
                    rawRecord.m_TotalBytes);
        }

        // Free the memory allocated for the raw record.
        if (rawRecord.m_TotalBytes > 0 && rawRecord.m_pBytes)
            delete rawRecord.m_pBytes;

        return retval;
}
```

## Reading and Writing Records

If you know the record ID or index of a record, you can retrieve the record directly using the SyncReadRecordById or SyncReadRecordByIndex functions, which have the following prototypes:

```
long SyncReadRecordById (CRawRecordInfo &rInfo);
long SyncReadRecordByIndex (CRawRecordInfo &rInfo);
```

Before calling these functions, you will need to fill in the m_RecId or m_RecIndex member of the CRawRecordInfo object that you pass to the functions. Also, as in the previous example that uses SyncReadNextModifiedRec, you should allocate a buffer to receive the record's data and point the CRawRecordInfo object's m_pBytes pointer to the buffer.

Writing to records may be accomplished using the SyncWriteRec function, whose prototype looks very similar to that of all the other record-handling functions in the Sync Manager API:

```
long SyncWriteRec (CRawRecordInfo &rInfo)
```

To write a record, you need to fill a buffer with the record data to write, point the CRawRecordInfo object's m_pBytes pointer at the buffer, and set m_RecSize and m_TotalBytes to the length of the record's data in bytes.

## Deleting Records

The Sync Manager API provides a number of functions for deleting records from databases. The most basic function, SyncDeleteRec, deletes a single record from a database, given a now-familiar CRawRecordInfo parameter:

```
long SyncDeleteRec (CRawRecordInfo &rInfo)
```

> All of the Sync Manager deletion functions, whether they begin with **SyncDelete** or **SyncPurge**, immediately and permanently remove a record or records from a database instead of just marking them for deletion. Be very careful that your conduit code has properly archived deleted records before removing them from the handheld.

Aside from deleting a single record, the Sync Manager also provides functions for deleting a lot of records at once. The SyncPurgeAllRecs function wipes out all the records contained in a database, given a handle to the open database:

```
long SyncPurgeAllRecs (BYTE fHandle)
```

If you want to be a little more selective in your mass deletions, you can pass a handle to an open database and a category index to SyncPurgeAllRecsInCategory to delete all the records contained in a specific category within that database:

```
long SyncPurgeAllRecsInCategory (BYTE fHandle,
                                 short category)
```

Even more selective, and probably the most useful, is the SyncPurgeDeletedRecs function, which removes only the records in the database that are marked for deletion. Typically, you call this function after archiving records to the desktop to clean up the handheld database.

```
long SyncPurgeDeletedRecs (BYTE fHandle)
```

## Maintaining a Connection

If your conduit needs to perform an action that could take a while to finish, such as retrieving data over a network, you need to ping the Sync Manager every once in a while so it will keep its connection open and not time out. The SyncYieldCycles function sends messages that keep the connection alive, and it also gives the HotSync application a chance to update its progress indicator and process user events, such as a click the of Cancel button. The prototype for SyncYieldCycles looks like this:

```
long SyncYieldCycles (WORD wMaxMiliSecs)
```

The wMaxMiliSecs parameter specifies the maximum number of milliseconds to spend servicing events. Because the HotSync application does not need a lot of time to process its events, any value higher than 1 would just be a waste of time; in fact, the current implementation of SyncYieldCycles just ignores this value anyway. Just use a value of 1.

> You can call SyncYieldCycles without significantly affecting performance because there usually are no events in the HotSync application's queue to process. PalmSource recommends calling SyncYieldCycles at least once every seven seconds during lengthy operations that might cause a timeout. Sprinkling SyncYieldCycles calls liberally throughout your code is a good idea.

# Summary

In this chapter, you learned how to build conduits using the Palm MFC Base Classes, the Palm Generic Conduit Base Classes, and low-level Sync Manager API calls. After reading this chapter, you should understand the following:

❑ The Conduit Wizard provides the easiest way to start any conduit project in Visual C++.

❑ Every conduit must implement certain required entry points, including OpenConduit, GetConduitInfo, GetConduitName, and GetConduitVersion; in addition, every conduit also should implement the optional CfgConduit and ConfigureConduit entry points.

❑ Creating a conduit based on the Palm Generic Conduit base classes involves describing a desktop record format, implementing storage and retrieval of records on the desktop, implementing conversion of records between your desktop format and the generic CPalmRecord format, and synchronizing the application info block.

❑ Creating a conduit based on the Palm MFC Base Classes is a matter of subclassing the base monitor, table, schema, record, and link converter classes, and then overriding selected methods of these classes to produce the desired behavior in your conduit.

❑ Among other things, the Sync Manager API provides functions for registering and unregistering a conduit, opening and closing handheld databases, iterating over records, reading and writing records, deleting records, and keeping a connection to the handheld alive.

# Programming Navigation Hardware

Many Palm Powered handhelds now sport hardware features that provide one-handed navigation capabilities. The most common examples of this are the "5-way" navigation button found on palmOne Tungsten, Zire, and Treo handhelds, and the Jog Dial found on Sony CLIÉ handhelds. These hardware enhancements are designed to allow the user to navigate through applications and data with only one hand.

This chapter describes the major navigation aids present in the most current handheld models and includes information on how to program your application to respond correctly to usage of the navigation hardware.

## Programming the palmOne 5-Way Navigation Button

With the introduction of the Tungsten, Zire, and Treo models from palmOne, handhelds began to support a new 5-way navigation button. By incorporating up, down, left, right, and select operations in a single thumb-controlled button cluster, the 5-way navigation button greatly reduces the number of scenarios in which handheld users must take out and use a stylus for program and data navigation. This further enables one-handed usage of handhelds by users on the go.

The 5-way navigation button is found on most handheld models produced by palmOne, including the Tungsten, Zire, and Treo. The usage model for the 5-way button is as follows:

❑   The left and right buttons move the current focus horizontally.

❑   The up and down buttons move the current focus vertically.

❑   The center button either simulates a "tap" on the currently focused object, or it can be used to toggle the state of the current focused object.

*The functions, constants, documentation, and other information regarding 5-way navigation are actually not part of the standard Palm OS SDK provided by PalmSource. 5-way navigation is part of the palmOne SDK provided by palmOne to developers who wish to enhance their Palm OS applications to support features and capabilities found on palmOne's handhelds and smartphones. Access to the 5-way SDK is provided to members of palmOne's "Plugged In" program. Information on the Plugged In program can be found on pluggedin.palmone.com.*

# Object Focus and Application Focus

When an object on a form (such as an input field) is set as the current object for input or selection, it is said to have object focus. Application forms can be said to be in one of two states:

❑   Object focus mode is seen when an object on your form has the current focus — in this case the 5-way button is used to jump, or navigate, from object to object on a form.

❑   Application focus mode is seen when no object has the current focus — in this case the 5-way button is used as a page-up/page-down navigation aid on the form itself.

# Understanding Tab Order

Tab order is perhaps a strange term to use for devices that generally do not have a Tab key, but the term clearly has a meaning borrowed from the PC world, in which pressing the Tab key on a dialog box moves the current focus from one dialog box element to the next. Similarly, forms on a 5-way enabled Palm OS application can be said to have a tab order, which defines how the user moves from one form object to the next using the navigation button.

You can set the tab order for your form by creating a special kind of resource called a navigation resource (fnav). If no navigation resource is found, the system determines the proper default tab order for your form, as well as which form objects can receive the input focus. While your application can function reasonably on a 5-way device without an fnav resource, it is recommended that you provide a navigation resource to achieve the best user experience.

*For information on how to create "fnav" resources in CodeWarrior and PODS, please refer to the palmOne SDK.*

# Handling Navigation Events

Five-way button actions flow through Palm OS to your program as navigation events. Although the keyDown event is of most interest, you can also detect keyUp and keyHold events. The relevant events, helper functions, and character codes are defined in palmchars.h.

If your form is in object focus mode, you will receive one of the following character codes in the keyDown event: vchrRockerUp, vchrRockerDown, vchrRockerLeft, vchrRockerRight, or vchrRockerCenter.

If your form is in application focus mode, you will receive a vchrPageUp or vchrPageDown instead of the vchrRockerUp and vchrRockerDown character codes.

The following event handler code can be used to determine which button was pressed by the user:

```
switch (event->eType)
{
    case keyDownEvent:
        if (EvtKeydownIsVirtual(event))
        {
            switch (event->data.keyDown.chr)
            {
                case vchrPageUp:
                    // Up button was pressed
                    handled = true;
                    break;
                case vchrPageDown:
                    // Down button was pressed
                    handled = true;
                    break;
                case vchrRockerUp:
                    // Up button was pressed (object focus)
                    handled = true;
                    break;
                case vchrRockerDown:
                    // Down button was pressed (object focus)
                    handled = true;
                    break;
                case vchrRockerRight:
                    // Right button was pressed
                    handled = true;
                    break;
                case vchrRockerLeft:
                    // Left button was pressed
                    handled = true;
                    break;
                case vchrRockerCenter:
                    // Center button was pressed
                    handled = true;
                    break;
            }
        }
}
```

# Detecting the Presence of 5-Way Navigation Buttons

If your code needs to detect the presence of the 5-way navigation button, you can call `FtrGet` and check for the hsFtrIDNavigationSupported feature. This call also returns a version that can be used to differentiate which 5-way implementation is present.

```
Err     error;
UInt32  keyboardType;

error = FtrGet (hsFtrCreator, hsFtrIDNavigationSupported,
                &version);
if (!error )
{
```

```
      // 5-way is present
   if (version == 1)
   {
           // older implementation (ex. Treo 600)
   }
   else
   {
           // newer implementation (ex. Treo 650, Tungsten T5)
   }
}
```

## Designing Your Forms for 5-Way Navigation

What is the proper navigation behavior to implement for your application's forms? As usual, one of the best ways to make sure that your application is intuitive to palmOne handheld users is to study the behavior of the built-in applications such as Calendar and Address Book when used with 5-way navigation.

Further information on design considerations and style guidance is forthcoming from palmOne as part of its palmOne SDK as of this writing.

# Programming the Sony Jog Dial

Sony's CLIÉ line of handhelds has traditionally incorporated a navigational aid that predates the 5-way navigation button, called the Jog Dial. The Jog Dial is a small wheel mounted on the side of a handheld that can be used to perform one-handed up and down scrolling actions. The Jog Dial also incorporates selection and a Back button, making it a convenient way to navigate through programs and data.

Sony's Jog Dial is very intuitive in usage:

❑   Move the wheel up to move a selection highlight up or left.

❑   Move the wheel down to move a selection highlight down or right.

❑   Press the wheel to select the highlighted item.

A navigation wheel makes it possible to navigate through an application and view its data without pulling out the stylus to tap on the screen. Navigation wheels are ideal for tasks such as scrolling through reading material, selecting records to view, and launching applications.

An example of navigation wheel operation, drawn from the Sony CLIÉ Address application, is shown in Figure 23-1. Scrolling the wheel moves a highlight in the list view, and pressing the wheel opens the highlighted address record for viewing.

Sony devices also include a Back button, which is normally tied to the concept of reverse navigation, or canceling out of an operation. For example, pressing the Back button in the record view of the Sony Address application takes you back to the list view, allowing you to select another record. Typically, if an application is already at its highest-level view, such as the list view in Address, pressing the Back button exits the program and starts the application launcher.

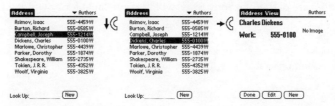

**Figure 23-1**

Detecting Jog Dial events on a Sony CLIÉ is very simple. When the user rotates or pushes the Jog Dial, the operating system generates an appropriate keyDown event, which your application can look for in its event handling code. Sony has defined virtual character constants for every action the user might take with the Jog Dial and its associated Back button, as you can see in the following table.

| Constant | Value | Description |
|---|---|---|
| vchrJogUp | 0x1700 | Occurs when the Jog Dial is rotated up. |
| vchrJogDown | 0x1701 | Occurs when the Jog Dial is rotated down. |
| vchrJogPushRepeat | 0x1702 | Occurs when the Jog Dial is held down. The first vchrJogPushRepeat event occurs 50 system ticks after the Jog Dial is first pressed in; then the event occurs repeatedly every 12 ticks until the user releases the Jog Dial. Note that vchrJogPushRepeat events are not generated if the dial is rotated while held down. |
| vchrJogPushedUp | 0x1703 | Occurs when the Jog Dial is pressed in and rotated up at the same time. |
| vchrJogPushedDown | 0x1704 | Occurs when the Jog Dial is pressed in and rotated down at the same time. |
| vchrJogPush | 0x1705 | Occurs when the Jog Dial is pressed in. |
| vchrJogRelease | 0x1706 | Occurs when the Jog Dial is released. |
| vchrJogBack | 0x1707 | Occurs when the Back button is pressed and released. |

These character constants are defined in the header file SonyChars.h. However, it is not necessary to directly include SonyChars.h in your application. Sony provides the header file SonyCLIE.h, which in turn includes many other header files for various Sony features, among them the character constants in SonyChars.h.

> The **Chars.h** file in Palm OS 5 SDK defines the constants **vchrSonyMin** and **vchrSonyMax**, which are also defined in **SonyChars.h**. If you include both header files in a project, conflict between the constant names will cause problems when you build your application. As a workaround, you can comment out the lines in **Chars.h** that define **vchrSonyMin** and **vchrSonyMax**.

The Sony header files are part of the Sony SDK, which is available for download from Sony's developer program Web site.

Responding to Jog Dial events is a simple matter of looking for the appropriate keyDown events. The following code snippet demonstrates how to respond to Jog Dial events:

```
switch (event->eType)
{
    case keyDownEvent:
        if (EvtKeydownIsVirtual(event))
        {
            switch (event->data.keyDown.chr)
            {
                case vchrJogUp:
                    // Jog Dial was rotated up.
                    handled = true;
                    break;

                case vchrJogDown:
                    // Jog Dial was rotated down.
                    handled = true;
                    break;

                case vchrJogPush:
                    // Jog Dial was pressed in.
                    handled = true;
                    break;

                case vchrJogRelease:
                    // Jog Dial was released.
                    handled = true;
                    break;

                case vchrJogPushRepeat:
                    // Jog Dial was held down.
                    handled = true;
                    break;

                case vchrJogPushedUp:
                    // Jog Dial was pushed in and rotated
                    // up.
                    handled = true;
                    break;

                case vchrJogPushedDown:
                    // Jog Dial was pushed in and rotated
                    // down.
                    handled = true;
                    break;

                case vchrJogBack:
                    // Back button was pressed and
                    // released.
                    handled = true;
                    break;
```

```
            }
        }
    }
```

*On Sony CLIÉ models that support JogAssist, it is impossible to handle the* vchrJogBack *event without first masking it; see the next section for details on JogAssist masking. In any case, you should probably think twice about overriding Sony's default handling of the Back button. The Back button is intended to allow a user to cancel a current action or to jump back to a previously viewed form. Changing the behavior of the Back button to anything else could be very confusing to the user.*

Because Sony may in the future release Palm Powered handhelds that do not have Jog Dials, knowing that your application is running on Sony hardware is not a guarantee that the handheld has a Jog Dial. Also, Sony has released two styles of Jog Dials—one with and one without a Back button. To check for the presence of a Jog Dial and whether or not it is accompanied by a Back button, use the FtrGet routine:

```
SonySysFtrSysInfoP  infoP;

if (! FtrGet(sysFtrCreator, sonySysFtrNumSysInfoP,
            (UInt32 *) infoP))
{
    if (infoP)
    {
        switch (infoP->jogType)
            {
                case sonySysFtrSysInfoJogTypeNone:
                    // No Jog Dial exists on this handheld.
                    break;

                case sonySysFtrSysInfoJogType1:
                    // Jog Dial exists, but no Back button.
                    break;

                case sonySysFtrSysInfoJogType2:
                    // Jog Dial and Back button exist.
                    break;
            }
    }
}
```

Passing sonySysFtrNumSysInfoP to FtrGet retrieves a pointer to a SonySysFtrSysInfoType structure. The SonySysFtrSysInfoType structure is defined in the Sony header file SonySystemFtr.h, and it contains a wealth of information regarding the status and abilities of a Sony handheld. Among the information contained in the structure is the jogType field, which indicates what kind of Jog Dial is present on the handheld.

## Understanding JogAssist

Many Sony handhelds include a feature called JogAssist, which allows the Jog Dial to perform useful functions, even in applications that were not written to handle the Jog Dial. JogAssist intercepts Jog Dial events and translates them into other events that applications can use, allowing one-handed operation in programs that were never designed for the Sony CLIÉ.

Arguably the most useful feature of JogAssist is its handling of Jog Dial rotation. If a scroll bar is present on the currently visible form, then rotating the Jog Dial is equivalent to tapping the arrows on the top and bottom of the scroll bar. In most applications, this scrolls data up or down a line at a time. If the user presses down on the Jog Dial and rotates it, JogAssist generates events equivalent to tapping on the gray areas above and below the scroll car, which in most applications scrolls data a page at a time. If the current form lacks a scroll bar, rotating the Jog Dial up generates a `keyDown` event containing a `vchrPageUp` character, and rotating the Jog Dial down generates a `keyDown` event containing a `vchrPageDown` character. Pressing the hardware scroll buttons normally generates `vchrPageUp` and `vchrPageDown`, behaviors that many applications support, even those without scroll bars.

JogAssist also controls how the Back button behaves. The general idea behind Back button behavior is that when the user presses the Back button, either the current operation should be canceled, or the application should return to its previous view. JogAssist makes this happen by scanning the current form for buttons that have specific text in their labels, and when it finds an appropriate button, JogAssist simulates a tap on that button. From highest priority to lowest priority, these are the button labels that JogAssist looks for when the Back button is pressed:

1. Cancel, Previous
2. No, Close
3. Done
4. Yes, OK

If JogAssist finds two buttons at the same priority label on the same form, it chooses the button with the lowest control index on that form. For example, assume a form contains buttons labeled Done, Cancel, and Previous, with index values of 1, 2, and 3, respectively. When the user presses the Back button, JogAssist will select the Cancel button because its index of 2 is less than the Previous button's index of 3. JogAssist never even considers the Done button, despite its lower index because Done is a lower priority than either Cancel or Previous.

If there are no buttons with suitable captions on the current form, pressing the Back button exits the current program and returns the user "back" to the application launcher.

JogAssist also allows for one-handed selection of controls on a form, navigation and selection from pop-up and regular lists, and selection of menu items from a form's menu bar. All of these features are context-sensitive, which means that, for example, `vchrJogBack` has a different meaning in a pop-up list than it does in a menu. For an exhaustive list of the actions JogAssist takes in various circumstances, consult *Programmer's Companion for Sony CLIÉ Handheld*, which is included in Sony's CLIÉ SDK.

## Working Around JogAssist

JogAssist is wonderful in that it allows very good Jog Dial navigation in older applications that don't contain built-in Jog Dial support. However, if you design your application specifically to make use of the Jog Dial, JogAssist can get in the way. JogAssist intercepts all Jog Dial events and processes them before your application's form event handler gets a chance to handle such events, so by the time your application gets input from the Jog Dial, what used to be a `vchrJogUp` character may have been changed into `vchrPageUp`. To make matters worse, CLIÉ users have the option of selectively disabling JogAssist for any application, so you can't rely on input from the Jog Dial to be consistently altered by JogAssist.

Fortunately, the bright developers at Sony designed a way to work around just such a problem. Any CLIÉ that supports JogAssist also supports the ability to turn off JogAssist processing of Jog Dial events. The process of turning off JogAssist is called *JogAssist masking*. To disable JogAssist, follow these steps:

1. Create a mask that tells JogAssist which Jog Dial events it should leave alone.

2. Retrieve the JogAssist mask pointer by using `FtrGet`.

3. Save the old value of the mask pointer.

4. Set the JogAssist mask pointer to point to your JogAssist mask.

5. Retrieve the JogAssist mask owner by using `FtrGet`.

6. Save the old mask owner.

7. Set the JogAssist mask owner to be your application.

8. When your application exits, restore the system mask pointer and mask owner to their original values.

### Creating a JogAssist Mask

A JogAssist mask is an array of `UInt16` values. Each member of the array has a specific meaning, depending upon both its position within the array and upon what type of mask you are creating.

There are two types of masks you can define for disabling JogAssist. Type 1 allows you to selectively disable JogAssist in specific forms in your application. This is particularly useful if you perform special Jog Dial handling in only one or two forms in your application because it allows Jog Assist to function normally in the rest of the application, which means that your program will behave in similar fashion to other applications installed on the user's CLIÉ. Type 2 masks Jog Dial events throughout your application.

Figure 23-2 depicts a Type 1 mask.

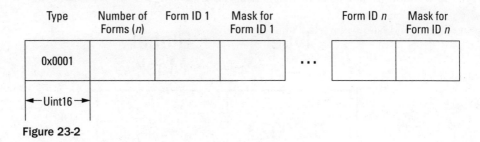

| Type | Number of Forms (*n*) | Form ID 1 | Mask for Form ID 1 | | Form ID *n* | Mask for Form ID *n* |
|---|---|---|---|---|---|---|
| 0x0001 | | | | ... | | |

←—Uint16—→

**Figure 23-2**

The first array element in either type of mask is a value defining whether the mask is Type 1 or Type 2. In a Type 1 mask, this first element has the value `sonyJogAstMaskType1`. A Type 1 mask's next element contains the number of forms for which you wish to provide masking. The next two array elements contain the form ID number of a form in your application, followed by a bit field that specifies which Jog Dial events to mask in that particular form. For every additional form you want to mask, the array contains another two elements, which contain another form ID and bit field pair.

The following table shows the constants that make up the masking bit field.

| Constant | Value | Description |
|---|---|---|
| sonyJogAstMaskUp | 0x0001 | Masks vchrJogUp |
| sonyJogAstMaskDown | 0x0002 | Masks vchrJogDown |
| sonyJogAstMaskPushedUp | 0x0004 | Masks vchrJogPushedUp |
| sonyJogAstMaskPushedDown | 0x0008 | Masks vchrJogPushedDown |
| sonyJogAstMaskPush | 0x0010 | Masks vchrJogPush |
| sonyJogAstMaskRelease | 0x0020 | Masks vchrJogRelease |
| sonyJogAstMaskPushRepeat | 0x0040 | Masks vchrJogPushRepeat |
| sonyJogAstMaskBack | 0x0080 | Masks vchrJogBack |
| sonyJogAstMaskAll | 0x00FF | Masks all the Jog Dial events |
| sonyJogAstMaskNone | 0x0000 | Masks none of the Jog Dial events |

The following snippet of code sets up a Type 1 mask that disables JogAssist processing of vchrJogUp and vchrJogDown in form ID 1000 and disables all JogAssist processing in form ID 1001:

```
UInt16  mask[] = { sonyJogAstMaskType1,
                   2,
                   1000,
                   sonyJogAstMaskUp | sonyJogAstMaskDown,
                   1001,
                   sonyJogAstMaskAll
                 };
```

A Type 2 mask is much shorter and easier to define. Figure 23-3 depicts a Type 2 mask.

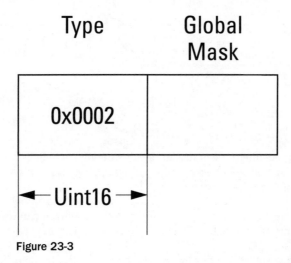

Figure 23-3

The first element of a Type 2 mask is the value sonyJogAstMaskType2. The second array element contains a bit field that defines the Jog Dial events that should be masked throughout your application. The following example sets up a Type 2 mask that disables JogAssist processing of vchrJogUp, vchrJogDown, vchrJogPush, and vchrJogRelease events throughout all of an application's forms:

```
UInt16  mask[] = { sonyJogAstMaskType2,
                   sonyJogAstMaskUp | sonyJogAstMaskDown |
                   sonyJogAstMaskPush |
                   sonyJogAstMaskRelease
                };
```

Regardless of whether you use a Type 1 or a Type 2 mask, be sure to create your JogAssist mask as a global variable. The JogAssist masking mechanism works by assigning an operating system pointer to point to your own mask. When the operating system generates a Jog Dial event, JogAssist looks at this pointer to find where the mask is located. If your mask is defined within a function in your application, once that function exits, your mask goes out of scope and ceases to exist, and JogAssist no longer has a mask to work with. If JogAssist cannot find a mask, it continues processing all Jog Dial events as it normally would.

## Retrieving and Setting the JogAssist Mask Pointer

Once you have defined a mask, you need to tell JogAssist where it is located. To do this, you must first retrieve the system JogAssist mask pointer using the FtrGet routine. The best place to do this is in your application's StartApplication routine, where your program handles startup tasks.

Before setting up the JogAssist mask pointer, your application should check to make sure that the handheld running your application supports JogAssist. Use the FtrGet routine for this purpose:

```
SonySysFtrSysInfoP  infoP;

if (! FtrGet(sonySysFtrCreator, sonySysFtrNumSysInfoP,
         (UInt32 *) &infoP))
{
    if (infoP && (infoP->extn &
              sonySysFtrSysInfoExtnJogAst))
    {
        // JogAssist is supported on this device.
    }
}
```

Once you have determined that JogAssist is supported, you can retrieve the JogAssist mask pointer, as in the following example:

```
if (! FtrGet(sonySysFtrCreator, sonySysFtrNumJogAstMaskP,
         (UInt32 *) &maskPP))
{
    // Save the current JogAssist mask so it may be
    // restored on exit.
    gOldJogAstMaskP = *maskPP;

    // Set the JogAssist mask to its new value.
    *maskPP = mask;
}
else
    maskPP = NULL;
```

The `maskPP` and `gOldJogAstMaskP` variables in the preceding code are global variables, defined as follows:

```
UInt16  **maskPP = NULL;
UInt16  *gOldJogAstMaskP = NULL;
```

Calling `FtrGet` with a second argument of `sonySysFtrNumJogAstMaskP` sets `maskPP` to point to the location of the system's JogAssist mask pointer. Your application should save the old value of the mask pointer so it may be restored when your application exits. Once you have the old mask pointer safely backed up, you can set the system's mask pointer to point to your application's JogAssist mask.

## Retrieving and Setting the JogAssist Mask Owner

Sometimes it is possible for Palm OS to activate another application while yours is running, as in the case of performing an Address lookup. The JogAssist mask you set up in your application remains active during such a sub-launch, which may cause unexpected behavior for the user in the sub-launched application when your mask prevents JogAssist from processing certain Jog Dial events. To avoid this problem, you can assign your application as the owner of the current JogAssist mask, which tells JogAssist to pay attention to the mask only when your application is the one currently running.

Like everything else related to JogAssist masks, you set the mask owner using the `FtrGet` routine. You will need to know your application's card number and database ID, which may both be retrieved using `SysCurAppDatabase`. The following code sets the mask owner to the currently running application:

```
if (!FtrGet(sonySysFtrCreator, sonySysFtrNumJogAstMOCardNoP,
            (UInt32*) &ftrCardNoP) &&
    !FtrGet(sonySysFtrCreator, sonySysFtrNumJogAstMODbIDP,
            (UInt32*) &ftrDbIDP))
{
    // Save the old mask owner to restore later.
    gOldFtrCardNo = *ftrCardNoP;
    gOldFtrDbID = *ftrDbIDP;

    // Set the mask owner.
    SysCurAppDatabase(ftrCardNoP, ftrDbIDP);
}
else
{
    ftrCardNoP = NULL;
    ftrDbIDP = NULL;
}
```

The `gOldFtrCardNo`, `gOldFtrDbID`, `ftrCarNoP`, and `ftrDbIDP` variables are all globally defined as follows:

```
UInt16   gOldFtrCardNo = NULL;
LocalID  gOldFtrDbID = NULL;
UInt16   *ftrCardNoP = NULL;
LocalID  *ftrDbIDP = NULL;
```

Once you have the mask pointer and mask owner set, Jog Assist will leave masked Jog Dial events alone so your application can process them. To give you an overview of the entire process of setting up JogAssist masking, the following code shows an entire `StartApplication` routine (and the global variables it relies upon) that masks `vchrJogUp` and `vchrJogDown` events in a single form.

```
#define frmMain  1000

// Global variables
UInt16  *gOldJogAstMaskP = NULL;
UInt16  gOldFtrCardNo = NULL;
LocalID  gOldFtrDbID = NULL;

UInt16  **maskPP = NULL;
UInt16  *ftrCardNoP = NULL;
LocalID  *ftrDbIDP = NULL;

UInt16  mask[] = { sonyJogAstMaskType1,
                   1,
                   frmMain,
                   sonyJogAstMaskUp | sonyJogAstMaskDown
                 };

static int StartApplication(void)
{
    SonySysFtrSysInfoP  infoP;


    // Check to see if JogAssist is available on this
    // device.
    if (! FtrGet(sonySysFtrCreator, sonySysFtrNumSysInfoP,
             (UInt32 *) &infoP))
    {
        if (infoP && (infoP->extn &
                    sonySysFtrSysInfoExtnJogAst))
        {
            if (! FtrGet(sonySysFtrCreator,
                        sonySysFtrNumJogAstMaskP,
                        (UInt32 *) &maskPP))
            {
                // Save the current JogAssist mask so it may
                // be restored on exit.
                gOldJogAstMaskP = *maskPP;

                // Set the JogAssist mask to its new value.
                *maskPP = mask;
            }
            else
                maskPP = NULL;

            // Set JogAssist owner mask
            if (!FtrGet(sonySysFtrCreator,
                        sonySysFtrNumJogAstMOCardNoP,
                        (UInt32*) &ftrCardNoP) &&
                !FtrGet(sonySysFtrCreator,
                        sonySysFtrNumJogAstMODbIDP,
                        (UInt32*) &ftrDbIDP))
            {
                // Save the old mask owner to restore later.
                gOldFtrCardNo = *ftrCardNoP;
                gOldFtrDbID = *ftrDbIDP;

                // Set the mask owner.
```

```
                    SysCurAppDatabase(ftrCardNoP, ftrDbIDP);
            }
            else
            {
                ftrCardNoP = NULL;
                ftrDbIDP = NULL;
            }
        }
    }

    // Launch the main form.
    FrmGotoForm(frmMain);
    return 0;
}
```

## Restoring the Mask Pointer and Mask Owner

When your application is preparing to exit, it needs to restore the JogAssist mask pointer and mask owner to their original values. This task should be accomplished in your application's StopApplication routine. Because your program should already have the system mask pointer and mask owner stored in global variables, it is a simple matter to restore the original values saved by the application's StartApplication routine. The following sample StopApplication routine restores the mask pointer and mask owner to the values saved by the StartApplication function from the preceding block of code:

```
static void StopApplication(void)
{
    FrmCloseAllForms();

    // Restore the original JogAssist mask.
    if (gOldJogAstMaskP)
    {
        *maskPP = gOldJogAstMaskP;

        // Restore the original JogAssist mask owner.
        *ftrCardNoP = gOldFtrCardNo;
        *ftrDbIDP = gOldFtrDbID;
    }
}
```

# Summary

This chapter discussed hardware found on handhelds to support one-handed navigation and showed how to program an application to take advantage of such hardware. You should now know the following:

❑  Navigation hardware is implemented in most models as either 5-way navigation buttons (palmOne) or Jog Dial (Sony).

❑  Navigation events are handled by trapping the keyDown event, which your application may then process in its regular event handling routines.

❑  The FtrGet routine may be used to detect the presence of a 5-way navigation button or Jog Dial support.

❑  If you want to add special support for Sony's Jog Dial, you may need to override JogAssist's handling of Jog Dial events by supplying a JogAssist mask and mask owner.

# 24

# Odds and Ends

This chapter is a collection of useful Palm OS programming techniques that you may not need to use as frequently as those described elsewhere in this book. Many of the things mentioned in this chapter are not for the timid, and you will need to be comfortable with both Palm OS and with your development tools before diving too deeply into this part of the book.

## Creating Large Applications in Palm OS Garnet

To save space within an application, Palm OS Garnet uses 16-bit memory references, which limits it to relative jumps of 32K. If an application tries to call a function that is located more than 32K away within the same code resource, the jump will fail. For many Palm OS applications, this is not a problem because many applications consist of a single code resource less than 32K in size. For larger applications, however, it may be necessary to extend the processor's jump distance, using techniques described next in the section "Breaking the 32K Barrier."

Even if you are able to break the 32K jump limit, the HotSync architecture puts an absolute limit of slightly under 64K for any resource, which includes the code resources that make up a Palm OS application. If you need to make a Palm OS application with code resources that total larger than 64K in size, you need to break your application into multiple code resources, a process known as *segmenting* your application. The "Segmenting Applications" section later in this chapter describes how to go about breaking your program into smaller bits to work around the 64K limit.

> *Palm OS Cobalt removes the need to segment your application to overcome size limitations in earlier versions of Palm OS. Large Palm OS Protein applications do not need to use multiple segments.*

# Breaking the 32K Barrier

An application larger than 32K in size may generate one or more "16-bit reference out of range" errors at compile time if one function in the application calls another that is more than 32K away in the compiled code. To work around this problem, you have several options:

- ❏ Change the link order of the application's source files.
- ❏ Rearrange your source code.
- ❏ Use the Smart code model in CodeWarrior.
- ❏ Create "code islands" by linking pieces of code that are more than 32K apart.

## Changing Link Order

In CodeWarrior, you may be able to prevent an "out of range" error by rearranging the order in which CodeWarrior links your application's source files. The Segment view in the project window allows you to change the link order; Figure 24-1 shows the Segments view for a typical application.

Figure 24-1

To figure out which source files to relocate in the Segments view, take a look at the "16-bit reference out of range" errors produced during compilation. These errors will let you know which functions are attempting to call functions that are more than 32K away. Find the source files that contain each of the offending routines and drag those source files closer to one another in the Segments view.

The same reordering process can be performed using PODS by shuffling the order of your source files in the project's makefile. It might take a bit of experimentation to come up with an order that works, however.

*This technique is effective only to a certain point. The larger and more complex your application is, the greater the chance that you will not be able to resolve "out of range" errors simply by rearranging the link order. If that is the case, you need to either try one of the other methods in this section or consider segmenting your application.*

## Rearranging Your Source Code

It also is possible to work around some jump limitations by simply rearranging your source code within each source file. Try to group functions that call one another closer together within a source file.

Like changing the application's link order, reordering your source code is effective only to a certain point. Also, this way of circumventing the 32K jump limit can lead to code that is hard to maintain. If you or some other developer makes changes to the source at a later date, the program may suddenly stop compiling for seemingly mysterious reasons as you shift the source code around in its file.

## Using the Smart Code Model

In CodeWarrior, you can enable the Smart code model option, which tells the compiler to use 32-bit jumps, rather than the usual 16-bit jumps, for references that are out of range. To accomplish this task, the compiler and linker have to add a fair amount of code to your application to produce each 32-bit jump, so this option can lead to code bloat very quickly if your application needs to make a lot of long-distance jumps.

> **If your application is hovering just under 64K in size, this option can actually bloat the code enough that it will no longer fit in a Palm OS code resource, in which case you are better off segmenting your application.**

To enable the Smart code model, open the project's target settings panel with the Edit ⇨ *target* settings menu command, where *target* is the name of your project. Under Code Generation in the Target Settings Panels list, select the 68k Processor list item, which will change the settings panel to look something like Figure 24-2. In the Code Model drop-down, select Smart to enable the Smart code model.

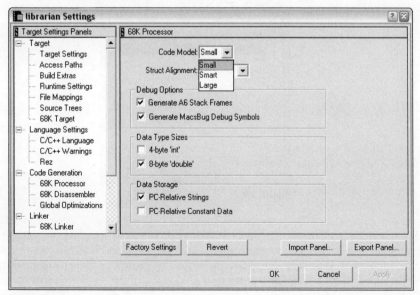

Figure 24-2

## Creating Code Islands

If you have only a few function calls that are out of range, you can work around the 32K jump limit by creating code islands, also known as *jump islands*, in your application code. A *code island* is simply a small function, located within 32K of both a calling function and the distant function that needs to be called, whose only purpose is to call the function that is normally out of range. Such code islands give a long-distance jump a place to "land" before moving on to the actual function the jump is trying to call.

Just as with rearranging your code, code islands can become a maintainer's nightmare. Be sure to carefully comment both the code island and any calls to the code island to prevent you or another developer from breaking the jump by adding excess code between the calling function and the island, or between the island and the function it calls.

# Segmenting Applications in Palm OS Garnet

If your Palm OS Garnet application is larger than 64K, you will need to build it as a *multisegment application*. A multisegment application is made of more than one code resource, or *segment*. This section describes how to create a multisegment application using CodeWarrior and the Palm OS Developer Suite (PODS).

> *Palm OS Cobalt removes the need to segment your application to overcome size limitations in earlier versions of Palm OS. Large Cobalt applications do not need to use multiple segments.*

## Segmenting Applications with CodeWarrior

If you know from the start that you are creating an enormous application, you can use CodeWarrior's project stationery for a multisegment application. When you first create a new project, select Palm OS Multi-Segment App from the New Project dialog box, pictured in Figure 24-3, and CodeWarrior creates a multisegment project for you, including all the linker settings required to properly build the project.

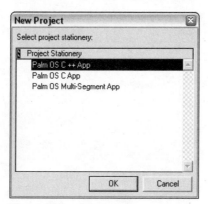

Figure 24-3

By default, CodeWarrior's Palm OS Application Wizard produces a project whose settings are appropriate for compilation as a multisegment application. Unless you choose "Single-segment C application" in the wizard's Application Type drop-down list, the project generated by the wizard is ready for you to add new code segments to, as described in the following paragraphs.

You can control the different code resources that make up a large project in the project window's Segments view. Figure 24-4 shows the Segments view for a typical multisegment application.

Figure 24-4

The first segment in a large application is segment 0, which the linker creates to hold startup data and code that the application uses at runtime to set up the other segments in the application. Segment 0 does not contain any source code that you can change so it does not appear in the Segments view.

Segment 1, which must appear first in the Segments view, is where the source file containing the application's `PilotMain` function should go. Also, any functions called directly from `PilotMain` during anything other than the `sysAppLaunchCmdNormalLaunch` or `sysAppLaunchCmdGoTo` launch codes must be part of the first segment.

> *The requirement that such functions must be in the first segment stems from the fact that the system keeps pointers to code resources in the application's global variable space. When global variables are available, which happens during the `sysAppLaunchCmdNormalLaunch` and `sysAppLaunchCmdGoTo` launch codes, code outside segment 1 is accessible. If global variables are not available, there is no way for the system to access functions outside the first segment. Functions that `PilotMain` calls when global variables are not available must, therefore, be part of the first segment because without a global variable space there is no way for the system to call code outside segment 1.*

Along with the source containing `PilotMain` and its related functions, the first segment also must contain a reference to the file `PalmOSRuntime_xx_A5.lib`, where *xx* is either `4i` or `2i`, depending upon settings in the 68K Processor panel, shown earlier in Figure 24-2. If the 4-Byte Ints check box is selected, the `4i` library should be used; otherwise, the `2i` library should be included.

Later segments in the application may contain any other application code. PalmSource recommends that you use each segment to contain code that implements related features. For example, a form's event handler and the routines it calls would fit nicely into a single segment.

To figure out exactly which source files can be located outside segment 1, do the following:

1.    Comment out the code in your `PilotMain` function that handles the `sysAppLaunchCmdNormalLaunch` and `sysAppLaunchCmdGoTo` launch codes.

2.    Open the target settings dialog box and select 68K Linker from the Target Settings Panels list to display the 68K Linker panel. Check the Generate Link Map check box. Click Save and close the dialog box.

3.    Rebuild your application.

CodeWarrior creates a file named *project*.map, where *project* is the name of your project that shows the link map for your application. Within the link map, references to files in segment 1 that begin with the phrase `Code:` must remain located in segment 1.

> *You can ignore functions in the link map that begin and end with a double underscore (\_\_); these are system functions.*

To add another segment to the application, select Project ⇨ Create New Segment. The Segment Info dialog box, shown in Figure 24-5, appears.

**Figure 24-5**

Enter a name for the segment in the Name text box, and then click OK. The Segment Attributes in the Segment Info dialog box have no meaning for Palm OS development; CodeWarrior ignores these settings when building a Palm OS application. You can add source files to a particular segment by selecting the segment in the project window and then selecting Project ⇨ Add Files from the menu bar. Moving source files from one segment to another is a simple matter of clicking and dragging them around the project window.

> *To rename a segment, double-click its name in the Segments view. The Segment Info dialog box appears, allowing you to change the segment's name. Segment names are entirely for your convenience; CodeWarrior does not build segment names into a `.prc` file in any way.*

## Converting a Small Application to a Large Application

As you add new features to an application during its lifetime, you may find that an application that once fit nicely into the 64K limit has grown too large to be a single-segment application. Fortunately, it is not very difficult to convert a small application into a multisegment application. Follow these steps:

1. Select the Targets tab in the project window to display the Target view.

2. Choose Project ➪ Create New Target. The New Target dialog box, shown in Figure 24-6, appears. Give the target a name, and choose the option to Clone an existing target. Pick a target from the existing project from the drop-down list, and then click OK.

**Figure 24-6**

3. In the Target view, pick the newly created target from the drop-down list so it is the current target for the project.

4. Select Edit ➪ *target* settings, where *target* is the name of the target you just created, or double-click the new target's name in the project window.

5. Select 68K Linker from the Target Settings Panels list. Ensure that the Link Single Segment check box is not selected. Click the Save button and close the dialog box.

6. Select the Segments tab in the project window to display the Segments view.

7. Replace the `StartupCode.lib` library with `PalmOSRuntime_2i_A5.lib` or `PalmOSRuntime_4i_A5`, depending upon your project's 4-Byte Ints setting in the 68K Processor panel.

8. Add segments to the application and rearrange the source code files in the project window until you have the code in the desired segments. Keep in mind that certain files must be located in the first segment in the list: the runtime library, any source file containing `PilotMain`, and any source file containing routines that `PilotMain` calls when processing any launch code other than `sysAppLaunchCmdNormalLaunch` or `sysAppLaunchCmdGoTo`. If `PilotMain` and its associated function calls are located in the same source file with other application code, you may need to create a new source file and separate the code into the new file before you can rearrange the link order.

## Segmenting Applications with the Palm OS Developer Suite

Creating multisegment 68k applications in PODS is supported but is not nearly as easy to accomplish as in CodeWarrior.

*In PODS, the term "multisection" is used instead of the traditional "multisegment" terminology.*

PODS 1.0 does not offer a project-level mechanism for breaking your Palm OS Garnet project into multiple segments. Rather, PODS relies on a special definition file called `Sections.def`, which lists out the segments you wish to maintain in your project. These sections must then be referenced as part of each function implemented in your source code. This method of handling segments is inherited from the original PRC-Tools 68K gcc component, which required explicit segmentation through a sections file.

To understand how this works, imagine a Palm OS Garnet project "BigApp," which you wish to set up with three segments. To accomplish this, the following would need to be implemented:

1.  In the PODS makefile for the project, include the statement

```
MULTIPLE_CODE_SECTIONS = TRUE
```

2.  Add to your project a file named Sections.def. This file should contain two lines as follows:

```
application { "BigApp" BIGAPP }

multiple code { "segment1" "segment2" "segment3" }
```

3.  Create a header file called Sections.h, which defines a name for each of your segments that can be referenced at compile time from your source code. This step ties the "section name" from Sections.def to a header-defined name. For BigApp, this header file would contain the following:

```
#ifndef _SECTIONS_H
#define _SECTIONS_H

#define CODESEGMENT1    __attribute__ ((section ("segment1")))

#define CODESEGMENT2    __attribute__ ((section ("segment2")))

#define CODESEGMENT3    __attribute__ ((section ("segment3")))

#endif
```

4.  In your source code, annotate each function with the name of the section definition representing the segment you wish the function to belong to. It is important to recognize that segment assignments are done at the function level, not the source file level, so each and every function needs to be annotated, or it will be assigned to the default first segment. Given a function foo() that we wish to have assigned to the second code segment of BigApp, the code would look like the following:

```
void foo(void) CODESEGMENT2;
```

Because segment assignments need to be set on a function-by-function basis, this mechanism clearly requires some forethought when planning your application development. The PODS segmentation method also makes sharing common toolbox source code across multiple Palm OS applications problematic because the number of segments and ordering in each Palm OS project are likely to be different. If you are planning to develop a large application that must be compatible with Palm OS Garnet, you may wish to consider the segmentation issue before choosing CodeWarrior or PODS as your development environment.

# Adding Custom Fonts to Palm OS Garnet Applications

The fonts that come with Palm OS are typically sufficient for most applications, but they do have their limitations. For one thing, the default fonts all have proportional spacing, which makes them particularly unsuitable for displaying things such as computer source code, which is much easier to read in a monospaced font. If you want some kind of decorative font for use in a game, you also are out of luck with the default fonts because they are very simple sans-serif fonts, designed to be easy to read and, at the same time, occupy as little screen space as possible.

*The custom font techniques described here apply to Palm OS Garnet only. Palm OS Cobalt ARM applications do not support the NFNT resource type. Developers interested in creating custom fonts for use on Palm OS Cobalt must instead create scalable "fttf" resources, which are wrappers around a TrueType font specification. Refer to the Palm OS Cobalt developer documentation for more information on adding a custom TrueType font to a Palm OS Cobalt handheld.*

You can create your own custom fonts for Palm OS Garnet. A font is a resource of type NFNT. On Palm OS 3 through Palm OS Garnet, you can use an NFNT resource in an application by calling FntDefineFont. You can use a custom font only from within the application that holds the font resource. The FntDefineFont function's prototype looks like this:

```
Err FntDefineFont (FontID font, FontPtr fontP)
```

The font parameter is an application-specific identification number for the font. Values less than fntAppFontCustomBase (defined in Font.h as 128) are reserved for system use so a custom font must have an ID equal to or greater than fntAppFontCustomBase. The fontP parameter takes a pointer to the locked font resource. As an example, the following lines of code lock a custom font resource and set it up for use in an application:

```
#define fntCustom fntAppFontCustomBase

FontType  *fontCustom;

fontCustom = MemHandleLock(DmGetResource('NFNT',
                          MyCustomFont));
FntDefineFont(fntCustom, fontCustom);
```

Once you have called FntDefineFont to define the custom font's ID, you can use that font ID as you would any other font ID. When the application exits, the system uninstalls the font so your application will need to reinstall it by calling FntDefineFont each time the application runs.

*You must keep the custom font resource locked until the application either quits or no longer needs to use the font.*

On versions of Palm OS prior to 3.0, the FntDefineFont function does not exist, but you can still use custom fonts with a little judicious hacking. By setting the user interface global variable UICurrentFontPtr, you can trick the system into using your custom font:

```
void *fontOld;
void *fontCustom;

// Save the current font.
fontOld = UICurrentFontPtr;

fontCustom = MemHandleLock(DmGetResource('NFNT',
                          MyCustomfont));
UICurrentFontPtr = fontCustom;

// Perform any drawing operations that use the custom font.

// Unlock the pointer to the custom font.
MemPtrUnlock(fontCustom);

// Restore the original font.
UICurrentFontPtr = fontOld;
```

There are limitations to using custom fonts. Constructor does not allow you to assign a custom font to form elements when you are building resources so if you use the CodeWarrior IDE to create your application, you will not be able to assign a custom font to anything on a form at design time. You can work around this problem at runtime, however, by setting the font of form elements programmatically before displaying the form. The FldSetFont function sets the font for a text field, and the PalmOSGlue library has functions for changing the fonts of other form elements, including CtlGlueSetFont for controls and LstGlueSetFont for lists.

Using custom fonts in form elements is much simpler if you build your resources with PilRC. Simply specify the font ID of the custom font when designing your form resources, as in the following example:

```
BUTTON "New" ID MainNewButton AT (1 147 26 12) FONT 128
```

## Creating a Custom Font

As of this writing, CodeWarrior's Constructor tool is not able to create custom fonts, but PilRC can. There also are a few shareware and freeware applications, for both Windows and the Mac OS, for creating new fonts on the desktop in a graphical environment, or for converting existing desktop fonts into resources that you can compile into an application using either CodeWarrior or the PRC-Tools.

Unfortunately, even with a good desktop font creation tool, Constructor still cannot use custom fonts in form elements. PilRC, on the other hand, is perfectly capable of building forms that contain custom fonts, provided the font definition comes first in the .rcp file, before any use of the custom font in a form. Another requirement for build-time use of custom fonts in PilRC is that the application whose forms contain the custom fonts must be running on Palm OS 3.0 or later.

It is possible to include fonts created with PilRC in a CodeWarrior project by using the PilRC Plugin. Constructor provides no way to use a PilRC custom font when creating forms, but the runtime techniques described earlier in this chapter work perfectly in a program built by CodeWarrior. See the sidebar "Using the PilRC Plugin with CodeWarrior" in Chapter 6 for more details about adding PilRC resources to a CodeWarrior project with the PilRC Plugin. Note that the PilRC Plugin is not required for CodeWarrior 9 users because it is now called from within the IDE.

The PilRC directive for creating a font resource looks like this:

```
FONT ID resourceID FONTID fontID "fontFile"
```

The `fontID` should be the same font ID number that you pass to the `FntDefineFont` function (a number between 128 and 255, inclusive), and `fontFile` specifies a text file that defines the font. For example, the following line creates a font resource from a font definition file called `myfont.txt`:

```
FONT ID 1000 FONTID 128 "myfont.txt"
```

A font definition file is a standard ASCII text file, consisting of some header information followed by the definitions for individual characters, or glyphs, that make up the font. The header for a font looks like this:

```
fontType 36864
ascent ascentValue
descent descentValue
fRectWidth fontWidth
fRectHeight fontHeight
```

The `fontType` is a magic number that is present in all the default Palm OS fonts. David Turnbull, the author of the font compiler in PilRC, created the compiler by reverse-engineering the existing default Palm OS fonts, so the `fontType` number is something of a mystery; rest assured, your font should work fine if you include `fontType 36864` at the head of the font definition.

Both `ascent` and `descent` are values that you do not have to take on faith. The `ascent` value is the number of pixels that make up the part of each glyph above the font's baseline, where the bottoms of most characters are. Most characters in a font sit directly on or above the baseline, but some, such as *q* and *y*, typically have a part (known in conventional typography as a descender) that dips below the baseline. The `descent` value specifies how many pixels are below the baseline in each glyph. A font's total height is equal to the ascent plus the descent.

The `fRectWidth` and `fRectHeight` values are entirely optional. These two header lines define the width and height of the font, respectively. If you omit `fRectWidth`, PilRC uses the width of the widest character in the font. If you omit `fRectHeight`, PilRC uses the height of the first character in the font.

As an example, the following header section defines a font with an ascent of 9 and a descent of 2, for a total height of 11:

```
fontType 36864
ascent 9
descent 2
```

Following the header are the definitions for individual glyphs in the font. Each glyph definition begins with the word `GLYPH`, followed by either the ASCII number of the character this glyph represents or the actual character itself, surrounded by single quotes. For example, the following `GLYPH` statements are equivalent, both representing a space character:

```
GLYPH 32

GLYPH ' '
```

*To define a glyph for the single quote character ( '), use GLYPH 39; using GLYPH ' ' ' will not work.*

Following the GLYPH line are several lines that define what the bitmap image of the glyph looks like. A bitmap line consists of hyphen (-) or period (.) characters to represent pixels that are turned off, and any other characters to represent pixels that are turned on. For example, the following glyph defines a letter *A*:

```
GLYPH 'A'
----------
----#-----
---#-#----
---#-#----
--#---#---
--#####---
-#-----#--
-#-----#--
###---###-
----------
----------
```

Keep in mind that all the glyph definitions in your font should be exactly the same number of lines high. Even a tiny character, such as a period, needs to have empty pixels above and below it so its height is the same as that of other glyphs in the font. For example, the following period glyph would work with the *A* defined previously:

```
GLYPH '.'
---
---
---
---
---
---
---
##-
##-
---
---
```

*To make a font more readable, include a pixel of blank space to the right of each glyph to keep the characters from running into one another. You also should leave a pixel of blank space at the top of each character, so descending parts of glyphs do not collide with the tops of tall letters on the next line of text.*

The last character in a font definition file must be GLYPH -1, which the system uses as a placeholder for characters that are not defined in the font. Typically, GLYPH -1 is drawn as a rectangle, as in the following example:

```
GLYPH -1
----------
##########
#--------#
#--------#
#--------#
#--------#
#--------#
#--------#
##########
----------
----------
```

# Creating a User Interface Dynamically

For most applications, the user interface elements on a form are static; there is no need to move them around at runtime. Even if you have an element that you want to hide or show only in response to user input, the best way to accomplish this is to include the element as part of a form's normal resources and then make it disappear and reappear at runtime by invoking the FrmHideObject or FrmShowObject functions. Vanishing form elements can be very confusing to a new user and usually make for a bad user interface.

If your application does need to create new forms at runtime or add elements to existing forms, note that Palm OS version 3.0 and later offers functions for creating a user interface dynamically — while an application is running. An example of an application where this might be useful is a database program that allows the user to create custom input forms.

The FrmNewForm function allows you to create a new form in Palm OS Garnet and Palm OS Cobalt, and it has the following prototype:

**Palm OS Garnet**

```
FormType *FrmNewForm (UInt16 formID, const Char *titleStrP,
    Coord x, Coord y, Coord width, Coord height,
    Boolean modal, UInt16 defaultButton, UInt16 helpRscID,
    UInt16 menuRscID)
```

**Palm OS Cobalt**

```
FormType *FrmNewForm (uint16_t formID, const char *titleStrP,
    Coord x, Coord y, Coord width, Coord height,
    Boolean modal, uint16_t defaultButton,
    DmOpenRef dbHelpRsc, uint16_t helpRscID,
    DmOpenRef dbMenuRsc, uint16_t menuRscID)
```

The difference between Palm OS Garnet and Palm OS Cobalt versions of FrmNewForm is that as with most UI functions, Palm OS Cobalt requires that you provide a DmOpenRef for the specific database that contains the requested resource. Thus the helpRscID and menuRscID parameters now each require a DmOpenRef parameter as well.

As a return value, FrmNewForm gives you a pointer to the newly created form, or 0 if the call did not succeed. The most common reason that FrmNewForm, or any of the dynamic UI functions, might fail is lack of available memory.

*Unlike a normal form resource, there is no need to call* `FrmInitForm` *with a dynamically created form.*

The following table describes each of the parameters to `FrmNewForm`.

| Parameter | Description |
|---|---|
| formID | ID to assign to the form. |
| titleStrP | Pointer to a string to use for the form's title. |
| x | Horizontal coordinate of the form's upper left corner. |
| y | Vertical coordinate of the form's upper left corner. |
| width | Width of the form in pixels; must be 1–160, inclusive. |
| height | Height of the form in pixels, must be 1–160, inclusive. |
| modal | If `true`, the form ignores pen events outside its borders. |
| defaultButton | ID of the form's default button, which the system simulates tapping if the user switches applications while the form is displayed. |
| dbHelpRsc | `DmOpenRef` database handle. Specifies the resource database that contains the help text resources referred to by the `helpRscID` parameter. (Palm OS Cobalt only.) |
| helpRscID | ID of a string resource that contains help text for the dialog box; only modal dialog boxes can have help text. |
| dbMenuRsc | `DmOpenRef` database handle. Specifies the resource database that contains the menu resources referred to by the `helpRscID` parameter. (Palm OS Cobalt only.) |
| menuRscID | ID of the menu bar resource that should be attached to the form. Note that you cannot dynamically create menu resources, so if you want menus for a dynamically generated form, you must attach the form to pre-existing menu resources. |

When creating any form or UI object dynamically, be careful not to use an ID that already exists for another object. A good way to avoid reusing ID numbers is to reserve a block of numbers that are used only for dynamic UI. When the application starts, set a global variable to the first number in this pool of ID numbers, and any time you create a new object, increment the variable so you will never use the same number twice. Here is a quick example:

```
#define DYNAMIC_UI_START 6000
UInt16 gNextID = DYNAMIC_UI_START;
// When creating a new object, increment gNextID:
newLabelPtr = FrmNewLabel(form, gNextID++, text,
                          x, y, stdFont);
```

An application may add user interface elements to forms that it creates dynamically, or to existing static forms, using a variety of functions. The only UI element that an application cannot create dynamically is a table. Also, some of the routines for creating user interface elements are restricted to certain versions of Palm OS. The following table lists the functions for creating individual form elements, along with the earliest version of Palm OS that supports the function and what element each function creates.

| Function | Minimum Palm OS Version | UI Element(s) |
|---|---|---|
| CtlNewControl | 3.0 | Controls: buttons, push buttons, repeating buttons, check boxes, pop-up triggers, or selector triggers |
| CtlNewGraphicControl | 3.5 | Graphic controls: buttons, push buttons, repeating buttons, pop-up triggers, or selector triggers |
| CtlNewSliderControl | 3.5 | Slider |
| FldNewField | 3.0 | Text field |
| FrmNewBitmap | 3.0 | Form bitmap |
| FrmNewGadget | 3.0 | Gadget |
| FrmNewGsi | 3.5 | Graffiti shift indicator |
| FrmNewLabel | 3.0 | Label |
| LstNewList | 3.0 | List |

As an example of a typical member of this group of functions, here is the prototype for CtlNewControl:

**Palm OS Garnet**
```
ControlType *CtlNewControl (void **formPP, UInt16 ID,
    ControlStyleType style, const Char *textP, Coord x,
    Coord y, Coord width, Coord height, FontID font,
    UInt8 group, Boolean leftAnchor)
```

**Palm OS Cobalt**
```
ControlType *CtlNewControl (void **formPP, uint16_t ID,
    ControlStyleType style, const char *textP, Coord x,
    Coord y, Coord width, Coord height, FontID font,
    uint8_t group, Boolean leftAnchor)
```

All of the UI creation functions share the same first parameter: formPP. The formPP parameter is a pointer to a pointer to the form where the new element should be installed. Unlike many pointers to pointers in Palm OS, formPP is not actually a handle. To accommodate the addition of another user interface element, the system may need to move the entire form structure in memory, which makes the original value of formPP, as you pass it to the function, invalid. Fortunately, if the dynamic UI functions need to move the form, they return the form's new location in the formPP parameter. Be sure to always use the new value returned in formPP and discard whatever value you originally passed in for the formPP parameter.

A pair of other parameters are shared by all the dynamic UI functions; x and y always specify the coordinates of the upper left corner of the user interface element, relative to the form that contains it. Most of the functions also have width and height parameters, which contain the width and height of the element, in pixels. Many of the functions also have an ID or id parameter, which is where you specify the ID number that you will use to refer to the element elsewhere in your application.

When creating a control with CtlNewControl or CtlNewGraphicControl, you need to specify exactly what type of control you want by supplying the style parameter. Values for style come from the ControlStyleType enumerated type, which looks like this:

```
enum controlStyles {
    buttonCtl,
    pushButtonCtl,
    checkboxCtl,
    popupTriggerCtl,
    selectorTriggerCtl,
    repeatingButtonCtl,
    sliderCtl,
    feedbackSliderCtl
};
typedef enum controlStyles ControlStyleType;
```

*Not all of the members of ControlStyleType are available for use with CtlNewControl or CtlNewGraphicControl. In particular, sliderCtl and feedbackSliderCtl may be used only with the CtlNewSliderControl function, and CtlNewGraphicControl cannot have a style type of checkboxCtl.*

Before closing a form containing dynamic UI elements, you need to call FrmRemoveObject to remove each dynamic object. The FrmRemoveObject function has the following prototype:

**Palm OS Garnet**
```
Err FrmRemoveObject (FormType **formPP, UInt16 objIndex)
```

**Palm OS Cobalt**
```
Status_t FrmRemoveObject (FormType **formPP, uint16_t objIndex)
```

The formPP parameter of FrmRemoveObject works in the same fashion as the formPP parameter of the UI element creation functions. This formPP also is not a handle, and you should discard whatever value you pass for formPP in favor of the value returned in formPP by the FrmRemoveObject function. When FrmRemoveObject removes a UI element, it does not free any memory associated with the object itself, such as the string data attached to a text field. The FrmRemoveObject function does shrink the memory chunk allocated to a form's data structure because the function frees the memory occupied by the object within the form structure itself.

Also, keep in mind that the FrmRemoveObject function's objIndex parameter requires the index of an object, not its ID number. As with any user interface object, you can retrieve the index by passing the object's ID to the FrmGetObjectIndex function.

*For more efficient removal of several form objects, remove them in descending index order (that is, call FrmRemoveObject on objects with higher index values before removing objects with low index values). Removing objects in this order reduces the amount of shuffling that FrmRemoveObject must do when filling in the hole left by the removed object's data because higher-indexed objects are at the end of the form's data structure.*

A common problem when programming a dynamic user interface is accidentally using invalid pointers to controls and forms. During debugging, you can use `CtlValidatePointer` and `FrmValidatePtr` to ensure that pointers are valid before trying to use them. The prototypes for these two functions look like this:

```
Boolean CtlValidatePointer (const ControlType *controlP);

Boolean FrmValidatePtr (const FormType *formP);
```

Both functions return `true` if the pointer you pass to them is a valid pointer to a control or a form. Use these functions only for debugging, however; leaving them in a released application adds bloat to the code.

# Localizing Applications

Creating applications that can display text in multiple human languages is easily one of the most challenging tasks in software development. Not only do you need to be careful to put display text only in the application's resources instead of hard-coding it, but there also are major problems in creating an application that can support both the standard ASCII text sufficient for the display of most Western languages and the multiple-byte character encoding used for most Asian languages. In addition to text differences, different countries also format numbers and dates differently, further adding to the confusion.

Fortunately, the folks at PalmSource have provided tools and functions within Palm OS to make the often arduous task of localizing an application much easier. The text and international managers, available in most versions of Palm OS since version 3.1 including Palm OS Garnet and Palm OS Cobalt, offer functions for working with localized strings and characters.

## Using the Text and International Managers

Since Palm OS 3.1, PalmSource has included the text and international managers as part of the operating system. Before using any text or international manager functions, check for the existence of the international manager with the `FtrGet` function:

```
UInt32  value;

Err error = FtrGet (sysFtrCreator, sysFtrNumIntlMgr,
                    &value);
```

If the international manager is installed, `value` will be a non-zero value, and the error return value will be `0`. The text and international managers are inseparable companions, so once you ascertain that the international manager exists, you can be certain that the text manager is also available.

The international manager detects the character encoding used by the system and uses this information to set up the text manager. Application code hardly ever interacts with the international manager directly; the manager operates in the background most of the time.

The text manager provides functions for manipulating strings and character data, regardless of what character encoding is in use on the system. In particular, text manager functions allow you to safely deal with both single- and multiple-byte character sets using the same set of text-handling functions. If you stick with using text manager calls instead of directly modifying text data, you should not need to change your application's code to handle different styles of character encoding.

Many of the "functions" included in the text manager are multiple-byte-aware versions of the C standard library character macros. For example, the text manager's TxtCharIsDigit macro duplicates the effects of the isdigit macro, but unlike isdigit, TxtCharIsDigit knows about multiple-byte character encoding, so it can properly determine whether a multiple-byte character is a digit. For more information about the various character macros, see the section "Using Character Macros" in Chapter 10.

## Comparing and Finding Text

Two particularly useful functions in the text manager are TxtCompare and TxtCaselessCompare, which allow you to compare the contents of two text buffers. The TxtCompare function is a case-sensitive comparison, and TxtCaselessCompare ignores case. The prototypes for TxtCompare are nearly identical; here is the prototype for TxtCompare:

**Palm OS Garnet**
```
Int16 TxtCompare (const Char* s1, UInt16 s1Len,
    UInt16* s1MatchLen, const Char* s2, UInt16 s2Len,
    UInt16* s2MatchLen)
```

**Palm OS Cobalt**
```
int16 TxtCompare (const char* s1, uint16_t s1Len,
    uint16_t* s1MatchLen, const char* s2, uint16_t s2Len,
    uint16_t* s2MatchLen)
```

Both functions return a value less than zero if the text in s1 occurs before the text in s2 alphabetically. The return value is greater than zero if s2 comes before s1 in alphabetical order, and the return value is exactly 0 if both text buffers are equal. Along with the pointers to the two text buffers, you also should supply the lengths of the respective buffers in the s1Len and s2Len parameters.

*Both s1 and s2 must point to the start of a valid character, which means either the first byte of a multiple-byte character, or a single-byte character. Pointing to the middle of a multiple-byte character will lead to unpredictable (and messy) results. This is true of text input parameters for any text manager function.*

The TxtCompare and TxtCaselessCompare functions return the length in bytes of the text that matches exactly between s1 and s2 in the s1MatchLen and s2MatchLen parameters. The byte lengths in s1MatchLen and s2MatchLen might differ because some character encodings, such as Shift-JIS for the Japanese language, can represent the same character as both single- and multiple-byte characters. If you are not interested in the amount of matching text between the two text buffers, pass NULL for s1MatchLen and s2MatchLen.

Another function in the text manager is TxtFindString, which finds an occurrence of one string inside another. The search that TxtFindString performs is case-insensitive, and it makes a fine multiple-byte-aware replacement for FindStrInStr when you are implementing the global find facility. For more information about implementing global find, take a look at the section "Implementing the Global Find Facility" in Chapter 16.

The prototype for `TxtFindString` looks like this:

**Palm OS Garnet**
```
Boolean TxtFindString (const Char* inSourceStr,
    const Char* inTargetStr, UInt32* outPos,
    UInt16* outLength)
```

**Palm OS Cobalt**
```
Boolean TxtFindString (const char* inSourceStr,
    const char* inTargetStr, size_t* outPos,
    size_t* outLength)
```

The `inSourceStr` parameter should point to the string that should be searched, and `inTargetStr` should point to the string in `inSourceStr` that you want to find. If `TxtFindString` finds `inTargetStr` within `inSourceStr`, the function returns `true`; otherwise, `TxtFindString` returns `false`. On a successful find, `TxtFindString` returns the byte offset of the beginning of `inTargetStr` within `inSourceStr` in the `outPos` parameter and the length of the matching text in `outLength`. The `TxtFindString` function sets the values of `outPos` and `outLength` to 0 on an unsuccessful search.

## Modifying Text

The `TxtTransliterate` function allows you to convert all the characters in a text buffer from one form to another. For example, `TxtTransliterate` may be used to change all the characters in a text buffer to uppercase. The prototype for `TxtTransliterate` looks like this:

**Palm OS Garnet**
```
Err TxtTransliterate (const Char* inSrcText,
    UInt16 inSrcLength, Char* outDstText,
    UInt16* ioDstLength, TranslitOpType inOp)
```

**Palm OS Cobalt**
```
status_t TxtTransliterate (const char* inSrcText,
    size_t inSrcLength, char* outDstText,
    size_t* ioDstLength, TranslitOpType inOp)
```

The `inSrcText` parameter points to the source text buffer you want to modify, and `inSrcLength` specifies the length of that buffer in bytes. You also need to supply a pointer to an output buffer via `outDstText` and specify the maximum length of that buffer in `ioDstLength`. When `TxtTransliterate` returns, it modifies the value in `ioDstLength` to reflect the actual length of the transformed text in `outDstText`.

You control exactly what `TxtTransliterate` does to the text in `inSrcText` by specifying an operation code in the `inOp` parameter. Operation codes are specific to the character encoding currently in use on the handheld, but two operations are always available: `translitOpUpperCase`, which converts all the text to uppercase, and `translitOpLowerCase`, which converts the text to lowercase. Both case conversion operations are useful for reducing a string to a single case for faster case-insensitive comparison with another string. The Palm OS header file `TextMgr.h` defines a base number for operations that are character encoding–specific:

```
#define translitOpCustomBase 1000
```

Within the header files for specific character encodings, other transliteration operations use `translitOpCustomBase` as a base value. For example, the following operations are defined in `CharShiftJIS.h` for Shift-JIS encoding:

```
#define translitOpFullToHalfKatakana \
        (translitOpCustomBase+0)
#define translitOpHalfToFullKatakana \
        (translitOpCustomBase+1)
#define translitOpFullToHalfRomaji   \
        (translitOpCustomBase+2)
#define translitOpHalfToFullRomaji   \
        (translitOpCustomBase+3)
#define translitOpKatakanaToHiragana \
        (translitOpCustomBase+4)
#define translitOpHiraganaToKatakana \
        (translitOpCustomBase+5)
#define translitOpCombineSoundMark   \
        (translitOpCustomBase+6)
#define translitOpDivideSoundMark    \
        (translitOpCustomBase+7)
#define translitOpRomajiToHiragana   \
        (translitOpCustomBase+8)
#define translitOpHiraganaToRomaji   \
        (translitOpCustomBase+9)
```

Along with the regular operation codes, you also can combine the `translitOpPreprocess` mask constant with any code using the bitwise OR operator (`|`). This causes `TxtTransliterate` to find out how much space is required for the transformed string without actually placing the string in the output buffer; the space required is returned in the `ioDstLength` parameter. If you are not sure whether you have enough space allocated to contain the transliterated text, call `TxtTransliterate` using the `translitOpPreprocess` mask before making the actual call. Here is an example:

```
UInt16  buf1Length, buf2Length, outputSize;
Char    *buffer1, *buffer2;


// Point buffer1 at the source text, allocate an output
// buffer, and point buffer2 at the output buffer.

buf1Length = StrLen(buffer1);
buf2Length = StrLen(buffer2);
outputSize = buf2Length;

TxtTransliterate(buffer1, buf1Length, &buffer2,
    &outputSize, translitOpLowerCase |
    translitOpPreprocess);

if (outputSize > buf2Length) {
    // Increase the size of the buffer2 buffer so it can
    // hold outputSize bytes of data.
}
```

```
TxtTransliterate(buffer1, buf1Length, &buffer2,
    &outputSize, translitOpLowerCase);
size_t  buf1Length, buf2Length, outputSize;
char    *buffer1, *buffer2;


// Point buffer1 at the source text, allocate an output
// buffer, and point buffer2 at the output buffer.

buf1Length = StrLen(buffer1);
buf2Length = StrLen(buffer2);
outputSize = buf2Length;

TxtTransliterate(buffer1, buf1Length, &buffer2,
    &outputSize, translitOpLowerCase |
    translitOpPreprocess);

if (outputSize > buf2Length) {
    // Increase the size of the buffer2 buffer so it can
    // hold outputSize bytes of data.
}

TxtTransliterate(buffer1, buf1Length, &buffer2,
    &outputSize, translitOpLowerCase);
```

## Retrieving Characters from a Text Buffer

It can be difficult to do something as simple as retrieving a single character from a text buffer if the buffer contains multiple-byte characters. This phenomenon also makes it difficult to iterate through a text buffer a character at a time, which is necessary for many kinds of text modification. With the proper functions from the text manager, this becomes much easier.

The TxtGetChar function retrieves a single character from a text buffer, given an offset into the buffer in bytes. Here is the prototype for TxtGetChar:

**Palm OS Garnet**
```
WChar TxtGetChar (const Char* inText, UInt32 inOffset)
```

**Palm OS Cobalt**
```
Wchar32_t TxtGetChar (const char* inText, size_t inOffset)
```

As with other text manager functions, you are responsible for ensuring that the offset specified in inOffset points to the beginning of a valid character and not to the middle of a multiple-byte character.

If you need to iterate through a text buffer, use the TxtGetNextChar and TxtGetPreviousChar functions, which look like this:

**Palm OS Garnet**
```
UInt16 TxtGetNextChar (const Char* inText, UInt32 inOffset,
    WChar* outChar);
UInt16 TxtGetPreviousChar (const Char* inText,
    UInt32 inOffset, WChar* outChar);
```

**Palm OS Cobalt**
```
uint16_t TxtGetNextChar (const char* inText, size_t inOffset,
    wchar32_t* outChar);
uint16_t TxtGetPreviousChar (const char* inText,
    size_t inOffset, wchar32_t* outChar);
```

These functions start at the offset specified in inOffset and return either the next or previous character in the outChar parameter. The function return value is the size in bytes of the appropriate character.

*Using the TxtGetPreviousChar function can be slower than using TxtGetNextChar because TxtGetPreviousChar sometimes has to work its way backward through the text buffer byte by byte until it finds an unambiguous beginning of a multibyte character.*

If you want to know only the size of the next or previous character, pass NULL for the outChar parameter in TxtGetNextChar or TxtGetPreviousChar. Alternatively, you can use the TxtNextCharSize and TxtPreviousCharSize macros as follows:

```
TxtNextCharSize (inText, inOffset)
TxtPreviousCharSize (inText, inOffset)
```

Like the TxtGetNextChar and TxtGetPreviousChar functions, TxtNextCharSize and TxtPreviousCharSize return a UInt16 value indicating the size in bytes of the appropriate character.

The nature of multiple-byte characters also makes it difficult to find where you need to truncate a text buffer to fit within a certain size. Use the TxtGetTruncationOffset function to determine where a text buffer should be chopped so it will fit a given number of bytes of memory:

**Palm OS Garnet**
```
UInt32 TxtGetTruncationOffset (const Char* inText,
    UInt32 inOffset)
```

**Palm OS Cobalt**
```
size_t TxtGetTruncationOffset (const char* inText,
    size_t inOffset)
```

The return value from TxtGetTruncationOffset is the offset into inText where the buffer may be safely truncated at an intercharacter boundary; the return value is always less than or equal to the inOffset parameter's value.

Finally, the TxtWordBounds function provides an easy way to find the beginning and end of an actual word in the middle of a text buffer, given an offset into the buffer that points to the beginning of a valid character. The prototype for TxtWordBounds looks like this:

**Palm OS Garnet**
```
Boolean TxtWordBounds (const Char* inText, UInt32 inLength,
    UInt32 inOffset, UInt32* outStart, UInt32* outEnd)
```

**Palm OS Cobalt**
```
Boolean TxtWordBounds (const char* inText, size_t inLength,
    size_t inOffset, size_t* outStart, size_t* outEnd)
```

The `inText` parameter points to the start of the text buffer, `inLength` indicates the length of the buffer, and `inOffset` is the offset around which you want to find a word. The function returns `true` if it finds a word at `inOffset`, or `false` if `inOffset` is at a punctuation or whitespace character. Whitespace characters are those that return `true` when passed to the `TxtCharIsSpace` macro. For example, if you have a string (in ASCII encoding) that contains the string `Find me a word.`, passing an offset of 6 to `TxtWordBounds` will result in `outStart` and `outEnd` values that point to the start and end of the word `me` because an offset of 6 characters into the string is located at the `e` character in the word `me`.

## Determining Character Encoding

The text manager also contains functions for determining the minimum required encoding to represent a particular character or string. The `TxtCharEncoding` function finds the minimum required encoding system necessary to represent a given character, and `TxtStrEncoding` finds the encoding required to represent a string. Prototypes for these functions look like this:

**Palm OS Garnet**
```
CharEncodingType TxtCharEncoding (WChar inChar);
CharEncodingType TxtStrEncoding (const Char* inStr);
```

**Palm OS Cobalt**
```
CharEncodingType TxtCharEncoding (wchar32_t inChar);
CharEncodingType TxtStrEncoding (const char* inStr);
```

The `CharEncodingType` return value from these functions is an enumerated type defined in the Palm OS header file `TextMgr.h` as follows:

```
typedef enum {
    charEncodingUnknown = 0,  // Unknown to this version of
                              // the Palm OS

    charEncodingAscii,        // ISO 646-1991
    charEncodingISO8859_1,    // ISO 8859 Part 1
    charEncodingPalmLatin,    // Palm OS version of CP1252
    charEncodingShiftJIS,     // Encoding for 0208-1990 +
                              //  1-byte katakana
    charEncodingPalmSJIS,     // Palm OS version of CP932
    charEncodingUTF8,         // Encoding for Unicode
    charEncodingCP1252,       // Windows variant of 8859-1
    charEncodingCP932         // Windows variant of ShiftJIS
} CharEncodingType;
```

The minimum coding required for a character is the encoding that requires the fewest bytes. Also, Palm OS supports only a single character encoding at one time, so `TxtCharEncoding` and `TxtStrEncoding` will always return a value equal to or less than the current encoding used by the system, or `charEncodingUnknown` if the character is completely unrecognizable to the current system.

These functions are not a reliable way to determine the current encoding that the system is using. For that purpose, use `FtrGet` to retrieve the current encoding:

**Palm OS Garnet**
```
UInt16 encoding;
Err error = FtrGet(sysFtrCreator, sysFtrNumEncoding,
                   &encoding);
```

Palm OS Cobalt

```
uint16_t encoding;
status_t error = FtrGet(sysFtrCreator, sysFtrNumEncoding,
                        &encoding);
```

The `error` value should be 0, and `encoding` will contain the `CharEncodingType` value for the system's current character encoding.

## Compiling with the PalmOSGlue Library

Even though the text and international managers are not built into Palm OS until version 3.1, you can add these useful managers to applications that support earlier versions of Palm OS, as early as version 2.0. The way to add text and international manager support is to link the PalmOSGlue library into your application.

The PalmOSGlue library contains all the functions in the text manager, but they are named differently: Any function beginning with `Txt` in the text manager starts with `TxtGlue` in the PalmOSGlue library. For example, an application using the PalmOSGlue library should call `TxtGlueCompare`, not `TxtCompare`. See the "Using PalmOSGlue" sidebar in Chapter 8 for more details about linking the PalmOSGlue library with your application.

# Using the File Streaming API

Although the 64K limit on database size in Palm OS Garnet is not a problem for most applications, it can pose a bit of a challenge for applications that must deal with large amounts of data, such as image viewers or long-document readers. For applications that need to handle arbitrarily long data in Palm OS Garnet, Palm OS provides the file streaming API, which is available in Palm OS version 3.0 and later.

For Palm OS Cobalt developers, the 64K database size limit no longer exists, but for some types of applications it may still be advantageous to make use of the standard file I/O function call interface that is provided by file streaming. The file streaming API should not be confused with file storage on an expansion card. To read and write data on an expansion card, use the VFS manager, which is discussed in Chapter 17.

A *file stream* is a block of data with no upper limit on its size, other than the available memory on the handheld. File streams are similar to files on a desktop computer, and they provide permanent storage for data because the mechanism underlying the file streaming API uses standard Palm OS databases for storage. However, the HotSync Manager cannot transfer file streams to the desktop computer during a HotSync operation; you must first convert the file stream data to regular records.

*The performance of the file streaming API is considerably slower than the performance of the data manager. If your application makes extensive use of individual records within its database, the file streaming API may be too slow to provide acceptable performance. File streaming does not work well for data that contains many records because of the overhead of parsing the file stream for those records. Instead, file streaming should be used for data that may be read front-to-back in one pass, such as large images.*

*If your application requires high performance when storing and reading large amounts of data, consider using feature memory instead. For example, applications that play video or audio may find the file streaming API too slow. Feature memory uses memory manager routines for reading and data manager routines for writing, both of which are much faster than the file streaming API. However, feature memory does not persist across system resets, so it is best used for temporary buffers rather than for permanent storage. For more information about using feature memory, see Chapter 15.*

The file streaming functions are based on the `stdio` functions from the C standard library, so if you are used to using `stdio` for handling files, most of the file streaming API will operate exactly as you expect it to. Although there are differences between the file streaming functions and those in the `stdio` library, many of the functions in the file streaming API have direct analogs in `stdio`. The table that follows shows the connections between file streaming functions and their counterparts in `stdio`.

| File Streaming Function | stdio Analog |
|---|---|
| FileClearError | clearerr |
| FileClose | fclose |
| FileEOF | feof |
| FileError | ferror |
| FileOpen | fopen |
| FileRead | fread |
| FileRewind | rewind |
| FileSeek | fseek |
| FileTell | ftell |
| FileWrite | fwrite |

## Opening File Streams

To open an existing file stream or create a brand new one, call `FileOpen`. The `FileOpen` function has the following prototype:

**Palm OS Garnet**
```
FileHand FileOpen (UInt16 cardNo, Char* nameP, UInt32 type,
    UInt32 creator, UInt32 openMode, Err* errP)
```

**Palm OS Cobalt**
```
FileHand FileOpen (const char* nameP, uint32_t type,
    uint32_t creator, uint32_t openMode, status_t* errP)
```

On a successful call, `FileOpen` returns a handle to the newly opened or created file stream. An application should pass this handle to other file streaming functions to perform other operations on the file stream. You can pass a pointer to a variable to receive any errors generated by `FileOpen` in the `errP` parameter. If you are not interested in receiving error values, pass `NULL` for the `errP` parameter. You also can retrieve errors produced by `FileOpen` using the `FileError` function, which is described later in this chapter in the section "Retrieving File Stream Errors."

The `cardNo` parameter is the number of the card containing the file stream; use 0 for this parameter because no current Palm OS handheld actually supports more than one memory card. Point the `nameP` parameter at a string that holds the name of the file stream. This filename follows the same rules as regular Palm OS database names; it may be a maximum of 31 characters in length, and it should be unique among all the database names on the handheld.

Use the `type` and `creator` parameters to specify a database type and creator ID for the file stream. Unlike a regular database, type and creator ID are not required for file streams; you can use them to restrict `FileOpen` to opening only existing file streams that were created with a specific type and creator ID. If you pass 0 for the `type` and `creator` parameters, `FileOpen` treats them as wildcards when opening an existing file stream.

When you're creating a new permanent file stream, a 0 value for `type` will result in a file stream with the constant value `sysFileTFileStream` (defined as `strm` in the Palm OS header file `SystemResources.h`) for its database type. If you specify `fileModeTemporary` for `openMode` and 0 for `type` when creating a new file stream, `FileOpen` creates the new file stream with a database type of `sysFileTTemp` instead, which is defined as `temp` in `SystemResources.h`.

A 0 value for `creator` when `FileOpen` is creating a new file stream causes the function to use the current application's creator ID as the new file stream's creator ID.

The `openMode` parameter is where you tell `FileOpen` what mode it should use when opening a file stream. Possible values for `openMode` are a one primary mode constant, combined using a bitwise or operator (|) with one or more secondary mode constants. The following tables outline the primary mode constants and show the secondary mode constants and what they mean.

| Constant | Description |
|---|---|
| `fileModeReadOnly` | Opens a file stream for read-only access. |
| `fileModeReadWrite` | Opens or creates a file stream for read/write access, first deleting any existing file stream that has the same name as the new file stream. |
| `fileModeUpdate` | Opens or creates a file stream for read/write access, preserving any existing version of the file stream. |
| `fileModeAppend` | Opens or creates a file stream for read/write access, writing new data to the end of the file stream. |

**Be sure to use only one of the primary mode constants. They are mutually exclusive, and you will get an error if you try to combine them.**

| Constant | Description |
|---|---|
| fileModeDontOverwrite | Prevents the fileModeReadWrite mode from throwing away any existing file stream with the same name as the new file stream. This constant may be used only with the fileModeReadWrite primary mode constant. |
| fileModeLeaveOpen | Leaves the file stream open when the application exits. Most applications should not use this option. |
| fileModeExclusive | Prevents other applications from opening the stream until this application has closed it. |
| fileModeAnyTypeCreator | Ignores the type and creator parameters when opening or replacing an existing file stream. |
| fileModeTemporary | Automatically deletes the file stream when it is closed. |

As an example, the following code creates a new file stream and opens it for reading and writing, discarding any existing file stream that has the same name as the new file stream:

**Palm OS Garnet**

```
FileHand  newStream;

newStream = FileOpen(0, "MyNewFileStream", 0, 0,
                  fileModeReadWrite, NULL);
```

**Palm OS Cobalt**

```
FileHand  newStream;

newStream = FileOpen("MyNewFileStream", 0, 0,
                  fileModeReadWrite, NULL);
```

This call to FileOpen opens a file stream for updating, which prevents the removal of an existing file stream that has the same name as the new file stream. The file also is opened in exclusive mode to prevent other applications from modifying the file stream until the current application closes the stream:

**Palm OS Garnet**

```
newStream = FileOpen(0, "MyUpdatedFileStream", 0, 0,
                  fileModeUpdate | fileModeExclusive,
                  NULL);
```

**Palm OS Cobalt**

```
newStream = FileOpen("MyUpdatedFileStream", 0, 0,
                  fileModeUpdate | fileModeExclusive,
                  NULL);
```

Finally, this example creates a temporary file stream, suitable for use in situations where you need a place to cache large amounts of data that will not fit within the system's dynamic memory space:

**Palm OS Garnet**

```
newStream = FileOpen(0, "MyTempFileStream", 0, 0,
                     fileModeReadWrite | fileModeTemporary,
                     NULL);
```

**Palm OS Cobalt**

```
newStream = FileOpen("MyTempFileStream", 0, 0,
                     fileModeReadWrite | fileModeTemporary,
                     NULL);
```

## Closing File Streams

When you have finished using a file stream, close it with `FileClose`. The `FileClose` function has the following prototype:

**Palm OS Garnet**

```
Err FileClose (FileHand stream)
```

**Palm OS Cobalt**

```
status_t FileClose (FileHand stream)
```

The `stream` parameter is the same handle returned from `FileOpen` when it opens the stream. Not only does `FileClose` close a file stream, but it also destroys the stream's handle for you. If you specified the `fileModeTemporary` secondary mode constant when opening the file stream, `FileClose` deletes the file stream as well. The `FileClose` function returns 0 if it successfully closes the file stream, or one of the error codes described in the next section if there is an error.

## Retrieving File Stream Errors

The `FileError` function allows you to retrieve read and write errors for a particular file stream. Whenever an error occurs, an error indicator remains set on the file stream until the stream is closed by `FileClose`. You can use `FileError`, which has the following prototype, to test for read and write errors:

**Palm OS Garnet**

```
Err FileError (FileHand stream)
```

**Palm OS Cobalt**

```
status_t FileError (FileHand stream)
```

The `FileError` function returns 0 if there is currently no error set on the file stream, or it returns an error code describing the error. Several file streaming error codes specify everything from a lack of memory to a generic I/O error.

Instead of calling `FileError`, you also can use `FileGetLastError` to retrieve an error code:

**Palm OS Garnet**

```
Err FileGetLastError (FileHand stream)
```

**Palm OS Cobalt**

```
status_t FileGetLastError (FileHand stream)
```

The major difference between `FileError` and `FileGetLastError` is that the latter function clears the error code value, unless the error is an end-of-file or I/O error.

You also can explicitly clear the error value with the `FileClearerr` function:

**Palm OS Garnet**
```
Err FileClearerr (FileHand stream)
```

**Palm OS Cobalt**
```
status_t FileClearerr (FileHand stream)
```

The `FileClearerr` function clears all file stream errors, including those that `FileGetLastError` cannot clear.

## Deleting File Streams

To delete a file stream, call the `FileDelete` function:

**Palm OS Garnet**
```
Err FileDelete (UInt16 cardNo, Char* nameP)
```

**Palm OS Cobalt**
```
status_t FileDelete (char* nameP, uint32_t creator)
```

You may use `FileDelete` to remove a closed file stream only.

If you want to just truncate a file stream at a certain length, use `FileTruncate`:

**Palm OS Garnet**
```
Err FileTruncate (FileHand stream, Int32 newSize)
```

**Palm OS Cobalt**
```
Status_t FileTruncate (FileHand stream, int32_t newSize)
```

The `newSize` parameter specifies how large the truncated file stream should be. Be sure to keep `newSize` smaller than the current total size of the file stream.

## Setting Position in a File Stream

Every file stream has a current position, which is an offset into the stream that is used for reading and writing data. If you need to change the current position, use the `FileSeek` function, whose prototype looks like this:

**Palm OS Garnet**
```
Err FileSeek (FileHand stream, Int32 offset,
    FileOriginEnum origin)
```

**Palm OS Cobalt**
```
status_t FileSeek (FileHand stream, int32_t offset,
    FileOriginEnum origin)
```

The offset is the number of bytes to seek, relative to whatever origin you specify. The origin may be one of the following constants:

❑ fileOriginBeginning: Beginning of the file stream.

❑ fileOriginCurrent: Current position in the file stream.

❑ fileOriginEnd: End of the file stream; this position is one byte past the last byte in the file stream.

If you need to find out where the current position is within a file stream, call the FileTell function:

**Palm OS Garnet**
```
Int32 FileTell (FileHand stream, Int32* fileSizeP,
                Err* errP)
```

**Palm OS Cobalt**
```
int32_t FileTell (FileHand stream, int32_t* fileSizeP,
                  status_t* errP)
```

The return value from FileTell is the current position, expressed as the offset in bytes from the start of the file stream. If you provide a pointer for the fileSizeP parameter, you also can retrieve the current total size of the file stream in bytes. Pass NULL for fileSizeP to ignore the file stream size information.

You also can reset the position in a file stream back to the beginning of the stream with the FileRewind function:

**Palm OS Garnet**
```
Err FileRewind (FileHand stream)
```

**Palm OS Cobalt**
```
status_t FileRewind (FileHand stream)
```

The FileRewind function also has the side effect of clearing all error codes from the file stream, allowing you to start with a clean slate.

## Reading and Writing File Stream Data

Reading data from a file stream may be accomplished by calling the FileRead function, which reads data into a buffer:

**Palm OS Garnet**
```
Int32 FileRead (FileHand stream, void* bufP, Int32 objSize,
    Int32 numObj, Err* errP)
```

**Palm OS Cobalt**
```
int32_t FileRead (FileHand stream, void* bufP, int32_t objSize,
    int32_t numObj, status_t* errP)
```

The bufP parameter points to the beginning of a buffer you have allocated to receive data from the file stream. The FileRead function reads data in discrete objects, each of which is objSize bytes long. You specify in the numObj parameter the total number of objects to read. When FileRead returns, it places the total number of whole objects read from the file stream in its return value.

*You may use FileRead to read data into a buffer only. If you want to read data from a file stream directly into a memory chunk or record, use FileDmRead, which is described later in this section.*

As FileRead reads in data, it moves the current position in the file by the number of bytes actually read. If insufficient data is left in the file stream to meet the amount you specified using the objSize and numObj parameters, FileRead will result in a fileErrEOF error code, indicating that the end of the file has been reached. You can retrieve this error value from the errP parameter, or by calling FileError, FileGetLastError, or FileEOF.

The FileEOF function specifically checks the error status for the fileErrEOF error, indicating that the current position in the file stream is at the end of the file. The prototype for FileEOF looks like this:

**Palm OS Garnet**
```
Err FileEOF (FileHand stream)
```

**Palm OS Cobalt**
```
status_t FileEOF (FileHand stream)
```

If the current position is at the end of the file, FileEOF returns a non-zero value; otherwise, FileEOF returns 0.

Typically, FileEOF is used with FileRead as part of a loop, allowing data retrieval until the end of the file stream is reached. As an example, the following code loops through a file stream, reading data from the stream ten characters at a time until FileRead hits the end of the file:

```
while(! FileEOF(stream))
{
    count = FileRead(stream, buffer, sizeof(Char), 10,
                     NULL);
    buffer += count;

    // Total up actual bytes read.
    total += count;
}
```

If you want to read data from a file stream directly into a memory chunk or record in a database, use the FileDmRead function:

**Palm OS Garnet**
```
Int32 FileDmRead (FileHand stream, void* startOfDmChunkP,
    Int32 destOffset, Int32 objSize, Int32 numObj,
    Err* errP)
```

**Palm OS Cobalt**
```
int32_t FileDmRead (FileHand stream, void* startOfDmChunkP,
    int32_t destOffset, int32_t objSize, int32_t numObj,
    status_t* errP)
```

The `startOfDmChunkP` parameter points to the start of the memory chunk that you want to write data to, and `destOffset` indicates the offset in bytes within that chunk at which `FileDmRead` should begin writing data. Otherwise, `FileDmRead` operates exactly like `FileRead`.

Writing to a file stream requires use of the `FileWrite` function:

**Palm OS Garnet**
```
Int32 FileWrite (FileHand stream, void* dataP,
    Int32 objSize, Int32 numObj, Err* errP)
```

**Palm OS Cobalt**
```
int32_t FileWrite (FileHand stream, void* dataP,
    int32_t objSize, int32_t numObj, status_t* errP)
```

Similar to `FileRead`, the `objSize` and `numObj` parameters tell `FileWrite` how large each write it makes should be and how many writes to attempt. The `dataP` parameter is a pointer to a buffer containing the data to write to the file stream. The `FileWrite` function returns the number of whole objects written to the file stream.

If insufficient storage space is available to contain all of the data `FileWrite` has been asked to write, the function writes as much data as possible before quitting, which means that the last object written to the stream might be cut off in the middle.

# Summary

This chapter showed you some of the less-often-used parts of Palm OS and how to program them. After reading this chapter, you should know the following:

❑   Palm OS Garnet applications larger than 32K may require some programming or linking tricks to avoid the 16-bit jump limit built into the Palm OS Garnet operating system.

❑   Because no single resource in Palm OS may be larger than 64K, you must segment large Palm OS Garnet applications in order to compile and run them properly.

❑   Applications that target Palm OS Cobalt applications do not require multiple segments.

❑   You may create and add custom bitmap fonts to Palm OS Garnet applications.

❑   It is possible to create forms and most user interface elements at runtime, although for most applications it is completely unnecessary, not to mention more difficult to code than using resources created at build time.

❑   The text and international managers provide a wealth of functions and macros to help you deal with localizing an application to use different methods of character encoding, particularly multibyte character sets.

❑   The file streaming API allows applications to use standard file I/O functionality to read and write Palm OS databases.

# Glossary

**5-Way Navigation**

A method of one-handed navigation on handheld devices, enabled by a special group of five buttons (left, top, right, bottom, and center).

**68K**

Short form of Motorola 68000, the family of processors used on Palm OS handhelds prior to Palm OS 5.

**active form**

Form that receives all user input. There can be only one active form at a time in Palm OS.

**active window**

Window where all drawing occurs. There can be only one active window at a time in Palm OS.

**alert**

Modal dialog box that presents the user with a short piece of text information.

**API**

Application Program Interface, a set of functions and data structures that give a developer access to certain features of an operating system or program.

**app info string list**

Resource that holds the initial category names for an application.

**application info block**

Structure in a Palm OS database that contains category names and other information about the database as a whole, as opposed to information about the database's records.

# Glossary

**Application Launcher**

Program in the Palm OS ROM that allows users to launch applications installed on a Palm OS handheld.

**application preferences**

See *preferences*.

**archive**

To mark a record as deleted but leave its data intact. An archived record then may be stored on the desktop computer by a conduit during the next HotSync operation.

**ARM**

Advanced RISC Machines, a processor family used on Palm OS 5 handhelds.

**auto-off timer**

A timer in the Palm OS that, after a certain time has gone by without any user input, causes the system to enter sleep mode to conserve power.

**autoshifting**

A feature of text fields that automatically sets Graffiti input into shift mode for the first letter entered in the field, as well as the first letter after a sentence-ending punctuation mark (., ?, or !).

**backlight**

A common feature on Palm OS handheld screens that allows the screen to be seen in the dark.

**backup conduit**

A default conduit installed as part of the standard Palm Desktop software that automatically makes desktop backup copies of databases that are not handled by their own conduits.

**baseline**

Bottom of those characters in a font that do not have descenders. For example, *a* and *z* sit on the baseline, while *p* and *y* dip below the baseline.

**beaming**

Transfer of data or applications between two devices via infrared.

**big-endian**

Byte order in which the most significant byte in a multibyte data type is stored at the lowest address, or "big end first." For example, the four-character sequence `byte` would be stored as `byte` on a big-endian system. Many processor families, including the Motorola 68000 series used in some Palm OS devices, use big-endian byte order. The term big-endian derives from Jonathan Swift's *Gulliver's Travels*, in which the Big Endians were a political faction that broke their eggs from the large end ("the primitive way") and rebelled against the Lilliputian King who required his subjects (the Little Endians) to break their eggs from the small end. See also *little-endian*.

**bitmap**

A resource type that can store an image for display on the Palm OS screen.

**bitmap family**

A resource type containing multiple bitmap images at different color depths, designed to allow a single image to display properly on handhelds with different screens.

**blitter**

The part of Palm OS that is responsible for the display of pixels on the screen. The process of translating drawing routine calls into the actual pixels that must be modified on the screen is called "blitting."

**Bluetooth**

An open standard for short-range wireless networking. Bluetooth has a range of 10 meters (or up to 100 meters with a power boost), and it communicates via radio in the unlicensed 2.4 GHz band.

**built-in applications**

Applications that come preinstalled in a Palm OS handheld's ROM. More specifically, this term usually refers to the four major applications: Date Book, Address Book, To Do List, and Memo Pad.

**busy bit**

A flag which indicates that an application or system process is busy modifying a record. While a record's busy bit is set, other applications and processes cannot open the record.

**button**

User interface object useful for launching frequently used commands and switching between different views in an application.

**byte order**

The order in which a computer stores multibyte integers. See also *big-endian, little-endian*.

**callback**

A function passed as an argument to another function, which the second function calls to perform some sort of task. A number of Palm OS routines take pointers to callback functions, which allows a developer to customize how the Palm OS routine works by changing the implementation of the callback.

**catalog resource**

A resource available from the catalog window in Constructor.

**catalog window**

A window in Constructor offering a choice of resources. Resources in the catalog window are all user interface objects that may appear within a form.

**category**

A user-defined group of records in a Palm OS application. The Palm OS data manager allows applications to sort records into 15 categories.

**CDK**

Conduit Development Kit, a set of tools and source code available from PalmSource for creating conduits.

# Glossary

**CDMA**

Code Division Multiple Access, a technology for simultaneous transmission of wireless communications over a shared section of the radio spectrum. CDMA assigns a code to each individual stream of communication and then spreads the communication across the spectrum. On the receiving end, CDMA reassembles a communications stream by looking at the code that is assigned to each piece of data in the spectrum. CDMA is widely used in North America.

**character encoding**

A method of representing text characters as data. Most European languages may be represented using the ASCII character encoding, where only a single byte is required to denote a text character. Many other languages, including most Asian languages, contain more symbols than a byte can hold (a byte is limited to 256 different values), so such languages must use multibyte character encoding systems.

**check box**

User interface resource that displays a check box and, optionally, a text string. A check box may have a value of 1 if selected (checked) or 0 if unselected (empty).

**chunk**

A contiguous memory area. Chunks may be movable, in which case they are referenced by handles; or fixed, in which case they are referenced by pointers.

**classic database**

Palm OS database that is created using the traditional Database Manager "Dm" API. Classic databases are accessed using a lower level programming API than the newer Schema databases.

**clipping region**

A defined region of a drawing surface which constrains drawing within that region.

**close-wait**

A state of the Palm OS net library, during which an application has requested that the net library be closed. While in the close-wait state, the net library runs a countdown from a user-defined length of time. If the countdown reaches zero before an application requests that the net library open again, the net library closes and the system frees resources taken by the network protocol stack. If an application does request that the net library be opened before the countdown runs out, the net library stays open and leaves the close-wait state.

**Cobalt**

Palm OS Cobalt, also known as Palm OS 6.*x*, is an advanced version of Palm OS written from the ground up to support ARM processors and advanced graphics, multimedia and other functionality.

**code island**

A small function designed to bridge the gap between functions that are more than 32K away from one another in compiled application code. Also called a *jump island*.

**code section**

Term used in PODS to specify a segment. See *segment*.

**CodeWarrior**

*IDE* and compiler system made by Metrowerks. CodeWarrior for Palm OS Platform is the version of CodeWarrior designed specifically for Palm OS development, although other versions of CodeWarrior exist to create applications for Mac OS, Windows, and many other platforms. CodeWarrior for Palm OS Platform allows Palm OS application development in C or C++.

**color depth**

The number of bits used to represent a pixel's color. Different versions of Palm OS and different kinds of Palm OS hardware support different color depths, ranging from 1-bit (monochrome) to 16-bit (65,536 colors).

**color table**

A count of the number of available colors, followed by an array of structures that define each individual color's red, green, and blue values.

**command bar**

See *menu command toolbar*.

**command shortcut**

A single character assigned to a menu item that, when entered after a Graffiti *command stroke*, executes the associated menu item as if that item had been selected from the menu.

**command stroke**

A special Graffiti stroke that precedes activation of a *command shortcut*. The user makes a command stroke by drawing a diagonal line from the lower left to the upper right within the Graffiti input area.

**conduit**

A plug-in module called by the *HotSync Manager* to synchronize a specific handheld application's data with the desktop.

**Conduit Configuration tool**

Tool that allows a developer to register and unregister conduits with the *HotSync Manager*.

**Conduit Switch tool**

Command-line tool that allows a developer to save and restore the settings of conduits that have been registered with the *HotSync Manager*.

**Conduit Wizard**

Tool installed in Microsoft Visual C++ by the *CDK* that generates a skeleton conduit project based on a developer's specifications.

**Constructor**

Visual resource creation tool that comes with *CodeWarrior* for Palm OS Platform.

**control**

One of several user interface resources in Palm OS. Controls consist of buttons, push buttons, check boxes, repeating buttons, sliders, feedback sliders, pop-up triggers, and selector triggers.

**control group**

A group of mutually exclusive push button or check box controls. Only one member of a control group can be selected at a time; selecting one "unselects" all the others.

**Copilot**

Emulator program created by Greg Hewgill for testing Palm OS applications. PalmSource used Copilot as the basis for *POSE*.

**creator ID**

Four-character code that uniquely identifies a Palm OS application, shared library, or feature. To ensure that each code is unique, developers must register each creator ID with PalmSource.

**cursor**

A reference to a subset of records in a database table matching supplied selection criteria. A cursor is the primary method for navigating schema database record sets.

**custom drawing routine**

An application-defined callback function that draws individual items within a list or individual columns within a table.

**custom load routine**

An application-defined callback function assigned to a table column that loads data into that column's text fields.

**custom save routine**

An application-defined callback function assigned to a table column that saves data from that column's text fields.

**DAL**

Device Abstraction Layer, a portion of Palm OS 5 that isolates the operating system code from the actual hardware. Hardware manufacturers can provide a different DAL to allow Palm OS to run on different types of hardware.

**database**

A list of memory chunks in a handheld's storage RAM, along with some header information to describe the database itself. Databases may contain either records or resources.

**date picker**

System dialog box that presents the user with a calendar, from which the user may select a day, week, or month.

**debug ROM**

See *ROM image*.

**default directory**

A location on a secondary storage volume where files with a specific extension or MIME type should go. The default directory for a particular file type is dependent on the manufacturer of the handheld and the expansion slot driver that manufacturer provides.

**descender**

The part of a text character that extends below a font's baseline. The tail on a *q* or a *y* is a descender.

**dialog box**

A pop-up form that either presents information to the user or allows the user to enter some sort of data. The form can be dismissed when the user taps a button.

**digitizer**

The hardware in a Palm OS handheld's screen that detects pressure from a stylus. The digitizer hands the coordinates where the stylus contacts the screen to the operating system, which translates a user's taps and drags into pen events.

**dirty bit**

A flag that indicates a record was changed and should therefore have its changes saved to the desktop computer (or the handheld if the dirty record is on the desktop computer) during the next HotSync operation.

**dotted decimal notation**

A system for expressing IP addresses in a more human-readable fashion, in which each byte of the IP address is written as a decimal number, separated by periods. For example, the hexadecimal IP address D8F0933D would be expressed as 216.240.147.61 in dotted decimal notation.

**double buffering**

A technique for speeding up screen updates, in which a program performs drawing in a memory buffer instead of on the screen itself, and then the program copies the contents of the buffer all at once to the display. Double buffering is often used to create smooth animation in games.

**doze mode**

Power mode that a Palm OS handheld spends most of its time in when it is "on." In doze mode, the processor is running but not processing instructions. Doze mode requires much less power than running mode, and switching from doze mode to running mode takes less time than switching from sleep mode to running mode.

**DragonBall**

A family of Motorola processors used on Palm OS handhelds prior to Palm OS 5. See also *Motorola 68000*.

**draw state**

The collective drawing properties for a window including, but not limited to, its font, foreground and background colors, and transfer mode.

**draw window**

The window where all drawing occurs. There can be only one draw window at a time in Palm OS.

**dynamic heap**

Memory heap where Palm OS applications store their global and temporary variables.

**dynamic RAM**

Area of a Palm OS handheld's RAM devoted to implementing the dynamic heap.

**dynamic user interface**

Method of creating forms and user interface elements at runtime, instead of from resources compiled into an application.

**Eclipse**

The visual *IDE* used for creating and managing projects in the Palm OS Developer Suite (PODS).

**edit mode**

Mode in which the user is editing a text field in a table.

**Edit view**

Screen in Librarian, the built-in Address Book, and many other applications that allows the user to edit the fields and properties of a single record.

**enter event**

Event generated when the user touches the stylus to the screen within the bounds of a user interface object.

**event**

A structure used to communicate that something has happened between different parts of the system and an application. An event structure contains information about the type of event (for example, entry of a Graffiti character) and information about that event (for example, the actual character entered).

**event handler**

A system or application function that receives events and responds to them according to their type and what data they contain. An error handler returns `true` if it completely handles an event, or `false` to allow the event to "fall through" to another event handler.

**event loop**

Central part of a Palm OS application that retrieves events from the *event queue* and dispatches them to the appropriate event handlers.

**event queue**

A first in, first out (FIFO) list of events, which both system and applications may add to. An application's event loop retrieves events from the event queue.

**exchange library**

A shared Palm OS library that provides data exchange services. Exchange libraries provide an interface between a method of data transmission, such as *SMS* or *Bluetooth*, and the Palm OS exchange manager APIs.

**exit event**

Event generated when the user touches the stylus to the screen within the bounds of a user interface object, drags the stylus outside the object, and then lifts the stylus.

**expansion slot**

A slot found in virtually every modern Palm OS handheld, which can read and write data on SD or MMC expansion cards.

**extended gadget**

A *gadget* resource with a callback function for handling the gadget's drawing and user interaction.

**fast sync**

Style of record synchronization used by a conduit when a handheld is being synchronized with the same desktop computer it was synched with during its previous HotSync operation. A FastSync can reliably use the *dirty bit* in each record to determine which records need to be processed, ignoring those records that have not been modified.

**feature**

A 32-bit value published by the system or an application to indicate the presence of a particular software or hardware element.

**feature creator**

The unique creator ID of the application that publishes a particular feature.

**feature memory**

A special technique for using features to store data that must persist between executions of an application, such as alarm data.

**feature number**

An application-defined, 16-bit value that distinguishes features that share a creator ID from one another.

**feature set**

A particular set of Palm OS functions and data structures, the presence or absence of which may be determined by checking for a particular feature.

**feature table**

A list of registered features. The Palm OS maintains two features tables: one in ROM for system features and one in RAM for application-published features.

**feedback slider**

A slider control that returns events continuously while the user holds the stylus down on the control.

**FEP**

Front-End Processor, a text-entry method used for some languages (like Japanese) with large, complex character sets.

**field**

A user interface element that displays text and allows the user to edit that text.

**file linking**

An optional conduit feature that, when implemented, allows the conduit to update data on a handheld from a linked desktop file source.

**file pointer**

The position within a file from which data is read or to which data is written. Most traditional file system APIs provide a "tell" function for reporting the current position of the file pointer and a "seek" function for setting the file pointer's position. Usually, the act of reading or writing data also moves the file pointer.

**file stream**

A block of data with no upper limit on its size that an application may read data from and write data to by using the file-streaming API.

**fill pattern**

An $8 \times 8$ pixel pattern that may be used by certain Palm OS drawing functions.

**focus**

A state possessed by either a text field or a table that contains editable text fields, in which that field or table receives all key events. A field or table in such a state is said to "have the focus." Text fields that have the focus display a blinking insertion point.

**form**

A visual and programmatic container for user interface elements. A given form usually represents a single screen or dialog box in an application.

**form bitmap**

A bitmap image that is attached to a specific form.

**form layout window**

A Constructor window that shows a form's layout and allows developers to position and edit user interface objects contained within the form.

**fragmentation**

A situation that occurs when very little contiguous memory is available because occupied memory chunks are scattered throughout a memory heap.

**frame**

The border around a button or window. Window frames are always drawn outside the rectangular region that makes up the window proper.

**gadget**

A customizable user interface object that, while providing little behavior of its own, gives a developer a framework for a new object that acts differently from the existing Palm OS user interface elements.

**Garnet**

Palm OS Garnet is the code name for Palm OS 5.*x*, the most current version of the operating system derived from the original version of Palm OS. It provides some support for native ARM application code but is not designed from the ground up as a fully ARM-native operating system like Palm OS Cobalt.

**global find facility**

A Palm OS feature that allows the user to search for a string of text in every application on the handheld that supports the find facility.

**GPRS**

General Packet Radio Service, an addition to the *GSM* wireless communication system that supports continuous flow of *IP* data packets. GPRS simplifies applications such as Web browsing and file transfer because it is always connected; there is no need for a GPRS-enabled device to dial up and connect to a service to initiate data transfer.

**Graffiti**

A software system that converts a special shorthand into text, used on most Palm OS handhelds to allow text data entry.

**Graffiti area**

Region across the bottom of a Palm OS handheld screen dedicated to receiving Graffiti input. The left side of the Graffiti area is for entering letters, and the right side is for entering numbers. On some models, notably the HandEra 330 and the Sony CLIÉ PEG-NR70, the Graffiti area is "virtual," drawn onto the display by software instead of silk-screened onto the handheld. A virtual Graffiti area can be hidden to allow more display space on such units.

**Graffiti shift indicator**

A small icon, usually located in the lower-right corner of a form, that indicates the current Graffiti shift state, which may be punctuation, symbol, uppercase shift, or uppercase lock. On Palm OS handhelds that support Asian languages, the Graffiti shift indicator has many more states to facilitate entry of multiple character sets.

**graphics context**

An intelligent buffer that accepts drawing commands from an application and handles rendering onto the actual target window.

**Gremlin**

A facility of the *Palm OS Emulator* that allows the Emulator to randomly poke at an application in a reproducible manner — a testing technique that can uncover obscure bugs that might be missed by more structured testing.

**Gremlin horde**

A facility of the *Palm OS Emulator* that allows a developer to queue up a whole bunch of Gremlins and assault an unsuspecting application en masse.

**GSM**

Global System for Mobile communications, a digital cellular phone networking technology. GSM was first adopted in Europe but it has gained support throughout the world.

**handle**

A pointer to a movable chunk of memory. It also is sometimes used to refer to the memory chunk itself.

**hard reset**

A system reset that clears the contents of both dynamic and storage RAM, usually reserved for recovering from a catastrophic system crash.

**hardware button**

One of the physical buttons on a Palm OS handheld, used for turning the handheld on and off, scrolling, and launching applications.

**hierarchy window**

A Constructor window that shows the hierarchy of objects within a form, useful for the selection of objects that are covered by other objects in the form layout window.

**host byte order**

The *byte order* used by a specific host computer for storage of IP addresses. Depending on the system architecture of the host, host byte order may or may not need to be translated into *network byte order* for the host to communicate via TCP networking.

**HotSync log**

A text file maintained by the *HotSync Manager* that conduits use to communicate errors and other useful information to the user.

**HotSync Manager**

An application that runs on the desktop computer and oversees the process of synchronizing a Palm OS handheld with the desktop, calling conduits to perform most of the actual synchronization tasks.

**"i" icon**

See *tips icon*.

**icon**

A resource holding a small graphic image, used to represent an application in the application launcher.

**icon family**

A resource type containing multiple icons at different color depths, designed to allow a single image to display properly on handhelds with different hardware configurations.

**IDE**

Integrated Development Environment, any of a class of programs that combine source code editors, debuggers, compilers, or other development tools into a single interface.

**increment arrow**

A repeating button containing an arrow symbol and lacking a border, usually used to allow scrolling through records in an application.

**in-place editing**

A method of changing text information that allows the text undergoing editing to be stored directly in storage RAM rather than in a temporary buffer in dynamic RAM. In-place editing is ideal for large pieces of text, such as Memo Pad records or the Note field attached to many application's records.

**insertion point**

The place in an editable text field where newly entered text appears, represented onscreen by a blinking cursor.

**insertion sort**

A sorting algorithm optimized for sorting an array that is mostly sorted already, useful when only a few array members are out of order and need to be placed in their proper locations.

**International Feature Set**

A feature set present in some versions of Palm OS that provides functions for manipulating text in a localization-friendly manner, as well as facilities for dealing with localized date, time, and number formats.

**IR**

Infrared.

**IrDA**

Infrared Data Association, an industry consortium that creates standards for communicating between devices using infrared beams.

**jog-dial**

A scrollable wheel, usually located on the side of a handheld, which provides one-handed navigation capability for Sony CLIÉ and other handheld models.

**jump island**

See *code island*.

**key event**

An event generated when the user enters a Graffiti character or presses a hardware button.

**label**

User interface resource that contains static text for display in a form.

**large icon**

The larger of two icon resources an application may have, displayed in the Icon view of the default Palm OS application launcher.

**launch code**

A special code sent to an application's *PilotMain* function, requesting an application to start and display its interface, or to perform some small task and exit without showing its interface, such as setting an alarm.

**Librarian**

Sample application that maintains a database of books, used throughout this book to demonstrate some Palm OS programming techniques.

**link converter class**

Class used in conduits based on the Palm MFC Base Classes to convert records from their handheld format to a desktop format, and vice versa.

**list**

User interface object that displays multiple rows of data in a single column, from which a user may make a selection. Lists come in two varieties: static, which take up screen space on a form, and pop-up, which are displayed only when the user taps a pop-up trigger.

**list item**

A single row within a list.

**List view**

Screen in Librarian, the built-in Address Book, and many other applications that displays a summary of the records contained in the application's database. From the List view, the user may select a record for closer inspection in the *Record view*.

**little-endian**

Byte order in which the least significant byte in a multibyte data type is stored at the lowest address, or "little end first." For example, the four-character sequence byte would be stored as ybet on a little-endian system. Some processor families, including Intel CPUs, use little-endian byte order. See also *big-endian*.

**local ID**

An offset from the beginning of a memory card to a chunk within that memory card.

**lock count**

A count of the number of times a particular memory chunk has been locked. Only when a chunk's lock count is 0 may the system move that chunk to a new location.

**logical port number**

A generic identifier for a kind of port on a Palm OS handheld.

**masked record**

A private record that shows up in an application's list of records but whose data is obscured by a gray bar. This method of hiding a private record is available only in Palm OS 3.5 and later.

**menu**

A user interface element that allows a user to launch a command by selecting the command from a drop-down list at the top of the screen, much as in a desktop GUI. Menus may be opened by tapping the Menu silkscreen button—or in Palm OS 3.5 and later, by tapping a form's title bar.

**menu bar**

Bar across the top of the screen that contains one or more menus. Each form may have exactly one menu bar.

**menu command toolbar**

Bar that appears across the bottom of the screen in Palm OS 3.5 or later when the user enters a command shortcut. A menu command toolbar contains buttons that may be tapped to launch the most commonly accessed menu commands, obviating the need to navigate through the menus and their respective items.

**menu item**

A single command listed in a menu.

**MFC**

Microsoft Foundation Classes, a set of C++ classes for building Windows applications.

**MIC**

Message Integrity Check, a system that detects tampering and transmission errors in data sent securely from a Palm OS handheld to a wireless network.

**MIDI**

Musical Instrument Digital Interface, a system for encoding both music and musical instrument definitions.

**mirror image synchronization**

Style of synchronization that allows modification of records on both the desktop and the handheld, keeping both databases up to date with each other and resolving conflicts where a record was modified on both platforms.

**modal**

Term describing a form or window that ignores taps outside its borders. Modal dialog boxes must be dismissed before the user can do anything else in the current application. The Select Font dialog box available in most of the built-in applications is a modal dialog box.

**monitor class**

Class used in conduits based on the Palm MFC Base Classes to control the synchronization process.

**Motorola 68000**

Processor architecture used on Palm OS handhelds prior to Palm OS 5, often shortened to Motorola 68K or simply 68K. Specifically, pre–Palm OS 5 devices contain Motorola MC68328 DragonBall, MC68EZ328 DragonBall EZ, MC68VZ328 DragonBall VZ, or MC68SZ328 DragonBall Super VZ processors.

**multibit icon**

An icon resource that can contain both monochrome and grayscale icons.

**multibyte character encoding**

Method of representing characters in a language that uses more than one byte to represent each character. Multibyte character encoding is essential for many Asian languages that contain more than 256 symbols—the maximum number that may be represented using single-byte encoding.

**multiline field**

A text field that allows more than one line of text to be entered. Typically, multiline fields may be scrolled. The *Edit view* in the Memo Pad application is composed chiefly of a multiline field.

**multisegment application**

An application composed of multiple code resources or segments. Palm OS programs not written for Palm OS Cobalt that are larger than 64K must be multisegment applications.

**native coordinate system**

The coordinate system used by the Palm OS blitter. The native coordinate system on a handheld is based on the actual physical pixels of the display hardware. In a native coordinate system, there may be more than one pixel per standard coordinate. See also *blitter*; *standard coordinate system*.

**native synchronization logic**

Logic implemented by the Palm OS base conduit classes to perform mirror image synchronization of records.

**no-notification reset**

A system reset that does not send a `sysAppLaunchCmdSystemReset` launch code to applications to let them know a reset was just performed. No-notification resets are useful if an application crashes upon receiving the `sysAppLaunchCmdSystemReset` launch code, thereby preventing the system from starting properly after a reset.

**notification (both Palm OS and HotSync)**

In Palm OS, a mechanism — similar to launch codes but more efficient — that allows applications registered to hear about certain events to receive notice when those events occur. In relation to HotSync operations, notification is how the *HotSync Manager* tells a desktop application when a HotSync operation is about to start and when it has finished, allowing the desktop application to prevent record modification while the sync is taking place.

**notifier DLL**

A dynamic link library that the *HotSync Manager* calls to notify a desktop application about the start or end of a HotSync operation.

**object ID**

Another name for *resource ID*. Some Palm documentation also uses object ID to refer to numbers that Constructor assigns internally to resources that it creates.

**object index**

Sequential number assigned to every user interface object contained by a form.

**offscreen window**

A drawing window that exists only in memory. Drawing to an offscreen window does not modify what is displayed onscreen.

**one-directional synchronization**

Synchronization style where data travels only from the desktop to the handheld, or vice versa.

**PACE**

Palm Application Compatibility Environment, an emulation layer that Palm OS 5 uses to provide backward compatibility for Palm OS applications compiled to run on the Motorola 68000 architecture.

**Palm Generic Conduit Base Classes**

Set of C++ classes designed to build conduits that can synchronize a Palm OS application with any arbitrary data source on the desktop.

**Palm Image Checker**

Tool for checking images to make sure they are acceptable for WCA and Web clipping use.

**Palm MFC Base Classes**

Set of C++ classes based on the Microsoft Foundation Classes designed to build conduits that can synchronize a Palm OS application with a data source on the desktop in MFC-serialized format.

**Palm OS Emulator**

A handheld emulator that simulates most aspects of an actual Palm OS handheld's hardware and software on the desktop. Also called *POSE* (and occasionally Poser), Palm OS Emulator is an invaluable debugging tool.

**Palm OS Resource Editor**

The visual resource editor supplied with PODS for designing forms and other user interface elements

**Palm OS Simulator**

A Windows program that simulates the Palm OS environment.

**Palm OS Simulator libraries**

A series of libraries that allow a Palm OS application to be compiled as a standalone Macintosh application for testing on a Mac OS computer. The Palm OS Simulator libraries should not be confused with *Palm OS Simulator* or *Palm OS Emulator*.

**palmOne**

Formerly known as Palm, Inc., prior to splitting into palmOne and PalmSource. It is the handheld device manufacturer responsible for creating and marketing the most popular handheld device in the world.

**PalmRez**

A post-linker in CodeWarrior that combines linked object code with other resources to form a Palm OS executable, or .prc file.

**PalmSource**

Spun off from Palm, Inc., the company responsible for developing and licensing the Palm operating system.

**path**

In Palm OS Cobalt's graphics model, a path is a set of lines, arcs, and curves used to draw on a surface.

**PC ID**

A pseudo-random number generated by the *HotSync Manager* to uniquely identify a desktop computer.

**.pdb file**

Desktop form of a Palm OS record database.

**pen event**

An event generated when the user taps on or drags the stylus across the screen.

**PilotMain**

Entry point function for a normal Palm OS application.

**PODS**

Palm OS Developer Suite, the official Palm OS development environment provided free of charge by PalmSource.

**pop-up list**

A list resource, normally hidden, that appears in response to a tap on a pop-up trigger.

**pop-up trigger**

A space-saving user interface element that displays the current selection from a hidden pop-up list and, when tapped, displays the list.

**port ID**

A value passed to most New Serial Manager functions to allow them to identify an open serial port.

**POSE**

Acronym for *Palm OS Emulator*.

**.prc file**

Desktop form of a Palm OS application or resource database.

**preferences**

A database maintained by Palm OS that stores settings for the system and applications. System preferences hold settings that control how the operating system behaves. Application preferences may be used by any application that needs to store small pieces of data, which should persist between invocations of an application but that are too small to merit being stored in a full-fledged record database.

**primary storage**

Data storage in the storage RAM portion of a Palm OS handheld. See also *secondary storage*.

**private record**

A record with its secret bit set, which applications can hide or mask, requiring that the user enter a password to display it. Palm OS does not enforce record privacy; it is up to individual applications to check the user's private records preferences to determine whether or not those records should be displayed.

**project**

The basic unit of application organization in CodeWarrior. A project contains references to the source files, resources, and settings required to build an application.

**project resource**

A resource displayed in Constructor's project window including, but not limited, to forms, alerts, icons, bitmaps, and menus.

**project stationery**

A CodeWarrior template that provides the basic skeleton and settings required for a particular kind of application.

**project window**

In CodeWarrior, a window that lists all the files, segments, and targets that make up a project. In Constructor, a window that lists major resources such as forms and alerts, as well as some application-wide resource settings.

**protection count**

A count maintained for a database to prevent the database from being deleted, which allows an application to keep a record or resource in the database locked without leaving the database open. When a database's protection count reaches 0, the database is no longer protected and can be deleted.

**public key cryptography**

A powerful system of data encryption in which a public key is used to encrypt data, which then can be decrypted only by the private key that goes with the public key. Owning the public key does not provide any way to find out the private key, so the public key may be safely distributed via insecure means.

**push button**

User interface object similar to radio buttons on other platforms, usually used in a group to allow selection of one and only one item in the group.

**RAM**

Random Access Memory, a type of memory that loses its data when it loses power. Palm OS handhelds store most of their data in RAM, including third-party applications and application data.

**record**

A relocatable memory chunk in storage RAM that holds one piece of an application's data, such as an Address Book entry or a memo. Records within a database may be scattered across a single memory card, allowing the system to move them around as needed to free up storage memory for other records and resources.

**record class**

Class used in conduits based on the Palm MFC Base Classes to access database records.

**record database**

A database containing records, as opposed to a resource database.

**Record view**

Screen in Librarian, the built-in Address Book, and many other applications that displays a detailed, read-only view of an entry's data.

**rectangle**

Structure defining a rectangular screen region, containing the coordinates of the region's upper-left corner and the region's width and height in pixels.

**rectangle frame**

Hollow rectangular screen region that surrounds a particular rectangle. Rectangle frames are always drawn outside the rectangle structure that defines them.

**repeat event**

Event generated repeatedly while the user holds the stylus down within the bounds of a repeating user interface object, such as a repeating button. The scroll arrows in the lower-right corner of the built-in applications are repeating buttons that generate repeat events.

**repeating button**

Button-like user interface object that sends repeat events while the user holds the stylus on it. Repeating buttons are often used to create *increment arrows*.

**resource**

A memory chunk in storage RAM that has a particular type and ID number. Resources are usually used to store user interface elements like forms and buttons.

**resource database**

A database containing resources, as opposed to a record database. A Palm OS application is a resource database containing executable code resources.

**resource fork**

Part of a Mac OS file that contains resources, as opposed to a data fork, which contains data. On Windows, CodeWarrior mimics the data fork of a file with an empty file and then creates the resource fork in a separate directory.

**resource ID**

Application-defined number that identifies a particular resource within a resource database. Within a resource database, resources that share the same type must have unique resource ID numbers.

**resource type**

Four-character code that identifies what kind of data a resource contains, such as tBTN for a button or code for executable code.

**Rez**

CodeWarrior tool that generates resources based on text file resource definitions.

**RISC**

Reduced Instruction Set Computer, a processor architecture that reduces chip complexity by using simpler instructions. The ARM processors in Palm OS 5 handhelds are RISC processors.

**RGB**

Red-Green-Blue, a numeric value that defines a particular color by specifying the amounts of red, green, and blue in the color. RGB values are most often expressed as a six-digit hexadecimal number, where the first pair of digits represents red, the second pair green, and the last two blue. In this scheme, 0x000000 is black, 0xFFFFFF is white, and 0xFF0000 is bright red, just to name a few of the more than 16 million colors possible using this notation.

**ROM**

Read-Only Memory, a type of memory that cannot be written to but that retains its contents when it loses power (as opposed to RAM). The Palm OS system software and built-in applications are stored in ROM.

**ROM applications**

See *built-in applications*.

**ROM image**

A file containing all the data and code packed into the ROM of an actual Palm OS handheld, in a format suitable for use in *Palm OS Emulator*. ROM images may either be retrieved from an actual Palm OS handheld or downloaded from PalmSource. Some ROM images, called debug ROMs, contain special debugging code that generates warnings when an application does something that goes against PalmSource's coding recommendations. For example, debug ROMs check that developers do not directly access user interface object structures.

**RS-232**

Electronics Industries Association standard that defines how the most common type of serial port should operate. The serial port on a Palm OS handheld is compatible with RS-232.

**running mode**

Power mode that a Palm OS handheld enters only briefly when actually processing instructions.

**schema class**

Class used in conduits based on the Palm MFC Base Classes to serve as a template for reading records out of a table object.

**schema database**

A new type of Palm OS database found in Palm OS Cobalt that employs relational database concepts to enable row/column data access.

**scroll arrow**

See *increment arrow*.

**scroll bar**

User interface object that allows the user to scroll text fields and tables, while providing visual feedback about the approximate position of the cursor within a text field or table.

**scroll car**

A dark bar in a *scroll bar* that indicates the currently displayed data's approximate position within a text field or table by its vertical position within the scroll bar and that indicates how much of the field or table data is currently visible by its height. The scroll car also allows movement through a field or table when the user drags it up and down in the scroll bar.

**secondary storage**

Data storage on removable, add-on memory. Palm OS secondary storage is similar to a desktop computer file system, including a serial interface that allows access to data only one bit, byte, or block at a time. See also *primary storage*.

**secret record**

See *private record*.

**segment**

A single code resource within a Palm OS application. Large, multisegment applications may contain several segments.

**select event**

Event generated when the user touches the stylus to the screen within the bounds of a user interface object and then lifts the stylus while still within the object's bounds.

**selection**

In a list, the highlighted list item. In a table, the table item that the user most recently tapped. In a control group, the push button or check box that is currently "on."

**selector trigger**

User interface element that contains text surrounded by a gray box, which displays a dialog box allowing the user to select a new value to display within the box.

**separator bar**

Special menu item that draws a line between other menu items in order to group them meaningfully.

**serial port**

A port for the transmission of serial data. Palm OS handhelds use a serial port to connect to a desktop computer and other devices that support the RS-232 serial standard. Although the port on the handheld itself is serial, many Palm OS handhelds come with a cradle that converts the serial signals to USB signals for connection to a desktop computer's USB port.

**serial receive buffer**

Buffer that contains incoming serial data.

**serial send buffer**

Buffer that contains outgoing data queued for serial transmission.

**silkscreen button**

One of the buttons printed to the sides of the Graffiti area on a Palm OS screen. Most Palm OS hand-helds have Applications, Menu, Calculator, and Find buttons; Japanese models have additional buttons to control the front-end processor (FEP). On some models, notably the HandEra 330 and Sony CLIÉ PEG-NR70, the silkscreen buttons are "virtual." They are not printed on the hardware; instead, the system draws virtual silkscreen buttons on the bottom part of the screen. See also *FEP*.

**Simulator**

See *Palm OS Simulator*.

**single-line field**

A text field that can contain only a single line of unscrollable text.

**skin**

Custom bitmap image that may be applied to *Palm OS Emulator* to make it look like different pieces of real Palm OS hardware.

**sleep mode**

Power mode that a Palm OS handheld is in when the unit is "off." Most systems on the handheld are shut down in sleep mode, including the display, digitizer, and processor.

**slider**

User interface element similar to a scroll bar, but arranged horizontally.

**slow sync**

Style of record synchronization used by a conduit when a handheld is being synchronized with a different desktop computer from the one it was synched with during its most recent HotSync operation. A SlowSync cannot reliably use the *dirty bit* in each record to determine which records need to be processed, so it compares every desktop record with every handheld record to resolve conflicts between them.

**small icon**

The smaller of two icon resources an application may have that are displayed in the List view of the default Palm OS application launcher.

**smartphone**

A handheld device that combines the advanced features of a PDA with the wireless voice and data capabilities of a cellular telephone.

**SMF**

Standard MIDI File, a musical data format used by some of the Palm OS sound routines.

**SMS**

Short Message Service, a service that allows mobile phones to send short text messages (usually between 140 and 160 characters in length) over the mobile phone network's control channel instead of over the usual voice channel. Some Palm OS handhelds with embedded mobile phones are able to send and receive SMS messages.

**soft reset**

A system reset that clears the contents of dynamic RAM, leaving storage RAM intact.

**sort info block**

Structure at the beginning of a Palm OS database originally intended to hold information about how a database's records should be sorted. Current and previous implementations of the *HotSync Manager* do not back up the sort info block, so sorting information is best stored in the application info block.

**Sound Manager**

A set of programming interfaces for Palm OS Garnet and Palm OS Cobalt that provides basic sound and WAVE file playing capabilities.

**SSL**

Secure Sockets Layer, a data security layer in common use on the Web for encrypting data that needs to be transmitted securely between a browser and a server.

**standard coordinate system**

The coordinate system used for drawing on Palm Powered handhelds that do not support the High-Density Display feature set. The standard coordinate system maps exactly one pixel to each standard coordinate. See also *native coordinate system*.

**storage heap**

Memory heap containing resources and persistent data.

**storage RAM**

Area of a Palm OS handheld's RAM devoted to storing applications and application data.

**string list**

Resource that contains a number of strings, packed together one after another.

**stylus**

Blunt, pen-like object that comes with Palm OS handhelds, which allows the user to interact with applications by tapping and dragging on the screen and by entering text in the Graffiti area.

**switching depth**

Number of events a particular *Gremlin* will generate before *Palm OS Emulator* switches to another Gremlin in a *Gremlin horde*.

**Sync Manager API**

Set of functions and data types used for direct communication between a conduit and a Palm OS handheld.

**system preferences**

See *preferences*.

**system resource**

Application resources created by the compiler and linker, such as executable code resources.

**system tick**

Unit of time used by a Palm OS handheld's real-time clock. The actual unit is device-dependent, but on most Palm OS handhelds, ticks occur 100 times per second.

**table**

User interface object well suited to allowing the user to edit values directly within the table's columns and rows and capable of containing many other types of user interface elements, such as text fields and check boxes.

**table class**

Class used in conduits based on the Palm MFC Base Classes to store records in a linear format.

**table item**

One cell in a table object.

**tap**

Handheld equivalent of a mouse click, where the user "taps" the stylus on the screen to select a user interface element.

**target**

In CodeWarrior, a particular group of source file and compile settings in a project, designed to produce a specific kind of output. This kind of target is often used for localization, with each country or language having its own target within the same project file. Targets are also useful to separate debug builds of an application from release builds. In a makefile, a target is the file or files generated by a particular rule.

**thumb**

The moveable part of a slider control that indicates what value is currently represented by the slider. A user may hold the stylus down on the thumb and drag it left or right to adjust the value represented by the slider. The thumb also jumps toward the stylus by a preset increment when the user taps the slider control on either side of the thumb.

**tick**

See *system tick*.

**time picker**

System dialog box that allows the user to select a time of day.

**tips icon**

Small "i" in a circle, located in the upper-right corner of some modal dialog boxes and alerts. When tapped, it displays another dialog box containing help text for the original dialog box.

**title bar**

Region at the top of a form that contains the form's title.

**tracing**

A debugging technique in which a program reports its progress to a debugging window or a log file as it runs. Tracing is particularly useful for debugging communications code, which, because of its dependence on timing, is difficult or impossible to debug using breakpoints in a source-level debugger.

# Glossary

**transaction-based synchronization**

Style of synchronization where the desktop computer must perform some sort of processing between each record synchronization. For example, a conduit might retrieve data from a Web site and update a handheld application's database from such information.

**transfer mode**

One of a number of techniques for drawing bitmaps, fonts, or simple graphics primitives onto the screen or onto an offscreen window. Transfer modes can be used to create various special effects, such as color inversion and transparency.

**typed data object**

A stream of data that includes identifying information about the stream's contents. The Palm OS exchange manager identifies typed data objects by creator ID, file extension, or MIME type.

**UART**

Universal Asynchronous Receiver and Transmitter, a microprocessor that controls a computer or handheld's interface to its serial devices.

**UIAS**

User Interface Application Shell. On Palm OS Garnet and earlier, it is responsible for managing applications that display a user interface.

**usable**

A descriptive term of a form object that allows user interaction and is drawn onscreen. An unusable object is effectively not there from a user's perspective because it does not appear on the screen and the user cannot do anything with it.

**user ID**

A pseudo-random number generated by the *HotSync Manager* to identify a handheld uniquely.

**VFS**

Virtual File System, a set of Palm OS APIs for handling data on removable *secondary storage* media.

**virtual key event**

Key event that does not contain a regular text character, used to represent or trigger system events such as turning on the backlight or extending the antenna on a Palm VII.

**volume**

A logical storage unit, usually containing a file system for storing data.

**window**

A rectangular region, either onscreen or off, that can receive pen events and defines a drawing region. All forms are windows, but not all windows are forms.

**Wireless Internet Feature Set**

A feature set present in some versions of Palm OS that provides functions for manipulating text in a localization-friendly manner, as well as facilities for dealing with localized date, time, and number formats.

# Index

# X

# Z